Audubon Wildlife Report 1988/1989

Audubon Wildlife Report 1988/1989

William J. Chandler
Editor

Lillian Labate
Assistant Editor

Chris Wille
Project Manager

The National Audubon Society
New York, New York

ACADEMIC PRESS, INC.
Harcourt Brace Jovanovich, Publishers
San Diego New York Berkeley Boston
London Sydney Tokyo Toronto

Academic Press Rapid Manuscript Reproduction.

ACADEMIC PRESS, INC.
1250 Sixth Avenue
San Diego, California 92101

United Kingdom Edition published by
ACADEMIC PRESS INC. (LONDON) LTD.
24-28 Oval Road, London NW1 7DX

LIBRARY OF CONGRESS CATALOG CARD NUMBER: 86-643440

ISSN 0885-6044

ISBN 0-12-041001-X (alk. paper)
ISBN 0-12-041002-8 (paperback)

PRINTED IN THE UNITED STATES OF AMERICA
88 89 90 91 9 8 7 6 5 4 3 2 1

Contents

Part Three. Conservation Challenges

Part Four. Species Accounts

Part Five. Appendices

Foreword

Wildlife conservation depends on people. But more than that, it depends on the effectiveness of people. Warm bodies and dedication are no longer enough.

The intricate problems and issues that now surround wildlife are not solved by clamor. They lend themselves more and more to reasoned compromise, where inescapable relationships between the needs of humans and wild creatures are aired, and decisions are made with deep understanding that all living things have similar ecological requirements.

To be effective, wildlife conservationists, managers, and program administrators must understand the maze of agencies, laws, lawmakers, and processes through which they routinely are forced. This boiling cauldron of democracy is especially frustrating to the parade of new activists and professionals entering the wildlife conservation scene. These dedicated people—whether they be congressional staff, federal or state personnel, or active members of a private conservation group—often need help to become acclimated fast. The *Audubon Wildlife Report* serves that purpose.

Every year, the report unravels a piece of the puzzle, covering the primary agencies involved with natural resource conservation, as well as major policy and management issues. This year, the focus is on the National Marine Fisheries Service (NMFS), an agency responsible for managing much of the country's sport and commercial oceanic fisheries. It is an agency little known to most people and is a constant target for severe budget reduction by the Reagan Administration. Oceanic fishery stocks are in trouble. So is NMFS. If you care whether stocks of redfish, bluefin tuna, billfish, and other marine species survive, you must learn what NMFS is all about.

Aside from governmental agencies, the 1988/1989 report explores implications of the Farm Act, struggles between development and wildlife interests over Platte River water, illegal trade in wildlife, effects of plastics and similar debris on marine fisheries, and other timely subjects. Also included are discussions of several species whose management illustrates the types of challenges faced by wildlife conservation in modern times. Some of these species are endangered, others are expanding their range and population.

In essence, the *Audubon Wildlife Report 1988/1989* is a tool that can make people more effective wildlife conservationists. It offers the insight and knowledge to help ensure a future for wild things. And well that it does, because a world with no room for wildlife has conceded the demise of humankind.

Lonnie Williamson
Vice-President
Wildlife Management Institute

Preface

This is the fourth edition of the *Audubon Wildlife Report*. Like earlier volumes, its central focus is federal wildlife conservation policy.

While the report's focus remains the same, its scope of coverage continues to evolve. Whereas earlier editions furnished extensive background information on the history, legal authorities, and administrative structure of federal wildlife agencies and programs, this volume provides more in-depth treatment of significant problems, issues, and developments involving wildlife. The following subjects are covered:

- Restoring North American waterfowl to desirable levels of abundance.
- The impact of plastic debris on marine wildlife.
- Protecting biological diversity in national forests, parks, and public lands.
- Recent court decisions that provide new interpretations of wildlife law.
- Restoring the Everglades ecosystem.
- The exploitation of wildlife in international commerce, with a case study of the orchid trade.
- The potential benefits of the 1985 Farm Act for wildlife.
- The implication for wildlife of continued water development in the Platte River Basin.
- Highlights of federal agency wildlife budgets for fiscal year 1988.

These chapters will bring the reader abreast of the latest developments and provide enough comprehensive background material for a real understanding of the depth and complexity of the most urgent conservation challenges.

Several important features of earlier reports have been retained in this volume as well. These include a thorough discussion of federal natural resource management issues, 14 chapters on the status of individual plant and animal species, and directories of key federal wildlife officials.

This year's featured agency is the National Marine Fisheries Service, an agency little known to most conservationists. The service has a colossal task: managing fish and marine mammals in one-fifth of the world's most productive marine waters. To accomplish this job, the fisheries service has both a budget and staff that is about one-fifth that of the National Park Service.

There are signs that many stocks of U.S. marine fish may be seriously depleted; some even commercially extinct. According to the NMFS chapter author, mainline conservation organizations have been noticeably absent in fishery politics. This situation merits close attention.

The species accounts are a popular component of the *Audubon Wildlife Report*, and with good reason. These chapters provide the reader with the latest information on a species' natural history, significance, historical and current status, management, and future needs. This information is valuable to both the professional and layman alike.

Two things caught my attention when I reviewed the species chapters. First, our basic knowledge of many species—including those deemed highly important—is riddled with gaps. Second, basic conservation needs of some of the species covered here are not being met. Indeed, the resources spent on their behalf can only be described as woefully inadequate.

Such observations raise fundamental questions about the biological research enterprise in the United States, the establishment of wildlife management priorities and budgets, and the overall coordination of research and management to address the nation's most pressing biological conservation needs. Readers' thoughts on these matters would be appreciated as we formulate future topics for treatment in the report.

Correspondence regarding any subject matter in the report, or lack thereof, should be sent to: Editor, Audubon Wildlife Report, National Audubon Society, 950 Third Avenue, New York, NY 10022.

William J. Chandler
Editor

Acknowledgments

Publication of this report would not have been possible without the generous support of the following individuals, foundations, and corporations:

James R. Dougherty Foundation
Joy R. Hilliard
Olin Corporation
Nathaniel P. Reed
Peter W. Stroh
The Stroh Foundation
The Williams Companies

Researching and writing a report of this magnitude requires the expertise and efforts of many people. Nearly the entire National Audubon Society staff was involved in some way, but special notes of appreciation are due: Alex Antypas, Fredrick Baumgarten, Kristin Berry, Jan Beyea, Louis Botsford, Faith Thompson Campbell, David Cline, Susan Drennan, Tom Exton, Natalie Goldstein, Maureen Hinkle, Carol Hyatt, Ron Klataske, Elizabeth Layne, Mercedes Lee, Cynthia Lenhart, Les Line, Susan Martin, Pete Myers, Daniel McClain, Ed Pembleton, Elizabeth Raisbeck, Anne Schwartz, Fran Spivy-Weber, Ann Stevens, Larry Thompson, Whitney Tilt, and Katherine Yagerman. Special thanks also to Mary McCarthy, for her expertise at unraveling computerese; Margaret McWethy, for her painstaking effort of producing all the figures for this volume; Roger Di Silvestro, former editor of the report, for his continuing advice and support; and to Jean Thomson Black, for her liaison with Academic Press, Inc.

The editors would also like to acknowledge and thank Carse Pustmueller, National Audubon Society; Scott Ellis and Robert Sanz, Environmental Research and Technology, Inc.; and John VanDerwalker, Platte River Whooping Crane Habitat Maintenance Trust, as well as various staff members from the following agencies: Bureau of Land Management, Bureau of Reclamation, Environmental Protection Agency, U.S. Fish and Wildlife Service, U.S. Forest Service, National Park Service, National Marine Fisheries Service, U.S. Army Corps of

Engineers, and the U.S. Department of Agriculture. In addition, we'd like to thank: Canadian Wildlife Service, Wildlife Management Institute, International Association of Fish and Wildlife Agencies, National Fish and Wildlife Foundation, Ducks Unlimited, California Department of Fish and Game, California Waterfowl Association, and the Natural Resources Defense Council.

Contents of Previous Volumes

Audubon Wildlife Report 1985

Audubon Wildlife Report 1986

Audubon Wildlife Report 1987

Part One

The Featured Agency

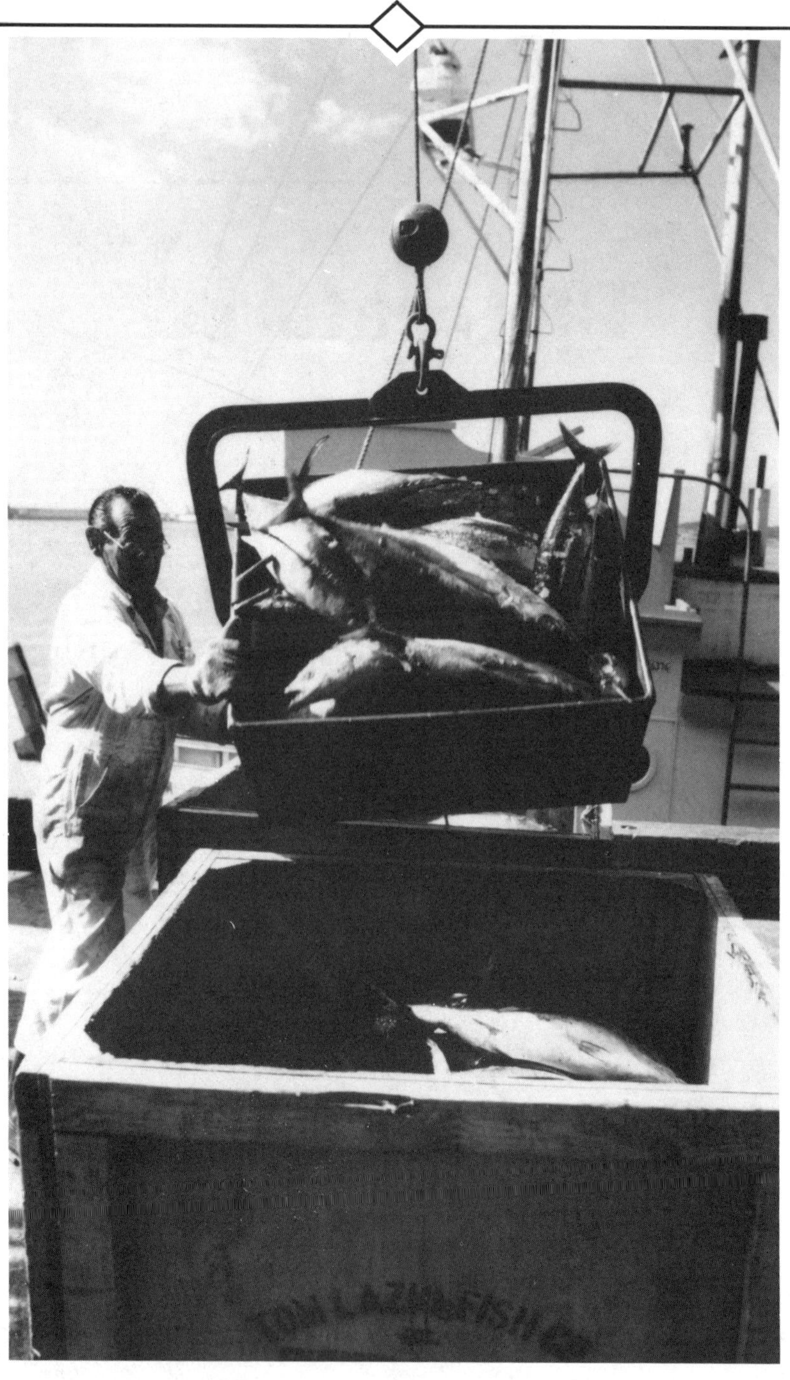

The National Marine Fisheries Service, an agency within the Department of Commerce, has the lead responsibility for managing two million square miles of ocean and all the living resources therein. *Alan Pitcairn/Grant Heilman Studios.*

The National Marine Fisheries Service

Alfred D. Chandler

> Well, if you ask me, the National Marine Fisheries Service is one of those agencies whose whole is less than the combined total of its composite parts.
>
> A Congressional Staff Member
> Sept. 25, 1987

INTRODUCTION

When the United States extended its fisheries jurisdiction from 12 miles to 200 miles offshore in 1977, it assumed authority over one-fifth of the world's most productive marine waters. The nation's new oceanic empire covers more than two million square miles[1] and includes thousands of creatures, including fish, mammals, and reptiles. Some of these species are highly migratory, moving in and out of U.S. jurisdiction; others are permanent residents.

All marine resources within U.S. jurisdiction are the common property of the nation. They are held in trust for present and future generations, partly by individual states and partly by the federal government. The management of the marine environment is a colossal task. At the federal level, Congress has given lead responsibility to the National Marine Fisheries Service (NMFS), an agency within the National Oceanic and Atmospheric Administration (NOAA) of the Department of Commerce.

Over the past few years, NMFS' performance has been heavily criticized. During 1987 confirmation hearings for Secretary of Com-

1. By way of contrast, the surface area of the U.S. is 3.62 million square miles.

merce C. William Verity, Jr., Senator John Breaux (D-LA) told the nominee that he thought the NMFS was "very weak . . . at least at the Washington, D.C., level." Similar criticism can be heard from the agency's constituency—commercial and sports fishermen, conservationists, state fish and game agencies—from its parent organization, NOAA, and even from its own staff members.

A quick inventory of the status of the nation's living marine resources under NMFS' protective umbrella shows that the dissatisfaction appears justified. Fishery resources of both commercial and recreational value are under serious pressure in all major fishing areas. Striped bass, haddock, Atlantic cod, yellowtail flounder, redfish, swordfish, scallops, Spanish mackerel, king mackerel, red snapper, Pacific Ocean perch, certain stocks of chinook and coho salmon, Greenland turbot, Atka mackerel, Alaska king crab, and various rockfish from Alaska all may be considered resources under stress. Questions also have arisen over the health of certain species of marine mammals under NMFS jurisdiction, including the northern fur seal, the Stellar sea lion, and California harbor porpoises.

Matters are not much better when one surveys the state of the nation's marine habitat. From New England to Texas, and from Southern California to the Bering Sea come hundreds of reports of heavy-metal pollution, ocean dumping, wetland destruction, environmentally harmful dredging, PCB and DDT contamination, and fish habitat destruction. In 1986 and 1987 Congress held hearings on pollution and fish contamination in California, New Jersey and Maine. The Office of Technology Assessment (OTA) published a 312-page study detailing the alarming extent of pollution in marine waters (U.S. Congress 1987a). The Coast Alliance, an *ad hoc* group of nonprofit conservation organizations, documented contamination of fish and shellfish in the waters off New England (Simon and Hague 1987).

While no one blames NMFS solely for the depressing situation, observers wonder what exactly the agency can and should do to keep matters from deteriorating further. Others wonder whether the current marine management system is inherently flawed and needs drastic restructuring to deal with today's problems.

This chapter explores the National Marine Fisheries Service: its obligations, its relationships to other agencies, and its relationship to its constituencies and to Congress. It covers the issues that NMFS confronts. It examines NMFS' internal spirit and its frustrations. Finally, it reviews the agency's budget and attempts to explain why funds are spent as they are. The chapter is divided into five parts: marine resources; legislative authorities; organization and administration; political pressure and agency direction; and budget and issues.

MARINE RESOURCES OF THE UNITED STATES

The Geography

The nation's marine jurisdiction spreads across more than two million square miles. Bordering the continental United States, jurisdiction includes all marine waters between the coastline and 200 miles offshore (see Figure 1). Off Alaska, it embraces the Beaufort Sea, the Chukchi Sea, the eastern Bering Sea, and the Gulf of Alaska. In the Pacific, it incorporates thousands of square miles around the Hawaiian Islands, as well as the waters surrounding American Samoa and other U.S. territories scattered across the central and western Pacific. In the Caribbean, it takes in the waters surrounding the Virgin Islands and Puerto Rico.

Fishery Resources

This extraordinary domain encompasses a wealth of fishery resources. Hundreds of valuable species live in it. In the Bering Sea alone, the federal government estimates the exploitable biomass of finfish and flatfish at more than 37.5 billion pounds. In addition to fish and shellfish, U.S. marine waters are home to significant populations of

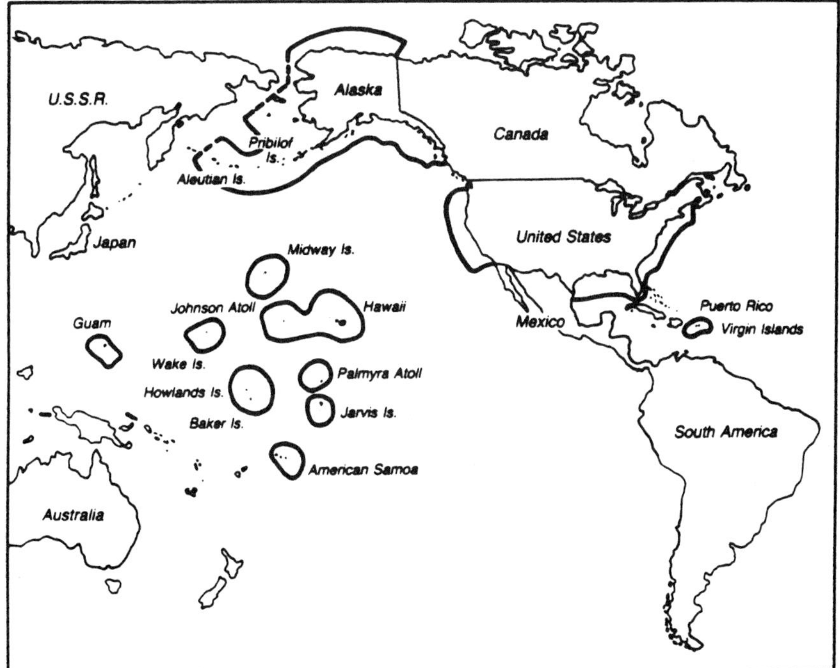

Figure 1. Fisheries of the United States, 1976. Source: U.S. Department of Commerce, NMFS, NOAA, April 1977.

marine mammals and other species, including whales, seals, sea lions, walruses, porpoises, manatees, sea otters, and sea turtles. Although not creatures of the sea, hundreds of species of sea birds and such land animals as polar bears rely almost exclusively on marine life for their survival.

The Users

From bathing to whale watching, the marine environment offers millions of Americans an extraordinary range of recreational opportunities. It is estimated that the 17 million people who annually participate in sport fishing catch about 700 million pounds of fish. Equally important, the various forms of sea life constitute an important source of food, and other marine-related products such as fish meal and oil. Marine fish and shellfish provide employment for more than 350,000 commercial fishermen and processing workers. In 1986, the total commercial fish and shellfish catch taken from U.S. waters was nearly 10.7 billion pounds, about one-third of which was consumed domestically.

Management Needs

With proper management, the nation's living marine resources can be maintained indefinitely and perhaps even increased. Yet, like the buffalo and passenger pigeon, many of these resources can be destroyed in a relatively short period if their harvest is uncontrolled or their habitat needs neglected.

The abundance and distribution of some fish and shellfish species can vary dramatically from year to year. Variations result from natural environmental fluctuations and from human actions. Predicting these shifts can be extremely difficult due to the complex interrelationships between species and their environment. Nevertheless, it is critical that such predictions be made. The failure of fisheries scientists to accurately estimate stock populations can result in the severe depletion of a species, which in turn can be economically devastating to the commercial and recreational fishing industries. The decline of a particular species also can affect the health of other species throughout the food chain.

Exacerbating the uncertainty of population estimates is the fact that the vast majority of fish and much of the shellfish harvested in the United States is available to U.S. fishermen on a "first come, first serve" basis. Although management agencies generally require some form of licensing for fishermen, these licenses are rarely limited in number. Managers, consequently, are required to control fishing indirectly by setting harvest levels or quotas, by imposing extensive seasonal and gear restrictions, or by implementing fishery area openings and closures. Management strategies combining all three approaches are common. In extreme cases, such as in the Pacific halibut fishery, seasons have been reduced to days and even hours.

Many believe that unrestricted access to the nation's fisheries has led to an economically inefficient and overcapitalized fishing industry that is prone to overfishing. Others say that stock depletion is primarily the result of an unimaginative management system so enmeshed in bureaucracy that it is incapable of responding to resource crises when they occur.

The Habitat

Harvesting fish is only one of the ways that humans affect the health of marine resources. Far more dangerous—because it is more difficult to measure—is the piecemeal degradation and destruction of fishery habitat. The range of human impacts is vast. It includes runoff from agricultural lands containing soil from eroding fields and pesticides, timber clear-cutting, water diversions, obstruction of critical fish passageways, landfill sites, coastal land development, sewage discharges, toxic contamination from industrial waste discharge, acid rain, outer-continental-shelf development, and ocean dumping.

One indicator of the impact that these environmental alterations may be having on the health of the nation's marine resources is the decreased level of seafood landings made within three miles of shore (see Figure 2). Until 1982, almost twice as many fish were caught within the nation's territorial sea (which extends from the nation's coastline to three miles) as were caught in the U.S. Exclusive Economic Zone (EEZ), which extends from 3 to 200 miles from shore. Since 1984, inshore landings have dropped 25 percent. Prolonged overfishing is certainly a factor in this decline, but it is not the only factor. Over the past half decade, few inshore fishermen, sport or commercial, have escaped tough new harvest restrictions. Yet there is little indication that depressed stocks are rebounding.

The Atlantic seaboard has been particularly affected by catch declines. Whereas the nation as a whole has seen dockside landings rise since 1982, the New England harvest has fallen by 18 percent and the Southeast harvest is down 42 percent. It is no coincidence that these two areas have suffered more cumulative coastline destruction and water pollution than any other region in the country. In the Northeast, no single habitat-altering activity can be singled out for blame; wetlands loss, sewage, and industrial waste can be cited equally as culprits. In the Southeast, on the other hand—and especially in Florida—loss of wetlands may well be the single most critical factor in catch declines (see Figure 3).

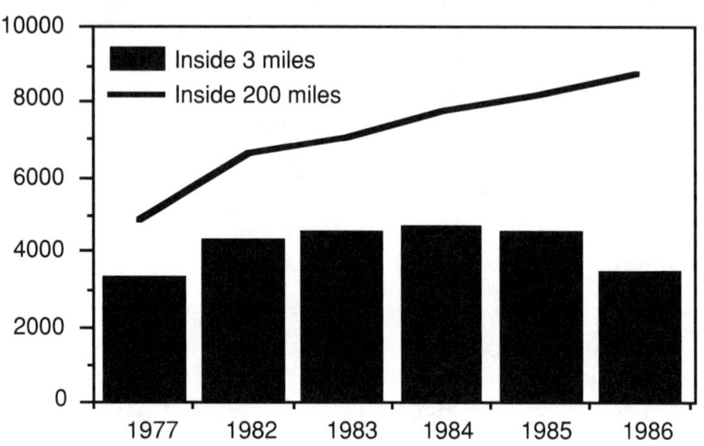

Figure 2. Source: NMFS.

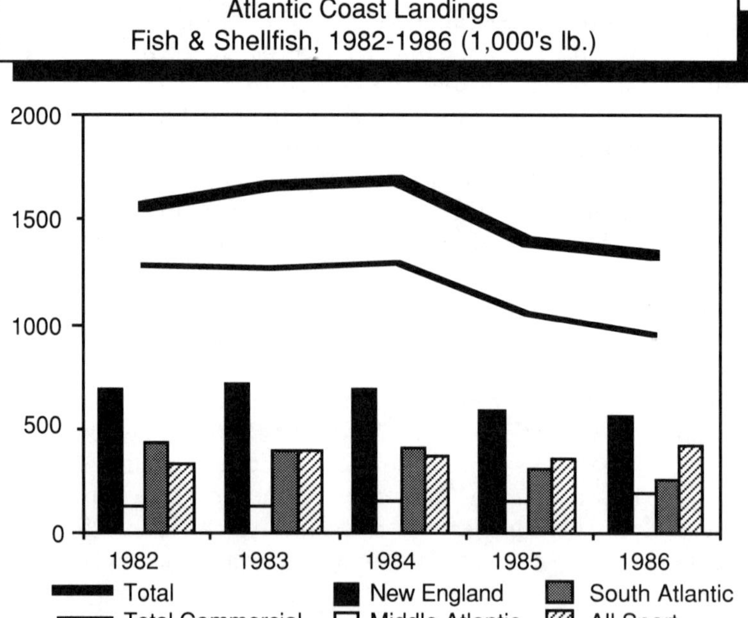

Figure 3. Source: NMFS.

Table 1
Regional Estuarine Dependency[a] as Established by the National Marine Fisheries Service.

Percentage	Region
98	Gulf of Mexico
94	Southeast Atlantic
76	Alaska
52	Pacific Northwest
41	Northeast Atlantic
18	California
1	Pacific Islands

[a] A region's fishery estuarine dependency is measured by the level of fish in that region that either spawn or spend a significant proportion of their life in coastal estuaries. For example, estuaries provide shrimp, the major commercial species in the South Atlantic and Gulf of Mexico, with critical nursery habitat.

Bays, estuaries and rivers that are replenished and cleansed by wetlands contribute significantly to the spawning and rearing of hundreds of estuarine, anadromous, and oceanic species caught by U.S. fishermen (see Table 1). In 1780, the nation had an estimated 11 million acres of coastal wetlands; today NMFS estimates that approximately half of those acres remain. Wetlands are lost through dredging, filling, or impounding. The U.S. Army Corps of Engineers is required to issue permits for any such activity affecting the navigable waters of the U.S. (see Figure 4). In recent years, about one half of all the dredge and fill permits issued in the nation were for the Southeast. Although NMFS officials review permit applications and suggest ways to dimin-

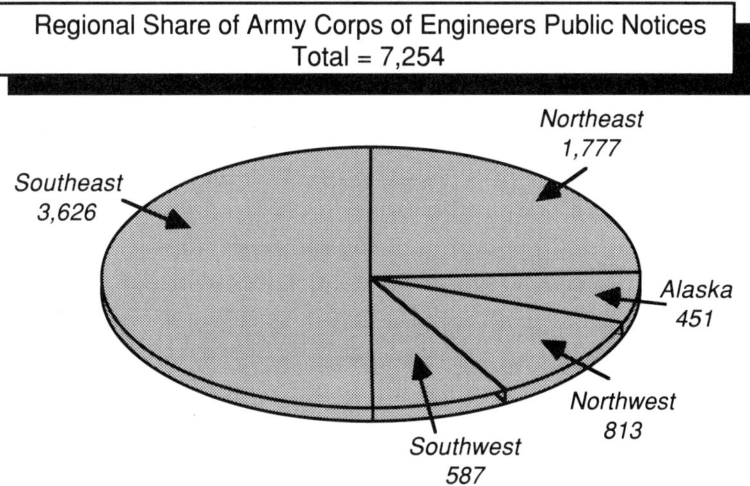

Figure 4. Source: NMFS.

ish impact on critical marine habitat, the agency reports that 40 percent of its recommendations are either rejected by the Corps or ignored by the permit holder.

Management Authorities and Responsibilities

While NMFS has been assigned primary federal responsibility for maintaining the health and productivity of the nation's marine fish and shellfish resources, it does not have sole authority. From the coastline to three miles offshore (in the nation's territorial sea), management rests with individual state governments. From 3 to 200 miles, in the EEZ, NMFS has sole authority. When a species ranges into both areas, the lead management role generally goes to the governing body with jurisdiction over the greatest part of the resource over the greatest period of time. For example, NMFS takes the lead in managing the west coast hook-and-line salmon fishery, although it is executed in both state and federal waters. On the other hand, the management lead in the east coast fishery for bluefish has been secured by states working through an interstate compact.

Although resources within the EEZ are managed by NMFS, the agency is not responsible for designing the management strategies it must enforce. Fishery management plans for species caught within the EEZ are prepared by regional councils comprised of public officials (both federal and state) and private citizens, including representatives from both the commercial and recreational fishing industries.

Regarding marine mammals and protected species, NMFS' authority is paramount whether those species reside in state, federal, or international waters. However, in its desire to mitigate the impact of marine mammal protection on fishermen, the agency has proceeded cautiously in asserting its responsibilities regarding protected marine mammal species.

NMFS' authority to protect coastal and ocean habitats vital to marine resources is extremely limited. Although federal law calls for the agency to review human activities affecting marine resources and to determine their impact, NMFS has no authority to veto a project, even when it determines that the project would severely damage a fishery. While the Environmental Protection Agency does, under certain conditions, have veto power to prevent harmful activities (such as ocean dumping), it has never exercised this authority.

Generally, whatever protection has been accorded to coastal, and to a lesser degree offshore, marine habitat has come from state programs established under the Coastal Zone Management Act (16 U.S.C.A. 1451 *et seq.*) or under state laws. In sum, NMFS lacks the necessary powers to protect habitats vital to the fishery resources it manages.

LEGISLATIVE AUTHORITIES FOR MARINE RESOURCE MANAGEMENT

Out of 103 NOAA legislative authorities listed in a 1982 compendium, 72 are either wholly or partly assigned to NMFS. Eight of these legislative authorities are reviewed in this section. They were chosen because knowledge of them is basic to understanding the service and its role as steward of the nation's marine resources. Other statutes will be discussed elsewhere in the chapter as appropriate, but some will receive no mention at all, not because they are unimportant or have had no impact, but because neither space nor time allows.[2]

The Magnuson Fishery Conservation & Management Act (16 U.S.C.A. 1801 *et seq.*)

Of all the bills relating to fisheries, none has had a greater impact on NMFS than the Magnuson Fishery Conservation and Management Act of 1976 (FCMA).[3] FCMA extended the nation's marine management jurisdiction from 3 to 200 miles offshore and mandated the accelerated development of the nation's offshore fishing industry.

With extended jurisdiction came immense responsibilities. A vast amount of new biological, economic, and sociological data were needed to carry out the act's management requirements. Additional enforcement capability was also required. Lawyers and administrators were necessary to develop new regulations and ensure that they complied with a novel set of fishery management standards spelled out in the law. The task was formidable. According to some agency observers, NMFS' attempt to successfully implement all the law's requirements was largely responsible for the agency developing a fishery management and development bias to the detriment of its other legislative responsibilities such as the protection of habitat and marine mammals.

FCMA took effect in early 1977. The act established a national program for the conservation and management of all fishery resources, except tuna, within the EEZ. The EEZ extends from the seaward boundary of the coastal states to 200 nautical miles from the shore.[4] The act was designed to promote the expansion of the U.S. fishing industry by giving it priority access to fisheries that previously had

2. For a full review of NMFS' statutory mandates see Memorandum from Kip Robinson and Beverly Carter, Office of Congressional Affairs, NOAA (1982).

3. The act was named after Senator Warren G. Magnuson of Washington, who was its leading Democratic supporter in the upper chamber. In the House, the battle for passage was led by second-term Congressman Gerry Studds, a Democrat from southeastern Massachusetts who nows chairs the Fisheries, Wildlife and the Environment Subcommittee of the Merchant Marine and Fisheries Committee.

4. Except for Texas, Florida, and Puerto Rico, the seaward boundaries of most coastal states extend to three miles offshore. The jurisdiction of these three former Spanish colonies extends to three nautical leagues, or approximately nine nautical miles.

been the almost exclusive domain of foreign fishing fleets. In particular, Congress wished to expand the U.S. share of the bottomfish catch off Alaska.

The Councils. FCMA created eight regional fishery management councils to prepare fishery management plans for their respective regions. The eight councils are: New England (with headquarters in Saugus, Massachusetts), Mid-Atlantic (Dover, Delaware), South Atlantic (Charleston, South Carolina), Caribbean (Hato Rey, Puerto Rico), Gulf (Tampa, Florida), Pacific (Portland, Oregon), North Pacific (Anchorage, Alaska), and Western Pacific (Honolulu, Hawaii).

The primary federal representative on each council is the NMFS regional director with responsibility for the council's geographic area. States are represented by their principal official with marine fishery management responsibility (usually the fish and wildlife agency director). Citizens are appointed by the Secretary of Commerce from a list of individuals nominated by state governors. According to the act, these individuals must be "knowledgeable and experienced with regard to the conservation and management, or the recreational or commercial harvest of the fishery resources of the geographical area concerned." When making appointments the Secretary of Commerce is urged to "ensure a fair apportionment, on a rotating or other basis, of the active participants (or their representatives) involved in the fisheries under council jurisdiction." Before nominating candidates, a governor must consult with commercial and recreational fishing interests regarding his nominees' qualifications (16 U.S.C.A. 1852a).

Each council is advised by a scientific and statistical committee consisting of fishery scientists (generally marine biologists, although economists and sociologists are eligible), and an advisory panel made up of individuals informed about each fishery under a council's jurisdiction. To manage council activities, FCMA authorizes council members to appoint an executive director and staff. NMFS provides scientific, legal, and administrative support to each council.

The principal mission of the councils is to prepare fishery management plans for their regions. The plans must be developed in accordance with seven national standards.

1. Conservation and management measures shall prevent overfishing while achieving, on a continuing basis, the optimum yield from each fishery.
2. Conservation and management measures shall be based upon the best scientific information available.
3. To the extent practicable, an individual stock of fish shall be managed as a unit throughout its range, and interrelated stocks of fish shall be managed as a unit or in close coordination.

4. Conservation and management measures shall not discriminate between residents of different states. If it becomes necessary to allocate or assign fishing privileges among the various United States fishermen, such allocation shall be a) fair and equitable to all such fishermen; b) reasonably calculated to promote conservation; and c) carried out in such a manner that no particular individual, corporation, or other entity acquires an excessive share of such privileges.
5. Conservation and management measures shall, where practicable, promote efficiency in the utilization of fishery resources; except that no such measures shall have economic allocation as its sole purpose.
6. Conservation and management measures shall take into account and allow for variations among, and contingencies in, fisheries, fishery resources, and catches.
7. Conservation and management measures shall, where practicable, minimize costs and avoid unnecessary duplication.

Optimum Yield. In devising a management plan for a fishery, a council must first determine that fishery's maximum sustainable yield (MSY). MSY is an estimate of the largest amount of fish (usually by weight) that can be annually harvested from a given stock or population under current known environmental conditions. It is a largely theoretical number based on biological and/or catch data. To establish a stock's MSY, scientists need information on its abundance over an extended period. This allows them to calculate an average that takes periods of exceptionally high and low populations into account. MSYs are usually presented as a range of values (for example, 14,000 to 18,000 tons) around a point estimate (for example, 16,000 tons). The calculations used to determine MSY vary in keeping with the data available. For long-standing fisheries with abundant information (such as Atlantic cod), a variety of methodologies exist to compute MSY. Conversely, minor fisheries with minimal data (such as Bering Sea squid) may simply have an MSY equal to the highest recorded catch.

Using the estimate for MSY, councils are required to determine an optimum yield (OY) for each fishery. OY is equal to that level of harvest that provides the greatest overall benefit to the nation. Councils set optimum yields in two different ways. They can define it as a numerical cap (number of fish which may be harvested annually),[5] in

5. In its bottomfish management plan for the Bering Sea and Aleutian Islands, the North Pacific Fishery Management Council has set the oy as a range from 1.4 to 2.0 million metric tons. Within that oy, it establishes separate catch levels (total allowable catch) for pollock, cod, yellowfin sole, Greenland turbot, arrowtooth flounder, other flatfish, sablefish, Pacific Ocean perch, other rockfish, Atka mackerel, squid, and other species.

a fishery under a management plan, or they can set it at whatever level is eventually caught under the established management measures required by a plan.[6] In setting an optimum yield, councils must consider both food production and recreational fishery benefits, but can favor neither.

Since OY can be based on social, and economic, as well as biological conditions, it has a great deal of inherent flexibility. It can equal the entire MSY or a small portion of it. Under some circumstances, it can even be greater than MSY. This flexibility gives council members extraordinary power in establishing the type of fishery that they feel is best for the nation. For example, in Alaska, the North Pacific Fishery Management Council ended a Japanese tanner crab fishery by setting the OY equal to the maximum amount of fish that the domestic fleet could catch and process, although this amount was less than the amount of crab that biologists estimated could be caught without adversely affecting the stock.

Councils must frequently allocate annual OY among competing fishing groups. Many consider this to be the councils' single most difficult chore, because by definition the OY must be fairly distributed among all people affected by the fishery. "All people" can include commercial fishermen (domestic and foreign), sport fishermen, processors, distributors, consumers, foreign governments, and a host of manufacturing and service industries. Since these groups often have conflicting views about how the resource can best be used, council members must regularly make decisions based as much on common sense and instinct as on biological data and professional knowledge. NMFS provides guidelines to help members in these decisions (50 CFR 602/603 [1986]). These guidelines are currently under revision.

Fishery Management Plans. Fishery management plans govern both foreign and domestic fishing. Each plan must contain 1) a description of the fishery; 2) an assessment of the present and future conditions of the fishery; 3) a determination of OY; 4) a determination of the portion of the optimum yield that U.S. fishermen expect to harvest and U.S. processors plan to process; 5) a determination of the portion of OY that can be made available to foreign fishermen; and 6) an assessment of the extent to which U.S. processors will utilize the U.S. harvest. Other provisions that may be written into a management plan at a council's discretion include requirements for domestic permits and fees, data collection programs, designation of fishing zones and periods, limits on size of catch and fishing gear used, limits on the number of fishermen

6. In its lobster plan, the New England Fishery Management Council has set OY as equal to what fishermen catch. Fishermen, however, must comply with a host of gear and size restrictions designed to ensure that enough lobsters survive to sustain the population.

Table 2
Implemented Management Plans.

Plan	Council	Regulation
Alaska High Seas Salmon	North Pacific	50 CFR Part 674
Alaska King Crab	North Pacific	50 CFR Part 676
Alaska Tanner Crab	North Pacific	50 CFR Part 671
American Lobster	New England	50 CFR Part 649
Atlantic Billfish and Sharks	Secretary	50 CFR Part 611
Atlantic Sea Scallops	New England	50 CFR Part 650
Atlantic Squid, Mackerel and Butterfish	Mid-Atlantic	50 CFR Part 655
Atlantic Surf Clam and Ocean Quahog	Mid-Atlantic	50 CFR Part 652
Bering Sea Groundfish	North Pacific	50 CFR Part 675
Bering Sea Herrings	Secretary	50 CFR Part 611
Bering Sea Snails	Secretary	50 CRF Part 611
Caribbean Shallow Water Reef Fish	Caribbean	50 CFR Part 669
Caribbean Spiny Lobster	Caribbean	50 CFR Part 645
Gulf of Alaska Groundfish	North Pacific	50 CFR Part 672
Gulf of Mexico Reef Fish	Gulf of Mexico	50 CFR Part 641
Gulf of Mexico Shrimp	Gulf of Mexico	50 CFR Part 658
Gulf of Mexico Stone Crab	Gulf of Mexico	50 CFR Part 654
Coastal Migratory Pelagics	Gulf and South Atlantic	50 CFR Part 642
Gulf and South Atlantic Corals	Gulf and South Atlantic	50 CFR Part 638
Gulf and South Atlantic Spiny Lobster	Gulf and South Atlantic	50 CFR Part 640
Northeast Multispecies	New England	50 CFR Part 651
Northwest Atlantic Hake Fisheries	Secretary	50 CFR Part 611
Northwest Atlantic Foreign Trawl Fisheries	Secretary	50 CFR Part 611
Pacific Billfish and Oceanic Sharks	Secretary	50 CFR Part 611
Pacific Groundfish	Pacific	50 CFR Part 663
Northern Anchovy	Pacific	50 CFR Part 662
Western Pacific Seamont Groundfish	Western Pacific	50 CFR Part 683
Snapper-Grouper	South Atlantic	50 CFR Part 646
Swordfish	South Atlantic	50 CFR Part 630
Washington, Oregon, and California Salmon	Pacific	50 CFR Part 661
Western Pacific Precious Corals	Western Pacific	50 CFR Part 680
Western Pacific Spiny Lobster	Western Pacific	50 CFR Part 681

Source: National Fisheries Institute 1987.

permitted in each fishery, and assessments of the plan's impact on naturally spawning stocks of anadromous fish. At the end of 1987, 32 plans had been implemented (see Table 2).

After obtaining public comment and advice, the regional council submits its management plan to NMFS for approval. NMFS has

110 days to allow for additional public comment and to review the plan on behalf of the Secretary of Commerce. NMFS ensures that the plan is consistent with the national standards, the provisions of FCMA, and other applicable law. Moreover, if a management plan is needed but has not been prepared by the appropriate council, NMFS may prepare and implement one (such plans are referred to as Secretariat).

Once a fishery management plan is approved, the Secretary of Commerce issues regulations implementing it. The secretary also may promulgate regulations to address emergencies involving any fishery either on his own initiative or when recommended by a unanimous council vote. Emergency regulations remain in effect for 90 days and can be extended one additional 90-day period. All plan regulations are enforced with the help of the Coast Guard and state officials. Civil and criminal penalties for violations of a plan include forfeiture of vessels, gear, and catch.

State Authority. A state's authority to regulate fishing in its territorial Sea was unchanged by FCMA. However, if state action or inaction adversely affects the implementation of an approved federal fishery management plan, the Secretary of Commerce may preempt state authority and regulate that portion of the fishery within state waters pursuant to the management plan. FCMA also allows foreign vessels into a state's internal waters[7] to buy and process fish caught by U.S. fishermen operating in those waters, so long as the vessel's country of origin has signed a governing international fishery agreement (see below) or is covered by some other international fishing agreement, and the governor determines that fish processors within that state will not buy all the fish which state management authorities designate as available for harvest.

Foreign Agreements. FCMA allows foreign vessels to fish in the EEZ only for that portion of the OY for each fishery that will not be harvested by U.S. vessels. Foreign fishing for this surplus fish is allowed only if: 1) the nation has an existing international fishing agreement or has signed a governing international fishery agreement (known as a GIFA) with the U.S.; 2) the nation extends reciprocal fishing privileges to U.S. vessels; and 3) foreign vessels have valid permits issued by the Secretary of Commerce. By signing a GIFA, foreign nations recognize the sovereign rights of the U.S. in the EEZ

7. A state's internal waters differ from its territorial sea. Internal waters are those marine waters *inside* a state's territorial sea. Simplified, internal waters are demarcated by drawing a line from one point of land to another—called the baseline (for example, the waters inside Alaska's southeastern panhandle are its "internal waters" not its "territorial sea"). Foreign vessels involved in commercial fishing operations cannot operate in a state's territorial sea under any circumstances.

and agree that its citizens will obey all applicable rules and regulations (see Table 3).

The surplus fish available to foreign vessels is called the total allowable level of foreign fishing (TALFF) and it is determined by the appropriate council. The Secretary of State, in cooperation with the Secretary of Commerce, determines how TALFF is divided among eligible nations. Under a *quid pro quo* policy known as "fish and chips;" the United States gives a foreign government a portion of its surplus resources – "the fish" – based on how much it values what that country offers the U.S. fishing industry in return – "the chips." In making its allocations, the State Department considers a nation's 1) tariff and other import barriers to fishery products, 2) level of exports to

Table 3
Governing International Fisheries Agreements

Country	Date signed	Date entered into force	Expiration date
Bulgaria			
(Original)	12/17/76	2/28/77	7/01/83
(Renegotiated)	9/22/83	4/12/84	7/01/88
People's Republic of China	7/23/85	–	7/01/90
European Economic Community			
(Original)	2/15/77	6/09/77	9/30/84
(Renegotiated)	10/01/84	11/18/84	7/01/89
(now includes Spain and Portugal)			
Faroe Islands			
(Original)	9/05/79	1/18/80	7/01/84
(Renegotiated)	6/11/84	11/20/84	7/01/89
German Democratic Republic			
(Original)	10/05/76	3/04/77	7/01/83
(Renegotiated)	4/13/83	7/20/83	7/01/88
Iceland	9/21/84	11/16/84	7/01/89
Japan			
(Original)	3/18/77	11/29/77	12/31/82
(Renegotiated)	9/10/82	1/01/83	12/31/87
Republic of Korea			
(Original)	1/04/77	3/04/77	7/01/82
(Renegotiated)	7/26/82	4/28/83	7/01/87
(Renegotiated)	–	10/27/87	7/31/89
Poland			
(Original)	8/02/76	2/28/77	12/31/85
(Renegotiated)	8/01/85	1/01/86	7/01/91
Taiwan[a]			
(Original)	9/15/76	2/28/77	7/01/82
(Renegotiated)	6/07/82	7/01/82	7/01/87
U.S.S.R.			
(Extended)	11/26/76	2/28/77	12/31/88

Source: NMFS
[a] No plans for new GIFA (as of November 1987).

the United States of products made from fish caught within the U.S. EEZ, 3) contribution to the growth of the U.S. fishing industry, 4) domestic consumption needs, 5) fisheries enforcement cooperation, 6) cooperation in resolving fishing gear conflicts between its fishermen and fishermen from the U.S.,[8] 7) cooperation in transferring fishing technology to the U.S. seafood industry, 8) traditional fishing patterns within the EEZ, 9) cooperation in fisheries research, and 10) other appropriate matters. Half the total amount of fish allocated to a foreign nation is withheld at the beginning of each year and released later provided the foreign nation is complying with the fish-and-chips policy.

Also considered in determining foreign catch allocations is whether a particular country's citizens are conducting whaling operations or engaging in trade that diminishes the effectiveness of the International Whaling Commission (IWC). Any nation doing so must be certified by the Secretary of Commerce as hampering the IWC's conservation work and be penalized by the loss of at least one half of the uncaught portion of its catch allocation. While several nations have been certified (including the Soviet Union in 1985, Norway in 1986, and Japan in 1988) none have suffered serious consequences. [9]

Permits are required for each foreign vessel that will catch, process, or otherwise support fishing operations in the EEZ. Foreign fishing activity is regulated through area and season closures, gear restrictions, and catch quotas as specified in each permit. No permit is valid for more than a year. FCMA requires U.S. observers on all foreign fishing and processing vessels to monitor compliance with all U.S. regulations. Permits are also required for foreign vessels that buy U.S.-caught fish directly from U.S. fishing boats while still in the EEZ.[10] These over-the-side transfers (known as joint ventures) may only be approved if U.S. fish processors do not have the capacity to handle the fish, or if they do have the capacity do not intend to fully use it. If a joint-venture permit is approved, the amount of U.S.-

8. Gear conflicts occur when one type of fishing gear interferes with another. For example, a trawler that is towing its net on the ocean's bottom can conflict with a longline that passively sits on the bottom waiting for fish to take the bait attached to its many hooks. "Passive" fishing techniques (where the fish comes to the gear) include gill nets, set nets, longlines, and pots (or traps). "Active" techniques (where the gear goes to the fish) include trawling and seining. Conflicts generally occur when active and passive fishing techniques are employed on the same fishing grounds.

9. Norway had no allocation to lose. When certified, the USSR and Japan had already had their access to U.S. waters seriously diminished, thus severely lessening any impact the penalty might have had.

10. Much of this fish is bought by foreign fishing companies to supply the internal demands of their own country. Some, however, is processed into fillet blocks and returned to the United States, where it is reprocessed into frozen portions (used in fish sandwiches and packaged frozen food).

harvested fish received by foreign vessels is limited to the portion of the OY that will not be used by U.S. processors. Large scale joint-venture operations are conducted off Alaska for pollock, cod, yellowfin sole, and Atka mackerel, and along the Pacific Coast for Pacific whiting. Smaller operations are carried out in the Atlantic for squid, mackerel, silver hake, and river herring.

Foreign vessels fishing in the EEZ pay permit registration fees and poundage fees for fish caught. Permit registration fees cover the administrative cost of processing foreign permit applications. The poundage fee is based upon the off-the-boat value of the species caught, and varies with each fishery (see Table 4).

Foreign fishing vessels are also assessed a surcharge based on their total vessel fees; surcharge receipts are deposited into the Fishing Vessel Gear Damage Compensation Fund to refund damage incurred by U.S. fishermen from foreign fishing. Another surcharge goes into the Foreign Fishing Observer Fund to cover all costs of providing U.S. observers on foreign vessels.

Fish and Wildlife Act of 1956 (16 U.S.C.A. 742a *et seq.*)

The Fish and Wildlife Act of 1956 established a comprehensive national fish and wildlife policy. The act originally authorized the Secretary of the Interior to develop measures for "maximum sustainable production of fish"; to make economic studies and recommend measures to insure stability of the domestic fisheries; to undertake promotional and informational activities to stimulate consumption of

Table 4
Foreign Poundage ($1/Metric Ton) for Alaska Species.[a]

Species	1984	1985	1986	1987	Proposed 1988[b]
Atka mackeral	42	52	66	113	181
Cod, Pacific	66	73	102	137	220
All Flatfish	59	34	56	87	127
Pacific ocean perch	89	100	142	186	299
Other groundfish	62	39	54	101	163
Pollock	28	32	43	82	145
Sablefish (GOA)	148	159	260	379	610
Sablefish (BSA)	148	64	137	200	321
Rockfish	68	94	165	310	498
Snails	40	66	91	122	196
Squid (Pacific)	23	59	80	67	115

Source: North Pacific Management Council

[a] Any country assessed the higher fee under the two-tier fee system legislated last spring will pay about 75 percent more than the fees shown in the table.

[b] Published in the *Federal Register* on November 4, 1987; comment period ended December 4, 1987.

fishery products; and to take steps required "for the development, management, advancement, conservation, and protection of fishery resources."

The act established the U.S. Fish and Wildlife Service (FWS) within the Department of the Interior to be composed of 1) the Bureau of Commercial Fisheries responsible for commercial fisheries, whales, seals, sea lions, and related matters; and 2) the Bureau of Sport Fisheries and Wildlife responsible for migratory birds, game management, wildlife refuges, sports fisheries, certain marine mammals, and related matters. In 1970, when Congress created the National Oceanic and Atmospheric Administration and established the National Marine Fisheries Service (NMFS) as one of its divisions (the Bureau of Commercial Fisheries became NMFS), the Fish and Wildlife Act provided NMFS' basic missions.

Endangered Species Act (16 U.S.C.A. 1531 *et seq.*)

The Endangered Species Act provides protection for endangered and threatened species of fish, animals, and plants, and their critical habitats. The act prohibits the taking, importing, exporting, and transporting in interstate commerce of any endangered or threatened species, with limited exceptions. Implementation of the law is shared by NMFS and FWS. NMFS is responsible for marine species, FWS for freshwater and terrestrial species. (See the 1986 *Audubon Wildlife Report* for a detailed description of the Endangered Species Program.)

The act requires the Secretary of the Interior to publish, and when necessary revise, a list of endangered or threatened species. The act sets procedures for NMFS and FWS to follow in the listing process, and requires that they develop and implement recovery plans for species listed as threatened or endangered.

Section 7 of the Endangered Species Act prohibits any federal agency from taking any action that would threaten the existence of a listed species or its needed habitat. The law requires federal agencies to consult with either NMFS or FWS, depending on the species affected, to determine the impact of any proposed action on listed species. A proposed project may be canceled or redesigned to mitigate the harm it causes. NMFS conducts several hundred consultations each year with federal development agencies that sponsor activities affecting the habitat of marine resources.

Marine Mammal Protection Act of 1972 (16 U.S.C.A. 1361 *et seq.*)

The Marine Mammal Protection Act (MMPA) establishes a moratorium (with certain exceptions) on the taking of marine mammals and a ban on the importation of marine mammal products. The FCMA amended the act to extend its requirements throughout the EEZ.

Responsibility for implementing the law falls principally to NMFS; FWS has authority over a few marine species such as sea otters and polar bears. NMFS issues permits for the incidental taking of marine mammals caught during commercial fishing operations.

Fish and Wildlife Coordination Act (16 U.S.C.A. 661 *et seq.*)

The Fish and Wildlife Coordination Act authorizes FWS and NMFS to assist federal, state, and other agencies in developing, protecting, rearing, and stocking fish and wildlife on federal lands. The act requires interagency consultation to assure that fish and wildlife are given equal consideration when a federal or federally authorized project is proposed that controls, modifies, or develops the nation's waters. NMFS reviews a wide variety of projects under the act, including the Army Corps of Engineers dredge-and-fill permits for U.S. waterways, ocean dumping permits, hydroelectric power project proposals, federal water projects, and outer-continental-shelf mineral leasing activities.

National Environmental Policy Act (42 U.S.C.A. 4331 *et seq.*)

The National Environmental Policy Act requires that any federal agency proposing an action that significantly affects the human environment must prepare an environmental impact statement. The act's basic purpose is to ensure that federal officials give appropriate consideration to environmental values in policy formulation and administrative actions, and that the public is provided adequate opportunity to review and comment on all proposed action. NMFS staff reviews appropriate environmental impact statements and provides recommendations to mitigate any expected impact on living marine resources and their habitat.

Marine Protection, Research and Sanctuaries Act of 1972 (33 U.S.C.A. 1401 *et seq.* and 16 U.S.C.A. 1431 *et seq.*)

The Marine Protection, Research and Sanctuaries Act establishes a program administered by the Environmental Protection Agency to regulate dumping of materials into ocean waters. Under Section 103, the Corps of Engineers evaluates proposed projects that involve the transportation and dumping of dredged material in most coastal waters and in the open ocean. NMFS, with assistance from FWS, provides environmental advice to the Corps during the review of Section 103 activities. The Environmental Protection Agency can prohibit the use of any disposal site on environmental grounds, but it has never exercised this power (U.S. Congress 1987a).

Clean Water Act of 1977 (33 U.S.C.A. 1251 *et seq.*)

The Clean Water Act sets standards and requires permits for the discharge of pollutants into the nation's waters. Also, Section 404 of the law requires the U.S. Army Corps of Engineers to issue permits for the disposal of dredged or fill material in most of the nation's wetlands and water bodies, including coastal waters within state territorial seas. The permit applicant or project sponsor is responsible for finding appropriate disposal sites. The Corps evaluates permits to determine if they should be issued. The Environmental Protection Agency may veto the use of any proposed site, and other agencies, including NMFS, provide comments and recommendations on the permit request.

ORGANIZATION AND ADMINISTRATION

To fulfill its legislative responsibilities, NMFS in 1987 had the equivalent of 2,310 full-time personnel and a budget of about $170 million (see Figures 5a, 5b, 6a, and 6b). Its staff of scientists and administrators are scattered in offices and laboratories located in more than 45 cities in 20 states and the District of Columbia. Personnel are attached either to the central office, a regional office, or a fisheries center. The central office, now located in Washington, D.C., is scheduled to move to Silver Spring, Maryland.

Regional Offices

NMFS has five regional offices: Alaska, Northwest, Southwest, Southeast, and Northeast. The Northeast Region (headquartered in Glou-

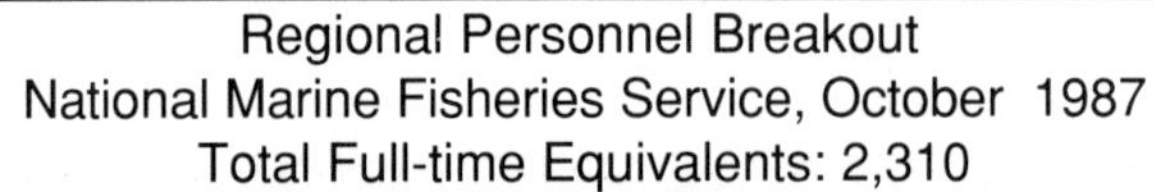

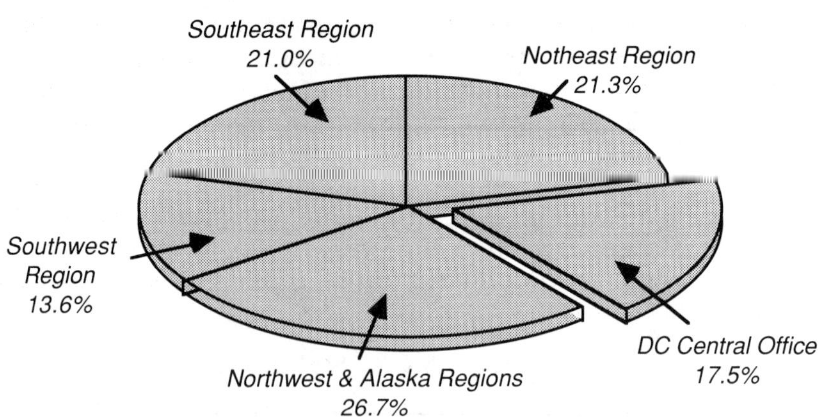

Figure 5a. Source: NMFS.

Regional Funding Breakout
National Marine Fisheries Service, October 1987
Total = $166.8 Million

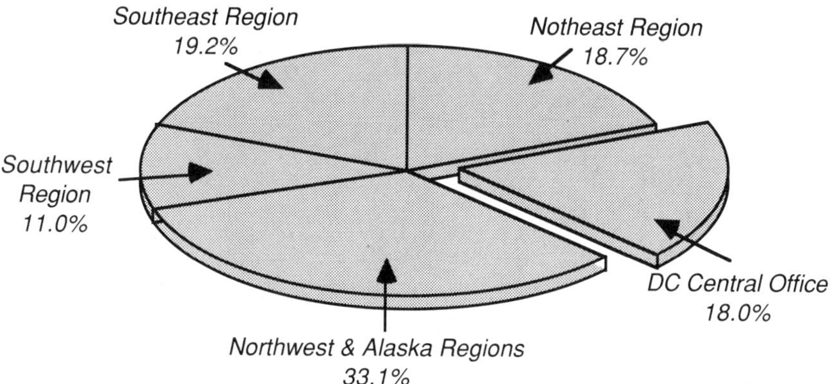

Figure 5b. Source: NMFS.

cester, Massachusetts) includes the Atlantic states from Maine to Virginia, as well as the Great Lakes states. The regional office supervises activities in many important fishing grounds, principally the Georges Bank and the Gulf of Maine. Some of the region's most valuable resources are American lobster, cod, haddock, flounder, and

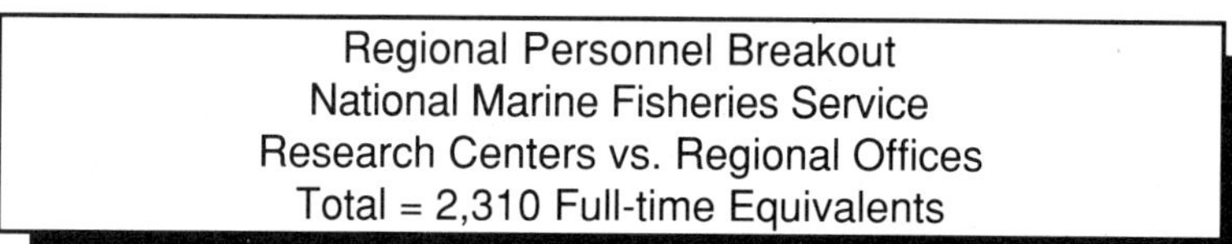

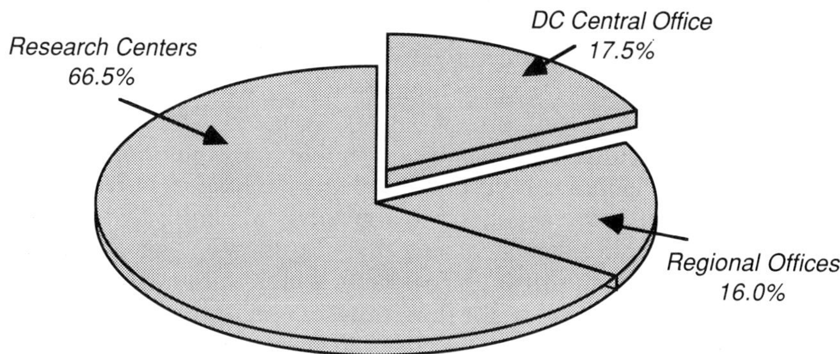

Figure 6a. Source: NMFS.

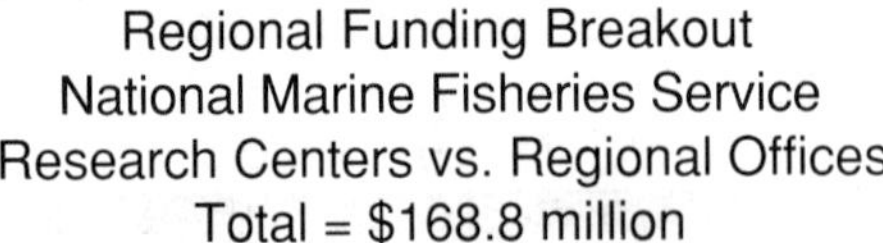

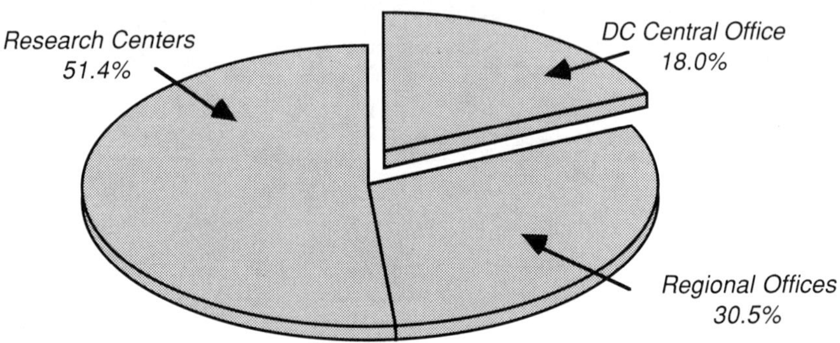

Figure 6b. Source: NMFS.

scallops. All of these resources have been subject to commercial fishing for more than three centuries. Since the passage of FCMA, the Northeast office has frequently been at odds with commercial fishermen over the status of the area's marine resources and over the best way to manage them. The region is also characterized by some of the nation's most heavily polluted waters and by conflicts between sport and commercial fishermen over such species as bluefin tuna and swordfish.

The Southeast Region (St. Petersburg, Florida) extends from North Carolina to Texas and along the Mississippi, Missouri, and Arkansas rivers. For years the region's principal task has been to manage the shrimp fishery. With an annual value of $448.8 million (1982–1986 average), shrimp provide about 18.5 percent of the value of the nation's entire commercial catch; only the salmon fishery in the Pacific Northwest and Alaska has a comparable worth. The Southeast Region also includes what was for years the nation's largest volume fishery: menhaden. In 1986, 2.4 billion pounds of menhaden (which is reduced into meal and oil for export to Europe and Africa) were landed. In recent years, the region has been preoccupied with long-term feuds between sport and commercial fishermen, especially in Florida and Texas. However, its attention has also been drawn to new struggles such as preserving rapidly diminishing coastal wetlands and sea turtles.

The Southwest Region (Los Angeles, California) primarily supervises California fisheries, but also has management responsibility for fisheries in Hawaii and the Pacific Trust Territories. Until recently, the Southwest office focused principally on tuna. However, changes in world trading patterns have almost eliminated the tuna processing business in southern California. In 1986, tuna landings were barely 40 million pounds, with a value of only $15.5 million. The U.S. tuna fleet now lands most of its catch in Puerto Rico, American Samoa, and a variety of foreign ports in the western Pacific where labor costs are lower and tax incentives greater.

Because of the decline in tuna landings, the region has turned its attention to other species, such as salmon, rockfish, bottomfish, anchovies, and mackerel (southern California). The office has become increasingly involved in protected species issues, particularly the impact of gill nets on sea birds, harbor porpoises, and some species of whales. Assisting the development of local fisheries in the Pacific Trust Territories has also been given a higher priority.

The Northwest Region (Seattle, Washington) takes in the Columbia River Basin, Puget Sound, and the Oregon and Washington coasts. Its attention has always been focused on salmon. Although the region's salmon resources (particularly the runs on the Columbia River and its tributaries) have been drastically reduced by dams and other human developments, the harvest pressure placed on the remaining stocks by U.S. and Canadian fishermen (sport, commercial, and Native American) still demands a great deal of the region's attention.

The Northwest office has also has become involved with marine mammal issues, particularly those related to mammal predation on wild salmon stocks. Finally, since the Pacific Northwest acts as the home port for much of the Alaska fishing fleet, the region has been a major conduit for federal grants to spur development of vessels and fleets capable of entering those Alaska fisheries that have been long dominated by foreigners.

The Alaska Region (Juneau, Alaska) covers many of the world's most valuable fisheries. The state of Alaska regulates the world's largest remaining fishery for wild salmon, and the NMFS regional office is responsible for managing two of the world's most productive bottomfish grounds: the Bering Sea and the Gulf of Alaska. In 1988, U.S. fishermen are expected to harvest almost five billion pounds of bottomfish—including pollock, Pacific cod, yellowfin sole, Greenland turbot, Atka mackerel, rock sole, arrowtooth flounder, sablefish, and halibut—from these waters. This equals roughly 57 percent of all fish and shellfish caught globally by U.S. fishermen during 1986, and approximately 83 percent of domestic landings. In addition to bottomfish, Alaska waters (primarily the eastern Bering Sea and the Gulf of Alaska) support major crab and herring fisheries for which NMFS has oversight.

No other NMFS regional office has greater marine mammal responsibilities. Alaskan waters support major populations of seals, sea lions, and whales—all of which interact in one way or another with the region's fishermen. The only two federally sanctioned marine mammal hunts also occur in Alaska. Northern fur seals are harvested by the Aleuts of the Pribilof Islands, and bowhead whales by the Eskimos.

Fisheries Centers

NMFS has four fisheries centers: the Northwest and Alaska Fisheries Center in Seattle, Washington; the Southwest Fisheries Center located in La Jolla, California; the Southeast Fisheries Center in Miami, Florida; and the Northeast Center in Woods Hole, Massachusetts (see Appendix F). Each center directs several satellite labs, each generally with a specialized function (see Table 5). The centers perform all of NMFS' research work on fisheries, protected species, habitat, marine ecology, and food science. They also conduct gear development research. Center scientists work closely with other NOAA scientists, particularly those in the National Ocean Service, as well as scientists from the academic community and the private sector.

Organizational Problems

NMFS has gone through five major reorganizations since it was created in 1970, most recently in 1983 and 1987. The recurring problem has been establishing lines of authority between regional offices, fisheries centers, and the central office. The issue of debate has been whether NOAA should structure NMFS as:

- five semi-autonomous regional units, each charged with establishing distinct research and management priorities, and all loosely overseen by a central administrative support staff; or
- a centralized agency imposing a national research and management program through regional offices, which would be allowed some implementation flexibility to account for regional idiosyncrasies; or
- an agency run by a team of senior central administrators capable of balancing central office and regional strengths.

Table 5
NMFS Laboratories.

Northeast	Southeast	Southwest	Northwest and Alaska
Narragansett, R.I.	Pascagoula, MS	Honolulu, HI	Manchester, WA
Millford, CT	Panama City, FL	Tiburon, CA	Auke Bay, AK
Sandy Hook, N.J.	Galveston, TX	Monterey, CA	Kodiak, AK
Oxford, MD	Charleston, S.C.		
Gloucester, MA	Beaufort, N.C.		
Washington, D.C.	Bay St. Louis, MI		

By selecting the first option, NOAA would place responsibility for NMFS programs in the hands of regional administrators, specifically regional directors and center directors. By choosing the second option, NOAA would give that task to administrators in the NMFS central office or in NOAA itself. Each option has its advantages.

The autonomy option allows NMFS to make full use of the local acumen developed by regional administrators. If they are doing their job properly, regional directors will be acutely sensitive to the needs of fishermen and other user groups in their geographic area. Moreover, regional directors sit on local regional fishery management councils and are thus intimately involved with the research needs and management requirements of most of their region's fisheries. They are likely to be equally familiar with local politics and state fishery management strategies. The need to balance local, state, regional, and federal demands makes the regional director particularly well placed to implement programs that must allow for compromise.

Much the same can be said about the directors of fisheries centers. What differentiates center directors from regional directors is that as scientists, center directors can better isolate themselves from the political pressures to which regional directors are subject. Center directors can place their full attention on 1) determining the biological status of the resources within their jurisdiction, and 2) recommending catch levels that will not overtax the fishery resource. Simply put, fish are the constituency of center directors, whereas the regional director must also answer to fishermen.

By pursuing the centralization option, NOAA could assemble information and experience from every region and cull from it lessons to guide the establishment of effective national strategies for protecting the nation's marine resources. It could ensure both consistency of implementation and ensure that actions in one region not set precedents that restrict opportunities in other regions. Moreover, the central office has much greater access to marine and fishery-related information and data collected by other federal and international agencies.

The third option, a balanced management scheme, offers the best of both worlds. In it, power resides in an elite corps of senior administrators based either in NMFS itself, or in NMFS and NOAA. Under this option the key person is the NOAA Assistant Administrator for Fisheries, who directs NMFS. The assistant administrator, a political appointee, is responsible for ensuring that the agency implements the general policies established by the President. He or she must also be cognizant of the main themes inherent in all management and scientific issues confronting the agency, and thus should be able to give the agency its overall direction and focus.

However, to achieve its goals, the leadership must successfully convince agency personnel that it is as sensitive to the necessities of compromise as to the needs for consistency. Put another way, agency leaders must be simultaneously practical and principled. Only by such a feat can they effectively use headquarters and field personnel. Such a balancing act demands tremendous management skills and finely tuned instincts, good communications, and excellent cooperation; without these skills, a balanced agency can easily be derailed.

The Burden of Diversity

While all natural resource agencies grapple with organizational issues, NMFS has a further complicating element: the burden of diversity. There are hundreds of recreationally and commercially valuable species of fish and shellfish, and many more hundreds with potential value. With the large number of species comes the problem of variation. Most species are characterized by unique biological traits that affect management strategies. For example, managers generally do not allow fishermen to target immature fish for fear of destroying a stock's reproductive capacity. But the life spans of different species vary tremendously; hence, detailed knowledge of them is mandatory in order to properly regulate a fishery in which more than one species may be caught.

"It seems like nothing in this area can be applied universally," says one veteran NMFS planner. "What the scientists learn about salmon can't be applied to shrimp, and what they learn about shrimp can't be applied to cod."

Exacerbating matters is a similar diversity among fishermen. Little uniformity exists in why, how, or when fishermen catch fish, or what they hope to do with their catch. Fishing methods are numerous, including hand trolling with hook and line, power trolling with hook and line; jigging with hook and line; longlining; dredging; purse seining; lampara netting; reef netting; set netting; drift gillnetting; bottom gill netting; pair trawling; midwater trawling; bottom trawling; pot or trap fishing; and harpooning. Moreover, within each of these methods are countless regional and local variations in techniques and equipment.

Not only do fishermen's methods vary, but so do their relationships to various fisheries. As with farming, commercial fishing efforts range from part-time and seasonal operations through full-time, year-round family-owned-and-operated companies, to large integrated multinational food corporations. Unlike farming, however, fishing also encompasses a large recreational component including weekend anglers, professional guides, and multimillion dollar charter boat operations. Complicating matters still further is that many recreational fishermen sell their catch (sometimes legally, sometimes not). Subsistence fishermen are also a component of the fishing population.

These fishermen depend on local fisheries for their basic survival; they play a particularly strong role in Alaska.

The diversity of fish species, fishing techniques, and fishermen presents fishery managers with an almost infinite variety of situations, each calling for a unique combination of biological, economic, and sociological information. In other words, says a NMFS official, "what works in New England might create havoc in Alaska." So, he asks, "where are the areas of commonality which can be transferred between regions?" In fact, many would contend such areas do not exist and that any search for commonalties to be applied in management will result only in frustration. Indeed, a number of observers argue that the propensity of federal managers to seek answers transferable among regions (and fisheries) has resulted in the nation's inability to effectively manage its marine resources.

The Gordon Solution

Under a 1983 reorganization, the agency's former director, William G. Gordon, tried to resolve the debate over organizational structure by creating a balanced management structure. His strategy was to create a collegial approach to policy development and implementation with the NMFS central office serving as the final arbiter. To accomplish this, he first reduced the span of control of his own office, giving day-to-day operational decisions to two newly created deputy assistant administrators, one for management and one for science.

The management chief was given responsibility for all management and conservation activities, including authority over the regional offices and their directors. The science chief was given oversight over all science and technology, including authority over the fisheries centers and their directors. A third deputy assistant administrator was appointed to evaluate all programs (and to be a general utility person). The three deputies and Gordon were to give NMFS its leadership and direction.

According to many NMFS administrators, the Gordon plan successfully reduced the assistant administrator's span of control, particularly at the headquarters level. However, it also placed a high priority on effective coordination, communication, and cooperation. While Gordon's three deputies were all skilled in their fields and ready to offer leadership, they were unsuccessful in fulfilling their new day-to-day responsibilities while simultaneously coordinating or communicating their actions with one another. At times this caused NMFS to charge off in too many directions; at other times, too few. According to sources familiar with NMFS, the arrangement frequently led to miscommunication and misunderstandings. In the field, commercial and recreational fishermen frequently received one set of signals from the regional director and another set from the center director. In the end, instead of clarifying lines of communications, the structure established by Gordon muddied them.

The Evans Solution

At an industry-sponsored conference in mid-December 1986, Gordon's replacement, Dr. William E. Evans, announced he would make the agency more responsive to its "constituents" by removing Gordon's "bureaucratic layers" (that is, Gordon's management and science deputies). Evans said his reorganization would be characterized by "streamlining" (see Figure 7). In effect, the Evans reorganization opted for regional authority, while simultaneously attempting to ensure that regions followed general guidelines established by senior NOAA administrators.

Under the Evans' plan, regional directors have access to the assistant administrator's office through the deputy assistant administrator. Center directors no longer answer directly to Washington, but report through the regional director.[11] Administrative authority for the central office was given to a new executive director, and a senior scientist was slated for appointment to oversee the direction and content of the agency's research and to coordinate with other senior NOAA scientists.

By placing fisheries centers under the authority of the regional director, Evans says he intends to better serve NMFS constituents by "integrating" regional activities. Perhaps more important, this move could also afford center directors increased protection from local political pressures. Under the Gordon structure, center directors became the senior regional officials accountable for NMFS research. If a regional fishing lobbying group was upset by an agency research decision, it brought its political weight to bear against the center director. Under the Evans reorganization, this burden will be borne by the regional director. Conversely, if Evans' reorganization gives regional directors the final say in establishing research priorities, it could result in NMFS placing an increasingly heavy emphasis on short-term investigative work needed to resolve immediate crises rather than the long-term basic research that many scientists believe is essential if NMFS is ever to implement effective multispecies fishery management.

The Central Office versus the Regional Offices

While the chain of command at the NMFS regional level is becoming clear, it remains less certain what the final impact of the Evans

11. One side effect from this restructuring may be the eventual division of the Northwest and Alaska Fisheries Center into separate regional centers in Seattle and Auke Bay, Alaska.

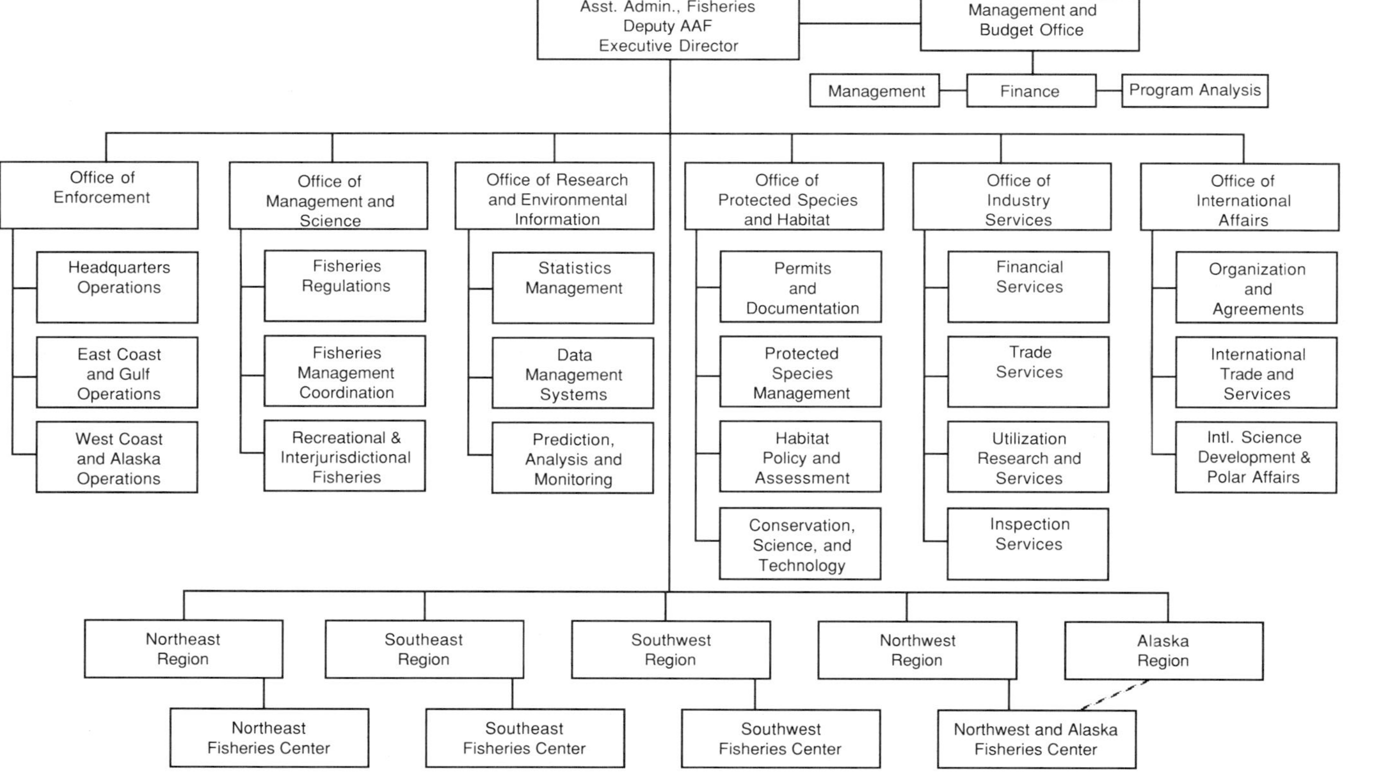

Figure 7. Source: NMFS.

reorganization will be on the struggle for influence between regions and the central office. In the new structure, regional directors are on a par with "office" directors, all of whom are based at NMFS' Washington, D.C., headquarters. Office directors oversee the implementation of NMFS policies and procedures as established by the President through the Secretary of Commerce, the Administrator of NOAA, and his Assistant Administrator for Fisheries. Each office director has a bailiwick composed of related functions. (For example, the Office of Protected Species and Habitat includes separate divisions of Permits and Documentation, Protected Species Management, Habitat Policy and Assessment, and Conservation, Science, and Technology; divisions are divided into branches.) Each is also responsible for ensuring that regional offices properly implement national policy.

In the past, according to both NMFS staff and agency observers, the central office's exercise of its oversight authority has led to conflicts with regional offices. Nowhere has this been more evident than in the review of fishery management plans developed by regional councils under Fishery Conservation and Management Act (FCMA). "The difficulty," according to a veteran industry observer, "is that the central office must deal with consistency, principles, and precedents, while the field staff is trying to solve problems and manage fish. While the two aren't incompatible, they often clash." Another observer points to the problem as one of "sensitivity." "The central office," he says, "is frequently unattuned to the political pressures under which regional councils devise their plans. Regional offices, on the other hand, are rarely attuned to the realities of administrative procedures which are an inescapable part of the implementing process in Washington."

In an attempt to resolve these tensions, a NOAA-appointed committee recommended that the plan review process be made both shorter and tighter (King Mackerel Committee 1987). The committee further recommended that:

> the Regional Office, as the primary contact with the Councils should be fully accountable for processing and submitting Council and agency documents for approval . . . Even minor or technical changes made in Washington should require consultation with the Region.

While it is becoming clear that NOAA wants NMFS regional offices to take the lead in deciding how national policy should be implemented, it is equally evident that regions have not been given increased authority to create policy. In fact, the opposite seems to be happening. More than ever, policy decisions are being made by the assistant administrator and his superiors at NOAA. Indeed, since the 1985 appointment of Anthony J. Calio as its administrator, NOAA has become increasingly involved in NMFS' day-to-day management decisions and responsibilities. This trend shows no signs of changing despite Calio's resignation in September 1987.

Central Office Reorganization

Evans has also reorganized the NMFS central office. Three of the existing offices—Enforcement, Industry Services, and Protected Species and Habitat—remain relatively unchanged. The former Office of International Fisheries has become the Office of International Affairs, and has assumed responsibility for a new Division of International Science, Development, and Polar Affairs.

Greater changes have come with the abolition of the old offices of Fisheries Management, Resource Investigations, Data and Information Management, and Utilization Research. Utilization Research has been absorbed into the new Office of Trade and Industry Services. Resource Investigations and Data and Information Management are absorbed into an Office of Research and Environmental Information. Whether this rearrangement will have any functional impact on NMFS services remains to be seen.

AGENCY POLITICS

To a significant degree, all government agencies reflect the needs and desires of their politically active constituents. As the political power of a constituency changes, the agency's services to that constituency also change. This relationship can be traced in three ways: 1) by reviewing an agency's legislative authorities; 2) by tracking its politically appointed leadership; and 3) by examining its funding history. Legislative authority provides a general measure of the constituency's power in Congress. Agency appointments reflect the constituency's influence over the current administration. And budget share is indicative of the constituency's overall political influence.

NMFS is no exception to these general rules. The influence of constituency may best be illustrated by tracing the ascendancy of fishery management—regulating the level of harvest and, when necessary, allocating fishery resources among fishermen—over all other NMFS functions.

The Ascendancy of Fishery Management

When Congress established NMFS in a 1970 reorganization plan, it had no intention of altering the mix of missions assigned previously to agencies entrusted with marine fisheries oversight. Generally, the mix included programs designed to protect, manage, and develop fisheries of national importance. For example, under the Fish and Wildlife Act of 1956, FWS, through its Bureau of Commercial Fisheries, had been authorized to conduct continuing investigations and disseminate information concerning: 1) the production of fishery products and their flow to the marketplace; 2) the availability, abundance, and biological requirements of fish and wildlife resources; 3) the competitive economic positions of the various U.S.-produced fishery products (*vs.* imports); and 4) the improvement of seafood production and marketing practices. Furthermore the bureau was to: 1) develop and recommend measures to ensure the maximum sustainable production of fish and fishery products; 2) conduct educational and extension services relative to commercial and sport fisheries; 3) study the economic condition of the industry, and develop special promotional and informational activities to stimulate consumption where surplus exists; and 4) take steps for the development, advancement, management, conservation, and protection of fisheries resources.

Indeed, in many ways the NMFS of the mid-1970s resembled the Bureau of Commercial Fisheries of the late 1950s. Its primary emphasis remained fisheries-related research: mainly fisheries biology, fishing gear technology, and seafood product development. Most of the work was done in field laboratories scattered throughout the country. Regional offices were maintained to administer federal grants-to-states programs and to collect fishing and fish processing statistics. The central office's chief role was to support the field staff.

Over the next decade, however, NMFS underwent a radical transformation. By 1987 almost two-thirds of its budget and more than half of its employees were either directly or indirectly supporting fishery management; nearly three out of every four enforcement dollars were earmarked to ensure compliance with fishery management regulations. In comparison, NMFS was spending barely three percent of its budget on habitat conservation and protection; only slightly more went to perform the many tasks required by the Marine Mammal Protection Act and the Endangered Species Act. "There's no question," says one veteran NMFS analyst, "the agency is focusing practically its entire effort on attempting to effectively implement the [FCMA]. Everywhere else all we're doing is hanging on."

The simplest explanation for this emphasis on fishery management has been the lack of funding to do anything else. "We're trying to do a good job, but we've been given flawed tools," says one NMFS veteran. "Essentially what's happened between 1970 and 1987 is that Congress has created a $100 job and given us $10 to do it."

There is much truth in that statement. Congress has burdened NMFS with a host of new responsibilities but has not increased NMFS' budget accordingly. "There's no way NMFS can do everything we're demanding of them on the budget we're giving them," says one congressional staffer. For example, between 1970 and 1986, the agency's budget for research, operations and facilities increased from just under $50 million to just over $160 million. Using 1972 constant dollar values, NMFS officials say that works out to a hike of only 40 percent (or less than 2.5 percent annually in real growth) (see Figure 8).

Another explanation for NMFS' heavy focus on fishery management is that NMFS senior administrators have led the agency in that direction. Between 1977 and 1986, the leadership of NMFS was in the hands of men whose primary interest was implementing FCMA. Only under Dr. William E. Evans, a former chairman of the Marine Mammal Commission, has this leadership pattern shown any sign of changing.

Terry L. Leitzell, the Assistant Administrator for Fisheries from 1978–1980, was a former State Department lawyer. As such, he was keenly aware that foreign governments would demand access to the U.S. 200-mile zone to fish for species they had caught prior to 1977 that could not be fully harvested by U.S. fishermen. To enhance the ability of the U.S. commercial fishing industry to compete in these same fisheries, Leitzell placed a high priority on implementing FCMA provisions designed to promote expansion of the domestic fleet.

Leitzell was followed by William G. Gordon (1981–1986), a career fishery manager. Leitzell had brought Gordon to Washington, D.C., in 1978 to run the agency's newly reorganized Office of Resource Conservation and Management. Throughout his tenure, Gordon's attention was focused on fishery management, and he effectively enhanced this function during a time of general budgetary retrenchment. For example, in the last Gordon budget, fisheries management positions increased by nine percent while overall agency personnel slots fell by eight percent.

A third explanation for the ascendancy of fishery management is that it is the one area in which NMFS has regulatory clout—in this case, the power to significantly alter the manner in which commercial and recreational fishermen conduct their activities. Consequently, from the viewpoint of NMFS administrators, it is the arena that warrants the most attention. Prior to passage of FCMA, the management of marine fisheries outside the U.S. territorial sea was generally left to toothless international organizations or guided by hard-to-enforce bilateral agreements negotiated by the State Department. After the passage of FCMA, hundreds of thousands of square miles of ocean came under U.S. jurisdiction. Although Congress left untouched state control over the territorial sea and created federal-state regional councils to devise fishery management plans, it gave NMFS the bulk of the authority to manage offshore fisheries.

Conversely, when it came to marine habitat protection, NMFS was practically impotent. In 1970, its small authority rested in the Fish and Wildlife Coordination Act and the newly enacted National Environ-

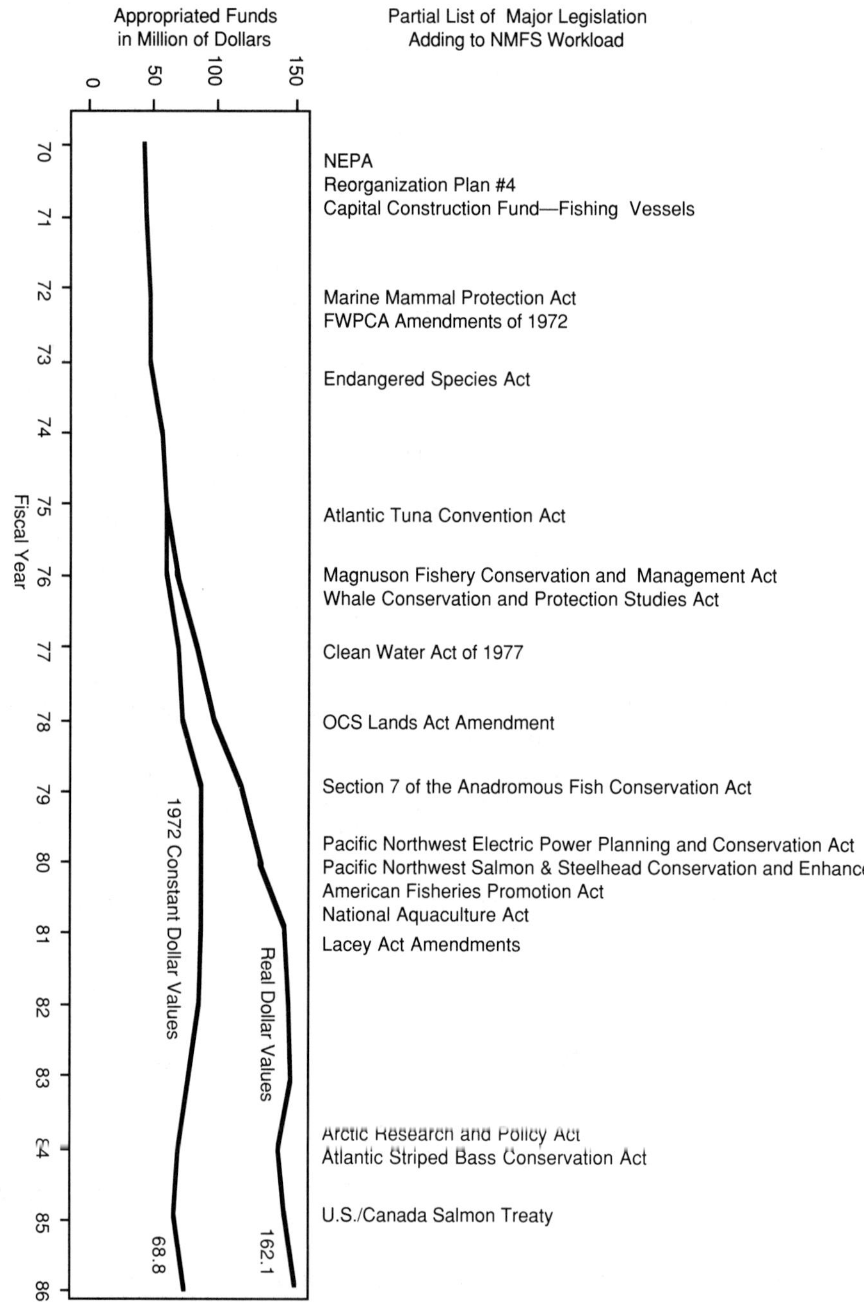

Figure 8. NMFS budget correlated with addition of new responsibilities. Source: NMFS.

mental Policy Act (NEPA). While the Coordination Act gives NMFS the power to review federal projects (or projects that need federal approval) and to propose ways to reduce a project's impact on marine habitat, NMFS' recommendations are not binding. Instead, the project agency decides which recommendations to accept and to what degree a project will be modified. NMFS can dispute an agency's decision by appealing to a higher level of authority within the project agency, but that agency's officials still make the final decision (see the *Audubon Wildlife Report 1985* for a more complete discussion of the Coordination Act). Project-sponsoring agencies must also consider the environmental impacts of a project under NEPA. But once again, although NMFS or a regional fishery management council can complain about the adverse impacts a project will have on fishery habitat, neither body has the authority to force the permitting agency to incorporate its recommendations.

Nor were NMFS' powers appreciably enhanced with the passage of the Marine Protection, Research and Sanctuaries Act of 1972,[12] the Clean Water Act of 1977, or recent amendments to FCMA. During the 1970s, NMFS gained one bona fide weapon for its habitat protection efforts. Under Section 7 of the Endangered Species Act, NMFS can halt an action that threatens the continued existence or critical habitat of a listed species. This tool, however, has only limited use in the habitat preservation battle because only a few of the species under NMFS' authority have been listed.

It is also arguable whether the agency would readily employ its veto power. Some critics allege that NMFS is extremely reluctant even to list species due to the impact such listing could have on fishermen. For example, it might be useful to protect critical salmon habitat from small hydroelectric dams or clear-cutting by listing one particular species of salmon as threatened (for example, the Salmon River sockeye or the Sacramento River winter chinook), but such action could equally restrict the activities of fishermen dependent on other nonthreatened salmon species.

A fourth reason for NMFS' predilection for fishery management is that, since the turn of the century, the federal government has consistently been more concerned with protecting fisheries for economic reasons than with protecting fish or their ecosystems (see Addendum 2). "The agency's sympathies have always been with the fishermen—not the porpoises or turtles or what have you," says

12. Title III of the Marine Protection, Research and Sanctuaries Act does authorize the Secretary of Commerce to designate and protect marine sanctuaries. While of much potential importance to protecting marine habitat generally, NMFS has only a minor role in the program. The lead has been given to NOAA's National Ocean Service.

one retired NMFS veteran. "But that was only natural; the fishermen were our constituency. We were supposed to be on their side, not making their lives miserable."

Political Dominance of the Commercial Fishing Industry

A final, and perhaps most critical, reason that fishery management gained such prominence is that economically affected groups—fishermen and related industries—effectively dominate the political process. How the fishermen achieved dominance is inextricably tied to FCMA and its passage.

According to a number of longtime observers, until the mid-1970s, NMFS had only one prominant constituency: the commercial fishing industry. The two most powerful—and most organized—lobbying groups were the Pacific tuna fleet and the Gulf of Mexico shrimp industry. Also vocal, but less influential, were the Alaska salmon canners. The rest of the industry lobby was made up of individuals who represented local associations or *ad hoc* industry groups. Neither sport fishing groups nor conservation organizations were noticeably effective in marine fisheries policymaking at the national level.

When the Stratton Commission (see Addendum 2) recommended changes in marine resource management in 1969, Congress was impelled to respond. After much discussion, Congress decided to create a new oceans and atmosphere agency—NOAA. Having reached that decision, the next question was whether NOAA should be independent or under the auspices of an existing department or agency. To help settle the matter, congressional staff called commercial fishing industry representatives to a meeting near Washington, D.C. For two days the group wrestled with the issue. Finally, it was decided to locate NOAA within the Department of Commerce. According to one participant, Commerce won over Interior not because Commerce had anything particularly special to offer, but because the chairman of the Senate Commerce Committee, Warren G. Magnuson (D-WA), was a friend of the commercial fishing industry and could best protect the industry if NOAA was a Commerce agency. "Maggie [Magnuson] was clearly ready to fight for the industry when it came time to battle for programs and funding," he said.

While there was some support for making NOAA an agency of the Department of the Interior, virtually no one favored independent status as Stratton had advised. Again the concern was political, not theoretical. In the words of one longtime congressional staffer, "If NOAA had gone independent, it would have gotten lost in the woodwork. When you're battling for a piece of the pie on [Capitol] Hill, it can make all the difference to have an established niche in which to fit, to have the entrenched strength of a department to stand behind you." For the commercial fishing industry, the experience was a lesson in practical politics that it never forgot: without entrenched well-placed congressional support, legislative victories can be of limited value.

For six years after NMFS' creation, the commercial fishing industry was preoccupied with two developments: 1) a growing national concern over the well-being of marine mammals and endangered species; and 2) increasing debate over whether the U.S. should extend its fisheries jurisdiction to 200 miles offshore as several other nations had done. NMFS would be significantly affected by both developments.

It was the tuna industry's killing of porpoises during the course of fishing operations that sparked passage of the Marine Mammal Protection Act. The debate over how these killings could be prevented was closely monitored both by NMFS and the commercial fishing industry. Because NMFS already had authority over most marine creatures, and because its primary function was marine fisheries research, Congress had no particular reason not to give NMFS the authority over the majority of marine mammals covered by the act. When Congress passed the Endangered Species Act in 1973, it again decided to give NMFS jurisdiction over threatened and endangered marine species, despite some opposition from the Interior Department. It is noteworthy that NMFS, unlike FWS, assumed these new responsibilities without additional funding.

Concurrent with the marine mammal and endangered species debates was growing industry concern over whether the United States would expand its fisheries jurisdiction to 200 miles. The shrimp and tuna industry opposed such a move: both fished off foreign shores and were afraid they would lose access to those fishing grounds if the United States extended its management jurisdiction to shut out foreigners. On the other hand, coastal fishermen from the mid-Atlantic to the Gulf of Maine and from the north coast of California to Alaska were becoming increasingly concerned about the growing number of large foreign trawlers and factory ships fishing just beyond the United States' territorial sea, and supported a 200-mile jurisdiction.

This foreign presence was not new. The Japanese had been fishing in the Bering Sea since before World War II. In 1964, to protect the interests of the U.S. fleet, Congress prohibited foreign vessels from fishing within the nation's three-mile territorial sea and from fishing for certain fishery resources of the nation's continental shelf, such as crabs. Two years later, under the so-called Bartlett Act, a nine-mile contiguous zone was established. Only those nations already fishing inside this zone would be allowed to continue their efforts, but even they would be required to negotiate bilateral fishing agreements.

These actions, however, had little affect on the level of foreign fishing, particularly for bottomfish.[13] The most popular fishing grounds for these species are New England's Georges Bank, the Gulf of Maine, the central Pacific Coast, the Bering Sea and the Gulf of Alaska. Foreign fishing for bottomfish was conducted by ocean-going vessels (many of which had processing factories on board), most of which used otter trawls to catch fish (hence the name "trawler"). The trawl nets, which were dragged either on or near the ocean's bottom, were tremendously efficient. A single vessel could catch several hundred thousand pounds of fish in a day. In 1972, Japanese and Soviet boats caught over four billion pounds of pollock (a cod-like white-fleshed fish) in the Bering Sea alone.

The U.S. fleet competing against these foreign vessels consisted mostly of small, independently owned vessels, including bottomfish "draggers"(a synonym for trawler), crab boats (pot fishermen), and salmon "trollers" (hook-and-line fishermen). Few of these boats were equipped to range far from shore and none could compete with the foreign factory fleets. Their owners and their crews were universally convinced that the foreign fleets made it impossible for U.S. fishermen to make a living. It was this economic distress that resulted in the industry's demand for "kicking out" the foreigners.[14] By the early 1970s commercial fishermen began to realize that they had to organize themselves better for Congress to take their concerns seriously. First came the formation of a number of regional associations. Then, in 1973, industry leaders founded the National Federation of Fishermen.[15]

The members of these new associations were primarily vessel owners. Many of them received substantial, if often indirect, assistance from NMFS-administered federal vessel subsidies and loan guarantees. These programs were designed to encourage U.S. fishermen to move into nontraditional fisheries (and to partially compensate them for legislation requiring that U.S. fishing boats over five tons be built in

13. "Bottomfish" is a generic term used by the fishing industry to refer to all fish that live either on or close to the ocean's bottom. It has come to include such species as cod, haddock, pollock, hake, and whiting as well as various types of flounders, soles, and rockfish (as many as 50 commercially distinct species spread across the nation's 200-mile zone). Bottomfish are frequently referred to as "groundfish."

14. Those interested in learning more about the foreign factory fleets and their impact (at least in the North Atlantic) are encouraged to read Warner, *Distant Water, The Fate of the North Atlantic Fishermen* (1977), and Boeri and Gibson, *Tell it Good-Bye, Kiddo* (1976).

15. The seafood industry (wet fish processors, cooked fish processors, importers, wholesalers, and distributors) had been well organized for years, both regionally and nationally. In Washington, this group is primarily represented by the National Fisheries Institute. Established in 1945, the institute currently represents more than 1,000 companies and has an annual budget of close to $2 million.

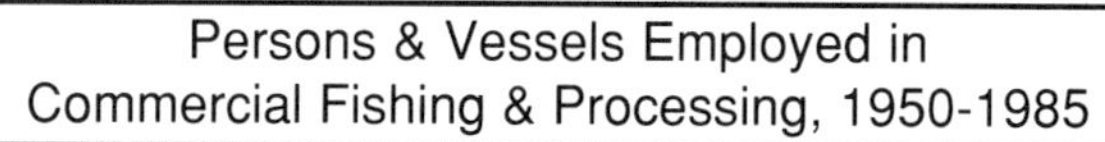

Persons & Vessels Employed in
Commercial Fishing & Processing, 1950-1985

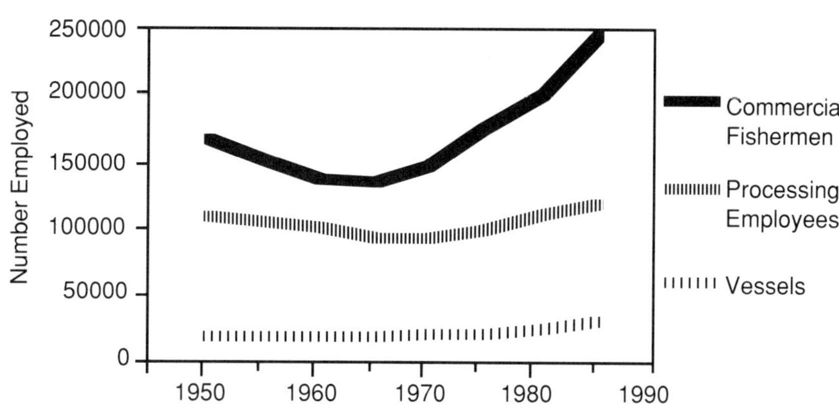

Figure 9. Source: NMFS.

the United States). The effect of the subsidies and guarantees was to encourage new vessel construction. New vessels meant new fishermen. Between 1965 and 1975 the number of U.S. fishermen jumped to 168,000, an increase of 30 percent (see Figure 9). As the ranks of fishermen swelled, so to did the political clout of the fishermen's associations.

The lobbying over FCMA was extraordinarily intense. The majority of U.S. commercial fishermen worked passionately for its passage. Consequently, when the bill was enacted in 1976, the fishermen and their organizations claimed a major share of the victory. The fishing industry responded to the legislation by embarking on a five-year spending spree. In 1976, 58 new vessels were constructed for the New England fishing fleet. In 1977, 97 were built. In the Pacific the number grew from 230 vessels to 411. Nationally, vessel construction jumped 68 percent.[16] The build-up continued unabated between 1977 and 1980. In 1980, 164 vessels were added to the New England fleet and 598 were added to the Pacific fleet.

Not only were more boats being built, but they were bigger and more powerful, a clear sign that FCMA's development aspects were already having an impact. In 1976, less than 12 percent of new vessel construction was for craft over 100 tons. Four years later, almost 19 percent of the vessels built were over 100 tons. Large boats enabled the U.S. commercial fishing fleet to move farther offshore into areas once exclusively dominated by foreigners.

16. Unless otherwise noted, fishery statistics used in this chapter come from various volumes of U.S. Department of Commerce, *Fisheries of the United States.*

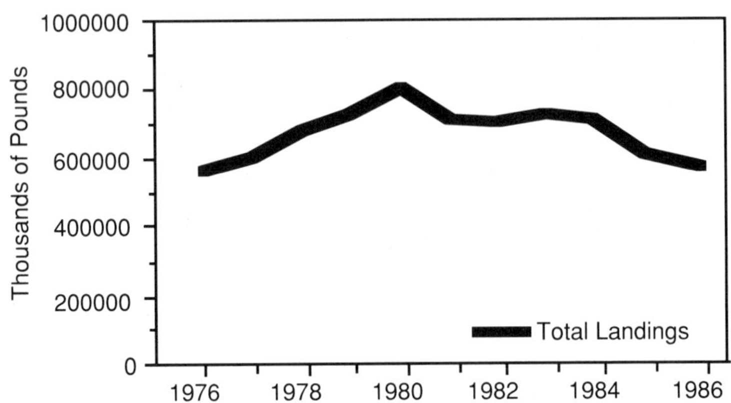

Figure 10. Source: NMFS.

The U.S. catch also began to rise. This increase was most immediately noticeable in New England, where processors were immediately able to buy whatever amount of fish could be landed.[17] Between 1976 and 1980, the New England catch jumped 44 percent (see Figure 10). Cod landings more than doubled (see Figure 11). The major reason for

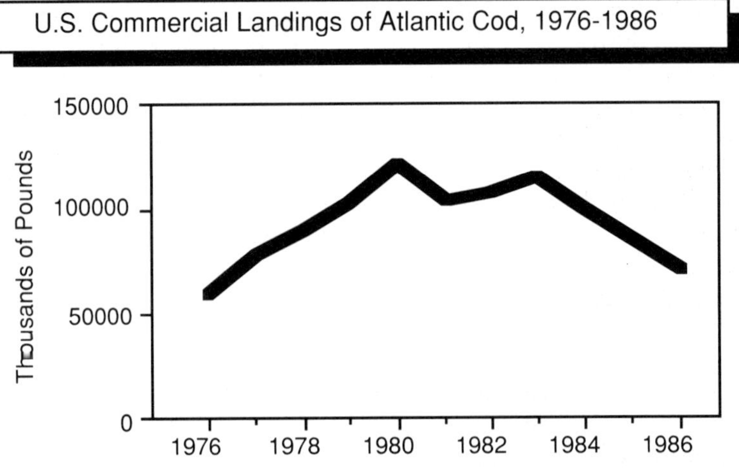

Figure 11. Source: NMFS.

17. Unlike the North Pacific, where U.S. processors were unprepared to buy those fish that had been caught primarily by foreigners. The Alaska processing industry was limited primarily to salmon, crab, and shrimp.

this unrestrained growth in harvests was the ability of fishermen and their organizations to place their allies on the New England Fishery Management Council. The New England industry had worked hard for FCMA, and its representatives knew well the powers the law gave to regional councils. By getting sympathetic members on the body that regulated their fisheries, the industry correctly determined that it could insulate itself from NMFS scientists who might argue for lower catch levels. Seeing the success of the New England fishermen, other associations followed their lead. By 1980 no other marine-related group had greater influence on the regional councils than the seafood industry.

During the same period, commercial fishermen and seafood processors continued to pressure their congressional allies for additional legislation to help them achieve FCMA's fishery development goals. The fishermen's first success came in 1978 when they convinced Congress to allow them to sell their catch, while still at sea, to foreign factory ships—as long as the amount sold was surplus not needed by U.S. processors. In 1980, the seafood industry scored another victory with the passage of the American Fisheries Promotion Act (16 U.S.C.A. 1801 note). Among other things, the Act: 1) required foreign vessels still fishing in the U.S. zone to carry observers; 2) raised the cost of foreign fishing fees required under FCMA; 3) extended the fishing vessel loan guarantee program to cover shoreside plants; 4) authorized the appointment of six U.S. fisheries trade officers to help develop export markets; and 5) ordered NMFS to design and administer a competitive grants program ($12.1 million was appropriated in the first year) to fund development projects, particularly those designed to assist the industry to enter offshore fisheries still dominated by foreign fleets.[18]

In sum, between 1970 and 1980 the commercial fishing lobby grew from a handful of small, scattered associations (dominated by tuna and shrimp) to a well-organized network of associations capable of sustained and effective congressional lobbying. This development did not go unnoticed by the National Marine Fisheries Service. Agency per-

18. This was the Saltonstall-Kennedy (S-K) fund. The program as initially established in 1939 was designed to purchase and distribute surplus fishery products. In 1954, it was expanded into a development program funded by an amount equal to 30 percent of the gross revenue collected by U.S. Customs on imported marine products. For the next 25 years, the income generated went directly to NMFS. However, in 1980 Congress directed the Secretary of Commerce that S-K funds were "only" to be used for "the purpose of 1) providing financial assistance in carrying out fisheries development projects and 2) implementing a national fisheries research and development program," (U.S. Congress 1980). In the American Fisheries Promotion Act, Congress directed the secretary to make grants from S-K funds to assist persons in carrying out fisheries development projects. In consequence, six regional fishery development foundations have been established around the country (New England, Mid-Atlantic, Gulf and South Atlantic, Great Lakes, West Coast, and Alaska).

sonnel began to court the industry to benefit from its new-found political clout. A number of scientists and administrators even resigned their positions to take up industry jobs. While NMFS never became wholly dominated by the seafood industry, its personnel did respond with increasing promptness to industry calls.

Rise of the Sport Fishing Industry

Recently, the dominance of the seafood and commercial fishing industries over NMFS and the regional councils has been challenged by sport fishermen and their associated industries. As a group, recreational fishermen have never enjoyed the political power of their commercial counterparts. This is chiefly because most sport fishing occurs within the territorial sea and is therefore a responsibility of state government. During the FCMA debate, however, recreational interests, anxious over the impact of foreign fishing on species of recreational interest such as Atlantic bluefin tuna, had argued fervently for the act's passage. Their involvement was rewarded by language highlighting their concerns and needs along with those of commercial fishermen. Congress declared that both commercial and recreational fishing were major employers and significant contributors to the nation's economy, and that FCMA would "promote" both groups "under sound management and conservation principles."

Although sport and commercial fishermen both wanted FCMA, they generally supported its passage for opposite reasons. Most commercial fishermen wanted to "kick the foreigners out" to better exploit local fisheries; sport fishermen wanted to impose a new conservative management regime that would reduce the impact of all commercial fishing on valuable recreational species. During the first few years after the act was passed, the interests of sport fishermen were clearly overshadowed by those of the commercial fishery lobby. As a result, spokesmen for the recreational fishing industry realized that to protect their interests, they too would have to spend more money on national organization, education, and lobbying.[19] The lead was assumed by the Sport Fishing Institute.[20] The institute was supported in its task by

19. To this effect, an annual Marine Recreational Fisheries Symposium was established in 1976 sponsored by the Sport Fishing Institute, the National Coalition for Marine Conservation and the International Game Fish Association. The Sport Fishing Institute publishes the proceedings.

20. The Sport Fishing Institute was at this time the recreational sector's only permanent Washington-based operation. SFI is not a grassroots organization; established in 1949, it is maintained with funds from tackle manufacturers and other industries associated with sports fishing. The Sport Fishing Institute staff place the association's current annual budget at approximately $800,000. The other organization consistently active in general marine issues was the National Coalition for Marine Conservation. The coalition, however, does not maintain a Washington, D.C., staff. A newly formed group

individual editors of angling publications, regional charter boat associations,[21] and small groups of sportsmen primarily interested in big game fish.

The task of organizing the host of recreational marine anglers was daunting. A major stumbling block was simply getting an accurate grasp of the number of sport fishermen, how often they fished, and what they fished for. Luckily for the Sport Fishing Institute, this information was equally important to NMFS fishery managers, who needed it to complement their commercial data. Both sets of information would be critical to regional councils in their efforts to set proper fishing levels and seasons in their fishery management plans. Soon the institute and others were working closely with NMFS to assist in its marine recreational fishery survey efforts.

As these connections were being made, the recreational community also launched a successful effort to get a share of the NMFS-controlled development grant money made available under the 1980 American Fisheries Promotion Act (see footnote 18). The House report that accompanied the act specifically stated that recreational fishing was a sector of the fishing industry and that, as such, it should receive a minority share of development funds. Starting at a token $71,000, recreational funding grew rapidly. Since 1982 it has averaged $450,000 annually. (Overall development program funding, meanwhile, dropped from $12.7 million in 1982 to $6.1 million in 1987.)

As important as the money is to sport fishing, it is equally important that the recreational industry had to work directly with NMFS officials to convince them of the merit of development projects linked to sport fishing. Increased contact with NMFS in such areas as fishery development and management was critical to the recreational community's long-range goal of gaining a voice within NMFS equal to that of the commercial fishing and seafood industries. The recreational community's willingness to work with mid-level NMFS staff was especially important as it gave their lobbyists an increasingly sympathetic ear within the agency. One reward was NMFS' adoption of a policy statement committing the agency to implementing federal law as it applied to recreational fishing. (Some see the need for such a statement as a NMFS admission that it was not giving equal weight to sport fishing concerns.)

Another reward has been NMFS' willingness to work with FWS in the latter agency's efforts to design a National Recreational Fisheries Policy.[22] According to one observer, however, the most important sign

---

which has quickly gained some prominence nationally is the United Sport Fishermen Association, which does maintain a Washington lobbyist.

21. The charter boat operators often found themselves pulled between the recreational and commercial camps. Both sides have sought for their affections.

22. The policy is expected to be promulgated in 1988. Its purpose, in the words of

that NMFS is finally serious about giving sport and commercial fishing equal weight is the recent creation by Dr. Evans of an informal policy development group comprised of representatives of the marine recreational fishing industry whose goal is to "neutralize" the commercial fishing bias of "many of [NMFS'] decision makers," in the words of one sport fishing lobbyist.

Gaining "sport fish seats" on regional councils was almost as important as gaining a voice within NMFS. To do this, sport fishing groups lobbied state legislatures and governors to have governors nominate their candidates. In the Southeast, where marine recreational forces are the strongest, such lobbying has paid the greatest dividends. As an illustration, in 1982 recreational fishermen managed to get two nationally recognized spokesmen for the commercial industry off the South Atlantic Regional Fishery Management Council and replace them with strong proponents of sport fishing (*National Fisherman*, December 1982). By 1987, recreational interests dominated two of the nine councils and had achieved parity or near parity on five others (see Table 6). Overall, sport fishermen have gained a third of all regional council seats, while the commercial industry has 42 percent.

Conflicts Between Commercial and Recreational Fishermen

By 1987, the two NMFS constituencies with the greatest investment in the regional council process on Capitol Hill and within NMFS were the commercial fishing and seafood industry and the marine recreational fishing community. Both groups placed fishery management and development as top priorities. Since both groups have opposing management philosophies, competition between them has become increasingly intense, involving both the courts and Capitol Hill.[23] The most recent example was the struggle over a replacement for the retiring director of NMFS' southeast region. Each group had its candidate and went to congressional and administration allies to promote its selection. When NOAA finally selected the candidate supported by recreational groups, commercial lobbyists successfully generated enough support to prevent his appointment.

The fundamental issues dividing sport and commercial fishermen are resource access and resource share. But battles over access and

Frank H. Dunkle, FWS director, is to "strengthen and advocate the advancement of recreational fisheries in this country" (Dunkle, July 1987).

23. This opposition is best illustrated by comparing the general management philosophies held by each group. For its part, the commercial sector wants to harvest any given stock at the maximum level possible. The sports sector, on the other hand, opts for management programs designed to *maintain* populations at their maximum sustainable levels, even if that means allowing large numbers of fish to go uncaught. Pacific salmon, Gulf redfish, and Atlantic swordfish are examples of federally managed fisheries where conflict exists between commercial and sport fishermen.

Table 6
Composition of Regional Fishery Management Councils.

Council	Commercial		Recreational		Environmentalist		Consumer		Academic/Scientist/ Consultant		Other		Total Council Appointments
	1985	1987	1985	1987	1985	1987	1985	1987	1985	1987	1985	1987	
New England	8	7	2	3	—	—	—	—	1	1	—	—	11
Mid-Atlantic	5	3	5	5	—	—	—	—	—	1	2	3	12
South Atlantic	1	1	5	4	—	—	—	—	—	1	1	1	8
Caribbean	—	1	2	1	—	—	—	—	1	—	1	1	4
Gulf of Mexico	5	5	4	4	2	2	—	—	—	—	—	—	11
Pacific	4	4	1	3	1	1	—	—	1	—	1	—	8
North Pacific	6	5	—	—	—	—	—	—	—	—	1	2	7
Western Pacific	3	3	3	3	3	—	—	—	1	1	1	1	8
TOTAL	32	29	22	23	3	3	—	—	4	3	8	7	69

Source: National Fisheries Institute 1987.
Note: State and federal officials hold 41 seats on the eight regional fishery management councils, bringing the total number of council members to 110.
Note: Totals differ because vacancies currently exist on the following councils: South Atlantic, Caribbean, and Western Pacific.

allocation are not unique to these groups. Off Alaska, for example, various commercial organizations are engaged in bitter contests over access to fisheries, involving similar litigation and lobbying. As the battle between user groups has intensified, many observers have questioned whether NMFS and the councils, in their desire to satisfy every demand for a piece of the resource pie, have lost sight of their fundamental responsibility to protect the health of fish stocks.

That this concern was left unexamined for so long is partly because few conservation or environmental groups with large memberships actively work in the fisheries arena. Those that do, such as the National Wildlife Federation, Greenpeace, and the Center for Environmental Education, have extremely small programs. It took the collapse of king mackerel stocks to shake NOAA out of its complacency on the resource protection issue.

The king mackerel fishery takes place in the southeast Atlantic and in the Gulf of Mexico. The mackerel is extremely valuable to both sport and commercial fishermen, and for many years the two groups have argued over catch and allocation levels. Under FCMA, the job of allocation was given to both the South Atlantic and the Gulf of Mexico regional councils because the fishery took place in both councils' areas of jurisdiction. Commercial and sport groups have lobbied council members intensely.

In 1982, the two councils, acting on the advice of NMFS scientists, set the king mackerel harvest limit at 37 million pounds. Two years later, again based on NMFS resource survey data, they lowered it to 14.2 million pounds. After another two years, it became clear that the scientists had grossly overestimated the king mackerel biomass. Harvest levels were again cut drastically, this time to a token 2.9 million pounds.

The entire experience was marred by delays, miscommunications, and charges of misconduct on the part of NMFS officials. To sort out what happened, NOAA established the King Mackerel Committee to review events. The committee concluded that overfishing had occurred for several reasons. First, NMFS biologists were guilty for not explaining to council members that the stock assessment data upon which they were basing catch levels was filled with uncertainties. Second, council members were cited for being more concerned about the immediate economic well-being of fishermen than the long-term health of the mackerel resource. Finally, the committee pointed to "terrible communication within NMFS" and "an inefficient system for processing emergency [regulations]."

If acted upon, the committee's report would mark a major, and perhaps long overdue, change in U.S. fishery management. The committee prefaced its recommendations with a plea that "the Councils, NOAA and NMFS adopt a more conservation-oriented management philosophy." This would be achieved partly by requiring NMFS scientists to do more than simply give council members their "best estimate" as to a stock's size. Instead, scientists should inform councils of all the uncertainties inherent in their estimates. Not supplying council members with the latter information, the committee said,

> leads to undue optimism on the part of Council members. The scientists must present the downside risks clearly enough so that the Council managing the stock can make a reasonable judgement which adequately takes into account uncertainties. This will require Council members to take a less simplistic view of fishery management and will increase the burdens placed upon the Council staff. In addition, NMFS should instill in the Councils a better appreciation for management under uncertainty through its management philosophy and its leadership. Council members, for their part, should give greater weight to their role as public trustees of a national resource and less weight to their role as representatives of a particular segment of the users of the resource.

Whether NMFS acts on the report is another story. While some support for implementing the recommendations may come from recreational and commercial fishermen, it is doubtful that either group will put together a major lobbying campaign to see that the committee's proposals are realized. Nor is it likely that sufficient pressure will come from conservation groups. First, such groups have never taken up the cause of fish in the past. Second, and perhaps more important, few conservation groups have invested enough time with NMFS to understand how it works or to know how to influence it.

Conservation Organizations and NMFS

This is not to say that environmental and conservation-oriented groups have not been active on certain marine issues. The Natural Resources Defense Council and other groups have dedicated considerable resources to preventing unwise energy development on the Outer Continental Shelf, and the Environmental Policy Institute and others have recently focused much needed attention on ocean pollution and seafood. The Center for Environmental Education, the Environmental Defense Fund, and others have worked tirelessly to protect endangered sea turtles from being caught and killed in shrimp nets. The National Wildlife Federation has shown a long-term commitment to habitat conservation and regeneration.[24] Greenpeace has worked to protect marine mammals and marine birds killed during fishing operations of Japan's high seas salmon fleet.

However no conservation organization has mounted a comprehensive, sustained campaign to strengthen the fisheries conservation

24. A combined effort in 1985 by National Wildlife Federation and California's commercial salmon fishermen to better safeguard habitat through amendments in FCMA received little encouragement from either industry or conservation groups.

efforts of NMFS. This omission may result from a belief held by many in the conservation community that such an effort would be pointless. These individuals have written off NMFS as an industry service agency uninterested in resource protection. While this analysis is to a large degree justified, it also must be understood that NMFS' bias toward the fishing industry in not necessarily innate. As noted earlier, the commercial and recreational fishing industries have spent years working to orient NMFS to their needs.

Until the conservation community begins to emulate the long-term political strategies that have been so successfully employed by commercial and recreational fishermen, it will be difficult for recommendations such as those made by the King Mackerel Committee to be implemented. It will be even more difficult for conservation groups to pressure NMFS to conserve critical marine habitat and species that are not directly related to fishery management programs.

BUDGET AND ISSUES

Budget Overview

Like every federal agency, NMFS prepares an annual budget. This budget is reviewed by NOAA, the Department of Commerce, and the Office of Management and Budget before it is submitted to Congress for approval. On Capitol Hill, the authorizing committees with jurisdiction over the agency conduct hearings.[25] At that time committee members may recommend changes in the budget to the appropriations and budget committees. Eventually, the budget committees determine a ceiling for each agency's spending; the appropriations committees then determine precisely, item by item, how each agency's budget allocation is spent.

Since the last year of the Carter Administration, NMFS—like most other federal agencies—has operated under a persistent cloud of budget uncertainty. Each year, the White House has proposed that NMFS programs be "zeroed out" and facilities closed; year after year Congress has disagreed. It has been the position of the Reagan Administration that many of the services provided by NMFS exclusively benefit the

25. Merchant Marine and Fisheries in the House and Commerce, Science and Transportation in the Senate. In the Merchant Marine and Fisheries Committee, fisheries is handled by the Subcommittee on Fisheries, Wildlife Protection and the Environment. The Senate has no fisheries subcommittee. Fisheries specialists are attached to the National Ocean Policy Study which is chaired by the Commerce committee chairman. The study was a creation of Warren Magnuson who, as Commerce Committee chairman, wanted to ensure himself full fishery oversight authority.

fishing industry, and thus should be paid for by the industry. Administration officials have been particularly steadfast in their attempt to abandon most of NMFS' industry services programs, particularly those relating to marketing and promotion.

For the most part, Congress has responded to industry lobbying and restored the majority of programs targeted for cuts. Despite much talk of fiscal austerity, Congress continued this pattern in 1987. In the final version of the NOAA FY 1988 budget, congressional appropriation committees restored virtually every presidential cut (many with significant increases), and added several new programs of their own.[26] In total, NMFS received a 5.1 percent increase for FY 1988 over its FY 1987 budget.

However, under a deficit reduction measure, agreed to late in 1987 by the Reagan Administration and Congress, NMFS' budget will be reduced 5.8 percent. The cuts will be made on a program-by-program basis, and will affect newly created as well as existing programs. Also, together with other federal agencies, NMFS is being asked to make 1988 pay increases without supplemental funding. This could, in effect, add up to an additional two to three percent cut as funds are diverted from programs to salaries.

Phased Budget For FY 1988

Due to the support of Congress, NMFS continues to operate with approximately the same goals, facilities and personnel levels as when the Reagan presidency began. However, the president's proposed FY 1988 budget contained one new wrinkle: phased funding for the agency. In its initial budget, NMFS asked for only $99.5 million—a massive 38.7 percent reduction from FY 1987 levels. However, additional funding of $28.97 million was to be requested later if Congress passed legislation establishing a marine user fee to fund a new Marine Fisheries Conservation Assurance program. This program would have:

- required sport fishermen to purchase a $6 federal permit to fish in marine waters;
- required an annual $25 federal stamp to buy or sell certain fish;
- collected fees equal to one percent of the sales value received by fishermen for those fish being sold commercially; and,
- required an annual $25 federal stamp to fish for species declared "game fish."

26. New programs included $500,000 to manage fisheries on Georges Bank, $38,000 for research into Oregon Harbor Seals and Sea Lions, $40,000 for research into improving vessel safety, $250,000 for an endangered species recovery plan, $350,000 for Interstate Fishery Commissions, $1 million for menhaden-surimi research, and $15,000 for a feasibility study into establishing a seafood consumer research institute.

NMFS said the assurance program would generate $99 million in new revenue. Of this amount, half would be allocated to coastal states to cover the costs of collecting the fee, and to replace the existing $9 million Grants-to-States program the Administration proposed to eliminate.[27] Of the balance, NMFS would get $29 million,[28] and the remaining $20.5 million would be deposited into the general treasury. After two years, the $6 stamp would increase to $7, and all other fees would double. Whether any of the additional $30 to $40 million in revenue generated by such increases would go to NMFS was left open.

Under the Administration plan, the additional funds raised by the fees would be used to restore fish survey work (an activity supported by industry) and habitat conservation programs (strongly supported by the environmental community). This may have been done to gain constituency support; if so, it failed. Even conservation groups opposed the proposal unless accompanied by guarantees that the fees generated would be dedicated to fisheries programs. Congress, in turn, ignored the entire proposal.

Equating the Budget to the Programs

The NMFS budget document (Department of Commerce, 1987d) is highly useful in determining the agency's objectives, program emphases, and willingness to deal with key resource problems and issues. The document shows levels of funding by functional task and justifies why a particular function or program implementing that function should have its funding increased, decreased, or left unchanged. Members of Congress respond to the administration's budget proposal depending on personal predilections, "horse trading" with other members, and constituent lobbying.

The entire budget process—the document itself, congressional hearings, and the public and private maneuvering of affected interest groups—offers tremendous insight into how a particular program is performing and what its future is. How a program fares in the budget process illustrates the political strength of each constituent group connected to it. Programs that generate political support (whether on the Hill, in the administration, or from the public) are almost always rewarded with sustained or even increased funding. Ineffectively supported programs may not disappear, but they often lose a portion of their funding.

The budget process should not be underestimated. An adequately funded program will have a better a chance of success than an

27. These grants had been originally established to assist states in anadromous and other marine fishery research and development programs.

28. Of this amount, $26.4 million would provide additional funding for information collection and analysis activities. Another $2.57 million would go to supplement conservation and management operations.

underfunded one. Similarly, an adequately funded program will be in a better position to respond to unexpected developments or problems that arise. Consequently, any discussion of marine problems and issues must consider budget levels of the functions and programs intended to deal with those issues.[29]

The NMFS Budget Accounts

In its budget document, the Administration projected that, disregarding any cuts or changes from the FY 1987 work load, $178 million would be required to operate NMFS in FY 1988 (in budget language this level is known as the FY 1988 base.) The $178 million includes funding for approximately 1,900 permanent positions (or their equivalent). Of these, NMFS estimates that slightly less than 80 percent are in the field. The rest work in the agency's central office in Washington, D.C.

NMFS divides its budget into eight accounts. The most important of these is called Operations, Research and Facilities (ORF). In budget language ORF is an "activity," or primary budget item. The account covers all the day-to-day expenses necessary to operate the agency. The other seven accounts include a variety of development, compensation, and management funds established by Congress. In the FY 1988 base, ORF constitutes 95.3 percent or $169.6 million of NMFS' budget (see Table 7). The other seven accounts make up the rest, about $8.4 million.

ORF is divided into three subaccounts. These are known as "subactivities" in the budget (see Figure 12). The Information Collection and Analysis subactivity includes the agency's environmental, biological, and technical research programs. The Conservation and Management Operations subactivity covers a wide variety of management programs. The State and Industry Assistance Programs subactivity covers a collection of grant programs.

Each subactivity is further divided into "line items." A line item is further divided into "sub-line accounts" covering the specific programs conducted by NMFS.

Information Collection and Analysis

Information Collection and Analysis budget subactivity is funded at $103.7 million, with 1,186 permanent positions attached to it (see Figure 13 and Table 8). The three line items under this subactivity include Resource Information, Fishery Industry Information, and Infor-

29. Readers should be aware of the caveat that program funding levels provided in this chapter are "good faith" estimates as submitted to Congress by NMFS. NMFS officials say actual spending levels may vary to some extent.

Table 7
NMFS Programs over $5 Million, FY 1988 Base (in Millions)

Program	Funding
Resource Surveys	$ 23.4
Anadromous Fisheries Research	17.3
Fishery Ecology	14.7
Fishery Biology	9.5
Columbia River Hatchery	8.3
Product Quality and Safety	8.2
Regional Management Councils	7.7
Protected Species Biology	7.6
Basic Fishery Statistics	7.3
FCMA Enforcement	6.1
Data Management	6.1
Resource Analysis	6.0
Fishery Management Plan Review and Implementation	5.4
Subtotal	127.6
26 Other NMFS Programs	42.0
TOTAL ORF Budget	$169.6

mation Analysis and Dissemination. Generally, personnel funded under the Information Collection and Analysis account are marine biologists, environmental scientists, economists, gear technicians, computer analysts, and statisticians. The majority work in NMFS' fishery research centers.

Resource Information. This line item is funded at $75.6 million and includes 828 permanent positions. Activities are designed to collect, analyze, and disseminate biological and environmental data about the nation's living marine resources and their environment.

Resource Surveys. Surveys are a subline item funded at $23.4 million. They provide the basic information needed for all fisheries and species management decisions. The surveys are NMFS' biggest investment. At this funding level, they equal almost a seventh of the agency's ORF account (see Figure 14).

NMFS uses vessels and aircraft to collect biological and environmental information on the composition, abundance, and distribution of living marine resources of commercial, recreational, or ecological significance. During each of the last three years, NMFS has surveyed 111 species of fish and 28 species of marine mammals. From these surveys NMFS estimates the total population for each species. These "stock assessments" are produced by combining information

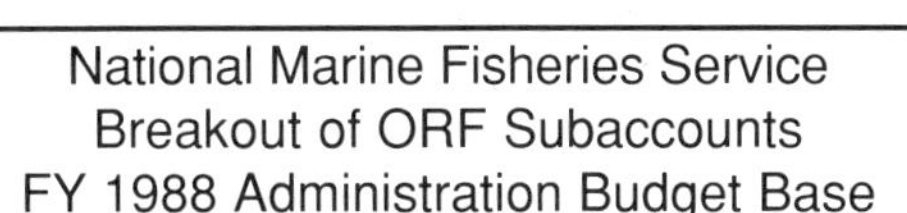

National Marine Fisheries Service
Breakout of ORF Subaccounts
FY 1988 Administration Budget Base
Personnel = 1,877 Permanent Positions

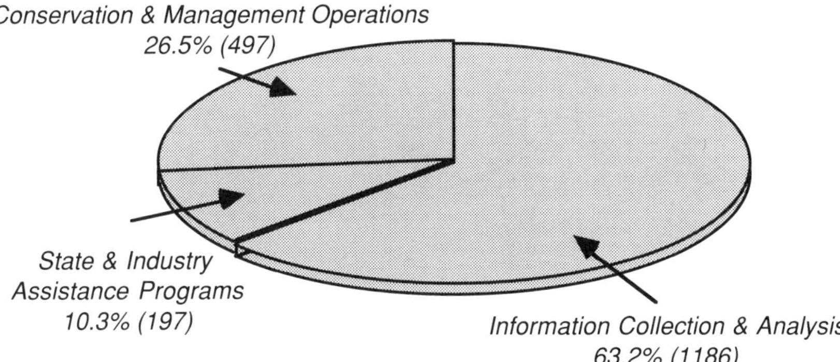

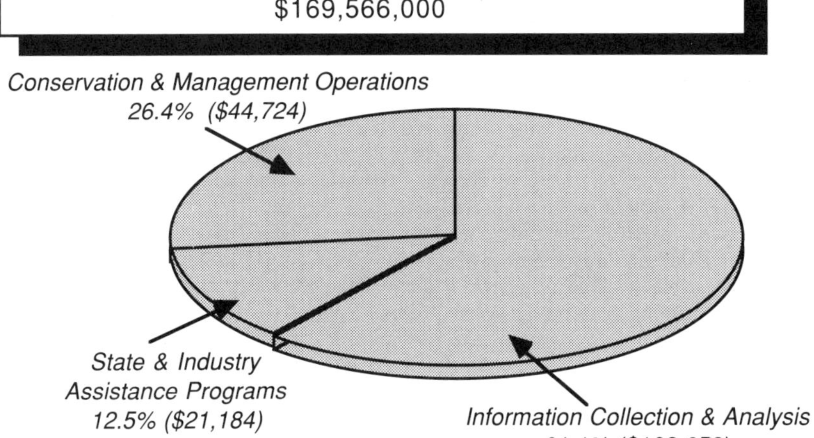

Figure 12. Source: NMFS.

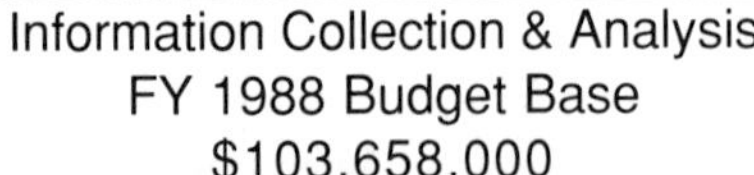

Information Collection & Analysis
FY 1988 Budget Base
$103,658,000

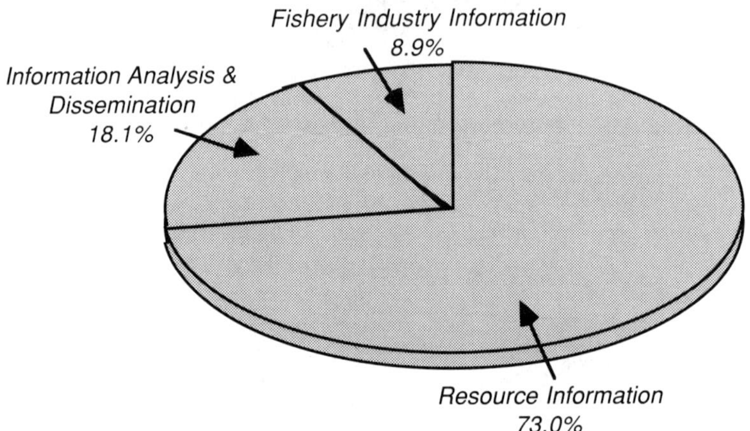

Figure 13. Source: NMFS.

from surveys with data collected from the fishing industry.[30] A combination of NOAA and chartered commercial vessels is used to gather the information NMFS needs.[31] Some information is also obtained under contract from states, universities, and private organizations. Finally, NMFS performs cooperative surveys with foreign governments.[32]

30. Generally, industry data is the best "hard" evidence available to scientists. This data includes the volume (and value) of fish landed, the number of vessels and the amount (and type) of gear employed. By combining this information, scientists can determine the rate of fishing success (as well as the overall catch volume). This rate is known as the catch per unit of effort; a declining rate can signal a stressed stock, even while total landings are increasing. Catch data is collected through "fish tickets." These reports are usually delivered to state fish and game officials at the port of landing. Some states base landing taxes on the volume of fish reported on tickets. While industry catch data is vital, scientists do not like to rely upon it exclusively. Fishermen respond to a host of demands that can skew data in the eyes of a researcher. For example, market demand determines which species are caught. Fishermen may throw back thousands of pounds of unwanted fish in their search for one particular species. Fishing strategies also effect results. For example, fishermen will generally stick to areas where they have had good results. Prospecting new areas is always risky, and only occasionally rewarding.

31. NOAA's National Ocean Service, not NMFS, is responsible for the operational costs incurred during survey work. NOAA maintains a fleet of 23 ocean-going research vessels ranging in length from 86 to 303 feet. The Atlantic Marine Center is in Norfolk, Virginia; the Pacific Marine Center is in Seattle, Washington. Vessels are also based in Pascagoula, Mississippi, San Diego, California, Honolulu, Hawaii, and Juneau, Alaska.

32. Independent foreign survey work is also taken into consideration. NMFS also uses *ad hoc* data provided by merchant ships and satellite overflights to track highly migratory species and environmental conditions.

Table 8
NMFS FY 1988, Information Collection & Analysis Programs (in Millions)

Program	Funding
Resource Information	
Resource Surveys	$23.4
Fishery Biology	9.5
Protected Species Biology	7.6
Fishery Ecology	14.7
Anadromous Fiseheries Research	17.3
Stock Enhancement & Disease Research	3.0
Fishery Industry Information	
Basic Fisheries Statistics	7.3
Industry Economic Data	1.9
Information Analysis & Dissemination	
Data Management	6.1
Fisheries System Analysis	3.3
Information Dissemination	1.8
Protected Species Analysis	1.6
Resource Analysis	6.0
TOTAL	$103.7

Data is collected on such subjects as species' growth and death rates, age structure, distribution and migrations, physiological requirements, and diseases. Surveys generally have focused on individual species or species groups.

Ecosystem Management. NMFS' current administrator, Dr. Evans, has directed the agency to develop an ecosystem-oriented management approach with the intent of improving the agency's ability to understand the various and complex interactions between all marine species present in a particular area (see Figure 15). For example, a critical task will be to better document predator-prey relationships and the workings of marine food chains so that the total impact of fishing in the ecosystem (including other species) can be comprehensively understood and taken into account when setting catch levels.

According to one NMFS scientist, "There's nothing particularly new about an ecosystem approach. During the 1950s and 1960s, we took this sort of broad-spectrum approach to our research." The new twist is that under Evans, the regional directors have been requested to develop, by March 1988, seven regional ecosystem program plans (U.S. Department of Commerce 1987c).

"The purpose is to orient the NMFS science and management programs to an approach which considers living marine resources and their use within an ecosystem context. I envision that this approach-will allow us to develop a [much improved] forecasting capability," Evans told his staff (Evans, Sept. 29, 1987).

NMFS Information Collection & Analysis
"Resource Information" Line Item
FY 1988 Administration Budget Base
($75,639 million)

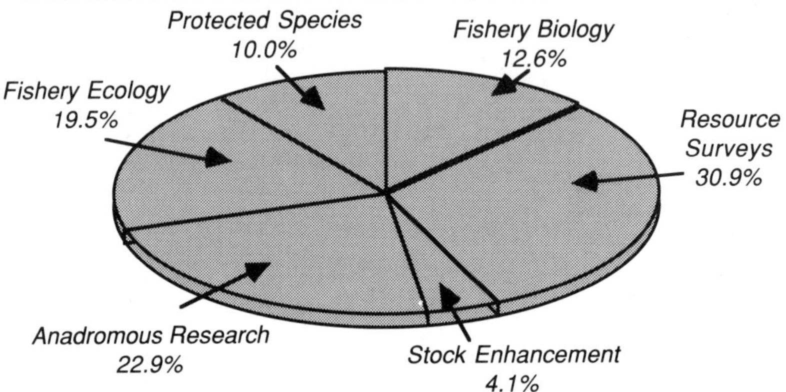

Figure 14. Source: NMFS.

Although NMFS scientists say they are delighted to take the broad ecosystem approach to surveys desired by Dr. Evans, they question whether the demands made by FCMA will make it possible. "FCMA brought a real demand for species—not ecosystem—management," says one scientist. With FCMA, he explains, came the demand for fishery management plans. These plans demand species-by-species analysis and data. For the past decade, NMFS scientists have designed surveys to provide data on those species that: 1) are covered under existing fishery management plans (whether approved or preliminary); 2) are designated by Congress for special attention;[33] or 3) have come under unexpected stress or have received public attention.

"What's needed," says a NMFS scientist, "is some slack somewhere in the system; otherwise we won't be able to do ecosystem research. Any research agency worth its salt ideally spends up to a quarter of its time doing basic research—the resource surveys with a broad spectrum." Currently, agency scientists are forced to spend virtually all their time supplying data to answer specific fishery management concerns.

33. Two particular programs in this area are Marine Fisheries Initiative (MARFIN) and Southeastern Area Monitoring and Assessment (SEAMAP). These programs are projects favored by Senator John Breaux and Representative Trent Lott (R-MS) and were designed by his staff to provide alternative fisheries to the Gulf of Mexico shrimp industry.

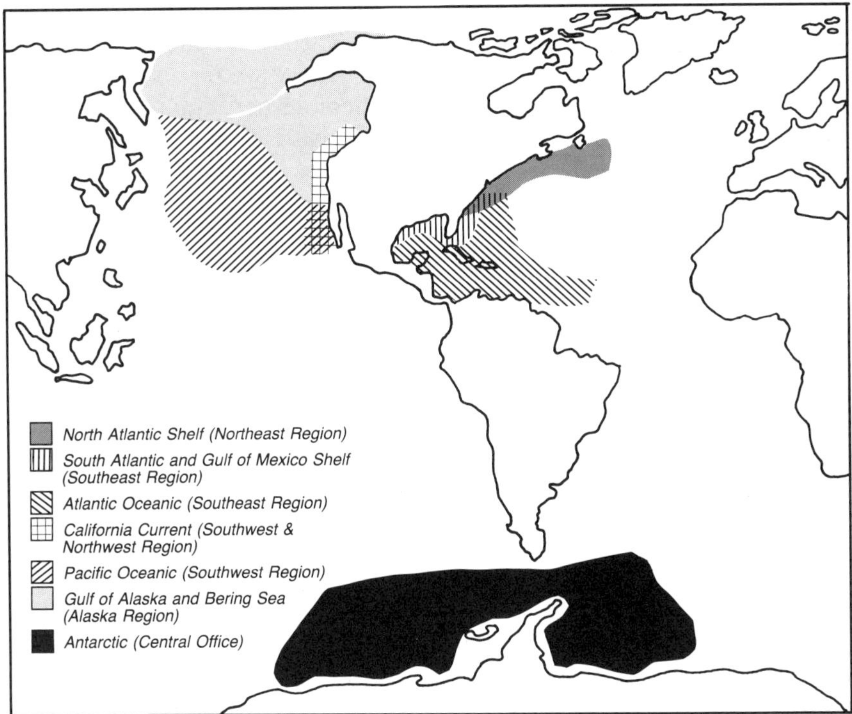

Figure 15. General location of the seven regional marine ecosystems within U.S. jurisdiction and/or containing living marine resources of interest to the United States. Source: NMFS.

Red Drum Crisis. Funding is only part of the difficulty. NMFS scientists also are faced with constant time-allocation dilemmas. As an example, scientists cite the 1986–1987 Gulf of Mexico redfish crisis. In this emotionally charged issue, sport anglers used their political muscle to pressure NMFS to all but shut down a growing offshore commercial fishery for red drum. The fishery had developed overnight in response to strong consumer demand for "blackened" redfish, the latest fad in restaurants. Anglers were concerned that this popular sport fish would be devastated by commercial overfishing. Their anxieties were intensified due to the lack of any limit on redfish harvests.[34]

34. There was no limit because there was no management plan. There was no management plan because until 1986 there had been no significant fishing of redfish outside of state territorial waters. The issue became further clouded when some members of the Gulf of Mexico Fishery Management Council argued that the council

Before any reasonable management plan could be devised, federal managers needed to determine the size of the redfish biomass, its maximum sustainable yield, and whether stocks were actually endangered. NMFS scientists were pulled off other jobs to develop the needed data. "It was a case of running just to catch up," says one scientist, adding that it was "not the only time this has happened."

Yet for all the "running," many fishermen question whether NMFS' research—which led to a ban in the EEZ of "directed" commercial fishing for redfish and limited recreational fishermen to 325,000 pounds and a one-fish-per-trip bag limit—was accurate.[35] This doubt is based in the belief (held by most commercial fishermen and some scientists) that traditional fishery surveys are, at best, a stab in the murk. "The ocean's a black box, and inside that box there are too many variables to allow for really reliable survey results," says one industry observer. He lists these variable as "things like water temperature, surface temperature, current variations, tide, and wind."

Many believe that the traditional fish survey, which may go over the same spot on the same date for 20 years *and* employ the same net moving at the same speed, does little more than give an interesting history of the presence or absence of marine life in that one particular area. Indeed, the only way to determine whether survey findings have any link with actual fish stock conditions is to allow commercial fishing and study the resulting catch. With enough vessels searching, one or two may discover that a stock shown by a survey to be declining has simply moved elsewhere. Similarly, by searching beyond the survey area, fishermen may find an as yet unsurveyed stock of the same species. On the other hand, fishermen may come up with only small, scattered catches, thus confirming the depressed stock condition suggested by the original survey and further aggravating matters. Although extraordinary advances in fish-finding technology (based on sonar) have transformed the ocean from a black box to a colorful, dotted screen, extrapolating a stock's health and size from limited survey data remains, at best, an uncertain business.

---

should leave redfish management to the states (Texas, Alabama, and Florida generally ban the commercial catch of redfish). Florida aggravated the situation by arresting one of its citizens for breaking a state law which prohibited the possession of fish caught in a purse seine; the individual arrested had legally made his catch of redfish in federal waters. The case remains under litigation.

35. A "directed" commercial fishery refers to those fisheries in which fishermen target specifically on particular species. In directed fisheries, fishermen usually catch other species "incidentally." These species are called bycatch. In the initial NMFS plan regulating redfish harvest, commercial fishermen targeting on shrimp or other species were allowed to retain 300,000 pounds of redfish as bycatch. In a later amendment, NMFS closed the sport fishery and required that commercial fishermen return all incidentally caught redfish to the ocean.

Fishery Biology. Funded at $9.5 million, fishery biology provides the other basic component of NMFS' fishery resource research work. Surveys can give an idea as to whether a species' biomass is increasing or declining only because biologists have discovered methods to analyze each survey's catch, and built models that permit extrapolations and projections to be made from catch data. To accurately analyze the catch from each survey tow, information is needed on fish mortality and growth rates, age structure, distribution and migration, physiological requirements, and disease. Considering the number of species of commercial and recreational value, the research task is daunting.

For example, concern has been growing over the increasing popularity of shark as a food fish. When properly cleaned, handled, and prepared, many species of shark make exquisite eating. With the demand for exotic foods on the rise, fishermen have been catching more shark. However, scientists know relatively little about how to determine shark age or about shark reproduction. By the time answers are found, a significant portion of the breeding stock could be lost due to overfishing. NMFS scientists are quick to point out that they cannot do research on "peripheral" species that may face future difficulties when funding is barely sufficient to cover today's many priorities.

Protected Species Biology. The Protected Species Biology program is funded at $7.6 million. NMFS has been active in protected species research since the passage of the Marine Mammal Protection Act and the Endangered Species Act in the early 1970s. Current priorities include work on 1) the bowhead and east coast (particularly right) whales;[36] 2) protected species abundance, distribution, migrations, and bioprofiles; 3) Pacific Coast marine mammal population trends and the impact of human activity on mammal populations (for example, whale watching and commercial gillnetting); and 4) fur seal research (including the entanglement research program). Other research focuses on sea turtles in the South Atlantic and Gulf of Mexico, harbor porpoise and monk seals off California, and bottlenose dolphins in the Gulf of Mexico and South Atlantic.

Marine Mammal/Fishermen Conflicts. In FY 1987, NMFS began a five-year eastern tropical Pacific dolphin monitoring program. The study is the result of long-time congressional concern over the impact of tuna seining on porpoises.[37] During reauthorization hearings in 1984, Congress expressed concern over the agency's ability to accurately assess the health of porpoise stocks caught "incidentally" in the

36. See the chapter on the North Atlantic right whale in this volume.

37. The terms dolphin and porpoise are frequently interchanged. Porpoise has become the acceptable generic term for the common, coastal spotted and eastern spinner dolphins taken in the eastern tropical Pacific tuna seine fishery.

yellowfin tuna fishery.[38] The issue is of more than academic interest; many vessels in the economically distressed U.S. tuna fleet depend on access to southeastern Pacific tuna for economic survival. Under the Marine Mammal Protection Act, the fleet has permission to kill incidentally 20,500 porpoise.[39] When that number is reached, the U.S. fishery is closed.[40] Those vessels incapable of sailing to alternative grounds in the western Pacific and Indian oceans must return to port, tie up, and send their crews home.

As the tuna-porpoise debate approaches its 20th year, a new marine mammal/fishery problem may soon arise: the continuing decline of northern fur seals and Stellar sea lions. This issue is already putting pressure on NMFS' protected species scientists. If the issue continues to develop as expected, it could result in a major confrontation between conservation groups and some Bering Sea commercial fishermen. If this happens, it will be a classic example of government fishery development efforts directly conflicting with federal conservation efforts.

Every year since 1984, the Marine Mammal Commission has recommended that NMFS designate the Pribilof Islands (Alaska) stock of North Pacific fur seals as "depleted" under the Marine Mammal Protection Act.[41] NMFS finally agreed to start the designation process

38. "The Merchant Marine and Fisheries Committee notes the failure of existing methods to produce determinations of current and historic stock status of sufficient precision to be of merit in rational regulation of incidental take of marine mammals. The Committee intends that the study provide a basis for a rational method for determining if marine mammal stocks are being adversely affected by incidental take . . . In addition . . . assessments of affected porpoise stocks . . . should not rely on methods that require calculations which are dependent on extensive extrapolation from a limited data base (U.S. Congress, House 1984)."

39. In the eastern tropical Pacific, porpoise travel together with yellowfin tuna. By setting their nets around porpoise (which travel on the surface), fishermen can usually be assured of catching tuna which travel beneath the porpoise. In 1972 (the year the Marine Mammal Protection Act was passed), NMFS estimated that 368,600 porpoises were either killed or seriously injured in the fishery. By 1983 that number had fallen to 9,600. This achievement was due to combined NMFS–industry effort to devise a way to release incidentally trapped porpoises from set nets. Called "backing down," the technique demands much skill and coordination. It also requires a special small mesh panel in the part of the net over which the porpoise escape (the small mesh prevents the porpoise from catching their snouts in the webbing below the waterline where they would die from lack of oxygen). For more on the tuna industry see Orbach 1977.

40. The fishery was closed for the first time in 1986. Whether the incidental kill actually reached the 20,500 limit continues to be debated. NMFS estimated the kill would reach 20,728 by late October. The industry argued that the NMFS estimate was askew due to inadequate observer data (a few sets with abnormally high mortality rates extrapolated across the entire fishery). The events of 1987 appear to uphold those concerns. With significantly increased observer coverage (and thus decreased necessity for extrapolation), the Porpoise Rescue Foundation estimates that 1987 porpoise mortality will be approximately 13,000.

41. A marine mammal species is "depleted" if it is below Optimum Sustainable Population (OSP). NMFS has defined it as "a population size which falls within a range

in 1986. During 1987, the North Pacific bottomfish fleet—which has developed largely under the encouragement of FCMA—began to realize that increased fur seal protection might affect its fishing activities.[42] Because some interaction (although the degree remains largely undetermined) occurs between several Bering Sea fishing fleets and fur seals, it is possible that the "depleted" status (which prohibits any form of harassment) could restrict fishing freedom.

With the Marine Mammal Protection Act up for reauthorization in 1988, the issue of marine mammal interactions with commercial fishermen is bound to put intense political pressure on NMFS. The fishing industry says that the act is inconsistent with FCMA, and should be changed.[43] The industry would like to see the act amended to allow for the taking of marine mammals by government authorities to preserve fish stocks important to sport and commercial fishermen, and it will also ask that commercial fishermen be allowed to catch a small number of "depleted" marine mammals while conducting otherwise legal fishing operations.[44] The ensuing debate will undoubtedly highlight the lack of information currently available on the effect of fishing gear on marine mammals, with the result that congressional funding of NMFS' three-year-old entanglement research program will be continued (see the "Plastic Debris and Its Effects on Marine Wildlife" chapter of this volume).[45]

Shrimp Fishing and Turtle Conservation. Another area of conflict that has involved the NMFS protected species biology program is the impact of shrimp trawling on various sea turtle populations in the Gulf of Mexico. This decade-old battle matches conservation groups against South Atlantic and Gulf of Mexico shrimp fishermen. While no

---

from the population level of a given species or stock which is the largest supportable within the ecosystem to the population level that results in maximum net productivity." For more on the evolution of the optimum sustainable population, see Bean 1983.

42. In an effort to increase their lobbying effectiveness, elements of the West Coast fishing industry came together in late 1987 to form Americans for Marine Eco-Balance.

43. In a 1983 *Federal Register* notice NOAA concluded that "it is clear that the Magnuson Act's emphasis on achieving OY precludes the exclusively protectionist point of view that forms the basis of the MMPA [Marine Mammal Protection Act]."

44. The issues and options have been extensively discussed in a document prepared by state and federal wildlife officials under the auspices of the Pacific Marine Fisheries Commission (Pacific Marine Fisheries Commission 1987).

45. This program grew out of anxieties over the impact of marine debris, and particularly discarded and lost fish nets, on marine life. Initially (in 1982), concerns were limited to northern fur seals, but by the mid-1980s those apprehensions had spread to include monk seals, sea lions, whales, and harbor porpoises. A formal program investigating the subject was established in FY 1985 with $1 million in congressional funding. Despite administration opposition, Congress has continued the program, although at the slightly reduced level of $750,000.

one questions that sea turtles are killed by the shrimp fishery, debate centers on the number of annual deaths and how to prevent them. NMFS scientists estimate that about 11,000 sea turtles are killed annually by shrimp nets. Industry estimates are much lower, ranging from 600 to 2,800.

Of the turtles killed, about 90 percent are loggerheads. The other four affected turtle species include Kemp's ridley, hawksbill, green sea, and leatherback. Loggerheads are listed as threatened under the Endangered Species Act. The four others are classified as endangered; of these, the biological health of the Kemp's ridley turtle is of the greatest concern.

In an attempt to devise a politically acceptable solution for conserving turtles short of shutting down the shrimp industry, NMFS developed a device that, when attached to a trawl net, prevents turtles from being swept into the net. The apparatus was formally introduced in 1981 and quickly became known as the TED ("turtle excluder device"). With the TED, NMFS thought that it had discovered a mitigation strategy that would be as successful as the one devised to prevent porpoise kills in the tuna industry.

In its efforts to convince fishermen to use TEDs, NMFS first had to fight the widely held conviction among shrimpers that under most conditions TEDs substantially decrease shrimp landings. To offset this belief, NMFS first promoted the device by arguing it would increase shrimpers' efficiency by decreasing the level of unwanted bycatch (such as jellyfish). On experimentation, however, fishermen found this to be the exception, rather than the rule.[46] Industry trade journals report that, at best, TEDs have worked inconsistently.

The NMFS protected species staff has been ineffectual in gaining a sympathetic ear from the shrimp industry. NMFS has been criticized for failing to coordinate its TED development work with similar research being conducted by industry, state, and academic groups. Fault has also been found in NMFS' decision to focus its testing of the TED in the Cape Canaveral area of Florida. While the area is known for its high turtle concentrations, few shrimpers feel that the waters and conditions there are representative of the entire Southeast region.

One final criticism has been directed at NMFS' erroneous assumption that one type of TED would be effective throughout the shrimp industry. While a single technological innovation may have been able to solve the tuna-porpoise problem, a simple technological fix was less

46. Such excluder devices were not new to the shrimp industry. Shrimpers along the Atlantic, Louisiana, and Texas coasts have long had seasonal problems with bycatch species such as jellyfish, horseshoe crabs, stingrays, and sharks. To deal with the problem they developed excluder devices (known locally as shooters). For a thorough discussion of TED development and the role of academia and industry see M. L. Edward's account in *National Fisherman*, July 1987 (Vol. 68, No. 3), pp. 37-41.

likely for shrimp fishermen. Unlike the shrimp industry, the tuna fleet is homogenous. Tuna seiners fish for the same fish in the same way. In contrast, there are several distinct shrimp fleets in the South Atlantic and Gulf of Mexico whose methods vary depending on season and geographic location. Shrimping off Padre Island, Texas, for example, bears little resemblance to shrimping in the shallow waters of North Carolina's Pamlico Sound. Thus, even if NMFS devises a TED acceptable to shrimpers who fish in one area, the same TED could be impractical in other waters.

NMFS' failure to take regional variations into account aggravated its already difficult problem of convincing shrimpers that using TEDs would not cut earnings. By 1986, after five years, NMFS had made no appreciable headway in getting shrimpers to voluntarily purchase and deploy TEDs. This delay became unacceptable to conservation groups. Led by the Center for Environmental Education, the conservation community served notice in August 1986 that unless NOAA acted immediately to require TEDs on shrimp trawlers it would take the issue to court.

Conservation groups refused to accept industry arguments that turtle hatcheries could make up for any turtle deaths related to fishing, contending that hatchery technology for turtle culture is unreliable. For their part, shrimp fishermen argued that mandatory use of TEDs would kill more turtles than it saved.[47] Finally, hoping to avoid a political battle, NOAA turned to arbitration.[48] Meetings were held during the fall of 1986. An agreement was reached to require TEDs on all shrimp boats using trawls longer than 30 feet after January 1, 1989. That compromise fell apart when grassroots opposition developed from fishermen who had not been represented by industry representatives on the arbitration panel.

Congress supervised the next round of negotiations. The result was a complex set of rules that exempted vessels under 25 feet from using TEDs as long as their tow time remained under 90 minutes.[49] Certain restrictions were to be delayed for up to 15 months. This compromise almost collapsed when it was realized that no TED had been designed to accommodate "flat" trawls used by North Carolina shrimpers. With the support of their congressman, Merchant Marine

47. During its TED trials, NMFS drowned at least one turtle.

48. It was the first time NOAA had employed such a tactic to resolve a fishery dispute. The agency selected for its negotiator a former Alaska labor leader who sat as a member of the North Pacific Fishery Management Council. The negotiations included a core group of conservationists and a selection of industry leaders who represented about 15 percent of the 6,000 vessel shrimp fleet.

49. The final TED regulation includes a dozen implementing variations (depending on where and when the shrimp fishing takes place, the distance fished from shore, and the size of the vessel employed). The complexity illustrates the regional diversity of the shrimp fleet.

and Fisheries Committee Chairman Walter Jones, these boats were exempted as well. One final wrinkle—a two-year implementation delay in inshore waters pending completion of further biological research—was added to legislation reauthorizing the Endangered Species Act, which passed the House late in 1987; this measure still must be approved by the Senate in 1988.

Whether any group can claim victory is arguable. The struggle split the shrimp industry in two. Inshore shrimpers (who make up about 90 percent of the fleet) got a virtual blanket release from the regulations; offshore shrimpers, while receiving certain seasonal and area exemptions, are generally required to use TEDs. Conservation groups hope the compromise will save those turtles most prone to capture by shrimp nets. While conservationists argue that half a victory is better than none, it is far from clear whether the regulations—even if they can be enforced—will do much to stop the continued decline in sea turtle populations. Some truth lies in the fishermen's argument that the real villain in this story is not fishermen's greed, but the ongoing degradation and destruction of turtle habitat.

Fishery Ecology. The fishery ecology program is funded at $14.7 million. NMFS studies the effects of natural and human-induced changes on marine habitats to determine their impacts upon the abundance, distribution, and physiological functions of species with commercial, recreational, and scientific significance. NMFS also investigates the effects of dams, power plants, effluents, dumping, dredging, and logging on fish, marine mammals, and endangered species. Increased understanding resulting from research on recruitment dynamics, pollutant effects, and other forces altering the ecosystem should help managers identify (if not lessen) nonfishing causes of mortality.

With the new Evans initiative for ecosystem management, fishery ecology has grown in significance, but not in funding.[50] Accurate prediction of fishery yields is difficult because of the variability of environmental factors that influence species abundance. Environmental changes can impact fish and shellfish at any point during their life, and may affect the distribution and availability of stocks in traditional migratory routes, feeding and spawning concentrations, and fishing grounds. This in turn drastically influences the supply of fish available to fishermen and marine predators (for example, marine mammals and sea birds).[51]

50. Since FY 1985, annual funding for fishery ecology has remained static. Funding for resource surveys, on the other hand, has grown 40 percent.

51. The most dramatic recent example of this sort of impact was the abnormally strong warm water current El Niño, which the West Coast experienced in 1983. That year, California king salmon landings dropped from 764,000 to 274,000 pounds. Three years later, landings approached record levels.

Base program activities in Fishery Ecology include critical work on the effects of microbial and other contaminants on fish and shellfish. Much of the work in this field is being done at NMFS' Sandy Hook laboratory in New Jersey. Located on a sand spit just south of the entrance to New York harbor, researchers there are developing scientific data on the distribution of toxins and the effects of environmental factors on clams, scallops, crab, hake (an abundant low-cost finfish), striped bass, bluefish, and various species of bottomfish. Particular emphasis has been placed on determining the levels of the contaminant PCBs (polychlorinated biphenyls) in various species.

The Fishery Ecology Program also conducts estuarine research, particularly at NMFS' Beaufort, North Carolina, laboratory. The lab's work is of special interest to conservation groups. Beaufort researchers are working to better document the functional importance of wetland habitat to fishery resources and to develop predictive models to assess the effects of large-scale wetlands loss on estuarine-dependent species such as striped bass, bluefish, menhaden, and shrimp. Conservationists believe this research will benefit biologists and coastal planners throughout the U.S. in their efforts to conserve fishery habitat in the U.S. coastal zone.

The desire to develop an effective predictive model is understandable, especially as budgets are tightened and NMFS' manpower is increasingly restricted. Coastal wetlands loss continues at an alarming pace and threatens important stocks of fish and other marine resources. NMFS estimates that 70 percent of the nation's fishery resources depend on estuaries at some stage in their life cycle for reproduction, shelter, food, migratory corridors, and so on. Estuarine-dependent species contribute $5.5 billion to the U.S. economy and support 17 million recreational fishermen, who generate an additional $7.5 billion of economic activity. Regardless of the ecological and economic importance of coastal wetlands, in the United States they continue to be dredged and filled at an annual rate of about 100,000 acres, according to NMFS habitat specialists.

Other habitat research under way includes investigations of ocean dumping, at-sea burning of hazardous wastes, the actual and potential impacts of offshore mineral and oil extraction, the relationship between natural and human-made factors in the decline of marine resources in Chesapeake Bay, and the role of dredging in microbial contamination of certain marine species.

Anadromous Fisheries Research. Anadromous research is funded at $17.3 million.[52] The vast majority of salmon research is

52. This big ticket item reflects in part the political power of salmon, and in part the political influence of the Pacific Northwest congressional delegation. It is the classic

performed in Washington, Oregon, and Alaska, where salmon is the most important commercial species. A limited amount of work is carried out in New England on Atlantic salmon. Research addresses salmon production and the quality of smolts released from hatcheries. NMFS staff also explores ways to improve the production efficiency of salmon hatcheries in the Pacific Northwest and Alaska. Other research is conducted in support of U.S. obligations under the U.S.-Canada Pacific Salmon Treaty[53] and to investigate the interception of U.S. salmon by the Japanese high-seas gillnet fishery.[54] Extensive work to implement the treaty is also done in cooperation with the states of Alaska, Washington, Oregon, and Idaho, Indian tribes, and the Pacific Salmon Commission (located in Vancouver, British Columbia). Many of these activities are overseen by a NMFS field office in Portland, Oregon.

NMFS also works to restore depleted Atlantic salmon stocks. This involves stock-identification work through tagging analysis. Agency scientists work closely with the North Atlantic Salmon Commission (located in Edinburgh, Scotland).

Stock Enhancement and Disease Research. The Stock Enhancement and Disease Research program primarily involves research on aquaculture and is funded at $3.1 million. Stock enhancement and disease research is conducted at NMFS fisheries laboratories to support management decisions affecting the long-term availability of certain fish and shellfish. Nonsalmon research and development activities include selective breeding of oysters and other shellfish, studying hatchery disease problems, determining nutritional requirements of shellfish larvae, developing new techniques for culturing larvae, and spawning and rearing scallops and surf clams. Research also includes culturing Kemp's ridley turtles to assist in species recovery.

---

example of how one segment of an industry can use effective political lobbying to its advantage. For more than 20 years, the salmon industry has enjoyed the powerful patronage of two chairmen of the Senate Commerce Committee, two chairmen of the Senate Interior Committee, a chairman of the Senate Appropriations Committee, a chairman of the Senate Finance Committee, and a Senate Minority Whip.

53. The treaty establishes a framework for bilateral management of Pacific Coast salmon stocks from the northern tip of the southeastern Alaska panhandle to the Oregon Coast and up the Columbia River. The Yukon River is also included (see the *Audubon Wildlife Report 1987* for details on the treaty).

54. This issue has been wedded to the anti-gill net initiative launched by Greenpeace (with support from other conservation groups). The marriage is one of convenience—not love. The salmon industry and the Alaska native groups are eager to increase the numbers of salmon returning to Alaskan rivers; Greenpeace and others are concerned over the loss of life suffered by seabirds and marine mammals caught incidentally in the Japanese salmon and squid nets (described as "curtains of death" by Senator Ted Stevens, an Alaska Republican).

Other activities include catfish farming at Stuttgart, Arkansas, a freshwater aquaculture facility partially supported by the Department of the Interior, and operational support for the Marine Science Center in Newport, Oregon.

Fisheries Industry Information. Collection of fishing industry data is funded at $9.2 million and supports 111 permanent positions. It is broken out as a separate line item in the budget. Eighty percent of the funds in this function are dedicated to compiling basic fishery statistics. This information is critical in both management and development efforts undertaken by NMFS and other agencies and organizations. The remaining 20 percent goes to collect social and economic data required by FCMA to help determine optimum yield (OY) for fish stocks.

Information is collected on commercial and recreational harvesting, processing and selling of fish and shellfish. This data includes: 1) the volume and value of catch in domestic and foreign fisheries by species, region, state, and method of gear; 2) the incidental take or harvest of nontarget species; 3) fishing effort and costs associated with harvesting; 4) the volume and value of processed fishery products from domestic landings and imports; 5) cold storage holdings of fishery products; 6) production of industrial fish products; 7) imports and exports of fishery products; 8) consumption of fishery products; and, 9) the number of marine recreational fishermen and their catches (by fishery), effort, and expenditures.

The type of data needed is determined through discussions with the industry, state and regional management bodies, and other federal agencies. Fishing effort and location data are collected from logbook records in some fisheries, from interviews of fishermen in others, and occasionally from on-board observers. Samples of commercial and recreational catches are also collected for biological and statistical analysis.

The availability and detail of fishing data gathered by NMFS varies tremendously from state to state. This disparity is due to the wide range of statistical support services that state fishery agencies are able to provide. Generally, West Coast state agencies are better funded and better staffed than their Gulf of Mexico and Atlantic counterparts. This is illustrated by the number and distribution of the 44 NMFS statistics offices. Despite the fact that more than half the nation's commercially caught fish are landed in U.S. Pacific ports, NMFS funds only four statistics offices throughout this region. On the other hand, in Florida, where less than five percent of the nation's commercially caught fish is landed, NMFS maintains seven offices (New Smyrna Beach, Miami, West Palm Beach, Key West, Fort Myers, St. Petersburg, Appalachicola, and Panama City). Louisiana, Texas, and Massachusetts each have five.

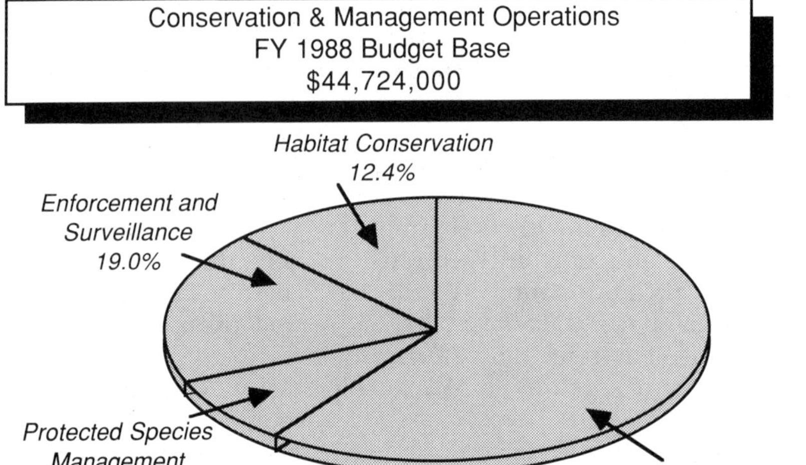

Figure 16. Source: NMFS.

Information Analysis and Dissemination. The Information Analysis and Dissemination budget line item is funded at $18.8 million and supports 247 permanent positions. The function of this program is to interpret all data collected under the Resource Information and Fisheries Industry Information programs. The analyses provided are critical to the makers of management policy, whether they are at the federal, regional or state level. The resource survey data is frequently used as a primary information source by conservation groups as well as by industry. Researchers analyze biological, environmental, economic and statistical information on marine resources to: 1) characterize various species by components such as growth rates, food requirements, habitat requirements, interrelationships, and behavioral characteristics; 2) assess the present and future status of stocks of value to the commercial and recreational sectors of the industry; 3) identify the consequences of natural and human-induced environmental changes on the production and abundance of marine resources; and 4) manage the impacts of fishery management measures on the resource and the industry.

Conservation and Management Operations

The Conservation and Management Operations subactivity is funded at $44.7 million and has 497 permanent positions attached to it (see Figure 16 and Table 9). The NMFS objectives under this account are to: 1) develop and implement domestic and international fishery manage

Table 9
NMFS FY 1988,
Conservation & Management Operations Programs (in Millions)

Program	Funding
Fishery Management Programs	
Regional Fishery Management Councils	$7.7
Fishery Management Plan Review and Implementation	5.4
International Fisheries Management	2.8
Interjurisdictional Fisheries Management	2.8
Columbia River Hatchery Program	8.3
Protected Species Management	
Permits & Recovery Program	1.7
Porpoise Observer	1.6
Pribilof Island Program	.4
Habitat Conservation	
Management & Project Planning	2.3
Environmental Impact Analysis	3.2
Enforcement & Surveillance	
Magnuson Act Enforcement	6.1
Protected Species Enforcement	2.4
TOTAL	44.7

ment measures needed for the optimum utilization of marine resources; 2) develop the U.S. fishing industry to be fully capable of utilizing those resources; 3) secure for the domestic industry the best terms possible for access to foreign and international fishery resources; 4) assist states in managing marine resources in their territorial waters; 5) conserve populations of marine mammals and endangered species affected by fishing and other marine activities (for example, offshore oil drilling, whale watching); 6) conserve the habitats of marine resources and associated ecosystems needed to sustain those resources at optimum levels; and 7) ensure compliance with management regimes for fishery resources, marine mammals, and species listed as threatened or endangered. Generally, personnel attached to NMFS' conservation and management operations are administrators, lawyers, enforcement officers, and management and development specialists. However, due to NMFS history as a research agency, many NMFS officials working in the management arena were trained originally as biologists. The majority of operations personnel work in regional offices.

Fisheries Management Programs. Fisheries Management Programs, a budget line item, is funded at $26.9 million and has 223 permanent positions attached to it (see Figure 17). NMFS, together with the eight

NMFS Conservation & Management
"Fishery Management Programs" Line Item
FY 1988 Administration Budget Base
$26,880 million

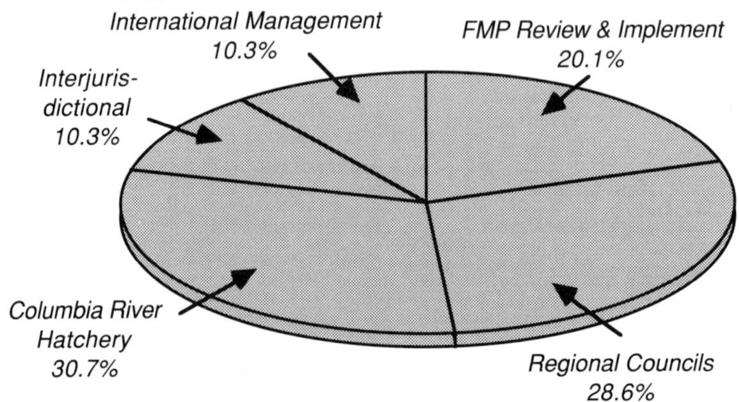

Figure 17. Source: NMFS.

regional fishery management councils, works with the states, industry, and other organizations "to provide stability and growth to the living marine resources of the United States and to the domestic fishing industry" (U.S. Department of Commerce 1987d). In practice, this means that fisheries must be managed to avoid overfishing and depletion while at the same time harvests are set at their optimum yield. In 1986, over 20,000 domestic and 430 foreign vessels fished within the nation's EEZ; they harvested almost 6.65 billion pounds of fish and shellfish. In addition, other fishery resources, such as tuna, shrimp, bottomfish, anchovies, scallops, and salmon, that range within and beyond the EEZ, are harvested by the fishing fleets of the U.S. and many other countries.

Regional Fishery Management Councils. Regional councils are funded at $7.7 million. NMFS provides the councils with technical and administrative assistance and financial support to assist them in developing, monitoring, and amending fishery management plans. Each year regional councils review up to 1,000 applications for fishing permits from foreign countries, conduct over 100 public hearings and meetings, and determine the yields and total allowable level of foreign fishing (TALFF) for each fishery under their management jurisdiction.

Catch Level Regulations. The major issue facing the councils in 1988 is a NMFS-proposed regulation terminating council responsibility for setting maximum harvest levels.[55] NMFS has taken this position out of its concern over the reaction of council members to lobbying from industry interest groups eager to maintain, if not increase, their harvest share. Many believe this pressure results in unjustifiably high harvest levels, as in the previously discussed case of king mackerel. While both NMFS and NOAA officials are actively encouraging council members to be more cautious in setting harvest levels, agency officials fear that persuasion alone will not protect marine resources from the social, economic, and political pressures that impel industry demands for fish.[56]

The proposed regulation incorporates a recommendation of the NOAA Fishery Management Study (Department of Commerce, 1986b), produced by the so-called blue-ribbon panel of 11 "wise men" invited by NOAA Administrator Anthony J. Calio to advise him on how to improve the nation's fishery management system. The study concluded that both conservation and fish allocation "decisions can [not] be made by the same body and still assure the integrity of the [harvest ceiling] determination. [The study] intends the [harvest ceiling] to be scientifically determined and inviolable for the period for which it is established. Accordingly, the study recommends that NOAA determine the [harvest ceiling] for each fishery at the national level and the Councils be responsible for making allocations."

NMFS has proposed that the management authority of councils be limited to allocating fish harvest levels set solely by NMFS. NMFS would seek advice from all sources (councils, states, academia, industry), and go through a public review process. However, the final decision-making authority would rest with the central office of NMFS.

NMFS's goal would be to set levels to protect stocks from overfishing. In theory, this approach would establish national controls to protect stocks from the inevitable local political pressures under which the councils must operate. The only significant change from the current council method would be reduced public involvement. Although a diminished public role could decrease the risk of councils setting harvest levels optimistically high, it would dramatically increase the responsibility and power of NMFS' resource assessment staff, who in turn would have to be adequately protected from industry pressure.

55. Under current regulation (discussed above under optimum yield), councils set both the maximum annual harvest level and, if they deem necessary, quotas or allocations within that harvest level to fishermen using different gear types (for example, trawl net *vs.* longline) or fishing for different reasons (for example, sport *vs.* commercial).

56. One tactic that NOAA might use to influence council decisions is to recommend that the Secretary of Commerce only appoint nominees who support conservative fishery management strategies. While conservative stock management is supported by some commercial fishermen, it is widely urged by recreational fishermen.

Another concern is that the harvest ceiling that NMFS would provide would depend upon which biological yield theory its scientists use. Some theories could result in harvest levels far higher than would ordinarily be set by councils. This situation is well illustrated by the debate over pollock harvest levels in the Bering Sea.[57] In 1986, NMFS estimated the pollock biomass to be 21.6 billion pounds; the NPFMC set the catch level at 2.87 billion pounds which was equal to 13.3 percent of the biomass. In a recent resource assessment document, however, NMFS scientists suggested that "exploitation rates of 10 to 13.6 percent may actually be conservative for a species like pollock. Based on the fishing strategy derived from yield per recruit theory, the optimal fishing rate may be as high as 22 percent" (Bakkala 1987).

A 22 percent exploitation rate would increase the pollock harvest from the 1987 level of 2.65 billion to 4.56 billion pounds. What is startling, however, is that the NPFMC's scientific and statistical committee recommended that the council consider an exploitation rate of 30 percent or 6.22 billion pounds. Ironically, a major portion of the domestic fishing industry fought against the scientific and statistical committee recommendation (as has Greenpeace, which is concerned over the impact of increased fishing on marine mammals and seabirds).

The case was argued at the December North Pacific council meeting. Despite the arguments of NMFS' Alaska Region director, the council voted to keep its conservative management strategy regardless of the advice of its scientific advisors. Many in the industry, as well as a number of state officials, are convinced that letting the councils set harvest levels is preferable to authorizing NMFS to do it alone. They contend that despite fierce pressure from fishermen, the current council system includes adequate checks and balances to ensure the well-being of the resource.

Not surprisingly, the proposed regulation is receiving uneven support. It is seen by many regional council supporters as yet another move by NMFS to limit the authority vested in the councils by FCMA. Whether NMFS can convince the Reagan Administration to adopt the proposed change remains to be seen; what finally happens is likely to be determined as much by politics as by good science.

Fishery Management Plan Review and Implementation. The Fishery Management Plan Review and Implementation program is funded at $5.4 million. NMFS reviews the fishery management plans developed by the regional councils to ensure compliance with FCMA, and implements these plans through promulgation and enforcement

57. In the United States, pollock is the primary ingredient in the so-called seafood analog products (imitation crab, shrimp, scallops, etc.). It is also is used heavily by fast food restaurants for fish sandwiches. Fish sticks are also frequently made from pollock. Many companies are also selling pollock in frozen fillet form and as a course in frozen dinners.

of appropriate regulations. The relationship between NMFS and the councils in the review process has never been cordial. It is the councils' position that Congress intended them to be "independent entities with specifically designed tasks and responsibilities. Unfortunately, administrative interpretation of the [FCMA] continues to put us into a subordinate or advisory role to [the Department of Commerce]" (U.S Congress, Senate, 1985). To clarify their position, the councils asked Congress in 1986 to highlight council independence from NMFS legislation reauthorizing FCMA (Pub. Law 99–659). Although Congress did not comply with this request, it made substantive changes to FCMA in an attempt to both accelerate the plan review process and ensure better communications.[58] The revision of current regulations regarding plan implementation should be complete by early 1988.

International Fisheries Management. International Fisheries Management is funded at $2.8 million. Most of the U.S. fisheries extending beyond the EEZ of the United States are managed by international organizations under several treaties and international agreements. Currently, nine international fishery management agreements involving 50 nations cover species such as halibut, tuna, and salmon. NMFS monitors significant fishery activities in foreign countries to determine their effects on U.S. interests. For example, NMFS monitors fisheries in the Soviet Union, Canada, and Mexico to determine what impact the management decisions of those nations could have on U.S. fisheries and fishermen. NMFS also collects information on foreign fishing policies, practices, and programs through the translation and review of technical literature, discussions with foreign and international fishery officials, and communications with overseas missions.

Foreign fishing effort within the U.S. zone is also assessed. This information is used by NMFS and the Department of State in negotiating and implementing international fishery agreements. It is also used for determining which foreign countries will be allowed to harvest the EEZ fishery resources left unused by the domestic fleet.[59]

58. Congressmen tend to view councils as constituents, and thus will go to bat for them. It is also worth remembering that Congress created the councils, and has a tendency to treat them as favored children ("We are inclined to be a little predjudiced about our babies," said Senator Ted Stevens [U.S. Congress, Senate, 1985]). Although it also created NMFS, Congress treats the agency more like an unwanted, but useful, stepchild. This may be the result of the councils' ability to play to Congress at a time when NMFS has frequently been forced to take an adversary role due to the policies of the Reagan Administration.

59. In 1987, twelve nations had signed governing international fisheries agreements (GIFA) with the U.S. They included: Bulgaria, the People's Republic of China, the European Economic Community, the Faroe Islands, the German Democratic Republic, Iceland, Japan, the Republic of Korea, Poland, the Soviet Union. In 1986, Italy, Spain, the

NMFS/NOAA participates annually in numerous negotiations with foreign governments and international fishery commissions.

Unregulated International Fisheries. For much of the seafood industry the major international fisheries issues for 1988 will be foreign fishing in the international waters of the Bering Sea and U.S. fishing in international waters off eastern Canada. Both issues arise from the global extension of fisheries jurisdiction to 200 miles. After 1977, the Bering Sea became almost exclusively a U.S.-Soviet lake. One pocket of international water—known as the doughnut hole—remained outside of both nation's 200-mile zone. As the opportunity to fish for pollock in Soviet and U.S. waters declined, Japanese, Korean, Chinese and Polish fishing companies increasingly turned their attention to the doughnut hole. By 1987, the U.S. estimated that the catch in the unregulated pollock fishery in Bering Sea international waters exceeded two billion pounds. Many U.S. industry representatives became increasingly concerned that this harvest could have a deleterious effect on the health of pollock stocks in U.S. waters. Soviet representatives expressed similar concern.

Some have suggested that Congress unilaterally extend U.S. management authority into the area. Currently, the State Department has the matter under discussion with Soviet officials. The most likely outcome will be formation of an international management commission. In the meantime, U.S. officials are doing what they can to place fishing observers on vessels trawling in the doughnut area.

The situation is further complicated because a handful of U.S. trawlers from New England are involved in an unregulated fishery in the North Atlantic. The U.S. vessels have joined a large multinational fleet fishing the waters at the tail of the Grand Banks, just beyond Canada's 200-mile limit. Except for the U.S., the national governments of every vessel of this fleet are members of the North Atlantic Fisheries Organization (NAFO). The international organization was established to prevent North Atlantic fleets from overfishing stocks of cod and other bottomfish.[60] The U.S. had not joined NAFO because since the 1930s, few U.S. fishermen had taken part in the Grand Banks trawl fishery. However, with fishing opportunities dwindling on U.S. grounds,[61]

German Democratic Republic, Japan, Poland, Korea, and China conducted fisheries off the Northeast, Pacific, and Alaska coasts. Their combined catch equaled 1.3 billion pounds, a 50-percent decline from 1985.

60. NAFO was resurrected from the ashes of the International Commission for North Atlantic Fisheries. The inability of the commission to control fishing effort was a major incentive for the United States and Canada to extend their respective jurisdictions.

61. In 1984, the World Court decided that the oceanic boundary between the United States and Canada should be a line equidistant from both coasts. This closed to U.S. fishermen grounds where they had fished for centuries (for example, the tip of Georges Bank, Browns Bank, and parts of the Gulf of Maine).

U.S. trawlers began once again to make the long trip to the Grand Banks. At one point late in 1987, the participating U.S. fleet had grown to 18 vessels. When the Canadians requested that the U.S. join NAFO, the New England fishing industry argued that membership was an unnecessary cost at a time when budgets were already tight.

The U.S. refusal to join the North Atlantic Fisheries Organization appears to signal Canada and other nations that the U.S. will not consult with them about U.S. fishing activities in international waters. The stance also makes it awkward for U.S. negotiators who are trying to achieve some sort of fishery management in the Bering Sea doughnut. "For the U.S. to demand international management in the Bering Sea while it ignores international management in the Atlantic just isn't acceptable," says one fisheries staffer on Capitol Hill. Others ask why the two issues need be merged. "We've never let inconsistency get in our way before," said a different congressional aide.

Interjurisdictional Fisheries. Interjurisdictional Fisheries are funded at $2.8 million. The coastal states are responsible for conserving and managing the commercial and recreational fisheries within their territorial waters, which for most states extend three miles offshore. Approximately two-thirds of the U.S. commercial harvest and more than three-quarters of the recreational catch occur in state waters. Because many fish species move constantly between state and federal waters, if stock conservation is to be effective, it is critical that state and federal officials coordinate management strategies. NMFS provides technical and financial assistance to the coastal states and to interstate marine fisheries commissions[62] to conserve and manage fisheries and to participate in the activities of the regional fishery management councils.

Interjurisdictional Conflict. The United States may be unique among nations in that the federal government continues to share authority for marine fisheries management with its coastal states. Those observers who believe that the federal government should be responsible for fishery management "from the beach to 200 miles," assert that power-sharing has resulted in inconsistent and frequently inadequate management. For example, they say, had the federal government had full marine management jurisdiction, the overfishing of striped bass along the East Coast could have been prevented without months of interstate debate and congressional threats of federal inter-

62. Three interstate fishery compacts have been authorized by Congress: Gulf States Marine Fisheries Commission, Atlantic States Marine Fisheries Commission, and Pacific States Marine Fisheries Commission. The commissions were established prior to the creation of the EEZ as a vehicle for interstate management. Since FCMA, their management opportunities have been limited. All three conduct important interstate fisheries research.

vention. Others contend that state governments are more sensitive to local demands and requirements. No one denies that multiple jurisdictions have led to turf battles, and that these struggles have resulted (and continue to result) in costly legal and political battles.

The debate over which level of government (state or federal) should take the fishery management lead will continue as long as responsibilities are shared. The previously discussed redfish controversy is one illustration of how the controversy manifests itself. Other interjurisdictional disputes have involved fisheries for king mackerel off Florida, salmon off Oregon and California, and crab off Alaska. The recurring theme in all these fights is the concern of one group of fishermen that another group will gain preferential treatment in the struggle to gain access to limited resources. In Florida, commercial fishermen fear that state management favors sport fishermen. In Alaska, Seattle-based crab fishermen worry that as "outsiders" they would be discriminated against under a state management program. In California and Oregon, state managers have agreed with industry arguments that federal salmon management plans have been unduly restrictive.

Columbia River Hatchery Operations. The Columbia Fishery Hatchery Operations program is funded at $8.3 million and pays for the operation of hatcheries located in the Columbia River basin. The hatcheries were authorized by Congress to help mitigate the losses of salmon and steelhead habitat caused by federal dams. The hatcheries release between six to eight million smolts annually.[63] The Pacific Northwest congressional delegation has protected federal funding of the hatcheries from cutback attempts by the administration.

NMFS also contributes biological and technological advice, as well as research assistance to salmon management plan development authorized under the Pacific Northwest Electric Power and Planning Conservation Act (16 U.S.C.A. 839) and the Pacific Northwest Salmon and Steelhead Conservation and Enhancement Act of 1980 (16 U.S.C.A. 3301). It reviews fish ladder and screen designs, assists in water budget and fish transportation activities, and implements provisions of the U.S.-Canada Pacific Salmon Treaty designed to protect salmon stocks harvested by fishermen from both nations.

Protected Species Management. The Protected Species Management budget line item is funded at $3.8 million, with 60 permanent

63. The authorizing legislation is the Columbia River Basin Fishery Development Program (also known as the Mitchell Act). It is ironic that the need for this program was largely due to the success of Senator Warren Magnuson in winning funding for dam construction. The paradox is, that while it can be argued that the Washington Democrat was the great protector of U.S. fishermen in their struggle against foreign competition, he was also the great destroyer. For more on the destruction of the great Columbia River salmon runs see Netboy 1980 and Seufert 1980.

positions. NMFS is required under the Marine Mammal Protection Act (MMPA), the Endangered Species Act, and the Fur Seal Act to investigate and minimize the effects of human activities that detrimentally affect species protected by those laws.

NMFS shares its MMPA responsibilities with the U.S. Fish and Wildlife Service (FWS). Included under NMFS' protective umbrella are more than 100 species, including whales, porpoises (dolphins), seals, and sea lions.[64] NMFS develops and implements procedures to reduce mortality of marine mammals during domestic and foreign commercial fishing operations, outer-continental-shelf development, and other activities affecting these animals. NMFS also processes applications for the taking or importing of marine mammals for scientific purposes and conducts public hearings on these applications. Since 1972, 770 scientific research and public display applications have been received and 569 permits have been issued. Approximately 60 applications for permits are processed annually.

NMFS is responsible for implementing several international agreements concerning marine mammals, including the International Convention for the Regulation of Whaling (IWC). It participates in numerous international negotiations concerning these and other marine mammal agreements.

NMFS is also responsible for the management, conservation, and, where possible, restoration of marine species listed as threatened or endangered under the Endangered Species Act. As it does under the Marine Mammal Protection Act, NMFS shares its endangered species responsibilities with FWS. Under the act, NMFS's protected species managers responsible for whales, seals, porpoises, sea lions, sea turtles, commercially harvested species of mollusks and crustaceans whose life is spent in estuary waters, and aquatic life forms that reside most of their life in marine waters or spend part of their life in estuaries and the remainder in marine areas.[65]

NMFS and FWS work together in listing, protecting, and controlling the importation of listed species into the United States. NMFS promulgates and administers regulations; reviews state laws, regulations, and management programs for compliance with federal regulations; monitors certificates allowing limited interstate commerce in certain whale oil and scrimshaw products; and issues permits for scientific research and propagation activities.

In addition, NMFS develops recovery programs for listed species under its jurisdiction. To date, it has completed a group recovery plan

64. Some marine mammals are under the authority of FWS, including the West Indian manatee, sea otter, marine otter, walrus, polar bear, and dugong.

65. FWS has responsibility for reptiles (sea turtles only on land), noncommercially harvested mollusks and crustaceans, mammals (except pinnepeds and cetaceans), birds, amphibians, all other aquatic life forms, and all other species which spend the major portion of their life on land or in fresh water.

for four Atlantic sea turtle species, and separate plans for the Hawaiian monk seal and the leatherback sea turtle. Plans for the California harbor porpoise, humpback whale, right whale, and Olive ridley sea turtle are in progress. NMFS also consults with other federal agencies and provides biological opinions under Section 7 of the act to assist federal agencies in minimizing the possibility that their activities will jeopardize the continued existence of listed species or habitat critical to those species.

The two major problems currently under NMFS investigation are the impacts of plastic debris on marine wildlife (see the "Plastic Debris and Its Effects on Marine Wildlife" chapter in this volume) and fishing gear entanglement. While the fishing gear entanglement program traditionally focused its research on *discarded* netting, it will be placing increased attention on entanglement caused during fishing operations. It will also focus attention on the growing anger among fishermen over marine mammals feeding on their catch and destroying their gear.

Preventing Fishery Impacts on Protected Marine Species. As an area of concern to conservation groups, the interaction between fishermen and marine mammals (and other protected species) has expanded significantly beyond the tuna-porpoise and shrimp-turtle issue. Since 1984, Greenpeace has intensified its opposition to high seas salmon and squid gill net fisheries conducted in the Pacific by nations such as Japan and Taiwan. The Sea Shepherd Conservation Society joined the gill net battle in 1986 with plans to directly interfere with the fishing operations of the foreign fleets. The Center for Environmental Education expanded the area of coverage with broad new research into the entanglement issue (O'Hara and Atkins 1986). The center is focusing particular attention on gill net fisheries, but is also concerned about the impact of Alaska bottomfish fishery on seals and sea lions. Another area of conflict between fishermen and mammals has developed in the Alaska longline fishery for black cod. For the past several years, vessels in this fishery have suffered financial losses from killer whales feeding on their catch. To date, no reliable method has been found to keep whales off fishermen's gear.

Understandably, as these issues grow in concern to conservationists, they receive increased attention from the fishing industry. As a result, fleet representatives are currently working with conservation groups to find solutions to the killer whale-black cod problem in Alaska and to the incidental catch of mammals and seabirds by gill nets in California. However, if NMFS is to protect marine mammals from death or harassment due to fishing gear, it must come up with management measures capable of effective implementation. The challenge is immensely difficult. In the case of tuna fishing and porpoises, it took years of intense public pressure, lobbying and ultimately congressional action (including designated funding) before NMFS established an effective program. The Porpoise Observer Program is based on extensive research, and most importantly, the placing of observers on most tuna boats to monitor porpoise mortality. Its annual funding is $1.6 million.

Whether the tuna boat observer program can be transferred to other fisheries is doubtful. First, the cost is high. In the case of tuna, without close to 100 percent observer coverage, the program would not work. While the NMFS budget dedicates $1.65 million for porpoise observers, boat owners say the amount only partially covers the expense of having observers on board. Second, placing observers on the majority of fishing vessels may not be practical. Tuna seiners are large, with relatively ample accommodations. Their facilities are exceptional in the industry. The only equivalent may be the 15 to 20 factory trawlers currently operating in the Bering Sea fishery for bottomfish. Elsewhere, the U.S. fleet most likely to interact with marine mammals and endangered species is characterized by tight living quarters (if they exist at all) and frequently tighter operating budgets. Despite these obstacles, NMFS is struggling to develop a national fishing vessel observer policy.[66]

The cost of training, transporting, and providing for observers, combined with the inability of most fishing vessels to carry them, may explain why NMFS has preferred developing conservation strategies based on new or alternative gear technology, such as the TED.[67] However, even if additional funding can be found to perfect TED technology and convince fishermen to use it,[68] the strategy may yet fail without on-board observers to monitor the effectiveness of TEDs and to ensure their use. Another delicate issue is whether observers should have enforcement powers added to their role as monitors—powers that are vehemently opposed by the fishing industry.

Permit and Recovery Plans. The Permit and Recovery Plans program is funded at $1.7 million. NMFS has been severely criticized

66. The marine mammal issue is not the only reason NMFS is now developing a national observer policy. For over a decade, NMFS scientists have relied heavily on data supplied by observers placed aboard foreign fishing and processing vessels operating in the EEZ. As the U.S. industry replaces foreign operations, that data is being lost since FCMA does not require observers on U.S. ships. With most foreign fishing soon to be a thing of the past, NMFS is striving to come up with new ways to get reliable fishing data.

67. State agencies have adopted a similar strategy. California, for example, has funded alternate gear programs through its fish and game department.

68. Conservation groups lobbied hard, but unsuccessfully, for Congress to add $900,000 to the NMFS budget for an intensified "dock-side" TED education and information program. The House State, Justice, and Commerce Appropriations Committee did add $250,000 for "endangered species recovery plans," which presumably could be spent for such a program.

Table 10
Species Listed by NMFS under the Endangered Species Act.[a]

Species	Year listed	Status of Recovery Plan
Gulf of California harbor porpoise	1985	in preparation
Guadalupe fur seal	1985	no plan
Caribbean monk seal	1967	no plan
Hawaiian monk seal	1976	completed 4/1/83
Mediterranean monk seal	1970	no plan
Blue whale	1970	no plan
Bowhead whale	1970	no plan
Finback whale	1970	no plan
Gray whale	1970	no plan
Humpback whale	1970	in preparation
Right whale	1970	in preparation
Sei whale	1970	no plan
Sperm whale	1970	no plan
Leatherback sea turtle	1970	completed 10/23/81
Green sea turtle	1970	completed 9/19/84[b]
Hawksbill sea turtle	1970	completed 9/19/84[b]
Kemp's ridley sea turtle	1970	completed 9/19/84[b]
Loggerhead sea turtle	1978	completed 9/19/84[b]
Olive ridley sea turtle	1978	in preparation
Shortnose sturgeon	1967	no plan
Totoaba	1979	no plan

Source: National Wildlife Federation
[a] All species except the Guadalupe fur seal and the Loggerhead sea turtle are listed as endangered.
[b] Group recovery plan for the Atlantic sea turtles.

by conservation groups for not diligently executing its responsibilities under the Endangered Species Act. During public testimony before the Senate on the act's reauthorization, the National Wildlife Federation argued that "not only is [NMFS] ill-suited to fulfill its obligations under the [act], but is disinterested in the need to protect and recover those threatened and endangered species for which it is responsible" (National Wildlife Federation 1987a). The organization justified this claim by pointing out that NMFS had listed only two species since 1980. Worse, of the 21 listed species under its jurisdiction, NMFS has approved recovery plans for only six (see Table 10).

Three things explain NMFS' poor performance, according to one senior FWS official familiar with the situation: lack of money, lack of interest, and lack of constituent pressure. According to this source, "In 1986 [FWS] had over $11 million for recovery plans; NMFS had less than $1 million. Secondly, small programs don't attract the best people. And finally the active NMFS constituency, fishermen, generally look at protected species as a nuisance—not a mission."

Habitat Conservation. The Habitat Conservation line item is funded at $5.5 million and has 85 permanent positions. Protecting marine habitat is essential if the nation wishes to preserve the fish and wildlife that depend upon it. To this end, the NMFS habitat conservation program works to fulfill the agency's responsibilities for habitat protection mandated by the National Environmental Policy Act, the Endangered Species Act, and the Fish and Wildlife Coordination Act (FWCA).

Limited Habitat Authority. The current status of estuarine wetlands is not reassuring. Louisiana is losing 60 square miles of wetlands annually. California has lost 90 percent of its original 3.5 million acres of inland and coastal wetlands. The Columbia River Basin has lost a third of its historic salmon, steelhead, and sturgeon spawning grounds. Connecticut has lost two-thirds of its coastal marshes. The litany of destruction is seemingly endless.

Equally troubling is the belief among many NMFS habitat preservation specialists that the Reagan Administration views their efforts more as an unavoidable irritant than as a vital service. "Our program is clearly [at] the bottom of the heap," lamented one official. "NOAA doesn't even seem to want anyone to know about us." The result, he says, is that "NMFS is out chasing fires and missing the earthquake."

The habitat program's weakness is that although it can make recommendations, it generally has no authority to stop another agency from issuing permits to private parties to conduct activities that destroy wetlands or to stop federal development agencies engaging in such activities. Except in cases involving endangered species, NMFS can at best appeal a decision to higher levels within the bureaucracy of the federal agency sponsoring the harmful activity. Despite its lack of authority to veto harmful projects, NMFS is frequently successful in convincing permit applicants and federal development agencies to minimize a project's environmental impact, according to NMFS officials. "Developers are fully aware that we can use our review authority to create long and costly delays," one NMFS habitat specialist said. Finally, he adds that the NMFS review process can be a critical source of information to conservation or other groups who plan to legally object to a permit's approval.

A good example of NMFS' efforts to protect habitat centers on a Navy proposal to relocate a carrier battle group at Everett, Washington. To make this Puget Sound port ready for its vessels, the Navy needs state and federal permits to dredge three million cubic yards of material from Everett harbor, one million cubic yards of which is seriously contaminated with toxic substances.[69] The Navy planned to tow the dredged material into water 400 feet deep and dump it.

69. NMFS scientists have identified 30 "priority contaminants" listed by the Environmental Protection Agency in the material to be dredged. They have also identified several species of fish living in the contaminated area that suffer severely from tumors.

Dumped contaminated matter would be covered by "clean" material. NMFS objected to the proposal, contending that no "capping" project of this magnitude had ever been carried out. It was also possible, said NMFS, that bottom-burrowing creatures would create holes through which the contaminated material would eventually seep.

Despite these concerns, the state issued a water quality permit approving the Navy's proposal. When it appeared that the district office of the Corps of Engineers would also issue a Section 404 dredging permit (under the Clean Water Act), NMFS requested that the permit decision be elevated to the Corps division level. At this level, the Corps agreed to approve the permit, but only under stringent sampling and monitoring requirements that could shut the project down if contamination began leaking into Puget Sound. Unhappy with that compromise, the Navy elevated the decision to Washington, D.C., where the Corps eventually decided to return the matter to the district level for a final decision. At that point, NMFS bowed out of the process.

However, during the two-year period over which these events occurred, enough information was gathered by environmental groups to file a suit to prevent the dumping of dredged material into Puget Sound. After some initial reluctance, the federal government decided to allow NMFS officials to testify about their concerns. By early 1988, the Corps had yet to issue the Navy a 404 permit.

While determined NMFS opposition can create procedural headaches and costly delays to permit applicants, NMFS officials want more specific authority to block projects with serious habitat-degrading potential. To this end, NMFS officials strongly support a set of proposed Department of Commerce amendments to the Fish and Wildlife Coordination Act now under review by the White House. The most critical proposal is a provision that would require future federal actions to be consistent with approved resource management plans (such as fishery management or wildlife refuge management plans). The proposed procedure is modeled after the consistency provision of the Coastal Zone Management Act (16 U.S.C.A. 1456(c)(d)). Due to opposition from other federal agencies, however, many NMFS officials doubt whether the Reagan Administration will support the proposal.

Management and Project Planning. The Management and Project Planning program is funded at $2.3 million. NMFS supplies federal agencies with information and recommendations about the environmental impact of developments and projects that could affect the habitats of valuable marine species. This consultation is mandatory as authorized under the Fish and Wildlife Coordinating Act, the National Environmental Policy Act, the Clean Water Act of 1977, and the Marine Protection, Research and Sanctuaries Act of 1972. The recently amended FCMA also strengthens NMFS review authority.[70]

Typical subjects for review are construction projects of the Bureau of Reclamation and the Army Corps of Engineers; projects to create industrial and residential waterfront property that require Corps of Engineers' permits for dredging and filling; hydropower plant construction projects requiring Federal Energy Regulatory Commission licenses; and facilities requiring discharge permits (for example, sewage and industrial effluents) from the Environmental Protection Agency.

Environmental Impact Analysis. The Environmental Impact Analysis program is funded at $3.2 million. To assess potential environmental impacts, NMFS annually reviews approximately 8,000 permit applications filed with the Corps of Engineers under Section 404 of the Clean Water Act. In 1986, these applications covered over 40,000 acres of coastal habitat with an annual fisheries value in excess of $8 million. The vast majority of these applications involved projects in NMFS' Southeast Region.

In an attempt to evaluate the NMFS permit review program, two NMFS habitat conservation specialists reviewed 5,385 permits affecting 184,187 acres (Mager and Thayer 1986). Forty-four percent of the permit requests were for dredging, 28 percent were for impounding, 25 percent were for filling, and 3 percent were for draining. NMFS approved permits for 26.3 percent of the total acreage involved without objection, and made conservation recommendations on the other 74 percent. To offset habitat losses, NMFS recommended that an additional 97,640 acres of wetlands be restored and 12,766 acres be artificially created.

Mager and Thayer then followed up on 857 permits for which NMFS had made conservation recommendations. They discovered that half of the recommendations had been accepted and 24 percent partially accepted. They then investigated 425 of these in an attempt to measure permit-holder compliance. It was just under 80 percent (see Figures 18a–c). Extrapolated, these findings indicate that two out of every five recommendations made by NMFS to preserve habitat are either rejected by the Corps or ignored by the permit holder.

In addition to reviewing permits for ocean dumping and coastal wetland dredging and filling, NMFS provides technical assistance on fisheries matters important to state coastal zone management plans,

70. Under Section 302(i) of FCMA, councils have new authority to review proposed public works and private developments in need of federal permits. The language requires that should a council request information or make recommendations concerning any state or federal activity which in the council's view might affect habitat, the agency responsible for the activity must provide a detailed response to the council's concern in writing within 45 days.

Treatment of 857 permits which included recommendations made by NMFS Southeast Region to the Corps of Engineers, 1981-1986

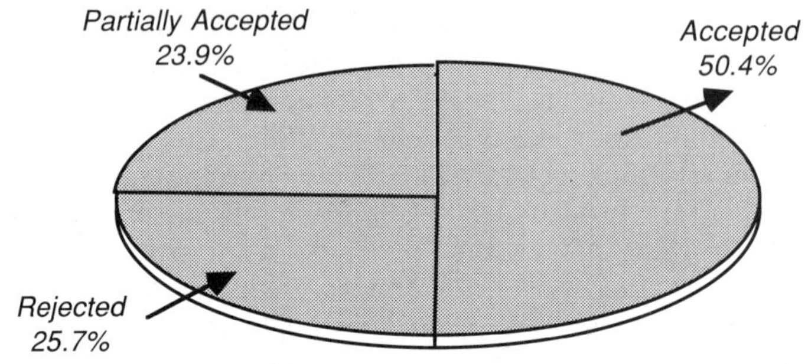

Figure 18a.

Survey of 425 projects with Corps of Engineers' permits in the NMFS Southeast Region to determinecompliance with permit stipulations, 1981-1986

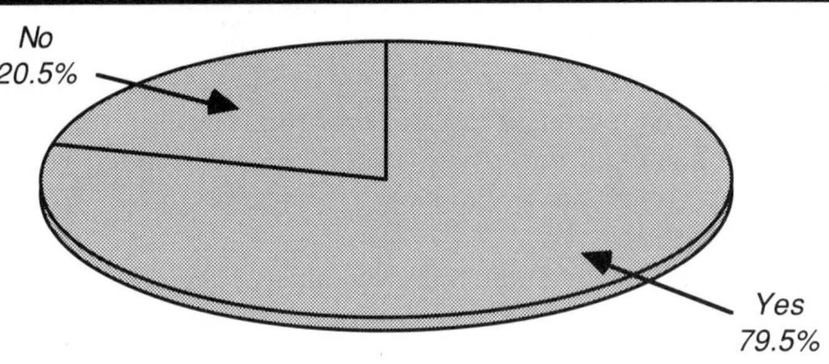

Figure 18b. Source: NMFS.

fishery management plans, special area management plans, proposed marine and estuarine sanctuaries, and outer-continental-shelf oil and gas exploration and production.

Enforcement and Surveillance. The Enforcement and Surveillance line item is funded at $8.5 million and funds 129 permanent positions. Effective management is predicated upon enforcement of marine resource laws. NMFS enforcement agents investigate violations of laws and regulations under FCMA, the Marine Mammal Protection Act, the Endangered Species Act, and the Lacey Act[71] (as well as under other

71. The Lacey Act Amendments of 1981 (16 U.S.C.A. 3401) have made this legislation the most convenient tool available to enforcement agents. The purpose of the

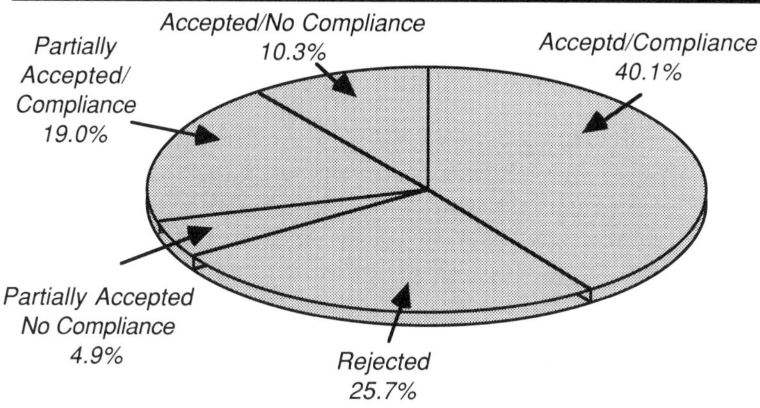

Figure 18c. Source: NMFS.

federal statutes and international agreements relating to living marine resources). Enforcement activities are designed to reduce the illegal take of all marine resources. If necessary, agents are authorized to seize nonmarine-related contraband (for example, drugs). NMFS enforcement agents are allowed to employ the full range of investigative techniques, including the purchase of evidence and information. Agents manage funds for covert operations and undercover activities.[72] Surveillance activities also provide information concerning catches and fleet movements that can be used in international negotiations, as well as for managing domestic and foreign fisheries.

The enforcement budget has survived the Reagan Administration unscathed. It is scheduled to receive a 10 percent increase in FY 1988. Yet it is clear the office is too small to effectively fulfill its responsi-

---

Act is to deter illegal trade in protected species by improving civil and criminal penalties for violations of federal, state, and foreign laws. Due to the severity of its penalties, the seafood industry regards the increasing use of Lacey in the regulation of seafood sales as pernicious. What the industry finds most upsetting is the requirement that violators are supposed to know whether the fish they are selling was taken, possessed, transported, or sold in violation of any underlying law. The law has been used to prosecute fish dealers who unwittingly bought striped bass that had been illegally caught, and suppliers who shipped legally caught, but inadequately marked, fish into a state where its harvest was illegal. It has also been used to prosecute fishermen who illegally caught shrimp in Mexico, and may soon be used against U.S. fishermen fishing in Canadian waters.

72. NMFS has been involved in a number of "sting" operations over the past years primarily to prevent the sale of fish caught illegally. Illegal salmon sales by native Americans was the focus of a Columbia River operation; striped bass sales were the target of a Chesapeake Bay investigation.

bilities. "We've got about 92 field agents,"[73] said one enforcement agent based in the NMFS central office. "They're all working flat out. It's crazy. We run them until they're burned out. There's no way we could do it without personnel support from the state agencies, the Coast Guard, and Customs [Service]. To be really honest, half of our arrests are accidental in that they come in the process of routine patrol work. The other half come from informants."

Magnuson Act Enforcement. The FCMA program is funded at $6.1 million. Almost three-quarters of the office's budget goes to enforcing FCMA. The office is responsible for ensuring that both foreign and domestic fishing vessels operate legally. Activities include the enforcement of fishing limits, seasons, area closures, gear restrictions and fish size limitations.[74] FCMA enforcement activities involving fishing vessels are planned and conducted together with the U.S. Coast Guard, which provides aerial and surface patrol craft.[75] NMFS also charters aircraft to supplement Coast Guard support and enters into cooperative agreements with state enforcement agencies. Shoreside activities require the purchase or lease of government unmarked cars for performing undercover operations and investigations.

The work is daunting. "We've got one agent in Louisiana. It's up to him to enforce closures on red drum (that is, potential "blackened" redfish) and Spanish mackerel. It's up to him to enforce the quota on a three-month bluefin tuna season – and remember we're talking about a $15-a-pound item. Remember, too, he's got the state and [Food and Drug Administration] on him to make sure contaminated oysters don't get onto the market. And the closest help he has is in Corpus Christi, Texas, or Appalachicola, Florida," said a NMFS official.

Protected Species Enforcement. The Protected Species Enforcement program is funded at $2.4 million. NMFS investigates importation or interstate transportation of parts or products of protected species. In this they work closely with officials from the U.S. Customs Service. All sales of scrimshaw are monitored. In 1987, 35 sealskin

73. Twenty-six agents in the Northeast Region, 19 in each the Southeast and Alaska regions, and 14 each in the Northwest and Southwest regions.

74. Under the recently approved Northeast Multispecies Fisheries Management Plan it is illegal for fishermen or fish dealers to have in their possession cod, haddock, or pollock under 19 inches, witch flounder under 14 inches, yellowtail or American plaice under 12 inches, or winter flounder under 11 inches. Imported fish (which come mostly from Canada) are included in the restrictions. During the regulations' first three months, about a half dozen seizures were made.

75. During the first 11 months of 1987, the Coast Guard boarded 477 fishing vessels in the EEZ off Alaska. Of those vessels, 69 percent were U.S. owned. It issued 59 FCMA violations, 11 to U.S. vessels. Over the same period, the Coast Guard expended 540 cutter days and 1,416 aircraft patrol hours on fisheries enforcement.

Table 11
NMFS FY 1988,
State & Industry Assistance Programs (in Millions)

Program	Funding
Grants to States	
Interjurisdictional Fisheries Management	$ 4.0
Disaster Aid	2.0
Anadromous	3.0
Fisheries Development	
Fisheries Trade	1.5
Product Quality & Safety	8.2
Menhaden Research	1.0
Fish Oil Research	1.0
Gulf Underutilized Species	1.0
Fish Inspection Program	0.35
Mahi Mahi Export Program	0.1
TOTAL	$21.2

coats were seized after an investigation disclosed the skins did not come from the Pribilof harvest as had been claimed.[76]

Enforcement personnel are so overextended that to monitor the new TED requirements that went into effect October 1, 1987 in Florida's Cape Canaveral area, the Southeast region had to pay for an agent from the Northwest region to come down for 90 days of temporary duty. He will work with just one other NMFS agent to ensure that the local shrimp fleet (from 100 to 200 vessels) complies with the new regulations.

State & Industry Assistance Programs

The State & Industry Assistance Programs budget subactivity is funded at $21.2 million and includes 194 permanent positions (see Table 11 and Figure 19). This conglomeration of programs has been under constant attack by President Reagan's budget-cutters. However, because each has a core constituency ready to fight for its continuation, the cuts have been denied and new programs have been added by Congress.

Grants to States. The Grants to States budget line item is funded at $9 million. No permanent positions are attached to it. It includes three grant programs.

76. The Aleuts of the Pribilof Islands (in the Bering Sea) conduct the only approved seal hunt in the United States. Until 1985 the Aleuts conducted a commercial hunt. Since then, the hunt has been classified as subsistence. This has meant that Aleuts can no longer sell seal pelts for commercial use.

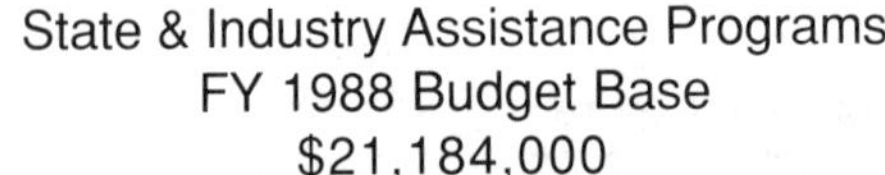

State & Industry Assistance Programs
FY 1988 Budget Base
$21,184,000

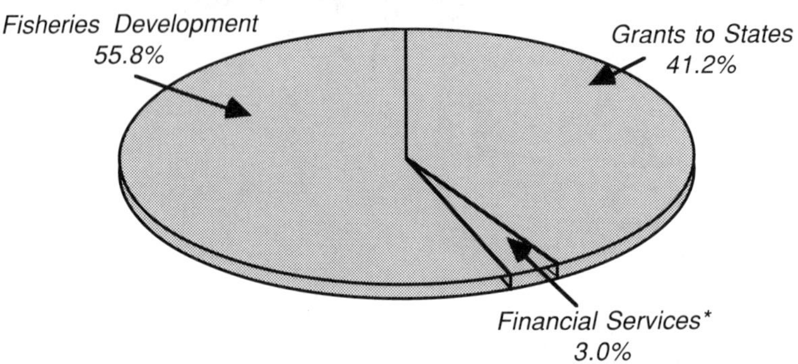

*Administration of these programs is no longer handled by NMFS.

Figure 19. Source: NMFS.

Interjurisdictional Fisheries Management. Commercial Research and Development is funded at $4 million. Until 1987, it was authorized under the Commercial Fisheries Research and Development Act (16 U.S.C.A. 779). However, effective October 1, 1987, it was replaced by the Interjurisdictional Fisheries Act of 1986 (PL 99–659, Title III). The act apportions funds under a complex formula among states based on commercial fishing activity. Funds are to be spent on either research or development projects with a connection to those fisheries covered by interjurisdictional fishery management plans, such as those developed by regional councils under FCMA or by interstate compacts (for example, striped bass and menhaden).

Disaster Aid. The Disaster Aid program is funded at $2 million. The program was designed to assist states suffering economic hardship due to a natural disaster to its fishery resources.

Anadromous Grants. Authorized under the Anadromous Fish Conservation Act (16 U.S.C.A. 757) and funded at $3 million, the 20-year-old Anadromous Grants program gives NMFS the authority to enter into cooperative agreements "to conserve, develop, and enhance" the nation's anadromous fishery resources subject to depletion from water resource development projects. It specifically includes $500,000 for striped bass research. The federal share of any project cannot exceed 50 percent. Funds can be spent on hatchery development or other research related to anadromous species including salmon, steelhead, herring, sturgeon, and striped bass.

Fisheries Development. The Fisheries Development line item is funded at $12.2 million, has 194 permanent positions assigned to it, and supports a variety of fishery research and development activities, as well as associated trade activities. It also provides for fishery product quality and safety programs.

Fisheries Trade. Fisheries Trade is funded at $1.5 million, and covers a host of industry-related activities including: 1) support for the expansion of export markets; 2) consumer services; 3) the market news publication service; 4) and fisheries trade policy analysis. The program supports fishery development personnel in Washington, D.C., and in each of the five regional offices.

Product Quality and Safety. The Product Quality and Safety program, which conducts research into the public health aspects of fishery product consumption, is funded at $8.2 million. It also researches new products that can be derived from fish and shellfish, particularly those species (such as pollock) that the fishing industry has been encouraged to develop under FCMA.

Menhaden Research. Menhaden Research is funded at $1 million. It was established to assist the menhaden industry to develop food products from its catch. Menhaden, a fish with a high oil content, is caught in large volumes; in 1986, 2.4 billion pounds were landed, mostly in Louisiana. Currently, menhaden processors reduce their catch into meal and oil, and export it, primarily to Europe. Menhaden products are used in products ranging from chicken feed to margarine.

Fish Oil Research. The Fish Oil Research program is funded at $1 million. NMFS has done extensive experimentation into methods of providing a standardized source of fish oil in forms suitable for medical research on the human health benefits of the Omega 3-fatty acids found in fish.

Gulf Underutilized Species. Funded at $1 million, the Gulf Underutilized Species program was established to assist fishermen in the Gulf of Mexico interested in diversifying into fisheries other than shrimp. NMFS is conducting both economic and technical feasibility studies. To date, the program's only success has been development of a limited fishery for butterfish.

Fish Inspection Program. Research into fish inspection is funded at $350,000. The Fish Inspection Program is part of a multiyear project with the seafood industry to design an effective seafood inspection program. Currently, the only inspection available to U.S. seafood companies is a voluntary program provided for a fee by NMFS.

Mahi Mahi Export Strategy. The Mahi Mahi Export Strategy, a market development program, is funded at $100,000. Congress has provided these funds to develop the market potential and design export strategies for this Hawaiian food fish.

ADDENDUM 1

The Fishery Management Plan Amendment Process

One way to understand why the U.S. fishery management process is so cumbersome and reacts so slowly to changing conditions is to walk through the procedure required to amend a fishery management plan.

For example, if a conservation organization wishes to restrict commercial trawl operations in an area of the eastern Bering Sea critical to the survival of Stellar sea lions, it would have to amend the Bering Sea/Aleutian Islands Groundfish Management Plan. To do this, the organization would first submit its proposed amendment to the North Pacific Fishery Management Council. Under the council's current calendar, all proposed amendments to its groundfish plan must be received before October 1.

Once submitted, the organization's proposal is reviewed, together with other proposals, by the council's groundfish plan team (consisting of scientists from the state and federal government and the academic community). A second critique is then performed by the Bering Sea groundfish plan amendment advisory group (consisting of members of the council, its scientific and statistical committee and its advisory panel).

Once it passes these two evaluations, the proposal is placed before the council at its January meeting. At this meeting the council votes whether to consider the proposed amendment. If a proposed amendment is included for further consideration, it then receives a more thorough analysis by the groundfish team and the advisory group.

At its April meeting, the council votes again on which proposals to consider and which to eliminate. If the proposed amendment is endorsed for further consideration, it then goes out to the public for further review. At its June meeting, the proposed amendment is discussed and voted upon by the council's scientific and statistical committee and its advisory panel. The council then takes oral public testimony, after which the members vote—assuming they request no further information.

If the Council approves an amendment to one of its plans, the proposal together with supporting documentation is forwarded to the Secretary of Commerce. To be complete, this "amendment package" must include:

1. the final amendment;
2. the proposed regulations and preamble;
3. notice of public availability of the amendment;
4. any source documents necessary to support the amendment;
5. a final environmental impact statement or environmental assessment as required under the National Environmental Policy Act and the Marine Mammal Protection Act;
6. a draft regulatory impact review combined with an initial regulatory flexibility analysis as required under Executive Order 12291 and the Regulatory Flexibility Act;
7. a request for information collection as required under the Paperwork Reduction Act;
8. a Coastal Zone Management consistency determination as required under the Coastal Zone Management Act; and
9. an Endangered Species Act Section 7 biological evaluation as required by the Endangered Species Act.

In Washington, the NMFS and Secretary of Commerce review process takes another 145 days (5 days for transmission, 110 days for review, including a 60-day public comment period), and a 30-day "cooling off" period after publication in the *Federal Register*). Assuming all is in order, and no affected party attempts to halt the amendment through litigation, the proposal will become law 413 days after originally submitted.

ADDENDUM 2

A Brief History of the National Marine Fisheries Service—1871 to 1970

By the Act of February 9, 1871, Congress first recognized a federal interest in the conservation of fisheries by authorizing appointment of a Commissioner of Fish and Fisheries to study the decrease of food fishes of the seacoasts and lakes of the United States and to suggest remedial measures. The commissioner was appointed by the President, with the advice and consent of the Senate, from among the civil officers or employes of the Government and was to serve without additional salary. The sum of $5,000 was appropriated to carry out the required study. In 1888, the law was amended to authorize a salary of $5,000 per year for the commissioner and to require that he not hold any other office or employment under the authority of the United States or any state.

The Fish Commission and the Office of the Commissioner of Fish and Fisheries functioned as an independent establishment of the government from February 9, 1871 to July 1, 1903. The Act of February 14, 1903, which created the Department of Commerce and Labor, placed the Fish Commission and the Office of the Commissioner of Fish and Fisheries in that department. The same act transferred from the Department of the Treasury to the Department of Commerce and Labor jurisdiction, supervision and control over the fur seal, salmon, and other fisheries of Alaska. The combined agency was called the Bureau of Fisheries.

By the Act of March 4, 1915, the Department of Commerce and Labor was divided into two separate departments. The Bureau of Fisheries remained with the Department of Commerce until July 1, 1939, when 1939 Reorganization Plan No. 11 transferred the Bureau of Fisheries to the Department of the Interior. This plan also transferred the Bureau of Biological Survey from the Department of Agriculture to the Department of the Interior. The Bureau of Fisheries and the Bureau of Biological Survey were then consolidated into one agency, the Fish and Wildlife Service, by the 1940 Reorganizational Plan No. III.

By the terms of the Fish and Wildlife Act of 1956, approved August 8, 1956, Congress established the U.S. Fish and Wildlife Service within the Department of the Interior. The service consisted of two separate agencies, each with the status of a federal bureau: the Bureau of Commercial Fisheries and the Bureau of Sport Fisheries and Wildlife.

On October 9, 1970, yet another agency reorganization occurred under Reorganization Plan No. 4 of 1970 (84 Stat. 2090). This was a direct result of the Stratton Commission (Commission on Marine Science, Engineering, and Resources 1969). Named after its chairman, MIT president Julius A. Stratton, the Commission made a number of recommendations to Congress. In particular, the commission called for the creation of an independent oceans agency to coordinate the nation's marine programs, including the management of marine fisheries.

While many of the commission's recommendations went unheeded, Congress did agree that a new National Oceanic and Atmospheric Administration made good sense. Congress decided that most of the functions of the Bureau of Commercial Fisheries as well as the marine functions of the Bureau of Sport Fisheries and Wildlife should be transferred from Interior to the National Oceanic and Atmospheric Administration (NOAA). The National Marine Fisheries Service was constituted within NOAA to supervise marine fisheries programs.

REFERENCES

Atlantic Marine Fisheries Commission, Gulf Marine Fisheries Commission and Pacific Marine Fisheries Commission. May 1977. *Eastland Fisheries Survey: A Report to Congress.* Pacific States Marine Fisheries Commission, Portland, Oregon. 91 pp.

Bakkala, Richard G., Vidar G. Wespestad and Jimmie J. Traynor. June 1987. "Walleye pollock," pp. 11–30 *in* U.S. Department of Commerce, National Oceanic and Atmospheric Administration, National Marine Fisheries Service, *Conditions of Groundfish Resources of the Eastern Bering Sea and Aleutian Islands Region in 1986.* NOAA Technical Memorandum NMFS F/NWC-117, Northwest and Alaska Fisheries Center. Seattle, Washington. 187 pp.

Bartlett, Kim. 1977. *The Finest Kind, the Fisherman of Gloucester.* Avon Books. New York, New York. 251 pp.

Bean, Michael J. 1983. *The Evolution of National Wildlife Law.* Praeger. New York, New York. 449 pp.

Blackford, Mansel G. 1979. *Pioneering a Modern Small Business: Wakefield Seafoods and the Alaskan Frontier.* JAI Press. Greenwich, Connecticut. 210 pp.

Boeri, David and James Gibson. 1976. *"Tell it Good-Bye, Kiddo": The Decline of the New England Offshore Fishery.* International Marine Publishing Company. Camden, Maine. 154 pp.

Burke, William T. 1988. *Memorandum on Legal Issues in Establishing Fishery Management in the Donut Area in the Bering Sea.* Fisheries Management Foundation. Seattle, Washington. 21pp.

Capuzzo, Judith McDowell, Anne McElroy and Gordon Wallace. 1987. *Fish and Shellfish Contamination in New England Waters: An Evaluation and Review of Available Data on the Distribution of Chemical Contaminants.* Coast Alliance. Washington, D.C. 59 pp. (June)

Chambers, James. 1987. New Directions of NMFS's Habitat Conservation Research Program. Speech before the International Estuarine Research Conference. New Orleans, Louisiana. October 27.

Commission on Marine Science, Engineering and Resources (known as the Stratton Commission). 1969. *Our Nation and the Sea: A Plan for National Action.* Government Printing Office. Washington, D.C.

Dunkle, Frank. 1987. Letter of July 1987 to NOAA Assistant Administrator for Fisheries, William E. Evans.

Innes, Harold A. 1954. *The Cod Fisheries: The History of an International Economy.* University of Toronto Press. Toronto. 522 pp.

King Mackerel Committee. Unpubl. Report of the King Mackerel Committee [U.S. Department of Commerce, National Oceanic and Atmospheric Administration, Washington, D.C., January 7, 1987]. 35 pp.

Mager, Andreas, Jr. and Gordon W. Thayer. 1986. "National Marine Fisheries Service habitat conservation efforts in the Southeast region of the United States from 1981 through 1985." *Marine Fisheries Review* 48(3):1–8.

Marine Mammal Commission. 1987. *Annual Report of the Marine Mammal Commission, Calendar Year 1986.* Washington, D.C. 189 pp. (January 31)

Memorandum from Kip Robinson and Beverly Carter, Office of Congressional Affairs, NOAA, "List of Legislative Authorities for NOAA," September 1982.

Memorandum of September 29, 1987 from William E. Evans to Distribution regarding NMFS Ecosystem Program Development Plan.

National Advisory Committee on Oceans and Atmosphere. 1982. *Fisheries for the Future: Restructuring the Government-Industry Partnership.* Washington, D.C. 61 pp. (July)

National Audubon Society. 1987. *Audubon Wildlife Report 1987.* Academic Press, Inc., Orlando, Florida, and National Audubon Society, New York, New York. 697 pp.

National Fisheries Institute, Natural Resource Access Committee. 1987a. Examination of Resource Access Issues Affecting the U.S. Fish and Seafood Industry. National Fisheries Institute. Washington, D.C. 23 pp. (June)

——. 1987b. *Greenbook.* National Fisheries Institute. Washington, D.C.

National Wildlife Federation. 1987a. Statement of the National Wildlife Federation before the Subcommittee on Environmental Protection of the Senate Committee on Environment and Public Works on Reauthorization of the Endangered Species Act, S. 675. National Wildlife Federation. Washington, D.C. 37 pp. (April 7)

——. April 7, 1987b. Statement of the National Wildlife Federation before the Subcommittee on Commerce, Justice, State, and the Judiciary and Related Agencies of the House Committee on Appropriations on the Proposed Fiscal Year 1988 Budget of the National Marine Fisheries Service, National Oceanic and Atmospheric Administration. National Wildlife Federation, Washington, D.C. 37 pp.

Netboy, Anthony. 1980. *The Columbia River Salmon and Steelhead Trout: Their Fight For Survival.* University of Washington Press. Seattle, Washington. 180 pp.

New England Fishery Management Council. 1987. *Northeast Multispecies Fishery Management Plan.* New England Fishery Management Council. Saugus, Massachusetts. (September)

North Pacific Fishery Management Council. 1984. "Policy on Annual Management Cycles." (June).

——. 1986. Fishery Management Plan for the Bering Sea/Aleutian Islands Groundfish. North Pacific Fishery Management Council. Anchorage, Alaska.

O'Hara, Kathryn and Natasha Atkins. 1986. *Marine Wildlife Entanglement in North America.* Center for Environmental Education. Washington, D.C. 200 pp. (November)

Orbach, Michael K. 1977. *Hunters, Seamen, and Entrepreneurs: The Tuna Seinermen of San Diego.* University of California Press. Los Angeles, California. 304 pp.

Pacific Marine Fisheries Commission, *Ad Hoc* Technical Committee on Marine Mammals. 1987. *Report on Proposed Amendments to the Marine Mammal Protection Act.* Pacific Marine Fisheries Commission. Portland, Oregon. 55 pp. (September 1)

Palmer, Andrew. 1987. "Seafood safety: an environmentalist perspective." *American Environment* (July): 4–8.

Pepper, Donald A. 1978. Men, Boats and Fish in the Northwest Atlantic: A Case History of Fishery Management. Ph.D. thesis (unpublished). Wales Institute of Science and Technology

Proceedings of the Seventh Annual Marine Recreational Fisheries Symposium. 1982. Marine Recreational Fisheries 7. Sport Fishing Institute. Washington, D.C. 183 pp.

Proceedings of the Eight Annual Marine Recreational Fisheries Symposium. 1983. Marine Recreational Fisheries 8. Sport Fishing Institute. Washington, D.C. 236 pp.

Public Voice for Food and Health Policy. 1986. *The Great American Fish Scandal: Health Risks Unchecked.* Washington, D.C. (December)

Seufert, Francis. 1980. *Wheels of Fortune.* Oregon Historical Society. Portland, Oregon. 259 pp.

Simon, Anne W. and Paul Hague. 1987. Contamination of New England's Fish and Shellfish. Coast Alliance, Washington. D.C. 15 pp. (June)

U.S. Congress, House of Representatives, Committee on Merchant Marine and Fisheries. 1984. Marine Mammal Protection Act Authorization for Fiscal Years 1985–1988. Report to accompany H.R. 4997, 98th Cong., 2nd sess. H. Report 98–758. 17 pp.

——. 1980. Report to accompany H.R. 7039, 96th Cong., 2nd sess. H. Report 96–1138. Pp. 6893–6897.

——., Office of Technology Assessment. 1987a. *Wastes in Marine Environments,* OTA-O-334. Government Printing Office. Washington, D.C. 313 pp. (April)

——., Senate Committee on Commerce, Science, and Transportation, National Ocean Policy Study. 1985. Magnuson Fishery Conservation and Management Act Amendments. 99th Cong., 1st sess. [S. Hrg. 99–328].

——., Senate Committee on the Environment and Public Works, Subcommittee on Environmental Protection. 1987b. Statement of Senator George J. Mitchell. Portland, Maine. (September 8)

U.S. Department of Commerce, National Oceanic and Atmospheric Administration, National Marine Fisheries Service. 1975. National Plan for Marine Fisheries, Washington, D.C. 81 pp. (October)

——., National Oceanic and Atmospheric Administration, National Marine Fisheries Service. 1976. *Fisheries of the United States, 1975.* Washington, D.C. 100 pp. (April)

——., National Oceanic and Atmospheric Administration, National Marine Fisheries Service. 1977. *Fisheries of the United States, 1976.* Washington, D.C. 96 pp. (April)

——., National Oceanic and Atmospheric Administration, National Marine Fisheries Service. 1979. *Fisheries of the United States, 1978.* Washington, D.C. 120 pp. (April)

——., National Oceanic and Atmospheric Administration, National Marine Fisheries Service. 1981. *Fisheries of the United States, 1980.* Washington, D.C. 132 pp. (April)

——., National Oceanic and Atmospheric Administration, National Marine Fisheries Service. 1983. *Fisheries of the United States, 1982.* Washington, D.C. 117 pp. (April)

——., National Oceanic and Atmospheric Administration, National Marine Fisheries Service. 1985. *Fisheries of the United States, 1984.* Washington, D.C. 121 pp. (April)

——., National Oceanic and Atmospheric Administration, National Marine Fisheries Service. 1986a. Strategic Plan for National Marine Fisheries Service (Revised edition). Washington, D.C. (January 6)

——., National Oceanic and Atmospheric Administration. 1986b. *NOAA Fishery Management Study.* Washington, D.C. 63 pp. (June 30)

——., National Oceanic and Atmospheric Administration, National Marine Fisheries Service. 1987a. Chronology of NMFS Organizational Restructuring, 1970–1987. (Unpublished, October)

——., National Oceanic and Atmospheric Administration, National Marine Fisheries Service. 1987b. *Fisheries of the United States, 1986.* Washington, D.C. 119 pp.

——., National Oceanic and Atmospheric Administration, National Marine Fisheries Service. 1987c. Program Development Plan for Ecosystems Monitoring and Fisheries Management. Washington, D.C. 26 pp. (January)

——., National Oceanic and Atmospheric Administration. 1987d. Unpubl. Budget Estimates: Fiscal Year 1988.

——., National Oceanic and Atmospheric Administration, National Marine Fisheries Service. 1986b. *The Habitat Conservation Program of the National Marine Fisheries Service.* Washington, D.C. 56 pp.

U.S. Department of the Interior, U.S. Fish and Wildlife Service. Unpubl. Draft Outline: National Recreational Fisheries Policy [July 1, 1987].

University of Alaska, Alaska Sea Grant. 1984. *Proceedings of the Workshop on Biological Interactions Among Marine Mammals and Commercial Fisheries in the Southeastern Bering Sea.* Alaska Sea Grant Report 84–1. University of Alaska, Fairbanks. 300 pp.

Warner, William W. 1977. *Distant Water: The Fate of the North Atlantic Fisherman.* Little, Brown and Company. Boston, Massachusetts. 338 pp.

The author also made use of the following periodicals and newsletters:

Alaska Fisherman's Journal, Seattle, Washington, volumes 9–10.

Commercial Fisheries News, Stonington, Maine, volumes 14–15.

Flashes, National Fisheries Institute, Washington, D.C., various issues.

Friday, Pacific Coast Federation of Fishermen's Associations, Sausalito, California, various issues.

National Fisherman, Camden, Maine, volumes 59–68.

Pacific Packers Report, Seattle, Washington, various volumes.

Seafood Business, Camden, Maine, volumes 1–6.

Seafood Leader, Seattle, Washington, volume 7.

SFI bulletin, Sport Fishing Institute, Washington, D.C., nos. 379–387.

Alfred D. Chandler is the general partner of ADC Planning and Communications, a consulting firm in Brooklyn, New York. ADC specializes in analyzing fishery and other marine-related issues for corporate clients, trade associations, and other organizations interested in the marine environment.

Part Two

Federal Agencies and Programs

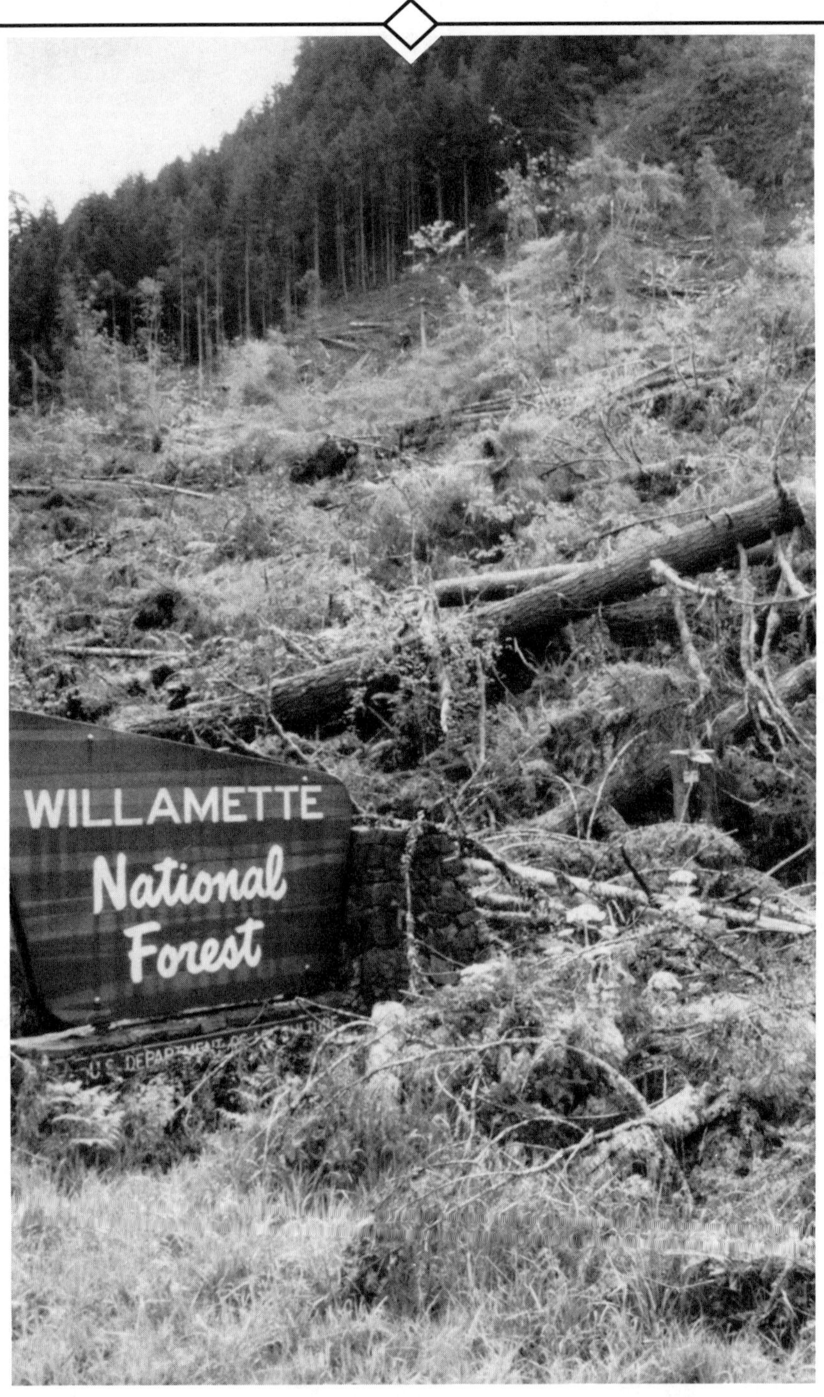

The Forest Service must manage its 191 million acres under the "multiple use" mandate, which includes timber harvesting and wildlife protection. Conflicts abound. *Chris Wille*

Wildlife Issues in National Forests

Frances A. Hunt

INTRODUCTION

The national forests are treasures that belong to every American, a priceless 191-million-acre inheritance that each generation can proudly pass on to the next. These lands support an abundance of natural resources, including thousands of wildlife and plant species, some found nowhere else but on national forests. In all, the National Forest System of 156 national forests and 19 national grasslands provides habitat for about 3,000 species of fish and wildlife and contains about half of the big-game and cold-water-fish habitat in the nation. Since these units are widely distributed, Americans who want to experience wildlife and wildlands firsthand do not have to go very far; virtually all residents of the coterminous United States live within 300 miles of one or more national forests or grasslands (see Figure 1).

Responsibility for the management and protection of the forest system has been given to the U.S. Forest Service, with the multiple-use mandate that the lands be used to achieve the most good, for the greatest number of people, over the long run. This ambitious charge has required Forest Service staff to juggle competing needs to a degree that would rival the most proficient circus performer's routine. The

Forest Service is pledged to balance the conflicting resource demands of a great variety of interests: forest-products companies seeking to harvest trees, biologists prescribing timber management to sustain wildlife species and their habitat, recreationists who may not care how timber is harvested so long as the cuts do not occur in prime recreation areas, and preservationists who oppose any tree cutting—not to mention the interests of hikers, hunters, fishermen, campers, and a bewildering array of other forest users.

Conflict and controversy surrounding the management of such a varied and valued resource is to be expected. Resource management conflicts have periodically sparked controversy since the days of John Muir and Gifford Pinchot. The debate over forest use, however, has intensified greatly since World War II. Prior to the 1950s, forest policy was largely the domain of a fairly isolated group of government land-management professionals. However, after the war's end, major national changes occurred. As America's population grew, new values, goals, and leaders arose—all of which have affected forest and wildlife management. In the late 1960s, conflicts associated with environmental demands, philosophies, and interests developed into confrontations. The 1970s saw a sharp rise in litigation by increasingly aggressive nonprofit groups. New environmental organizations appeared, and existing conservation groups grew more vocal. Increased public awareness and greater use of national forests for wildlife-related recreation and other noncommodity benefits, combined with ever-increasing demands for the production of timber, minerals, and other commodities, have fanned renewed debates over the appropriate role for national forests during the 1980s.

Although it is safe to say that all competing interests, including conservationists and the forest industry, support a "balanced" approach to forest management, it is also clear there is little agreement on what constitutes appropriate balance between commodity and noncommodity uses. Nevertheless, the illusive concept of balance frames nearly all national forest wildlife management debates and conflicts.

Today, a decade after passage of the National Forest Management Act, the Forest Service is completing the first 10- to 15-year forest plans required by that law for all forest system units. The forest planning process was designed to increase public input in forest management, while providing for balanced management of all forest resources. As the late Senator Hubert Humphrey, a principal sponsor of the act, declared during hearings on the legislation:

> The days have ended when the forest may be viewed only as trees and trees viewed only as timber. The soil and water, the grasses and the shrubs, the fish and the wildlife, and the beauty that is the forest must become integral parts of resource managers' thinking and actions (U.S. Congress, Senate 1979).

The forest planning process has focused debate and highlighted trade-offs between commodity and noncommodity resources as various resource groups have lobbied the Forest Service to "correct" the balance in favor of their particular interests. Timber industry groups nationwide have questioned the need to restrict timber harvesting to protect wildlife and have repeatedly warned that proposed reductions in timber harvest levels in some national forests will severely damage the forest industry and the communities that depend on it. Conversely, conservationists claim that projected logging activities will devastate fisheries and watersheds, fragment ecosystems, and harm threatened and endangered species of wildlife.

The planning process has proven to be immensely controversial and complicated but, as Daniel Poole, chairman of the board of the Wildlife Management Institute recently concluded,

> "For great numbers of America's wildlife, our irreplaceable public lands are the only game in town. The success or failure of wildlife on public lands in coming years depends on how well resource values and objectives are coordinated and implemented. Those who insist on getting a lion's share of the action can do serious harm to other public forest values and resources" (Poole 1987).

CURRENT DEVELOPMENTS AND ISSUES

Biological Diversity and Ecosystem Management

Ever since forest managers began managing forest wildlife, their basic strategy has been to manipulate the forest environment so as to provide the appropriate habitat for desired species. And although the requirements of many game animals have been met during timber harvest and management activities, many nongame species, such as the spotted owl and red-cockaded woodpecker, have been adversely affected.

Conservationists have become increasingly interested in the maintenance of nongame wildlife. Indeed, as the science of ecology has matured, it has become increasingly apparent that all living species of plants and animals contribute in some way to the healthy functioning of the environment. Since life began on Earth, an amazing variety of plant and animal species has evolved as a highly complex functioning system in response to environmental pressures and change. Ecologists use the term "biological diversity" to describe this incredible variety of ecosystems, individual species, and genetic material. And because human activities can erode or protect the diversity, health, and productivity of the Earth's ecosystems, many environmentalists have focused attention on the necessity of maintaining biological diversity in the National Forest System.

In recent years, people worldwide have begun to realize that the loss of natural diversity and the diminishment of natural ecosystems may indeed threaten the well-being of every citizen of the world. Interacting communities of plants and animals provide us with countless indispensible services, from the production of food, to the control of erosion, to the moderation of global climate.

For example, the world's forests are a rich and largely unexplored source of medicines. The National Cancer Institute has made progress in developing anticancer drugs from plants such as yews and mayapples from temperate forests. "Because of the biochemical diversity of life, many more potential medicines from plants, animals, and microorganisms await discovery. In addition to foods and medicines, biological diversity can also provide new sources of energy (such as fast-growing fuelwoods) and industrial raw materials" (Norse 1986).

As important as these natural benefits are, the protection of the Earth's natural diversity and functioning ecosystems is particularly essential for the protection of the global environment. Forests and other ecosystems help maintain the chemical composition of the atmosphere. Decomposers such as bacteria purify water contaminated with human wastes, dead plants, and animals. In short, "living things maintain the habitability of the Earth. Without the services performed by diverse, intact communities of plants, animals, and microorganisms, we would be starving, baking, gasping for breath, and drowning in our own wastes" (Norse 1986).

Arguments concerning the maintenance of biological diversity on most forests are fueled by conflicting attitudes about the appropriate balance of commodity versus noncommodity uses. For example, conservation groups have become increasingly concerned that sufficient areas of old-growth forests be maintained to protect the many species of plants and animals that are found only in association with such ecological communities. Scientists have sought to understand the functioning of the various natural communities found in the national forests in an attempt to learn how to protect these communities, yet still allow for commodity production.

New concepts have entered the realm of forestry as a result of these discussions and explorations. "Ecosystem management" is the term given to the management of natural areas based on the functional relationships that exist between their living and nonliving components: plants, animals, soil, water, etc. This management approach can be contrasted with the more traditional approach of managing forests for the singular purposes (timber, wildlife, etc.) which are valued by people at a particular time. Ecosystem management is seen as a way to protect biological diversity by maintaining functional ecosystems and their inhabitants. Forest fragmentation, which is the reduction of functional ecosystems and habitats into smaller, less-functional areas through development, timber management, and other human activities, can reduce biological diversity.

The protection of ecosystems and biological diversity is addressed in both legislation and regulations guiding forest management and is therefore a legally mandated goal of each national forest plan. Conservationists, however, have frequently questioned the Forest Service's success in achieving that goal.

The National Forest Management Act (16 U.S.C. 1601 *et seq.*) requires the Forest Service to protect the diversity of plant and animal communities found on national forest lands. The act mandates that timber harvests are to be conducted so as to ensure the protection of soil, watersheds, fish, wildlife, recreation, and aesthetic resources, and the regeneration of the timber resource. In addition, the regulations which guide implementation of the act state that forest planning will be based on the principles that "the national forests are ecosystems and their management for goods and services requires an awareness and consideration of the interrelationships among plants, animals, soil, water, air and other environmental factors within such ecosystems" (36 CFR 219.1). The regulations also require the agency to "provide for adequate fish and wildlife habitat to maintain viable populations of existing native vertebrate species," and to "preserve and enhance the diversity of plant and animal communities . . . so that it is at least as great as that which would be expected in a natural forest" (36 CFR 219.27).

In order to assure that forest plans meet the requirements set forth in the National Forest Management Act and other environmental statutes and regulations, each region of the Forest Service has developed specific management guidelines, known as minimum management requirements. These requirements, for example, specify certain minimum amounts of habitat that must be protected to maintain viable populations of forest wildlife. Viewed as unnecessary constraints on timber production by some and as inadequate to protect wildlife by others, minimum management requirements have proven to be a controversial tool of forest planning and wildlife management. It is the individual forest plans, however, that generally are the focus of debates concerning the appropriate management of specific forest resources; these debates are occurring around the country.

Old-growth Forests and the Spotted Owl

The spotted owl has become the focal point for a long-standing controversy surrounding the appropriate management of national forests in the Pacific Northwest. The northern spotted owl, a medium-sized owl native to the coniferous forests of the Pacific Northwest, is threatened by the harvest and fragmentation of its old-growth habitat;

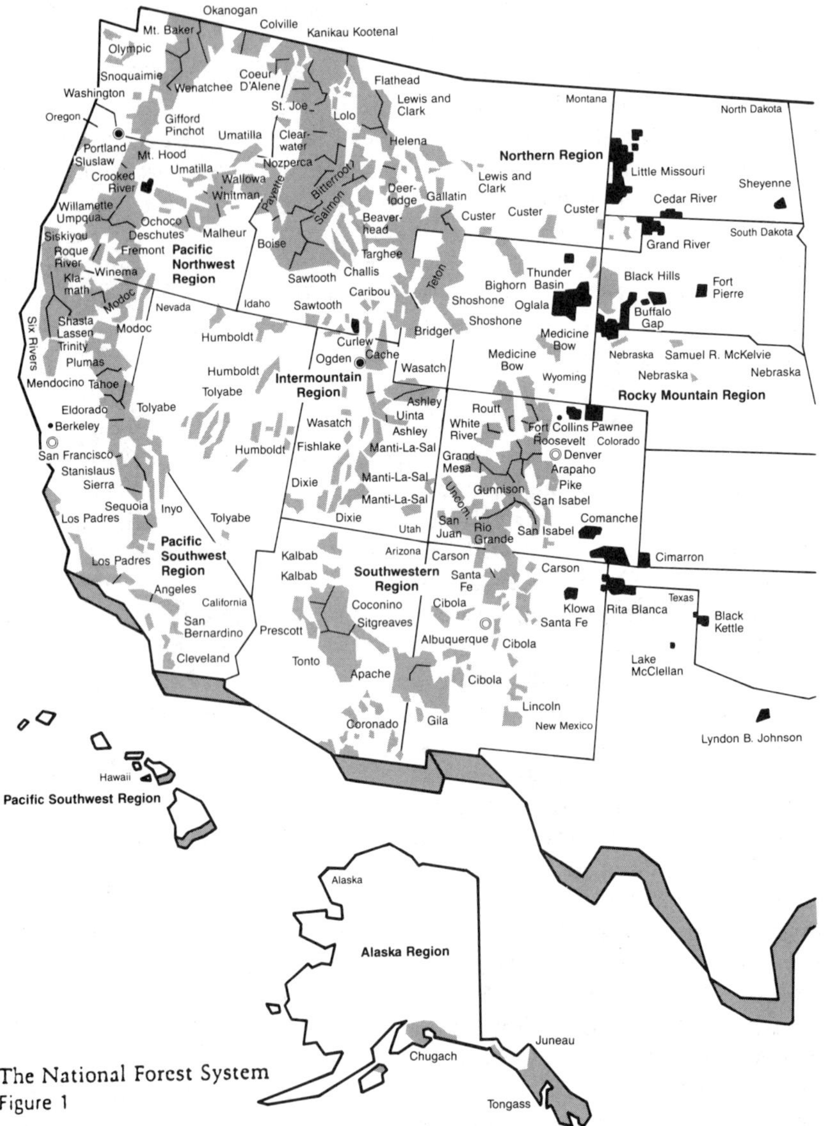

The National Forest System
Figure 1

an estimated 2,000 to 2,500 birds still survive in the region. Like the red-cockaded woodpecker, the spotted owl requires extensive tracts of old-growth trees for nesting and forage habitat. Consequently, the spotted owl's habitat requirements are at odds with the economic plans and practices of the region's forest industry.

Old-growth habitat for the owl has been reduced from some 15 million acres or more in the early 1800s to less than 5 million acres today. "With almost all suitable habitat eliminated from private lands

in the region, 96 percent of the owl's remaining habitat is on federal lands, and 76 percent is on national forests in Oregon and Washington" (Barton 1987). These publicly managed old-growth stands also represent a valuable, high-quality source of timber for the region's forest industry.

Although it is difficult to make reliable estimates of how much old-growth owl habitat is scheduled for harvest (individual forest managers often include acreages of "mature" stands in "old-growth" estimates) a recent report by the Wilderness Society claimed that the "rapid decimation of old-growth forests currently under way in the Pacific Northwest" is "probably the greatest threat to the biological wealth of the national forests" (Wilderness Society 1987). As the report notes, "A large portion of timber sold on the national forests comes from this region. While few draft [forest] plans and no final plans have been issued in this area, all indications point toward a continued policy of old-growth liquidation" (The *Audubon Wildlife Report 1987* contains more detailed information regarding the habitat requirements of the spotted owl and the conflict surrounding its management).

In 1984, four conservation groups appealed the Forest Service's 1984 regional guide which established standards and guidelines for forest plans in Oregon and Washington, arguing in part that the service's management provisions for the spotted owl were inadequate to maintain long-term viability of the bird. In March 1985, the deputy assistant secretary of Agriculture directed the Forest Service to prepare a supplemental environmental impact statement on the regional guide to give more adequate consideration to spotted owl management issues. In August 1986, the Forest Service released for public comment a draft of the supplemental environmental impact statement. Under the Forest Service's preferred owl management alternative—Alternative F—the number of habitat areas (550) targeted for protection of owl pairs in Oregon and Washington would not change. However, the draft did specify the need to protect up to 2,200 acres of old-growth for each pair's habitat over the 10- to 15-year life of the plan, thus increasing the total acreage allotted to each pair. While environmentalists criticized the proposal as still providing for too few protected habitat areas of too small a size, the forest industry countered that the proposal would overly restrict harvest of valuable timber (see the 1987 *Wildlife Report* for a more complete discussion of the draft supplemental environmental impact statement).

The final version of the statement is expected to be released in February 1988. Owl management guidelines are expected to closely resemble the preferred alternative in the draft supplemental impact statement. In the interim, the Forest Service has initiated additional spotted owl research as directed by Congress in the report on the FY 1987 Interior Appropriations bill (U.S. Congress, Senate 1987). Congress directed the agency to conduct monitoring and research on the suitability of various forest types as spotted owl habitat. Although it is still too early to assess the results of the program, providing better answers to questions about the habitat needs of the owl will require an accelerated and coordinated blend of research and management addressing two objectives: 1) the determination of biological requirements and ecological relationships of the spotted owl, and 2) the inventory and monitoring of owl populations and their habitat.

The Forest Service has drafted a five-year research plan, "The Spotted Owl Research, Development and Application Program," to meet these goals and to "provide guidelines for managing forests to ensure habitats for viable populations of spotted owls throughout their existing range" (U.S. Department of Agriculture 1987a). The program is intended to improve the Forest Service's effectiveness in managing spotted owls and their habitat by providing a single focal point for agency leadership on owl research and management in Oregon, Washington, and California. In addition, the program is intended to further cooperation and coordination with other agencies and groups—state fish and game agencies, local universities, conservation organizations, other federal agencies—involved in the effort.

Meanwhile, in response to the delayed release and expected content of the supplemental environmental impact statement, several environmental organizations petitioned the U.S. Fish and Wildlife Service (FWS) to list the spotted owl as either threatened or endangered under the Endangered Species Act. The first petition, a one-page letter submitted by Green World in January 1987, cited the 1986 National Audubon Society Report of the Advisory Panel on the Spotted Owl (National Audubon Society 1986) as evidence that FWS should list the owl as endangered. On July 23, 1987, FWS decided to launch a full-scale review of the owl's status.

In a separate petition dated July 31, 1987, 29 environmental groups urged FWS to list the owl as endangered throughout its range along the Olympic Peninsula of Washington and coastal Oregon, and as threatened elsewhere in the Cascade Mountains of the Pacific Northwest. The 25-page petition was signed by representatives of the Natural Resources Defense Council, the Wilderness Society, Defenders of Wildlife, and 24 Audubon chapters. The second petition apparently was drafted because of fears that the short Green World petition might be too weak, and because of concerns over the content of the draft supplemental environmental impact statement and continued logging in spotted owl areas.

Although the final outcome of the petition was still pending at the end of FY 1987, the Forest Service and FWS are negotiating a memorandum of understanding concerning owl management, which will preclude FWS' listing of the species. Although one environmentalist reported that FWS biologists close to the issue support the listing of the species, higher-level FWS officials are said to be less sympathetic to the need to expand protection of the owl and are therefore reluctant to grant the petition.

[**EDITOR'S NOTE:** On December 23, 1987, FWS announced that the agency had decided not to list the spotted owl as an endangered or threatened species. The owl's requirements, said the agency, could be addressed through better interagency cooperation—especially with the

National Park Service and the Bureau of Land Management—and improved management of existing programs.

Conservationists agree that better interagency cooperation and program management is needed, but maintain that the spotted owl should be listed. In addition, conservationists entered a new petition on behalf of the marbled murrelet, which, they claim, should be listed as threatened in Washington, Oregon, and California. The murrelet, a robin-sized seabird, apparently nests in coastal old-growth trees.]

Bureau of Land Management Spotted Owl Management. While public debate over the owl has focused primarily on national forests, research has shown that timber harvests on Bureau of Land Management (BLM) lands in western Oregon—the Oregon and California Grant lands—may also be a significant threat to the bird's survival. BLM lands may provide a critical link between owl populations in the national forests on the Oregon coast and in the Oregon Cascades, a link that may be necessary to maintain a self-sustaining breeding population. In a BLM report that was shelved by the Department of the Interior, but leaked to the National Audubon Society, researchers suggested that if current cutting levels continued on BLM lands for the next four years, habitat on these lands may not be adequate to provide this vital link. Under these circumstances, the report warned, there is a high probability that the spotted owl will have to be federally listed as threatened or endangered in four to six years, but by then little suitable habitat would remain for the owls on BLM lands.

In an attempt to protect old-growth owl habitat from proposed logging on BLM lands, the Wilderness Society, Natural Resources Defense Council, and other environmental groups, including several local Audubon chapters, filed an administrative appeal with the Department of the Interior's Board of Appeals on June 9, 1987, challenging BLM's timber harvest program in Oregon and California. The environmental groups charge that, at the current rate of logging, BLM will eliminate all old-growth forests under its management within the next four decades. The groups further allege that the logging program will violate federal statutes including the National Environmental Policy Act (42 U.S.C. 4321 *et seq.*), the Oregon and California Lands Act (43 U.S.C. 1181 *et seq.*), and eventually, the Endangered Species Act (16 U.S.C. 1531 *et seq.*).

Of particular interest is the Oregon and California Lands Act. The Interior department has interpreted that law as giving high priority to timber harvesting and as sharply constraining BLM's ability to set aside commercial timber lands for uses such as spotted owl habitat. The appeal challenges this interpretation. The environmental appellants have requested that the Board of Land Appeals order BLM to stay all sales of timber in stands older than 200 years within a 2.1 mile radius of each spotted owl habitat site.

After the Board of Land Appeals delayed responding to the appeal, environmental groups filed a legal appeal on October 19, 1987, with the U.S. District Court in Portland. In an effort to keep the case out of court, BLM has "voluntarily" agreed to stay timber harvests as requested by the environmental groups, pending the outcome of Interior's Board of Appeals decision.

Management of the Greater Yellowstone Ecosystem

Yellowstone National Park, the world's first national park, has been proclaimed one of America's "crown jewels." Located along the Continental Divide in northwestern Wyoming and adjacent parts of Montana and Idaho, the park is the centerpiece of the largest, intact ecosystem in the continental United States. The total land area of the Greater Yellowstone Ecosystem is about 14 million acres. The Forest Service manages some 10.2 million acres in six national forest units: Custer, Gallatin, Beaverhead, Shoshone, Targhee, and Caribou (see Figure 2). The National Park Service manages 2.6 million acres in Yellowstone National Park, Grand Teton National Park, and the John D. Rockefeller, Jr., Memorial Parkway connecting the two parks. FWS has three refuges in the area totaling 73,000 acres, and BLM oversees about 126,000 acres. The states of Idaho and Montana own 45,000 and 70,000 acres, respectively, and the remaining one million acres are privately owned.

The Yellowstone ecosystem supports grizzly bears, elk, cutthroat trout, bighorn sheep, deer, moose, mountain goats, trumpeter swans, and bald eagles. The area also is a haven for recreationists and sightseers; over two million people visit Yellowstone National Park each year. Logging companies, local mills, and entire populations of some communities point to the importance of national forest timber for their continued economic survival.

The complex mix of ownership and management philosophies has made management of the ecosystem and its wildlife difficult. The various agencies that manage pieces of the ecosystem have radically different cultures, histories, and legislative mandates. National parks, for example, were founded to preserve important natural resources, while national forests were established to promote the balanced *use* of forest resources. Wildlife such as elk and the threatened grizzly are therefore at least nominally protected within parks, but roam freely across the borders onto national forests and other adjacent lands where they may be subject to a variety of threats, including hunting and habitat disturbance. Coordinated management of the entire region is necessary for the continued health and productivity of the ecosystem;

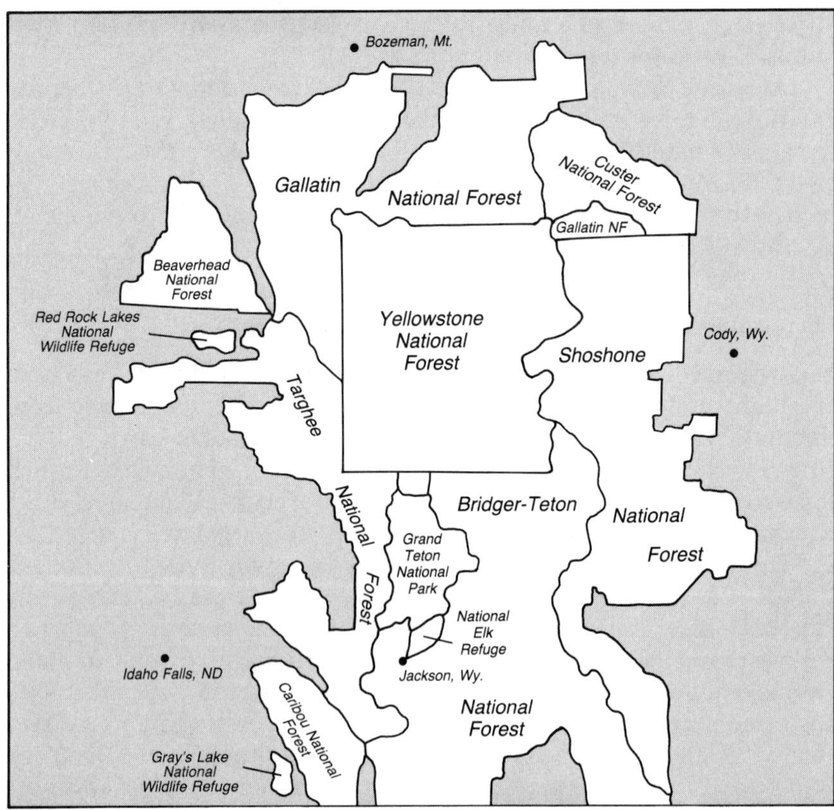

Figure 2. Federal lands in the Yellowstone Region. The Custer, Gallatin, and Beaverhead National Forests are administered by U.S. Forest Service Region 1; The Shoshone by Region 2; the Targhee and Caribou by Region 4. Source: The Wilderness Society.

hence management of the national forests will play a critical role in shaping the future of the ecosystem's resident wildlife species.

The Greater Yellowstone Coalition, a group founded in 1983 with some 40 environmental organizations as its members, has been a chief advocate of ecosystem management in the area:

> The ecosystem approach to resource management is a very logical and sensible approach to land management. From it would accrue many benefits, among them wildlife benefits, sustained yields of timber and forage, recovery of threatened and endangered species, economic stability through the marketing of the GYE's [Greater Yellowstone Ecosystem] principal economic product – which is tourism – and not the least of which is water, which benefits municipalities, industry, agriculture, fish, wildlife, and recreation in the northern Rockies (U.S. Congress, House 1985).

In spite of these purported benefits of ecosystem management, many conservationists claim that the national forests of the Greater

Yellowstone Ecosystem are being managed, not to conserve a uniquely intact ecosystem, but rather for the principal purpose of commodity production. The Wilderness Society and other groups have claimed that timber harvesting "drives most of the area's forest plans" (Franklin 1986). The society also notes that below-cost timber sales are the norm, and reports that between 1979 and 1984 all six national forests in Greater Yellowstone lost money on their timber-sale programs.

Conservationists are concerned that the current practices of clear-cutting timber in numerous small areas, and the construction of roads to facilitate these cuts, will fragment the forest's wildlife habitat and harm vulnerable wildlife species including the grizzly, elk, bighorn sheep and others. Furthermore, many groups have expressed concern that there is insufficient coordination of planning and land-management activities between the various federal agencies and states which manage the ecosystem. This lack of coordination is blamed for conflicting wildlife management strategies in different units of the region.

Forest Service managers have looked for ways to harvest timber and still protect wildlife. As Shoshone National Forest Supervisor Stephen Mealey has stated, "We'll be careful to pay more attention to wildlife cover and visual quality in timber-sale design." However, Forest Service actions to protect wildlife have drawn negative reactions from the forest industry. For example, proposals to decrease timber harvests on some forests to satisfy wildlife conservation needs have led the forest products industry to charge that the agency, in the words of Richard Reid, executive vice-president of the Inland Forest Resource Council, has demonstrated a "bias against commodity uses of public land that violates the principles of multiple-use" (Franklin 1986).

A 1987 report by the Congressional Research Service (Library of Congress 1987) documented both the management conflicts arising in the Greater Yellowstone area and the cooperative efforts of the various agencies to coordinate management. The report confirmed the lack of an effective, coordinated, "ecosystem management" approach in the Greater Yellowstone Ecosystem. Insufficient coordination of management and information was cited as a problem for wildlife management, particularly in the case of the grizzly bear.

Given the progress on reintroducing both peregrine falcons and whooping cranes in the region, the Congressional Research Service concluded that the ecosystem now lacks only one large vertebrate, the wolf. However, the report stated that human activities have reduced the populations of many other animals, including grizzly bears, eagles, and elk, and said that further population declines were likely.

The Congressional Research Service concluded that the most significant development impacts on the ecosystem resulted from roads and other human intrusions. Roads can degrade water quality, upon which many animals depend. In addition, human activities were found to disturb many animal species, including elk, bighorn sheep, and especially grizzly bears. Despite these effects, road construction and other access decisions are made on a case-by-case basis, rather than in an integrated manner that takes into account the cumulative environmental effects of all types of access.

In gauging the effect of human development on wildlife, the status of the grizzly bear is considered an indicator of the overall health of the ecosystem. This is because the areas heavily used by bears also provide important habitat for many other species. While the grizzly population may be an appropriate indicator of the effects of human activities on the ecosystem, the existing data on grizzly bear mortalities was, nevertheless, found to be both incomplete and inconsistent. The Congressional Research Service did identify seven areas with concentrations of grizzly bear deaths—known as "mortality clusters." The report called for improved data on grizzly bear mortality, as well as focused management efforts to reduce grizzly bear deaths in these areas, and thus improve the species' chance for survival in the Yellowstone ecosystem.

The report also examined the special management zones ("Management Situation" zones) created by the Forest Service to predict grizzly bear requirements and to plan forest management activities to reduce adverse impacts on the species. These zones were found to be inadequate to assure continued grizzly survival because they do not accurately identify important habitat areas or actual areas used by grizzlies.

Recreation was identified as the most important economic activity occurring on federal lands. Excluding the substantial phosphate mining in the Caribou National Forest, nearly two-thirds of the jobs supported by the region's national forests are recreation-related. Conversely, the Congressional Research Service reported that, "Many of the commodity resource programs in GYE national forests—timber harvesting, water developments, grazing, and energy and mineral development—are of minor importance. The jobs in these industries (except phosphate mining) are few, compared to recreation-related jobs."

Finally, the report documented the many interagency committees, task forces, and working groups that have been organized to provide better communication and coordination between the various entities managing the ecosystem. The report concluded that the existing coordinating committees are not sufficiently comprehensive in either membership or approach, and therefore are inadequate for providing complete, coordinated management of the ecosystem.

The Forest Service, which gave no high-level official reaction to the document, has claimed that bear mortality information is actually maintained better than the report alleged. Meanwhile, the Greater Yellowstone Coalition and other conservation groups have praised the report as a validation of their concerns for the management of the ecosystem. Although it seems unlikely that this report will generate legislation mandating either the ecosystem management approach or improved cooperation between Greater Yellowstone Ecosystem management agencies, it does provide conservationists with new ammunition for their fight for more holistic management of this ecosystem.

Southern Appalachian Mountain Ecosystem

Although conflict over the management of the Greater Yellowstone Ecosystem is perhaps the most visible ecosystem controversy, it is by no means the only one. The Southern Appalachian Mountain Ecosystem, composed of the Great Smoky Mountain National Park, and the Chattahoochee-Oconee, Cherokee, Pisgah-Nantahala, and Jefferson national forests, is an extensive ecosystem with a wide variety of valuable forest and wildlife resources. Although management controversies have not reached the same level of national visibility and intensity as they have in Yellowstone, the proximity of the Great Smokies to a large, highly educated, mobile population practically ensures that its management will become more hotly contested in the coming years. Forest management can therefore be expected to play an increasingly integral and visible role in the maintenance of the region's biological diversity.

The Southern Appalachian Mountain Ecosystem contains several varied forest types and associated wildlife habitats, which principally vary with altitude. The ecosystem supports southern pine forests at lower altitudes and spruce-fir forests at the crest of the Appalachians. The treeless southern Appalachian Mountain "balds" (high-elevation areas which have been historically maintained at early successional stages by fire, grazing, or timber harvests) are a unique, and highly prized component of the ecosystem (Hillman interview).

Wildlife populations also are diverse. Black bear, a species which requires large home ranges and is generally intolerant of disturbance from humans, is the region's most prized wildlife inhabitant. Turkeys, northern flying squirrels, and golden eagles also occupy the area. Certain of the region's extirpated species, such as the river otter and peregrine falcon, may eventually be re-established; others, such as elk, bison, and the grey wolf, have habitat requirements far in excess of the acreage still available in the ecosystem (Cook interview).

As in the Yellowstone ecosystem, the mixed management of the Southern Appalachian Mountain Ecosystem has led to the development of interagency cooperative efforts to improve management of the area. Chief among these is the Southern Appalachian Resource Management Commission, composed of both federal and state agencies and university representatives. Commission members meet only once every two years, indicating that the level of cooperation is somewhat less than that found in Yellowstone.

Red-cockaded Woodpecker

The red-cockaded woodpecker, an inhabitant of large stands of old pine (80 to 150 years old) with sparse understories, has been at the center of a continuing forest management debate involving old-growth management, timber production, and biological diversity in the Southeast.

The woodpecker—a colonial-nesting bird federally listed as endangered—excavates nesting cavities in older, fungus-weakened trees, predominantly longleaf and loblolly pine. Nesting habitat for a colony usually requires 1 to 30 mature pines within a 1,500-foot radius. Each colony also requires at least 50 acres of 60-year-old pine forests—and a greater area of younger trees—for use as foraging habitat.

Since the woodpecker requires a forest that has a diversity of stand ages, it is threatened by the widespread harvest of mature softwood forest stands and subsequent reharvesting on shorter rotation schedules.

A recent Wilderness Society report summarizes the status of the endangered bird:

> Red-cockaded woodpeckers are vanishing because of habitat loss; commercial logging has claimed 13 percent of its habitat over the past 30 years. The habitat loss continues despite the listing of the [species as endangered]. Efforts to conserve this species have been controversial and recovery efforts have lagged because the woodpecker's special ecological requirements collide with modern forestry practices. The currently widespread commercial practice of even-aged timber management and short rotations—trees grown for 25 to 40 years, then all removed for pulpwood at once—is incompatible with the woodpecker's need for mature trees. Formerly abundant from Texas to New Jersey and as far inland as Tennessee, the red-cockaded woodpecker now depends for its survival primarily on management of 18 national forests in 7 states (Norse 1986).

Pine Beetle Control. As reported in the *Audubon Wildlife Report 1987* the red-cockaded woodpecker has been a complicating factor in a controversial southern pine beetle suppression program conducted by the Forest Service. The pine beetle is a native bark beetle which periodically attacks pines from Texas to Virginia. Unlike the woodpecker, the beetle thrives when forest diversity is reduced to even-aged stands of overmature southern pines, the prime target of beetle attacks. The beetle kills pine trees by burrowing into the living (cambrial) tissue found just under the bark, thereby disrupting the flow of nutrients between the leaves and roots. The beetle can also infect the tree with blue stain fungus, which further damages the tree by cutting off the flow of water from the roots.

According to Forest Service reports, "An outbreak—a large, rapidly increasing beetle population—began in east Texas in 1982. Since then destructive outbreaks have occurred in Arkansas, Louisiana, Mississippi, and Alabama. In these states, the beetles have killed about 250,000 acres of southern pine trees which would have yielded 1.5 billion board feet of timber" (U.S. Department of Agriculture 1987b). The Forest Service response has been to treat beetle-infested trees to minimize the impact of the outbreak. Treatments, which include the harvest, removal, and chemical spraying of trees, are applied directly on national forests and other federal lands, and on state and private lands under cooperative cost-share agreements. Two types of pesticides, lindane and chlorpyrifos, are used to control the beetle. Both are sprayed onto the outer bark of infected trees, after harvest, and kill the beetle on contact or if ingested.

Although timber harvest is seldom allowed in wilderness areas, the Wilderness Act (16 U.S.C. 1131 *et. seq.*) does authorize the Forest Service to take such measures as necessary to control fire, insects, and disease. Environmental groups argue that the Forest Service beetle control program violated the Wilderness Act because the program had never proven to be efficacious, as the law requires. They also claimed that the agency had failed to comply with the environmental assessment requirements of the National Environmental Policy Act.

On the basis of these concerns, environmental organizations brought two lawsuits to prevent the Forest Service from cutting trees in designated wilderness areas as part of its efforts to control the beetle, claiming that timber harvesting endangers the red-cockaded woodpecker by reducing habitat and disturbing nesting colonies. The Forest Service claimed that beetle control was actually necessary to protect woodpecker colonies, as beetle-killed trees were not considered suitable woodpecker habitat.

In 1985, preliminary injunctions curtailing the beetle suppression program in wilderness were issued in Texas (*Sierra Club v. Block*, 614 F. Supp. 488 [D. Tex. 1985]) and in Arkansas, Louisiana, and Mississippi (*Sierra Club and the Wilderness Society v. Block*, 614 F. Supp. 134 [D.D.C. 1985]). In the latter case, the Forest Service was directed to prepare an environmental impact statement on the pine beetle suppression program. Further legal action on these suits was delayed pending the completion of the agency's final environmental impact statement on the beetle control program. Subsequent to the issuance of the final environmental impact statement in February 1987, the court ruled in favor of the Forest Service on one lawsuit; the decision on the second is still pending.

The Forest Service had also requested a formal biological opinion from FWS as to whether the failure to cut trees to protect red-cockaded woodpecker habitat (as part of the beetle suppression program) would violate the Endangered Species Act requirement that federal agencies not jeopardize either the continued existence of endangered species or their critical habitat. While the environmental impact statement was being prepared, FWS ruled that the Forest Service would in fact jeopardize the red-cockaded woodpecker if it took no beetle control actions of any kind on any national forest land (U.S. Department of the Interior 1986). In spite of the broad nature of this ruling, which was far more general than the specific wilderness/red-cockaded woodpecker/ beetle issues at hand in litigation, the Forest Service, in its pine beetle environmental impact statement, claimed that FWS supported its pine beetle suppression program in wilderness areas (Honnold interview).

The environmental impact statement did contain new restrictions on the control of southern pine beetles in wilderness areas. Basically, no cutting will be allowed in wilderness areas except within one-fourth mile of the boundary of the wilderness. Further, infested wilderness areas will only be cut if adjacent state and private land is determined to be susceptible to and threatened by a beetle outbreak spreading from wilderness lands. Under these restrictions, Sierra Club attorneys estimated that 90 percent of wilderness areas infested with the beetle would be off-limits for harvesting (Honnold interview).

Only one wilderness area was found to have both a beetle outbreak and a population of red-cockaded woodpeckers: the Kisatchie Hills Wilderness in Louisiana. Following the release of the environmental impact statement, the Forest Service decided to take no further beetle control activities in that area, one-third of which had already been logged to control the beetle. Several woodpecker nest sites were destroyed in the process.

Following the release of the environmental impact statement in February, the judge for the Arkansas, Louisiana, and Mississippi case made a summary judgement ruling in favor of the government. The judge found that the control program, as outlined in the final environmental impact statement, would not violate the Wilderness Act. While this judgement concluded the Arkansas case, the Texas suit, which was filed in a different appeals court district, was still active at the close of FY 1987 and the litigants were awaiting a trial date or summary judgement. In spite of the ruling on the Arkansas case, the plaintiffs hope that the judge for the Texas case will reach a different interpretation of either the relevant statutes or of the facts of the case, and will rule to restrict the agency's control of the beetle in wilderness areas in Texas.

Whatever the outcome of the Texas suit, the issue of pine beetle control, and its ramifications for biological diversity, red-cockaded woodpeckers, and other forest resources, will no doubt flare-up repeatedly in the years ahead. Although it is unlikely that the pine beetle, a natural forest component, will ever be erradicated, controlling the severity of pine beetle outbreaks may ultimately depend on increasing the diversity of southern forests. Diversity is also key to the survival of the red-cockaded woodpecker, which requires variously aged forest stands to nest and feed.

Tongass National Forest

Alaska's Tongass National Forest, the nation's largest national forest, covers 500 miles of coastline and islands of Southeast Alaska and averages 100 miles wide. Noted for its abundant fish and wildlife populations, the forest supports the greatest concentrations of bald eagles and grizzly bears in the United States. The Tongass is also home to significant populations of black bear, Sitka black-tailed deer, mountain goats, wolves, and a variety of birds and furbearers. The freshwater fisheries of southeast Alaska, including a salmon fishery vital to the local economy, largely depend on the streams and lakes within the Tongass (Franklin 1987). These fish and wildlife populations depend on the continued health of the forest's old-growth stands of spruce and cedar, which also represent a valuable resource to the state's timber industry.

In recent years, controversy has surrounded the management of the Tongass. This controversy intensified with the passage and implementation of the Alaska National Interest Lands Conservation Act (ANILCA) (16 U.S.C. 3210 *et seq.*). The act sought to guide protection and development of Alaska's natural resources by designating wilderness, national parks, wildlife refuges; encouraging the development of the forest products industry; and guiding conservation and management of the Tongass National Forest. The unique, subsidized timber management program that the act created for the Tongass was the focal point for much of the conflict during 1987.

The Tongass is managed in accordance with unique provisions incorporated into Section 705 of ANILCA. Under this section, Congress set a goal of supplying 4.5 billion board feet of timber per decade to the forest industry dependent on the Tongass. The Forest Service has interpreted this direction as a mandate to offer 450 million board feet of timber per year, regardless of the actual demand for the timber. Between 1980 and 1986, the Forest Service made available for sale an average of 474 million board feet of timber per year, while only an average of 261 million board feet were actually purchased. No other national forest has this type of mandated timber-sale program.

To support attainment of the sale goal, Congress established the Tongass Timber Supply Fund to provide at least $40 million annually to the Forest Service for construction of logging roads, preparation of harvest sites, and administration of timber sales. This $40 million is automatically provided each year outside of the regular appropriations process; hence the Tongass timber program is less subject to the effects of the changing political, economic, or environmental conditions which annually affect other Forest Service budgets and programs.

ANILCA also exempted the Tongass from Section 6(k) of the National Forest Management Act, which directs the Forest Service to designate those lands on each national forest that are physically and economically unsuitable for commercial timber production. No other national forest is exempt from this requirement.

The unusual status of the Tongass resulted from a congressional bargaining process surrounding, in part, ANILCA designation of 5.4 million acres of wilderness within the Tongass. Although the forest industry claims that the compromise was, and continues to be, necessary to sustain historic timber harvest levels and thus preserve the local economy, environmentalists counter that the wilderness designations made on the Tongass actually contained very little of the forest's highest quality timber and related high-quality wildlife habitat.

The Tongass also has a unique relationship with two large neighboring pulp mills, which have unusually lengthy, 50-year contracts to purchase pulpwood from the forest. As part of these contracts, the mills can purchase spruce and cedar stumpage for one percent or less of its previously appraised value (Franklin 1987). While the forest industry claims that these special contracts provided necessary incentive to attract the mills to Southeast Alaska, environmentalists have charged the corporations holding these contracts with wasteful logging operations that degrade the forest environment.

Fueling the controversy surrounding the forest's timber management program is the fact that the old-growth forest stands that produce the highest quality and volume of timber are also the stands that provide the most important wildlife habitat, especially during the winter. Environmentalists, the local fishing and tourism industry, and the Alaska Department of Fish and Game have frequently criticized the Forest Service's logging and roading programs as damaging to the many old-growth dependent species on the Tongass, including Sitka black-tailed deer, moose, and wolves. The timber industry, meanwhile, rejects the notion that the forest is being devastated, and points to recent record harvests of fish and game (U.S. Department of Agriculture 1986) (see the 1987 *Wildlife Report* for a more detailed account of the conflict surrounding the Tongass timber program).

On March 10, 1987, Representative Robert J. Mrazek (D-NY) and Senator William Proxmire (D-WI) introduced identical legislation (H.R. 1516, S. 708) to place the management of the Tongass on a more equal footing with other national forests. The bills call for the outright repeal of the 4.5 billion board feet timber goal (which the Forest Service has controversially interpreted as a mandate) and would fold all Tongass-related funding into the annual appropriations process. Further, the bills would repeal the forest's exemption from Section 6(k) of the National Forest Management Act. Although the proposed legislation stopped short of terminating the two 50-year timber purchase contracts, Rep. Mrazek urged the committee to address that possibility when it considers his legislation.

Reaction to these proposals was swift and predictable. Speaking for the Southeast Alaska Conservation Council, a grassroots environmental group, K.J. Metcalf stated, "This legislation would be a major step toward resolving the senseless resource management situation on our nation's largest national forest. Smokey Bear would roll over in his grave if he knew what was happening in the Tongass. [These reforms are] needed to bring order back to Tongass management" (Metcalf 1987).

Forest Service Chief Dale Robertson, on the other hand, urged Congress to postpone any major legislative remedies until after the 1979 Tongass Land Management Plan revision is completed in 1989 or 1990. As Robertson testified, "ANILCA designated wilderness and established a timber management program. Both relied heavily on information developed for the 1979 TLMP [Tongass Land Management Plan]. We are doing our best to carry out the intent of Congress and fulfill our land stewardship responsibilites. We believe that a major change in management direction by Congress is not appropriate at this time" (Robertson 1987).

Representing the forest industry, Don Finney of the Alaska Loggers Association called on Congress to uphold its compromise agreement concerning ANILCA's wilderness set-asides and the special timber harvest and funding considerations granted to the Tongass. "From our perspective, the attempt to repeal Section 705 is simply a bad faith effort to renege on a compromise . . . which was critical to [the passage of] ANILCA" (Finney 1987).

In the fall of 1987, Representative Mrazek continued his effort to reform timber management on the Tongass by introducing legislation (H.R. 3556) to terminate the 50-year contracts; no hearings had been held at the end of the fiscal year. Meanwhile, Representative George Miller (D-CA) is drafting legislation to expand wilderness designations within the Tongass, but the congressman had not introduced a bill by the end of FY 1987.

National Forests in Florida

Biological diversity preservation concerns also are at the heart of an ongoing controversy surrounding the three national forests in Florida—

Apalachicola, Osceola, and Ocala. In February 1986, eight conservation organizations, including National Audubon Society and the National Wildlife Federation, appealed the one forest plan for these forests on three grounds: an overemphasis on timber production, inadequate protection of biological diversity, and failure to maintain and recover the endangered red-cockaded woodpecker.

Conservation groups say that the forest plan emphasizes timber production to the direct detriment of other resource uses. They note that while annual timber sale levels are scheduled to almost double (from 14.1-million cubic feet to 24.6-million cubic feet) over the life of the plan, there is no projected increase in acreage for red-cockaded woodpecker colony sites, no projected increase in the acreage of pines to be managed for red-cockaded woodpeckers, no increase in wilderness projections, and no long-term increase in dispersed recreation targets (National Wildlife Federation 1986).

The appeal also charges that the plan fails to provide for and maintain a diversity of plant and animal communities. The longleaf pine forest (with its associated wiregrass and other native groundcover) is considered to be one of the coastal plain's most biologically diverse and important communities. After harvest of longleaf pine stands, natural forest regeneration provides habitat for the red-cockaded woodpecker, gopher tortoise, and songbirds. The forest plan, however, calls for mechanical site preparation and planting for reforestation, which according to the appellants, would severely reduce the distribution and abundance of many species associated with longleaf stands.

Finally, environmentalists fear that implementation of the plan would harm one endangered species—the red-cockaded woodpecker—and do little to promote the recovery of three other federally listed threatened or endangered species: the indigo snake (threatened), the Florida panther (endangered), and the wood stork (endangered). The Endangered Species Act not only requires federal agencies to avoid jeopardizing the continued existence of a species, it also directs them to take affirmative actions to increase populations of threatened and endangered species. The appellants maintain that Forest Service management strategies for the red-cockaded woodpecker are based on outdated information, and represent, at best, the very minimum standards necessary to protect the bird (see the *1987 Audubon Wildlife Report* for more information on agency management of the red-cockaded woodpecker). In the case of the indigo snake, panther, and wood stork, environmentalists say that the plan does not fulfill the government's legislative mandate to take positive actions to aid these species' recovery.

At the end of FY 1987, the appeal of the Florida national forests plan was still pending. The appellants received an oral hearing before a representative of the chief of the Forest Service in April 1987. At that time, conservationists indicated that they were willing to work with the agency to achieve a compromise on the plan, but reserved the option to move forward with their legal appeal if these negotiations proved unsuccessful. Since then, discussions have taken place between the two sides and the Forest Service drafted an amendment to the plan. Although this amendment would evidently satisfy certain of the environmentalists' concerns regarding the regeneration of longleaf pine stands, it fell far short of resolving issues surrounding management of red-cockaded woodpeckers and the other threatened and endangered species. Discussions continued, however, and conservationists were optimistic that an agreement would be reached by early 1988.

Chequamegon National Forest

Conservationists have proposed a unique approach to the protection of both biological diversity and timber production on the Chequamegon National Forest in Wisconsin. By urging the designation of relatively large blocks of the forest as "biological diversity preserves" while intensifying timber management on other areas, conservationists devised a potentially precedent-setting approach to forest management.

After being ravaged by logging and subsequent fires in the early 1900s, the lands for the Chequamegon National Forest were acquired during the Depression of the 1930s. The 846,000-acre forest now supports aspen, northern hardwoods, maple, yellow birch, and basswood. Swampy areas of the forest support hemlocks and related species, and scattered pines, balsams, and spruce still remain. White-tailed deer are common—perhaps overly so—and grouse, bear, woodcock, and rabbits also entice hunters to the forest.

While praising the work of the Forest Service in restoring the Chequamegon, conservationists appealed the forest's new land management plan on the grounds that it would seriously affect the future biological diversity of the area. The plan targets some 95 percent of the forest for timber harvest on short to moderately long cutting rotations. Wilderness areas and other nonharvested research areas account for only about five percent of the forest, and conservationists point out that these areas are fragmented into small, isolated patches. Without the maintenance of large unharvested areas elsewhere in the forest, it is feared that the diverse native animals and trees that require large undisturbed tracts of old-growth forest will suffer, while those species that do well at the edges or forests, or in otherwise disturbed areas, will gain an undesired advantage. Deer, for example, are favored by such "edge" environments, and conservationists fear that the timber harvests would so increase the deer population as to endanger certain of the tree species (hemlock, Canada yew, and white cedar) on which deer browse (Solheim *et al.* 1987).

The Wisconsin Conservation Task Force, National Audubon Society, Sierra Club, and other conservation organizations have promoted the concept of "zoning" the forest. These groups advocate intensified timber harvests on parts of the forest and the designation of other areas as "diversity maintenance zones." Instead of the patchwork of disturbed (harvested) lands and small, old-growth stands that conservationists say the forest plan would create, large chunks of nonharvested land would provide sufficient habitat for a diversity of plants and animals. Unlike wilderness areas, however, diversity zones would be open to a wider range of multiple uses, with the exception of timber harvest. Since the conservation groups support intensified harvests outside of the diversity maintenance zones, the diversity preservation goal could be attained without a net loss of timber production from the forest as a whole.

The diversity zones were chosen to include the forest's important vegetative communities and to provide a biological buffer zone for a wilderness area, several rare plant sites, and proposed research natural areas. Two separate areas were chosen, totaling about 140,000 acres or 17 percent of the forest. These areas are believed to be of sufficient size to maintain biological diversity by preventing forest fragmentation and its related problems.

A compromise that would both maintain biological diversity and historic timber-sale levels seemed almost too good to be true, and at the end of FY 1987 it appeared that might indeed be the case. Although conservationists claim that the Chequamegon Forest staff originally agreed to the proposal, documents obtained in response to a Freedom of Information Act request indicated that the regional forester's office criticized and eventually overruled the Chequamegon forest supervisor's decision (Solheim *et al.* 1987).

Local forest industry representatives also objected to the creation of diversity maintenance zones. A long-time advocate of increased harvests on the forest, the timber industry feared that the diversity zones were thinly disguised wilderness areas, and claimed that their establishment would diminish timber productivity. The industry contended that the Forest Service had underestimated the demand for wood products from the Chequamegon and that the forest was scheduled to produce an inadequate supply of timber.

Conservationists appealed the rejection of their compromise plan and received an oral hearing before the chief of the Forest Service on October 15, 1987; no final decision has yet been made. If the administrative appeal is rejected, conservation groups may continue their struggle for diversity maintenance zones by filing a lawsuit on the plan.

OTHER WILDLIFE DEVELOPMENTS AND ISSUES

Rise to the Future

In March 1987, the Forest Service unveiled a new initiative—Rise to the Future—designed to increase the agency's emphasis on fisheries management within the national forests. Although the Forest Service has long maintained a fisheries program, numerous critics, both inside and outside of the agency, believed the program lacked visibility and direction; hence, they encouraged the establishment of a national fisheries program with concrete goals. The new program was developed by a task force of agency personnel, in cooperation with the American Fisheries Society and other conservation organizations.

The national forests contain about 128,000 miles of streams and rivers; 2.2-million acres of ponds, lakes, and reservoirs; and 16,500 miles of coasts and shorelines. National forest waters annually produce large harvests of fish for sport, commerce, and subsistence use. In California, Oregon, Idaho, and Washington, for example, over 50 percent of all salmon and steelhead trout habitat occur in 15,000 miles of national forest streams found in that region (U.S. Department of Agriculture 1987c).

There is a great recreational demand for sport fishing in national forests; current fishing use throughout the system is estimated at 46.5-million-angler-days yearly with a net related economic activity value of $1.2 billion. As access to private lands for fishing declines, particularly near urban areas, demand for fishing opportunities on forest system lands is expected to increase.

Rise to the Future was designed to integrate fisheries concerns more fully within the agency's ongoing land management and research efforts by more clearly identifying the objectives of the fisheries program at national, regional, forest, and district levels. If the program is successful, its supporters also hope it will help increase the status of fish and wildlife professionals within the agency. According to one Forest Service staff member, "Wildlife and fisheries biologists are not really part of the organization, rather, they were thrust upon the agency by the requirements of the National Environmental Policy Act."

To help achieve the integration of fisheries concerns, the new program calls for a number of improvements, including: the inclusion of fisheries projects in forest plan implementation schedules that are used to develop annual budgets; the use of best management technologies to improve habitat management; the strengthening of fish-management partnerships with states, other agencies, and the private sector; and the use of valid estimates of fishery values, supplies, and demands.

Research needs are also addressed, as Rise to the Future document notes, "because the current Forest Service fish habitat research program is small compared to the extent of the fisheries resource and the technical knowledge required to manage this resource." The agency readily admits that, "In no forest experiment station are fish habitat needs being fully addressed." Research areas identified for emphasis include: fish habitat requirements; land use relationships and effects; habitat enhancement; and the economic and recreational values of fisheries.

Rise to the Future has been charged with an ambitious mandate to address more adequately fisheries management and research issues as part of the Forest Service's multiple-use mandate. Early indications bode well for the success of the initiative. In FY 1988, Congress appropriated additional fisheries funds, including $1 million earmarked for Rise to the Future, and the Agriculture Department has indicated its intention to request a tripling of the fisheries habitat improvement budget for the agency in FY 1989. Furthermore, Forest Service leaders seem solidly in support of the program, and are requiring the involvement of each of the agency's nine regional offices in the effort.

Below-Cost Timber Sales

Below-cost timber sales continued to receive limited attention in 1987. Below-cost timber sales (sales so-named because the Forest Service spends more to grow and manage the trees than it receives in sale income), are often opposed by fish and wildlife interests on environmental grounds; timber harvests and associated roads can adversely impact both wildlife populations and their habitat.

During 1987, the agency continued to refine and implement a new timber sales accounting system, which had been prepared at the request of Congress for use in identifying uneconomic sales. When first released in draft form in 1986, the new system received widespread criticism from the Natural Resources Defense Council, other environmental and conservation groups, the forest products industry, and Congress. At the end of FY 1987, the House and Senate appropriations committees were at odds over funding the implementation of the system, with the House supporting funding for only part of the new procedures and the Senate pushing for full funding. The final congressional report accompanying the FY 1988 Interior Appropriations bill directed the Forest Service to implement part of its system and continue to refine other aspects of the proposal.

The continuing controversy and general lack of confidence in the new system indicates that the new procedures, even if implemented, will do little to help resolve the below-cost timber-sale issue. Moreover, many observers point out that the basic issue at hand is not so much one of choosing correct accounting procedures, as it is one of determining management priorities for the resources of the National Forest System. Absent a major shift in our society's attitudes toward our forests, this underlying debate concerning overall forest management priorities is likely to escalate in years to come.

REFERENCES

Barton, Katherine. 1987. "Wildlife and the U.S. Forest Service," pp. 267–289 *in* R.L. DiSilvestro ed., *Audubon Wildlife Report 1987*. National Audubon Society. New York, New York. Academic Press, Inc. Orlando, Florida.

Cook, Robert. Telephone interview with the author. Washington, D.C. November 20, 1987.

Finney, Don. Statement before the Public Lands, National Parks, and Forest Subcommittee, U.S. Senate Energy and Natural Resource Committee. Oversite Hearings on Tongass National Forest. November 5, 1987

Franklin, Karen E. 1986. "The Process at Work: Greater Yellowstone." *American Forests* 92:25

——. 1987. "Turmoil in the Tongass." *American Forests* 93: 36–44.

Hillman, Loren. Telephone interview with the author. Washington, D.C. November 20, 1987.

Honnold, Doug. Telephone interview with the author. Washington, D.C. November 5, 1987.

Library of Congress, Congressional Research Service. 1987. Greater Yellowstone Ecosystem: An Analysis of Data Submitted by Federal and State Agencies. Government Printing Office. Washington, D.C.

Metcalf, K.J. Statement before the Public Lands, National Parks, and Forest Subcommittee, U.S. Senate Energy and Natural Resource Committee. Oversite Hearings on Tongass National Forest. November 5, 1987.

National Audubon Society. 1986. Report of the Advisory Panel on the Spotted Owl. New York, New York.

National Wildlife Federation. Unpubl. Appellants'Reply to the Forest Service's Response to the Statement of Reasons for Appealing the Land and Resource Management Plan for Florida. August 28, 1986.

Norse, E. A. *et al.* 1986. Conserving Biological Diversity in Our National Forests. The Wilderness Society. Washington, D.C.

Poole, Daniel A. 1987. "The public lands: bust or boon for wildlife?" *American Forests* 23:20.

Robertson, Dale. Statement before the Public Lands, National Parks, and Forest Subcommittee, U.S. Senate Energy and Natural Resource Committee. Oversite Hearings on Tongass National Forest. November 3, 1987.

Solheim, S.L. *et al.* 1987. "Maintaining biological diversity in national forests: applying island biogeography concepts in forest planning." *Forest Watch* 8:9–14.

U.S. Congress, House, Committee on Interior and Insular Affairs. 1985. Hearings, Greater Yellowstone Ecosystem. 99th Cong., 1st sess. Serial No. 99–18.

U.S. Congress, Senate, Committee on Agriculture, Nutrition and Forestry. 1979. Compilation of the Forest and Rangeland Renewable Resources Act of 1974. 96th Cong., 1st sess.

U.S. Congress, Senate, Committee on Appropriations. 1987. Department of Interior and Related Agencies Appropriations Bill, 1988. 100th Cong., 1st. sess. (Report No. 100–165).

U.S. Department of Agriculture, Forest Service. 1986. Status of the Tongass National Forest: 1985 Report. Admin. Doc. Number 153. Washington, D.C.

U.S. Department of Agriculture, Forest Service. 1987a. Unpublished Five Year Plan, Spotted Owl Research, Development, and Application Program.

——. 1987b. Final Environmental Impact Statement for the Suppression of the Southern Pine Beetle, Southern Region. Atlanta, Georgia.

——. 1987c. Unpublished Rise to the Future.

U.S. Department of Interior, Fish and Wildlife Service. 1986. Unpublished Biological Opinion of December 12, 1986 from James W. Pullman, Jr. to John Alcock.

Wilderness Society. 1987. *Forests of the Future?* Washington, D.C.

Frances Hunt is director of resource policy with the American Forestry Association.

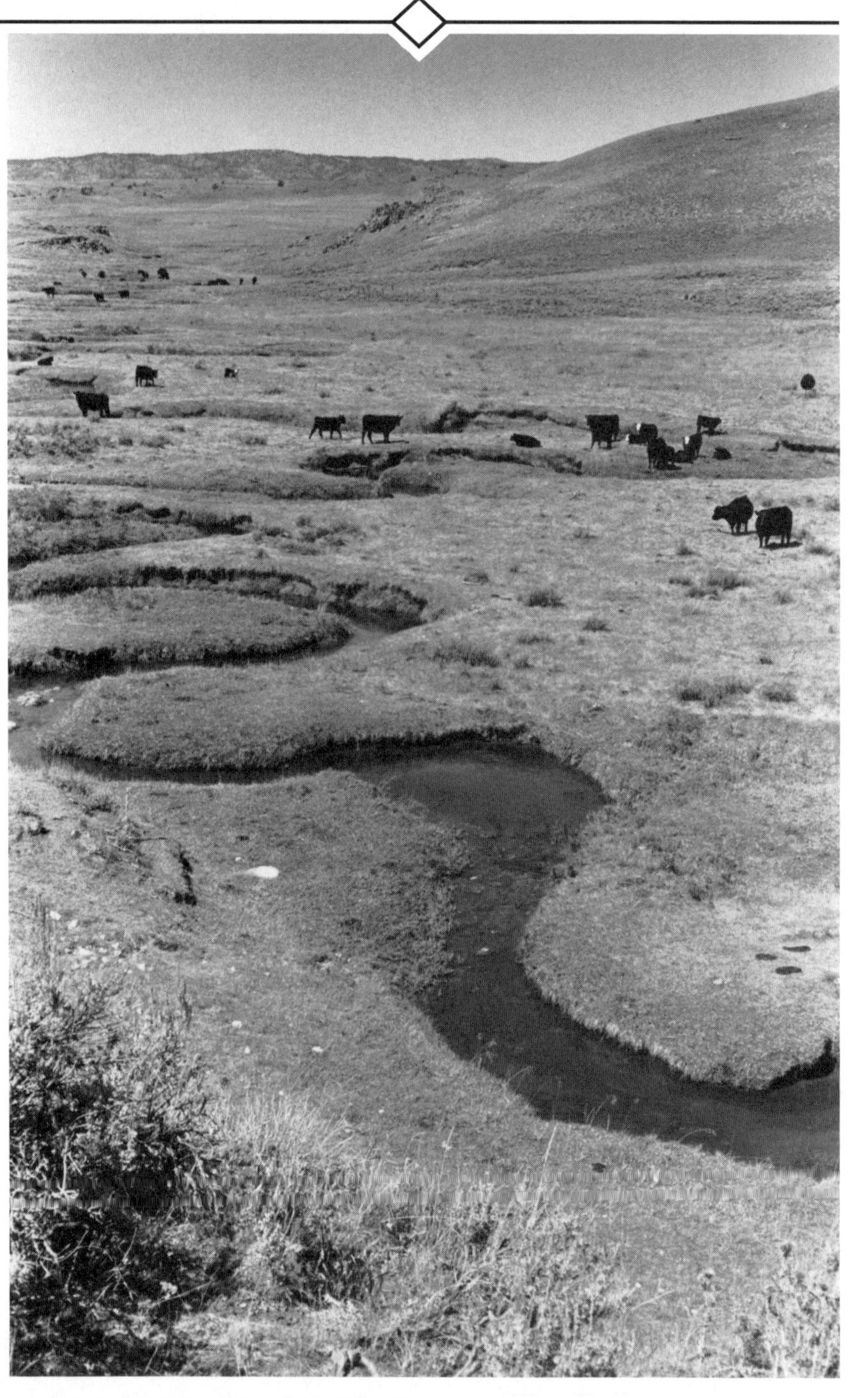

The Bureau of Land Management has responsibility for some 300 million acres, primarily in the West and Alaska. The regulation of privately held grazing permits is one of BLM's most contentious issues. *Chris Wille*

Wildlife and the Bureau of Land Management

Karen Franklin

INTRODUCTION

Publicly owned lands administered by the Bureau of Land Management (BLM), an agency within the Department of the Interior, comprise more area than all other federal lands combined. Commonly known as "the public lands," most of the 334 million acres under BLM jurisdiction are found in 12 western states: Alaska, Arizona, California, Colorado, Idaho, Montana, Nevada, Oregon, Washington, New Mexico, Utah, and Wyoming. (see Figures 1 and 2). In addition to its 334 million acres of exclusive jurisdiction (surface and subsurface rights), the Bureau also has jurisdiction over the mineral rights on another 398 million acres.

Although the agency oversees many kinds of terrain, most of it is considered rangeland. Some 96 percent of BLM lands outside Alaska are classified as rangelands—roughly 170 million of 177 million acres. BLM also manages mountainous regions, wetlands, glacial areas and tundras, forests, and deserts.

A variety of ecosystems still remain in nearly pristine condition on BLM land. Alaskan lands managed by BLM comprise approximately 95 million acres of primitive backcountry, and include some prime fish and wildlife habitat. Little grazing occurs there and as a result,

WASHINGTON
Total BLM acreage: 312,514
WSA acreage: 5,518

MONTANA
Total BLM acreage: 8,087,071
WSA acreage: 453,076

OREGON
Total BLM acreage: 15,697,724
WSA acreage: 2,613,850

IDAHO
Total BLM acreage: 11,906,460
WSA acreage: 1,934,707

WYOMING
Total BLM acreage: 18,408,734
WSA acreage: 568,412

COLORADO
Total BLM acreage: 8,362,137
WSA acreage: 819,897

UTAH
Total BLM acreage: 22,137,652
WSA acreage: 3,308,992

CALIFORNIA
Total BLM acreage: 17,151,663
WSA acreage: 7,272,710

ARIZONA
Total BLM acreage: 12,232,171
WSA acreage: 2,115,308

NEW MEXICO
Total BLM acreage: 12,899,533
WSA acreage: 1,129,160

WSA — Wilderness Study Area
BLM Lands

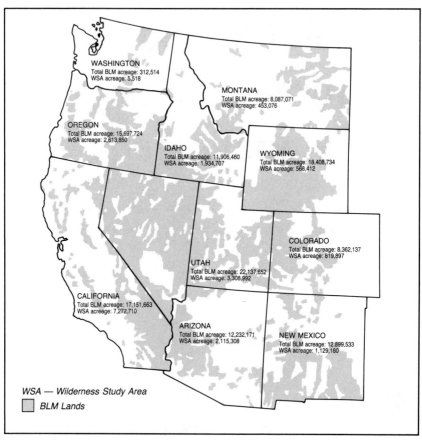

Figure 1. Source: The Wilderness Society.

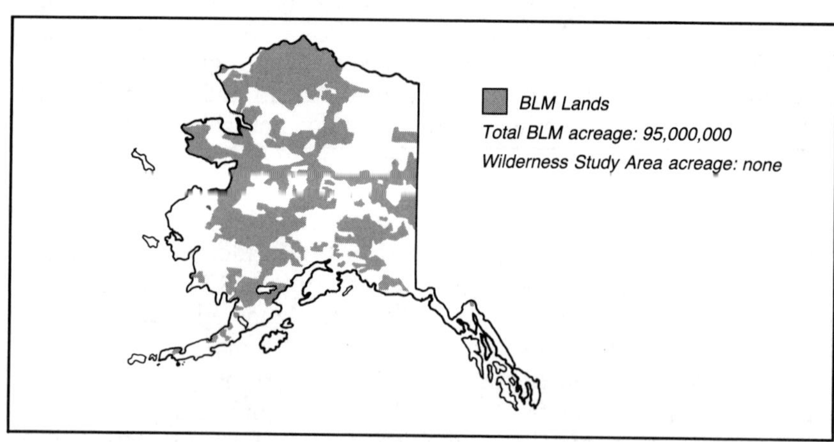

Figure 2. Source: The Wilderness Society.

environmental concerns over Alaskan BLM lands have remained relatively low to date.

BLM land supports an abundant, diverse variety of wildlife. Some 3,000 species depend on bureau land for their last strongholds of habitat, including many declining species such as the desert tortoise, northern spotted owl, grizzly bear, and desert bighorn sheep. Approximately 127 federally listed threatened and endangered species, in addition to more than 800 candidates for protected status, occur throughout the public lands (see Table 1).

Since the agency's birth in the 1940s, BLM operations have focused largely on commodity development, an entrenched priority that has been vigorously reinforced by the Reagan Administration. Grazing has remained the most intensive and widespread management activity, and the most controversial. After grazing, minerals production accounts for the heaviest consumptive land use. BLM also administers timber harvests, utility rights-of-way, and water allocation; it sets aside small parcels of land to preserve for scientific, scenic, recreational, cultural, and wilderness qualities; and it manages fish and wildlife habitat areas, including wild horse and burro range.

Table 1
Estimated Populations and Habitat of Threatened and Endangered (T/E) Species on Public Lands, Fiscal Year 1986.

Administrative State	T/E species[a]		Estimated habitat[b]		Recovery plans implemented[c]
	Plants	Animals			
	Number	*Number*	*Thousands of acres*	*Miles*	*Number*
Alaska	–	5	100	–	1
Arizona	9	15	450	300	13
California	6	16	300	6	12
Colorado	7	7	937	200	6
Idaho	1	6	81	302	7
Montana	–	7	356	–	6
Nevada	7	20	36	339	3
New Mexico	10	7	10	10	3
Oregon	1	7	95	11	4
Utah	12	13	2,160	446	7
Wyoming	–	7	1,215	–	6
Eastern States	16	13	50	–	4
TOTAL	–	–	5,790	1,614	72

Source: *Public Lands Statistics, 1986.* U.S. Department of the Interior, BLM

[a] Numbers of species cannot be added because many species occur in more than one state. Bureau-wide, there are 82 animal and 45 plant species listed as threatened and endangered.

[b] Terrestrial, wetland, and riparian habitat are measured in acres; aquatic habitat is measured in miles.

[c] Cumulative total

The Federal Land Policy and Management Act of 1976 (FLPMA) (43 U.S.C.A. 1701 *et seq.*) stipulates that BLM consider both the renewable and nonrenewable values of its resources equally in land-use decisions, a mandate referred to as "multiple-use." The act requires BLM to prepare land-use plans with public participation to ensure habitat conservation, range recovery, and other protection measures. The law makes fish and wildlife management a high-priority use of the public lands. It mandates land inventories, recommendations to Congress for wilderness designations, and the establishment of areas of critical environmental concern for special protection. FLPMA also authorizes the agency to allocate 50 percent of grazing fee revenues to range improvements.

Due to its multiple-use mandate, much of BLM's work now involves resolving conflicts among interest groups with vastly different ideas about managing the public lands. Despite FLPMA, environmental groups vehemently criticize BLM for overemphasizing commercial land uses, and accuse the agency of disregarding its responsibility to conserve the public resources under its charge.

For example, grazing advisory boards, made up entirely of ranchers, have counseled the agency on rangeland management decisions since 1934 and are extremely influential. This arrangement has drawn intense criticism from conservationists who charge that BLM caters to the special interests of the livestock industry. In response to such accusations, Congress established multiple-use advisory councils under FLPMA to provide input on resource management issues. The councils theoretically consist of representatives of a variety of user groups, but according to the National Wildlife Federation and the Natural Resources Defense Council, the bureau has allowed stockmen to dominate the advisory councils.

The agency's shift away from its commodity orientation has indeed been sluggish—sometimes to the point of inertia—due largely to the political priorities of both the Reagan Administration and Congress. President Reagan's appointment of a rancher and grazing-permit holder, Robert Burford, to head the agency set a tone for reduced emphasis on land and habitat conservation (U.S. Congress, House 1986).[1] Subsequent changes in regulations, staffing, budget priorities, and internal policies have resulted in more influence on the agency by the livestock industry than had previously existed under President Jimmy Carter. In addition, the Sagebrush Rebellion of the early 1980s, though unsuccessful on many counts, resulted in a policy of less

1. A 1986 congressional report, "Federal Grazing Program: All Is Not Well on the Range," prepared by the House Government Operations Committee, includes a lengthy discussion on the propriety of director Burford heading the agency, and suggests that the director lacks objectivity in policy-making. His position with the bureau appears to be a conflict of interest, the report says.

federal control over lands in the West. Throughout the history of public land management, congressional committees overseeing federal land laws and practices also have typically been dominated by westerners, which has slanted management priorities toward livestock and mining interests. Environmental organizations have been unable to change this bias primarily because they have historically focused less attention on BLM lands than on other conservation issues.

In addition to FLPMA, BLM is guided by a number of congressional mandates that determine its management direction:

- The Public Rangelands Improvement Act of 1978 (43 U.S.C.A. 1901 *et seq.*) established the goal of resource recovery on BLM land and set up an experimental grazing fee formula intended to ensure range and habitat improvements and a fair market price for grazing on public lands.
- A 1974 amendment to the Sikes Act (16 U.S.C.A. 670 *et seq.*) authorized federal-state cooperative programs for improved fish and wildlife management strategies on all federal lands, including those of BLM.
- The National Environmental Policy Act of 1969 (42 U.S.C.A. 4331–44) requires environmental analyses of proposed management activities and solicitation of public participation in preparation of environmental impact statements.
- The Endangered Species Act of 1973 (16 U.S.C.A. 1531 *et seq.*) subjects the bureau to all laws and mandates enacted to protect federally listed threatened or endangered species, and requires BLM to develop and implement species recovery plans and to ensure that no management activity jeopardizes the survival of any listed species.

BLM ORGANIZATION AND STRUCTURE

Decision-making in BLM

Land-use policies in BLM are established by four governing tiers: the national office, the state offices, the districts, and resource areas (see Figure 3). The national office consists of many divisions which develop priorities and policies for each land use, such as rangelands, minerals, forestry, and wildlife, and issue policy statements to the state directors. The state directors amass national directives and make all the final land-use judgments in their jurisdictions; they oversee all the management activities in their states and report yearly to national headquarters. State directors are also responsible for preparing budget requests for their operations.

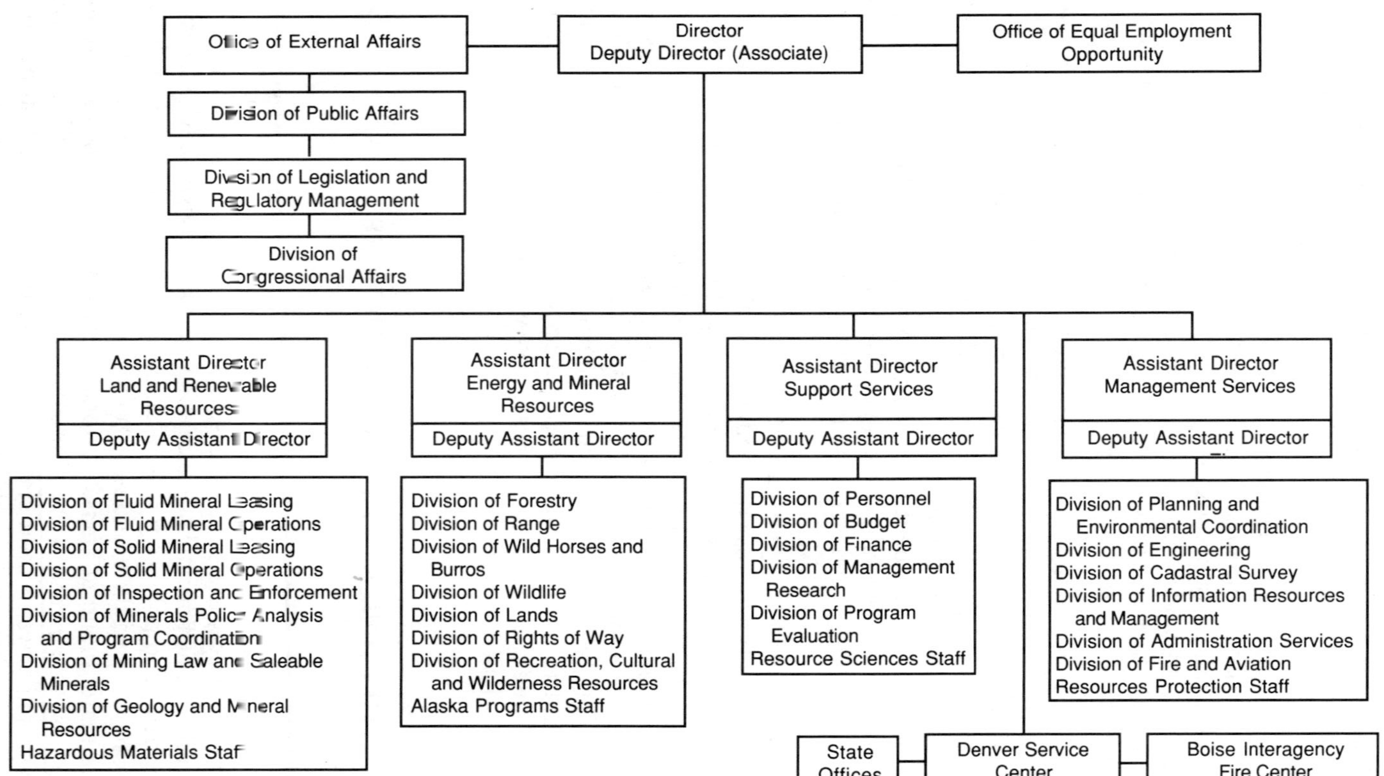

Figure 3. Source: BLM, 1987.

Each state is divided into districts, headed by district managers. Districts are further segmented into resource areas, each with its own manager. Site-specific land-use decisions primarily take place at the resource area level, and are approved by the district manager.

Nearly all BLM decision-making occurs at the state and local levels with virtually no oversight by the national office. This highly decentralized management structure severely limits opportunities for citizens to hold BLM accountable to the law or its own stated objectives. Furthermore, the agency cannot guarantee consistency or cohesion in implementing its programs on a national scale. Although the national office routinely hands down policy statements and program guidelines to the states, national division chiefs lack the power to oversee or enforce their directives. National policies are typically uncoordinated among headquarters divisions, and often are issued in such a disjointed way that they cancel each other.

As a result, it is up to the state directors to sift through national policies, determine their own priorities, and make tradeoffs, independent of the national perspective. Wildlife and conservation objectives commonly get shortchanged in the process because of the strong influence local ranchers exert on BLM's district and area managers. In southern Utah, for example, a BLM manager recently proposed to increase the number of cattle grazing in his resource area, a plan "which goes against everything we know about managing the [threatened] desert tortoise," explained a BLM official. State and national directors are not always apprised of such clear land-use conflicts, he said. Although state directors are required to submit management data to national headquarters annually, what information they report essentially is left to their discretion, according to agency officials.[2] Therefore, BLM cannot accurately determine the consequences of the policies it executes. Furthermore, no accountability mechanism exists within the agency to ensure that field managers comply with multiple-use laws and principles.[3]

Land-Use Planning

BLM's planning process requires local managers to consider the many competing values of all resources in making land-use decisions. FLPMA mandates "resource management plans" (RMPs) developed in cooperation with user groups, the public, and pertinent state and

2. While the fish and wildlife division instructs the state directors on reporting requirements, the small staff of the Washington office cannot ensure that the states comply with national guidance, one official explains.

3. Tracking management activity state by state is difficult, if not impossible, says an agency planning analyst. But at least one wildlife division official disagrees: "We have one of the best evaluation programs," says Division Chief J. David Almand.

federal agencies, to set multiple-use management priorities for 151 resource areas.[4] "BLM's job is to find ways to accommodate the increasingly competitive demands on these lands while protecting [them] and ensuring their long-term productivity," says an agency booklet, *BLM Planning: A Guide to Resource Management Planning on the Public Lands* (U.S. Department of the Interior 1983).

In theory, resource management plans allocate resources, establish utilization practices and standards, map out resource protection measures, and set up monitoring schedules for individual resource areas. Each is accompanied by an environmental impact statement. At several points during the planning process, BLM solicits participation and comment from interested land users, environmental groups, and the public. Participants typically include ranchers, mining interests, utility companies, loggers, community planners, recreationists, wildlife advocates, and conservationists. Planning involves such steps as identifying the issues needing resolution, collecting data, formulating and choosing alternatives, approving the plan, and monitoring its implementation.

By September 30, 1987, BLM had completed and implemented—to various degrees—44 resource management plans, covering 64 million acres, 19 percent of BLM-managed land. In addition, five plans were complete but not yet implemented, and ten plans remained in draft form. In total, only 59 out of 151 resource areas have been subject to the planning process.

In some cases, land-management planning in the bureau has resulted in improved conditions for wildlife, BLM officials say. Between 1976 and 1986, for example, the pronghorn antelope population on the public lands increased from 190,000 to 275,000; the number of elk rose from 96,000 to 135,000 in the same 10-year period. BLM has taken the credit, claiming "certain species have benefited as a result of improved resource management."

According to conservationists, BLM's approach to planning contains several flaws. Nevertheless, although FLPMA mandated preparation of resource management plans, it is not BLM policy to develop them systematically. Instead, BLM is continuing to use its older, often outdated, and typically more general "management framework plans" (MFPs), prepared prior to FLPMA's enactment. "There is no specific date by which all MFPs will be replaced by RMPs, [nor any guarantee that] we will even replace all of them," explained a BLM planning analyst. The agency initiates RMPs only when "pressing resource conflicts" emerge—area and district managers usually make that judgment.

4. See BLM booklet *BLM Planning: A Guide to Resource Management Planning on the Public Lands* and the 1985 and 1987 *Audubon Wildlife Report* for more detailed explanations of BLM land-use planning.

Consistent with its overall approach to decision-making by field personnel, BLM's national office has adopted a hands-off policy toward planning. Although the national office issues policy goals and directives to incorporate into planning objectives, state directors use their discretion in applying those goals to their jurisdictions. In effect, national policies are voluntary at the field level (see Table 2).

Resource management plans often embrace only broad, theoretical goals. Implementation strategies show up only in site-specific "activity plans," such as "allotment management plans" for grazing and "habitat management plans" for wildlife. At the activity plan level, there is far less opportunity for public input and review.

Budget and Staff Shortages

BLM manages approximately 46 percent of all federally owned land. Despite the enormity of its charge, budgets and staff levels have remained low throughout the agency's history. Chronic shortages partly explain the bureau's decentralized structure—neither the personnel nor the money exists for the national office to oversee field activities rigorously. Historically, BLM lands were the least desirable of the public-domain acreage, which also helps explain BLM's low priority status for federal appropriations.

The agency's budget priorities lean heavily toward commercial development, such as grazing and minerals production. Funding for range management rose substantially in the last four years, from roughly $40 million in 1984 to $54 million in 1987. Similarly, the budget for fluid energy minerals management increased from approximately $43.5 million in 1984 to $48.5 million in 1987. In contrast, the wildlife and fisheries budget has remained between $13.5 million in 1984 and $16 million in 1987, despite a considerable increase in demand for habitat protection. Funding for multiple-use planning has held steady at about $9 million annually.

BLM's budget figures alone reveal little about the quality of the agency's overall wildlife management activities; many expenditures

Table 2
Resource Management Plan Management Structure

BLM Director:	Assumes responsibility for planning; issues national policies and guidance; develops procedures and budget priorities.
State Director:	Approves RMPs in his jurisdiction; issues drafts to the public and the Environmental Protection Agency; gives statewide guidance and oversight.
District Manager:	Supervises RMP process; provides budget and staff support; sometimes issues district guidance to area managers.
Area Manager:	Prepares, implements, and monitors RMP.

Source: *BLM Planning: A Guide to Resource Management Planning on the Public Lands.* U.S. Department of the Interior, BLM 1982.

for habitat protection and conservation are hidden in budgets of divisions other than wildlife and fisheries. Costs for resource development projects may include such components as conservation efforts, consultation with biologists, endangered species protection activities, and environmental impact analyses. For example, the minerals budget would fund all wildlife inventories and follow-up monitoring associated with mining activities on the public lands.[5]

This system makes it difficult, if not impossible, to determine the bureau's total expenditures for various conservation measures agencywide. For example, the cost of analyzing a proposed oil well's impact on an endangered species would be budgeted as a minerals program expense. (These analyses are required by Section 7 of the Endangered Species Act.) As a result of this accounting method, BLM could theoretically spend no money on such analysis and no one would know it.[6]

The only wildlife and fisheries expenditures that can be tracked in budget documents are those specifically allotted to the wildlife division, such as recovery projects for endangered species or habitat management plans. However, these distinct wildlife activities make up a small proportion of the total workload of agency biologists.

BLM's staffing priorities more clearly reflect the agency's emphasis on commodity development than does its budget. As of mid-1987, the number of biologists totaled 239 full-time equivalent positions, compared with 1,332 full-time equivalent personnel in range conservation, engineering, geology, and forestry (see Table 3).

In mid-1987, the agency employed only eight botanists,[7] despite the occurrence of 45 plant species on BLM land that were federally listed as threatened or endangered. Only 16 recovery plans for listed plants had been implemented, yet the Endangered Species Act obligates the agency to protect from extinction all listed species under its jurisdiction.

Biologists are distributed unevenly throughout BLM's states, districts, and resource areas. In July 1986, the latest date for which composite figures are available, 13 out of 151 resource areas had no wildlife biologists. Only 10 resource areas had fisheries biologists, despite a bureau policy to make protection of aquatic areas a top priority. Even more alarming, 5 out of 55 districts were without wildlife biologists and 39 districts had no fisheries biologists. Four out of 12 states had no fisheries biologists.

Such thin distribution of wildlife expertise requires small teams—often just one person—to take on planning, inventories, monitoring,

5. Depressed funding levels have kept such activities to a minimum.

6. According to a BLM official, not only do budget documents fail to reflect the bureau's Section 7 consultation work, there are no records of money or time spent on such activities within the agency.

7. At that time, one botany job remained unfilled.

Table 3
BLM Staff Distribution, Mid-1987
(Full-Time Equivalents)

Staff Position	FTEs
Biologists	239
Wildlife	207
Fisheries	24
Botanists	8
Range Conservationists	442
Engineers	177
Mining	74
Petroleum	103
Geologists	307
Foresters	406

Source: Based on figures provided by BLM's Office of Public Information, 1987.

habitat improvements, and mitigation measures for millions of acres, a task too overwhelming to be done adequately in nearly every case. The field biologists' inability to accomplish those objectives does not reflect their competence or commitment, however, which has been highly praised. Rather, their impossible workload clearly reveals the development-oriented political priorities in Washington.

THE BLM WILDLIFE PROGRAM

BLM is responsible for managing fish and wildlife habitat on the public lands, a task overseen by the Division of Wildlife and Fisheries. BLM field biologists work cooperatively with state governments to maintain viable population levels of both game and nongame wildlife species, including plants.

Specifically, bureau biologists advise local managers on the incorporation of wildlife and plant management into all land-use activities; establish and implement wildlife and plant protection measures; and inventory and monitor resources as required by land management plans and congressional mandates. The activities of field biologists to date have focused on providing consultation on commercial projects such as forestry, grazing, and minerals production. Additional habitat protection measures, identified in resource management plans, are typically limited to critical needs—such as habitat for a threatened or endangered species. As one BLM biologist put it, "Wildlife is not a high-priority program."[8]

8. Some staff predict that BLM's wildlife programs will take on more importance in the future.

Fish and Wildlife 2000: A Plan for the Future

In mid-1987, the wildlife division launched a more proactive approach to habitat management by issuing a policy aimed at expanding BLM efforts to protect wildlife and fisheries on the public lands. "Fish and Wildlife 2000: A Plan for the Future" is intended to achieve "a proactive program rather than a reactive one, which is all we've had so far," explained a BLM official (U.S. Department of the Interior 1987a).

The report outlines many strategies to improve BLM's overall approach to wildlife and fisheries management. For example, under the new policy, "candidate" species for listing under the Endangered Species Act would be protected to prevent their addition to the threatened and endangered list. Attention to wetlands and riparian areas also would be improved, and a more supportive working environment for the agency's biologists would be provided. Should the strategy work, it will be the first time in BLM history that the wildlife program actively pursues habitat protection objectives.

The plan's goals and objectives also include:

- Providing and increasing habitat to ensure "optimum" populations and natural diversity, with specific management objectives for big game, upland game, waterfowl, raptors, and riparian areas.
- Enhancing and restoring fisheries habitats for "high-value" species.
- Minimizing conflicts between bureau development and conservation activities regarding threatened and endangered plants, fish, and wildlife; improving habitat conditions to prevent further listings; and maintaining rare and vulnerable habitats through planning and cooperation with other land agencies and private groups.
- Increasing awareness of fish and wildlife values within the agency by improving the "organizational environment" and by enhancing the professional and technical expertise of BLM's wildlife resources.
- Improving the cooperation between the wildlife program and all other BLM activities by giving higher priority to multiple-use values of BLM resources.
- Enlisting cooperation of public groups, scientists, educational institutions, and other federal agencies to improve public support of the agency and staff morale in regard to wildlife programs. Strategies include conducting "outreach" programs; encouraging staff scientists to publish papers in professional journals; nurturing relationships with community groups, other federal agencies, states, and conservation organizations to promote multiple-use principles; and seeking private investments in BLM wildlife programs.

Interdisciplinary teams are being set up to establish strategies to ensure implementation of the plan, and some have already made progress. In October 1987, a desert tortoise management team issued an instruction memorandum to the state offices with recommendations for managing the species. The strategy included considering the tortoise equally with other resources in planning; ensuring a viable, sustained population; and monitoring selected habitats. The national office has requested state-level implementation plans by March 31, 1988 (U.S. Department of the Interior 1987b).[9]

Environmental organizations have reacted to "Fish and Wildlife 2000" with caution. While conservationists approve of the plan's goals, they regard "2000" as highly idealistic. In essence, they allege, the plan is largely a public-relations document. Although the report cites specific objectives, it provides no mechanism to ensure their incorporation into resource planning or day-to-day management, and no such vehicle currently exists. Some observers say the plan appears to be little more than the wildlife division's wish list.

The plan's language is vague and ambiguous, offering no assurance that fish and wildlife objectives will take on any new importance within BLM. An example: "When competition exists between wildlife and other uses, BLM will strive to maintain optimum habitats by mitigating adverse impacts whenever possible."

In effect, the plan is voluntary and subject to the discretion of each state director.[10] The degree to which each wildlife goal should be achieved has not been established. Both the pace and timing for the plan's implementation are determined by the state directors, who will weigh the priorities laid out in the report with other land-use demands, other BLM programs, and the needs of their constituents.

"What we're after is educating and obtaining a commitment from our field managers—establishing a sense of ownership and commitment in getting these goals realized," explained an agency official. But indications are that the policy does not mesh with BLM's overall land-use goals, particularly grazing and mining.[11] Implementation of the policy depends entirely on available funding and staffing, currently held at minimum levels, and "other bureau workloads," according to the report. Funding for most of the plan will come from the wildlife

9. A full chapter in this *Audubon Wildlife Report* is devoted to a discussion about desert tortoise management.

10. However, the division of wildlife and fisheries has instructed all of the state directors to develop similar documents for their jurisdictions, and will use the "2000" document in budget requests.

11. A wildlife and fisheries official contends that a high degree of cooperation exists between the various divisions in seeing the policy through, particularly with regard to riparian management. But at least one agency planner remains skeptical, explaining, "Each program office is an advocate of its own program. The trade-offs occur at the field."

and fisheries division's budget; generally the wildlife division has little impact on most commodity management activities that affect wildlife. Finally, there is no indication that low budget trends for the wildlife division will be reversed in the near future.[12]

Plant Protection

Even the wildlife division's commitment has been called into question by some conservation organizations with regard to protecting sensitive or endangered plants. In 1986, the division withdrew proposed regulations that would have put tighter controls on collecting plants on the public lands. Conservation groups object to the lack of formal regulations on two grounds. First, although many collectors sell wild plants for profit, the government does not control the use of these public resources for private gain. Second, lack of regulations poses a danger of depletion or extinction of some highly sought-after plants.

According to the Natural Resources Defense Council, the absence of formal rules already has caused worrisome declines of some species. For example, since the 1970s, plant collectors have put heavy pressure on wild cactus species because they cannot easily be reproduced in greenhouses. For that reason, wild cacti are in high demand among consumers and serious collectors. BLM does not oversee plant collection on BLM land, nor does it conduct regular plant inventories. Therefore, the agency cannot quantify the damage collectors have caused or make accurate plant population projections for future management decisions.

BLM argues that an effort to protect plants is reflected in the voluntary "Fish and Wildlife 2000" plan, and that formal regulations are both unnecessary and not useful. The report calls for increased internal attention to plant protection and more education about plant conservation at the field level. "There was no consensus about how the regulations ought to fit into our plant program," said J. David Almand, chief of the division of wildlife and fisheries, "plus the number of botanists had declined to the point where we realized we'd be passing regulations that we had no power to implement" (Almand 1987a).

Protecting Endangered Species

The wildlife and fisheries division is working on several initiatives in addition to the "2000" plan aimed at improving its endangered species

12. The division of wildlife and fisheries views the document as "a historic milestone," which will effectively turn around the bureau's approach to wildlife management. According to Division Chief J. David Almand, the plan will improve the division's credibility both inside and outside the agency; will help raise the status of fish and wildlife programs; and will provide a clearer sense of direction and purpose for bureau biologists (Almand 1987a).

Table 4
Threatened, Endangered, and Candidate Species on BLM Lands, Mid-1980s.

	Number of species
Listed species	
Fish	34
Mammals	16
Birds	22
Reptiles	7
Amphibians	2
Invertebrates	45
Candidate species	
Plants	620
Animals	250

Source: BLM, "Fish and Wildlife 2000: A Plan for the Future." Department of the Interior 1987.

Table 5
Recovery Plans

	Animals	Plants	Total
Number of plans	57	16	73
Plans being implemented	40	16	56
Species lacking plans	25	29	54
Plans being developed	6	6	12

Source: BLM, "Fish and Wildlife 2000: A Plan for the Future." U.S. Department of the Interior 1987.

program for both plants and animals (see Tables 4 and 5). After nearly eight years of drafting, a national policy aimed at protecting species on BLM land from reaching endangered or threatened status was approved in mid-1987 (U.S. Department of the Interior 1987c). The wildlife and fisheries division also recently launched a training program to educate district and area managers about their legal obligation to protect federally listed species.[13]

In mid-1987, a policy aimed at recovery of threatened and endangered species was pending (U.S. Department of the Interior 1987d). If approved, the policy will require BLM field staff to participate on recovery teams, to review and implement recovery plans, and to ensure that all BLM management activities affecting threatened or endangered species comply with approved recovery objectives. Although the Endangered Species Act already requires BLM to participate in recovery

13. The Endangered Species Act was passed in 1973, some 15 years preceding the training program.

efforts on the public lands, "there's been a reluctance on the part of the state directors to put BLM staff on recovery teams because of a [false] perception that recovery is the Fish and Wildlife Service's job," an agency official said. BLM's draft policy is stronger than Fish and Wildlife Service regulations implementing Section 7 of the Endangered Species Act. Those regulations state that, except in unusual circumstances, federal actions that hinder recovery, but do not threaten a species' survival, are not prohibited by the act and hence may take place.[14] By late 1987, the BLM draft policy was under review at the field offices; final approval was not expected until at least March 1988.

The wildlife division's attempts to further the protection of threatened and endangered species necessitates bucking the bureaucratic tide. "Trying to get endangered species programs implemented isn't easy. There's very little compliance [within the agency] with the Endangered Species Act," an agency insider says. He explains:

> It's difficult when the whole tone of our administration is contrary to that. Endangered species are an obstacle to what the bureau wants to accomplish. Local managers have 15 ranchers in their office every day to talk about cows and fences. Rarely do they have Audubon or Defenders walk in to talk about elk or bald eagles.

GRAZING AND RIPARIAN LANDS MANAGEMENT

Livestock grazing accounts for the most intensive and widespread commercial use of BLM land. Historically, grazing issues have triggered the most heated, frequent controversies of all BLM policies, a trend that persists today. In 1987, as in past years, BLM was embroiled in several emotional issues involving range condition, grazing regulations, grazing fees, and riparian area management.

Range Condition

The condition of public rangelands has seriously deteriorated throughout this century, largely due to grazing practices (Meiners 1986).[15] BLM and professional livestock organizations contend that although the

14. A chapter on the federal Endangered Species Program in the 1987 edition of the *Audubon Wildlife Report* discusses the extent to which FWS' regulations allow federal activities to affect endangered species.

15. Analysis of current range condition is included in a 1986 congressional report, "Federal Grazing Program: All Is Not Well on the Range," as well as in "Our Ailing Public Rangelands," a 1985 report by the Natural Resources Defense Council and the National Wildlife Federation. The General Accounting Office anticipates releasing another report on public range condition in early 1988.

range still remains badly damaged, it is steadily improving (Brooks 1987). According to many cattlemen, however, the public range provides far poorer grazing lands than do privately owned rangelands. The conservation community echoes that sentiment, pointing out that degraded rangelands have lasting detrimental impacts on wildlife populations and habitats (see Table 6).

The Federal Land Policy and Management Act requires BLM to monitor and compile information on range condition, but the agency has not consistently done so. As a result, management decisions within the grazing program are often based on flawed or outdated data, which effectively prevents the BLM from accurately assessing the damage livestock are causing on public rangelands.

Inadequate data have also precluded Congress from effectively evaluating range condition in order to determine policy. To remedy that problem, the House Committee on Interior and Insular Affairs recently requested a study from the General Accounting Office assessing the condition of the public rangelands. Attempting to compile and update what is currently known, General Accounting Office researchers have asked range conservationists in the bureau and the Forest Service for their professional judgments on range condition and management trends. The report is due in early 1988 and will likely include recommendations for range improvement. But it is unclear whether

Table 6
Percent of Acreage in Range Condition Classes by State, Fiscal Year 1986.

Geographic state	Percent by range condition[a]				Unclassified or unsuitable[b]
	Excellent	Good	Fair	Poor	
Arizona	4	24	52	20	–
California	1	44	43	10	2
Colorado	3	16	43	28	10
Idaho	3	23	31	22	21
Montana	5	60	23	1	11
Nevada	6	26	42	23	3
New Mexico	1	24	48	23	4
Oregon	4	26	50	17	3
Utah	4	29	38	13	16
Wyoming	5	45	37	6	7
Bureau-wide	4	30	41	18	7

Source: *Public Land Statistics, 1986.* U.S. Department of the Interior, BLM.

Note: Ecological site inventory is available for approximately 52 percent of the public lands. This table reflects this percentage, plus range condition estimates based on earlier inventories and professional judgement. Ecological site inventories are currently being conducted to fill in data gaps.

[a] Expressed in degrees of depletion from the potential, or climax, plant community: Excellent = 0–25% depletion (moderate); Good = 26–50% depletion (material); Fair = 51–75% depletion (severe); Poor = 76–100% depletion (extreme).

[b] This category includes rangelands that have been classified as unsuitable for livestock grazing and/or where neither data nor estimates are available.

the findings will be considered definitive for decision-making, or in what way they will affect future management direction.

Proposed Grazing Regulations

In 1987, BLM issued a draft of proposed changes in grazing regulations that would hand much of the decision-making on range management over to the livestock industry (52 *Federal Register* 19032 1987). A federal district court in California ruled against similar regulations on several grounds in 1985 (*NRDC v. Hodel,* 618 F. Supp. 848 [E.D. Cal., 1985]), but the bureau has reintroduced them nevertheless, apparently in an effort to further the Reagan Administration's agenda to develop the public lands for commercial purposes.

Among the changes, the new regulations would eliminate the criteria of "grazing capacity" and "forage allocation" in making range management decisions. Both concepts have been used historically to determine acceptable livestock levels and to ensure sufficient food for both wildlife and livestock in range-use planning.[16]

According to the new rules, instead of adjusting stocking levels to meet grazing capacity standards, BLM would limit overgrazing by using the subjective criteria of "undue or unnecessary degradation." BLM's division of rangeland resources contends that the grazing capacity estimate (also called carrying capacity) is determined by inventories that are conducted too infrequently to be meaningful. The new rule proposes to rely entirely on five-year monitoring studies of range condition, and to make adjustments in stocking levels as "undue and unnecessary degradation" occurs. But the new rules would not require monitoring projects to analyze the effects of grazing on soil erosion, wildlife habitat, or riparian conditions.

Conservationists take issue with the new language, calling it too broad and vague, and suggesting it would sanction range degradation. Such a policy defies several congressional mandates, they charge, including the Taylor Grazing Act of 1934 (43 U.S.C.A. 315 *et seq.*), the Federal Land Policy and Management Act of 1976, and the Public Rangelands Improvement Act of 1978. "The proposed rules may, in essence, eliminate all meaningful restrictions on grazing," according to comments on the draft regulations submitted by the National Wildlife Federation. Barring the use of carrying capacity criteria could result in overgrazing, range deterioration, and increased desertification (Alberswerth *et al.* 1987).

The cattle industry supports BLM's position that the grazing capacity concept is too inflexible and does not reflect range conditions

16. "Grazing capacity" estimates how many animals can graze on an allotment per specified time period; "forage allocation" determines the distribution of available food on an allotment to wildlife and livestock.

as accurately as does monitoring. Understaffing within the agency, however, has resulted in inadequate and infrequent range evaluation, say environmentalists. The Natural Resources Defense Council (NRDC) called monitoring "a fatally flawed basis for making range management decisions" and a "bankrupt policy," citing budget shortages, inadequate and inconsistent data, and in some cases, lack of monitoring altogether. Furthermore, conservationists say that monitoring is typically used as a vehicle to delay grazing reductions.[17]

Another change in the regulations would establish a Cooperative Management Agreement program between stockmen and the bureau, which would allow ranchers to manage their grazing allotments virtually independently of BLM oversight. (The 1987 edition of the *Wildlife Report* details the recent history of BLM attempts to establish Cooperative Management Agreements.) In theory, the program would recognize ranchers who practice effective range conservation by allowing them the freedom to continue their good management practices on their own.

BLM says it would offer such agreements only to permit-holders with track records that show range improvement. Not only would the agreements allow those permittees to continue their good grazing techniques, but they would also provide an incentive to all permit-holders to practice good management, according to agency officials. The bureau would retain sole authority to determine initial stocking levels and prepare allotment management plans.

Conservationists oppose the creation of cooperative management agreements on the grounds that they would empower a small number of ranchers to make decisions that affect the public. The proposed program provides no opportunity for public participation, and could violate the Federal Land Policy and Management Act by shutting out nonranchers from management decisions, according to NRDC. Furthermore, conservation groups believe the new regulations would allow not only stockmen with good records to enter into cooperative management agreements , but also ranchers who hold permits on badly degraded land. "BLM has created a process by which livestock operators rule the range," says NRDC.

Several additional changes in the proposed rules would further limit BLM's ability to manage public rangelands for multiple use, according to conservation groups. For example, the new regulations would restrict BLM's authority to modify grazing permits to meet multiple-use objectives, and they would give too much decision-making discretion to low-level field employees, says NRDC. "In general, the proposed rules seek to institutionalize the current admin-

17. See 1987 comments by the Natural Resources Defense Council *et al.* for more discussion about this point.

istration's view that livestock grazing should be the dominant use of the public lands," says a joint statement issued by NRDC, the National Audubon Society, and the Wilderness Society (Edelson *et al.* 1987).[18] These organizations further charge that although adoption of the regulations would represent a significant change in public policy, BLM failed to prepare an environmental impact statement analyzing the potential effects on wildlife habitat.

The International Association of Fish and Wildlife Agencies also opposes the rules because they would "weaken the land use planning process" and emphasize grazing "regardless of the needs and uses of fish and wildlife," says a 1987 resolution passed by the association. The resolution further charges that BLM did not give proper consideration to fish and wildlife resources in developing the proposal (International Association of Fish and Wildlife Agencies 1987).

BLM began evaluating public comments on the draft grazing regulations in the spring of 1987. In light of the 1985 court ruling against nearly identical rules, bureau officials have declined to predict when or if the proposed changes would be adopted.

Grazing Fees

For years, the cattle industry and the environmental community have battled over fees the federal government charges for using public grazing lands. (Both the 1986 and 1987 editions of the *Audubon Wildlife Report* discuss the history of grazing fee debates in depth.) Since 1985 the fee has remained at $1.35 per animal-unit-month,[19] based on an experimental formula established by the Public Rangelands Improvement Act (PRIA). BLM has retained the fee despite a 1986 study in which the Forest Service and BLM appraised the average market value of federal grazing lands at $6.35 per animal-unit-month (U.S. Congress, House 1986).

Current fee levels have not covered the administrative costs of the grazing program, and hence have caused ongoing losses to the Treasury. According to the House Government Operations Committee, "The difference in the appraised market value and the actual grazing fees paid under PRIA average $75 million per year in Government revenue foregone" (U.S. Congress, House 1986).

Congress intended PRIA's fee formula to be temporary, and scheduled its expiration for 1985. The legislators did not renew it, but

18. These comments, as well as those prepared by the National Wildlife Federation, provide comprehensive analysis of the proposed grazing regulations from the conservationist point of view. See August 18, 1987, comments from the Natural Resources Defense Council and August 19, 1987, comments from the National Wildlife Federation.

19. An animal-unit-month is the amount of forage it takes to feed one cow in one month.

in 1986 President Reagan promulgated an executive order directing the secretaries of Agriculture and Interior to permanently adopt the fee formula (E.O. 12548, Feb. 14, 1986). Both departments approved the PRIA formula, with a new provision that established a floor of $1.35 per animal-unit-month.

NRDC filed suit against both departments over the renewed formula, contending that the fee was not established in accordance with public participation provisions of several laws;[20] that the Federal Land Policy and Management Act required fees of fair market value; and that an environmental impact statement should have been prepared to determine the environmental feasibility of the formula (*NRDC v. Hodel,* Civil Action No. S-86–0548 EJG [E. D. CA]).

On October 13, 1987, the court upheld the authority of the secretaries to adopt the formula, ruling that fair market value was not the only factor to consider in determining federal grazing fees. However, the judge agreed with NRDC that failure to collect public comments had violated the law, and ordered both departments to start the rule-making process again. That procedure involves proposing a fee formula in the *Federal Register,* soliciting and evaluating public comments, incorporating the necessary changes, and approving a new grazing fee formula. The new formula and the departments' responses to the public comments, are due out in early 1988.

The court called the Interior and Agriculture departments' environmental assessments of the fee formula "after the fact rationalization[s] that did not comply with [their] congressional mandate to consider environmental factors on an equal basis with other, more traditional concerns when establishing grazing fees." Neither department was ordered to conduct a comprehensive environmental impact statement on the fee formula, but they were required to conduct a more adequate environmental analysis of whatever fee formula they propose.

Independent of the NRDC case, three bills have been introduced in the House of Representatives during the 100th Congress (1987–88) to address the fee issue. One would maintain the status quo, while the other two would raise grazing fees via a new formula. Either of the latter two bills, if passed, would eliminate the Secretary of the Interior's discretionary authority, upheld in the *NRDC v. Hodel* decision, to establish a grazing fee.

H.R. 1899, introduced by Representative Ron Marlenee (R-MT), would make permanent the current formula but would eliminate the $1.35 floor, essentially allowing the fee to be set according to ranchers' ability to pay. The other two bills—H.R. 2621, introduced by Repre-

20. The Administrative Procedures Act (5 U.S.C.A. 553 *et seq.*), the Federal Land Management and Policy Act, and the National Environmental Policy Act.

sentative Mike Synar (D-OK), and H.R. 1481, introduced by Representative George Darden (D-GA)—would substantially raise the fee level to resemble fair market prices. Synar's bill also would redistribute use of the grazing receipts to provide for more funding of riparian improvements and better implementation and enforcement of land management plans.

The House Subcommittee on National Parks and Public Lands held oversight hearings on the grazing fee issue September 22, 1987, during which the three bills were discussed. Arguing for higher fees, environmentalists favored H.R. 2621 and H.R. 1481. They maintained that low grazing fees benefit few western stockmen; only seven percent of western ranchers hold permits to graze cattle on public land (see Table 7). Conservationists further argued that low fees encourage overgrazing, which results in degradation of the public lands, and that higher fees would provide more money for conservation of the range (Wald *et al.* 1987).

Table 7
Number and Percent of Livestock Producers in the 16 Western States with Forest Service and BLM Grazing Permits, 1983.

State	Total producers[a]	Number of producers with federal grazing permits		Total federal	Adjusted federal[b]	Federal percentage of total[c]
		FS	BLM			
Arizona	3,792	625	931	1,556	1,323	35
California	26,579	953	1,009	1,962	1,668	6
Colorado	16,127	1,842	1,908	3,750	3,188	20
Idaho	15,980	1,640	2,383	4,023	3,420	21
Kansas	47,008	—	11	11	11	*
Montana	15,822	1,308	4,032	5,340	4,539	29
Nebraska	39,555	114	39	153	153	*
Nevada	1,786	320	716	1,036	881	49
New Mexico	9,189	1,285	2,626	3,911	3,324	36
North Dakota	18,548	—	100	100	100	*
Oklahoma	58,236	28	11	39	39	*
Oregon	21,811	762	1,357	2,119	1,801	8
South Dakota	27,000	416	474	890	756	3
Utah	8,757	1,683	1,887	3,570	3,035	35
Washington	20,147	232	474	706	600	3
Wyoming	6,428	886	1,004	1,890	1,607	25
TOTAL	336,765				26,445	8

Source: "All Is Not Well on the Range," 1986. U.S. House of Representatives, Government Operations Committee.

[a] 1982 Census of Agriculture, Table 11, pp. 218–224. Number of farms with cattle and calves.

[b] Fifteen percent of permittees have both FS and BLM grazing.

[c] Percent of producers/state with federal permits.

* = less than 1 percent

BLM favored H.R. 1899, which would retain the below-market fee rates, as warranted by economic conditions. J. Steven Griles, the Interior Department's assistant secretary for land and minerals management, who oversees BLM, argued that raising the fee would detrimentally affect the western livestock industry, which already had suffered economic decline; the increased fee would put many ranchers out of business, he said. Griles also opposed earmarking fee revenues for riparian management, as H.R. 2621 would do, favoring instead the current policy which allows BLM to allocate range improvement funds to "the most important uses," as determined by the bureau.[21] "Riparian areas should not be singled out over other public land areas for special funding," he told the subcommittee.

In reply to questions by committee members, Griles claimed that the range is not overgrazed and that the fee has no bearing on the number of livestock grazing on public land. That number is solely determined through land-use plans and monitoring, Griles said (Griles 1987a).

Like the administration, cattlemen supported H.R. 1899 largely on economic grounds. According to industry spokespersons, livestock operators who use public lands for grazing incur higher costs for range improvements than ranchers who lease private lands. Though the BLM often pays for the materials used for range improvements, the permittees supply the labor to install and maintain them (Eppers 1987). Limited grazing seasons, remote pastures, and wildlife management also burden permit holders with additional expenses. Neither H.R. 1481 nor H.R. 2621 compensates for those added production costs, testified cattle industry representatives (Brooks 1987).

In addition, industry spokespersons argued that higher fees would lessen the economic feasibility of grazing on public lands, and therefore reduce the monetary value of ranchers' current grazing permits. Stockmen rely on permit values both to determine the overall worth of their ranches and to take out loans. Finally, permittees get less for their money, argued industry representatives, and therefore should pay less. "Private land is better quality and is worth a higher fee—on private lands you get a much better deal," said Patty McDonald, executive director of the Public Lands Council, an organization that represents permit holders (McDonald interview).

21. Currently, 50 percent of grazing receipts go into the Range Betterment Fund (also called the Range Improvement Fund) to make range improvements for the primary benefit of livestock, such as watering facilities, fences, corrals, and other structures. Although monies from the fund also could be used for wildlife projects, such as the improvement of riparian areas, such cases are rare, according to environmental groups. Ranchers argue that many of the range improvement projects have spill-over benefits for wildlife. H.R. 2621 would specifically earmark at least 25 percent of the range improvement fund for environmental protections.

Because of the extremely emotional and polarized nature of the fee controversy, it is highly improbable that members of Congress will take a stand on any of the bills during 1988, a presidential election year. None of the proposals has emerged as the lead bill, and in all likelihood all three will remain pending in committee until after the election. Observers are not predicting what will happen after that. Conservationists point out, however, that the grazing fee controversy has doggedly and relentlessly been brought before Congress for years; hence congressional inaction has failed to make the issue disappear.

Riparian Management and the Grazing Program

BLM's livestock policy is intimately connected with a longstanding controversy on how to restore disappearing riparian habitat in the West. Though the streamsides and lakeshores that make up riparian zones comprise less than one percent of BLM lands, they are widely regarded as among the most important and productive ecological communities on the public lands. Riparian lands also have valuable aesthetic qualities and provide outdoor recreation opportunities (Crouse 1987) (see Table 8).

Healthy riparian systems provide numerous benefits to wildlife and the environment. They filter and purify groundwater; prevent erosion and sedimentation; moderate temperatures and climatic con-

Table 8
Lakes, Reservoirs, Fishable Streams, Riparian Land, and Wetlands on Public Lands, Fiscal Year 1986.

Administrative state	Lakes	Reservoirs	Streams	Riparian	Wetland
	Thousands of acres	*Thousands of acres*	*Miles*	*Thousands of acres*	*Thousands of acres*
Alaska	3,874	–	65,000	6,563	15,848
Arizona	1	28	500	85	1
California	41	9	735	88	119
Colorado	1	19	1,822	42	2
Idaho	10	39	3,580	57	11
Montana	26	22	1,132	143	40
Nevada	23	5	1,134	83	84
New Mexico	2	3	176	18	7
Oregon	56	30	7,136	172	74
Utah	5	8	2,300	78	29
Wyoming	8	29	1,327	123	33
Eastern States	–	–	–	26	37
TOTAL	4,047	192	84,842	7,478	16,285

Source: *Public Land Statistics, 1986.* U.S. Deparment of the Interior, BLM.
Note: estimated data.

ditions; and provide fish and wildlife habitat. They also offer an important source of food, water, and shade to both wildlife and livestock (Braun 1986).

Heavy use of riparian areas by cattle and sheep has resulted in extensive land degradation, a fact BLM has acknowledged in several of its resource management plans (Meiners 1986).[22] The damage includes decreased streamside vegetation; compacted soil; broken down streambanks; lower water quality; loss of food, cover, and water for wildlife; higher degrees of surface runoff; loss of fish habitat; and adverse impacts on aesthetic and recreational values (Braun 1986).

The Arizona Game and Fish Department has reported that nearly 110 species of animals in the state could face extinction if current grazing levels on riparian lands continue, testified Steve Johnson, southwest representative of Defenders of Wildlife, during congressional hearings on grazing fees (Johnson 1987). "Since livestock is by far the most common form of land use in both Arizona and the other western states, it is not surprising that grazing abuse is a leading cause of riparian decline," he said.

BLM's national administrators recently declared the recovery of riparian systems a high priority in a policy issued in early 1987 (U.S. Department of the Interior 1987e). The statement identifies riparian zones as "unique, important ecosystems" and maps out a management direction: achieve "healthy, productive ecological condition," ensure that plans recognize the importance of riparian areas and improve them, and give special attention to monitoring.[23]

Implementation of the policy, like all prescriptions issued from the national office, is entirely subject to the priorities and judgments of the state directors. According to one BLM official, "We can check on how things are going [in the state offices] from time to time, but we really don't have any plans to do that in the future. Obviously, there are a lot of politics involved in trying to get these programs through – being able to work with your constituents is how these people got to be state directors in the first place."

22. A 1986 affidavit by environmental consultant (and former veteran BLM range manager) William R. Meiners, supporting the Natural Resources Defense Council in the lawsuit filed against the departments of Interior and Agriculture over grazing fees, cites several examples of such plans. Quotes are taken from "Grazing Supplement to the Draft Resource Management Plan/EIS for the Lander Resource Area, Lander Wyoming" (1985), and others. Meiners' statement also includes a good summary of the effect of grazing on riparian lands, as well as arguments in favor of raising grazing fees. See Affidavit of William R. Meiners In Support of Plaintiffs' Motion for Summary Judgment, *NRDC et al. v. Hodel et al.*, Civil No. S-86–0548 EJG, October 20, 1986.

23. BLM's Wildlife and Fisheries Division has also cited riparian management as a high-priority activity in its recent report "Fish and Wildlife 2000: A Plan for the Future," a discussion of which appears earlier in this chapter.

Improved riparian management almost necessarily entails putting additional burdens on livestock operators, which presents the biggest roadblock to implementing the policy. Suggested management methods include hiring herders to relocate cattle during certain times of year, rotating pastures, fencing off streambanks, removing livestock for extended periods, and constructing alternative sources of water. Those management techniques can add costs—both cash and labor—to ranching operations, and are not likely to receive the support of the livestock industry. As a result of resistance by local ranchers, it is unlikely that the new riparian policy will change BLM's current course—particularly because it could threaten the grazing program. In fact, in states operating under heavy pressure by livestock operators, such as Nevada, BLM field managers have yet to consider riparian protection a viable management objective, according to one bureau official.

Some states are establishing model riparian management programs, however. In Wyoming, for example, ranchers have employed cattle herders to move livestock away from streams to upland areas, which has resulted in hundreds of miles of riparian land improvement, according to BLM. In Oregon and Montana, livestock operators have begun using riparian areas seasonally for grazing. Such programs are not typical on BLM land, but agency officials contend that the new policy has resulted in "greatly improved awareness of riparian problems and management options, both within BLM and the outside conservation community."

BLM also has adopted a demonstration program in each district to show how to restore riparian zones.[24] The demonstration projects employ various management methods such as fencing off stream banks to solve the problems specific to each riparian site. Each district has set up at least one demonstration project so far, and the riparian lands involved are in various stages of recovery. The projects are needed to teach ranchers, agency field personnel, and the public the extent to which riparian areas can recover using careful management techniques, according to BLM. "We want to show people what can be done. That's essential in convincing ranchers to use lower-impact grazing methods," a bureau wildlife official explained.

The Government Accounting Office has undertaken a study of riparian management on public lands at the request of the House Committee on Interior and Insular Affairs. "The real issue is how to get scientists on the ground to design riparian improvements on a site-by-site basis, and to monitor those systems," says a Government Accounting Office official. A draft of the results is expected to be released in

24. The wildlife and fisheries division of the national office is promoting the idea of setting up riparian demonstration projects in each resource area, a plan the Oregon and Idaho state offices have agreed to undertake.

early 1988. According to preliminary findings, western cattlemen do not oppose riparian improvements, but also do not want livestock reductions on their allotments. "The degree of conscientiousness and far-sightedness of cattlemen determines whether they will put these management techniques to work," the official said.

MINERALS MANAGEMENT

BLM is the principal federal agency responsible for administering mining activities and minerals exploration on the public lands. In addition to the 334 million acres over which the bureau presides, the agency oversees minerals and energy development on 398 million acres of federal, state, and private holdings.[25] BLM minerals resources include large deposits of coal, oil, and gas, in addition to uranium, geothermal energy sources, shale, phosphate, sodium, lead, zinc, gold, and silver.

BLM's minerals policies have been the source of much conflict between industrial and environmental interests. Conservationists charge that BLM's minerals programs, like its grazing activities, reflect a disproportionate bent toward commodity development and have negative impacts on wildlife. For example, mining still occurs in wilderness study areas, parcels the bureau has selected to evaluate for possible inclusion in the National Wilderness System.[26] According to the Wilderness Act of 1964 (16 U.S.C.A. 1131 *et seq.*), wilderness areas must contain specific characteristics such as pristine scenery, unique opportunities for solitude, and the absence of roads. The bureau contends that mining—as well as roadbuilding, grazing, and other commercial activities—can proceed in wilderness study areas provided that it does not degrade the land or that the land can be restored to its original condition.

Resource management plans prepared by BLM typically make large areas, including important wildlife habitat, available for oil and gas development, according to David Alberswerth, the National Wildlife Federation's director of public lands and energy division. "The agency's theory is that they can mitigate the impacts," he says. However, BLM officials argue that according to the Federal Land Policy and Management Act, the purpose of resource management plans is to provide land for development as well as for wildlife habitat, and that impact mitigation is proper.

25. The bureau administers on-shore mining on all federal lands, and holds subsurface mineral rights on many state and private lands.

26. As of 1983, wilderness study areas have been closed to new leasing and minerals development activities, according to BLM. Development activities allowed in these areas prior to that date have continued. The *Audubon Wildlife Report 1987* discusses BLM's management activities in wilderness study areas.

Oil and gas leases have also been offered within areas of critical environmental concern over the objections of state wildlife agencies.[27] Furthermore, the bureau has issued leases prior to the development of resource management plans, effectively rendering after-the-fact planning irrelevant, according to Alberswerth. Although the vast majority of leases have been issued in compliance with land-use plans, most comply only with the older management framework plans. Management framework plans do not require as comprehensive an environmental analysis as do resource management plans.

Oil and Gas Leasing Reform Bills of 1987

The methods by which BLM issues leases for development of oil and gas have received much attention and criticism in recent years. Only areas known to have mineral deposits are offered competitively—approximately 10 percent of existing leases. Some observers contend that too many tracts have been leased noncompetitively and the public has not received a fair economic return. Critics also charge that the current system does not adequately protect against fraud and abuse, and that BLM sidesteps environmental laws.

In the past year, much of the attention regarding BLM's minerals program focused on two bills under consideration in Congress: the Federal On-shore Oil and Gas Leasing Reform Act of 1987 (H.R. 2851), introduced by Representative Nick Rahall (D-WV), and the Federal On-Shore Competitive Oil and Gas Leasing Act of 1987 (S. 1730), introduced by Senator Dale Bumpers (D-AR). H.R. 2851 has been approved for inclusion in the House budget reconciliation bill (H.R. 3545).

Both bills would require BLM to offer all leases initially by competitive oral bid. Those that do not receive an acceptable bid would become available for noncompetitive leasing for a specified period of time. The House bill would allow BLM to offer leases noncompetitively for one year after the oral bidding closed; the Senate proposal would allow noncompetitive leasing for three years before the next bidding cycle.

The House bill includes several additional provisions aimed at ensuring environmental safeguards in oil and gas exploration and development. For example:

- Leases would only be allowed on lands already identified for minerals development in resource management plans. The plans would need to include development projections, likely environmental consequences, and any stipulations to protect the environment during oil and gas activities.

27. The Federal Land Management and Policy Act did not establish areas of critical environmental concern solely as wildlife habitat, and BLM has the authority to issue leases in such areas, a policy upheld by the Interior department's Board of Land Appeals.

- Public notice would be required in the *Federal Register* 60 days before offering lands for competitive leasing, and 30 days before modifying lease terms.
- Leases would be prohibited on wilderness study areas.
- Yearly rental rates on 10-year leases would be raised from $1 to $2 per acre for the first 5 years, and to $3 for the last 5 years.

The oil and gas industry opposes both measures, particularly the House bill, on several grounds. Doubling the rental rate (perceived by the industry as primarily a revenue-generating measure) would hurt both independent operators and the overall goals of the program, industry spokespeople say. The new rates would effectively cut in half the companies' inventories and restrict the bureau's ability to generate royalties on future production, according to Ken Wonstolen, executive director of the Independent Petroleum Association of Mountain States (Wonstolen interview).

Some 5,000 independent companies, compared with less than 10 giant oil and gas conglomerates, rely on noncompetitive leases for their exploratory and development activities, particularly in areas with unproven drilling potential. Making all leases competitive would put them at a disadvantage because the big companies would likely outbid them, according to Wonstolen.

Industry spokesmen also oppose the environmental restrictions in the House bill. They argue that the Endangered Species Act, the National Environmental Policy Act, the Federal Land Policy and Management Act, and an array of other laws already provide enough environmental guidance on oil and gas development. "We agree that the agencies don't comply well with existing laws," Wonstolen says, "but those problems should be dealt with administratively or through laws already in place." Because environmental stipulations currently are placed on both leases and drilling permits, the industry believes removing wilderness study areas and areas of critical environmental concern from leasing consideration would be unnecessary and detrimental to energy production. Wonstolen adds, "As a national policy, it makes more sense to know what we'd be giving up when we decide to designate an area as wilderness," particularly in light of the country's reliance on foreign oil.

Wonstolen objects to the House bill's requirement to project development activities in resource management plans. "It's not possible to guess oil and gas potential before you even go in and explore, and few leases actually result in drilling," he says. The industry favors instead conducting environmental analyses between the exploration phase and actual drilling, at which point a more accurate projection could be made (see Table 9).

Table 9
Oil and Gas Leases on Federal Lands in Producing Status as of September 30, 1986.

Geographic state	Number of producible leases[a]	Number of acres in producing status
Alabama	11	1,442
Alaska	34	62,763
Arkansas	161	88,259
California	305	72,932
Colorado	3,861	2,788,506
Florida	1	2,188
Kansas	63	22,060
Kentucky	13	17,484
Louisiana	118	116,164
Maryland	2	2,498
Michigan	25	14,092
Mississippi	166	54,956
Missouri	1	1,329
Montana	1,518	801,087
Nebraska	19	7,843
Nevada	43	12,962
New Mexico	5,260	4,791,756
North Dakota	429	377,700
Ohio	30	7,318
Oklahoma	663	106,043
Pennsylvania	5	2,693
South Dakota	97	68,548
Texas	62	38,642
Utah	879	691,020
Virginia	1	2,165
West Virginia	48	90,951
Wyoming	4,808	2,457,427
TOTAL	18,623	12,700,808

Source: *Public Land Statistics, 1986.* U.S. Department of the Interior, BLM.
[a] Includes leases in actual and allocated production.

BLM, favoring the Senate measure, also opposes the additional planning requirements of the House bill, which would impose a January 1, 1991 deadline by which to include leasing activity in resource management plans. Planning provisions for oil and gas development are already part of the bureau's internal guidance, and the new law "would botch up our priorities," an official from the fluid minerals leasing division said. "The planning schedule would be yanked around to accommodate oil and gas and our other management objectives would suffer. We're trying to manage for multiple use." Not only would planning priorities shift as a result of the law, "we'd have to shut down our leasing program for several years until environmental studies were up to standard," he said.

But higher environmental standards, as well as reforms in noncompetitive leasing procedures, are badly needed, say conservationists. Competitive bidding on all leases would result in less fraud and speculation and a more fair return to the public, as well as limiting leases only to those needed by the industry, according to the National Wildlife Federation. Moreover, "if the land management agencies are not directed to take such actions as proposed in [this] measure by Congress, they will continue to conduct federal leasing programs in a manner which presumes all environmental problems can be addressed later," testified Karl Gawell of the National Wildlife Federation on July 28, 1987, before the House Subcommittee on Mining and Natural Resources (Gawell 1987). "We believe this approach— lease now, plan later—courts confrontation, management problems, litigation, and unnecessary expense for both the public and the industry."

The National Wildlife Federation further charged that BLM's leasing practices evade environmental laws in several ways and do not provide adequate impact analysis. In the Pinedale, Wyoming, Resource Area, the draft plan proposed to lease all land not already under lease for oil and gas production, despite that land's importance to wildlife, the federation contends. "This zeal to lease every acre of federal land regardless of the impacts of development is sadly typical of BLM's current planning and decision-making," Gawell testified.

Once a lease is issued, BLM cannot preclude exploration or development, but must ensure mitigation of resulting impacts on the environment. Conservationists charge that bureau staff and budget levels do not always allow full enforcement of environmental stipulations, such as mitigation measures. Furthermore, the agency can approve exceptions to environmental stipulations without informing or consulting the public.

That policy is expected to improve somewhat. On June 12, 1987, BLM issued new guidance on oil and gas leasing, exploration, and development, which requires public involvement in modifications of leases that were originally drawn up with public input (43 C.F.R. 3101.1–3). Lease stipulations established as part of resource management planning, therefore, could not be modified without public participation. However, the new rule will apply only to a fraction of existing leases; stipulations established without public input, such as most of those in management framework plans, will not be subject to the new guidance. [**EDITOR'S NOTE:** Congress took final action on leasing reform late in 1987 when it added leasing provisions to the omnibus spending bill for the federal government (H.J. Res. 395). According to *The Washington Post* (December 12, 1987), the new law requires the Department of the Interior to offer all oil and gas leases by competitive bid. The final measure did not include the environmental planning requirements sought by conservationists. Instead, the law requires studies of the problem by the General Accounting Office and the National Academy of Sciences. However, several provisions favored by conservationists were included in the leasing reform measure. Such provisions deny new leases to any party that does not reclaim land after drilling; permanently bans leases in wilderness study areas; and authorize the Forest Service to veto BLM leasing decisions affecting national forests.]

SPECIAL MANAGEMENT AREAS

Since the enactment of the Federal Land Policy and Management Act in 1976, BLM has undertaken the task of designating and managing areas of critical environmental concern (ACECs) and studying potential sites to recommend to Congress for wilderness status.[28] Both the ACEC and the wilderness programs have been attacked by environmental groups, who charge that the BLM is identifying such areas too slowly and administering them inadequately. New guidelines on defining and designating ACECs had been expected in 1987. However, the bureau "is still tinkering with them," said a BLM planner. Final rules might emerge in 1988, but according to some agency sources the rules could be delayed indefinitely.

BLM also administers various "special status" lands to protect or enhance specific resources. Such areas include wild and scenic rivers, national recreation areas, national scenic trails, natural resource areas, national conservation areas, outstanding natural areas, and others. Those areas account for a small percentage of BLM land and overall have been the subject of little conflict. However, a controversy has emerged over the California Desert Conservation Area, regarding a proposal to remove much of the management responsibility from BLM to better protect the area's scenic and scientific resources.

California Desert Protection Act of 1987

BLM presides over nearly half of the 25-million-acre California Desert Conservation Area, a patchwork of lands managed by the bureau, the National Park Service, the Department of Defense, and state and private owners (see Table 10). For several years, conservation organizations have criticized BLM for inadequately protecting the desert's natural areas.

28. The law defines areas of critical environmental concern as areas requiring special management to protect their cultural, historic, scenic, or wildlife resources.

Table 10
Ownership of California Desert

Ownership	Acreage (in millions)
Federal	
Bureau of Land Management	12.1
National Park Service	2.6
Defense Department	3
State	1
Private	6

Source: Wilderness Society.

BLM land in the California Desert provides habitat for many critical wildlife species, 25 of which are federally listed as threatened or endangered. The conservation area also contains some outstanding scenic, cultural, and historical resources; and it provides opportunities for remote camping and backpacking. In addition, the desert is important for mining, off-road vehicle use, hunting, and some grazing. The Federal Land Policy and Management Act directed BLM to consider the California Desert a fragile ecosystem that scars easily and heals slowly and to protect it accordingly.

Conservationists contend that BLM's 1980 management plan for the California Desert does not go far enough in protecting the resource. Critics say that in the last seven years, the plan has been weakened by amendments and its implementation has been seriously flawed. In particular, conservationists charge that development activities called for in the plan have taken priority while protection measures have been postponed or ignored.

The California Desert Protection Act (S.7) was introduced by Senator Alan Cranston (D-CA) in 1987 to enhance protection of the desert, in part by removing management responsibility for certain desert lands from the bureau. The bill would transfer three million acres of BLM land to the National Park Service, adding acreage to Death Valley and Joshua Tree national monuments and changing their status to national parks; and it would convert BLM's East Mohave National Scenic Area into a 1.5-million-acre national park. Additionally, the measure would designate 81 separate areas of BLM land—some 4.5 million acres—as wilderness. It is the first wilderness proposal involving large areas of BLM land.[29]

The Wilderness Society, a principal supporter of the bill, cited several needs for the legislation in testimony offered to the Senate Subcommittee on Public Lands, National Parks, and Forests on July

29. See the *Audubon Wildlife Report 1987* for an extensive discussion on the process by which BLM is recommending areas for wilderness designation and current management direction for those areas.

23, 1987. Primarily, BLM has failed to protect the desert's pristine resources, allowing damaging activities to occur in areas of critical environmental concern and wilderness study areas, according to the society. For example, areas of critical environmental concern have been damaged by authorized motorcycle races, illegal off-road vehicle (ORV) use, and sand and gravel excavations, all of which have "denuded hillsides, endangered cultural resources, and impaired wildlife habitat." Bulldozing, cyanide storage, water diversion, and "extensive excavation" have been allowed in potential wilderness sites, the society further charged. At least 100 of the 137 wilderness study areas in the desert have been affected by surface disturbance (Schifferle 1987).

The Interior department maintains that the bureau has managed wilderness study areas properly. According to department officials, land uses that would irreversibly impair those areas have been denied, while strict mitigation and reclamation standards have been placed on all other uses (Griles 1987b). However, BLM has failed to prevent unauthorized activities in wilderness study areas, say conservationists, which has resulted in damage to both natural and cultural resources.

Officially, BLM opposes the Desert Protection Act. Backed up primarily by mining interests, BLM officials testified in congressional hearings that the bill would detrimentally impact minerals development activities in the desert. According to J. Steven Griles, the Interior department's assistant secretary for land and minerals management, studies to determine minerals potential in the desert's wilderness study areas are scheduled to occur before the bureau makes final wilderness recommendations to the president. "Minerals studies are not being conducted for an additional 6 million acres that S.7 proposes to add to the National Wilderness System or the National Park System," Griles said; prohibiting development on those lands prior to assessing their potential would not be in the public interest.[30]

The bill also would negatively affect recreation and transportation in the desert, according to BLM. It would close off more than 2,000 miles of "key access" roads, which would affect off-road vehicle users and overall transportation routes in the desert, Griles said. The Wilderness Society disagreed, contending that 30,000 miles of roads would still allow access to backcountry, and that the vast majority of ORV areas would also remain open under the proposed bill.

Fifty-five percent of the grazing on the desert would be eliminated by the bill, according to BLM. Little grazing occurs in the area compared with the huge allotments on other BLM lands, but the legislation would place some grazing lands in national parks, and

30. Conservationists point out that for more than 100 years the California Desert has been explored for mineral deposits extensively, and that more is known about its minerals qualities than most other regions on the continent.

permits would not be renewed.[31] In addition, excluding hunting and shooting from three million acres would concentrate such activities in other areas of the desert, BLM officials argue.

Despite the bureau's official position, some insiders contend that S.7 would accomplish more for wildlife and conservation than the current BLM land-use plan. For example, the plan prescribes protection measures for only 15 out of 25 species of threatened and endangered animals. "We would have ended up just trashing the other 10," a BLM official says. He adds, "We've been lax in implementing the good parts of the plan – I'd like BLM to have some nice areas to manage, but if we can't do it right we should give them up to some other agency." Enough data on the California Desert were available to make good management decisions – which is not always the case for BLM land – but the bureau did not take advantage of them, he said.

The desert tortoise provides a good example: "We monitor the populations there and watch them decline. The local manager says 'I don't know if the data is conclusive, but let's get some more information.' With that kind of attitude, I say let's give it up to the Park Service."

REFERENCES

Alberswerth, David, Kathleen C. Zimmerman, and Wendy Tarlow. 1987. Letter of August 19, 1987 to Director of Bureau of Land Management, Robert F. Burford, commenting on proposed grazing regulations.

Almand, J. David. 1987a. Changing Perspective for Renewable Resources: Wildlife and Fisheries. Unpublished paper. November 18.

——. 1987b. Interview with the author. Washington, D.C., September 9.

Braun, Richard. October 1986. "Livestock grazing in riparian zones: ensuring fishery protection in federal rangeland management." *Anadromous Fish Law Memo.* 37:1–19. October.

Brooks, C.E. 1987. Testimony of Constance E. Brooks, Mountain States Legal Foundation on Behalf of the National Cattlemen's Association, the National Wool Growers Association, and the Public Lands Council. Oversight hearings on grazing fees conducted by the Subcommittee on Public Lands, Committee on Interior and Insular Affairs, House of Representatives. September 22.

Crouse, Michael R. 1987. New Approaches to Riparian Area Management on Public Lands. Paper giving Bureau of Land Management perspectives presented to Eighth Annual Meeting of the Society of Wetlands Scientists, Seattle, Washington, May 26–29.

Edelson, David B. and Johanna Wald. 1987. Comments of the Natural Resources Defense Council, the Wilderness Society, and the National Audubon Society on Proposed Amendments to the Grazing Regulations, 43 C.F.R. Part 4100. May 20.

Eppers, Bud. 1987. Statement by Bud Eppers for the National Cattlemen's Association on H.R. 2621, H.R. 1481, and H.R. 1899 Before the National Parks and Public Lands Subcommittee of the House Interior and Insular Affairs Committee. Oversight hearings on grazing fees, House of Representatives. September 22.

31. Less than one percent of California's total beef production depends on rangelands in the desert.

Gawell, Karl. 1987. Statement of Karl Gawell, Legislative Representative, Public Lands and Energy Division [National Wildlife Federation], Before the Subcommittee on Mining and Natural Resources, Committee on Interior and Insular Affairs regarding H.R. 933 and H.R. 2851. July 28.

Griles, J. Steven. 1987a. Statement of J. Steven Griles, Assistant Secretary for Land and Minerals Management, Before the Senate Committee on Energy and Natural Resources, Subcommittee on Public Lands, National Parks and Forests, on S. 7, the California Desert Protection Act of 1987. July 21.

——. 1987b. Statement of J. Steven Griles, Assistant Secretary, Land and Minerals Management, U.S. Department of the Interior, Before the Subcommittee on National Parks and Public Lands, Committee on Interior and Insular Affairs, U.S. House of Representatives, on H.R. 1481, H.R. 1899, and H.R. 2621, Bills to Establish Grazing Fees for Domestic Livestock on the Public Rangelands. Oversight hearings on grazing fees, House of Representatives. September 22.

International Association of Fish and Wildlife Agencies. 1987. "Resolutions." Adopted at 77th Annual Convention, Winston-Salem, North Carolina. September 17.

Johnson, Aubrey Stephen. 1987. Testimony of Aubrey Stephen Johnson, Southwest Representative, Defenders of Wildlife, Before the Subcommittee on National Parks and Public Lands, Committee on Interior and Insular Affairs, U.S. House of Representatives, on Grazing Fee Legislation. Oversight hearings on grazing fees, submitted on behalf of Defenders of Wildlife and the National Audubon Society. September 22.

McDonald, Patty. 1987. Interview with the author. Washington, D.C. November 5.

Meiners, William R. 1986. Affidavit of William R. Meiners in Support of Plaintiffs' Motion for Summary Judgment. Submitted by Natural Resources Defense Council, *NRDC v. Hodel,* Civil Action No. S-86–0548-EJG [E.D. CA]. October 20.

Schifferle, Patricia. 1987. Statement of Patricia Schifferle, The Wilderness Society Regional Director for California and Nevada, Before the Public Lands, National Parks and Forest Subcommittee of the Senate Energy and Natural Resources Committee on the California Desert Protection Act, S. 7. July 23.

U.S. Congress, House of Representatives. 1986. Committee on Government Operations. "Federal Grazing Program: All Is Not Well on the Range." 99th Cong., 2nd Sess., [House Report 99–593].

U.S. Department of the Interior, Bureau of Land Management. 1983. *BLM Planning: A Guide to Resource Management Planning on the Public Lands.* Government Printing Office. Washington, D.C. Pp. 574–232.

——. 1986. *Public Land Statistics.* Washington, D.C.

——. 1987a. "Fish and Wildlife 2000: A Plan for the Future."

——. 1987b. Instruction Memorandum 88–31 dated October 15, 1987.

——. 1987c. Instruction Memorandum 87–684 dated August 27, 1987.

——. 1987d. Draft revision, Section 6840, BLM Manual dated November 27, 1987.

——. 1987e. Instruction Memorandum 87–274 dated February 17, 1987.

Wald, Johanna and David Alberswerth. 1985. *Our Ailing Public Rangelands: Condition Report 1985.* National Wildlife Federation and Natural Resource Defense Council. Washington, D.C. December.

——. and Faith T. Campbell. 1987. Testimony of the Natural Resources Defense Council Before the Subcommittee on National Parks and Public Lands of the House Committee on Interior and Insular Affairs.' Oversight hearings on grazing fees, House of Representatives. September 22.

Wonstolen, Ken. 1987. Interview with the author. Washington, D.C. November 10.

Karen Franklin is a Washington, D.C., freelance writer who covers natural resources and the environment, among other issues.

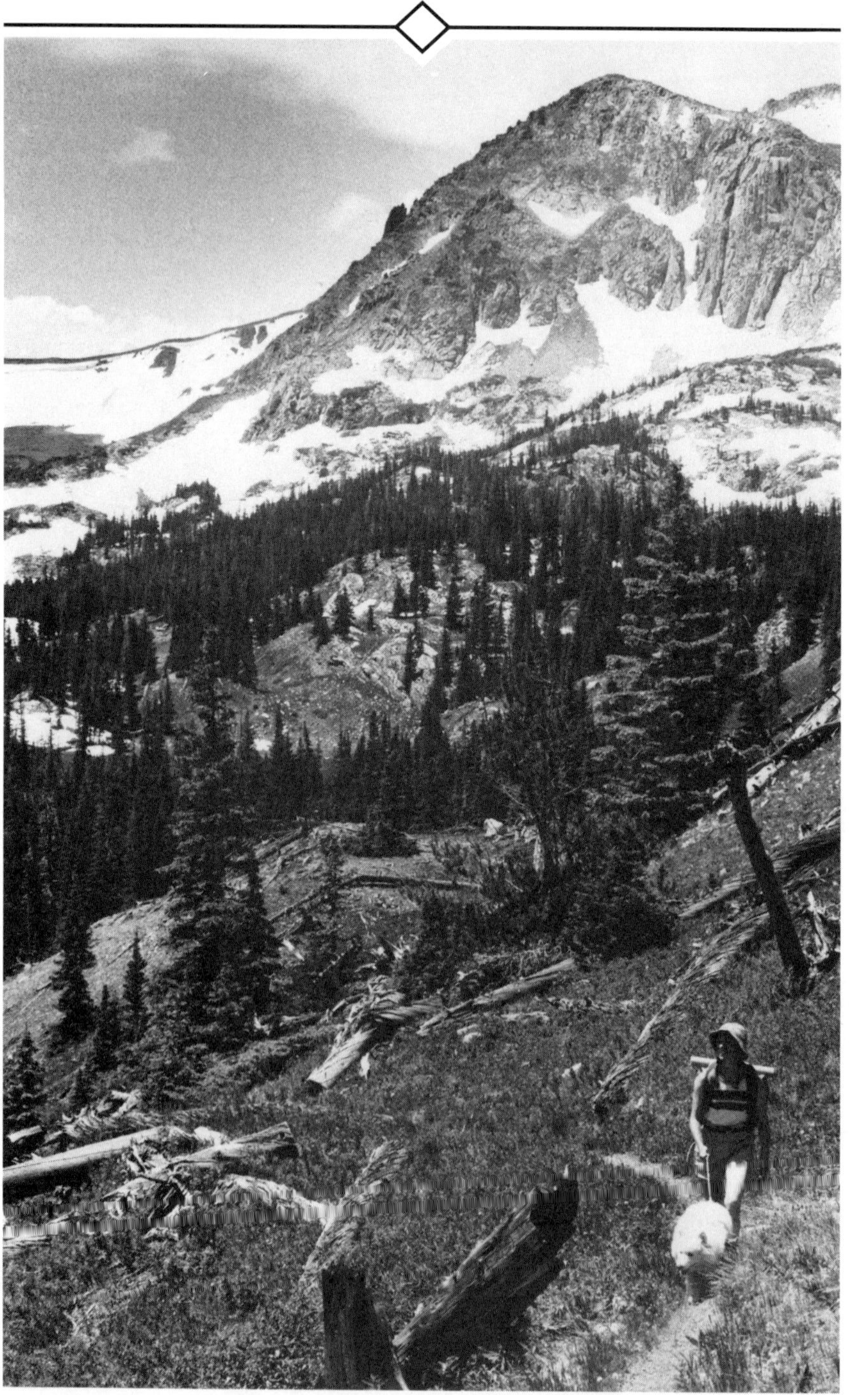

The National Park Service must protect wildlife from people and vice versa. An ongoing controversy is whether nature or NPS should manage wildlife. *Kent and Donna Dannen*

Wildlife Issues in National Parks

R. Gerald Wright

INTRODUCTION

National parks occupy a unique position in American society. Parks are a vacation destination for millions of Americans every year and the National Park Service (NPS) is held in high esteem by the American public. NPS manages 337 areas totaling over 75 million acres. These range from small, single-acre historic sites to the vast wilderness of the 13.2 million-acre Wrangell St. Elias National Park and Preserve in Alaska.

Along with encompassing some of the nation's most spectacular scenic treasures, parks have assumed a major role in the conservation and protection of wildlife in the United States. For example, park lands provide critical nesting habitat for species like the trumpter swan. In addition, a large proportion of the continental U.S. populations of grizzly bears, Roosevelt elk, gray wolf, and bison are found in national parks. It is estimated that between one-third and one-half of the rare and endangered species in the United States occur within units of the national park system.

Unfortunately, the status of many wildlife species in parks is not known. There is no complete inventory of all of the animal species found in the national park system; there is not even adequate information on population numbers or trends of major species. There are two principle reasons for this lack of data. First, the task of determining the population status of most wildlife species is extremely difficult, especially in the remote, often mountainous terrain typical of parks. Second, population surveys are generally low priority tasks, particularly for nonproblem species; hence, the funds and personnel are not made available to conduct them.

Large as it is, the national park system incorporates less than three percent of the total U.S. land area; by itself it cannot guarantee the preservation of all pristine ecosystem types or wildlife species that occur in America. Parks not only suffer from the strains of increasing visitation, but also from a myriad of phenomena emanating both from within and without. Many of these, such as air pollution, acid rain, pesticide contamination, and water pollution, may originate far beyond park boundaries and are difficult to control. Of equal concern, lands around the parks which formerly buffered them from human intrusion, as well as providing important habitat for park wildlife at certain times of the year, are being lost as they are developed, mined, timbered, or grazed.

The Historical Evolution of Wildlife Management in NPS

The prominent role NPS now plays in preserving wildlife is a dramatic change from the way things were when the first parks were established. Only a little more than a century ago, vast numbers of wild animals roamed the plains and the forested wilderness that covered much of the United States. The great numbers of animals and the seemingly limitless supply of other resources spawned a philosophy of resource exploitation. Few individuals were concerned with preserving natural resources for the future. As a result, there was substantial public opposition to the idea of setting aside lands for national parks and forests when such designations restricted or ended human economic uses. Nor was there even concern about protecting most species of wild animals from human activities.

Wildlife management in the nation's first parks was complicated by several factors. Wildlife management as a scientific discipline did not exist, and there were few trained resource professionals. The laws that govern NPS also provided little guidance in establishing policies for managing wildlife. Original policies dealing with wildlife were derived from the 1916 Organic Act which states that NPS' role is:

> to conserve the scenery and the natural and historic objects and the wildlife therein and to provide for the enjoyment of the same in such manner and by such means as will leave them unimpaired for the enjoyment of future generations (16 U.S.C.A. 1).

The act also stated that:

> . . . the director of the National Park Service may also provide in his discretion for the destruction of such animals and of such plant life as may be detrimental to the use of any of said parks, monuments, or reservations (16 U.S.C.A. 1).

The Organic Act, combined with a highly decentralized management structure, left much to the interpretation of park managers; hence, during its first several decades, NPS' wildlife management philosophies varied widely. For example, predators in parks were killed to protect large herbivorous species. Later herbivores were killed by NPS to protect the range. Prior to the 1940s, bears were fed at formal interpretive shows for the enjoyment of visitors. Later, NPS regulations specifically prohibited the feeding of bears. Policies dealing with nonnative or alien species have been equally vacillatory.

The only real consistency in the NPS wildlife program was that it emphasized the management and protection of the so-called heroic species—elk, deer, bison, antelope, black bear, and mountain goat—to the neglect of the rest of the faunal community. Only recently has management emphasis shifted from a single-species orientation to a concern for all species, and more importantly, to the protection and understanding of natural ecological processes such as fire and predation which help shape the park environment. Current management policies reflect this orientation:

> The Service will perpetuate the native animal life of the parks for their essential role in natural ecosystems. Such management, conformable with the general and specific provisions of law and consistent with the following provisions, will strive to maintain the natural abundance, behavior, diversity, and ecological integrity of native animals in natural portions of parks as part of the park ecosystem (National Park Service 1978).

This policy, combined with continued high public interest in wildlife, is compelling park management to consider all species, not just the popular, rare, or problem animals.

Current Management Trends

There have always been significant differences between the ways wildlife is managed in national parks and on other public lands. NPS is unique among federal land-management agencies because, in most units, NPS retains exclusive legal jurisdiction over resident wildlife regardless of state game laws. Since its establishment, NPS has interpreted its 1916 authorizing legislation to mean that animal life in parks is protected from hunting, removal, destruction, or harassment.

This interpretation has undergone few legal challenges even though few parks have authorizing legislation that specifically bans sport hunting.

As the park system grew, many different types of units came under NPS jurisdiction, including national monuments, preserves, historic sites, battlefields, lakeshores, and recreation areas. Until the late 1970s, wildlife management policies on these units were not consistent. As a result of 1978 revisions in the 1916 Organic Act, however, NPS has taken steps to manage park wildlife resources in a uniform manner throughout the system without regard to the unit's classification.

Visitor Interactions with Wildlife. Due to lack of hunting pressure, wildlife is generally more abundant and approachable in national parks and monuments than on other public lands.[1] As a result, national parks have become renowned for the opportunities they offer to view wildlife in a natural setting; observing wildlife is a major part of park visitor experience. The visitor has always had an important influence on the way park wildlife has been managed. However, the point at which the needs of wildlife are balanced with those of park visitors and administrators has varied throughout the history of NPS.

In the early days, providing the opportunity to see wildlife was seen as an important way to draw visitors, and hence much needed public support for parks. Displays of animals were set up in several parks because of the frequent disappointment expressed by visitors who had failed to see wildlife. Park officials sometimes used elaborate and, by today's reasoning, absurd measures to ensure that visitors could see and even pet "beneficial" animals. For example, bear feeding shows were established at garbage dumps in several western parks in the 1920s and 1930s. A small "petting zoo" was established by the first NPS director, Stephen Mather, at Wawona in Yosemite in the mid-1920s to display the most common animals in the park. Today, NPS strives to better balance the needs of wildlife with the demands of visitors.

Wildlife Research. It is difficult to measure the value of wildlife to park visitors or to society as a whole. Opinions are mixed relative to contemporary Americans' attitudes toward wildlife. Kellert and Westervelt (1982) feel that public interest in animals has diminished somewhat since 1970. This opinion is contradicted by the observations of Scheffer (1976) and Shaw and Cooper (1980), who see a growing

1. Congress has authorized sport hunting in 52 units of the park system. These are primarily National Recreation Areas (NRA), National Seashores, and National Preserves. Limited sport hunting is also permitted in Grand Teton National Park because the legislation creating the park specifically authorized elk hunting in certain zones of the park under a special permit. Trapping is authorized in only four National Rivers and National Recreational Areas.

spiritual and emotional interest in wildlife, and less emphasis on consumptive uses; the growth of the animal rights movement tends to support their viewpoint. In addition, the limited social science studies done in parks and formal and informal observations of park visitors and their interactions with wildlife by the author support the conclusion that wildlife is one of the most significant resources of parks.

The lofty status that wildlife enjoys in the visitor's eye and in NPS promotions unfortunately is not matched by monetary or personnel support for wildlife research. Less than two percent of the total NPS budget has been devoted to research over the past several years, with only a fraction of that going to wildlife studies. Likewise, there are only about 30 individuals employed by NPS who are classified as research biologists and who deal with wildlife issues; yet there are about 7,500 permanent employees. While it is true that resource management personnel in parks are often involved with wildlife monitoring or management tasks, the time devoted to these activities is limited due to other job demands. Consequently, wildlife management duties are often disjointed.

The Biological Resources Division within NPS' Office of Science and Technology maintains nominal oversight of research policy in the NPS. However, wildlife research is conducted primarily at the park and regional level. Large parks such as Yellowstone, Everglades, Yosemite, and Great Smoky Mountains maintain a resident research staff that is directly responsible to the park superintendent. Research in other parks, particularly those in the Western and Pacific Northwest regions, is conducted through Cooperative Park Studies Units. These units are composed of NPS scientists stationed at, or affiliated with, a university in the region and who are responsible to the chief scientist in NPS' regional office. This structure provides the individuals with a broader base for acquiring scientific information and expertise and generally provides a more cost-effective way of using limited scientific personnel. For example, Cooperative Park Studies Unit scientists are available to help smaller parks which have no in-house scientific staff.

Research Initiatives. Several programs have been initiated in 1986–1987 that should help strengthen an understanding of wildlife needs and add greater credibility to NPS' science program. NPS is finally showing increasing interest in a long-neglected activity: monitoring the condition of park resources and establishing permanent baseline inventories. Such measures are needed for accurate documentation of long-term changes in park resources. A natural resources inventory and monitoring task force was organized early in 1987 by NPS' Associate Director for Science and Technology to examine the policy and rationale of gathering, analyzing, and managing baseline inventory data and long-term monitoring of the natural resources of parks. This task force, made up of NPS resource management, science, and management personnel, is now involved in drafting NPS-wide standards and guidelines for inventory and monitoring, and will shortly begin a survey of the status of NPS inventory and monitoring procedures and activities. A draft report on NPS inventory and monitoring standards and guidelines is scheduled for distribution in late 1987 or early 1988.

While new baseline studies are important, so are historical data. Unfortunately, most parks have a poor track record in information management; managers often know little about what research has historically been done in parks or where the data are located. A program was initiated in 1987 to address that problem. Over the next three years, the Cooperative Parks Study Unit at the University of Idaho will compile information on all resource studies done in parks in the Pacific Northwest Region in microcomputer data bases; these data will be available to all parks.

Finally, the 1986 action plan of NPS Director William Mott recommended that a panel of outside experts be convened to review natural resource management policies. Although not explicitly stated, it is believed that the scope of this committee will be to recommend management policies for all natural resources for the next several decades. While most NPS wildlife researchers would appreciate a renewed focus on resource issues, they are not unanimous in endorsing an outside committee. When a similar review board was convened in 1962, NPS had little in-house scientific expertise and by necessity had to rely on outside experts. Today that is not the case. NPS-affiliated scientists argue that they have the solutions to many wildlife problems in the parks if only management would listen to them. To date, no action has been taken on appointing the advisory panel, and some insiders suspect that this is because of disagreements within the bureaucracy over who should be appointed to the committee.

In order to do a better job of protecting the ecosystems and species within park boundaries, Director Mott, in 1986, organized a special task force to review NPS' role in conserving biological diversity and to serve as a forum for ideas on ways to strengthen NPS' capability to meet this challenge.[2] The report of the task force, which will include a plan for preserving biological diversity in parks, is scheduled to be released late in 1987.

NPS has also launched a series of projects designed to develop methods to assess the status of biological diversity in units of the park system. One component of that effort will be an inventory and analysis (compiled on 1:200 million scale base maps), of the natural vegetation

2. The task force is led by Dr. Christine Schoenwald-Cox, CPSU, University of California, Davis.

types represented in land areas administered by 11 federal land-management agencies. A more detailed assessment of representative ecosystem types that are not preserved currently in the national park system is to be completed in 1988. Presumably, this assessment will be used as a guide to help identify new areas to be included in the system, but it should be noted that NPS conducted a similar study in 1972 which received very little recognition or use.[3] Whether the new initiative will fare better is open to question.

A second component of Director Mott's initiatives includes studies to evaluate how park resources are affected by development activities on adjacent, nonpark lands. This effort recognizes the growing ecological differences between parks and adjacent areas in terms of species distributions and habitat quality. NPS seeks to better understand how these differences influence such factors as the exchange of genetic material between park and nonpark wildlife populations.

ISSUES IN THE PARKS

During 1987, NPS confronted several wildlife management issues that were the subject of considerable controversy and public concern. The continuing problem with alien species in several parks is typical of these. The first part of this section discusses the concept of alien species and examines in detail the research and management programs being undertaken or contemplated to control mountain goats at Olympic National Park.

As in past years, conflicts between park visitors and wildlife remains a significant concern. NPS often goes to great lengths to protect both humans and wildlife by minimizing the interactions between the two. In the case of dangerous animals such as bears, this is often justified. However, separation also prevents visitors from learning more about wildlife. These conflicting policies are explored in a subsequent section.

The 1986 publication of Alston Chase's book, *Playing God in Yellowstone*, served to focus national publicity on the alleged deficiences of NPS natural resource management activities, particularly at Yellowstone. Of special concern is the debate over whether park wildlife should be actively managed or allowed to be regulated by nature. The last section explores this controversial issue.

3. *Part II of the National Park System Plan: Natural History*. National Park Service, 1972.

The Management of Alien Species

The terms *alien, exotic,* and *nonnative*[4] are commonly used to describe plant and animal species that inhabit areas in which they did not evolve or migrate to naturally. Typically, alien species are introduced into areas in two ways: 1) by direct human introduction, either purposeful or accidental; or 2) by human-induced changes in the environment that facilitated the establishment and survival of the species.[5]

There are four general categories of alien animal species. First are those animals which, upon introduction to a new environment, find it inhospitable and soon disappear or barely continue to survive without continued reintroductions. Second, there are alien species that establish viable populations in a new area, but do not play a major role in the ecological community. They have a negligible impact on native species and the net effect of these aliens is a slight increase in the complexity of the community.

A third category of alien species are those which find their new environment to be much less limiting than their original habitat. Such a species, generally because of freedom from factors that held its numbers in check in its native habitat, may rapidly expand and proliferate to the point where it threatens the existence of some native plants and animals. When the damage to "valuable" native species becomes severe enough, the alien species often becomes the target of long-term, expensive, and sometimes controversial control or eradication programs.

A fourth category of aliens are those species that are capable of hybridizing with native species. These aliens are potentially the most troublesome of all because their impact is more difficult to detect, and the loss of pure, native genotypes is permanent. Examples include the hybrids resulting from the introduction of Rocky Mountain elk into Roosevelt elk ranges, of plains buffalo into mountain buffalo ranges, and of hatchery-reared trout into streams and lakes populated by native trout.

Whenever alien species cause economic disruption or threaten human health, natural resources, or valuable native species, there is generally widespread support for programs to control or eliminate

4. I have chosen to use the term "alien" to designate such species. This decision is based on the opinions of several biologists (for example, Smith 1985, Stone interview) who feel that the other terms do not convey to the public the ecological dangers posed by such species. For example, the word "exotic" is not appropriate as it often connotes species that are intriguing or unusual but not destructive to native ecosystems.

5. Technically species are classified as aliens only when their existence in an area can be traced to some human influence. This definition can create ambiguities. It separates species which may, for example, inhabit remote islands as a result of natural wind-born introduction from those carried to the same island directly by humans or by human introduced plants or animals.

them. Conversely, when such species are viewed as beneficial because of their aesthetic, economic, or recreational values, their propagation is supported. In many states, alien species are stocked or transplanted by state fish and wildlife agencies and form an important part of the sport hunter's bag or catch.

National Park Service Policies. NPS has a different and somewhat unique perspective on alien species. NPS' basic management philosophy is to keep parks free of artificial controls and influences. Thus, alien species have no place in parks, a fact that is clearly recognized in park management policies. However, park officials also realize that the elimination or even control of highly mobile, ubiquitous species such as the European starling and Norway rat is impossible. Thus, despite the lofty ideals of management philosophy, control of alien species, both plant and animal, is generally limited to only the most troublesome species.

The decision to attempt to keep parks free of alien species was reached early in the history of NPS. In 1921, the American Association for the Advancement of Science (AAAS), acknowledging that the "liberating of game animals not native to the region, impairs or destroys the natural conditions and native wilderness of parks," passed the following resolution:

> Be it resolved, that the [AAAS] strongly opposes the introduction of nonnative plants and animals into the national parks and all other unessential interference with natural conditions, and urges the National Park Service to prohibit all such introductions and interferences (Grinnell and Sheldon 1925, p. 353).

Today, almost all parks have problems with some alien animal species. These problems primarily include habitat damage such as soil compaction, destruction of vegetation, and erosion, and threats to significant or rare plant species. Many parks have elaborate, expensive programs to deal with the adverse impacts caused by specific species. It is difficult to estimate the amount of money spent on alien species control programs because in most parks such programs involve a variety of divisions including research, resource management, and maintenance. Control programs include the use of park rangers or deputized personnel to kill problem species, live-capture and transplantation of alien animals to areas outside the parks, construction of boundary fences to keep alien species out, and live capture of animals that can be domesticated.

Many control efforts have proven or are proving to be quite successful. For example, the Hawaiian parks have come a long way in solving their problems with feral pigs and goats through fencing and lethal control programs. The numbers of burros in Grand Canyon and Death Valley have been greatly reduced by live capture and removal programs. However, other control efforts such as those for feral pigs in the Great Smokies National Park have proven extremely difficult to carry out and represent little more more than holding actions.

Public support for alien control programs in parks varies considerably depending on the species. Many problem species are the result of purposeful unsanctioned introductions by local "sportsmen" seeking to use the park as a reservoir of breeding stock. Attempts to eliminate these animals thus engender considerable local hostility. Killing animals that the general public views as "cute" or otherwise valued can also generate adverse publicity, particularly among animal rights and humane groups. Their opposition to lethal controls was one of the principal reasons NPS adopted an expensive live-trapping and adoption program to remove unwanted burros from western parks.

Sensitivity to such protests has often limited the ability of NPS to control alien species except by expensive methods such as live capture and removal. While such programs have spared NPS public wrath, they have engendered professional criticism both open and covert. Allen *et al.* (1981, p. 20), for example, pointed out that:

> The much publicized catching and live removal of animals . . . is conditioning the public to believe that these expensive methods are the proper way to control nuisance animals. The National Park Service will never have money to handle most jobs in that manner. We wonder also about the priorities of a society in which contributions can be raised to rescue feral domestic burros at $1,000 each while nearly all the wild horses of the Earth . . . are declining to extinction.

Mountain Goats in Olympic National Park. The current situation with the mountain goat (*Oreamnos americanus*) in Olympic National Park finds NPS struggling to develop a plan to eliminate this animal, and epitomizes all of the problems that alien species can cause in parks as well as the difficulties NPS has in explaining and carrying out its policies.

Mountain goats are native to many of the mountainous areas of northwestern North America (see Figure 1). However, due to the isolation of the Olympic Mountains from the Canadian Rockies and the Cascade Range, mountain goats never colonized the Olympics. Surveys of the region in 1897 and 1899 by eminent biologists found no evidence of mountain goats. In 1909, the mountainous area of the peninsula was designated as Mount Olympus National Monument under U.S. Forest Service management.

According to local sources, a group of local sportsmen were responsible for bringing the mountain goat to the Olympic area. They considered the mountains suitable for establishing a herd of mountain goats for hunting purposes. Accordingly, in 1925, four adult mountain goats were brought from the Selkirk Mountains of British Columbia and released in the northern foothills of the Olympic Mountains near

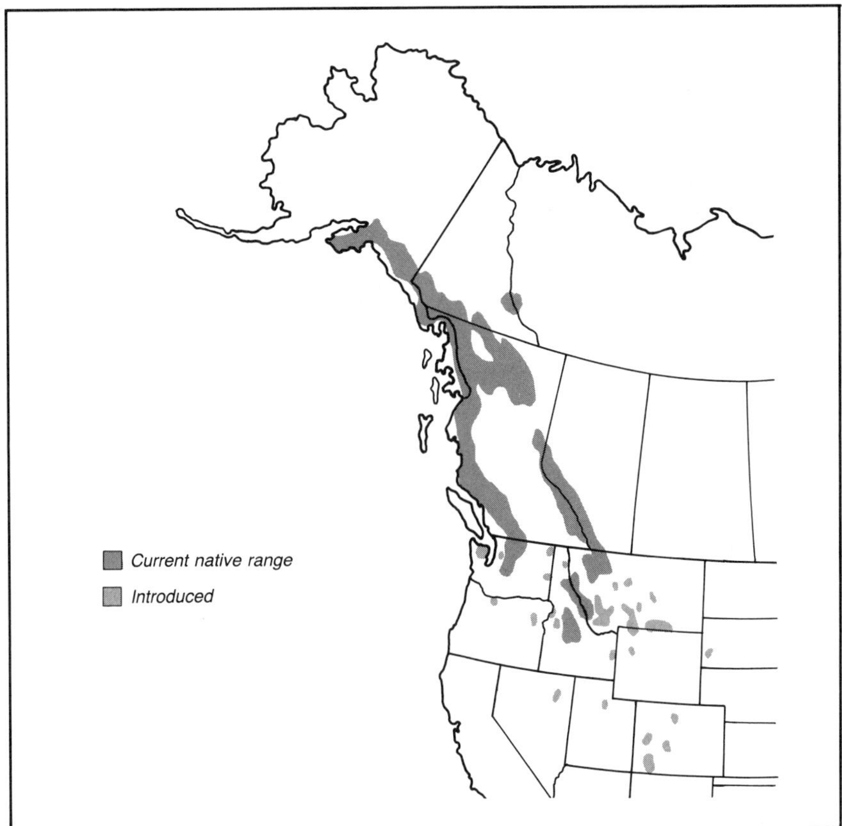

Figure 1. Distribution of mountain goats in North America, showing location of native and transplanted populations. Source: Chadwick, D.H. 1983. *A Beast the Color of Winter.*

Lake Crescent. Additional releases in 1927 (and probably 1929) brought the total number of transplanted individuals to about 12.

In 1933, jurisdiction of the National Monument was transferred to NPS. In 1938, Olympic National Park was established and the mountain goat was protected from sport hunting; hence, the goats had few checks on their population. The great majority of goats resided in the park rather than on the more marginal, adjacent Forest Service lands where sport hunting occurred. The wolf had been extirpated from the peninsula by this time. Other predators had been controlled by local game agents and their numbers were probably small. By the 1960s, a thriving mountain goat population existed over much of the northern and eastern parts of the park.

Concern that the goats were damaging subalpine vegetation caused NPS to initiate studies of the mountain goats in the 1970s. Research studies examined the impacts of the mountain goat on plant communities and soils. Erosion due to the goats' wallowing was documented, and plant communities near those wallows were shown to have been changed considerably. Mountain goat grazing reduced the dominance of several species in the climax subalpine plant communities. There was also concern that some species of unique endemic plants would eventually be eliminated. The first large scale aerial census of mountain goats, conducted in 1983, estimated the population at between 1,000 and 1,350 (Houston *et al.* 1986).

The park undertook its first management control actions in 1980 when 17 goats were removed. In 1981, the park began a three-year experimental management program to test the available options to control goat numbers. To date more than 200 goats have been live-captured and removed from the park. Most of these goats have been given to the game departments of surrounding states for restocking ranges.[6] Another 300 animal have been captured, marked and released in the park as part of the ongoing research effort. A variety of capture techniques have been tested including drop nets, drive nets, net guns, snares, and the use of tranquilizer darts.

Several factors have combined to make control of the mountain goats in Olympic an extremely sensitive issue. First, mountain goats are very popular and probably the most visible large mammal in the park. They are easily seen by backpackers (sometimes to the point of being an annoyance) and by motorists from the Klahhane Ridge overlook. Mountain goats are also a particularly attractive animal and mountain goat kids are nothing short of adorable. Second, the ecological damage that the goats are causing is not readily apparent to the causal observer. Changes in plant dominance and species composition are factors plant ecologists deal with; they are not things which generally alarm the average visitor. Third, many pro-goat people view NPS' policy on alien species control as inconsistent. They ask why some parks have alien English sparrows or ring-necked pheasant but Olympic cannot have mountain goats. The fact that mountain goats are native in similar terrain in areas as close as 25 miles from the park also causes consternation. Finally, the state of Washington, which administers the sport hunting of goats on lands surrounding the park, is concerned that a control program in the park will ultimately eliminate goat hunting on lands adjacent to the park.

NPS also faces several complications in any goat-control program it might undertake. The Olympic Mountains are largely roadless, incredibly rugged, and often have long periods of harsh weather. All of the control options tested would require the use of helicopter in most

6. An ironic twist to this story is that some of the mountain goats given to the state of Idaho and stocked in the southeastern portion of the state have apparently been seen in Grand Teton National Park, an area which was also never previously occupied by mountain goats.

areas of the park and their cost would be prohibitively expensive. (Cost estimates for helicopter removal are approximately $500 per animal.) Shooting goats from the air would be by far the most cost efficient and expedient method of reducing or eliminating the population, but would be politically unpalatable.

The unacceptability of traditional population control techniques has led to a search for other control methods, including sterilization (Hoffman and Wright 1987). Two fertility control techniques have been tested on free-ranging mountain goats in the park. Females have been treated with silastic implants of melengestrol acetate, a synthetic hormone that inhibits estrous. This treatment is estimated to be effective for three to four years. Males were chemically vasectomized using a sclerosing agent (lactic acid) injected into the epididymus. This treatment renders the male permanently sterile, apparently without changing courtship and reproductive behavior. Beginning in 1982, 12 females have been captured and sterilized. Subsequent monitoring of these females over four years of the study has indicated that only three kids were produced. This was a significantly lower reproduction rate than that observed in nontreated females.

Five males were captured and sterilized in 1985. An attempt was made to choose the largest males in a particular area to ensure social and therefore sexual dominance. Unfortunately, these males dispersed more widely than anticipated making it difficult to measure their influence on the reproductive success of female goats in the research area. The reproductive success of female goats in the male-capture area was apparently not lowered. It appears from these findings that too few males were sterilized to have an effect on reproduction, particularly if the males disperse throughout a wide area. Given the uncertainties with respect to male dispersal and reproductive behavior, the number of males that would need to be sterilized in order to lower the reproduction rate is not known at this time.

Because it involves the live-capture of mountain goats, sterilization is an expensive option. New sterilization techniques presently in development and testing may soon eliminate the need for capturing an animal to be treated, thus removing the most expensive and difficult step in sterilizing wild animals. Should this occur, it would provide NPS with a humane and politically viable control option to deal with what has thus far been an extremely difficult problem to solve.

Visitor Interaction with Wildlife

History of Wildlife Viewing in Parks. In the early years, there were many valid if misguided attempts by NPS officials to provide wildlife viewing opportunities for visitors. In fact, many of the first public programs dealing with wildlife in the United States took place in parks. These programs often emphasized "good" and "bad" animals. Ungulates, particularly deer, were good, predators were bad. The popular bear feeding shows at Yellowstone apparently began at the Fountain Hotel in the late 1800s, when the kitchen garbage was dumped each evening at six o'clock behind the hotel. In the 1920s, bleachers were set up at several sites around the dumps in Yellowstone, so that the visitors could watch the bears feed and fight. Organizers sometimes put out choice foods like bacon in order to encourage fights among bears.

In the early 1920s, a bear feeding area was set up in the Giant Forest in Sequoia National Park. Originally the site was a garbage pit, but by 1921 it had become a popular place to observe bears in the evening. In time bleachers were erected to facilitate viewing. The popularity of these shows led the superintendent to point out that "there is no doubt that the bears are our biggest show in the park" (National Park Service 1922). The shows were frequently accompanied by talks by ranger-naturalists on various aspects of the park. However, there was a gradual recognition by NPS officials that these shows were harmful and degrading to the animals or dangerous to the public or both; hence, they were terminated in the early 1940s.

For several years prior to 1930, Yellowstone held an annual bison round-up at the Buffalo Ranch in the park which ultimately was deliberately staged as a visitor attraction. Several southwestern parks such as Zion and Grand Canyon maintained seasonal zoos containing common park animals for the purpose of better educating park visitors. However, since World War II, there has been a steady trend to minimize wildlife-visitor interactions in parks and a subsequent decline in visitor viewing programs.

The Current Situation. Today, the observation of wildlife is a major part of the visitor experience in many parks, even in those areas originally established to protect primarily scenic or historic values. The traffic jams that result when even the most common large mammal is spotted along park roads leaves little doubt that park wildlife is an important recreational value. One survey estimated that more than 49 million Americans participated in some form of wildlife observation in 1975, and membership in animal-related organizations has grown tremendously in recent years (Whitter 1977).

Identifying people's preferences for different species is not always easy. Preferences may vary with viewing situations; and the same person may not only respond differently to various species but to the same species in different environments. There are few quantitative data available to specifically measure the recreational value of different species of park animals. However, many individuals who have observed park visitors have made qualitative judgements. Brown *et al.* (1980)

found that seeing the larger animals added more enjoyment to the experience of backcountry park visitors. Flewelling and Johnson (1981) found that sighting wolves or bears improved visitor satisfaction on backcountry trips in Denali National Park.

Hastings (1986) conducted an extensive survey of more than 4,000 visitors to Cades Cove in Great Smoky Mountains National Park Even though this area is noted for its living history exhibits and scenery, he found that the expectation of seeing wild animals was a major reason for visiting the cove for 73 percent of the respondents, and a minor reason for another 19 percent of visitors. Furthermore, more than 92 percent of all visitors reported that actually seeing wildlife was very important to their enjoyment of their trip to Cades Cove. He concluded that with its yearly visitation of over six million, Cades Cove was one of the more important areas in the southeastern United States for viewing wildlife in a natural setting.

Hasting's survey not surprisingly showed that people generally preferred mammals and birds over reptiles, amphibians, and invertebrates. The animal most visitors wanted to see was the black bear, although the white-tailed deer was also popular. The survey also showed that most visitors supported the reintroduction of some animals such as the elk, river otter, and bison, but were less enthusiastic towards the reintroduction of wolves and mountain lions. NPS' actions to remove alien species like the wild boar met with mixed reaction. Almost one half of the respondents felt that the boars should not be removed from the park.

Most surveys on park visitors and wildlife have shown that the average visitor is relatively uninformed about park animals. Visitors are generally more informed about animals that inflict human injury or disease, but even then pertinent biological knowledge often is lacking.

The lack of data concerning the wildlife knowledge of visitors and their viewing preferences is unfortunate as there seems to be a great potential for wildlife to serve as an interpretive tool to enhance the visitor's biological knowledge and ecological awareness (Wright 1984). In addition, interactions with wildlife can provide people with thrills not experienced in daily living. Hastings (1982), for example, found that minor damage to camping gear (for example, a water bottle riddled by bear teeth), could not only lead to improved respect and understanding of a species, but could serve as a "trophy" and as a reminder of an experience worth relating to others.

In recent years, NPS policy emphasizing natural regulation of wildlife populations (see the next section) has reduced or eliminated some wildlife viewing opportunities in many of the larger parks. For example, management policies that attempt to disperse animals from roadsides, campgrounds, and other visitor use areas also reduce the visitor's chances of seeing animals. The same is true of road and trail closures to protect the habitats of human-sensitive species. Interpretive programs often do an inadequate job of acquainting visitors with park wildlife or informing them about NPS management policies and human actions which threaten different species. In light of current park policies, one could argue that the pendulum has swung too far and that NPS has been remiss in not living up to the second part of its mandate, which is to provide for the enjoyment of the wildlife resources of the parks by providing more opportunities for people to observe and learn about wild creatures and their biological relationships.

Current Problems. The feeding of animals by visitors remains one of the most common ways visitors interact with wildlife. Although feeding of any wildlife in parks is illegal and discouraged where possible, such rules are difficult to enforce and are generally not enforced uniformly among parks. Most park staff are tolerant of visitors feeding small mammals and birds. In most cases, such activities are considered to be deleterious only to an individual or one group of individuals and not to the population as a whole. Furthermore, the impacts of feeding are generally viewed as minor such as causing unnatural behavior or higher than normal densities of animals in certain areas.

Most actions taken to lessen visitor/wildlife interactions have been executed to minimize conflicts and potential injury or death to visitors and to protect sensitive wildlife species. Some, however, have argued that this trend has gone too far and that there are few formal wildland-management plans that provide for adequate resource management and sufficient wildlife viewing opportunities. For example, most management efforts have involved alterations of habitat in order to provide cover or otherwise buffer human impacts on wildlife.

Attempts to develop plans that allow for viewing wildlife in its natural environment will not be easy without making parks artificial environments. Thus, while visitors come to the parks often for the expressed purpose of seeing animals, national parks are not intended to be zoos without cages. Visitors must be made aware that parks were established as sanctuaries for all animals and that the parks are areas where the animals must have a natural existence. Knowledge of the viewing habits of visitors and the tolerances of various species to different levels of human interaction is a first step in carrying out this mission.

The reaction of individual wildlife species to human activities most likely reflects their previous experiences with humans. The tendency of a species to avoid humans may be reinforced by specific forms of harassment including hunting. In contrast, an absence of overt harassment (the situation in parks), frequently results in a species' habituation to human presence.

Such factors often place wildlife managers in conflicting situations. In most parks, management seeks to protect wildlife from harassment, although a lack of harassment may cause some species such as black bears to reduce avoidance behavior and bother visitors. To avoid this, park employees may in some cases deliberately harass wildlife in order to keep them distant from visitors.

Today, individual parks attempt to balance the species' needs with the desires of visitors to see wildlife. NPS strives to minimize complete habituation to humans, which leads to unnatural, nuisance, or dangerous behavior. On the other hand, most park managers recognize that a complete avoidance of humans by park animals would be detrimental to visitor satisfaction and possibly erode political support for parks. Often, the species which managers try to separate from visitors are the animals the visitor is most interested in seeing.

There are, however, several exceptions to this balancing philosophy. The NPS staff on Isle Royale, Michigan, for example, is committed to protecting the eastern timber wolf from human disturbance. Although in some areas where wolves have had little or no contact with humans, they exhibit no outright fear, on Isle Royale wolves continue to show pronounced avoidance behavior towards humans despite a 30-year history of protection. Researchers feel that a fear of humans seems to be acquired early in a wolf's life; on Isle Royale this fear has probably been culturally transmitted from the island's first wolf to the present generation. The management goal of the NPS is to perpetuate this fear, because it enhances the public perception of the wolf as elusive, wilderness creature, and prevents the spectacle of wolves foraging for food in campgrounds or running off with backpacks. To assist in maintaining wolf isolation, park trails purposely avoid known denning areas or critical habitat, and a winter closure of the park was put into effect in 1975. In addition, no research is permitted which involves the handling of wolves (for example, attaching radio-transmitters) or closely approaching the denning areas.

As a result of these policies, there are few wolf sightings (an average of 12 to 24 per year) by visitors. The fact that most visitors are denied one of the few opportunities in the continental United States to view this unique species in a natural setting probably makes their visit less satisfactory. Some might argue that the average park visitor does not possess the experience or skills needed to find and see such elusive species as the wolf even if given the opportunity. In general, this may be true. However, others argue that visitors to Isle Royale are different; they seek the chance to see wolves and often possess the prerequisite skills to find them. Nevertheless, what is clear is that NPS' wolf management policy at Isle Royale does not teach the visitor much about wolves and probably does not generate much new support for the wolf's survival elsewhere.

The bear management policy at Glacier National Park also is designed to protect the bears by encouraging shyness and avoidance of humans as a characteristic behavior. This policy recognizes that shyness may not be a completely natural behavior, but an historic artifact of selective pressures against bears with aggressive traits. This selective pressure is maintained by removing individuals that exhibit aggressive behavior toward humans.

Little is known of the tolerance of most species towards humans in parks. Pedevillano and Wright (1987) conducted research to gain such information for mountain goats, a species which shows a mixed tolerance to humans. Mountain goats inhabit mountainous and rocky terrain usually remote from human developments. Increasingly, however, resource exploitation activities and recreational use have brought them into close association with humans.

In Glacier National Park, mountain goats have traditionally used a mineral lick which necessitated their crossing a major national highway. Visitors aware of the crossing point often congregate to observe the goats. In 1975, a decision was made to widen and upgrade the highway. An environmental impact analysis revealed that the resulting high-speed traffic would not only threaten the goats, but also endanger the visitors who stopped to watch them. To mitigate these effects, fencing was placed along the highway to restrict goat movement and two tunnels were constructed under the highway to allow the mountain goats to safely cross the highway to reach the lick. At the same time, the park constructed a special observation platform to allow visitors to unobtrusively observe mountain goats on the lick. These modifications were completed in 1981.

Pedevillano and Wright examined how well the mountain goats adjusted to these new crossing devices and how much disturbance visitors on the observation platform caused mountain goats on the lick. Both the tunnels and observation platform were very successful. Almost 100 percent of the goats used the tunnels, and visitors on the observation platform did not appear to disturb goats at the lick. Although expensive, this project shows that with proper planning, it is possible to develop methods which provide both for the safety and well-being of certain park animals while enhancing visitor enjoyment.

Conflicts Between Bears and Visitors. The tremendous emphasis on bear management is unique among wildlife species found in national parks. Although figures are not available, more money has probably been spent in managing bears than for any other animal in national parks. Bear management techniques are probably more advanced within NPS than in any other land- or resource-management agency.

Bears have also received the majority of the attention in programs to reduce conflicts between wildlife and visitors in parks. The reasons for this are twofold: 1) bears have historically been among the most sought-after-animals in parks; and 2) they are at the same time one of the most dangerous animals in parks. In general, problems with bears appear to stem from two behavioral attributes. One is that protection from human harassment causes bears to lose their natural avoidance behavior of humans. The other is that bears often associate people with food. Hence, managers have repeatedly sought ways to reduce contact between bears and visitors and to develop methods of preventing bears from obtaining food carried or discarded by humans.

The increased use of park backcountry areas which occurred in the 1960s and 1970s greatly increased the opportunity for contact between grizzly bears and people. Martinka (1982) found a direct positive relationship between the number of park visitors and the number of confrontations with bears. He concluded that unless certain factors changed, the pattern of increased confrontations with rising visitation could be expected to continue.

It has been postulated that habituation of grizzlies to human presence in parks may be an important factor influencing the number of confrontations or injuries. Habituation is defined as a decline in an animal's natural responses following repeated exposure to an inconsequential stimulus (Jope 1985). Changes in grizzly bear behavior in parks have been documented in a number of studies. These shifts were often related to changes in the distribution of visitors. Jope described the loss of a grizzly bear's fear response in certain areas in Glacier that were heavily used by visitors. She theorized that habituation reduced the number of charges made by bears during encounters with humans, thereby decreasing the injury rate to hikers. McCullough (1982), however, pointed out that because habituation reduced the avoidance response to people, close encounters were more frequent with habituated bears, which in turn increased the probability of injury.

Damage to hiking equipment caused by bears, particularly black bears, is much more common than human injury and appears to be far more pervasive than is commonly realized by park managers. Most damage occurs as bears tear apart containers, packs, or other equipment seeking food. Such problems have spawned a series of investigations, primarily in the California parks, to look for better ways to inform visitors of potential bear problems and to safely store food in backcountry camps. Park staff have been experimenting with bear-proof food storage lockers placed in backcountry camps and with different methods of caching food in other areas. One of the most promising developments has been the use of cylindrical tubes of PVC which can be sealed on the ends and used for storing food while backpacking. These devices seal in food odors and are virtually impervious to tampering by black bears. In a pilot test program, visitors are able to check out or rent these devices from park offices.

These technological developments are being complemented by tougher enforcement of food storage policies in the backcountry. Yosemite, for example, has adopted strict policies regarding proper food storage methods. The level of enforcement of this rule has varied from verbal warnings to arrest or impoundment of property.

Such measures alone, however, may not be sufficient if bear confrontations continue to increase. Better visitor dispersion techniques may provide another means of eliminating conflicts in some areas. Such techniques include selective closures of areas in the park for certain time periods or allowing use only when bears are least likely to be present; rerouting trails of these areas; and relocating campgrounds outside prime bear habitat areas. A recent study in the Two Medicine drainage of Glacier National Park mapped both grizzly habitat and backcountry use. The study revealed that a large percentage of hikers were concentrated in the best bear habitat. It was determined that potential conflicts could be minimized by limiting human use to daylight hours, the time period when bear use was low (Baldwin *et al.* 1985).

Another management technique has been to condition black bears to avoid humans and their food by frightening the bears with noise from cracker shells or by shooting them with rubber shot.[7] Denali and Katmai national parks have also experimented with chemical repellants that could be applied by backpackers.

Winter Use of Parks. The growing winter use of parks, particularly by cross-country skiers and snowmobile users, is causing a new set of problems for park wildlife and managers alike. Parks like Yellowstone are experiencing an explosive growth in winter visitation. During winter, park animals are often under a great deal of physiological stress due to the cold and low food supplies. The added trauma caused by visitor disturbance may drive animals out of preferred habitats and in some cases result in the death of individual animals. Currently, a research study is under way at Yellowstone to examine such impacts. The study may result in zoning winter use to specific areas or trails in the park.

Natural Regulation of Wildlife in the National Parks

The Theory of Natural Regulation. The idea that wildlife populations in national parks should be allowed to exist with little or no

7. Denali National Park has been experimenting with soft plastic slugs fired from a 12-gauge shotgun to discourage bear raids on backcountry camps. The slugs, which sting but do not actually injure the bears, are fired by hidden observers when an identified problem bear approaches a research camp. Since bears often raid camps at night or when hikers are away during the day, the objective of this effort is to convince the bear to associate the unpleasant experience with the camp rather than with people (Dalle-Molle and Van Horn 1987).

human interference has been accepted for over half a century. This concept, now referred to as "natural regulation," was first articulated by Wright *et al.* who stated that the aim of park management should be:

> that every species shall be left to carry on its struggle for existence unaided, as being to its greatest ultimate good, unless there is real cause to believe that it will perish if unassisted (1933 p.147).

The concept has been reinforced by NPS officials like Director Conrad Wirth, who said that in certain units of the national park system "natural processes are permitted to function with the least possible control or manipulation" (Wirth 1962).

Natural regulation was given professional credibility with the publication of the report of the Special Advisory Board on Wildlife Management which recommended that:

> biotic associations within each park be maintained, or where necessary recreated, as nearly as possible in the condition that prevailed when the area was first visited by white man (Leopold *et al.* 1963, p.31).

In practice, however, the concept has been widely ignored. Dating from the late 1930s, many western parks had active programs to regulate the numbers of ungulates—primarily Rocky Mountain elk and mule deer—in order to keep their numbers at some desired level of carrying capacity. Programs to reduce the numbers of ungulates in parks were based on the premise that these animals were too numerous for their own good and were destroying their range; hence, the herds eventually would starve without human intervention.

Concern that park ungulate populations were too large was based on several factors. First, predator species such as the wolf had been eliminated in parks, thus removing a natural control on population size. Second, many managers were convinced that some western parks, such as Yellowstone and Rocky Mountain, had not been used as winter range by large numbers of ungulates before European man arrived. Their contention was that these parks were not used as ungulate wintering areas until development on adjacent nonpark lands eliminated ungulate use of migration routes and traditional wintering areas outside the parks, thereby concentrating more animals in the parks than the habitat could support.

Evidence in support of this viewpoint came from a variety of sources. These included periodic censuses which reported larger than normal numbers of a given species, instances of high overwinter mortality, decreases in the numbers of other associated species such as bighorn sheep and white-tailed deer attributed to competition with other ungulates, and determinations that habitat was being damaged or soil erosion was occurring. Most of these judgments were based on qualitative or spotty observations rather than on quantitative or long-term measurements

Of foremost concern to park managers was the suspected degradation of the winter range. Parks such as Yellowstone, Rocky Mountain, Sequoia, Yosemite, Zion, and Mount Ranier all had reports allegedly documenting habitat degradation dating from the early 1930s. Interest in the condition of park winter range increased due to the drought conditions and series of mild winters experienced in many Rocky Mountain parks in the mid- and late-1930s. Most scientists examining the situation reported substantial habitat damage; these accounts were accepted for many years with little question (Rush 1932, Cahalane 1941).

As a result, NPS initiated a concerted effort to decrease the number of ungulates in certain parks. Common methods included transplanting individuals to other parks or natural areas, zoos, and Indian reservations; killing animals in the park (generally providing the carcasses for food for welfare or institutional use); and cooperating with state wildlife departments to increase the sport harvest of animals on lands adjacent to the parks. Opportunities to place transplants rapidly diminished, however, and killing in the park became the only reliable way to assure population reduction.

Large numbers of elk were killed in Yellowstone and Rocky Mountain, particularly in the late 1950s and early 1960s. These actions generated much adverse criticism. Opposition came both from animal lovers and sportsmen's groups, the latter feeling that the reductions could best be handled through sport hunting.

The growing public concern over population reduction programs in the parks provided the impetus for the establishment in 1962 by the Secretary of the Interior of the Special Advisory Board on Wildlife Management in the National Parks. Although the report issued by this committee advocated continued regulation of "excess" animals in the parks through shooting by park personnel, growing public pressure resulted in the cessation of most population control programs in the late 1960s. In 1969, a long-term research program was begun at Yellowstone to test a series of hypotheses on whether natural factors such as predation, weather, and fire could satisfactorily regulate ungulate populations. This study also examined the effects of ungulates on vegetation. The aim of these studies was to determine if reductions were actually needed or if natural ecosystem processes were sufficient to keep ungulate numbers at desired levels without periodic culling.

Throughout the 1970s and early 1980s, a growing number of studies advanced the idea that parks were not static entities and that there was no reason to think, as many early investigators did, that the condition of park ecosystems should remain the same year after year (Despain *et al.* 1986). Houston (1982) compared historic and contemporary photographs of representative landscapes in Yellowstone and concluded that there were relatively few changes in natural biotic conditions in Yellowstone that could be attributed to native ungulates. Gruell's (1973) assessment of conditions in southern Yellowstone and the surrounding area reached similar conclusions.

The photographs showed that most of the range sites that were considered to be overgrazed by earlier investigators looked the same way in the 1870s and 1880s, presumably before European man began to tamper with the area. In addition, the studies suggested that early investigators were generally unfamiliar with the history of human and livestock use on certain sites, and underestimated the effects of drought, fire suppression, domestic livestock, and soil influences on the range conditions they observed.

These findings led to a new management approach for ungulates which relied on natural processes to regulate herd size. Park managers decided to let the combined action of periodic adverse weather conditions, food limitations, and predators[8] regulate animal numbers. Only when these processes failed would other regulatory mechanisms such as increased hunting outside park boundaries and selective culling in the park be used.

The new management practices were set in the framework of an experimental management plan that was to be tested and refined (Cole 1971). In keeping with this approach, an intensive vegetation sampling and monitoring program was begun in the late 1960s. In the following years, a natural fire management program was developed which dictated the instances and areas where natural fires would be allowed to burn without suppression while their effects were studied. Long-term research programs were also initiated to study and monitor elk and bison populations and their effects on plant communities.

The cessation of control programs in Yellowstone had an immediate effect on the elk and bison populations in the park; both populations entered a period of steady increase which continues today. Elk populations have increased at least fourfold in the last 20 years and bison populations have almost doubled.

Current Wildlife Controversies. The validity of the concept of natural regulation is again being questioned. The fact that the elk population has shown no sign of stabilizing has again raised concern over deterioration of winter range. As bison numbers have increased, they have begun to move outside the park, causing concern among ranchers over the threat of transmission of brucellosis to their cattle.

Chase (1986) implied that the adoption of the natural regulation philosophy was done only to avoid criticism of animal-control operations; in his words it "was an attempt to make a scientific virtue out

8. Despain *et al.* (1986) points out that "scientific evidence tempts one to conclude that the wolf had a relatively minor role in controlling elk numbers on the northern range . . . "

of a political necessity" (Chase 1986, p. 47). Chase further implied that the NPS policy gave a blank check to nature and that NPS had forfeited its management responsibilities. What would managers do, he asked, if after allowing the ecosystem to operate naturally, some species such as the grizzly or bighorn sheep got into trouble? "Would they stand silently by, wringing their collective hands, as a wild and rare species went to oblivion?" (Chase 1986, p. 41).

In this instance, Chase clearly misses the point. Rather than being a politically expedient policy, the basic premise of natural regulation has been a part of NPS management philosophy throughout the agency's existence.

A more valid criticism of the use of the natural regulation strategy in Yellowstone is its diminution of the role predators play in regulating ungulate numbers. Unfortunately, determining the role that predation historically played in most continental U.S. parks is extremely difficult. Large-scale control programs in the early 1900s totally exterminated some predators and reduced other species to very low levels. In many cases, predator species have never recovered from this persecution. In areas where predator control was not very effective, such as Alaska and Canada, predators such as wolves have an important role in keeping populations in balance with the carrying capacity of their habitat.

Until a viable population of wolves can be reintroduced or naturally recolonize some of the Rocky Mountain parks, no one really will have the ability to study their relationship to ungulate herd size. Thus, the degree to which the major national parks in the continental United States can support naturally regulated populations of large ungulates and predators remains open to question. The recent recolonization of the North Fork drainage of Glacier National Park by wolves moving down from Canada offers a chance to study ungulate-predator relationships, but it is far too early to draw any conclusions. Scientists from the University of Montana are currently monitoring the wolf population and park staff initiated a prey availability study in the North Fork. It is hoped that the wolves will be permitted to become firmly established without harassment or threats by individuals living near the park.

Island Biogeography. Historically, parks were rarely designed with ecological boundaries adequate to protect park wildlife. In the past few years, there has been much interest in finding ways to design parks that will optimize the protection of wildlife and other natural resources within them. Some investigators have taken their lead from the theories of island biogeography first espoused by MacArthur and Wilson (1967). Proposed originally for oceanic islands, island biogeographic theory is being applied to parks which are seen as analogous islands of natural habitat surrounded by lands of human-altered habitat.

As applied to parks, island biogeographers make two points: 1) the total number of different species that can be maintained in a park is directly related to park size; and 2) parks that are isolated from similar ecological areas by different habitat will lose species more rapidly due to lower immigration and higher extinction rates.

The first point is highly contentious, with arguments focusing on whether a group of small parks will preserve more or less species than would a single large park of equal total area (Soule and Simberloff 1986). Proponents of large parks argue that such parks are more likely to have a diversity of habitat. Random environmental events such as fire, flood, drought, and disease would be less able to impact the whole park at once, thus assuring that some habitat and the species associated with it could survive. As noted in NPS' State of the Parks Surveys (see *Audubon Wildlife Report 1986* for a discussion of the survey), wildlife in many parks is threatened by a variety of environmental problems—poaching, fires, pesticides, and alien species encroachment. Larger parks may provide a greater buffer area against such intrusions, thereby making wildlife preservation easier. In addition, larger parks generally have a greater size to boundary length ratio than smaller parks, and thus may be less likely to be affected by external threats (Wright and Machlis 1986).

Critics have challenged these ideas on theoretical, empirical, and statistical grounds. They argue that designing parks based solely on island biogeography theory ignores other relevant factors in park design such as how diverse the habitat actually is in a given area, the severity of human development both in and around the park, and the colonizing ability of different species.

Unfortunately, the debate on the merits of island biogeography principles has remained largely theoretical; rarely have the principles been applied in actual park design. In the United States, as in most of the world, park design is driven primarily by political and economic considerations rather than ecological ones; this is not likely to change. As early as 1933, Wright and others recognized this factor in their pioneering wildlife surveys, concluding that parks were ". . . artificial units . . . [whose] boundaries . . . frequently fail to include terrain which is vital to the park animals during some part of their annual cycles" (Wright *et al.* 1933). They ranked the inability of parks to function as complete biological units as the most important wildlife problem in parks. The fact that parks are incomplete biological units continues to be the most important factor affecting management of park wildlife. The ramifications are seen in the difficulties in managing wide-ranging grizzly bears in the Greater Yellowstone Ecosystem, and the problems inherent in wolf reintroduction in parks such as Yellowstone, Glacier, Rocky Mountain, and Olympic.

Some individuals have argued that the inadequate size of parks has led to a serious depletion of the number of species in some parks. Newmark (1987) attempted to catalog the number of natural and human-influenced extinctions that have occurred among the major groups of mammals in western national parks since their establishment. Using island biogeographic theory as a foundation, Newmark showed that smaller parks had significantly more natural, post-park establishment extinctions than larger parks. He concluded that the loss of mammalian species would continue in those parks isolated by altered habitat on surrounding lands unless park managers intervened or the parks were enlarged or both. Newmark's article received considerable publicity and served to highlight the fact that parks are indeed threatened. It was criticized by NPS personnel because of the accuracy of the data and their interpretation, and because it did not clearly distinguish between natural and human-caused extinctions.

It is clear that the issue of optimum park size and shape for wildlife protection will remain a volatile one in the future as more and more habitat on lands external to parks is converted to human use. It seems equally clear, however, that achieving a consensus on how to approach this problem will be difficult. NPS lacks the jurisdiction to regulate activities or developments originating on lands outside park boundaries (Keiter 1985). Yet because of the agency's preservation mandate, and in view of the magnitude of the external treats posed to park resources, NPS cannot ignore the problem.

In the past few years several bills have been introduced in Congress to address the problem of external threats to parks. In 1982 and 1983, the House of Representatives passed a Parks Protection Act designed to address this problem, but the Senate failed to act on it. In 1984, Senator John Chafee introduced (Amendment no. 2807 to S 978) The Wildlife and the Parks Act, which was to protect park wildlife against habitat loss on federal lands adjoining national parks. However, the legislation was never reported by the Senate Environment and Public Works Committee and was not reintroduced.

NPS has been criticized for its failure to support active legislation giving it more control over activities on lands external to parks. Some critics also believe that NPS has been negligent in pursuing the research and resource management initiatives needed to document or monitor the impact of threats to parks. The recent renewed emphasis under Director Mott on programs to monitor vital environmental parameters and on the collection of baseline data needed to track changes in environmental conditions is an indication that this problem is finally being recognized. The results of these efforts may be very important in convincing politicians of the need for either enlarging the parks or effectively protecting the habitat adjacent to them.

REFERENCES

Allen, D.L., L. Erickson, E.R. Hall, and W.M. Schirra. 1981. "A review and recommendations on animal problems and related management needs in units of the National Park System." *The George Wright Forum.* 1(2):9–32.

Baldwin, S.B., B. Butterfield, R.G. Wright, and G E. Machlis. 1985. Habitat Mapping in the Two-Medicine Area of Glacier National Park Combining Information Gathering Techniques. University of Idaho Cooperative Park Studies Unit Report. SB-85–2. 110 pp.

Brown, P.J., G.E. Haus, and B.L. Driver. 1980. "Value of Wildlife to Wilderness Users." Proceedings 2nd. *Conference on Scientific Research in the National Parks* 6:168–179.

Cahalane, V.H. 1941. "Wildlife Surpluses in the National Parks." *Transactions of the North American Wildlife Conference* 6:355–361.

Chase, A. 1986. *Playing God in Yellowstone.* Atlantic Monthly Press. Boston, Massachusetts.

Cole, G.F. 1971. "An Ecological Rationale for the Natural or Artificial Regulation of Native Ungulates in Parks." *Transactions of the North American Wildlife Conference* 36:417–425.

Despain, D., D. Houston, M. Meagher, and P. Schullery. 1986. *Wildlife in Transition.* Roberts Rinehart Inc. Boulder, Colorado.

Dalle-Molle, J.L. and J.C. Van Horn. 1987. Successful Bear-People Conflict Management in Denali National Park, Alaska. Paper presented at Conference on Human-Bear Interactions. Yellowknife, Yukon Territory.

Flewelling, B. and D. Johnson. 1981. Wildlife Experience and Trip Satisfaction in the Backcountry. A preliminary summary of Denali backcountry survey data. University of Washington Cooperative Park Studies Unit.

Grinnell, G.B. and C. Sheldon (eds). 1925. "Resolution of the American Association for the Advancement of Science," pp. 353 in *Hunting and Conservation: The Book of the Boone and Crockett Club.* Yale University Press. New Haven, Connecticut.

Gruell, G.E. 1973. An Ecological Evaluation of Big Game Ridge. U.S. Forest Service Publication, Intermountain Region.

Hastings, B.C. 1982. Human-Bear Interactions in the Backcountry of Yosemite National Park. M.S. thesis. Utah State University. Logan, Utah.

——. 1986. Wildlife-related Perceptions of Visitors in Cades Cove Great Smoky Mountains National Park. Ph.D. dissertation. University of Tennessee. Knoxville, Tennessee.

Hoffman, R.A. and R.G. Wright. 1987. *A Comparison of Population Control Techniques for Mountain Goats in Olympic National Park, Using Field Sterilization Procedures and Computer Modeling.* University of Idaho Cooperative Park Studies Unit Report. B-87–1. 81 pp.

Houston, D.B. 1982. *The Northern Yellowstone Elk.* MacMillan Publishing Company. New York, New York.

——., B B. Moorhead and R.W. Olsen. 1986. "An aerial census of mountain goats in the Olympic Mountain Range, Washington." *Northwest Science* 60:131–136.

Jope, K.L. 1985. "Implications of grizzly bear habituation to hikers." *Wildlife Society Bulletin* 13:32–37.

Kellert, S.R., and M.O. Westervelt. 1982. "Historical trends in American animal use and perception." *Transactions of the North American Wildlife and Natural Resource Conference* 47:649–664.

Keiter, R.B. 1985. "On protecting the national parks from the external threats dilemma." *Land and Water Law Review* 20:355–420.

Leopold, A.S., S.A. Cain, C.M. Cottom, I.N. Gabrielson and T.L. Kimball. 1963. "Wildlife management in the national parks." *Transactions of the North American Wildlife Conference* 28:28–45.

MacArthur, R.H., and E.O. Wilson. 1967. *The Theory of Island Biogeography.* Princeton University Press. Princeton, New Jersey.

Martinka, C.J. 1982. "Rationale and options for management in grizzly bear sanctuaries." *Transactions of the North American Wildlife and Natural Resources Conference* 47:470–475.

McCullough, D.R. 1982. "Behavior, bears, and humans." *Wildlife Society Bulletin* 10:27–33.

Newmark, W.D. 1987. "A land-bridge island perspective on mammalian extinctions in western North American parks." *Nature* 325:430–432.

Pedevillano, C. and R.G. Wright. 1987. "Mountain goat visitor interactions in Glacier National Park." *Biological Conservation* 39:1–11.

Peek, J.M., D.G. Miquelle and R.G. Wright. 1987. "Are bison exotic in the Wrangell St. Elias National Park and Preserve?" *Environmental Management* 11:149–153.

Rush, W. 1932. *Northern Yellowstone Elk Study.* Montana Fish and Game Commission.

Scheffer, V.B. 1976. "The future management of wildlife biology." *Wildlife Society Bulletin* 4:51–54.

Shaw, W. and T. Cooper. 1980. "Managing wildlife in national parks for human benefits." *Proceedings of the 2nd Conference on Scientific Research in National Parks* 6:189–198.

Smith, C.W. 1985. "Impact of alien plants on Hawaii's native biota," pp. 180–250 *in* C.P. Stone and J.M. Scott eds., *Hawaii's Terrestrial Ecosystems Preservation and Management.* University of Hawaii Press. Manoa, Hawaii.

Soule, M.E. and D.S. Simberloff. 1986. "What do genetics and ecology tell us about the design of nature reserves?" *Biological Conservation* 35:19–40.

Stone, C. 1987. Interview with the Author. Hawaii Volcanos National Park, Hawaii. June 4.

U.S. Department of Interior. National Park Service. 1922. *Superintendent's Annual Report.* Sequoia National Park.

U.S. Department of the Interior. National Park Service. 1978. *Management Policies.* Government Printing Office. Washington, D.C.

Whitter, D.J. 1977. Black Bear Management in Great Smoky Mountains National Park. Report to the Superintendent. Great Smoky Mountains National Park.

Wirth, C.L. 1962. "Wildlife conservation and management." *National Parks Magazine* 36(172):15–17.

Wright, G.M., J. Dixon and B. Thompson. 1933. A Preliminary Survey of Faunal Relations in National Parks. *National Park Service Fauna Series* 1. Government Printing Office. Washington, D. C.

Wright, R.G. 1984. "The challenges for interpretation in the new Alaskan parks." *Journal of Interpretation* 9:39–46.

——, and G.E. Machlis. 1986. "National park size and threats to their wildlife: any relationship!" *Proceedings of the 3rd Conference on Scientific Research in the National Parks.* In Press.

R. Gerald Wright is associate professor and Project Leader of the Cooperative Park Studies Unit at the College of Forestry, Wildlife and Range Scientists, University of Idaho, Moscow.

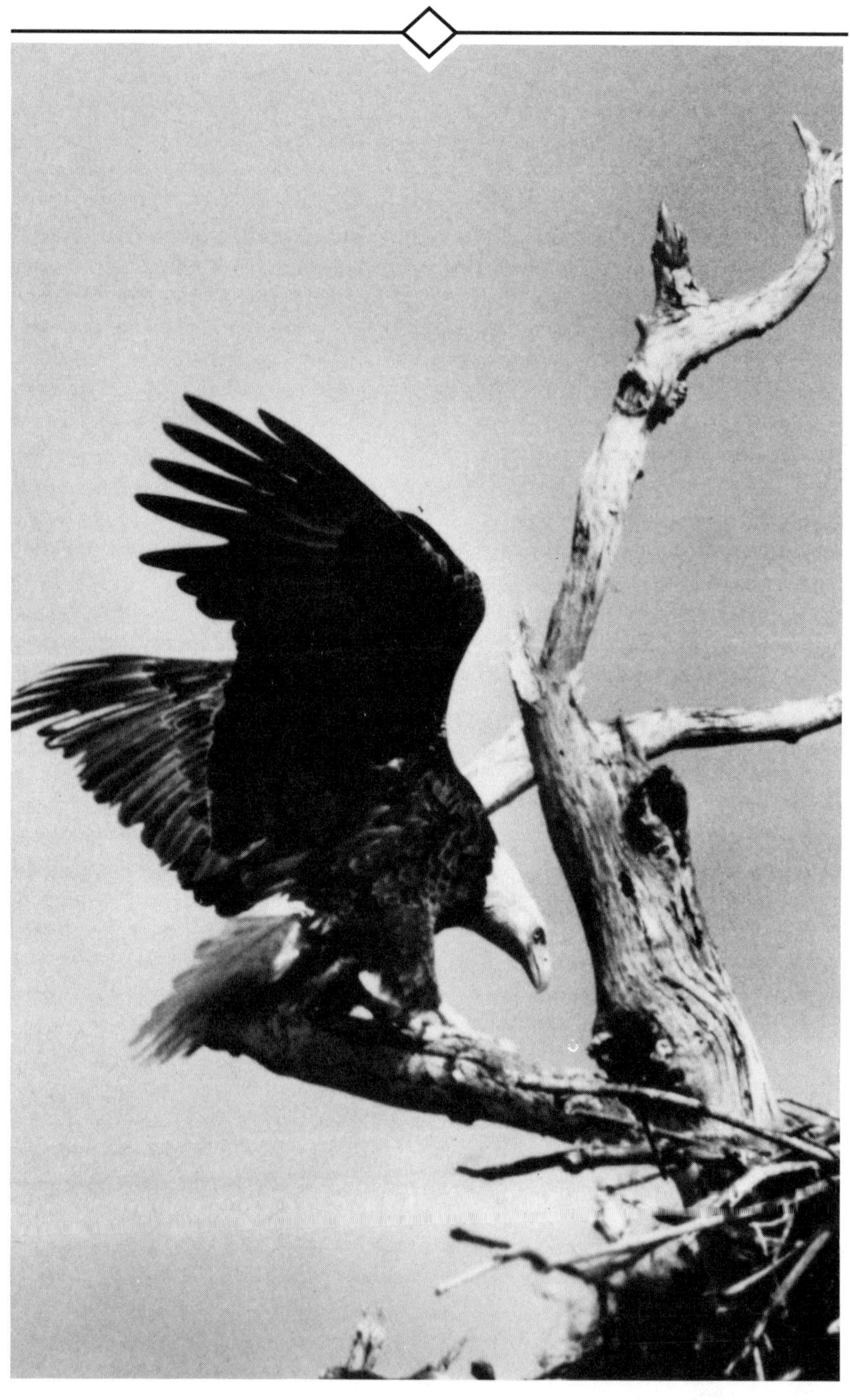

Several courts have debated whether American Indians have the right to hunt eagles despite federal and state endangered species laws. *Les Line/National Audubon Society*

Recent Legal Developments Affecting Wildlife Conservation

Michael J. Bean

INTRODUCTION

The creation of a vacancy on the United States Supreme Court in 1987, and the monumental battle over the nominee initially selected to fill it, Judge Robert Bork, served as a striking reminder of the importance that courts play in American society. This has been particularly true in the area of environmental protection. In large measure, the growth of the modern environmental movement took place contemporaneously with the opening up of the courts to citizen-initiated lawsuits. Litigation, and the decisions of the courts, remain important components of wildlife policy.

This chapter examines the most significant court decisions of the past year that affect wildlife and governmental programs for wildlife conservation. The initial section covers several recent cases that illustrate both the potential and the limits of citizen-initiated lawsuits to force governmental compliance with environmental laws. Subsequent sections examine the nature of the restraints imposed by wildlife conservation laws on private development and on Native Americans, and cases brought in the United States to protect wildlife outside U.S. borders; the final section explores current judicial attitudes toward wildlife law enforcement.

CITIZEN SUITS: OPPORTUNITIES AND LIMITS

The crucial role environmental organizations can play in the implementation of wildlife laws by bringing citizen lawsuits is well illustrated by the case of *Sierra Club v. Marsh* (816 F.2d 1376 [9th Cir. 1987]). The case concerned a combined federal highway and flood-control project in San Diego County, California. Completion of the project would have destroyed, among other things, more than 40 acres of marshland used by the California least tern and the light-footed clapper rail, both listed as endangered under the federal Endangered Species Act (16 U.S.C.A. 1531 *et seq.*).

When the U.S. Army Corps of Engineers, which is responsible for the flood-control portion of the project, consulted with the U.S. Fish and Wildlife Service (FWS) about the effects of the project on the two birds, FWS concluded that the project was likely to jeopardize the birds' continued existence unless certain mitigating actions were undertaken. Principally, FWS specified that the Corps would have to acquire and protect 188 acres of privately owned marshland in order to mitigate the damage caused by the project. This mitigation would not increase the amount of marsh habitat available for the birds, but would ensure that certain other lands used by the birds would be protected from future development. The Corps agreed to buy the land. To speed the transaction, the Corps contracted with the county to buy the land and transfer it to the Corps or to a Corps-designated agency within one year.

However, San Diego County failed to carry out its part of the agreement. More than a year after its contract with the Corps had been made, the county entered into an agreement with the owner of the 188 acres to acquire the land subject to a variety of deed restrictions that, in the opinion of FWS, eliminated the lands' value as habitat for the endangered birds. These restrictions included an access easement for construction of streets, utility lines, walkways, and other installations on a portion of the mitigation property. Moreover, the landowner's agreement to transfer the land was further conditioned on the Corps' willingness to issue permits for the development of other nearby land owned by the same landowner. Since these events constituted significant new information that called into question FWS' determination that the project would not jeopardize the survival of the endangered birds, FWS requested the Corps to reinitiate consultation. The Corps refused and pressed ahead with the project.

In September 1986, nearly two years after the contract had been negotiated by the Corps and the county, the Sierra Club and the League for Coastal Protection brought suit against the Corps under Section 11(g) of the Endangered Species Act (16 U.S.C.A. 1540[g]), which authorizes citizen suits to enjoin violations of the act. The two environmental groups challenged the Corps' continued work on the project despite noncompliance with FWS' condition that the mitigation lands be acquired. The plaintiffs asserted that the failure to acquire the land meant that the Corps had not ensured that its project would not jeopardize the continued existence of the two endangered species; hence, the Corps was in violation of Section 7 of the act (16 U.S.C.A. 1536). The plaintiffs also alleged that the Corps' refusal to reinitiate consultation with FWS was unlawful because such renewed consultation was clearly required under FWS regulations implementing the consultation requirements of Section 7.

The district court refused to grant the Sierra Club's request for a preliminary injunction stopping further work on the project. That refusal was appealed to the United States Court of Appeals for the Ninth Circuit and was reversed. In its arguments before the appeals court, the Corps fought the injunction effort on the grounds that it had filed its own legal claim to compel the county to transfer the disputed 188 acres as provided in the original contract, and that it was premature to judge whether its effort would succeed. The court, noting that the Corps' claim was filed only after the Corps was sued by the Sierra Club, reasoned that "the risk that the [Corps] might not prevail must be borne by the project, not by the endangered species . . . [A]ny delay caused by the County's breach must be of construction, not of mitigation" (816 F.2d at 1386). Thus, the court enjoined further work on that part of the project affecting the birds until the Corps acquired the mitigation lands.

In regard to the procedural claim, the court concluded that the county's failure to transfer the mitigation lands free of encumbering easements was new information that indicated that the effects of the project on the birds might be different from what was originally assumed. Hence, reinitiation of consultation with FWS was warranted. The court agreed to enjoin work on the entire project, unless the Corps agreed to reinitiate consultation.

The recalcitrance of the Corps of Engineers in dealing with FWS was a factor that seemed to affect significantly the court's perception of the issues in the *Sierra Club* case. The Corps not only had refused FWS' request to reinitiate consultation, but had never explained the reasons for its refusal until after it had been sued. Without the stimulus of a citizen suit authorized by the Endangered Species Act, the Corps would have been able to ignore indefinitely the protestations of FWS.

Unfortunately, citizen suits are not always available to force a federal agency to carry out its responsibilities. An illustrative example, also involving the Corps, is *Harmon Cove Condominium Ass'n v. Marsh* (815 F.2d 949 [3d Cir. 1987]).

In *Harmon Cove*, the Corps had issued a permit, under Section 404 of the Clean Water Act (33 U.S.C.A. 1344), authorizing a condominium developer to dredge and fill portions of the Hackensack River in New Jersey in order to build a new condominium complex. The Clean Water Act generally prohibits the discharge of pollutants into wetlands and water bodies. Section 404, however, authorizes the Corps to issue permits that allow the placing of dredged or fill material in such areas. The permit issued in the *Harmon Cove* case included a number of conditions, among them requirements that the developer maintain a marina area associated with the condominium complex and prevent damage to piers and embankments from wave wash. Differences soon arose between the developer and those who bought units in the condominium. The condominium owners believed that the developer had failed to live up to the conditions in its Corps permit and several times requested the Corps to enforce compliance with those conditions. The Corps refused.

Finally, the condominium association sued the Corps to compel it to enforce compliance with the condition of its permit. The United States Court of Appeals for the Third Circuit held that the Corps had complete discretion to decide whether to enforce permit conditions and that the exercise of its discretion is not subject to judicial review. In so holding, the court invoked the general principle that an order compelling a federal agency to take a particular action is an extraordinary remedy that can be applied only when the agency's duty is so clear-cut under law that no exercise of discretion on the agency's part is warranted. The court also held that the Clean Water Act conferred no right upon the condominium association to sue the developer. Thus, the association was left without any remedy under the act against either the developer, who was unwilling to live up to the conditions in the permit, or the Corps, which was unwilling to insist on compliance with those conditions. Since Section 404 of the Clean Water Act is the principal federal regulatory authority for protecting wildlife-rich wetlands from inappropriate development, this case underscores the risk that environmental interests may take in relying upon seemingly stringent conditions in Corps-issued permits to protect wetlands.

PRIVATE DEVELOPMENT AND THE RESTRAINTS OF FEDERAL WILDLIFE LAW

The "Incidental Taking" of Endangered Species

Many laws designed to promote the conservation of wildlife significantly affect the development of privately owned land. Sometimes these effects come about in indirect and unsuspected ways. Illustrative is the prohibition in the federal Endangered Species Act against the "taking" of any endangered species. As used in the act, "taking" encompasses not just activities deliberately intended to result in the death or capture of a protected animal, such as hunting or trapping, but *any* activity that may harm or kill the animal. Thus, a landowner who clears the trees and other vegetation from property, in order to prepare it for development, may commit a prohibited taking if an endangered bird happens to nest in one of the trees or if the eggs or larvae of a protected butterfly are crushed in the process.

Rather than simply prohibit such incidental takings associated with otherwise lawful activities as the Endangered Species Act had ineffectively done before[1], Congress amended the act in 1982 to require compensating conservation measures when an incidental taking unavoidably occurs. The impetus for the amendment, which authorizes FWS to issue incidental taking permits in such circumstances, was a major real estate development project on San Bruno Mountain near San Francisco that was certain to result in the taking of some endangered mission blue butterflies.[2] The notion behind an incidental taking permit is that major land developers, in return for the guarantee of no criminal or civil liability for incidentally taking endangered species, will undertake conservation actions beneficial to the species that have been indentified in formal habitat conservation plans. Such plans are to entail long-term commitments of resources, typically including the dedication of a portion of project lands for the purpose of conserving the affected species.

The first incidental taking permit that FWS issued—for development of San Bruno Mountain—was at issue in *Southwest Diversified Inc. v. City of Brisbane* (652 F. Supp. 788 [N.D. Cal. 1986]). The San Bruno permit had been issued to the developer on the basis of a formal habitat conservation agreement for conserving the mission blue butterfly to which FWS, the developer, and a number of local zoning and governmental authorities all were parties. The developer agreed to set aside a portion of project lands as butterfly habitat and to manage it in perpetuity.

After the permit was issued, the City of Brisbane, where the development was to occur, enacted new, more restrictive zoning ordinances that affected the developer's plans. The developer sued the city in federal court, alleging that because of the issuance of the federal incidental taking permit and the related agreements upon which it was based, he had a "vested right" to proceed with the development as

1. In practice, incidental takings of endangered species were never prosecuted either because FWS had no way of knowing when they occurred or was disinclined to prosecute such takings because no criminal intent on the "taker's" part could be proven.

2. See the *Audubon Wildlife Report 1987* for more information on the mission blue butterfly.

contemplated in the permit. The federal court abstained from ruling on the developer's claims, stating that the question of vested right was an issue of state, not federal, law; hence, the issue should be resolved in the state courts. If the federal permit does not confer vested rights upon would-be developers, and the state court also denies vested rights, the enthusiasm of developers to apply for incidental take permits may be dampened. However, irrespective of the vested rights issue, an incidental take/conservation plan permit still will assure participating developers that future activities planned under the permit will not be challenged by the federal government.

At present, incidental take permits have been issued, or are being developed, for major real estate developments in or near Palm Springs, California (affecting the Coachella Valley fringe-toed lizard), San Diego (affecting Bell's least vireo), and North Key Largo, Florida (affecting the American crocodile and several other endangered species). The process of negotiating these permits has typically brought together development, planning, and conservation interests in an effort to reconcile development and conservation needs over a somewhat broader area than has generally been the case with respect to local land-use planning efforts. While this process has both its supporters and its critics, most agree that it represents a rather novel approach to natural-resource planning.

One aspect of the opinion in the *Southwest Diversified* case raises a warning to environmental interests. In a footnote to the opinion, the court said that "[o]nly the government may seek to enforce a section 10(a) [i.e., an incidental taking] permit" (652 F. Supp. at 799 n. 12). Precisely what the court meant by this is difficult to discern. If the court meant that citizens are unable to invoke the act's citizen suit provision against a permittee for failure to comply with one of the conditions of an incidental taking permit (an interpretation consistent with that in *Harmon Cove*), such construction would represent a significant and potentially debilitating result for environmental interests. That interpretation would go well beyond the facts of the *Southwest Diversified* case, however, because the suit was not brought by an environmental group trying to enforce conditions in the FWS permit, but rather was the initiative of a developer trying to enforce the terms of the permit issued to him.

Regulating the Filling of Wetlands

Section 404 of the Clean Water Act is one of the most important federal regulatory efforts governing private land development and its impacts on fish and wildlife habitat. Section 404 requires the Corps of Engineers to regulate the discharge of dredged and fill material into wetlands and other water bodies. Although the *Harmon Cove* case, discussed earlier, represents a setback for conservation interests under the 404 program, two other cases decided early in 1987 represent important gains. In one, *United States v. Akers* (651 F. Supp. 320[E.D. Cal. 1987]), a California ranch owner sought to make major modifications to a nearly 3,000-acre wetland area that served as an important wintering area for Pacific Flyway waterfowl. The Corps advised him that a permit under Section 404 was required before he could undertake the project. The rancher began work without seeking the needed permit. The United States sued. Due to the area's importance to waterfowl, National Audubon Society and the National Wildlife Federation intervened in support of the government's position.

The issue that the *Akers* court had to decide was whether Section 404 of the Clean Water Act applies to human-made wetlands as well as to natural wetlands. The Clean Water Act refers simply to "waters of the United States" without limitation. The Corps' regulations make clear that such waters include wetlands, but define that term to include only areas that "under normal circumstances" support a prevalence of vegetation typically adapted for life in saturated soils (33 C.F.R. 323.2 1987). Akers argued that the wetlands on his ranch resulted from irrigation and flood-control structures that he had built; hence, the land in question did not support wetland vegetation under normal circumstances. The court disagreed, reasoning that the language of the regulations was meant to preclude Corps regulation of areas where wetland vegetation was infrequently found. Since the evident purpose of the federal law is to reach broadly so as to encompass as many activities affecting the hydrological cycle as possible, the court concluded that human-made wetlands are subject to the requirements of Section 404.

A second important case involving the scope of Section 404 was *Monongahela Power Co. v. Marsh* (809 F. 2d 41 [D.C. Cir. *cert. denied,* 108 F. ct. 68 [1987]). In this case, the Federal Energy Regulatory Commission (FERC) had licensed the construction of a private hydroelectric facility on the Blackwater River in the Canaan Valley area of West Virginia, an area rich in wetlands. Since the facility would destroy 7,000 acres of wetlands, the project sponsors[3] also applied to the Army Corps of Engineers for a permit under Section 404 of the Clean Water Act. The Corps, however, denied the permit application on the grounds that the project's environmental impacts were too severe. The power companies then sued, alleging that the Corps had no jurisdiction to require Section 404 permits for FERC-licensed facilities.

3. The sponsors are the Monongahela Power Company, the Potomac Edison Company, and West Penn Power Company.

Interestingly, the issue of Corps jurisdiction had been decided in favor of the Corps more than a decade earlier in a well-known case in a different Court of Appeals—*Scenic Hudson Preservation Conference v. Callaway* (370 F. Supp. 162 [S.D.N.Y. 1973]), *aff'd per curiam* (499 F.2d 127 [2d Cir. 1974]). In *Monongahela,* the power companies sought to avoid the *Scenic Hudson* result by arguing that intervening events[4] had negated the Corps' claim of jurisdiction. The Court of Appeals for the District of Columbia Circuit found this argument unconvincing.

The court was also unwilling to imply a general exemption from Section 404 for all FERC-licensed projects. The power companies had argued for an exemption on the grounds that FERC requires license applicants to submit environmental information as part of the license process. This environmental information is comparable to the information that the Corps must consider under the so-called 404(b)(1) guidelines that govern its review of dredge-and-fill permit applications. The court characterized the FERC information requirements as "unchanneled, precatory invitations for information" that "were designed merely to assist license applicants in submitting information . . . , while [the Clean Water Act guidelines] are standards governing decisions by the Corps on permit applications" (809 F.2d at 52).

The power companies have asked the Supreme Court to review the Court of Appeals decision. If the decision is upheld, private FERC-licensed hydroelectric projects affecting wetlands will be subject to the environmental review provided under Section 404. This may not stop many new hydroelectric projects, however, since the Corps' pro-environment decision denying a permit for the West Virginia project was rather unusual when it occurred in 1978; it would be equally unusual today, as the *Harmon Cove* and *Sierra Club v. Marsh* cases suggest.

NATIVE AMERICANS AND FEDERAL WILDLIFE LAW

One of the most active areas of litigation in recent years involves Native American hunting and fishing rights and their regulation under state and federal wildlife conservation laws. In general, most American Indian tribes claim a right to hunt and fish on their reservations—and

4. Specifically the enactment of federal legislation in 1977 that transferred hydroelectric licensing functions to FERC from the old Federal Power Commission, and a 1976 Supreme Court decision (*Train v. Colorado Public Interest Research Group,* 426 U.S. 1) that pertained to the regulation of nuclear waste under a different provision of the Clean Water Act.

sometimes on nonreservation areas also—as a result of the treaties by which they ceded their claims to nonreservation lands. Such hunting and fishing rights are often spelled out explicitly in the language of the treaties; the courts have also implied such rights from treaties otherwise silent on the matter. The question that has been frequently litigated of late is the extent to which treaty-secured hunting and fishing rights are subject to state or federal regulation in the interest of wildlife conservation.

Most of the litigation to date has concerned state regulation and, in general, American Indians have been quite successful in asserting that their rights are paramount. In 1986, however, the Supreme Court issued a major opinion involving Indian treaty rights and federal conservation authority. In *United States v. Dion* (476 U.S. 734, *enforced*, 800 F. 2d 77 [8th Cir. 1986]), the Supreme Court upheld the supremacy of two important federal wildlife conservation laws—the Bald Eagle Protection Act (16 U.S.C.A. 668 *et seq.*) and the Endangered Species Act—against a claim by a Yankton Sioux Indian that he had a treaty-secured right to hunt eagles irrespective of the hunting prohibitions within those laws. (The *Dion* case is discussed extensively in the *Audubon Wildlife Report 1987*).

The *Dion* decision left a number of important questions undecided. One of these is whether a claim of Indian religious rights—as distinct from treaty rights—would be paramount to the requirements of the two federal statutes. In addition, since the *Dion* court's holding with respect to the Endangered Species Act was inextricably linked to its reasoning with respect to the Bald Eagle Protection Act, the question was left open whether the *Dion* decision would apply to endangered species other than the bald eagle.

Both of these questions were soon addressed in other cases in lower federal courts. In *United States v. Thirty Eight (38) Golden Eagles* (649 F. Supp. 269 [D.Nev. 1986, *aff'd. memo.*, 829 F. 2d 41, 1987]), the district court for the state of Nevada upheld the validity of the Bald Eagle Protection Act against a claim by an American Indian that the act's requirement that Indians obtain a permit in order to take or possess eagles for religious purposes was unconstitutional. That decision, handed down only three months after *Dion*, is at odds with the decision of another federal court in a New Mexico decision just five months earlier, *United States v. Abeyta* (632 F. Supp. 1301[D.N.M. 1986]). The court in the New Mexico case held that the same requirement to secure a federal permit to take or possess eagles violated the First Amendment rights of religious freedom of American Indians. Since the lower federal courts have been unable to articulate a consistent resolution of this contentious issue, a definitive ruling must await a decision from a higher tribunal.

One of the more widely noticed prosecutions of an American Indian for a wildlife offense was the trial of a Seminole Indian, James Billie. Billie was charged with killing a Florida panther, one of the most endangered mammals in the world. He contended that he had acted legally in that he was hunting on the Seminole Reservation, where he had a treaty-protected right to hunt. He also contended that the panther was to be used in a religious ritual and that his action was therefore protected by the First Amendment to the Constitution. Both of these contentions raised issues that had been left undecided by the Supreme Court in the *Dion* case. For a time, many observers believed the Billie prosecution was likely to find its way to the Supreme Court. However, in August 1987, the federal jury trying Billie became deadlocked. Soon after, a separate state prosecution against Billie resulted in acquittal, reportedly because the jury believed the state's efforts to preserve vital evidence had been mishandled. In the wake of the acquittal, the federal government decided not to retry Billie. As a result, the question whether Indian religious freedom claims prevent prosecution under the Endangered Species Act remains unresolved.

Some light may be shed on the question of the relationship between Indian religious rights and federal conservation laws by a decision expected from the Supreme Court in its 1987–88 term. The court will review the decision of the Court of Appeals for the Ninth Circuit in *Northwest Indian Cemetery Protective Ass'n v. Peterson* (795 F.2d 688[9th Cir. 1986]), *cert. granted, Sub. non. Lyng v. Northwest* (107 S. Ct. 1971 [1987]). In that action, several American Indians and an allied association challenged various aspects of the U.S. Forest Service's plans for the management of California's Six Rivers National Forest. The Ninth Circuit held that the plans to permit timber harvesting and build a road in a portion of the forest deemed sacred by several Indian tribes unconstitutionally burdened the Indians' free exercise of religion. In several earlier cases, however, other courts of appeals rejected similar Indian claims with respect to federal land-management activities that allegedly interfered with the Indians' religious use of sacred areas. In all of these cases, the principal legal questions are whether the federal action does, in fact, seriously interfere with religious practices, and if so, whether there is a compelling governmental interest that justifies such interference. Further elaboration by the Supreme Court of what constitutes a compelling governmental interest sufficient to override Indian religious objections to use of public lands can be expected in the *Northwest* case.

The wildlife rights of Native Americans do not derive exclusively from the Constitution and treaties; some have their origin in conservation statutes as well. The Marine Mammal Protection Act (16 U.S.C.A. 1361 *et seq.*), for example, exempts Native Americans on the Alaskan coast from the act's prohibitions against the taking of, and trade in, marine mammals. Any exempted taking must be for the purposes of subsistence or for creating and selling "authentic native articles of handicraft and clothing." The meaning of this authenticity requirement was the subject of litigation in *Katelnikoff v. Dep't of Interior* (657 F.Supp. 659[D. Alaska 1986]).

At issue in *Katelnikoff* were regulations issued by the Secretary of the Interior which limited the handicraft exemption to items that were commonly produced on or before the 1972 enactment of the Marine Mammal Protection Act. The plaintiff, an Aleut, made and sold a variety of distinctly modern curios from sea otter pelts. Some of her stock was seized by FWS on the grounds that it was not of a type produced prior to 1972 and therefore not authentic native handicraft within the meaning of the act and the regulations. She brought suit to recover her goods and to have the regulations declared invalid. The thrust of her claim was that the statute defined "authentic native articles of handicraft and clothing" solely in terms of the methods of manufacture; the regulations, she insisted, exceeded the secretary's statutory authority by imposing the added requirement that the items be of a type commonly produced prior to enactment of the federal law. The court upheld Interior's regulations, noting that the law's legislative history indicated congressional solicitude for "the protection of an extant industry rather than an encouragement to expand into new enterprises," particularly since such an expansion would "necessarily [be] accompanied by greatly increased takings of marine mammals" whose protection was "Congress' overriding purpose in enacting the act" (657 F. Supp. at 663, 665).

Congressional concern for preserving the subsistence cultural traditions of Alaskan natives is also found in the 1980 Alaska National Interest Lands Conservation Act (P.L. No. 96–487). Among other things, Section 810 of the act requires federal land managers to assess carefully the impact of their decisions on the subsistence users of Alaska's natural resources. The Supreme Court had its first opportunity to consider this requirement in 1987 in *Amoco Production Co. v. Village of Gambell* (107 S.Ct. 1396[1987]).

In this case, the Alaskan Native Villages of Gambell and Stebbins sought to enjoin the Secretary of the Interior from going forward with the leasing of outer-continental-shelf areas in Norton Sound and the Navarin Basin of the Bering Sea for oil and gas exploration. The villages contended that the secretary had failed to comply with the requirement of the Alaska National Interest Lands Conservation Act's Section 810 to consider carefully the impacts of such leasing on subsistence users who take marine mammals and seabirds that could be adversely affected by the lease program. In a double setback for subsistence interests, the court held that Section 810 does not apply to federal oil and gas leasing decisions on the Outer Continental Shelf. The court also held that even where Section 810 does apply, courts are free to balance environmental considerations against economic ones in determining whether to enjoin violations of the Section 810 subsistence requirement. (In so ruling, the Supreme Court refused to extend to the *Amoco* case its holding in *TVA v. Hill* (437 U.S. 153 [1978]) that courts are without any authority to balance economic and environmental concerns when violations of the Endangered Species Act occur.)

PROTECTING FOREIGN WILDLIFE

The problem of declining wildlife exists throughout the world. Scientists predict that the most severe loss of species in the years ahead will occur in the forested areas of the tropics. Dr. Norman Myers (1986), for example, has asserted that deforestation in the tropics during the next two decades could cause the extinction of several hundred thousand species of plants and animals.

The United States and its citizens are not mere passive observers of wildlife problems abroad, rather, they often are linked directly to those problems. The United States is one of the world's major markets for international trade in wildlife (see the "International Trade" chapter in this volume for more details). The United States is also one of the major sources of assistance for developing countries, and often finances projects that exact a heavy toll on the environment and wildlife of the developing world.

A variety of federal agencies carry out activities that significantly affect wildlife in other countries. U.S. foreign assistance to developing nations is channeled through the Agency for International Development. Multinational institutions like the World Bank and its regional counterparts funnel even larger sums from the United States and other donor countries to the Third World. The United States participates in these multinational institutions through the Treasury Department, whose representative casts the U.S. vote for or against the projects that these institutions are asked to fund. Even agencies like the Bureau of Reclamation and the Army Corps of Engineers provide technical assistance to foreign nations with respect to water-resource development and other projects. Conservation organizations concerned about the environmental effects of these activities have mounted a longstanding effort to ensure that environmental considerations are taken into account for these projects just as they are for federal projects in the United States.

Applying the Endangered Species Act in Foreign Countries

In *Defenders of Wildlife v. Hodel* (658 F. Supp. 43 [D.Minn 1987]), Defenders and two other organizations sought to ensure that the requirements of Section 7 of the Endangered Species Act are applied to the activities of U.S. agencies abroad. Section 7 requires all federal agencies to ensure that their actions do not jeopardize the continued existence of any threatened or endangered species. Section 7 also imposes a duty on federal agencies to consult with FWS on ways to protect a listed species from being jeopardized by agency projects or actions.

Despite the Supreme Court's far-reaching interpretation of Section 7 in 1978 in *TVA v. Hill,* which said that Section 7 applies to *all* federal actions, FWS in 1986 promulgated regulations that, in at least one respect, significantly narrowed the court's holding (51 *Federal Register* 19930[June 3, 1986]). Specifically, the regulations provided that Section 7 requirements—both substantive and procedural—do not apply to the overseas activities of federal agencies. Thus, under FWS regulations, the Agency for International Development or any other federal agency is not barred by Section 7 from providing funds or assistance for foreign projects that jeopardize the survival of an endangered species or even cause its extinction. Moreover, the Agency for International Development is not even required to consult with FWS to determine what effect its action might have on endangered species. On these points, the 1986 regulations marked a complete about-face from FWS' own prior regulations, which had interpreted Section 7 to apply to the activities of federal agencies abroad.[5]

The suit filed by Defenders of Wildlife with the U.S. District Court for Minnesota sought judicial declaration that FWS' reversal of its prior regulations was unlawful because it imposed a limitation on Section 7's scope that was not authorized by the statute itself. However, rather than consider the merits of the issue, the court held that the plaintiffs could not press their suit because they did not meet constitutional requirements for "standing."

"Standing" is a jurisprudential concept that determines when a person or organization has a sufficient interest in the outcome of a controversy to initiate a lawsuit concerning it. The court seemed to attach the most significance to the fact that the plaintiffs focused their attack on the regulations without seeking to enjoin any specific federal activity abroad that allegedly threatened any endangered species. Thus, the court reasoned, the relief Defenders sought (invalidating the regulations) was unlikely to redress the injury they claimed to suffer (actual harm to endangered species).

While a future plaintiff may be able to raise the same issues raised in this case in the context of a challenge to a specific federal action

5. Although the regulations were not changed until 1986, the conclusion that Section 7 did not apply to federal activities abroad was originally reached in a 1981 legal opinion by the Solicitor's of the Department of Interior.

abroad, the absence of any requirement in the current regulations to consult with FWS about the impacts of federal actions overseas makes it difficult, if not impossible, to determine what impact those actions might have on endangered species. It is possible that this practical difficulty will be recognized by the United States Court of Appeals for the Eighth Circuit, which will hear the appeal, and that the court will not deny standing to Defenders solely because it lacks information regarding species impacts that can only be provided by the federal government.

State Initiatives to Protect Foreign Species

Concern over the potential inadequacy of federal laws to promote the conservation of foreign wildlife in international trade has increasingly motivated the states to take action. In so doing, however, state actions raise a host of legal questions because extensive federal regulation of trade in wildlife under the Endangered Species Act and the Convention on International Trade in Endangered Species (CITES) has been accompanied by uncertainty as to what role, if any, is left to the states. What has long been clear is that the states cannot authorize trade that the Endangered Species Act or CITES prohibits. Less clear is whether the states can impose trade controls more restrictive than federal ones. The uncertainty stems in part from the established legal doctrine that, under certain circumstances, pervasive federal regulation in a given area preempts the states from any regulatory authority in the same area. Compounding this uncertainty is the lack of clarity in Section 6 of the Endangered Species Act, which specifies the types of state regulation allowed or preempted. As a result, the limits of state authority over wildlife trade have often been the subject of litigation.

In 1984, the state of New York enacted a Wild Bird Law (N.Y. Envt'l Conservation Law, sec. 11–1728) prohibiting the sale within the state of wild birds that were not bred in captivity. The law was aimed primarily at the pet industry, since about 90 percent of all imported birds are destined for the pet trade, and most of those are wild-caught rather than captive-bred. The major impetus for the law was not concern that birds in the legal pet trade were in danger of extinction (the Endangered Species Act already prohibits the importation of endangered and threatened birds), but rather concern over the often shockingly high mortality rate of wild-caught birds during the course of capture and transport (Nilsson 1984).

In *Cresenzi Bird Importers, Inc. v. State of New York* (658 F. Supp. 1441[S.D.N.Y., *aff'd.*, 831 F. 2d 410 [2nd Cr. 1987]), several commercial bird importers attacked the legality of the state law. They alleged that the state was without authority to prohibit the sale of imported birds because of the pervasive federal regulation of the international wildlife trade. The importers' claim was made more difficult because they had to distinguish their situation from that of another wildlife importer who several years earlier had unsuccessfully challenged a California law prohibiting the importation and sale of certain nonendangered wildlife (*H.J. Justin & Sons, Inc. v. Deukmejian*, 702 F.2d 758[9th Cir., *cert. denied*, 464 U.S. 823 1983]).

The New York importers advanced an argument not considered in the California litigation. They argued that since they were licensed wildlife importers under Section 9(d) of the Endangered Species Act (which requires the licensing of all wildlife importers and exporters, whether or not they deal in species protected by that act), their licenses constituted "an exemption or permit" that authorized trade. Since, under Section 6(f) of the act, states may not prohibit trade that is authorized under an exemption or permit, the importers argued, the New York law was invalid. The court rejected this argument, holding that the exemption or permits contemplated by Section 6(f) do not include the general type of trading licenses that they held. Thus, the court concluded that nothing in the Endangered Species Act preempted the state of its authority to enact the law in question. The court also rejected a similar preemption argument advanced by the New York importers based on federal quarantine laws.

Another strictly constitutional argument advanced by the *Cresenzi* importers was that the New York law unduly interfered with interstate commerce. A long history of Supreme Court cases over the past century probes the fine line that separates unconstitutional state interference with interstate trade from lawful state regulation of such trade. Among other things, those cases require that, to be constitutionally permissible, state regulation must serve a "legitimate purpose." The importers contended that the law's purpose was to affect activities wholly outside the state and thus did not serve any legitimate local purpose. The court rejected that contention by holding that a state "has an interest in cleansing its markets of commerce which the Legislature finds to be unethical" and "may constitutionally conserve wildlife elsewhere by refusing to accept local complicity in its destruction." The significance of the *Cresenzi* case is that it has galvanized environmental and humane interests to look to state legislatures for wildlife trade controls more restrictive than those of the federal government. Measures similar to the New York Wild Bird Law were introduced in 1987 in both Pennsylvania and New Jersey.

A final case with important implications for the conservation of wildlife beyond U.S. borders is *Federation of Japan Salmon Fisheries Cooperative Ass'n v. Baldridge* (Civ. No. 87–1351[D.D.C. June 15, 1987]). In this action, Alaskan natives and environmentalists challenged the secretary of Commerce's issuance of a Marine Mammal Protection Act permit authorizing Japanese fishermen to take Dall's porpoises "incidentally" while fishing for salmon in the U.S. Exclusive Economic Zone off Alaska. The Marine Mammal Protection Act generally prohibits the killing of any marine mammal, but allows for permits authorizing the incidental capture of marine mammals during commercial fishing operations if such incidental killing can be shown to have no adverse effect on the species caught.

Dall's porpoises are the predominant, but not exclusive, type of marine mammal caught in the nine-mile long driftnets set by Japanese boats; approximately 2,000 Dall's porpoises are caught each year within waters subject to U.S. jurisdiction. Other marine mammals, including northern fur seals, are also caught in Japanese nets, but because the numbers involved are much lower than for the porpoise, the secretary's permit focused exclusively on the porpoise.

Both the environmentalists and Alaskan natives disputed the secretary's authority to ignore the other species, and the court agreed. The court issued a preliminary injunction enjoining the issuance of the disputed permit because the secretary had failed to make any findings with respect to the impact of the anticipated taking on the several other species of marine mammals that were likely to be taken, albeit in smaller numbers.

The legal issue in the case was not complex or novel, but the case is nonetheless important because it threatens the future of the Japanese salmon driftnet fishery off Alaska. This fishery has been the subject of much controversy, not merely because of its impact on marine mammals, but because of its interception of salmon of North American origin and because it is believed to be one of the major sources of plastic debris that entangles and kills marine life in the North Pacific (see the chapter on "Plastic Debris and and Its Effects on Wildlife" in this volume). The case is now on appeal before the United States Court of Appeals for the District of Columbia Circuit. A ruling is likely to occur before the start of the next fishing year in June 1988.

WILDLIFE LAW ENFORCEMENT

Ultimately, the success of many wildlife conservation laws depends on the effectiveness with which they are enforced. In part, the effectiveness of law enforcement is directly dependent on the number of enforcement officers employed. The few dozen FWS port inspectors responsible for enforcing wildlife trade laws are deluged with tens of thousands of wildlife shipments yearly. Because there are so few inspectors, most wildlife shipments are never actually examined by an FWS inspector. Probably no more than one-tenth of the illegal wildlife trade is discovered.

There is another aspect of law enforcement that is impossible to quantify, but which can also have a profound influence on the effectiveness of the enforcement effort: The perception by law-enforcement officials of the seriousness of wildlife violations. Historically, one of the problems hampering effective enforcement has been that many judges (and often prosecutors) do not regard wildlife offenses as particularly serious. Many public prosecutors have seemed reluctant to pursue wildlife cases, particularly since most infractions—even violations of the Endangered Species Act—are merely misdemeanors. Also, judges too have often been disinclined to impose stiff penalties when convictions occur.

A case before a three-judge panel of the United States Court of Appeals for the Third Circuit in late 1986 well illustrates the range of judicial attitudes regarding wildlife violations and some of the obstacles prosecutors face in persuading courts that wildlife offenses are in fact serious. The narrow issue in *United States v. Engler* (806 F.2d 425 [3rd Cir. 1986], *cert. denied,* 107 U.S. 1900[1987]), concerned what most might consider to be a minor legal technicality. Under the Migratory Bird Treaty Act (16 U.S.C.A. 703 *et seq.*), the hunting of a protected migratory bird in violation of federal regulations is a misdemeanor. The government need only prove the fact of unlawful hunting to establish a misdemeanor violation and secure conviction; it is not necessary to prove that the violator knew that he/she was breaking the law when he/she committed the violation. The selling of a protected migratory bird, alive or dead, however, is a felony. Notwithstanding the more serious nature of a felony, a violator may be convicted for breaking the law even without prior knowledge of it.

Edward Engler was convicted by a federal jury of the felony of selling migratory birds to undercover FWS agents. In a post-trial motion, Engler raised a constitutional claim to set aside his conviction. Even though the government had introduced evidence in the trial showing that Engler knew he was unlawfully selling birds, Engler argued that the statute's failure to require any criminal intent for a felony conviction was unconstitutional. The basis of his contention was that constitutional due process requires a prosecutor to prove that a defendant acts with some degree of criminal intent whenever a severe punishment may be imposed, and that Congress' failure to include a criminal intent element in the crime of selling migratory birds violated that constitutional requirement. Engler found support for his contention in a ruling of the Sixth Circuit that was handed down shortly after his trial (*United States v. Wulff* (758 F.2d 1121P[6th Cir. 1985]). The trial court agreed and set aside his conviction. The government appealed.

The three judges who heard the appeal all agreed that Engler's conviction should be reinstated, but they were unable to agree on the rationale for doing so. The majority opinion, by Judge Aldisert, rested upon the rather tenuous argument that whereas most crimes punishable as felonies require some element of criminal intent, the crime of selling migratory birds is a special sort of offense. It belongs in the special category of "public welfare" offenses that seriously harm the public good and for which the ordinary person is presumed to understand that activities harming the public welfare are wrong.[6] The application of this theory to Engler's activity is proper, Judge Aldisert believed, because the preservation of migratory birds is "a national interest of very nearly the first magnitude."[7]

Judge Leon Higginbotham agreed with the result but not with the reasoning. In his view, "the sale of bird parts is neither a public welfare offense nor conduct that an average person would realize was criminal, much less felonious" (806 F.2d at 441). He acknowledged that the protection of birds was "a legitimate issue of public concern," but concluded that it could "hardly be equated with" the concerns underlying the sort of public welfare laws for which the courts had sanctioned strict criminal liability in the past. In short, Higginbotham echoed the view that wildlife offenses are typically perceived as trivial, not serious matters, and was unwilling to convict Engler of a felony if criminal intent is not required by the statute. However, Higginbotham then decided to uphold Engler's conviction by virtue of an implied congressional intent to include criminal intent as part of the act's standards for a felony conviction.

The differences between Judges Aldisert and Higginbotham, as well as their collective disagreement with the Sixth Circuit in *Wulff*, might have been resolved had the Supreme Court reviewed the case, as Engler asked it to do. On April 20, however, the Supreme Court declined review, leaving the *Engler* opinions as telling examples of the ambivalence with which the judiciary regards the importance of wildlife law enforcement.

REFERENCES

Myers, N. 1986. "Tackling Mass Extinction of Species: A Great Creative Challenge." University of California Horace Albright Lectureship in Conservation 1986.

Nilsson, G. 1984. Importation of Birds into the United States 1980–1984. Animal Welfare Institute. Washington, D.C.

Michael J. Bean is a senior attorney and chairman of the wildlife program for the Environmental Defense Fund. He is the author of The Evolution of National Wildlife Law.

6. Public welfare offenses include such things as possession of drugs or possession of a firearm without a permit.

7. Aldisert borrowed this phrase from Justice Oliver Wendell Holmes' opinion upholding the constitutionality of the Migratory Bird Treaty Act more than half a century earlier (*Missouri v. Holland*, 252 U.S. 416P[920]).

Most geese, such as these Canadas, are holding their own, but duck populations continue to slide. Biologists hope that the North American Waterfowl Management Plan will stop the decline. *Ron Nichols/SCS*

Conserving North American Waterfowl: A Plan for the Future

William J. Chandler

INTRODUCTION

In 1986, Canada and the United States launched an ambitious program to restore and maintain waterfowl populations at levels that existed in the 1970s. This undertaking, described in the *North American Waterfowl Management Plan* (U.S. Department of the Interior 1986a), represents "the best opportunity we will ever have" to halt the decline of many species of ducks and geese, according to officials of the U.S. Fish and Wildlife Service (FWS) and Canadian Wildlife Service (CWS).

Waterfowl managers are particularly concerned about duck species that breed in the prairie and parkland regions of the U.S. and Canada. The estimated breeding population of these species dropped 18 percent between 1979 and 1986. While goose populations generally are in good shape, several goose species that breed in the arctic regions of Alaska and Canada have either decreased in numbers or are below optimum population size. These include the Pacific brant, western mid-continent white-fronted goose, and the dusky, cackling, and Aleutian populations of the Canada goose. This chapter will focus on duck species since they constitute the principal restoration objective of the North American plan.

"Revising or modifying activities that destroy or degrade waterfowl habitat is imperative to the future . . . [of North American waterfowl]," states the plan. However, many other issues must be addressed concurrently with habitat conservation efforts, including harvest regulations, pollution, predation and disease.

The timing of the plan's release is opportune for one particular reason: The farm economy in both the United States and Canada is in a slump. Grain crops are in surplus. Farmers are retiring cropland from production and are little inclined to bring new lands, including wetlands, into production.

Waterfowl managers see this as an opportunity to work hand-in-hand with farmers to ensure that lands retired from production are managed to benefit both the farmer and waterfowl. In short, the agricultural crisis has made the farmer more receptive to the gospel of wildlife conservation. And it is the farmer who holds the key to waterfowl conservation, because he owns most of the land in the major duck-breeding regions of the continent: the prairies and parklands of the United States and Canada. In addition, agricultural lands provide vital feeding grounds for wintering populations of ducks and geese.

While the waterfowl plan calls for the continued acquisition of key habitat areas, its major thrust is to preserve, through voluntary changes in land management practices, waterfowl habitat on 3.6 million acres of privately owned land in Canada and 1.9 million acres in the United States. This is the first time a voluntary program of this scope ever has been attempted by the two federal conservation agencies.

STATUS OF NORTH AMERICAN DUCK POPULATIONS

Annual Population Survey

Each year FWS, CWS, and cooperating states and provinces conduct aerial and other surveys of duck-breeding grounds in the prairie-parkland region of the United States and Canada and in parts of Alaska and northern Canada to assess environmental conditions, numbers of breeding ducks, and the number of new ducks added to the population in the current breeding season. These data are used to estimate the total fall-flight population of species that breed in the survey area.[1] Approximately two-thirds of all ducks in the fall flight are produced in the prairie-parkland region. Canada and the United States annually

1. Surveyed areas do not include most black ducks, gadwalls, and other forest-nesting species. However, the survey does cover the breeding habitat with the largest variety of species and largest total number of breeding ducks.

promulgate waterfowl hunting regulations that are designed to achieve a duck harvest level consistent with maintaining a breeding population of sufficient size for the following year. Kill levels are adjusted for individual species as appropriate.

Breeding Population Trends

The estimated breeding population of North American ducks in the surveyed area declined significantly from 1979 through 1985. The 1985 breeding population, 30.8 million, is the lowest recorded since FWS and CWS began conducting the breeding-ground survey in 1955. Populations of certain species were especially low. The mallard count of 5.4 million breeding ducks and the pintail count of 2.9 million are the lowest ever recorded for these species. Also hard hit were the American wigeon and blue-winged teal[2] (see Table 1).

In response to this situation, FWS changed its hunting regulations for the 1985–86 season so as to reduce the total number of ducks killed by hunters in the fall by approximately 25 percent from the 1984 harvest level of 12.5 million. Similar regulations again were promulgated for the 1986–87 and 1987–88 seasons[3] (see Table 2). Canada also took steps to reduce hunting pressure on ducks.

Either as a result of these harvest cut-backs or environmental changes or both, the breeding population increased slightly to 35 million in 1986 and held steady at about that level in 1987 (see Table 3). Nevertheless, the 1987 breeding population was still 12 percent below the long-term average for the 1955–1986 period. Some individual species also remained significantly depressed, including the mallard (19 percent below its long-term average size), the pintail (44 percent), and the blue-winged teal (26 percent) (see Figures 1 to 5).

The Black Duck. The black duck, which breeds in the eastern United States and Canada, has been in a long-term decline since 1955. Although winter population surveys showed some increase in black duck population between 1985 and 1986 in both the Atlantic and Mississippi flyways, the increase was short-lived. The 1987 survey indicates that black duck numbers decreased 17 percent from 1986 and are 14 percent below the 10-year average. The Atlantic Flyway population index for black ducks—194,100—is the lowest ever recorded. The Atlantic population decreased 14 percent from 1986, the Mississippi population 23 percent (see Figure 6).

2. Statistics in this chapter are derived from FWS publications, especially the annual *Status of Waterfowl and Fall Flight Forecast* (U.S. Department of the Interior 1987a).

3. According to FWS' Office of Migratory Bird Management, the 1985 harvest level was 9.5 million ducks, the 1986 kill, 9.3 million.

Table 1
Breeding P●pulation Estimates for 10 Species of Ducks, 1955–87 (in Thousands).[a]

Year	Mallard	Gadwall	American wigeon	Green-winged teal	Blue-winged teal	Northern shoveler	Northern pintail	Redhead	Canvasback	Scaup
1955	10,[illegible]45	1,106	3,333	2,076	6,436	1,965	9,251	733	595	7,100
1956	11,[illegible]11	1,202	3,712	1,898	6,267	2,084	10,124	928	692	6,595
1957	10,[illegible]46	1,102	3,208	1,293	5,449	1,744	6,856	684	600	6,535
1958	12,[illegible]04	687	3,372	1,618	5,799	1,515	6,889	524	713	6,040
1959	10,[illegible]92	683	3,779	3,153	5,300	1,649	7,228	641	481	8,220
1960	8,[illegible]06	873	3,165	1,630	4,303	1,859	5,769	542	575	5,566
1961	8,[illegible]90	1,422	3,219	2,216	4,833	1,625	4,860	437	396	6,764
1962	6,[illegible]44	1,610	2,721	1,119	3,890	1,633	4,299	664	385	6,398
1963	7,[illegible]60	1,578	2,209	1,754	4,587	1,435	4,361	396	523	6,564
1964	6,[illegible]74	1,223	2,630	2,051	4,943	1,685	4,111	560	658	6,326
1965	5,[illegible]48	1,692	2,695	1,526	4,628	1,607	4,301	568	505	5,383
1966	7,40[illegible]	1,976	2,901	2,219	5,616	2,272	5,777	747	683	5,421
1967	8,205	1,638	2,637	1,944	4,715	2,244	5,870	846	556	5,877
1968	7,586	2,098	2,783	1,805	3,697	1,811	4,225	502	557	5,971
1969	8,065	1,837	3,192	1,991	4,514	2,150	6,390	759	530	6,338
1970	10,[illegible]79	1,698	3,752	2,259	5,633	2,269	7,004	834	601	6,930
1971	9,843	1,733	3,425	2,352	5,426	2,052	6,291	693	441	6,149
1972	9,857	1,776	3,428	2,407	5,673	2,505	7,875	489	429	9,527

1973	8,781	1,198	3,665	2,444	4,866	1,657	5,114	754	696	7,535
1974	7,392	1,562	3,003	2,221	5,437	2,060	7,165	613	493	7,045
1975	8,109	1,672	2,862	2,038	6,441	1,994	6,387	974	706	7,846
1976	8,637	1,478	2,699	1,844	5,023	1,818	6,045	946	686	6,973
1977	8,226	1,546	2,678	1,952	4,626	1,616	4,971	688	702	7,490
1978	7,695	1,593	3,808	2,978	4,497	2,162	5,664	833	423	7,125
1979	8,444	1,889	3,388	2,920	5,278	2,555	6,070	774	606	9,135
1980	8,003	1,459	3,857	2,925	4,903	2,050	5,420	1,146	688	7,690
1981	6,757	1,479	3,555	2,515	4,076	2,403	4,227	825	594	7,253
1982	6,684	1,690	3,159	2,247	3,879	2,540	4,112	674	543	6,549
1983	7,107	1,536	2,923	2,574	3,381	2,237	4,086	866	528	8,788
1984	5,974	1,799	3,979	1,804	3,870	2,222	3,664	849	569	8,402
1985	5,475	1,410	2,506	1,873	3,756	1,925	2,935	701	411	6,235
1986	6,303	1,590	2,446	2,588	4,664	2,403	3,201	956	442	6,252
1987	6,691	1,705	2,734	3,041	3,618	2,229	3,137	767	478	6,261
Goals[b]	8,700	1,600	3,300	2,300	5,300	2,100	6,300	760	580	7,600
1955–86 Average	8,252	1,495	3,147	2,132	4,888	1,992	5,642	723	563	6,938
Percent Change in 1987 from:										
1986	+6	+7	+12	+18	-22	-7	-2	-20	+8	NC
1955–86 Ave.	-19	+14	-13	+43	-26	+12	-44	+6	-15	-10

Source: U.S. Department of the Interior 1987a.

[a] All duck indexes adjusted for visibility bias.

[b] Breeding duck population goals, from *North American Waterfoul Management Plan* (Fish and Wildlife Service, Canadian Wildlife Service 1986).

Table 2
Estimated Annual U.S. Duck Harvest[a] by Flyway, 1952–1985. (in thousands).

Year	Pacific Flyway[b]		Central Flyway		Mississippi Flyway		Atlantic Flyway		United States
	Harvest	Percent	Harvest	Percent	Harvest	Percent	Harvest	Percent	Total[b]
1952	4,770	33.1	3,112	21.6	5,164	35.8	1,365	9.5	14,411
1953	4,401	33.1	3,031	22.8	4,577	34.4	1,289	9.7	13,298
1954	3,837	33.1	2,303	19.8	4,143	35.7	1,319	11.4	11,602
1955	4,025	28.4	3,033	21.4	5,343	37.8	1,751	12.4	14,153
1956	3,603	27.4	2,997	22.8	5,054	38.5	1,488	11.3	13,142
1957	4,356	28.3	3,835	24.9	5,708	37.1	1,494	9.7	15,394
1958	4,285	33.1	2,626	20.3	4,733	36.6	1,289	10.0	12,934
1959	2,182	31.4	1,315	18.9	2,743	39.5	704	10.1	6,943
1960	2,510	31.5	1,452	18.2	3,129	39.3	868	10.9	7,959
1961	2,066	38.7	788	14.8	1,747	32.7	738	13.8	5,339
1962	1,948	45.9	428	10.1	1,129	26.6	742	17.5	4,247
1963	2,832	39.0	1,012	14.0	2,505	34.5	905	12.5	7,255
1964	2,530	30.2	1,321	15.8	3,537	42.2	994	11.9	8,382
1965	2,975	33.7	1,219	13.8	3,618	41.0	1,021	11.6	8,833
1966	3,570	29.7	2,135	17.7	4,902	40.7	1,423	11.8	12,030
1967	4,438	34.7	2,240	17.5	4,770	37.3	1,345	10.5	12,792
1968	3,095	38.3	1,237	15.3	2,384	29.5	1,372	17.0	8,088

1969	4,108	31.6	2,597	20.0	4,493	34.6	1,802	13.9	13,000
1970	4,480	28.1	2,996	18.8	6,455	40.6	1,986	12.5	15,917
1971	4,049	29.0	2,795	20.0	5,381	38.6	1,724	12.4	13,949
1972	3,964	29.2	2,966	21.8	5,005	36.8	1,650	12.1	13,586
1973	3,306	27.8	2,447	20.6	4,592	38.6	1,547	13.0	11,892
1974	3,657	28.6	2,218	17.3	5,193	40.6	1,733	13.5	12,801
1975	4,091	26.4	2,934	18.9	6,603	42.6	1,858	12.0	15,487
1976	4,256	28.0	2,805	18.5	6,041	39.8	2,093	13.8	15,195
1977	3,193	23.7	2,440	18.1	5,956	44.2	1,882	14.0	13,470
1978	4,099	26.7	2,969	19.3	6,340	41.3	1,946	12.7	15,355
1979	3,476	24.1	2,707	18.8	6,383	44.3	1,849	12.8	14,415
1980	3,310	25.0	2,106	15.9	5,900	44.5	1,936	14.6	13,252
1981	2,774	22.7	2,040	16.7	5,476	44.9	1,904	15.6	12,194
1982	2,986	25.2	2,238	18.9	5,026	42.3	1,621	13.7	11,872
1983	3,158	24.4	2,147	16.6	5,926	45.9	1,692	13.1	12,923
1984	2,568	20.4	2,326	18.5	5,838	46.4	1,844	14.7	12,576
1985	2,225	24.1	1,503	16.3	4,124	44.7	1,366	14.8	9,218
1952–85:									
Average	3,445	29.0	2,244	18.9	4,703	39.6	1,487	12.5	11,879

Source: Office of Migratory Bird Management, U.S. Fish and Wildlife Service.

[a] Retrieved kill of all species combined based on questionnaire survey data summarized as follows: 1952–60 by state of duck-stamp purchase; 1961–85 by state of harvest.

[b] Includes Alaska during the periods 1952–55 and 1965–85.

Table 3
Duck Breeding Population Estimates in Survey Area (Plus Estimated Breeding Populations in Six States Not in Survey Area (in Thousands).

Survey Area	1986	1987	Percent Change
Alaska—Old Crow Flats	4,327	4,426	+ 2
N. Alberta—NE. British Columbia—Northwest Territories	7,498	8,604	+15
N. Saskatchewan—N. Manitoba—W.Ontario[a]	3,278	3,845	+17
S. Alberta	2,685	3,190	+19
S. Saskatchewan	6,244	5,553	−11
S. Manitoba	1,990	1,368	−31
Montana	601	838	+39
Wyoming[b]	356	340	− 4
Colorado[b]	105	125	+19
North Dakota	3,138	3,008	− 4
South Dakota	3,771	2,564	−32
Nebraska[b]	69	120	+74
Minnesota[b]	534	615	+15
California[b]	106	114	+ 8
Wisconsin[b]	332	370	+11
TOTAL	35,034	35,080	NC

Source: U.S. Department of the Interior 1987a.
[a] W. Ontario was surveyed in 1986 and 1987.
[b] State not in survey area, but which estimates breeding duck population within its territory.

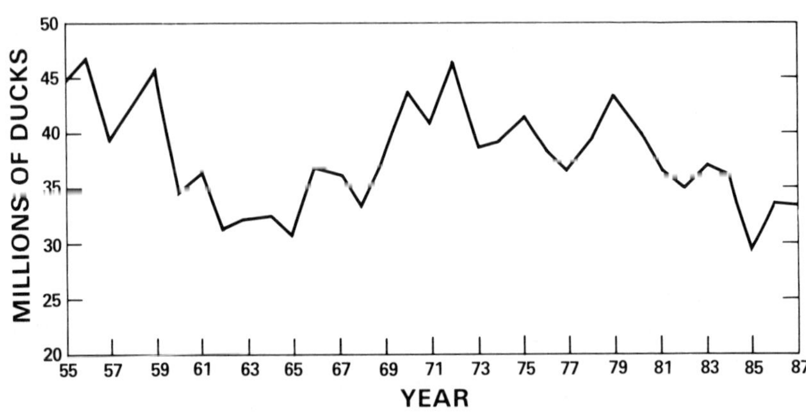

Figure 1. Estimated duck breeding population in survey area. Source: *Status of Waterfowl and Fall Flight Forecast* 1987.

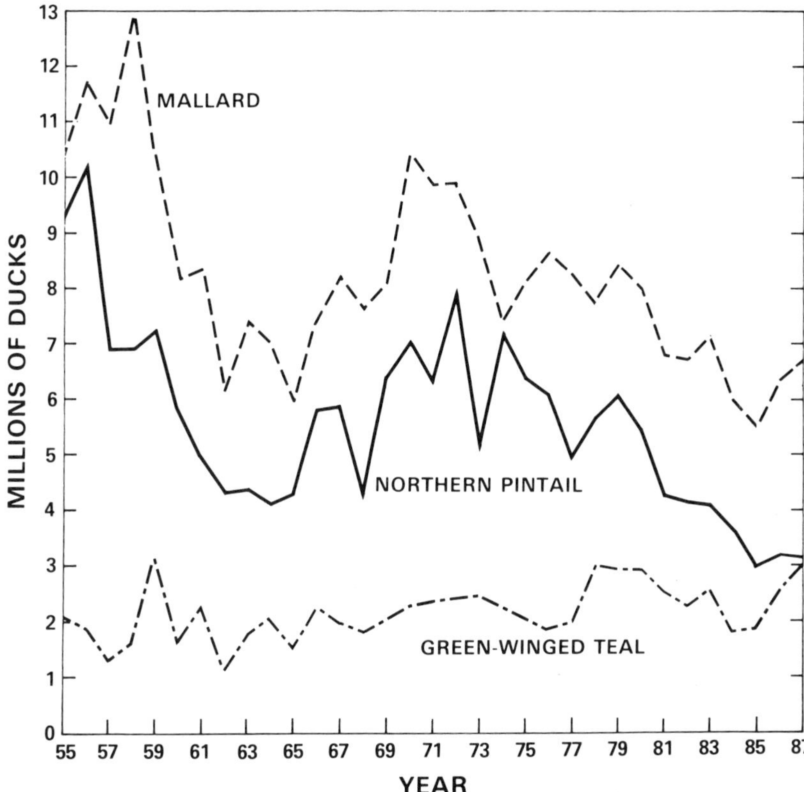

Figure 2. Estimated breeding population in survey area: mallard, northern pintail, and green-winged teal. Source: *Status of Waterfowl and Fall Flight Forecast* 1987.

Hunting regulations designed to reduce the harvest of black ducks have been in effect since 1983 in the United States and since 1984 in Canada.[4] However, the population trend continues downward. Several factors are thought to contribute to the decline, including habitat degradation and loss, hybridization with mallards (which have invaded or been purposefully introduced into black duck range),[5] and perhaps overharvest. The exact relationships of these factors in the decline are not well understood and are the subjects of ongoing research. (For further information on the species, see "The Black Duck," *Audubon Wildlife Report 1986*.)

4. Harvest cut-backs have been greater in the United States than Canada according to FWS officials.

5. Some state wildlife agencies have sponsored the release of captive bred mallards in black duck areas because of the popularity of mallards among hunters. New York and Pennsylvania once conducted such releases, but no longer do; Maryland still releases large numbers of mallards annually.

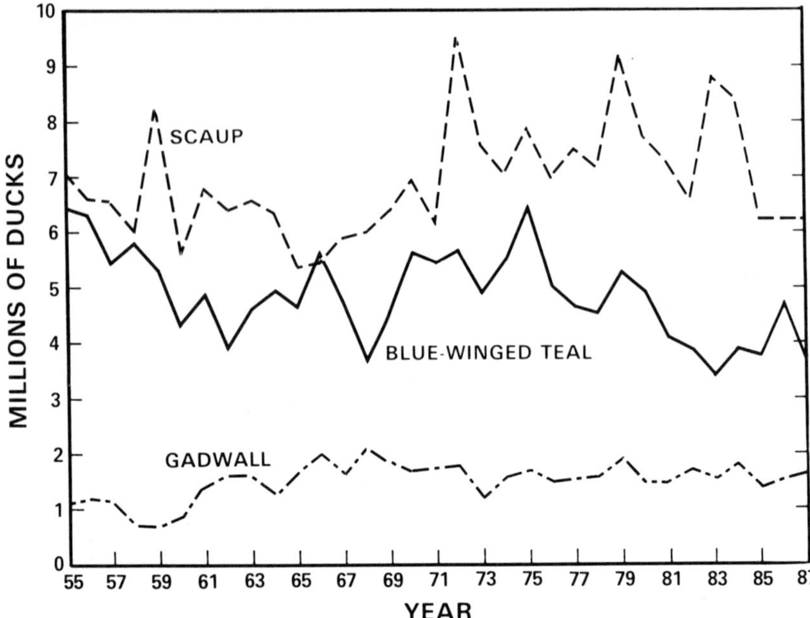

Figure 3. Estimated breeding population in survey area: greater and lesser scaup (combined), blue-winged teal, and gadwell. Source: *Status of Waterfowl and Fall Flight Forecast* 1987.

Causes for Decline

A number of interacting factors influence the population size of ducks, including climate and weather, the quantity and quality of habitat available, nest success and recruitment, and mortality from hunting, predation, and disease. According to FWS biologists, the primary reasons for the 1979–85 breeding population decline are the multiyear

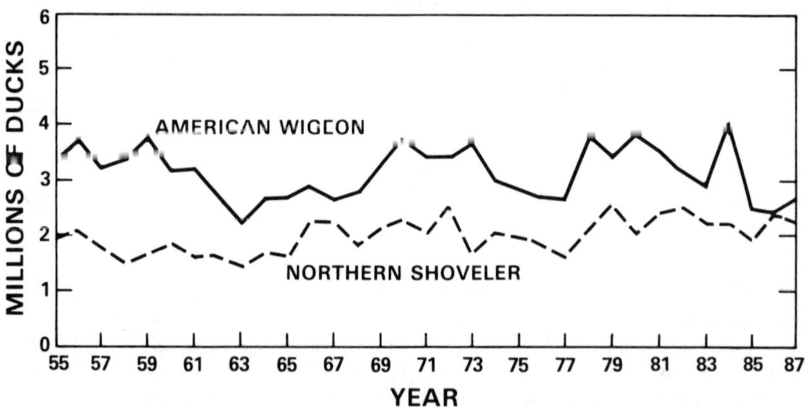

Figure 4. Estimated breeding population in survey area: american wigeon and northern shoveler. Source: *Status of Waterfowl and Fall Flight Forecast* 1987.

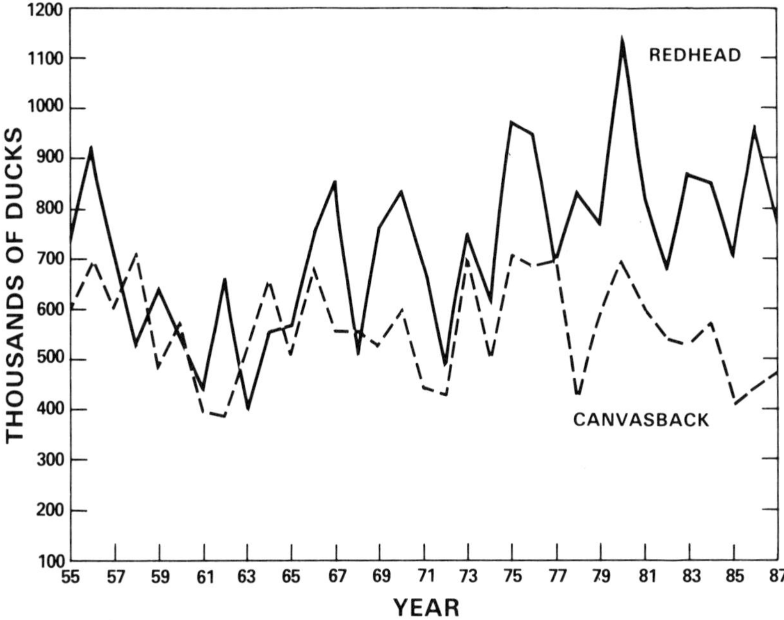

Figure 5. Estimated breeding population in survey area: redhead and canvasback. Source: *Status of Waterfowl and Fall Flight Forecast* 1987.

drought that has occurred in large portions of the prairie-parkland breeding area and the degradation and permanent loss of breeding habitat.

Also implicated in the decline is the poor nest success and low recruitment experienced by certain prairie-nesting species. When wet

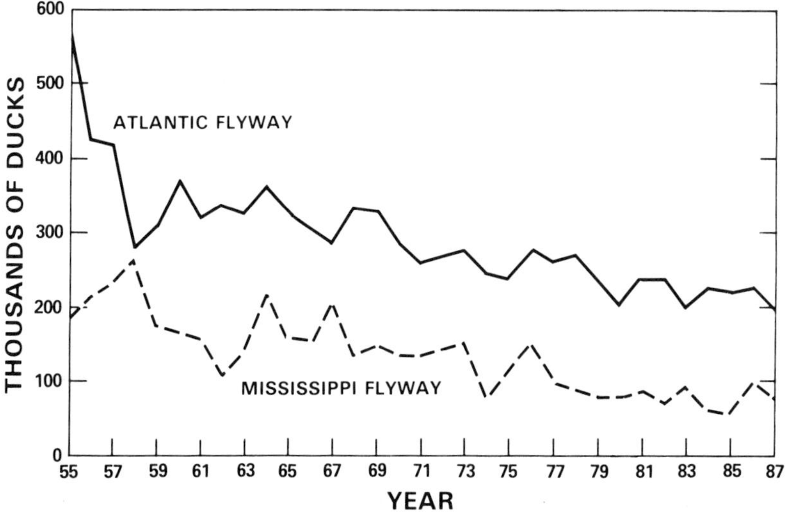

Figure 6. Trends in black duck populations in the Atlantic and Mississippi flyways (midwinter surveys). Source: *Status of Waterfowl and Fall Flight Forecast* 1987.

lands and associated uplands used by ducks for nesting cover are degraded or destroyed, ducks and their eggs are highly susceptible to predation from foxes, skunks, coyotes, ground squirrels, raccoons, and birds of prey. Abnormally high predation levels mean that fewer eggs are hatched and fewer new birds recruited into the population.

Drought. Some of the wetlands used by ducks for breeding, feeding, nesting, and rearing young are ephemeral, others permanent. Generally, the more ponds of all types there are in the breeding area and the longer those ponds remain wet, the more likely it is that ducks will have a good production year.

Duck populations are known to fluctuate with cyclical precipitation levels in the prairie-parkland region. When droughts occur, populations decline; when precipitation increases, populations increase. Previous major declines in duck numbers such as those that occurred in the 1930s and from 1958 to 1965 have been associated with drought periods.

Once the current drought cycle ends, populations again are expected to increase. Yet there is justifiable concern among waterfowl managers that population levels may not reach those achieved in the 1970s because other factors besides precipitation are now operating to suppress populations to a greater extent than previously. Such factors include large-scale degradation and loss of breeding habitat and low recruitment of new ducks into the population due to increased predation.

Habitat Destruction. Waterfowl habitat has been severely altered by humans. According to FWS, less than half of the nation's original wetlands acreage remains. Wetlands have been destroyed to accommodate numerous human activities, including agriculture, industry, flood control, navigation, recreation, and settlement.

Even though the ecological, economic, and scientific values of wetlands have been well-documented, neither the United States nor Canada have federal laws that categorically prohibit the drainage of wetlands. Wetlands loss in the United States continues at an estimated rate of 300,00 to 450,000 acres per year. Eighty-seven percent of all wetlands losses from the mid-1950s to the mid-1970s were due to agriculture (Tiner 1984).

Equally important is the destruction of prairie grasslands located near wetlands which provide nesting cover for species like the pintail and mallard. Loss of remaining tracts of prairie grasslands in the north central United States continues at a rate of about 2 percent annually; in the last decade, one-third of the remaining grasslands was converted to cropland (U.S. Department of the Interior 1986a).

Duck-breeding habitat in the prairie-parkland region is especially susceptible to destruction by agriculture because the soils, topography, and climate of the region are highly favorable to grain production. Agricultural development of the prairies has severely affected waterfowl habitat. For example, North and South Dakota have lost 4 million acres of wetlands; Minnesota, 9 million acres; Iowa has lost 95 percent of its original wetlands acreage (Tiner 1984). Such losses have:

> . . . interrupted the natural relationships that have evolved between ducks and their environment. Losses of upland nesting cover and small ephemeral prairie wetlands have concentrated ducks and their predators in remaining patches of suitable habitat. As a result, in much of the prairie pothole region, recruitment of young is inadequate to maintain or build certain waterfowl population levels even in years of favorable water conditions (U.S. Department of the Interior 1986a).

Habitat Loss in Canada. Breeding habitat loss in Canada also has been substantial, though not quite as pervasive as in the United States. Nevertheless, the trend in agricultural practices and land conversion in the prairie-parkland region of Canada does not bode well for ducks. Some examples:

- In the prairie provinces of Alberta, Saskatchewan, and Manitoba, the total area annually cultivated increased by 25.7 percent between 1951 and 1981; pasture lands increased by 129.1 percent. At the same time, the amount of unimproved land decreased by 28.9 percent, and wooded areas by 66.9 percent.
- Total wetlands loss in the three provinces is estimated to be 40 percent of the original wetlands acreage. In some locales, the loss is much greater (Turner *et al.* 1987).

A recent study of about 10,000 wetlands in 65 study areas in the prairie provinces found that 57.2 percent of wetlands basins and 73.9 percent of the margin land contiguous to the basins was in degraded condition when the study began. A five-year (1981 to 1985) monitoring of land-use practices at the 10,000 sites showed an increase in degradation of both wetlands and margin lands due to haying, grazing, burning, draining, filling, clearing, or cultivation. At the end of the study, 59.3 percent of the wetlands and 84.2 percent of the margins were degraded. Most of the land-use practices that degraded habitat—haying, burning, cultivating—were transitory in nature; if discontinued, the affected lands would restore naturally. However, when such activities are conducted annually, their effects are, in essence, permanent.

Actual drainage of wetlands at the 65 study sites was low. The drainage rate in Saskatchewan was 0.19 percent, Manitoba, 0.25 percent, and Alberta, 0.53 percent. However, researchers note that such rates "should not instill complacency because wetland consolidation and subsurface drainage programs are currently being promoted in prairie-Canada" (Turner *et al.* 1987).

Nest Success and Recruitment. Degradation and loss of breeding habitat have a variety of impacts on ducks. At a simplistic level, loss of quantity means less acreage for duck nesting and rearing of young, hence fewer ducks. In addition, as ducks are crowded into fewer, smaller sites, or are forced to nest on lands with inadequate nesting cover, other factors, such as predation, operate to reduce population size.

In a study of nest success on 17 study areas in 3 Canadian provinces from 1982 to 1985, FWS researchers estimated mallard nest success[6] for the study areas. They found that the nest success rate averaged just 12 percent for the 1,500 to 1,600 mallard nests studied. For individual study areas the success rate ranged from 2 percent to 29 percent; in only seven instances did the nest success rate for particular study areas exceed 15 percent (Greenwood *et al.* 1987). According to FWS scientists, the mallard population must have a nest success rate above 15 percent to experience *any* population growth;[7] a rate lower than 15 percent means that the population will decrease.

Predation. Predators can have a significant influence on the nest success of ground-nesting ducks; they catch and kill nesting hens and eat eggs. The species composition of the predator community and the abundance of those species varies from area to area and over time. The eight species known to prey on prairie-nesting ducks are the coyote, red fox, raccoon, striped skunk, badger, Franklin's ground squirrel, American crow, and black-billed magpie. Of these, the red fox is believed to cause the most harm. In the prairie nest success study, five or more predators were present in each study area each year, and "at least three species were abundant-to-common in each area every year. There was little annual change in composition and abundance of predators on most areas studied more than one year" (Greenwood *et al.* 1987).

Nearly 75 percent of all mallard nests studied were destroyed by predators. In addition, predators had destroyed one or more eggs in 6 percent of abandoned nests and are believed to have killed the nesting hen on other abandoned nests. Nest success was highest in study areas characterized by a large block of native grassland used for pasture, numerous wetlands, and a predator community dominated by coyotes.

6. According to a FWS biologist, nest success is the one phenomenon associated with recruitment which may be reliably studied with current methodologies. Nest success is the percentage of nests that have one or more eggs that hatch.

7. This rule-of-thumb is based on the detailed FWS study of a population of mallards in a particular area of North Dakota.

> Large pastures not only allow ducks to space their nests widely, thereby possibly reducing the chance of detection by predators, but also may influence the make-up of the predator community. For instance, large pastures may afford protection to the coyote, a species that does well in prairie environment, but that is vulnerable to human-inflicted mortality . . . The red fox is also highly adapted to living in prairie, but where the two species are sympatric, coyotes tend to exclude red foxes from large blocks of habitat . . . The red fox is probably the most serious predator on upland-nesting ducks in the prairie pothole region . . . and its absence is a benefit to nesting ducks. All of the large pastures in our study areas were occupied by coyotes and had few red foxes; however, red foxes were common in most areas of cropland. The predator communities on our study areas comprised many of the same species that are held responsible for low nest success in the prairie pothole region in the United States (Greenwood *et al.* 1987).

FWS biologists also suspect, but have not yet demonstrated, that the coyote limits or excludes raccoons, a voracious egg predator. In earlier times, raccoons were confined to wooded river valleys and did not occupy open prairies. But young raccoons seeking to establish a home territory have been attracted to prairie lands due to the farms there that provide them with shelter (trees and brush) and food sources.

Drought may accentuate the adverse impact of predators on ducks because it changes the availability and quantity of a predator's usual food sources. For example, ducks like the mallard that tend to return to the same site each year for nesting may become more sought after as a food source by predators when other prey decline in abundance due to drought.

Migrating and Winter Habitat. While sufficient breeding habitat is vital to population maintenance, ducks also require adequate "stop-over" habitat during migration and suitable habitat for wintering in the United States and Mexico. FWS has established several hundred refuges to protect both migration and wintering sites favored by waterfowl. Although it is generally believed that migration and wintering habitat are better protected than breeding habitat, the degradation or loss of wetlands in stopover sites and wintering zones is a significant problem in all flyways. Some examples:

- About 60 percent of all ducks and geese in the entire Pacific Flyway winter in the Central Valley of California. More than 95 percent of the valley's original wetlands have been destroyed. Approximately 281,000 acres of wetlands still exist, of which about 90,000 are still unprotected.
- In the lower Mississippi alluvial plain, a U.S. Department of Agriculture study (Heimlich and Langer 1986) estimates that

398,000 acres of wetlands are potentially convertible to agricultural use. Federal and state waterfowl managers have determined that at least 366,000 acres of wetlands in the alluvial plain should be acquired to help sustain wintering populations of mallards, pintails, and other waterfowl. In addition, another 386,000 acres of coastal wetlands need protection.

- Along the Atlantic coast, waterfowl managers say that another 60,000 acres of black duck habitat—50,000 acres in the United States and 10,000 in Canada—must be protected for migration and wintering purposes.

If ducks do not have adequate resting and feeding sites during migration and while wintering, they become vulnerable to several mortality factors. First, the general physical condition of the flock deteriorates, and its members may starve or succumb to disease. Second, as the quantity of wetlands declines, birds are crowded into remaining areas, which makes them more prone to diseases such as avian cholera and botulism. Third, crowding also makes birds more vulnerable to being shot by hunters. Fourth, inadequate diet caused by crowding birds into areas with insufficient food supplies can cause some individuals to fail to reproduce the following breeding season.

To maintain desired populations of waterfowl, wildlife managers may take a variety of actions to either increase the total number of birds added to the population each year or to decrease the total number of birds that die each year from hunting and other causes. According to FWS biologists, the primary requirement for duck population growth is adequate breeding, migration, and wintering habitat. However, as total habitat is reduced, managers have sought ways to increase duck production on remaining habitat to compensate. Duck production techniques include the planting of vegetation for nesting cover, construction of nest structures, provision of water and food sources, and the control of predators.

Hunting Mortality. According to FWS, the hunting of waterfowl, while directly controllable, is not a threat to most duck populations as long as kill levels do not exceed a certain percentage of a species' population. FWS-sponsored studies of the relationship between hunting mortality and natural mortality indicate that many birds killed by hunters would otherwise die of natural causes anyway (disease, weather, starvation, etc.). However, FWS research has not been able to identify definitively at what point the total hunter-kill becomes great enough to reduce the breeding population the following spring more than would occur under natural conditions (without hunting).

The North American Waterfowl Management Plan

The recent decline in duck breeding populations during a drought period has once again focused the attention of wildlife managers on goals, objectives, and strategies for waterfowl management. As a result, FWS and CWS have come up with a new assessment of waterfowl problems, needs, and solutions. That assessment is embodied in the North American Waterfowl Management Plan.

The North American Waterfowl Management Plan is a statement of needs, goals, objectives and strategies required to perpetuate waterfowl populations at desired levels. The plan commits the United States and Canada to maintaining an average annual continental duck-breeding population of 62 million birds which, states the plan, is the minimum number needed "to meet public demand."[8] This continental objective was derived by summing the estimated average breeding population for each of 29 duck species during a period of years (1970 to 1979) when duck production ranged from excellent (1970 to 1972) to average (1973 to 1979) relative to other years[9] (see Table 4).

Some ducks are more sought after by hunters than others. The most important sport species are dabbling ducks (nine species) and, to a lesser extent, the diving ducks (six species). The highest breeding densities of both diving and dabbling ducks occur in the prairies and parklands of the United States and Canada.

Population levels of 6 of the 10 most common species in the survey area are substantially below the plan's continental population objectives (see Table 5). These shortfalls will have to be made up through a combination of actions, including habitat conservation, increasing the production of ducks on publicly owned refuges and other areas, and control of hunter harvest levels.

Habitat Strategy and Objectives

According to the North American plan, the major threats to both duck and geese populations continue to be degradation and loss of habitat in breeding, migration, and wintering areas. Duck populations are especially at risk: "Loss of nesting cover, wetland drainage, and degradation of migration and wintering habitat have contributed to long-term downward trends in some important duck populations." The plan

8. In the case of ducks, public demand is virtually identical with hunter demand. Nonhunters such as bird watchers and wildlife enthusiasts also benefit from waterfowl populations but nonconsumptive demand is hard to measure and has been little studied.

9. Note that the continental breeding population objective of 62 million is different than the breeding population estimate FWS makes for the surveyed area. The continental population is the sum of the breeding population in the surveyed area plus the estimated duck population in all other unsurveyed areas.

Table 4
Estimated Average Population of Breeding Ducks in North America, 1970–1979. (in thousands).

Species	Surveyed Areas[a] U.S.	Canada	Total	Unsurveyed areas	Continental estimate
Dabbling ducks					
Mallard	2,066	6,675	8,741	1,926	10,667
Pintail	2,332	3,927	6,259	745	7,004
Black duck		88	88	1,340	1,428
Gadwall	512	1,102	1,614	380	1,994
Wigeon	956	2,315	3,271	216	3,487
Green-winged teal	482	1,889	2,371	740	3,111
Blue-winged and cinnamon teal	1,719	3,571	5,290	856	6,146
Shoveler	654	1,415	2,069	100	2,169
Wood duck				3,230	3,230
Diving ducks					
Redhead	221	539	760	120	880
Canvasback	119	459	578	64	642
Lesser and greater scaup	1,333	6,243	7,576	322	7,898
Ring-necked duck	16	533	549	419	968
Ruddy duck	216	316	532	120	652
Sea ducks					
Hooded, red-breasted and common merganser	9	578	587	915	1,502
Bufflehead	82	805	887	195	1,082
Common and Barrow's goldeneye	126	603	729	740	1,469
Harlequin				165	165
Oldsquaw	600	828	1,428	1,275	2,703
King and common eider	22	1	23	2,443	2,466
Black, white-winged and surf scoter	346	1,065	1,411	579	1,990
TOTAL	11,811	32,952	44,763	16,890	61,653

Source: *North American Waterfowl Management Plan* (U.S. Department of the Interior 1986a).
[a] Includes data from Strata 1–50 and the six states that contribute information to the annual *Status of Waterfowl and Fall Flight Forecast.*

states that "Reversing or modifying activities that destroy or degrade waterfowl habitat is imperative to the future success of waterfowl management" and calls for "creative action" to achieve that end.

To produce 62 million breeding ducks annually, waterfowl habitat must resemble that of the 1970s in terms of types, quantity, and quality. To achieve that goal, the plan calls for protecting another 5.60 million acres of land – 1.93 million in the United States, 3.67 million in Canada – in addition to waterfowl areas that already are protected. The acreage to be protected lies within five "priority habitat ranges."

Table 5

	Population status in survey area (in thousands)	Plan goal (year 2000)
Mallard	6,691	8,700
American wigeon	2,734	3,000
Blue-winged teal	3,618	5,300
Northern pintail	3,137	6,300
Canvasback	478	580
Scaup (greater and lesser)	6,261	7,600

Two of these ranges lie wholly within the United States and three include lands in both the United States and Canada (see Figure 7).

Specific land-protection goals within the priority ranges are as follows:

1. To restore mallard and pintail breeding habitat in the mid-continent region to 1970–1979 levels by protecting and improving 3.6 million additional acres in Canada and about 1.1 million additional acres in the United States for duck production. These estimates are based on a ratio of three acres of upland nesting cover per acre of water.
2. To protect 686,000 additional acres of mallard and pintail migration and wintering habitat in the lower Mississippi River-Gulf Coast region, and increase the carrying capacity for wintering birds on lands and waters already acquired for waterfowl.
3. To improve the quality of publicly managed habitat, and protect and restore 80,000 additional acres of wintering habitat for pintails and other waterfowl in the Central Valley of California.
4. To protect 60,000 additional acres of breeding and migration habitat in the Great Lakes-St. Lawrence lowlands for black ducks and other waterfowl in Canada and 10,000 additional acres in the United States.
5. To protect and enhance migration and wintering habitat for black ducks by:

   a. protecting 50,000 additional acres of migration and wintering habitat on the east coast of the United States;
   b. protecting 10,000 additional acres on the east coast of Canada;

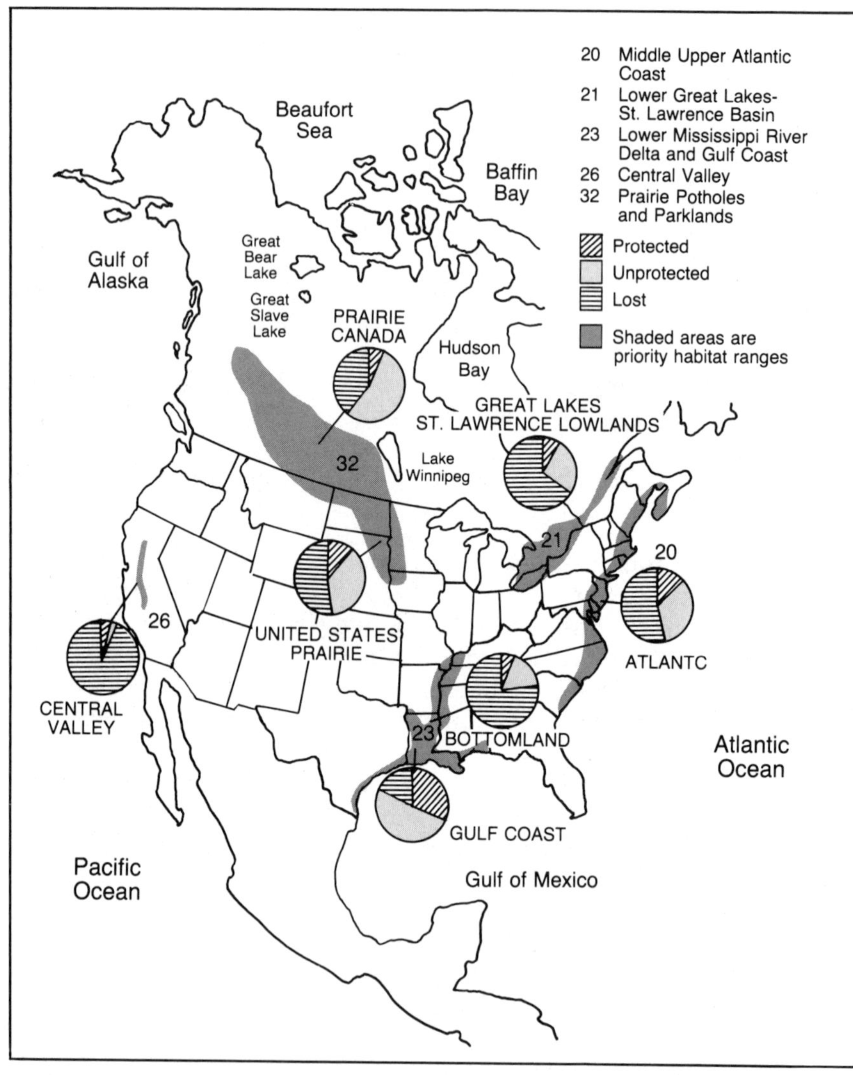

Figure 7. Status of the habitat in key priority habitat ranges. Source: *North American Waterfowl Management Plan* (U.S. Department of the Interior, 1986a).

c. improving habitat quality of other areas in the region; and

d. producing a 25 percent increase in carrying capacity of 382,500 acres of land managed for waterfowl use by wildlife agencies in the eastern United States (U.S. Department of the Interior 1986a).

About 14 percent of the 3.6 million Canadian acres scheduled for protection will be purchased in fee title or conservation easements; the rest will remain privately owned. Lands in the United States will be protected through a combination of acquisition, voluntary agreements with private landowners, and other methods (see following section).

According to the plan, "The major requirement for waterfowl conservation in North America is to influence land-use practice on extensive areas across the continent." In other words, CWS and FWS officials must devise strategies to get private landowners to manage their property in ways that are compatible with waterfowl needs.

This approach represents a major change in FWS' habitat conservation strategy. Prior to the plan's creation, FWS had protected land principally through acquisition of fee title or conservation easements. While substantial waterfowl habitat has been protected in this manner, FWS' acquisition program has never been funded at a level sufficient to save enough wetlands fast enough. The plan acknowledges that it will never be possible to buy all the land needed to protect sufficient duck habitat. Thus ways must be found to induce private landowners—principally farmers—to manage their lands so as to maintain their value to waterfowl.[10]

Land Protection Methods

FWS and CWS will continue to purchase lands and conservation easements in cases where acquisition is the most effective protection measure. However, other protection methods will be used to save the largest amount of habitat. In the United States, these methods include use of land management and conservation provisions of the 1985 Food Security Act (also known as the Farm Act), voluntary land management agreements with landowners, and economic incentives and disincentives.

Acquisition. FWS acquires waterfowl habitat under two principal authorities. The Migratory Bird Hunting and Conservation Stamp Act (16 U.S.C.A 718) requires waterfowl hunters to purchase a duck stamp each season they hunt. Stamp-sale receipts are placed in a migratory bird conservation fund. Fund monies are used exclusively for purchasing land and easements for the benefit of waterfowl.

Since the fund was established in 1934, Congress has created other sources of revenue for the fund, including direct appropriations (authorized by the Wetlands Loan Act), refuge entrance fees, and import duties on firearms and ammunition. In FY 1988, FWS estimates it will collect $37.5 million from all sources for the fund. All lands purchased become components of the National Wildlife Refuge System.

In 1986, Congress passed the Emergency Wetlands Resources Act (P.L. 99–645) to improve federal wetlands conservation programs. A

10. The outright prohibition of land-use practices that destroy wetlands vital to migratory waterfowl is an approach that has yet to receive serious consideration.

provision of that law amends the Land and Water Conservation Fund Act to authorize the appropriation of monies from the fund to federal and state agencies for wetlands acquisition. Acquisitions by federal agencies must be consistent with a national wetlands priority plan to be prepared by the Secretary of the Interior, who has delegated this responsibility to FWS.[11] In drawing up the plan, the secretary must consider the values of all wetlands, not just those which support waterfowl populations.

FWS expects to issue a draft wetlands priority plan in 1988. The plan will provide general guidelines and criteria for federal and state agencies to follow in selecting specific wetland sites for protection. Meanwhile, in FY 1988, Congress appropriated $6 million to FWS from the Land and Water Conservation Fund (LWCF) specifically for waterfowl habitat acquisition in support of the North American Waterfowl Management Plan. This is the first appropriation FWS has received for wetlands protection through the LWCF.

In sum, both migratory bird conservation fund revenues and LWCF appropriations will be used by FWS to purchase lands targeted for acquisition by the North American Waterfowl Management Plan.

Federal Farm Act. A number of land conservation provisions were included in farm program legislation enacted by Congress in 1985. According to FWS officials, the Farm Act (16 U.S.C.A. *et seq.* 3801) offers significant new avenues to deal with wetlands loss in agricultural areas. More than 85 percent of wetlands loss between the 1950s and 1970s was due to agricultural conversion. Three provisions of the act could provide significant benefits for waterfowl: the so-called swampbuster provision, the Conservation Reserve Program, and the farm debt restructure provision.

Swampbuster. Under the swampbuster provision, farmers lose federal farm program benefits on all of their land if, after December 23, 1985, they convert wetlands to cropland that produces a commodity crop. The intent of the provision is to reduce the production of commodities already in surplus and to save wetlands.

Final regulations implementing the program were not published until September 17, 1987 (52 *Federal Register* 180), so it is much too early to tell how well the program is working. According to FWS, more than five million acres of wetland in the coterminous 48 states have moderate-to-high conversion potential (see Table 6). FWS officials hope the swampbuster program will be particularly useful in protecting breeding habitat in the prairie states and wintering habitat, especially bottomland hardwoods, in the lower Mississippi Valley.

11. Plan contact: Mr. Dale Pierce, Branch of Special Projects, U.S. Fish and Wildlife Service, Broyhill Building, Room 500, 18th and C Streets, N.W., Washington, D.C. 20240.

Table 6
Conversion Potential of Wetlands in Critical Problem Areas, 1982.[a]

Area	High	Medium	Unlikely	Other[a]	Total
			1,000 acres		
South Florida palustrine wetlands	62	321	1,566	1,455	4,470
Prairie pothole emergent wetlands	98	472	1,540	2,103	4,888
Nebraska sandhills and rainwater basin	26	105	479	173	859
Lower Mississippi alluvial plain	96	302	1,724	1,415	4,264
Coastal pocosins	18	271	2,578	3,183	7,754
Western riparian	2	33	166	1,125	1,441
TOTAL	302	1,504	8,053	9,454	23,676
TOTAL nonfederal	813	4,371	28,467	25,986	78,384
			Percentage		
Percentage of nonfederal	37	34	28	36	30

Source: R.E. Heimlich, and L.L. Langner. 1986. "Swampbusting: Wetland Conversion and Farm Programs." (U.S. Department of Agriculture). Washington, D.C.

[a] Includes wetlands with no conversion potential and where conversion potential was not estimated.

The administrative structure for implementing the swampbuster program may prove the greatest hurdle in ensuring that the program provides maximum benefits for waterfowl and other fish and wildlife. While FWS worked with the Agricultural Stabilization and Conservation Service (ASCS) and Soil Conservation Service (SCS) in designing regulations for the program, it is up to the two Agriculture department agencies to determine when violations occur and to withdraw farm benefits. According to FWS officials, ASCS and SCS personnel will have to place wetlands conservation above their traditional mission of crop production.[12]

FWS provides technical assistance in the field to ASCS and SCS on certain aspects of swampbuster implementation. Also, when FWS field staff during the normal course of their duties see drainage activity that may violate the law, they report this information to the local ASCS county office for further investigation. However, if ASCS and FWS disagree over whether a violation of the law has occurred, FWS has no right to appeal the decision to a higher authority or to a neutral third party.

According to Ann Robinson, regional soil and water conservation coordinator of the Izaak Walton League, one of the greatest flaws in the swampbuster program is the provision in the implementing regulations that lets farmers self-certify whether they are growing crops on

12. For many years, federal laws administered by ASCS and SCS directly promoted the drainage of wetlands.

lands that were drained after the law took effect and whether they are planning future drainage activities. ASCS will spot-check "a representative number" of farms in each state each year to ensure compliance with the law, but many are skeptical this will occur (*Land Letter*, January 15, 1988).

Another potential flaw is the role played by ASCS county committees in program enforcement. Violations of swampbuster will be determined by the county committee, yet that committee is composed of locally elected farmers who will be required to pass judgment on the drainage activities of their neighbors and associates.

Conservation Reserve. Under the Conservation Reserve Program, farmers who retire highly erodible land from crop production for 10 years receive annual rent payments from the Department of Agriculture. Up to 45 million acres may be retired under the program.[13] Participating farmers must plant permanent cover such as grasses or trees on retired acres. The farmer is paid 50 percent of the cost of planting cover on his land by the ASCS, the agency charged with implementing the program. (See "The 1985 Farm Act and Its Implications for Wildlife" in this volume.)

The legislation creating the reserve did not give FWS an explicit role in program implementation. Nevertheless, FWS views the reserve as having high potential to benefit fish and wildlife, especially migratory birds. Although the primary intent of the reserve is to reduce crop surplus and prevent soil erosion on erosion-prone land, FWS officials say the program also has tremendous potential for conserving wetlands.

> Many of the highly erodible land areas contain interspersed wetlands. These wetlands thus become part of the set-aside effort. Of special importance is the fact that the cost sharing of cover establishment may include the utilization of surface water as an appropriate soil erosion reduction option. The Conservation Reserve can thus serve as a means to protect existing wetlands as well as providing an avenue through which drained wetland basins could be restored. Uplands, in proximity to such wetlands basins, that receive erosion stabilization . . . in the form of vegetative cover . . . provide vital nesting cover for waterfowl and protect the . . . basins from siltation (U.S. Department of the Interior, Fish and Wildlife Service 1987b).

FWS has conducted experimental projects in North Dakota, South Dakota, and Minnesota to demonstrate the feasibility and value of working with farmers participating in the reserve to also conserve wetlands. In one project, FWS provided personnel and equipment to help landowners refill drained wetlands. FWS also provided supplementary cash payments to certain farmers on an experimental basis to

13. According to the Department of Agriculture, about 23 million acres had been retired into the reserve as of January 1988.

induce them to retire into the reserve land with significant waterfowl habitat value and to secure special land management rights that enable FWS to maximize waterfowl production.

In summary, FWS is working in tandem with the Conservation Reserve Program to maintain and restore waterfowl habitat, especially in the prairie region. For instance, FWS officials in Minnesota have established a goal of restoring 700 wetland basins in 1988. FWS officials say that the wildlife benefits derived from the reserve could be even further magnified if:

1. the Department of Agriculture would place a priority emphasis on the restoration of wetlands in suitable basins, in lieu of the establishment of vegetative cover in such basins;
2. FWS had additional funds to expand its own reserve-related conservation work; and
3. state fish and wildlife agencies and nonprofit conservation organizations also implement waterfowl conservation projects in areas where lands are retired from production.

Easements for Debt. A third provision of the Farm Act, which deals with debt restructure for farmers who hold loans from the Farmers Home Administration (FmHA), provides opportunities to save or restore wetlands throughout the nation. Under Section 1318 of the act, FmHA may grant partial debt relief to a borrower who has defaulted on a loan made prior to the law's enactment, in exchange for a 50-year easement on that portion of his land that has conservation values (for example, wildlife, outdoor recreation). The easement may be assigned by FmHA to FWS, a state agency, or a nonprofit conservation organization for enforcement of its terms. No easement will be accepted by FmHA unless it can be assigned to another party for enforcement.

A final regulation implementing Section 1318 is expected to be issued in 1988.[14] According to an FmHA official, the implementation process will work as follows: When a borrower becomes delinquent on loan repayment and wishes to reduce his debt, an environmental review team of federal, state, local, and conservation-group representatives will examine the parcel in question, make recommendations regarding the land's conservation values and the portion of the property that should be protected with an easement, and identify who will enforce the easement. If FmHA agrees that an easement is appropriate, it will place a 50-year restriction on the property and lower the farmer's debt by an amount equal to the value of the acreage controlled by the easement.

14. A draft rule was issued in the *Federal Register,* January 15, 1987, but withdrawn.

Easements on Repossessed Lands. Another provision of the Farm Act, Section 1314, authorizes FmHA to grant, sell, or donate easements, restrictions, and development rights for conservation purposes on repossessed lands held in FmHA's landinventory[15] to state or local government agencies or private nonprofit organizations. The Agricultural Credit Act of 1987 (P.L. 100–233) broadened FmHA's flexibility in disposing of inventory land by authorizing the outright transfer of inventory land (or interests in such land) to federal and state agencies for conservation purposes. To be eligible for transfer, the land must be determined to be "suitable" or "surplus," and 1) have a "marginal value for agricultural production," 2) be "environmentally sensitive" or 3) have "special management importance."

Thus, FmHA can protect the environmental values of land in its inventory in two ways.

- Any land that is resold for agricultural use can have perpetual restrictions placed in the deed to conserve wetlands for waterfowl or other wildlife.
- Inventory land with significant wildlife values such as lands contiguous to existing federal or state refuges, parks, and forests, or lands with waterfowl habitat value, can be donated to an appropriate agency either in fee or easement.

Another way FmHA can protect the environmental value of inventory land is under authority of presidential executive orders on "Floodplain Management" (E.O. 11988) and "Protection of Wetlands" (E.O. 11990). These orders enable FmHA to place restrictions in the deeds of properties sold from the inventory that protect the property's wetland and floodplain values in perpetuity.

Finally, FmHA has signed a memorandum of understanding with FWS which gives FWS the opportunity to screen all new loan applications that could adversely affect wetlands or other significant wildlife habitat. FmHA and FWS are developing procedures at the field level to screen loan applications submitted to state FmHA offices so that FWS field personnel can make recommendations as to which applications should be rejected or modified on environmental grounds.

Voluntary Agreements. The theory behind the utility of voluntary agreements in conserving waterfowl is that certain land management practices can simultaneously provide benefits to the farmer and to waterfowl. For example, for years Ducks Unlimited Canada has sponsored the construction of small water management structures and systems on farms in the prairie provinces of Canada to maintain or create wetlands. In return for giving Ducks Unlimited Canada a free

15. The inventory contained approximately 1.6 million acres in January 1988. Land in the inventory has been repossesed from defaulted FmHA-loan holders.

easement to install and operate the structures, the farmer may alleviate a flooding problem or obtain water for irrigation or livestock.

FWS also believes that techniques for improving soil conservation and pasture management can provide significant benefits to both the farmer and waterfowl. For example, conservation tillage enables farmers to reduce soil loss from wind and water erosion and reduce the costs of crop production associated with traditional tillage methods. No-till farming

> adds benefits to wildlife in addition to improved water quality. Waste grains left on the surface with crop residues from zero-tilled fields provide extensive feeding areas for wildlife during the winter months and during migration periods. Many . . . [types] of ground nesting birds utilize crop residues on zero-tilled agricultural fields as nesting sites. Rodents and insects living in retained crop residues provide food sources for many avian and mammalian predators. From the viewpoint of increased wildlife habitat diversity in heavily farmed regions, zero-till . . . methods of crop production is one of the better alternatives to provide multiple conservation benefits to a profit motivated agricultural industry (Dornfield *et al.* 1985).

FWS conducted a pilot program in three western Minnesota counties to get farmers to switch to fall-seeded, no-till grain crops. Spring tillage is detrimental to waterfowl that nest in the region because it leaves little cover where birds can safely lay and hatch their eggs. Even no-till spring plantings are harmful because farm equipment destroys nests and birds. Predators, who are raising young at the same time, are forced to use the same remaining habitat patches as birds. Waterfowl loss to predators in these counties may exceed 90 percent.

FWS, in cooperation with local soil and water conservation districts and private organizations, worked to develop more nesting sites for birds by increasing the number of zero-tilled fields where fall crops are planted. Farmer reaction to the experimental program was positive.

According to FWS officials, ducks and other ground-nesting birds use the stubble left in no-till winter wheat and winter rye fields as nest sites. "While nest densities in the grain fields are generally lower than nearby non-use grass fields, nest success appears to be higher. We believe that mammalian predators spend less time hunting in the grain fields than they do in grass cover, thus fewer nests in the grain are destroyed" (Dornfield *et al.* 1985).

Economic Incentives. The North American Waterfowl Management Plan notes that economic inducements may be necessary to convince some private landowners to manage their waterfowl habitat in appropriate ways. This is especially true in cases where farmers are unwilling or unable to manage their land so as to benefit waterfowl. However, the plan gives few details about the types of incentives envisioned. This is a subject that will be examined in more detail as the plan evolves. The two basic forms of incentives are direct payments and tax incentives.

Direct Payments. Direct payments include in-kind assistance and cash payments. The work performed by FWS personnel to help restore wetlands under the conservation reserve program is one example of in-kind assistance.

The principal federal example of direct payments for wetlands habitat protection is the Water Bank Program (16 U.S.C.A. 1301, *et seq.*) administered by the Agricultural Stabilization and Conservation Service. Under the program, landowners who agree not to degrade or destroy waterfowl habitat on their property for a period of 10 years receive annual rental payments from the federal government. (For more on the Water Bank, see "Federal Wetlands Protection Programs" in *Audubon Wildlife Report 1986.*)

In 1984, FWS initiated a pilot program in Minnesota to pay landowners to restore drained wetlands.[16] The program restored 1,460 acres of wetlands in its early phase; an additional 3,700 acres of uplands contiguous to the restored areas were seeded in permanent vegetative cover for erosion control and waterfowl nesting habitat. Ninety participating farmers were paid an average of $64 per acre per year to allow FWS use of their land for a 10-year period. The development costs for wetlands restoration work were paid for by Ducks Unlimited, as was the cost of seeding vegetation on land surrounding the wetlands.

The pilot program showed that farmers will cooperate to restore wetlands and conserve waterfowl if they are paid to do so. In addition, FWS officials say the pilot program demonstrated that drained wetlands, even those which have been dry for years, can be successfully restored:

> Ducks returned to the ponds when the first runoff event filled them. Response of aquatic plants and aquatic invertebrates . . . was immediate . . . Two years after restoration, it is difficult to tell that a wetland had ever been drained, even some that had been drained for more than 70 years (Madsen undated).

Tax Incentives. The provision of tax benefits to private landowners who manage their property for wildlife conservation purposes is another way for governments to conserve waterfowl habitat. The plan offers no particular suggestions for tax measures at this time, but this matter is likely to receive more serious scrutiny as plan implementation evolves.

16. The pilot program is one of several efforts conducted under FWS' Mid-Continent Waterfowl Management Project to increase duck production. For further details see *1986 Annual Report: Mid-Continent Waterfowl Management Project* (U.S. Department of the Interior 1986b).

At the federal level, donations of land and perpetual conservation easements are deductible from gross income. However, not all owners of wetlands may wish to donate a perpetual easement on their wetlands or grasslands for personal or financial reasons; hence, other incentives must be found.

Several states have experimented with tax incentives. Minnesota and Iowa, for example, require no property tax on qualifying wetlands. In addition, Minnesota once provided a tax credit (against total tax due) for property owners who maintain wetlands, but the credit was terminated in 1987 as part of a move to balance the state's budget.

IMPLEMENTATION OF THE NORTH AMERICAN WATERFOWL PLAN

Philosophy

The North American plan commits FWS and CWS to a 15-year period of cooperative planning and management of shared waterfowl populations. The plan also calls for heavy involvement of the private sector and other government agencies in implementing and funding the plan. Indeed, the primary source of implementation funding, says the plan, "must be private organizations and individuals who enjoy and benefit from achieving and maintaining [waterfowl populations]. Major governmental budget increases for waterfowl management, especially in the United States, should not be anticipated in the near future, given competing demands and projected budget levels."

Due to its vast, ambitious scope, implementation of the plan will require a higher degree of cooperation between the public and private sector than has existed in the past if plan objectives are to be met by the year 2000. The plan calls for the establishment of "joint venture" committees to plan and implement specific projects in support of plan objectives:

> Joint venture projects should be implemented through facilitating agreements negotiated and agreed to by all those wishing to participate. A joint venture action group [committee] should be established for each joint venture. The planning, ongoing management funding, implementation method and evaluation of joint ventures should be set out as a proposal which would detail the contributions of private organizations, individuals, states, provinces, territories and official proposed budgets of the two governments. Each [proposed] project should be forwarded to the North American Waterfowl Management Plan Committee for its review and recommendation (U.S. Department of the Interior 1986a).

A joint venture project may focus on a particular species, a priority habitat area, or a functional matter such as research.

National Management Committee

The plan establishes a North American Waterfowl Management Committee to provide leadership and guidance to all parties involved in implementation. The committee is composed of 12 government representatives: two FWS officials, four state officials (one from each flyway), two CWS officials, and four provincial officials. The chairmanship rotates each year between CWS and FWS members. For 1988, the committee chairman is Harvey Nelson,[17] a former FWS regional director, who has been involved in waterfowl management throughout his career. In 1988, FWS Director Frank Dunkle appointed Nelson executive director for the North American Waterfowl Management Plan, a newly created position within FWS. Both FWS and CWS have appointed "coordinators" to serve as liaisons with the plan committee. The Canadian coordinator, Jim Patterson, also is a committee member. The U.S. coordinator is Harvey Nelson.

According to the plan, the responsibilities of the plan committee are as follows:

1. Serve as a forum for discussion of major, long-term, international waterfowl issues and problems, and translate those discussions into recommendations for consideration by the cooperating countries.
2. Update the North American Waterfowl Management Plan in 1990 and every five years thereafter.
3. Review the scientific and technical data on the status and dynamics of waterfowl populations and their habitats as they relate to the aims of the plan.
4. Review and monitor progress toward achieving goals contained in the plan.
5. Review management plans for waterfowl populations requiring coordinated international action, and make recommendations for additions or revisions.
6. Review scientific and technical data to determine whether other waterfowl populations require coordinated international action.
7. Review joint venture drafts to ascertain that they further the intent of the plan.
8. Consider and, if needed, recommend additional actions to the federal governments of Canada and the United States.

In sum, the committee's powers are advisory. It does not have authority to require actions by either CWS or FWS, nor does it replace any existing waterfowl management organizations in either Canada or

17. Nelson's address: Executive Director for the North American Waterfowl Management Plan, Fish and Wildlife Service, Federal Building, Fort Snelling, Twin Cities, MN 55111; Phone (612) 725–3737.

the United States. However, recommendations of the committee will obviously receive serious attention from the directors of each nation's wildlife agency.

Private Sector Implementation Committees

Implementation committees will be established in both countries at the national level to coordinate private sector involvement in plan implementation and to work with the plan committee. In the United States prospective members of the implementation committee include, among others, the National Fish and Wildlife Foundation, The Nature Conservancy, National Wildlife Federation, and Ducks Unlimited. Implementation committee members will conduct a variety of activities in support of plan objectives including fundraising, public relations, lobbying, and habitat protection and management, depending on their respective skills and interests. The National Fish and Wildlife Foundation[18] has made plan implementation a top priority and is working to coordinate private fundraising efforts for land-protection.

Joint-Venture Committees

Since the plan was signed in May 1986, several joint venture projects have been launched or are under development with the approval of the plan committee:

Canadian Prairie Habitat. The principal objective of this project is to make agreements with private landowners in the three prairie provinces to place 3.6 million acres of wetlands-uplands complexes under management for waterfowl production. These complexes are scattered throughout 19 million acres of land that have high waterfowl production capability but low agricultural potential. The complexes would be actively managed to achieve a mallard nest success rate of 30 to 40 percent.

Black Duck. The black duck joint venture will attempt to systematically address the decline of the black duck population. New methodologies will be developed to estimate breeding population trends, improve winter surveys, and identify distinct populations. In addition, research is needed on such subjects as nest success, interaction with the mallard, and mortality factors.

Arctic-Nesting Geese. The goal of this joint venture is to increase the populations of several Pacific Flyway populations of geese and to maintain other populations at desired levels. A significant amount of research must be conducted to determine the status of these species.

18. Contact: Mr. Charles Collins, Executive Director, National Fish and Wildlife Foundation, Department of the Interior, Room 2725, Washington, D.C. 20240.

An additional six habitat conservation joint-venture projects are being developed for the priority duck habitat regions in the United States: Prairie Pothole-U.S., Lower Mississippi Valley, Gulf Coast, Atlantic Coast, Great Lakes, and California Central Valley. According to FWS officials, additional joint-venture projects will undoubtedly be established later as implementation proceeds. Potential candidates for joint venture status include the canvasback duck and waterfowl research.

Canadian Prairie Habitat Joint Venture

The plan calls for the protection and enhancement of 3.6 million acres in prairie Canada at a cost of at least $1 billion over 15 years. Since duck hunters in the United States depend upon Canadian-produced ducks,[19] the plan recognizes the need for large sums of money raised in the United States to be spent for habitat protection in Canada.

To demonstrate the willingness of U.S. organizations to finance habitat protection in Canada, several organizations have worked together to raise U.S. funds for a "first-step" project proposed by the Canadian Prairie Habitat Joint Venture Committee. A total of $8.2 million was raised as follows:

- Ducks Unlimited donated $1 million to be matched by 10 or more states.
- The International Association of Fish and Wildlife Agencies worked with 11 member states to raise $1 million.
- The National Fish and Wildlife Foundation, a federally chartered organization, which can receive 50–50 matching funds through congressional appropriations, requested and received $2 million from Congress in FY 1988 to match the $2 million raised by Ducks Unlimited and the states; the foundation also contributed $175,000 of its own privately raised funds.
- A consortium of public and private Canadian organizations contributed $4 million to match the U.S. contribution.

The $8.2 million will be spent to protect 8,400 acres of upland nesting area associated with marshes in the Quill Lakes lowland in Saskatchewan, and for nest cover enhancement at Whitford-Rush Lakes in Alberta and White Water Lake in Manitoba. The cost of land acquisition is estimated at $250 per acre; the establishment of dense cover crops, $110 per acre. A consortium of organizations is already at work acquiring and developing the marshes of the Quill Lakes area for waterfowl. These include Ducks Unlimited, Wildlife Habitat Canada,

19. U.S. hunters kill about 80 percent of all ducks harvested each year in both countries.

Saskatchewan Natural History Society, Saskatchewan Wildlife Federation, Ducks Unlimited Canada, and the governments of Saskatchewan and Canada.

U.S. Habitat Joint-Venture Committees

The habitat joint-venture committee is the workhorse of the implementation structure. Each of the six U.S. committees is responsible for identifying specific lands for protection or management, determining which committee members will protect and manage the sites, and deciding who will pay for these efforts. The committees will be composed of interested parties from both the government and private sectors.

FWS is the lead organization in the joint venture structure. Overall supervision of joint-venture work will be provided by the appropriate FWS regional director through a project coordinator whom the regional director appoints. The coordinator in turn will organize a technical advisory group to assist in all phases of habitat and waterfowl protection and management.

No U.S. habitat committee was fully organized and operational at the start of 1988. However, since the committees will be doing the lion's share of plan implementation, it is important to have a tangible understanding of how they will work. The California Central Valley habitat joint-venture project is illustrative.

California Central Valley Joint Venture. Wetlands in the Central Valley are vital to Pacific Flyway populations of ducks and geese. According to a FWS habitat protection concept plan prepared for the region, "Nowhere in the United States are so many waterfowl dependent on so few acres of wetlands" (U.S. Department of the Interior 1987c).

About 60 percent of the flyway's total population of wintering waterfowl reside in the Central Valley. The valley is the sole wintering area for the endangered Aleutian Canada goose and the tule white-fronted goose. It also accommodates 80 to 90 percent of the flyway's wintering populations of the cackling Canada goose, the Wrangle Island and western populations of the lesser snow goose, the Ross' goose, and the pintail duck. Ninety-five percent of the valley's wetlands have been destroyed during the last 100 years. About 280,000 wetland acres remain, of which 90,000 acres are still unprotected.

Unprotected areas are subject to loss from conversion to agricultural use. An estimated 8,000 to 10,000 acres of wetlands were lost between 1978 and 1987. This slow attrition is expected to continue. In addition, changes in agricultural crops and practices on dry land acres where ducks and geese feed could have a negative effect on waterfowl populations.

The North American Waterfowl Management Plan calls for protecting 80,000 acres of the existing unprotected wetlands in the Central Valley. According to the concept plan these lands would be protected principally through acquisition of easements. The cost of acquisition would be paid for by FWS, but state and private groups may also share some of the costs. Easement acquisition costs are expected to average $750 an acre, for a total of $60 million.

In addition, the concept plan proposes to protect another 120,000 dry acres of land on which wetlands can be restored or created. This objective was established in conformance with a state of California law[20] passed in 1979, which directed the California Department of Fish and Game to develop a program to prevent wetlands loss, increase the wildlife value of existing wetlands, and create additional wetlands. Altogether, the resolution called for a 50-percent increase in total wetland acreage throughout the state by the year 2000.

In 1983, the California Department of Fish and Game issued a plan identifying the drainage basins in the valley where 120,000 acres of dry land could be converted to wetlands. The plan states that 75 percent of the lands should be acquired in easements and 25 percent in fee title. According to a state wildlife official, a comprehensive strategy to implement the restoration plan is in preparation. Meanwhile, some progress has already been made in setting up various implementing structures.

Since the department does not have condemnation authority, the entire state effort depends upon the voluntary cooperation of landowners. The California Waterfowl Association helped establish an "agriculture outreach" group to explore ways to protect land through easements or other means. Methods being considered include making annual payments to farmers who modify their agricultural practices to benefit waterfowl (for example, not disking rice fields in the fall so that birds can feed on waste grain); working with farmers to enhance waterfowl benefits of lands retired under federal agricultural programs; and paying farmers annual rental fees for restoring wetlands on their property for a period of 10 years.

The state legislature has created a statewide California Waterfowl Habitat Program through which landowners may receive cash payments to enhance and restore wetlands under 10-year contracts. The program is modeled after the Federal Water Bank Program. A $100,000 appropriation was made to set up a special fund for making the rental payments. Wildlife interests hope to secure an additional $2 million for the fund in 1988 from the California legislature, and will seek additional sums in the future so that payments to cooperating landowners can be financed from the fund's interest earnings.

20. Senate Concurrent Resolution 28.

In addition, a 1983 ballot initiative, Proposition 19, provided $85 million for wetlands protection; $30 million was allocated to the Coastal Commission for coastal wetlands protection and $55 million to the California Department of Fish and Game. The department budgeted $30 million for protecting, enhancing, and developing new wetlands in the Central Valley; much of this already has been spent. Another land protection initiative has been placed on the ballot for 1988 by a consortium of conservation organizations. The $750-million measure includes $38 million for wetlands: $13 million for San Francisco Bay, and $25 million for the Central Valley.

In conclusion, significant advances should be made in protecting waterfowl habitat in the Central Valley in 1988. California wildlife officials say interest in the program is high and increasing. "We're even getting calls from legislators," said one state official. The formation of a formal joint venture committee will help move matters along. Committee members are likely to be representatives from the same organizations that are on the agriculture outreach group. These include the California Waterfowl Association, National Audubon Society, Rice Growers Association, private landowners, University of California Extension Service, Department of Fish and Game, Fish and Wildlife Service, Bureau of Reclamation, Agricultural Stabilization and Conservation Service, and Soil Conservation Service.

CONCLUSION

The North American Waterfowl Management Plan makes fundamental changes in the strategy for protecting and managing the continent's ducks and geese. First, the plan sets a desired population size for different species of ducks and distinct populations of geese, and commits resource managers in both countries to achieve these objectives. While both nations have set population goals before—some independently, some cooperatively—the plan represents the first-ever commitment by both nations to do what it takes to maintain a breeding population of 62 million ducks and desired levels of geese in the face of developmental forces that have depressed many species, especially ducks, since 1955. In essence, the plan says that the current gradual attrition of certain waterfowl species must stop.

Second, the strategy is comprehensive in its approach. It addresses all phases of waterfowl management: harvest regulations, habitat protection, population management, and research.

Third, the strategy directly addresses a fundamental problem that has not been adequately dealt with previously: the destruction of waterfowl habitat on privately owned lands, especially farm lands in duck breeding areas. Acknowledging that neither FWS nor CWS will ever be able to buy sufficient land in fee title or easement to support desired population levels, the plan calls for a massive new initiative to change land-use practices on tens of thousands of farms in the United States and Canada so that both the farmer and waterfowl benefit. This voluntary approach to conserve large amounts of habitat is unprecedented.

Fourth, the plan challenges all interested parties in both the government and private sector to work cooperatively to bring about the plan's objectives. This will require highly sophisticated leadership and coordination by the wildlife services of each nation. While FWS and CWS have worked cooperatively with other federal agencies, state and local governments, and private organizations prior to the plan, the scale of operations envisioned is much grander than any carried out before. During the 15-year implementation period, public and private organizations will have to raise $1.5 billion just for the land protection portion of the plan.[21] In addition, tens of millions of dollars will be spent on land and waterfowl management.

Yet, all involved in the plan's preparation and implementation believe funding needs can be met if everyone puts his or her shoulder to the wheel. Indeed, the "cost of failure" in the words of one observer, "is too great to consider" because it "could mean that . . . the next generation will miss the thrill of seeing a sunrise from a duck blind" (Washburn 1987).

REFERENCES

Dornfield, Rick, Tim Bremicker and Ray Norrgard. 1985. Paving the Way for No-till, or Many Hands Make Light Work. Paper presented at the 40th Annual Meeting of the Soil Conservation Society of America, August 4–7, St. Louis, Missouri.

Greenwood, Raymond J., Alan B. Sargeant, Douglas H. Johnson, Lewis M. Cowardin, and Terry L. Shaffer. 1987. "Mallard Nest Success and Recruitment in Prairie Canada." *Transactions of the 52nd North American Wildlife and Natural Resources Conference.* Wildlife Management Institute. Washington, D.C.

Heimlich, R.E. and L. L. Langer. 1986. Swampbusting: Wetland Conversion and Farm Programs. U.S. Department of Agriculture. Washington, D.C.

Madsen, Carl R. Undated. Wetland Restoration in Western Minnesota. Unpublished paper. U.S. Fish and Wildlife Service. Fergus Falls, Minnesota.

Tiner, R. W. 1984. Wetlands of the United States: Current Status and Recent Trends. U.S. Department of the Interior. Washington, D.C.

Turner, Bruce C., George S. Hochbaum, F. Dale Caswell and Daniel J. Nieman. 1987. "Agricultural Impacts on Wetland Habitats on the Canadian Prairies, 1981–85." *Transactions of the 52nd North American Wildlife and Natural Resources Conference.* Wildlife Management Institute. Washington, D.C.

U.S. Department of the Interior, Fish and Wildlife Service and Environment Canada.

21. Many knowledgeable observers predict that land protection costs will be higher.

1986a. *North American Waterfowl Management Plan.* Washington, D.C.

——., Fish and Wildlife Service. 1986b. *1986 Annual Report: Mid-Continent Waterfowl Management Project.* Twin Cities, Minnesota.

——., Fish and Wildlife Service, and Canadian Wildlife Service. 1987a. *1987 Status of Waterfowl and Fall Flight Forecast.* Washington, D.C.

——., Fish and Wildlife Service. 1987b. Farm Bill Related Wetland Protection and Restoration Opportunities. Unpublished document, September 29, 1987. Washington, D.C.

——., Fish and Wildlife Service. 1987c. Draft Concept Plan for Waterfowl Wintering Habitat Preservation, An Update, Central Valley. Portland, Oregon.

Washburn, Lowell. 1987. "Blue Print for Recovery." *Outdoor Highlights* 15:22. Illinois Department of Conservation. Springfield, Illinois.

William J. Chandler is president of W. J. Chandler Associates, a government relations and research firm in Washington, D.C., which specializes in natural resource policy. He is the editor of this volume and has been the research director of previous wildlife reports.

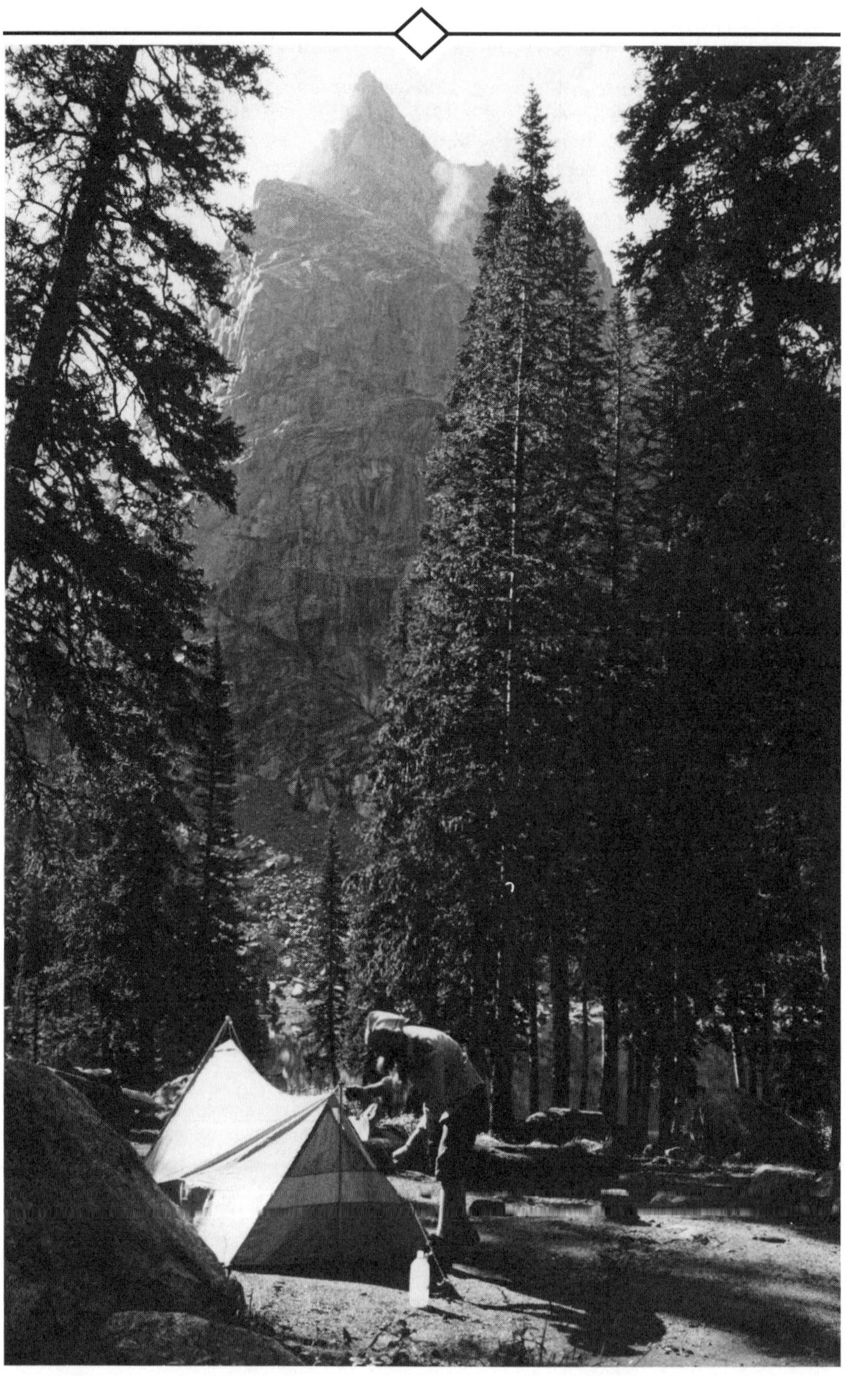

Federal and state government agencies have withdrawn millions of dollars from the Land and Water Conservation Fund to buy and manage parks and refuges. The fund must be improved to keep up with increasing outdoor recreation needs. *Kent and Donna Dannen*

The Land and Water Conservation Fund: Past Experience, Future Directions

Michael Mantell, Phyllis Myers, and Robert B. Reed

INTRODUCTION[1]

For the past quarter century, the Land and Water Conservation Fund (LWCF) has been one of the most significant federal funding mechanisms for the protection of land in national and state parks, wildlife refuges, forests, and other reserved areas, and for outdoor recreation use by state and local governments (16 U.S.C.A. 460l-5 *et seq.*) (see Figure 1). A brief list of accomplishments since the LWCF was established in 1964 shows how important it has been to land conservation in the United States:

- State and local governments have matched (in varying proportions) more than $3.2 billion in federal LWCF grants to plan, acquire, and develop more than 32,000 projects providing parks and outdoor recreation facilities in some 14,000 communities (Myers 1987).

1. Much of this chapter is adapted from: The Conservation Foundation, *National Parks for a New Generation: Visions Realities, Prospects 1985*; and Phyllis Myers, *State Grants for Parklands, 1965–1984: Lessons for a New Land and Water Conservation Fund.* The Conservation Foundation, Washington, D.C. 1987.

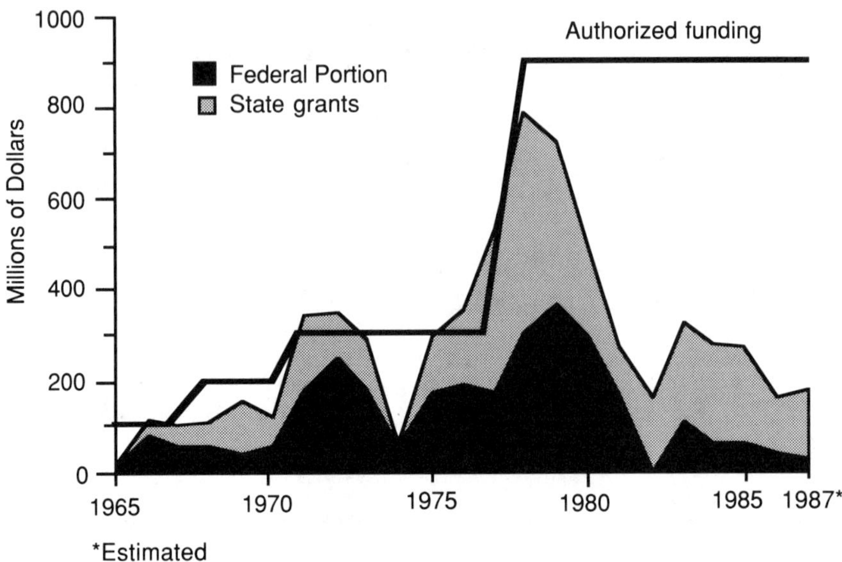

Figure 1. History of Land and Water Conservation Fund appropriations, 1965-1987. Source: NPS.

- By the end of FY 1986, the National Park Service had spent $2.1 billion in LWCF money to acquire 1.6 million acres of land for national parks (see Figures 2 and 3) (U.S Department of the Interior 1987a). During 1965 to 1983, money from the LWCF to the service averaged about 25 percent of the park service's total annual appropriations reaching as high as 40 percent in some years (Conservation Foundation 1985).
- Between 1967, when it first received LWCF grants, and 1986, the Fish and Wildlife Service spent over 350 million LWCF dollars (U.S. Department of the Interior 1987b) to acquire 390,000 acres of land (U.S. Department of the Interior 1987c) (see Figures 2 and 3).
- From 1965 to 1986, some 3.2 million acres (U.S. Department of the Interior 1987a-d, U.S. Department of Agriculture 1987a) of recreational land were purchased by federal agencies with $3.6 billion of LWCF money (see Figure 3) (U.S. Department of Agriculture 1987b).
- The LWCF has also paid for pre-acquisition-related work, such as identifying parcels and landowners and searching title, to decrease the time before purchase (Conservation Foundation 1985).

Creation of a federal recreation grants program was a major recommendation of the Outdoor Recreation Resources Review

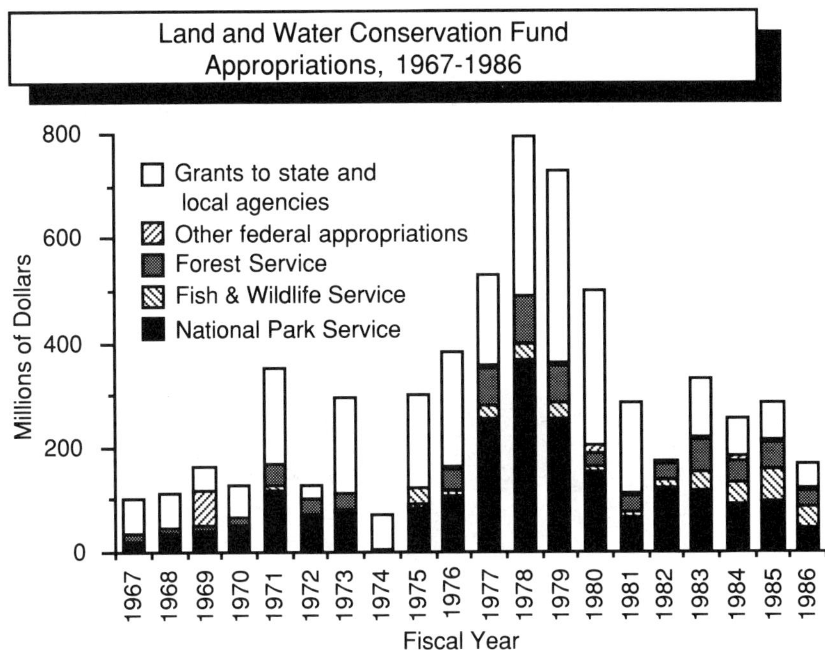

Figure 2. Sources: NPS, FWS, USFS, BLM.

Commission, established in the late 1950s to determine the nation's needs for outdoor recreation through the remainder of the century, and to recommend policies to address those needs. Chaired by Laurance S. Rockefeller, the commission's 1962 report, *Outdoor Recreation for America*, presciently foresaw that rising affluence, the automobile, and a shortening work week would make a leisure boom inevitable. To meet the nation's outdoor recreation needs, the commission recommended that all levels of government should provide continuing recreational funds in amounts substantially greater than were then being spent (Myers 1987). Endorsing a strong federal responsibility to help meet demand for outdoor recreation, the commission recommended that:

> A Federal program of grants-in-aid should be established promptly to provide matching funds to the States to stimulate recreation planning and to assist in acquiring lands and developing facilities for public outdoor recreation (Siehl 1981).

When established in 1964, the LWCF had strong bipartisan support in Congress and the enthusiastic backing of conservation and recreation groups. Forty-nine states endorsed the bill (Myers 1987).

Despite its origins and accomplishments, the ability of LWCF to continue providing money at the levels needed for federal land acquisition and state and local park and recreation programs is uncertain.

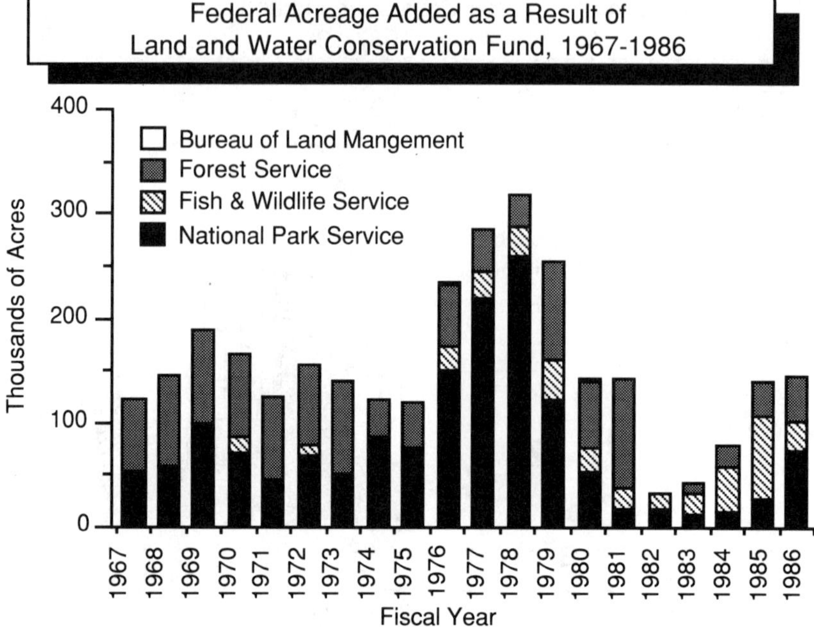

Figure 3. Sources: NPS, FWS, USFS, BLM.

Although Congress reauthorized LWCF for another 25 years at the end of 1987 (Pub. Law 100–203), fiscal constraints, skepticism about federal programs, the changing context for outdoor recreation, and markedly reduced LWCF appropriations over the last seven years raise serious questions about the fund's ability to respond to the next generation of land conservation needs. Yet no other action Congress takes can fundamentally shape the extent and condition of land conservation as much as the reform of the fund.

Debate over how the fund should be restructured has already begun. Recommendations about LWCF were the cornerstone of a report issued in early 1987 by the President's Commission on Americans Outdoors, the successor to the Outdoor Recreation Resources Review Commission. Chaired by former Governor Lamar Alexander (R-TN), this 15-member body urged the creation of a "dedicated trust . . . providing a minimum of $1 billion a year" for outdoor recreation expenditures (President's Commission on Americans Outdoors 1987). Bills have been introduced in the 100th Congress that embody the recommendations of the President's commission in various ways; other measures make changes in the way money from the fund is allocated.

In shaping a new LWCF, several key questions must be addressed. These include:

- What would a new fund do?
- How can it be best structured to take account of past experience and future needs?
- How will it be funded and administered?

This chapter will examine each of these questions.

THE LWCF: ITS STRUCTURE AND ACCOMPLISHMENTS

How LWCF Functions

The LWCF was intended to provide a predictable, sizable flow of earmarked funds that would be insulated from the year-to-year competition for congressional appropriations. Indeed, some members of Congress apparently believed that the LWCF would operate more like a true trust fund, with revenues earmarked for the LWCF held in a separate account that could not be used for other purposes; Congress would simply appropriate money from the fund as it was needed. Thus, the flow of revenues into the LWCF would be removed from the political process, while use of fund money would not.

In practice, the LWCF does not operate, and has never operated, as a trust fund in the same way as the Highway Trust Fund does. Revenue in the LWCF may be (and is) used for other purposes and funds cannot be spent without advance approval from the applicable appropriations committees in Congress. Neither is it simply another authorized program that receives appropriations from the general fund because the "fund" does exist, even if only on paper. Instead, the LWCF lies somewhere in between, and this hybrid character has confused discussion of the fund—even in Congress (U.S. Department of the Interior 1984). Yet the fund's existence has seemingly made it easier for Congress to appropriate money for federal land acquisition—nearly $3.6 billion in 22 years (see Figure 2).

The key to understanding the LWCF is that there are essentially two LWCF accounts—a receipts account and an appropriations account for distributing state grants and money for federal land acquisition programs. The receipts account grows by $900 million each year, less whatever is appropriated to the appropriations account. The receipts account, however, is merely a bookkeeping account. Although $1.8 billion was nominally in that account at the end of fiscal year 1982, there is, in fact, no distinct fund, no money lying idle or invested in government securities which can be drawn against. Instead, the money "in" the LWCF receipts account is really part of the general treasury fund and is included in the federal budget as an "offsetting receipt" (Conservation Foundation 1985).

The LWCF's "carryover" feature makes it a hybrid betwen a trust fund and a plain authorization. Unlike most other federal appropriations, once money is transferred to the fund's appropriations account, it is considered a "no-year appropriation" and is available for use indefinitely. This feature is both a cause of and cure for variations in annual appropriations from the LWCF. If, for example, a federal land agency accumulates a large reserve of appropriated but unspent LWCF funds, Congress may reduce its LWCF appropriations in a given year and instruct the agency to use up the surplus. At the same time, the carryover feature blunts the destabilizing effect of wild fluctuations in annual appropriations on land acquisitions. Figure 2 illustrates this relationship by showing the park service's LWCF appropriations and the total amount available for expenditure (that is, the annual appropriation plus carryover from the previous year). For example, $23.6 million remained unobligated at the end of fiscal year 1973. Fiscal year 1974 saw widespread budget cuts due to the recession, and Congress appropriated only $910,000 of LWCF money. By fiscal year 1975, carryover funds were down to $3.7 million, and LWCF appropriations rose to nearly $80.2 million (Conservation Foundation 1985).

Fund Structure

Originally, the LWCF received revenues from the sale of surplus federal property, the motorboat fuel tax, and user fees from recreation activities on federal lands. When these sources proved less bountiful than anticipated, Congress amended the act in 1968 to provide a minimum annual income to the fund of $200 million. The shortfall between revenues from the above sources and the $200 million floor would come from subsequent appropriations from the government's general fund and, if necessary, from oil- and gas-lease revenues on the Outer Continental Shelf. Congress raised the floor to $300 million annually in 1970 and to $900 million in 1977 (16 U.S.C.A. 4601-5(c)(1)). Approximately 90 percent of LWCF receipts now come from Outer Continental Shelf oil- and gas-lease revenues.

The state share of the LWCF provides matching grants to state governments for acquisition and development of recreational facilities; states have the option of using the money themselves or passing a portion on to local governments. The federal share of the LWCF, however, provides money primarily for the acquisition of recreation lands administered by the National Park Service, Bureau of Land Management, Fish and Wildlife Service, and the Forest Service.

In order to receive its share of federal grants, each state prepares a State Comprehensive Outdoor Recreation Plan inventorying all federal, state, county, and local recreational lands and facilities; analyzing present and projected recreation demands; and laying out a program for implementing the plan. Grants are not entitlements—each project must be approved by federal officials in the context of its relationship to the needs and priorities identified in the state's plan.

The LWCF was amended in 1986 by the Emergency Wetlands Resources Act (Pub. Law 99–645) to allow acquisition of wetlands. Acquisition of wetlands under the LWCF was formerly prohibited because it was originally assumed that acquisition of these key wildlife areas would come from the Migratory Bird Conservation Fund, which derives its revenue from duck-stamp receipts. Some may argue that alternate funding sources for wetlands acquisition remain adequate, but such sources have failed to halt the continuing loss of wetland areas. The act principally encourages states to acquire wetlands with LWCF money by directing them to assess and consider these areas in their Comprehensive Outdoor Recreation Plan. The act also enables the Fish and Wildlife Service to broaden LWCF acquisition efforts for the refuge system. As a result of the Emergency Wetlands Resources Act, an additional $6 million was appropriated through the LWCF to the Fish and Wildlife Service in FY 1988 to implement the North American Waterfowl Management Plan (Graves interview), a cooperative agreement between the United States and Canada to conserve wetlands used by ducks and geese (see "Conserving North American Waterfowl" in this volume).

Federal Accomplishments

The LWCF has been the key to expanding the protection of wildlife habitat, scenic and historic resources, and outdoor recreation lands at the federal level. The national park and wildlife refuge systems have been the principal federal beneficiaries of the fund's outlays. Figure 3 depicts the growth in acreage of federal lands obtained through the fund. Figure 2 illustrates how the expenditures of the fund have been allocated to federal agencies since its origin.

These figures also illustrate the drop-off in support for federal land acquisition and related LWCF activities since 1981. Since that time, the Reagan Administration has recommended greatly reduced LWCF expenditures; only determined action by Congress and conservation organizations have kept appropriations flowing. For example, in FY 1988, the administration requested $16 million for park service land acquisition efforts from the LWCF and nothing for state grants; Congress responded with an appropriation of $43.5 million and $16.5 million, respectively.

State and Local Accomplishments

The blend of federal, state, and local assistance in the LWCF was an integral element of its design and political appeal in the 1960s. The fund initiated a new period in the partnership between the federal government and state and local governments over parklands. Stephen Mather, the first director of the National Park Service, nurtured the formation of state parks because he believed they played an essential complementary role in protecting the nation's natural resources and providing recreation. During the Depression, the federal government spent millions of dollars to deploy armies of men to work in state and local parks to restore resources and national spirit. Federal assistance under the LWCF helped meet a new generation of needs, providing grants on a matching basis to support state and local programs.

By providing matching support for land acquisition and recreation development to states and localities, the LWCF promotes conservation of some valuable habitats. This is particularly true for state-level expenditures,which have tended to focus on acquisition of relatively large tracts of natural land.

Given the importance of the LWCF to state and local parklands, how have these grants been used? A study by the Conservation Foundation of these grants showed that, between 1965 and 1984, projects funded by the LWCF state grants program totaled almost $2.86 billion. These projects fall into categories: "land acquisition," "facilities development," "facilities redevelopment" (involving substantial rehabilitation or modernization), and "combination" projects, which involve both land acquisition and facilities development or redevelopment.

As Table 1 shows, over a 20-year period about one-third of the state grants—$883 million—was spent to help buy 2,540,555 acres of parkland. An additional estimated $76 million was spent to help acquire 218,153 acres in combination projects. Of this acreage, a small amount, conservatively estimated at 13,920 acres, has been protected by the purchase of less-than-fee interests, including scenic and conservation easements, in 65 projects totaling about $15 million.

About two-thirds of LWCF grants have helped fund the development or modernization of recreational facilities including picnic areas; sports and play fields; trails; swimming, boating, and fishing areas; campgrounds; passive parks; ice skating rinks and other winter sport areas; and so on. Planning grants account for approximately one percent of the funds.

Trends in State Spending. The most dramatic spending trend with state grants is the sharp drop in appropriations which began in the late 1970s and accelerated after 1980. Between 1970 and 1980, Congress appropriated an average of $230 million annually for state grants; between 1981 and 1984, average annual appropriations dropped 61 percent to $89 million.

Table 1
LWCF state grants: Summary of obligated projects,[a] 1965–1984

Project type	Amount	Percent of total	Number of projects	Acreage
Acquisition[b]	$ 882,547,039	31	6,543	2,540,555
Development[c]	1,497,161,558	52	20,846	4
Redevelopment[d]	110,893,423	4	1,270	n.a.[e]
Combination[f]	329,452,167	12	2,701	218,153
Planning	38,120,,087	1	388	0
TOTAL	$2,858,174,274	100	31,748	2,758,712

Source: U.S. Department of the Interior, National Park Service, Recreational Grants Division.

[a] State grants from the Land and Water Conservation Fund for the District of Columbia, Puerto Rico, Mariana Islands, Guam, American Samoa, and the Virgin Islands are excluded from this analysis.

[b] Acquisition projects involve buying land.

[c] Development projects involve construction of capital facilities.

[d] Redevelopment projects involve substantial rehabilitation and modernization of capital facilities.

[e] n.a. = not available.

[f] Combination projects involve both land acquisition and development or redevelopment.

Aggregate amounts, however, do not tell the whole story. As Table 2 shows, the proportion spent on land acquisition projects has declined over time while the proportion spent on all types of facilities development has increased. (The share for new capital development projects has been relatively stable, but redevelopment and combination projects have increased.) Because the decline in the proportion of total grant funds used to buy land began before the cutback in funds, this

Table 2
LWCF D'State Grants: Obligated Projects by Type of Project,[a] Selected Years, 1970–1984 (in Thousands).

Project	1970	1975	1980	1984
Acquisition[b]	19,395 (41%)	56,216 (36%)	74,664 (32%)	22,652 (22%)
Development[c]	24,069 (52%)	82,467 (52%)	105,512 (45%)	53,192 (53%)
Redevelopment[d]	0	161 (.1%)	15,274 (6%)	13,705 (14%)
Combination[e]	2,824 (6%)	17,422 (11%)	39,449 (17%)	8,748 (9%)
Planning	466 (1%)	1,771 (1%)	1,846 (1%)	2,650 (3%)
Total[f]	$46,754	$158,037	$236,744	$100,946

Source: U.S. Department of the Interior, National Park Service, Recreation Grants Division.

[a] State grants from the Land and Water Conservation Fund for the District of Columbia, Puerto Rico, Mariana Islands, Guam, American Samoa, and the Virgin Islands are excluded from this analysis.

[b] Acquisition projects involve buying land.

[c] Development projects involve construction of capital facilities.

[d] Redevelopment projects involve substantial rehabilitation and modernization of capital facilities.

[e] Combination projects involve both land acquisition and development or redevelopment.

[f] Due to rounding, total may not add up to 100%.

Table 3
LWCF state grants: Obligated projects by SMSA[a] location, selected years,[b] 1970–1984.

Year	Total obligated projects ($1000s)	Percent grant funds		Number of acres acquired		
		SMSA	Non-SMSA	SMSA	Non-SMSA	Total
1970	$ 46,754	59%	41%	15,379 (29%)	37,616 (71%)	52,996
1975	158,037	61%	39%	31,153 (32%)	66,379 (68%)	97,532
1980	236,744	64%	36%	49,428 (43%)	64,975 (57%)	114,403
1984	100,946	50%	50%	8,760 (13%)	56,482 (87%)	65,242

Source: U.S. Department of the Interior, National Park Service, Recreational Grants Division.
[a] Standard Metropolitan Statistical Area.
[b] State grants from the Land and Water Conservation Fund for the District of Columbia, Puerto Rico, Mariana Islands, Guam, American Samoa, and the Virgin Islands are excluded from this analysis.

shift represents a choice by states and local government which is at least in part independent of the level of federal assistance.

Up until 1980, the majority of state grant funds were spent within metropolitan areas. However, historically, more land has been acquired outside of metropolitan areas (see Table 3). Again, this is a long-term trend that probably reflects the higher costs of buying urban land as well as the greater ease of buying lands on the metropolitan fringe or in more remote areas.

Since 1980 both the proportion of land bought and funds spent within metropolitan areas has declined. State officials attribute this to reduced funding levels in general and to federal urging that states spend grant funds more quickly. "We have had to back off complex projects in urban areas," a Massachusetts official commented, explaining that environmental reviews, appraisals, and acquisition arrangements are all more difficult in populated areas than in rural areas (Myers, 1987).

State versus Local Spending. State grants can be spent directly by a state or passed through to local governments. How much has been spent by each level of government? Does this affect what the money is used for? Are there discernible recent trends?

Figure 4 shows the division of funds between states and local governments for two periods, 1977–1980 and 1981–1984. Overall, despite a dramatic drop in the amount of federal grants (1981–1984), the division of funds between states and local governments was about the same in both periods: a little over one-third was sent by states, the rest by localities. Although there were changes from one period to the next in individual states, the overall division of funds was stable[2] (see Figure 5).

2. Maryland and Hawaii passed through more money to local governments after 1981, for example, while New York and Alabama retained more at the state level.

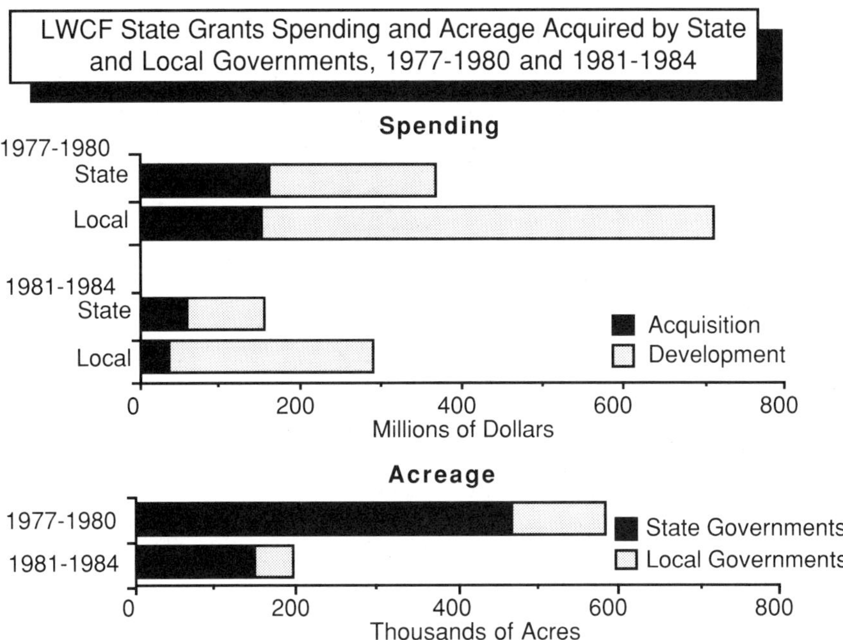

Figure 4. Sources: U.S. Department of the Interior, National Park Service, Recreation Grants Division.

The government unit that spends the money has considerable effect on what is done with it. Compared to local governments, states have been far more likely to buy land for parks than to develop facilities. Although states obligated only about half as much money as localities between 1977 and 1980, states spent about as much on acquisition as did localities (see Figure 4). States accounted for 80 percent of the recreational acreage acquired with the assistance of federal funds in this period. Local governments accounted for most of the development projects—73 percent. (This calculation combines development, redevelopment, and combination projects). After 1981, states continued to account for most of the land purchases; both states and local governments, however, spent a higher proportion of their grant funds on facilities development.

ASSESSING THE FUND'S OPERATION

Without question, the LWCF has made a significant contribution to America's outdoor legacy. Nevertheless, enormous needs exist at the federal level to meet the backlog of lands authorized for acquisition but not yet purchased, and to enable federal land-managing agencies to

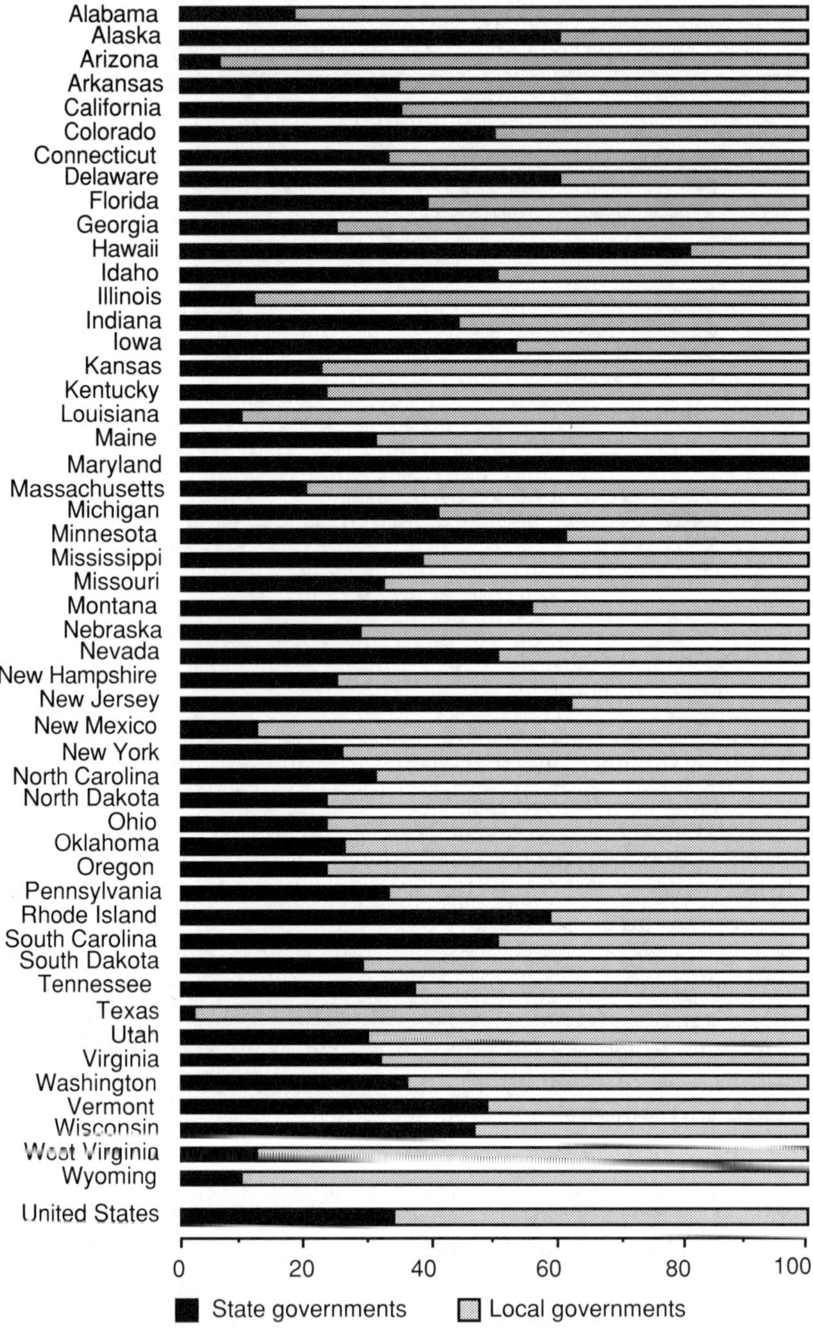

Figure 5. LWCF state grants: division of funds between state and local governments, 1977-1980. Source: The Conservation Foundation based on National Park Service data.

continue saving unprotected examples of America's landscape and ecosystems. The same is true at state and local levels where important resources get protected and where federal dollars leverage and catalyze valuable investment that protects resources and benefits recreational users across the country. What is needed now is consensus for a new kind of fund that can deal with land protection issues well into the 21st century.

Despite its successes, the LWCF has not escaped serious criticism. Some say that because the fund is not totally insulated from yearly political squabbles, it is subject to the whims of the political process. Moreover, appropriations from the LWCF have fallen far short of authorized levels; critics point out that the unstable funding level makes it difficult for federal agencies and, especially, states, to plan for future recreational needs. A more subtle complaint at the federal level is that the fund has spurred new park authorizations by giving Congress and others a false sense of having a huge pot of money to draw from when, in fact, no LWCF money is sitting idly by, waiting to be used.

Other shortcomings have been noted as well. Federal agencies may have trouble in some cases providing public access to acquired lands without purchasing easements from private landowners, for which funds may not be provided (Anderson interview). States are faced with having to comply with detailed planning and reporting requirements, some of which are claimed to be unnecessarily onerous and not entirely related to planning intentions. While conceived to foster a partnership among different levels of government, the fund has not provided for coordinating the activities and priorities of different public land systems. State Comprehensive Outdoor Recreation Plans were intended, in large part, to fulfill this need, but have fallen short for a variety of reasons.[3]

Most significantly, a vocal and effective constituency commensurate with the fund's importance—especially at the state and local levels—has not developed. Administration and congressional leaders continually observe that constituent support for the program is noticeably absent during budget deliberations, precisely the time when such support should be at a peak. Perhaps most revealing is the absence of virtually any fanfare or media attention when the LWCF was recently reauthorized for 25 years. For a program that has spent billions of dollars on thousands of projects throughout the country, the lack of a visible, forceful constituency to support its continued existence and funding is indeed troublesome.

3. Although State Comprehensive Outdoor Recreation Plans have strengthened planning at the state level, they lay out broad principles and directions, providing only general guidance to localities.

The structure of the LWCF, especially the state grants program, accurately reflected the needs and opportunities of the time. A new fund needs to respond to not only perceived shortcomings, but also to the significant differences that exist today. These include:

- A large number and diversity of private groups, such as land trusts, working creatively to conserve, manage, and interpret outdoor resources.
- The complexity of new concepts in recreational resource conservation, such as greenways and trails, which rely on mixed public and private ownership and the purchase of less-than-fee interests in land to protect special places close to where people live.
- Increased interest in protecting fragile natural areas, including wildlife habitat and wetlands where conventional forms of recreation may not be feasible.
- Increased interest in historic and cultural resources.

THE CURRENT DEBATE

While the LWCF was recently reauthorized without change for another 25 years, serious debate is shaping up in Congress over its reform. In simply extending the fund's life for another generation, conservation leaders in Congress sought to move the debate from whether there should in fact be a LWCF to how the fund should be structured and administered. As a result, issues such as the role and purpose of the fund, sources of revenue, and the institutional mechanism for administering it are likely to receive the most attention.

The President's Commission on Americans Outdoors set the stage for this debate with its recommendations released in early 1987 (President's Commission on Americans Outdoors 1987). Basically, this presidentially appointed group recommended the establishment of a true trust fund as a successor to the LWCF. The commission envisioned a fund big enough to disburse at least $1 billion a year to federal, state, and local agencies for outdoor recreation needs.[4]

The commission called for the creation of a new quasi-public institution to "stimulate grassroots leadership and promote innovation and excellence." Recognizing the tremendous contribution of private groups and the role partnerships play in stimulating investments in natural and recreational resources, the commission recommended that

4. Two commissioners—Senator Malcolm Wallop (R-WY) and Representative Barbara Vucanovich (R-NV)—did not support any fixed level of federal funding, preferring to leave questions of funding up to the annual budget process in Congress.

small portion of the new fund's proceeds be set aside for local cooperative conservation efforts. A new institution was also proposed—a sort of national endowment for conservation modeled after the National Endowment for the Arts and Humanities—to catalyze and promote innovative action at the local level.

Major national environmental, recreational, and historic preservation groups convened shortly after the release of the report to develop common principles for legislation and a strategy to build on the momentum created by the report. Led by the National Parks and Conservation Association and the Wilderness Society, the group adopted 13 consensus points in May 1987 as the basis for legislative action. The points embodied, and in some cases went beyond, the commission's recommendations:

1. In order to ensure a consistent, stable source of funding for conservation, recreation and historic preservation purposes, a fund should be established, called the "American Heritage Trust." The trust should guarantee a minimum return of $1.75 billion annually and be either a dedicated Treasury account (like the Highway Trust Fund) or a true trust fund which derives revenue from invested principal.
2. The trust should be divided into two funds including a traditional Land and Water Conservation Fund (LWCF) and Historic Preservation Fund (HPF). The Land and Water Conservation Fund portion should embrace those activities included in the Urban Parks and Recreation Recovery Program. The percentage of money available to each fund will be fixed.
3. The trust should rely primarily on existing LWCF and HPF revenue sources, particularly outer continental shelf oil- and gas-leasing revenue, to maintain the philosophy that as we deplete our nonrenewable resource base, a portion of the revenue should be reinvested to permanently protect other public resources. The existing unappropriated balances of the two funds should also be tapped as a source of funding. Additional sources of funding to augment the trust should be examined.
4. The trust should provide a fixed level of income, the total amount of which will not be subject to congressional appropriation. With regard to the federal side of the Land and Water Conservation Fund, Congress will determine the allocation for federal agencies and projects.
5. The federal share of the Land and Water Conservation Fund would be used solely for land acquisition; the state and local side could be used for acquisition, development, rehabilita-

tion/renovation, planning, research, and inventories. There should be a congressionally encouraged emphasis on acquisition at the state and local level.

6. A portion of the Land and Water Conservation Fund should be set aside for an innovation grants program. Federal, state, and local agencies and nonprofit organizations will be eligible to apply on a competitive basis for these innovation grants.
7. Legislation establishing the trust should specify the allocation among the accounts. Within the LWCF, the allocation between the federal and state/local sides should be specified in accordance with the guidelines below. Within the HPF, the allocation among the states, local governments, and the National Trust for Historic Preservation should be specified.
8. Forty percent of the total amount in the Land and Water Conservation Fund should be available to federal agencies, with 5 to 10 percent of this set aside for innovative federal programs in accordance with criteria established by the endowment. The federal government should be encouraged to use the technique of greenlining countryside parks to foster land conservation.
9. Sixty percent of the Land and Water Conservation Fund should be available to state and local governments on a matching basis. No less than 5 percent and no more than 10 percent of this amount should be available for innovation grants in accordance within criteria established by the endowment. States are encouraged to pass at least 50 percent of their funds on to local governments.
10. Two congressionally chartered public endowments should be established. The endowments will be responsible for administering the nonfederal side of the Land and Water Conservation Fund and Historic Preservation Fund, as well as the innovation grants program. The endowments will establish criteria for eligibility for innovation grants. They will create a national focus on conservation, recreation, and historic preservation within the federal government. The endowments could also have functions related to information and encouraging public participation, and would assume an advisory role with regard to Congress and the president. Administrative costs for the endowments will come out of the trust.
11. For the states to be eligible for funding from the LWCF, they must have completed a comprehensive inventory of states' and localities' resource and recreation needs.
12. There should be an effective means for nonprofit organizations to participate in the Land and Water Conservation Fund program. Thus, for all eligible LWCF activities, private non-

profit organizations should be eligible to participate fully in the program. A minimum of 5 percent of the total amount available to state and local governments shall be spent in this manner, with the state and local governments' share of LWCF contributing 90 percent of the project funds and nonprofits contributing 10 percent. Nonprofit organizations should work from state-sanctioned priority lists based on comprehensive resource and recreation needs inventories for states and localities.

13. States are encouraged to establish similar state-level funds for conservation, recreation, and historic preservation purposes.

LEGISLATIVE DEVELOPMENTS

During the 100th Congress (1987–1988) several bills have been introduced or are awaiting introduction that propose some fundamental changes in the way the LWCF operates. Varying proposals are offered in terms of the source of revenues, how they would be allocated, the institutional framework for administering them, and the role of Congress in appropriating future sums.

Source of Funds

Several options exist for funding a restructured LWCF. Potential revenue sources include an excise tax on recreation equipment, new recreation user fees, revenues derived from onshore federal resource development activities, park bonds, and an income tax check-off. Both user fees and an excise tax are based in part on the "user pays" principle, whereby the beneficiaries of parks and recreation facilities bear at least a portion of the costs in providing them. User fees, of course, already contribute to the LWCF (although they did not from 1968 to 1980). Park bonds and income tax check-offs have been used successfully by states. Rhode Island, Massachusetts, and New Jersey are among states that passed major land initiatives in November 1987, for example, to fund open-space acquisition. Moreover, more than two-thirds of the states offer tax check-offs that allow individuals to contribute money toward wildlife or habitat protection programs from any refund due on their income tax return; such check-offs generated a total of $9.85 million in 1986 (Wildlife Conservation Fund of America 1987).

Most measures currently under consideration by Congress continue to rely heavily on outer continental shelf oil- and gas-leasing receipts as the primary source of revenue for the LWCF. Senator John Chafeee (R-R.I.) and Representative Chester G. Atkins (D-MA) (S. 1338, H.R. 3736, 100th Cong.) have introduced companion bills to establish a $1 billion per year trust fund—called the "Outdoor American Conservation Fund"—that would derive its revenues from a mix of offshore oil- and gas-lease receipts, the sale of conservation bonds, and a new national real estate transfer tax on large dollar transactions.

The Nature Conservancy has urged Congress to "provide authority for a special, one-time issuance of American Heritage Bonds" by a new federally chartered corporation. This quasi-public corporation would also help manage the proceeds of the bond sale as a permanent endowment (Flicker 1987). The corporation would issue $10 billion of American Heritage Bonds; the proceeds would be invested as a permanent endowment that will generate about $1 billion annually, to be used solely for LWCF purposes.

Under the conservancy proposal, the Department of the Interior would continue to manage the LWCF program, and Congress would continue to determine funding priorities through the appropriations process. Outer Continental Shelf leasing revenues, as currently allocated, would be dedicated to debt service for the life of the bonds and the conservancy anticipates that full repayment could occur within 10 to 15 years of issuance. The Nature Conservancy envisions a 25-year time frame to fully capitalize the fund. Total costs to the federal government are estimated to be $4 to 6 billion, assuming debt service for the bond would be $10 to 12 billion over the next decade and that $6 billion of the LWCF's unexpended balance would be deauthorized.

Congressman Morris K. Udall (D-AZ), the influential chairman of the House Interior Committee, has introduced a bill (H.R. 4127, 100th Congr.) that would establish a dedicated trust fund, the "American Heritage Trust," funded by current revenue sources. Interest on fund receipts would be reserved exclusively for use in land acquisition and recreation development. The new trust would incorporate both the LWCF and the Historic Preservation Fund, although these funds would continue to operate independent of each other. Under Representative Udall's proposal, the unappropriated balances of the LWCF would be invested in Treasury securities and funds would accrue annual interest from it. The interest would be automatically appropriated, subject to obligation limitations for LWCF purposes.[5]

Arctic National Wildlife Refuge Proposal and the LWCF. Senator J. Bennett Johnston (D-LA), who chairs the Senate Energy and Natural

5. **EDITOR'S NOTE:** Udall's bill, H. R. 4127, was introduced March 9, 1988, as this volume went to press.

Resources Committee, has introduced legislation (S 735, 100th Cong.) to restructure how receipts from oil and gas drilling in units of the National Wildlife Refuge System are allocated. Fifty percent of the money received from these oil and gas leases is to be distributed to the state in which the refuge unit is located; 25 percent would go into the LWCF; and the remaining 25 percent into the general treasury. Critics of the bill largely view it as a way for Louisiana and Alaska to reap large dividends from oil drilling on refuges in those states where energy supplies are relatively abundant. The proposed drilling in the Arctic National Wildlife Refuge (ANWR) in Alaska's north slope would generate large amounts of leasing revenue if oil is found.

The Alaska refuge drilling proposal is enormously controversial because it would occur in a pristine wilderness area and have effects on a major caribou herd and other wildife. Many conservationists who oppose drilling in the refuge are concerned that allocation of 25 percent of the refuge's oil revenues to LWCF could help win support for allowing the drilling to take place. Because of his position as chairman of the Senate Energy and Natural Resources Committee, Senator Johnston strongly influences legislation covering both energy development and LWCF. Linking the two issues in S.735 has divided the conservation community. Some organizations feel the potential revenue to enhance LWCF from oil exploration and recovery in the Arctic Refuge is sufficiently attractive to compensate for damage that may occur to the refuge. Others strongly feel that the threats to wildlife and the loss of wilderness values from energy development in the refuge outweigh any benefits gained through additions to the LWCF. Debates over ANWR and the LWCF are two important issues that probably deserve attention and consideration on their own merits independently. Senator Johnston's influence, however, increases the prospect of linking the future of the LWCF to oil production and is likely to result in a more heated debate over LWCF reform than would occur if the issues were considered separately.

Allocation

Some legislative proposals modify the current way LWCF appropriations are to be allocated. The Chafee-Atkins proposal would allocate 40 percent of the proceeds to the federal government, 55 percent as grants to states and the remaining 5 percent to a newly created "National Endowment for Open Space." Of the federal share, the bill provides that no single agency can receive more than 50 percent of the money available in any one year. States are required to grant a minimum of 50 percent of their share to localities and nonprofit, local land trusts—the first time fund revenues to states would be directly available to private organizations. Under the Chafee-Atkins proposal, federal dollars for state grants would be available on a 50-percent matching basis for land acquisition projects and on a 35-percent rotating basis for planning, improvement, and rehabilitation projects.

Under Representative Udall's proposal, money from the trust would be divided primarily between federal acquisition and grants to state and local governments, with a smaller percentage dedicated to funding projects included in the Urban Parks and Recreation Recovery Program. Federal land acquisition and state grants programs would each receive at least 30 percent of the annual proceeds; 10 percent could be matched by states to serve as principal for state heritage trusts; 10 percent would be used for purposes of the Urban Park and Recreation Act; and the remaining 20 percent would be allocated to any of the eligible users, as Congress sees fit. As with the Chafee-Atkins proposal, private organizations would be eligible to receive state grants.

Institutional Framework

The administration of the fund, including the need for a new institution, is one of the most interesting aspects of the LWCF debate. The President's Commission on Americans Outdoors prompted interest in this topic with its proposal for a new institution to provide federal seed money to stimulate innovative action at the grassroots level. This idea has been embodied in the bills introduced by Senator Chafee and Representative Atkins, both of which would establish a National Endowment for Open Space to provide grants-in-aid to public agencies and private nonprofit groups for a variety of specified purposes. Key considerations regarding the need for a new implementing structure include the following:

- Should a new institution be created in a time of severe budget deficits?
- If so, how much money should it be given to administer each year?
- Can adequate steps be instituted to ensure public accountability?
- How broad should its mandate be?

Since its inception, the LWCF has been administered through several different agencies in the Department of the Interior. Following a recommendation by the Outdoor Recreation Resources Review Commission, a federal Bureau of Outdoor Recreation was created within the Interior department to help administer the LWCF, provide technical assistance to state and local governments in their use of grants, and prepare a National Outdoor Recreation Plan. Under President Carter the bureau was transformed into the Heritage Conservation and Recreation Service, which assumed responsibility for administering the LWCF. During the first year of the Reagan Administration, Secretary of the Interior James Watt abolished the Heritage Conservation and Recreation Service and transferred its LWCF responsibilities to the National Park Service.

Several critics believe that park service administration of the LWCF is unwise because the service has an inherent conflict of interest: like other federal land agencies, the park service wants as much LWCF money as it can get for its own land acquisition needs. States, in particular, complain about a lack of attention given to them since the park service began administering the fund. At the same time, growing discontent over the politicization of the park service by the Reagan Administration and the service's reported lack of attention to historic preservation have fueled interest in seeing the park service removed from Interior and the historic preservation functions split off from it.

Members of the coalition of national environmental, recreation, and historic preservation organizations that reached consensus on the 13 points for a new LWCF have expressed divergent views about the structure and responsibilities of a new LWCF institution. Some continue to support the concept of an independent organization recommended by the President's commission in the Chafee-Atkins bills.

Recent proposals by some organizations, however, go far beyond the idea of a quasi-public entity to administer an innovative grants program. Seeing the opportunity through a revamped LWCF to get at longer-term problems with the National Park Service and its administration of park units, LWCF grants, and historic preservation programs, some groups have broadened their concept of a new institution to include virtually all of the functions of the National Park Service. A few organizations have proposed the formation of a new quasi-public "Heritage Agency," which would be responsible for administering both a new "Heritage Trust Fund," and the state grant, historic preservation, and park system responsibilities of the National Park Service under three separate directorates reporting to a common chairperson and board.

The specifics of the Heritage Agency proposal will undoubtedly change over time to reflect differing views and changing strategic opportunities. Nonetheless, some type of new organization is likely to be included in a concrete legislative proposal. More importantly, the current institutional debate points to deep-seeded discontent with how the LWCF has been administered in the past.

Type of Trust Fund

To many conservationists, the most important issue facing the LWCF is whether it can be converted into a true trust fund, no longer subject to annual congressional appropriations. It has often been proposed that a true trust fund be established as a fund distribution mechanism. As discussed, several current proposals envision a trust amassing capital of $10 billion over the next decade or so. With revenues raised in various ways and invested in U.S. Treasury notes at 10 percent interest, such a trust would yield $1 billion per year. Thus, the fund would provide more money annually than has ever been appropriated from the LWCF. Most significantly, the money flow would be steady and reliable, because it would be insulated from the annual congressional appropriations process.

A basic objection to trust funds is that they limit Congress's ability to set annual priorities, particularly in times of fiscal austerity. Yet the value of parks and refuges to society is beyond question, as is the need to assure a steady source of funds to plan and provide for the needs of future generations.

If there is an additional justification for a park and recreation land trust fund, it lies mainly in the source of the revenues. Because general tax revenues have no close relation to parkland, some find little justification for a parkland trust financed by such revenues. But private and federal resource development activities diminish the nation's natural environment and frequently permanently preclude alternative uses of the land or water. Thus, it makes sense that some of the federal revenues gained from consumption of the nation's natural resources should be used to preserve other natural resources.

There is considerable debate among those knowledgeable with the workings of Congress, the budget process, and other so-called trust funds as to whether any fund could be completely insulated from the politics of annual appropriations. Yet regardless of the shape of its financial mechanism, a future LWCF needs to be structured so as to create and maintain a powerful constituency. Strong political support is needed both to reform the LWCF and to keep the dollars flowing. Even if a true trust fund were created, political support outside of Washington, D.C., will be necessary to keep it that way under pressure from opponents and other needy government programs, or when up for legislative renewal. Whatever the legislature does one year, it can undo the next.

The design of a new federal funding mechanism to support the next generation of land conservation efforts is one of the most important issues facing the conservation community. The outcome will have a long-lasting influence on the availability and quality of landscapes, wildlife habitat, and recreational experiences. Conservationists need to be prepared to answer hard questions about the effectiveness of the program—how the fund has made a difference—and explain how their proposals will address new needs and opportunities efficiently and wisely. Establishing a new fund is more than a search for money; it is a strategy to develop new alliances and support conservation programs into the 21st century.

ADDENDUM

Obtaining a LWCF Grant—The Rules of the Road for Localities

In general, three steps are involved for a locality to obtain a state LWCF grant: development of a project proposal; submission of the proposal to the state for review by the state liaison officer for the LWCF; and approval of state-submitted proposals by the National Park Service.

Formal requirements guide the overall process. However, within each state, there are variations in how the process works depending on the relationship among parties, the ability of local governments to put together matching funds, how the regional office of the National Park Service interprets the regulations, and clarity and dispatch of decisions about funding availability and priorities.

Because each proposed project must receive state approval, local proposals that are consistent with state priorities and requirements have the greatest chance of being funded. The state, in its liaison role, typically notifies local and county planning boards of grant application requirements and deadlines, which may be a year in advance of fund disbursement. If such notice does not occur, localities may request information from the state liaison officer. Liaison officers are authorized to represent their states in administrating the LWCF program and usually are ranking officials in state parks, recreation, or natural resource agencies.

State recreation priorities are established in the State Comprehensive Outdoor Recreation Plan, which each state prepares every five years in order to be eligible for LWCF grant assistance. The priorities defined by the plan, based on an inventory of recreational land and facilities and an assessment of need, guide the selection of projects for further funding consideration. In general, the state plan serves as a starting point in the state "open project selection process," an evaluation system established by each state and subject to approval by the National Park Service. The process is supposed to ensure that eligible sponsors have an opportunity to participate in and benefit from the LWCF program, and that competitive evaluation of projects reflects state recreation priorities. The plans are usually written broadly enough to accomodate unforeseen opportunities not specifically addressed.

The park service administers and disburses LWCF state and local grants through its regional offices. While service officials follow a standard procedure for determing each state's annual LWCF allocation, the amount available to localities varies from state to state. Because LWCF grant funds have been so reduced in recent years, many local projects do not get funded. Most of the projects approved by the state are funded by the service, if they otherwise meet technical requirements, since liaison officers usually know how large their allocation will be in a given year.

Private land conservation organizations, such as The Nature Conservancy and the Trust for Public Land, have successfully participated in LWCF projects by providing a land donation to match the state's share or acquiring land for a project that the state intends to repurchase. However, the difficulties reportedly encountered by many private groups in finding out what funds are available, what deadlines exist, and in aligning their projects with state priorities have limited wider participation.

REFERENCES

Anderson, Oscar. Interview with author. Washington, D.C., January 14, 1988.

——. 1987. *State of the Environment: A View toward the Nineties.* The Conservation Foundation. Washington, D.C.

Flicker, John. 1987. Letter of September 22, 1987 to U.S. Congressman Morris K. Udall.

Graves, Robert. Interview with author. Washington, D.C., January 13, 1988.

Myers, Phyllis. 1987. *State Grants for Parklands 1965–1984: Lessons for a New Land and Water Conservation Fund.* The Conservation Foundation. Washington, D.C.

The Conservation Foundation. 1985. *National Parks for a New Generation: Visions, Realities, Prospects.* The Conservation Foundation. Washington, D.C.

The President's Commission on Americans Outdoors. 1987. *The Report of the President's Commission—Americans Outdoors: The Legacy, the Challenge.* Island Press. Washington, D.C.

Siehl, George H. 1981. The Land and Water Conservation Fund: Origin and Congressional Intent. Report No. 81–98ENR. Congressional Research Service. Washington, D.C.

U.S. Dept. of Agriculture, Forest Service. 1987a. Land and Water Conservation Fund, Acquired Land. Washington, D.C.

——., Forest Service. 1987b. Land and Water Conservation Fund: Adjusted Appropriations by Fiscal Year. Washington, D.C.

U.S. Department of the Interior, National Park Service. 1984. Federal Recreation Fee Report, 1983. Washington, D.C.

——., National Park Service. 1987a. Purchases by Fiscal Year, Land and Water Conservation Fund. Washington, D.C.

——., Fish and Wildlife Service. 1987b. Land and Water Conservation Fund, History of Obligations. Washington, D.C.

——., Fish and Wildlife Service. 1987c. Summary of Land Obligations. Washington, D.C.

——., Bureau of Land Management. 1987d. Land and Water Conservation Fund Acquisitions. Washington, D.C.

Wildlife Conservation Fund of America. 1987 "Fish and Wildlife Agency Funding 1987." Wildlife Conservation Fund of America. Columbus, Ohio.

Michael Mantell is director of the Land, Heritage, and Wildlife Program; Phyllis Myers is senior associate; and Robert Reed is a research fellow at The Conservation Foundation in Washington, D.C.

Part Three

Conservation Challenges

The main stem of the Platte River in Nebraska is an essential stopover for sandhill cranes and thousands of other migrating birds. The river has lost much of its flow to water-development projects; future projects may reduce its usefulness to wildlife. *Nebraska Game and Parks Commission*

WILDLIFE AND WATER PROJECTS ON THE PLATTE RIVER

Thomas G. Shoemaker

INTRODUCTION

Since 1967, the Platte River Basin in Colorado, Wyoming, and Nebraska (see Figure 1) has been the scene of continued and often intense controversy between conservationists and water development interests. The theme of the conflict is a common one in the arid west: an ongoing struggle between a conservation community that wants water left in the river to benefit wildlife versus a development community that wishes to divert water to meet growing agricultural and municipal needs.

The focus of the controversy is a 225-mile reach of the North Platte and Platte rivers, between the towns of Sutherland and Duncan, Nebraska (see Figure 1). Of special concern is the 80-mile "Big Bend" segment between Overton and Chapman. The Big Bend is one of the most important migratory bird habitats in North America. While more than 240 bird species have been recorded there, the Big Bend is especially valued as habitat for several species that depend on the river's wide, open channel and nearby wetlands: sandhill crane (*Grus canadensis*), waterfowl, the threatened piping plover (*Charadrius melodus*), and three endangered species—whooping crane (*Grus amer-*

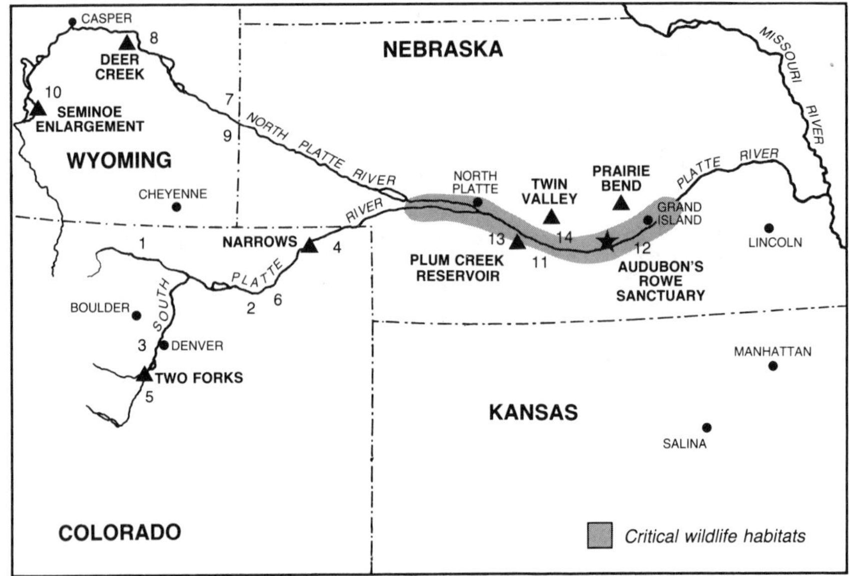

Figure 1. The Platte River basin in Colorado, Wyoming, and Nebraska. Numbers 1 to 14 show the general location of water development sites (see Table 1).

icana), least tern (*Sterna antillarum*), and bald eagle (*Haliaeetus leucocephalus*) (Currier *et al.* 1985). A 54-mile section of the Big Bend, from Lexington to Denman, was designated critical habitat for the whooping crane by the U.S. Fish and Wildlife Service (FWS) (43 *Federal Register* 21784 [1978]). FWS also has designated two sections of the river as Category 1 Resource areas: the 20-mile section between Sutherland and North Platte was recognized for its "unique and irreplaceable" value to sandhill cranes; and the 80-mile section between Overton and Chapman was similarly recognized for its value to sandhill cranes and white-fronted geese (*Anser albifrons*) (U.S. Department of the Interior 1987a).[1]

At issue is the cumulative effect of past and future water development on habitats used by these species. The Platte and its tributaries have been manipulated to provide water for agriculture, power generation, and domestic and industrial uses since 1838 (Eschner *et al.* 1983). Past water development has depleted annual instream flow volumes in central Nebraska by nearly 70 percent, which in turn has profoundly changed the character of the river (Williams 1978). What was once an unvegetated river described as "a mile wide and an inch deep" is now, in many places, a series of narrow channels meandering through a dense floodplain forest. The result, according to conserva-

1. Category 1 Resources are defined by the FWS Mitigation Policy (48 *Federal Register* 7644 [1981]) as "unique and irreplaceable resources." The mitigation goal for these areas is "no loss of existing habitat value."

tionists, is a dramatic reduction in the availability of suitable habitat for the migratory birds that depend on the river and adjacent wetlands, birds that the United States is obligated to protect under international treaties with Canada, Mexico, and the Soviet Union, and federal laws including the Migratory Bird Treaty Act (16 U.S.C.A. 703 *et seq.*) and the Endangered Species Act of 1973 (16 U.S.C.A. 1531 *et seq.*).

Conservationists believe that new water developments will result in further habitat deterioration which would diminish survival prospects for the threatened and endangered species and reduce waterfowl and sandhill crane populations. In their view, new water developments should not be permitted until the instream flow levels needed to sustain the Platte's habitats have been quantified and legally guaranteed. In contrast, water development interests contend that additional reservoirs and diversion projects are necessary; failure to develop additional water supplies, they maintain, endangers the economic well-being of Colorado, Wyoming, and Nebraska.

Past Conflicts

These contrasting views have led to a series of battles between conservationists and water development proponents that has lasted more than 20 years. Four projects in particular set the stage for the controversy that continues today.

The Mid-State Reclamation Project. The conflict between water development and wildlife interests on the Platte began in earnest in 1967 when Congress authorized federal participation in the Nebraska Mid-State Reclamation project. This Bureau of Reclamation (BuRec) proposal would have diverted more than 50 percent of the remaining streamflow in central Nebraska to irrigate 140,000 acres (Wallenstrom 1976a, U.S. Department of the Interior 1981a). FWS opposed the project unless it was modified to guarantee specific instream flows to maintain whooping crane, sandhill crane, and waterfowl habitat. Project proponents rejected this alternative, resulting in a prolonged controversy. The project was finally defeated in a local referendum in 1975 (Wallenstrom 1976a).

The Grayrocks Project. During 1978, controversy erupted over the Grayrocks Dam and Reservoir that were proposed for the Laramie River, a tributary of the North Platte in Wyoming. The dam and reservoir projects were components of the $1.6 billion Missouri Basin Power Project. The state of Nebraska, National Wildlife Federation, National Audubon Society, and Nebraska Wildlife Federation sued the federal Rural Electrification Administration and the Corps of Engineers, contending, in part, that these agencies had failed to properly consider the impacts of the project on whooping crane critical habitat in Nebraska (*Nebraska v. Rural Electrification Administration, 12 ERC 1156[1978]).* The court ruled that the Rural Electrification Administration had failed to prepare an adequate environmental impact statement and had also failed to comply with Section 7 of the Endangered Species Act, which requires federal agencies to consult with FWS regarding potential effects of their projects on endangered species.

The controversy was settled in a complex agreement in December 1979. While the dam was allowed to proceed, the agreement restricted the amount of water it could use and required the project sponsors to establish a $7.5-million trust fund for use in monitoring and maintaining whooping crane habitats (MacDonnell 1985). The money was used to fund the Platte River Whooping Crane Habitat Maintenance Trust (Platte River Trust), a nonprofit organization that is now devoted to the conservation of migratory bird habitat on the Platte.

The Wildcat Project. The Wildcat project extended the controversy to the South Platte River in Colorado. The Riverside Irrigation District and Public Service Company of Colorado proposed a joint project to develop a 60,000 acre-foot reservoir to supply cooling water for Public Service's Pawnee Power Plant as well as supplemental irrigation water. The U.S. Army Corps of Engineers denied an application for a 404 permit for the project after FWS issued a biological opinion in 1982 that concluded that the flow depletions resulting from the project would jeopardize the continued existence of the whooping crane and adversely modify the species' critical habitat (MacDonnell 1985).

In its biological opinion, FWS recommended that these impacts could be avoided either by guaranteeing flow releases during certain times of the year or by managing habitat for whooping cranes in Nebraska. Project sponsors rejected these alternatives and challenged the Corps' decision. The court upheld the Corps' decision of Endangered Species Act review requirements to the 404 permit process (*Riverside Irrigation Dist. v. Andrews*, 568 F. Supp. 583 [D. Colo. 1983], affirmed by *Riverside Irrigation Dist. v. Andrews*, 758 F. 2nd 508 [10th Cir. 1985]). These decisions have indefinitely delayed the project. The Public Service Company of Colorado subsequently obtained cooling water from existing diversion sources on the South Platte. However, project sponsors say they may still pursue development of a project on Wildcat Creek in the future.

The Narrows Unit. The Bureau of Reclamation's proposed Narrows Unit on the South Platte in eastern Colorado is a $377-million, 1.1 million acre-foot reservoir, the principal purpose of which is to supply irrigation water to 287,000 acres of land (U.S. Department of the

Interior 1985). In 1983, FWS issued a biological opinion that concluded that projected streamflow depletions would jeopardize the continued existence of the whooping crane and adversely modify its critical habitat (U.S. Department of the Interior 1983a). FWS recommended that the proposed operation of the project be modified to provide water releases to maintain specified instream flows in central Nebraska. BuRec rejected this alternative.

Faced with an impasse, BuRec and FWS initiated a joint study to develop other alternatives to allow the project to proceed without adversely affecting whooping crane habitat. The Platte River Management Joint Study now involves BuRec, FWS, the states of Colorado, Wyoming, and Nebraska, and representatives of both water development and environmental organizations. As explained in detail in the section entitled, "The Search for a Solution," the alternative water management plans have not yet been developed.

Current Status

The result of these past conflicts on the Platte is essentially a stalemate between wildlife and water development interests. New water projects have not been allowed to proceed without first implementing alternatives that would offset the effects of flow depletions. Development proponents have consistently rejected these alternatives and instead delayed their projects. Although additional streamflow depletions have not yet occurred from new projects, conservationists have made virtually no progress toward their goal of legally protecting instream flows in the Platte River. The fundamental question, "Can the Platte River basin sustain additional water development and its critical wildlife habitats?" remains unanswered after more than two decades of scientific research, negotiations, and legal battles.

The controversy over the Platte River has evolved into one of the most complex and long-standing natural resource issues in the west. Current events promise only to increase the intensity of the debate. As the controversy moves into its third decade, it can be characterized by four major themes:

- *Increased Competition.* The pressure for new water development is greater now than ever before. At the same time, conservationists and wildlife managers believe more strongly than ever that the Platte is already overdeveloped. Conservation organizations have expanded their activities and increased their commitment to protecting the river's unique habitats.
- *Scientific Debate.* The Platte River ecosystem is extremely complex. Despite years of research, considerable uncertainty remains regarding the interrelationships between flows in the river and the well-being of migratory birds.

- *Political and Legal Debate.* Efforts to protect instream flows on the central Platte occur within a legal context that did not allow protection of instream flows until 1984. While water laws now allow protection of instream flows, legal and political impediments remain that make it difficult to achieve such protection on the Platte.
- *The Search for a Solution.* Paradoxically, even as the debate becomes more intense, the opposing interests are attempting to devise water management plans that meet both the needs of wildlife and humans. Although no firm plans have been devised, potential solutions are being explored.

The remaining sections of this chapter explore these themes in greater detail.

THE COMPETITION FOR WATER

Water for Human Use

The waters of the Platte River basin have been prized by humans for many years. Direct diversion of water began in the basin in 1838 (Eschner *et al.* 1983). By 1885, demand for irrigation water exceeded the reliable supplies of natural flows. Municipalities, irrigation districts, and private entities responded to the shortage of water by building storage reservoirs to capture peak spring runoff for use during later periods of low flow. Today, literally thousands of diversion structures and more than 194 storage reservoirs capture nearly 70 percent of the Platte River's natural flow (Williams 1978, Eschner *et al.* 1983)[2] One of the most extensive water supply systems in the west, the Platte provides water for an estimated 2.5 million people, 2.8 million acres of irrigated cropland, and more than 400 megawatts of hydroelectric power generating capacity (U.S. Department of the Interior 1982).

The demand for water continues to increase throughout the Platte River basin, resulting in proposals to capture the remaining "excess" (unallocated) flows with new diversions and storage reservoirs. During 1987, 14 surface water development proposals were active at some stage of planning or permitting (See Table 1 and Figure 1) (Faanes, in press). These projects reflect the diversity of current water demands in the basin. The Narrows Dam and Reservoir, a traditional large dam project to provide water for new irrigation, is still under consideration despite the previously noted conflicts. The Two Forks, Colorado, and Deer

2. This figure refers to reservoirs with capacity greater than 5,000 acre-feet. Numerous smaller reservoirs are also present.

Table 1
Summary of Current Water Development Proposals in the Platte River Basin.

Project name	Loc.	Project Proponents	Cost	Features	Purposes	Depletion	Status
COLORADO							
Cache la Poudre	1	Northern Colorado WCD	$1.5 billion	200,000 a-f reservoir 350,000 a-f reservoir 50,000 a-f reservoir 2,100 MW hydroelectric	P: 2,100 MW M & I 282,000 people A: NA	NA	Pre-feasibility studies ongoing through 1989.
Narrows Unit	2	BuRec Lower S. Platte WCD Central Colorado WCD	$377 million	1,333,000 a-f reservoir	A: 287,070 ac	89,000 a-f	Delayed indefinitely pending resolution of T & E species conflicts.
Senac Reservoir	3	City of Aurora	$28 million	31,000 a-f reservoir	M & I: NA	15 a-f	Under construction
South Platte/ Frenchman Creek	4	BuRec, Central Yuma County GWD Frenchman GWD Marks Butte GWD Sandhills GWD Upper Republican GWD Frenchman Valley GWD H and RW ID Frenchman-Cambridge ID	NA	Diversion to existing reservoir	GW: NA	50,000 a-f	Feasibility studies began during 1987.
Two Forks	5	City of Denver 23 suburbs	$461 million	1,100,000 a-f reservoir	M & I: 1,564,000 people	14,800 a-f	Final EIS to be issued 1988. Permit decisions expected 1988.

(cont.)

Table 1 *(cont.)*

Project name	Loc.	Project Proponents	Cost	Features	Purposes	Depletion	Status
Wildcat	6	Public Service Co. Riverside ID	$25 million	60,000 a-f reservoir	P: NA A:NA	14,000 a-f	Permits denied 1983.Project delayed indefinitely.
WYOMING							
Corn Creek	7	WY Water Development Commission Corn Creek ID	$45 million	Irrigation diversion	A: 15,000 ac	32,500 a-f	Project delayed due to economic conditions
Deer Creek	8	WY Water Deverlopment Commission City of Casper	$52 million	66,000 a-f reservoir	M & I: 60,000 people	11,000 a-f	Final EIS issued 1987. Permit decisions expected 1988.
Horse Creek	9	WY Water Development Commission Goshen ID	$11 million	10,000 a-f reservoir	A: NA	6,000 a-f	Project delayed due to economic conditions.
Seminole Dam Enlargement	10	BuRec WY Water Development Commission City of Casper	$73 million	700,000 a-f enlargement of existing reservoir	M & I: NA	15,800 a-f	Feasibility studies ongoing until 1989.
NEBRASKA							
Catherland	11	Catherland RD	$82 million	120,500 a-f reservoir	A: 66,500 ac	125,000 a-f	Water rights approved 1987. Planning studies ongoing.
Groundwater Recharge Demonstration	12	BuRec Central Platte NRD	NA	Diversion to recharge basin	GW: NA	1,400 a-f	Not included in 1988 BuRec budget. Status uncertain.

Plum Creek	13	Upper Big Blue NRD Platte River Trust Central Nebraska Public Power and ID	$185 million	250,000 a-f reservoir	Instream flow maintenance	8,800 a-f	Included with Prairie Bend project; EIS due 1988.
Prairie Bend/ Twin Valley	14	BuRec Central Platte NRD Central Nebraska Conservation Association	$208 million	50,125 a-f reservoir 23,360 a-f reservoir 9,470 a-f reservoir 4 small reservoirs 16 recharge ponds	GW: 106,000 ac	102,000 a-f	EIS to be released during 1988.

Locations are shown on Figure 1.
ID = Irrigation District
GWD = Groundwater District
NRD = Natural Resource District
RD = Reclamation District
NA = data not available
A = Agriculture
GW = Groundwater Recharge
M = Municipal
I = Industry
P = Power Generation

Sources (by project number):
1 Northern Colorado Water Conservancy District 1986; Dreher interview.
2 U.S. Department of the Interior 1985
3 Kemper interview
4 Weidleman interview
5 U.S. Army Corps of Engineers 1986
6 Eastom interview
7 Purcell interview
8 U.S. Army Corps of Engineers 1987
9 Purcell interview
10 Mercer interview
11 Wallin interview
12 Andrews interview
13 Andrews interview
14 Andrews interview
All depletion estimates are from Faanes 1987.

Creek, Wyoming, projects would provide water for municipal and industrial use, reflecting the increasing human population in the basin. Final permitting decisions are currently pending on both of these projects.

Two other proposals, Prairie Bend and the South Platte-Frenchman Creek, reflect the close interrelationship between groundwater and surface water in the basin. Both of these projects would divert Platte River water to reservoirs where the water would be allowed to seep into the ground to recharge depleted aquifers. These projects would "rescue" lands currently irrigated by wells from reverting to dryland agriculture when natural ground water supplies are used up.

All told, the proposed projects would supply water for an additional 1.9 million people, 368,570 acres of newly irrigated cropland, 106,000 acres of land currently irrigated with groundwater, and 2,100 megawatts of hydroelectric generating capacity at a cost of approximately $3 billion (see Table 1).

Significantly, if the current proposals for surface water development were all completed, they would deplete present flow levels in the central Platte by 458,318 acre-feet[3] per year, or 46 percent of the current flow levels of 994,800 acre-feet (Faanes, in press). Local groundwater pumping would further reduce streamflow in the river. Although estimates of future conditions vary, a BuRec study projected that surface and groundwater development could reduce average annual streamflow in the Big Bend reach near Overton to 399,700 acre-feet per year—about 40 percent of current flow levels, and only 15 percent of historic flows of 2.6 million acre-feet (U.S. Department of the Interior 1982).

THE NEED FOR WATER FOR MIGRATORY BIRDS

Habitat Changes on the Platte.

One of the complexities of the controversy over use of the Platte's waters is the *indirect* threat to migratory birds posed by water development. Unlike other controversies where water development would directly inundate wildlife habitat, consumptive use of the Platte leads to changes in the quality and availability of habitat which, in turn, may harm migratory birds. Conservationists' concern for the Platte is that the cumulative effects of water development will change the river so dramatically that it will become unsuitable for the endangered, threatened, and migratory birds that occur there each year.

This concern is based on habitat changes that have accompanied past water development. One such change has been the conversion of

3. An acre-foot is the amount of water required to cover an acre of land one foot deep, about 325,851 gallons.

native sandhills, prairie, and lowland grasslands to agricultural land. In the 80-mile river reach between Overton and Chapman, corn, milo, and other crops have been planted on about 229,000 acres—55 percent of the total land area within 3.5 miles of the river (Currier *et al.* 1985).

Accompanying the increase in cropland has been a loss of 73 percent of the native grassland, nearly 274,000 acres along the Overton to Chapman reach (Currier *et al.* 1985). Much of the native grassland that still remains occurs in lowland "wet meadows" along the river channel. Often, these areas have not been plowed because of high water tables that saturate soils during portions of each year. Because groundwater levels in these areas are closely linked to the amount of water in the river, conservationists are concerned that additional development may lower groundwater levels and contribute to further habitat losses (Currier *et al.* 1985, U.S. Department of the Interior 1981a).

The second major change that has accompanied past water development is the dramatic alteration of the river channel. Early accounts and photographs characterize the central Platte as an extremely wide, shallow river, generally free of vegetation within the braided channel. In many areas the river now flows in narrow channels that meander through a dense forest of cottonwoods and willows (See Figures 2a and 2b). The open river channel is nearly completely gone between Sutherland and Overton. Downstream from Overton, changes have been less pronounced and the river still retains some of its wide, unvegetated

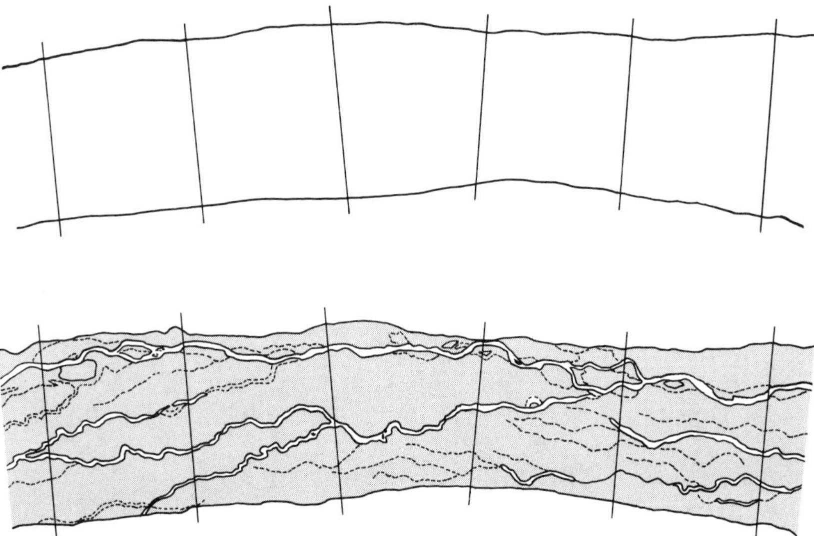

Figure 2a. Examples of the changes in the channel of the Platte River, near Cozad, Nebraska, in 1860 (top) and in 1979 (bottom). Shaded areas are vegetated.

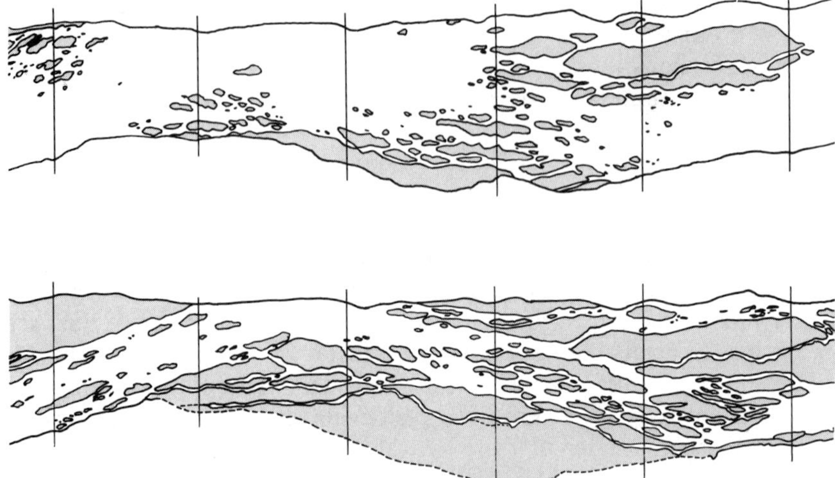

Figure 2b. Changes in the channel farther downstream at Grand Island, Nebraska, in 1938 (top) and later in 1979 (bottom). Shaded areas are vegetated. Source: Eschner *et al.* 1983.

character. Even in this area, 26,000 acres of open channel—67 percent of the original channel present in the 1840s—have been replaced by riparian forest (Currier *et al.* 1985).

There is intense scientific debate regarding the exact reasons for the changes in the river channel that have occurred in the past. (This debate is summarized in a later section of this chapter.) The prevailing explanation for the changes is that reductions in the magnitude of peak flows led to the narrowing of the river channel and the growth of vegetation on sandbars and the river banks (Currier *et al.* 1985, O'Brien and Currier 1987). Consequently, conservationists and wildlife managers believe further reductions in streamflow may result in further losses of channel area due to encroachment of vegetation.

Conservationists are also concerned that water development may substantially change flow conditions, such as water depth or velocity, that determine the suitability of the open channel habitats of the Platte for migratory birds. Though their habitat needs vary and they use the river at different times of the year, each of the species of concern depends on the availability of flowing water. Exactly how each species depends on the river is summarized in following sections.

Sandhill Crane. The Platte River is best known for the spectacular concentrations of sandhill cranes that occur there each spring. Between February and April, approximately 540,000 sandhill cranes stage on the central Platte, midway through their northward migration (U.S. Department of the Interior 1981a). The cranes funnel into the Platte

Valley from wintering grounds in Texas, New Mexico, and Mexico. They rest and feed on the Platte for four to six weeks and then migrate north to their breeding grounds in Canada, Alaska, and the Soviet Union. During the peak of staging, nearly 80 percent of the world population of sandhill cranes is found along the Platte. Nearly 400,000 birds occur within a 45-mile stretch of river between Kearney and Grand Island, 60,000 occur within a 9-mile reach between Overton and Elm Creek, and 90,000 occur in a 20-mile reach of the North Platte between Sutherland and the town of North Platte (Currier *et al.* 1985). These sections of the Platte and North Platte rivers are designated by FWS as Category 1 Resources, "unique and irreplaceable" habitats for sandhill cranes (U.S. Department of the Interior 1987a).

While on the Platte, sandhill cranes use three major habitat types. Wide, shallow sections of the river provide night roost sites protected from predators and human disturbance. Native grasslands and wet meadows near the river are a source of earthworms, snails, and other invertebrate foods which supply protein and calcium – nutrients essential to reproduction (U.S. Department of the Interior 1981a). Extensive corn fields throughout the valley provide an abundant supply of waste corn, a high energy food. During their four to six week stay, the cranes gain fat reserves that will sustain them through their remaining migration and partially through the nesting season (U.S. Department of the Interior 1981a).

Although sandhill cranes still occur in large numbers on the Platte, conservationists are very concerned about the potential effects of water development on the species. While agriculture has provided food for the cranes to eat, it has also replaced native grasslands and wet meadows that the birds also need. Wet meadows are now in short supply.

Most importantly, the past changes in the river channel have already resulted in the loss of two-thirds of the crane's open channel roosting habitat (U.S. Department of the Interior 1981a). Sandhill cranes prefer to roost in sections of the river that are over 500 feet wide; they rarely roost in areas narrower than 150 feet (U.S. Department of the Interior 1981a). As the river channel has narrowed, the cranes have abandoned much of their former range along the Platte, resulting in very high densities in the remaining roost sites. These crowded conditions increase the birds' vulnerability to harm from hailstorms or other natural and human-caused hazards, and to disease outbreaks.

Concern that new water development will exacerbate deteriorating habitat conditions underlies conservationists' insistence that instream flows be guaranteed on the Platte. Biologists believe that three different factors must be considered for sandhill cranes. First, flows necessary to maintain a wide, unvegetated channel are needed to provide roost sites. Second, instream flows may be needed to maintain proper habitat conditions in the wet meadows and native grasslands. Finally, specific flow levels are important to provide the proper water depth and width for roosting sites during the migration season.

Whooping Crane. The whooping crane emerged as a species of major concern on the Platte River during the controversy over the Mid-State Project. The species has remained at the forefront ever since, in part due to its beauty, rarity, and legal protection under the Endangered Species Act. The whooping crane was federally listed as endangered in 1967 (32 *Federal Register* 4001); a 54-mile reach of the Big Bend segment of the Platte was designated by FWS as critical habitat for the species in 1978 (43 *Federal Register* 21784). This reach, between Lexington and Denman, is one of four migration stopover areas designated as critical habitat within the migration route of the Wood Buffalo-Aransas whooping crane flock. All other stop-over areas designated as critical habitat are protected as state or national wildlife refuges.

The Wood Buffalo-Aransas whooping crane flock is one of two whooping crane populations in the wild. This population of 132 birds (1988 data) winters at Aransas National Wildlife Refuge on the Gulf Coast of Texas and nests at Wood Buffalo National Park in the Northwest Territories of Canada (Lewis interview). This is the only wild population of whooping cranes that currently produces young. The second population, the Gray's Lake flock, migrates between Bosque del Apache National Wildlife Refuge in New Mexico and Grey's Lake National Wildlife Refuge in Idaho. The Gray's Lake population was established by an experimental program begun in 1975 (U.S. Department of the Interior 1986). So far, breeding has not occurred in this population.[4]

The Platte River bisects the 2,600-mile migration corridor of the Wood Buffalo-Aransas cranes. Whooping cranes occupy some of the same habitats on the Platte as the sandhill cranes: they roost in wide, shallow sections that provide protection from predators and human disturbance and feed in nearby wetlands and cornfields (U.S. Department of the Interior 1981a, Currier *et al.* 1985). Whereas sandhill cranes occur on the Platte each year in large numbers and for a period of weeks, whooping cranes occur irregularly, as individuals, in pairs, or small flocks, and stay for short stopovers of one to seven days (U.S. Department of the Interior 1981a, Johnson 1981).

Water development interests ask how the river can be critical habitat and why it should be protected if the cranes do not use it each year. FWS defends its critical habitat designation by noting that the whooping crane population remains extremely small; migration is the most precarious period of the species' annual cycle; the river provides

4. See the *Audubon Wildlife Report 1986* for a review of the status of the whooping crane.

a dependable source of food and safe roost sites for migrating cranes; and there is a long history of whooping crane use of the Big Bend reach of the Platte (Buterbaugh 1987a). In addition, whooping cranes invariably roost in wetlands during migration stopovers (Howe 1987); both riverine and standing water wetlands are becoming scarce throughout the whooping crane migration corridor (Lingle 1987).

Because whooping cranes roost in even wider river sections than sandhill cranes, biologists believe the changes in the Platte River channel may already be causing whooping cranes to avoid the Platte. There is evidence that whooping crane use of the Platte has declined since the 1950s when the changes in the river channel became substantial, although use may now be increasing in certain managed areas (Johnson 1981, U.S. Department of the Interior 1981a). In any case, there has apparently been increased use by whooping cranes of wetland areas in the Rainwater Basins, about 20 miles south of the river (Johnson 1981). Biologists view this change with great alarm because avian cholera outbreaks have regularly occurred since 1975 in the Rainwater Basins; more than 300,000 ducks and geese have died as a result (Currier *et al.* 1985, Johnson 1981, Buterbaugh 1987a). Transmittal of this disease to the whooping crane, biologists say, represents a very serious threat to the survival of the species. As a result, conservationists strongly believe that conditions must be improved and instream flows must be protected in the Platte to provide habitat suitable for whooping crane use.

Least Tern. The Platte River supports a significant breeding population of least terns, a small colonial nesting bird. Least terns nest along the Atlantic, Gulf, and Pacific coasts and on the major river systems in the interior of the United States. Populations of the species in California were listed as endangered by FWS in 1970 (32 *Federal Register* 16047). The interior least tern populations were classified as endangered during 1985 (50 *Federal Register* 21784).

The interior populations of least tern were once widely distributed on the major river systems in the central United States, including the Colorado, Red, Rio Grande, Arkansas, Missouri, Ohio, and Mississippi river systems from Montana south to the Gulf Coast. By 1985, when the interior populations were listed as endangered, the total breeding population of only 1,400 to 1,800 birds was restricted to about 20 areas within their former range. More than 50 percent of the total population occurred in three areas: 350 to 450 birds on the Mississippi River from Osceola, Arkansas, to Cairo, Illinois; 180 to 300 terns at Salt Plains National Wildlife Refuge in Oklahoma; and 160 to 240 birds on the Platte River in Nebraska (50 *Federal Register* 21785–21786 [1985]). Current population estimates total nearly 4,000 adult birds, 438 (11 percent of the total population) of which nest on the Platte between Kearney and the mouth of the Platte (Buterbaugh 1987a).

The overall population decline of interior least terns is attributed to the widespread loss of nesting habitat throughout their range due to past water developments. Interior least terns nest on unvegetated sandbars or islands within wide river channels. In many areas, island nest sites were destroyed by channelization or permanently inundated by reservoirs. On the Platte (and elsewhere) nesting sites were lost as streamflow reductions led to the narrowing of the river channel and encroachment of woody vegetation on islands and sandbars (50 *Federal Register* 21784 [1985]). Vegetation encroachment on the Platte has reduced the terns' range by nearly 30 percent. Terns once nested on the entire mainstem Platte from North Platte to its confluence with the Missouri River (a distance of 325 miles); they no longer nest in the 95-mile reach between North Platte and Kearney (Bailey 1985, Buterbaugh 1987a).

Human manipulation of natural river flows poses three other indirect threats to nesting terns (Buterbaugh 1987a). Water depletions may reduce the width or depth of water surrounding nesting islands, and thus increase the terns' vulnerability to predation by coyotes, dogs, or other terrestrial predators, and to disturbance by humans. Extreme depletions may de-water the river sufficiently to kill the small fishes, such as sand shiner (*Notropis stramineus*) and Plains killifish (*Fundulus zebrinus*), that are the terns' only food. Water management activities may also shift the timing of peak flow periods, resulting in higher than normal river flow during the nesting season. High summer flows may prevent nesting, or inundate nests after they have been established. These phenomena are all believed to have contributed to the decline of least terns throughout their interior range, and all of them have been documented on the Platte during recent years (Bailey 1985, Buterbaugh 1987a).

Biologists believe a year-round flow regime needs to be guaranteed to protect the Platte River populations of least tern. This regime would include spring peak flows to maintain bare sandbars within a wide river channel. Biologists also believe summer flows should be regulated to maintain areas of open water around sandbar nest sites, without becoming so high that nests are inundated. Finally, sufficient flow needs to be maintained year-round to assure adequate populations of prey fish.

Piping Plover. The Platte River in Nebraska is also considered a key habitat for the piping plover, a small shorebird that occurs on the Atlantic Coast from Newfoundland south to North Carolina; in the Great Lakes region; and in the Northern Great Plains from southern Alberta, Saskatchewan, and Manitoba south to the Platte in Nebraska (Haig and Oring 1987). Although historic population size is unknown, biologists believe piping plover numbers have declined significantly since 1900. Plovers have been extirpated from Illinois, Indiana, New

Hampshire, inland New York, Ohio, Pennsylvania, and Wisconsin. Current populations are estimated to total only 3,500 to 4,200 adult birds: 28 in the Great Lakes region; 1,370 to 1,435 on the Atlantic Coast; and 2,137 to 2,684 birds on the Northern Great Plains (Haig and Oring 1987). The Great Lakes population is classified as endangered by FWS, and the Atlantic and Great Plains populations are listed as threatened (50 *Federal Register* 50726).

As of 1987, 164 piping plovers nested on the Platte River in Nebraska, 102 on the central Platte between Kearney and Duncan, and 62 on the lower Platte east of Duncan (Buterbaugh 1987a). The Platte River population is one of the largest concentrations of plover remaining anywhere; it represents four to five percent of all piping plovers in the world, and six to eight percent of the threatened population of the Northern Great Plains of the United States and Canada (Buterbaugh 1987a, Haig and Oring 1987). In their review of the species in the *Audubon Wildlife Report 1987*, Haig and Oring (1987) identified acquisition and strict protection of Platte River habitats used by piping plovers as needed steps toward preserving the species.

On the Platte River, piping plovers nest on sandbars within the river channel and forage for invertebrates along moist, sandy shorelines. They prefer sites that are "wide, free of woody vegetation, and isolated from human activities" (Buterbaugh 1987a). As a result of these habitat preferences, the threats to piping plovers posed by water development projects mirror those described previously for least terns. Encroachment of woody vegetation onto islands in the river channel has led to the abandonment of former nesting areas in the 65-mile river reach between North Platte and Lexington (Bailey 1985). Piping plovers are also vulnerable to artificial control of both high and low water levels. As with the least tern, artificially high water levels may inundate nest sites, and low water levels may increase the risk of predation and human disturbance.

Biologists also believe that instream flow levels need to be maintained to conserve the breeding populations of piping plovers on the Platte. Instream flow needs being investigated for plovers are identical to those discussed for the least tern, except that the requirements to maintain forage fish populations apply only to the least tern (Buterbaugh 1987a).

Waterfowl. The central Platte River valley provides essential wintering and migration habitat for waterfowl in the Central Flyway. Each year, the Platte's open channel and adjacent croplands attract seven to nine million ducks and geese (Currier *et al.* 1985). These include:

- Up to to 3.2 million mallards (*Anas platyrhynchos*), between 15 and 40 percent of the mid-continental population (Pustmueller *et al.* 1986).

- As many as 1.3 million northern pintails (*Anas acuta*), between 5 and 30 percent of the mid-continental population (Pustmueller *et al.* 1986).
- About 300,000 white-fronted geese, nearly all of the mid-continental population of this species (U.S. Department of the Interior 1987a).

Ducks and geese are attracted to the Platte by the presence of open water during the early spring when most other wetland areas remain frozen. Waste corn in nearby agricultural lands provides an abundant food supply that enables the birds to increase the fat reserves needed to sustain them on migration. This is especially important to white-fronted geese. Like sandhill cranes, these geese stage annually on the Platte for several weeks and gain nutritional reserves that sustain them partly into the nesting season (U.S. Department of the Interior 1981a). The 80-mile section of river between Overton and Chapman was designated a Category 1 Resource by FWS, reflecting the "unique and irreplaceable" value of the habitat in this area for white-fronted geese (U.S. Department of the Interior 1987a).

Past water development on the Platte has had mixed effects on waterfowl habitat. The abundant supply of corn is a partial result of the development of irrigation supplies. Also, some ice-free areas are maintained during the winter by releases from reservoirs and power plants. On the other hand, the replacement of the open channel habitat by floodplain forest has decreased the available habitat by about two-thirds (U.S. Department of the Interior 1981a). The greatest waterfowl concentrations occur where river flows are highest and the channel is widest.

Biologists are concerned that further reductions in streamflow may dramatically increase the risk of disease outbreaks in the waterfowl populations on the Platte. Ducks and geese generally occupy the Platte early in the spring migration season in February and March. As wetlands in the Rainwater Basins south of the river thaw, the birds move to them. Avian cholera epidemics have occurred frequently in the Rainwater Basins since 1975, with estimated losses of up to 300,000 birds between 1975 and 1983 (Currier *et al.* 1985). Biologists believe avian cholera outbreaks have been avoided on the Platte because the river's flowing water dilutes the concentration of disease organisms and carries them downstream. Additional flow reductions, however, could significantly increase the risk of disease:

> A serious threat could exist for both cranes and waterfowl if habitat conditions along the Platte deteriorate and flows during spring are reduced until slackwater conditions develop. With the combination of high population densities and high levels of association between populations in a nonflowing channel environment, avian cholera outbreaks likely would

> involve virtually all species, for example waterfowl, cranes, and eagles, with little prospect for control . . . (U.S. Department of the Interior 1981a).

Conservationists believe it is critical to maintain instream flows for waterfowl. These would include flows to maintain channel width, to keep the river open during winter and early spring, and to disperse birds during spring staging periods.

Bald Eagle. The Platte River basin in Nebraska is valued as winter habitat for the endangered bald eagle. The Platte provides ample roost sites in the riparian forest and abundant populations of fish and wintering waterfowl, primary foods for wintering eagles. Between November and March, an average of 200 bald eagles (about one-half of the average statewide population) are found along the North Platte, South Platte, and Platte rivers (Lingle and Krapu 1986). The Platte River population represents about two percent of the total population of 8,300 bald eagles estimated to winter in the 48 contiguous states (Lingle and Krapu 1986).

Past water development has had mixed effects on bald eagle wintering habitat. Reservoir development has expanded the area of available habitat. Water discharges from reservoirs and from power generation sites have helped maintain ice-free conditions in some areas, allowing eagles access to fish and waterfowl. Development of the floodplain forest has expanded the availability of large cottonwoods which are used as roost and perch sites.

Despite these benefits, conservationists identify two main concerns regarding the potential effects of future water development on bald eagle habitat. First, because fish are a preferred food source for the birds, year-round flows must be adequate to support a fishery (Currier *et al.* 1985, U.S. Department of the Interior 1981a). Second, wildlife managers believe that streamflow levels must be of sufficient volume during winter to maintain ice-free areas where the birds can fish (Bailey 1985, Buterbaugh 1987a).

The Severity of the Conflict

Water development plans depend greatly on economic conditions, population growth, electrical demand, and political conditions, so it is difficult to predict exactly how future development may influence water levels on the Platte. On the other hand, quantifying instream flows needed by wildlife is a complex challenge and the subject of intense scientific debate. These uncertainties make it difficult to precisely quantify the gap between human demand for water and that required to maintain wildlife habitat.

Nevertheless, the estimates that have been made suggest the gap may be very wide. As illustrated in Figure 3, preliminary estimates of

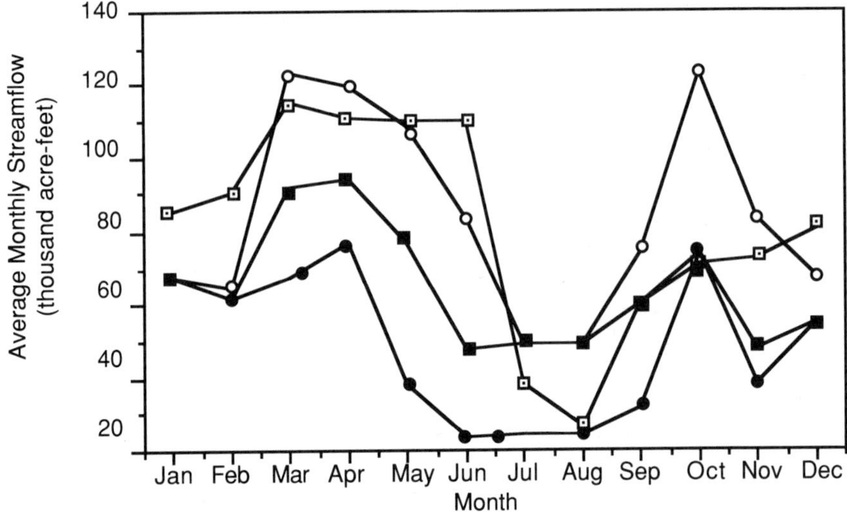

Figure 3. Comparison of current instream flow levels and instream flow regimes recommended by various organizations.

the year-round flow regime needed for migratory birds indicate that existing river flows may already be insufficient. A particular flow regime recommended by the Platte River Trust exceeds current flows during most months; lower estimates developed by FWS exceed current summer flows.

Hypothetical estimates of future river flows developed by BuRec (U.S. Department of the Interior 1982) indicate that the gap between wildlife and water interests may widen considerably if additional groundwater and surface water development occurs (see Figure 4). The bureau's estimates suggest that future developments in the basin may reduce water volumes well below even the least restrictive estimates of the instream flows needed for migratory birds. Although these projections will certainly change, they underscore the severity of the conflict on the Platte and explain the intensity of the controversy that has continued for so long.

THE SCIENTIFIC DEBATE

Intense scientific debate over the ecological connections between water development and wildlife on the Platte began when FWS and

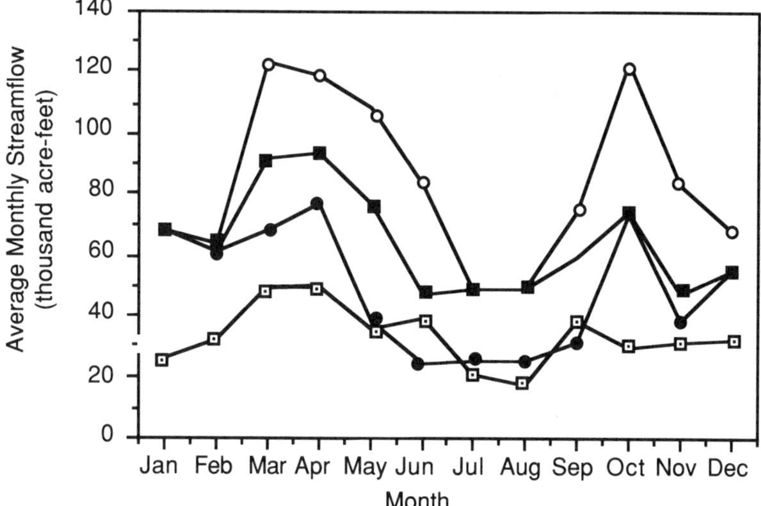

-□- Estimated future flow levels (U.S. Dept. of the Interior 1982)
-●- Streamflow regime recommended by BuRec (Woodward unpubl. data)
-■- Streamflow regime recommended by FWS (Buterbaugh 1987a)
-○- Streamflow regime recommended by Platte River Trust (Lowell 1987)

Figure 4. Comparison of estimated future flow levels and instream flow regimes recommended by various organizations.

conservation groups first claimed in 1967 that additional water development threatened the river's unique migratory bird habitats. While the changes in the Platte's habitats were easily observed, establishing why and when they occurred, how they affected migratory birds, and how future development may affect remaining habitats has proved to be a daunting challenge.

Over the years both government and private research studies have provided crucial information in three main areas: 1) documenting use of the Platte by sandhill cranes and other species (Currier *et al.* 1985, Frith 1974, U.S. Department of the Interior 1981a); 2) demonstrating the changes in the hydrology of the river and the resulting effects on the river channel in various reaches (Eschner *et al.* 1983, Currier *et al.* 1985, Kircher and Karlinger 1983, Williams 1978); and 3) highlighting the increasing competition for water throughout the basin (Faanes, in press, U.S. Department of the Interior 1982, U.S. Department of the Interior 1983b). The ecological interrelationships at issue are extremely complex, however, and scientists continue to research and debate several key aspects of the river's ecology.

The Need to Protect the Platte

Despite the well-documented use of the Platte by significant migratory bird species, water development and wildlife interests continue, after

20 years, to dispute the need for protection. Not surprisingly, this debate focuses on the threatened and endangered species that development interests are obligated to protect because of the strict requirements of state and federal endangered species legislation.

Ever since FWS designated portions of the Platte as critical habitat for the whooping crane, opposing biologists have scrutinized the same limited data on crane migration ecology and have developed arguments supporting both the view that the Platte is essential to the survival of the species, and that it is not. Conservationists believe the large number of whooping crane sightings on the Platte supports the claim that the river is of great importance; water development interests claim those records are biased by the fact that biologists look harder to find whoopers on the Platte. Developers say the fact that whooping cranes do not use the Platte during each migration proves that the river is not critical to the species (EA Engineering, Science, and Technology, Inc. 1985). As a second example, water developers cite the whooping cranes' frequent use of the Rainwater Basins south of the Platte as evidence that the river is not critical to whooping cranes. Wildlife officials and conservationists say that cranes use the Rainwater Basins because of deteriorating habitat conditions on the Platte. Furthermore, the risk of exposure to avian cholera which is rampant in the Rainwater Basins is precisely why the Platte is so critical, say conservationists (Buterbaugh 1987a, U.S. Department of the Interior 1981a).

There is also considerable controversy regarding the importance of the Platte River to interior least terns and piping plovers. Water development interests maintain that these species do not depend entirely on the river channel. They correctly note that terns and plovers both nest on bare sand areas created by sand and gravel mining operations near the river, and contend that these sites provide abundant habitat outside the river channel. Environmentalists counter with two points: 1) the terns that do nest on spoil sites still depend on the river channel for their food supply; 2) both species experience high mortality at sandpits and poor reproductive performance due to human disturbance and predation (Bailey 1985, Buterbaugh 1987a).

Quantifying Instream Flow Needs

Currently, the most intense scientific debate centers on efforts to quantify the instream flows needed to create and sustain suitable habitat conditions for the migratory bird species of concern. Although the need to maintain a year-round minimum streamflow is clear, at least to conservationists, precise definition of how much water is needed, in which parts of the river, and during what time periods, has proved elusive. The preliminary estimates that have been made so far differ both in terms of timing and magnitude. As previously illustrated (see Figures 3 and 4), total annual flow estimates range from approximately 582,891 acre-feet per year according to BuRec (Woodward unpubl. data), to 1,012,360 acre-feet according to the Platte River Trust (Lowell 1987).

All parties readily admit that their estimates need to be refined through further research. Since 1985, participants in the Platte River Management Joint Study have worked to try to reach a consensus on this issue. Their approach attempts to isolate the three primary "functions" or "benefits" provided by instream flows: 1) "habitat flows" defined as the quantity and timing of water flow required to meet the needs of cranes and other migratory birds during the periods when they use the Platte; 2) "channel maintenance flows" needed to maintain a wide, unvegetated river channel in the areas where these conditions currently exist; and 3) "wet meadow maintenance flows" that determine the condition of wetland foraging habitats adjacent to the river. Together, these different types of flows constitute the year-round flow regime needed to sustain continued use of the Platte by endangered, threatened, and other migratory birds.

Habitat Flows. Although the concept of habitat flows to benefit cranes and other migratory birds is simple enough, quantifying those flows is a surprisingly complex process. So far, work has focused on developing a series of analytical tools that will allow biologists to analyze how changes in water volume affect the availability of suitable habitat. A computerized hydrologic model had been developed that predicts how alterations in streamflow will affect habitat conditions (such as water depth or water width) in specific river reaches.[5] Work is continuing on a series of "species models" that define how changes in habitat conditions affect the area of suitable habitat in each river segment (Fannin and Nelson 1986, Shenk and Armbruster 1986, Ziewitz 1987).[6]

While most participants agree that the methods adopted are the best ones available for defining instream "habitat flows," implementing the methodologies has proved difficult. In particular, efforts to develop the species models suffer from a lack of quantitative data on the habitat requirements of the species of concern. This lack of data, in turn, leads to heated debate over model assumptions and the instream flow regimes that those models generate.

For example, assumptions used to develop a model for whooping crane roost sites have been the subject of controversy since 1986. Observations that cranes generally roost in water shallower than eight

5. Hydrologists are applying the FWS' Incremental Instream Flow Methodology (Bovee 1982).

6. The species models follow the conceptual framework of FWS' Habitat Suitability Index Models which are developed to apply FWS' Habitat Evaluation Procedures.

inches suggest that water depth may be an important factor in roost site selection (Shenk and Armbruster 1986). In one version of the whooping crane model, it is assumed that cranes select a specific roost site based on the depth of water at that location. On the central Platte, flows of approximately 1,100 cubic feet per second (cfs) maximize the availability of areas of uniform shallow depth (EA Engineering, Science, and Technology, Inc. 1987). In a second version of the model, a more complex assumption is made: optimum habitat occurs when a shallow roost site is surrounded by deeper river channels. On the central Platte, these conditions are most abundant when instream flows are about 2,000 cfs (Ziewitz 1987).

Thus, different model assumptions yield dramatically different estimates of the proper instream flow levels. Not surprisingly, water development interests prefer the assumption that yields the lower instream flow requirement, while conservation interests prefer the interpretation that suggests more water should be retained in the river. Unfortunately, conclusive resolution of this type of debate is difficult to achieve. Habitat preferences are difficult to define with certainty, especially when data are as limited as they are for the whooping crane. Moreover, model assumptions are always subject to challenge because, by design, they attempt to simplify complex ecological and behavioral patterns. Similar controversies will undoubtedly plague efforts during 1988 to develop habitat models for other species.

Channel Maintenance Flows. Disputes are rampant over the flow regime needed to maintain the wide, unvegetated river channels that still remain. Although numerous authors attribute the dramatic changes in the Platte River channel to changes in river flow, considerable uncertainty exists regarding the specific causes of channel narrowing and vegetation encroachment. The problem is especially difficult to resolve because the flow regime has been altered in several ways, the changes have not been uniform, and significant alterations of the river system occurred before the installation of flow measurement devices (Eschner *et al.* 1983). Thus, scientists face the task of explaining ecological changes that probably resulted from several interrelated factors and began before any records were kept.

Here also, two countervailing theories are advanced, each leading to opposite positions regarding the need to reserve instream flows. Water development interests advance the "dessication theory," which holds that willows and cottonwoods failed to establish themselves in the river channel in the past because the river went completely dry during long periods of the summer (Smith 1984). These periods of no-flow are believed to have dessicated the trees and shrubs, preventing development of significant forest stands. According to this theory, water development "evened out" the flow in the Platte, creating a perennial flow more conducive to plant growth; these conditions allowed vegetation to invade the river channel. Once established, trees and shrubs stabilized on river banks and instream islands, which forced the river into narrow meandering channels.

The other, prevailing "scouring flow" theory is similar to that first advanced in the 1970s—that the changes in the river channel are best explained by the systematic reduction in peak flows, combined with changes in the volume of sediment carried by the river (Eschner *et al.* 1983, O'Brien and Currier 1987, Williams 1978). This theory maintains that willows and cottonwoods routinely germinated on sandbars in the river channel during the summer growing season. However, high flows and the movement of sediment during the following spring runoff period shifted the seedlings from the channel. According to this theory, upstream water developments may have affected the channel in three ways. Reductions in the magnitude of peak flows decreased the area of the river channel affected by the "scouring flows." Decreases in the frequency of peak flow events limited the ability of the river to remove woody vegetation; within two to three years after establishment, seedlings may stabilize sandbars or the river bank sufficiently to prevent removal by subsequent high runoff (O'Brien and Currier 1987). Finally, some researchers believe upstream reservoirs may also have trapped much of the supply of sediment that historically washed through the system (Milhouse interview, O'Brien and Currier 1987). In turn, the river eroded the bed and began to shift from a wide, braided form to a narrow, meandering channel (O'Brien and Currier 1987).

Most hydrologists say the dessication theory is at best, only a partial explanation for the changes in the river. They say the scouring flow concept corresponds more closely with accepted theories regarding the behavior of braided river systems. However, even if the scouring flow concept is accepted, there still is no consensus on the magnitude and frequency of peak flows needed to maintain a wide river channel. Recent reviews of the subject by the Platte River Trust (O'Brien and Currier 1987) and FWS (Buterbaugh 1987a) estimated that peak flows need to be about 8,000 cfs (about the current average peak), but admitted a possible range of more than fourfold, from 3,800 cfs to 16,900 cfs (O'Brien and Currier 1987). Moreover, hydrologists stress that the shape of the river channel is determined by a complex and poorly understood interaction between peak flows and sediment characteristics.

In 1979, FWS stated that "further studies are needed to determine precisely the water stream flow and channel condition necessary to maintain the present sandbars and open water areas" in the central Platte. The statement remains valid today. According to one FWS official, a comprehensive program to address fully the interactions between streamflow, sediment volume, and channel shape would require three to five years and approximately $500,000. As of December 1987, BuRec and FWS planned to continue limited investigations based on existing data. At the same time, the Platte River Trust was planning its own analysis program, also using existing data.

Wet Meadows Maintenance. Wildlife interests believe that instream flow reservations must be made to protect the wet meadows adjacent to the Platte River channel. A study conducted by the U.S. Geological Survey (Hurr 1983) on wet meadows owned by the Platte River Trust near Grand Island found that "changes in the stage of the river rapidly affect groundwater levels" in the adjacent wet meadows. This close hydraulic connection means that the plant and animal communities of the wet meadows are dependent on streamflows in the river and may be affected by reduced flows caused by water development projects.

So far, the relationship between instream flows and wet meadow habitats has not received much attention or debate. Both wildlife and water development interests say the issue is important, but admit that not enough research has been done to determine if a significant conflict exists. FWS, BuRec, and National Audubon Society all plan to initiate research programs during 1988 to better define the relationships between the river channel and adjacent wet meadows.

Alternatives to Maintaining Instream Flows

The debate over instream flows is fueled primarily by wildlife interests who believe that instream flows must be reserved as part of any long-term plan to protect the Platte's migratory bird habitats. Water development interests, however, believe other management alternatives should be considered. As expressed by one Colorado water attorney: "It seems fundamental that nonflow conservation alternatives which minimize or eliminate the need to compete for water, as between instream and consumptive uses, should be given the first priority by fish and wildlife managers" (Hobbs 1985).

One alternative being used on the Platte is to mechanically remove woody vegetation that has encroached upon the river channel. National Audubon Society and the Platte River Trust both began research on methods of restoring deteriorated habitat shortly after they acquired sanctuary lands on the Platte River. They found that the open channel habitat can be temporarily restored by removing the woody vegetation with large machinery, such as a bulldozer or brush hog, and then discing the area to loosen root systems (Currier 1987, Strom 1987). Removing trees and shrubs facilitates the river's natural tendency to erode islands and redistribute sediments in the river channel during subsequent high flow periods.

The effectiveness of these management measures has been proven by the fact that whooping cranes, sandhill cranes, and least terns have subsequently used sites from which woody vegetation had been cleared (Strom 1987, Currier 1987). Although both wildlife and water development interests regard the successful restoration efforts as positive, they disagree over how much emphasis such efforts should receive. Water development interests identify mechanical clearing of vegetation as a means of obviating the need for high volume channel maintenance flows (Pitts 1985). National Audubon and the Platte River Trust, however, stress that habitat manipulation is not a replacement for instream flow maintenance (Strom 1987, Currier 1987). They emphasize that mechanical clearing of vegetation requires repeated efforts and works only if it is followed by periods of high flow and scouring.

POLITICAL-LEGAL CONFLICT

Even if the scientific issues could be resolved, it is likely that the conflict between water development and wildlife interests on the Platte would continue due to the presence of an equally complex set of unresolved political and legal issues. These issues stem from existing laws and institutions that support the desires of both wildlife and water development interests: while federal wildlife protection statutes support the maintenance of instream flows to provide habitat for migratory birds, state water allocation laws and procedures impede achievement of that goal.

Wildlife Protection Statutes

No federal or state statutes currently exist that specifically protect the Platte River as a unique migratory bird habitat. Thus, wildlife managers and conservationists have sought protection for the Platte's habitats and related instream flows through the provisions of existing wildlife laws. Applicable statutes include the federal Endangered Species Act (16 U.S.C.A. 1531 *et seq.*), Nebraska's Nongame and Endangered Species Conservation Act (Nebraska Revised Statutes 37–430 *et seq.*), the Fish and Wildlife Coordination Act (16 U.S.C.A. 661 *et seq.*), and the Migratory Bird Treaty Act (16 U.S.C.A 703 *et seq.*). These laws each offer some impetus for conserving the Platte's water and land resources; however, the Endangered Species Act has so far proven the strongest protection tool.

Endangered Species Act of 1973. While conservation interests contend that the Platte River and related areas constitute a unique ecosystem that deserves protection, the conflict has centered on threatened and endangered species that occur in the region. This emphasis originated from the fact that the Endangered Species Act provides the strictest protective requirements that could be applied to the situation. The wording of the law is unambiguous. Section 7(a)(2) requires all federal agencies to consult with FWS to "insure that any action authorized, funded, or carried out" by them "is not likely to jeopardize the continued existence of any endangered or threatened species or result in the destruction or adverse modification" of designated critical habitats. During the formal consultation process that implements these requirements (51 *Federal Register* 19926–19963 [1986]), FWS reviews plans for a proposed project and prepares a biological opinion regarding the anticipated impacts on threatened or endangered species. If FWS concludes that the project will "jeopardize the continued existence" of a protected species or "adversely modify" critical habitat, the proposed project cannot go forward without implementing actions to avoid the adverse impact or, under very limited circumstances, obtaining an exemption from the law's protective stipulations.

The act's protective requirements have been central to conservationists' efforts to maintain instream flows on the Platte. The controversy over the Grayrocks's project firmly established the applicability of the federal Endangered Species Act to water management issues on the Platte (*Nebraska v. Rural Electrification Admin.*, 12 ERC 1156 [1978]). The conflict over the Wildcat Project re-enforced this position when the courts ruled that the U.S. Army Corps of Engineers must consult with FWS regarding potential effects on endangered species before issuing construction permits under Section 404 of the Clean Water Act (*Riverside Irrigation Dist. v. Andrews*, 568 F. Supp. 583 [D. Colo. 1983] and *Riverside Irrigation Dist. v. Andrews*, 758 F. 2d 508 [10th Cir. 1985]).

Since 1978, FWS has repeatedly concluded that additional flow depletions resulting from proposed developments in the Platte River basin would jeopardize the continued existence of the whooping crane, or would result in the adverse modification of whooping crane critical habitat (Buterbaugh 1987a, MacDonnell 1985). FWS has also consistently ruled that the adverse effects on protected species may be avoided by 1) offsetting predicted water depletions during key time periods, or 2) in some cases, removing existing woody vegetation from sections of the river channel to offset the incremental habitat loss projected to result from streamflow alterations.

While the Endangered Species Act has proven to be a powerful tool in the fight to conserve the Platte's valuable wildlife habitats, the protection it provides is by no means absolute. For example, the act has repeatedly been reviewed by Congress in response to intense political pressure from both wildlife and water development interests. Congress did not originally anticipate conflicts such as those that have occurred on the Platte and has twice amended the law to deal with such controversies. Partly due to the conflict over the Grayrocks Dam and Reservoir, the 1978 amendments to the act created an exemption process for projects meeting certain criteria. In 1982, Congress also recognized the conflicts between water development and wildlife conservation by adding Section 2(i)(2), which states that "federal agencies shall cooperate with state and local agencies to resolve water resource issues in concert with conservation of endangered species." Other proposals to limit the influence of the Endangered Species Act over water use are always a possibility and may be considered when the law faces reauthorization during 1988, or in subsequent years.

Even if the Endangered Species Act remains unchanged, its protective provisions are subject to varying interpretations. One example where this has occurred is in the definition of "cumulative impacts" to be considered by FWS when assessing the effects of a proposed federal action. FWS originally adopted a broad interpretation, similar to that used in analyses conducted under the National Environmental Policy Act. A 1978 Solicitor's Opinion took the position that FWS should take a broad approach in the consultation process:

> The focus of Section 7 consultations should not be limited to the individual impacts of the activity under review. Rather, consultation should also look at the cumulative impacts of all similar projects in the area (U.S. Department of the Interior 1978).

This interpretation was withdrawn in 1981 and replaced by a new policy that strictly limits the scope of the analysis performed by FWS:

> The impact of future federal projects should each be addressed sequentially rather than collectively, since each must be capable at some point of individually satisfying the standards of Section 7. Section 7 provides a "first-in-time, first-in-right" process whereby the authorization of federal projects may proceed until it is determined that further actions are likely to jeopardize the continued existence of a listed species or adversely modify its critical habitat (U.S. Department of the Interior 1981b).

While this interpretation may simplify the consultation process on individual projects, it avoids the central concern in the Platte River basin. At issue on the Platte are the cumulative effects of past and future water developments. While the overall effects of water development are readily observable, the incremental effects of individual projects on habitat are extremely difficult to distinguish, as previously discussed.

A second area in which interpretation of the Endangered Species Act's protective provisions has become important is in the definition of what constitutes "jeopardy" to a listed species. During 1987, FWS issued biological opinions on the proposed Two Forks and Deer Creek projects, which conservationists believe departed from the strong positions the agency had taken since 1978. In both cases, FWS found that, under some conditions, the projects would reduce the volume of water in the river below estimated minimum thresholds during the whooping crane spring migration period (Buterbaugh 1987a, 1987b). In contrast to past cases, FWS found that the Deer Creek and Two Forks projects would not jeopardize the continued existence of the whooping crane or adversely modify the species' critical habitat. These conclusions were based on the applicants' commitments, before the biological opinions were issued, to clear vegetation from the river channel in Nebraska to offset the loss of habitat predicted to occur due to flow depletions[7] (Buterbaugh 1987a, 1987b).

Although FWS has previously included habitat manipulation as a means of reversing a "jeopardy" biological opinion, conservationists believe these recent rulings establish a new, and unfortunate, precedent. In the past, FWS had always concluded that flow depletions would jeopardize the whooping crane; offsetting water releases and habitat manipulation options were considered as alternatives to protect crane habitat and avoid a jeopardy ruling. Conservationists believe that habitat manipulation is needed on the Platte to restore deteriorated habitats, but cannot be relied on to maintain the habitats that currently exist (Currier 1987, Strom 1987). Moreover, they believe the Two Forks and Deer Creek biological opinions open the door for future developments to include habitat manipulation as a component of proposed projects, and thereby avoid scrutiny of the effects of flow depletions.

An even stronger difference of opinion regarding what level of impact constitutes jeopardy to a protected species developed during 1987 after FWS issued its biological opinion on the potential effects of the Two Forks project on least terns and piping plovers (Buterbaugh 1987a). FWS found that operation of Two Forks during an extremely dry year would completely de-water a 116-mile section of the Platte between Overton and Duncan for an extended period during June, the peak of the least tern and piping plover nesting season. According to FWS, this flow depletion would have the following effects:

> In the impacted reach, fish life will probably cease to exist and juvenile terns will starve or adults will be forced to abandon nests, or both chicks and adults will be killed by predators. The same is true for piping plovers because no-flow conditions will eliminate their forage of invertebrate organisms.

7. According to FWS estimates, the Two Forks project would destroy 221 acres of open channel, the Deer Creek project, 24 acres. Conservationists question the accuracy of these estimates.

Despite the projected reproductive failure of the tern and plover populations in this reach, FWS concluded that Two Forks would not jeopardize the continued existence of these species because the projected loss "represents only a small fraction of one year's reproduction, assuming that the population remains at or near current levels (Buterbaugh 1987a)."

FWS did find that Two Forks would result in the "incidental take" of least terns and piping plovers and required project sponsors to implement "reasonable and prudent measures" to minimize the extent of the adverse impact. FWS regulations specify that reasonable and prudent measures cannot significantly alter the project's basic design or purpose (51 *Federal Register* 19962 [1986]). In this case, Two Forks' sponsors were required to: 1) develop an "early warning system" to give FWS sufficient time to implement public education and predator-control programs to limit the loss of tern and plover nests in the event of a severe water depletion, and 2) make a one-time contribution of $50,000 to offset the costs of these programs.

Environmentalists were uniformly outraged by FWS biological opinions on both the Two Forks and Deer Creek projects. They felt the opinions represented a "sudden and unexplained shift" in long-standing FWS policy. The Two Forks and Deer Creek biological opinions, they said, did not consider the alternative of requiring replacement flows, and the conservation measures specified did not adequately protect the threatened and endangered species. National Audubon's President, Peter A. A. Berle, stated that "It is clear that the Fish and Wildlife Service has abdicated its responsibilities under the Endangered Species Act" (Berle 1987). National Audubon and others charged that FWS yielded to political pressure from water developers.

FWS officials bristle at charges of political influence. They contend the Two Forks and Deer Creek opinions do not represent a change in policy, but are the best response to the circumstances of these particular projects. In both opinions, FWS maintained that flow maintenance measures were considered, but were eliminated due to the "legal and institutional problems which would have had to be overcome for implementation of any flow-related measures" (Buterbaugh 1987a, 1987b). In their opinion, the specified measures represent the best means of offsetting projected impacts (Bowman interview).

Nebraska Nongame and Endangered Species Conservation Act.

Nebraska's Nongame and Endangered Species Conservation Act fulfills an important need by requiring scrutiny of proposed projects in Nebraska that may not require federal approval. The state statute closely parallels federal law by requiring state agencies to consult with the Nebraska Game and Parks Commission to ensure that state agency actions will not jeopardize the existence of state-listed species (Vaughn

1987). The commission has consistently issued biological opinions that concluded that further depletions of instream flows in the central Platte would jeopardize the continued existence of whooping cranes, least terns, or bald eagles within Nebraska.

As with the federal statute, the Nebraska law is subject to political pressure and varying interpretations that weaken its protective force. A current controversy surrounding the proposed Catherland project illustrates this concern. The Catherland project is a proposal by the Catherland Reclamation District to divert 125,000 acre-feet of water per year from the central Platte near Overton to irrigate 66,500 acres of cropland in the Little Blue River basin in south central Nebraska.

During 1985, the commission reviewed the district's application to the Nebraska Department of Water Resources to obtain the necessary water rights for the project. The commission found that the proposed depletions would jeopardize the continued existence of the whooping crane, bald eagle, and least tern. Despite this opinion, the director of the Water Resources Department granted the water rights during 1986, allowing the District to proceed with the project (Jess 1986). In granting the water rights, the water resources director disagreed with the commission's finding and said that it is "inconceivable" that the project would jeopardize the species.

Conservationists were obviously concerned by this decision. They questioned whether the water resource director's decision to treat the commission "as a witness and its biological opinion as mere testimony" in the water rights hearings fulfills the statutory requirement for consultation (Aiken 1987). While much conflicting evidence regarding the probable effects on endangered birds was presented in the hearings, environmentalists believe the burden of proof should rest with water developers to conclusively prove that their proposals will not jeopardize the listed species (Meyer interview, Vaughn 1987). The director of water resources himself had previously taken that position in similar hearings on the Enders project, a project in western Nebraska in which water rights were denied (Vaughn 1987). National Wildlife Federation and the Nebraska Wildlife Federation appealed the director's decision to the Nebraska Supreme Court during the summer of 1987. In December, the court requested that additional briefs and oral arguments be presented during February 1988.

Other Statutes. The Fish and Wildlife Coordination Act plays an important role in efforts to protect the Platte because it requires federal water development agencies to consider the impacts of their proposals on all fish and wildlife and not just those listed as threatened or endangered.

Under the law, water development agencies must give "equal consideration" to fish and wildlife values in planning water projects, consult with FWS and state wildlife agencies regarding impacts to fish and wildlife, and consider substantive mitigation measures to limit adverse impacts within final project plans. FWS has designated two areas of the Platte as Category 1 Resources for sandhill cranes and white-fronted geese, which establishes a mitigation goal of "no loss of existing habitat values" for proposed projects.

The Coordination Act has had mixed impacts on efforts to protect instream flows in the Platte. FWS did include as mitigation for the proposed Narrows project minimum streamflow recommendations to maintain suitable habitat for sandhill cranes and other species (U.S. Department of the Interior 1985). Because the Narrows project has been indefinitely delayed due to conflicts concerning endangered species, project proponents have not stated whether they will agree to the recommendations. Unlike the mandatory protection requirements of the Endangered Species Act, the Coordination Act allows the project sponsor discretion in adopting or rejecting mitigation recommendations.

Significantly, FWS did not include any mitigation measures to benefit nonendangered species in Nebraska in its Fish and Wildlife Coordination Act Report on the proposed Two Forks project (U.S. Department of the Interior 1987a). FWS concluded that the impacts associated with Two Forks would be "insignificant," despite the fact that they "remain seriously concerned about the cumulative impacts of past, present, and future flow depletions and vegetative encroachment on fish and wildlife resources of the Platte River system in Nebraska" (U.S. Department of the Interior 1987a).

Conservationists also believe that the Migratory Bird Treaty Act requires protection of the Platte's valuable habitats. The act implements international treaties which obligate the United States to protect migratory birds, including those of concern on the Platte. However, the statute only protects the birds themselves—their nests, feathers, and body parts—and not the habitats on which they depend.

State Water Laws

Ultimately, protection of instream flows to maintain migratory bird habitat within the Big Bend segment of the Platte must be accomplished through laws and institutions which are used to allocate water among the many water users in the basin. FWS' recent reluctance to require water developers in upstream states to implement alternatives to maintain minimum instream flow levels in Nebraska is a revealing commentary on the prospects of protecting instream flows within the existing legal and political framework. In its biological opinion on Two Forks, for example, FWS stated that "there are legal and institutional problems which would have had to be overcome for implementation of any flow-related measures" (Buterbaugh 1987a). The phrase "legal and institutional problems" has become a convenient reference to a host of issues related to state water laws which, at the very least, slow efforts to guarantee a year-round streamflow regime to provide habitat for migratory birds. These issues are rooted in three basic concepts of water basin law: jurisdiction over water use, equitable apportionment among the states, and the prior appropriation doctrine. These concepts, and the difficulties they pose for instream flow maintenance, are described here.

State Jurisdiction. One of the basic concepts of water law in the United States is that individual states have jurisdiction over water management. Thus, each state has its own system of water laws and its own procedures for allocating water among competing interests. Water laws apply only within the boundaries of individual states, regardless of the number of states with jurisdiction over a particular river or stream.

One of the several difficulties associated with this rule is that the states have developed a parochial attitude that ignores the fact that rivers and water management needs cross state lines. Thus, the need to maintain instream flows to benefit wildlife in Nebraska is regarded as "Nebraska's problem" or the "federal government's problem" despite the fact that water use in the South Platte and North Platte rivers in Colorado and Wyoming determines how much water flows into the Platte in Nebraska.

In this semi-arid region, water is considered the most valuable, and most limited, natural resource. Thus, states jealously guard "their share" of the waters of the Platte River basin and strongly resist efforts perceived to threaten their ability to develop available water supplies. While wildlife interests view the Endangered Species Act as an important tool to protect instream flows in the Platte, water developers have come to regard it as an unwarranted intrusion by the federal government in state allocation procedures. Some argue that FWS requirements for instream flow releases (on the Platte and elsewhere) unfairly, and perhaps illegally, restrict the state's right to allocate water as it sees fit. Conservationists counter that the Endangered Species Act supersedes state laws, however, neither position has been tested in court.

Finally, state jurisdiction over water creates logistical difficulties for those who wish to preserve instream flows in the Platte. Because water laws of individual states apply only within their boundaries, there is no guarantee that water released for instream flow purposes in Wyoming or Colorado would be used for the same purpose in Nebraska.

Equitable Apportionment. A second key concept of water law is that the total water supply of a river should be apportioned equitably among the states according to each state's needs. This is accomplished by mutual agreement in an interstate compact, or by a decree of the U.S. Supreme Court when the states are unable to agree. Both situations apply in the Platte River basin. The waters of the South Platte River are apportioned by an interstate compact signed by Nebraska and Colorado in 1923. The waters of the North Platte River are apportioned among Wyoming, Nebraska, and Colorado by a U.S. Supreme Court decree of 1945 and a 1953 court stipulation. All of these compacts and decrees were enacted decades before the conflict between wildlife and water development emerged. Thus, efforts to guarantee instream flows in the central Platte occur within a legal context in which wildlife concerns have never been formally considered.

As noted above, Colorado and Wyoming regard efforts to guarantee instream flows to benefit endangered species in Nebraska as an improper infringement of their rights. Any plan for the Platte, in their view, must acknowledge their right to develop all of the water allocated to them under applicable compacts and decrees (Herschler 1983, McDonald 1983). Colorado's remaining undeveloped share of the South Platte River, for example, is estimated to be approximately 335,000 acre-feet annually—about one-third of the present average flow in central Nebraska (U.S. Department of the Interior 1982).

Conservationists correctly point out that times have changed since the compact and decrees were enacted, and that the apportionment of water among the states should be reconsidered. In an argument already used to support reallocation of water in California and other states, conservationists contend that water is a public resource managed by the states as a public trust; instream flows for wildlife and other purposes are now recognized as a critical public value that the states must protect.

A long-standing dispute between Nebraska and Wyoming may soon offer an unprecedented opportunity to incorporate the instream flow needs of whooping cranes and other other migratory birds into the mix of water demands considered in apportioning waters of the North Platte River. The two states have disagreed for many years over the correct interpretation of the Supreme Court Decree and Stipulation covering the North Platte. In 1986, both states initiated legal action to resolve the ongoing dispute. In October, the state of Wyoming filed suit in state district court to enjoin further diversions in BuRec's North Platte system, which supplies water to a series of reservoirs in Nebraska (and eventually the Platte). Wyoming contends that BuRec has never applied for the right to divert water to these projects and therefore is violating Wyoming water law. Immediately following this action, Nebraska filed suit in the U.S. Supreme Court for enforcement of the 1945 and 1953 decrees. Nebraska contends that present and future water developments in Wyoming, including the proposed Deer Creek project, violate the terms of the existing court decrees.

Neither case was originally aimed at the question of instream flows for migratory birds in Nebraska. However, in a surprise move in January 1988, Nebraska amended its original petition and specifically requested that the court: 1) consider the need to maintain instream flows in Nebraska to preserve "critical wildlife habitat" and 2) modify the previous decree to reflect current environmental laws and public values (Simms 1988). In support of its case, Nebraska presented an argument that echoes what environmentalists have maintained for decades:

> The preservation and regulation of flows of the North Platte and its tributaries for the protection of critical wildlife habitat presents a basin-wide problem, necessitating affirmative action not simply by the State of Nebraska, but also by the states of Wyoming and Colorado and the United States (Simms 1988).

The Supreme Court granted Nebraska's original motion early in 1987, and in June 1987 appointed a Special Master to hear the case. As of February 1988, neither the Supreme Court nor the Special Master had ruled on Nebraska's request to modify the decree to reflect the instream flow needs of wildlife. Nor had the Special Master ruled on requests by National Audubon Society and the Platte River Trust that these organizations be allowed to intervene to represent wildlife interests. Ultimately, the significance of *Nebraska v. Wyoming* will depend on the boundaries that the Supreme Court puts on the case. If the court agrees to consider modifying the decree, the case presents a unique opportunity to change the rules of water use on the Platte.

Prior Appropriation Doctrine. The third key concept of water law is the prior appropriation doctrine. In simple terms, the prior appropriation doctrine has historically provided (emphasis added):

> that any person who *diverts* water from a stream and applies it to a *beneficial use* obtains a water *right* for that amount of water. This water right will be superior to all who come later in time, and is junior to all who came earlier (Meyer undated).

This doctrine sets the ground rules for water use in the Platte River basin. As historically implemented, the only legal use of water was to divert it from the stream and use it for domestic, municipal, agricultural, or commercial purposes. Thus, during most of the history of the conflict between wildlife and water development on the Platte, instream flow reservations to benefit fish and wildlife were not even considered a legal use of water.

However, water law has been evolving throughout the West. Colorado implemented an instream flow statute in 1973, Nebraska in 1984, and Wyoming in 1986. The Platte River basin states are now able to grant instream flow rights and have broadened the definition of beneficial use to include fish and wildlife habitat values. However, these are recent developments that so far have not dramatically altered traditional views or institutions.

Although the enactment of instream flow laws represents an important victory, conservationists believe the laws are not strong enough to achieve the year-round flow regime needed on the Platte. For example, where instream flows have already been depleted below levels needed to sustain fish or wildlife, as some believe is the case on the central Platte, there is no means of reallocating water use. Prior water rights remain senior to new instream flow rights, despite the fact that the instream flow rights could not be obtained until very recently.

Also, Nebraska statutes (Nebraska Revised Statutes 46–2, 108 *et seq.*) treat instream flow rights differently from rights granted for traditional consumptive uses. One difference is that instream flow rights may be withdrawn if they conflict with new water development projects; hence, instream rights lack the same degree of protection afforded water rights for other uses. Also, only state natural resources districts or the Game and Parks Commission may apply for instream flow appropriations. Thus, organizations such as National Audubon, The Nature Conservancy, or the Platte River Trust, which have made major commitments to habitat protection on the Platte, are unable to obtain instream flow rights that would allow them to fully manage the lands they acquired to benefit cranes and other species.

The final barrier posed by the instream flow statute is institutional. As with other water rights, instream flow rights must be granted by the Nebraska Department of Water Resources. Given the director's 1986 position that diversion of 125,000 acre-feet per year by the Catherland project would not affect whooping cranes, least terns, or bald eagles, conservationists believe it is unlikely he would approve applications to obtain instream flow rights for these species of wildlife in the Big Bend reach of the Platte.

THE SEARCH FOR A SOLUTION

The Platte River Management Joint Study

Neither side in the conflict has been willing to accept a continuing impasse that prevents further water development in the basin and fails to protect the essential habitats of the central Platte. As a result, both wildlife and water interests have participated in the Platte River Management Joint Study, a program intended to find a mutually agreeable plan for resolving the conflict. The joint study began in 1983 as a cooperative effort by FWS and BuRec to develop a plan that would allow the Narrows Project to proceed without jeopardizing the continued existence of the whooping crane (U.S. Department of the Interior 1984). Because of the potential for conflicts with other species and other development proposals, the scope of the program was expanded during 1985. BuRec and FWS remain the lead agencies but representatives from many groups having a stake in the basin are now participating in the study: the states of Nebraska, Wyoming, and Colorado; the Army Corps of Engineers and other federal agencies; water development interests; and the environmental community. The study is also supposed to be expanded to include all of the species of concern and water development throughout the basin. To date this has not occurred.

The goal of the study is to develop a land and water management plan that would allow: 1) additional water development to proceed in compliance with the protective requirements of the Endangered Species Act, and 2) assure adequate habitat for the endangered, threatened, and other migratory bird species that depend on the Platte, without conflicting with existing water laws. If realized, this goal would set specific objectives regarding the amount of habitat needed on the Platte, define alternative methods for achieving those objectives (including the maintenance of instream flows and other methods), and establish the steps and responsibilities for implementing the habitat management plan (U.S. Department of the Interior 1987b). In so doing, the plan would help resolve the ongoing controversy by defining the actions to be taken to protect the Platte and by setting standards for evaluating the impact of future development proposals.

Both wildlife and development interests initially approached the study optimistically; a representative of the Colorado Water Congress even went so far as to call the process a model "for resolving potential conflicts between implementation of the Endangered Species Act and achievement of other long-standing national goals" (Pitts 1985). After nearly three years, however, this optimism has given way to frustration with the slow progress of the effort. Completion of the study was initially set for March 1986 and later postponed until September 1987 (U.S. Department of the Interior 1987b). As of December 1987, none of the 16 major tasks were completed and no firm completion date had been set, although participants "hoped" to finish the work during 1988 (Weidleman interview).

One factor contributing to the lack of progress is the fact that the Platte River Management Joint Study was not set up as a separate project within the budgets or work schedules of either FWS or BuRec. Funding for the study has come from planning funds allocated to BuRec's proposed Narrows and Prairie Bend projects ($500,000 in FY 1986, $200,000 in FY 1987, and $500,000 in FY 1988 for all activities related to those projects). Work on the study has consequently taken second priority to the tasks directly associated with ongoing planning for the Narrows and Prairie Bend projects (Weidleman interview). Similarly, FWS staff time during 1987 was consumed by Prairie Bend planning studies and by the Section 7 consultation processes for the Two Forks and Deer Creek projects (Bowman interview). Environmentalists maintain that the study should have been given priority over efforts that advance individual water projects. But the agency representatives contend they had no alternative because none of the water project sponsors were willing to postpone or delay their project schedules in deference to the study (Bowman interview, Weidleman interview).

A second reason for the slow pace is simply that the problems are very complex. Development of a comprehensive management plan requires resolution of difficult ecological questions regarding the relationship of the various species to a complex ecosystem. As previously described, the relationships are imperfectly understood and hotly debated. Aside from the scientific questions, participants also face difficult legal questions regarding the means to implement potential solutions.

Finally, participants acknowledge that progress is also slow because the program is both a research program and a forum for discussion and negotiation. Since these processes are not separated, work that should be "strictly technical" is colored by politics. Research data are evaluated according to how they affect the eventual outcome (that is, do they imply a need for more or less water committed to instream flows) rather than any technical standard. With negotiations occurring at each step, progress is indeed slow, and consensus appears impossible (Pustmueller interview, Weidleman interview). The recent legal actions between Wyoming and BuRec and between Nebraska and Wyoming only increase the adversarial atmosphere. Most participants now express pessimism that the Platte River Management Joint Study will successfully achieve its goals.

Private Conservation Initiatives

While private organizations have been active on the Platte for many years, many have recently increased their commitment in response to the growing number of water development proposals. For example, during 1986, National Audubon Society established protection of the Platte as one of its top conservation priorities and began a nationwide campaign to secure permanent protection for the river's key habitats. Similarly, American Rivers Inc., added the Platte to its list of "endangered rivers" and began a series of actions to promote the conservation of the Platte's land and water. These actions enhance the ongoing efforts of the Platte River Trust, National Wildlife Federation, Nebraska Wildlife Federation, and other groups, which continue action in several arenas.

Conservation organizations maintain that positive actions to protect the Platte's migratory bird habitats need not be delayed until the exact details of a comprehensive plan are known. Many of the elements of such a plan are apparent, they say, and can be implemented while research and negotiations continue. These groups are proceeding independently to implement steps which they feel are needed to conserve the Platte's special bird habitats.

Protection Status. While the Category 1 Resource and critical habitat designations assigned to the Platte by FWS are important, conservationists believe the Platte deserves broader protection. Given its importance to many migratory bird species, conservationists believe that a national wildlife refuge should be established along the central Platte. Such designation would permanently protect essential habitats, would add additional impetus to the argument to preserve instream flows, and would provide long-term funding for research and habitat management.

The idea of a Platte River National Wildlife Refuge is not new. In April 1974, FWS announced plans to purchase a 15,000-acre national wildlife refuge on the Platte River near Grand Island. Local landowners who feared that the lands would be acquired through condemnation vigorously opposed the proposal (Wallenstrom 1976b). The refuge proposal was subsequently dropped. Since then, FWS has continued to evaluate the prospects of establishing a national wildlife refuge. According to FWS officials, a federal refuge is needed on the Platte, but there are no active plans for establishing one (Bowman interview).

Conservationists believe the prospects for establishing a federal refuge may be better now than in the past. At the same time, they are also investigating other options that would provide additional legal recognition of the river's importance. Among the options under investigation are designation of critical habitat areas for the least tern and piping plover, recognition under the Wild and Scenic Rivers Act, and designation of the Platte as a "Wetland of International Importance" under the 1986 RAMSAR Treaty.

Habitat Acquisition and Management. Rather than wait for governmental action, three organizations have begun to acquire and manage lands to benefit wildlife. Since 1979, The Platte River Trust has acquired 7,000 acres of land that are managed to benefit migratory birds. Together with The Nature Conservancy, the Trust plans to acquire an additional 18,000 acres. National Audubon Society also owns and manages the 2,000-acre Lillian Annette Rowe Sanctuary located on the Platte River near Kearney. Audubon plans to acquire and manage additional lands, but has not yet set a specific acquisition goal.

Public Information and Education. Private organizations have also increased efforts to increase public understanding of the significance of the Platte to migratory birds and of the complexity of the threat posed by additional water development. During 1987, many organizations published articles about the Platte in their newsletters or magazines. National Audubon continues to hold its annual river conference in March and the Rowe Sanctuary conducts field trips year-round and trips to its viewing blinds during spring migration. In addition, National Audubon began work on a television special for national broadcast during 1989. Within Nebraska, the Nebraska Water Education Foundation began a public information campaign and the Nebraska Wildlife Federation initiated a door-to-door canvass throughout the state. These and other efforts are all intended to increase public support for private and governmental programs to conserve the Platte's migratory bird habitats.

Toward Basin-wide Water Development

Conservationists stress that all of their efforts to protect and manage Platte River habitats will be in vain without guarantees of water flowing in the river (Currier *et al.* 1985, Strom 1987). Ironically, this aspect of protection is the only one which they cannot achieve independently, because Nebraska law does not allow private parties to hold instream flow rights. Despite this limitation, conservation groups are actively investigating alternatives for improving current water management to better meet the needs of wildlife and traditional water users. The key to resolving the conflict on the Platte, in their view, is "basin-wide management," an approach that is gaining acceptance throughout the West (Currier *et al.* 1985). This relatively new philosophy was described by Colorado's former director of natural resources as follows:

> Another step that needs to be taken to encourage efficient water use is the more cooperative utilization of water resources. The dog-eat-dog competition that has characterized the operation of the prior appropriation doctrine has to be put behind us. We need to move toward basin-wide management of all water resources. This means using reservoirs jointly; it means exchanges for use and re-use of water; and it means a variety of measures that will achieve maximum use of water as it passes through the system (Getches 1985).

Water development interests agree that basin-wide management offers considerable promise for meeting the many water demands in the Platte River basin. Past water development has achieved an annual capacity of more than 7,000,000 acre-feet in the basin's many reservoirs. Those reservoirs currently operate independently. Most participants in the water controversy feel intuitively that the water needs of wildlife, agriculture, industry, and municipalities could be better met if a system-wide management scheme were implemented.

When this intuitive belief will be made operational, however, is uncertain. The scope of the Platte River Management Study includes evaluation of alternative water supply options that fit within the definition of "basin-wide management." However, the study has not yet begun to define alternatives in detail, much less to evaluate and implement them. When that effort occurs, it will also be constrained by the lack of a comprehensive hydrological model that accounts for all existing water sources and diversions in the basin. There are currently no firm plans for developing such a model. Although a fully comprehensive basin-wide management plan may be distant, several recent developments give some indication of the types of proposals that may be included in a future plan.

Exchanges and Transfers. Environmentalists have frequently suggested that proposed depletions could be offset by exchange or purchase of water from other sources; this method of maintaining instream flows has been discounted due to the "legal and institutional barriers" previously discussed. However, BuRec recently proposed a water exchange to partially offset the depletions of the proposed Narrows project (U.S. Department of the Interior 1987c). According to the proposal, BuRec would release water from Narrows Reservoir during October and November to the Central Nebraska Public Power and Irrigation District system in Nebraska. In exchange, the system would schedule offsetting releases from Lake McConaughy during spring, to provide habitat flows during the time when whooping cranes may occur on the central Platte.

No formal review has been conducted to determine if this proposal would offset the projected adverse impacts of the Narrows project; environmentalists remain seriously concerned about the effects it may have on sediment supply in the central Platte. However, the proposal is significant because it demonstrates that, at least in BuRec's opinion, the legal and institutional barriers to water exchanges are surmountable:

> In conjuction with the 10,000 acre-foot release from Narrows Reservoir, legal and institutional arrangements would be negotiated with the appropriate state and private organizations within the states of Colorado and Nebraska to arrange for the adjusted operation of Lake McConaughy to supply minimum Platte River streamflows in the spring (U.S. Department of the Interior 1987c).

The concept demonstrated by this recent BuRec proposal is significant because such exchanges and transfers may have wide applicability for improving instream flow conditions for wildlife (Pustmueller interview).

Modified Operation of North Platte River System. Any long-term strategy to meet instream flow requirements in the central Platte Valley is also likely to include modifications in the operating rules of existing water developments. Conservationists believe the operating practices of BuRec's existing system of eight reservoirs in the North Platte basin (with a total storage capacity of 3,000,000 acre-feet) should be carefully examined to determine if the system may be operated more efficiently to meet existing water demands and, in turn, freeing water for instream flows.

BuRec has completed preliminary studies to determine if modified operating practices may be used to increase the yield of irrigation water (U.S. Department of the Interior 1985). These studies indicated that existing yields may be increased by 40,000 to 80,000 acre-feet per year, if existing legal and institutional constraints are ignored. No studies have been completed to determine how BuRec operating practices could be modified to better meet wildlife needs, but conservationists believe they should be, especially since the agency announced during 1987 that it would redirect its mission from dam-building projects to "water conservation, environmental protection and restoration, and improved water management practices" (Wille 1987).

Modified Operation of Nebraska Projects. Conservationists also believe the operating practices of the Nebraska Public Power District and the Central Nebraska Public Power and Irrigation District systems in western Nebraska could be modified to better meet the instream flow needs of wildlife in the Big Bend of the Platte. These privately operated projects are fully integrated to supply water for hydroelectric generation and irrigation of 127,000 acres of upland crops in western Nebraska (Bentall 1982). The Central Nebraska system includes Lake McConaughy, a 1.6 million acre-foot reservoir in the North Platte, which is the largest storage reservoir in the basin and the closest one to the Big Bend. The system also includes the Tri-County Supply Canal, which diverts about 80 percent of the Platte's flow, just below the confluence of the North Platte and South Platte (Bentall 1982). Return flows from the Tri-County system re-enter the river just west of Overton; the high volume of water returned there is believed to be partly responsible for maintaining the open channel habitats which remain downstream from Overton.

Currently, instream flow requirements are not considered in the operation of the Central Nebraska Public Power and Irrigation District or the Nebraska Public Power District projects. Wildlife interests believe that the habitat requirements of cranes and other migratory birds should be added to the list of criteria that determine the operating rules of the system. This belief is bolstered by a preliminary study sponsored by the Platte River Trust that suggests that alternative rules could improve the delivery of water to the key migratory bird habitat without significantly affecting irrigation supplies or hydroelectric power generation (Shen *et al.* 1985).

Both the Central Nebraska Public Power and Irrigation District and the Nebraska Public Power District systems are licensed by the Federal Energy Regulatory Commission (FERC) under the Federal Power Act. Interest in these systems is becoming increasingly intense because their 50-year federal licenses expired during 1987; both systems must eventually obtain new long-term licenses from FERC. The long-term licensing of the projects is significant for several reasons. Relicensing is a major federal action subject to the National Environmental Policy Act and the Section 7 consultation provisions of the Endangered Species Act. Also, Congress included provisions in the Electric Consumers Protection Act of 1986 that require FERC to give "equal consideration" to the protection and enhancement of fish and wildlife habitats when it grants operating licenses for new or existing projects.[8]

Conservationists regard the relicensing process for the Central Nebraska Public Power and Irrigation District and the Nebraska Public Power District projects as a precedent-setting test of these new requirements, significant not only on the Platte, but nationwide. Many environmental groups, FWS, and state agencies plan to intervene in the relicensing process; however, the schedule for the proceedings is uncertain. Applications for relicensing submitted by project operators have twice been rejected by FERC as deficient.

Meanwhile, FERC granted both projects annual operating licenses when the 50-year licenses expired in 1987. In granting the annual licenses, FERC denied a formal request from FWS to consult over the license's effect on endangered species. FERC also denied petitions from the Platte River Trust and American Rivers Inc., requesting that FERC immediately begin to evaluate and apply license conditions that force equal consideration of migratory bird habitat needs in operating the projects. Both groups have appealed the ruling, requesting that FERC prepare an environmental impact statement and hold evidentiary hearings to consider future operating procedures. As of December 1987, FERC had not ruled on the appeal.

Incorporating Habitat Needs into New Developments. Another approach under consideration is to actually incorporate the habitat

8. See the *Audubon Wildlife Report 1987* for further discussion of the fish and wildlife provisions of the Electric Consumers Protection Act.

needs of migratory birds into the planning process for new water development projects. BuRec is trying this approach in its current planning efforts for the Prairie Bend/Twin Valley project in central Nebraska. This project would include instream diversions from the Platte near Overton to supply a system of reservoirs to be used to recharge groundwater. It also would include two major features specifically intended to benefit the migratory birds that depend on the central Platte.

One of these features would be a storage reservoir specifically operated to augment instream flows for the birds. In the plan, the proposed 250,000 acre-foot Plum Creek reservoir would be constructed on a tributary immediately above Overton. The reservoir would capture and store flows in excess of instream flow requirements for release during periods of low flow.

The second feature is a plan to acquire and manage 14,000 acres of land to benefit migratory birds. This proposal would add to the land acquisition efforts of the Platte River Trust, The Nature Conservancy, and National Audubon. It would effectively create the system of protected areas that wildlife interests believed are needed.

Environmentalists express mixed emotions about the Prairie Bend/Twin Valley proposal. While interested in the wildlife-oriented parts of the plan, they are unsure if the other components of the project are needed. A proposed plan and environmental impact statement on the Prairie Bend/Twin Valley Unit are expected to be released during 1988. Until these have received public and agency review, it will not be known if either the overall project, or its wildlife components, make environmental or economic sense.

THE OUTLOOK

At no time in the history of the Platte River controversy have so many events of such importance occurred during a relatively short period of time. How these events will affect future water management in the basin is uncertain, especially given the fact that current developments in all arenas—scientific, political, and legal—hold both promise and disappointment for those who believe that conservation of the Platte is essential.

The efforts of scientists to quantify instream flow needs is encouraging. Despite the intense debate surrounding this work, there is promise of improved understanding of the effects of water management on habitat conditions. However, research tends to generate new questions as it provides answers. It seems likely that the scientific efforts will refine the instream flows needed on the Platte, but there may be no single conclusive answer. Even if research was definitive, there would still remain political and legal impediments to obtaining instream flows.

Political events are also mixed. The efforts of National Audubon Society and other organizations demonstrate a heightened commitment to conservation of the Platte. At the same time, interest in new water development continues throughout the basin. These opposing interests guarantee continued, intense controversy. While it is significant that the Platte River Management Joint Study has brought the opposing interests together, achieving a negotiated solution seems less likely today than when the program began nearly three years ago. The impasse is just as great as before, while the atmosphere is more adversarial. Yet a similar effort on the Colorado River also languished for several years before finally producing a plan for resolving conflicts between water development and endangered fish.

Thus, it appears that the courts will once again play a pivotal role. The U.S. Supreme Court case in *Nebraska v. Wyoming* may well be the most significant development in decades, but this depends on the bounds placed on the case. Even if wildlife concerns are considered, a decision may take years. The pending decision on the Catherland project by the Nebraska Supreme Court will set the tone for conservation efforts within Nebraska. Other litigation has not been initiated, but it seems possible that the courts will be asked to scrutinize the Section 404 permits that will be required for the Two Forks and Deer Creek projects. In addition, the relicensing decision for operation of Kingsley Dam and Lake McConaughy may be litigated.

In the end, the future of the endangered, threatened, and other migratory birds that use the Platte River cannot be predicted. The only certainty is that the events transpiring now will influence the debate for years to come.

REFERENCES

Aiken, J.D. 1987. "New directions in Nebraska water policy." *Nebraska Law Review* 66: 8–75.

Andrews, Roger. Interview with the author, January 1988.

Bailey, W.J. 1985 Biological Opinion, Little Blue—Catherland Project. Letter of February 8 from William J. Bailey, Nebraska Game and Parks Commission to Michael Jess, Nebraska Water Resources Department.

Bentall, R. 1982. "Nebraska's Platte River a graphic analysis of flows." Nebraska Water Survey Paper 53. Conservation and Survey Division. The University of Nebraska-Lincoln. 47 pp.

Berle, P.A. 1987. "Final biological opinion on Two Forks dam is weaker than draft opinion." Press release, 21 October. National Audubon Society. New York, New York.

Bovee, K.D. 1982. "A guide to stream habitat analysis using the instream flow incremental methodology." *Instream Flow Information Paper* No. 12. U.S. Fish and Wildlife Service. Western Energy and Land Use Team. Fort Collins, Colorado. 248 pp.

Bowen, C.M. 1979. "Grayrocks—a new approach to mitigation." pp. 434–438 *in* G.A. Swanson, technical coordinator, *The Mitigation Symposium: A National Workshop on Mitigating Losses of Fish and Wildlife Habitats.* General Technical Report RM-65, U.S. Department of Agriculture, Rocky Mountain Forest and Range Experiment Station. Fort Collins, Colorado.

Bowman, David. Interview with the author, November 1987.

Buterbaugh, G.L. 1987a. Biological opinion on the Platte River off-site effects of the Denver Water Department's Two Forks project. Letter of October 14 from Galen L. Buterbaugh, Regional Director, Region 6, U.S. Department of the Interior, Fish and Wildlife Service to Colonel Steven G. West, District Engineer, Omaha District, U.S. Army Corps of Engineers.

——. 1987b. Biological opinion on the Platte River off-site effects of the Wyoming Water Development Commission's proposed Deer Creek Dam and Reservoir Project. Letter of July 20 from Galen L. Buterbaugh, Regional Director, Region 6, U.S. Department of the Interior, Fish and Wildlife Service to Colonel Steven G. West, District Engineer, Omaha District, U.S. Army Corps of Engineers.

Currier, P.J., G. R. Lingle, and J.G. VanDerwalker. 1985. *Migratory Bird Habitat on the Platte and North Platte Rivers in Nebraska.* The Platte River Whooping Crane Critical Habitat Maintenance Trust. Grand Island, Nebraska. 177 pp.

—— 1987. Reclamation of Crane Roosting Habitat on the Platte River and Restoration of Riverine Wetlands. Unpublished manuscript. The Platte River Whooping Crane Critical Habitat Maintenance Trust. Grand Island, Nebraska.

Dreher, Karl. Interview with the author, January 1988.

EA Engineering Science, and Technology, Inc. 1985. *Migration Dynamics of the Whooping Crane with Emphasis on Use of the Platte River in Nebraska.* EA Engineering Science, and Technology, Inc. Lincoln, Nebraska.

——. 1987. Critique of Spring and Fall Habitat Maintenance Flows Proposed by the Bureau of Reclamation for the Central Platte River. EA Engineering Science, and Technology, Inc. Lincoln, Nebraska. 24 pp.

Eastom, Fred. Interview with the author, January 1988.

Eschner, T.R., R.F. Hadley, and K.D. Crowley. 1983. "Hydrologic and morphologic changes in channels of the Platte River basin in Colorado, Wyoming, and Nebraska: a historical perspective." *Geological Survey Professional Paper* 1277-A. Government Printing Office. Washington, D.C. 39 pp.

Faanes, C.A. "Factors influencing the future of whooping crane habitat on the Platte River in Nebraska." *Proceedings of the 1988 Crane Workshop, Naples, Florida.* U.S. Department of the Interior, Fish and Wildlife Service. Grand Island, Nebraska. In press.

Fannin, T.E. and P. Nelson. 1986. Habitat Suitability Index Curves for Channel Catfish, Common Carp, Sand Shiner, Plains Killifish, and Flathead Chub Developed by Consensus Discussion for Use in the Instream Flow Incremental Methodology on the Central Platte River. Unpublished report. U.S. Fish and Wildlife Service, Wyoming Fishery and Wildlife Cooperative Research Unit, University of Wyoming, Laramie. 64 pp.

Frith, C.R. 1974. The Ecology of the Platte River as Related to Sandhill Cranes and Other Waterfowl in South Central Nebraska. M.S. thesis. Kearney State College. Kearney, Nebraska. 115 pp.

Getches, D. 1985. Excerpt from luncheon address at the 1985 conference: Western Water Law in Transition. University of Colorado Law School. Boulder, Colorado.

Haig, S.M. and L.W. Oring. 1987. "The piping plover," pp. 509–519 *in* Roger L. Di Silvestro ed., *Audubon Wildlife Report 1987.* National Audubon Society. New York. Academic Press Inc. New York. 697 pp.

Herschler, E. 1983. Letter of 27 June to James Flannery, U.S. Department of the Interior.

Hobbs, G.J. 1985. Federal environmental law and state water law: accomodation or preemption?" Paper prepared for the *Natural Resources and Environment* publication for the American Bar Association, June 1985. Davis, Graham, and Stubbs, P.C. Denver, Colorado.

Howe, M.A. 1987. "Habitat use by migrating whooping cranes in the Aransas-Wood Buffalo corridor," pp. 303–311 in *Proceedings of the 1985 Crane Workshop*. Platte River Whooping Crane Habitat Maintenance Trust. Grand Island, Nebraska. 415 pp.

Hurr, R.T. 1983. "Ground-water hydrology of the Mormon Island crane meadows wildlife area near Grand Island, Hall County, Nebraska." *Geological Survey Professional Paper* 1277-H. Government Printing Office. Washington, D.C. 12 pp.

Jess, J.M. 1986. "Order of approval in the matter of applications A-15145, A-15146, A-15147 and A-15148 assigned to the Catherland Reclamation District. Water Divisions 1-A, 1-B, and 1-C." Department of Water Resources. Lincoln, Nebraska.

Johnson, K.A. 1981. "Whooping crane use of the Platte River, Nebraska—history, status, and management recommendations," pp. 33–43 *in* J.C. Lewis ed., *Proceedings 1981 Crane Workshop*. National Audubon Society. Tavernier, Florida.

Kemper, Doug. Interview with the author, January 1988.

Kircher, J.E. and M.R. Karlinger. 1983. "Effects of water development on surface-water hydrology, Platte River Basin in Colorado, Wyoming, and Nebraska upstream from Duncan, Nebraska." *Geological Survey Professional Paper* 1277-B. Government Printing Office. Washington, D.C. 49 pp.

Lewis, James. Interview with the author, January 1988.

Lingle, G.R. 1987. "Status of whooping crane migration habitat within the Great Plains of North America," pp. 331–340 in *Proceedings of the 1985 Crane Workshop*. Platte River Whooping Crane Habitat Maintenance Trust. Grand Island, Nebraska. 415 pp.

Lingle, G.R. and G.L. Krapu. 1986. "Winter ecology of bald eagles in southcentral Nebraska." *Prairie Naturalist* 18:65–78.

Lowell, A.D. 1987. Motion of Platte River Trust for Leave to Intervene as Plaintiff, Memorandum in Support of Motion and Complaint in Intervention. Unpublished document. Brand & Lowell. Washington, D.C.

MacDonnell, L.J. 1985. *The Endangered Species Act and Water Development Within the South Platte Basin*. Completion Report No. 137. Colorado Water Resources Research Institute. Colorado State University. Fort Collins, Colorado. 122 pp.

McDonald, J.W. 1983. Letter of 29 July to Mr. James Flannery, U.S. Department of the Interior.

Mercer, Derwood. Interview with the author, January 1988.

Meyer, C.H. undated. Western Water Allocation: New Players in an Old Game. Rocky Mountain Natural Resources Clinic. National Wildlife Federation. Boulder, Colorado. 16 pp.

——. Interview with the author, January 1988.

Milhouse, Robert. Interview with the author, November 1987.

Northern Colorado Water Conservancy District. 1986. Cache La Poudre Basin Study Summary Report. Northern Colorado Water Conservancy District. Loveland, Colorado.

O'Brien, J.S. and P.J. Currier. 1987. Channel Morphology, Channel Maintenance, and Riparian Vegetation Changes in the Big Bend Reach of the Platte River in Nebraska. The Platte River Whooping Crane Critical Habitat Maintenance Trust. Grand Island, Nebraska. 49 pp.

Pitts, T. 1985. "Conflict resolution: western water law and the Endangered Species Act," *The Environmental Forum* July 1985. Pp. 37–39.

Purcell, Michael. Interview with the author, January 1988.

Pustmueller, Carse. Interview with the author, December 1987.

——., *et al.* 1986. Letter of December 11 to Regional Director, U.S. Fish and Wildlife Service, Galen Buterbaugh.

Shen, H.W., K.L. Hiew, and E. Loubser. 1985. The Potential of Modified Flow-Release Rules for Kingsley Dam in Meeting Crane Habitat Requirements—Platte River, Nebraska. Completion Report No. 138, Colorado Water Resources Research Institute. Colorado State University. Fort Collins, Colorado. 43 pp.

Shenk, T.M. and M.J. Armbruster. 1986. Whooping Crane Habitat criteria for the Big Bend of the Platte River. Unpublished report. U.S. Fish and Wildlife Service, National Ecology Research Center. Fort Collins, Colorado. 34 pp.

Simms, R.A. 1988. Brief in Support of Motion to Amend Petition for an order enforcing decree and for injunctive relief. Unpublished document. Department of Justice, State of Nebraska, Lincoln.

Smith, B.A. 1984. Environmental Quandary Over Water Management. Unpublished paper presented to the Nebraska Water Resources Association, June 5, 1984. EA Engineering, Science, and Technology, Inc. Lincoln, Nebraska. 25 pp.

Strom, K.J. 1987. "Lillian Annette Rowe Sanctuary—managing migratory crane habitat on the Platte River, Nebraska," pp. 326–330 in *Proceedings 1985 Crane Workshop.* Platte River Whooping Crane Habitat Maintenance Trust. Grand Island, Nebraska.

U.S. Army Corps of Engineers. 1986. Denver Metropolitan Water Supply Draft EIS. U.S. Army Corps of Engineers, Omaha District. Omaha, Nebraska.

——. 1987. Final Environmental Impact Statement for Regulatory Permits, Deer Creek Dam and Reservoir, Wyoming. U.S. Army Corps of Engineers, Omaha District. Omaha, Nebraska.

U.S. Department of the Interior. 1978. Memorandum, Cumulative impacts—Section 7 of the Endangered Species Act, from Solicitor, Department of the Interior to Director, Fish and Wildlife Service, July 19, 1978. U.S. Fish and Wildlife Service. Washington, D.C.

——. 1981a. *The Platte River Ecology Study, Special Research Report.* Fish and Wildlife Service, Northern Prairie Wildlife Research Center. Jamestown, North Dakota. 187 pp.

——. 1981b. Memorandum, Cumulative Effects to be Considered under Section 7 of the Endangered Species Act, from Associate Solicitor, Conservation and Wildlife, to Director, Fish and Wildlife Service, August 27, 1981. U.S. Fish and Wildlife Service. Washington, D.C.

——. 1982. Water Use and Management in the Upper Platte River Basin. Bureau of Reclamation, Lower Missouri Region. Denver, Colorado. 87 pp.

——. 1983a. Narrow Unit Biological Opinion—Whooping Crane. Memorandum of January 20 1983 from Regional Director, Region 6, U.S. Department of the Interior, Fish and Wildlife Service, to Regional Director, Lower Missouri Region, Bureau of Reclamation.

——. 1983b. *Summary Report, Upper Platte River Study.* U.S. Department of the Interior. Washington, D.C. 122 pp.

——. 1984. Platte River Management Joint Study—Narrows Option. Unpublished document. Bureau of Reclamation, Lower Missouri Region. Denver, Colorado.

——. 1985. Final Supplement to the Final Environmental Statement, Pick-Sloan Missouri Basin Program, South Platte Division, Narrows Unit, Colorado. Bureau of Reclamation, Lower Missouri Region. Denver, Colorado.

——. 1986. *Whooping Crane Recovery Plan.* U.S. Department of the Interior, Fish and Wildlife Service, Albuquerque, New Mexico. 283 pp.

——. 1987a. Fish and Wildlife Coordination Report for the Two Forks Reservoir and William's Fork Gravity Collection System Projects, Colorado. U.S. Department of the Interior, Fish and Wildlife Service, Region 6. Denver, Colorado. 177 pp.

——. 1987b. Revised Work Plan for Platte River Technical Steering Committee. Unpublished document. Platte River Management Joint Study, Bureau of Reclamation. Loveland, Colorado.

——. 1987c. Draft Biological Assessment, Narrows Unit—Colorado, Pick—Sloan Missouri Basin Program. U.S. Department of the Interior, Bureau of Reclamation. Eastern Colorado Projects Office. Loveland, Colorado.

Vaughn, D.C. 1987. "The whooping crane, the Platte River, and endangered species legislation." *Nebraska Law Review* 66: 175–211.

Wallenstrom, R.L. 1976a. "The history and present status of the Mid-State project," pp. 139–140 *in* J.C. Lewis, ed., *Proceedings of the International Crane Workshop.* Oklahoma State University Publishing and Printing.

——1976b. "The Platte River National Wildlife Refuge," pp. 140–143 *in* J.C. Lewis, ed. *Proceedings International Crane Workshop.* Oklahoma State University Publishing and Printing.

Wallin, Jerry. Interview with the author, January 1988.

Weidleman, Roger. Interview with the author, November 1987.

White, W. 1985. "Interstate compacts and endangered species: Wyoming's approach." Paper presented at the workshop on the Endangered Species Act and Western Water Law, 25 September 1985. Colorado Water Congress. Denver, Colorado.

Wille, C.M. 1987. "Dam-building agency says it will now push conservation." *Audubon Activist* 2(2): 13.

Williams, G.P. 1978. The Case of the Shrinking Channels—the North Platte and Platte Rivers in Nebraska. Geological Survey Circular 781. U.S. Department of the Interior, Geological Survey. Arlington, Virginia. 48 pp.

Woodward, Duane. Interview with the author November 19, 1987.

Ziewitz, J.W. 1987. Whooping Crane Riverine Roost Habitat Suitability Model: Discharge Versus Habitat Relationship in the Big Bend of the Platte River. Unpublished report. Platte River Whooping Crane Habitat Maintenance Trust, Grand Island, Nebraska. 21 pp.

Thomas G. Shoemaker is a science and environmental writer based in Ft. Collins Colorado. He is president of the Ft. Collins Audubon Society.

A customs official examines confiscated endangered species products. International trade in pets, specimens for collectors, ivory, furs, shells, hides and other wildlife products threatens many species. *U.S. Fish* and *Wildlife Service.*

International Wildlife Trade

Ginette Hemley

INTRODUCTION

International commercial trade in wildlife and wildlife products directly affects the survival of species throughout the world. A complex issue involving thousands of species, dozens of countries, and ever-changing regulatory schemes, wildlife commerce has become the subject of extensive debate in both conservation and political circles. In recent years, populations of familiar fauna such as rhinoceroses, elephants, and crocodilians have plummeted as a direct result of their exploitation for commercial trade, prompting worldwide trade-control initiatives. Controversy has surrounded efforts to protect other traded species, largely due to the lack of accurate scientific data on their biological status. Initiatives to control wildlife commerce have taken on added importance as other ecological threats such as habitat loss continue to accelerate. Unfortunately, most attempts to legally regulate wildlife trade have met with limited success, and illegal wildlife commerce remains a serious problem worldwide.

International trade in wildlife and wildlife products can generally be broken down into two types: commerce in food items such as marine fisheries resources and timber for human consumption, and trade in live plants and animals or their products for everyday use and ornamentation. Wildlife food and commodity items that are covered by specific laws and regulations are largely excluded from treatment in this chapter. The other category, which can generally be characterized as consumer items primarily of a luxury nature, is the principal focus here. From an international perspective, it is the commerce in wildlife consumer items—live animals and plants, furskins, hides, and ivory, for example—that present some of the greatest challenges to nations seeking to protect some of the world's most threatened species.

International commercial trade in wildlife is not a new phenomenon. Furs and ivory, for example, have been traded and bartered for centuries for their practical and aesthetic value to man. Whales have been exploited since the Middle Ages for meat, oil, and whalebone. At the turn of this century, the millinery trade in Europe and the United States posed a serious threat to the survival of certain egrets, birds of paradise, parrots, and other avifauna with colorful and decorative plumage. Only in recent decades have improvements in transportation and shipping techniques allowed for a large-scale international wildlife business to develop. Rapid air transport has provided the basis for a flourishing commerce in live wild animals and plants. These changes, along with the general affluence brought with the post-World War II economic boom and the use of increasingly efficient capture and hunting techniques, have combined to make the international wildlife trade a profitable, expanding enterprise.

Commerce wildlife trade, including both plants and animals, has an estimated value of at least $5 billion (World Wildlife Fund 1986a). The bulk of all traded wildlife enters the world market from the tropical and subtropical regions of Africa, Southeast Asia, and South America (see Table 1). Most wildlife commodities in trade are consumed by the industrialized nations of the European Economic Community (EEC), Japan, and the United States. Some nations, such as the United States and Canada, are both consumers and producers, while others, like several in the EEC, are principally consumers and trans-shippers, importing raw materials for manufacture and domestic use or to re-export to other countries.

The United States is the world's largest wildlife market, importing and exporting about $1 billion worth of wildlife and products each year. About three quarters of this value involves imports; the remaining one-quarter is exports and re-exports (U.S. Department of the Interior unpubl.). In an average year, the United States imports some 12,000 to 14,000 live primates, primarily for biomedical research; 5 to 10 million raw furskins; 6 to 8 million pieces of carved African elephant ivory; 800,000 live birds; 15 to 20 million finished reptile leather products; 125 million live ornamental fish; over 1 million cacti; and 500,000 orchid plants, among many other products (see Table 2). Imported

Table 1
Major Wildlife Exporters and Importers[a]

Exporters	Importers
Argentina	Canada
Bolivia[b]	China
Brazil[b]	European Economic Community
Central African Republic	Hong Kong
China	Japan
Congo	Singapore
Guyana	Taiwan
Honduras	United States
Indonesia	
Mexico[b]	
Paraguay[b]	
Peru	
Philippines	
Senegal	
South Africa	
South Korea	
Sudan	
Taiwan	
Tanzania	
Thailand	
Turkey	
United States	
U.S.S.R	
Zaire	

Source: World Wildlife Fund 1986a, U.S. Department of the Interior (unpublished).
[a] Based on U.S. imports and export of select wildlife trade items, including primates, furskins, ivory, birds, reptile skins, coral, and cacti.
[b] Countries that prohibit most wildlife exports. Most trade in species taken from these nations is illegal and must be "laundered" through other countries.

items carrying the greatest dollar value are fur and reptile skins and products. Raw furskins from North American mammal species[1] are the most-valued export commodity. (See the chapter in this volume on the orchid trade.)

The precise number of species affected by international trade is not documented, but thousands of different animal and plant species have been reported in commercial trade in recent years. While this shows the overall diversity of the commerce, the volume of trade and its impact varies widely with the species and type of trade.

In general, the commerce in wildlife products is more voluminous than the trade in live wildlife, but involves fewer species. For example, more than 20 species of wild furbearing mammals are commonly traded in North American fur markets, but as much as half of the total

1. These species include mink, beaver, muskrat, raccoon, coyote, fox, otter, bobcat, lynx, marten, fisher, and several other species.

Table 2
U.S. Imports of Wildlife in a Typical Year[a]

Primates	12,000 to 14,000 live (mostly for biomedical research) Declared value: \$1.2 million
Furs	6 million raw furskins 500,000 to 1 million manufactured products Declared value (estimated): \$800 million
Ivory	4 to 6 million worked or carved products 5,000 raw tusks Declared value: \$20 to 30 million
Birds	800,000 live (including about 250,000 parrots) Declared value: \$15 million
Reptiles	300,000 to 500,000 live 2 to 4 million skins 15 to 20 million manufactured products Declared Value: \$200 to 250 million
Ornamental Fish	125 million Declared value: \$25 to 30 million
Shells	12 to 15 million raw shells 50 million manufactured products Declared value: \$13 to 13 million
Corals	1,000 to 1,500 tons of raw corals 2 to 3 million manufactured products Declared value: \$5 to 6 million
Cacti	1 to 2 million whole plants Declared value: NA
Orchids	300,000 to 500,000 whole plants Declared value: NA

Source: World Wildlife Fund 1986a, U.S. Department of the Interior (unpublished).
[a] Figures included are based on the average number of imports recorded from 1980 to 1985. They represent reported trade and should be considered minimum.
NA = not available

production value involves only 3 species: raccoon, muskrat, and beaver (Prescott-Allen and Prescott-Allen 1986).

Similarly, one study showed that about 80 percent of all reptile skins and products imported by the United States during a three-month period consisted of only seven species (Hemley 1983). By contrast, as many as 500 species of live ornamental fish may be imported into the United States in a given year (Hemley and Gaski unpubl.), with as much as 85 percent of the trade involving fewer than 25 species (Conroy 1975). This can be compared with the trade in live reptiles for the pet market; during one year, at least 300 species were imported into the United States (TRAFFIC(U.S.A.) unpubl.).[2] It is

2. Two facets of the wildlife trade, the fur and ornamental fish trades, rely heavily on captive-bred specimens. The most valuable fur species on the North American market is mink, 95 percent of which is captive-produced (Prescott-Allen and Prescott-Allen 1986). Similarly, an estimated 95 percent of all imported ornamental fish are captive-bred freshwater species produced primarily on Southeast Asian fish farms (Hemley and Gaski unpubl.).

important to point out that much of the attraction to and thus demand for live exotic wildlife as opposed to products stems from the sheer diversity of species of available,i.e. the more unique a species is, the more attractive it seems to the buyer. This quality of "uniqueness" is often associated with a species' rarity; thus, more truly rare species are generally involved in the live wildlife trade than in the wildlife products trade.

Historically, the overall impact of trade on a particular species can be partially gauged by examining trade trends.

Unfortunately, because international wildlife trade was largely unregulated until the 1970s, little reliable historical data exist for most species. The information that does exist suggests that there has been a tendency in some cases to exploit a species to the point of commercial extinction, then shift the commerce to a different species, which itself eventually becomes depleted, and so on.

This pattern can be readily seen in the crocodilian skin trade. During the 1950s and early 1960s, so great was the demand for exotic leathers that 5 to 10 million crocodilian skins were traded internationally each year. Intense hunting pressure drastically reduced populations of species with the most valuable skins, such as the American (*Crocodylus acutus*) and Orinoco (*C. intermedius*) crocodiles of Latin America. As these species became scarce, hunters turned to the rougher-skinned black (*Melanosuchus niger*) and broad-snouted (*Caiman latirostris*) caimans, also found in the region. When these species later became depleted, traders shifted their attention to the smaller and less-desirable spectacled caiman (*Caiman crocodilus*) (King 1978). By the late 1960s, all of these species except the spectacled caiman were considered endangered.

Today, the number of species for which trade represents the most significant threat to their survival is open to debate. For many taxa, commercial exploitation for trade is a secondary or tertiary threat after habitat loss and local or subsistence exploitation. However, with the rate of environmental degradation, especially in the developing world, generally increasing as a result of expanding human populations, the rate of exploitation for trade is also likely to be increasing simply because humans are coming into closer contact with commercially valuable species.

It is difficult to gauge what proportion of the international wildlife trade is illegal, but estimates put the figure at one-quarter to one-third of the total trade (World Wildlife Fund 1986a). Thus, on a worldwide basis, the illegal trade may be on the order of \$1 to \$2 billion worth of goods per year. According to the U.S. Fish and Wildlife Service (FWS), illegal wildlife imports into the United States alone may be valued at \$100 to \$250 million annually (U.S. Department of the Interior unpubl.). These illegal imports include wildlife and products that are not reported in import records but escape U.S.

Customs detection as a result of inadequate inspection, document fraud, or outright smuggling.

Of the U.S. wildlife imports that are reported in trade records, a significant portion may be illegal although they are not detected as such. "Laundering" is a frequent practice used in the wildlife trade, whereby a species' name or country of origin is deliberately or mistakenly falsified on trade documents. Due to the complex trade routes associated with much of the commerce, especially manufactured products, it is often difficult to trace the actual origin of the goods to verify whether they were taken legally. Similarly, species are sometimes declared as originating in countries where they do not occur or where they exist in insignificant numbers; inadequate local enforcement allows these claims to go unchecked. The ivory, live bird, and reptile skin trades have been especially prone to laundering practices.

THE INTERNATIONAL WILDLIFE TRADE CONTROL SYSTEM: CITES

Worldwide concern over the threat international commerce poses to the survival of species in the wild reached a peak in 1973 with the signing of the Convention on International Trade in Endangered Species of Wild Fauna and Flora, or CITES (27 U.S.T. 1086, March 3, 1973). The treaty came into force in 1975 after ratification by the United States and 9 other countries; today 95 nations, including most major wildlife producer and consumer countries, have become parties to the convention.

Trade Control Provision

The purpose of CITES is to protect certain species from the threat international trade poses to their survival. It achieves this by establishing lists of species at risk and, depending on their status in the wild, prohibiting or limiting their export and import. Special permits are required for transactions in species covered by CITES; these are issued by member nations and serve to track the trade. Every two years, CITES parties meet to review treaty implementation worldwide and amend the protected species lists. CITES is generally regarded as both a protectionist treaty and a trade treaty in that it prohibits commercial trade in species in danger of extinction, but allows controlled trade in other less-threatened species (Lyster 1985). Enforcement is left to individual parties, making the treaty's effectiveness very much dependent on the goodwill of its member nations. Close communication among the parties is also crucial to the convention's success.

The most widely accepted international wildlife conservation agreement in existence, CITES is characterized by a number of unique features. Key among these is the degree to which nongovernmental organizations (NGOs) are allowed to participate in its activities.[3] CITES' roots are closely associated with NGOs, particularly the International Union for Conservation of Nature and Natural Resources (IUCN), which played an important role in the convention's initiation and drafting. The treaty also provides for the establishment of a permanent secretariat to oversee its implementation at the global level and to coordinate communications among the parties.[4]

CITES categorizes species at risk into two principal groups and restricts their trade accordingly. Those species threatened with extinction that are or may be affected by trade are included in Appendix I and cannot be traded for commercial purposes; those species that are not necessarily threatened with extinction, but that may become so unless their trade is regulated, are listed in Appendix II and may be traded commercially under certain conditions and with special permits. In addition, Appendix III includes species legally protected within the borders of a treaty nation that have been determined by that country to need international trade control. For example, India lists several protected native snake species in Appendix III because they are considered threatened by trade for the international leather market.

Appendix I currently lists about 675 species, including some of the most endangered plants and animals in the world. The great apes, great whales, all species of rhinoceros, most of the large cats, numerous parrots, all sea turtles, most crocodilians, and several species of cacti, orchids, and cycads are among the taxa covered by the convention's strictest trade prohibitions. Appendix II contains at least 27,000 species—about 2,350 animals and some 24,000 plants—including all primates, cats, parrots, crocodilians, cacti, and orchids not already included in Appendix I, the African elephant, various

3. Article XI of the treaty expressly allows for nonvoting participation by approved NGOs at the biennial conferences of the parties. In addition, NGOs have made important technical and financial contributions to CITES through formal participation in and support of special CITES working groups and meetings, seminars, publications, and biological studies. Some observers conclude that NGO involvement in CITES has been key to whatever success the convention has achieved (Kosloff and Trexler 1987).

4. Based in Lausanne, Switzerland, the CITES Secretariat works with a small professional staff and a core budget of over $1 million. The secretariat acts as a clearinghouse for information by providing parties and NGOs with relevant administrative, legal, and trade information. It is also responsible for developing scientific and technical studies authorized by the parties, for reviewing statistics on the annual trade by member nations, and for organizing the biennial conferences of the parties. The secretariat's funding originally came from the United Nations Environment Programme, but is now drawn from annual contributions of the parties.

snakes and lizard species, poison-arrow frogs, certain butterfly and coral species, and numerous other taxa.

Decisions to add, delete, or transfer species from one list to another are made at the biennial meeting of the signatories, also known as "meeting of the conferences of the parties." Such changes must be formally proposed by one or more individual parties, and are actual amendments to the appendices of the treaty, which require the approval of two-thirds of the parties present and voting at the meeting.

The CITES trade control mechanism involves a system of permits administered by the trading parties. Both the importing and exporting party must issue a permit for any specimen (live or dead) traded. Because commercial trade is not allowed for Appendix I species, most of the legal transactions involve zoological or scientific specimens or, in some cases, noncommercial souvenirs or hunting trophies.[5] For trade in Appendix II species, the exporting or re-exporting party is required to issue a permit for each transaction. For both Appendix I and II species, special exemptions are made for captive-bred specimens, personal accompanying baggage items, pre-convention items, and certain other specimens and transactions.

The conditions under which a CITES permit may be issued are the basis of the convention's implementation activities. Upon acceding to CITES, party states are required to designate scientific and management authorities whose principal task is to determine when CITES-listed specimens under their jurisdiction may be traded. In some cases national laws more restrictive than CITES, which the convention allows for, preclude the authorization of any trade in CITES-listed species from those countries. For example, national laws in Australia and Brazil ban most commercial wildlife exports, so relatively few CITES permits are issued in those countries. In general, however, CITES-authorized trade is based on the premise that the responsible government has determined that: 1) the transaction will not be detrimental to the survival of the species in the wild; 2) the specimen in question was legally taken in its country of origin; and 3) the risk of injury, damage to health, or cruel treatment during trade will be minimal.

5. For example, import permits are regularly issued in the United States for noncommercial souvenir or trophy specimens of two species listed on Appendix I, leopard (*Panthera pardus*) and southern white rhino (*Ceratotherium simum simum*). In 1983, the CITES parties adopted a special quota system for noncommercial trade in leopard, and certain African CITES parties now allow a limited number of exports. Hunting trophies of southern white rhino are frequently imported from South Africa, where the species is managed for sport hunting.

CITES in Practice: Problems in Applying International Trade Controls

CITES parties are bestowed with tremendous responsibility when they join the convention. Not only are they required to establish a fairly sophisticated system for issuing permits, tracking trade, and enforcing CITES rules, but they also must collect a good deal of biological information on the status of certain species. Status determinations are important for native species listed on Appendix II, which can be traded commercially if such trade is determined harmless by the exporting party. In reality, the task of making such "no-detriment" findings is overwhelmingly difficult, especially for wildlife-producer countries in the developing world that lack the resources to undertake extensive biological surveys or to conduct sophisticated wildlife research.

The result is that much of the commercial trade in Appendix II species is simply "rubber-stamped" because of the lack of information to show that trade may or may not be detrimental. This problem has been compounded by the fact that certain parties have not even designated scientific authorities to review trade levels and potential impacts. In addition, it often is difficult for government authorities to determine the actual origin of the specimens involved and thus verify their legality; the range of most Appendix II species extends across numerous national boundaries and such species are often subject to varying degrees of legal protection in different countries. Specimens are often smuggled out of countries where they are legally protected into neighboring countries where CITES export permits can be obtained. In some cases, government compliance in such illegal transactions has added to the enforcement difficulties. When specimens reach their destination, customs inspectors have no way of determining the true country of origin; rather, they must rely solely on the permit declaration.

The Ivory Debate. Nowhere have wildlife trade control problems and challenges been more apparent than in the elephant ivory trade. Indeed, few international conservation issues have been as widely debated or have cost CITES so much time and resources as the commerce in ivory taken from the African elephant (*Loxodonta africana*).

Listed on Appendix II in 1977, the African elephant is regarded by CITES as a renewable wildlife resource of considerable economic importance to both African producer countries and ivory consumer nations, particularly those of the Far East that have used ivory for centuries.[6] CITES controls are intended to restrict trade to a level that

6. The other elephant species, the Asian elephant (*Elephas maximus*) was once heavily exploited for its ivory, but is now considered an endangered species and listed on CITES Appendix I.

does not harm wild populations. In some countries, especially in southern Africa, ivory trade is well-controlled and elephant populations are managed and relatively stable. In certain other countries, however, CITES controls and elephant population management programs are largely ineffective. Overall, the total number of African elephants has declined steadily during the last decade. The latest estimates put the entire elephant population at about 765,000 animals, down from over a million in the late 1970s (African Elephant and Rhino Specialist Group 1987, Douglas-Hamilton 1987).

Experts have argued over the actual role trade in ivory has played in the elephant's demise, with some maintaining that the species' decline is due primarily to poaching which has stemmed from the growing number of elephant/human conflicts associated with Africa's rapidly expanding human population. However, most agree today that while elephants and humans often compete for suitable living space, there is also a tremendous incentive to poach purely for profit.

The recent dramatic drop in elephant numbers is linked to the large-scale illegal ivory trade that took place in the 1970s. This illegal trade was spurred by the tremendous increase in the prices paid for raw ivory, which jumped from $7 per kilo in 1970 to $74 per kilo in 1978 as a result of inflation and general worldwide monetary instability (Anonymous 1980).[7] Ivory, like precious metals, is often used for investment and as a hedge against inflation because of its long-standing value and durability. As the price of ivory rose, elephant killing, particularly in Kenya and Zaire, increased dramatically. Poaching of elephants was facilitated by the increased availability of automatic weapons, a by-product of growing civil and guerrilla warfare throughout Africa. High kill-rates were purportedly promoted by corrupt government officials in some instances. As the situation worsened, some countries, including Kenya and Zaire, banned ivory exports (Caldwell 1984). Trade patterns then shifted as ivory was laundered through countries that continued to allow exports, namely the Central African Republic, Congo, and Sudan.

Reacting to the illegal trade problem, CITES members began in the early 1980s to adopt specific measures to halt the illicit export of tusks. These efforts culminated in 1986 with the implementation of a special CITES ivory-trade control system. Designed by the African ivory producer nations together with the principal ivory consuming nations of the Far East, Europe, and the United States[8], the new system is generally considered the most sophisticated mechanism ever developed to monitor international trade in a wildlife commodity.

7. Raw ivory currently sells for about $100 to $130 per kilo wholesale (Douglas-Hamilton 1987, Thomsen, pers.commun.).

8. The United States is principally an importer of worked or carved ivory.

The framework of the system is a series of annual tusk export quotas that are set by individual countries, based on elephant population estimates. All tusks authorized for export are specially marked, and their trade is tracked through a special unit in the CITES Secretariat. Ivory consuming nations have agreed to accept only specially marked tusks from treaty nations that have recognized quotas, or from non-treaty nations that have agreed to work with the system. The total number of tusks sanctioned for trade under the system was about 93,000 for 1986, and 117,000 for 1987, which included some tusks that had been stockpiled (CITES 1986a and 1987a).

At the July 1987 CITES conference in Ottawa, Canada, the ivory trade situation was reviewed. To the surprise of many, illegal ivory trade during 1986—the first year the new ivory trade control system was in effect—had remained substantial. A report issued at the meeting by the IUCN African Elephant and Rhino Specialist Group estimated that only 22 percent of the ivory that entered world trade during 1986 was traded within the quota system; hence most of the ivory that entered the world market that year was illegal. The illegal trade included the tusks of about 89,000 elephants, including some tusks from elephants killed in previous years. The report went on to say that according to the latest surveys, the African elephant population may have declined by 36 percent since 1981 (African Elephant and Rhino Specialist Group 1987).

The disturbing news issued at the 1987 CITES meeting has reactivated the ivory debate in the U.S., causing some conservationists to scrutinize CITES' approach to ivory trade control. Many animal protection organizations believe that a complete U.S. ivory import ban, as called for in legislation introduced in Congress several times in the last ten years, is critical to stopping the decline of African elephant numbers. They argue that the compromise measures embodied in the CITES ivory-control system go too far in trying to appease all sides, rendering the system largely ineffective. They point out that CITES continues to be undercut by countries such as Burundi, the United Arab Emirates, and Singapore, all of which which have been implicated in large-scale illegal ivory trade in recent years[9]. They also argue against the special treatment some nonparty countries have received that have allowed them, for all practical purposes, to enjoy the benefits of CITES while remaining officially outside of the convention. For example, Burundi has been allowed a one-time opportunity to trade its ivory stockpiles to CITES members, even though these tusks are known to be from illegal sources.

9. Burundi is not yet a CITES party, and the United Arab Emirates recently withdrew from CITES, the first party to ever do so.

Supporters of the CITES ivory trade control system such as World Wildlife Fund are firm in their belief that the system is the most realistic means of keeping the African elephant from becoming an endangered species eligible for listing on Appendix I. They maintain that the CITES measures, combined with increasingly sophisticated data on elephant population numbers and trends, offers the first means of determining the full extent of the ivory trade, both legal and illegal. They point out that to control illegal trade over the long run, stockpiles must be fully accounted for. They further argue that the system is still in its infancy; because the African elephant is not an endangered species, the system should be given a realistic amount of time to work. A trade ban, they say, will not likely be effective at this time because the illegal trade is too well-established and the worldwide investment in ivory is too great.

The CITES ivory trade control system will be reviewed again at the 1989 biennial CITES meeting. U.S. conservationists currently following the plight of the African elephant are generally taking one of two approaches to the issue: supporting a complete U.S. ban on commercial imports of elephant products through passage of special federal legislation, or supporting efforts to improve the CITES ivory trade control system in the hopes that illegal ivory trade will be significantly reduced over the next two years. One reform being considered is the creation of an excise tax on imported elephant products to generate funds for elephant conservation and for strengthening ivory trade controls.

Continuing Commercial Trade in Endangered Species

International trade in Appendix I species is scrutinized to a greater degree by the CITES parties than trade in Appendix II species simply because the taxa affected are generally recognized as in danger of extinction and usually are strictly protected in their countries of origin. Overall, there is much less international commerce today in species now considered endangered than there was in those same species two decades ago.

For example, since CITES came into effect in 1975, there has been a noticeable decline in the trade of skins of certain large cat species that were once heavily utilized by the fur industry, but were protected by inclusion on Appendix I. Although reliable world trade figures are lacking, the U.S. market is probably a fair gauge of the decline in the cat skin trade. In 1968, import records show that about 1,300 cheetah (*Acinonyx jubatus*), 9,600 leopard (*Panthera pardus*), 13,500 jaguar (*P. onca*), and 129,00 ocelot (*Felis pardalis*) skins were imported into the United States for the fur industry (King 1978). Ten years later, after most large cat species were listed on Appendix I, trade records revealed only three such products imported into the United States: one leopard trophy, one tiger (*P. tigris*) and one snow leopard (*P. uncia*) garment (U.S. Department of the Interior 1979). While this change can be partly attributed to CITES *per se,* it is more likely the combined result of an increase in legal trade prohibitions at the national level in both exporting and importing countries (including enactment of the Endangered Species Act), changes in fashion design and public opinion, and the difficulty in finding increasingly scarce animals.

However, not all commercial trade in endangered species has ceased. Some species listed on Appendix I, in particular rhinos and sea turtles, have continued to suffer from excessive legal and illegal international trade. Some of the trade has been facilitated by special exemptions allowed by the convention; in other cases lax law enforcement is the problem.

The Rhinoceros Trade. For rhinos, continued exploitation for trade has been particularly devastating. Rhino horn is marketed in parts of Asia where it is valued as a medicinal product, and in the Middle East, primarily North Yemen, where it is carved into traditional dagger handles or "jambias." Eighty-five percent of the world's population of five rhino species has disappeared since 1970 largely as a result of poaching for this trade (Martin 1987). Fewer than 11,000 animals remain worldwide. The black rhino (*Diceros bicornis*) of east and southern Africa has had its population reduced almost 75 percent by poaching during the last seven years; fewer than 4,000 animals exist today (Martin 1987).

The cause of this enormous decline is linked to the increasing demand for rhino horn in certain markets: the Middle East, where purchasing power greatly expanded with the oil boom in the 1970s, and Asia, where growth in general affluence has led to a dramatic rise in imports in general. North Yemen, a non-CITES country with a total human population of about 2.3 million, has consumed approximately half the world's rhino horn since 1970. Trade has declined somewhat in the 1980s, partly as a result of economic troubles in that region. Some countries, including North Yemen, have recently stepped up efforts to control imports. Since 1985, the last major rhino consumers – South Korea, Taiwan, Macau, and Singapore – have officially banned rhino horn trade, although only Singapore has joined CITES. Illegal trade to other CITES member nations, notably China, Hong Kong, and Thailand, continues (Martin 1987).

In spite of the tightening of trade controls in some consumer nations, poaching of the black rhino in its last stronghold – the Zambezi Valley of Zimbabwe – continues at an alarming rate. Horn is taken primarily by poachers based in neighboring Zambia and then transported to Burundi for shipment to the Middle East or Asia (Martin

1987). Although the Zimbabwe government has launched a major anti-poaching effort, the profit made from the sale of one black rhino horn (about $1,500 per horn in the Far East) (Fitzgerald in prep.) virtually guarantees that illegal hunting and trade will continue.

The Sea Turtle Trade. Sea turtles also have been affected by continuing large-scale illegal trade, in spite of the listing of all seven species on Appendix I. In contrast to rhinos, however, it is more difficult to gauge the full impact of this trade. Sea turtles are long-lived and inherently difficult to study, spending most of their lives at sea. While several species have a global distribution, they tend to form discreet populations, many of which have been the targets of intense exploitation for their meat, oil, skin, eggs, and shell. Females are often hunted when they come to shore to nest and are especially vulnerable. Japan is the world's largest importer of sea turtle products and is the driving force behind much of the continuing commercial trade. Most of Japan's trade focuses on the hawksbill turtle, whose carapace is carved into traditional and contemporary jewelry and ornaments. Japan's hawksbill shell, or "bekko" trade, involves the annual slaughter of an estimated 28,000 turtles. In recent years, imports have come primarily from Indonesia, Panama, Cuba, Singapore, and the Philippines. Japan also imports a significant number of stuffed juvenile hawksbill and green turtles for use as wall ornaments, primarily from Indonesia, and a sizeable volume of sea turtle skin and leather from the olive ridley turtle, primarily from Ecuador and Mexico. Most of Japan's suppliers of sea turtle products are parties to CITES, and many of these claim that all exports to Japan have been illegal (Milliken and Tokunaga 1987).[10]

Continuing international commercial trade in hawksbill, green, and olive ridley sea turtles has been spurred largely by Japan's refusal to abide by CITES for these species by entering "reservations." This action—allowed for under Article XXIII—underscores an inherent weakness in CITES' structure. By entering a reservation on a species, a party is not bound by regular CITES trade restrictions for that species. This general exemption provision, which is not uncommon in international conservation agreements, has in effect allowed commercial trade of some Appendix I species to continue, notably certain sea turtles and other reptiles.[11]

10. Recent debates over the sea turtle trade have centered not on Japan's voluminous imports, but rather on requests for CITES exemptions for commercial trade in "farmed" or "ranched" turtles. These proposals have failed principally because operations such as the Cayman Turtle Farm in the Cayman Islands have not met the strict CITES criteria for commercial captive-production, and because wildlife trade controls by countries seeking exemptions, such as France (for its green turtle ranch in the Reunion Islands), are so poor.

11. Twelve CITES parties currently hold reservations on various CITES listings:

Japan's continuing trade in Appendix I species and her general failure to implement CITES properly for Appendix II species has caused considerable concern in the international conservation community. Because Japan is a major wildlife consumer, the implications of this trade and its potential impact on certain species worldwide are enormous. But, out of respect for national sovereignty, CITES participants have failed to address this issue in a meaningful way. Rather, the treaty parties have chosen to take up other, less confrontational CITES implementation activities.

Controversy Over Species Listings

One activity that is generally perceived by many CITES parties as a means of strengthening the convention is the routine addition of species to the various CITES appendices. In some cases, decisions to add species to the appendices have not been based on any demonstrated threat of trade to a particular species. Although the quality of data to support a species' addition to (or removal from) the CITES appendices has come under closer scrutiny in recent years, the degree to which decisions by the conferences of the parties reflect biological data has varied widely. In general, parties have favored adding species to the appendices not always on the basis of sound scientific data, but often because of political pressure and special interests at home. In addition, certain listings have been facilitated by a provision in the convention that allows for the inclusion of species not directly threatened by trade, but for which trade control is deemed necessary to protect other, "similar" listed species. The same restrictions apply to trade in species listed under these "look-a-like" criteria as to trade in species listed because of the direct impact of commerce.

A number of CITES listings have been controversial because of the lack of scientific data to support the decisions, and the added administrative burden each new listing poses to each party's management and scientific authorities. In particular, controversy has surrounded the listings of entire families or other higher taxa, such as the 1977 listing in Appendix II of all species in the cat family Felidae that were not already covered by the convention, and the similar 1981 listing of all parrot species in the order Psittaciformes.

The U.S. opposed the 1977 Felidae listing because of its lucrative export trade of bobcat pelts (*Felis rufa*), the harvest of which is largely regulated by state wildlife agencies. In 1979, the species' Appendix II listing took on particular importance when the U.S. scientific author-

Austria, Botswana, Brazil, Chile, Japan, Liechtenstein, Norway, Peru, Singapore, Sudan, Switzerland, and the Soviet Union. Japan maintains reservations on twelve Appendix I species, more than any other party.

ity's no-detriment finding for the export of bobcat skins was challenged by Defenders of Wildlife. Concern arose over the quantity of bobcat skins taken in 34 states and the Navajo reservation that were approved for export by the U.S. Scientific Authority in accordance with guidelines developed by that office the previous year. While the government's no-detriment finding included general population trend, total harvest, and harvest distribution information, it lacked specific information on different populations of bobcat that Defenders said was necessary to show that trade would not be harmful to the species overall. In *Defenders of Wildlife v. Endangered Species Scientific Authority* (659 F.2d 168, (D.C. cir.), the plaintiff argued that both the guidelines for making no-detriment findings and the actual findings for bobcat skin exports in 1979 were not in accordance with the convention's requirements.

In 1981, after the pelt exports from the 1979 trapping season had been made, a federal appeals court ruled in favor of Defenders. The court held that the use of population trend data to make no-detriment determinations for hunting levels was unlawful because it did not provide sufficient data on the total bobcat population or on the number to be killed in each state. In 1982, however, the court's decision was overruled by an amendment to the Endangered Species Act that relieved the government of any responsibility of making population estimates to substantiate a no-detriment finding (see Lyster 1985; Bean 1983). This issue—the amount and quality of evidence a scientific authority requires in order to determine whether or not a proposed export will be detrimental to the survival of a species—has never been formally addressed by the CITES parties.

Although the species involved are less valuable than the bobcat from an economic standpoint, the 1987 addition to Appendix II of all poison arrow frogs in the genera *Dendrobates* and *Phyllobates* and the entire hummingbird family Trochilidae, raise similar questions. Proponents of these listings, which totalled about 400 species, argued that although not all of the species are traded in numbers that warrant monitoring, enforcing trade controls for the truly threatened species is made easier if all similar species are covered by the same restrictions. Opponents argued that the trade threats to most of these species is relatively small, and that it would be extremely difficult to enforce the convention for such listing because of the lack of identification guides needed to monitor trade and the inherent difficulty of making no-detriment findings. Many parties have begun to argue strongly that, if the convention is to be fully effective for the species most threatened by trade, more time and resources must be devoted to ensuring proper enforcement of trade controls for species known to be at risk and less to the inclusion of new species on the appendices for which there is little demonstrated trade threat.

Lack of an Enforcement Framework

CITES has occasionally been criticized as having "no enforcement teeth." This is partly because the treaty itself does not establish an enforcement framework, as with other international agreements, enforcement is left up to the individual parties. The convention does not outline sanctions for violations; it only requires parties to take "appropriate measures" to enforce its provisions and to penalize trade that violates the treaty. Enforcement is largely dependent on the goodwill of the parties. This is no doubt one reason that relatively little time has been devoted to issues of a purely enforcement nature at biennial CITES meetings.[12] Although this forum probably offers one of the best opportunities for reviewing enforcement problems and pressuring countries into better compliance with the treaty, it has yet to be used effectively for these purposes. However, there are signs that this may be changing.

The convention assigns the CITES Secretariat responsibility for monitoring treaty implementation at the global level. The secretariat has carried out this activity somewhat more ambitiously in the last three years than previously, although relatively few staff resources are devoted to enforcement tasks on a full-time basis. A report prepared by the Secretariat for the 1985 conference of the parties in Buenos Aires, Argentina outlined a series of failed attempts on the part of the Secretariat to improve CITES implementation in Bolivia, Paraguay, and the European Economic Community. Bolivia, a major exporter of parrots, monkeys, and reptile skins, was particularly identified as an illegal trade center where forged and stolen permits were frequently used, often for wildlife smuggled into Bolivia from other countries (CITES 1986b).

The report led to a recommendation by the CITES Standing Committee to the parties to prohibit all CITES trade with Bolivia, leaving it up to individual nations whether or not to pursue this action (CITES 1986c).

The Bolivia issue arose again at the 1987 CITES conference when the Secretariat reported on that country's slight improvements, but this update was accompanied by a broader report on "alleged infractions" by other CITES parties as well. The first of its type, the report cited numerous apparent CITES violations by both producer and consumer parties during the previous two years, including instances of commercial trade in Appendix I species, trade in Appendix I or II species without proper

12. In fact, most of the formal discussion at biennial CITES meetings has centered on defining the sometimes vague provisions of the convention, particularly with regard to trade exemptions. A substantial amount of time and resources has been devoted to defining such clauses as "primarily commercial purposes," "in-transit shipment," "pre-convention acquisition," and "ranching."

documents, use of forged permits, and failure to take action against illegal trade (CITES 1987b). Although the Secretariat's intention was to stimulate constructive dialogue on these problems, the effort failed largely because CITES delegates, especially from parties that were mentioned in the report, strongly opposed such discussion. Interestingly, the United States was not mentioned in the report. Many parties and observers were encouraged by this rather frank presentation of fundamental compliance problems, although it is clear that a more effective means of addressing them is needed. As a result of the Ottawa discussions, the CITES Standing Committee is developing a formal strategy, long overdue, for regular review of treaty infractions.

Annual Reports: A Means of Measuring Compliance

One way of measuring a party's compliance with the convention is by reviewing the annual report each member is required to prepare on its trade in CITES-listed species. These reports can provide useful information on trade trends and patterns because they list each transaction in a particular species, noting its country of origin, the type of item traded, purpose of the transaction, and other relevant details. These reports can assist investigations into violations and can also help assess the impact of trade on a species.

In general, reporting has improved considerably in the last few years. However, in a recent review of annual reports for 1985, the degree of correlation between import and export declaration by trading countries was found to be astoundingly low. Overall, only 16 percent of export shipments were identical to those reported by the importing country. Reporting correlation was much worse for plants in trade than for animals (CITES 1987c). In addition, some parties, principally developing nations[13], have never filed an annual report, while other consumer countries such as Japan continue to file incomplete reports. Although reporting problems have been regularly reviewed at the biennial CITES meetings, little has been done to improve the situation and reporting appears to remain a low priority for many CITES parties. Representatives from some management authorities note that they lack the staff and financial resources to produce annual reports.

The EEC Report Controversy. In a controversial move that could have important implications for trade monitoring and reporting worldwide, the EEC Commission recently began submitting CITES annual reports for EEC-wide CITES trade, in effect replacing the individual nation reports previously submitted by certain EEC members. The

13. These are Algeria, Bahamas, Belize, Cyprus, Egypt, Guyana, Honduras, Hungary, Iran, Israel, Jordan, Morocco, Nigeria, Portugal, Trinidad and Tobago, and United Arab Emirates.

EEC report contains only external trade information, and does not cover intra-community trade. This new reporting procedure was initiated after the 1983 adoption by the CITES parties of an amendment to the treaty, now pending ratification, that would allow the EEC to become a party to CITES and thus allow for uncontrolled trade in CITES species within the EEC.[14]

Conservationists worry that this new reporting procedure, if it replaces individual reporting by CITES parties in the EEC, could potentially mask illegal imports into the community because not all EEC member states are CITES parties, even in nations that are parties enforcement of CITES is not uniform.

Meanwhile, the EEC has moved steadily towards a harmonized implementation system, with the entry into force in 1984 of EEC regulations laying out a framework for wildlife import and export controls for the EEC member states. While these regulations include a number of measures that are more restrictive than CITES and are directly binding on EEC members, they do not impose penalties for violations, leaving this to individual member states (Thomsen and Brautigam in press). Further, they relieve member states from national obligations to report on CITES trade with other EEC members.

Critics have questioned this action, arguing that EEC members who are also party to CITES are required under the convention to report on trade with all other countries, at least until the amendment is ratified by the necessary majority of parties (World Wildlife Fund 1986b). As of January 1, 1987, only 12 of the 54 required CITES parties had ratified the amendment (Thomsen and Brautigam in press). In 1987, the U.S. Congress postponed voting on ratification of the amendment pending full review of CITES implementation in the EEC. Underlying Congress' decision was strong evidence that certain EEC CITES members such as France and Italy were not implementing the convention properly and were allowing significant illegal wildlife trade to go unchecked (World Wildlife Fund 1986b).

WILDLIFE TRADE CONTROLS IN THE UNITED STATES

The United States has developed one of the world's most sophisticated systems to control the import and export of wildlife and wildlife products. At the heart of this system are two important laws—the Endangered Species Act and the Lacey Act— that together give the

14. Some observers contend that Article XIV(3) of the Convention allows for this. The article states that CITES shall "in no way affect the provisions of or obligations deriving from (other international agreements) . . . creating a union or regional trade agreement establishing or maintaining a common external customs control . . . ".

federal government broad authority to control wildlife trade and to assist other countries in their efforts to protect native wildlife from illicit trade. As the world's leading importer of wildlife and wildlife products, the United States has the potential to strongly influence international trade control and efforts to stem illegal exports from countries of origin. However, this power is not effectively employed, and trade control continues to be frustrated by an inadequate number of trained personnel, conflicting priorities within the federal government, and the sheer magnitude of growing trade volume.

The Endangered Species Act of 1973 (16 U.S.C.A. 1531 *et seq.*) provides the statutory authority for much of the wildlife trade control practiced in the United States. The act authorizes control over trade in endangered and threatened species, prescribes a basis for monitoring trade in other species, and provides for implementation of CITES.

The act generally prohibits U.S. import and export of species listed as endangered or threatened.[15] Exceptions may be granted for trade for scientific purposes or to enhance propagation or survival of the species. The act also authorizes the development of special regulations to allow commercial trade in threatened species under certain conditions. Since 1973, special rules have been adopted for threatened species such as African elephant, certain kangaroos, and American alligator, allowing their commercial import and export to continue.

The Secretary of the Interior, through the U.S. Fish and Wildlife Service (FWS), has primary responsibility for implementing the act, including its broad trade provisions. In addition to establishing a framework for issuing Endangered Species Act and CITES permits, FWS has developed an import/export control system that requires all commercial shipments of wildlife and wildlife products, regardless of the species involved, to enter and leave the country through one of nine designated ports.[16] This allows FWS to concentrate its limited inspection staff at relatively few ports around the country. In addition, all commercial wildlife imports and exports, as well as certain noncommercial raw wildlife products and hunting trophies, must be reported on a special FWS declaration form ("3–177"). Finally, FWS requires any business engaged in wildlife imports or exports valued at more than $25,000 per year to purchase a $250 annual license. These same businesses are subject to inspection fees for certain shipments (50 CFR 14). Currently, FWS licenses about 3,200 commercial wildlife traders (Striegler, pers. commun.).

15. Species protected specifically by the Endangered Species Act are prescribed separately from those protected by CITES. Some species are covered by provisions of both; about 50 percent of the species listed by the act are also listed by CITES (U.S. Department of the Interior 1986).

16. These are Chicago, Dallas-Ft. Worth, Honolulu, Los Angeles, Miami, New Orleans, New York, San Francisco, and Seattle.

While FWS has primary authority for enforcing endangered species trade controls, several other federal agencies share some of this responsibility and add to the complexity of the control system (see Figure 1). Endangered and threatened plant trade enforcement falls primarily to the Animal and Plant Health Inspection Service (APHIS) of the U.S. Department of Agriculture, which checks to see that imported plants are free of disease and noxious weeds, are accompanied by the required phytosanitary certificates and, when applicable, CITES permits. APHIS also is charged with overseeing the import of live birds, which are required to undergo disease screening and quarantine. The National Marine Fisheries Service is responsible for trade control of certain marine species, notably those protected by the Marine Mammal Protection Act and certain marine species listed under the Endangered Species Act. Finally, with its general responsibility for overseeing all imports, the U.S. Customs Service is usually the first to encounter incoming wildlife shipments. Customs usually checks for a completed wildlife declaration form, and then contacts FWS for inspection and clearance.

The other federal statute of considerable importance in controlling wildlife trade is the Lacey Act (18 U.S.C.A. 42–43; 16 U.S.C.A. 3371–3378). Originally passed in 1900 primarily to control illegal interstate commerce of wildlife and to prevent the importation of "injurious" species, the Lacey Act has since been amended to cover foreign species protected in their countries of origin. Under the Lacey Act, it is illegal to import wildlife or wildlife products taken, transported, or sold in violation of foreign law. In practice, enforcement of the Lacey Act falls largely to the FWS by virtue of its oversight of all wildlife imports.

Both the Endangered Species Act and the Lacey Act provide for civil and criminal penalties, as well as broad authority for making seizures of illicit goods. Under the Endangered Species Act, a criminal violation is a misdemeanor, with a maximum penalty of $20,000 and/or one year in prison. Certain criminal violations under the Lacey Act are felonies, subject to a maximum penalty of $20,000 and/or five years in prison. Civil offenses for both the Endangered Species Act and Lacey Act carry a maximum penalty of $10,000, which may be imposed by the Secretary of the Interior.[17]

Trade Controls in Practice: The CITES Bureaucracy

Under the authority of the Endangered Species Act, the Secretary of the Interior has delegated CITES scientific and management authority

17. In 1984, Congress increased the possible fines for all crimes, both misdemeanors and felonies, in the Omnibus Crime Control Act. This act, which applies to most federal offenses, increases the potential maximum fine for certain misdemeanors to $100,000 for organizations and $25,000 for individuals (see Kosloff and Trexler 1987).

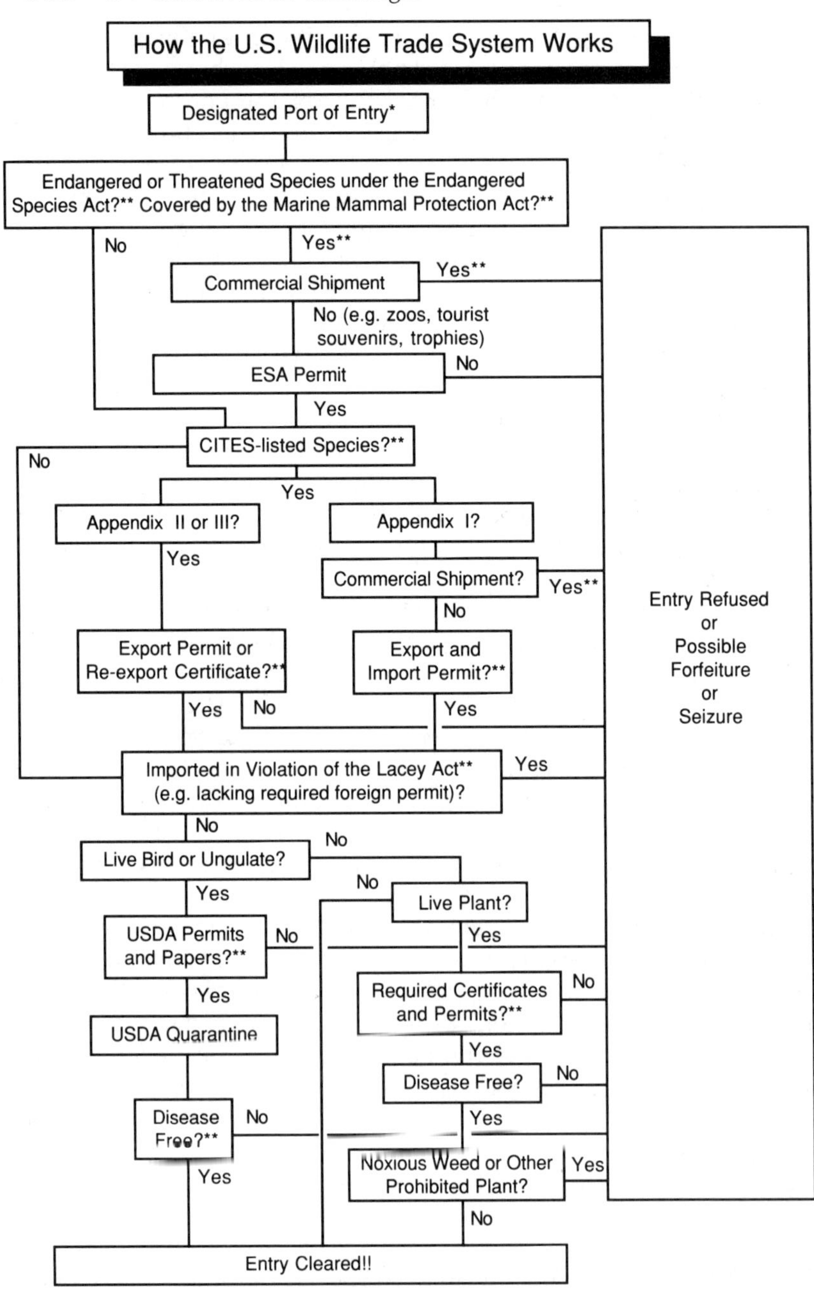

* All commercial shipments must enter through one of nine designated ports of entry.
**Special exemption or procedures may govern these steps. Please contact your local Fish and Wildlife Service Office or the Wildlife Permit Office for details.

Figure 1. Source: TRAFFIC (U.S.A), World Wildlife Fund.

responsibilities to FWS. Three offices under three different FWS assistant directors have distinct roles in CITES administration. The Office of Management Authority under the assistant director for Fish and Wildlife Enhancement has primary responsibility for international CITES communications, general CITES permit policymaking, and preparations for the biennial CITES conferences. The Office of the Scientific Authority in the research division (Region 8) reviews endangered species and Appendix I permit applications, and oversees rulemaking for CITES listing changes. The Division of Law Enforcement under the assistant director for Refuges and Wildlife is responsible for enforcing all U.S. wildlife trade laws and for carrying out investigations and inspections. While the separation of these responsibilities may be logical from an organizational standpoint, it has sometimes led to confusion and conflict in resolving CITES-related problems.

The Division of Law Enforcement is more involved with the practical application of CITES than any other FWS unit. The division maintains a team of wildlife inspectors and agents, who are posted at certain ports around the country. Wildlife inspectors, who numbered 60 in 1987, are trained in basic CITES and U.S. law enforcement techniques, as well as wildlife identification. In FY 1985, the inspection program, including trade-related investigations, cost FWS about $1.8 million dollars and amounted to about 10 percent of the total Law Enforcement budget (U.S. Department of the Interior 1985).

Weaknesses in the U.S. Wildlife Trade Control System

Insufficient Inspection Capability. Although FWS' inspection program has grown steadily in the last few years, a number of factors still preclude thorough review of all wildlife imports and exports. The sheer volume of trade is one major problem. Inspectors are faced with the overwhelming task of checking the more than 90,000 *reported* wildlife shipments that now enter and leave the country annually (see Figure 2), including a review of all paperwork accompanying those shipments. In reality, fewer than one in four shipments is physically inspected, and some of these are only partially examined (U.S. Department of the Interior unpubl.). Many shipments are cleared on the basis of paperwork alone.

In addition, inspectors are required to log all shipment-related data, which takes up 20 to 30 percent of their actual work time and leaves less opportunity for physical inspection. While logging data is necessary for collecting information and compiling CITES annual reports, much of the task could be accomplished by trained clerks or support staff. Inspectors are also responsible for issuing many CITES permits and for checking wildlife trade licenses, which further adds to their administrative workload.

While reporting of wildlife shipments is steadily improving as a result of the growing FWS program and better compliance among traders (Roeper, pers. commun.), an unknown number of imports and exports continue to go completely unchecked. Although an estimated 90 percent of all known wildlife shipments pass through international airports (U.S. Department of the Interior 1985), some shipments enter at nondesignated ports or as containerized cargo at sea ports, which are generally not staffed or readily accessible by FWS. Sea ports handle a tremendous volume of cargo in general. In addition, wildlife cargo traveling by truck across the Canadian and Mexican borders may go unreported, especially when vehicles cross the borders at night. When shipments enter or leave by any of these routes, FWS is forced to rely on Customs inspection and interdiction, the effectiveness of which varies significantly around the country. Even at the designated ports, FWS inspectors do not work around the clock, and shipments may arrive or depart during unmanned hours (Dixon 1986).

Lack of Information and Directives for Inspectors. Lack of enforcement information and directives on specific trade problems also impedes consistent enforcement. Wildlife inspectors frequently do not have quick access to information on foreign laws that they need to

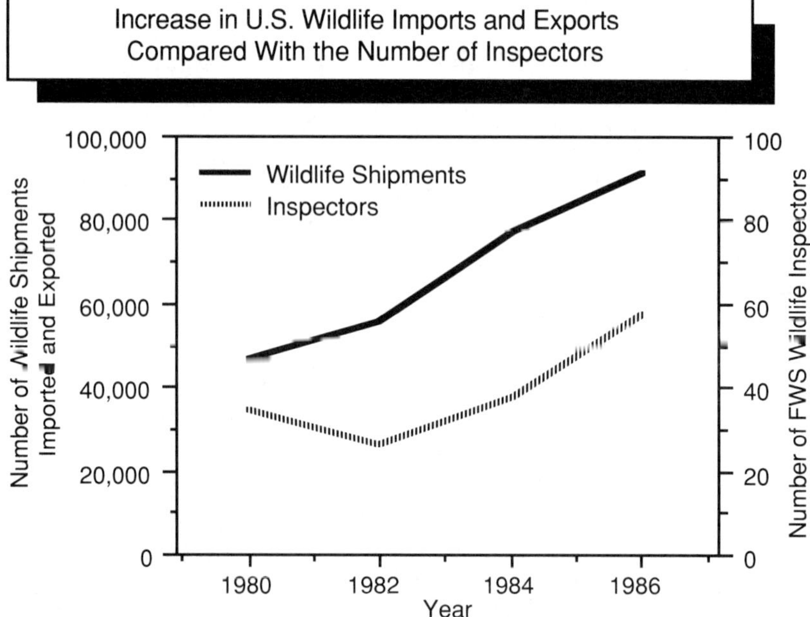

Figure 2. Source: U.S. Department of the Interior, unpublished.

enforce the Lacey Act, or to notifications issued by the CITES Secretariat relating to specific international trade issues. Most of this information must filter down from the central Law Enforcement office in Washington through the regional FWS office before arriving at the ports, a process that can take weeks or even months. The problem is sometimes complicated by the fact that port inspectors are generally required to take orders from the regional FWS office, not Washington. Some FWS officials in Washington also note that it has been difficult to compile a master list of foreign wildlife laws because many laws are difficult to interpret and sometimes require extensive research. Further, the office primarily responsible for international CITES communication, the Office of Management Authority, has very little direct contact with inspectors in the ports, even though it has frequent contact with foreign management authorities and the CITES Secretariat. As a result, much of the information needed to facilitate enforcement at the ports never leaves Washington.

Proliferation of Nondesignated Ports. During the last two years, the inspection program has taken on a slightly new orientation. While only nine ports of entry are officially designated to handle commercial shipments of wildlife entering or leaving the country, an increasing number of shipments are being allowed to pass through nondesignated ports.

FWS regulations adopted in early 1986 established a system of "user fees" for commercial wildlife traders, that effectively increased the cost of import/export licenses from $50 every two years to $250 every year; the regulations also outlined a procedure for collecting inspection fees (50 CFR 14). The new fees are intended to allow FWS to recover part of the costs incurred for compliance inspection of commercial traders and shipments, and to allow expansion of the inspector program.

While the Endangered Species Act authorizes the establishment of user fees in order to facilitate enforcement, in imposing them the FWS has made an effort to accomodate commercial traders, especially those dealing in live wildlife, by expanding inspection services to allow for more frequent passage of shipments through nondesignated ports that were previously not available for wildlife inspection services. These ports, most of which have been staffed by inexperienced wildlife inspectors, generally lack the infrastructure and support system of the designated ports and are thus less equipped to intercept illegal shipments.

Deterrent Value of U.S. Enforcement

The effectiveness of U.S. law enforcement efforts is partially reflected in the total number of seizures and forfeitures of illegal wildlife shipments, penalties assessed for violations, and successful prosecutions that have taken place in recent years. The most current summary information available is for 1984. That year, 1,815 CITES violations were reported and 1,597 investigations were opened.[18] These resulted in total fines of $5,800 and 1,460 days of jail terms. Civil actions resulted in $126,253 in penalties assessed and collected. The value of the specimens forfeited or abandoned to the government as a result of civil actions was declared to be about $1.1 million (U.S. Department of the Interior 1986).

Considering the enormous value of the U.S. wildlife trade and the overall proportion that may be illegal, these total penalties are woefully small. While limited enforcement capability is largely to blame, in some cases, so is enforcement reluctance. The incentive to enforce wildlife trade laws, or lack thereof, has no doubt been influenced by judicial attitudes, and perceived attitudes, toward violations. Some observers have noted that the courts have been reluctant to impose penalties for "innocent conduct," in spite of the strict liability and strengthened criminal and forfeiture provisions of the Endangered Species Act and Lacey Act. In addition, the FWS has shown reluctance in enforcing the Lacey Act in some cases because of the lack of ample, substantive proof of violation of a foreign law which FWS believes may be necessary to convince courts to impose penalties (Kosloff and Trexler 1987).

What actually substantiates "proof" of foreign law in a court may not be the principal impediment; obtaining a foreign government's assistance in wildlife trade investigations may actually be more of an obstruction (Kosloff and Trexler 1987). The FWS has experienced occasional difficulty in obtaining verification of a foreign country's wildlife laws and regulations. However, improving international communication with CITES management authorities should lessen this problem. In addition, a recent project initiated by World Wildlife Fund with financial support from the U.S. departments of the Interior and Justice has helped fill the void of information on foreign wildlife laws. This project is documenting and summarizing the requirements of wildlife trade laws of Latin American, Asian, and African countries, and making this information available to wildlife and customs inspectors, management authorities, prosecutors, and traders (Fuller *et al.* 1985).

An important forfeiture case recently decided in Florida should help bolster FWS enforcement efforts. In *United States v. 3,210*

18. According to one source, violations involving CITES-listed species were treated as violations of one or more laws: Lacey Act, Endangered Species Act, Migratory Bird Treaty Act, or Marine Mammal Protection Act. Approximately 80 percent of Endangered Species Act violations involved CITES species. About 25 percent of the Migratory Bird Treaty Act and Marine Mammal Protection Act violations may have included CITES species, but these were prosecuted under the Lacey Act (U.S. Department of the Interior 1986).

Crusted Sides of Caiman crocodilus yacare (636 F. Supp. 1281, 1285–86, [S.D. Fla. 1986]) , the court accepted certified translations of Bolivian decrees as proof that some skins of the subspecies, which is listed under the Endangered Species Act, had been exported illegally from Bolivia and thus violated the Lacey Act. The court also determined that because part of the shipment was illegal, the entire shipment of 10,870 skins (valued at over $1 million) was forfeitable. Even though the cargo was en route to Europe, the court considered the shipment an import into the United States under the Endangered Species Act's broadest definition of that term.

In an effort to enforce the Lacey Act more consistently, FWS began in 1985 to issue "Notices of Information" on foreign wildlife laws (50 *Federal Register* 34015 [1985]). These notices serve as FWS policy with regard to the requirements of foreign wildlife trade laws. To date, seventeen notices have been published (52 *Federal Register* 16459 [1987]), ranging in subject from species-specific trade restrictions to foreign wildlife export bans. On two occasions these notices imposed complete U.S. wildlife import prohibitions from two countries, the Philippines and Singapore, because of those countries' failure to provide information on the validity of export documentation for shipments that had arrived at U.S. ports. In the case of the Philippines, the foreign government responded swiftly, no doubt because of the lucrative Philippine export trade in live tropical fish, shell and coral products, and snakeskin goods. The U.S. import ban was lifted one week later, after FWS received confirmation on the validity of certain documents and permit issuing authorities (50 *Federal Register* 39851 and 50 *Federal Register* 41747 [(1985]).

The U.S. ban on imports from Singapore had broader implications. A major trade center for wildlife and wildlife products, Singapore for years has been suspected of acting as a transhipping and "laundering" point for protected wildlife. The U.S. import ban imposed in September 1986 was prompted by questionable shipments of skins of pangolin (*Manis*, spp.), a CITES-listed mammal whose hide is sometimes made into leather products. Although pangolins are protected throughout most of their Southeast Asian range, Singapore had continued to issue export documents for shipments to the United States.[19] Failing to receive a response to queries on the legality of the skins of pangolin and other species, FWS decided that *all* wildlife imports from Singapore were suspect and invoked a complete import ban. The threat of a possible court injunction by the U.S. pet industry caused FWS to lift the ban almost immediately for Singapore's voluminous non-CITES tropical fish exports, most of which involve captive-bred fish.

19. Although Singapore was not party to CITES at the time, the convention requires comparable documentation for imports from nonparty nations.

Negotiations entered into between the U.S. and Singapore governments to determine under what conditions the ban would be fully lifted led to major changes in Singapore's wildlife trade policy. In discussions led primarily by the U.S. State Department, the government expressed concern over Singapore's continuing trade in endangered species products, particularly rhino horn, and the country's failure to join CITES. Although the United States had no legal authority to make lifting the ban conditional upon Singapore's enactment of specific legislation, Singapore officially outlawed rhino horn trade one month later, and acceded to the convention within two months. The United States lifted the trade ban with Singapore in January 1987 (Anonymous 1987).

THE IMPACT OF U.S. DEMAND ON THE WORLD'S WILDLIFE RESOURCES: CASE ANALYSES

An average of almost 250 shipments of wildlife have entered the United States daily in recent years (U.S. Department of the Interior unpubl.). Most of these shipments do not contain species that are specifically protected by U.S. law or CITES. In fact, the U.S. has been fairly effective at restricting imports of endangered species such as sea turtles, large cats, and marine mammals. Although the United States is still considered the world's largest wildlife consuming country, Japan, by comparison, probably conducts the most extensive trade in endangered species (Milliken, pers. commun.).

On a shipment-by-shipment basis, most U.S. imports consist of nonendangered species of furbearers, reptiles, tropical fish, birds, and other wildlife. In 1984, only about one in five shipments imported into the U.S. contained CITES-listed species (U.S. Department of the Interior 1986). Even though the trade volume of CITES-listed species is comparably low, U.S. imports involve species that are considered threatened. There is considerable concern about many of these species because of their questionable status in the wild and the failure of many supplying countries to implement CITES properly. Of particular note are U.S. imports of elephant ivory, live parrots, and crocodilian skin products.

Elephant Ivory Trade

The United States is not a major importer of raw ivory from the African elephant, as compared to Hong Kong and Japan. However, the United States may be the second largest importer of worked ivory after Japan

(Barzdo 1984). Most of the four to six million pieces of processed or carved ivory imported annually come from Hong Kong. From 1984 to 1986, U.S. elephant product imports, including raw and worked ivory and leather, averaged about $29 million in value per year. These products may have an annual retail value in the United States of more than $100 million (Thomsen 1987).

Although the African elephant is listed as threatened under the Endangered Species Act, a special rule allows the import of ivory and other products provided they originate in a CITES member nation (50 CFR 17.40). Worked ivory imports from Hong Kong, which supplies over 90 percent of all such items, are generally accompanied by re-export documents that specify the country of origin. However, because of the difficulty of verifying this information once a tusk is worked into smaller pieces, it is almost impossible to establish the actual legality of these imported goods under either the Endangered Species Act or the Lacey Act. FWS must simply accept or reject legality claims made by Hong Kong. In reality, these claims are rarely questioned, and most ivory shipments are allowed entry into the U.S.

In 1986, 75 percent of all worked ivory imports from Hong Kong were declared as originating in countries that prohibited the export of raw ivory well before 1986: Congo, Kenya, Sudan, and Zaire (Thomsen 1987, Caldwell 1984). FWS inspectors allowed these shipments to enter the United States. The U.S. enforcement effort is complicated by the fact that ivory is sometimes stockpiled in Hong Kong for periods before carving and export, which clearly complicates U.S. enforcement efforts.

The legality of U.S. imports of raw ivory is also questionable, in spite of the fact that procedures for controlling this trade have been clearly laid out both in U.S. regulations and CITES notifications. An average of about 4,200 individual tusks, including noncommercial hunting trophies, were imported into the United States annually from 1983 to 1986. A number of these imports apparently originated in countries that did not authorize such exports, notably the Central African Republic and Zaire. Of particular concern are the 1986 imports of almost 600 tusks from Zaire. According to the CITES Secretariat, several of these shipments were apparently accompanied by irregular, possibly forged, permits, but were allowed into the United States unchallenged. While a FWS investigation of this matter has since been opened, it appears that wildlife inspectors in the ports were not fully informed of the latest ivory trade procedures and foreign export laws; although the inspectors were lax in examining the permits, they also were not properly equipped to intercept those shipments (Thomsen 1987).

Live Parrot Trade

The import of live birds for the pet and aviculture trade also presents the government with special problems. The possibility of introduction into the wild of ecologically harmful exotic (alien) species is a constant concern. And, as with all live animal cargo, special care and handling must be exercised to ensure proper treatment and avoid injury to, and mortality of, specimens during shipment and inspection. Birds imported into the United States are required to undergo a 30-day quarantine period, which may further prolong the biological stress associated with shipment. On average, about 20 percent of all imported birds are either dead on arrival or die during quarantine as a result of disease and stress (Nilsson 1985).

Parrots are among the most popular of all cage birds kept in the United States and constitute about one-third of the 800,000 or so live exotic birds imported each year, most of which are wild-caught. The annual retail turnover in the United States of parrots, both wild and captive-bred, is an estimated $300 million (Meyers, pers. commun.). CITES considers the parrot group as a whole potentially threatened by trade, listing all 329 species in the order Psittaciformes on the appendices, including 51 species and subspecies on Appendix I.[20] Yet, in spite of CITES protection, as many as 60,000 parrots may have entered the U.S. illegally in 1984, according to a recent estimate (Dixon 1986). This does not include the additional 100,000 or so parrots that may be smuggled across the Mexican border each year (Carr, pers. commun.).

Although the Mexican border presents almost insurmountable control problems, weaknesses in a federal enforcement system that relies heavily on close communication and coordination among disparate agencies enhances the continuance of illegal trade. A study undertaken in 1985 concluded that, while the government is generally successful at detecting and destroying diseased imported birds, efforts to intercept protected species are lacking (Dixon 1986). A number of problems were documented. The Department of Agriculture's Animal and Plant Health Inspection Service personnel responsible for identifying and screening quarantined birds often lacked the necessary training and supervision to perform their jobs adequately, and evidence suggested that some of the technicians and veterinarians overseeing imports showed "favoritism" towards certain bird importers, many of whom own the quarantine stations where birds are inspected. In addition, the study found that most parrot shipments are not physically inspected by FWS because of insufficient personnel, arrival of shipments during off-hours, or lack of notice of a shipment's arrival time. Also, interagency disagreements were found to occur over such matters as payment of quarantine costs for seized birds (Dixon 1986).

Live birds also present special problems when it comes to legal investigations. The federal government often has difficulty finding

20. Two species widely bred in captivity, the budgerigar (*Melopsittacus undulatus*) and the cockatiel (*Nymphicus hollandicus*) are excluded from the CITES Appendices.

adequate housing facilities and care for imported birds and other live wildlife that is seized for violations of trade law. FWS has an agreement with the American Association of Zoological Parks and Aquariums to help find housing for confiscated live wildlife, but it is often difficult to place large shipments, especially of the more common species.

Problems in the parrot trade are not restricted to importing countries such as the United States. As with much wildlife commerce, exporting countries and species in trade shift constantly as a result of illegal-trade crackdowns and changing export policies. Some of the most dramatic changes have taken place in Latin America, which as a region supplies more than half of all U.S. parrot imports (Jorgenson and Thomsen 1987).

At least 96 of the 141 parrot species native to the Neotropics were imported into the United States from 1981 to 1985. In the early 1980s Bolivia was the leading supplier, exporting one-third of all parrots received from Latin America and 90 percent of all macaws traded to the United States (Jorgenson and Thomsen 1987). Bolivia came under heavy international criticism in the early 1980s for its corrupt wildlife trade practices. At the 1983 CITES meeting in Gaborone, Botswana, two of Bolivia's endemic parrots, the caninde macaw (*Ara glaucogularis*) and the red-fronted macaw (*Ara rubrogenys*) were listed on CITES Appendix I. Faced with uncontrolled trade and growing international criticism, Bolivia banned export of all live wildlife in 1984 (Fuller *et al.* 1985). As Bolivia's reported share of the parrot supply subsequently declined, Argentina became the leading supplier. In 1985, Argentina exported an unprecedented 72,000 parrots to the United States (see Figure 3) (Jorgenson and Thomsen 1987).

The species involved in the trade also have changed markedly. The decline in imports of macaws (mainly *Ara* spp.) as a result of Bolivia's ban can be contrasted with the sharp increase in U.S. imports of amazon species (*Amazona* spp.). Of particular note is the dramatic rise in imports of blue-fronted amazon parrot (*Amazona aestiva*), which reportedly increased tenfold in five years, from about 2,500 birds in 1981 to 25,500 in 1985 (Jorgenson and Thomsen 1987). Although the species is considered an agricultural pest in parts of Argentina, the primary source country, preliminary studies suggest the species is also suffering from extensive destruction of nesting habitat (Bucher, pers. commun.). Imports of another species, the yellow-crowned amazon (*Amazona ochrocephala*) reportedly quadrupled during that same period (from about 2,700 in 1981 to 11,000 in 1985), with most birds coming from Honduras. Parrot exports from Honduras, the only major exporter in Central America, are of growing concern since trade appears to focus primarily on four species (Jorgenson and Thomsen 1987) and there appear to be a number of irregularities with the country's CITES administration (Menghi, pers.commun.).

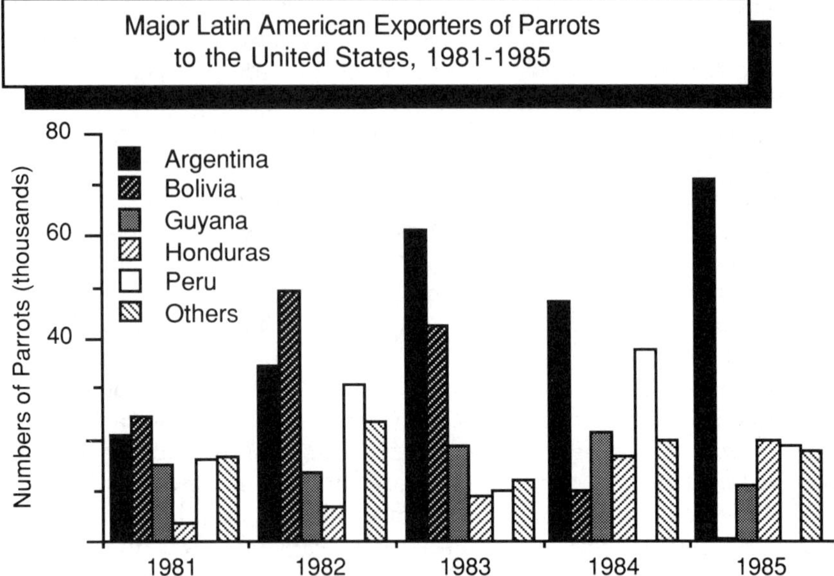

Figure 3. Source: Jorgenson and Thomsen, 1987.

The parrot trade remains strong, although international trade controls continue to tighten. The 1987 Ottawa CITES conference transferred three species to Appendix I: the palm cockatoo (*Probosciger aterrimus*) of Southeast Asia, and the military (*Ara militaris*) and hyacinth (*Anodorhynchus hyacinthinus*) macaws of Latin America. The hyacinth macaw in particular has been an important species in the U.S. bird market, although virtually all birds traded in recent years have been captured illegally in Brazil and smuggled to neighboring countries like Bolivia for export. Trade in the hyacinth macaw, both internally within Brazil and internationally, have caused a drastic reduction in the species' numbers: only an estimated 2,500 to 5,000 remain in the wild (Munn *et al.* 1987). But the incentive to trade illegally remains strong: a hyacinth macaw will sell for about $50 at the point of capture, and will command $5,000 to $10,000 in the U.S. market today (Thomsen, pers. commun.).

State Regulation. Inadequacies in federal import controls for live birds have recently caused state legislators to take the issue into their own hands. Prompted largely by humane groups, in 1986 New York banned the sale of imported wild-caught birds. Similar bills have been introduced in at least seven other states (Thomsen and Hemley 1987). While these actions have brought much-needed attention to the troubled bird trade, state bans may not be effective in arresting the trade problems unless a model law and enforcement system are followed. It is also clear that without improvements at the federal level, illegal bird imports will continue.

Crocodilian Skin Trade

Like exotic birds, crocodilian species have been subject to extensive exploitation and trade. The United States has always been a driving force behind the trade, importing thousands of luxury items such as crocodile and alligator shoes, handbags, wallets, and belts each year. At the time the demand for these goods peaked in the 1950s and 1960s, numerous species became endangered. Laws subsequently enacted afforded protection to many species, but by that time numerous crocodilians were already extremely rare. CITES eventually extended protection to all 21 species in the order Crocodylia, listing most of them on Appendix I.

World trade, however, remains strong. As a result of strict protection and management, some species have recovered and can now be traded under CITES. But U.S. law is stricter than the convention, and most species are still prohibited from import under the Endangered Species Act.[21] As a result, U.S. commerce focuses on the spectacled caiman (*Caiman crocodilus*), one of the few species listed on Appendix II. Heavy hunting pressure and rampant smuggling have made the caiman trade one of the most troublesome facets of the wildlife commerce today.

FWS has been fairly successful at keeping most Appendix I crocodilian products out of U.S. market, but an unprecedented one-half million products made from the spectacled caiman were imported in 1986. Most of these came from Italy, a leading exotic leather manufacturing center. While these imports may appear to meet U.S. requirements, many do not. An estimated one-third of the products imported were probably made from skins illegally exported from their countries of origin. In addition, many were probably made from the Endangered Species Act-listed *Caiman crocodilius yacare*, which is often passed off as being another nonprotected subspecies (Gaski and Hemley 1988).

Most Latin American countries, as a result of past depletion of other species, prohibit caiman hunting and export. Yet as many as one million caiman skins leave South America each year (King, pers. commun.); most are smuggled out of Brazil, Paraguay, Bolivia and Colombia and shipped primarily to the EEC and Japan. Manufactured

21. Certain Appendix II crocodilians, such as the the saltwater crocodile and New Guinea crocodiles from Papua New Guinea, and the Nile crocodile from Zimbabwe, may be imported and are traded under specially controlled ranching schemes. In addition, the American alligator is legally hunted and exported under special U.S. regulations.

products are then re-exported to the United States, often with permits listing false countries of origin. In the last three years, Venezuela is the only country to have exported a significant number of legal skins (Gaski and Hemley 1988).

As with much of the wildlife trade, U.S. authorities lack the personnel, forensics techniques, and sometimes the incentive needed to intercept illegal caiman shipments. It is often extremely difficult for inspectors to identify the type of skin and species used in manufactured products, and few experts are available to assist with these tasks. A new FWS forensics laboratory recently opened in Portland, Oregon is working to develop reptile skin identification techniques, including chemical and protein analyses for skin products. New methods are sorely needed to assist inspectors with efficient, accurate identification of protected and endangered crocodilians.

Complex trade routes associated with the caiman trade also stymie U.S. enforcement efforts. As with ivory, the Lacey Act gives the government authority to require proof from the country of origin that the skins were legally shipped, but this is rarely done for manufactured products. FWS generally takes countries like Italy at their word. But realistically, only until trade in the whole skins is better regulated by stricter monitoring and skin-tagging requirements will FWS be in an effective position to verify the legality of imports. Currently, skin laundering by the manufacturers is simply too easy, and tracking the source of products too arduous (Gaski and Hemley 1988).

One species in the crocodilian skin trade, the American alligator (*Alligator mississippiensis*) of the southern United States, has become a true model for controlled exploitation and commerce. Decimated by overhunting during the heyday of the crocodilian trade, the American alligator was federally listed as endangered in 1967. But strict law enforcement and habitat protection have allowed the species to steadily recover. Last year all U.S. alligator populations were formally removed from the endangered species list (52 *Federal Register* 21059 [1987]). Since 1979 when the species was transferred from Appendix I to Appendix II, trade has continually increased. Hunting limits are set by the states, with most skins coming from Louisiana and, recently, Florida. A record 31,000 skins with a declared value of $4.6 million were exported in 1986, primarily to Italy and France (Hemley 1988). All alligator skins traded are required to have special tags, and the states and FWS keep detailed records on harvests and trade.

The American alligator is a true conservation success, and is one of the few, heavily traded CITES species not subject to extensive illegal trade. But the investment in the alligator's recovery and management has been enormous. Few wild species have been as extensively studied. Hunting controls are as well-enforced as for any species, and the export control system is more sophisticated than most. Few other countries have been able or willing to make the sort of commitment to conserving a commercially valuable species as the U.S. has done for the alligator. Most of the world's wildlife-producer countries probably will never be able to do so without increased support and financial assistance from the richer wildlife-consuming nations.

THE FUTURE OF INTERNATIONAL WILDLIFE TRADE CONTROL

Thirteen years after coming into force, CITES remains an important, visible conservation tool. Much of the administrative framework has been set up, and most of the convention's provisions have been well-studied and defined. But enforcement everywhere is seriously lagging, and a solid body of information on the status of most species, especially the heavily traded Appendix II taxa, still is lacking. Some parties do not yet have a full understanding of the convention, and others disagree on some of its fundamental operative principles. Also, nonparty countries, although fewer in number, continue to undercut the convention's efforts and financial investment.

Like most international conservation initiatives, CITES suffers most from lack of financial support. The private sector, both nonprofit and commercial, has come to play a key role in this regard, but some parties, most notably the Soviet Union, have yet to pay their prescribed annual dues. Recently, funds contributed by wildlife-user industries have allowed for studies to be undertaken on certain species, which should help set realistic guidelines for export levels. For example, reptile leather exporters are currently funding a five-year study of the heavily traded tegu lizard (*Tupinambis* spp.) in Argentina in order to develop a management plan for that valuable species. In a similar effort, traders are funding a study of the spectacled caiman (*Caiman crocodilus*) in Bolivia, Brazil, and Paraguay.

This information will only be useful if enforcement mechanisms are effective. As long as profits earned far outstrip penalities imposed, illegal trade will continue. Compounding this problem is the fact that some countries still lack basic implementing legislation for CITES. Many others need improved legislation with stronger sanctions for violations.

A number of other fundamental changes are needed if wildlife trade controls are to be effective at the international level. CITES, through the secretariat, should devote more effort to on-the-ground implementation issues to help ensure that individual parties are properly equipped to enforce and administer the convention. In addition, CITES parties should identify the species at greatest risk from excessive and illegal trade—both Appendix I and Appendix II taxa—and focus on strengthening trade controls for those species in particular. In general, less time should be devoted to adding new species to the appendices—except in cases where there is a clear-cut threat—until trade controls for the species currently covered by the convention improve.

Wildlife trade policies must be strengthened everywhere, but especially in major consumer nations like Japan. International public and political pressure against persistent violators like Japan must be increased in order to elevate these issues to the highest levels of government in those countries. To achieve this, the CITES parties, through the secretariat and the biennial CITES meetings, should make discussion of enforcement and infractions their highest priority.

The United States has one of the most sophisticated systems in the world for controlling wildlife trade and implementing CITES, yet the likelihood that a shipment will enter or leave this country illegally remains relatively high because of weaknesses in the system. The volume of trade is simply too large to allow for complete inspection and interdiction of illegal shipments, especially when one of the agencies closest to the front lines of trade, the customs service, is forced to contend with higher priorities such as illegal shipment of drugs, weapons, and computers. The limited inspection capability of the small FWS inspection program also suffers from problems ranging from high personnel turnover as a result of the limited career growth potential for inspectors, to lack of clear directives for trade enforcement priorities.

Clearly, FWS must make wildlife trade control a higher priority if the government is to intercept the thousands of wildlife shipments that continue to enter this country illegally each year. The inspection program must be greatly expanded. Wildlife inspectors' positions should be upgraded, and more clerical staff should be hired to assist with processing the voluminous amount of trade data. Information on wildlife trade problems and foreign laws should be distributed more frequently to the ports. In general, the FWS inspection program should be more closely coordinated with the activities of FWS' management authority office.

The greatest responsibility for controlling international wildlife trade lies with the consumer countries, foremost among them the United States. The developing world will always look to these countries for assistance and cooperation in enforcing their own wildlife protection laws. Until U.S. efforts at regulating trade, punishing offenders, and increasing awareness improve, illegal trade will continue. The next 5 to 10 years will be critical to determining how effective the international wildlife trade control system can be in reducing the impact of trade on the world's threatened species.

REFERENCES

Anonymous 1980. "Elephants and the trafficking in ivory." *IUCN Bulletin.* 11(1&2):13. Gland, Switzerland.

——. 1987. "Singapore becomes 94th party to CITES." *TRAFFIC(U.S.A.).* 7(2&3):33. World Wildlife Fund. Washington, D.C.

African Elephant and Rhino Specialist Group. 1987. "Elephant population estimates, trends, ivory quotas and harvests: report to the CITES Secretariat from the African Elephant and Rhino Specialist Group of IUCN." Doc. 6.21 (annex 2). Presented at the Sixth Meeting of the Conference of the Parties, Ottawa, Canada, 1987.

Barzdo, J. 1984. "The worked ivory trade." *Traffic Bulletin* 6(2):21. Cambridge, United Kingdom.

Bean, M. 1983. *The Evolution of National Wildlife Law.* Praeger Publishers. New York, New York.

Caldwell, J. 1984. "Recent developments in the raw ivory trade of Hong Kong and Japan." *Traffic Bulletin* 6(2):16–20. Cambridge, United Kingdom.

CITES. 1986a. Ivory Notification to the Parties No. 9. Secretariat of the Convention. 19 September 1986. Lausanne, Switzerland.

——. 1986b. "Report of the Secretariat: International Compliance Control," pp. 287–289 in *Proceedings of the Fifth Meeting of the Conference of the Parties.* Secretariat of the Convention. Lausanne, Switzerland.

——. 1986c. Notification to the Parties No. 413. 28 November 1986. Secretariat of the Convention. Lausanne, Switzerland.

——. 1987a. Ivory Notification to the Parties No. 21. Secretariat of the Convention. 25 September 1987. Lausanne, Switzerland.

——. 1987b. "Interpretation and Implementation of the Convention: Review of Alleged Infractions." Doc. 6.19. Presented at the Sixth Meeting of the Conference of the Parties, Ottawa, Canada, 1987.

——. 1987c. "Report on National Reports under Article VIII, para. 7, of the Convention." Doc. 6.17. Presented at the Sixth Meeting of the Conference of the Parties, Ottawa, Canada, 1987.

Conroy, D.A. 1975. "An evaluation of the present status of world trade in ornamental fish." *FAO Fisheries Technical Paper* no. 146. Rome, Italy.

Dixon, A. 1986. *Evaluation of the Psittacine Importation Process in the United States.* TRAFFIC(U.S.A.), World Wildlife Fund. Washington, D.C.

Douglas-Hamilton, I. 1987. "African elephants: population trends and their causes." *Oryx* 21(1):11–24. London, United Kingdom.

Fitzgerald, S. In prep. *The International Wildlife Trade: Whose Business Is It?* World Wildlife Fund. Washington, D.C.

Fuller, K., Swift, B., Jorgenson, A., Brautigam, A. 1985. *Latin American Wildlife Trade Laws.* TRAFFIC(U.S.A.), World Wildlife Fund. Washington, D.C.

Gaski, A. and G. Hemley. 1988. "The ups and downs of the crocodilian skin trade." *TRAFFIC(U.S.A.)* 8(1). World Wildlife Fund. Washington, D.C.

Hemley, G. 1983. "Reptile skin trade dependent on few species." *TRAFFIC(U.S.A.)* 5(2):1–12. World Wildlife Fund. Washington, D.C.

——. 1988. "Alligator exports boom in 1986." *TRAFFIC(U.S.A.)* 8(1). World Wildlife Fund. Washington, D.C.

——. and Gaski, A. Unpubl. Travelling Tropicals: A Study of the U.S.-International Ornamental Fish Trade." TRAFFIC(U.S.A.), World Wildlife Fund. Washington, D.C.

Jorgenson, A. and Thomsen, J. 1987. "Neotropical parrots imported by the United States, 1981–1985." *TRAFFIC(U.S.A.)* 7(2&3):2–4. World Wildlife Fund. Washington, D.C.

King, W. 1978. "The wildlife trade," pp. 253–271 *in* Brokaw, ed., *Wildife in America.* Council on Environmental Quality. Washington. D.C.

Kosloff, L. and Trexler, T. 1987. "The Convention on International Trade in Endangered Species: no carrot, but where's the stick?" *Environmental Law Reporter* 17(7):10222–10236.

Lyster, S. 1985. *International Wildlife Law.* Grotius Publications Ltd. Cambridge, United Kingdom.

Mack, D. 1983. "Foreign wildlife trade laws: reaction to unregulated trade," pp. 158–162 in *Annual Conference Proceedings of the American Association of Zoological Parks and Aquariums.*

Martin, E. 1987. "Status of the rhino populations and associated trade in rhino products." Doc. 6.25 (annex 1). Presented at the Sixth Meeting of the Conference of the Parties, Ottawa, Canada, 1987.

Milliken, T. and Tokunaga, H. 1987. The Japanese Turtle Trade, 1970–1986. TRAFFIC-(Japan) report to the Center for Environmental Education. Tokyo, Japan.

Munn, C.A., Thomsen, J.B., Yamashita, C. 1987. Population Survey and Status of the Hyacinth Macaw (*Anodorhyncus hyacinthinus*) in Brazil, Bolivia, and Paraguay. Report to the Secretariat of the Convention on International Trade in Endangered Species of Wild Fauna and Flora. Lausanne, Switzerland.

Nilsson, G. 1985. *Importation of Birds into the United States, 1980–1984.* Animal Welfare Institute. Washington, D.C.

Prescott-Allen, C. and Prescott-Allen, R. 1986. *The First Resource: Wild Species in the North American Economy.* Yale University Press. New Haven, Connecticut.

Thomsen, J. 1987. *Recent U.S. Imports of Certain Products from the African Elephant.* TRAFFIC(U.S.A.), World Wildlife Fund. Washington. D.C.

——. and Brautigam, A. In press. "CITES in the European Economic Community: who benefits?" *Boston University Journal of International Law.* Boston, Massachusetts.

——. and Hemley, G. 1987. "Bird trade . . . bird bans." *TRAFFIC(U.S.A.)* 7(2&3):1–24. World Wildlife Fund. Washington, D.C.

TRAFFIC(U.S.A.). Unpublished. Live Reptiles Imported into the U.S. in 1980. World Wildlife Fund. Washington, D.C.

U.S. Department of the Interior, Fish and Wildlife Service. 1979. *CITES: Annual Report for 1978.* Washington. D.C.

——., Fish and Wildlife Service. 1985. *Division of Law Enforcement End of Year Report -FY 1985.* Washington, D.C.

——., Fish and Wildlife Service. 1986. *CITES: Annual Report for 1984.* Washington, D.C.

——., Fish and Wildlife Service. Unpublished. Wildlife Import/Export Declaration Data. Washington, D.C.

World Wildlife Fund. 1986a. TRAFFIC(U.S.A.) Wildlife Trade Factsheets. Washington, D.C.

——. 1986b. *The EEC Annual CITES Report for 1984: A Preliminary Assessment of the Implementation of CITES in the European Economic Community.* Washington, D.C.

Ginette Hemley is the director of TRAFFIC(U.S.A.), the trade-monitoring program of the World Wildlife Fund.

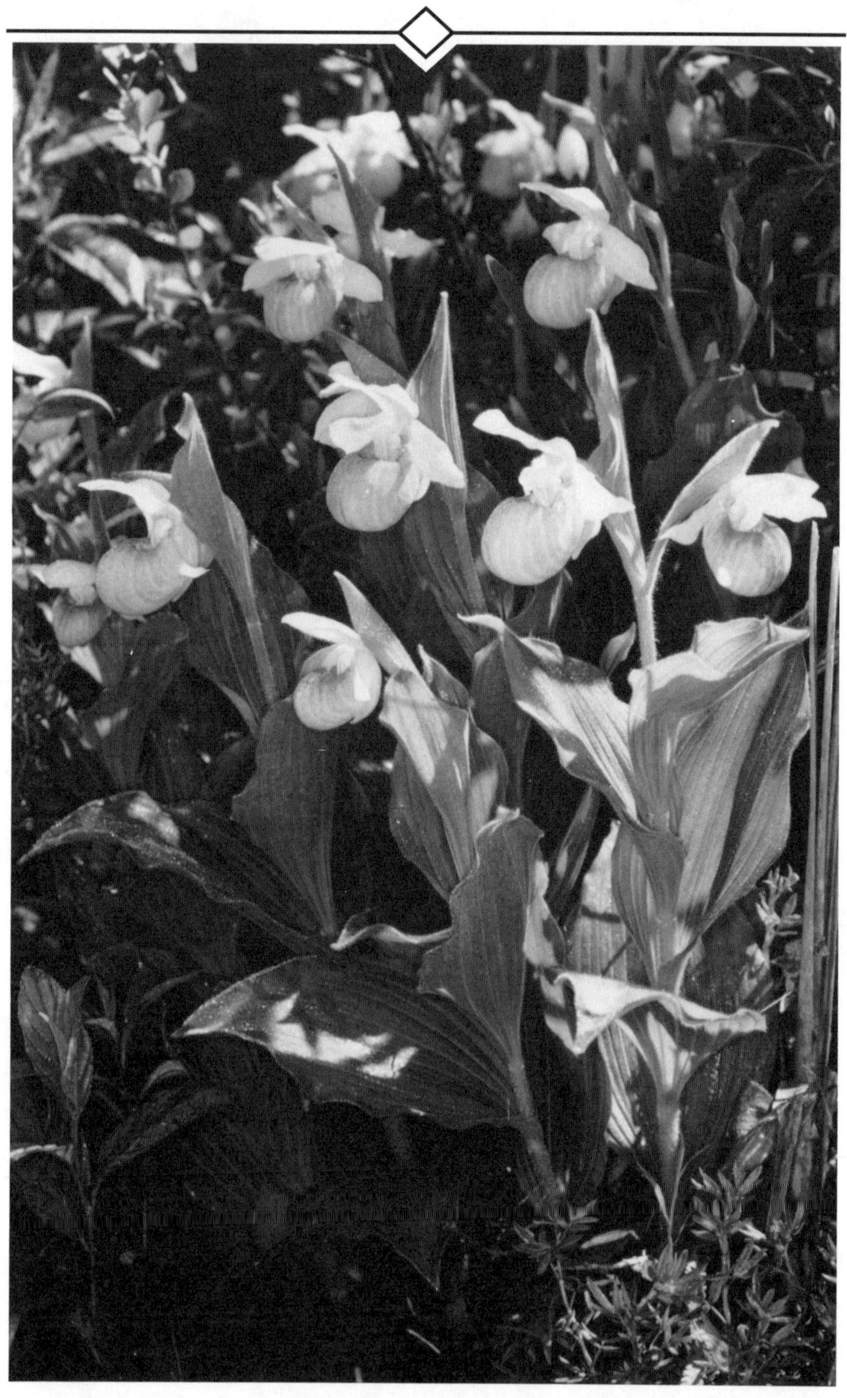

International trade in both wild and hothouse-grown orchids is a huge business, but, because record-keeping and enforcement of regulations are so difficult, no one knows what effect the trade is having on wild populations at large. *Kerry S. Walter*

The International Orchid Trade

Linda R. McMahan and Kerry S. Walter

SPECIES DESCRIPTION AND HISTORICAL PERSPECTIVE

The orchid family contains an estimated 25,000 to 35,000 species and is the largest family of flowering plants; approximately one-tenth of all higher plant species are orchids. Orchids are among the most popular plants in horticulture, representing to many the very embodiment of exotic lands and tropical rain forests. Orchid plants vary tremendously in size, from less than one-quarter inch in length to over 90 feet; the flowers borne on these plants range from one-eighth of an inch in diameter to more than 10 inches.

Although widespread throughout the world (Antarctica is the only continent lacking native orchid species), orchids are especially numerous in the tropics; in some tropical countries, such as Costa Rica, there are more species of orchids than any other flowering plant family. In the temperate zone, most orchids are terrestrial, but in the tropics and subtropics, they are predominantly epiphytic, with as many as 88 percent of the species growing on trees instead of in the ground (Walter 1983).

Because of the unusual shapes, colors, and fragrances of its flowers and its often great beauty, the mystique of the orchid family is unsurpassed by any other group of plants. There is no better group than the orchids to represent the plight of rare plants in international trade, for trade in orchids is common and problematic.

Although it is impossible to determine when they were first transported or traded internationally, orchids have been known and admired for more than 2,000 years by European cultures and for much longer in China. The famous seventeenth century herbalist John Parkinson illustrated and described a temperate North American lady's-slipper orchid (most likely *Cypripedium acaule*) as occurring in Europe as early as 1640. At least one tropical American orchid, *Brassavola nodosa*, was in cultivation in Holland as early as 1698. By 1737, two North American lady's-slippers (*Cypripedium reginae* and one of the two subspecies of *C. calceolus*) were cultivated in England. Two years later, in 1739, *Vanilla planifolia* (the source of a perfume and the flavoring agent vanilla, which became known to European culture after the conquest of Mexico by Cortes in 1519) was cultivated in England (Reinikka 1972).

However, early trade in orchids was nothing compared to what happened in the late nineteenth century during the Victorian "orchid craze." Long before there were any international regulations concerning trade, horticultural firms from Britain and continental Europe sent out collectors to ship back the newest and the best orchids from tropical lands. The industry soon became cutthroat, with collectors often deliberately falsifying the origin of their finds or even destroying the native habitat so as to confuse and confound collectors from rival firms. The industry became so fanatical that one collecting expedition was reported to have felled 4,000 trees in Colombia in order to ship back 10,000 plants of *Odontoglossum crispum*, a particularly desirable orchid species. Although the days of such massive exploitation are over, a similar mentality unfortunately persists today among some modern-day collectors.

SOURCE OF STATISTICS ON RECENT INTERNATIONAL TRADE IN ORCHIDS[1]

Species-specific international recordkeeping for orchid trade began in 1975 with the implementation of the Convention on International

1. The numbers used here are from reports of world trade by CITES parties provided by the Wildlife Trade Monitoring Unit (1987), computer printouts of U.S. trade from 1977 through 1979 compiled by the International Convention Advisory Commission (1981), and our own analysis of U.S. Annual Reports for CITES, 1980 through 1985. Copies of the CITES reports were provided by TRAFFIC(U.S.A.), the trade monitoring unit of the World Wildlife Fund. U.S. Customs reports for 1947–1986 are also courtesy of TRAFFIC(U.S.A.).

Trade in Endangered Species of Flora and Fauna (CITES). The first trade records became available for the year 1976. Although their value was somewhat limited because of incomplete recording of data in the early years, these records are an important tool for analyzing international trade in orchids and other wild plants and animals. If the exporter or importer declares the species properly, the permit forms record the species, subspecies, or varietal level. Another tool used in this report is U.S. Customs Service records of U.S. imports kept from 1947 until the present. These records list import totals by country of origin and declared dollar value, but do not list the specific taxa imported.

CITES covers *all* members of the plant family Orchidaceae on one or more of its appendices. This high number of listed orchid species makes it difficult to keep track of them internationally, a fact long lamented by those involved in orchid conservation. Appendix I, intended to include very rare plants and animals, contains only a handful of orchid species.[2] Any legal trade in wild collected specimens listed on Appendix I must benefit the species in some way, such as trade for scientific research. Both importing and exporting countries must grant permits before trade in Appendix I species is allowed. Trade in artificially propagated Appendix I plants is less restrictive than trade in wild plants.

For taxa listed on Appendix II, which includes all remaining orchids, the exporter must obtain a permit from the country of origin before shipping the plants internationally. The permit will, under ideal circumstances, record the species and state their origin as wild or artificially propagated. If the collections are from the wild, the agency in charge of granting export permits is responsible for determining that the export will not harm the survival of the species in the wild.

It is difficult to assess trade in rare, threatened, and endangered species because so little is known about the true rarity of orchids in nature. The International Union for Conservation of Nature and Natural Resources (IUCN) tracks 3,828 taxa of orchids, of which 906 are considered "threatened." The total number of all plant taxa, orchids and otherwise, is 45,928, of which 18,566 taxa are considered threatened internationally. Thus, orchids constitute five percent of the rare taxa and eight percent of the total taxa monitored by IUCN. One of the stated goals of the IUCN Species Survival Commission Orchid Specialist Group is to gather data on the plants' status worldwide (Stewart 1986). Until the survey is completed, no large-scale analysis of the trade is possible, and statements such as " . . . 10,000 species [of tropical orchids] are endangered" (Koopowitz 1986) will be speculative.

2. These species are: (*Cattleya skinneri, Cattleya trianae, Didiciea cunninghamii, Laelia jongheana, L. lobata, Lycaste virginalis* var. *alba, Paphiopedilum druryi, Peristeria elata, Renanthera imschootiana,* and *Vanda coerulea.*

All orchid species are placed on Appendix II of CITES except 10 that are listed on Appendix I. While Appendix I should include species that are extremely rare, in reality, decisions to list some Appendix I orchids were made on political, not biological, bases. For example, certain nations requested Appendix I listing for their national flowers. There are much rarer orchids (some now extinct) that never have appeared on Appendix I. The Orchid Specialist Group of the IUCN Species Survival Commission has proposed that all Appendix I orchids be moved to Appendix II, citing as its main reason the difficulty of distinguishing one orchid from another when the flower is not available for inspection.

CHARACTERISTICS OF THE ORCHID TRADE

Orchids have long been popular items in international trade. The most current international trade volume—from 1985 records—is reported as 3.3 million plants. Trade volume numbers are undoubtedly low due to the inadequate reporting procedures. Figures tracking the volume of the orchid trade from 1976 to 1985 have shown increases over the years that are due in part to increased reporting efficiency; however, the increases may also mean that trade is increasing as well (see Table 1). About 2,400 species, subspecies, and varieties of orchids were reported in trade in 1985. CITES trade records were available only through 1985, the latest year for which data is computerized.

Table 1
Recorded International Trade in Orchids from 1976 through 1986 Based on CITES Reports.

Year	Number (in thousands)				
	World imports (Excl. U.S.)	World exports (Excl. U.S.)	U.S. imports	U.S. exports	Minimum total trade[a]
1976	11	1	0	0	11
1977	129	1	n.d.[b]	2	131
1978	63	4	n.d.	3	66
1979	398	59	71	31	500
1980	3	146	144	36	326
1981	570	332	208	116	894
1982	426	604	257	160	1,021
1983	1,713	821	320	347	2,380
1984	1,125	1,779	395	299	2,473
1985	1,687	1,445	690	968	3,345

[a] Estimated by adding the higher of World Imports or World Exports plus U.S. Imports and U.S. Exports. Actual total trade is undoubtedly higher (see text).

[b] No data available.

CITES trade data are useful in analyzing the orchid trade. However, the poor quality of reporting hampers assessment of how such trade is affecting wild populations. Particularly significant is the recording of only 37 percent of the total trade to the species level and the large number of orchids declared as of "unknown" origin rather than as "wild" or "artificially propagated."

There are at least three major reasons why trade records still fall short in providing accurate data on trade volume: 1) some countries exporting orchids, such as Mexico, are not yet members of CITES and therefore do not report their own exports; data must be gathered from the importing country's reports; 2) many countries, including the United States, sometimes still record trade as numbers of shipments, bags, cartons, or boxes, further obscuring the actual number of individual plants in trade; and 3) many orchids are still smuggled illegally across national boundaries.

In addition to adult plants, there are large numbers of vials, meristem cultures, flasks, seedlings, and community pots in recorded international trade. This shows the continued, and perhaps growing, interest in trading artificially propagated material rather than plants collected from wild habitats, a practice increasingly called for in the orchid press (Bailes 1985, Cribb 1987b, Koopowitz 1986, Steele 1975, Stewart 1987). However, trade in wild specimens still appears strong, especially in desirable taxa.

Trends in orchid trade shift quickly, often before they can be identified; trade data lag about two years behind actual trade. Rapid trade shifts occur for exporting countries as well as for the kinds of species traded. Volatility of trade makes the conservationists' job difficult because of their inability to predict trends that may affect conservation of the species in the wild.

THE ORCHID TRADE IN 1985

In 1985, 3.3 million orchids, 18,000 shipments of undeclared numbers, 14,000 flasks or meristem cultures, 243,000 seedlings, and 6,000 community pots were reported as traded internationally. Recorded trade included about 2,400 orchid species or varieties in some 380 genera (of the estimated 25,000 to 35,000 species grouped into approximately 720 genera).

Trade Routes

Although orchid trade in 1985 occurred between nearly all 96 parties to CITES, the United States and Japan accounted for over 60 percent of the exports; Japan accounted for about 60 percent of the imports (see Table 2). The United States and European countries are also major orchid importers. In 1985, the major exporting region of the world appeared to be Asia; the most active countries were Thailand, Taiwan, China, and Japan.

Species Traded in Large Numbers

Although only a little over one-third (36 percent) of all orchids reported to be in trade were identified to species, subspecies, or variety, it is possible to calculate minimum numbers of traded plants of these taxa. Of the 2,400 taxa reported as traded in 1985, 84 were reported as being traded in numbers of 1,000 or more plants. Thirteen of these species had recorded trade of 10,000 or more plants (see Table 3).

Many of the species declared in volumes exceeding 10,000 were terrestrial orchids, including those in the genera *Cypripedium*, *Habenaria*, and *Paphiopedilum*. The same is true for species declared as traded in numbers higher than 1,000 but lower than 10,000 (see Table 4), although many popular tropical epiphytes, such as *Brassavola nodosa* and *Oncidium carthagenense*, were also recorded as traded in high numbers.

Popular species with trade recorded as predominantly from wild sources include: *Ascocentrum ampullaceum* and *A. miniatum* from Thailand, *Dendrobium aggregatum*, *D. scabrilingue* and *D. thyrsiflorum*, also from Thailand, *Oncidium luridum* from Mexico, and *Rodriguezia secunda* from Suriname.

Table 2
Major Exporting and Importing Countries of Orchid Plants, Listed in Estimated Percentage of Total Trade.[a]

Exporting		Importing	
Country	Estimated percent	Country	Estimated percent
United States	31	Japan	60
Thailand	28	United States	17
Netherlands	21[b]	Taiwan	5
Taiwan	5	French Polynesia	5
Denmark	4	Korea	5[c]
China	3	Netherlands	4
Japan	2	Denmark	4[c]

[a] Estimates were based on analysis of shipments of over 1,000 plants. Shipments of this size accounted for 88 percent of World Imports (excluding U.S.), 92 percent of World Exports (excluding U.S.), 73 percent of U.S. Imports, and 80 percent of U.S. Exports.

[b] Although the Netherlands was reported as the exporting country by many importing nations, the country itself did not record a high number of imports. Based on export figures, we estimate that the Netherlands ranks just below the U.S. and Thailand.

[c] Both Denmark and Korea were recorded as the destination by exporting countries to a much higher degree that either reported receiving orchid plants. Based on export figures, Denmark and Korea's imports are estimated to be roughly four and five percent of the trade, respectively.

Table 3
Orchid Species Recorded in Trade in Numbers Exceeding 10,000 Plants.

Scientific name	Minimum number traded[a]	Declared source[b]	Major exporting country	Major importing country
Bletilla ochracea	23,000	none	China	Japan
Bletilla striata	61,000	a.p.	Japan	Netherlands
Bletilla yunnanensis	55,050	none	China	Japan
Bulbophyllum transarisanese	10,003	none	Taiwan	Japan
Cymbidium goeringii	34,162	none	China	Japan
Cypripedium japonicum	12,736	none	Taiwan	Japan
Cypripedium macranthum	17,574	none	Taiwan	Japan
Habenaria radiata	25,000	none	Japan	United States
Habenaria rhodocheila	19,287	none	Thailand	Japan
Paphiopedilum callosum	35,302	none	Thailand	F.R. Germany
Paphiopedilum niveum	11,563	none	Thailand	Japan
Pleione formosana	213,486	none	Taiwan	Japan
Pleione maculata	15,410	a.p.	India	Japan

[a] The minimum numbers were compiled by adding the larger world exports or imports to the total U.S. imports and exports.

[b] The source listed here is for either the largest shipment or the greatest number of shipments. "None" means no source was declared or appeared on the printouts; a.p. means declared as "artifically propagated."

Those orchid species declared primarily as artificially propagated were: *Angraecum philippinensis* (Philippines); *Cypripedium cordigerum, C. debile,* and *C. himalaicum* (India); *Dendrobium fimbriatum, D. formosum, D. nobile, D. parishii,* and *D. pierardii* (India); *Paphiopedilum barbatum* (Malaysia); *P. fairrieanum, P. hirsutissimum, P. spicerianum, P. sukhakulii,* and *P. venustum* (India); and *Pleione hookeriana and P. praecox* (India). All others were declared as either artificially propagated or of unknown source.

It is interesting to note the history of wild-collected plants of *Paphiopedilum fairrieanum* in the trade. This plant was first exhibited before the Horticultural Society in England in 1857. Four years later, plants collected in Assam were sent to the Calcutta Botanic Gardens. The species was offered in trade until 1875, but then disappeared from nursery catalogs. By 1904, only one small plant remained in cultivation in England, and four seedlings were growing in the Jardin de Luxembourg. In December 1904, Frederick Sander, the "Orchid King," offered a reward of 1000 pounds sterling for the rediscovery of *P. fairrieanum*; the rediscovery was announced on March 25, 1905. On September 15, Sander offered 179 plants for sale, and by the end of that year, many plants were being collected and offered for sale. Pradhan (1969) reported that this species was becoming scarce in the wild because of overcollecting, forest fires, and goats (Cribb 1987b, Swinson 1970).

Table 4
Orchid Species Recorded as Traded in Numbers Greater Than 1,000, but Less Than 10,000 Plants.

Scientific name	Number	Scientific name	Number
Aerides multiflora	1,269	*Doritis pulcherrima*	2,409
Aerides odorata	1,377	*Epidendrum alatum*	3,942
Angraecum philippinensis	1,644	*Epigeneium sanseiense*	1,000
Arundina graminifolia	1,072	*Habenaria medioflexa*	4,500
Ascocentrum ampullaceum	3,340	*Holcoglossum quasipinifolium*	7,481
Ascocentrum miniatum	7,352	*Laelia purpurata*	1,657
Ascocentrum pumilum	8,617	*Laelia sincorana*	1,009
Brassavola digbyana	4,598	*Liparis caespitosa*	1,012
Brassavola nodosa	4,286	*Liparis cordifolia*	2,912
Brassia maculata	1,557	*Oncidium carthagenense*	3,124
Broughtonia sanguinea	1,011	*Oncidium cebolleta*	2,451
Calanthe caudatilabella	1,610	*Oncidium luridum*	1,113
Calanthe arisanensis	1,802	*Paphiopedilum* x *ang-thong*[a]	1,192
Calanthe elliptica	7,220	*Paphiopedilum barbatum*	2,019
Calanthe gracilis	1,522	*Paphiopedilum bellatum*	6,856
Calanthe kintaroi	1,000	*Paphiopedilum concolor*	3,808
Calanthe plantaginea	1,509	*Paphiopedilum exul*	1,115
Calanthe reflexa	1,635	*Paphiopedilum fairrieanum*	2,467
Calanthe tricarinata	6,363	*Paphiopedilum hirsutissimum*	1,986
Cymbidium ensifolium	2,054	*Paphiopedilum parishii*	3,724
Cymbidium faberi	5,750	*Paphiopedilum spicerianum*	2,532
Cymbidium kanran	9,230	*Paphiopedilum sukhakulii*	8,456
Cypripedium cordigerum	1,597	*Paphiopedilum venustum*	3,724
Cypripedium debile	2,510	*Paphiopedilum villosum*	2,697
Cypripedium himalaicum	1,511	*Phaius tankervilliae*	4,281
Dendrobium aggregatum	2,172	*Pleione hookeriana*	1,622
Dendrobium falconeri	1,251	*Pleione praecox*	6,296
Dendrobium fimbriatum	1,055	*Pleione yunnanensis*	1,100
Dendrobium formosum	1,182	*Rhynchostylis coelestis*	1,460
Dendrobium nobile	1,462	*Rhynchostylis gigantea*	1,772
Dendrobium parishii	1,571	*Rhynchostylis retusa*	1,519
Dendrobium peirardii	1,198	*Rodriguezia secunda*	1,076
Dendrobium scabrilingere	1,020	*Sophronitis coccinea*	1,655
Dendrobium thyrsiflorum	1,036	*Thrixspermum formosanum*	1,764

[a] There is question as to whether this taxon should be treated as a natural hybrid or simply as a variant within *P. godefrovae* (Cribb 1987b).

CURRENT COLLECTION PRESSURES ON ORCHID SPECIES

There have been countless complaints in the orchid literature about CITES regulations and their curtailing of legitimate "salvage" operations; it is often stated that orchid collectors have an absolutely minimal effect on species compared to extinctions caused by tropical forest destruction (Beckner 1979, Catling 1980, Kennedy 1975, Dun sterville 1975). The devastation caused by rapidly increasing clear-cutting cannot be denied, but neither can the deleterious effects of fervid collecting of horticulturally valuable specimens. In addition to the pressures from habitat destruction, genera such as *Cattleya* and *Laelia* in Brazil and *Pleione* in China, as well as species such as *Vanda (Euanthe) sanderiana* from the Philippines, have been or continue to be decimated by overcollecting.

Although most overcollecting occurred in the nineteenth century, there are many recent examples of local, if not regional and even global, extirpation of orchid species by overzealous collectors (Cribb 1987a, 1987b, Dunsterville 1975, Hagsater, pers. commun.). Cribb (1987a) cites the example of *Cypripedium calceolus*, a taxon reduced in Great Britain since 1945 to a single individual, largely through systematic collecting. In another case, wild-collected plants of another new species of *Paphiopedilum—P. henryanum—* have already been advertised in quantity in the pages of the *American Orchid Society Bulletin* only two or three months after these species were described. Yet another example shows how a recently described relative from South America, *Phragmipedium besseyae*, has been systematically stripped from the three or four known localities; it is presently being advertised for $350 a growth.

Similar stories may be told of the "new" species of *Paphiopedilum—P. micrantha, P. malipoense,* and *P. armeniaca*—recently reported from China. When it was first offered in the trade, *P. micrantha* fetched prices of $500 per growth; now, however, prices have fallen to only a few dollars a growth because of the tremendous numbers of plants illegally coming out of China. It appears that the plants are smuggled into Hong Kong from near the China-Vietnam border and then into Taiwan, Singapore, and Thailand. Once inside these borders, CITES permits are issued indicating that the plants are artificially propagated. Thus, such false certification makes possible the import of these plants into the United States, as well as into other CITES signatory countries. It is estimated that some 35,000 wild-collected plants were exported through Hong Kong in the six-month period up to April 1986 (Cribb 1987b).

Some of the Asiatic "moth orchids," especially the Bornean species *Phalaenopsis amabilis* and *P. gigantea* (Bailes 1985), are under severe collection pressure. Dunsterville (1975) tells of a rapid extirpation of the rare Venezuelan form of *Lycaste denningiana* from an abundant but easily accessible colony after word of its discovery got out. *Paphiopedilum rothschildianum* is probably the rarest species in its genus, with only two sites known, both on the lower slopes of Mount Kinabalu in northeastern Borneo, and both inside a national park. The original description of *P. rothscildianum* cited New Guinea as the area of origin, a falsification of the facts undoubtedly designed to throw off rival collectors. Although all of the reported trade in this

Table 5
U.S. Trade in Orchid Plants in 1985 (in Thousands).

	Purpose		Declared Source		
Category	Commercial	Noncommercial	Wild	Artificially propagated	Unknown
Imports	674	16	87(13%)	464(67%)	139(20%)
Exports	968	<1	<1(0%)	968(100%)	0

species was reported from artificially propagated material, the plant is now virtually extirpated from the wild.

However, not all news concerning rare orchid species is bleak. Perhaps the best publicized success story involves *Epidendrum ilense*, a species discovered in 1976 and known from only four plants collected from a patch of recently cut forest in Ecuador. The four plants survived at the Marie Selby Botanical Garden and were micropropagated there. This strange and showy orchid, although almost surely extinct in the wild, is now widespread in the orchid trade. Seedlings have recently been reintroduced into Ecuador.

THE UNITED STATES AS EXPORTER AND IMPORTER

The United States is one of the major importers of orchids in the world. In 1985, according to information in the CITES report, the United States imported about 690,000 orchid plants (see Tables 1 and 5). In general, U.S. CITES reports provide detailed information; however, data analysis is limited by the high number of plants that remain reported only to the family or genus level.

Recorded Exports and Imports of Wild Orchids

About 300 species with one or more shipments declared as "wild" entered the United States in 1987. Declared wild imports accounted for about 87,000 plants, representing 13 percent of total recorded imports. Thailand, Mexico, Peru, and Suriname were the main countries exporting wild orchids to the United States in 1985 (see Table 6).
Many shipments declared as wild were reported only as "Orchidaceae" or to the genus level. This high number of plants not recorded to species, as well as the high number declared as "unknown" rather than as "artificially propagated" or "wild," makes analysis of the effect of the trade on wild species particularly difficult and is of grave concern to conservationists.

Table 6
Countries Exporting Wild Orchid Plants to the United States in Large Numbers.

Country	Approximate number[a] (in thousands)
Thailand	40
Mexico	19
Peru	10
Suriname	8
Panama	2
Paraguay	1

[a] Plants declared as "wild" in the U.S. CITES report for 1985.

The United States is also a major exporter of orchids. Most exports are recorded as artificially propagated plants, seedlings, or vials of seedlings or cultures of orchid taxa not native to the U.S., primarily tropical epiphytes. There was little recorded trade in U.S. native species for 1985, but this has not always been the case. Analysis of data for 1980 U.S. exports (Anonymous 1982a) revealed recorded exports of more than 10,000 terrestrial orchids (see Table 7), representing 20 percent of the reported exports for that year. The trade in U.S. native species is primarily focused on the lady's-slipper orchids of the genus *Cypripedium* (a close relative of the tropical lady's-slipper, *Paphiopedilum*, whose members are often strikingly beautiful). Most of these, 63 percent, were sent to the Netherlands; another 17 percent went to Japan.

Table 7
Recorded Exports of Selected U.S. Terrestrial Orchids from 1979 to 1985.

Species	Numbers of recorded exports by year					
	1980	1981	1982	1983	1984	1985
Cypripedium acaule [b](pink lady's-slipper)	4,248	0	0	8,550	750	2
C. arietinum [b](ram's-head lady's-slipper)	3,080	0	0	0	0	0
C. calceolus [b](yellow lady's-slipper)	1,989	1	0	0	7,550	6
C. reginae [b](showy lady's-slipper)	741	0	0	0	3	0
Others	309	30	0	72	112	36
TOTAL	10,397	31[a]	0[b]	8,622	8,420	44

[a] 1981 export figures record exports of 2,000 *Cypripedium* "hybrids" that may be unrecorded species or nonnative lady's-slippers of the genus *Paphiopedilum*, a genus once called *Cypripedium*.
[b] 1982 reports record U.S. exports of 3,450 *Cypripedium* "hybrids."

Because many North American *Cypripedium* species do not survive transplantation even under the best conditions, many conservationists are concerned about the future of these species. International disease- and insect-control regulations require that plants be shipped "bare root," without any attached soil. Plants shipped in this manner may grow and bloom for one to three years, but rarely survive for longer periods. The 1980 shipments were clearly illegal since they had occurred under permits to ship artificially propagated plants. Most of the kinds of terrestrial orchids shipped during that year are still nearly impossible to propagate artificially, and no commercial nursery was known to be propagating terrestrial orchids on this scale.

U.S. exports of terrestrial orchids, which are more difficult to propagate, have continued in subsequent years, declared properly as "wild." Such trade is legal if the United States has determined that the export will not harm the species in the wild; however, conservationists charge that it is unethical to export and sell wild plants that are doomed to fail in horticultural settings.

Longer-Term Trends In U.S. Imports

In 1947, the U.S. Department of Commerce began recording U.S. imports of orchid plants, breaking them down by country of origin and including a declared value. Although the U.S. Customs records do not track at the species level or below, they do provide a glimpse of the orchid trade before CITES data became available, thus revealing some longer-term trends in orchid imports. Just as the CITES data show the volatility of the trade in orchids, the U.S. Customs records reveal quick shifts in countries supplying orchids to the United States and in trade volume year to year.

Between 1948 and 1971 (see Figure 1), orchid imports hovered between a few thousand plants and 150,000 plants per year. Imports then soared to more than 400,000 in 1975, an increase most likely due to a general increase in interest in house and garden plants (Gibson *et al.* 1980, Anonymous 1982b, McMahan 1985). This general surge, lasting from 1975 to 1977, was followed by a drop to levels only slightly above what they had been in 1971. Since 1978, orchid imports have again shown increases, with figures for 1986 approaching the record peak of 1975.

By tracing imports from a few selected countries since 1948, it can be seen how quickly trends in supplying countries can change (see Figure 2). Even in periods of fairly steady trade, the importing countries shift dramatically. In the 1980s, the Netherlands emerged as a major supplier of orchids, most likely of artificially propagated origin. Asian countries, particularly Taiwan and Thailand, are also important suppliers; many Asian orchid imports are of wild origin.

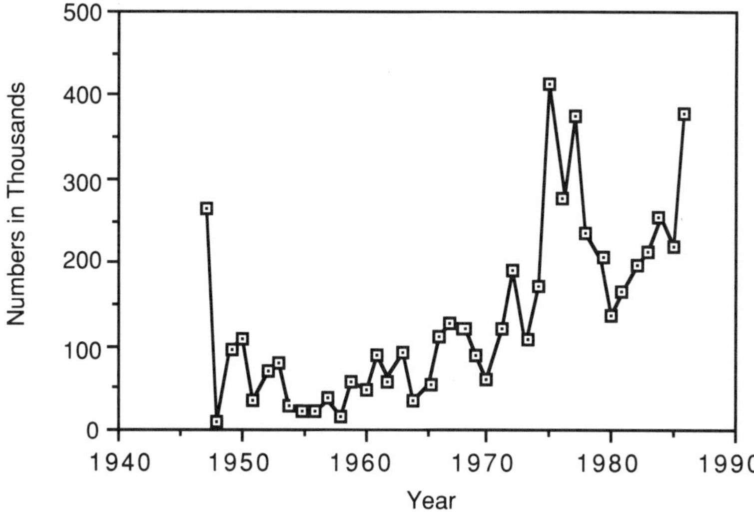

Figure 1. U.S. Orchid Imports, 1947-1987, according to records of the U.S. Customs Service.

In general, European countries have been less important suppliers of orchids in the 1970s and 1980s than they were in earlier decades (see Figure 3.). Latin America and the Caribbean currently supply only about 17 percent of U.S. imports. Asia has grown as an export region, supplying about half of the trade in the 1970s and 1980s, as compared to about one-fourth of the trade in the prior two decades.

CONCLUSIONS

After analyzing the trade data available for orchids, the authors were discouraged that information on orchids in trade is far from complete and sometimes incorrect or misleading. This poor recording of the orchid trade is disheartening when we realize that CITES has been in effect for 12 years.

Faced with loss of species diversity worldwide, conservationists need at their disposal all the tools possible to help conserve animals and plants. When speaking of orchids, the CITES tool has been a poor one to date. If CITES is to work for orchids, both enforcement and information processing must improve dramatically.

While it is true that CITES trade data on orchids provide information needed to learn trends and to monitor overseas trade, what is needed is detailed information on the species traded and whether plants traded are wild or artificially propagated. Only with this

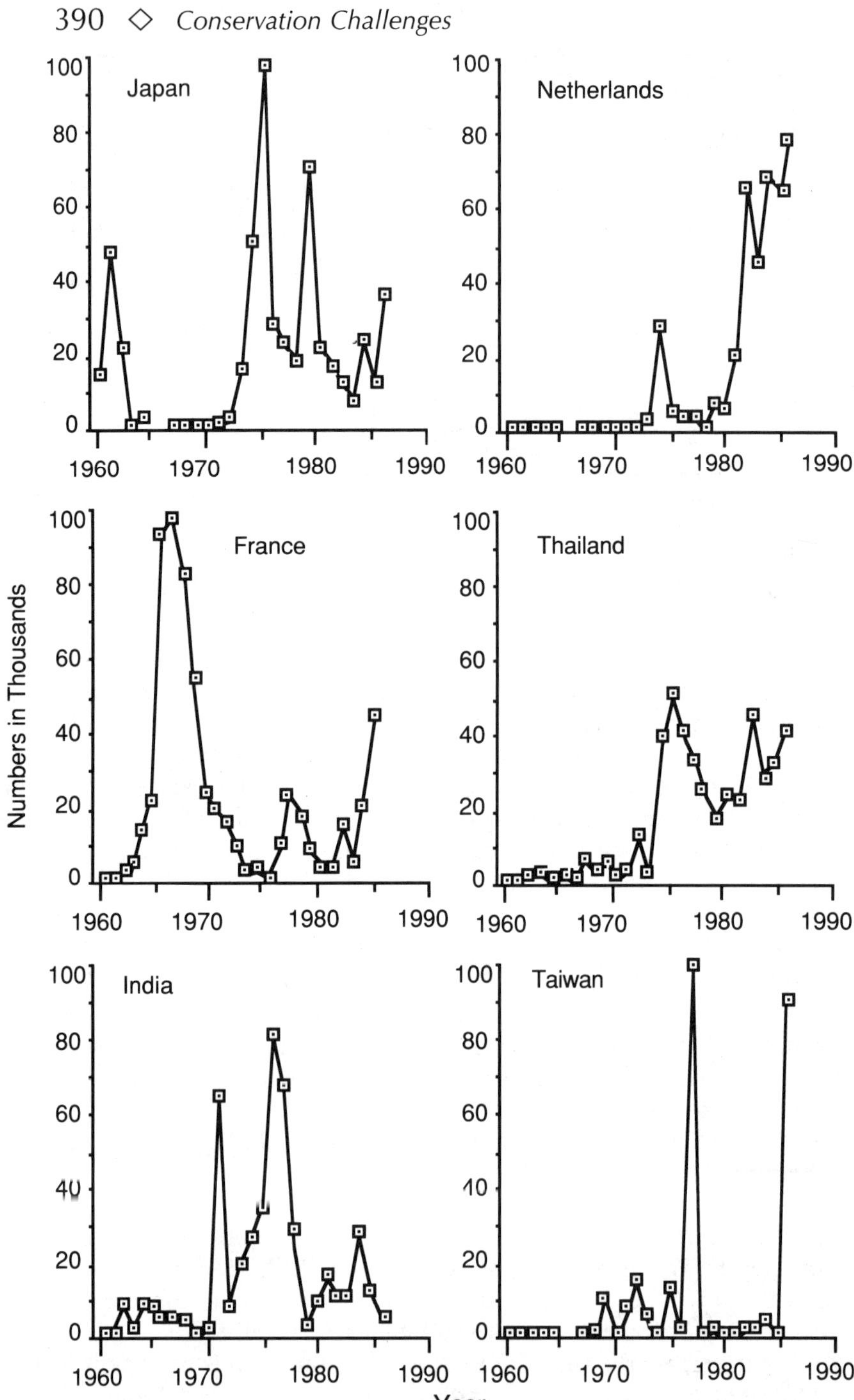

Figure 2. Imports of orchids from selected countries, 1960-1986, according to records of the U.S. Customs Service.

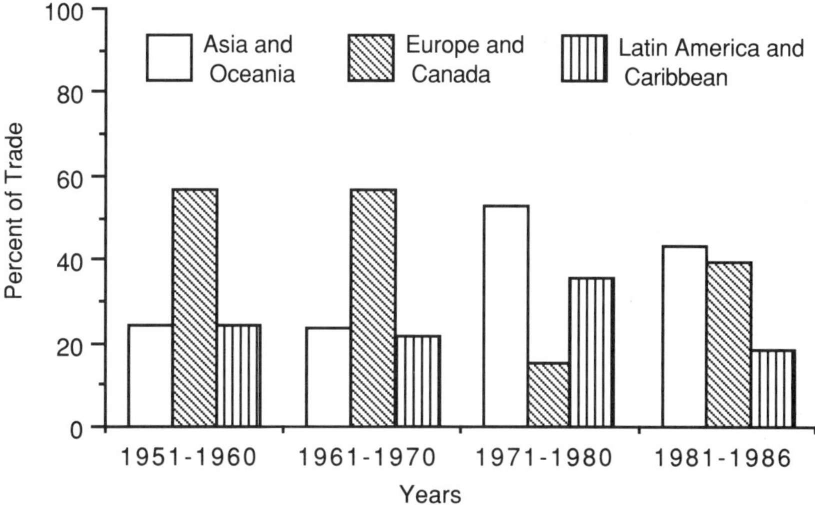

Figure 3. Changes in percent of U.S. orchid imports from regions of the world based on records of the U.S. Customs Service.

information will CITES truly help conserve orchid diversity rather than simply help document its decline.

REFERENCES

Anonymous. 1982a. "Terrestrial orchids in trade." *TRAFFIC(U.S.A.).* 4(1):6.

——1982b. "U.S. is major importer of orchids." *TRAFFIC(U.S.A.).* Vol. 4(2):7.

Anonymous. 1986. "IUCN Species-Survival Commission—Orchid Specialist Group." *Orchid Research Newsletter* 8:5–7.

Bailes, C. 1985. "Orchids of Borneo and their conservation," pp. 111–114 in *Proceedings of the Eleventh World Orchid Conference.* Miami, Florida.

Beckner, John. 1979. "Are orchids endangered?" *American Orchid Society Bulletin* 48(10):1010–1017.

Catling, Paul M. 1980. "Endangered Orchids?—Another viewpoint." *American Orchid Society Bulletin* 49(3):220–222.

Cribb, P. J. 1984. "The golden slipper orchid of Yunnan." *The Garden* 109(9):352–353. Journal of the Royal Horticultural Society.

——1987a. "Beautiful, Yes, But ... " *American Orchid Society Bulletin* 56(8):828–830.

——1987b. *The Genus Paphiopedilum.* Royal Botanic Gardens, Kew in association with Timber Press. Portland, Oregon. 222 pp.

Dunsterville, G. C. K. 1975. "A letter to orchid conservationists." *American Orchid Society Bulletin* 44(10):882–885.

——1985. "Conservation in an overpopulated world." *American Orchid Society Bulletin* 54(10):1189–1193.

Gibson, T., McCarten, N., Campbell, F., and McMahan, L. 1981. *International Trade in Plants: Focus on U.S. Exports and Imports.* TRAFFIC(U.S.A.). Washington, D.C.

Hagsater, Eric. 1976. "Can there be a different view on orchids and conservation?" *American Orchid Society Bulletin* 45:18–21.

International Convention Advisory Commission. Computer printouts of U.S. CITES data from 1977 through 1979.

Kennedy, G. C. 1975. "Orchids and conservation—a different view." *American Orchid Society Bulletin* 44(5):401–405.

Koopowitz, H. 1986. "A gene bank to conserve orchids." *American Orchid Society Bulletin* 55(3):247–250.

McMahan, L. 1985. "U.S. Customs data on orchids."*TRAFFIC(U.S.A.)* 6(2):15–17.

Pradhan, G. M. 1969. "*Paphiopedilum fairrieanum* [sic]." *Orchid Review* 77:256–257.

Rands, Ray J. 1975. "*Phragmipediums*—and their future." *American Orchid Society Bulletin* 44(3):235–238.

Reinikka, Merle A. 1972. *A History of the Orchid.* University of Miami Press. Coral Gables, Florida. 316 pp.

Replogle, Rod. 1973. "Orchid red-tape." *American Orchid Society Bulletin* 42(9):798–800.

Stewart, Joyce. 1986. "Orchid conservation at the international level." *American Orchid Society Bulletin* 55(3):242–246.

——1987. "Orchid conservation: Survival and maintenance of genetic diversity of all orchids throughout the world." *American Orchid Society Bulletin* 56:822–827.

Steele, Helen. 1975. "Species orchid seed—Conservation and distribution." *American Orchid Society Bulletin* 44(6):514–515.

Swinson, A. 1970. *Frederick Sander: The Orchid King. The Record of a Passion.* Hodder & Stoughton. London, England. 252 pp.

U.S. Department of Interior. CITES Annual Reports for the Years 1980 through 1985.

Walter, Kerry S. 1983. "Orchidaceae (Orquideas, Orchids)," pp. 282–292 *in* D.H. Janzen ed., *Costa Rican Natural History.* University of Chicago Press. Chicago and London.

Wildlife Trade Monitoring Unit, Conservation Monitoring Centre, International Union for Conservation of Nature and Natural Resources. 1987. Printout of Recorded CITES Trade from 1976 through 1985, excluding the United States.

Linda McMahan is director of Botanic Garden Programs at the Center for Plant Conservation and a member of the IUCN/SSC North American Plant Specialist Group.

Kerry S. Walter is director of Botany and Information Systems and is also a member of the IUCN/SSC Orchid Specialist Group.

The oceans have been used as dumps for centuries, but modern refuse has created a major hazard for wildlife. Thousands of sea lions (seen here) and seals die each year after becoming tangled in plastic debris. *Dr. Charles W. Fowler/NMFS*

Plastic Debris and Its Effects on Marine Wildlife

Kathryn J. O'Hara

INTRODUCTION

Marine pollution is not a new concern. The world's oceans long have been used as a receptacle for various types of wastes including oil, organic chemicals, heavy metals, sewage, and solid wastes. In addressing the many pollutants entering the marine environment, however, solid wastes generally have been considered to be a mere problem of aesthetics. As recently as 1985, a three-year federal plan that established marine pollution research priorities in the United States categorized the effects of marine litter as a low priority concern (U.S. Department of Commerce 1985). However, during 1987, a presidential task force, a federal workshop, a dozen congressional bills, several national and international conferences, and more than a quarter of a million citizens across the nation all focused on a relatively new marine pollution issue: plastics debris and its impacts.

A major reason for this heightened concern is that plastic debris is causing widespread mortality of marine mammals, turtles, fish, and birds. Recent studies in Alaska indicate that each year as many as 30,000 northern fur seals become tangled in plastic debris, primarily fishing nets and strapping bands, and die. For other species, including sea turtles, seabirds, and fish, there is increasing worldwide documentation of ingestion of plastic debris. The ingestion of discarded plastic bags and sheeting by sea turtles is one example. Evidently, sea turtles deliberately eat these floating items that they mistake for jellyfish or other natural prey. At least 50 of the world's 280 species of seabirds also have been known to ingest plastic debris. Ingested plastic may lodge in an animal's intestines and stomach, blocking digestion and preventing assimilation of nutrients; it can also create false feelings of satiation, causing an animal to stop eating and starve or lose strength and succumb to other natural forces.

Another adverse effect of plastic debris is "ghost fishing," the ability of lost or discarded plastic fishing nets and traps to continue catching large numbers of commercially valuable finfish and shellfish for years after they have been lost. In New England, for example, it is estimated that more than 500,000 lobster pots are lost yearly; these lost traps continue to catch millions of pounds of valuable lobster that is never retrieved for human use.

Sources of plastic debris include both vessels that follow a centuries-old practice of dumping garbage at sea, and several land-based sources that discharge plastic materials via storm and sewer drains and other outlets. Plastic fishing gear, cargo sheeting, and galley wastes from ships are becoming increasingly prevalent in marine areas. Plastics generated from land-based sources include sewage-associated wastes such as plastic tampon applicators, disposable diapers and plastic resin pellets from manufacturing plants.

While the total amount of plastic debris in the oceans is unknown, it tends to be concentrated along coastlines where there is heavy vessel traffic and commercial fishing activity and numerous land-based sources of plastic debris. The ubiquity of plastics in the world's oceans is demonstrated by their presence on remote islands in Antarctica and notable concentrations in mid-ocean gyres such as the Sargasso Sea.

Several important initiatives prior to 1987 documented what is presently known about the plastic debris problem. In 1984, at the request of the U.S. Marine Mammal Commission, the National Marine Fisheries Service (NMFS) organized an international workshop to identify the scientific and technical aspects of the debris problem and its impacts on marine species. Later that year, Congress appropriated $1 million to NMFS to develop a comprehensive research and management program addressing the issue. Over the past three years, NMFS' Marine Entanglement Research Program has provided additional documentation on the extent of the problem.

In 1986, the Environmental Protection Agency commissioned the Center for Environmental Education to prepare a report on the plastic debris problem in the marine and Great Lakes waters of the United

States. The study helped to redirect attention from general "marine debris" to those problems caused specifically by plastic items. The study showed that plastic debris is a nation-wide problem for marine wildlife. It also identified the major ocean and land-based sources of plastic debris, but indicated that the total amount of debris generated by these sources in unknown. Finally, the study noted the absence of appropriate laws to address the plastic debris problem.

By 1987, the problems caused by plastic debris and the primary sources of the debris were no longer debatable. Even though the total number of animals killed by debris each year is unknown, and the amount of debris generated by all sources has not been quantified, sufficient information has been collected to show that the problem is increasingly serious, but preventable by human action. Hence, government officials, conservationists, and industries that generate or use plastics have focused their efforts on finding practical solutions.

No single agency or program has exclusive responsibility for controlling the disposal of plastics in the marine environment. Instead, a variety of authorities coexist in numerous agencies to carry out different programs pertaining to ocean dumping, water quality, solid-waste management, species protection, and fisheries management. NMFS has taken a leading role in addressing ocean sources of debris. But the diversity of types, sources, and problems caused by plastic debris dictates that other federal agencies must also be involved.

In 1987, two major efforts were undertaken to identify current federal agency activities, or lack thereof, and to address the plastic debris problem. In response to a Senate letter addressed to the president on April 2, 1987, the Energy and Natural Resources Group of the Domestic Policy Council charged the National Oceanic and Atmospheric Administration with preparing a report on what is being done by federal agencies to address the plastic debris problem and with making appropriate recommendations. A final report is expected in April 1988. In June 1987, the National Marine Pollution Program Office of the National Oceanic and Atmospheric Administration convened a workshop on persistent plastic debris to identify further research needs. The results of this workshop will be used in the development of the next five-year federal plan for ocean pollution research, which must be sent to Congress by September 1988.

Furthermore, recognizing that existing pollution control authorities are inadequate, legislators have introduced bills at the local, state, and federal levels to address the plastic debris problem. In 1987, the United States stepped up its efforts to ratify an international treaty, Annex V of the International Convention for the Prevention of Pollution from Ships, which would prohibit the disposal of garbage, and plastic items in particular, by all ships at sea.

THE PROBLEM OF PLASTIC DEBRIS

Until recently, the problems caused by various types of human-made marine litter were not obvious; metal and glass garbage dumped into the ocean sank, and paper and cloth wastes decayed. During the 1930s and 1940s, however, plastics began to replace these traditional materials. By 1960, annual U.S. plastics consumption was 6.3 billion pounds. In 1970, this figure rose to 19 billion pound; by 1985, nearly 47 billion pounds of plastic was produced in the United States (Society of the Plastics Industry 1986).

The success of plastics lies in the diversity of its applications. The convenience of plastic for consumer products and packaging is demonstrated by the fact that plastic packaging has more than doubled over the past 10 years (Society of the Plastics Industry 1986) and is expected to reach approximately 22.6 billion pounds by the year 2000 (Chem Systems, Inc. 1987) (see Figure 1). By the 1970s, lightweight plastic fishing nets, ropes, and lines had virtually replaced those made of hemp, linen, cotton, and manila. Its strength also made plastic an ideal substitute for materials used in packaging heavy cargo. In 1984, some 300 million pounds of plastic were used in shipping sacks and pallet shrink wrap (Society of the Plastics Industry 1986). Above all, plastics are durable. A simple, plastic six-pack ring used for carrying beverage cans persists in the environment for several hundred years before it decomposes (Paul 1984).

Ironically, the very qualities of plastics that have contributed to their success—their light weight, strength, and durability—have made

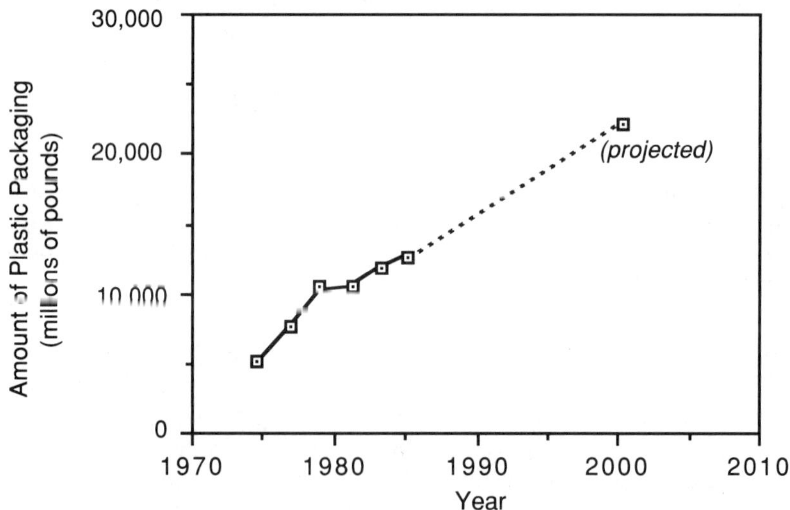

Figure 1. Growth in plastics packaging in the United States 1975-2000. Sources: Society of the Plastics Industry 1986, Chem Systems, Inc. 1987.

them the most problematic component of marine litter. Plastic articles presently make up more than one-half of all human-made debris items found at sea and on coastlines (Dahlberg and Day 1985, Center for Environmental Education 1987b). But not even the visible prevalence of plastic debris in the marine environment has been a major factor in bringing this issue to the forefront. Rather, it was the adverse impacts of plastics on marine wildlife that captured national attention. Photographs appearing in various media have shown seals and sea lions garroted by fishing nets, gulls and geese strangled by six-pack rings, and a sea turtle wedged between the legs of plastic lawn chair. It is now believed that the increased use and subsequent disposal of plastics in marine areas is causing widespread mortality among a number of marine species either through entanglement or by ingestion.

Entanglement

Entanglement in plastic debris poses a serious threat to a number of marine species, both at the individual and population levels. Marine mammals, sea turtles, seabirds, and fish have been found entangled in the loops and openings of fishing nets, strapping bands, and other plastic items. Once ensnared, an individual may be unable to swim or feed, or may incur open wounds that lead to infection. In some cases, entanglement may result from random encounters with debris. For example, an animal may not be able to see or otherwise detect plastic debris, especially fishing gear that is designed to be nearly transparent in water (Balazs 1985). However, there appear to be a number of biological factors that increase the risk of entanglement for certain species.

Floating plastics, like natural ocean debris such as sargassum weed and logs, attract fish, crustaceans, and other species seeking shelter and concentrated food sources. Marine mammals, turtles, and birds are also attracted to floating debris where they may become entangled when attempting to feed. Predators such as seals and seabirds have increased chances of becoming entangled when attracted to their normal prey entangled in discarded fishing gear. Finally, pinnipeds haul out and rest on natural debris such as floating kelp mats, logs, and other debris (Fiscus and Kajimura 1965, 1967), while young seals are attracted to floating debris as objects of play. If such debris include plastics, entanglement can result.

Seals and Sea Lions. Due to their behavioral characteristics, seals and sea lions may be the most prone to entanglement. At least 15 of the world's 32 species of seals have been observed to become entangled in plastic debris including the northern fur seal (Fowler 1985, 1987, Scordino 1985), South African or Cape fur seal (Shaughnessy 1980),

New Zealand fur seal (Cawthorn 1985), South American sea lion (Ramirez 1986), northern sea lion (Calkins 1985), California sea lion, northern elephant seal, and harbor seal (Stewart and Yochem 1985, 1987), Antarctic fur seal, Juan Fernandez fur seal, southern fur seal, grey seal, southern elephant seal, harp seal (Fowler 1987a), and the federally listed, endangered Hawaiian monk seal (Henderson 1984, 1985).

The effects of entanglement on an individual animal may vary. Most northern fur seals have had items of debris around their necks and shoulders (Fowler 1986b). This kind of entanglement, if constricting, may directly impair swimming or feeding. Entangling debris also increases drag during swimming (Feldkamp 1983). Consequently, an entangled seal must use more energy to swim and therefore must consume more food to compensate. Drag caused by entangling debris, however, also inhibits high-speed swimming required for pursuit of prey and may lead to starvation of an entangled animal. In other cases, abrasion from entangling debris may cause wounds that are susceptible to infection.

Entanglement of breeding animals can also adversely affect their young. In field studies on St. Paul Island, Alaska, 9 out of 17 female northern fur seals observed entangled in debris never returned to their pups after foraging at sea. The other entangled seals took twice as long to return as compared to unencumbered female seals (Fowler 1987b).

Sea Turtles. Sea turtles are also prone to entanglement in plastic debris. In the first comprehensive assessment of this problem, Balazs (1985) compiled a list of 60 cases of sea turtle entanglements worldwide that involved green, loggerhead, hawksbill, olive ridley, and leatherback turtles. The most common form of entanglement involved monofilament fishing line. Other cases involved (in decreasing frequency) rope, trawl nets, gill nets, and plastic sheets or bags. As is the case for pinnipeds, entangled sea turtles are unable to carry out basic biological functions such as feeding, swimming, or surfacing to breathe; constricting debris may also cause lesions or even necrosis of flippers.

Seabirds. In contrast to the increasing documentation of pinniped and sea turtle entanglement in plastic debris, the impact of plastics on birds consists of anecdotal accounts. There has been no attempt by any agency to collect extensive data on bird entanglement deaths caused by debris. The entanglement problem tends to be overshadowed by the magnitude of seabird mortality related to active fishing operations. For example, the Japanese salmon gill-net fishery, in which more than 1,600 miles of drift gill net is set each night, is reported to drown over 250,000 seabirds in U.S. waters each year during a two-month fishing season (King 1984). Seabirds are also attracted to lost or discarded nets and have been found entangled in large pieces of lost gill nets that continue to ghost fish at sea (Jones and Ferroro 1985).[1]

Birds also become entangled in monofilament fishing lines and other plastic objects. On the west coast of Florida, the staff of the Suncoast Seabird Sanctuary each year finds hundreds of brown pelicans entangled in fishing line (Suto interview). Many of these occurrences result when birds attempt to eat bait from fishing hooks. An entangled bird trailing line may either be immediately immobilized, or become snagged on a tree or power line, unable to break free. Other items, such as plastic six-pack rings, get stuck on the necks of marine birds and waterfowl when they attempt to dive or feed through the rings. Osprey and other birds actively collect pieces of nets and fishing line for nest material; this can lead to strangulation of both adults and juveniles.

Other Species. The extent of entanglement among species of cetaceans is only in the beginning stages of analysis. Many species have been reported entangled in nets or trap lines; but such occurrences have generally been attributed to collisions with active fishing gear (O'Hara *et al.* 1987).

Debris on coastlines is also known to entangle terrestrial species. For example, foxes and rabbits have been observed entangled in nets and other plastic items (Fowler and Merrell 1986). In one case, the skeletal remains of 15 reindeer were found in a Japanese gill net (Beach *et al.* 1976).

Ingestion

Along with increasing reports of wildlife entanglement caused by plastic debris, there has been increased documentation of a problem that is less obvious: the ingestion of plastics by marine animals. Several factors may increase the likelihood of plastic ingestion by certain species. For example, winds and currents that tend to concentrate food sources such as fish and plankton, also concentrate debris. For some species, floating items may actually resemble authentic food items. Seabirds, for example, are thought to mistake small pieces and fragments of plastics for planktonic organisms, fish eggs, or even the eyes of squid or fish (Day *et al.* 1985). Plastics covered with fish eggs or encrusting organisms such as algae and bryozoans may even "smell" or "taste" like authentic food items. It has been suggested that hungry animals are less likely to discriminate between natural foods and look-alike debris (Balazs 1985).

1. A gill net is suspended by floats and is designed to entangle fish or other species that are not small enough to pass through the webbing. Drift gill nets are not stationary but drift freely with ocean current. Twenty-one species of seabirds are killed in Japanese drift gill nets. The majority of these are either short-tailed shearwaters or tufted puffins.

Sea Turtles. Perhaps the most highly publicized case of plastic ingestion has been the consumption of plastic bags or sheeting by sea turtles that are thought to mistake these items for jellyfish, squid, and other prey. In a comprehensive review of this subject, Balazs (1985) reported five species of sea turtles known to ingest plastic: green loggerhead, leatherback, hawksbill, and Kemp's ridley. Of the items ingested, plastic bags and sheets were the most common (32 percent of 79 cases) followed by tar balls (20.8 percent), and plastic particles (18.9 percent). On Long Island, New York, a researcher reported that 11 of 15 dead leatherback turtles washed ashore during a two-week period had ingested four eight-quart-sized bags, while one had eaten 15 bags (Anonymous 1983). Another of the leatherback turtles had ingested 590 feet of heavy-duty monofilament fishing line (Sadove 1980).

However, it is impossible to define what specific types of plastics pose the greatest threat to sea turtles because of the diversity of objects being digested. For example, one 12-pound juvenile hawksbill turtle found in Hawaii had ingested 1.8 pounds of plastic consisting of a plastic bag, golf tee, shreds of bag and sheeting, pieces of monofilament fishing line, a plastic flower, part of a bottle cap, a comb, chips of polystyrene, and dozens of small round pieces of plastic (Balazs 1985).

Recent studies suggest that small turtles that concentrate to feed in the open ocean at areas of convergence (where opposing currents collide and are forced downward) are particularly prone to ingesting plastic(Carr 1987). The downwelling in these areas not only concentrates food for turtles, but also plastic debris. For all turtle species, with the exception of the leatherback (which is rarely seen in the immature stage), reports of immature turtles that have ingested debris are more frequent than reports of adults (Balazs 1985). Carr (1987) noted that plastic pellets found in the stomachs of dead juvenile sea turtles are similar in size and shape to sargassum weed, which concentrates in areas of convergence and provides both shelter and food for turtles.

The effects of plastic ingestion on sea turtle longevity and reproductive potential is presently unknown. It is thought that ingested plastics may cause mechanical blockage of the digestive tract, starvation, reduced absorption of nutrients, and ulceration. Buoyancy caused by plastics could also inhibit diving activities needed for pursuit of prey and escape from predators (Balazs 1985).

Seabirds. The ingestion of plastic debris by seabirds has received increasing attention in recent years. The first documentation of plastic ingestion by a bird, a Laysan albatross, was in the 1960s (Kenyon and Kridler 1969). Today, at least 50 of the world's 280 seabird species are known to ingest plastic debris (Day *et al.* 1985).

The tendency to ingest plastic debris appears to be closely related to bird feeding habits, with diving birds having the highest incidence of plastic ingestion. Most bird species also exhibit selective preferences for certain types of plastic based on debris color, shape, or size. For example, the parakeet auklet, which feeds primarily on planktonic crustaceans, was found to ingest large amounts of light-brown plastic particles that are similar in size and shape to its crustacean prey.

The most common plastic materials ingested by all species of seabirds are resin pellets, the raw form of plastic after it has been synthesized from petrochemicals. Resin pellets, however, are not as abundant as other debris items in the ocean. In studies of plastic items in the North Pacific, only 0.5 percent of the plastic pieces retrieved were pellets (Day *et al.* 1986). Yet pellets make up about 70 percent of the plastic eaten by seabirds (Day 1980). Hence, researchers speculate that seabirds selectively choose plastic resin pellets over other debris (Day 1980, Day *et al.* 1985).

Some birds also feed plastic debris to their young, including the Laysan, black-footed, and wandering albatrosses, and Leach's storm-petrel. For the Laysan albatross, the incidence of plastic ingestion by chicks appears to be increasing. In 1966, analyses of dead chicks found in Hawaii showed that 74 percent had plastics in their stomachs (Kenyon and Kridler 1969). In a recent study, all of the 300 Laysan albatross chicks examined on Midway Islands of Hawaii (located over 1,000 miles northwest of the nearest populated Hawaiian islands) had plastic debris in their stomachs, including plastic fragments, toys, bottle caps, balloons, condoms, and cigarette lighters (Sievert interview).

Many birds naturally digest and regurgitate hard, nonfood items such as fish bones, squid beaks, and bottom substrate materials. According to some researchers, large quantities of ingested plastics may cause intestinal blockage, a false feeling of satiation, or may reduce absorption of nutrients, thus robbing the animal of needed nutrition (Day *et al.* 1985). Suffocation, ulceration, or intestinal injury could result from jagged edges on plastics or the grinding of these items against intestinal walls.

Long-term effects of plastics ingestion may include physical deterioration due to malnutrition, decreased reproductive performance, and the inability to maintain energy requirements (Day *et al.* 1985). It has also been suggested that many plastic pigments are toxic and that plastics may serve as vehicles for the absorption of organochlorine pollutants from sea water which could then be transferred to marine wildlife (Carpenter *et al.* 1972).

Other Species. Far less is known about the ingestion of plastic debris by marine mammals. At least nine species of cetaceans have been found to ingest plastics, primarily in the form of bags and sheeting (Center for Environmental Education 1987c). Since most of this information was obtained by studying dead animals that had been stranded, the actual cause of death is uncertain. In Texas, however, a stranded pygmy sperm whale, which was taken into captivity, presumably died from ingestion of plastic garbage bags, a bread wrapper, and a corn chip bag (Center for Environmental Education 1987b). Analyses of sperm whale stomach contents at an Icelandic whaling station from 1977 to 1981 revealed plastic drinking cups and children's toys as well as large pieces of fishing nets. Since sperm whales readily ingest and subsequently regurgitate the hard parts of prey, principally fish bones and cephalopod beaks, small pieces of plastic are thought to pose no significant problem. But in one case, an ingested fishing net weighing 139 pounds was considered to be large enough to cause eventual starvation of the sperm whale (Martin and Clarke 1986).

Mate (1985) attributed the deaths of a northern elephant seal and a Stellar sea lion to choking on styrofoam cups. There have also been reports from Florida of plastic ingestion by the West Indian manatee, an endangered species. In 1985, a manatee apparently died from ingesting a piece of black plastic sheeting, possibly a bag, which had lodged in its digestive tract (Florida Department of Natural Resources 1985). In 1981, a manatee was reported to have ingested a plastic rope measuring over five feet in length (Possert interview).

Population Effects: The Northern Fur Seal

Since plastic debris has only recently been considered a problem worthy of research, very little is known about its broader impacts on the overall population of different species. To date, extensive research on population impact has been carried out for only one species—the northern fur seal. This research strongly suggests that plastic debris can be a major cause for the population decline of a species.

The Pribilof Islands of Alaska are home to a population of approximately 827,000 northern fur seals, 71 percent of the estimated total world population of this species (Fowler interview). Studies show that the Pribilof population of northern fur seals is less than half that observed 30 years ago, and is declining at an annual rate of four to eight percent (Fowler and Merrell 1986). Entanglement in plastic debris is a contributing factor to this decline.

The history of entanglement for the northern fur seal demonstrates the adverse impacts plastic fishing gear and other items can have on an animal population. In the 1930s, researchers reported the occasional entanglement of northern fur seals. Such reports documented seals entangled in rubber bands cut from inner tubes, pieces of cord, strings, and rawhide. Following World War II, seals were observed entangled in rubber rings, presumably of military origin (Fowler 1987b).

An increasing frequency of entanglement was noted in the early 1960s, at a time when fishing efforts increased in the North Pacific and Bering Sea and synthetic fiber fishing gear was in wide use. In 1969, U.S. fur seal managers began to document the number of entangled seals seen during the annual commercial seal hunt then allowed on the Pribilof Islands. Young animals, between two and three years of age, appear to be the most prone to entanglement because of their curious and playful nature. Comparisons of 20 years worth of entanglement data with changes in birth rates and high levels of juvenile mortality now support the conclusion that entanglement in plastic debris contributes significantly to the decline of the Pribilof northern fur seal population (Fowler 1987b). (Figure 2 shows the decline in the number of fur seal pups born from 1976 to 1987.) A similar decline in numbers has occurred for mature animals, such as harem bulls (see Figure 3).

The most common items of debris known to entangle northern fur seals are generated by commercial fishing operations. Two-thirds of the debris observed on seals consists of trawl net fragments. Strapping

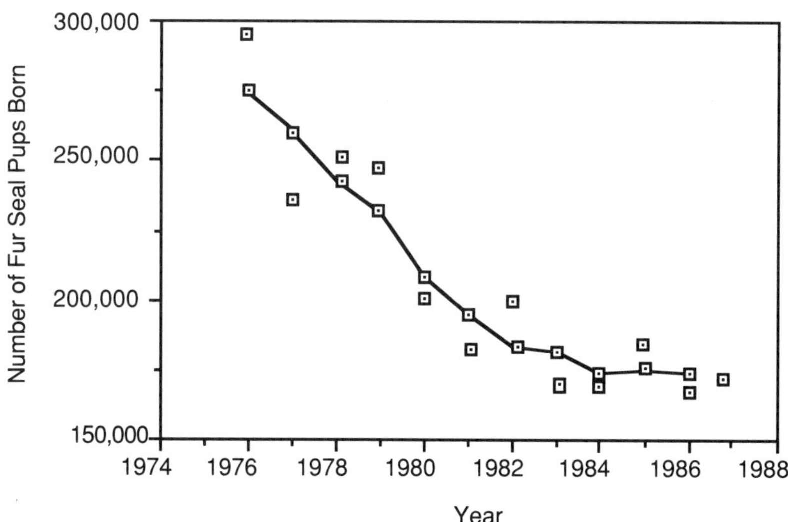

Figure 2. The estimated number of fur seal pups born on St. Paul Island, Alaska 1976-1987. The number of pups born each year is influenced by many natural factors such as disease and predation. In order to reduce the effects of this normal interannual variability, an average was calculated for each three-year period. For example, the annual number of pups born during the period of 1977-1979 is obtained as an average and plotted for the year 1978. The solid line represents this running mean of three. Other points not connected by a line represent actual number of pups born per year. Source: National Marine Fisheries Service.

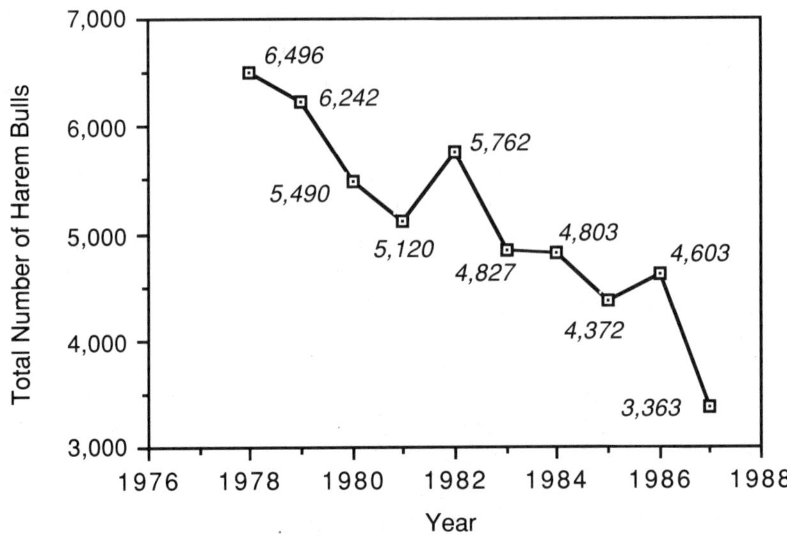

Figure 3. The total number of harem bulls on St. Paul Island, Alaska, 1978-1987. Source: National Marine Fisheries Service.

bands used for binding boxes of bait and other goods are also common. An individual fur seal from the Pribilof Islands is expected to encounter an estimated 3 to 25 pieces of trawl net in an average year. Of these pieces, 30 percent are expected to be of a size capable of causing entanglement (Fowler 1987b).

While entangled seals usually are observed with only small fragments of net or pieces of debris, these seals represent only those individuals that have survived entanglement. The limited number of entangled seal observations seals at sea have involved larger net fragments, in which most of the seals were dead (Fowler and Merrell 1986). It is not known how many seals may become entangled and die, and subsequently drop out of these larger nets at sea without ever being observed. However, from existing information it is estimated that 30,000 northern fur seals die each year from entanglement (Fowler interview).

Impacts on Ecosystems

Although plastic debris has been shown to cause widespread mortality of marine wildlife and to be a major cause for the decline of at least one marine species, the magnitude of this problem for marine species in general is unknown. However, many species that appear to have the greatest degree of interaction with plastics are endangered or threatened with extinction including the Hawaiian monk seal, brown pelican, Kemp's ridley, hawksbill, leatherback, green and olive ridley sea turtles. While plastic debris may not be a major causal agent in the decline of these species, it is certainly a contributing factor.

The broader impacts of plastics on marine ecosystems is purely speculative at this time. The bioaccumulation of plastics via food chains, for example, may be a problem based on observations of secondary and tertiary ingestion of plastics by certain species: bald eagles preying on parakeet auklets with plastics in their stomachs (Day *et al.* 1985); Antarctic skuas preying on broad-billed prions in the South Atlantic (Bourne and Imber 1982); and short-eared owls in the Galapagos Islands preying on blue-footed boobies, which in turn had ingested fish containing plastic pellets (Anonymous 1981b).

One scientist has proposed that floating plastics may present a new habitat niche for encrusting marine species, namely bryozoan species (Winston 1982). Others have suggested that diatoms, hydroids, and bacteria attached to plastic debris could absorb PCBs from seawater and pass along these concentrated sources of pollutants to animals that ingest the pellets (Carpenter *et al.* 1972).

A major problem that could ultimately affect marine ecosystems is ghost fishing—the ability of lost or discarded fishing gear to continue to catch finfish and shellfish species indefinitely. Unfortunately, this is a difficult problem to study and there are few quantitative data on the subject.[2] Gill nets containing fish, crabs, and other economically important species have been found years after they have been lost (Carr *et al.* 1985, High 1985).

Ghost fishing also occurs in commercial trap fisheries when fish and shellfish enter traps that are never retrieved; trapped species (either alive or dead) may become bait that attracts yet other animals. Lost king crab traps have been reported to contain as many as 100 live, market-size crabs per trap (Smolowitz 1978a). Black cod (sablefish) pots recovered after one month have been found to contain up to 32 snow crabs and an average of 12 sablefish per pot (High 1976). In New England, more than 500,000 lobster traps are lost in a single year. It is estimated that these traps catch over one million pounds of lobster annually (Smolowitz 1978b). In 1986, the U.S. lobster catch was approximately 46 million pounds (U.S. Department of Commerce 1987). The cumulative effects of lost gear, in combination with the trend to use more plastic-coated wire or plastic traps, presents considerable hazards for fish and crustaceans.

2. Since domestic fishermen are not required to report lost fishing gear, there is presently no way to determine and monitor the total amount of lost fishing gear and its potential impacts on U.S. fishery resources.

SOURCES OF PLASTIC DEBRIS

Sources of plastic debris have been typically grouped in two major categories: ocean-based and land-based sources. The amount of plastics generated by these sources is presently unknown. Most of the quantitative estimates of debris in the marine environment provide information only on isolated concentrations in relatively localized areas. These concentrations of plastics are influenced by a multitude of controlling factors including tides, winds, and currents which concentrate debris in some areas, yet help keep other areas free of debris. The types and quantities of plastic debris found in a particular area may also be closely related to the proximity of debris sources and hence cannot be used to estimate total quantities in the ocean. For example, in areas of Alaska adjacent to major fishing grounds, pieces of lost or discarded fishing gear make up the majority of debris items (Merrell 1985). Near heavily populated metropolitan areas such as New York, plastics generated from land-based sources are most prevalent (Center for Environmental Education 1987c).

Although the lack of information on total quantities of plastics in the ocean could be addressed by additional studies, the expense and usefulness of such studies is questionable. To determine the amount of debris in waters that cover 70 percent of the world's surface is virtually impossible. In terms of the effects of plastics on marine wildlife, the likelihood of entanglement and ingestion may be more related to natural behavior patterns, winds and currents that tend to concentrate debris, and the characteristics of debris items, than to the sheer quantity of plastics in the environment.

Ocean Sources

Present estimates of the amount of debris generated by various ocean sources are based largely on a study conducted by the National Academy of Sciences over a decade ago. At that time it was estimated that ocean-going vessels and petroleum rigs and drilling platforms dumped 6.4 million metric tons of garbage into the sea every year—nearly 700 tons per hour (National Academy of Sciences 1975). This figure includes all solid cargo and crew waste material (paper, glass, metal, rubber, and plastics) that were assumed to be disposed of by the world's commercial fishing and merchant shipping fleets, passenger cruise liners, military vessels, oil drilling rigs and platforms, and recreational boaters, as well as debris washed to sea by major storms. Approximately 89 percent of the total trash generated by ocean sources—or 5.7 million tons—was estimated to come from the world's merchant shipping fleet. Of this amount, almost 98 percent by weight is in the form of cargo-associated wastes, including dunnage, pallets, wires, and plastic covers. (Other ocean sources and estimated amounts of litter are given in Table 1)

According to the academy, not only is the majority of all ocean litter concentrated in the Northern Hemisphere, but assuming that ocean trash is generated in proportion to the Gross National Product, the United States could be a source of approximately one-third of all the trash in the world's oceans.

While the academy provided information on the amount of plastics generated by some ocean sources, the use of plastics has increased markedly since the time of the study; hence, those estimates significantly underrepresent the amount of plastic debris today. Plastic beverage bottles, for example, were just coming into production in the late 1970s (Anonymous 1987).

Today, the disposal of wastes into the ocean from vessel sources continues essentially because it is inexpensive and convenient. Alternative means of handling shipboard wastes such as incinerators, grinders, and compactors are costly. Small vessels do not have the space for large waste-processing equipment. For larger vessels, such equipment is often not durable enough to handle shipboard shock and vibration, or is considered to be a potential safety hazard. Furthermore, vessels that store garbage on board require adequate disposal facilities on shore, but many ports both in the United States and abroad reportedly do not have such facilities (Horsman 1987).

In the United States, on-shore disposal of wastes from ships is complicated by the fact that vessels entering U.S. waters from destinations outside of the United States and Canada are required to

Table 1
Total Litter Estimates at Sea Generated by Ocean Sources.

Source	Amount of litter (metric tons/year)	Percent plastics (by weight)
Merchant shipping		
Crew	110,000	0.7
Cargo	5,600,000	*
Commercial fishing		
Crew	340,000	0.7
Gear	1,000	100
Recreational boating	103,000	*
Military	74,000	0.7
Passenger Vessels	28,000	1.8
Oil drilling and platforms	4,000	*
Accidents	100,000	*
TOTAL	6,360,000	

* = No estimates made on the percentage of plastics.
Source: National Academy of Sciences 1975.

incinerate, sterilize, or grind any garbage (including plastic packaging) that has come in contact with food, and dispose of it at a facility approved by the U.S. Department of Agriculture's Animal and Plant Health Inspection Service (APHIS). This regulation is designed to prevent the introduction of foreign agricultural pests and diseases such as swine fever or hoof-and-mouth disease. But there is some question as to the availability, convenience, and cost of APHIS-approved facilities. Recently, the American Association of Port Authorities surveyed their members to assess the existing availability of facilities for disposing APHIS-regulated wastes. The survey showed that approximately 60 percent of the association's 79 members can dispose of regulated wastes at or near their ports (Stromberg 1987). According to the Department of Agriculture, however, only 32 out of more than 100 deepwater U.S. ports presently have APHIS-approved facilities (Caffey 1987).

Cost of disposal may be an even greater factor in determining the ultimate fate of shipboard wastes. According to testimony provided by a major waste-management company in the United States (Greco 1987), a vessel with a 50-person crew on a 10-day voyage may generate approximately 2,000 pounds of solid wastes. To dispose of this amount on land may cost anywhere from $30 to $75 depending on various factors including local fees, transportation costs, and land-fill fees. However, if this same amount of waste has to be steam sterilized or incinerated to meet APHIS disposal regulations, the costs could range between $500 to $1,000 (a rate of $.25 to $.50 per pound). A captain of a merchant ship may find it difficult to justify such expenditures when garbage can be dumped at sea free of charge. Consequently, in many situations, garbage, including plastics, is routinely dumped overboard before entering a port. In 1986, of the 73,164 vessels arriving in U.S. ports from foreign origins, only 1,832 ships (less than three percent) offloaded garbage. Horsman (1985) estimated that the world's fleet of merchant vessels dumps at least 450,000 plastic containers, 4,800,000 metal containers, and 300,000 glass containers into the sea each day.

Land-Based Sources

Far less is known about the amount of plastics generated by land-based sources that eventually find their way into marine areas. It is also not known what portion of the solid wastes entering marine areas from land-based sources is plastic. In New York City, 7.4 percent by weight of all wastes from the residential and commercial sectors consists of plastics, 9.2 percent is metal, and 5.7 percent glass (Environmental Defense Fund 1985). Since plastics are lightweight, these figures do not give a clear indication of the volume of plastics in the solid waste stream. For example, during a recent survey of beach debris in Texas, approximately 66 percent of 382,878 items collected were made from plastic materials (Center for Environmental Education, ms. in prep.).

In some cases, plastic debris generated by land-based sources is easily identified as emanating from a particular source. For example, plastic resin pellets, a worldwide contaminant of the oceans, are suspected to originate from plastics processing and manufacturing plants. Studies in the early 1970s reported that pellets were found in river sediment samples taken downstream from U.S. plastics factories, suggesting that plastics are directly discharged into river systems by these industries (Hays and Cormon 1974). The industry, however, says that pellets presently found at sea could be the remnants of a problem that once existed for the plastics industry, but has since been corrected (at least in the United States), through better equipment and waste treatment procedures (Freeman 1987). With the installation of pellet collection traps, precautions in handling, and thorough cleansing of freight cars used to ship resin pellets, one major resin plant reclaims 500 pounds of resin—approximately 5 million pellets—each day; these pellets, if unreclaimed, would otherwise escape into marine areas (Dow undated). However, the pellet pollution problem has not been assessed carefully; hence, it is not known whether pellet loss or discard is still a problem at the manufacturing level for U.S. industry, or if pellets enter marine areas during transportation and handling.

Plastics associated with municipal sewage treatment systems and ocean dumping of sewage sludge are also readily identifiable. They include plastic tampon applicators, condoms, and thin pieces of plastic sheeting from sanitary napkins and disposable diapers. In metropolitan areas, primarily along the North Atlantic coast, sewer systems that are combined with stormwater runoff systems generate large amounts of plastic debris via outfalls in marine areas (Swanson *et al.* 1978). During times of heavy rainfall such systems often become flooded, resulting in the discharge of sewage and floatable plastics directly into marine areas. Other municipal wastewater treatment plants discharge plastic debris directly from both primary and secondary sewage treatment plants. Ocean dumped sewage sludge, a by-product of the treatment process, is also a source of plastic debris; this is especially true in the New York Bight, where nine municipalities use a sewage sludge dump site located 12 miles off the New Jersey coast. Although plastic items are routinely skimmed during the sewage treatment process, approximately five percent escape screening and wind up in treated sludge that is dumped. In the late 1970s, an estimated 1,000 plastic tampon applicators were dumped with sewage sludge in the New York Bight per day. Today that amount is considerably higher. Although the Environmental Protection Agency has mandated that sewage sludge disposal be moved to a site 106 miles offshore by 1988, ocean dumping of plastics will still occur no matter where the dumping site is located until these items are removed at treatment plants.

Municipal solid waste disposal practices are also a source of plastic debris (Swanson *et al.* 1978). In some jurisdictions, garbage is emptied at collection sites onto barges and transported to landfills located along coastal waterways. An example is the Fresh Kills landfill on Staten Island, New York, which receives 700 tons of trash a day. Lightweight litter such as plastic packaging is frequently blown off the barges and into the water. Such litter is also blown off landfills and into surrounding waters.

Another possible source of plastic debris is garbage barges that illegally dump solid wastes in marine areas. In mid-August of 1987, a garbage slick almost 50 miles long caused the closure of many New Jersey beaches when medical wastes such as plastic pill bottles, intravenous tubes, and hypodermic needles, in addition to tons of household trash, washed ashore. One suspected source of this debris was a garbage barge.

Beach goers also contribute their share of plastic debris. For example, in Los Angeles County, California, beach goers leave approximately 75 tons of trash each week. Thus, beach goers' contribution to the debris problem could be substantial (Cahn 1984).

EXISTING LEGAL CONTROLS

At present, no single federal agency has sole authority to control plastic debris pollution. Instead, a variety of federal, state, and local agencies have legal authority pertaining to different aspects of the problem (see Table 2). Federal statutes that address ocean dumping are primarily administered by the Environmental Protection Agency. Wildlife protection laws are administered by the departments of Commerce and Interior, and pollution enforcement capabilities lie largely with the Department of Transportation through the U.S. Coast Guard. Moreover, prior to December 1987, existing legal authorities governing ocean dumping and protection of marine species did not specifically address the problem of plastics in the marine environment. This section describes why the need for adequate legislation became a major focus in 1987.

Laws to Control Ocean Dumping

Several analyses have demonstrated an overall lack of authority to control the plastic debris problem, particularly in the case of vessel

Table 2
United States Laws Potentially Applicable to the Problem of Plastic Debris

Statutes	Regulatory Authority	Administering Agency
Laws to Control Ocean Dumping		
Marine Protection, Research and Sanctuaries Act (Ocean Dumping Act) (33 U.S.C. 1401)	Regulates dumping of all types of materials and prevents or strictly limits ocean dumping of materials which have adverse effects on human health, welfare, or amenities, or the marine environment; implements the London Dumping Convention	EPA issues permits; Army Corps of Engineers permitting authority; Coast Guard surveillance
Act to Prevent Pollution from Ships (33 U.S.C. 1901)	Prohibits discharge of oil and other hazardous substances into navigable waters; implements the MARPOL Protocol	Coast Guard enforcement; EPA develops mechanisms and procedures for handling hazardous substances
Fishery Conservation and Management Act (16 U.S.C. 1801)	Provides a program to conserve and manage the fishery resources found in U. S. waters	NMFS
Rivers and Harbors Act of 1899 (33 U.S.C. 407) (The Refuse Act)	Prohibits discharge of refuse matter into navigable waters out to three miles but does not include refuse from storm and sewer drains	Coast Guard and Department of Justic administer; Army Corps of Engineers has permitting authority
Laws to Control Pollution		
Clean Water Act (33 U.S.C. 1251, 1262, 1311)	Regulates discharges of any pollutant into navigable waters	EPA
Resources Conservation and Recovery Act (42 U.S.C. 6901)	Regulates disposal of solid wastes	EPA
Toxic substances Control Act (15 U.S.C. 2601)	Regulates chemical substances and mixtures that may prevent unreasonable risk of injury to health or environment	EPA
Laws to Protect Wildlife		
Marine Mammal Protection Act (16 U.S.C. 1361)	Ensures that species and population stocks of marine mammals do not diminish beyond the point where they cease to be a significant functioning element in the ecosystem of which they are a part	Commerce, NMFS, Interior, FWS
Endangered Species Act (16 U.S.C. 1361)	Provides a program for the conservation of endangered and threatened species	Commerce, NMFS, Interior, FWS
Migratory Bird Treaty Act (16 U.S.C. 703)	Prohibits the taking of migratory birds, including seabirds	Interior, FWS

generated wastes (Bean 1984, 1987, Center for Environment Education 1987c, Gosliner 1985). For example, the Convention of the Prevention of Marine Pollution by Dumping of Wastes and Other Matter, commonly known as the London Dumping Convention (26 U.S.T. 2403, December 29, 1972), is an international treaty that prohibits the transport of materials at sea for the purpose of dumping. The convention regulates discharges of wastes from vessels that transport wastes generated on land for disposal at sea. While the dumping of plastics is prohibited under Annex I of the treaty, excluded from this prohibition is the "disposal at sea of wastes or other matter incidental to, or derived from the normal operations of vessels . . . " Hence, the large amounts of plastic waste generated by crew members during the course of vessel operations is not regulated.

The Marine Protection, Research and Sanctuaries Act (33 U.S.C.A. 1401), also known as the Ocean Dumping Act, prohibits all U.S. vessels from transporting materials to sea for the purpose of dumping except under permit from the Environmental Protection Agency. Since this act implements the London Dumping Convention, it too has been interpreted to regulate only those wastes specifically taken to sea for the purpose of dumping (Center for Environmental Education 1987c).

The Act to Prevent Pollution from Ships (33 U.S.C.A. 1901) prohibits the discharge of oil or other hazardous substances into navigable waters of the United States. This act implements the International Convention for the Prevention of Pollution from Ships, or the MARPOL Protocol. The MARPOL Protocol, which resulted from a 1973 conference of the United Nations International Maritime Organization, consists of five categories or annexes which state the regulations governing specific types of pollution. Annexes I-IV address the prevention of pollution from oil, hazardous chemicals, sewage, and other potentially harmful substances. Annex V contains regulations specifically dealing with garbage from ships, including the intentional discard of fishing gear, packing materials, dunnage, and food wastes. A key feature of Annex V is its prohibition of the "disposal of all plastics, including but not limited to synthetic ropes, synthetic fishing nets and garbage bags." However, Annex V is an optional annex that must be ratified by at least 15 nations whose fleets jointly constitute 50 percent of the world's shipping tonnage before it becomes legally enforceable. Until December 1987, the United States had ratified only Annexes I and II; hence, the Act to Prevent Pollution from Ships was not applicable to plastics.

The Fishery Conservation and Management Act which regulates fishing by foreign and domestic fishermen in the United States prohibits the disposal of fishing nets at sea, but applies only to foreign fishermen. According to Bean (1987) "it is clearly within the authority conferred by the Act to impose such a prohibition on domestic fishermen."

Finally, the Rivers and Harbors Act of 1988 (33 U.S.C.A. 407) prohibits the disposal of any refuse matter, including garbage, from any source into the navigable waters of the United States. While the act contains no provisions specific to plastics, it is likely that plastics disposal is covered under the term "refuse" as long as it is not "flowing from streets or sewers" (Center for Environmental Education 1987c). According to the U.S. Coast Guard, however, this statute is difficult to enforce because a violation carries only a very small criminal fine (Kime 1986). In addition, the act only covers U.S. marine waters within three miles of the coast.

Laws to Control Pollution

In terms of land-based sources, plastics were overlooked when pollution laws were passed. The Clean Water Act, for example, focuses on municipal and industrial wastes discharged into water bodies; plastics are not specified as a "pollutant" by the act, nor do they constitute a "discharge from a point source" except in the case of resin pellets or sewage-associated wastes (Center for Environmental Education 1987c).

In the case of effluent from plastics manufacturing and processing plants, the Environmental Protection Agency has authority under Section 402 of the Clean Water Act to regulate such discharges. However, according to Bean (1987), discharge of solid waste is not regulated in the effluent guidelines established specifically for the plastics manufacturing industry. Guidelines for state implementation of the act encourage enforcement against point source discharges of floating debris in amounts that are unsightly or deleterious. Therefore, it would appear that states have the authority to regulate pellet discharges. Based on assertions of the plastics industry, most pellets that enter marine areas are lost during transportation and not manufacture.

The Resource Conservation and Recovery Act (42 U.S.C.A. 6901) controls the disposal of wastes, particularly hazardous substances, in landfills. Plastic is not covered under the act's definition of "hazardous." Finally, the Toxic Substances Control Act (15 U.S.C.A. 2601) designed primarily to regulate harmful chemicals, has been considered by some as a possible means of controlling harmful plastic debris since the act provides an array of control measures ranging from labeling and use restrictions to outright bans. At present, however, plastic is not a "chemical" as defined by the act.

Laws to Protect Marine Wildlife

Other laws, such as the Endangered Species Act, the Marine Mammal Protection Act, and the Migratory Bird Treaty Act, which protect marine wildlife, do not provide sufficient authority to control plastic debris pollution. While these laws prohibit the taking (including killing) of protected species, proving that the taking occurred because of plastic debris is extremely difficult. In the case of entanglement, for example, not only would the source of the debris item, such as a fishing net, have to be identified, but the discard of such debris would have to be proven to be deliberate. Recent attempts to identify the source of net fragments found on beaches in Hawaii were complicated by the large variations in gear used among different countries and even within specific fisheries (Henderson *et al.* 1987). Finally, even if a net that had entangled a protected species could be traced to a particular user, it would be difficult to determine whether it was deliberately disposed of at sea.

Annex V of the MARPOL Protocol

In 1987, attention focused on what is presently the most promising legal tool for prohibiting disposal of plastics at sea, the International Convention for the Prevention of Pollution from Ships or the MARPOL Convention. Until recently, 28 countries representing 48 percent of the world's gross merchant shipping tonnage had ratified Annex V. On November 5, 1987, the U.S. Senate gave its unanimous consent to ratification of Annex V; the president signed it later that month.U.S. ratification would provide the necessary shipping tonnage (50 percent of the world's fleets) to bring this treaty into force internationally within the next 12 months. However, despite urgings from the U.S. Coast Guard and environmental groups, the State Department did not deposit the instruments of ratification at the December 1987 meeting of the Marine Environment Protection Committee of the U.N. International Maritime Organization. The State Department's delay was due to a department policy which states that U.S. implementing legislation has to be passed before the instruments of ratification can be deposited with the International Maritime Organization.

Subsequently, the shipping tonnage of Annex V signatories was recalculated and it appeared that even after U.S. ratification became final, there would still be a shortfall. But during the last few days of 1987, implementing legislation was passed by the Senate and signed by the president (see "Legislative Developments"). U.S. ratification of Annex V was deposited with the International Maritime Organization on December 31, 1987, and will take effect on December 31, 1988.

CURRENT DEVELOPMENTS

NMFS Marine Entanglement Research Program

With mounting evidence of the problems caused by marine debris, the Marine Mammal Commission recommended in 1982 that the

National Marine Fisheries Service (NMFS) convene a workshop to address the issue; the commission provided the initial funding to plan the event. NMFS agreed and the Workshop on the Fate and Impact of Marine Debris was held from November 27 to 29, 1984, in Honolulu, Hawaii. Workshop objectives were: 1) to review the state of knowledge on the fate and impact of plastic debris to determine the extent of the problem; 2) to identify and make recommendations on possible mitigating actions; and 3) to identify and make recommendations on future research needs.

Workshop participants pointed out the need for a mechanism to improve the exchange of ideas, data, and scientific techniques on the debris problem. It was specifically recommended that NMFS designate a program coordinator for plastic debris activities. Subsequently, in 1984, as part of the reauthorization of the Marine Mammal Protection Act of 1972, Congress appropriated $1 million to NMFS to consult with the Marine Mammal Commission and to develop a comprehensive research and management program addressing the plastic debris issue. In April 1984, a member of the Northwest and Alaska Fisheries Center staff was designated to manage NMFS' Marine Entanglement Research Program.[3] Appropriations for this program were subsequently reduced to $750,000 in 1986 and remained at that same level in 1987.

The goals of the program were developed from the recommendations of the 1984 workshop. Major projects currently conducted under the Marine Entanglement Research Program include:

1. education and public awareness efforts to increase the knowledge of both industrial and commercial contributors about the plastic debris problem, its impacts and control;
2. research and monitoring to assess information on the origin, amount, distribution, fate, and effects of plastic debris in marine areas; and
3. mitigation projects directed toward reducing the amount of nondegradable materials entering the marine environment (Coe and Bunn 1987).

(A listing of specific activities under each of these categories for the period 1985–1987 is provided in Table 3)

Over the past three years the majority of Marine Entanglement Research Program funds have been used for research and monitoring projects. The Marine Entanglement Research Program staff has made a conscious effort not to expend a large portion of funds to quantify the amount of debris entering marine waters, but rather to document the impacts of debris on certain marine species. Education projects to date

3. Mr. James M. Coe, NOAA/National Marine Fisheries Service, Marine Entanglement Research Program, 7600 Sand Point Way, NE, BIN C15 700, Seattle, Washington, 98115.

Table 3
National Marine Fisheries Service Marine Entanglement Research Program Tasks from 1985 to 1987

Fiscal Year 1985 Activities

Education

Education Program Development and Implementation for the North Pacific Region ($144,000)
West Coast/New England Coast Beach Cleanup Northern Fur Seal Entanglement ($6,100)
Hawaiian Workshop on the Fate and Impact of Marine Debris ($50,000)

Scientific and Technical Information

Northern Fur Seal Entanglement Research ($106,000)
Northern Sea Lion Entanglement Debris Research ($85,000)
Establishment of a Reference Collection on Marine Debris ($48,000)
Beach Accumulation and Loss Rate Estimation in Alaska ($35,000)
U.S. Fishery Observer Data Analyses on Marine Debris for the Joint Venture Groundfish Fishery ($23,000)
Squid Gill net Fishery Survey ($100,000)
Hawaiian Islands Endangered Species Monitoring ($13,000)
Dynamics of Derelict Gill net ($27,000)
Sea Turtle Debris Ingestion ($27,000)
Seabird Debris Ingestion ($30,000)
At-Sea Debris Survey Methodology ($20,000)
Stranding Program Information Expansion ($8,000)
Aerial Techniques for Debris Assessments ($8,000)

Mitigation

Disposal Methods Development ($66,000)
Research on the Use of Degradable Materials ($49,000)
Program Management ($54,000)

Fiscal Year 1986 Activities

Education

Marine Debris Education Continued and Expanded to Atlantic and Gulf of Mexico ($112,000)

Scientific and Technical Information

Alaskan Beach Debris Survey Methodology ($35,000)
Survey of High Seas Squid Driftnet Fisheries ($95,000)
Hawaiian Island Engangered Species Monitoring (cont'd, $15,000)
Fur Seal Responses to Derelict Fishing Gear ($35,000)
Entanglement Rates of Female Northern Fur Seals ($25,000)
Northern Fur Seal and Sea Lion Pup Entanglement Assessment ($35,000)
Debris Ingestion by Hawaiian Seabirds ($20,000)
Dynamics of Gillnet Gear ($15,000)
Benthic Debris Impacts ($19,800)
Cetacean Ingestion ($23,000)
Infrared Spectrophotometric Anaylsis of Derelict Fishing Gear ($37,000)

Mitigation

Disposal Methods Development ($97,000)
Fur Seal Rookery Cleanup ($5,000)
Photodegradation Processes ($24,000)
Program Management ($73,700)

Table 3 (cont.)

Fiscal Year 1987 Activities
Education
Marine Debris Education (cont'd, $120,000)
North Pacific Education Program Evaluation ($15,000)
Marine Debris Teaching Unit Development for Project Wild ($15,000)
Development of Manual on Procedures for Monitoring Plastic Debris on Beaches and at Sea ($2,000)
Scientific and Technical Information
High Seas Squid Fishery Impacts (cont'd, $150,000)
Hawaiian Monk Seal Entanglement Protection and Evaluation ($10,000)
Dynamics of Gillnet Gear ($15,000)
Northern Fur Seal Entanglement Studies ($45,000)
Channel Islands Pinniped Entanglement Monitoring ($5,000)
Alaska Beach Litter Index (cont'd, $30,000)
Sampling Survey of Impacts of Marine and Coastal Debris and Entanglement on Sea Turtles ($12,000)
Anaylses of Sea Turtle Stomachs Collected from Strandings on the Atlantic Coast ($20,000)
Composition and Weathering of Derelict Trawl Web Collected from Alaskan Beaches ($21,000)
Marine Debris in Upwelling and Frontal Zones in the Gulf of Mexico ($31,000)
Assessment of Floating Plastic Particles ($21,000)
Completion of Hawaiian Seabird Plastic Ingestion Impacts ($18,700)
Support for Pacific Fisheries Conference on Marine Debris ($5,000)
Mitigation
Plastics Research Steering Group Meeting ($2,000)
Assessment of Vessel Refuse Reception Problems in Alaskan Ports ($25,000)
Recycling Fishing Gear ($48,000)
Program Management ($80,000)

Source: Coe and Bunn 1987.

have primarily focused on commercial fishing, merchant shipping, and the plastics industries. Mitigation projects have been directed primarily at assessing existing shipboard waste disposal technologies and port waste reception facilities, and conducting research on degradable plastics and recycling systems.

So far, NMFS' program has brought about a greater understanding of both the extent of the problem and the methods by which it may be reduced through education and technology. However, the diversity of types and sources of plastic debris, and of the harm they cause, dictates that more than just one federal agency play a role in solving the problem. In general, the few initiatives that have been undertaken by other federal agencies, such as studies of seabird plastics ingestion conducted by the Fish and Wildlife Service, have been largely conducted through cooperative agreements with the Marine Entanglement Research Program. During the course of its existence, the program has progressively taken on an increasing number of projects within its funding constraints that are outside of NMFS' traditional responsibilities. For example, while initial education efforts primarily targeted commercial fishermen, recent projects have focused on groups such as offshore petroleum workers whose industry is regulated by the Minerals Management Service, and the plastics industry, which could conceivably be regulated by the Environmental Protection Agency.

In 1987, the following efforts were initiated to define roles for other federal agencies.

Interagency Task Force on Persistent Marine Debris

On April 2, 1987, a letter signed by 30 U.S. senators was sent to the president requesting "assistance in developing a coordinated strategy to resolve the increasingly serious and complex problems resulting from the presence of plastic debris in the marine environment." Major points brought out in the letter included the need to "focus and coordinate the various efforts of the federal government to develop solutions to the marine plastic debris problem." The letter called for the establishment of an interagency task force that would set forth a plan of action to reduce the plastic debris problem as well as research and development efforts and additional legislation as warranted.

Subsequently the Energy and Natural Resource Group of the Domestic Policy Council charged the National Oceanic and Atmospheric Administration with producing a report on current federal efforts and making recommendations to address the problem. Recognizing that the authority to deal with the issue lies with many agencies, the National Oceanic and Atmospheric Administration is preparing the report with the assistance of an *ad hoc*, interagency steering committee made up of representatives from the departments of Agriculture (Animal and Plant Health Inspection Service), Commerce (National Oceanic and Atmospheric Administration), Defense (Navy), Health and Human Services (Food and Drug Administration), Interior (Fish and Wildlife Service, Minerals Management Service, and National Park Service), State, Transportation (Coast Guard), the Environmental Protection Agency, Council on Environmental Quality, the Office of Management and Budget, and the U.S. Marine Mammal Commission. The objective of this task force is to provide an evaluation of the federal government's role in resolving the plastic debris problem. A final report from the task force is due in April 1988.

Persistent Marine Debris as a High Priority Issue for the National Marine Pollution Program Office

The National Ocean Pollution Planning Act of 1978 (33 U.S.C. 1701) calls for the establishment of a comprehensive, coordinated, and effective federal program for ocean pollution research, development, and monitoring. As required by the act, the National Oceanic and Atmospheric Administration in consultation with other agencies, prepares a five-year federal plan for the National Marine Pollution Program every three years. The National Marine Pollution Program office is assigned responsibility within the National Oceanic and Atmosphere Administration for updating the five-year plan and coordinating the implementation of plan recommendations.

In June 1987, the National Marine Pollution Program Office convened a workshop to set national priorities for research on the five most important marine pollution problems; "persistent plastic debris" emerged as one of the top five along with nonpoint source pollution, habitat loss and modification, discharge of sewage effluents, and discharge of industrial wastes.

Significant research topics for plastic debris identified by the workshop include: methods for handling vessel wastes; identification of the source and effects of plastic pellets, particles and fragments in the marine environment; identification of the source of land-based litter, the means by which it gets into the oceans and its fate thereafter; and investigation into the effects of ghost fishing and ways to alter or regulate fishing gear to reduce its adverse impacts in the marine environments. These recommendations will be used in the development of the next five-year Federal Plan for Ocean Pollution Research, Development, and Monitoring due in September 1988.

Other Agency Developments

The Minerals Management Service, which overseas all offshore petroleum development in the United States, issued a special directive to all Gulf of Mexico lessees and operators advising them to develop and use training aids and awareness programs specifically focused on the plastic debris problem. The Minerals Management Service has also organized a special task force made up of environmental groups and industry representatives to address the problem of plastic debris in the Gulf of Mexico.

In September 1987 the Navy formed an advisory committee consisting of congressional staff members and environmental group representatives to help outline recommendations on how naval vessels can comply with Annex V's prohibitions of the dumping of plastics by vessels.

LEGISLATIVE DEVELOPMENTS

In response to growing concern over the problems caused by the disposal of plastics in the marine environment and inadequate controls, a hearing was held in August 1986 before the House Subcommittee on Coast Guard and Navigation. The federal government's role in this issue was elucidated in testimony provided by the National Oceanic and Atmospheric Administration, the Marine Mammal Commission, and the U.S. Coast Guard, which has authority to enforce existing prohibitions on pollution from vessels in U.S. waters. The environmental community's concerns were raised in testimony by the Center for Environmental Education, the Environmental Defense Fund, and the Oceanic Society. Industry's perspective was provided in testimony of the Society of the Plastics Industry and by a spokesman for the commercial fishing industry. In general, all witnesses recognized the problems caused by plastics and agreed on the need for stricter controls on the disposal of plastics at sea. All groups pointed to the need for expeditious U.S. ratification of Annex V.

Later in 1986, four bills were introduced in Congress directing studies and action to solve the plastic debris problem and reduce entanglement of marine wildlife: S. 2596 sponsored by Senator John Chafee (R-RI) and a companion bill H.R. 5422 sponsored by Rep. Leon Panetta (D-CA), and S. 2611 sponsored by Senator Ted Stevens (R-AK) and a companion bill H.R. 5108 sponsored by Rep. Charles Bennett (D-FL). Although none of these bills reached the floor, the momentum for legislative action carried over to the 100th Congress (1987–1988), during which ten bills were introduced as of January 1, 1988. The strongest of these measures were H.R. 940 sponsored by Rep. Gerry Studds (D-MA), S. 534 and S. 535 sponsored by Senator John Chafee (R-RI) who was the first in Congress to introduce legislation to address the plastic debris problem, and S. 633 sponsored by Senator Frank Lautenberg (D-NJ). After substantial negotiations between the Senate Environment and Public Works and Commerce Committee, Senate Science and Transportation Committee, House Merchant Marine and Fisheries Committee, and House Public Works and Transportation Committee, a compromise bill, H.R. 3674, was passed by the Senate on December 20 and signed by the president on December 29, 1987 (P.L. 100–220). Among other things, H.R. 3674 included authority to implement the provisions of Annex V, to assess and mitigate the negative effects of plastics in the environment, and to improve efforts to monitor, assess, and reduce the adverse effects of driftnets.

H.R. 3674, Title II—The Marine Plastic Pollution Research and Control Act of 1987

The primary purpose of the Marine Plastic Pollution Research and Control Act is to implement the provisions of Annex V in the United States by an amendment to the U.S. Act to Prevent Pollution from Ships. The act prohibits the disposal of plastics from vessels at sea effective on December 31, 1988, the date on which Annex V is enforceable in the United States. Unfortunately, most laws governing ocean-based activity have major enforcement problems. Since it is impossible to patrol ocean waters (more than two-thirds of the earth's surface), it is necessary to provide incentives for complying with the law, and to provide vessel waste handling and reception facilities that are both easily accessible and economically practical. Such strengthening measures were incorporated into H.R. 3674.

The law requires each vessel to display placards to notify crew and passengers of the requirements of Annex V. It also requires each vessel to keep a log book on garbage disposal. (A similar log is required for oil under regulation 20 of Annex I of the MARPOL Protocol). Each time vessel garbage is offloaded at port, or handled onboard by incineration or some other means, an entry in the log is required.

H.R. 3674 also requires a U.S. vessel to develop and use a shipboard waste management plan to be approved by the Coast Guard. The plan would specify how the ship plans to comply with the provisions of Annex V. In addition, while Annex V applies only to ships of countries which are signatories to the MARPOL Protocol, the law gives the Coast Guard additional authority to prosecute any vessel operator who dumps plastics within 200 miles of the U.S. coast. Under current international and domestic law, public vessels are exempt from MARPOL restrictions, but the act directs all federal agencies, including the Navy and Coast Guard, to bring their vessels into full compliance with Annex V regulations within the next five years. The law also directs the Department of Transportation to ensure and certify that ports and terminals have adequate facilities for collecting shipboard wastes.

H.R. 3674 requires a study to determine and control the adverse effects of plastics in the environment. Specifically, it directs the Environmental Protection Agency, in consultation with the National Oceanic and Atmospheric Administration, to undertake a major study of two components of the plastic waste problem: the effects of plastics on the marine environment and plastics in the solid-waste stream. The study will include: an assessment of improper disposal practices of plastics from both ocean and land-based sources; evaluation of the feasibility and desirability of substitutes for those plastic items that occur most frequently and pose the greatest threats in the marine environment; evaluation of methods to reduce the impacts of plastics in solid waste, including recycling incentives such as deposits on plastic containers; tax laws that would favor the use of recycled plastic over virgin plastic material in manufacturing; and an evaluation of the efficiency and feasibility of making plastics degradable. A final report from the Environmental Protection Agency is due in June 1989.

H.R. 3674 requires a report by the National Oceanic and Atmospheric Administration to Congress due by September 30, 1988. The report must include: identification of harmful plastics in the marine environment, their effects on living marine resources, and analysis of degradable plastics, and recommended legislation to prohibit, tax, or regulate sources of plastic materials that enter the marine environment.

A three-year public outreach education program, conducted by Commerce and in consultation with the Environmental Protection Agency and the Department of Transportation, is mandated to begin on April 1, 1988. Through workshops, public service announcements, posters, and other materials, the agencies will educate recreational boaters, fishermen, and other marine user groups on the harmful effects of plastic pollution and the need to reduce such pollution and to recycle plastic materials. The agencies will also encourage the formation of volunteer groups of "Citizen Pollution Patrols" to assist in monitoring, reporting, cleaning up, and preventing plastic pollution of the ocean and shorelines.

The law further requires the Environmental Protection Agency to study plastic waste and other forms of pollution in the New York Bight, including an assessment of land-based sources of plastics and municipal sewage sludge dumping practices. A report containing recommendations to Congress is due in 1988 and a plan for restoration of the New York Bight is due within three years. Appropriations authority for a New York Bight Restoration Plan was set at $3 million during fiscal years 1988–1990.

Lost or abandoned driftnets were also addressed in H.R. 3674 under Title IV. The purpose of this title is to assess and minimize the adverse effects of driftnets in the marine environment. The National Oceanic and Atmospheric Administration is directed to arrange for cooperative international monitoring and research programs with foreign countries that conduct high seas driftnet fishing operations in the north Pacific Ocean in order to assess the impacts of driftnets on marine resources. Aside from the problem of incidental take pertaining to driftnet fisheries, the law also addresses the problems caused by lost or discarded driftnets. Under Annex V, fishing nets that are deliberately discarded constitute pollution whereas nets that are accidentally lost do not. At present, distinguishing between lost and discarded nets is extremely difficult. Two possible means of addressing this problem were originally proposed at the 1984 Workshop on the Fate and Impact of Marine Debris: paying bounties for lost nets and creating net marking systems that would provide the means for tracing lost or discarded gear back to a particular vessel.

H.R. 3674 directs the National Oceanic and Atmospheric Administration to evaluate the feasibility of establishing a driftnet marking, registry, and identification system to provide a reliable method for identifying the origin of lost or abandoned driftnets. It also directs the agency to evaluate the feasibility of establishing a bounty system to pay persons who retrieve lost or abandoned driftnets and other plastic fishing gear from U.S. waters. A report on these matters is due to Congress in June 1989.

State Initiatives

Traditionally, garbage has been viewed as an aesthetic problem, and in this context regulation has been left largely to state and local authorities. Many states have litter laws but enforcing them is difficult. Recently, several states have begun to address the problems caused by garbage, and plastics in particular, at the manufacturing level.

To date, 11 states have enacted legislation that requires all plastic six-pack ring carriers sold in the state to be photodegradable.[4] These states include Alaska, California, Connecticut, Delaware, Maine, Massachusetts, New Jersey, New York, Oregon, Rhode Island, and Vermont. Several other states have similar legislation pending. With the exception of California, New Jersey, and Rhode Island these laws have been enacted as part of state beverage container deposit laws.

In 1987, a Maine legislator, Representative James Mitchell, tried to take plastic six-pack ring control one step further when he proposed legislation that would ban the sale of both degradable and nondegradable six-pack rings in the state (L.D. 1224 "An Act to Ban the Use of Plastic Connectors for Containers.") Although Maine law requires all plastic ring connectors to be photodegradable, according to Mitchell, the plastic rings are not decomposing in a reasonable period of time and therefore still present a threat to wildlife and remain a prevalent component of litter. Although Mitchell's bill was rejected in committee, the legislation did amend the state's beverage law to require degradable ring connectors for all containers, not just beverage containers. The law was signed by the governor in June 1987.

In realizing the potential impacts of lost gear on fishery resources, the state of Maine also recently implemented regulations requiring that a biodegradable vent be placed in all lobster traps to minimize the impact of ghost fishing. Other states have begun considering bans on plastic items. In New Jersey, for example, the banning of nondegradable plastic egg cartons has been considered. Bills have been introduced in New Jersey and Massachusetts banning the sale and distribution of nondegradable tampon applicators. Suffolk County, New York has

4. The photodegradable ring, developed in the early 1970s, breaks apart upon exposure to ultraviolet light from the sun. As the plastic breaks down, wind and rain cause the carrier to crumble into smaller and smaller pieces. The amount of time for this process varies from one area of the country to another and from season to season. In general, a ring will degrade within three months.

proposed a ban on all nondegradable packaging materials. Michigan successfully banned all nondegradable fast food packaging materials last year and Berkeley, California, is considering a similar ban.

An Oregon legislator recently introduced a bill requiring warning labels on all plastic products that do not degrade within two weeks in the marine environment or in a landfill. The bill specifically listed foamed polystyrene containers and packaging, plastic bags, plastic container rings, plastic fishing supplies, and durable plastic industrial containers as products that would have to be labeled. Although the bill passed the Senate, it died in a House committee.

Industry Initiatives

Unlike many pollution problems, the issue of plastic debris in the oceans is unique in terms of the intensity of attention given to this issue over a relatively short period of time. Another unusual aspect of the issue has been the high degree of industry cooperation in solving the problem.

A considerable amount of effort on the part of industry groups has been directed at reducing their contribution to the problem of plastics in the marine environment. For example, primarily due to the successful educational efforts under NMFS' Marine Entanglement Research Program, commercial fishermen on the Pacific Coast have become increasingly aware of plastic debris as a problem of economics, safety, and reputation. The fishing industry may be negatively affected by ghost fishing and by vessel disablement caused by plastic debris. In addition, many of the pictures appearing in various media have highlighted the effects of lost or discarded fishing gear on marine wildlife thereby creating bad publicity for the industry as a whole.

Some fishermen now are demonstrating an outstanding willingness to help mitigate their contribution to the problem. In late 1987, a coalition of commercial fishermen sponsored a North Pacific Rim Fishermen's Conference on Marine Debris. Approximately 60 representatives from the fishing industries of the United States, Canada, Japan, the Republic of China and the Republic of Korea attended this five-day meeting. The goal of the conference was to devise a plan to reduce the amount of debris originating from commercial fishing vessels operating in the north Pacific Ocean. Topics discussed included the nature and magnitude of the debris problem, the legal framework, actions and programs currently being undertaken by the fishing industry to address the problem, and technical problems and solutions. As a result of the conference, a set of guidelines and resolutions has been adopted by the fishing industry to address debris problems.

The plastics industry could be the most severely affected by the increasingly negative attention given to plastic debris. However, the industry has moved to help reduce the problem.

The Society of the Plastics Industry (SPI) is a trade organization of more than 1,900 members representing all segments of the plastics industry in the United States, including resin producers, distributors, machinery manufacturers, plastics processors, and moldmakers. In November 1986, SPI held a meeting with representatives of major resin companies to discuss the problems caused by resin pellets in marine areas. In addition, SPI is conducting a comprehensive survey of industry practices concerning resin pellets. Information gathered thus far indicates that most pellet escapement may have resulted from past industry practices (such as inadequate screening of factory effluent) that have now been corrected (Freeman 1987).

In addition, the Society of the Plastics Industry, in cooperation with the Center for Environmental Education and the National Oceanic and Atmospheric Administration, has developed a national public education campaign to address improper disposal of plastics in the marine environment. The first phase of this campaign involved the development of public service announcements for trade publications of the commercial shipping, commercial fishing, and plastic industries with accompanying brochures targeted at each group. Many of the major trade journals for these groups have agreed to feature these ads during 1988.

With the increasing attention to the problems caused by plastic debris, several conservation groups and scientists have begun to explore degradable plastics as a possible solution. In June 1987, the Society of the Plastics Industry sponsored the Symposium on Degradable Plastics to disseminate information about research being done within and outside of the plastics industry to make plastics degradable and to explore the technical, economic, and social dimensions of this subject. According to one scientist who is examining the feasibility of using degradable plastics in the manufacture of fishing gear, "currently available technologies for rendering plastics photodegradable can be immediately utilized with minimal developmental effort, to neutralize the hazard posed by some of the disposable (plastic) items . . . " (Andrady 1986). However, plastic breaks down at a different rate at sea than on land. In addition, the effects of degradable plastics on the marine environment is not known.

Citizen Awareness and Participation

Public attention to the debris problem has been increased through statewide beach cleanup projects sponsored by federal and state agencies, environmental organizations, and other groups. In the fall of 1987, 19 states held beach cleanups during a period designated as COASTWEEKS.

In total, more than 26,500 volunteers covered over 1,900 miles of U.S. coastline and collected more than 700 tons of trash (see Table 4).

Table 4
COASTWEEK 1987 Beach Cleanup Results by State

State	Volunteers participating	Miles cleaned	Tons of debris collected
Alabama	127	3	*
California	4,000	1,000	75
Connecticut	15	1	0.1
Delaware	700	50	1.5
Florida	1,232	50	4
Georgia	20	5	0.5
Hawaii	2,726	*	36.8
Louisiana	3,300	85	200
Maine	350	31	3
Massachusetts	391	39.5	1.9
Mississippi	100	5	3.5
New Hampshire	112	3	2
New Jersey	1,250	100	40
New York	80	2	1.5
North Carolina	1,000	150	10
Oregon	2,600	120	17
Rhode Island	450	40	*
Texas	7,132	154	306.5
Washington	1,000	100	6
TOTAL	26,585	1,938.5	708.8

* = Data not available
Source: Center for Environmental Education 1987a

In addition to increasing public awareness some cleanup projects have provided detailed information on the types of debris in the marine environment. For example, data on debris items collected during the Center for Environmental Education's Texas beach cleanup show that at least 15,000 pieces of plastic debris were traceable to fishing operations, consisting mainly of pieces of fishing nets, lines, and buoys. Debris that originated from dumped vessel wastes included bottles with labels from Arabia, Argentina, China, Denmark, England, France, Germany, Italy, Jamaica, Japan, Singapore, Sweden, Thailand, and Venezuela.

CONCLUSION

In 1988, both international and domestic laws will be in place prohibiting the disposal of plastics from vessels at sea. The laws will clearly define the role of federal agencies in this issue and identify future research needs of critical importance. However, there are no overnight solutions to the plastic debris problem.

Available information shows that plastic debris negatively affects individual marine animals, but relatively little is known about the broader implications for total species populations, with the exception of the northern fur seal. In addition, while entanglement in plastic debris causes obvious problems, the effects of plastic debris ingestion on marine wildlife is poorly understood. Ongoing long-term research is necessary to evaluate the effects of plastic debris on marine wildlife, particularly in the case of threatened and endangered species.

During the next few years, there will also be a continued interest in alternative materials such as degradable plastics. Research will be necessary to determine the feasibility of using these materials, particularly in marine areas.

In addition, while legislative measures will soon be in place to prohibit the disposal of plastics from vessels at sea, effective implementation of the laws will be a gradual process. Hence, continuation and expansion of education efforts is necessary to increase awareness and initiate changes in attitudes about the problem of plastic debris from both ocean and land-based sources.

Finally, plastic debris is not a problem unique to the United States; international cooperation will be required if the problem is to be adequately resolved. For example, while the U.S. plastics industry is becoming increasingly aware of the problems caused by resin pellets in marine areas, only 30 percent of all plastic resin is manufactured in the United States (Freemen 1987). Therefore, even if the United States strictly controlled all plastics dumped by its merchant shipping fleet, only five percent of the world's gross shipping tonnage would be covered.

In December 1987, the U.S. delegation to the International Maritime Organization presented draft guidelines to assist parties to the MARPOL Protocol in effective implementation of Annex V. Not only the United Nations, but many other organizations such as the Commission of the European Economic Communities, the Intergovernmental Oceanographic Commission, the International Union for the Conservation of Nature and Natural Resources, Commission for the Conservation of Antarctica and Living Marine Resources, and countless other academic, professional, and governmental bodies have research projects under way or are considering studies that will target the occurrence and impacts of persistent plastics in the oceans. These efforts should be coordinated in order to ultimately solve the problems posed by plastic pollution.

According to James M. Coe, program manager of NMFS' Marine Entanglement Research Program, a second international conference on plastic debris is scheduled for late March, 1989. Identifying international solutions to the global problem of plastic debris will be a subject of major importance.

A final factor that must be considered is that plastics were developed in response to increasing consumer demands for more durable plastic products. However, it is now becoming increasingly clear to the public that the United States is facing a solid waste crisis. Simply put, Americans are generating too much solid waste that is both costly and difficult to dispose of. As the crisis and debate intensifies, it is certain that consideration will be given both to reducing the waste per capita and to developing environmentally benign disposal solutions. As one of the most visible and persistent forms of waste, plastic packaging and other products are likely to draw ever-increasing attention.

REFERENCES

Andrady, A.L. 1987. *Research on the Use of Degradable Fishing Gear and Packaging Materials.* National Marine Fisheries Service, Northwest and Alaska Fisheries Center. NWAFC Processed Report 87–03. 49pp.

Anonymous. 1981. "Galapagos tainted by plastic pollution." *Geo* 3:137

——. 1987. "1970s: Plastics beverage bottles may sweep glass from the market." *Plastics World* 45(10):155–156.

Balazs, G.H. 1985. "Impacts of ocean debris on marine turtles: entanglement and ingestion," pp. 387–429 *in* R.S. Shomura and H.O. Yoshida eds., *Proceedings of the Workshop on the Fate and Impact of Marine Debris.* November 27–29, 1984. Honolulu, Hawaii. U.S. Department of Commerce, NOAA Technical Memorandum. NMFS NOAA-TM-NMFS-SWFC-54.

Beach R.J., T.C. Newby, R.O. Larsen, M. Penderson and J. Juris. 1976. "Entanglement of an Aleutian reindeer in a Japanese fish net." *Murrelet* 57(3):66.

Bean, M.J. 1984. *United States and International Authorities Applicable to Entanglement of Marine Mammals and Other Organisms in Lost or Discarded Fishing Gear and Other Debris.* A report to the Marine Mammal Commission, October 30. 56 pp.

——. 1987. "Legal strategies for reducing persistent plastics in the marine environment."*Marine Pollution Bulletin* 18(6B):357–360.

Bourne, W.R.P. and M.J. Imber. 1982. "Plastic pellets collected by a prion on Gough Island, central South Atlantic Ocean." *Marine Pollution Bulletin*13:20–21.

Caffey R.B. 1987. Testimony before the Subcommittee on Fisheries and Wildlife Conservation and the Environment, Committee on Merchant Marine and Fisheries. U.S. House of Representatives. July 23.

Cahn, B. 1984. "Muck and sand." *Los Angeles Magazine*, August 1984.

Calkins, D.G. 1985. "Stellar Sea Lion entanglement in marine debris," pp. 308–314 *in* R.S. Shomura and H.O. Yoshida eds., *Proceedings of the Workshop on the Fate and Impact of Marine Debris.* November 27–29, 1984. Honolulu, Hawaii. U.S. Department of Commerce. NOAA Technical Memorandum NMFS NOAA-TM-NMFS-SWFC-54.

Carpenter, E.J., S.J. Anderson, G.R. Harvey, H.P. Milkas and B.B. Peck, 1972. "Polystyrene spherules in coastal waters." *Science* 178(4062):749–750.

Carr, A. 1987. "Impact of nondegradable marine debris on the ecology and survival outlook of sea turtles." *Marine Pollution Bulletin* 18(6B):352–356.

——., H.A., A.W. Hulbert and E.H. Amaral. 1985. "Underwater survey of simulated lost demersal and lost commercial gill nets off New England," pp. 438–447 *in* R.S.

Shomura and H.O. Yoshida eds., *Proceedings of the Workshop on the Fate and Impact of Marine Debris.* November 27–29, 1984. Honolulu, Hawaii. U.S. Department of Commerce. NOAA Technical Memorandum NMFS NOAA-TM-NMFS-SWFC-54.

Cawthorn, N.W. 1985. "Entanglement in and ingestion of plastic litter by marine mammals, sharks, and turtles in New Zealand waters." pp. 336–343 *in* R.S. Shomura and H.O. Yoshida eds., *Proceedings of the Workshop on the Fate and Impact of Marine Debris.* November 27–29, 1984. Honolulu, Hawaii. U.S. Department of Commerce. NOAA Technical Memorandum NMFS NOAA-TM-NMFS-SWFC-4.

Center for Environmental Education. In prep. *1987 Texas Coastal Cleanup Report.* Washington D.C.

——. 1987a. "COASTWEEKS." *The Entanglement Network Newsletter.* November 1987. Number 2. p. 2.

——. 1987b. *1986 Texas Coastal Cleanup Report.* Washington, D.C. 52 pp.

——. 1987c. *Plastics in the Ocean: More than a Litter Problem.* Washington, D.C. 128 pp.

Chem Systems, Inc. 1987. *Plastics: A.D. 2000.* The Society of the Plastics Industry, Inc. Washington, D.C. 136 pp.

Coe, J.M. and A.R. Bunn. 1987. *Description and Status of Tasks in the National Oceanic and Atmospheric Administration's Marine Entanglement Research Program for Fiscal Years 1985–1987.* National Marine Fisheries Service, Northwest and Alaska Fisheries Center. NWAFC Processed Report 87–15. 39 pp.

Dahlberg, M.L. and R.H. Day. 1985. "Observations of man-made objects on the surface of the North Pacific Ocean" pp. 198–212 *in* R.S. Shomura and H.O. Yoshida eds., *Proceedings of the Workshop on the Fate and Impact of Marine Debris.* November 27–29, 1984. Honolulu, Hawaii. U.S. Department of Commerce. NOAA Technical Memorandum NMFS NOAA-TM-NMFS-SWFC-54.

Day, R.H. 1980. The Occurrence and Characteristics of Plastic Pollution in Alaska's Marine Birds. M.S. thesis. University of Fairbanks. Fairbanks, Alaska.

——., D.H.S. Wehle and F.C. Coleman. 1985. "Ingestion of plastic pollutants by marine birds," pp. 344–386, *in* R.S. Shomura and H.O. Yoshida eds., *Proceedings of the Workshop on the Fate and Impact of Marine Debris.* November 27–29, 1984. Honolulu, Hawaii. U.S. Department of Commerce. NOAA Technical Memorandum NMFS NOAA-NMFS-TM-NMFS-SWFC-54.

Dow Chemical. N.D. *Waste Reduction Always Pays.* Wrap sheet. Dow Chemical U.S.A. Midland, Michigan.

Environmental Defense Fund. 1985. *To Burn or Not to Burn: the Economic Advantage of Recycling Over Garbage Incineration for New York City.* 80 pp.

Feldkamp, S.D. 1983. *The Effects of Net Entanglement on the Drag and Power Output of Swimming Sea Lions.* Final report to the National Marine Fisheries Service Contract Number: NOAA-82abc-02743.

Fiscus C.H. and H. Kajimura. 1965. *Pelagic Fur Seal Investigations, 1964.* U.S. Fish and Wildlife Service. Special Scientific Report to Fisheries No. 522.

——. and H. Kajimura. 1967. *Pelagic Fur Seal Investigations, 1965.* U.S. Fish and Wildlife Service. Special Scientific Report to Fisheries No. 537.

Florida Department of Natural Resources. *Summary of Manatee Deaths – 1985.* Results of the Manatee Recovery Program. Bureau of Marine Research. St. Petersburg, Florida.

Fowler, C.W. 1987. Interview. National Marine Fisheries Service, Northwest and Alaska Fisheries Center. Seattle, Washington. December 17.

——. 1985. "An evaluation of the role of entanglement in the population dynamics of Northern fur seals on the Pribilof Islands," pp. 291–307 *in* R.S. Shomura and H.O. Yoshida eds., *Proceedings of the Workshop on the Fate and Impact of Marine Debris.* November 27–29, 1984. Honolulu, Hawaii. U.S. Department of Commerce. NOAA Technical Memorandum NMFS NOAA-TM-NMFS-SWFC-54.

——. 1987a. "A review of seal and sea lion entanglement in marine fishing debris." Paper presented at the North Pacific Rim Fishermen's Conference on Marine Debris. October 13–16, 1987. Kailua-Kona, Hawaii.

——. 1987b. "Marine debris and the northern fur seal: a case study." *Marine Pollution Bulletin* 18(6B): 326–335.

——. and T.R. Merrell. 1986. "Victims of plastic technology." *Alaska Fish and Game* 18(2):34–37.

Freeman, L.R. 1987. Testimony before the Subcommittee on Fisheries and Wildlife Conservation and the Environment, Committee on Merchant Marine and Fisheries. U.S. House of Representatives. July 23.

Fry, D.M., S.I. Fefer and L. Sileo. 1987. "Ingestion of plastic debris by Laysan albatrosses and wedge-tailed shearwaters in the Hawaiian Islands." *Marine Pollution Bulletin* 18(6B):339–343.

Gosliner, M. 1985. "Legal authorities pertinent to entanglement by marine debris," pp. 15–33 *in* R.S. Shomura and H.O. Yoshida eds., *Proceedings of the Workshop on the Fate and Impact of Marine Debris. November 27–29, 1984. Honolulu, Hawaii. U.S. Department of Commerce. NOAA Technical Memorandum NMFS NOAA-TM-NMFS-SWFC-54.*

Greco, J.R. 1987. Testimony before the Subcommittee on Fisheries and Wildlife Conservation and the Environment, Committee on Merchant Marine and Fisheries. U.S. House of Representatives. July 23.

Hays, H. and G. Cormons. 1974. "Plastic particles found in tern pellets, on coastal beaches, and at factory sites." *Marine Pollution Bulletin* 5:44–46.

Henderson, J.R. 1984. "Encounters of Hawaiian monk seals with fishing gear at Lisianski Island, 1982." *Marine Fisheries Review* 46(3):59–61.

——. 1985. "A review of Hawaiian monk seal entanglements in marine debris," pp. 326–335 *in* R.S. Shomura and H.O. Yoshida eds., *Proceedings of the Workshop on the Fate and Impact of Marine Debris.* November 27–29, 1984. Honolulu, Hawaii. U.S. Department of Commerce. NOAA Technical Memorandum NMFS NOAA-TM-NMFS-SWFC-54.

——., S.L. Austin and M.B. Pillos. 1987. Summary of Webbing and Net Fragments Found on Northwestern Hawaiian Island Beaches, 1982–1986. National Marine Fisheries Service, Southwest Fisheries Center Administrative Rep. H-87–11. 15 pp.

High, W.L. 1976. "Escape of Dungeness crabs from pots." *Marine Fisheries Review* 38(4):19–23.

——. 1985. "Some consequences of lost fishing gear," pp. 430–437 *in* R.S. Shomura and H.O. Yoshida eds., *Proceedings of the Workshop on the Fate and Impact of Marine Debris.* November 27–29, 1984. Honolulu, Hawaii. U.S. Department of Commerce. NOAA Technical Memorandum NMFS NOAA TM NMFS SWFC 54.

Horsman, P.V. 1985. "Garbage kills." *BBC Wildlife*:391–393. (August 1985).

Jones, L.L. and R.C. Ferroro. 1985. "Observations of net debris and associated entanglements in the North Pacific Ocean and Bering Sea, 1978–84," pp. 183–196 *in* R.S. Shomura and H.O. Yoshida eds., *Proceedings of the Workshop on the Fate and Impact of Marine Debris.* November 27–29, 1984. Honolulu, Hawaii. U.S. Department of Commerce. NOAA Technical Memorandum NMFS NOAA-TM-NMFS-SWFC-54.

——., R.J. Tarpley and S. Fernandez. 1986. "Cetacean strandings along the Texas coast, U.S.A." Paper presented at the 11th International Conference on Marine Mammals, April 2–6 1986. Guaymas, Mexico.

Kenyon, K.W. and E. Kridler. 1969. "Laysan albatross swallow indigestible matter." *Auk* 86:339–343.

Kime, J.W. 1986. Testimony before the Subcommittee on Coast Guard and Navigation, Committee on Merchant Marine and Fisheries. U.S. House of Representatives. August 12.

King, W.B. 1984. "Incidental mortality of seabirds in gillnets in the North Pacific," pp. 709–715 *in* J.P. Croxall, P.G.H. Evans and R.W. Schreiber eds., *Status and Conservation of the World's Seabirds.* International Council for Bird Preservation. ICBP Technical Publication No. 2

Martin, A.R. and M.R. Clarke. "The diet of sperm whales (*Physeter macrocephalus*) captured between Iceland and Greenland." *Journal of the Marine Biological Association of the United Kingdom* 66:779–790.

Mate, B.R. 1985. "Incidents of marine mammals encounters with debris and active fishing gear," pp. 453–457 *in* R.S. Shomura and H.O. Yoshida eds., *Proceedings of the Workshop on the Fate and Impact of Marine Debris.* November 27–29, 1984. Honolulu, Hawaii. U.S. Department of Commerce. NOAA Technical Memorandum NMFS NOAA-TM-NMFS-SWFC-54.

Merrell, T.R. Jr. 1985. "Fish nets and other plastic litter on Alaska beaches," pp. 160–182 *in* R.S. Shomura and H.O. Yoshida eds., *Proceedings of the Workshop on the Fate and Impact of Marine Debris.* November 27–29, 1984. Honolulu, Hawaii. U.S. Department of Commerce. NOAA Technical Memorandum NMFS NOAA-TM-NMFS-SWFC-54.

National Academy of Sciences. 1975. "Marine litter," pp. 405–433 in *Assessing Potential Ocean Pollutants.* A report of the Study Panel on Assessing Potential Ocean Pollutants to the Ocean Affairs Board. Commission on Natural Resources, National Research Council, National Academy of Sciences. Washington, D.C.

O'Hara, K.J., Atkins, N. and S. Iudicello. 1987. *Marine Wildlife Entanglement in North America.* Center for Environmental Education. Washington, D.C. 219 pp.

Paul, T. 1984. "A plague of plastics." *Alaska Fish and Game* 16(3):2–5.

Possert, E. Interview. U.S. Fish and Wildlife Service. Jacksonville, Florida. April 8, 1986.

Ramirez, G.D. 1986. *Rescue of Entangled South American Sea Lions (*Otaria flavescens*).* Center for Environmental Education. Washington, D.C. 16 pp.

Sadove, S. 1980. "Marine turtles." *SEAN Bulletin* 6(7):15.

Scordino, J. 1985. "Studies on fur seal entanglement, 1981–1984, St. Paul Island, Alaska," pp. 278–290 *in* R.S. Shomura and H.O. Yoshida eds., *Proceedings of the Workshop on the Fate and Impact of Marine Debris.* November 27–29, 1984. Honolulu, Hawaii. U.S. Department of Commerce. NOAA Technical Memorandum NMFS NOAA-TM-NMFS-SWFC-54.

Shaughnessy, P.D. 1980. "Entanglement of Cape fur seals with man-made objects." *Marine Pollution Bulletin* 11:332–336.

Sievert, P. Interview. U.S. Fish and Wildlife Service. National Wildlife Health Center. Madison, Wisconsin. January 14, 1987.

Smolowitz, R.J. 1978a. "Trap design and ghost fishing: An overview." *Marine Fisheries Review* 40(5–6)L2–8.

Society of the Plastics Industry. 1986. *Facts and Figures of the U.S. Plastics Industry.* Washington, D.C. 134 pp.

Suto, B. Interview. Suncoast Seabird Sanctuary. Indian Beach, Florida. November 25, 1986.

Stewart, B.S. and P.K. Yochem. 1985. "Entanglement of pinnipeds in net and line fragments and other debris in the Southern California Bight," pp. 315–325 *in* R.S. Shomura and H.O. Yoshida eds., *Proceedings of the Workshop on the Fate and Impact of Marine Debris.* November 27–29, 1984. Honolulu, Hawaii. U.S. Department of Commerce. NOAA Technical Memorandum NMFS NOAA-TM-NMFS-SWFC-54.

——. and ——. 1987. "Entanglement of pinnipeds in synthetic debris and fishing net and line fragments at San Nicholas and San Miquel Islands, California, 1978–1986." *Marine Pollution Bulletin* 18(6B):336–339.

Stromberg, E. 1987. Testimony before the National Ocean Policy Study and Senate Committee on Commerce, Science, and Transportation. U.S. Senate. July 29.

Swanson, R.L., H.M. Stanford, J.S. O'Connor,*et al.* 1978. "June 1976 pollution of Long Island beaches." *Journal of Environmental Engineering Division, ASCE* 104(EE6), Processed Paper 14238 December 1978:1067–1085.

U.S. Department of Commerce, National Oceanic and Atmospheric Administration, National Marine Pollution Program Office. 1985. *National Marine Pollution Program Plan—Federal Plan for Ocean Pollution Research, Development, and Monitoring, Fiscal Years 1985–1989.* Rockville, Maryland. 350 pp.

——, National Oceanic and Atmospheric Administration, National Marine Fisheries Service. 1987. *Fisheries of the United States, 1986.* Washington, D.C. 119 pp.

Winston, J.E. 1982. "Drift plastic—an expanding niche for a marine invertebrate?" *Marine Pollution Bulletin* 13(10):348–351.

Kathryn O'Hara is a marine biologist with the Center for Environmental Education in Washington, D.C. The Center is a conservation organization dedicated to protecting marine wildlife and their habitats.

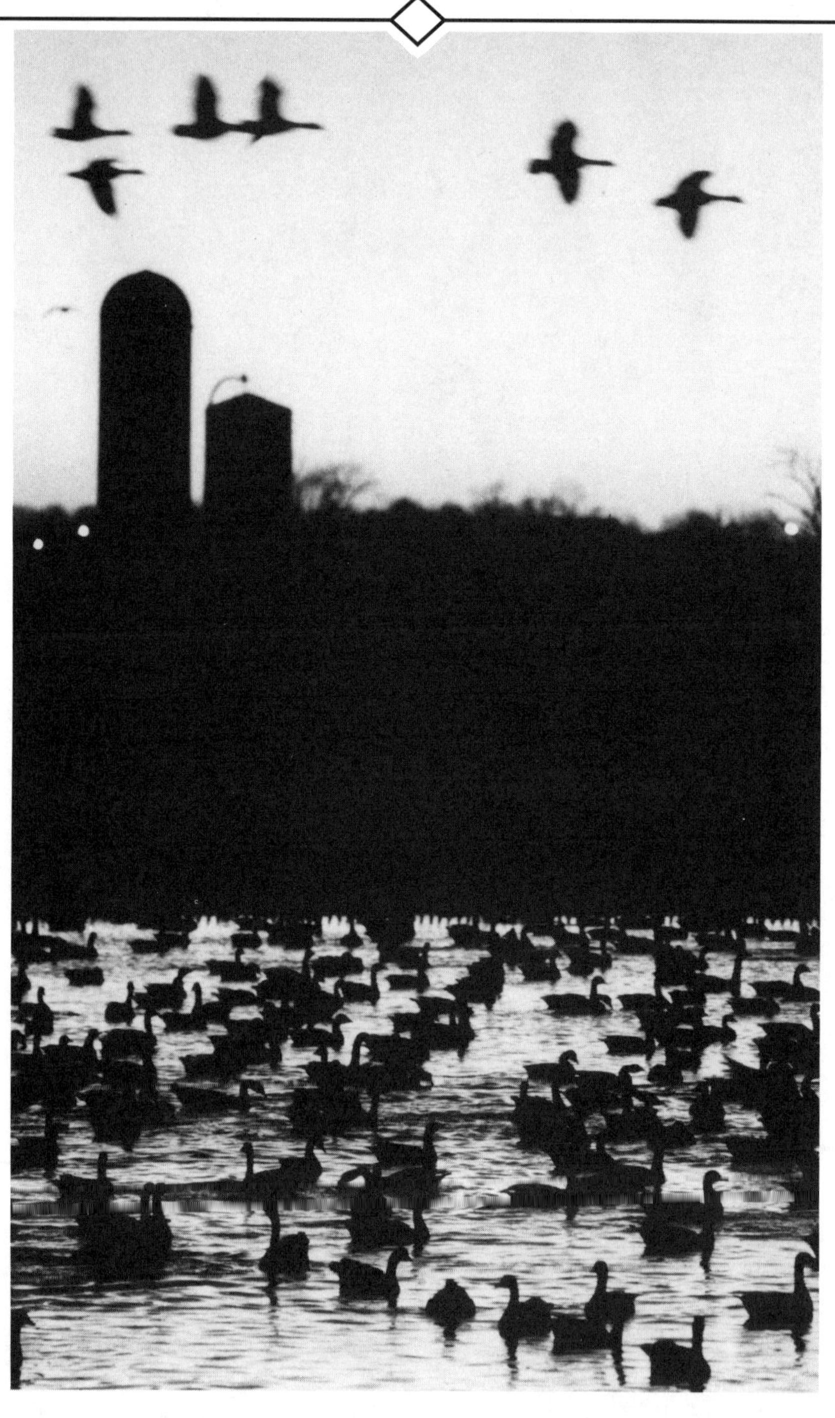

Wildlife, said Aldo Leopold, "rides on the farmer's coattails." The 1985 Farm Act has far-reaching soil and wildlife conservation provisions. *Michael Johnson/SCS*

The 1985 Farm Act and Its Implications for Wildlife

Alfred Berner

INTRODUCTION

The Food Security Act of 1985 (P.L. 99–198), better known as the 1985 Farm Act, has added a new dimension to farm-subsidy programs that began more than half a century ago. For the first time in the 54-year history of federal farm legislation, a farmer may be denied federal farm benefits for improperly managing certain noncropland and cropland acres. In addition, the 10- to 15-year Conservation Reserve Program, which pays farmers to retire farmland to improve soil and water resources was created.

If the act is implemented as Congress intended, this new approach to federal farm programs will significantly reduce soil erosion, improve water quality, and increase the diversity and abundance of wildlife. Understanding the special importance of the Farm Act for wildlife requires some knowledge of past farm programs and their impacts on this natural resource.

Impacts of Agriculture and Farm Programs on Wildlife

Over the last half century, sweeping land-use changes caused by agriculture have significantly affected a wide array of wildlife species

Table 1
Population Changes in Selected Grassland Bird Species in Illinois from 1957 to 1958 and 1978.

Species	Percent change, 1957–1958 to 1983
Upland sandpiper	-92
Bobolink	-97
Meadowlarks (two species)	-84
Dickcissal	-96
Grasshopper sparrow	-96
Savannah sparrow	-98
Henslow's sparrow	-94

Source: Graber and Graber 1983.

(U.S. Department of Agriculture 1987a). The impacts have varied from favorable to detrimental, depending on the species in question (Allen 1956, Graber and Graber 1963, 1983, Berner 1978, 1984b, 1987). During the last 25 years, however, the impacts on many species have been negative rather than favorable (Farris and Cole 1981, Edwards *et al.* 1982, Graber and Graber 1983, Warner *et al.* 1984, Warner and Etter 1986). For example, researchers in Illinois documented dramatic declines (greater than 90 percent) in several species of grassland birds (see Table 1). A survey of 14 midwestern states by Farris and Cole (1981) found that between 1958 and 1978 pheasants had declined an average of 66 percent, cottontail rabbits 55 percent, and bobwhite quail 48 percent.

Habitat changes caused by the specialization and intensification of agriculture are responsible for severe population declines. Critically needed grassland, wetland, and brushland habitats are still being converted to produce already abundant row crops and grains. Enlargement of fields to grow monoculture crops reduces the diversity of habitats within the normal home range of many species of wildlife. Increased use of agricultural pesticides degrades habitat by reducing plant and insect diversity.

Federal commodity[1] programs, in particular, have contributed much to habitat decline. Lands retired under some federal commodity programs have provided varying amounts of good wildlife habitat. Past programs that retired land under multiyear contracts or required the planting of grass or legume cover on retired acreage or both created significant amounts of quality nesting cover. However, during the last 25 years, multiyear retirement programs were discontinued in favor of

1. A commodity crop is considered any crop planted and produced by annual tilling of the soil, including tilling by one-trip planters (for example, corn, oats, wheat, and milo) and sugarcane.

annual programs.[2] Some regulation of annual programs encouraged the recruitment of land to produce more commodity crops, which caused the destruction of critical habitats (for example, wetlands and prairie grasslands). Other regulations permitted the development of significant amounts of unsafe habitat by allowing late-seeding and requiring destruction (by mowing, disking, or plowing) of cover on retired acres during the nesting season, which destroyed much nesting and brooding wildlife.

Past Farm Acts – A Historical Perspective

In the 54-year history of federal farm programs, some form of land retirement occurred in all but 15 years (1943 to 55 and 1980 to 81). In addition, some form of subsidy was paid in all but 8 years (1948–55). Despite overproduction in most years since 1934, the federal government has supported the expansion of the cropland base and increased yields through financial assistance programs (such as the Agricultural Conservation Program [ACP]), federal agencies (such as the Bureau of Reclamation), and the Agriculture Extension System.

The combination of the Great Depression and the economic conditions in the Dust Bowl prompted Congress in 1934 to legislate the nation's first cropland retirement program for the purpose of stabilizing the farm economy and creating farm markets (Edwards 1984). The Cropland Adjustment Act of 1934 stimulated the retirement of between 17 and 20 million acres of cropland annually during its two-year existence (see Figure 1). Although dramatic soil erosion was evident, hence the term "Dust Bowl," the Department of Agriculture did not require the seeding of cover crops on the retired acres.

The lack of improvement in the farm economy and continued extensive soil loss led to passage of the Soil and Water Conservation Act of 1935 and the Soil Conservation and Domestic Allotment Act of 1936. Congressional intent for the Soil and Water Conservation Act was so stated: "The wastage of soil and moisture resources on farmlands, grazing lands, and forestland of the nation, resulting from soil erosion, is a menace to the national welfare and it is . . . the policy of Congress to provide permanently for the control and prevention of soil erosion" (Sampson 1981). The Soil Conservation Service was created within the Department of Agriculture to develop and execute a continuing program of soil and water conservation.

In passing the Soil Conservation and Domestic Allotment Act, Congress sought to provide ways to help farmers adjust to the new

2. Assistance to farmers under the annual programs have included payments for retiring cropland (paid diversion), payments for growing certain crops, low-interest loans using stored crops as collateral, crop disaster insurance, and deficiency payments, which paid the difference between a target price and the prevailing market price.

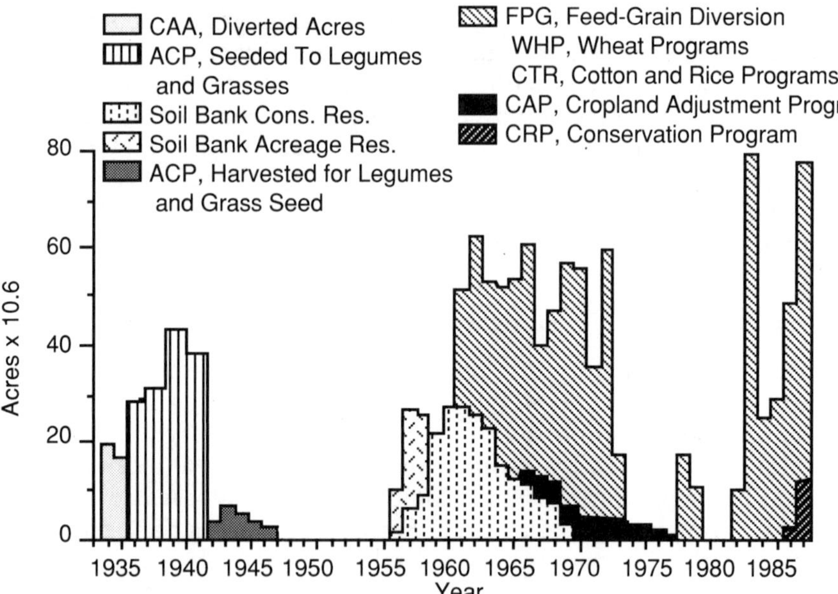

Figure 1. Distribution and comparative magnitude of the acres in the U.S. of the various USDA cropland retirement programs, 1934-87.

economic realities brought about by drought, the Depression, and the increasing mechanization of farming. The act created the Agricultural Stabilization and Conservation Service (ASCS) to administer all farmer assistance programs (Sampson 1981). The basic roles of the Soil Conservation Service and the Agricultural Stabilization and Conservation Service have not changed substantially since the agencies were created.

The first responsibility of the Agricultural Stabilization and Conservation Service was to implement the Agricultural Conservation Program of 1936, which, like the Cropland Adjustment Act, was aimed at strengthening the rural economy through paid cropland retirement. Unlike the Cropland Adjustment Act, however, the Agricultural Conservation Program also addressed soil protection needs by paying farmers to grow soil-conserving crops (for example, grass, legumes, or grass-legume mixtures) instead of soil depleting crops (for example, corn, oats, and wheat).

From 1936 through 1942, about 36 million acres were retired annually and seeded with prescribed cover crops. During this seven-year period, more than 250 million acres of cropland were affected by the annual ACP contracts (see Figure 1). Wildlife species that required undisturbed grasslands during part of their reproductive cycle found these conditions favorable. In the midwestern states, populations of the ring-necked pheasant, which had been introduced only about 20 years earlier, reached record highs (Edwards 1984).

Increased demand for agricultural commodities due to post-World War II reconstruction, and the Korean conflict eliminated the need for paid cropland retirement programs from 1943 to 1956. By 1956, however, overproduction and reduced farm income prompted Congress to create yet another cropland retirement program. The Soil Bank program differed from its predecessors by providing not only an annual land retirement option, the Acreage Reserve, but also a multiyear retirement feature called the Conservation Reserve with three-, five-, or ten-year contract options (see Table 2 and Figure 1).

In the early 1960s, the Soil Bank Program was phased out in favor of two annual cropland-retirement programs: the Emergency Feed Grain Program of 1961 and the Wheat Program of 1962. A shift to annual programs was considered necessary because the acreage payments provided under the Conservation Reserve were too low to induce participation by farmers in the more productive agricultural areas; hence, it was difficult for the Department of Agriculture to control overproduction to the degree desired. Also, it was believed by some that multiyear programs reduced the opportunity to respond quickly to changing market conditions. The history of land retirement programs, however, has not borne out the imperative for this degree of flexibility: cropland has been retired under an annual commodity program in 24 of the last 32 years (see Figure 1 and Table 2).

In 1966, a new program, the Cropland Adjustment Program, was developed to retire cropland under 10-year contracts. Unfortunately, the program was undermined by the more financially lucrative annual feed grain and wheat programs that still were operative.

Since 1961, federal commodity programs have primarily rewarded farmers for the annual retirement of cropland from production (see Figure 1). Farmers enrolled in these programs received governments benefits such as direct land rental payments, crop insurance, low interest loans, crop storage payments, and crop deficiency payments (see Table 3).

Because of the annual nature of these programs and the wide variety of agricultural management practices across the nation, the Agricultural Stabilization and Conservation Service has provided little guidance on appropriate management of retired lands. The option of adopting more restrictive guidelines within these federal frameworks is left to state and county committees composed entirely of local farmers eligible to participate in the programs. This system of local self-regulation has resulted in environmentally questionable management practices. For example, committees may allow the late seeding of cover crops or require no cover crop. Many committees require the early destruction of the cover (between June 1 and July 15) and allow the plowing of established cover in the fall. Without vegetative cover, the soil is exposed to erosion for 9 to 12 months. Also, the required

Table 2
Acres of Cropland (in Millions) Retired in the U.S. under Various USDA Farm Programs[a] from 1956 to 1987

	Soil Bank							
Year	AR	CR	FGP	WHP	CTR	CAP	CRP	Total
1956	12.2	1.4						13.6
1957	21.4	6.4						27.8
1958	17.2	9.9						27.1
1959		22.5						22.5
1960		28.7						28.7
1961		28.5	25.2					53.7
1962		25.8	28.2	10.7				64.7
1963		24.3	24.5	7.2				56
1964		17.4	32.5	5.1				55
1965		14	34.7	7.2				55.9
1966		13.3	34.7	8.2	4.6	2.0		62.8
1967		11	20.3		4.9	4		40.2
1968		9.2	32.4		3.3	4		48.9
1969		3.4	39.1	11.1		3.9		57.5
1970		0.1	37.4	15.7		3.8		57
1971		<0.1	18.2	13.5	2.1	3.4		37.2
1972		<0.1	36.6	20.1	2.0	2.8		61.5
1973			9.4	7.4		2.8		19.6
1974						2.7		2.7
1975						2.4		2.4
1976						2.1		2.1
1977						1.0		1.0
1978			8.3	9.6	0.3			18.2
1979			4.8	8.2				13
1980								
1981							0.0	8.8
1982			3.3	5.8	2			11.1
1983			39.3	30	8.6			77.9
1984			5.1	18.6	3.3			27
1985			7.1	18.8	4.8			30.7
1986[b]			19.3	20.9	4.9		2	47.1
1987[b]			29.5	20.5	5		14	69

Source: U.S. Department of Agriculture 1970, 1973, 1976, 1986.

[a] Acreage Reserve (AR); Conservation Reserve (CR); Emergency Feed Grain Program (FGP); Wheat Program (WHP); Cotton and Rice (CTR); Cropland Adjustment Program (CAP); Conservation Reserve Program (CRP).

[b] Acreages for 1986 Conservation Reserve Program are preliminary estimates.

untimely destruction of seeded cover during the nesting season has proven detrimental to wildlife (Montag 1974, Berner 1973, 1984a, 1984b, 1987).

Since 1956, some land has been retired under a commodity program every year except 1980 and 1981 (see Figure 1). Even in those two years, however, some farmers were being subsidized (with deficiency payments) without being required to retire any land from production. During this 32-year period (1956 to 1987), low crop prices precipitated by overproduction, which in turn lowers farm income,

Table 3
U.S. Department of Agriculture Benefits Provided to Participating Farmers under the Food Security Act of 1985.

Commodity price support payments
Production adjustment payments
Farm storage facility loans
Disaster payments
Payments for storage of CCC grain
Federal crop insurance
FmHA loans

Source: Robinson 1987.

continues to be the norm. The desire of Congress to increase farm income and stabilize the farm economy has been the principal impetus for farm subsidy programs. Yet, while administering various costly land retirement programs (see Table 1) aimed at reducing production, the Department of Agriculture has implemented other Congressionally established programs that promoted the development and planting of additional cropland acreage and increasing yields (for example, financial and technical assistance for wetland drainage and woodland clearing through the Agriculture Conservation Programs and P.L. 83–566, and education and crop research through the Agricultural Extension Program). Moreover, liberal ASCS regulations permit farmers to add most of these newly developed cropland acres to their commodity crop base acreage,[3] adding to the dilemma of overproduction and allowing increased farm program benefits to such farmers.

Other federal agencies, such as the Bureau of Reclamation and the Army Corps of Engineers, also aid farmers in developing additional cropland with little concern for water quality, wildlife habitat, and sound soil conservation. Such actions occur while federal and state wildlife agencies simultaneously attempt to preserve critical habitat, particularly wetlands, through land acquisition and other means. Likewise, the technical assistance arm of the Department of Agriculture—Soil Conservation Service—attempts to reduce soil erosion through the development and implementation of conservation plans on individual farms, while commodity programs continue to stimulate production on marginal land and converted wetlands.

Despite the Soil Conservation Service's efforts, and expenditures of more than $18 billion through various ASCS conservation programs since 1936, evaluations by both the Government Accounting Office

3. Base acreages are the official record of the amount of each commodity grown on a farm in past years. This record determines the amount of land that must be retired to qualify the farmer for the various program benefits. The methods for calculating the various crop base acreages can be found in the Food Security Act of 1985 under Title X, Section 1031.

(U.S. Government Accounting Office 1983) and the National Wildlife Federation indicate that soil and wildlife conservationists are losing the battle.

The obvious conflicts between and within various federal agencies and programs, the deteriorating economic and environmental conditions on our nation's farms since the late 1970s, and the large and costly Payment-in-Kind land retirement program of 1983 have all heightened public awareness of the need for reform (Berner 1984b). In a concerted effort to influence the 1985 Farm Act, fish and wildlife conservation and environmental organizations banded together with farmland conservation groups to include strong resource conservation provisions in the bill. Their combined effort resulted in passage of the strongest conservation provisions ever enacted in farm legislation. Unfortunately, the act also perpetuates annual cropland retirement programs and other policies that will continue to have significant detrimental impacts on wildlife and other natural resources.

PERTINENT PROVISIONS OF THE 1985 FARM ACT

Overview

Various provisions of the Food Security Act of 1985 affect the management of hundreds of millions of acres of farmlands (see Table 4). Two conservation provisions attempt to discourage farmers from converting wetlands and uncultivated, highly erodible lands to cropland for commodity crop production. The "conservation compliance" provision requires the farmers to implement Soil Conservation Service-approved conservation plans on highly erodible croplands by 1990. Another provision provides for the Conservation Reserve Program, which pays farmers to remove highly erodible lands from crop production for up to 15 years and plant them with grasses, trees or other permanent vegetative cover. Other sections authorize Department of Agriculture assistance in developing plans and implementing practices to protect water resources, conserve soil and water, promote dryland farming, and provide loans for managing softwood timber on marginal lands.

Acreage Reduction Programs, provisions that pay farmers to annually idle land to reduce production of certain commodity crops, are less discussed by conservationists, but have as great an impact on natural resources. Also, the Farm Act authorizes the Farmers Home Administration (FmHA) to grant or sell conservation easements to government or private nonprofit organizations on lands acquired by the agency through loan default or liquidations. Also, conservation easements on

Table 4
Location of Various Provisions in the Food Security Act of 1985 that Will Have an Impact on Wildlife Habitat and Abundance.

	General Commodity Provisions
Title X	
Subtitle A	
Section 1010	Multiyear set-aside
Section 1011	Supplemental set-aside and acreage limitation authority
Section 1015	Special grazing and haying program
Subtitle B	Uniform Base Acreage and Yield Provisions
Section 1031	Acreage base and program yield system for the wheat, feed grains, upland cotton, and rice programs
Title XII	Conservation
Subtitle A	Definitions
Subtitle B	Highly Erodible Land Conservation
Section 1211	Program ineligibility
Section 1212	Exemptions
Sectin 1213	Soil survey
Subtitle C	Wetland Conservation
Section 1221	Program ineligibility
Section 1222	Exemptions
Section 1223	Consultation with the Secretary of the Interior
Subtitle D	Conservation Reserve
Section 1231	Conservation Reserve
Section 1232	Duties of owners and operators
Section 1233	Duties of Secretary
Section 1234	Payments
Section 1235	Contracts
Section 1236	Base history
Subtitle E	Administration
Section 1241	Use of Commodity Credit Corporation
Section 1242	Use of other agencies
Section 1243	Administration
Section 1244	Regulations
Subtitle F	Other Conservation Provisions
Section 1251	Technical assistance for water resources
Section 1252	Soil and water resources conservation
Section 1253	Dryland farming
Section 1254	Softwood timber
Title XIII	Credit
Section 1314	Disposition and leasing of farmland
Section 1318	Farm debt restructure and conservation set-aside
Title XVII	Agriculture Stabilization and Conservation Committees
Subtitle B	Conservation committees
Section 1711	Local committees
Section 1712	County committees

critical habitats can be traded by landowners in return for debt reduction. These provisions restricting incompatible uses (for example, draining wetlands) may preserve essential wildlife habitats in some regions.

The wildlife benefits of the act are contingent on how effectively its provisions discourage the conversion of wetland, grassland, and forest to cropland, and how the cover on the lands retired under the Conservation Reserve Program and the Acreage Reduction Programs is managed. Of course, success in meeting these objectives depends on how well the programs are administered by the Agricultural Stabilization and Conservation Service.

Sodbuster, Swampbuster, and Conservation Compliance

The most innovative provisions of the Farm Act's conservation title attempt to discourage farmers from converting grasslands and forests on highly erodible land (sodbuster), and wetlands (swampbuster), to the production of commodity crops. Under conservation compliance, farmers are also encouraged to control erosion on highly erodible lands already in crop production.

Under swampbuster, farmers who drain wetlands for commodity crop production are ineligible for all Department of Agriculture benefits provided in the 1985 Farm Act (see Table 3). Benefits are lost not only on the converted land but on all the lands that the farmer wants to enter into the program. Basically, this provision states that, as of December 23, 1985, the public will no longer subsidize the conversion of wetlands to croplands used to grow commodity crops. Similarly, under the sodbuster provision, farmers who till previously uncultivated land for commodity crop production stand to lose all commodity benefits unless they are acting in accordance with an Soil Conservation Service-approved conservation plan. Unfortunately, the law will not stop the conversion of these lands to other uses, such as housing, nor will it affect the commodity croplands of farmers not participating in federal farm programs.

The act's conservation provisions have significant potential for preserving important wildlife habitats such as wetlands, native grasslands, and woodlands. As much as 146 million acres of grasslands (pasture and range), and 74 million acres of forests (see Figure 2 and Table 5) (U.S. Department of Agriculture 1987a), and 5.1 million acres of wetlands (see Table 6) (U.S. Department of Agriculture 1987b) that have a potential of being converted to cropland would be protected under sodbuster and swampbuster. Highly erodible land, defined as land with an Erosion Index (EI)[4] of 8 or greater, affects an estimated 118

4. Erosion Index (EI) is a numerical rating that expresses potential erodibility of a soil, by wind or water, in relation to the soil tolerance value without consideration of

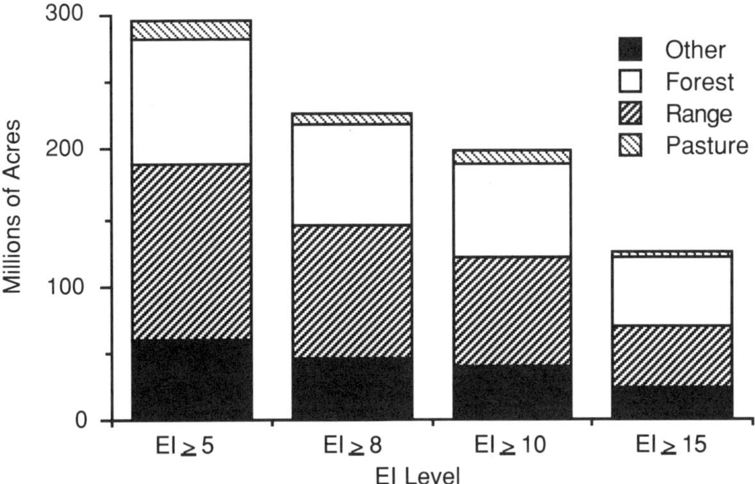

Figure 2. Comparative impact of various erosion potential classes on acres available in four categories of noncropland with low to high potential of conversion to cropland in the U.S. Lands with zero potential for conversion were excluded (Department of Agriculture 1987a).

million acres of cropland that will be subject to conservation compliance regulations. Regulations that once required reducing soil loss to "T,"[5] now require that highly erodible croplands be farmed in accordance with an approved Soil Conservation Service management plan that "substantially" reduces soil loss by the year 1995 (U.S. Department of Agriculture 1987a); this still means that lands may be eroding at rates in excess of three times the tolerable level. Under the original regulations, substantial acreage would have had to be converted to grasslands or trees to assure compliance. Presently, however, these acres will still be cropped using conservation tillage (which may enhance winter food availability for wildlife), and various other soil conservation practices, such as terracing and strip cropping.

Conservation Reserve Program

The Conservation Reserve Program is the portion of the Farm Act most discussed and heralded by conservationists and perhaps most benefi-

---

applied conservation practices or management. The higher the value, the greater the potential for erosion. These numbers are calculated using the Wind Erosion Equation or the Universal Soil Loss Equation.

5. "T" is defined as the average annual loss, in tons/acre, that a particular soil can tolerate and still permit economical and indefinite crop production. This allowable loss can vary from less than one ton to about seven tons/acre depending on the crop grown and the rate of organic replacement.

Table 5
Acreages of Various Land-Use Types by Varying Levels of Erosion Potential in the United States (in Millions). Data for Noncroplands Exclude Those with Zero Potential of Conversion to Cropland.

		Erosion potential			
Land-use type	Total	>5	>8	>10	>15
Pasture	179	63	47	41	28
Range	354	130	99	80	45
Forest	282	95	74	65	48
Other	27	10	7	6	4
Subtotal	842	298	227	192	125
Cropland	444	188	118	89	49
TOTAL	1286	486	345	281	174

Source: U.S. Department of Agriculture 1987a.

Table 6
Acres of wetlands in the United States. Forty-eight contiguous states that have high or medium potential for conversion to cropland.

State	Acres	State	Acres
Alabama	400,900	Nebraska	156,300
Arizona	23,500	Nevada	6,900
Arkansas	121,500	New Hampshire	1,600
California	102,400	New Jersey	8,000
Colorado	22,400	New Mexico	2,700
Connecticut	12,000	New York	170,800
Delaware	83,700	North Carolina	278,100
Florida	535,400	North Dakota	298,200
Georgia	173,100	Ohio	169,300
Idaho	57,100	Oklahoma	22,500
Illinois	103,400	Oregon	117,500
Indiana	45,000	Pennsylvania	90,800
Iowa	27,300	Rhode Island	400
Kansas	1,200	South Carolina	179,000
Kentucky	74,600	South Dakota	98,000
Louisiana	144,300	Tennessee	157,700
Maine	18,100	Texas	101,200
Maryland	68,200	Utah	11,100
Massachusetts	12,100	Vermont	3,100
Michigan	224,600	Virginia	51,100
Minnesota	393,900	Washington	99,500
Mississippi	279,200	West Virginia	5,300
Missouri	27,300	Wisconsin	122,600
Montana	68,500	Wyoming	12,400
TOTAL			5,183,800

Source: U.S. Department of Agriculture 1987b.

cial to wildlife. This program requires the Secretary of Agriculture to contract with farmers and ranchers to retire between 40 and 45 million acres of highly erodible cropland by 1990.[6] Under contracts, the landowners receive annual rental payments established through a bidding process. Participating farm owners and operators must establish approved vegetative cover (native grasses, trees) on the retired lands, receiving 50 percent of the planting costs from the U.S. Department of Agriculture. The cover must be maintained for the life of the contract. By law, the length of contracts cannot be less than 10 or more than 15 years; in implementing the law, the Secretary of Agriculture has selected the minimum, 10-year option. This 10-year cover maintenance provision has the potential of temporarily replacing a significant portion of grass and woodlands lost over the last 25 years.

Miscellaneous Conservation Provisions

Other provisions provide for the development of plans and technical assistance for protection of water resources, conservation of soil and water resources, and promotion of energy and water conservation through dryland farming.[7] Development of plans for improved soil and water conservation can have wide-ranging benefits. Some of the provisions in this section, however, may not be entirely positive. For example, one section states that planning and technical services provided to property owners, state and local governments, and other agencies will "enable property owners to reduce their vulnerability to flood hazards that may also affect water resources." This might allow continued financial assistance to those who farm floodplains that in many cases are still wetlands.

Promotion of energy and water conservation through dryland farming may lead to a reduction in the amount of irrigated land and to increased black summer fallow (no cover) or no-till practices on the lands. The type of habitat created or eliminated by dryland farming will dictate the degree of impact on wildlife abundance and diversity. The intent and potential effects of these sections on soil, water, and wildlife resources should be closely scrutinized by conservationists.

The act also authorizes re-amortizing loans using future revenues from softwood timber crops on marginal land previously used as cropland or pasture. Under this provision, up to 50,000 acres of monotypic softwood timber may be planted on marginal farmlands.

6. As of April 1988, 23 million acres had been accepted into the Conservation Reserve Program. An additional 4.5 million acres were bid into the reserve on the sixth, and most recent, signup; final figures are not available on the portion that will be accepted into the program.

7. Dryland farming entails the use of moisture-conserving farm practices to produce crops in arid regions without irrigation.

Planting of pine plantations usually has limited positive benefits for wildlife because the newly forested stands lack the vegetative diversity required by most wildlife species.

Potential Effects of the Conservation Provisions on Wildlife

The policy changes discussed above could have significant wildlife benefits. Sodbuster and swampbuster could, potentially, prevent conversion of more than 225 million acres of grasslands, forests, and wetlands to cropland. Moreover, by 1990 the 40 to 45 million acres of highly erodible croplands retired under the Conservation Reserve Program, representing up to 12 percent of our nation's cropland, will have been planted with trees or grasslands and should remain undisturbed for a period of 10 years. Implementation of the conservation compliance provision could potentially affect the management practices on more than 118 million acres of highly erodible cropland. The noncroplands—native grasslands, wetlands, and woodlands—preserved from conversion will aid in maintaining habitat diversity and associated wildlife populations.

If these programs are effectively implemented, more than 25 percent of our nation's farmland presently in row crops such as corn and soybeans, or closely sown grain crops such as wheat or oats, will be converted back to grassland, wetlands, and trees, or farmed to substantially reduce soil erosion. However, because of the varying erodibility of soil, the land affected by the conservation provisions is not evenly distributed across the country (see Figure 3). Therefore, the effects on habitat, and ultimately on wildlife diversity and abundance, will vary greatly among states; in some cases there will be notable differences within a single county.

Precisely how wildlife populations will respond to these massive land-use changes remains to be seen. However, knowledge of the effect of past land-use changes on various wildlife populations supports some general conclusions.

Not all wildlife species will be favorably affected by the projected land-use changes. Those species that have thrived in light cover provided by row crops will be negatively affected. In some cases, the replacement of the few cropped acres with a cover type (such as grass or trees) already in adequate abundance in the area may eliminate a needed food source (for example, prairie chickens in Nebraska's Sandhills, bobwhite quail in southern Iowa). In general, however, the array of wildlife species and their abundance will increase substantially. Wildlife species favorably affected will be those whose habitat requirements include undisturbed grassland and wetland areas or trees and shrubs. These same species have been most negatively affected by the conversion of these cover types to cropland over the last 25 years.

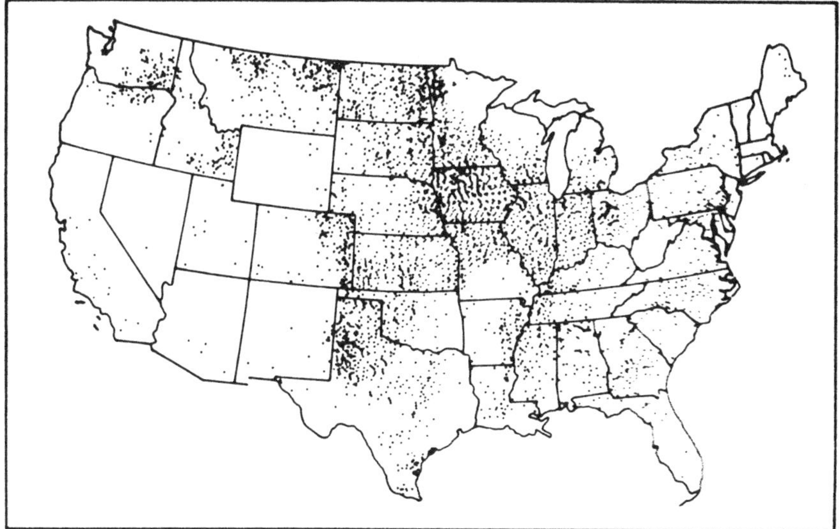

Figure 3. Cropland where sheet and rill erosion or erosion is greater than "T." (See footnote and text.) Each dot represents 50,000 acres. (Taken from Department of Agriculture 1987d, pp 4–7.)

In the case of birds, studies indicate that the diversity of breeding bird species in various grassland types and marshes are two to five times greater than in row crops and up to three times greater than in small grain crops such as wheat or oats (see Table 7) (Good and Dambach 1943, Graber and Graber 1963, Wiens and Dyer 1975).[8] Although the array of species differs, the total number of bird species occurring in small plantings (less than three acres) of various tree and/or shrub species is similar to that found in grasslands. The diversity of bird species in stands of large trees with dense undergrowth is estimated to be 10 times greater than that found in grain crop cover (Graber and Graber 1963, Emmerich and Bohs 1982, Berner and Cooper 1981).

In addition to the diversity of species, breeding bird densities also vary with cover type.[9] Grassland cover similar to that expected to be planted on Conservation Reserve Program (CRP) acres averages more than seven times the breeding bird densities found in row crops and five times that found in small grain crops (see Table 7). Marshes dominated by grasses, sedges, and cattails have breeding densities more than 13 times greater than grain crop fields. In small plantings (less than three acres) of various tree and/or shrub species, breeding

8. Diversity of breeding birds is defined as the average number of breeding species per unit area of a given cover type (for example, species/100 acres of grassland).

9. Breeding bird density is defined as the number of breeding birds per acre of a particular habitat type.

Table 7
Mean Number of Breeding Birds and Species per 100 Acres in Various Farmland Habitats in Illinois, 1957–1958. (Data Summarized from Graber and Graber 1963).

Cover type	Breeding Birds		All Species
	Species	per 100 acres	
Corn	3	n.d.	66
Soybean	3	n.d.	53
Fallow (plowed)	0	0	86
Fallow (w/volunteer)	13	105	219
Oats	10	113	178
Wheat	5	30	100
Pasture (grazed)	17	113	219
Pasture (ungrazed)	7	n.d.	228
Mixed hay	14	328	408
Red clover	10	210	371
Sweet clover	4	n.d.	381
Alfalfa	9	138	294
Marshland	18	n.d.	595
Shrublands	17	n.d.	401
Forest (w/understory)	n.d.	n.d.	215
Forest (w/o understory)	n.d.	n.d.	397

n.d. = no data

bird densities are 10 to 20 times greater than those found in croplands; densities in large stands of trees with dense undergrowth are up to four times that of grain fields.

In addition to increasing the abundance of common bird species, the restoration of habitat types critical to the survival of less common species may have notable effects on the recovery of declining populations. For example, in response to a substantial increase, 60 to 120 acres per square mile, in grass and grass/shrub cover provided by the Conservation Reserve Program in northwestern Minnesota (and perhaps in parts of the Dakotas and Montana), depressed native populations of both prairie chicken and sharp-tailed grouse are expected to increase three to five times their present levels in the next five years. (Berg, pers. commun.).

The relationship of cropland retirement programs to changes in wildlife populations has been most thoroughly documented for the ring-necked pheasant. According to Edwards (1984), pheasant populations throughout the midwestern states increased significantly in response to the acreage retired and seeded under the Agricultural Conservation Program between 1936 and 1942. A similar response of pheasant populations to the Conservation Reserve portion of the 1956–1961 Soil Bank Program was documented (Schrade 1960, Fouch 1963, Dahlgren 1966, Bartman 1969, Erickson and Wiebe 1973, Trautman 1982, Berner 1987). The land retired under the reserve contributed significantly to the number of young produced (Bartman 1969, Trautman 1982), and the amount of land affected the rates at which populations increased (Schrade 1960). Two- to three-fold increases in pheasant abundance were documented in South Dakota and parts of Minnesota and Michigan (Fouch 1963, Dahlgren 1966, Berner 1987). Similar responses by the pheasant population were observed in areas with significant amounts of multiyear CAP acres (Machan and Feldt 1972).

In addition to birds, a wide variety of other vertebrates such as small mammals, reptiles, and amphibians, will be favorably affected by the preservation and improvement of wetland, woodland, and upland grassland habitats through the conservation provisions of the 1985 Farm Act. Also, fish populations should respond positively to improved water quality resulting from reduced soil erosion and reduced pesticide and fertilizer use (Robinson 1987). Experts estimate that the Conservation Reserve Program will annually reduce erosion by 760 million tons, stream sedimentation by over 200 million tons, pesticide use by 61 million pounds, and fertilizer use by 1.44 million tons.[10]

Concern with Final Regulations

Definition of terms is a part of all legislation and usually receives little attention. In this case, however, definitions will determine the effectiveness of the Farm Act's conservation provisions, particularly sodbuster and swampbuster.

On September 17, 1987, the final regulations for sodbuster and swampbuster were issued.[11] In general, most conservationists believe that the results were better than anticipated. However, many natural resource professionals still have concerns about the regulations. In particular, concern is focused on the criteria for determining highly erodible lands and the acceptable erosion rates on the lands being cropped that will still allow large soil losses, and on various determinations in the swampbuster regulations that may allow drainage to continue at unacceptable levels.

The selection of an Erosion Index of 8 or greater as the criterion for highly erodible lands excludes an estimated 80 million acres of cropland with an EI in the 5 to 7 range; such lands have the potential of eroding at rates between 8 and 20 tons per acre per year. Selection of

10. Unfortunately, an estimated five billion tons of topsoil will continue to be lost from private land each year despite this significant effort. Also, the reduction in pesticide and fertilizer use still represents less than five percent of the present application.

11. For additional clarification of these terms, refer to the final U.S. Department of Agriculture rules for "Highly Erodible Land and Wetland Conservation" in the *Federal Register*, September 17, 1987.

EI 8 leaves another 68 million acres of pasture, range, and forest lands unprotected from conversion to environmentally damaging commodity crop production (see Table 5).

In the past, the U.S. Department of Agriculture has aided in the exploitation of natural resources by encouraging the conversion of wetlands and other critical habitats through liberal cropland expansion policies and financial assistance (Harmon 1987). By not combining the EI values for wind and water erosion as the criteria for highly erodible lands, the agency continues to foster such environmental damage.[12]

Originally, the U.S. Department of Agriculture allowed farmers to continue farming with erosion losses of up to 2T only if "economic considerations" prohibited full compliance. Under the current rules, local technical guideliness promulgated by SCS will determine which erosion control methods are used to substantially reduce soil loss. This ruling, however, will allow continued cultivation of lands that will continue to erode at rates greatly exceeding the original limitations; some lands will continue to erode at 60 or more tons per acre and still be eligible for farm program benefits (Soil Conservation Service 1988). Estimates indicate that at least 10 percent of the nation's highly erodible lands could continue to be cropped while eroding at excessive rates under this loophole (Nelson 1987). Moreover, this ruling pertains not only to highly erodible lands presently cropped, but also to those that might be sodbusted. Although some lenience may be acceptable concerning lands presently being cropped, under no circumstances should sodbusted lands or CRP lands be exempted from the original, more rigorous restrictions.

One of the swampbuster regulatory provisions of concern to conservationists is the "third party exemption" that exempts farmers from swampbuster sanctions if the wetland conversion was carried out by a third party. This exemption provides continued opportunities for drainage without loss of benefits. The final regulations are unclear as to who has the responsibility for proving that a farm program participant was not involved in swampbusting. At issue is whether the burden of proof falls on the government or on the farmer to determine whether the farmer was involved in drainage activities.

12. An explanation by the U.S. Department of Agriculture on why they decided not to combine the wind and water EI values in determining overall EI values states:

> Furthermore, it has been determined that the EI value for wind and water erosion should not be combined. While both wind and water erosion may occur on the same field, both erosion types do not necessarily occur on the same acre nor do both types of erosion occur at the same time of year. Thus, whichever is the most prevalent type of erosion, either wind or water, will be used to establish the EI value. If that value exceeds 8 or more, the soil unit is classified as "highly erodible." About 1.4 million acres of the Nation's cropland have EI values between 5 and 8 for both wind and water combined, which is less than 1.3 percent of all the highly erodible cropland in the United States" (U.S. Department of Agriculture 1987c).

Another concern with the swampbuster regulations is the lack of clear definitions for "minimal effects" of drainage on wetlands and the criteria for determining whether farmers have "committed substantial funds" in determining "commencement" of drainage projects before the December 1985 deadline. The final rules still leave much open to to local determination. More specific criteria would minimize the discretion available to county ASCS committees in determining whether a particular wetland drainage project is to be allowed.

Swampbuster is further weakened by the allowable completion date of 1995 for already "commenced" drainage; drainage critical to the survival of a farm operation should be completed before 1990.

Final rules and regulations for the Conservation Reserve Program, available since February 11, 1987, contain at least one section of concern to conservationists. Under "contract modifications," the Commodity Credit Corporation may modify a CRP contract at any time through mutual agreement with the participating farmer. This allows the corporation to decrease the program acreage and permit the production of any agricultural commodity during a crop year on all or part of the land subject to the contract. There are no provisions for mandatory consultation with natural resource agencies or the Soil Conservation Service regarding such modifications, except "when modifications to a CRP contract involve a technical aspect of the participant's conservation plan." In this case, the concurrence of the Soil Conservation Service, state forester (where applicable), and conservation district is necessary.

Plans for Documenting Impacts

Beginning in 1988, between 30 and 40 states will participate in a CRP evaluation project coordinated by the National Ecology Center of the U.S. Fish and Wildlife Service in Fort Collins, Colorado. The project will evaluate changes in habitat quantity and quality for three regionally selected wildlife species that would be affected by the cover developed on CRP fields. The midwest states, for example, have selected the meadowlark, cottontail rabbit, and ring-necked pheasant. In addition, individual states will evaluate the impacts of CRP lands on selected wildlife populations through use of existing population surveys. If funds permit, the site evaluation process will be repeated at least every other year; impacts of other Farm Act provisions (for example, ARP acres and conservation compliance) on wildlife abundance and habitat may also be measured. Information gathered will be useful in making management recommendations for future agricultural programs.

Proposed Modifications of the Conservation Reserve Program

Presently, amendments to the 1985 Farm Act are being proposed in both houses of Congress. Of particular interest are those advanced by

Senator Sam Nunn (GA). Senator Nunn's bill (S. 1521) would make several substantial changes that would have positive environmental impacts. This bill would expand the present CRP minimum from 40 to 60 million acres and set a maximum of 65 million acres. It would also expand land eligibility criteria for the program and authorize additional benefit options to make the program more competitive with annual retirement programs.

Future funding for the Conservation Reserve Program would be secured by mandating the Secretary of Agriculture to use the facilities, services, authorities, and funds of the Commodity Credit Corporation to carry out the program's sections, rather than annual appropriations. Also included is a provision for a groundwater pilot program that would expand the use of the program to retire irrigated lands contributing to overdraft of groundwater and contamination of underground aquifers by fertilizers and pesticides.

Of some concern, however, as suggested by Benbrook (1986), is the provision in the Nunn bill that allows haying and grazing on retired land to occur during the contract period. Such activities would allow disturbance and destruction of cover during the nesting season and remove desirable residual cover. Another provision would mandate the secretary to implement the softwood timber program and expand the program maximum from the present 50,000 acres to 200,000 acres. While this will probably keep the lands in timber production for longer than 10 years, monoculture pine forests have limited wildlife diversity.

COMMODITY PROGRAMS' IMPACTS ON WILDLIFE

Lands retired under annual commodity programs have not lived up to their potential (Joselyn and Warnock 1964, Nelson and Chesness 1964, Gates and Ostrom 1966). As previously mentioned, the lack of adequate cover on many of these retired acres and the destruction of the cover crops during the bird nesting season on the remainder have proven detrimental to wildlife populations (Berner 1973, 1984b, 1987; Castrale 1984).

The bulk of the acres eligible for conservation compliance and the Conservation Reserve Program are in the less fertile, erodible regions of the country. Many wildlife species, especially the pheasant, thrive in areas with fertile soils (Allen 1956, McIntosh and Evans 1984). Although highly fertile areas will not, in most cases, be significantly affected by the Conservation Reserve Program and conservation compliance, they will be affected by annual federal commodity programs now and in the future (U.S. Department of Agriculture 1987d).

In farmland areas where there are significant amounts of land qualifying for the Conservation Reserve Program, participation in the reserve has been limited because of the financial attractiveness of the Acreage Reduction Program (ARP) and the loss of base acres under CRP contracts. Contract bids under the Conservation Reserve Program were higher than previously anticipated because farmers would receive greater benefits from enrolling the same acres in the Acreage Reduction Program. Taff and Runge (1986) provide an in-depth discussion of the conflicts between these two programs and a possible solution to the dilemma of higher-than-expected CRP bids and lower-than-expected enrollment rates.

General Commodity Provisions

The primary purpose of commodity programs is to stabilize farm income by providing income subsidies and reducing crop surpluses through land retirement. To reduce production, the Secretary of Agriculture may enter into annual or multiyear contracts on acres retired from production. A participating farmer is entitled to program benefits according to his/her base acreage and the average yield of the crop grown. In general, the more base acres and yield per acre a farmer can accrue, the greater the program benefits derived up to the maximum established by Congress: $50,000 in deficiency and land retirement payments per farm unit. Also, the secretary may establish a special haying and grazing program on the acres retired under the Acreage Reduction Program (except for wheat), which may be of substantial financial benefit to some program participants.

The impact of the commodity programs on land use is indicated by the more than 30 million acres retired under the Acreage Reduction Program in both 1986 and 1987; these acres are in addition to the 23 million acres contracted under the Conservation Reserve Program as of September 1987. The more than 50 million acres retired in both 1986 and 1987 are comparable to many previous years, but exceed the average annual acres (32.5 million acres) retired under the various land retirement programs for the period 1956–1985 (see Table 2).

The disturbance allowed on the ARP acres through both haying and grazing in 1986 and grazing in 1987 greatly reduces the value of these acres as good wildlife habitat; haying was also allowed in 1987 in some states under an emergency provision.

The U.S. Department of Agriculture predicts that crop surpluses will continue through the year 2000 and beyond. Because of this, it is likely that, in addition to the Conservation Reserve Program, significant cropland acreage—more than 20 million acres—will be retired under annual Acreage Reserve Programs to control crop production (U.S. Department of Agriculture 1987d). Despite the probability of retiring significant amounts of prime cropland on an annual basis, the prognosis for wildlife is mixed. If present policies continue to promote inadequate cover and untimely disturbance of cover for wildlife on ARP acres, wildlife species such as pheasants, bobolinks, and cottontail rabbits will be harmed. Also, the positive effects of the Conservation Reserve Program may be reduced somewhat by the unsafe nesting and brood rearing habitat created by the Acreage Reduction Programs (Berner 1987).

A few minor changes in the cover management on ARP acres, however, would produce significant wildlife benefits. Present management of ARP acres emphasizes the control of commodity crop production to the detriment of soil, water, and wildlife benefits. The lack of multiyear agreements in Acreage Reduction Programs is ostensibly for program flexibility, yet land has been retired under annual Acreage Reduction Programs in most years since 1956; in only eight years were no lands retired (see Figure 1 and Table 2).

Because ARP agreements are annual, farmers are not willing to pay to seed perennial grass-legume cover crops (Berner 1984b). Moreover, because ASCS committees are composed of farmers eligible for Acreage Reduction Programs, the committees opt to maintain maximum flexibility in establishing the cover requirement, cover crop seeding dates and rates, and cover destruction dates with minimal consideration of natural resource benefits. It makes little sense to allow this to continue while agencies in the U.S. government (for example, the U.S. Fish and Wildlife Service and other programs within the U.S. Department of Agriculture) struggle to preserve and protect wildlife habitat.

Wildlife Response to Cover Management on ARP Acres

The manner in which lands retired under annual acreage retirement plans are managed has significant effects on nesting wildlife such as pheasants. When ARP acres are seeded early in the spring to an annual cover crop (small grains), or are already in perennial cover crops (grass-legumes) and left undisturbed during the nesting and brooding season or for several years, pheasant populations have increased significantly (Joselyn and Warnock 1964, Gates and Ostrom 1966, Nomsen 1972, Berner 1984b).

Present management regulations for ARP acres, however, encourage practices proven to be detrimental to nesting wildlife (Nelson and Chesness 1964, Harmon 1968, Trautman 1982, Castrale 1984, Berner 1984b, 1987). Management regulations are developed by state and county Agriculture Stabilization and Conservation Service committees within the broad guidelines set by the ASCS national office; these guidelines do not require seeding of ARP acres and permit late seeding of annual cover crops (Berner 1973, 1984a; Montag 1974). The regulations also require early destruction of cover crops and volunteer vegetation on unseeded fields. Disturbance dates vary across the nation but usually occur about midway through the bird nesting and brooding season.

Although Castrale (1984) found a wide variety of wildlife using ARP lands in Indiana, the reproductive success of the birds and small mammals using these acres for nesting and/or brooding was limited due to untimely disturbance of the cover crops. An analysis of 24 years of pheasant population data (1960 to 1983) for southcentral Minnesota indicated that pheasant populations in non-ARP nesting cover decline as ARP acres increase (Berner 1987). Pheasant production averaged 30 percent lower in years with an Acreage Reduction Program than in years without a program (Berner 1984b).

With only minor revisions in the management of ARP acres, wildlife populations throughout our nation's most productive farmlands could benefit with little if any increased expense to the farmer (Berner 1984b, Warner and Etter 1985). In many cases, the changes could save farmers money. Negative impacts on wildlife can be reversed by requiring that acres retired under an annual Acreage Reduction Program be seeded to an annual cover crop (small grains) and not mowed, disked, or plowed for a period of at least 90 days. This 90-day period should encompass the reproductive season of the principal wildlife species in the area (for example, in Minnesota from May 1 through August 31). In areas where cover is needed for wintering wildlife, a portion of these acres should be seeded to cover crop such as forage sorghum and left undisturbed through the winter.

Population increases similar to those expected in areas affected by the Conservation Reserve Program and conservation compliance provisions could be expected if ARP acres are retired for three or more years in succession (Nomsen 1972, Klonglan 1973, Berner 1984b). Indeed, implementing the multiyear ARP provisions could result in significant improvements in soil, water, and wildlife benefits of Acreage Reduction Programs by creating significant acreages of undisturbed perennial grassland habitats.

Value for Wildlife of Conservation Easements on Farmers Home Administration (FmHA) Lands

The 1985 Farm Act provides for "granting or selling of easements for conservation purposes to units of local and state government or a private nonprofit organization" on lands owned by FmHA and for lowering the debts of farmers who give 50-year easements for conservation purposes.

Taking full advantage of the conservation easement provisions on FmHA lands will significantly improve the quality of the habitat in certain regions. Existing native grassland, wetlands, and riparian habitats, in particular, will be preserved and improved under these conservation easement provisions.

ADMINISTRATION OF PROGRAMS

The administration provisions in the 1985 Farm Act are the key to how well program objectives are met. One special concern is that funding for the Conservation Reserve Program is not assured after September 30, 1987, but must be appropriated annually. However, once the bids are signed the contracts must be honored for the full 10 years. While establishment of regulations governing the conservation provisions is left to the discretion of the Secretary of Agriculture within the broad definitions provided in the act, wildlife agencies such as the Fish and Wildlife Service or state departments of natural resources have little real influence on implementation of rules. In implementing Conservation Reserve Programs, the secretary is required to consult with the Soil Conservation Service, U.S. Forest Service, U.S. Fish and Wildlife Service, state forest and fish and wildlife agencies, land-grant colleges, and local, county, and state ASCS committees. Reform is inevitably slow and recalcitrant bureaucrats need support and education to help them reverse 50 years of handing out agricultural benefits.

ASCS Committees

Selection and election of the ASCS committees (state, county, and local) that establish management policies for land retired under commodity and conservation provisions is a very important consideration. As with all farm acts since 1947, the only voting members of these committees are landowners and producers who are eligible to participate in commodity programs. The Secretary of Agriculture appoints a three-member committee for each state. In each county, a maximum of three local committees of three members each is elected by the eligible producers in that county. County committees are then selected from the members of the elected local committees. There is no provision in the 1985 Farm Act for voting input from natural resource professionals (soil, water, and wildlife) and other interested parties, despite the effects that Department of Agriculture programs have on these natural resources.

RECOMMENDATIONS

Although the 1985 Farm Act provides significant opportunities to reduce soil erosion and improve wildlife habitat and water quality across the nation, many of the consequences of agriculture on our natural resources need to be addressed. Conservationists must remain vigilant as the Farm Act is implemented, so that its gains are not weakened or lost during the regulations and enforcement process or bargained away in new farm legislation. [**EDITOR'S NOTE:** In late 1987 and early 1988, some farmers, especially from North Dakota, mounted an attack on the swampbuster and sodbuster programs. At press time, it was not clear how well the programs would withstand the onslaught.] In addition to a constant vigilance, the following proposed modifications should be incorporated into new farm legislation.

In view of the enormous impact of farm programs on natural resources, steps must be taken to include biologists, soil conservationists, and other conservation-oriented persons as voting members on ASCS committees. To balance representation, the present committee structure should be changed to include equal representation between the producers and natural resource interests. This proposed change in committee structure would facilitate developing Acreage Reduction Program land-management regulations that provide the highest degree of benefits—both economic and environmental.

Another crucial change needed in the basic framework of federal farm programs is reform of the "base acreage" concept. This problem has been graphically described by Mekelburg (1983) and nicely summed up by Jahn and Harmon (1987):

> Another longstanding procedure in agricultural policy requiring change is the use of "base acreage" for individual commodities—such as corn, wheat, etc.—to determine how many taxpayer dollars a landowner will be paid each year. As one Nebraska farmer stated recently, his "base acreage" is his ticket to the federal treasury.
>
> The official record of acreage of a crop grown on a farm in past years is used to qualify a landowner for target prices, low-interest loans on commodities produced, and deficiency payments, etc. made available to landowners yearly by the federal government. In essence, government payments substitute for free-market financial incentives and encourage production of crops, even in an era of commodity surpluses. Instead of the market encouraging or discouraging crop production, the calculated and ensured taxpayer-funded government payments continuously stimulate bringing land into crop production and maximizing yields per acre. These actions push trends in the wrong direction and contribute to mounting surpluses that must be stored at additional cost to taxpayers.
>
> The base acreage/target price/deficiency payment/storage payment system encourages grassroots decisions that move uses of land away from, rather than toward, an integrated commodity/conservation agricultural program. That system should be realigned if taxpayer costs for the

multibillion-dollar agricultural programs are to be reduced and much needed integrated conservation/commodity programs are to be broadly installed to place agricultural land use on a sustainable basis.

Modifying federal farm program legislation to address environmental problems, however, cannot deal with all the problems facing wildlife on farmlands. Conversion of prime farmlands (highly productive land with an EI of three or less) to irreversible uses like housing and shopping malls must be addressed at both state and federal levels. According to Sampson (1981), more than 16 million acres of existing and potential cropland were converted to urban uses between 1967 and 1975; more than 6.5 million of these were prime farmland. These actions create added impetus to convert noncropland areas, many of which are valuable wildlife habitats, to cropland. Also, with the farming of less productive lands, more marginal and perhaps highly erodible acres will have to be farmed to maintain previous production levels from prime levels.

An existing law, The Farmland Protection Policy Act (7 U.S.C.A. 4201c) attempts to prevent the federal government from subsidizing the conversion of prime cropland to nonagricultural uses. Governments at all levels, however, must address this problem in the near future. Programs must be developed that promote sustainable crop production and farmland improvement while protecting wildlife populations and water quality. Conservationists will again have to play an important role in providing critical input for balanced solutions to the nation's farm crisis.

REFERENCES

Allen, D.L. 1956. *Pheasants in North America.* Stackpole Co., Harrisburg, Pennsylvania, and Wildlife Management Institute. Washington, D.C. 490 pp.

Bartman, R.M. 1969. "Pheasant nesting on soil bank land in northern Utah." *Journal of Wildlife Management* 33:1020–1023.

Benbrook, C.M. 1986. "The science and art of conservation policy." *Journal of Soil and Water Conservation* 41:285–291.

Berg, W. 1987. Personal communication, September.

Berner, A.H. 1973. "Summarization and analysis of the 1972 set-aside acre management survey in the Midwest." *Minnesota Game Research Quarterly Progress Reports* 32:207–263.

——. 1978. "Agriculture and wildlife: critical need for planning." *Naturalist-Environmental Planning Issue*:29–32. (Autumn and Winter).

——, and C. Cooper. 1981. 10-row Farmstead Shelterbelts: Potential as Wildlife Habitat. Presented at the 43rd Midwest Fish and Wildlife Conference. Wichita, Kansas.

——. 1984a. "Committee report on the 1983 set-aside program." *Proceedings of Perdix III*. Pp. 193–197.

——. 1984b. "Federal land retirement program: a land management albatross." *Transactions of the North American Wildlife and Natural Resources Conference* 49:118–130.

——. 1987. "Federal pheasants: impact of federal agricultural programs on pheasant habitat, 1934–85" *in* W.R. Edwards and G. Burger eds., *Symposium on Pheasants: Symptoms of Wildlife Problems on Agricultural lands.* 49th Midwest Fish and Wildlife Conference, December 8, 1987. North Central Chapter of the Wildlife Society. (In press).

Castrale, J.S. 1984. "Wildlife use of cultivated fields set aside under the Payment in Kind (PIK) program." *Proceedings of Indiana Academy Science* 93:173–180.

Dahlgren, R.B. 1967. "What happened to our pheasants in 1966?" *South Dakota Conservation Digest* 34(4):6–9.

Edwards, W.R., S.P. Havera, R.E. Labisky, S.L. Etter, and R.E. Warner. 1982. "The abundance of cottontails (*Sylvilagus floridanus*) in relation to land use in Illinois (U.S.A.) 1956–1978, with comments on mechanisms of regulation," pp. 761–789 *in* K. Myers and C.D. MacInnes eds., *Proceedings of the International Lagomorph Symposium,* August 12–16, 1979. University of Guelph. Guelph, Ontario, Canada. 983 pp.

——. 1984. "Early ACP and pheasant boom and bust!– a historical perspective with rationale." *Proceedings of Perdix III.* Pp. 71–83.

Emmerich, J.M., and P.A. Vohs. 1982. "Comparative use of four woodland habitats by birds." *Journal of Wildlife Management* 46:43–49.

Erickson, R.E., and J.E. Wiebe. 1973. "Pheasants, economics and land retirement programs in South Dakota." *Wildlife Society Bulletin* 1:22–27.

Farris, A.L., and S.H. Cole. 1981. "Strategies and goals for wildlife habitat restoration on agricultural lands." *Transactions of the North American Wildlife and Natural Resources Conference* 46:130–135.

Fouch, W.R. 1963. Evaluation of the Effect of Conservation Reserve of the Soil Bank on Wildlife. Michigan Job Completion Report Research Project, Segment W-40-R-17–7. 9 pp.

Gates, J.M., and G.E. Ostrom. 1966. "Feed grain program related to pheasant production in Wisconsin." *Journal of Wildlife Management* 30:612–617.

Good, E.E., and C.A. Damaach. 1943. "Effect of land use practices on breeding bird populations in Ohio." *Journal of Wildlife Management* 7:291–297.

Graber, R.R., and J.W. Graber. 1963. "A comparative study of bird populations in Illinois–1906–1909 and 1956–1958." *Illinois Natural History Survey Bulletin* 28(3):383–528.

Graber, J., and R. Graber. 1983. "Declining grassland birds." *Illinois Natural History Survey Report* 227:1–2.

Harmon, K.W. 1968. The Economics of Land-use Changes in Larimer County, Colorado and Their Possible Effects on Pheasants. PhD thesis. Colorado State University. Fort Collins, Colorado. 150 pp.

——, and M.M. Nelson. 1973. "Wildlife and soil conservation in land retirement programs." *Wildlife Society Bulletin* 1:28–38.

——. 1987. "History and economics of farm bill legislation and impacts on wildlife management and policies," *in* Proceedings of Regional Symposium on Ecological, and Economic Impact of the Conservation Reserve Program on Landowners and Professional Managers, September 16–18, 1987. Denver, Colorado. (In press).

Jahn, L.R., and K.W. Harmon. 1987. "Wildlife and the land." in *1987 Yearbook of Agriculture.* U.S. Documents. Washington, D.C. (In press).

Joselyn, G.B., and J.E. Warnock. 1964. "Value of federal feed grain program to production of pheasants in Illinois." *Journal of Wildlife Management* 28:547–551.

Klonglan, E.D. 1973. Iowa pheasants affected by federal farm programs. Iowa Conservation Commission. 4 pp.

Land Letter (Chandler, W.J., ed.) 1987. "Conservationists lose ground in farm credit debate." *Land Letter* 6(19):1–2.

Machan, W.J., and R.D. Feldt. 1972. "Hunting results on cropland adjustment program land in northwestern Indiana." *Journal of Wildlife Management* 36:192–195.

McIntosh, M. and R. Evans. 1984. "Soil: The body of life." *Missouri Conservationist* 8:15.

Mekelburg, M.E. 1983. "New approaches to commodity programs and conservationgoal." *Journal of Soil and Water Conservation* 38:324–325.

Montag, D.G. 1974. "Summarization and analysis of the 1973 set-aside acre management survey in the Midwest." *Minnesota Wildlife Research Quarterly Progress Reports* 34:76–95.

Nelson, E. 1987. Personal communication, October.

Nelson, M.M., and R.A. Chesness. 1964. The Effect of Long-term Land Use Trends and the Feed Grain Program on Pheasants in Minnesota. Presented at 26th Midwest Wildlife Conference. 20 pp.

Nomsen, R.C. 1972. "Pheasant nesting and production on the Hancock County wildlife research area." *Iowa Wildlife Management and Research Quarterly Progress Reports* 2(1):1–4.

Robinson, A.Y. 1987. "Saving soil and wildlife: the promise of the Farm Act's conservation title." *Izaak Walton League of America Bulletin.* 63 pp.

Sampson, R.N. 1981. *Farmland or wasteland: A Time to Choose.* Rodale Press. Emmaus, Pennsylvania. 422 pp.

Schrader, T.A. 1960. "Does soil bank aid pheasants?" *Minnesota Conservation Volunteer* 23(134):34–37.

Soil Conservation Service. 1988. Personal Communication, January.

Taff, S., and C.F. Runge. 1986. Supply control conservation and budget constraint: conflicting instruments in the 1985 Farm Act. Staff Paper P86–33, University of Minnesota. Institute of Agriculture, Forestry and Home Economics. St. Paul, Minnesota. 21 pp.

Trautman, C.G. 1982. "History, ecology and management of the ring-necked pheasant in South Dakota." *South Dakota Department of Game, Fish, and Parks Bulletin* 7. 118 pp.

U.S. Department of Agriculture. 1970. Final Report of Conservation Reserve Program: Summary of Accomplishments– 1956–1972. Agricultural Stabilization Conservation Service. Washington, D.C. 17 pp.

——. 1973. Summary of Acreage Diverted Under Government Program Except CCP, 1956–1972. Agricultural Stabilization Conservation Service, Washington, D.C. 13 pp.

——. 1976. U.S. Land Use Summary, Crop Years 1968–1975. Agricultural Stabilization Conservation Service. Washington, D.C. 49 pp.

——. 1986. U.S. Land Use Summary, 1976–1985. Agricultural Stabilization Conservation Service. Washington, D.C. 49 pp.

—— 1987a. Environmental Assessment and Final Regulatory Impact and Flexibility Analyses for the Highly Erodible Land Conservation Provisions of the Food Security Act of 1985. Soil Conservation Service. Washington, D.C. 55 pp.

——. 1987b. *Environmental Assessment and Final Regulatory Impact and Flexibility Analyses for the Wetland Conservation Provisions of the Food Security Act of 1985.* Soil Conservation Service. Washington, D.C. 62 pp.

——. 1987c. *Summary of Comments and Rationale for the Final Regulations for Highly Erodible Land and Wetland Conservation.* U.S. Department of Agriculture. Washington, D.C. 15 pp.

——. 1987d. *The Second RCA Appraisal: Soil, Water, and Related Resources on Nonfederal Land in the United States—Analysis of Condition and Trends.* U.S. Department of Agriculture. Washington, D.C. 377 pp.

U.S. General Accounting Office. 1983. *Agriculture's Soil Conservation Programs Miss Full Potential in the Fight Against Soil Erosion.* U.S. General Accounting Office. Gaithersburg, Maryland. 79 pp.

Warner, R.E., S.L. Etter, G.B. Joselyn, and J.A. Ellis. 1984. "Declining survival of ring-necked pheasant chicks in Illinois agricultural ecosystem." *Journal of Wildlife Management* 48:82–88.

——., and ——. 1985. "Farm conservation measures to benefit wildlife, especially pheasant populations." *Transactions of the North American Wildlife and Natural Resources Conference* 48:82–88.

——, and ——. 1986. "The dynamics of agriculture and ring-necked pheasant populations in the corn belt." *U.S.A. World Pheasant Association Journal* 11:76–89.

Wiens, J.A., and M.I. Dyer. 1975. "Rangeland avifaunas: their composition, energetics, and role in the ecosystem," pp. 146–182 *in* D.R. Smith, technical coordinator, *Proceedings of the Symposium on Management of Forest and Range Habitats for Nongame Birds, May 6–9, 1975.* Tucson, Arizona. U.S. Department of Agricultural Forest Service Technical Report. WO-1. 343 pp.

Alfred Berner is the research group leader for the Department of Natural Resources' Farmland Wildlife Populations and Research Center in Madelia, Minnesota.

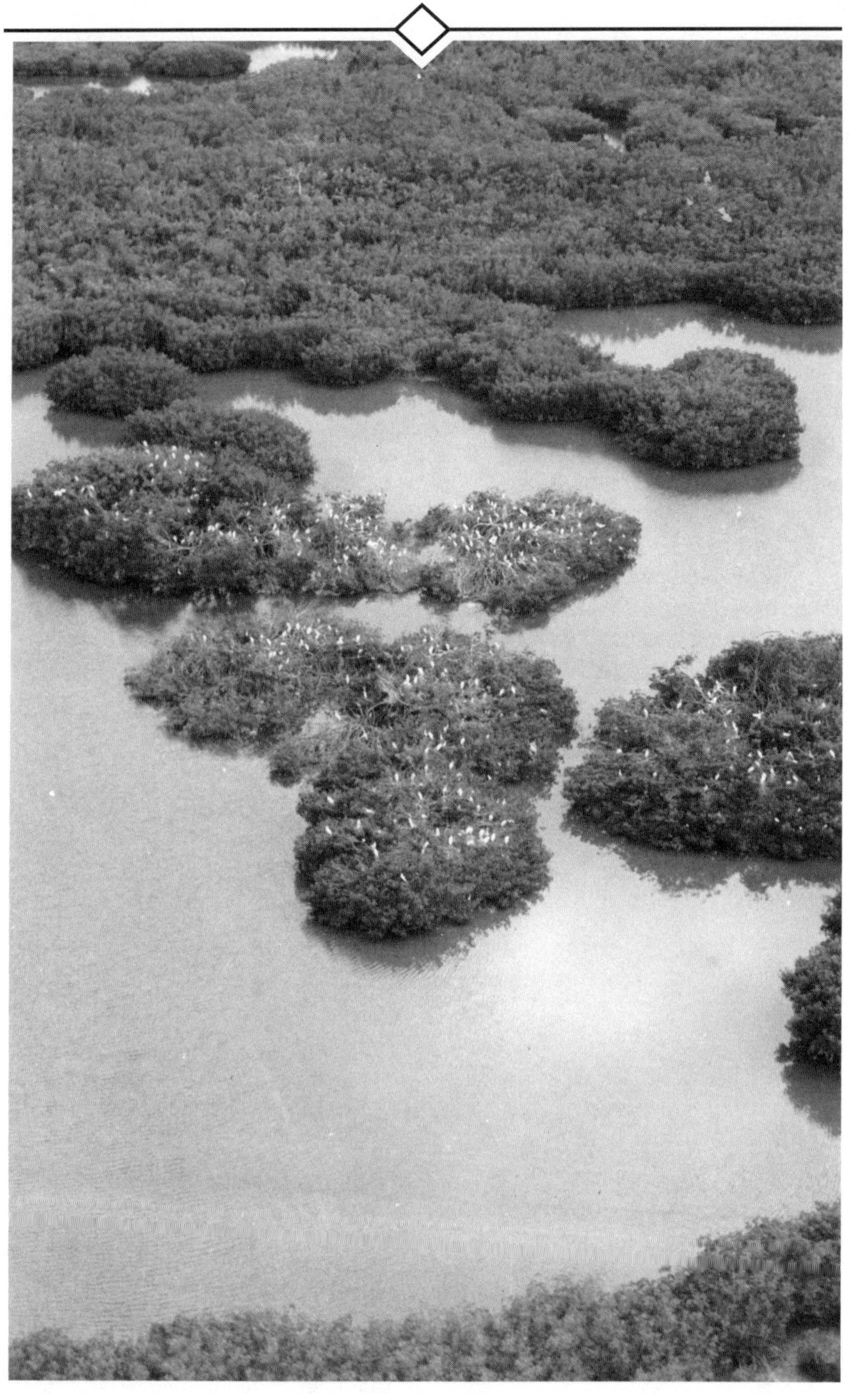

Natural water flow in the Everglades has been disrupted and the entire ecosystem changed to the detriment of both people and wildlife. Ambitious efforts are under way to stop and even undo the damage. *National Park Service*

Restoring the Everglades

Estus Whitfield

INTRODUCTION

The Everglades and its interrelated system of lakes, rivers, marshes, freshwater swamps, mangrove forests and coastal estuaries covers almost the entire Florida peninsula south of Lake Okeechobee (see Figure 1). This vast hydrological system is more accurately known as the Kissimmee-Lake Okeechobee-Everglades system.[1] The Upper Kissimmee chain of lakes south of Orlando are the headwaters of the Kissimmee River, largest tributary to Lake Okeechobee. From Lake Okeechobee, the Everglades historically extended south 100 miles to the mangrove forests along the south and southwest coasts; and from the Atlantic coastal ridge on the east coast to some 40 miles west where the Everglades merged with the Big Cypress Swamp which covered most of lower southwest Florida.

The Everglades is the largest freshwater marsh in the world. Its sawgrass marshes, interspersed with hardwood tree islands, grow on a layer of peat (or muck) that varies in depth from over 10 feet near Lake

1. Kissimmee River Basin—3,000 square miles; Lake Okeechobee—730 square miles; Everglades—3,900 square miles, historically and approximately 2,000 square miles today; Big Cypress Swamp—2,400 square miles.

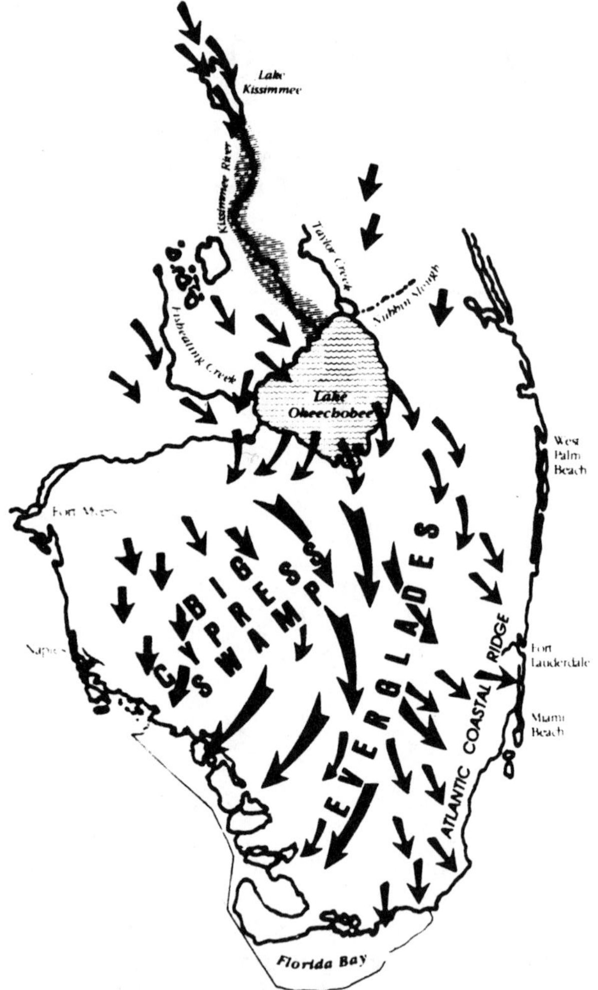

Figure 1. Historic water flow of the Kissimmee River—Lake Okeechobee Everglades System. Source: Office of the Governor, State of Florida.

Okeechobee to only a few inches to the west and south. Underlaying the peat is a bedrock of limestone. In the southeastern part of the peninsula, the bedrock forms the Biscayne Aquifer, which is among the most permeable aquifers on earth. The Biscayne Aquifer is the sole source of fresh water for South Palm Beach, Broward, Dade, and Monroe counties (Fernald and Patton 1984).

The climate of south Florida—characterized by warm rainy summers and mild dry winters—combines with the gently sloping topography of the land and the very slow north-to-south flow of water to support a variety of water-oriented ecological systems. The resultant rivers, lakes, freshwater marshes, wet prairies, sloughs (strands), cypress swamps, hardwood hammocks, salt marshes, mangrove forests, and marine coastal waters make the Everglades among the richest and most diverse biological areas in the world. For example, the Fakahatchee Strand in the western portion of the Big Cypress Swamp has the largest stand of Florida royal palms and the only natural association of royal palm-bald cypress in existence. The strand is also the only North American location for at least twelve species of plants; harbors 25 plant species classified as threatened or endangered under the federal Endangered Species Act; contains a greater density of native orchids than any other comparable area on the continent; and supports at least 10 threatened or endangered species of animals.

During the May-to-September rainy season, when most of south Florida's 54 inches of rainfall occurs, the entire Everglades system once filled with water (see Figure 2.). Historically, the Upper Kissimmee Basin's chain of lakes would fill and overflow one to another through sloughs and depressions. Overflows from Lake Kissimmee, along with rainfall and runoff in the lower Kissimmee River Basin, would push the river out of its banks and fill the 2-mile-wide floodplain. The narrow, 98-mile-long meandering river became a 48-mile-long, 2-mile-wide sheet of water flowing slowly into Lake Okeechobee.

The lake in turn would fill and overflow at its southern rim. Excess lake water would pour into the Caloosahatchee River to the west and the Everglades to the south. When this overflow spilled into the already rain-swollen Everglades, a solid sheet of water would form from the Kissimmee Basin to the gulf. (Gleason 1974). With a land elevation decline of 15 feet from north to south over the 100 miles (less than one inch per mile between the lake and the gulf), the water flowed south at a rate of about a foot per day through the Everglades. The Atlantic Coastal Ridge prevented outflow except where the Miami, New, and Hillsborough rivers and some other streams broke through to the ocean. Higher lands in the Devil's Garden and the Big Cypress Swamp prevented flow to the west. Near where Tamiami Trail (U.S. 41) is today, the bulk of the flow curved southwest and eventually entered the estuaries of the gulf between Cape Sable and Everglades City. East of Cape Sable, near present-day Homestead, Florida, the flow curved east into Florida Bay and Biscayne Bay. Similiarly, rainfall in the Big Cypress would overfill the thousands of depressions, cypress heads, and sloughs and flow overland through the sloughs, or strands, south into the Ten Thousand Islands area of the Gulf.

More than a hundred years of drainage have severely damaged the Everglades system. Dredging, filling, and draining for agricultural and urban development destroyed large portions of the historic Kissimmee River, Everglades, and Big Cypress Swamp. Natural water flow has been altered by levees, canals, and roads; changes in the water regime have played havoc with the life cycles of fish, birds, and other wildlife species. Wading bird populations, including white ibis, snowy egrets, and great egrets, drastically declined in Everglades National Park. Between 1930 and 1980 the wood stork population declined from approximately 4,000 mating pairs to about 400 pairs (Fairchild Tropical Garden July 1983). Alligators also declined significantly. The Florida panther neared extinction with just 30 to 50 animals confined to the park and to Big Cypress National Preserve and surrounding areas. The white-tailed deer herd of the Everglades suffered recurring disaster due to extreme high water periods in the water conservation areas. In the Kissimmee River Valley, 75 percent of the river marshes were lost due to channelization. The waterfowl population of the Kissimmee declined by 90 percent, bald eagle nesting by 74 percent, and six species of fish were lost from the river.

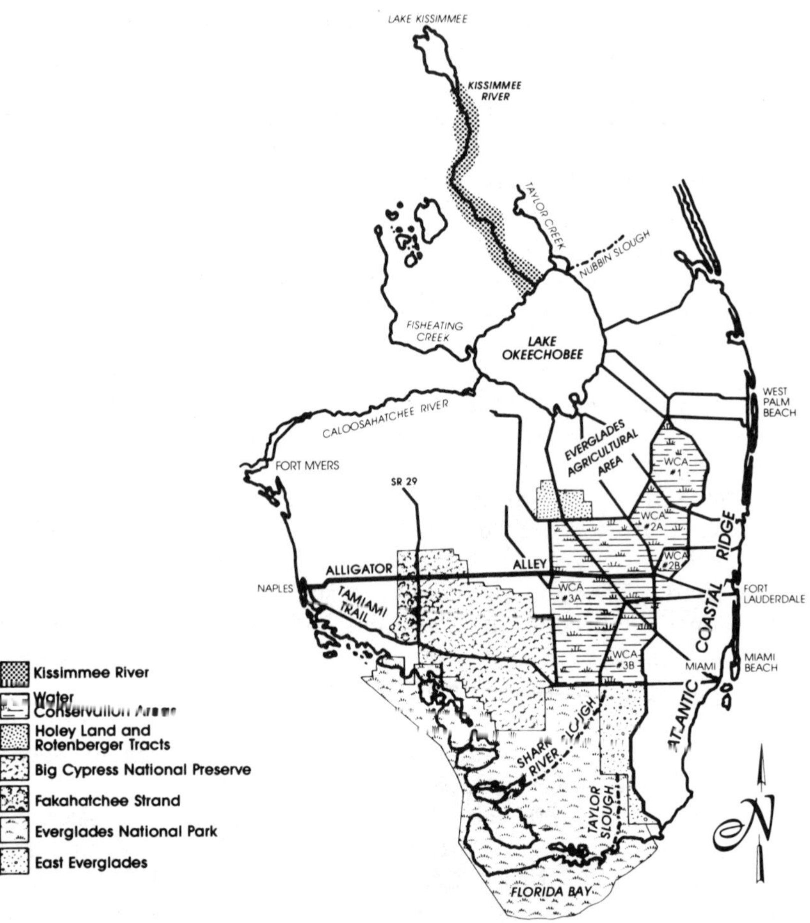

Figure 2. Kissimmee River—Lake Okeechobee Everglades System. Source: Office of the Governor, State of Florida.

History of Drainage Efforts

Early writings about the Everglades in the 1820s describe it as a very inhospitable, watery wasteland. At that time, almost all of the Florida peninsula south of Lake Okeechobee was almost continuously inundated except during occasional drought years. In the Coconut Grove area of Miami, water reportedly reached within three miles of the Atlantic shoreline during its lowest level and periodically poured over the ridge (Blake 1980).

Interest in draining the Everglades predated Florida's statehood. In 1845, the first state legislature declared the Everglades "wholly valueless"and asked the U.S. Congress to appoint engineers to examine and survey the region in hope of reclaiming it (Resolution No. 12, December 10, 1845). It was thought at the time that if southwest outlets such as the Miami, New, and Hillsborough rivers were opened, the Everglades would drain into the ocean, lowering water levels by ten feet. Florida legislators envisioned millions of acres of "new" land on which to grow tropical fruits, hemp, sugar, cotton, rice, and tobacco, but nothing was done.

Politicians fumbled around for nearly 40 more years before successful drainage of the Everglades began. At statehood (1845), the federal government granted Florida 500,000 acres of land. Under the Swamp and Overflowed Lands Act of 1850, the federal government gave another 20.3 million wetland acres to Florida for the purpose of reclamation.

In an effort to encourage development in general, Florida pledged its only asset—land—to guarantee interest on railroad bonds sold to the public by private railroads. The Civil War bankrupted the railroads and bond holders demanded payment from the state in the form of land. In desperation, Florida sought private investors to help alleviate its financial crisis; the state enlisted the help of Hamilton Disston, an heir to a Philadelphia saw and file manufacturing company (Blake 1980).

Disston had a dream—to drain the Everglades and build an urban and agricultural empire on the reclaimed land. The state sold him four million acres of land for $.25 an acre and promised to give him half of any additional land he could drain. In 1882, Disston dredged a canal to connect Lake Okeechobee with the Caloosahatchee River. He later dug canals that connected several of the lakes in the upper Kissimmee chain and dredged portions of the Kissimmee River. He thus opened the lakes in the upper Kissimmee Basin for navigation to the Gulf of Mexico via Lake Okeechobee and the Caloosahatchee River. Disston also developed a 1,000-acre sugar cane plantation and a sugar mill at St. Cloud, Florida, and developed Tarpon Springs, Gulfport, and a community near Orlando before his financial failure and death in 1896 (Blake 1980).

No serious drainage was undertaken following Disston's efforts until, in 1907, the state legislature created the Everglades Drainage District as a state agency with taxing authority. This district's purpose was to drain the Everglades for agricultural and urban use. By 1913, 225 miles of drainage canals had been dug including the Miami River, North New River, and South New River canals.

In 1927, the Everglades Drainage District's work totaled 440 miles of canals, 47 miles of levees, and 16 locks and levees, including a peat dike around the southern rim of Lake Okeechobee. Five large canals connected Lake Okeechobee to the Atlantic, and the Caloosahatchee had been thoroughly channelized (C&FFCS 1949–1957).

In 1926 and 1928, major hurricanes swept through South Florida; 2,000 lives were lost south of Lake Okeechobee when the muck dike gave way. Following the 1928 disaster, the state appealed to the U.S. Army Corps of Engineers for help. The Everglades Drainage District had gone broke, so in 1929 the state legislature created the Okeechobee Flood Control District to cooperate with the Corps in flood-control work. By 1949, the district had constructed most of the major drainage works that exist today.

A powerful hurricane in 1947 again caused serious flooding in South Florida, and once again the Corps was called in to help. The following year Congress approved a water control plan (U.S. Congress, House 1948) that created the Central and Southern Florida Project.[2] The purposes of the project were to provide flood protection and water supply for east coast cities, prevent saltwater intrusion, enhance fish and wildlife, store surplus water, and improve navigation. The plan called for creating 1,340 square miles of conservation pools with encircling dikes to protect the urban east coast from flooding, diking Lake Okeechobee, constructing flood-control works on the Kissimmee and St. Johns rivers and various other drainage works. Allocation of the projected benefits of the Central and Southern Florida project was 35.4 percent for flood control, navigation, and preservation of fish and wildlife, and 64.6 percent for increased land use. Interestingly, while the impetus for the project was hurricanes, flooding, and saltwater intrusion, the major benefit was increased land use—agricultural and urban development (Central and South Florida Flood Control District 1949–1955). The project was designed and built by the Corps.

Today, there are more than 1,400 miles of canals and levees, 125 major water control structures, 18 pumping stations, 13 boat locks, and several hundred minor structures in the Everglades region. Virtually every natural stream in South Florida has been turned into a canal, and

2. The Central and Southern Florida Flood Control District, covering 16,000 square miles, was established by the state legislature in 1949 to work on the project with the Corps.

Lake Okeechobee has been brought under rigorous regulation. All major decisions relating to water control such as regulation of the water level of Lake Okeechobee are made by the Corps. Maintenance and day-to-day routine operations are conducted by the South Florida Water Management District.[3]

EVOLUTION OF THE EVERGLADES PROTECTION MOVEMENT

A Dredge-and-Fill Mentality

From 1925 to 1945, South Florida's population grew from 250,000 to 500,000, while land in agriculture grew from 256,000 to 430,000 acres. From 1960 to 1975, the region's population grew from 1.8 million to 3.5 million and agricultural acreage increased from 630,000 to 942,000 acres. With this growth, the demand for flood control outstripped the capability of the drainage works. Flood-control projects stimulated development of wetlands and flood-prone areas, creating the need for further drainage. It was a cycle of drain, overbuild, and drain again.

In the late 1960s and early 1970s, conservation-minded individuals began to voice strong concern about Florida's dredge-fill-and-drain way of life that showed little regard for natural ecological systems. Fish, birds, and other wildlife were disappearing from the Everglades; what was once sawgrass and cypress swamps was now crop fields, roads, and lawns. Rivers and streams had all been turned into canals.

The Florida legislature enacted laws in the late 1960s and 1970s that are still regarded as models for water quality and wetlands protection, land and water resources planning and management, and environmentally sensitive land acquisition. While these laws helped, alone they were not enough. Florida still lacked a strong commitment to conserving the Everglades as an entire ecological system.

During the 1980s the conservation community, which had become well organized and represented by several effective spokespersons, strongly pressured state and local governments to take action. Art Marshall, a former U.S. Fish and Wildlife Service biologist, had spent several years championing a plan to restore the Everglades. Restoration of the Everglades gained wide support among South Florida conservationists, including Marjorie Stoneman Douglas, famous author and long-time conservationist; Marjorie Carr, president of the Florida Defenders of the Environment; Alice Wainwright of the National

3. The South Florida Water Management District was created in 1972 by Chapter 373, Florida Statutes. The district is successor to the Central and Southern Florida Flood Control District.

Audubon Society; Charles Lee, vice-president of the Florida Audubon Society; and especially Johnny Jones, president of the Florida Wildlife Federation.

In the spring of 1982, on the heels of two years of the worst drought in South Florida's recorded history, heavy spring rains filled the Everglades as they have done for thousands of years. The deer herd, which had thrived during the drought and grown to over 5,000 animals, was imperiled. With over two feet of water covering the Everglades water conservation areas, only a few hundred acres of dry land—the higher tree islands and levees—existed for the deer to occupy.

With starvation an imminent prospect for deer, in July 1982 the Florida Game and Fresh Water Fish Commission scheduled a meeting to approve an emergency deer hunt to kill most of the deer. While the hunt proceeded, fierce local and national reaction against the hunt prompted then-Governor Bob Graham to appoint a committee of state and federal officials to develop recommendations for a coordinated wildlife management plan that would be compatible with water management objectives.[4] The committee found that unless the deer herd was managed at much lower numbers than existed in early 1982, flood-related die-offs would recur. More significantly, the committee concluded that the deer crisis was symptomatic of major problems in the Everglades that were associated with disruption of the natural water regime caused by canals, levees, roads, and water regulation schedules. The committee's final report called for re-creation of a more natural water flow, acquisition of wetlands, and a study of ways to better manage the entire Kissimmee-Lake Okeechobee-Everglades system (Florida Governor's Office 1983).

When the Everglades Wildlife Management Committee held a public meeting on February 17, 1983, in Pompano Beach, over 200 people, including conservationists from around the state and nation, showed up. But rather than focus on deer management, they focused on the restoration of natural water flow through the Everglades system.

Governor Graham had become extremely concerned about the Everglades. In late 1982, he called a statewide meeting of conservationists, public officials, and natural resource managers to discuss the environmental problems of south Florida.[5] On March 4, 1983, Gover

4. The Everglades Wildlife Management Committee was appointed on August 10, 1982, and was made up of representatives of the Florida Governor's Office, Florida Game and Fresh Water Fish Commission, South Florida Management District, Florida departments of Natural Resources and Environmental Regulation, U.S. Department of Agriculture, Consumer Services, Army Corps of Engineers, U.S. Fish and Wildlife Service, and the National Park Service.

5. The "round table" meeting involved over 30 prominent conservationists and federal and state natural resource agency directors.

nor Graham directed his staff to assess the problems of the Everglades as a holistic system and to present him with a strategic plan to address significant problems over the next decade; the plan was to contain concrete, measurable objectives that would help restore the Everglades system. The problem assessment took four months. The staff's approach was straightforward. They asked: What is wrong? What needs to be done? What can be done? How do we get it done? The staff tried to be as innovative as as possible, yet it was clear that certain "givens" could not be changed. For example, the dikes surrounding Lake Okeechobee that provide flood protection to thousands of citizens and their property could not be removed. By late July 1983, the assessment was ready.

SAVE OUR EVERGLADES

On August 9, 1983, Governor Graham announced the Save Our Everglades program (see Figure 3). The goal of the program is to make the Everglades "look and function more like it did in 1900 than it did on August 9, 1983." Water flow restoration, water quality improvement, and land protection via public acquisition are essential elements of the program. Cost of implementation was estimated to exceed $300 million. The acquisition of some 50,000 acres of land in the Everglades region could cost $200 million and the cost of construction to restore the Kissimmee River and the Holey Land and Rotenberger tracts could cost $100 million or more. Cost estimates for cleaning up Lake Okeechobee, while not available, could be substantial. Implementation is expected to take another 10 to 15 years and will be accomplished through the cooperative efforts of the South Florida Water Management District, the Florida Game and Fresh Water Fish Commission, the Florida departments of Natural Resources and Environmental Regulation, the U.S. Army Corps of Engineers, Department of the Interior, and the Federal Highway Administration.

The governor promoted the program with personal visits to the White House and meetings with members of Congress, three Secretaries of the Interior, the Under Secretary of the Army for Civil Works, the Administrator of the Federal Highway Administration, and others. The governor and cabinet passed two resolutions supporting the program. Rarely, if ever, did the governor give an environmental speech without mentioning the Everglades program.

Progress on the program was monitored by the governor's staff. Almost daily contact was made with the various state and federal agencies to check on the status of activities. Verbal and written reports the governor were made by his staff as necessary to affect action, and quarterly progress reports were prepared by the governor's office and made available to the public.

The Everglades Coalition

On March 16, 1984, Governor Graham met with representatives of several national and state conservation organizations at the headquarters of the National Parks and Conservation Association in Washington, D.C. The governor presented the Save Our Everglades program and asked for assistance. The conservation organizations reacted by forming the Everglades Coalition. The initial member organizations were:

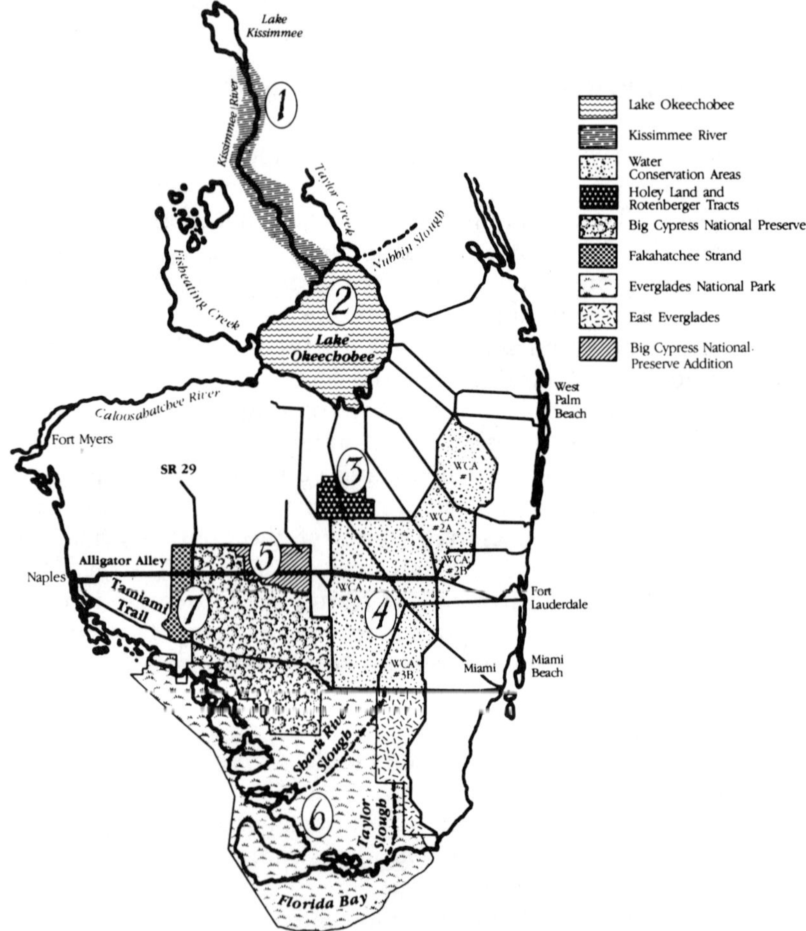

Figure 3. Land-use designations in southern Florida. Source: Office of the Governor, State of Florida.

American Rivers Conservation Council, Conservation Foundation, Defenders of Wildlife, Izaak Walton League, National Audubon Society, Florida Audubon Society, National Humane Society, National Parks and Conservation Association, National Wildlife Federation, The Nature Conservancy, Sierra Club, Trust for Public Land, Wilderness Society, Wildlife Management Institute, and Friends of the Everglades.

The coalition went to work immediately in promoting components of the program to various congressional committees and Members of Congress, the Assistant Secretary of the Army for Civil Works, the Secretary of the Interior, the Administrator of the Federal Highway Administration, and others. The coalition meets regularly to discuss strategies for implementing Save Our Everglades. Generally, Washington-based members of the coalition work on federally related aspects of the program, and Florida groups on state initiatives.

Project Coordination

On November 4, 1983, Governor Graham issued Executive Order 83–178 creating the Kissimmee River-Lake Okeechobee-Everglades Coordinating Council, made up of representatives from several state agencies and the water management district, to coordinate and promote the restoration and protection efforts. The Secretary of the Department of Environmental Regulation was directed to serve as chairperson, with assistance and guidance from the Office of the Governor. However, it was later decided that the governor's office could best affect multiagency coordination of the program with the Department of Environmental Regulation serving as task force and work group leader.

The program's specific objectives are:

- Restore the Kissimmee River and floodplain.
- Improve the water quality of Lake Okeechobee.
- Restore the natural values of the Holey Land and Rotenberger tracts.
- Improve the environmental characterisitics of Alligator Alley.
- Restore the natural hydrology of Everglades National Park.
- Protect the Florida panther.

Each of these objectives and progress toward their achievement is described in the sections that follow.

Restoring the Kissimmee River and Floodplain

Objective. The Save Our Everglades program calls for the restoration of the middle two-thirds of the river through the installation of weirs across the channel and the installation of earthen fill in the channel to force water back into the old river channel and onto the floodplain.

Background. The Kissimmee River was channelized between 1961 and 1971 by the Army Corps of Engineers as a part of the state-federal partnership in the Central and South Florida Flood Control Project. A 98-mile-long serpentine river was converted into a 48-mile-long, 200-foot wide, 30-foot deep channel with six water control structures and associated navigational locks.

Channelization of the river directly destroyed approximately 40,000 acres of river marshland and enhanced drainage of over 100,000 acres of wetlands throughout the basin. Retention time of run-off in the basin was drastically reduced and water receded from the basin eleven times faster than before channelization (Florida Department of Administration 1976). Wetland habitat was reduced by 75 percent. Waterfowl populations declined by 90 percent and bald eagle nesting by 74 percent. Six species of freshwater fish disappeared from the river and two exotic (alien) species moved in after channelization. But the most worrisome result of channelization was its potential to affect both the quantity and quality of South Florida's water supply.

After channelization had been completed, the state requested the Corps to study ways of mitigating the adverse impacts caused by the project. The Corps initiated its study in 1979 but had not completed it when the Save Our Everglades was initiated in 1983.

Implementation Progress. On July 26, 1984, the South Florida Water Management District began construction of three steel sheet pile weirs[6] across the Kissimmee canal (C-38) along with culverts and a berm to divert water from the canal back into old river oxbows and historic marshlands. This demonstration project was intended to restore 12 miles of old river channel and 1,300 acres of river marsh. The project was completed in 1986 at a cost of $1.3 million to the water management district. During high water levels in the canal, several thousand acres of the historic floodplain are flooded by the project. Testing and maintenance of the project will continue until 1989 as part of the planning for further restoration work. Additional restoration planning and design work is being done by the University of California at Berkeley. In preparation for further restoration, the water management district is trying to purchase the 50,000-acre floodplain. Thus far, 19,000 acres are owned by the district.

In October 1985, the Corps completed its final environmental impact statement and feasibility report on the Kissimmee River

6. The weirs are located in the northern part of the canal about 12 miles south of Lake Kissimmee. Each weir has a 5-foot-deep, 60-foot-wide navigation notch to allow boat passage.

restoration (U.S. Army Corps of Engineers 1985). The report recommended no federal financial assistance for a restoration project because it would not produce a net contribution to national economic development. The state of Florida disagreed, saying that modification of the channelized river would enhance the environment of south Florida.

In 1986, Congress passed the Water Resources Development Act. Section 1135 of the law directs the Corps to undertake demonstration projects to modify existing projects for the benefit of the environment and the public interest. The Kissimmee project is a logical candidate for this program and received the strong support of the governor and the Florida congressional delegation for funding under Section 1135. The Everglades Coalition, led by the Sierra Club, carried out an intense and effective lobbying campaign in Congress and with the Assistant Secretary of the Army for Civil Works and the Corps' District Engineer in Jacksonville. In July 1987, the Corps announced that it had approved the Kissimmee project as eligible for funds under Section 1135. Senator Lawton Chiles (D-FL) was instrumental in earmarking $2 million in the FY 1988 federal budget for the Kissimmee Project. It is too soon to know whether Florida will succeed in completely restoring the Kissimmee or whether the Corps can be persuaded to assist in a greater capacity over the long term.

Cleaning Up and Preventing Pollution of Lake Okeechobee

Objective. Eliminate the pollution of Lake Okeechobee caused by agricultural and other activities on lands to the north and south of the lake and improve the quality of the lake.

Background. Lake Okeechobee, often called the "liquid heart"of south Florida, is the centerpiece of the flood control and water supply system—the Central and Southern Florida Project. Surrounded by a 35-foot dike, the lake no longer overflows into the Everglades. All water flow from the lake is released through locks and gates into canals according to a Corps water regulation schedule.

The lake was declared eutrophic by a 1976 state study (Florida Department of Administration 1976). Large nutrient loads, particularly nitrogen and phosphorus, were entering the lake from the dairy lands to the north and crop lands to the south. Taylor Creek and Nubbin Slough, a small tributary to the north, supplies 4 percent of the lake's water, but 30 percent of the phosphorus. The Everglades Agricultural Area to the south supplied up to 8 percent of the lake's water and 26 percent of the nitrogen.

Since 1976, some action had been taken to improve water quality. In accordance with a plan of the water management district, pumping of rich agricultural water from the crop fields in the south was reduced.

In a cooperative effort, the Department of Agriculture, the water management district, and landowners began installing retention basins, fences, and other "best management practices" on the dairies to the north to keep the phosphorus-rich cattle waste out of the lake. By August 1986, 20 dams had been constructed in the control effort.

While cleanup efforts were progressing, a huge algae bloom covered half the lake in the summer of 1985. Following the algae bloom, Governor Graham aaked the Department of Environmental Regulation to study the problem and recommend measures to protect and improve the lake. Consequently, the Secretary of the Department of Environmental Regulation established the Lake Okeechobee Technical Advisory Committee (LOTAC). The committee concluded that the lake was in jeopardy and that phosphorous inflows from dairy farms to the north must be greatly reduced. Subsequently, lake cleanup was added to the Save Our Everglades program.

Implementation Progress. On August 23, 1986, while touring the lake, Governor Graham issued Executive Order 86–150 directing clean up. The legislature appropriated $370,000 to begin the installation of "best management practices" on the 12 dairies in the lower Kissimmee Basin. In 1987, the legislature appropriated $4.8 million for "best management practices" on the dairies north of the lake. Also, in March 1987, the Department of Environmental Regulation adopted a stringent dairy rule requiring dairies in the area to retain runoff onsite and keep waste out of natural waters. Meanwhile, flood-control backpumping of nutrient rich water from the Everglades Agricultural Area into the lake had been significantly reduced under a 1979 water management district plan and a 1982 Department of Environmental Regulation permit to the water management district.[7]

Largely due to concern about Lake Okeechobee pollution, the 1987 legislature enacted the Surface Water Improvement and Management Act (CS/HB 1350, 1987). This law established a Lake Okeechobee Technical Advisory Committee (LOTAC II) to develop recommendations for protecting Lake Okeechobee and other parts of the Everglades.

A massive effort is now under way to clean up Lake Okeechobee, but it is too soon to judge the outcome. Several grand ideas are being evaluated by LOTAC II, such as diverting Taylor Creek and Nubbin Slough waters away from the lake into a large reservoir;[8] a two-mile wide flow-way from the lake through the Everglades Agricultural Area into Water Conservation Area 3; and pumping Taylor Creek and Nubbin Slough waters into the saline aquifer via injection wells. The

7. Under the 1982 Department of Environmental Regulation permit, water is pumped into the water conservation areas rather than the lake.

8. The feasibility of constructing a 10,000-acre reservoir 10 miles east of Taylor Creek is being studied by the Corps of Engineers.

effectiveness of the "best management practices" on dairy lands is yet to be determined. The diversion of runoff from the Everglades Agriculture Area into Water Conservation Area 1 (Art Marshall-Loxahatchee National Wildlife Refuge)[9] is causing conversion of the sawgrass marsh to cattails.[10]

Restoring the Holey Land and Rotenberger Tracts

Objective. Acquire all remaining private land in the Holey Land and Rotenberger tracts and install necessary water control measures (levees and structures) to help re-create a biologically productive Everglades.

Background. A 100-square-mile parcel of partially state-owned land is located adjacent to the northern boundary of Water Conservation Area 3, located about 15 miles south of Lake Okeechobee. This land, known as the Holey Land and Rotenberger tracts, had been degraded by overdrainage, peat fires, and the invasion of upland weeds and trees. The entire acreage was once part of the functioning Everglades system.

The eastern tract (Holey Land) contained 470 acres of privately owned land; the Rotenberger Tract had about 7,000 acres of private land and 4,470 acres were owned by the Seminole Indian tribe. These dried out, overdrained lands served no useful purpose to the Everglades.

Purchase of the remaining private and Seminole Indian land with Conservation and Recreation Land (CARL) acquisition funds would allow reflooding of these lands and restoration of more natural water flows. Acquisition and restoration plans jointly developed by the departments of Environmental Regulation and Natural Resources, the Game and Fresh Water Fish Commission and the water management district have been approved. The estimated cost for constructing the necessary levees was $6.3 million, to be funded 75 percent by the state and 25 percent by the water management district. One million dollars was appropriated for this project by the 1983 legislature.

Implementation Progress. The water management district began construction of containment levees around the Holey Land tract in March 1985; the project is now two-thirds complete. The levees will have flow-through capability and will allow water fluctuations from 0 to 2 feet on this parcel. Water levels will be controlled by the water management district in consultation with the Florida Game and Fresh Water Fish Commission.

As a mitigation measure for wetlands to be lost by I-75 construction, the Florida Department of Transportation contributed $1 million

9. The Fish and Wildlife Service leased Water Conservation Area 1 from the South Florida Water Management District and established the national wildlife refuge.

10. The Fish and Wildlife Service and the Florida Game and Fresh Water Fish Commission have documented that discharges from the Everglades Agricultural Area are causing cattails to replace native Everglades marsh.

to this project. The funds are being used to construct levees around the eastern 3,500 acres (known as the Toe-of-the-Boot), an area not previously included in the restoration.

Restoration of the Holey Land Tract (35,300 acres) will soon be a reality. Acquisition in the Rotenberger Tract has progressed. Some 4,470 acres of Seminole Indian land and 3,500 acres of other private land have been acquired. About 3,500 acres remain to be acquired to achieve full public ownership. No major obstacles stand in the way of restoration of both these tracts, which cover 100 square miles.

Managing the Everglades Deer Herd

Objective. Manage the deer herd through hunting regulations to maintain a population that will have sufficient food and shelter during extreme high water periods.

Background. The deer crisis of the spring and summer of 1982 left an estimated 1,200 deer dead of starvation, drowning, and disease. Another 723 undernourished animals were taken by hunters during a two-day hunt in July. Nineteen deer were rescued, but only six survived. Florida could ill afford a repeat of the deer fiasco.

As recommended by the Everglades Wildlife Management Committee, which studied the 1982 deer crisis, the Florida Game and Fresh Water Fish Commission decided to keep the deer herd size small in Water Conservation Areas 2 and 3. Controlling the number of deer to less than 3,000 would increase their chances of survival during high water by reducing intraspecific competition for limited food supplies. To achieve the population goal, the game and fish commission increased the fall/winter hunting quota and allowed the taking of does.

Implementation Progress. Since 1983, the Game and Fresh Water Fish Commission has effectively managed the deer herd in water conservation area's 2 and 3 with no major problems. The herd size has ranged between 2,500 and 3,000 animals. There have been no water-related mortalities.

Since 1983, the water management district and the Corps have managed the water conservation areas to allow for more natural fluctuation of water. Prolonged high water levels have not occurred. This has been the result of opening and closing the S-12 structures on the Tamiami Trail as necessary to allow water to flow from the water conservation areas into Everglades National Park in proportion to the rainfall in those areas.

Improving the Environmental Characteristics of Alligator Alley

Objective. Convert Alligator Alley (State Road 84) to Interstate 75 across the Everglades and in so doing enhance water flow through the Everglades; install wildlife crossings to protect the Florida panther and other animals.

Background. Alligator Alley, a two-lane road, was built in the 1960s from Fort Lauderdale to Naples through Water Conservation Area 3 and the Big Cypress Swamp. During construction of the road, inadequate attention was given to drainage concerns. The canal parallel to the road on the north side overdrained the land and shunted the water eastward. Sheetflow of water to the south of the road was blocked. The road had similar effects in the Big Cypress Swamp, blocking flow overland and through sloughs.

Alligator Alley has always been considered a death trap for animals. In any given 24-hour period large numbers of mammals and amphibians are killed by automobiles.

Plans for the conversion of Alligator Alley to I-75 had been postponed by the Florida Department of Transportation and the Federal Highway Administration due to environmental controversies. The Florida Department of Transportation was directed to complete design plans, including hydrological improvements for the eastern half (traversing Water Conservation Area 3) of the interstate by October 1984. The Department of Transportation and the water management district were also directed to assess the need for hydrological modifications to Tamiami Trail to restore natural flows to Shark River Slough.

Implementation Progress. Construction on I-75, utilizing the Alligator Alley roadbed for the westbound lanes, began in July 1986. The eastern portion in water conservation area 3 is nearing completion. Additional culverts are being installed and dams placed in the parallel canal to the north of the road to enhance water flow to the area south of the highway. Access for privately owned oil and gas resources and recreation will be provided.

When the interstate is constructed through the Big Cypress over the next few years, additional bridges and culverts will be installed to enhance water flow. To enhance panther and animal safety, 36 underpasses will be installed on the new highway. These underpasses will be located at strands and sloughs, which are the natural panther and animal travel routes. The travel habits of the panther have been documented through radio tracking studies by the Florida Game and Fresh Water Fish Commission over the past four years. Twenty-three of these underpasses will be funded totally by the state at a cost of $10,750,000 because the Federal Highway Administration will assist only in the construction of 13 of these structures. Ten-foot-tall fencing will span both sides of the highway between the animal crossings to prevent road kills from occurring. The underpass–fence combination will ensure the animals' safe movement from one side of the highway to the other.

Because access to private property along the Alley will be lost when the interstate is built, severance damages must be paid as a part of the cost of the highway (90 percent—Federal Highway Administration Agency—10 percent—Department of Transportation). Total severance costs are equal to about one-half the total value of the 88,000 acres of private land affected. The devaluation of the 88,000 acres resulting from interstate construction presents an opportunity to purchase those lands outright at about one-half their original value.[11]

The unique opportunity to cheaply acquire those lands in the upper Big Cypress watershed stimulated a proposal that the state of Florida and Department of the Interior jointly purchase them as part of a larger addition to the Big Cypress National Preserve. In 1985, the Florida Legislature amended the Big Cypress Conservation Act of 1973 (Section 380.055, F.S.) to expand the Big Cypress Area of Critical State Concern[12] by 128,000 acres (including the lands devalued by the highway project). On July 2, 1985, the governor and cabinet included the area on the state's CARL acquisition list. Subsequently, the governor and cabinet set aside $22.5 million of CARL funds for land acquisition in the Everglades, including the Big Cypress addition.

Federal legislation to expand the Big Cypress National Preserve by 128,000 acres through a joint federal-state purchase was introduced by Senator Lawton Chiles (S.2029) and Representative Thomas Lewis (H.R. 4090) on January 30, 1986. On July 28, H.R. 4090 passed the House with an amendment to expand the purchase to 136,000 acres.

In the Senate, S.2029 met opposition from the Department of the Interior and the Colliers family, principal land owners in the proposed addition to the preserve. The Interior Department opposed the bill principally because it wanted to obtain most of the acreage through an interstate land exchange. The swap would have involved 118,000 acres of privately owned land, including about 85,000 acres in the proposed addition, 15,000 acres in the Fakahatchee Strand, and about 18,000 acres in the Ten Thousand Islands area. Since interstate land swaps require congressional approval, the Interior Department and the Col-

11. Recreational access points will be provided along I-75. Alligator Alley is presently the only means of access to over one million acres of public land in the Everglades region. Access to oil and gas reserves will also be provided, lest over $1 billion in mineral interests would have to be purchased.

12. Area of Critical State Concern designation provides the state with stringent land and water use controls beyond that which otherwise exist in Florida law. This designation also gives the state authority to purchase the land using eminent domain.

liers tried to get the swap added to S.2029, but were unsuccessful. The entire measure died at the end of the 99th Congress.

Big Cypress acquisition legislation was reintroduced in Congress in 1987 as H.R. 184 (Representative Lewis) and S.90 (senators Lawton Chiles and Bob Graham).[13] S.90 passed both House and Senate in March and April of 1988, respectively. The legislation was sent to the president for signature (or veto) April 22, 1988. Florida has already invested about $15 million in panther protection and land acquisition in the proposed Big Cypress addition, in expectation of federal legislation.

Restoring the Natural Hydrology of Everglades National Park

Objective. Restore natural water flows into Everglades National Park and acquire additional land around the perimeter of the park and in the Big Cypress National Preserve to protect water flows.

Background. Two hundred miles south of the Kissimmee headwaters lies Everglades National Park, a 1.4-million acre expanse of marsh, cypress swamp, pine lands, hardwood hammocks, and mangrove estuaries. Historically, this area received about half of its water from local rainfall and half from overland flow from the north. Slightly over half the inflow came from the Big Cypress and the rest came from the Ever- glades. Biological communities and life cycles evolved around the slow rise and fall of water levels during the rainy summers and dry winters.

Water levels and flow were altered before the park was established in 1947. The previous 40 years of drainage had lowered Everglades water levels by several feet. The Tamiami Trail (U.S. 41) was constructed in the 1920s, with its accompanying drainage canal along the park's northern border.

By the mid-1960s, the water conservation areas in the Everglades were diked on the east and south sides, and the southern levee along Tamiami Trail was fitted with four structures[14] that totally controlled flow into the park from the water conservation areas. Water was held in the areas during the dry season (for water supply) and discharged during the wet season (to maintain flood-control storage capacity). As a result, the park suffered from extended dry seasons and extreme flooding.

13. Principal differences between the bills are: S.90 includes 146,000 acres, specific oil and gas regulatory provisions, and encourages hunting and fishing; H.R. 184 includes 136,000 acres, allows more liberal oil and gas development, and allows hunting and fishing.

14. These water control structures are named S-12 structures.

In 1968, the Corps and National Park Service agreed on a plan to guarantee the park 315,000 acre-feet of water per year on a monthly basis patterned on historical flow. However, this arrangement did not solve the problem of dry periods and flooding in the park. In 1983, the park reported that numbers of colonial wading birds had declined 90 percent since 1934; woodstorks had nested only five of the nine years between 1953 and 1961, and since 1962 they had nested successfully only during three years; ospreys had declined 58 percent in the Florida Bay over the previous 20 years; and brown pelicans had declined 40 percent between 1977 to 1987. Estuary-dependent species and fish had shown a noticeable decline. Alligators had lost most of their eggs over the previous five years. Invasions of exotic (alien) plants, especially Brazilian pepper, Melaleuca, and Australian pine, were replacing native species. The park service claimed that these adverse impacts resulted from the drastic alterations in the hydrology of the Everglades.

To correct hydrological problems, in 1983 the park service asked the South Florida Water Management District to fill in the canal associated with levee L-67 extension, which separates the park from the East Everglades,[15] and remove levee L-28 to allow natural flow from water conservation area 3 into the Big Cypress. The park also wanted to restore flow into the northeast Shark River Slough and establish a new water delivery schedule for the park. The park's request, coupled with the state's efforts to acquire large amounts of land on the east and northwest boundaries of the park was a good start toward restoring the Everglades' ecological values.

Implementation Progress. Restoration of the park began with the water management district's April 5, 1983, emergency order approving the park's request. In late 1983, the Corps undertook two projects. Earthen plugs were placed in the canal and openings were cut in the levees along the northern portion of levee (L-28), which separates Water Conservation Area 3 from the Big Cypress National Preserve. These gaps allowed water to flow into the Big Cypress Swamp. The park had requested complete removal of L-28, but the Corps did not want to eliminate its capability to restore the levee, if necessary, for water supply. The Corps also installed plugs in the canal (L-67 extension) that extends from Tamiami Trail along the eastern park border. The plugs were installed to force water from the canal into the sawgrass marshes so that it would flow through Shark River Slough.

Before canals and levees changed the hydrology, the East Everglades provided about half the water to the eastern portion of Everglades National Park. This 240-square-mile area includes the head-

15. The L-67 extension was built as a part of the 1968 water delivery plan for the park. However, the canal gushed into the park with no sheetflow effect.

waters of northeast Shark River Slough and Taylor Slough, the two principle flow-ways into the eastern park.

Since August 1983, the state and water management district has acquired 55,000 acres in the lower East Everglades in the Taylor Slough and C-111 basin.[16] About 75,000 acres of the northern East Everglades, which includes a portion of northeast Shark River Slough, are in private ownership. Although this area is not drained or protected from flooding, it is deprived of natural flow by levees and canals to the east, north, and west.

In 1984, Congress passed legislation sponsored by Congressman Dante Fascell (P.L. 98–181) that authorized the Corps to develop a new water delivery schedule for the park. The law also authorized an experimental water delivery program to northeast Shark River Slough and the East Everglades. Because the land to be flooded in the East Everglades is private and partially developed, the Corps also began developing plans for flood control works to protect residential and agricultural areas.

The experimental water delivery program began in mid-1984 and has considerably increased water flow into northeast Shark River Slough. The effect has been a doubling of the area over which water flows into the eastern half of Everglades National Park. A major feature of the new water delivery program is the "rain driven model" developed by the water management district. Under the model, water is delivered to the park in proportion to the amount and timing of rainfall that would otherwise have naturally flowed from the water conservation areas.

The experimental delivery program is authorized until January 1, 1989. Meanwhile, the Corps has completed a draft general design memorandum for the East Everglades that includes flood protection for the residential area and agricultural operations along the eastern edge of northeast Shark River Slough. The memorandum has not yet been officially released.

The undeveloped private property in the East Everglades is on the state CARL acquisition list and the water management district's, Save Our Rivers acquisition list. In January 1988, Governor Martinez proposed the expansion of Everglades National Park to include approximately 75,000 acres of the East Everglades. Secretary of the Interior Donald Hodel agreed to pursue expansion of the park.

The water management district and the Corps have nearly completed plans for restoration of C-111 to establish sheet flow from the lower East Everglades to Florida Bay. Another Interior-proposed land swap could be involved in this flow restoration effort. The swap

16. C-111, also known as the Aerojet Canal, was dug in the 1960s; it interrupts sheetflow into Florida Bay.

involves trading 5,000 acres of Aerojet General land in the C-111 basin to the Department of the Interior in return for several thousand acres of federally owned land in Nevada. If the swap occurs, the water management district has agreed to purchase the 5,000 acres from the Department of Interior; the Department would use the sale proceeds of $1.6 million to purchase land in the Key Deer and Lower Suwannee River national wildlife refuges. This swap is also pending in Congress. [**EDITOR'S NOTE:** The swap was passed by Congress (P.L. 100-275) in March 1988 and signed by the President.]

Aerojet, in January 1988, sold another 5,000 acres in the Taylor Slough basin to agricultural interests that had leased the land for farming for several years. The western 1,500 acres of this area, known as the Frog Pond, is flood prone, and crop growth during some portions of the year requires a lowering of water levels by pumping down adjacent canals. Lowering of the water levels in this area also lowers the water level for one to two miles inside the park. Park officials claim that this is adversely affecting Taylor Creek. The water management district plans to phase out Frog Pond drawdowns by 1990.

In May 1986, the Corps released a report describing methods of restoring natural conditions on large portions of Golden Gate Estates. The report suggested the plugging of canals and land acquisition as a means of restoring seasonal flooding on 30,000 acres and increasing finfish by 28 percent in Faka Union Bay. The Corps estimated the cost of construction to be $2.2 million, with no federal participation (Army Corps of Engineers 1986). Golden Gate Estates is on the CARL acquisition list, but there is strong local landowner opposition to acquisition and restoration. Meanwhile, the park service has received federal, state, and county approval to restore three canals in the Big Cypress National Preserve that affect the hydrology of the park.

Protect the Florida Panther and Acquire Portions of the Big Cypress Swamp and Fakahatchee Strand

Objective. Protect the Florida panther and other wildlife through the regulation of hunting and other activities and by the acquisition and management of land in the Big Cypress Swamp and Fakahatchee Strand.

Background. The Florida panther is on the brink of extinction. The Everglades National Park/Big Cypress Preserve and Fakahatchee Strand provide the only habitat for this rare mammal (see "The Florida Panther" in this volume). Despite this, federal and state acquisition programs in these areas have dragged on for years.

The best-documented threat to South Florida's existing panther population is the automobile. Twelve of twenty known panther deaths since 1972 were caused by automobiles. Four animals were killed on Alligator Alley from 1984 through 1986; three panthers have been killed in recent years on State Road 29, which passes through the Fakahatchee Strand. Alligator Alley, with 3,000 cars per day and increasing, represents a more serious threat. To a lesser degree Tamiami Trail is also a problem.

In late 1982, a proposal to extend an oil company road to connect Tamiami Trail to Alligator Alley set off a series of events. The Florida Game and Fresh Water Fish Commisson said that only about 20 Florida panthers existed and that further human intrusion into the panthers' habitat facilitated by roads would accelerate the animals' extinction.

The governor vetoed the proposal in 1983. This action quickly attracted the attention of major Big Cypress mineral and land owners, Collier Enterprises, Inc., and Barron Collier Company. Later in 1983, preliminary discussions began between the governor's staff and the Colliers on possible federal legislation to expand the Big Cypress National Preserve in concert with the conversion of Alligator Alley to I-75.

The 1983 legislature passed legislation to strengthen Florida's wetlands protection ability and specifically defined the Everglades and Big Cypress Swamp as wetlands to be regulated and protected. This legislation required that consideration be given to protection of fish and wildlife values when wetlands development permits are considered and that mitigation occur when such lands are developed. The 1983 legislature also created the Florida Panther Technical Advisory Committee. On July 19, 1983, the Governor and Cabinet assigned the Fakahatchee Strand high priority for acquisition under the CARL acquisition program. By January 1984, over 34,000 acres had been added to the Fakahatchee Strand CARL acquisition project, bringing this project to a total of 79,300 acres in state ownership or designated for future acquisition.

Implementation Process. The principal strategy for protecting the panther involves highway modification and land acquisition. Acquisition of land for the panther has multiple benefits including protection of water flow and quality to the Big Cypress National Preserve and Everglades National Park, regional water supplies, and plant and animal communities that include several threatened and endangered species.

The Florida Department of Transportation was directed to erect panther warning signs along State Road 29, Alligator Alley, and Tamiami Trail. The department also began exploring roadway design modifications to allow the panther safe crossing.

In April 1984, the governor announced plans to pursue joint state/federal acquisition of 165,000 acres in the Fakahatchee Strand and Big Cypress in conjunction with with I-75 construction. The U.S.

Fish and Wildlife Service (FWS) later revealed plans to establish a national wildlife refuge in the Fakahatchee Strand.

As plans progressed for I-75, FWS issued its biological opinion under Section 7 of the Endangered Species Act, stating that the construction of the highway would jeopardize the continued existence of the panther (Allen 1985). Consequently, animal and panther underpasses and fences were incorporated into the highway plans.

In 1985, the Florida Department of Transportation reduced nighttime speed limits to 45 miles per hour on Alligator Alley, Tamiami Trail, and State Road 29. Warning signs were erected on these roads and an additional highway patrolman was assigned to enforce speed limits.

In the Big Cypress National Preserve, the Florida Game and Fresh Water Fish Commission issued new regulations in May 1985, prohibiting the use of all-terrain cycles, motorcycles, and certain off-road vehicles for hunting, fishing, and frogging. The commission also prohibited the use of dogs for hunting in the preserve, except for the first nine days of hunting season; it also closed the Fakahatchee Strand to all hunting in 1986.

In April 1986, FWS, the National Park Service, the Florida Department of Natural Resources and the Game and Fresh Water Fish Commission formed an interagency task force on panther recovery. The task force released a recovery plan on June 22, 1987.

The commission has established a captive-breeding program for the panther utilizing the 7,000-acre White Oak Plantation near Jacksonville, Florida. The commission plans to release captively bred panthers back into the wild to increase the panther population.

Unprecedented efforts are being made to protect the Florida panther from extinction. The success of this work will not be determinable for years. The estimated number of panthers has increased to a maximum of 50, thanks principally to better estimation ability and not to recovery efforts.

OUTLOOK FOR THE FUTURE

The potential for restoring the Everglades is greater today than any time since the initiative began. The program has gained institutional stability and acceptance as more than a short-term fad. The tremendous public support from around the state and nation and the impressive interest and assistance from the Everglades Coalition have provided a solid foundation for the program. The Save Our Everglades program is strongly supported by the governor and cabinet of Florida and the Florida congressional delegation.

The election of former Florida Governor Bob Graham to the U.S. Senate in 1986 gives the state a strong advocate in Washington.

Governor Martinez has also stepped forward as a strong proponent of protecting and restoring the Everglades. During the 1987 legislative session, Governor Martinez proposed and signed state legislation to: 1) increase the state land acquisition fund (CARL) by over $200 million over the next nine years; 2) clean up polluted lakes, rivers and bays, especially Lake Okeechobee; 3) provide $4.8 million to clean up dairies north of Lake Okeechobee; and 4) provide eminent domain authority for acquiring Golden Gate Estates. He also supports the inclusion of the Kissimmee River in the Corps' plans for implementing Section 1135 river restoration demonstration projects, federal legislation to expand the Big Cypress National Preserve, and the restoration of water flow to Everglades National Park.

Governor Martinez publicly affirmed his strong commitment to protecting and restoring the Everglades on November 17, 1987, and asked for full cooperation of state agencies, the water management district, the Corps of Engineers and the Department of the Interior. On December 21, 1987, in answer to a request by Dade County, the governor rejected a proposal to construct an airport in the Everglades water conservation areas. This is the same airport that was planned and partially constructed in the Big Cypress Swamp in the 1970s before it was halted.

Governor Martinez on January 21, 1988 issued an executive order directing state agencies and the water management district to prevent development in the water conservation areas and protect the Everglades from harm. The order also directed the restoration of the Kissimmee River, the cleanup of Lake Okeechobee and the restoration of Golden Gate Estates. The following day the governor announced plans for expansion of Everglades National Park through joint state of Florida-Department of the Interior acquisition of the East Everglades.

Funding for a program as large and diverse as the Save Our Everglades program is difficult to project beyond any particular current budget year. Thus far the state legislature has funded all needs of the program. With the Everglades as a state priority, and with strong public and conservation community support, adequate funding is likely to continue at the state level. Yet program success still depends on substantial federal financial assistance, especially for the Kissimmee River restoration, Big Cypress National Preserve addition and Everglades National Park expansion and restoration.

Ultimately, the success of Save Our Everglades depends upon the continued support and active involvement of individual citizens and state and national conservation organizations. Without continued pressure from the public, Save Our Everglades, like any program, is susceptible to having its funds cut or its objectives scaled back.

REFERENCES

Allen, D.B. 1985. Letter of February 21, 1985 to Federal Highway Administration Division Administrator P. E. Carpenter.

Blake, N.M. 1980. *Land Into Water—Water Into Land.* University Presses of Florida. Tallahassee, Florida.

Central and Southern Florida Flood Control District. Unpublished. Central and Southern Florida Flood Control Project—Eight Years of Progress, 1949–1957.

Fairchild Tropical Garden. July 1983. *Garden Bulletin.* Miami, Florida.

Fernald, E.A. and Patton, D.J. 1984. *Water Resources Atlas of Florida.* Institute of Science and Public Affairs. Tallahassee, Florida.

Florida Department of Administration. 1976. Unpublished. Final Report on the Special Project to Prevent Eutrophication of Lake Okeechobee.

Florida Governor's Office. 1983. Unpublished. Report of the Everglades Wildlife Management Committee. (August).

Gleason, P.J. 1974. *Environments of South Florida: Present and Past.* Miami Geological Society. Miami, Florida.

Estus Whitfield is environmental advisor to the governor of Florida and has been involved in Everglades matters since 1971.

Part Four

Species Accounts

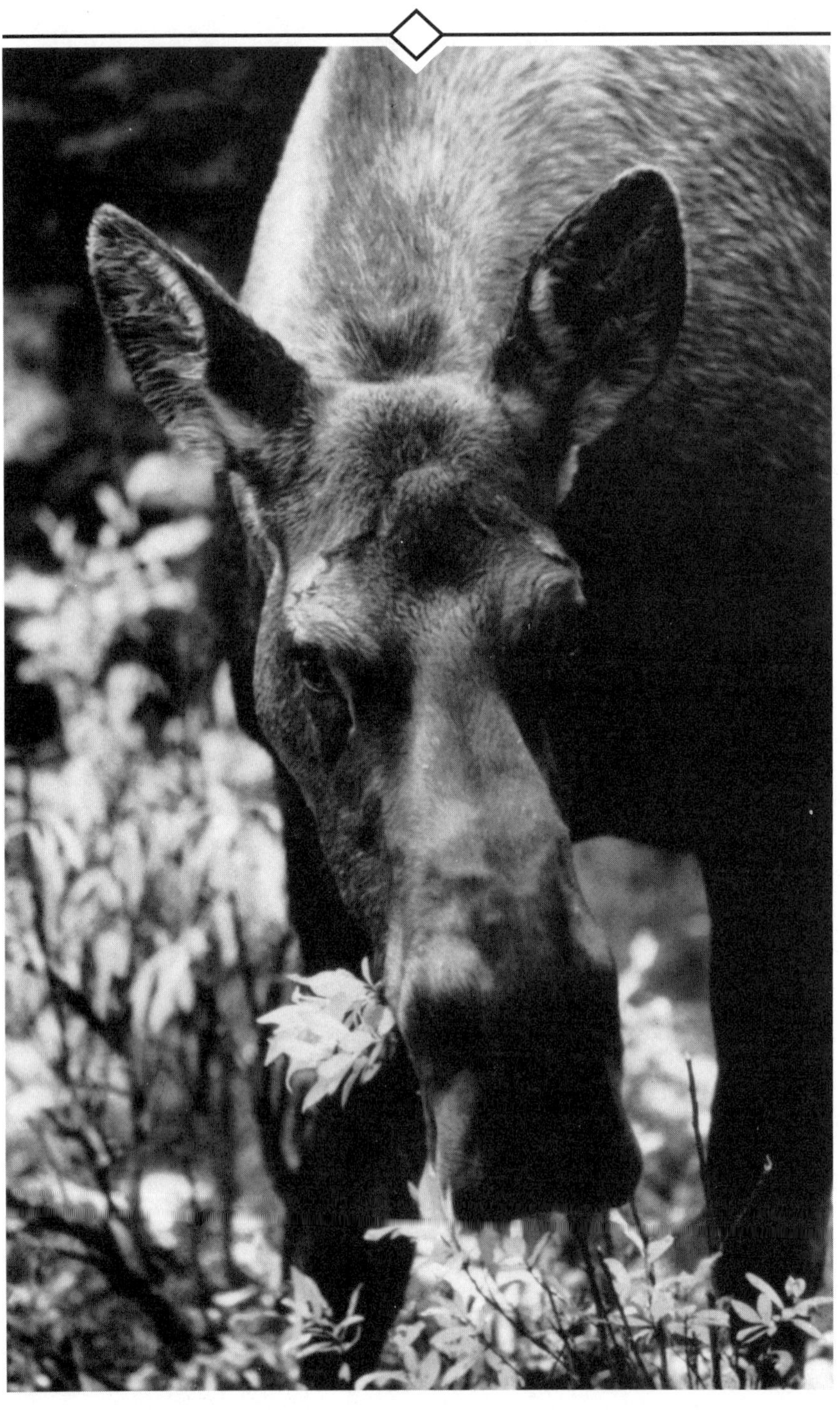

Moose populations in Alaska vary greatly due to snow conditions, habitat quality and quantity, predation, and hunting. *John Hyde*

The Moose in Alaska

Richard H. Bishop

Alaska Department of Fish and Game

SPECIES DESCRIPTION AND NATURAL HISTORY[1]

The moose (*Alces alces*) is the largest member of the deer family in the world, and the Alaskan race (*Alces alces gigas*) is considered the largest of all moose. Moose are long-legged and heavy-bodied, with a drooping nose, a "bell" or dewlap under the chin, and a small tail that is sometimes absent. They are golden brown to almost black in color, depending upon the season and the sex of the animal. The hair of newborn calves is generally red brown, fading to a lighter rust color within a few weeks. Newborn calves weigh 28 to 35 pounds and grow to more than 300 pounds within five months. The few adult males in prime condition that have been weighed indicate that 1,200 to 1,500 pounds is the usual range; adult females weigh 800 to 1,300 pounds.

The largest moose antlers in North America come from Alaska and the Yukon Northwest Territories of Canada. Only bulls have antlers. Large-antlered bulls are found throughout Alaska, but many of the largest have come from the western portion of the state. Moose occasionally produce trophy antlers when they are 6 or 7 years old, but

1. Adapted from the Alaska Department of Fish and Game *Wildlife Notebook Series.*

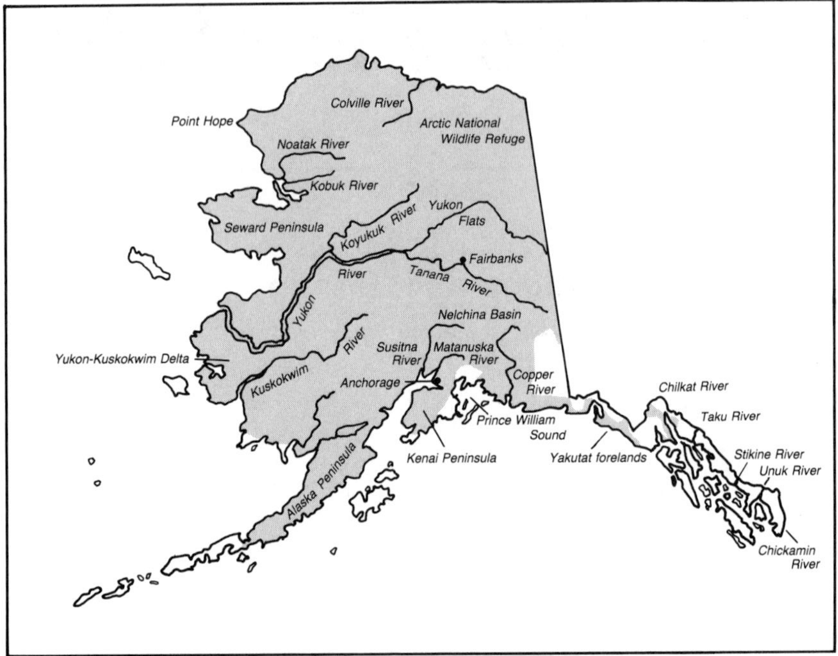

Figure 1. Moose distribution in Alaska. Source: LeResche *et al.* 1974.

the largest antlers are grown at 8 to 12 years of age. Antlers may begin to decline in size by age 13 or 14. In the wild, few moose live more than 16 years, although some cows have exceeded 20 years.

Distribution

In Alaska, moose occur in suitable habitat from the southeastern "Panhandle" to the Colville River on the Arctic Slope. In most of Alaska, they are usually most abundant in recently burned areas that contain willow and birch shrubs, in timberline plateaus, and along major rivers. In the last 30 years, moose have become very abundant in parts of the Arctic Slope and northwestern Alaska (see Figure 1).

Breeding

Moose breed, or "rut," in the fall, with peak activity in late September and early October. Cows generally first breed when they are 28 months old, but occasionally breed at 16 months. Calves are born from mid-May to early June after a gestation period of about 240 days. Cows have twins 15 to 60 percent of the time, and triplets may occur once in every 1,000 births. The incidence of twinning is related to nutrition; a cow is more likely to have twins when it is well fed. A cow defends her newborn calf vigorously against any intruder, including other moose.

Calves begin eating solid food a few days after birth and are weaned in the fall, when the mother begins breeding again. The maternal bond is not broken until calves are 12 months old, at which time the mother aggressively chases the offspring from her immediate area just before she gives birth. Both sexes are able to reproduce as yearlings at 15 to 16 months of age.

Adult males "spar" with each other during the rut by bringing their antlers together and pushing. The winner's prize is the female. Broken ribs and abscessed punctures are quite common, but usually heal satisfactorily. Occasionally, a bull dies as a result of a breeding fight, or two bulls will die as a result of locking antlers.

By late October, when adult males have exhausted both their summer accumulation of fat and their desire to rut, they begin feeding again. Most adult bulls shed their antlers in late November through mid-January. Yearling bulls may not lose their antlers until February or March.

Diet

During fall and winter, moose consume large quantities of willow, birch, and aspen twigs. In some areas with high population numbers, moose actually establish a "hedge" or browse line six to eight feet above the ground by eating most of the available branches of favored food species. Spring is the time of grazing and browsing, and moose eat a variety of foods, particularly sedges (*Carex* sp.), horsetail (*Equisetum* sp.), and various pond weeds, and grasses. During summer, moose feed on vegetation in shallow ponds, on forbs, and on leaves of birch, willow, and aspen.

Seasonal Movements

Most moose make seasonal movements to calving, rutting, and wintering areas. Some movements are only a few miles; others are up to 60 miles. Spring travel may involve long movements to lowlands with abundant ponds where calving occurs. In the fall, moose seek rutting areas often at timberline in adjacent mountains. Commonly, moose move back to lowlands during winter.

SIGNIFICANCE OF THE SPECIES

Throughout their range in Alaska, moose are of great ecological significance. When people think of "the north woods," moose invariably and rightly come to mind. Their numbers, size, distribution, and ecological role as plant eaters, and as prey, make moose one of the most important species in the boreal forest, or taiga. Only caribou (*Rangifer tarandus*) sometimes rival or surpass moose as the principal, large prey species in the taiga ecosystem.

In coastal tundra areas, caribou take precedence as large prey. In the mountains, Dall sheep (*Ovis dalli*) or mountain goat (*Oreamnos americanus*) are the main large prey species; while in the rain forests of southeastern Alaska, Sitka black-tailed deer (*Odocoileus hemionus sitkensis*) fulfill this role. Moose, however, overlap all of these species in distribution. Moose populations are well established along arctic and western coastal rivers and shrublands, in major river valleys and other suitable habitats in southeastern Alaska, and in subalpine areas of most mountain ranges. This broad distribution dramatizes the moose's adaptability.

Moose convert vast quantities of plant material into large, mobile units of animal protein, fat, and bone. In doing so, they provide a great resource to other species unequipped to sustain themselves by eating plants. Wolves, black bears (*Ursus americanus*), grizzly bears (*Ursus arctos*), and humans kill moose for food. People also use the skin, bones, and antlers for leather, implements, and handicrafts, although these by-products have been largely replaced by manufactured items.

Wolverines (*Gulo gulo*), red foxes (*Vulpes vulpes*), coyotes (*Canis latrans*), marten (*Martes americana*, shrews (Soricidae), various voles and lemmings (Microtinae), red squirrels (*Tamiasciurus hudsonicus*), bald eagles (*Haliaeetus leucocephalus*), ravens (*Corvus corax*), crows (*Corvus caurinus*), gray jays (*Perisoreus canadensis*), and chickadees (*Palus* sp.) all benefit by feeding on the remains of moose. In a land where food can be very scarce and unevenly distributed, moose remains assure the scavenger's prosperity for a short time.

When moose numbers decline, the moose predators and scavengers turn to other foods. If other foods are also scarce, predators and scavengers are likely to diminish. Fortunately, most of the species that depend on the moose for food are adapted to catching other prey or, like bears, to eating grasses, berries, and other plant material.

In earlier times, human populations in Alaska were highly dependent on fishing and hunting. Today, the wolf's well-being in vast areas of central Alaska is most closely linked with moose. Wolves are dependent on large plant eaters such as moose, caribou, and deer. As highly adaptable, efficient predators, wolves can live for a time on other foods. But when numbers of primary prey decline, wolves eventually follow. Wolves occasionally contribute to their own dilemma by reducing or suppressing the recovery of prey species such as the moose.

Moose are still prized as food by humans. Although commercially produced foods are widely available, Alaskans prefer moose and other wildlife for several reasons. In remote communities, the supply of alternatives to local foods is sometimes unreliable, and the cost is very high. For people in even more remote locations away from communities, there is no regular transportation and no stores. Commercially produced foods can be unavailable for long periods. In these situations, moose may be the most economically practical protein source.

For those living in towns, moose can also represent a significant economic benefit. A recent estimate for the Fairbanks area indicated that on average a moose would supply meat worth approximately $1,960. Since 1963, reported moose kills by hunters have ranged from 8,883 in 1971 to 3,286 in 1975; the reported 1986 take was 7,571 moose (Alaska Department of Fish and Game 1986). In addition, many people consider moose meat to be of higher quality than commercial beef because it has higher protein content, significantly lower fat content, and contains no synthetic substances.

Finally, moose is important to a wide cross-section of Alaskans who take great personal satisfaction in hunting and gathering. Hunting, trapping, and gathering foods and materials contribute to feelings of self-sufficiency and attachment to the land.

Moose are also a significant aesthetic resource. Their visibility, wide distribution, and adaptability to the incursions of people and development make them more viewable than most other Alaskan wildlife species.

HISTORICAL PERSPECTIVE

Moose populations have responded to Alaska's diverse habitats and ecological events in equally diverse ways. The following abstract concisely summarizes the moose's historic distribution in Alaska and accurately describes its general circumstances up to the present.

> Moose have been present in Alaska since mid- to late-pleistocene times. They probably survived in relatively small, disjunct groups wherever suitable habitat could be found throughout this period, when a tundra-steppe community dominated much of the Alaska refugium. With the close of the glacial period and proliferation of shrub and forest communities, they spread throughout much of Alaska. In more recent times, riparian and subalpine willow communities have provided a means of maintaining minimal populations able to exploit new range produced by fire and other disturbances; this pattern persists today. Very recent extensions of moose distribution have occurred in the geographic extremes of Alaska: in southeastern Alaska, where glacial recessions have allowed moose to expand along major river valleys crossing the coastal range, and in northwestern Alaska, where moose have become established on the western Seward Peninsula and north of the Noatak River. On the Arctic Slope moose seem to have been established for a longer time than on the western tundra areas, but are currently increasing in numbers. In

most of Alaska, moose numbers have risen and declined dramatically in local areas over the last 150 years, largely in response to creation and maturation of fire-caused seral range. Historical accounts that moose were absent from a particular locale most likely reflect only a period of very low numbers resulting from a prolonged absence of fires in that area. Extremely low densities of moose presently exist in some areas where extensive spruce stands are dominant. Thus, in most of Alaska, the purported variations in moose distribution have in reality been only variations in relative abundance (LeResche *et al.* 1974).

Southeastern Alaska

Southeastern Alaska, generally known as the panhandle, is the narrow strip of the state adjacent to the Canadian border and south and east of Cordova. In most of this region, moose were essentially unknown prior to 1875 (Alaska Department of Fish and Game 1985). Their subsequent distribution and numbers were restricted by limited habitat and occasionally by extremely deep, persistent snows. Major rivers, such as the Unuk, Stikine, Taku, Alsek, and Chilkat, which rise in Canada and cut through the glaciated coastal mountains, provided the moose with access to coastal areas (Klein 1965). Moose numbers in the Yakutat area, where more extensive habitat exists, irrupted in the 1960s and reached 4,000 to 5,000 by 1971–1972 (Alaska Department of Fish and Game 1973). The population crashed soon after when prolonged deep snows precluded access to adequate food. Predation by wolves, which had grown in numbers along with the moose, and by brown bears, retarded moose population growth. Moose numbers since have recovered to 700 to 800 animals (Alaska Department of Fish and Game 1985).

The U.S. Fish and Wildlife Service (FWS) transplanted moose to several sites in southeastern Alaska in the 1940s and 1950s. Small populations persist along the Chickamin River and at Berners Bay, and a small natural population is present at Thomas Bay. Near Cordova on the Copper River delta, transplanted moose thrived and numbered about 1,000 in 1983. Farther north and west, a few moose are found near Valdez and in western Prince William Sound on the Nellie Juan River. However, moose are absent elsewhere in Prince William Sound because it lacks good habitat and is largely isolated by extensive icefields (Alaska Department of Fish and Game 1973).

Southcentral Alaska

Southcentral Alaska is generally considered to be that part of the state lying south of the Alaska Range and including the Kenai and Alaska peninsulas, but not lands in southeastern Alaska. It is a large area with great variations in topography, weather, habitats, and ecological relationships. Generalizations about moose in this area are difficult to make. However, enough information exists to indicate that moose numbers have fluctutated dramatically in various parts of southcentral Alaska since the late 1800s. The accounts of explorers and naturalists suggest that moose, although present, were not abundant in much of southcentral Alaska around 1900 (Spencer and Chatelain 1953, Bishop and Rausch 1974). Reports indicate that moose numbers increased sporadically, mainly in response to wildfires and human-caused fires, land clearing, or other habitat disturbances (Spencer and Chatelain 1953).

On the Alaska Peninsula, moose had become common by 1900 (Peterson 1955); they were then very scarce for many years, but by the 1950s were again increasing. In general, their numbers increased during the 1950s and 1960s. Spencer and Chatelain (1953) speculated that this increase resulted from gradual revegetation following extensive volcanic activity between 1910 and 1930. On the Kenai Peninsula, a series of wildfires between 1900 and 1950 caused recurring periods of improved habitat and periodic increases in moose numbers. Interspersed with these increases were declines as vegetation matured and food species either grew too large to provide accessible browse or died out (Spencer and Chatelain 1953, Spencer and Haakala 1964). Wolves were not a factor because they had disappeared from the Kenai Peninsula around 1900 and did not return until the mid-1960s (Bishop and Rausch 1974).

In the Susitna and Matanuska River valleys, north of Anchorage, moose were at low numbers until the 1920s and 1930s, when fires and settlement created improved habitat. Moose populations in these areas reached some of the highest densities in the state during the 1960s. During the 1960s, moose in the Nelchina Basin, a large area northeast of the Matanuska Valley, underwent similar population fluctuations with moose reaching peak numbers about 1960. During the 1960s and early 1970s, severe winters and high wolf populations contributed to substantial population declines (Bishop and Rausch 1974). The Nelchina Basin shares with Interior Alaska long winters, periodic deep, peristent snow cover, and, in the 1960s and 1970s, substantial wolf populations and increasing brown or grizzly bear populations.

Overall, in southcentral Alaska, moose populations increased during the period from 1900 through 1960 in response to favorable habitat changes resulting from wildfire, human-caused fire and other disturbances, moderate winters in the 1940s and 1950s, and wolf control in the late 1940s through 1960.

Interior and Western Alaska

Interior Alaska includes the vast taiga between the Alaska Range and the Brooks Range. Dry continental climates, broad valleys, and rugged mountains characterize inland areas. Low, old mountains with diminishing forests and increasingly cool, wet, year-round climates occur near the western coast. Tundra and shrublands dominate the western coast, except in eastern Norton Sound, where strands of forest stretch down to the sea along rivers. Recurring wildfire modified, to the benefit of the moose, habitats in the dry Interior. Fires changed vast areas of maturing forest to young forest and shrub stands, thus providing prime food for browsing moose, hares, bud-eating grouse, and seed-eating lemmings and voles. Wolves, lynx (*Felis lynx*), and other predators or scavengers benefited from the subsequent increases in prey. Yet moose were virtually absent in great expanses of the Interior at the turn of the century, particularly along major waterways where fire impacts were limited.

Moose numbers gradually rose in the early 1900s until by the late 1930s they were common if not abundant in much of the Interior. In the late 1940s and 1950s, increases in moose occurred in response to new fire-caused range, moderate winters, systematic wolf control and, in some years, essentially unlimited aerial shooting of wolves (Bishop and Rausch 1974, LeResche *et al.* 1974). Increased government fire-control programs reduced benefits of wildfires beginning in the late 1940s. During the ensuing 40 years, fire control significantly reduced the total area rehabilitated by fire.

During the 1960s and 1970s, severe winters precipitated moose population "crashes" (Bishop and Rausch 1974, Gasaway *et al.* 1983). Coincidentally, wolf numbers, relieved of systematic control programs and of public aerial shooting in 1972, rapidly increased. Grizzly bear numbers also appeared to increase during the same period. Both species contributed to increased moose mortality. In some areas, excessive hunting contributed to more rapid moose declines. Despite hunting season restrictions or closures and a series of moderate winters, moose numbers in most areas continued to decline (Gasaway *et al.* 1983, Boertje *et al.* 1985). Exceptions to this were principally areas where wolf control programs were undertaken by the Alaska Department of Fish and Game after 1975 or where hunter/trappers were able to take significant numbers of wolves (Alaska Department of Fish and Game, unpubl. reports 1975–1984, Gasaway *et al.* 1983).

In western Alaska, moose numbers appeared to increase during the early 1900s through the 1950s, but did not reach the numbers found in the Interior. Peterson (1955) cites accounts from the turn of the century indicating that moose had recently reached the lower Yukon River near the limit of forest and tall shrub habitats. Moose did not become established on the coastal tundra of the Yukon-Kuskokwim delta, although individual animals wandered into the area and still continue to do so. However, hunting probably has precluded establishment of populations in the open country of the delta (Alaska Department of

Fish and Game 1985). Moose in the forested habitat of the lower Yukon, Innoko, and Kuskokwim rivers have often become very abundant during the last 30 to 40 years. Recurring winters of deep snows and subsequent severe spring floods have frequently reduced numbers dramatically.

Arctic and Northwestern Alaska

Coady (1980) reviewed records of moose observations north of the Brooks Range, in the Kobuk and Noatuk drainages and on the Seward Peninsula. He noted that evidence of moose being present before 1870 to 1880 was very scarce. Between 1880 and 1900, moose were killed occasionally on the Colville River by local people; early explorers rarely saw evidence of moose around the turn of the century. By the early 1950s, moose were common in many areas north of the Brooks Range and had reached coastal areas of the Seward Peninsula and Noatak River. Moose had reached the extreme western coast near Point Hope and Point Lay by 1960 (Coady 1980). In 1970 and again in 1977, extensive aerial surveys by the Alaska Department of Fish and Game found 1,550 to 1,700 moose on a large portion of the Arctic Slope with greatest concentrations along the Colville River (Coady 1980). Coady reviewed factors that may have affected numbers and distribution of moose and concluded that both were probably limited due to hunting by aboriginal people during the early years. Low moose populations south of the Brooks Range probably also limited immigration to the North Slope. During the 1960s and 1970s, moose numbers increased rapidly on the Seward Peninsula and moderately in more northern areas. Populations became well established along major rivers of northwestern Alaska and the Arctic Slope. Coady (1980) estimated that moose numbered 2,000 on the Arctic Slope at that time.

CURRENT TRENDS

Overview

Moose population trends vary considerably throughout the state. The major factors influencing these trends are weather, including snow conditions, habitat quantity and quality, predation, and hunting. Any combination of these factors may cause changes in moose numbers that are unique to one moose population or subpopulation in a relatively small geographic area for a short time. These factors, however, may be operating on a very broad scale, affecting many moose populations over vast areas and perhaps for long periods.

In May 1986, the Alaska Department of Fish and Game estimated the total Alaskan moose population to be 144,000 to 160,000. Techniques for estimating moose numbers vary considerably. The overall estimate represents a composite of the best data and best professional judgment of department game biologists from all over the state. The estimate is subject to change each year as environmental conditions change and as additional data are gathered. The following discussion reviews population trends in major geographic regions of the state.

Southeastern Alaska

Knowledge of moose population trends in southeastern Alaska varies. Small populations in the Chickamin and Unuk Rivers and at Thomas Bay are apparently secure, but are unlikely to increase significantly due to natural habitat limitations (Alaska Department of Fish and Game 1985). Somewhat larger populations on the Taku and Stikine rivers and at Berners Bay seemed to be increasing for a time, but more recently appear to have stabilized (Alaska Department of Fish and Game 1987).

Based on increased reports of moose and their tracks, it appears that moose may be expanding their distribution in the Juneau-lower Lynn Canal area. Moose are also moving into some of the clear-cut logging areas on large islands near the Stikine River. The permanency of this expansion is uncertain (Alaska Department of Fish and Game 1985, 1987).

Moose numbers in the Haines area are currently stationary and at full carrying capacity. Increased efforts are under way to assess the effects of hunting and of habitat changes due to logging.

Population levels in the Yakutat area are thought to be relatively stationary, with probable increases in some subpopulations. Because most moose populations in southeastern Alaska are small and habitat-limited, hunting opportunities are restricted by regulations.

In the Cordova-Copper River area, moose populations are generally stationary. Hunting is being used as a management tool to limit the size of one subpopulation in a effort to avoid overuse of limited habitat (Alaska Department of Fish and Game 1985).

Throughout the area surrounding northern Prince William Sound, moose numbers are low and stationary as a result of limited suitable habitat (Alaska Department of Fish and Game 1973, 1985).

Southcentral Alaska

Moose numbers on the western Kenai Peninsula declined as a result of severe winters in the 1970s. Since then, numbers increased in response to favorable winter conditions, low to moderate predation, and conservative hunting regulations. The trend in moose habitat quality has been downward, wolves have become fully re-established on the Kenai, and predation by black bears on moose calves has been significant (Franzmann *et al.* 1984). As a result, current moose populations in the western part of the Kenai Peninsula is of moderate density, but is declining. Moose numbers in the eastern part of the Kenai are stationary at low densities. (Alaska Department of Fish and Game 1985).

Moose numbers have increased in the Susitna Valley and areas west of Cook Inlet since the mid-1970s in response to favorable winter conditions, low to moderate predator populations, and conservative hunting regulations. In the lower Susitna drainages and west of Cook Inlet, the population recovery was substantial, but the current population level is probably one-third lower than the peak numbers reached in the 1960s. The current trend may be stationary as a result of declining habitat quality as vegetation in disturbed areas matures. Increasing predation by a growing brown/grizzly bear population is likely to be contributing to this stationary trend (Alaska Department of Fish and Game 1985, J. Faro, pers. commun.).

In the Matanuska Valley and Anchorage area, moose populations have also reached relatively high numbers. The population trend in the Anchorage area is considered to be upward, while the Matanuska Valley population seems to have leveled off at high numbers (Alaska Department of Fish and Game 1985). Overall, winter habitat quality in the Matanuska Valley has probably declined as vegetation has matured following fires and agricultural land clearing. Increased human occupancy for residential and recreational purposes has discouraged contemporary land clearing and fire. Community expansion has preempted moose habitat in some situations.

Moose populations on the northern and southern parts of the Alaska Peninsula appear to be stable, but in the central portion numbers are declining becuse of poor calf survival. Predation by brown/grizzly bears is the probable cause of chronically low calf survival in this area. In nearby drainages of northern Bristol Bay, moose numbers seem to be increasing slightly in most areas, but persistent hunting during closed seasons in some areas has held moose numbers at low densities. Again, moderate winter conditions since the mid-1970s seem to be a major factor in upward moose population trends (Alaska Department of Fish and Game 1985).

In the Nelchina Basin, moose numbers are at relatively high levels, and the population trend is a gradual increase (Alaska Department of Fish and Game 1987). Moose numbers have recovered in most areas from the severe winters of the 1960s and early 1970s. Overall population growth has probably been slowed by relatively stable habitat composition, but several mild winters and substantial hunting takes of brown/grizzly bears and of wolves by trapping have allowed the moose population to reach its present level. To the east in the eastern Copper River and Chitina River drainages, moose numbers are chronically low and have increased only slightly from the mid-1970s. Low numbers are probably a result of poor habitat quality, consistently deep snow in some areas, and continuing predation from moderate to high populations of brown/grizzly bears and wolves (Alaska Department of Fish and Game 1985, 1987).

Interior Alaska

Moose populations in most of the Interior are very low relative to population levels in the 1950s and 1960s and in comparison to many moose populations elsewhere in Alaska. Despite closed or very restrictive hunting seasons, populations generally have not recovered from the declines caused by severe winters, increased predator populations, and, in some accessible areas, excessive hunting during the early 1970s. In the upper Tanana and Yukon River drainages, moose numbers are very low. Exceptions occur in relatively small, isolated areas where wolf control was conducted in the early 1980s by the Alaska Department of Fish and Game and near Delta Junction, where hunting and trapping by the public has effectively, if temporarily, regulated wolf numbers. Predation by brown/grizzly bears, principally on calves, has contributed to low, decreasing moose populations in some areas. Farther west, in the area surrounding Fairbanks, moose numbers increased dramatically in response to mild winters, conservative hunting regulations, and to wolf control conducted between 1976 and 1986 (Gasaway *et al.* 1983, Alaska Department of Fish and Game 1985, 1987, unpubl. reports). In that area, predation by wolves was identified as the critical factor preventing moose population recovery.

Athough the extent of wolf control has been substantially restricted in recent years, in two large areas near Fairbanks (Game Management 20A and part of Game Management 20B), moose numbers increased substantially and continue to grow, but at a reduced rate (Alaska Department of Fish and Game 1985, 1987, unpubl. data). Moose numbers in much of the rest of the Interior are low. The Yukon Flats (along the Yukon River north of Fairbanks), the Tanana drainage west of the Parks Highway, the Yukon drainage west to the vicinity of Ruby, the northern two-thirds of the Koyukuk drainage, most of the Kuskokwim drainage, the Innoko drainage, and much of the lower Yukon drainage, support moose populations considerably below recent historic population levels and well below apparent carrying capacity of the various habitats. Moose numbers along the lower portion of the Koyukuk River are at higher levels. From the vicinity of Ruby downriver along the Yukon River, in the Innoko drainage and in much of the Kuskokwim drainage, a combination of deep snows and severe spring flooding in 1984–1985 resulted in poor survival of yearling and calf moose (Alaska Department of Fish and Game, unpubl. data). Moose numbers at best will remain stationary for a few years in areas affected by flooding, but may decline throughout the vast lowlands. Predation by wolves and possibly bears has further complicated the picture in some areas, such as the Nowitna River (Alaska Department of Fish and Game 1987). In certain areas, year-round hunting is a significant restraint on moose population growth (Alaska Department of Fish and Game 1985).

Arctic and Northwestern Alaska

Moose numbers on the Arctic Slope have apparently experienced minor variations, but the long-term trend appears to be one of stationary or slightly increasing populations in the western and central portions (Alaska Department of Fish and Game 1985, 1987). In the eastern portion, within the Arctic National Wildlife Refuge, moose numbers are apparently increasing in some drainages and remaining stationary in others (Alaska Department of Fish and Game 1985). Although it is not clear if habitat availability is limiting Arctic Slope moose populations, it is clear that winter habitat is confined to streamside stands of willows and some other shrubs or tree species (Alaska Department of Fish and Game 1985). As a result, substantial further short-term increases in moose numbers are unlikely. However, an increase in temperature of the Arctic Slope permafrost profiles over the last century suggests a possible long-term climatic warming trend. Such a trend may have encouraged increased browse production in the past. If a climatic warming trend occurs or persists in the future, it could possibly enhance food production for shrub eaters such as moose.

Moose numbers in the Noatak and Kobuk drainages appeared to have peaked by the early to mid-1970s and have become stationary. More recently, 1985 to 1986, this population appears to be increasing (Coady 1980, Alaska Department of Fish and Game 1985, 1987). In local areas, recent wildfires have enhanced moose food supplies, while in other areas browse appears to be heavily used. Also, hunting by local people tends to regulate moose numbers in several areas accessible from communities. However, individual moose have been seen in areas of less favorable habitat west of established concentrations (Alaska Department of Fish and Game 1985).

Moose on the Seward Peninsula increased spectacularly in distribution in the 1960s and in numbers during the 1970s, but the population appears to have become stationary in the last few years. It may be that moose numbers are approaching or exceeding overall carrying capacity. Hunting has been used as a tool to regulate moose numbers within habitat carrying capacity, but reproduction and physiological characteristics of moose suggest that numbers may be reaching habitat limitations despite substantial harvest (Alaska Department of Fish and Game 1985).

MANAGEMENT

Wildlife management in Alaska has become much more complex in the last 15 to 20 years. Overlapping and sometimes conflicting land- and resource-use goals have resulted from new state and federal laws, from changing land ownership status, and from increased human populations. State of Alaska land- and resource-use policies have changed in response to increased interest in mining, oil exploration and development, timber production, and agriculture. State lands newly acquired from the federal government as a condition of statehood have also been in demand for economic uses and as private residential or recreational lands. New land uses or disposals frequently are proposed in areas of prime wildlife habitat or public access (Bishop, pers. observ.). Rapid urban/suburban expansion in major communities has preempted moose habitat and caused difficulties for moose moving to seasonal ranges and for commuters who literally "bumped" into them.

Most recently, allocation of fish and wildlife resources has been complicated by federal and state laws which accord priority to subsistence uses of these resources. More than one lawsuit has questioned whether *any* restrictions can be placed on subsistence uses of wildlife by Alaska Natives. Other suits have questioned laws that appear to favor any one user group over another. An appeal for sovereign tribe status for Alaskan Native communities or groups, similar or analogous to that enjoyed by American Indians with whom the federal government has treaties, potentially adds to the confusion relating to management of fish and wildlife. Finally, there are increasing efforts by animal protection groups and some environmental organizations to constrain traditional fishing, hunting, and trapping wildlife management practices through state and federal regulatory processes and by proposing land-use restrictions such as park or wilderness designations. Clearly, one segment that has grown rapidly in Alaska consists of public and private bureaucracies somehow involved in attempting to influence fish and wildlife management.

Moose Management Plans

Despite growing complexity, several positive avenues of moose management are being pursued.

Classification or Legislative Designation of Lands as Wildlife Habitat. The state of Alaska is rapidly developing land-use plans for extensive areas. Where appropriate and feasible, lands are either classified as wildlife habitat or recommended for legislative designation as refuges, sanctuaries, critical habitat areas, wildlife ranges, public-use areas, or state parks. Such efforts are especially important to maintain wildlife habitat in areas with rapidly growing human populations such as Anchorage.

Wildlife Management. Because of the exceptional importance of wildfire as a beneficial ecological force in much of Alaska, wildlife biologists have long advocated that wildfires be allowed to burn if they posed no significant threat to human life or property. Such an approach was seen as a means of saving millions of dollars in fire-fighting costs as well. During the last five years, wildfire plans that cover virtually the entire state have been developed cooperatively among federal land-management agencies, the state, and major private landowners (principally Native regional and village corporations). As a result, the occurrence and influence of wildfire on large areas should become more like the natural fire regime which preceded extensive fire control efforts. The result should be increased productivity and diversity of wildlife habitats in substantial areas of the state, which will particularly benefit browsers and their predators and scavengers. In the long run, wildfire management plans are likely to be the most significant way to ensure that substantial populations of wildlife have places to live.

Habitat Manipulation. In selected key areas, habitat is being manipulated mechanically or by controlled fire to increase carrying capacity for moose. Principal efforts have been on the Kenai Peninsula and in the Matanuska Valley, but smaller efforts have been undertaken or planned in the Nelchina Basin and Interior Alaska. High cost and the relatively small areas treated limit the potential of this technique to areas of special importance or where wildfire cannot be tolerated.

Hunting Regulations. A great deal has been learned about the effects of various factors on moose populations over the last 30 years. A major result was improved ability to adjust hunting regulations to the well-being of the moose populations so that human use would not constitute a threat to moose populations. Hunting regulations in most areas are more conservative than they were 15 years ago.

Land-Use Regulations. To the extent possible, plans for various developments are modified to avoid unnecessary loss of moose habitat or disruption of important seasonal movements. Perhaps the best known example of past efforts in this regard are the structural changes in the Trans-Alaska Pipeline that accomodated moose and caribou movements. These requirements were formulated by state and federal wildlife biologists and appear to have been successful.

Predator Management. Predator management in the United States is one of the most interesting and controversial elements of wildlife conservation. Its history is largely one of overreaction by both scientists and the public based on what theory was currently in vogue. Emotionalism stimulated by extreme and opposing opinions has clouded the issue in one way or another, certainly for the last 75 years and probably much longer. Historically, the pendulum of scientific opinion has swung from blaming predators for most population problems to holding predators blameless for practically any of such problems. Unfortunately, in much of the United States, while the debate went on, large predators, such as wolves, grizzly bears, and mountain lions, were eliminated from much of their original range. Predator/prey relations among large mammals have been re-examined over the last 20 years with the result that neither of the extreme views formerly advocated have withstood scientific scrutiny.

As a result of recently completed, long-term studies, predators are recognized as potential limiting factors of prey populations under various circumstances, but not in all. In Alaska it became apparent that earlier wolf control programs had very likely contributed to high populations of moose and caribou 25 years ago (Davis *et al.* 1978, Gasaway *et al.* 1983). It also became apparent that when moose numbers declined due to other factors, wolves or bears or both in some cases were able to keep the moose population down or to depress it further; wolf control programs successfully reversed declining moose numbers in several areas. However, considerable controversy arose over these programs, at least in part because public opinion was conditioned by earlier, popularized scientific opinion that predation was not of consequence to prey populations. In addition, a great empathy for wilderness as a concept has recently emerged, with large predators symbolizing wilderness. As usually defined, the concept of wilderness does not allow for management of large predators. However, much of Alaska is wilderness where people depend to varying degrees on moose and other species for food.

At present, one wolf control program, which involves removal of wolves by state personnel, is authorized for a small area west of Fairbanks. Two other programs are authorized to officially encourage local people to attempt to take more wolves through conventional trapping techniques. Public opinion regarding these efforts, of course, is mixed. However public policy may evolve, it is clear that managing predators can help enhance prey populations under certain circumstances.

PROGNOSIS

The outlook for moose in Alaska is good. As a species, they will persist partly due to their adaptability, partly due to their popularity with people. However, moose population numbers may fluctuate greatly depending on factors ranging from weather conditions to public policy. Public policy affects matters as diverse as the regulation of industrial development to predation control.

Public policy may not always favor conservation and enhancement of moose or other wildlife because the economic and other benefits are neither calculated nor well known. A commodity like the moose, which does not have a recognizable commercial value like salmon, may be given scant consideration when land-use options are weighed. Nevertheless, by applying sound conservation practices, moose can continue to fulfill both their ecological role and benefit people. People, however, do not have the option of being neutral with regard to the well-being of moose; their activities will either be positive or negative.

RECOMMENDATIONS

Moose are ecologically secure in Alaska, but some populations in areas of marginal habitat may not persist. The principal questions regarding moose management relate to desired moose population levels and to allocation of moose among people, bears, and wolves. It is obvious that total allocations will be smaller if moose populations are low; hence these predators will be disadvantaged to some degree.

Increased human development will preempt habitat and management options on more lands, and most wildlife management options are already preempted on 25 million acres of National Park Service lands. On lands where management options have not been preempted, it seems prudent to conserve and enhance moose populations for the benefit of all members of the ecosystem by ensuring long-term habitat quantity and quality and by ensuring that significant moose populations persist to use those habitats. To sustain significant moose populations will probably require adjusting allocations of moose among people, bears, and wolves through hunting regulations and predator population management. Presently, allocation of moose in areas where populations are low tends to favor bears and wolves, which reduces the chances of increased moose numbers and allocations in the near future.

REFERENCES

Alaska Department of Fish and Game. 1973. *Alaska's Wildlife and Habitat.* R.E. LeResche and R.A. Hinman eds. Alaska Department of Fish and Game. Juneau, Alaska. 141 pp.

——. 1985. "Moose," *in* A. Seward ed., *Annual Report of Survey-Inventory Activities.* Vol. XV, Part VIII. Alaska Department of Fish and Game in Federal Aid in Wildlife Restoration Project W-22–3, Job. 1.0. Juneau, Alaska. 164 pp.

——. 1987. "Moose," *in* B. Townsend ed., *Annual Report of Survey-Inventory Activities.* Vol. XVII, Part VIII. Alaska Department of Fish and Game. Federal Aid in Wildlife Restoration Project W-22–5, Job. 1. Juneau, Alaska. 158 pp.

Ballard, W.B., J.S. Whitman and C.L. Gardner. 1987. "Ecology of an exploited wolf population in southcentral Alaska." *Wildlife Monograph 98.* 54 pp.

Bishop, R.H. and R.A. Rausch. 1974. "Moose population fluctuations in Alaska, 1950–1972." *Naturaliste Canadian* 101:559–593.

Boertje, R.D., W.C. Gasaway, S.D., DuBois, D.G. Kelleyhouse, D.V. Grangaard, D.J. Preston, and R.O. Stephenson. 1985. *Factors Limiting Moose Population Growth in Game Management Unit 20E.* Alaska Department of Fish and Game Federal Aid in Wildlife Restoration Program Report Project W-22–3, W22–4, Job 1.37R. Juneau, Alaska.

Coady, J.W. 1980. "History of moose in northern Alaska and adjacent regions." *Canadian Field Naturalist* 94:61–68.

Davis, J.L., R.E. LeResche and R.T. Shideler. 1978. *Size, Composition, and Productivity of the Fortymile Caribou Herd.* Alaska Department of Fish and Game Federal Aid in Wildlife Restoration Final Report Project W-17–6 and W-17–7. Juneau, Alaska. 69 pp.

Gasaway, W.C., R.O. Stephenson, J.L. Davis, P.E.K. Shepherd and O.E. Burris. 1983. "Interrelationships of wolves, prey, and man in Interior Alaska." *Wildlife Monograph no. 84.* 50 pp.

LeResche, R.E., R.H. Bishop and J.W. Coady. 1974. "Distribution and habitats of moose in Alaska." *Naturaliste Canadian* 101:143–178.

Peterson, R.L. 1955. *North American Moose.* University of Toronto Press. 280 pp.

Spencer, D.L. and E.F. Chatelain. 1953. "Progress in the Management of the Moose of Southcentral Alaska." *Transactions of the 18th North American Wildlife Conference.* Pp. 539–552.

——. and J.B. Hakala. 1964. "Moose and fire on the Kenai." *Tall Timbers Fire Ecology Conference* 3. 11–33. Tallahassee, Florida.

Richard Bishop is regional supervisor for the game division of the Alaska Department of Fish and Game. He is in charge of game division management and research in Interior Alaska.

The Florida panther, like all mountain lions, has declined dramatically. Only 30 to 50 Florida panthers remain, in fragmented habitat. *Robert C. Belden.*

The Florida Panther

Robert C. Belden
Florida Game and Fresh Water Fish Commission

SPECIES DESCRIPTION AND NATURAL HISTORY

The Florida panther (*Felis concolor coryi*), a subspecies of mountain lion, is characterized as being relatively dark in color, with short, stiff hair (Bangs 1899), and as having relatively longer legs and smaller feet (Cory 1896) than other subspecies. Contrary to popular belief, the Florida panther is not black. The unspotted coat of the adult is typically rusty reddish-brown on the back, tawny (deer-colored) on the sides, and pale gray underneath. The long cylindrical tail is relatively slender compared to other subspecies.

Panther kittens are gray with dark brown or blackish spots and have five bands around the tail. These spots gradually fade as the kittens grow older and are almost unnoticeable by the time they are six months old. At this age, their bright blue eyes slowly turn to the light-brown straw color of the adult.

Three other characteristics relatively common to this subspecies are white flecks of hair on the shoulder and neck and sometimes on the back of the head (Goldman 1946); a whorl of hair or "cowlick" in the middle of the back; and a distinctive kink in the end of the tail (Belden 1986). The white flecks are consistently present but vary in quantity.

This characteristic appears only on the adult pelage and seems to be age related. The white flecks are possibly the result of scar tissue forming at the site of a tick bite (*Ixodes* sp.) (Roelke, pers. commun.). The whorl is oblong or tear-shaped—from 0.16 to 1.2 inches long;it is present in both males and females at birth. The third from the last vertebrae in the tail is reduced in size, slightly curved, and angled at 90° from the preceeding vertebrae, resulting in a crooked tail. The last two vertebrae are also reduced in size, with the last one appearing vestigal. This occurs in both sexes and is also present at birth. Because these characteristics occur rarely in individuals of other subspecies and are found in combination in this subspecies, they are considered characteristic only of the Florida panther (Wilkons and Belden, unpubl. data).

Mature male Florida panthers weigh an average of 120 pounds and measure nearly seven feet from the nose to the tip of the tail. They stand approximately 24 to 28 inches at the shoulder. Females are considerably smaller with an average weight of 75 pounds and measure about six feet in length.

In general, the most distinctive feature of the skull is the shortened rostrum and the corresponding expanded and inflated nasals, which give the animal the appearance of having a prominant or "Roman" nose. The outer margins of the nasals are often free and pushed upward and tend to overlap the upper jaw or "maxilla" and frontal bones (Goldman 1946).

Taxonomy and Distribution

Charles B. Cory in 1896 first described the Florida panther as a separate geographic race of mountain lion, assigning it the name *F.c. floridana*. Four years later, Outram Bangs (1899) renamed the type *Felis coryi*. Bangs designated the panther as a separate species because he believed that it had been restricted to peninsular Florida and could no longer interbreed with any other form. After analyzing almost all available specimens in North American collections, Nelson and Goldman (1929) revised the taxonomic classifications of the *Felis concolor* group and assigned the Florida panther subspecific status with the designation *F.c. coryi* Bangs.

Breeding

The mountain lion is polyestrous. Breeding, pregnancy, birth, and care of postnatal young can occur yearlong, but over half the births occur during April, June, July, and August (Anderson 1983). The Florida panther's breeding season starts in October and continues through April, with the majority of conceptions occurring from November to March (Roelke *et al.* 1985, 1986).

Mountain lions usually breed approximately every other year and sometimes only at three-year intervals (Robinette *et al.* 1961, Young 1946). However, cases of two litters being produced within 12 to 15 months have been reported (Robinette *et al.* 1961, Hornocker 1970).

The age when a mountain lion first breeds is dependent not only on sexual maturity, but also on its being established on a territory (Hornocker 1970, Seidensticker *et al.* 1973). Sexual maturity has been reported as 24 months (Eaton and Velander 1977), with the animals breeding for the first time when they are two- to three-years old (Robinette *et al.* 1961, Young 1946). However, male panthers appear to reach sexual maturity after three years of age (Roelke *et al.* 1985).

Florida panthers are not monogamous. The males breed with all of the females whose ranges overlap theirs and females breed with males whose range overlaps with theirs. A female in estrous will alternate among two or three male panthers on several occasions; mating may occur over each of these several-day periods (Allen 1950).

Mountain lions in general have high copulation rates and low conception rates (Anderson 1983). Copulation rates of captive mountain lions have been reported as 50 to 70 per day over seven to eight days (Eaton 1976). This high rate may be because females are induced ovulators and, as with other large cats, the males generally tend to have a high percentage of abnormal sperm (Howard *et al.* 1984).

The gestation period of the Florida panther varies from 90 to 98 days (Allen 1950). For the species as a whole, the number of young per litter ranges from one to six, averaging two or three (Young 1946); in Florida, litter sizes have ranged from one to four.

Longevity and Mortality

The greatest cause of death in most mountain lion populations probably results from humans (Russell 1978), and this seems to be true for the Florida panther population as well. In the last 10 years, 13 panthers have been hit by motor vehicles on highways. Of these, 10 died. In this same period, 7 panthers were illegally shot; 5 of these died. In addition, 2 panthers died as the result of intraspecific aggression, 2 died of unknown causes, and 1 was a capture-related mortality.

Although age-specific mortality rates have not been determined, the pattern of mortality in Florida panthers seems to follow that of most mammals, with the highest mortality rates in the pre-reproductive young and the oldest classes (Dixon 1982). There is evidence of a 15- to 18-year life span in the wild for the Florida panther, but 8 to 12 years is considered old (Young 1946).

Circumstantial evidence based on behavioral data from radio-collared Florida panthers indicates that neonatal and early juvenile morality is occurring (Belden, unpubl. data). It is hypothesized that most of this mortality is due to starvation, diseases and parasites, and possibly to some extent by adult male panthers who kill and occasionally eat young kittens.

Diseases and Parasites. Although the effects of diseases and parasites on the Florida panther population is unknown at this time, the poor physical condition and anemia of many animals (particularly females) and exposure to infection by several potentially pathogenetic viral, bacteriologic, and parasite agents is of critical concern.

Feline panleukopenia or feline distemper is the most significant infectious panther disease documented (Anderson 1983). Antibodies to this virus have been detected in 85 percent of the Florida panthers tested (Roelke 1987); it is presumed that some degree of clinical disease and mortality has been experienced, particularly in kittens under one year of age (Roelke *et al.* 1985). At present, the majority of wild captured panthers and those held in captivity are inoculated against feline panleukopenia. Calcivirus, another pathogenic virus, has been detected in 50 percent of the panthers (Roelke *et al.* 1985). This virus is normally mild, but certain strains can cause severe oral lesions, pneumonia, or death (Roelke *et al.* 1985).

Twenty species of parasites have been detected in Florida panthers; all examined panthers have shown infections with at least six species. The two most prevalent and abundant parasites are the diplostomatid trematode (*Alaria marcianae*) and the hookworm (*Ancylostoma pluridentatum*) (Forrester *et al.* 1985). Although nothing is known about the pathogenicity or life cycle of this particular hookworm, it is know that other hookworm species can be extremely devastating to neonatal domestic kittens (Roelke *et al.* 1985). Hookworm parasitism in older panthers may contribute to chronic anemia and weight loss, particularly if the animal is already nutritionally stressed (Roelke *et al.* 1985).

Diet

An anaylsis of panther scats collected in south Florida showed the principal foods of the Florida panther to be white-tailed deer (*Odocoileus virginianus*), wild hogs (*Sus scrofa*), and raccoons (*Procyon lotor*). Panthers will, however, take almost any other prey of suitable size.

A positive relationship between body weight, physical condition, hematology values, serum iron, and female reproductive success has been shown (Roelke *et al.* 1985). These values are highly associated with the size of prey taken by panthers in the respective geographical areas studied (Roelke *et al.* 1986). Panthers living in an area where they fed primarily on small mammals were underweight, anemic, and had a very low documented reproductive rate. Those panthers on an adjacent area, however, that were deriving almost all of their diet from large prey were heavier, in better physical condition, and had a higher documented reproductive success (Roelke *et al.* 1986). These data indicate that although individual panthers may be able to subsist in areas with low large-prey densities, they are unable to reproduce. Without available large-prey items, females are apparently barely able to survive. For example, a female with three year-old cubs would require a deer approximately every three days to fulfill her energy needs and those of her young. The energy expended to catch small mammals would not equal that derived from them.

Stalking and Habitat Relationships

Mountain lions use vegetative cover and terrain while stalking their prey (Hornocker 1970, Logan and Irwin 1985); certain land types are more suitable than others for capturing deer. The mixed swamp and hammock forests of southern Florida are the habitats most used (Belden *et al.*, unpubl. data). These habitats have a more diverse woody flora than the other available habitat types (Duever *et al.* 1979.) and occur mostly in strands and islands surrounded by prairies and marshes. This extensive edge probably provides conditions suitable for stalking cover. Mixed swamp and hammock forests also contain a greater abundance of acorn-producing species and provide cover and food for the panther's primary prey—white-tailed deer, wild hogs, and raccoons (Belden *et al.*, unpubl. data). Killing success rate is also related to the density of the prey and its vulnerability as determined by the amount of cover provided by the vegetation and topography (Seidensticker *et al.* 1973).

Home-Range Area

The mean home area for adult male Florida panthers is between 168 and 196 square miles and between 68 and 74 square miles for adult females (Belden 1986, Maehr 1987). Because mountain lions are large, solitary carnivores at the top of the food web, they require large ranges to obtain the necessary prey to meet their energy needs (Ackerman 1982). Also, their social and reproductive behavior requires access to large contiguous areas of suitable habitat in order to maintain viable breeding populations (Seidensticker *et al.* 1973). Variability in home-area size is probably due to differences in prey density, prey size, topography, and foraging efficiency (Seidensticker *et al.* 1983, Hemker 1982, Murphy 1983).

SIGNIFICANCE OF THE SPECIES

Historically, the Florida panther has been viewed as a dangerous animal that needed to be exterminated, or at least, controlled because of its "threat" to livestock and people (see "Historical Perspective"). However, the mountain lion is a vital part of the ecological balance of a wildlife community, particularly in its relation to the control of deer density. Several studies have also suggested that mountain lions not only control deer numbers, but also tend to take a greater proportion of fawns and mature bucks (Ashman 1977, Dixon 1967, Hornocker 1970, Robinette *et al.* 1959, Russell 1978). Since fawns and mature bucks contribute least to the reproductive effort of the population, their removal stimulates productivity by reducing competition among the remaining animals (Dixon 1982).

Draining of swamps and development of deer and panther habitat diminish the quality and size of wild areas. However, people will only allow the panther to live in such areas. If Florida wildlands continue to be destroyed, the panthers that rely on them will eventually die-off. The presence of Florida panthers can therefore be considered to be an indication of the integrity of a wilderness area.

HISTORICAL PERSPECTIVE

When the first explorers came to the New World, mountain lions were one of the most widely distributed mammals, occurring from British Columbia to Patagonia and from the Atlantic to the Pacific coast. As one of 30 recognized subspecies, the original range of the Florida panther is considered to have extended from eastern Texas or western Louisiana through the southeastern states, including Arkansas, Louisiana, Mississippi, Alabama, Georgia, to parts of Tennessee and South Carolina (Goldman 1949) (see Figure 1).

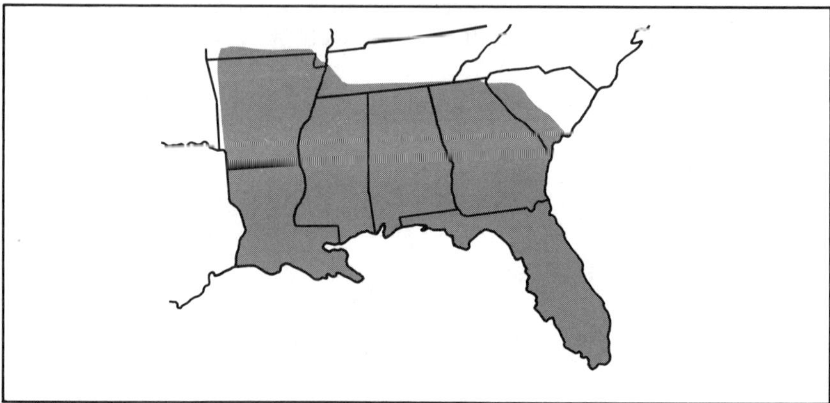

Figure 1. Historic range of the Florida panther.

The decline of the mountain lion began with the first European immigrants who settled in the New World. The animal not only killed livestock, but it was believed to be equally dangerous to people (Tinsley 1970); legends of its ferociousness spread throughout the frontier. Early settlers considered the animal a nuisance to their livelihood. As civilization advanced, mountain lions were destroyed at every opportunity and bounties were offered for their scalps. By the mid- to late-nineteenth century, the mountain lion had been extirpated from the vast majority of the eastern states and could only be found in a few inaccessible mountain ranges and coastal swamps.

In the eastern United States, the mountain lion was found only in central and south Florida, and possibly along some of the major river drainages in Louisiana by the late 1920s (Lowery 1936, Tinsley 1970, Young and Goldman 1946). As livestock raising and other human activity increased in those areas, intensified pressure was directed against the animal. Also, a deer eradication program was initiated in Florida during the 1930s to control the fever tick, but the resulting decrease in deer density caused panthers to stray from the safety of their normal haunts and to seek domestic prey. Greater persecution of the panther by ranchers resulted (Tinsley 1970).

Partial protection was given to the panther in 1950 by designating it a game animal and allowing it to be hunted only during the open season for deer. Animals that were found destroying livestock could be taken by special permit at any time. In 1958, the panther was removed from the native game list and given complete legal protection by the Florida Game and Fresh Water Fish Commission. The U.S. Fish and Wildlife Service (FWS) listed the Florida panther as endangered on March 11, 1967.

Even after panthers were legally protected from deliberate killing, human development continued to encroach on the diminishing panther habitat. As late as 1977, it was not known whether a viable or reproducing population of panthers still occurred in Florida, and if so, where the population would be found (Belden 1977).

In October 1976, the Florida Game and Fresh Water Fish Commission's Wildlife Research Laboratory commenced an investigation to locate and geographically delineate at least one population of Florida panthers. Breeding populations occurred in south Florida from Lake Okeechobee southward, primarily in the Big Cypress and Everglades regions (Belden 1978, Belden and Roboski 1984) (see Figure 2). Although periodic confirmed sightings have come from other areas, particularly along the St. Johns River (Belden and Frankenberger, unpubl. data), panther signs cannot be predictably found in areas other than the Big Cypress and Everglades regions (Belden *et al.* 1987).

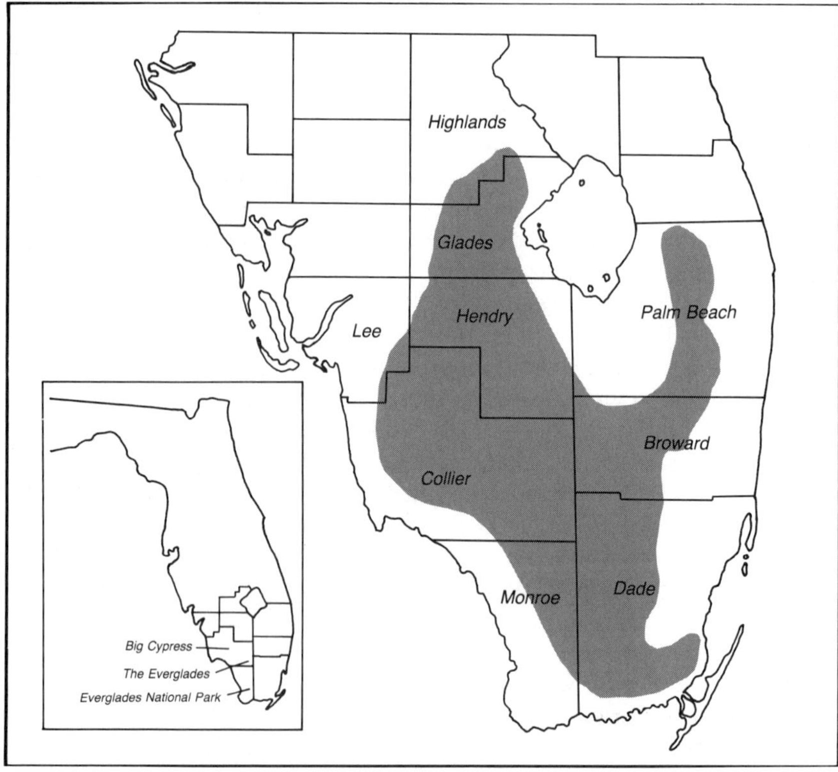

Figure 2. Current documented distribution of Florida panthers in nine southeast Florida counties in 1987. Inset: Map of Florida.

CURRENT TRENDS

The current estimate of the south Florida population of Florida panthers is 30 to 50 animals (Hines *et al.* 1987); hence, the panther may be teetering on the brink of extinction. The population shows a clumped pattern of dispersion, where approximately half the animals inhabit public lands. These public lands include: Fakahatchee Strand State Preserve, administered by the Florida Department of Natural Resources; Big Cypress National Preserve and Everglades National Park, administered by the U.S. National Park Service; Water Conservation Areas, administered by the South Florida Water Management District; and the Seminole and Miccosukee Indian Reservation, administered by the Bureau of Indian Affairs. The Florida Game and Fresh Water Fish Commission regulates recreational hunting in all these areas except Everglades National Park, which is closed to hunting, and Indian reservations. The other half of the panther population occurs on private lands to the north and west of these areas.

The major factor limiting the panther population in south Florida appears to be the availability of suitable habitat (Belden *et al.*, ms. in prep.). Field signs indicate that the number of animals residing on public lands south of Alligator Alley has decreased since 1981 (Robertson *et al.* 1985).

The present threats to the survival of the Florida panther are varied and interrelated. All of these threats, however, can be traced back to an increasing human population. Additional human demands on water and land place the needs of wildlife and people at odds. Panthers in south Florida are probably subjected to a higher intensity of human activity than any remaining mountain lion population.

Habitat Loss

The only reason the panther still remains in south Florida may be that, until recently, the Big Cypress Swamp/Everglades region was virtually impenetrable to humans. Only the most hardy individuals with specialized equipment could enter the area. When they did manage to enter, their range was limited by the amount of fuel that could be carried on their custom-made swamp buggies (Belden 1986).

Tamiami Trail (now U.S. Highway 41), built in 1928 to connect Miami and Naples, was the first road built through the area. Even with the road, the majority of the area remained inaccessible to humans. Alligator Alley (State Highway 84), built in 1966–1967 through the middle of the area, made access easier. Several major access roads have subsequently been built off Alligator Alley.

The Big Cypress/Everglades region has continued to shrink because of the increase in both access roads and more efficient off-road vehicles. The mobility of these vehicles has been further aided by a vast system of canals that has caused a general drying out of the region. Habitat disturbance has been such that relatively little wilderness remains (Belden 1986).

The majority of private lands that currently support panthers are made up of relatively large land holdings managed primarily for low density, free-ranging cattle. These lands appear to produce more deer and wild hogs (and subsequently panthers) than do adjoining public lands. This may be true because of better soils and hence better quality deer forage, a more diverse vegetative composition, and lower hunting pressure. However, inheritance taxes are forcing the break up of these large parcels; their subsequent conversion to intensive agriculture may eliminate the lands as suitable panther habitat in the near future. Winter freezes, which have killed many of the citrus groves in central Florida, have also increased the conversion of these private holdings because they are less susceptible to crop-killing frosts.

Although Florida has one of the most ambitious conservation land-acquisition programs in the nation, funds are limited. Meanwhile, development keeps chipping away at the remaining panther habitat. If the private lands are lost as panther habitat, the panther's survival will be entirely dependent on habitat situated on the less productive public lands (Alvarez 1986).

Recreational Demand and Prey Availability

The areas presently inhabited by panthers represent some of the wildest, least accessible wilderness remaining in south Florida. The very wildness of these areas is a lure to recreationists and poses a threat to their own preservation. Public use was an important consideration in the purchase of Big Cypress National Preserve. However, too much recreational use can diminish the wilderness character of the area and overhunting of white-tailed deer and wild hogs can be in direct competition with Florida panthers.

Captive Mountain Lions

The Florida Game and Fresh Water Fish Commission permits possession of other subspecies of mountain lions. It has been estimated that there are over 1,000 captive mountain lions in Florida alone (Capt. Barry Cook, pers. commun.). These animals pose a potential problem to the recovery of the Florida panther. Captive animals that have escaped or that are released create confusion over the Florida panther's true status and distribution, as well as posing a threat to the gene pool through hybridization (Belden 1986).

Public Attitudes

Public attitudes toward the Florida panther have improved greatly since the days of the early settlers, so much so that the panther has been named Florida's official state animal (Belden and Roboski 1984). However, the large private landowners and developers who have to deal with complex environmental regulations regarding the management of their lands, and hunters who must abide by the regulation of their sport, still view the panther as a nuisance and a threat to their livelihood or recreation.

MANAGEMENT

Several agencies, including the Florida Game and Fresh Water Fish Commission, Florida Department of Natural Resources, FWS, and the National Park Service, are responsible for the panther's recovery. Because of such overlapping and interrelated responsibilities, the

Florida Panther Interagency Committee was established in May 1986 to provide guidance and coordination on research and management activities involved in the implementation of the recovery plan. Agency directors who have the authority to make decisions regarding actions necessary for the panther's recovery serve on the committee. Many conservation organizations have also been extremely supportive of efforts to protect the panther, including National Audubon Society, Florida Audubon Society, and Florida Defenders of the Environment.[1]

Florida panthers are legally protected from harm under the federal Endangered Species Act of 1973, the Wildlife Code of the State of Florida, and State of Florida Panther Act of 1978. The laws and rules set forth in the Florida statutes and the rules of the Florida Game and Fresh Water Fish Commission appear adequate in terms of legal protection. However, managing a mountain lion population requires monetary resources and considerable time, energy, and expertise (Russell 1978). At present, almost $1 million is being spent yearly by various state and federal agencies to recover the Florida panther.

The Florida Panther Recovery Team was appointed by FWS in July 1976 to prepare and assist in coordinating the implementation of a recovery plan for the Florida panther. The final Florida Panther Recovery Plan was submitted in January 1981 and approved by FWS in December 1981 (U.S. Fish and Wildlife Service 1981). The plan was revised in June 1987 by the Technical Subcommittee of the Florida Panther Interagency Committee. The objectives of this committee, made up of two people selected from each agency, are to: 1) ensure technical coordination among agencies to recover the Florida panther; 2) provide technical staff support and advice to the Florida Panther Interagency Committee on pertinent issues; 3) provide recommendations to the Florida Panther Interagency Committee on specific recovery actions; and 4) revise the recovery plan as needed (U.S. Fish and Wildlife Service 1987).

The revised recovery plan is based on the best expert opinion available and outlines the steps for restoring the panther as a viable, self-sustaining element of the ecosystem (U.S. Fish and Wildlife Service 1987). The plan's three major objectives are: 1) identify, protect, and enhance existing populations by delineating them and analyzing their demographic condition; measures need to be taken to reduce mortality, enhance natality, and preserve and manage the panthers' remaining habitat; 2) establish positive public opinion and support for its management; 3) re-establish populations where feasible (U.S. Fish and Wildlife Service 1987).

1. The other conservation organizations are: National Wildlife Federation, Shakar Safari, Inc., Sierra Club, the Wildlife Society, The Nature Conservancy, and the Wilderness Society.

In 1983, the Florida Panther Technical Advisory Council was established. The council's mandate is to advise the Florida Game and Fresh Water Fish Commission on technical issues involving the Florida panther.

The Florida Panther Record Clearinghouse was established in 1976 by the Florida Game and Fresh Water Fish Commission for the collection of panther reports and their subsequent field investigation where practical. The clearinghouse has recently been expanded and its activities are now handled by the commission's five regional offices. Systematic field searches are carried out throughout the state in areas suspected of having panthers (Belden and Frankenberger 1985).

A study was initiated in February 1981 to determine the feasibility of capturing, radio-instrumenting, and tracking panthers in Florida. Subsequently, a full-scale radio-telemetry project was started in January 1982 (Belden 1986). Twenty-three panthers have been collared since the project's inception. Of these, 14 are still alive—6 in Everglades National Park (Bass and Jansen, unpubl. data) and 8 in Big Cypress National Preserve—and are being monitored (Maehr 1987). This work supplies data documenting habitat use, daily activities, home-range characteristics, social interactions, etc. Repeated field counts provide an opportunity to determine density, sex, age, and reproductive status, as well as the health of the population.

Because the management goal is to increase Florida panther populations to the fullest extent, the elimination of as many mortality factors as possible is desirable. Deaths must also be prevented to bar the loss of genetic variability that is highly threatened by low population size.

Panthers are generally struck and injured or killed by motor vehicles where highways and panther corridors intersect, during hours when visibility is impaired and when traffic occurs at high volumes, and where the panthers field of vision is restricted by narrow road shoulders. Specific management actions have been taken to help alleviate this type of mortality. Reduced speed zones along strategic segments of state roads 84 and 29 have been in effect since mid-1985. Large informational signs signaling the entrance into panther habitat are erected at each end of State Road 84. Also, brochures encouraging motorists to drive at reduced speeds and to be vigilant for panthers have been prepared for distribution at the toll booths at each end of the state road (Logan and Evink 1987). State Road 84 is currently being reconstructed as Interstate 75 with special features such as wildlife underpass crossings, bridge extensions, fencing, and shoulder expansions designed to help reduce panther highway mortality (U.S. Fish and Wildlife Service 1987). A major highway improvement project for State Road 29, undertaken by the Florida Department of Transportation, actually moved the road bed and widened the shoulders along critical segments.

Management efforts to increase natality, via increasing food supplies of deer and wild hogs, have centered on regulating hunting in Big Cypress National Preserve. The Florida Game and Fresh Water Fish Commission has lowered the permit quota and placed restrictions on access. Hunting pressure has also been reduced by limiting the use of all-terrain vehicles and by closing Eleven-Mile Road, a major access point.

The removal of illegal hunting camps by court order has helped to reduce hunting pressure even further. The commission also restricted hunting with dogs on Big Cypress to the first nine days of the general gun season and increased the minimum antler size for legal deer from one inch to five inches. There has been an overall decrease in hunter-days in Big Cypress National Preserve by approximately 30 percent and a 39-percent decrease in deer takes (McCown 1987b). The Florida Game and Fresh Water Fish Commission has completely closed hunting for deer and wild hogs in Fakahatchee Strand, on the western edge of Big Cypress National Perserve, because of problems with illegal trespass. The Florida Department of Natural Resources is presently establishing permanent food plots on the area in an attempt to increase the deer carrying capacity.

Research on panther natality is ongoing and includes a study of reproduction and general health (Roelke *et al.* 1985, 1986, Roelke 1987), food habits (Belden 1986, Belden and Maehr 1987, Belden *et al.*, unpubl. data, Bass and Jansen, unpubl. data), and the affects of deer hunting on the panthers (McCown 1987a, Land 1987, Smith, unpubl. data). The panther will be a featured species in a General Management Plan that the National Park Service is preparing for Big Cypress National Preserve; the plan outlines the management of all natural resources within the preserve (U.S. Fish and Wildlife Service 1987).

The Florida Department of Natural Resources field office in Naples accelerated acquisition of "inholdings" in Fakahatchee Strand State Preserve; it is also in the process of purchasing land along the perimeter of the state preserve that lies south of Alligator Alley and west of State Road 29, and is involved in acquisition actions for the Florida Panther National Wildlife Refuge. This new refuge (located north of Alligator Alley and west of State Road 29) will total approximately 32,000 acres. An environmental assessment on the acquisition of this tract has already been prepared (U.S. Fish and Wildlife Service 1987). As part of the I-75 Interstate Highway project, state and federal governments will purchase lands not needed for access to the highway. This extensive acquisition project will considerably increase the amount of acreage and panther habitat in public ownership (U.S. Fish and Wildlife Service 1987).

Reintroduction

In addition to efforts to manage panthers in south Florida, the Florida Game and Fresh Water Fish Commission has made a commitment to reintroduce Florida panthers into suitable areas within the state. Successfully introducing Florida panthers into such areas would help reduce the risk of extinction for the subspecies. This projects is divided into four phases: 1) determine where areas of suitable habitat exist; 2) determine the feasibility of using captive-raised offspring in the re-establishment of panther populations; 3) determine the feasibility of using translocated wild panthers in the re-establishment of the subspecies; and 4) introduce Florida panthers into unoccupied areas where feasible (U.S. Fish and Wildlife Service 1987).

The captive-rearing portion of the project has been initiated. A captive-breeding facility has been constructed at White Oak Plantation near Yulee, Florida. A male Florida panther, captured as a result of injuries sustained when a car struck him in 1984, and a female panther taken out of the Fakahatchee preserve in 1987 because of her poor health, are presently housed at this facility. Also, three wild-caught Texas females (*F.c. stanliana*) are at the facility for initial breeding trials with the Florida male. Hybrids resulting from these matings will be surgically sterilized and used in the reintroduction feasibility phase of the project.

Education

Education of the public concerning the panther and its management has been effectively achieved through the media, local and national environmental organizations, and school groups. A panther brochure was produced for distribution through Florida's school system and to the general public (Belden 1986); the Florida Panther Interagency Committee publishes the newspaper, "Coryi."

PROGNOSIS

It is probable that the Florida panther is involved in a slow, but rather certain extinction process and that genetically the population numbers are critically low. From a biological standpoint, habitat preservation and other management actions may reverse this process by bringing population numbers back to viable levels.

From a sociobiological standpoint, the survival of the Florida panther depends on public understanding and support, and the ability of individuals, organizations, and agencies to work together. Because of the panther's low numbers, some rather radical and artificial management measures may be required. These may include moving individual panthers between populations, in and out of captivity, and introducing them into new areas of unoccupied habitat. A well-coordinated and cooperative effort from all concerned will be needed to implement an effective management program.

Although bringing the Florida panther back from the brink of extinction will be difficult, its chances for survival are better now than ever. General public attitudes have shifted in favor of the panther, and agencies are working together as a team to assist the recovery. The Florida Panther Interagency Committee has aggressively promoted panther conservation actions over the last few years.

RECOMMENDATIONS

If the objectives of the recovery plan are to be accomplished, the federal and state agencies involved need to continue working closely and must be willing to compromise certain agency policies, where necessary, for the good of the panther (see "Management").

Although the modifications planned for highways 84 and 29 should greatly reduce the chances of panthers being killed on them, the projects are not expected to be completed until late 1990. Interim actions need to be implemented during this period to provide further protection to panthers that cross these highways.

Comprehensive land-management plans that address the enhancement of habitat conditions and other needs of the panther should be developed for each major management unit by the appropriate agency (U.S. Fish and Wildlife Service 1987). These areas should be managed to closely simulate wilderness conditions and to control human activity (Belden 1986). Increased law enforcement may be necessary in certain areas to curtail the illegal takes of deer and hogs out of season and above the legal limit during the season.

Deer hunting on public lands has been a sensitive issue for many years and this directly affects the panther. It is important to reach a compromise so that public support for the panther reintroductions will not suffer as a result of this ongoing conflict.

Residential and agricultural encroachment will have to be controlled through a combination of federal-state fee title acquisition, acquisition of conservation easements, and cooperation by large private landowners. The only practical means of arresting the rate of habitat loss may be land-use planning that accounts for both panther and human needs and corresponding mitigation policies (Russell 1978). A full range of economic incentives also needs to be considered for protecting panther habitat on private lands (U.S. Fish and Wildlife Service 1987). Legislation is needed to establish special funding and staffing to expedite complex small-parcel acquisition projects (Alvarez 1986). A cumulative impact model should be developed to assess and predict the impacts of hydrological changes, agriculture, air pollution, human population growth, roads, and recreation on Florida panther habitat (U.S. Fish and Wildlife Service 1987).

Current data must be gathered on panther population demographics, habitat preferences, social structure, activities, food habits, reproduction, diseases and parasites, and genetic variability. Also, research needs to continue on predator-prey relationships, the productivity, abundance, survival, habitat selection, and carrying capacities of panther-occupied habitat for white-tail deer and the effects of human-panther competition for available prey. Further study on the feasibility of reintroducing panthers into areas of suitable, but unoccupied habitat is necessary. Research on evaluating habitat manipulation techniques needs to be initiated as does a study on the abundance, productivity, survival, and habitat selection of wild hogs in areas where panthers occur.

Some system of marking (for example, tattooing) and careful record-keeping is needed to keep track of captive mountain lions within the historic range of the Florida panther. Owners should be made responsible for the continued upkeep of the mountain lions in captivity (Belden 1986).

REFERENCES

Ackerman, B.B. 1982. Cougar Predation and Ecological Energetics in Southern Utah. M.S. thesis. Utah State University. Logan, Utah. 103 pp.

Allen, R. 1950. "Notes on the Florida panther, *Felis concolor coryi* Bangs." *Journal of Mammalogy* 31:279–280.

Alvarez, K.C. 1986. Survival prospects for the Florida panther and some perspectives on strategy. Talk presented at Florida Defenders of the Environment Panther Conference. Tallahassee, Florida. April 1986.

Anderson, A.E. 1983. *A Critical Review of Literature on Puma* (Felis concolor). Special Report No. 54. Colorado Division of Wildlife. 91 pp.

Ashman, D. 1977. Mountain lion investigations. Performance Report P-R Project W-48–8, S&I, Job 5 and Study RV, Job 1. Nevada Fish and Game Department. 11 pp.

Bangs, O. 1899. The Florida Puma. *Proceedings of the Biological Society of Washington* 13:15–17.

Belden, R.C. 1977. "If you see a panther." *Florida Wildlife* 31:31–34.

——. 1978. "Florida panther investigation—a progress report," pp. 123–133 *in* R.R. Odom and L. Landers eds., *Proceedings of the Rare and Endangered Wildlife Symposium*. Georgia Department of Natural Resources Technical Bulletin. WL4. Athens, Georgia. 184 pp.

——. 1986. "Florida panther recovery plan implementation—a 1983 progress report," pp. 159–172 *in* S.D. Miller and D.D. Everett eds., *Cats of the World: Biology, Conservation and Management*. Proceedings of the Second International Cat Symposium. Caesare Kleberg Wildlife Research Institute. Kingsville, Texas. 501 pp.

——. and W.B. Frankenberger. 1985. Panther population survey. Annual Performance Report, Endangered Species Project E-1–09. Florida Game and Fresh Water Fish Commission. 9 pp.

——., T.C. Hines, and T.H. Logan. 1987. Florida panther captive breeding/reintroduction feasibility. Annual Performance Report, Endangered Species Project E-1–11. Florida Game and Fresh Water Fish Commission. 5 pp.

——. and D.S. Maehr. 1986. Florida panther food habits. Annual Performance Report E-1–10. Florida Game and Fresh Water Fish Commission. 2 pp.

——. and J.C. Roboski. 1984. "Florida panther status report," pp. 29–36 *in* J. Robinson and F. Lindszay eds., *Proceedings of the 2nd Mountain Lion Workshop.* Zion National Park. Springdale, Utah. 271 pp.

Cory, C.B. 1896. *Hunting and Fishing in Florida.* Estes and Lauriat. Boston, Massachusetts. 304 pp.

Dixon, K.R. 1967. Mountain lion predation big game and livestock in Colorado. Job Completion Report Project W-38-r-21. Colorado Game, Fish, and Parks Department. Fort Collins, Colorado. 23 pp.

——. 1982. "Mountain lion," pp. 711–727 *in* J.A. Chapman and G.A. Feldhammer eds., *Wild Mammals of North America.* The Johns Hopkins University Press. Baltimore, Maryland. 1,147 pp.

Duever, M.J., J.E. Carlson, J.F. Meeder, L.C. Duever, L.H. Gunderson, L.A. Riopelle, T.R. Alexander, R.F. Myers and D.P. Spangler. 1979. *Resource Inventory and Analysis of the Big Cypress National Preserve.* Final report to the USDI National Park Service. University of Florida Center for Wetlands. Gainesville, Florida. National Audubon Society Ecosystem Research Unit. Naples, Florida. Two volumes. 1,225 pp.

Eaton, R.L. 1976. "Why some felids copulate so much." *World's Cats* 3:73–94.

——. and K.A. Velander. 1977. "Reproduction in the puma: biology, behavior, and ontogeny." *World's Cats* 3:34–70.

Forrester, D.J., J.A. Conti and R.C. Belden. 1985. Parasites of the Florida Panther (*Felis concolor coryi*). *Proceedings of the Helminthology Society of Washington* 52:95–97.

Goldman, E.A. 1946. "Classification of the races of the puma," pp. 175–302 *in* S.P. Young and E.A. Goldman eds., *The Puma, Mysterious American Cat.* American Wildlife Institute. Washington, D.C. 358 pp.

Hemker, T.P. 1982. Population Characteristics and Movement Patterns of Cougars in Southern Utah. M.S. thesis. Utah State University. Logan, Utah. 66 pp.

Hines, T.C., R.C. Belden and M.E. Roelke. 1987. An Overview of Florida's Panther Research and Recovery Program. *Proceedings of the 3rd Symposium on Southeastern Nongame Wildlife.* September 1987. Athens, Georgia. In press.

Hornocker, M.G. 1970. "An analysis of mountain lion predation upon mule deer and elk in the Idaho Primative Area." *Wildlife Monograph* 21. 39 pp.

Howard, J.G., M. Bush, L.G. Simmons and D.E. Wildt. 1984. "Comparative Evaluation of Ejaculate Characteristics in Nondomestic Felids with Emphasis on Sperm Morphology." *Proceedings of the American Zoo Veternarians.* pp. 168–170.

Jansen, D.K. 1986. Big Cypress public use survey. Final Performance Report, Endangered Species Project E-1–10. Florida Game and Fresh Water Fish Commission.

Land, E.D. 1987. Big Cypress deer/panther relationships: deer mortality. Annual Performance Report E-1–11. Florida Game and Fresh Water Fish Commission. 6 pp.

Logan, K.A. and L.L. Irwin. 1985. "Mountain lion habitats in the Big Horn Mountains, Wyoming." *Wildlife Society Bulletin* 13:257–262.

Logan, T.H. and G. Evink. 1987. A Plan for Florida Panther Safety on Collier County Highways. Florida Panther Interagency Committee. 7 pp.

Lowery, G.H. Jr. 1936. "A Preliminary Report on the Distribution of the Mammals of Louisiana." *Proceedings of the Louisiana Academy of Sciences* 3:11–39.

Maehr, D.S. 1987. Florida Panther Movements, Social Organization and Habitat Utilization. Annual Performance Report E-1–11. Florida Game and Fresh Water Fish Commission. 21 pp.

Murphy, K.M. 1983. Characteristics of a Hunted Population of Mountain Lions in Western Montana. Final Performance Report, Montana P-R Project W-120-R-13 and 14. 48 pp.

McCown, J.W. 1987a. Big Cypress Deer/Panther Relationships: Deer Herd Health and Reproduction. Annual Performance Report E-1–11. Florida Game and Fresh Water Fish Commission. 21 pp.

——. 1987b. The Effects of Hunting and Habitat Quality on the Big Cypress National Preserve Deer Herd. Report to the Florida Panther Interagency Council. 21 pp.

Nelson, E.W. and E.A. Goldman. 1929. "List of the pumas with three described as new." *Journal of Mammalogy* 10:345–350.

Roelke, M.E. 1987. Florida Panther Biomedical Investigation. Annual Performance Report, Endangered Species Project E-1–11. Florida Game and Fresh Water Fish Commission. 39 pp.

——., E.R. Jacobsen, G.V. Kollias and D. Forrester. 1985. Medical Management and Biomedical Findings on the Florida Panther, *Felis concolor coryi*, July 1, 1983 to June 30, 1985. Annual Performance Report, Endangered Species Project E-1–9. Florida Game and Fresh Water Fish Commission.

——., E.R. Jacobsen, G.V. Kollias and D. Forrester. 1986. Medical Management and Biomedical Findings on the Florida Panther, *Felis concolor coryi*, July 1, 1985 to June 30, 1986. Annual Performance Report, Endangered Species Project E-1–10. Florida Game and Fresh Water Fish Commission. 65 pp.

Robertson, W.B., Jr., O.L. Bass Jr. and R.T. McBride. 1985. Review of Existing Information of the Florida Panther in the Everglades National Park, Big Cypress National Preserve and Environs with Suggestions for Need and Research. Unpublished Technical Report. Everglades National Park. 13 pp.

Robinette, W.L., J.S. Gashwiler and O.W. Morris. 1959. "Food Habits of the cougar in Utah and Nevada." *Journal of Wildlife Management* 23:261–273.

——. 1961. "Notes on cougar productivity and life history." *Journal of Mammalogy* 42:204–217.

Russell, K.R. 1978. "Mountain lion," pp. 207–225 *in* J.L. Schmidt and D.L. Gilbert eds., *Big Game of North America: Ecology and Management*. Stackpole Books. Harrisburg, Pennsylvania. 494 pp.

Seidensticker, J.C. IV., M.G. Hornocker, W.V. Wiles and J.P. Messick. 1973. "Mountain lion social organization in the Idaho Primative Area." *Wildlife Monograph* 35:1–60.

Tinsley, J.B. 1970. *The Florida Panther*. Great Outdoors Publishing Company. St. Petersburg, Florida. 60 pp.

U.S. Fish and Wildlife Service. 1981. Florida Panther Recovery Plan. Florida Panther Recovery Team. Atlanta, Georgia. 32 pp.

——. 1987. Florida Panther (*Felis concolor coryi*) Recovery Plan. Florida Panther Interagency Committee. Atlanta, Georgia. 75 pp.

Young, S.P. 1946. "History, life habits, economic status, and control, Part 1." pp. 1–173 *in* S.P. Young and E.A. Goldman eds., *The Puma, Mysterious American Cat*. The American Wildlife Institute, Washington, D.C. 358 pp.

Robert C. Belden is a Biological Scientist III/Coordinator with the Florida Game and Fresh Water Fish Commission and was formerly the team leader of the Florida Panther Recovery Team. Presently, he is the principal investigator for the Florida panther captive breeding/reintroduction feasibility studies.

The common barn-owl, one of the most widely distributed of all birds, is in widespread decline. *A. Cruickshank/VIREO*

The Common Barn-Owl

Carl D. Marti
Weber State College

SPECIES DESCRIPTION AND NATURAL HISTORY

The common barn-owl (*Tyto alba*) is the most widespread of all owl species (Burton 1984) and, in fact, is one of the most widely distributed of all birds. Versatility in the use of nest sites and in the selection of prey, and the ability to use human-modified habitats are undoubtedly significant factors contributing to the large geographic range of this species. Despite being common in some areas and often nesting close to human dwellings, the secretive nocturnal activity of the barn-owl renders it inconspicuous to most humans. Declining barn-owl populations in several areas have recently raised public awareness of the species. The barn-owl has been studied on all continents where it occurs; this chapter, however, will discuss primarily the North American race (*T.a. pratincola*).

In North America, barn-owls measure approximately 14 inches in length and have a wingspan of 43 inches. The North American race is the largest of all barn-owl subspecies, weighing nearly twice that of its smallest counterparts. As in most raptor species, female North American barn-owls are larger than males (Snyder and Wiley 1976), weighing an average of 20 ounces, while males average 16 ounces (Marti 1985).

Several of the smaller subspecies, however, may not be sexually dimorphic in size (Amadon 1942, De Groot 1983). Barn-owls have distinctly marked, heart-shaped facial discs, dark brown eyes, and no ear tufts. The back and upper sides of the wings are golden brown, marked with an intricate pattern of gray, dark brown, and white. The facial disc, breast, belly, and underwings are white, with brown and buff marks. Males are lighter on the underparts with fewer and smaller spots than females. Females usually have a buffy wash over the breast that extends to the feet and have more and larger breast spots. Occasionally males are almost entirely white on the face, breast, and underwings, and some females may be uniformly dark buff on the same areas. There is an overlap between the sexes, however, so that the differences in color are not 100 percent successful as a means of distinguishing between them. Some subspecies have little sexual dichromatism; in others, the degree of sexual difference in color varies among populations (Parkes and Phillips 1978).

Juvenile barn-owls are covered with whitish down that is gradually replaced with plumage indistinguishable from that of adults. Juveniles have their full plumage by the time they are 60 to 70 days old (Bunn *et al.* 1982).

The barn-owl usually can be easily distinguished from all other North American owls. Among large species, only the snowy owl (*Nyctea scandiaca*) and the white-phase of the great horned owl (*Bubo virginanus*) are also light-colored. The snowy owl, however, is much larger, and its distribution is usually farther north than that of the barn-owl. The short-eared owl (*Asio flammeus*) is similar in size and shape to the barn-owl, but is much darker on the ventral surface.

Taxonomy and Distribution

The common barn-owl is a member of the family Tytonidae. This family contains only 11 species and is the smaller of the 2 families in the order Strigiformes. Over the vast geographic distribution there is much variation in barn-owl size and coloration, resulting in the recognition of 36 subspecies or races (Howard and Moore 1980). The American Ornithologists' Union (1983), now considers the ashy-faced barn-owl (*T. glaucops*, formerly *T.a. glaucops*) to be a full species, and Parkes and Phillips (1978) have proposed two additional subspecies. North America is inhabited by a single race, (*T.a. pratincola*), (see Figure 1).

Barn-owls also occur over much of South America, Africa, Europe, India, southeast Asia, and Australia, and can be found on many islands in the Caribbean and East Indies as well as on several isolated oceanic islands. The species has been introduced successfully to the Hawaiian

Islands, Seychelles Islands (Long 1981), and Lord Howe Island (American Ornithologists' Union 1983). Within historic times, the species itself has apparently colonized Bermuda and Tasmania (Long 1981).

Barn-owls have a relatively low tolerance to cold and are absent from higher latitudes. Johnson (1974) found that the insulating ability of the barn-owls' feathers is much less than would be expected from a bird of its size. The sparsely feathered legs and bare toes are poorly suited for cold climates, allowing more heat loss than does the heavier plumage of other species. Piechocki (1960) reported that barn-owls had less fat reserve than several other owl species, another characteristic that may reduce their ability to survive lean periods in winter. Evidence of winter mortality among barn-owls in the northern United States and northern Europe indicates that this lack of adaptation to cold climates can have a heavy impact on populations in those areas (Marti and Wagner 1985).

Habitat and Home Range

Barn-owls are characteristic of open landscapes, inhabiting grasslands, marshes, savannas, and certain deserts and agricultural lands. The

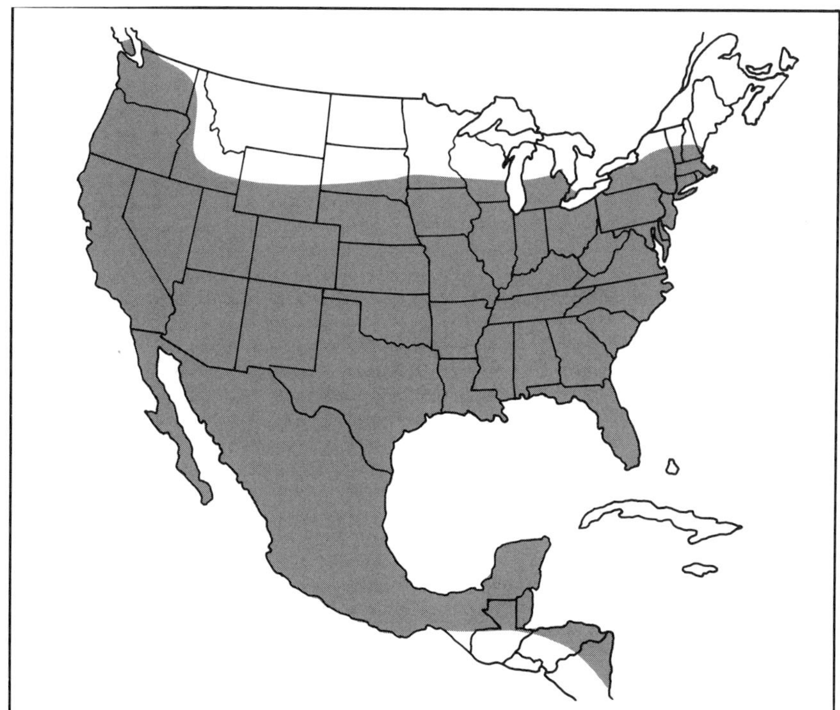

Figure 1. Distribution of the North American race of the common barn-owl.

birds' long wings and flight pattern are adapted to maneuvering in open spaces (Lack 1966). Barn-owls need relatively large cavities for roosting and nesting, but are quite adaptable in their choice of such cavities. Hollow trees, cliff crevices, and burrows in river banks are typical nest sites. Barn-owls are even known to excavate their own burrows in soft soil (Martin 1973). A variety of human-made structures are also used for nesting and shelter, including barns, church steeples, and abandoned houses and buildings. Additionally, barn-owls readily use nest boxes provided for them (Frylestam 1971, Marti *et al.* 1979, Juillard and Beuret 1983).

Good barn-owl habitat must have open areas inhabited by populations of small mammals in close proximity to suitable nest/roost sites. Barn-owls will travel moderate distances, however, from nests to hunting areas. Hegdal and Blaskiewicz (1984) reported that radio-tagged barn-owls sometimes flew up to five miles from their nests to hunt. The size of home ranges is not well known and probably varies considerably according to habitat characteristics and prey populations. Using radio telemetry, Hegdal and Blaskiewicz (1984) found home ranges averaging about 1,750 acres in New Jersey. The same technique used in Malaysia revealed barn-owl home ranges averaging only 300 acres (Lenton 1980). Some owls in both New Jersey and Malaysia apparently did all of their hunting in a very small area, ranging from approximately 15 to 50 acres. Barn-owls do not appear to defend their hunting areas and are territorial only at the nest site (Smith *et al.* 1974, Colvin 1984).

It is unresolved as to whether barn-owls are migratory. Most studies of marked barn-owls, conducted only in North America and Europe, have not found any evidence that migration occurs (Schneider 1937, Mikkola 1983, Marti, pers. observ.); no data are available for large areas of the species' distribution. Some reports of migratorial movements in North American barn-owls have been published (Stewart 1952, Mueller and Berger 1959, Bolen 1978), but the conclusions in these reports are based largely on circumstantial evidence. Juvenile barn-owls disperse, often widely, from their natal site (see "Reproduction"), and these movements could be easily be confused with migration.

Reproduction

Compared to most other birds of prey, barn-owls possess a very flexible reproductive regimen capable of high productivity. They are able to breed at an early age, have a large range in clutch size, can produce multiple broods per year, have a high dispersal of juveniles, find and use new resources quickly, and have a relatively short adult life span.

Barn-owls normally pair monogamously, but there are several reports of polygyny—one male paired with two females (Baudvin 1975, Schönfeld and Girbig 1975, Colvin 1984). Two females and one male nesting simultaneously in the same nest box has been observed (Marti 1987). Pairs will often nest in very close proximity to each other (Baudvin 1975, Smith *et al.* 1974, Marti, pers. observ.). Wilson *et al.* (1986) found 49 pairs breeding on a 750-acre study site in Mali, Africa.

Barn-owls commonly breed in their first year of life (Bunn and Warburton 1977, Colvin 1984, Marti, pers. observ.) and captive birds as young as six months old have produced fertile eggs (Trollope 1971). In North America, most nesting is done in the spring and summer, but barn-owls have been reported to nest in all months of the year (Stewart 1952, Otteni *et al.* 1972). One brood per year is usually produced, but it is not uncommon for a second brood to follow if prey populations are high and weather is favorable (Baudvin 1975, Lenton 1984, Marti, pers. observ.).

Barn-owls are capable of continuous breeding in captivity (Flieg 1972, Maestrelli 1973) and seemingly also in the wild (Wallace 1948, Wilson 1970). The number of eggs per clutch varies anywhere from 2 to 13 and may be related to prey abundance, although the mechanism for this relationship has not been investigated. The average number of eggs in a clutch also varies among populations—from 2.9 in Suriname (Haverschmidt 1962) and 3.1 in the Galapagos Islands (De Groot 1983) to 6.6 in Malaysia (Lenton 1984) and 6.9 in Utah (Marti 1985). There seems to be little correlation between clutch size and latitude.

Eggs are laid at intervals of two to three days (Epple 1983, Marshall *et al.* 1986), but incubation begins when the first egg is laid. As a result, the earlier eggs hatch first, causing a large discrepancy in size among siblings. This asynchrony, which occurs in almost all raptor species, is viewed as a mechanism to permit some members of the brood to survive if the parents cannot supply enough food for all the chicks (Lack 1966); hence, the larger, stronger members of the brood may be able to obtain food at the expense of their smaller nest-mates. Cannibalism among barn-owl siblings has been reported (Baudvin 1975, Colvin 1984, Lenton 1984). However, when food is abundant, nesting barn-owls have been observed to share food with their younger siblings (Epple 1979, Bunn *et al.* 1982, Marti, pers. observ.). Incubation takes about 30 days (Marshall *et al.* 1986) and is done entirely by the female (Bunn *et al.* 1982, Marti, pers. observ.). Once incubation begins, the female usually leaves the nest only briefly to defecate. The male brings food to her throughout this period. When the young can be left alone without brooding, the female begins to help supply food.

Nestlings are capable of flight when they are 60 to 65 days old (Smith *et al.* 1974, Bunn *et al.* 1984, Lenton 1984). In contrast to most birds, however, young barn-owls return to the nest site after fledging to roost and are still fed by the adults for some time. They gradually drift or are driven away from the nest over a period of several weeks. The total period of dependence on the parents is about 90 days. A female may begin a second clutch while the young of the first clutch are still being fed by the male (Ames 1967, Marti 1968, Bunn *et al.* 1982).

Once independent from their parents, juvenile barn-owls disperse from the natal area (Stewart 1952, Braaksma and De Bruijn 1976, Juillard and Beuret 1983). Banding studies have documented that this dispersal may be in any direction—determined largely by geographic features—and for distances up to 1,080 miles in North America (Soucy 1980) and 975 miles in Europe (Glutz von Blotzheim 1979). However, dispersal distances usually are not that great. Braaksma and De Bruijn (1976) found that 87 percent of barn-owls banded as nestlings were recovered within 60 miles of the nest site. Juvenile dispersal is a one-way movement apparently in search of suitable habitat. The distance may be affected by prey abundance (Schönfeld 1974) or time of fledging (Glutz von Blotzheim 1979). Once the post-fledging dispersal is over, most barn-owls are very sedentary. In northern Utah, barn-owls banded as breeding adults have not been observed to make permanent moves of over one mile from the nest/roost sites throughout the year (Marti, pers. observ.). Several birds banded as nestlings in the same population, however, have been observed to travel great distances—one as much as 800 miles.

Longevity and Mortality

Most wild barn-owls appear to have a short life span. Stewart (1952) reported that the average age at death of 220 barn-owls banded as nestlings was only 1.5 years in the United States. A similar finding was reported for Europe (Bairlein 1985). The greatest mortality appears to occur during the first winter of life when juveniles become independent from their parents. It has been estimated that the mortality rate may be as high as 75 percent in the first year (Frylestam 1972, Juillard and Beuret 1983). Barn-owls, however, are capable of much longer life spans. The oldest known wild barn-owl reached 34 years of age (Keran 1981), and a number of wild, banded barn-owls have lived anywhere from 8 to 11 years.

During their first year of independence, when juveniles attempt to perfect their hunting skills, starvation must be a common cause of death. Starvation coupled with exposure to very cold temperatures can also be a significant source of adult mortality. In northern

North America and Europe, severe winter weather has been observed to kill many barn-owls (Marti and Wagner 1985). Another major cause of barn-owl mortality in some places is collision with vehicles (Glue 1971, Smith and Marti 1976, Keran 1981). Very few field studies have evaluated the true effects of chemical hazards on barn-owls, but residues of chlorinated hydrocarbon pesticides have been detected in wild birds from several locations (Johnston 1978, Peakall and Kemp 1980, Henny *et al.* 1984). The number of owls tested was small in all cases and the residue levels showed individual variation. Polychlorinated biphenyls (PCBs) also have been detected in barn-owl eggs (Risebrough *et al.* 1968). Laboratory investigations have shown that pesticides can cause mortality and eggshell thinning in barn-owls, and their presence is of concern (Mendenhall and Pank 1980, Mendenhall *et al.* 1983).

Diet

Barn-owls feed primarily on small mammals, most of which are characteristically found in open habitats. Voles (*Microtus* spp.) are important in the diet in the northern portions of the barn-owl distribution in both North America (Wallace 1948, Marti 1974, Colvin and McLean 1986, Campbell *et al.* 1987) and Europe (Glue 1974, Cuisin and Cuisin 1979, De Bruijn 1979). In the southern United States, cotton rats (*Sigmadon hispidus*) are major prey (Baumgartner and Baumgartner 1944, Glasgow 1962, Trost and Hutchison 1963. Pocket gophers (*Thomomys* spp.) are commonly eaten in California (Fitch 1947, Selleck and Glading 1943). Elsewhere, barn-owls feed on many other kinds of small mammals; over 20 mammal genera have been reported from around the world as the most common prey in the species' diet (Marti 1985).

Barn-owls usually do not eat large numbers of birds, but on occasion have been found to do so (Brosset 1956, Görner 1978). They also eat arthropods, reptiles, and amphibians but in very small numbers.

Estimates of daily food consumption by North American barn-owls range from 2 ounces per day for a sedentary captive (Marti 1973) to 3.9 per day for wild barn-owls in Colorado (Marti 1970) and 5.3 ounces in California (Evans and Emlen 1947).

The scientific literature describing food habits of the barn-owl is abundant. Many major geographic areas of its worldwide range are represented, but the great bulk of these studies have been done in North America and Europe. Africa and Australia are reasonably well-represented, but South America, India, southeastern Asia, and the East Indies are not.

Hunting Behavior

Barn-owls usually hunt at night, beginning about one hour after sunset and ending about one hour before sunrise (Marti 1974, Colvin 1984), but some daylight foraging does occur (Haverschmidt 1970, Bunn *et al.* 1982). The birds hunt primarily on the wing, making low, quartering flights about 5 to 15 feet over the ground (Bunn *et al.* 1982). Occasionally, barn-owls will hover momentarily when they detect potential prey below. They also hunt from perches overlooking open grounds (Bunn *et al.* 1982). This hunting technique is reported to be common in Malaysia (Lenton 1984).

Barn-owls detect prey both visually and acoustically and have excellent low-light vision (Dice 1945, Marti 1974). There are times under natural conditions, however, when light levels fall below the owls' visual threshold (Dice 1945). Additionally, prey may conceal itself under vegetation or snow. Under these conditions, barn-owls detect prey by the sounds it makes. Payne (1962) showed that barn-owls have excellent hearing abilities and can locate prey entirely by sound.

Knudsen (1981) found that barn-owls have the most accurate ability to locate sound sources of any animal species tested. Barn-owls can also memorize complex sounds; this is a probable means of acoustically recognizing suitable prey and discriminating prey sounds from the background noise (Konishi and Kenuk 1975).

SIGNIFICANCE OF THE SPECIES

Because the barn-owl preys on small mammals, there have been several experiments to use the species for rodent control. Some success has been claimed in oil-palm plantations in Malaysia (Lenton 1980). Even though the introduction of barn-owls to the Hawaiian islands was for the purpose of controlling rodents, the success of this effort apparently has not been well evaluated. Two reports from the islands indicate that barn-owls fed mostly on introduced rodents (Tomich 1971, Baker and Russell 1980), but sample sizes were too small to adequately evaluate the diet there. Other investigators found evidence of barn-owl predation on seabirds in Hawaii (Byrd and Telfer 1980). In the Seychelles Islands, introduced barn-owls were reported to prey mainly on seabirds, including the endangered fairy tern (*Gygis alba*) (Penny 1974). Limited information from Platte Island in the Seychelles indicated that barn-owl predation on rats had significantly reduced crop damage (L. Chenseng, pers. commun.).

With their large broods and sometimes high population densities, barn-owls can consume large numbers of rodents. In North America, barn-owls often prey heavily on voles and pocket gophers—both agricultural pests. Little information is available on the impact that owls have on their prey populations, but Craighead and Craighead (1956) concluded that the raptor assemblages they studied could limit prey numbers.

HISTORICAL PERSPECTIVE

The secretive, nocturnal nature of barn-owls complicates studies of their population numbers. As a result, there are very few estimates of past or present barn-owl numbers other than for small areas where the species is under study. The scarcity of such information creates difficulty in determining trends in population status. Nevertheless, several major changes in barn-owl distribution and population density have occurred following European settlement of North America; both expansion and contraction of distribution have been documented. At the local level, barn-owl population densities have similarly both increased and decreased.

Clearing of forests in the upper midwestern United States appears to have created suitable barn-owl habitat where it had not previously existed (Lerg 1984, Colvin 1985). Barn-owls seemed to reach peak densities in the upper Midwest in the 1920s and 1930s (Colvin 1985). Beginning in the 1930s, barn-owl populations in Ohio declined, probably in response to changing agricultural practices that reduced populations of important prey (Colvin 1985). Nearly all of the midwestern states have experienced similar large-scale declines in barn-owls within the last 20 years.

Stewart (1980) documented a gradual invasion of the northwestern United States by barn-owls. The reason for this expansion is not clear but could also be related to agriculture. Increased irrigation in dry areas may have produced conditions more favorable to voles and other rodents. This increase in important barn-owl foods may have allowed the barn-owl to expand into previously unoccupied areas. The species has also extended its distribution or increased its population densities by using man-made structures in areas lacking natural nest sites. For example, Reese (1972) found barn-owls nesting in offshore duckblinds in Chesapeake Bay, and barn-owl density increased substantially in northern Utah farmlands in response to nest boxes made available for them (Marti *et al.* 1979). Range expansions and population increases of a similar nature were noted in Africa (Brown 1971) and Malaysia (Lenton 1985).

CURRENT TRENDS

The common barn-owl was placed on "The Blue List"[1] from 1972 to 1981 because its numbers were judged to be "down" or "greatly down"; the bird was listed as a "special concern bird" from 1982 to 1986 (Tate 1986). The most serious North American declines in barn-owl populations have been in the midwestern United States (Lerg 1984, Mumford and Keller 1984, Colvin 1985). As a result, six midwestern states have placed the barn-owl on their endangered species list.[2] Nine other states list it as a species of special concern (Anonymous 1984).[3] No widespread, catastrophic population reductions were observed in the western United States, but decreases in the barn-owl's central California populations were recently reported (Tate 1986).

Barn-owl declines in the Midwest have received much attention. To place this phenomenon in perspective, it must be realized that much of the affected area was, before being cleared for farming, too heavily forested to be good barn-owl habitat. Thus, larger barn-owl populations present in the Midwest in the early 1900s may have been the result of human-caused habitat change. What caused the midwestern declines in barn-owls is not understood fully, but Colvin's (1985) explanation is the best to date (see "Historical Perspective").

Mikkola (1983) believes that there has been a general decline of the species in Europe. Kragenow (1970) and Braaksma and De Bruijn (1976) attributed decreased populations in Germany and Holland to loss of nest sites, changes in agriculture, and a succession of bad winters. In the British Isles, declines in barn-owl populations seem to have started around 1900—a trend that is probably continuing today (Bunn *et al.* 1982).

Several factors have been implicated in barn-owl population declines. Pesticides are one possible cause, but only a few field tests on their effects have been conducted. More tests need to be done because laboratory studies have shown that there is a potential for contamination. Reduced availability of both natural (large, hollow trees) and man-made (open buildings) nest sites may also be a factor in the decline of some barn-owl populations. The loss of foraging areas and/or prey populations due to urban sprawl and changing agricultural practices are other factors potentially more dangerous because their impacts are difficult to mitigate. Barn-owl intolerance to severe winter weather is another possible factor for population declines in the colder parts of the bird's range. However, climatic changes would have to

1. "The Blue List," published by *American Birds*, documents the status of birds that may be or are declining in number or are otherwise of concern.

2. The six states are Illinois, Indiana, Iowa, Michigan, Missouri, and Wisconsin.

3. The nine states are Kentucky, Massachusetts, Mississippi, Nebraska, New York, Pennsylvania, South Carolina, Tennessee, and West Virginia.

continue over many years in order to have any long-term effect on population density and distribution. One isolated year of unusually severe weather may not have lasting effects on barn-owl populations because dispersal of juvenile barn-owls from adjoining areas and the owls' high reproductive rate have the potential to rapidly repopulate suitable areas (Stewart 1952, Marti and Wagner 1985).

MANAGEMENT

Management of barn-owls has been attempted in two ways: providing nest boxes and releasing captive-raised birds. Nest boxes have been successful in inducing barn-owls to nest in areas where favorable foraging habitat occurs, but where nest sites are limited. In northern Utah, densities of barn-owls nesting in boxes have been as high as 10 pairs per eight square miles (Marti, pers. observ.). It must be recognized that such high densities are not uniform for barn-owls in general. These high densities are probably the result of abundant nest sites close to high rodent populations. Numbers of nesting barn-owls also increased substantially in Switzerland with the addition of nest boxes (Juillard and Beuret 1983). In contrast, nest boxes have not been effective in areas where some other problem—for example, low prey density—exists (Colvin *et al.* 1984).

Several midwestern states have attempted restocking barn-owls after severe population declines. The largest effort was in Missouri, where 485 captive-raised birds were released over eight years in a cooperative program between the Missouri Conservation Department and the Tyson Research Center (J. Wilson, pers. commun.). Only three wild barn-owl nests could be attributed to the released birds. The Nebraska Game and Parks Department has conducted a limited restocking program in eastern Nebraska (J. Dinan and B. Hancock, pers. commun.), releasing about 150 birds in seven years. No evaluation of the success has been undertaken, but one to five pairs of owls per year have been known to nest in the release areas. It is unknown if any of the wild birds were from the release program. In Iowa, State Conservation Commission biologists released about 400 barn-owls over five years but have post-release sightings on only two of them (D. Reeves, pers. commun.). The Wisconsin Department of Natural Resources released about 150 owls in six years (S. Matteson, pers. commun.). Missouri, Iowa, and Wisconsin suspended their restocking attempts in 1987 pending an evaluation of the results. Illinois, Indiana, Iowa, Michigan, Missouri, Nebraska, Ohio, and Wisconsin have placed several hundred nest boxes for barn-owls. To date, very few of these have been used by the species.

Management of barn-owl foraging areas apparently has not been attempted. Successfully manipulating hunting grounds for the species' benefit is the most difficult aspect of barn-owl habitat management. Consequently, this may be the most potentially damaging problem. Maintenance of grasslands on public lands and planting and maintaining grasses on roadsides, along fencerows, and in other unused areas might be effective for maintaining foraging areas. Little information is available on how much hunting area is required and how close together such patches must be to support a viable barn-owl population.

PROGNOSIS

The barn-owl has shown considerable ability in coping with human changes in its environment—even to the extent of expanding its range. Its "ecological plasticity," or ability to adapt to varying environmental conditions, and its flexible reproductive strategy may help it cope with a human-dominated landscape. Several significant unknowns cloud the ability to predict the future for the barn-owl in North America: the shift to farming practices that are detrimental to the species and the extent to which pesticides and other chemical contamination will cause direct mortality or inhibit reproduction. Yet, based on the present state of knowledge, it appears likely that the barn-owl will maintain viable populations in most parts of its range. Nevertheless, it probably will continue to decline in areas where serious, but not fully understood, problems have already caused population reductions.

RECOMMENDATIONS

Attempting to restock birds in areas where they have declined does not seem to have been effective and is contraindicated unless factors causing the original decline can be first identified and corrected. Management of the species may be necessary in some areas. Placing nest boxes has been shown to be effective in building or rebuilding populations where natural sites are scarce. Nest boxes alone, of course, will not guarantee a viable barn-owl population. Adequate foraging habitat with sufficient prey populations is also necessary.

Chemical contamination is a potentially important but largely unexamined factor that may affect the barn-owl. Careful analysis of this hazard throughout the barn-owl's range is needed. Comparative studies between seemingly healthy and declining populations would be especially useful.

Accurate information on population numbers, especially breeding densities, is also needed in order to better understand the species' current situation, to predict future trends, and to manage the barn-owl wisely. These data are lacking for most of the barn-owl's range.

On a worldwide basis, there are major areas of the barn-owl's distribution where virtually nothing is known of its biology—particularly in South America and much of Asia. Natural history information obtained from those areas may someday help us better understand the barn-owl in all areas.

REFERENCES

Amadon, D. 1942. "Birds collected during the Whitney South Sea Expedition." *American Museum Novitates No. 1176.* American Museum of Natural History. New York.

American Ornithologists' Union. 1983. *Check-List of North American Birds,* 6th ed. Allen Press, Inc. Lawrence, Kansas. 877 pp.

Ames, P.L. 1967. "Overlapping nestings by a pair of barn owls." *Wilson Bulletin* 79:451–452.

Anonymous. 1984. "Status reports: state endangered and threatened raptor species." *Eyas* 7:17–20.

Bairlein, F. 1985. "Dismigration und Sterblichkeit in Suddeutschland beringter Schleiereulen (*Tyto alba*)." *Die Vogelwarte* 33:81–108.

Baker, J.K. and C.A. Russell. 1980. "Rat and mouse predation by owls on the island of Hawaii." *'Elepaio* 40:142–143.

Baumgartner, A.M. and F.M. Baumgartner. 1944. "Hawks and owls in Oklahoma 1939–1942: food habits and population changes." *Wilson Bulletin* 56:209–215.

Baudvin, H. 1975. "Biologie de reproduction de la Chouette Effraie (*Tyto alba*) en Cote d'Or: premier resultats." *Jean le Blanc* 14:1–51.

Bolen, E.G. 1978. "Long-distance displacement of two southern barn owls." *Bird Banding* 49:78–79.

Braaksma, S. and O. De Bruijn. 1976. "De kerkuilstand in Nederland." *Limosa* 49:135–187.

Brosset, A. 1956. "Le régime alimentaire de l'Effraye *Tyto alba* au Maroc oriental." *Alauda* 24:303–305.

Brown, L. 1971. *African Birds of Prey.* Houghton Mifflin. Boston, Massachusetts. 320 pp.

Burton, J.A. (ed.) 1984. *Owls of the World.* Tanager Books. Dover, New Hampshire. 208 pp.

Bunn, D.S. and A.B. Warburton. 1977. "Observations on breeding barn owls." *British Birds* 70:246–256.

——., A.B. Warburton and R.D.S. Wilson. 1982. *The Barn Owl.* Buteo Books. Vermillion, South Dakota. 264 pp.

Byrd, G.V. and T.C. Telfer. 1980. "Barn owls prey on birds in Hawaii." *'Elepaio* 41:35–36.

Campbell, R.W., D.A. Manuwal and A.S. Harestad. 1987. "Food Habits of the common barn-owl in British Columbia." *Canadian Journal of Zoology* 65:578–586.

Colvin, B.A. 1984. Barn Owl Foraging Behavior and Secondary Poisoning Hazard from Rodenticide Use on Farms. Ph.D dissertation. Bowling Green State University. Bowling Green, Ohio. 326 pp.

——. 1985. "Common barn-owl population decline in Ohio and the relationship to agricultural trends." *Journal of Field Ornithology* 56:224–235.

——., P.L. Hegdal and W.B. Jackson. 1984. "A comprehensive approach to research and management of common barn-owl populations." pp. 270–282 in *Proceedings of the Workshop on Management of Nongame Species and Ecological Communities.* Department of Forestry, University of Kentucky. Lexington, Kentucky.

Colvin, B.A. and E.B. McLean. 1986. "Food habits and prey specificity of the common barn-owl in Ohio." *Ohio Journal of Science* 86:76–86.

Craighead, J.J. and F.C. Craighead, Jr. 1956. *Hawks, Owls and Wildlife.* Stackpole Books. Harrisburg, Pennsylvania. 443 pp.

Cuisin, J. and M. Cuisin. 1979. "Le régime alimentaire de la Chouette Effraye (*Tyto alba* [Scopoli]) dans le canton des Riceys (Aube) et ses environs immédiats." *L'Oiseau et la Revue Francaise d'Ornithologie* 49:81–89.

De Bruijn, O. 1979. "Voedseloecologie van ide Kerkuil *Tyto alba* in Nederland." *Limosa* 52:91–154.

De Groot, R.S. 1983. "Origin, status and ecology of the owls in Galapagos." *Ardea* 71:167–182.

Dice, L.R. 1945. "Minimum intensities of illumination under which owls can find dead prey by sight." *American Naturalist* 79:385–416.

Evans, F.C. and J.T. Emlen. 1947. "Ecological notes on the prey selected by a barn owl." *Condor* 49:3–9.

Epple, W. 1979. "Geschwisterfütterung bei jungen Schleiereulen *Tyto alba.*" *Journal fur Ornithologie* 120:226.

——. 1983. "Gedehnte Legeabstande bei der Schleierule (*Tyto alba*). *Okologie der Vogel* 5:271–276.

Fitch, H.S. 1947. "Predation by owls in the Sierran foothills of California." *Condor* 49:137–151.

Flieg, G.M. 1972. "Unusual egg production of the barn owl (*Tyto alba*) in captivity." *Raptor Research* 6:104.

Frylestam, B. 1971. "Über Massnahmen zur Förderung der Brut von Schleiereulen (*Tyto alba*) in Südschweden." *Die Vogelwelt* 92:112–114.

——. 1972. "Uber Wanderungen und Sterblichkeit beringter skandinavischer Schleiereulen *Tyto alba.*" *Ornis Scandinavica* 3:45–54.

Glasgow, L.L. 1962. "The barn owl." *Wildlife Education Bulletin* 44. Louisiana Wildlife and Fisheries Commission. 7 pp.

Glue, D.E. 1971. "Ringing recovery circumstances of small birds of prey." *Bird Study* 18:137–146.

——. 1974. "Food of the barn owl in Britain and Ireland." *Bird Study* 21:200–210.

Glutz von Blotzheim, U.N. 1979. "Zur Dismigration junger Schleiereulen *Tyto alba.*" *Der Ornithologische Beobachter* 76:1–7.

Görner, M. 1978. "Schleiereule, *Tyto alba*, als Vogeljäger." *Beitrage zur Vogelkunde* 24:273–275.

Haverschmidt, F. 1962. "Beobachtungen an der Schleiereule, *Tyto alba*, in Surinam." *Journal fur Ornithologie* 103:236–242.

——. 1970. "Barn owls hunting by daylight in Surinam." *Wilson Bulletin* 82:101.

Hegdal, P.L. and R.W. Blaskiewicz. 1984. "Evaluation of the potential hazard to barn owls of talon (brodifacoum bait) to control rats and house mice." *Environmental Toxicology and Chemistry* 3:167–179.

Henny, C.J., L.J. Blus and T.E. Kaiser. 1984. "Heptachlor seed treatment contaminates hawks, owls, and eagles of Columbia Basin, Oregon." *Raptor Research* 18:41–48.

Howard, R. and A. Moore. 1980. *A Complete Checklist of the Birds of the World.* Oxford University Press. Oxford, England. 701 pp.

Johnson, W.D. 1974. The Bioenergetics of the Barn Owl, *Tyto alba.* M.S. thesis. California State University. Long Beach, California. 55 pp.

Johnston, D.W. 1978. "Organochlorine pesticide residues in Florida birds of prey, 1969–76." *Pesticides Monitoring Journal* 12:8–15.

Juillard, M. and J. Beuret. 1983. "L'amenagement de sites de nidification et son influence sur une population de Chouettes effraies, *Tyto alba*, dans le nord-ouest de la Suisse." *Nos Oiseaux* 37:1–20.

Keran, D. 1981. "The incidence of man-caused and natural mortalities to raptors." *Raptor Research* 15:108–112.

Konishi, M. and A.S. Kenuk. 1975. "Discrimination of noise spectra by memory in the barn owl." *Journal of Comparative Physiology* 97:55–58.

Knudsen, E.I. 1981. "The hearing of the barn owl." *Scientific American* 245:112–125.

Kragenow, P. 1970. "Die Schleiereule in den Nordbezirken der DDR." *Falke* 17:256–259.

Lack, D. 1966. *Population Studies of Birds.* Clarendon Press. Oxford, England. 341 pp.

Lenton, G.M. 1980. "Biological control of rats in oil palm by owls." *Tropical Ecology and Development*:615–621.

——. 1984. "The feeding and breeding ecology of barn owls *Tyto alba* in peninsular Malaysia." *Ibis* 126:551–575.

——. 1985. "History, distribution and origin of barn owls *Tyto alba* in the Malay peninsula." *Bulletin of the British Ornithologists' Club* 105:54–58.

Lerg, J.M. 1984. "Status of the common barn owl in Michigan." *Jack-Pine Warbler* 62:39–48.

Long, J.L. 1981. *Introduced Birds of the World.* Universe Books. New York. 528 pp.

Maestrelli, J.R. 1973. "Propagation of barn owls in captivity." *Auk* 90:426–428.

Marshall, J.D., C.H. Hager and G. McKee. 1986. "The barn owl egg: weight loss characters, fresh weight prediction and incubation period." *Raptor Research* 20:108–112.

Marti, C.D. 1968. "Double broods of the barn owl in Colorado." *Colorado Field Ornithologist* 3:7–8.

——. 1970. Feeding Ecology of Four Sympatric Owls in Colorado. Ph.D dissertation. Colorado State University. Fort Collins, Colorado. 106 pp.

——. 1973. "Food consumption and pellet formation rates in four owl species." *Wilson Bulletin* 85:178–181.

——. 1974. "Feeding ecology of four sympatric owls." *Condor* 76:45–61.

——. 1985. "The barn-owl (*Tyto alba*)—what do we know about it?" pp. 11–12 in *Symposium on the Biology, Status and Management of Owls.* Sacramento, California.

——. 1987a. "Polygyny in the common barn-owl." p. 5 in *Cooper Ornithological Society Annual Meeting Abstracts.* Snowbird, Utah.

——. and P.W. Wagner. 1985. "Winter mortality in common barn-owls and its effect on population density and reproduction." *Condor* 87:111–115.

——., P.W. Wagner and K.W. Denne. 1979. "Nest boxes for the management of barn owls." *Wildlife Society Bulletin* 7:145–148.

Martin, D.J. 1973. "Burrow digging by barn owls." *Bird-Banding* 44:59–60.

Mendenhall, V.M. and L.F. Pank. 1980. "Secondary poisoning of owls by anticoagulant rodenticides." *Wildlife Society Bulletin* 8:311–315.

——., E.E. Klaas and M.A.R. McLane. 1983. "Breeding success of barn owls (*Tyto alba*) fed low levels of DDE and dieldrin." *Archives of Environmental Contamination and Toxicology* 12:235–240.

Mikkola, H. 1983. *Owls of Europe.* Buteo Books. Vermillion, South Dakota. 397 pp.

Mueller, H.C and D.D. Berger. 1959. "Some long distance barn owl recoveries." *Bird-Banding* 30:182.

Mumford, R.E. an C.E. Keller. 1984. *The Birds of Indiana.* Indiana University Press. Bloomington, Indiana. 376 pp.

Otteni, L.C., E.G. Bolen and C. Cottam. 1972. "Predator-prey relationships and reproduction of the barn owl in southern Texas." *Wilson Bulletin* 84:434–448.

Parkes, K.C. and A.R. Phillips. 1978. "Two new Caribbean subspecies of barn owl (*Tyto alba*), with remarks on variation in other populations." *Annals of Carnegie Museum* 47:479–492.

Payne, R.S. 1962. "How the barn owl locates prey by hearing." *Living Bird* 1:151–170.

Peakall, D.B. and A.C. Kemp. 1980. "Organochlorine levels in owls in Canada and South Africa." *Ostrich* 51:186.

Piechocki, R. 1960. "Über die Winterverluste der Schleiereule (*Tyto alba*)." *Die Vogelwarte* 20:274–280.

Penny, M. 1974. *The Birds of Seychelles and Outlying Islands.* Collins. London, England. 160 pp.

Reese, J.G. 1972. "A Chesapeake barn owl population." *Auk* 89:106–114.

Risebrough, R.W., S.G. Herman, D.B. Peakall and M.N. Kirven. 1968. "Polychlorinated biphenyls in the global ecosystem." *Nature* 220:1098–1102.

Schönfeld, M. 1974. "Ringfundauswertung der 1964–1972 in der DDR beringten Schleiereulen (*Tyto alba guttata* Brehm)." *Jber. Vogelwarte Hiddensee* 4:90–122.

——. and G. Girbig. 1975. "Beiträge zur Brutbiologie der Schleiereule *Tyto alba* unter besonderer Berücksichtigung der Abhängigkeit von der Feldmausdichte." *Hercynia* 12:257–319.

Schneider, W. 1937. "Berigungs-Ergebnisse an der Mitteleurpäischen Schleiereule (*Tyto alba guttata* Brehm)." *Der Vogelzug* 8:159–170.

Selleck, D.M. and B. Glading. 1943. "Food habits of nesting barn owls and marsh hawks at Dune Lakes, California, as determined by the 'cage nest' method." *California Fish and Game News* 29:122–131.

Smith, D.G., C.R. Wilson and H.H. Frost. 1974. "History and ecology of a colony of barn owls in Utah." *Condor* 76:131–136.

——. and C.D. Marti. 1976. "Distributional status and ecology of barn owls in Utah." *Raptor Research* 10:33–44.

Snyder, N.F.R. and J.W. Wiley. 1976. "Sexual size dimorphism in hawks and owls of North America." *Ornithological Monographs* no. 20. American Ornithologists' Union. 96 pp.

Soucy, L.J. 1980. "Three long distance recoveries of banded New Jersey barn owls." *North American Bird Bander* 5:97.

Stewart, P.A. 1952. "Dispersal, breeding behavior, and longevity of banded barn owls in North American." *Auk* 69:227–245.

——. 1980. "Population trends of barn owls in North America." *American Birds* 34:698–700.

Tate, J. 1986. "The blue list for 1986." *American Birds* 40:227–236.

Tomich, P.Q. 1971. "Notes on the foods and feeding behavior of raptorial birds in Hawaii." *'Elepaio* 31:111–114.

Trollope, J. 1971. "Some aspects of behaviour and reproduction in captive barn owls (*Tyto alba alba*)." *Aviculture Magazine* 77:117–125.

Trost, C.H. and J.H. Hutchison. 1963. "Food of the barn owl in Florida." *Quarterly Journal of the Florida Academy of Sciences* 26:382–384.

Wallace, G.J. 1948. "The barn owl in Michigan." *Michigan Agricultural Experiment Station Technical Bulletin* no. 208. 61 pp.

Wilson, R.T., M.P. Wilson and J.W. Durkin. 1986. "Breeding biology of the barn owl *Tyto alba* in central Mali." *Ibis* 128:81–90.

Wilson, V.J. 1970. "Notes on the breeding and feeding habits of a pair of barn owls, *Tyto alba* (Scopoli) in Rhodesia." *Arnoldia* 4:1–8.

Carl D. Marti is a professor of zoology at Weber State College in Ogden, Utah. He has conducted a long-term study of the barn owl in Utah and Idaho.

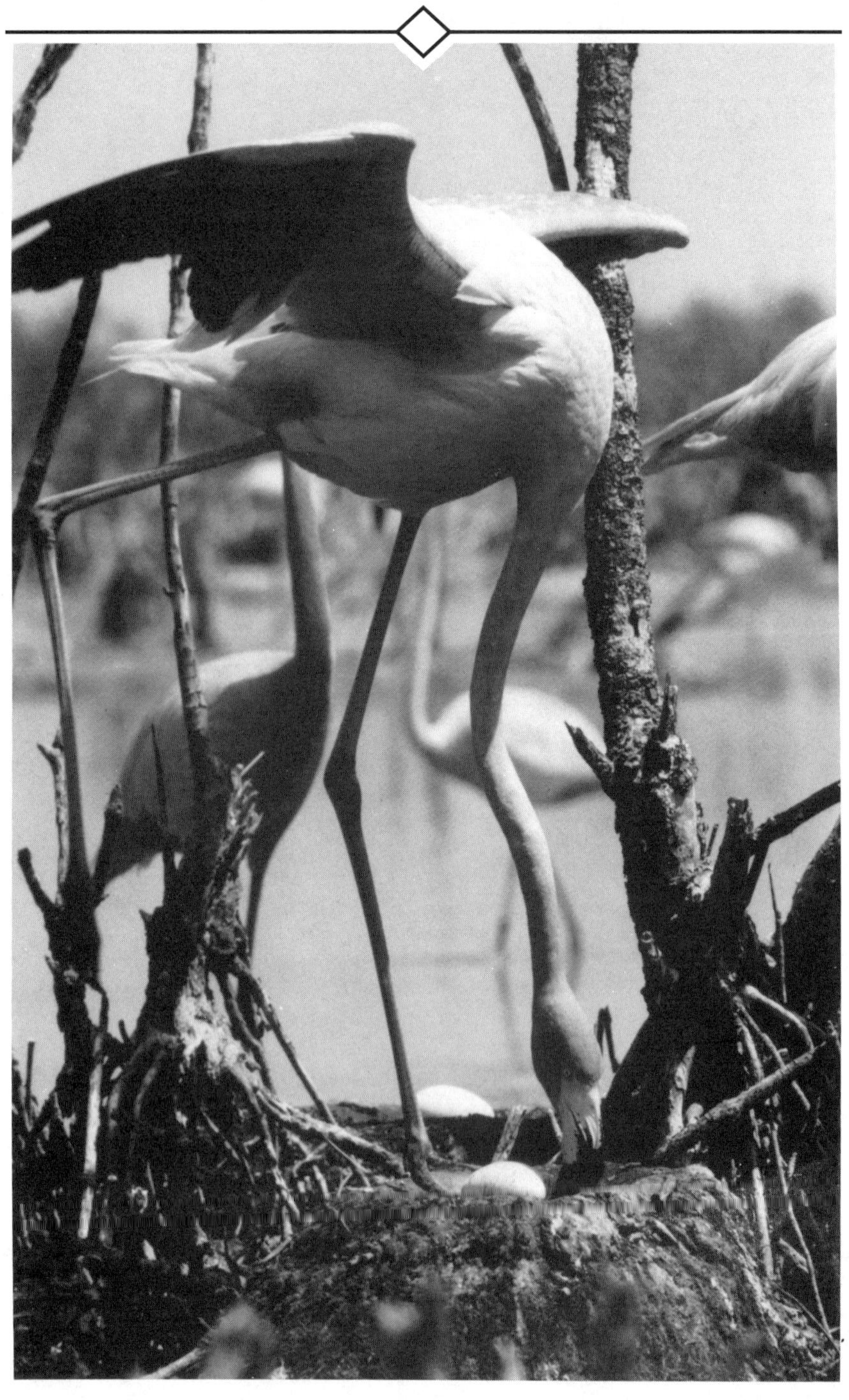

The instantly recognizable flamingo requires specialized habitat; populations have stabilized and in some cases increased. *Alexander Sprunt IV*

The Greater Flamingo

Alexander Sprunt IV

National Audubon Society

SPECIES DESCRIPTION AND NATURAL HISTORY

Flamingos are one of the few wild birds instantly recognized by people the world over. Their long necks and legs, bright color, and strange form have led to their use by humans in decoration and design since long before the dawn of history. For example, a flamingo is among the animals portrayed by Stone Age artists on the walls of a cave in Spain. Today flamingos are seen on every conceivable item from t-shirts to coffee cups. In spite of this notoriety, it is only in very recent times that flamingos have been studied and some understanding of their life cycle and needs has been gained.

Flamingos are the tallest of the wading birds, with very long legs and necks. Size varies considerably between the sexes and between individuals. Males are larger than females. Large males may exceed five feet in height when standing fully upright and weigh more than 8 pounds, while females weigh about 6.5 pounds (Rooth 1965). Their wingspread is about five feet which, with the long neck and legs extended, gives the impression of a flying cross. The Caribbean flamingo is the reddest of the flamingos; it is not really pink, but rather various shades of orange red or vermilion. The adult coloration is quite variable, changing from season to season and among individuals. The birds are usually deepest red on the neck and breast and on the upper surface and lining of the wings. The large flight feathers of the wings are black. The flamingo's long legs are reddish purple, and the bill is yellow to orange with a black tip.

One of the most striking features of the flamingo is its massive bill, which is bent sharply downward in the middle and is remarkable in many ways. In most birds the upper mandible is fixed, but in the case of the flamingo, which feeds with its head upside down, it is the upper mandible that is hinged and movable. The bill is actually a very efficient filter. It has lamellae along both edges that strain out edible particles as water is pumped in and out of the bill by the large muscular tongue. The tongue acts as a piston and is equipped with soft "spines" that move water into and through the bill. The greater flamingo has rather coarse lamellae and can thus take larger food items than the smaller species.

It takes at least three years for flamingos to attain full adult plumage. The first year their feathers are gray with tinges of pink on the wings and underparts. Second year flamingos are distinctly paler than adults, and in the third year they continue to show some paleness with brownish feathers, particularly on the hind neck and head.

The color of flamingos is produced by complex organic compounds called carotenoids (Fox 1975); unless its food contains good sources of these compounds, the bird loses its color. Captive flamingos in zoos are kept in excellent color by making sure that they receive an abundance of carotenoids.

Taxonomy

There are six forms of flamingos around the world, grouped in three genera. Some authorities recognize four species with two subspecies (Hartert 1915), while others give all six specific rank (Peters 1931). Ornithologists most familiar with the group are unanimous in their belief that five species is the proper number (Kear and Duplaix-Hall 1975). These are: the greater flamingo (*Phoenicopterus ruber*), Chilean Flamingo (*Phoenicopterus chilensis*), Andean flamingo (*Phoenicoparrus andinus*), James' flamingo (*Phoenicoparrus jamesi*), and lesser flamingo (*Phoeniconaias minor*). The greater flamingo has been divided into two subspecies, *P. ruber ruber* and *P. ruber roseus*. The latter is found in Europe, Asia, and Africa, while the nominate race is found almost exclusively in the Caribbean Basin. This form has been called by different authors the American, West Indian, or Caribbean flamingo and is the form treated here.

Taxonomists not only have trouble defining flamingo species but also do not agree on the relationship of flamingos to other birds. They have been variously placed with the herons, ibises, and storks (Ciconiiformes) by some authorities and with the ducks, geese, and swans (Anseriformes) by others. Even with the sophisticated analytical tools available to modern-day scientists, such as protein analysis and recombinant DNA, the picture is still unclear. It seems likely that shorebirds (Charadriiformes), storks, flamingos, and ducks and geese all had a common ancestor, but that flamingos probably are closer to storks than to any other group (Sibley *et al.* 1969). Due to this uncertainty, flamingos have been given their own order—Phoenicopteriformes—in the latest Check List of the American Ornithologists' Union (American Ornithologists' Union 1983).

Distribution

Flamingos require a rather specialized habitat and, because of this, their distribution is discontinuous. The Caribbean flamingo is divided into four populations which, at least at this time, have no known interchange of individuals. Each of the populations has one regularly used breeding site, but may also have satellite sites used at more irregular intervals.

The largest of these populations breeds primarily on Great Inagua in the Bahamas, but also uses the much larger islands of Cuba and Hispaniola. The second group is found on the Yucatan peninsula in Mexico. The third breeds on the island of Bonaire off the coast of Venezuela, but the birds spend much of their time on the north coast of South America ranging from Colombia to the Guianas. The fourth population is very small and the most isolated and is found in the Galapagos Islands, where it breeds in small colonies on several of the larger islands (see Figure 1).

Voice

Flamingos are highly gregarious and, like most other bird species found in groups, are quite vocal. The flamingo's voice is decidedly goose-like, with a variety of honking notes and a still larger vocabulary of lesser "conversational" tones. The most often heard call is a three-syllabled note that has given rise to the South American Indian name for this species, "Cho go go." This call is often given in flight as well as while feeding. When the birds are courting and feeding in large groups, they keep up a constant gabble that has been described as "eep-eep cak-cak, eep-eep cak-cak" (Allen 1956), with the females giving the higher pitched "eep-eep" and the males a lower pitched "cak-cak." The noise made by a large flock can be heard under certain conditions up to a mile or more. A warning call given by a bird that has discovered an intruder, is a long-drawn, low-pitched "kahaan."

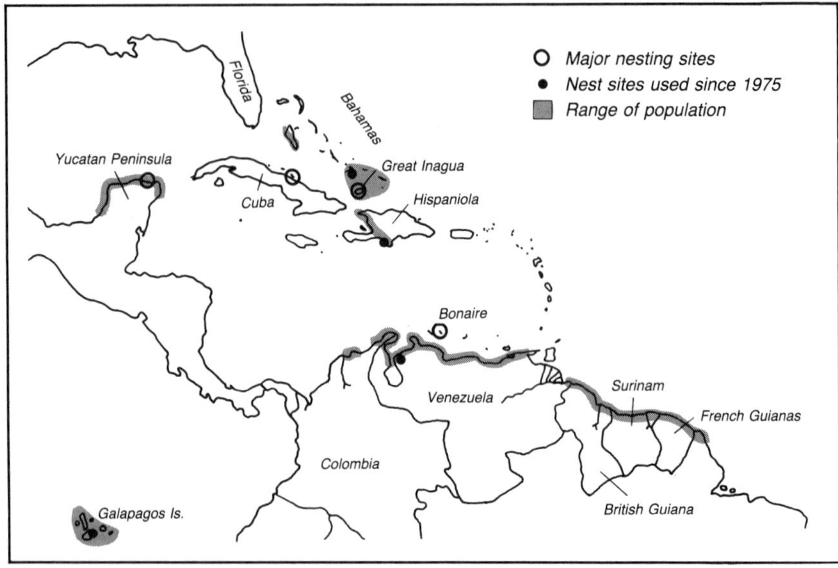

Figure 1. Range and major nesting sites of the greater flamingo.

Breeding

Flamingos are highly social birds, with all of their activities taking place in groups. Their courtship displays are no exception and have evolved into complex and highly ritualized behaviors. Both sexes take part in the displays, usually initiated by males. Displays may take place over a long span of time, beginning months before nesting and continuing after colonies have formed. The individual displays have been derived from comfort movements but have become stylized and exaggerated. They are stiffly performed and contagious, that is, when one bird performs them, others follow. A number of these displays have been described:

Head Flagging. In this display the birds, mostly males, stand in a group, usually from 10 to 30, in the alert posture with necks extended. A few then begin to call loudly and snap their heads from side to side. This may continue for several minutes.

Wing Salute. Head flagging is usually followed by the wing salute. The birds, still in the alert posture, suddenly spread their wings, with the primaries tightly closed, hold this posture for a few seconds and then fold them smartly. The impression that this creates is a flash of black against a red background. Several birds will often give this display either together or in turn. After this display, the birds usually give another.

Twist-Preen. In this movement, the bird loosens one wing, the neck is looped down over the back, and the head and bill are tucked under the wing for a second or two.

Inverted Wing Salute. This movement consists of the bird bowing forward with its neck extended and the wings half opened and held out with the bend of the wing pointed down. Again it is a flash of black and vivid red. This seems to be done more often by the females.

These movements are all performed by birds standing in a group. At times, the whole group will start to move in a display called marching. They move forward rapidly, some of the birds (mostly males) bowing their necks into a "hooking" posture as they charge along. They may change direction suddenly or even reverse and charge back.

The Caribbean flamingo has elaborated the marching display into one of the most spectacular sights in the bird world. At times, thousands of these big red birds will engage in mass marchings. When this happens, another display, called mock feeding, occurs. As the birds begin a mass march they seem to go into a trance-like state perhaps brought on by the sheer numbers of birds and the tremendous sound produced. They march along and suddenly, as if on cue, slow, drop their heads to a feeding posture, take a few steps, then raise their heads again and resume speed. A mass march is a sight and sound that is unforgettable once experienced.

Nesting

Courtship rituals lead to pair formation and copulation which may continue for several weeks before a colony is actually started. In zoos, flamingos may pair for years (Studer-Thiersch 1975), but information on pairing longevity is lacking for wild birds.

Flamingos generally nest in large groups of several hundred to several thousand nests. Smaller colonies of some 50 nests are occasionally found in satellite breeding sites, but only the isolated Galapagos population regularly nests in very small colonies.

Flamingo nests are usually built of mud or a calcareous clay, called marl, piled into a truncated cone and often containing bits of sticks, mangrove roots, rocks, or shell. Depending on the substrate and the water depth, nests are generally from 5 to 18 inches in height. Departure from this norm, however, is frequent. Nests have been found that consisted only of a ring of small stones built on a rock, while others used for several successive nestings may be 30 inches high. The top of the nest is slightly hollowed and usually about a foot in diameter.

Nests may be placed close together, at times more than one per square meter. Some colonies are a single mass of nests, while others are made up of a collection of smaller groupings. The birds continue to add to the nest during incubation, reaching out and down for mud to pile on the side of the nest.

Incubation of the single egg is shared by both members of the pair and takes 28 to 31 days (Allen 1956). Two eggs may be found in about one percent of nests, but whether both eggs are from the same female is unknown. In zoos, two females have been known to mate with the same male and to lay in the same nest (Studer-Thiersch 1975).

The hatching process takes from 24 to 36 hours after the egg is first pipped. The adult bird is quite restless during the hatching process, standing up often and watching the young bird in the egg. It may also nibble at the egg shell, but this does not actually seem to help the chick in the process.

Newly hatched flamingos are covered with a thick coat of white down with more or less gray shading on the head and back. Their legs and bills are orange pink and the bills are straight. The first five to eight days are spent on the nest. Both adults continue to brood the chick, which spends most of its time between the adult's wing and body with its head looking out above the bend of the wing. The chick is fed a liquid by both parents that is secreted by glands located in the upper digestive tract. The bright red liquid contains 15 percent fat, 8 to 9 percent protein, and 0.1 to 0.2 percent carbohydrate. It also contains high concentrations of canthaxanthin, a carotenoid, and 1 percent blood (Studer-Thiersch 1975).

The young birds grow rapidly. After they leave the nest, they form groups and roam about the colony site. They are fed at increasing intervals by the adults throughout the first month. By that time, the young birds are stocky, have replaced their white down with a thick gray coat, and their legs and bills have turned to a dark blackish gray. Their bills have started to bend downward, and they begin to feed in typical fashion. From this time on, the young are left alone more and more by the adults. Young birds form a large group and move about the area of the colony and nearby areas accompanied by a few "nursemaid" adults. From time to time, one of the parents will return and their young bird will come to them to be fed. When this happens, the adults call loudly, and the chick answers and comes running from the flock. Recognition seems to be primarily by voice. After about six weeks, the chicks' feathers and long bones start to grow rapidly. Flight is first attempted at about 73 or 74 days after hatching and actually achieved at 75 to 77 days (Allen 1956).

Mortality in any colony, under normal conditions, seems to average about 20 percent, but can be increased markedly by human disturbance, predators, or natural disasters such as flooding rains.

Diet

In the media, in advertising, and usually in art, flamingos are portrayed in lush tropical settings with palm trees, vines, flowers, and lots of greenery. Nothing could be further from the reality of the flamingos' actual habitat. They occupy salt flats and saline lagoons where they are exposed to sun and blasting wind. Flamingos are among the relatively few species that thrive in this sort of harsh setting. Their diet varies from locality to locality. Indeed, some authors (Rooth 1965) have suggested that in some areas the birds are almost monophagus, that they eat only one thing. In Bonaire, where Rooth did his work, the birds ate the larvae and pupae of the brine fly (*Ephydra gracilis*) almost exclusively. In other locations, flamingos eat a variety of small mollusks, crustaceans such as brine shrimp (*Artemia* sp.), aquatic insects, seeds, and small fish. One of the most important food sources eaten almost everywhere is highly organic mud, or perhaps more accurately, the rich algal mat that forms on top of the mud under hypersaline conditions. This is the crust which drys up and curls on the surface during dry conditions, but starts to grow again vigorously when water returns. The mat is made up of algae, diatoms, and bacteria and may contain protozoa, annelid worms, and the larvae and pupae of insects.

Feeding Behavior

Flamingos feed in several different ways. They may walk along and pick up single items, such as mollusks or small fish, as would a heron, but usually feed by filtering. This is also done in several ways. One of the most common can be termed treading or stamping, which is done in water up to a foot in depth. The bird puts its head down, turns in a circle with its head in the center, and treads to stir up the bottom, all the while filtering this "soup." This results in the formation of a shallow depression with a low mound of larger, inorganic debris in the center. These round depressions, or "ronds," and have often been mistaken for old nest mounds by inexperienced observers. In another filtering method, the birds walk slowly forward in water only a few inches deep, dragging their bills along the surface of the mud and filtering as they go. This results in a shallow meandering track through the algal mat. This method also is used in deep water, where the bird "tips up" while swimming, just as ducks, geese, and swans do. At times the Caribbean flamingo also feeds by swimming or walking in water up to its belly and filtering the surface. This method is much more rarely seen among greater flamingos than in the smaller flamingos, whose lamellae are adapted to much smaller organisms. In the case of the Caribbean birds, this method is probably most often used when feeding on brine shrimp.

Longevity

Different populations of flamingos start to breed at somewhat different ages. Those birds nesting on Inagua may begin at four, but the majority do not breed until age five.

A species in which individuals mature late and have only one young per year can be expected to have a long life span. Banding of flamingos has not been done long enough to determine the longevity of wild birds. The oldest banded bird known was marked as a chick in 1964 and observed on an egg in 1980, 16 years later. Flamingos have lived much longer in zoos. A bird in the Philadelphia Zoo died at age 44 (Kear and Duplaix-Hall 1975).

SIGNIFICANCE OF THE SPECIES

Flamingos represent a group of birds that has special needs and requirements for future survival. The flamingos' habitat—isolated areas with waters of high salinity or alkalinity—is not abundant throughout the world. Although flamingos have been sought by people for food and feathers over the years, the forbidding nature of their breeding areas minimized chances for contact with people. But as humans humans continue to spread into more and more remote parts of the world, this is no longer the case. Flamingos also need to congregate in large groups in order to carry out their elaborate breeding rituals successfully, a fact which makes sharply reduced populations more vulnerable.

In short, flamingos will have to receive special consideration in order to survive in a human-dominated world. The bird is a symbol of the beauty and complexity of the evolutionary process and as such should receive the consideration and protection of its only mortal enemy—humans.

HISTORICAL PERSPECTIVE

The Caribbean flamingo probably has never occurred in as large numbers as some of its relatives, such as the Old World greaters and lessers and the Chilean flamingo. It is a bird of the West Indian Islands and the immediate perimeter of the Caribbean Basin. In this area there can be only a limited amount of suitable habitat. It is clear that the flamingo was at one time much more widespread. In his pioneering work on the species, Robert P. Allen documented a great many breeding sites used by Caribbean flamingos in the past, many of them unoccupied for many years. It is difficult, however, to arrive at realistic estimates of the magnitude of the reduction in overall numbers. Using Allen's figures for the number of sites used in the past and with current knowledge of the extent and distribution of suitable habitat, it is probable that the present population numbers 40,000 to 60,000 birds, perhaps half the number of birds present before Europeans reached the New World.

CURRENT TRENDS

Since Allen's work in the 1950s highlighted the extreme vulnerability of a species—which has only three or four nesting sites, is easy to capture in numbers, and is sought for food by people—the situation of the Caribbean flamingo has improved. The three major breeding areas are now protected by law; warden protection is very good for two areas and seems adequate in the third. A fourth breeding area, on the north coast of Cuba has been active in recent years but knowledge of conditions there as well as information on the numbers of birds involved is lacking.

That overall protection efforts for the bird have been effective is shown by the fact that a number of breeding sites that were deserted in the past are active again. A small colony has reappeared on Acklins Island in the Bahamas, located about 80 miles north of Inagua. A second site, on the Beata Peninsula in the Dominican Republic, has also been used, at least occasionally, in the last decade. Recently, the most exciting news is that a group of birds from the southern Caribbean population has nested successfully in a site—Los Olivitos, on the north coast of Venezuela. This is the first breeding on the South American mainland in many years, and possibly since the early parts of this century. The population as a whole has at least stabilized and in some cases increased. In Yucatan, flamingos have shown a marked increase from 12,000 birds in 1971 to some 20,000 to 25,000 individuals in 1987.

MANAGEMENT

Warden protection to prevent shooting and disturbance of breeding colonies must be continued. Flamingos are highly vulnerable to disturbance of several kinds during the entire breeding season. Damaging disturbance can take many forms. Approach to breeding areas by humans is probably the most common. This can vary from inadvertent disturbance in the course of fishing or hunting to willful destruction of eggs and young for use as food. Tourism is growing in several parts of the flamingo's range. Approaching nesting colonies too closely or disruption of feeding flocks can result in the desertion of colonies. Predators need to be controlled in some areas. Feral hogs and wild dogs have been a problem on Inagua and must be guarded against. Low-flying aircraft, particularly "buzzing" by pilots, cause the birds to flush and, in the case of colonies, can cause extensive damage ranging from smashed eggs to trampled young.

Flamingos are a tourist attraction and as long as visitation is carefully controlled, particularly during the breeding season, the presence of flocks of flamingos can be a very real resource.

The most serious threat to the long-term survival of flamingos is the loss of suitable habitat. Probably the only reason that flamingos still persist over most of their original range is due to the inhospitable aspect of the areas where they are found. However, in the last half of this century, even this has changed. Human population pressure is pushing people into areas that were once remote and not easily exploited. This increasing human presence, coupled with machines that have allowed the use of flamingo habitat for the profitable production of salt, has resulted in new pressures on flamingo populations throughout the Caribbean. On Inagua, Bonaire, and in the Yucatan, salt production has taken over areas used in past years for nesting and feeding by flamingos. Where the area is large enough, salt production is not necessarily damaging to flamingos. The birds freely use some of the large shallow evaporating ponds for feeding, and such ponds may actually increase the amount of feeding areas available to them. There are, however, tradeoffs in this situation. Salt operations introduce more people into the area and unless care is taken to set aside protected, undisturbed areas for breeding, the operations can be seriously damaging.

Flamingos are birds adapted to hypersaline conditions and such conditions are often found in coastal lagoons quite close to the coast. Fishermen have influenced their governments to cut through the coastal barriers and dredge the lagoons to create harbors. This completely destroys the area for flamingos. Tourist accomodations and their attendant "improvements" are another threat to the harsh, and usually unattractive (to people), areas needed by the birds.

PROGNOSIS

The future of the Caribbean flamingo seems fairly well assured under present conditions. The absolutely essential factor, however, is the maintenance of the limited habitats available to the birds. If this can be accomplished, and protection of the colony sites continued, flamingos should survive for the foreseeable future.

RECOMMENDATIONS

Monitoring of all populations should be continued to provide early warning of problems in the habitat. Declining numbers, especially sudden drops in the numbers of young birds, are signs of possible habitat complications attributable to pollution, drainage, or a number of other conditions. Monitoring is presently being done by the Mexican and Netherlands Antillan governments and by private or semi-private organizations in the Bahamas and Venezuela.

A banding program has been carried out in the Bahamas and a similar program was started in Mexico in 1987. Banding a sample of the southern Caribbean population would help to answer some of the questions of movements, longevity, and so forth in that group. An expanded marking program, especially covering the Mexican and southern Caribbean flamingo populations, would be helpful in answering some of the still unknown parameters of the birds' biology. Careful monitoring of planned activities that would seriously alter essential habitat needs must be instituted and maintained.

Proper use of flamingo populations as tourist attractions would aid in their protection and would help supplement human activities in areas important to the birds, thus increasing local interest in protecting the resource. It is most important that nonscientists be permitted in the field with the birds so that they can learn of the birds' value and of the necessity of preserving the systems which support both the birds and themselves.

Research on the functioning of the ecosystems used by flamingos is a very real need. The biology of the birds is fairly well known, but the processes governing the conditions in their feeding and breeding grounds have not been addressed adequately; they should be in the future.

REFERENCES

Allen, Robert P. 1956. *The Flamingos: Their Life History and Survival.* Research Report No. 5. National Audubon Society. New York. 285 pp.

American Ornithologists' Union. 1983. *Checklist of North American Birds.* American Ornithologists' Union. Lawrence, Kansas. p. 59.

Fox, D.L. 1975. "Carotenoids in Pigmentation," pp. 162–182 *in* J. Kear and N. Duplaix-Hall eds., *Flamingos.* T. and A.D. Poyser. Berkhamstead, England.

Hartert, E. 1915. "Die Vögel der Paläarktischen," Fauna 2:1903–22. Friedlander, Berlin.

Kear, J. and N. Duplaix-Hall. 1975. *Flamingos.* Appendix 65. T and A.D. Poyser. Berkhamstead, England. p. 219.

Peters, J.L. 1931. *Checklist of Birds of the World.* Vol 1. Harvard University Press. Cambridge, Massachusetts.

Rooth, J. 1965. *The Flamingos of Bonaire.* Foundation for the Scientific Research in Surinam and the Netherlands Antilles, No. 41. Utrecht, Netherlands. 151 pp.
Sibley, C.G., K.W. Corbin and J.H. Haavie. n.d. "The relationship of the flamingos as indicated by the egg-white proteins and hemoglobins." *Condor* 71(2):155–179.
Studer-Theirsch, A. 1975. "Basle Zoo," pp. 121–130 *in* J. Kear and N. Duplaix-Hall eds., *Flamingos.* T. and A.D. Poyser. Berkhamstead, England.

Alexander Sprunt IV is vice-president and director of field research for National Audubon Society.

The desert tortoise, an increasingly rare inhabitant of the southwestern deserts, digs shallow burrows to escape extreme heat and cold. *Beverly F. Steveson*

The Desert Tortoise

Faith Thompson Campbell
Natural Resources Defense Council

SPECIES DESCRIPTION AND NATURAL HISTORY

The desert tortoise (*Xerobates* = *Gopherus* = *Scaptochelys agassizii*) is one of three species in the genus found in the United States. The shell of an adult desert tortoise measures from 8 to 13, or possibly 15, inches. The shell varies in color from grey to butterscotch to brown (Berry, pers. commun.); it also has distinct growth furrows. On younger tortoises, the center of each carapace scute is lighter than the margins (Stebbins 1985, Pritchard 1979). Males are larger than females.

Taxonomy and Distribution

The desert tortoise inhabits the Mojave, Colorado, and Sonoran deserts in the southwestern United States—which cover parts of Arizona, California, Nevada, and Utah—and adjacent Mexico as far south as southern Sonora. In the Colorado and Mojave deserts, the tortoise is found primarily on flats and bajadas. In the Sonoran Desert, it is found primarily on steep, rocky slopes.

Recent studies based on shell shape and variations in genetic makeup indicate that the species has three distinct populations in the

United States: the "California type" found in that state and southwestern Nevada; the "Sonoran type" found in Arizona south of the Grand Canyon; and the "Beaver Dam Slope type" found on that geologic formation in southwestern Utah and neighboring portions of Nevada and Arizona (Weinstein and Berry 1987).

Life Span

The species is long-lived, reaching from 60 to 80 years or more of age (Berry 1979). Slow to mature, the tortoise does not reach reproductive age until it is anywhere from 12 to 20 years old (U.S. Fish and Wildlife Service 1987c). Due to its slow maturation process, the species has a low reproductive potential and thus would require several decades to recover from a loss of a substantial proportion of the breeding population (Johnson 1984).

The desert tortoise depends on burrows for shelter during both winter hibernation and summer aestivation. Woodbury and Hardy found that tortoises on the Beaver Dam Slope used dens that are from 5 to 30 feet long during winter hibernation. The dens are usually dug in the gravelly banks of washes. During the summer, the tortoises may move up to the flats to some extent and use shorter dens dug beneath bushes as shelter from the sun (Carr 1983). Pritchard (1979) believes that in warmer climates, such as Arizona, the tortoise may rely on shorter burrows during the winter as well, which, he says, are often on the south sides of hills. He also believes that the long burrows now found in Utah were originally begun as short ones when that area had warmer winters (Pritchard 1979).

Diet and Habitat

The desert tortoise is a herbivore and depends on the relatively scanty vegetation of its desert home. Both survival and successful reproduction are apparently tied to annual plants that appear in the spring, when the tortoise emerges poorly nourished after its winter hibernation. The tortoises must find sufficient food to support growth; females must also fuel egg production.

The availability of annuals requires sufficient precipitation, which is an unreliable occurrence in the desert. Later in the year after the annuals have withered, and during times of drought, the tortoise finds essential food from dried annuals and perennial grasses and cacti (Bureau of Land Management 1978, Berry 1984). On Beaver Dam Slope, the desert tortoise feeds on annuals such as filaree (*Erodium cicutarium*) and red brome (*Bromus rubens*) and on perennials such as bush muhly (*Muhlenbergia porteri*) and rice grass (*Oryzopsis hymenoides*) (U.S. Fish and Wildlife Service 1983). The tortoise also eats cactus, primarily prickly pear (*Opuntia*).

Unfortunately, desert vegetation has undergone significant changes as the result of a century or more of livestock grazing. Perennial grasses, which once dominated large areas of the desert, have disappeared. The annual grasses that have partially replaced them are often nonnative species. Shrubs have also increased. These changes, which can be reversed only over decades, if at all, may have deprived the desert tortoise of important native food sources.

Breeding

Wild tortoises court and mate during spring, summer, and fall. Nesting begins in late April and may continue until the first week of July (Berry, pers. commun.). During the mating period, males are aggressive and try to overturn rivals. Clutches range from 2 eggs to as may as 13 eggs (Berry pers. commun., Pritchard 1979). Incubation usually lasts three to four months. Hatchlings are about two inches long and light in color, with dark scute borders (Pritchard 1979). Females may defend their nests from predators, such as gila monsters (Barrett and Humphrey 1986). However, they do not protect the hatchlings or offer parental care.

SIGNIFICANCE OF THE SPECIES

A large herbivore that is highly sensitive to human disturbance, the desert tortoise is an indicator of the health of its desert ecosystem. The tortoise, however, is more persistent than some of its former neighbors. The desert pronghorn, for example, has already disappeared from many of the areas in which populations of desert tortoises can be found (Berry 1984). It may be possible that other desert herbivores, such as the pronghorn and desert bighorn, are driven out much faster by hunting and intolerance of livestock diseases than by changes in the vegetation.

The desert tortoise is also an indicator species in a political and ecological sense. We can learn much about the current philosophy of the wildlife conservation movement by observing the willingness of responsible agencies to take the actions necessary to conserve this creature whose existence is in conflict with so many human activities. Such actions will almost certainly depend upon increased political pressure by a conservation community that still shows more interest in mammals and birds than in reptiles or "lower life forms."

HISTORICAL PERSPECTIVE

Berry (1984) estimates that in the 1870s, high densities of desert tortoises could be found on 6,000 square miles in the western Mojave

Desert, and that the tortoise was widespread and abundant in California until the 1950s. By 1980, the tortoise occupied only 2,300 square miles, in lower densities. It suffered a 60-percent reduction in range and a 90-percent reduction in numbers over little more than a century. Less is known about the species' status in the eastern Mojave, but there has apparently been little change in the extent of its range or abundance. In the Colorado Desert, the species has seemed to disappear in some areas and has declined in others (Berry 1984).

There are no historical data for desert tortoise densities in Nevada before the 1970s, but Berry believes that they must have been distributed much more continuously and at considerably higher densities over approximately the current range. The longest-studied population of desert tortoise is found on Beaver Dam Slope in the extreme southwest corner of Utah. Woodbury and Hardy set up a permanent study plot from 1936 to 1945, in which they estimated the density of adult tortoises to be 160 per square mile. Studies in the mid-1970s indicated that densities had fallen and estimated populations of 109 to 137 per square mile for all age classes (Berry 1984). Populations on the Beaver Dam Slope have since fallen by more than half.

There is little data on historic population levels and distributions in Arizona. The species appears to have been restricted to rocky slopes since before European settlement. These slopes are in essence islands surrounded by flatland area not used by the tortoise.

CURRENT TRENDS

There are no good estimates of the species' current population levels. In its draft management strategy for the desert tortoise, the Bureau of Land Management (BLM) gives the following population ranges for the species (U.S. Department of Interior 1987b) (see Table 1):

Table 1
BLM population estimates for the Desert Tortoise

State	Minimum	Maximum
Utah	500	3,500
Nevada	100,000	375,000
California	300,000	1,000,000
Arizona	100,000	950,000
TOTAL	500,000	2,328,500

Source: Bureau of Land Management (1987b).

BLM estimates "total occupied habitat" for the desert tortoise in the United States as 75,870 square miles.

Considerable caution should be used in evaluating these figures. BLM's population maps, on which these estimates are based, make no allowance for extensive areas of human disturbance within the tortoise's range. These disturbances, both individually and cumulatively, are causing severe decline in tortoise populations. Also, BLM's report does not consider recent documented declines, such as the probable 50-percent decline in tortoise populations in Utah and 30- to 70-percent reductions in some areas of California. Even the lower figures for range in the BLM report should be considered as overestimates(see Figure 1).

Although there is uncertainty about historic and current populations in Arizona and Mexico, there is consensus that the species is declining in the remainder of its range in the United States—California, Nevada, and Utah. In fact, the morphologically separable Beaver Dam Slope population found in the southwestern corner of Utah

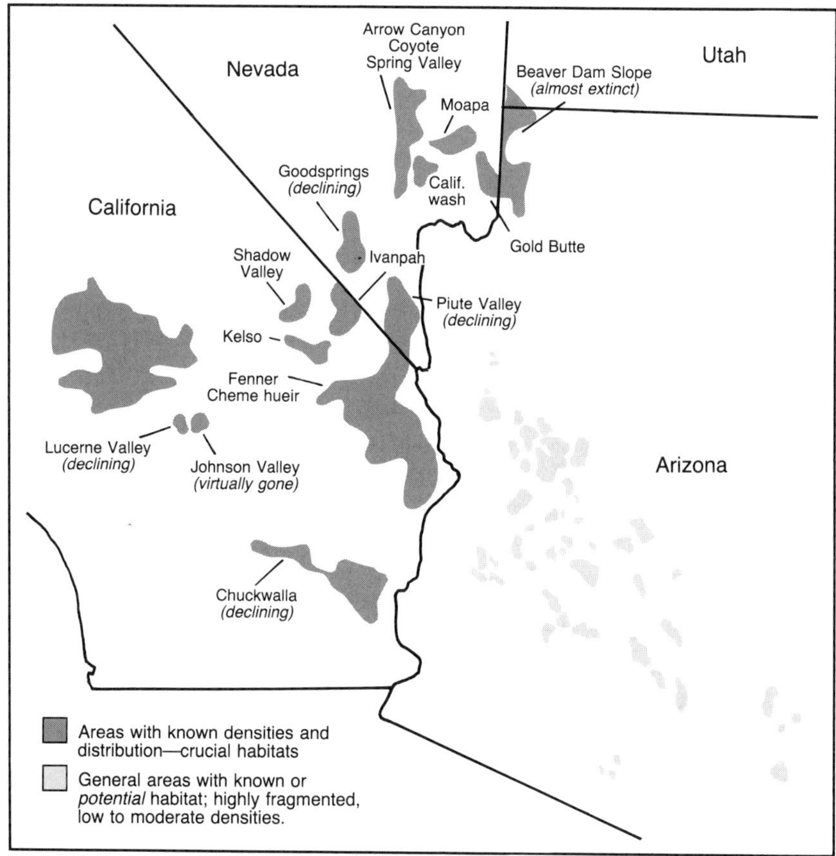

Figure 1.

and neighboring portions of Arizona and Nevada appears on the verge of extinction.

Recent studies indicate that the downward population trend is accelerating. Resurveys of eight desert tortoise study sites in the western Mojave Desert of California showed significant population reductions at seven of them (Berry, pers. commun.). For example, declines of 34 to 48 percent occurred at one plot on the edge of the Desert Tortoise Natural Area, a 21,320-acre protected area—made up of both BLM and privately owned lands—in eastern Kern County, California (Berry *et al.* 1986b). At another site at Fremont Peak, declines of 55 percent were recorded. At both sites, the heaviest mortality rates were among the juvenile and immature tortoises.

Populations at other sites in the western Mojave also show similar declines. The species is under severe pressure from deliberate shooting or vandalism at all sites, as well as from vehicle kills and continuing habitat destruction (Berry, pers. commun.). Populations at three sites in the eastern Mojave Desert and Colorado Desert that experience considerably less human disturbance show little change (Berry *et al.* 1986a).

Berry believes that similar population declines are taking place in Nevada, where the species is already confined to pockets; however, population surveys documenting this trend have been made at only one area in Piute Valley (Mortimer and Schneider 1983). Moreover, much of the tortoise habitat in the state lies in valleys currently sought for urban or industrial development. Pending land-use decisions could irretrievably eliminate those habitats for the tortoise.

The Utah segment of the Beaver Dam Slope type has already been listed by the U.S. Fish and Wildlife Service (FWS) as threatened. Despite this listing, its population has continued to plummet. Michael Coffeen of the Utah Department of Wildlife Resources carried out a study on a new plot considered representative of much of the critical habitat in 1985. He found very low densities, reversal of sex ratio (to favor males), and very high mortality rates. A 1986 survey by the Utah Department of Wildlife Resources in the Woodbury-Hardy plot indicated a 50-percent reduction in tortoise numbers since 1981. Coffeen postulated that two causes were heavy coyote predation and malnutrition (Berry, pers. commun.). Jarchow (1987) provided additional evidence for malnutrition from overgrazing by cattle. The available evidence shows that the small tortoise populations on neighboring portions of Arizona and Nevada are in similar distress. Thus, it may be too late to save this distinctive population of tortoise.

The Sonoran type found in Arizona south of the Grand Canyon is believed to be stable in its already small and fragmented habitats. However, there is no research to validate this.

MANAGEMENT

Any human use of the desert poses significant and direct threats to the tortoise, as well as other desert-dwelling species. Better controls can help minimize or mitigate such threats, but never eliminate them. The desert tortoise is especially vulnerable because it is a slow-moving creature and is easily victimized. Desert tortoise are collected for pets, accidentally or deliberately killed by vehicles that run them over, and killed by people who use them for target practice or who tip the tortoises over on their backs. Recent studies indicate the large toll these actions are taking on the species. Berry reports that in the western Mojave Desert of California, 20 percent or more of the dead tortoises found during her research work had been killed by gunshots, vandalism, or vehicles. Even in the center of the Desert Tortoise Natural Area, 15 percent of dead tortoises had been shot (Berry *et al.* 1986a, Berry *et al.* 1986b).

Any action that encourages or facilitates further human access to desert tortoise habitat potentially places the species at risk. For example, heavy use of the desert by off-road vehicles damages vegetation, wash banks and overhangs, and other parts of the habitat on which desert tortoises depend for food and shelter. Access is encouraged not only by purposeful development for recreation, but also by roads built for any purpose—access to oil and gas wells or mines, maintenance of utility corridors, and transportation.

Human activity in the desert has had another indirect effect: it has allowed the common raven (*Corvus corax*) to move into desert habitats from which it was formerly absent. Ravens feed from garbage dumps, drink water from stock watering troughs, and use fences, utility poles, and other structures for perches and nest sites (Berry, pers. commun.). Raven predation on young tortoises is causing alarming levels of mortality. A recent study at the Desert Tortoise Natural Area showed that almost 30 percent of recently dead tortoises had been killed by ravens.

Livestock Grazing and Other Activities on Desert Tortoise Habitat

Various economic activities contribute to the species' problems in ways other than merely encouraging more people to be in the area. Whatever the species' original diet, it is certain that the tortoise must now compete with livestock for the remaining forage. Sheep compete primarily for annuals, and cattle eat both annuals and perennials. For example, Coombs found an average 37-percent overlap in diet between tortoise and cattle (U.S. Fish and Wildlife Service 1983). Of course, livestock are considerably more mobile than tortoises and are able to compete for vegetation more efficiently. Also, cattle and sheep can reach plants that are too high or protected by rocks or shrubs and thus unavailable to the tortoise. Livestock also trample and crush both tortoises and burrows, trapping desert tortoises inside or outside, leaving them without shelter. Unfortunately, because research has not yet shown the extent to which such competition is a cause of the species' decline, most range managers are avoiding actions that will reduce livestock grazing pressure.

Reducing the numbers of cattle and sheep allowed on the range to ensure survival of the tortoise would be a somewhat costly effort, although not as great as might be imagined. Only seven percent of western ranchers graze livestock on public lands (U.S. Department of Agriculture and Interior 1986); the number of livestock grazing in areas where the desert tortoise reaches significant densities is much smaller. In California, between 2,300 and 6,370 square miles contain desert tortoises in densities greater than 20 animals per square mile. BLM manages about 70 percent of this land. In Nevada, only 800 square miles have similar densities. In Utah, tortoises are found on about 35 square miles. In Arizona, the tortoise occupies 300 square miles north of the Grand Canyon and scattered areas south of the canyon (Berry 1984). In the years since these estimates were published, desert tortoise populations have decreased in many of these areas, thus further reducing the acreages where livestock reductions that would be needed. From a national or regional perspective, the losses in numbers of livestock grazed would be minimal.

Mining operations crush tortoises, destroy habitat, and create pits in which the tortoises may become trapped; mining also increases the number of people and heavy vehicles in the vicinity. The amount of mining activity in desert tortoise habitat may increase in the near future as a result of the development of a new cyanide heap leaching technique that facilitates profitable extraction of gold from low-grade ore (Berry, pers. commun.).

The desert tortoise is being considered for listing under the Endangered Species Act. The population in southwestern Utah was listed as threatened in August 1980. In response to a petition by Defenders of Wildlife, Environmental Defense Fund, and Natural Resources Defense Council to list the remainder of the U.S. population of desert tortoises, FWS acknowledges that most studies indicate that the species is declining, particularly in the western Mojave Desert of California. However, FWS says that further study is needed to determine the species' status in Arizona and Mexico. FWS stated that it may consider listing those populations north and west of the Colorado River (in Nevada and California and the northern strip of Arizona) more promptly (U.S. Fish and Wildlife Service 1987), but this had not occurred as of February 1, 1988.

BLM administers 67 percent of all desert tortoise habitat and, in cooperation with state wildlife agencies, directly manages the species.

BLM has designated the desert tortoise as a "sensitive" species and claims to give it a high priority in its multiple-use planning and management. However, facts show that the agency has done little to curb the species' decline, and that what it has done to date has been insufficient.

BLM has funded most of the research done on the species, but has failed to fully implement the recommendations of that research. Budget cuts have forced survey intervals on 16 California monitoring plots to be stretched from the originally planned three-year interval to five to seven years (Berry *et al.* 1986a). This timing deprives BLM of population trend data at a time when it is most needed to influence land-use and listing decisions.

The Federal Land Policy and Management Act requires BLM to designate as Areas of Critical Environmental Concern (ACEC) those areas requiring special management to protect and prevent irreparable damage to important wildlife resources. As a BLM-recognized sensitive species under consideration for listing as endangered or threatened, at least parts of desert tortoise' habitat would seem to qualify for such designation. However, the ACEC program has not been used to help conserve the tortoise. Only two ACECs contain tortoise habitat: the Desert Tortoise Natural Area—created before the ACEC program was established—and the Chuckwalla Bench. None of the tortoises' crucial habitats[1] in Nevada, Utah, or Arizona has been designated an ACEC.

In California, BLM designated four major and four minor sites as crucial habitats for the tortoise. However, the tortoise is not adequately protected in any of these habitats. With the exception of Desert Tortoise Natural Area, the sites continue to be grazed by livestock.

BLM also allows continued heavy recreational use on some of these lands, even off-road vehicle races. The use of these vehicles is a problem that is spreading from the western Mojave to the eastern Mojave and Colorado deserts as well. In an attempt to curb the use of off-road vehicles in Desert Tortoise Natural Area, BLM in 1973 posted signs declaring the area closed to unauthorized vehicle use. Construction of a fence to exclude both vehicles and sheep was started in 1977, but the presence of privately owned inholdings within the natural area as well as other problems have prevented the fence from being completed.

In 1979, BLM developed a desert tortoise habitat management plan for Desert Tortoise Natural Area with three objectives: 1) maintain and protect natural populations of the tortoise and other desert species; 2)

1. According the BLM, a "crucial habitat" is one that is required by a given species as it fulfills its life cycle. In the case of the tortoise, all areas needed to maintain the population at current levels are considered crucial habitats, and are shown on BLM land-use maps.

gather baseline data; and, 3) develop a natural-history program to increase public awareness. An interpretive center was constructed to inform visitors about the tortoise. The Desert Tortoise Natural Area was formally established by Congress in 1980 as part of the California Desert Plan (Berry *et al.* 1986b).

Despite its initial promise, the Desert Tortoise Natural Area has not provided sufficient protection to ensure survival of the tortoise even within its borders. Although the unfinished fence has helped reduce habitat-damaging activities, off-road vehicles have caused damage to the habitat along the access road and near the parking area. Most disturbing is the high tortoise losses attributable to collecting, shooting, road kills, and other vandalism. In November 1987, BLM appointed its first full-time ranger for the natural area to help reduce the killing of tortoises. Closing the area to shooting—a step resisted by the California Department of Fish and Game—would also reduce unnecessary deaths (Berry, pers. commun.). Both California and Utah have outlawed collecting of tortoises.

BLM designated several very small crucial habitats in Nevada, but they do not hold much promise. The designation has had no real influence on land-use decisions in those areas. Berry (1984) suggested six fairly large-sized areas in Nevada as critical habitat; BLM designated small pieces of those areas. No protection is given to these areas. The areas are smaller than recommended and harmful activities such as cattle grazing and off-road vehicle use are allowed to continue within them. BLM has failed to consider the human impacts of these activities on lands adjacent to crucial habitats. BLM is now on the verge of trading some of the lands on which the habitats are located.

Arrow Canyon in Nevada has suffered from grazing by livestock and feral burros, fires, off-road vehicle races, and mineral exploration. Nevertheless, Berry considers it the most "protected" tortoise habitat area in Nevada (Berry 1984). Unfortunately, the canyon's accessible groundwater and other attractive attributes led Aerojet-General Corporation to seek ownership of the land to build rocket-testing facilities some time around 1986. FWS carried out a consultation (as required by Section 7 of the Endangered Species Act) to assess the impact of the proposed new land use on listed fish species and the desert tortoise. The draft opinion noted that the transfer of this land to Aerojet would affect 17,000 acres of "crucial, moderate-density" tortoise habitat and "would represent a major negative impact on one of the only six known areas in Nevada where tortoise populations are believed sufficient to maintain viable populations." Nevertheless, the final opinion downplayed these concerns and approved the transfer in late 1986 to early 1987 (Desert Tortoise Council 1987). Legislation to effect a land exchange with BLM is now pending in Congress and is expected to pass. Two other tortoise habitats, Goodsprings and Moapa, are threatened by recreational vehicles, urban development, or mining (Betty L. Burge, pers. commun.).

A fourth crucial habitat, Piute Valley, on the California border south of Lake Mead, is almost completely open to grazing and off-road vehicle recreation. Between 1979 and 1983, a large proportion of the tortoises in the area died. The Nevada Department of Wildlife attributed the deaths to the effects of overgrazing combined with drought and asked BLM to close the two pastures involved for 15 years (Nevada Department of Wildlife 1984a). A compromise was worked out under which annual grazing would be allowed at current stock levels from July 1 until the end of February—presumably before tortoises leave their winter burrows—if ephemeral forage levels reach 500 pounds (dry weight) per acre. The Nevada Department of Wildlife considered this level so high as to effectively preclude grazing for five years (Nevada Department of Wildlife 1984b). Despite this decision, cattle were reported to be still on the pasture in March 1985 (Johnson 1985a). Meanwhile, the cattlemen, working through a planning process which they dominate, had the forage level requirements reduced to 300 pounds per acre and extended the grazing period through April 10. The Nevada state office of BLM has been unable thus far to overcome local opposition to removing cattle to allow restoration of the habitat.

Given the likely outcome of the pending land-use decisions, the cattlemen's pressure at Piute Valley, and the small size of the two remaining habitats, it is probably too late to ensure viable populations of the desert tortoise in Nevada.

One population of the desert tortoise—in the southwestern corner of Utah—has been listed as a threatened species under the Endangered Species Act. In its *Wildlife 2000 Report*, BLM recognized its legal obligation under the act to "seek means to ensure recovery of listed species on BLM lands . . . [and] to ensure that any Federal action authorized, funded, or carried out is not likely to jeopardize the continued existence of [such] species or result in destruction or adverse modification of critical habitat" (U.S. Department of Interior 1987a). Furthermore, although BLM has been aware of the tortoise's dire plight in Utah for at least a decade, the agency has not acted to halt the species' decline.

BLM's 1978 Hot Desert Environmental Impact Statement described the desert tortoise population in Utah as "rapidly declining." The statement continued, "As evidenced by the difference in mortality and reproductive rates determined by Coombs (1977), the present density is too low and there is not enough reproduction to even maintain the population." The environmental impact statement proposed excluding cattle from a study plot of 3,040 acres, which more or less coincides with the Woodbury-Hardy 1936–1945 study area. The statement further noted the poor quality of the range and the unavoidable long-term decline of the 5,000 acres of tortoise habitat outside the proposed exclosure if grazing continued. It stated, "The short-term competition between cattle and the desert tortoise during the years the area is grazed in the spring could eventually lead to long-term decline of the tortoise population" (Bureau of Land Management 1978). Despite this recognition, BLM officials in Utah opposed listing the population under the Endangered Species Act, insisting that it had corrected past grazing abuses and was otherwise managing the species' habitat adequately to ensure survival.

Despite its own earlier criticism that the draft environmental impact statement was biased in support of continued grazing, FWS accepted BLM's recommendation and listed the population as threatened rather than endangered.

Although the designated critical habitat constitutes only four percent of the Hot Desert area administered by BLM, about two-thirds of the livestock grazing in the area takes place within the designated critical habitat. According to the draft recovery plan for the desert tortoise, grazing is particularly heavy in washes (U.S. Fish and Wildlife Service 1985), in which burrows are located and where the tortoise expends considerable energy to dig shelters from winter cold.

Until a new pasture rotation system was introduced in 1983, BLM allowed cattle on the two pastures in tortoise habitat until the end of May of each year, resulting in direct competition for important spring annual forage. The new rotation system called for these pastures to be grazed two out of four years or one out every three. Extensions to allow use of spring forage in years of good annual production have been granted often. FWS' acceptance of this practice is surprising, since the draft recovery plan specifically notes that the tortoises' reproduction and growth depend on occasional years of good annual forage production, and that extended livestock grazing during such years increases the risk to tortoises.

The evidence of desert tortoise malnutrition has mounted. A recent report by Jarchow (1987) concurs with BLM's 1978 findings on the competition for food between tortoise and cattle on the Beaver Dam Slope. "It is my opinion that a prolonged decline in nutrient availability since the studies by Woodbury and Hardy in the 1940s is a major cause of recent desert tortoise mortality witnessed on the Beaver Dam Slope." Desert Tortoise mortality in this study area is linked to the decline of bush muhly, a desert perennial that is heavily grazed by cattle.

Despite the Utah Department of Wildlife Resources' study that estimated a 50-percent decline in the Beaver Dam Slope population, BLM, in early 1987, accepted a request by the local ranchers to resume grazing higher numbers of livestock on the allotments in the desert tortoise habitat. BLM would also continue to allow grazing in the spring in wet years with good growth of annuals. As of March 1988, FWS, caught in the middle, had not yet issued its biological opinion on whether such a change in grazing would jeopardize the continued survival of the species.

Growing controversy over the status of the desert tortoise has awakened BLM's Division of Wildlife to the need to improve the agency's management of the tortoise. BLM's principal goal is to avoid stringent controls that should follow listing of the species under the Endangered Species Act. The division's new chief, David Almand, initiated preparation of a management plan in 1986. The process of preparing this management plan has been criticized by professional chelonian groups and conservation organizations because it does not involve any tortoise experts. The draft plan gave an erroneously optimistic view of the tortoise' current status and trends, recommended further research but few protective actions, did not recognize the likelihood that little funding would be available, and failed to convey any sense of urgency. The draft further recommended replacing the concept of "critical habitat" by a vague zone system. The new strategy, weak as it is, has encountered opposition from within BLM and has yet to be finalized.

RECOMMENDATIONS

No agency responsible for conserving the desert tortoise has yet fulfilled its responsibilities. FWS has failed to protect the population that is already listed as threatened and has not actively pursued the listing of the other populations. While it is true that FWS has a long list of species waiting to be listed, time is running out to ensure this species' survival. As a long-lived species, the tortoise can persist for decades despite extremely low levels of recruitment. However, if current trends are not reversed, the species will ultimately become extinct. The longer FWS delays taking action, the more difficult it will be to restore viable populations. The author believes that two nonbiological factors are responsible for the delay in listing: the possibility of political repercussions, if listing were to mean real changes in grazing and energy management and recreational use of the desert, and FWS reluctance to take on the workload of carrying out Section 7 consultations and other investigations for such a widespread species.

The recent hiring of a full-time ranger at the Desert Tortoise Natural Area may indicate that BLM personnel in the California Desert District, at least, now wish to do more. So far, there is little evidence that this change of heart reaches even to the California state office, much less to the other states or the national office.

Private landowners continue to act without regard for the tortoise's welfare, and this is an important factor. In California, over 80 percent of the habitat supporting tortoise populations higher than 250 animals per square mile is privately held. Southern Pacific Land Company owns about 300 square miles of land that supports tortoise densities of between 100 and 200 per square mile (Berry 1984).

To ensure survival of the tortoise throughout its remaining range, the following recommendations are offered to managers of those areas, both federal and private, that still support viable populations of desert tortoise:

1. Remove livestock competing for forage;
2. Curtail mining;
3. Prohibit off-road vehicle use;
4. Close the areas to shooting;
5. Patrol tortoise areas to ensure compliance with these prohibitions.

Other recommendations include the following:

1. BLM and other land-managing agencies in California should develop a program for controlling raven predation. Other predator control programs may be warranted on the Beaver Dam Slope.
2. Responsible state and federal agencies and private landowners should greatly increase funding for research on the species' status and habitat needs so as to identify other actions which should be taken. They should also increase efforts to educate the public about the tortoise and its vulnerability to a vast range of human activities. Law enforcement efforts within and outside habitat areas must be increased.
3. Listing of the species as endangered or threatened throughout the United States would assist in realizing these goals by outlawing killing or harming of the animal, by requiring federal agencies to avoid jeopardizing its existence, and by calling attention to the species' plight. However, listing is not a panacea.

REFERENCES

Barrett, S.L. and J.A. Humphrey. 1986. "Agonistic interaction between *Gopherus agassizii* (Testudinidae) and *Heloderma suspectum* (Helodermatidae)." *Southwestern Naturalist* 31(2):261–263.

Berry, K.H. 1979. "Tortoises for tomorrow." *The Nature Conservancy News.* November/December.

——. 1984. ed. The Status of the Desert Tortoise (*Gopherus agassizii*) in the United States. Report to the U.S. Fish and Wildlife Service from the Desert Tortoise Council on order no. 11310–0083-81. March.

——., L.L. Nicholson, S. Juarez, A. P. Woodman. 1986a. Changes in Desert Tortoise Populations at Four Study Sites in California. Prepared in 1986 for the U.S. Bureau of Land Management. Riverside, California. 20 pp + tables.

——., T. Shields, A.P. Woodman, T. Campbell, J. Roberson, K. Bohuski, A. Karl. 1986b. Changes in Desert Tortoise Populations at the Desert Tortoise Research Natural Area Between 1979 and 1985. Draft dated July 28, 1986. 25 pp. + tables.

Bureau of Land Management, Department of Interior. 1978. Final Hot Desert Grazing Management Environmental Statement.

——. 1987a. *Fish and Wildlife 2000: A Plan for the Future.* Approved by Director Robert F. Burford, May 21, 1987. 26 pp + appendices.

——. 1987b. *Management of Desert Tortoise Habitat.* Draft. An internal report to the Bureau of Land Management Chief Division of Wildlife in Washington, D.C. 55 pp.

Desert Tortoise Council. 1987. Position Statement of the Desert Tortoise Council, S 854, Nevada-Florida Land Exchange Authorization Act of 1987. June 7, 1987. 10 pp.

Jarchow, J.L. DVM. 1987. Report on Investigation of Desert Tortoise Mortality on the Beaver Dam Slope, Arizona and Utah. Prepared for Arizona Game and Fish Department, Arizona Strip District, BLM, Cedar City District, BLM, and Utah Division of Wildlife Resources. December 20.

Johnson, A.S. 1984. Comments on the Management of the Desert Tortoise in Arizona. August 23, 1984.

——. 1985a. Letter to Robert Jantzen, Director, U.S. Fish and Wildlife Service, May 8, 1985.

——. 1985b. Memorandum regarding Beaver Dam Slope population, October 23, 1985.

Mortimer, C. and P. Schneider. 1983. Population Studies of the Desert Tortoise (*Gopherus agassizii*) in the Piute Valley Study Plot of Southern Nevada. Nevada Department of Wildlife. Las Vegas, Nevada. March.

Nevada Department of Wildlife. 1984a. Letter to Aubrey Stephen [sic] Johnson, April 3, 1984.

——. 1984b. Letter to Aubrey Steven Johnson, May 4, 1984.

Pritchard, R.C. 1979. *Encyclopedia of Turtles.* T.F.H. Publications, Inc., Ltd. Neptune, New Jersey.

Stebbins, R.C. 1985. *A Field Guide to Western Reptiles and Amphibians.* Houghton Mifflin Company. Boston, Massachusetts.

U.S. Department of Agriculture and Department of Interior. Grazing Fee Review and Evaluation Final Report 1979–1985. February 1986. Cornell University Press.

U.S. Fish and Wildlife Service, Department of Interior. 1983. Biological Opinion on Beaver Dam Slope Grazing Management Plan. September 26, 1983.

——. 1985. Draft Recovery Plan. March 15, 1985.

——. 1987. "Endangered and threatened wildlife and plants; notice of findings on petitions and initiation of status review." 52 *Federal Register* 126:24485–88.

Weinstein, M.N. and K.H. Berry. 1987. Morphometric Analysis of Desert Tortoise Populations. Draft Bureau of Land Management Contract No. CA950-CT7–003. 39 pp. + annexes.

Faith Thompson Campbell specializes in species conservation issues at both the national and international level. She has been with the Natural Resources Defense Council since 1976.

The Eskimo curlew is the smallest and rarest of the four curlews that breed in North America. Photographs of the bird are equally rare. *Sally Hewitt*

The Eskimo Curlew

J. Bernard Gollop
Canadian Wildlife Service

SPECIES DESCRIPTION AND NATURAL HISTORY[1]

The Eskimo curlew (*Numenius borealis*) is the smallest and rarest of the four curlews that breed in North America. This shorebird is 12 to 14 inches in length, about the size of a northern flicker (*Colaptes auratus*); it is slightly larger than the lesser golden-plover (*Pluvialis dominica*), with which it frequently associates. The Eskimo curlew weighs between a half pound (Audubon 1967) and a pound (Swenk 1916).

The curlew's brown plumage is darkest on the crown, lighter on the back, and streaked underneath. Its bill is long and down-curving like its fairly common relative, the whimbrel (*Numenius phaeopus*), which is about one-third larger. The curlew also has a common Old World relative, the little curlew (*Numenius minutus*).[2] The little curlew migrates between Russia and Australia and has been seen once in North America in California (Lehman and Dunn 1985). Similarities

1. Most of what we know about the Eskimo curlew was written in the 19th century. Hence, much of what follows is written in the past tense.

2. Some scientists believe the little curlew and the Eskimo curlew are different species while others think that they are both subspecies of the same species.

among the three curlews makes positive identification of an Eskimo curlew difficult. The problem is greatest in the fall—when a young whimbrel's bill is shorter than an adult whimbrel's and its total length is only an inch longer than the Eskimo curlew's (Peterson 1980).

The primary feathers of the Eskimo and little curlew are unbarred; the whimbrel's are barred. This characteristic may be visible even on standing birds because they occasionally raise their wings above their backs. The wing linings of the Eskimo curlew are cinnamon; those of the little curlew are buffy. In addition, the crown of the Eskimo curlew is almost solid brown, while that of the other two species has a light brown stripe in the center (Gollop *et al.* 1986).

Distribution

Eskimo curlews were once found from arctic North America to southern South America. In the fall, curlews migrated south by way of the East Coast and the Atlantic Ocean to Brazil, Paraguay, Uruguay, Argentina, and Chile. They returned north in the spring via the interior of North America (see Figure 1).

Breeding

The Eskimo curlew (*Weekee-meneesew* to the northern Indians) probably nested in a narrow northwest-southeast band running across the Northwest Territories from Bathurst Peninsula to Point Lake, north of Fort Enterprise (see Figure 1). Although there are no known nesting records in northern Alaska, the bird probably bred there and may have bred in northeastern Siberia.[3] The Eskimo curlew's breeding habitat lies north of the treeline: "the Barren Grounds proper being the real habitat of the species during the season of nidification" (MacFarlane *in* Gollop *et al.* 1986).

Curlews arrived in the arctic about mid-May and began laying eggs early in June. They were not colonial. MacFarlane documented 38 of the 39 known nests.[4] He found 19 nests, each of which was ". . . a mere hole in the earth, lined with a few decayed leaves, and having a thin sprinkling of hay in the midst of them." The remaining 19 clutches were brought to him by "Eskimaux" (MacFarlane 1891, MacFarlane *in* Gollop *et al.* 1986).

The usual clutch was four eggs. The eggs had a ground color of "olive-drab, tending either to green, gray or brown . . . The markings,

3. This assumption is based on the fact that Eskimo curlews were seen during the breeding season in both places.

4. The first nest had been described by John Richardson in 1821 (Swainson and Richardson 1831).

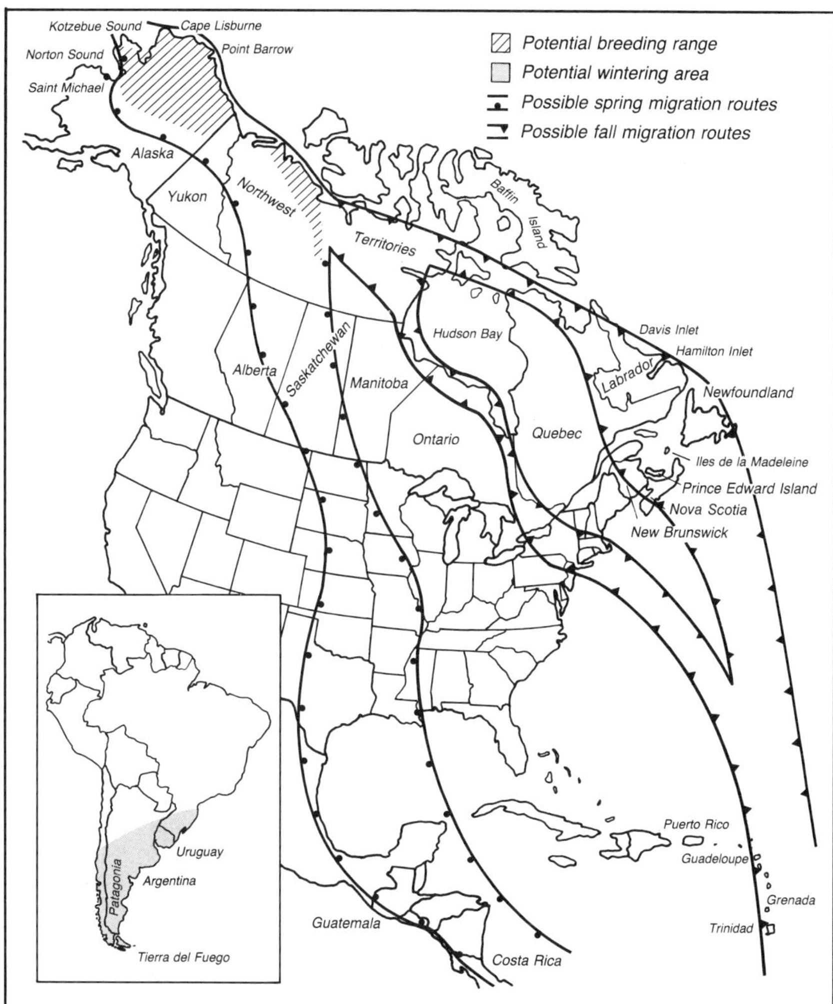

Figure 1. Migration routes and breeding range of the Eskimo curlew in North America. Inset: Potential wintering area of the Eskimo curlew in South America.

always large, numerous and bold," were dark brown (Coues 1874). While nests with eggs were found in July, hatching probably peaked the last week in June and the first week in July. The downy young have never been described. Although MacFarlane collected two downy young, neither reached the Smithsonian Institution, apparently due to wolverine (*Gulo luscus*) predation on his winter cache of specimens (Gollop *et al.* 1986). Nothing is known about the species between hatching and its late summer concentrations. Arctic foxes (*Alopex lagopus*) and jaegers (*Stercorarius* sp.) may have been the main predators.

Migration

Fall. Fall migration began with the birds flocking in July. These flocks flew along the entire arctic coast to Ungava, Quebec, then turned south down the Canadian coast, where they made their only known regular stop between their breeding and wintering grounds. In early August they began to concentrate in parts of a 150-mile stretch between Hamilton Harbour, Labrador, and Bras d'Or, Quebec.

In good weather, from mid-August to mid-September, the curlews left in large flocks, some stopping in Newfoundland and the Maritime Provinces. From these points, if not further north, they began an oceanic flight of some 2,500 to 3,000 miles toward South America (see Figure 1). In most years they apparently covered this distance nonstop, but storms occasionally drove them ashore in Maine, Massachusetts, and the West Indies. Great flights involving thousands of curlews, often with lesser golden-plovers mixed in, were reported in Maine from 1877 to 1879 (Palmer 1949). For Massachusetts, the years of abundance were 1808 and/or 1813, 1863, 1872 (or thereabouts), 1881, and 1883 (Gollop *et al.* 1986). It is interesting to note that the years do not coincide for the two states. The period for these flights was brief—from August 25 through September 5; the landings lasted from one to seven days.

Eskimo curlews occasionally landed on Bermuda, Barbados, and other islands, but the records are poorly documented (Hapgood 1887). The same is true for concentration areas which may have existed in northern South America. The location of the migrating flocks' first regular landing site after their oceanic voyage is unknown. There are August records from Alaska to Barbados.

Winter. The Eskimo curlew may have wintered in Paraguay and extreme southern Brazil, but the heart of its wintering grounds apparently was Uruguay and the southern half of Argentina and Chile (Barrows 1884, Wetmore 1927, Hellmayr 1932) (see Figure 1). The earliest known arrival date was the second week of September.

Spring. Spring migration began in late February or early March. The route the curlews took from Argentina to the Gulf Coast of the United States is unknown. There are no spring sighting reports for South America north of the wintering range; only two April records for Guatemala and northern Mexico; and one undated specimen from Costa Rica. The birds arrived in Texas the first week in March, became abundant and stayed there, in some years at least, until the first week in May (Oberholser 1974, Blankinship and King 1984). There are March sightings marking their occurrence from Argentina to Nebraska and May dates from Texas to Alaska (see Figure 1).

In Illinois and Nebraska, "prairie pigeons" (as the settlers called them) and golden-plovers were particularly attracted to burned prairies as new grass appeared. Later these birds followed the plow through corn and wheat fields and fed in tame meadows. Curlews apparently roosted on the prairie and were rarely seen near water in the midwestern states, although they roosted on beaches along the Atlantic coast.

Voice

The songs of most birds are difficult to describe, and the Eskimo curlew's song is no exception. The species' main call on the breeding grounds apparently resembled its name, and may have been what MacFarlane (1891) referred to as a "prolonged mellow whistle." Their flight call has been described as "an oft repeated, soft, mellow, though clear whistle, which may be easily imitated" (Coues 1861). While feeding, the curlews gave a "chirruping whistle" in Nebraska (Swenk 1916) and they "kept up a continuous, low piping noise" in South Dakota (Coues 1874). A call heard in Texas was "a *tee dee dee* note, usually either two or three syllables" (Bleitz 1962).

Diet

The bird fed largely on invertebrates, although in Canada and Alaska, crowberries (*Empetrum nigrum*) made up a significant part of its diet. On the breeding grounds, Richardson found that the Eskimo curlews ate ants, grubs, freshwater insects, and crowberries (Swainson and Richardson 1831). Along the Labrador coast, curlews fed on the shore before and after overnight roosting. Their favorite food was snails, but they also took worms and other invertebrates. In the morning, the curlews headed for nearby rocky uplands in search of crowberries. While feeding, they moved quickly across an area, picking up berries at a rapid rate. Soon they were coated from bill to tail with purple juice. When the stomach contents of three long-preserved birds from Massachusetts and New York were examined in 1938, it was found that field crickets (*Gryllus* and *Nemobius*) made up 52 percent, grasshoppers (*Acrididae*) 40 percent, and beetles, spiders, moths, and ants the remainder (Cottam and Knappen 1941). On northward migration, a favorite food was grasshopper egg pods (Swenk 1916).

SIGNIFICANCE OF THE SPECIES

Decimation of the Eskimo curlew created a significant void in the arctic environment that is now being filled by the whimbrel. T.W. Barry of the Canadian Wildlife Service found that by the 1980s whimbrels had expanded into parts of the Eskimo curlew range that they had not used in the 1860s (Gollop *et al.* 1986).

The significance of the species to people was primarily its palatability. In the earliest settlements in Labrador and adjacent Quebec, the Eskimo curlew was a gourmet addition to the settlers' and fishermen's diet of fish and mammals. The species was eaten fresh, or salted, or parboiled and bottled for winter food. During a 13-year stay in Labrador in the 1700s, George Cartwright (1792) and his men apparently shot some 500 curlews for their own consumption. In the 1880s, it became fashionable to ship them as gifts: "The Hudson's Bay people at Cartwright [Labrador] annually put up large numbers in hermetically sealed tins for use of the company's officials in London and Montreal . . . " (Carroll 1910).

On the East Coast in the 1880s, the curlews became the focus of market hunters in the fall. In the interior, they were shot in the spring largely at first for western markets, but began showing up in eastern markets about 1886. There are records of curlews being sold in Halifax, Montreal, Boston, Chicago, Detroit, New York, Omaha, Philadelphia, St. Louis, and Wichita. This list is undoubtedly incomplete. Prices varied from 6 to 75 cents, and later, $1.00 per bird. This price was "nearly double that of any other shorebird" (Cahoon 1888). On their wintering grounds, the "birds were offered for sale in the markets of Buenos Aires and were included on the bills of fare in the principal restaurants" (Wetmore 1927).

HISTORICAL PERSPECTIVE

The total population of the Eskimo curlew may not have been the millions that historical accounts imply. The species probably had a smaller summer range than that of other North American arctic-nesting, noncolonial gamebirds. Compared to species for which we have population data, the curlew's breeding distribution was most similar geographically to that of the noncolonial greater white-fronted goose. The goose's range is apparently much larger than that of the curlew's. However, nesting through most of the goose's range is scattered, with one or two dozen segments where densities reach only "a few pairs/sq. mi." (Palmer 1976). In the winter of 1984–1985, there were fewer than 400,000 greater white-fronted geese in North America (Anonymous 1986).

The curlew probably was not as abundant as the lesser golden-plover. The curlew may have had only half the breeding range of the plover and may have occurred in lower densities. MacFarlane (1891) shipped 170 plover clutches, but only 30 curlew clutches, to the Smithsonian Institution from 1862 to 1866. He commented that both were difficult to find.

Migratory concentrations of the Eskimo curlew were clearly impressive and may have given an exaggerated impression of their numbers. In 1833, Audubon reported that the birds "arrived [in Quebec] in such dense flocks as to remind me of the Passenger Pigeon [*Ectopistes migratorius*]"(Audubon 1967).

In Labrador they appeared "in flocks of every size, from three to as many thousands" and in "immense numbers" (Coues 1861). In Nebraska they flew over the prairie as "dense masses of birds extending for a quarter to a half mile in length and a hundred yards or more in width. When the flock would alight the birds would cover 40 or 50 acres of ground" (Swenk 1916).

Hunting

From the time of European settlement, the Eskimo curlew was hunted 11 months of the year. Major hunting pressure was exerted on the species in the 1880s. With the disappearance of the passenger pigeon, market hunters turned to Eskimo curlews, lesser golden-plovers, and upland sandpipers (*Bartramia longicauda*) to supply their ever-increasing demands. Curlews were abundant, easily killed, and their taste was described by Chappell (1818) as "far surpassing any of our English game in richness and flavour."

Fall Hunting. There is scanty documentation of large kills during fall migration, but those recorded are rather impressive. During the great flight of 1863, an estimated 7,000 to 8,000 curlews and golden-plovers were shot on Nantucket Island, Massachusetts. That number would have been higher if hunters had not had to leave the island to get more ammunition (Forbush 1916). In the 1872 flight on Cape Cod, two hunters reportedly shot 5,000 birds that were sold for six cents apiece (Forbush 1916). To place the impact of these fall kills in perspective, it must be remembered that the opportunity for such large harvests occurred only once in 10 or 15 years, when storm conditions forced migrating curlews to land. It is doubtful that such kills significantly affected total population size.

Spring Hunting. For about 15 years after 1880, the heaviest hunting pressure was in the spring, when the birds were a few weeks away from nesting. In the midwestern United States, the fields where curlews gathered were patrolled regularly and scanned with binoculars (Swenk 1916). Sometimes a gunner put himself in a line of flight where shooting only one bird from a flock caused the remaining birds to circle again and again until most or all had been shot. The procedure was repeated flock after flock. At other times, a horse and buggy was used to drive quickly near a group on the ground, as if to pass it by. Instead, the hunter stopped opposite the closely packed aggregation and fired into it. Describing a day's hunting, Bogardus (1874) wrote: "That afternoon I killed two hundred and sixty-four plover and curlew . . . This was done with a muzzle-loader. With a good breech-loader . . . I believe I could have killed five hundred birds that afternoon." There are several reports of 20 to 28 birds downed by a single shot.

Swenk (1916) described some of the hunting in Nebraska: "Hunters would . . . shoot the birds without mercy until they had literally slaughtered a wagonload of them, . . . Sometimes . . . their wagons were too quickly and easily filled, so whole loads of the birds would be dumped on the prairie . . . [and] . . . allowed to rot while the hunters proceeded to refill their wagons . . . "

The only record of market shipments was obtained by Mackay (1891) from two of several game dealers in Boston in 1890. He reported eight barrels of curlews, packed 300 to a barrel; and 12 barrels of Eskimo curlews and golden-plovers, packed 720 to a barrel. Shipments of these spring-shot birds to Boston lasted from about 1887 to 1896, when the curlew was reportedly in the midst of its decline.

Population Decline

The Eskimo curlew's decline was first reported from the Midwest (Banks 1977). In the early 1870s, Bogardus (1874) wrote that the golden-plover and curlew were not so common in Illinois as in the previous decade. Swenk (1916) noted that "the decade 1870–1880 witnessed the beginning of the diminution of these great flocks of Eskimo curlew" in Nebraska. The timing of the decline in Labrador is based on several reports, one by W.T. Grenfell: "The Curlew became scarce in the end of the eighties" (Townsend and Allen 1907). F.C. Bertau recalled that "during the first four or five of the ten years, that I was collector of customs on Labrador, they were very numerous indeed . . . they gradually diminished in numbers, until in 1890 or thereabouts they entirely disappeared" (Carroll 1910). Declines were not noticed in Massachusetts and Maine because flock landings did not occur in most years. The last eastern flight worth mentioning was in 1888 (Mackay 1892).

The Eskimo curlew's decline was undoubtedly due in some part to spring hunting, especially if the species' total population was not as large as its fall and spring aggregations might indicate. Banks (1977) speculated that the yearly take of curlews was in excess of two million birds but there may have been only half that many curlews leaving the breeding grounds. Banks has suggested that climatic conditions may have been a contributing factor to the bird's decline. A warming trend through the 1880s intensified and shifted the general atmospheric system northward. As a result, "the slightly altered angle of departure from Labrador, . . . led the birds along a flight line with a more easterly component than in previous decades, and some flocks missed South America and perished in the South Atlantic." (This explanation would probably be invalid if curlews used celestial navigation.) Banks added that both deteriorating habitat through wintering and spring migration ranges and heavier hunting pressure also increased mortality. However, those losses were initially offset by summer production, so that decreases were not noticeable on the East Coast as early as in the Midwest.

It is also possible that volcanic ash, abundant in the 1880s, caused cooler summers and reduced production during that decade (Banks 1977). Tree-ring studies in the Yukon, however, suggest that the 1880s were warmer than the previous three decades; furthermore, there is no indication of poor curlew production in the mid-1800s (Jacoby and Cook 1981). The biggest problem with such environmental speculation is explaining why the factors that brought the Eskimo curlew to the verge of extinction, and that continue to keep it there, did not similarly affect the lesser golden-plover, its close traveling associate between Canada and Argentina.

CURRENT TRENDS

The Eskimo curlew is one of the rarest native North American birds in the wild. Whether the known handful of remaining birds is still spread throughout its former breeding range or is concentrated only in a part of it is unknown. The species is no longer seen every year. A total of 18 birds has been reported in four years from 1982 to 1987, and there is some question about at least two of these birds. The curlew has been reported most frequently in Texas—with occurrences in 12 different years since 1945. These reports include the largest flock seen in more than 80 years, consisting of 23 birds on Galveston Bay in May 1981 (Gollop *et al.* 1986, Blankinship and King 1984).

From 1972 through 1984, T.W. Barry spent a few days each summer traveling on foot and by helicopter (from 1981 to 1984) along portions of MacFarlane's arctic collecting route from Anderson River to Langton Bay. In 1983 and 1984, he played taped calls of the little curlew to entice a response from Eskimo curlews, but only whimbrels reacted. Had his search been successful, the Canadian Wildlife Service was prepared to expand investigations (Gollop *et al.* 1986).

At least four apparently reliable Eskimo curlew sightings were reported in 1987: one on April 16, when Craig Faanes of the U.S. Fish and Wildlife Service studied a curlew with greater and lesser yellowlegs (*Tringa melanoleuca* and *T. flavipes*) near Grand Island, Nebraska; one on April 17 by John Arvin of Texas, who carefully described an Eskimo curlew, noting the cinnamon wing linings and unbarred flight feathers, as it flew by him at Sabine Pass on the Texas-Louisiana border; one on May 2, reported by Wayne and Martha McAlister of Texas who studied three Eskimo curlews for 40 minutes as the curlews moved among long-billed curlews (*Numenius americanus*), marbled godwits (*Limosa fedoa*) and Wilson's plovers (*Charadrius wilsonia*) in the Aransas National Wildlife Refuge in Texas; and one on May 24 by Inuk guide and longtime naturalist Billy Jacobsen who, with binoculars, watched an Eskimo curlew as close as 30 to 40 feet for 10 to 20 minutes, on a snow-free point on Lac Rendez-vous, Northwest Territories, where the species was common in the 1860s. When he started his skidoo, a second Eskimo curlew flushed, and the two birds flew off together.

MANAGEMENT

Like most shorebirds, the Eskimo curlew is protected from hunting in Canada, Mexico, and the United States under the Migratory Bird Treaty Act of 1916. Several other international conventions give the bird further protection, including the Convention on Natural Protection and Wildlife Preservation in the Western Hemisphere [1940], and the Convention on the International Trade in Endangered Species of Wild Fauna and Flora, or CITES [1974] (Gollop *et al.* 1986). The curlew was also designated an endangered species in 1967 by the U.S Fish and Wildlife Service and in 1980 by Canada (U.S. Fish and Wildlife Service 1986, Fraser 1980).

Part of the Eskimo curlew's historic breeding range has been protected by the Anderson River Migratory Bird Sanctuary, established by the Government of Canada in 1961.

Additional Eskimo curlew habitat is protected by the Kendall Island Migratory Bird Sanctuary in the Northwest Territories (Gollop *et al.* 1986); six curlews were reported there on July 10, 1985.

PROGNOSIS

The survival of this small, delicate, and difficult-to-find bird seems tenuous, whether the handful of remaining individuals travel the 19,000-mile round trip together or separately. Quantity and quality of habitat may not be a problem since there are so few birds left. So far, storms, civilization, and other sources of mortality apparently have not significantly affected the species in this century. Whether the bird will survive another hundred years if left alone is questionable. Few species with populations as small as the curlew's—possibly 50 birds—have been able to do so.

RECOMMENDATIONS

In August 1987, U.S. and Canadian biologists met in San Francisco to take the first step toward devising an Eskimo curlew recovery plan as required by the Endangered Species Act. They agreed that an attempt should be made to learn how to safely capture, maintain, breed, and rear the Eskimo curlew in captivity by experimenting first with the little curlew. The little curlew has been located and studied on its Russian breeding grounds and Australian wintering range (Labutin *et al.* 1982, Blakers *et al.* 1984).

In the meantime, Eskimo curlew numbers could be monitored on March and April concentration areas in Texas and Nebraska and on August sites in Labrador. At this time there would seem to be little point in undertaking any large-scale operation in the arctic that would risk causing nest desertion and loss to predators. However, if the little curlew proves amenable to artificial propagation, Eskimo curlews or their eggs could be taken for captive rearing and eventual release in the wild.

REFERENCES

Anonymous. 1986. North American Waterfowl Management Plan. U.S. Department of the Interior, Washington, D.C., and Environment Canada, Ottawa. 19 pp.

Audubon, J.J. 1967(1944). *The Birds of America.* Dean Amadon, ed. Volume 6. Dover publications. New York. 457 pp.

Banks, R.C. 1977. "The decline and fall of the Eskimo curlew, or Why did the curlew go extaille?" *American Birds* 31:127–134.

Barrows, W.B. 1884. "Birds of the Lower Uruguay." *Auk* 1:313–319.

Blakers, M., S.J.J.F. Davies and P.N. Reilly. 1984. *The Atlas of Australian Birds.* Melbourne University Press. Melbourne, Australia. 738 pp.

Blankinship, D.R. and K.A. King. 1984. "A probable sighting of 23 Eskimo curlews in Texas." *American Birds* 38:1066–1067.

Bleitz, Don. 1962. "Photographing the Eskimo curlew." *Western Bird Bander* 37:43–45.

Bogardus, A.H. 1874. *Field, Cover, and Trap Shooting.* C.J. Foster, ed. J.B. Ford. New York. 343 pp.

Cahoon, J.C. 1888. "The shore birds of Cape Cod." *Ornithologist and Oölogist* 13(10):153–156.

Carroll, W.J. 1910. "The Eskimo Curlew or doughbird." *Forest and Stream* 74:372.

Cartwright, George. 1792. *A Journal of Transactions and Events During a Residence of Nearly Sixteen Years on the Coast of Labrador.* 3 volumes. Newark, England. 287, 505, and 263 pp., respectively. (Canadian Institute for Historical Microreproductions. Microfiches 37493–37495.)

Chappell, Edward. 1818. *Voyage of His Majesty's Ship Rosamond to Newfoundland and the Southern Coast of Labrador.* J. Mawman. London, England. 270 pp.

Cottam, Clarence and Phoebe Knappen. 1941. "Eskimo Curlew food note corrected." *Auk* 58:256

Coues, Elliott. 1861. "Notes on the ornithology of Labrador." *Academy of Natural Sciences of Philadelphia Proceedings* 13:215–257.

——. 1874. *Birds of the Northwest: A Hand-Book of the Ornithology of the Region Drained by the Missouri River and its Tributaries.* Department of Interior. U.S. Geological Survey of the Territories. Miscellaneous Publication 3. 791 pp.

Forbush, E.H. 1916. *A History of the Game Birds, Wild-fowl and Shore Birds of Massachusetts and Adjacent States.* Massachusetts State Board of Agriculture. Boston, Massachusetts. 636 pp.

Fraser, J.A. 1980. "Department of Environment public notice. Schedule of endangered and threatened species." *Canada Gazette* Part 1. pp. 698–699. 2 February.

Gollop, J.B., T.W. Barry and E.H. Iversen. 1986. *Eskimo Curlew. A Vanishing Species?* Saskatchewan Natural History Society Special Publication 17. 159 pp.

Hapgood, Warren. 1887. *Shore Birds.* Forest and Stream Series 1. 45 pp.

Hellmayr, C.E. 1932. *The Birds of Chile.* Field Museum of Natural History Publication 308. Zoological Series 19. 472 pp.

Jacoby, G.C. and E.R. Cook. 1981. "Past temperature variations inferred from a 400-year tree-ring chronology from Yukon Territory, Canada." *Arctic and Alpine Research* 13:409–418.

Labutin, Y.V., V.V. Leonovitch and B.N. Veprintsev. 1982. "The Little Curlew *Numenius minutus* in Siberia." *Ibis* 123:1–18.

Lehman, Paul and J.L. Dunn. 1985. "A little known species reaches North America." *American Birds* 39:247–250.

MacFarlane, Roderick. 1891. "Notes on and list of Birds and Eggs Collected in Arctic America, 1861–1866." *U.S. National Museum Proceedings* 14:413–446.

Mackay, G.H. 1891. "The habits of the Golden Plover (*Charadrius dominicus*) in Massachusetts." *Auk* 8:17–24.

——. 1892. "Habits of the Eskimo Curlew (*Numenius borealis*) in New England." *Auk* 9:16–21.

Oberholser, H.C. 1974. *Bird Life of Texas.* E.B. Kincaid, Jr., ed. Volume 1. University of Texas Press. Austin, Texas. 530 pp.

Palmer, R.S. 1949. *Maine Birds.* Museum of Comparative Zoology at Harvard College Bulletin 102. 656 pp.

——. 1976. *Handbook of North American Birds.* Volume 2. Yale University Press. New Haven, Connecticut. 521 pp.

Peterson, R.T. 1980. *A Field Guide to the Birds East of the Rockies.* Houghton Mifflin. Boston, Massachusetts. 384 pp.

Swainson, William and John Richardson. 1831. *Fauna Boreali-Americana: or the Zoology of the Northern Parts of British America.* Part 2. *The Birds.* John Murray. London, England. 523 pp.

Swenk, M.H. 1916. "The Eskimo Curlew and its disappearance." *Smithsonian Institution Annual Report* 1915:325–340. (Reprint with additions of an article with the same name that appeared in the 1915 *Proceedings of the Nebraska Ornithologists' Union* 6:25–44.)

Townsend, C.W. and G.M. Allen. 1907. "Birds of Labrador." *Boston Society of Natural History Proceedings* 33:277–428.

U.S. Fish and Wildlife Service. 1986. Endangered and Threatened Wildlife and Plants. U.S. Department of Interior. Washington, D.C. 30 pp.

Wetmore, Alexander. 1927. Our Migrant Shorebirds in Southern South America. U.S. Department of Agriculture Bulletin 26. 24 pp.

J. Bernard Gollop, recently retired from the Canadian Wildlife Service, Environment Canada, is a coauthor of Eskimo Curlew. A Vanishing Species? *(Available from the Saskatchewan Natural History Society, Box 1121, Regina, Sask., Canada, S4P 3B4. [$9 Canadian])*

The author thanks M.D. Gilliland, B.C. Dale, and E.A. Driver for their help in preparing this chapter

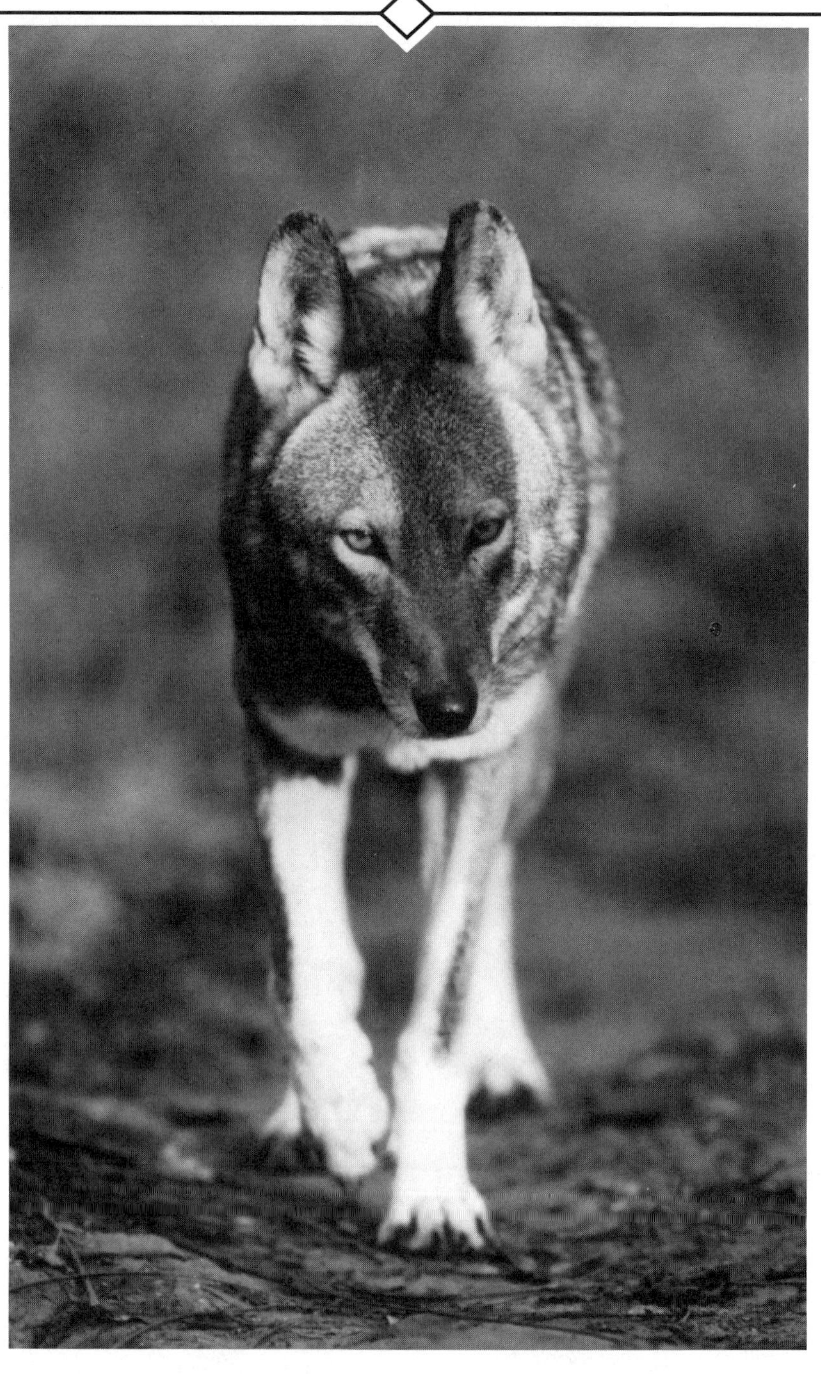

The red wolf once ranged across the southern states, but is now nearly extinct. Captive-raised animals are being reintroduced onto wildlife refuges. *Steve Maslowski/USFWS*

The Red Wolf

Warren T. Parker
U.S. Fish and Wildlife Service

SPECIES DESCRIPTION AND NATURAL HISTORY

The red wolf (*Canis rufus*) is intermediate in size between the larger gray wolf (*C. lupus*), which was found to the north and west, and the smaller coyote (*C. latrans*) of the western United States; it is a uniquely southern species. An adult female red wolf may weigh from 40 to 60 pounds, the adult male from 60 to 80 pounds. The red wolf is generally more lanky than the gray wolf, with long, slender legs that may be an adaptation to long-distance running and pursuing prey in river bottom swamps and wet coastal prairies.

The reddish color that is referred to in its scientific and common name was actually only typical in certain populations in Texas. Evidently, there was a considerable color variation throughout its range, including black, brown, gray, and yellow phases. The best taxonomic parameters for distinguishing red wolves from coyotes now invading the wolf's historic range are general body size, structure, and weight.

Taxonomy and Distribution

It is believed that the red wolf was represented by three subspecies—the eastern *C.r. Floridanus*, the western *C.r. rufus*, and an intermediate form *C.r. gregoryi*. The eastern and western subspecies became extinct during the first half of the twentieth century, but *C.r. gregoryi* persisted in isolated areas from Mississippi to eastern Texas. This last stronghold was slowly compressed over the years until only a few animals could be found in southwest Louisiana and southeast Texas by the early 1970s.

Despite early taxonomic squabbling, the red wolf is now considered by most authorities to be a true species. However, the red wolf's place in the evolutionary ladder of the family Canidae probably will always remain uncertain. Various climatic and competitive changes gradually forced the species southward and eastward into the area where they were first documented by Bartram (1791).

Home Range

The home range of a red wolf is undoubtedly dependent on the quality of the habitat where it resides. Habitat quality is determined by cover, prey availability, and terrain features. Telemetry studies of red wolves in Louisiana and Texas indicate that animals often traversed areas larger than required for the purpose of securing food. Shaw (1975), in a study of red wolf range in 1972, reported an average home range of 17 square miles for two female and five male animals. By systematic tracking of three adult animals for over a year, Riley and McBride (1972) estimated the home range of a red wolf to be from 25 to 50 square miles. In a telemetry study in 1974, recovery-program biologists concluded that male red wolves ranged over an area of about 45 square miles; the range of females was somewhat smaller, averaging 25 to 30 square miles (Carley 1975).

In the wild, red wolves are predominantly nocturnal, with the highest periods of activity being from 8:00 p.m. to midnight (Carley 1975, Shaw 1975). Another period of activity seems to be from 3:00 a.m. until dawn. During winter months, red wolves tend to be more diurnal.

Breeding

Red wolves breed only once a year, either in February or March. The gestation period is 60 to 63 days, and pups are born in April or May. While some females are capable of breeding at nine months of age, it is more common for them to breed in their second breeding season. It is generally agreed that male wolves are sexually immature until at least their third breeding season, when they are approximately 33 months old. Litter sizes in captivity range from 2 to 8 pups, with an average of 4.6 per litter.

Diet

The red wolf preys less on large ungulates than the gray wolf. Early accounts often refer to smaller animals being the mainstay of the wolf's diet. This was confirmed through an analysis of red wolf scats collected during an experimental nine-month release of a pair of red wolves on Bulls Island, South Carolina (Carley 1979). Marsh rabbits, small rodents, squirrels, muskrats and nutria, fish, insects, and plant material apparently are the red wolf's preferred foods. Rabbits and hares head the list. An occasional deer or domestic animal will be taken under the right circumstances. Livestock predation could be expected where chickens, sheep, goats, and unattended calves are permitted to run free.

SIGNIFICANCE OF THE SPECIES

In the precolonial era, the red wolf played a dynamic role as one of several predators in a variety of naturally occurring southern ecosystems. Wolves and cougars were efficient at culling the young, weak, or diseased from any prey population.

The demise of the red wolf is directly related to human fears and prejudices toward all predators. These same attitudes brought about the extinction of the eastern cougar, and also the gray wolf, in most of its original range. A favorable climate and a seemingly unlimited agricultural potential unleashed rapid human settlement in the southeastern United States. This movement from the Atlantic seaboard westward was only temporarily hindered by the the Appalachian Mountains. Once this barrier was crossed, expansion and settlement was rapid. Red wolf numbers dwindled as river bottoms were cleared and burned for crop poduction; as settlements and communities flourished into towns and cities; as highways and reservoirs were constructed; and as a once vast wilderness was tamed. The very presence of a few remnant red wolves under these circumstances brough down the wrath of state and county governments, as effective predator-control efforts in the 1950s and 1960s eliminated the species from most of its historical range.

The red wolf and the gray wolf both epitomize an image of wilderness that now exists in only a few areas of the lower 48 states. Although misunderstood by the American public, there is nevertheless a great deal of public interest and positive response toward present-day wolf restoration programs and projects. As Americans become more urban and sympathetic to environmental issues, this interest is likely to grow.

HISTORICAL PERSPECTIVE

American Indians respected and even revered the wolf, but Anglo-American settlers viewed predators as the enemy. The wolf was characterized as a symbol of the devil by early American settlers, and "no beast was more deserving of Christian wrath than the wolf" (Oakley 1986). Folk tales and American literature of the 18th and 19th centuries told of wolves devouring humans and rearing human children (Goldman 1944).

Audubon and Bachman (1851) were the first early naturalists to determine "that in the Southern United States there exists wolves structurally different from those in other regions" (Nowak 1979). Nowak also concludes that *C. rufus* evolved in the New World, while *C. lupus* arose in Eurasia, eventually crossing the Bering Land Bridge into North America. There is some evidence that supports the thesis that the red wolf actually represents the surviving line of primitive wolves that once ranged over North America a million years ago (Nowak 1972).

During the first half of this century, red wolves were extirpated from nearly all of their original range. The declines in red wolf populations were attributed to human persecution, including state and federal predator-control programs. Increases in human population and subsequent changes in land use, especially during the 1900s, were also important factors (Carley and Mechler 1983). But despite this, these animals were still common in some isolated areas of the Southeast until the early part of this century.

As red wolf numbers declined to remnant populations in Texas, Oklahoma, Arkansas, and Louisiana, the coyote moved rapidly into portions of the wolf's former range. By 1970, the red wolf had been forced into a small area of coastal habitat in southwestern Louisiana and southeastern Texas (McCarley and Carley 1979). This overlap of ranges resulted in hybridization between the two species and the breakdown of thousands of years of reproductive isolation between them (McCarley 1962, Nowak 1979).

On March 11, 1967, the U.S. Fish and Wildlife Service (FWS) listed the red wolf as endangered. The passage of the Endangered Species Act of 1973 further underscored the plight of the species. By the mid-1970s, FWS determined that the species could only be saved from extinction by a two-pronged effort: the establishment of a captive-breeding project and the location and rescue of as many pure red wolves as possible for the project. A Red Wolf Captive Breeding Program was established in November 1973 under contract with the Point Defiance Zoo in Tacoma, Washington (Carley and Mechler 1983). In concert with this effort, 40 wild-caught adult red wolves were supplied to the program. By 1980, with the capture of those animals for the project, the red wolf was considered to be extinct in the wild; any remaining wolves were presumed to be hybrids.

Of the 40 original animals that were captured in the mid-1970s in Louisiana and Texas, only 17 were pure red wolves. Minimum taxonomic standards—skull x-ray and electrophoretic and vocalization analyses—were used in the initial selection process (Carley 1975). The first litters of pups were born in May 1977 at the Point Defiance Zoo. By the early 1980s, the captive population had grown sufficiently to allow the transfer of excess wolves to private and public zoos for display and captive breeding. In 1987, there were six such facilities: Audubon Zoo, Louisiana; Alexandria Zoo, Louisiana; Burnet Park Zoo, New York; Texas Zoo, Texas; Wild Canid Survival and Research Center, Missouri; and Point Defiance Zoo, Washington. All animals are the property of the federal government and are cared for under a rigorous permit system.

Overall captive-breeding objectives are carefully controlled and regulated by the American Association of Zoological Parks and Aquaria's *Species Survival Plan* for the red wolf. FWS' red wolf coordinator meets yearly with the association's red wolf propagation group to develop breeding needs for the following breeding season. Once these yearly objectives are defined, the species coordinator oversees captive-breeding projects at the various cooperating facilities. Genetic vigor is carefully maintained by yearly interchange of animals from one facility to another through a computer-based breeding program developed by the association. Since its inception, the project has continued to aim toward eventual release of animals into the wild.

With the species secure in captivity, FWS turned its attention to re-establishing the red wolf in a portion of its historic range. Early experiments centered on developing acclimation, release, and recapture techniques. To ascertain the feasibility of the reintroduction strategy, two groups of wild-caught animals were released during 1976 and from 1977 to 1978 on Bulls Island, a 4,000-acre component of the Cape Romain National Wildlife Refuge in South Carolina (Carley 1979, 1981). These experiments demonstrated the feasibility of reintroducing adult, wild-caught red wolves into selected areas. Observations on the opportunistic nature of wild canids and their learning abilities show that re-establishing captive-born-and-reared wolves into the wild is also feasible.

CURRENT TRENDS

Several strategies have been suggested regarding the re-establishment of the red wolf. One calls for the use of islands along the southeast coast of the United States. A similar experiment using gray wolves was conducted on Coronation Island, southeast Alaska (Merriam 1964).

Unfortunately, most U.S. islands off the southeast coast are too small to support enough red wolves to bring about the genetic heterozygosity the species desperately needs. To minimize inbreeding, offspring of animals would have to be moved from one island to another.

The alternate and most desirable strategy is to re-establish mated pairs on mainland sites. In such areas, natural processes would be allowed to control the resulting wolf population. A population could become truly wild and self-sustaining and thus satisfy the objectives of the recovery plan (U.S. Fish and Wildlife Service 1984). A population would be considered re-established when offspring born in the wild are in turn producing young.

Re-establishment Projects

From 1982 to 1984, FWS considered reintroducing red wolves into the Tennessee Valley Authority's Land Between the Lakes in western Kentucky and Tennessee. This project was cancelled in 1984 when both state wildlife agencies withdrew their support because of opposition from several livestock groups.

In March 1984, a 118,000-acre tract of wooded wetlands in Dare and Tyrrell Counties, North Carolina, was donated to the U.S. government. These lands are now administered by FWS as the Alligator River National Wildlife Refuge. Major natural communities in the refuge include large expanses of nonriverine swamp forests, pocosins, and brackish and freshwater marshes.

Shortly after being transferred to the government, the refuge was assessed as a possible site to attempt a major red wolf re-establishment (see Figure 1). It was determined ideal for this purpose for at least five reasons:

1. The area is within the historic range of the species.
2. It is situated within a peninsula bounded to the south by an extensive agricultural area that wolves would be reluctant to cross.
3. There are no coyotes or feral dogs in the area.
4. The refuge and adjacent 47,000 acres of U.S. Department of Defense lands compose an area of suitable size with a large enough prey population to support the wolves (Potter 1982).
5. The refuge is isolated and sparsely settled—only two paved roads provide all-weather access. Approximately 1,500 people live in four small communities near the refuge.

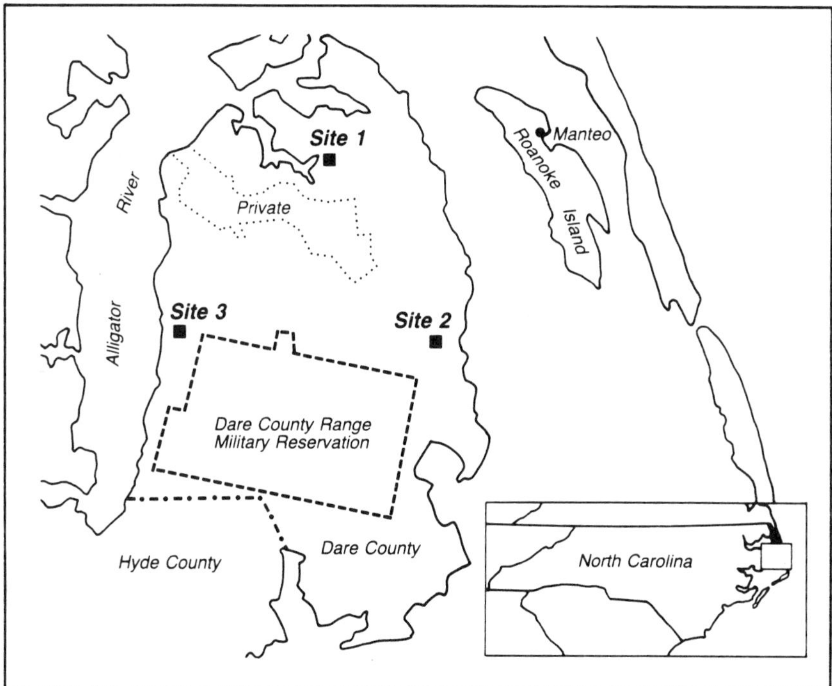

Figure 1. Red wolf reintroduction site in Alligator River National Wildlife Refuge. [As of press time, private lands had been purchased by FWS.]

During January and February 1986, FWS met with the North Carolina Wildlife Resources Commission, the Dare County commissioners, congressional delegations, conservation groups, the North Carolina Department of Agriculture, and others, to brief them on the proposed red wolf project. Four public meetings were held in the refuge area to solicit local response about the proposal. Opposition was minimal. Local and national media attention was significant and generally was positive and accurate. In late February 1986, FWS' southeast director, in consultation with the director of the North Carolina Wildlife Resources Commission, decided that the re-establishment should be attempted.

Selection of Wolves and Acclimation. The eight wolves selected for release were taken from FWS' certified captive-breeding stock. Age, health, genetics, reproductive history, behavior, and physical traits representative of the species were considered in the selection process.

Four widely separated, isolated areas of the refuge were chosen as acclimation sites. Work began on the four 2,500-square-foot pens in August 1986. A three-foot wide skirt of fencing was placed on the ground around the inside perimeter of the pen to prevent wolves from digging out.

On November 12, four pairs of wolves were shipped by air to Raleigh, North Carolina, and then flown by helicopter to Manteo. They were then driven in refuge trucks to the acclimation pens within Alligator River National Wildlife Refuge. FWS maintained 24-hour security and observation at the sites.

The wolves were fitted with motion-sensitive radio collars before being released into the pens. Early fitting of this collar permitted the animals to adjust to them and provided project personnel with experience in using telemetry equipment as well as with a means to track an animal if it escaped.

Because the original wild red wolves were either dead or unsuitable for release, the animals used in the project were first and second generation captive-born. Considerable effort was devoted to devising techniques that would enhance the probability of survival for these captive-born red wolves in the wild. Gradually weaning wolves from their dog-food diet to native meat was considered essential. In addition, their normal daily feeding schedule was drastically altered to feeding every third day to accustom them to a more natural feeding frequency. Human contact was rigidly controlled; the wolves were only handled during infrequent health checks and when the new collars were fitted. These capture collars, with both a transmitter and tranquilizer darts that, on radio command, inject and sedate an animal that requires recapturing, were fitted to each wolf before release (Mech *et al.* 1984).

Release and Monitoring. Late spring or early summer was selected as the best period for releasing the acclimated wolves. This would give them six to eight months to adapt to the area's climate and break any homing instincts they may have retained. The six-month adjustment period is believed to be largely responsible for the success of the 1977–1978 Bulls Island experiment (Carley 1981). Unfortunately, the release was delayed for three months while refinements were made in the capture collar. The project's acceptance by the local community was contingent upon the design of the tracking and tranquilizing capture collar; FWS wanted to avoid the problems that caused the withdrawl of state agency support for the Land Between the Lakes project mentioned earlier.

On September 14, 1987, one pair of red wolves was released into the wild. On September 30, the remaining three pairs of red wolves were released. These animals are being monitored carefully and appear to be adjusting well to their new home.

Since little is known about the ecology and life history of red wolves in a natural environment, there is obviously a great deal of information to be gathered and interpreted from this experiment. If all goes as planned, four more pairs will be released in the spring of 1988.

This will complete the basic red wolf reintroduction strategy at Alligator River National Wildlife Refuge. It is hoped that by the end of five years there will be 25 to 35 wolves within the refuge area.

Island Strategy. While the Alligator River project is considered by many to be a major accomplishment, its long term significance has yet to be measured. A potential weakness in the present red wolf program is the lack of available wild animals for translocation purposes. A feasible solution involves the temporary use of one or more islands within the National Wildlife Refuge System or National Park System in the southeastern United States. This strategy requires the use of a carefully selected captive pair of adult animals released after acclimation on an island for breeding and eventual capture of resulting wild offspring. The wild-caught offspring wolves would be then used in mainland translocations and possibly in the captive-breeding program.

Management Strategy and Legal Aspects. It was determined early on that the Alligator refuge and other red wolf reintroduction efforts would have to mesh with traditional human uses of an area. This was a critical determination because the ultimate recovery of the species depends on the re-establishment of at least three self-sustaining populations within its historic range (U.S. Fish and Wildlife Service 1984). If the first re-establishment effort required substantial changes in other management objectives to accomodate the red wolf, other federal land-management agencies would have little assurance that *their* mission and objectives would not be disrupted as well. The co-existence of the traditional land uses and the reintroduction of the red wolves were a paramount consideration in the Alligator River National Wildlife Refuge restoration project.

Because of the uncertainties involved with the release of a large predatory animal, the first five years of the Alligator River Refuge re-establishment project are viewed as highly experimental. During this period, key elements of the refuge will be monitored along with the wolves. If serious conflicts arise, the project could be terminated and the animals removed.

In order to permit re-establishments of endangered species like the red wolf, Congress amended the Endangered Species Act. Under the amended act, Congress provided for release of endangered and threatened animals under the designation of "experimental" if the release is deemed necessary for the eventual recovery of the species. The designated animals must be further defined as either "essential" or "nonessential" to the survival of the species. Red wolves selected for release in Alligator River National Wildlife Refuge are treated as an "experimental nonessential" population. The animals are accorded full protection under of Sections 7 and 9 of the Endangered Species Act while they and their offspring remain on the refuge (Parker *et al.* 1986). Animals that leave the refuge and enter private lands during the initial five-year phase will be captured by FWS and probably returned to the refuge or the captive-breeding program.

At the end of the fifth year, the project will be reviewed by FWS and the North Carolina Wildlife Resources Commission. A decision will then be made concerning its future. Public opinion on this matter will be solicited through a series of local public meetings sponsored by FWS.

If the reintroduction proves successful after five years, the wolves will remain as a threatened species on Alligator River National Wildlife Refuge and will be considered an integral component of the refuge ecosystem.

RECOMMENDATIONS

The Indian belief that people and wolves can coexist in harmony has only recently begun to be accepted by the rest of the American public (Nee and Oakley 1986). In modern America, the degree to which wolves can exist in the presence of humans is dependent on the attitudes of people living within and adjacent to a wolf reintroduction site. Nevertheless, potential release sites should not be excluded from consideration because of human presence, unless that presence poses a direct threat to the survival of the reintroduced wolves.

Efforts to re-establish various endangered species have recently been highlighted by the news media and various national environmental organizations. The California condor, the Florida panther, the northern Rocky Mountain wolf, and the red wolf are prime examples. Classic techniques of capture, acclimation, and release are often viewed with almost casual regard by the public. A technically sound reintroduction effort, however, is a complicated process that also has to be coupled with a great deal of background work regarding public attitudes and cooperation. Innovative ideas and strategies are often needed to maximize the technical impact of such efforts. The success of these reintroduction projects and their subsequent application to other species of concern would be a significant step forward in restoring hundreds of species to ecological health.

REFERENCES

Audubon, J.J. and J. Bachman. 1851. *The Quadrupeds of North America.* Volume 2. New York. 334 pp.

Bartram, W. 1791. *Travels.* Philadelphia. xxxiv + 522 pp.

Carley, C.J. 1975. *Activities and findings of the Red Wolf Recovery Program from Late 1973 to July 1, 1975.* U.S. Fish and Wildlife Service. Albuquerque, New Mexico. 215 pp.

——. 1979. Report on Successful Translocation Experiment of Red Wolves (*Canis rufus*) to Bulls Island, South Carolina. A paper presented at the Portland Wolf Symposium, Lewis and Clark College. Portland, Oregon. Pp. 1–23.

——. 1981. "Red wolf experimental translocation summarized." *Wild Canid Survival and Research Center Bulletin.* Part I, Winter 1980. Pp. 4,5,7. Part II, Spring 1981. Pp. 8–9. Eureka, Missouri.

——. and J.L. Mechler. 1983. *An Experimental Reestablishment of Red Wolves,* (Canis rufus) *on the Tennessee Valley Authority's Land Between the Lakes.* U.S. Fish and Wildlife Service. Asheville, North Carolina. 72 pp.

Goldman, E.A. 1944. "Classification of wolves," pp. 389–636 *in* S.P. Young and E.A. Goldman eds., *The Wolves of North America.* American Wildlife Institute. Washington, D.C.

McCarley, H. 1962. "The taxonomic status of wild *Canis* (Canidae) in the South Central United States." *Southwest Naturalist* 7:227–235.

——. and C.J. Carley. 1979. Recent Changes in Distribution and Status of Wild Red Wolves (*Canis rufus*). Endangered Species Report No. 4. U.S. Fish and Wildlife Service. Albuquerque, New Mexico. 38 pp.

Mech, L.D., R.D. Chapman, W.W. Cochran and U.S. Seal. 1984. "Radio-triggered anesthetic-dart collar for recapturing large mammals." *Wildlife Society Bulletin* 12:69–74.

Merriam, H.R. 1964. "The wolves of Coronation Island." *Proceedings of the Alaska Scientific Conference* 15:27–32.

Nee, J.A. and G. Oakley. 1986. "Wolf management," pp. 49–54 in *WOLF! A Modern Look.* Wolves in American Culture Committee. Boise, Idaho. Northward, Inc. Ashland, Wisconsin.

Nowak, R.M. 1972. "The mysterious wolf of the South." *Natural History* 81:51–53, 74–77.

——. 1979. *North American Quaternary* Canis. Museum of Natural History, University of Kansas Monograph 6. 154 pp.

Oakley, G. 1986. "Historic Overview," pp. 1–7 in *WOLF! A Modern Look.* Wolves in American Culture Committee. Boise, Idaho. Northward, Inc. Ashland, Wisconsin.

Parker, W.T., M.P. Jones and P.G. Poulos. 1986. "Determination of experimental population status for an introduced population of red wolves in North America. Final Rule." *Federal Register* 51(223):41790–41796.

Potter, E. 1982. *A Survey of the Vertebrate Fauna of Mainland Dare County, North Carolina.* North Carolina Biological Survey. Raleigh, North Carolina. 94 pp.

Riley, G.A. and R.T. McBride. 1972. A Survey of the Red Wolf (*Canis rufus*). U.S. Department of the Interior Special Science Report, Wildlife No. 162. Washington, D.C. 15 pp.

Shaw, J.H. 1975. Ecology, Behavior, and Systematics of the Red Wolf (*Canis rufus*). Ph.D. dissertation. Yale University. New Haven, Connecticut. 99 pp.

U.S. Fish and Wildlife Service. 1984. *Red Wolf Recovery Plan.* Edited by Warren T. Parker. U.S. Department of the Interior. Atlanta, Georgia.

Warren T. Parker is a biologist with the U.S. Fish and Wildlife Service's Asheville, North Carolina, office. He is the full-time coordinator and recovery team leader for the red wolf.

Indiana bats hibernate on the walls of caves, as shown here. Loss of cave habitat and other factors have caused major declines in the populations of this endangered species. *Merlin D. Tuttle/Bat Conservation International*

The Indiana Bat

Virgil Brack, Jr.
WAPORA, Inc.

SPECIES DESCRIPTION AND NATURAL HISTORY

The Indiana bat (*Myotis sodalis*) is a small, dull-grayish bat weighing less than one-third of an ounce, with a wingspread of approximately 10 inches. The Indiana bat's appearance is similar throughout its range; there are no subspecies (Hall 1962). The Indiana bat looks similar to several other species of bats from the genus *Myotis*, with which it has overlapping ranges. The little brown bat (*Myotis lucifugus*) and Keen's bat (*Myotis keenii*) are difficult to distinguish from the Indiana bat and a combination of relatively obscure characteristics is used to differentiate them. These include the number and length of toe hairs, the length and shape of a fleshy appendage at the ear canal, or "tragus," and the shape of the small bone supporting the tail membrane, or "calcar." A variety of other characteristics, such as pelage color, behavior, ear size and color, facial appearance, and overall size are useful in aiding identification, but these are inconclusive in themselves.

Taxonomy and Distribution

The similarity between the Indiana bat and related species has caused confusion over the years. Early in this century, Hahn (1908) reported populations of bats hibernating in caves of southern Indiana, but the three species of *Myotis* were not recognized as distinct. They were not described as separate species until 20 years later (Miller and Allen 1928).

Both the common and scientific names are descriptive of the bat. The common name refers to the location where the species was first described—Wyandotte Cave in Indiana. The latin name for the genus *Myotis* comes from "mouse ear," referring to the bat's appearance. *Sodalis*, the specific Latin name, means "companion," referring to the bat's propensity to hibernate in very compact clusters where each bat is compressed between several neighboring bats.

Barbour and Davis (1969) described the range of the Indiana bat as the eastern United States, from Oklahoma, Iowa, and Wisconsin, east to Vermont, and south to northwestern Florida (see Figure 1). However, since the bat is migratory, this description represents a composite range. The winter range is associated with regions of well-developed limestone caverns. Major populations of hibernating Indiana bats are found in Indiana, Kentucky, and Missouri. Smaller populations also occur in Alabama, Arkansas, Georgia, Illinois, Maryland, Mississippi, New York, North Carolina, Ohio, Oklahoma, Pennsylvania, Tennessee, Virginia, and West Virginia. About 85 percent of the population hibernates in only seven caves, and nearly 50 percent may hibernate in only two caves (Brady *et al.* 1983). Thus, although the winter range is

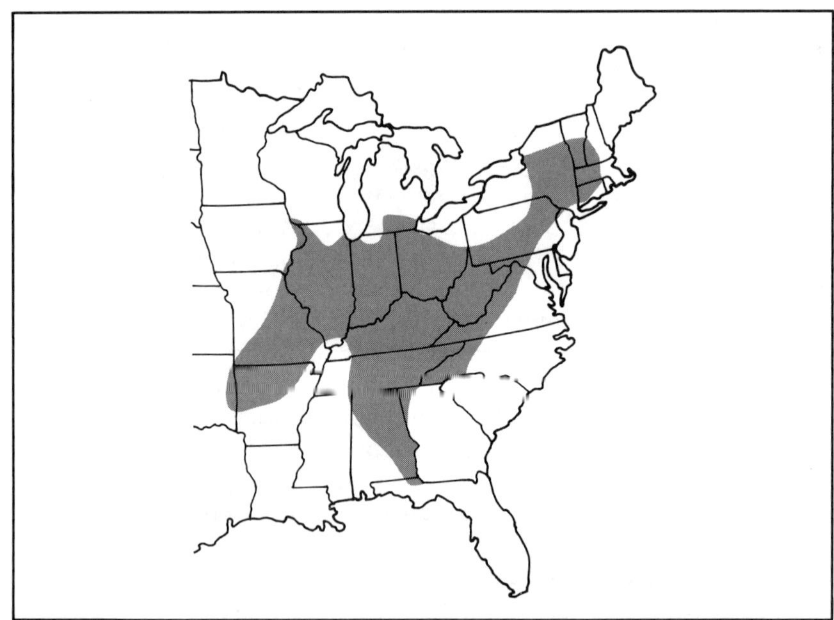

Figure 1. Distribution of the Indiana bat.

large, the species is restricted to about 135 hibernacula caves. There are large populations in only a very few caves and most hibernacula caves contain only a very few bats.

In summer, Indiana bats can be found hundreds of miles north of their hibernacula caves. Northern Indiana, southern Michigan, Illinois, northern Missouri, and southern Iowa have the most summer records of reproductive females and juveniles. In contrast, adult males can frequently be found in the cave regions. In Indiana there are no records of reproductive adult females or juveniles from the cave region during the summer and only a few scattered records of adult males north of the cave region (Brack 1983). In Indiana and Missouri, males frequently visit hibernacula caves during summer although they do not roost there (Brack 1983, Hall 1962, Brack and LaVal 1985, LaVal *et al.* 1977). These data indicate that males and females are largely seasonally separated, or "allopatric." However, because at least a few males migrate, the separation is not complete. Seasonal geographic segregation of the sexes is possible because mating occurs in autumn, prior to hibernation.

Breeding

Like many species of bats in temperate regions, the Indiana bat mates in autumn. Pairs of copulating bats have been observed in Missouri caves during late September and early October (LaVal and LaVal 1980). Female Indiana bats store sperm through winter hibernation, as do other *Myotis* species, and fertilization is delayed until spring. Females are pregnant when they arrive at the nursery roost. Unlike most other small vertebrates that maintain a constant body temperature, bats have a very low fecundity and produce only one young per year. In comparison, a similar sized field mouse usually produces several litters of offspring per year. It is not known with certainty if female Indiana bats mate their first autumn as juveniles.

The length of nursery roost occupation and the timing of reproductive phenology is probably dependent on seasonal temperatures and the thermal character of the roost (Humphrey *et al.* 1977, Brack 1983). Like many other bats, the Indiana bat is a thermal conformist and is able to expend only limited amounts of energy to warm itself and its young. If ambient temperatures fall significantly below the bats' normal body temperature for any prolonged period, its body temperature will drop correspondingly (Stones and Wiebers 1985). Since prenatal, neonate, and juvenile development are heavily temperature-dependent (Tuttle 1975), the gestation and development periods may vary among years. Temperature may also affect food availability.

Birth takes place in late June to early July. The young are large at birth and may be over one-half the length of an adult female. Lactating females have been caught as early as June 11 through July 29 in

Missouri, from June 26 to July 22 in Iowa, and from June 11 through July 29 in Indiana (LaVal and LaVal 1980, Bowles, pers. commun., Humphrey *et al.* 1977, Brack 1983). The young may be weaned in 25 to 37 days. Juveniles become volant, or able to fly, from early July to early August. Independent juveniles and post-reproductive females have been found at the caves as early as July 18 in Missouri and July 31 in Indiana, although most do not arrive until mid-August.

Habitat and Ecology

Winter. Caves suitable as hibernacula for the Indiana bat have cool, stable temperature regimes throughout the winter. These temperature regimes are a function of cave location and morphology (Humphrey 1978). Caves with entrances in a sinkhole tend to have a greater influx of cold air. The sink entrance may be a pit or karst window, or a downward sloping passage. Regardless of whether the entrance is in a sink, a downward trend to the cave passage is important to the influx of cold air. Air influx is also more likely if the cave has more than a single entrance, has a system that is voluminous, or has a large mouth and foreward passageways. Ultimately, the shape, topography, and location of the cave or mine, combined with the external climate, determine whether it will serve as a suitable hibernaculum.

The Indiana bat, like many other species of bats, mammals, and some birds, hibernates. Hibernation is a physiological-ecological adaptation to avoid extremes in temperatures or shortages of food and water. A winter's hibernation consists of many periods of hibernation, each terminated by spontaneous arousal. The Indiana bat's period of hibernation averages 13 days (Hardin and Hassell 1970). The duration of the period of hibernation between arousals is inversely related to temperature of hibernation; bats hibernate longer at lower temperatures (Brack and Twente 1985, Twente *et al.* 1985).

A hibernating bat's body temperature approximates cave temperatures. The lower the temperature, the lower the heart and respiration rates and metabolic demand, hence, the greater the efficiency of hibernation. Since prolonged exposure to temperatures below freezing will kill the bat, ideal temperatures are just above freezing. The Indiana bat has been found hibernating at temperatures between 29° and 63°F. At many hibernacula caves, specific locations are used repeatedly for hibernation. Temperatures at these locations most frequently range from 39° to 46°F (Clawson *et al.* 1980). These sites may represent optimal conditions for that cave. The species' winter distribution, with most of the population in a few caves, probably indicates that an appropriate temperature regime of cold without freezing is uncommon.

The Indiana bat hibernates in compact clusters of about 300 individuals per square foot. These clusters contain males and females in approximately equal numbers. However, females enter hibernation earlier in autumn than do males. Some females begin torpor—almost complete motor inactivity—in early October, but by late November all bats, including males, are hibernating.

Summer. When females emerge from hibernation, they migrate north to areas where nursery colonies are established. The details of migration and the ecology of nursery colonies have unraveled slowly, and a great deal is yet to be learned. The first summer record of a female from noncave regions was reported from central Indiana 30 years ago. Ten years later, several additional records had accumulated, strengthening the supposition that caves were not used by the Indiana bat for nursery colonies. Intensive studies in the early 1960s in Indiana and Missouri confirmed the lack of nursery colonies in caves, but failed to establish where the nursery sites were (Hall 1962, Meyers 1964). Later, pregnant female bats were caught in northwestern Missouri, outside the state's cave regions, and in Michigan.

The first Indiana bat nursery colony was found on August 3, 1971 when a dead American elm tree was bulldozed from a hedgerow near Noland Fork River, Indiana (Cope *et al.* 1974). The colony, estimated at 50 individuals, was housed behind a loose slab of bark. Bats were captured near this area in 1972 and 1973, and in 1974 another nursery roost was located (Humphrey *et al.* 1977). This colony was under the loose bark of a dead bitternut hickory. A nearby living shagbark hickory was used as an alternate roost when the temperature there was more favorable. Since then, several colonies have been found. One colony was behind the bark of a dead cottonwood tree along the Blue River, Indiana. The others were located in Illinois (Gardner, pers. commun.). Since the first colony was found in a riparian woodland, adult females and juveniles have been caught in riparian habitats in Missouri, Iowa, Illinois, Indiana, and Michigan, and in upland woodlots in Iowa, Illinois, and Indiana.

Nursery colonies, composed of several to 50 adult females and their young, may be occupied from mid-May to mid-September. The bats exit the roost to forage shortly after sunset. At the Blue River nursery roost, emergence varied between 38 and 71 minutes after sunset and emergence was generally earlier when more bats were leaving the roost (Brack 1983). The precise reason for this relationship is unclear, but it is probably related to an interaction of individuals in the roost or to the timing of foraging. For example, juveniles not yet proficient at foraging may require either more feeding time or may require that foraging be conducted when insects are most abundant. The Noland Fork colony increased its foraging habitat area from 3.6 acres in early summer to 11.2 acres after the young were volant (Humphrey 1977).

At the Noland Fork colony, bats foraged among the foliage of floodplain trees from 6.6 to 98.5 feet high. During early summer, foraging was restricted to riparian habitat. After the young became volant, foraging was extended to single trees and other floodplain forest edge. Forest, open pasture, corn fields, upland hedgerows, and treeless creeks were not used by the bats. Foraging habitat estimates were made using flashlights to spot reflective tape placed on the bats' forearm bands (Humphrey 1977).

In Missouri, adult male bats foraged predominantly in upland forest (LaVal *et al.* 1977). Foraging data were collected using a technique called light-tagging. A glass sphere filled with a glowing chemiluminescent material was attached to bats that were released. This sphere allowed the bats to be observed while they foraged.

Adult males and females and juveniles were light-tagged for foraging observations in late summer and early autumn in southern Indiana. No differences in foraging behavior were discerned between sex or age groups. Foraging was most frequent and prolonged around the tree crowns. The bats foraged less frequently and for shorter periods along forest edges and riparian strips. Bats only occasionally foraged over old fields and pastures. Bats traveled without foraging in areas free of obstruction, such as the open understory of both upland and riparian woodlands, above the canopy, and above vegetation of old fields and pastures (Brack 1983).

The foraging and roosting habitat of the Indiana bat may not necessarily be one and the same. Thus, while the Indiana bat forages predominantly around tree crowns, without regard to riparian location, the summer range encompasses many areas where the predominant remaining forested tracts are riparian. Nursery colonies have been found in both riparian and nonriparian habitats. Riparian habitats may provide a large proportion of available maternity roost sites because tree species composition, species diversity, and growth characteristics of riparian woodlands may be more conducive to roost-site production. Greater selective logging of upland woodlots and continued agricultural clearing of upland sites within the summer range may continue to concentrate roost availability in riparian habitat.

Migration and Autumn Swarming

In late summer, after the young are volant, bats migrate south to hibernacula caves. Distances traveled depend on the geographic association of summer roosts and winter caves, but several migrations of 200 to 300 miles have been documented. All bats from a summer nursery colony do not necessarily occupy the same hibernaculum cave, although individuals return year after year to the same hibernaculum. This strong philopatry to a specific hibernaculum may doom many individuals if the cave is degraded or destroyed (Humphrey 1978).

Bats begin to return to the caves about the beginning of August. Autumn activity at the caves, or "swarming," is characterized by many bats flying in and out of the cave, with relatively few bats roosting in the cave. Swarming activity is apparent from mid-August to late October with peaks in early September and mid-October (Cope and Humphrey 1977). Mating takes place during the swarming period and is followed by hibernation. Males initiate hibernation later than females. A probable advantage to this is that males have the opportunity to mate with females that arrive late to the caves.

Diet

There have been several food habit studies on various segments of the Indiana bat's population (Belwood 1979, Brack and LaVal 1985, Brack 1983). Many similarities in the diets of these groups were found regardless of habitat, geographic locale, season, sex, or age of the bats sampled. Since the Indiana bat forages high in the woodland canopy, it eats primarily terrestrial insects, not aquatic ones.

Insects are caught and consumed by the bat while on the wing. Insects include moths (Lepidoptera), beetles (Coleoptera), flies (Diptera), caddisflies (Trichoptera), stoneflies (Plecoptera), lacewings (Neuroptera), and ants (Hymenoptera). Moths and beetles are the largest part of most bat diets. Other types of insects are eaten occasionally. The bats sporadically eat large numbers of ants; in late summer the bats frequently eat the Asiatic oak weevil, an abundant introduced forest pest. The bat's diet may be less diverse early in the evening and late in the season when insects are more abundant; when there are more insects, bats frequently feed on just a few species rather than feeding on just what is available. The moon may influence insect prey availability and thereby influence the bat's diet.

Life Span and Mortality

The Indiana bat is relatively long-lived. One bat was recaptured 20 years after being banded as an adult of unknown age (LaVal and LaVal 1980). Several individuals 13 to 14 years old have been reported (Humphrey and Cope 1977). At the Noland Fork nursery roost there was approximately an eight percent mortality between birth and weaning. Adult life has two survival phases. The first phase, calculated from one to six years after banding, has an annual survival rate of almost 76 percent for females and almost 70 percent for males. The second phase, beginning at six years after banding, has a 36-percent survival rate for males, a 66-percent rate for females six to ten years after marking, and a 4-percent rate for females surviving more than ten years after marking. Because it is difficult to distinguish between juvenile and adult Indiana bats, researchers associate age with the time of banding.

Mortality may result from a variety of causes, including predation by birds, mammals, snakes, and perhaps frogs. There are no direct observations of predation at nursery colonies. Raccoons frequent many caves used by bats and prehistoric raccoon feces from Wyandotte Cave contained many *Myotis* bones. Snakes on the bars of gated caves have been observed catching bats leaving the cave. In a hibernaculum cave in Missouri, a mink had numerous prey caches that were predominantly Indiana bats. The Indiana bat is host to a variety of external and internal parasites (Mumford and Whitaker 1982) that probably contribute to mortality.

Human disturbance and vandalism and flooding have been documented at several Indiana bat caves. Juvenile gray bats (*Myotis griscens*), also an endangered species, have been found dead beneath their own maternity roosts in Missouri. Anaylsis of their brain tissue showed lethal concentrations of the pesticide dieldrin (Clark *et al.* 1978). The stress of migration has also proved lethal to the gray bat (Tuttle and Stevenson 1977).

SIGNIFICANCE OF THE SPECIES

The Indiana bat is strictly insectivorous, and some species of *Myotis* eat up to one-third of their weight in insects nightly. As the dominant nocturnal insect predator, bats occupy an important niche in the ecological community and can be considered the nocturnal equivalent of swifts and swallows. Although the value of these insectivorous birds is well established, the value of bats is less well known. The loss of the Indiana bat, or more drastically, the additional loss of other bat species with which the Indiana bat shares its range, would create an ecological imbalance.

Birds are a valued aesthetic resource, but this also can be increasingly said of the bat. Many people are beginning to appreciate the benefits of bats and enjoy the occasional glimpse of a bat silhouetted against the evening sky.

HISTORICAL PERSPECTIVE

The range of the Indiana bat is nearly the same as when the species was first described by Allen in 1928. The relatively late recognition of this bat as a distinct species may mean that the early abundance and distribution of the species will never be known. The bat's range includes 17 states of the northern Midwest and the middle and upper New England states. However, over 85 percent of the population winters in Indiana, Missouri, and Kentucky; summer records are virtually unknown except from northern Missouri, southern Iowa, Illinois, northern Indiana, and southern Michigan. It appears the eastern populations were always small in relation to midwestern populations, but they probably were substantially larger in the past.

CURRENT TRENDS

The U.S. Fish and Wildlife Service (FWS) listed the Indiana bat as endangered on March 11, 1967. Legal protection for the bat did not occur until passage of the Endangered Species Act of 1973. The earliest concerns for this species addressed its precarious existence, with 97 percent of the then-known populations hibernating in four caves. It was reasoned that these exceptional seasonal aggregations made the species extremely susceptible to human-caused perturbations and natural catastrophes.

The bat's precarious position was soon confirmed. From 1960 to 1975, known hibernating populations decreased by 28 percent (Humphrey 1978). Populations in Kentucky declined by 73 percent. The bat's endangered status stimulated the search for new hibernacula, which continues to the present. However, since individual Indiana bats return to the same hibernaculum each year, these finds of "new hibernacula" represent increases in the known percentage of the total population and not true population increases.

Using data gathered since 1960, and assuming no declines prior to discovery, the Indiana bat has experienced a 55-percent decline at Priority I hibernacula in the past 27 years (Clawson 1987) (see "Management"). The decline at Priority II hibernacula has been similar, although a cave in Indiana and another in Kentucky have shown recent increases. Therefore, despite endangered status and associated protection, particularly at hibernacula, the decline has continued.

Over the years a variety of factors have contributed to the loss. Vandals have harassed and killed bats by almost every imaginable means, including bb guns, shotguns, fireworks, torches, and bonfires; the bat has been killed one by one and in mass. Cave modifications restricting air flow have had radical effects on hibernacula populations. For example, at Coach Cave, Kentucky, a population that once numbered 100,000 declined to only 250 in 1987 after one of the entrances was closed by the construction of a building in the early 1960s.

Indiana bat populations declined by 60 percent at Bat Cave, Carter County, Kentucky, as a result of repeated cave visitation. Remedial steps have been implemented at this cave. At other caves, population declines have been linked to heavy recreational caving, although many users have attempted to avoid disturbing the bats.

Bat researchers have not been without blame either. A 27-year population increase from 512 to 22,920 bats at a Priority II cave in Indiana is attributed to the reduction of research activity. In this instance, the repeated removal of a large number of bats, and the associated disturbance from those removals, was more than the population could withstand.

Natural catastrophes can also decimate populations of the Indiana bat. Flooding at Bat Cave, Edmonson County, Kentucky, probably in 1937, killed 300,000 Indiana bats—the largest colony ever known (Hall 1962). Floods at other hibernacula have also been documented, although there were fewer deaths. After unusually long cold spells, numerous bats have been found dead beneath the hibernaculum roost in Bat Cave, Shannon County, Missouri (Humphrey 1978). While this roost is particularly appropriate during normal winters, the cave provides no thermally advantageous alternatives if the roost becomes too cold. Natural catastrophes may be impossible to guard against, but by virtue of their existence, they emphasize the importance of guarding against human-caused disturbances that augment natural population losses.

MANAGEMENT

The Indiana bat recovery plan was approved by FWS on October 14, 1983 (Brady *et al.* 1983). The objectives of the plan are: 1) to protect hibernacula, 2) to maintain, protect, and restore summer nursery habitat, 3) to monitor population trends through winter censuses, 4) to educate the public, and 5) to continue researching the bat.

The importance and priority of protection given to hibernacula have been weighted according to the number of over wintering bats. Priority I hibernacula have housed more than 30,000 bats since 1960; Priority II hibernacula have had more than 1,000 but less than 30,000 bats; Priority III hibernacula have not had more than 1,000 bats, but they require further investigation. Hibernacula of marginal significance requiring no further action are Priority IV. There are two Priority I hibernacula in Indiana, three in Kentucky, and three in Missouri.

A total of 11 caves and 2 mines have been classified as critical habitat—2 caves in Indiana, 2 caves in Kentucky, 5 caves and a mine in Missouri, a mine in Illinois, and 1 cave each in West Virginia and

Tennessee. This classification requires that "all Federal agencies must take such action as is necessary to ensure that actions authorized, funded, or carried out by them do not result in the destruction or modification of these critical habitat areas," as directed in Section 7 of the Endangered Species Act.

Hibernacula protection requires a multifaceted approach. The primary objective is to prevent unauthorized entry and disturbance. Methods include warning and informational signs, fences, or gates. The chosen method requires periodic monitoring of significant hibernacula, with violations reported to FWS. A second protection objective is to prevent hibernacula modifications that make the caves less desirable and to rehabilitate hibernacula that have been detrimentally altered.

Understanding the biology of this bat species is the key to effective management, but there are still many unanswered questions (see "Recommendations").

PROGNOSIS

Indiana bat populations were in decline prior to the organized monitoring of the species. Initially, protection and management were nonexistent, but in recent years there has been a mounting effort to protect, preserve, and manage the bat. Despite these efforts, however, the population has decreased by 55 percent at seven of the eight Priority I hibernacula.

It is obvious that no species can continue to sustain the long-term, large-scale population declines incurred by the Indiana bat. But the actions that must be taken to curtail the species' precipitous decline are not as obvious. While major strides have been taken to preserve and protect the bat, they have not mastered the forces of decline. Without dedication, research, and financial support from all levels of government, the bat faces extinction. With support, the bat may be able to survive. It will take continued research to identify problems contributing to the bat's decline and the design and implementation of management procedures to stop it.

Luckily for the Indiana bat, help is available from several sources. FWS is protecting hibernacula under its jurisdiction. The species' endangered status requires that federal projects and actions, including management plans for federally owned lands, consider any effects on the bat. Many state wildlife agencies, independently and in cooperation with FWS, are acting to protect the bat, especially at hibernacula. Private organizations are also contributing. The Nature Conservancy has purchased caves or protected them through voluntary agreements with private landowners. The Indiana Karst Conservancy's goal is the conservation and preservation of caves and their biota, particularly the bat. The National Speliological Society and its local chapters have contributed to bat conservation and cave management.

RECOMMENDATIONS

To date, most time, effort, and money spent to aid the Indiana bat has been directed towards protection, preservation, and management of winter hibernacula. This was essential to initiation of a conservation program, and it must be continued in the future. However, with many protected hibernacula, it is equally apparent that the nonhibernating habitat and ecology of the bat should receive similar attention. Further research is needed to identify the relationship of nursery colonies to specific habitats. Since most roosts are ephemeral, frequently being associated with dead or dying trees, it is not known how many alternate roosts must be available to assure retention of a colony within a particular area.

The fidelity to a site both of individuals within a nursery colony and of the colony itself is unknown. Studies of fidelty must consider the relationship of the movements of young at maturity, the formation of new colonies, the possible overlapping among colonies to roosting and foraging areas, and effects, if any, of human intrusion into the bat's summer habitat.

Summer woodland habitats, including nursery roosts and foraging areas, must be maintained and enhanced if the species is to survive. This will require continuing studies of habitat use and requirements. These studies may include monitoring of habitat availability and indicators of habitat quality, such as roost availability or perhaps water quality. Data acquisition on summer populations must continue. Since the potential for poisoning by toxic chemicals exists, dead bats and insects from foraging habitat should be tested.

Research should also focus on environmental contaminants. Gray bats and Mexican free-tailed bats have accumulated pesticides to toxic levels. The U.S. Environmental Protection Agency and the scientific community are realizing the enormous potential for subterranean pollution from pesticide applications on the surface. Bats are particularly at risk in karst areas, where potential for subterranean pollution is high.

Studies should continue on the winter ecology of the Indiana bat. Efforts to find unknown hibernacula and thus identify the total species population must also continue. This will allow protection priorities to be set and the entire species population to be monitored. We can only assume that unknown populations are declining at the same rate as known populations.

Ongoing protection of winter hibernacula must be strengthened, especially at Priority I hibernacula. Restoration of once viable hibernacula to their former status may require that structural modifications be eliminated or that use by people must be terminated.

Above all, human disturbance of the bats during hibernations must be eliminated. Theoretically, unauthorized visitation is easy to stop by placing informational signs at cave entrances. However, many people feel that access to caves is more important than the bat's welfare. Public education would help and could be achieved by a variety of personalized and mass-media methods. Finally, the Endangered Species Act provides for the prosecution of individuals who disturb or harm the bat, and this protective law should be enforced.

REFERENCES

Barbour, R.W. and W.H. Davis. 1969. *Bats of America.* University of Kentucky Press. Lexington, Kentucky. 286 pp.

Belwood, J.J. 1979. Feeding Ecology of an Indiana Bat Community with Emphasis on the Endangered Indiana Bat, *Myotis sodalis.* M.S. thesis. University of Florida. Gainesville, Florida. 103 pp.

Brack, V., Jr. 1983. The Nonhibernating Ecology of Bats in Indiana with Emphasis on the Endangered Indiana Bat, *Myotis sodalis.* Ph.D. dissertation. Purdue University. West Lafayette, Indiana. 280 pp.

——. and R.K. LaVal. 1985. "Food habits of the Indiana bat in Missouri." *Journal of Mammalogy* 66:308–315.

——. and J.W. Twente. 1985. "The duration of the period of hibernation of three species of vespertilionid bats. I. Field Studies." *Canadian Journal of Zoology* 63:2952–2954.

Brady, J.T., R.K. LaVal, T.H. Kunz, M.D. Tuttle, D.E. Wilson and R.L. Clawson. 1983. *Recovery Plan for the Indiana Bat.* U.S. Fish and Wildlife Service. 80 pp.

Clark, D.R., Jr., R.K. LaVal and D.M. Swineford. 1978. "Dieldrin-induced mortality in an endangered species, the gray bat (*Myotis grisescens*)." *Science* 199:1357–1359.

Clawson, R.L. 1987. "Indiana bats: down for the count." *Bats* 5:3–5.

——., R.K. LaVal, M.L. LaVal and W. Caire. 1980. "Clustering behavior of hibernating *Myotis sodalis* in Missouri." *Journal of Mammalogy* 61:245–253.

Cope, J.B. and S.R. Humphrey. 1977. "Spring and autumn swarming behavior in the Indiana bat, *Myotis sodalis.*" *Journal of Mammalogy* 58:93–95.

——., A.R. Richter and R.S. Mills. 1974. "A summer concentration of the Indiana bat, *Myotis sodalis*, in Wayne County, Indiana." *Indiana Academy of Science* 83:482–484.

Hahn, W.L. 1908. "Some habits and sensory adaptations of cave-inhabiting bats." *Biological Bulletin* 15:135–193.

Hall, J.S. 1962. "A life history and taxonomic study of the Indiana bat, *Myotis sodalis.*" *Reading Public Museum and Art Gallery, Scientific Publication* 12:1–68.

Hardin, J.W. and M.D. Hassell. 1970. "Observations on waking periods and movements of *Myotis sodalis* during hibernation." *Journal of Mammalogy* 51:829–831.

Humphrey, S.R. 1978. "Status, winter habitat, and management of the endangered Indiana bat, *Myotis sodalis.*" *Florida Scientist* 41:65–76.

——. and J.B. Cope. 1977. "Survival rates of the Indiana bat, *Myotis sodalis.*" *Journal of Mammalogy* 58:32–36.

——., A.R. Richter and J.B. Cope. 1977. "Summer habitat and ecology of the endangered Indiana bat, *Myotis sodalis.*" *Journal of Mammalogy* 58:334–346.

LaVal, R.K., R.L. Clawson, M.L. LaVal and W. Caire. 1977. "Foraging behavior and nocturnal activity patterns of Missouri bats, with emphasis on the endangered species *Myotis grisescens* and *Myotis sodalis*." *Journal of Mammalogy* 58:592–599.

——. and M.L. LaVal. 1980. "Ecological studies and management of Missouri bats, with emphasis on cave-dwelling species." *Missouri Department of Conservation Terrestrial Series* 8:1–53.

Miller, G.S., Jr. and G.M. Allen. 1928. "The American bats of the genera *Myotis* and Pizonyx." *U.S. National Museum Bulletin* 144:1–218.

Mumford, R.G. and J.O. Whitaker, Jr. 1982. *Mammals of Indiana*. Indiana University Press. Bloomington, Indiana. 537 pp.

Myers, R.F. 1964. Ecology of Three Species of Myotine Bats in the Ozark Plateau. Ph.D. dissertation. University of Missouri. Colombia, Missouri. 210 pp.

Stone, R.C. and J.E. Wiebers. 1965. "A review of temperature regulation in bats (Chiroptera)." *American Midland Naturalist* 74:155–167.

Tuttle, M.D. 1975. "Population ecology of the gray bat (*Myotis grisescens*): factors influencing early growth and development." *Occasional Papers Museum of Natural History, University of Kansas* 36:1–24.

——. and D. Stevenson. 1977. "An analysis of migration as a mortality factor in the gray bat based on public recoveries of banded bats." *American Midland Naturalist* 97:235–240.

Twente, J.W., J. Twente and V. Brack, Jr. 1985. "The duration of the period of hibernation of three species of vespertilionid bats. II. Laboratory studies." *Canadian Journal of Zoology* 50:877–883.

Virgil Brack, Jr., is a senior biologist and regional manager with WAPORA, Inc., an environmental consulting company. He has been studying bats for 10 years and completed his Ph.D. on the nonhibernating ecology of the Indiana bat.

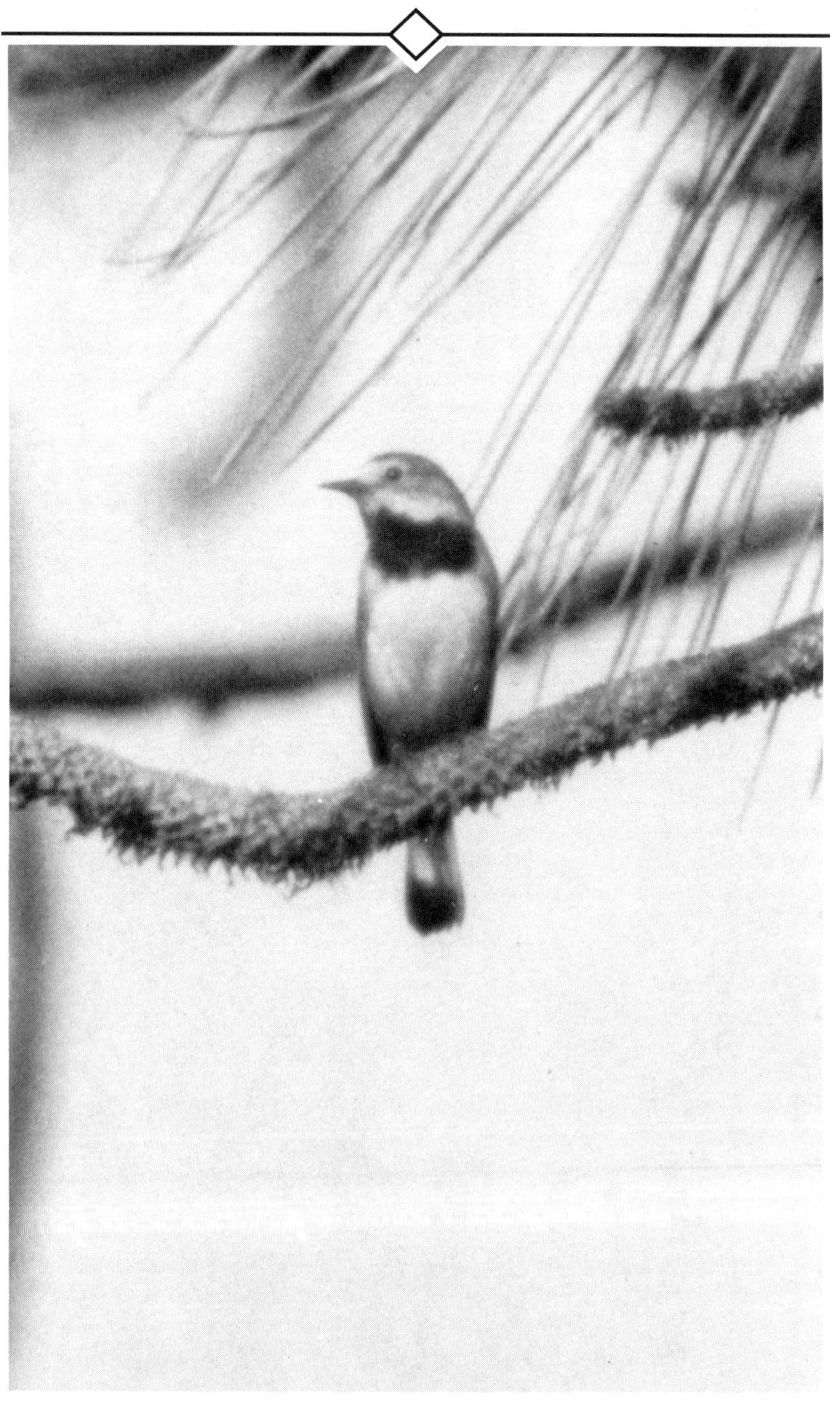

Much of what is known about the Bachman's warbler, perhaps the rarest passerine bird species in North America, was derived from historical accounts. *J. H. Dick/VIREO*

Bachman's Warbler

Paul B. Hamel
Tennessee Department of Conservation

SPECIES DESCRIPTION AND NATURAL HISTORY

Bachman's warbler (*Vermivora bachmanii*), perhaps the rarest passerine bird species in North America, is about four inches long, weighing probably 0.28 to 0.35 ounces. None have ever been weighed. The species is approximately the size of a Cape May warbler (*Dendroica tigrina*), but has a finer, more curved bill (Hamel 1986). Bachman's warbler is sexually dimorphic in plumage and in some morphological characters. Full adult plumage may not be acquired until the second prebasic molt (Hamel and Gauthreaux 1982).

Plumage colors[1] are as follows: The upperparts are yellowish olive-green; the wings are dark-brownish olive, hair-brown, or dark drab; the flanks are light drab or drab-gray; and the nape is olive-gray. Male underparts are spectrum yellow grading to lighter on the under-tail coverts, with a similarly yellow face and forehead, a black crown, and a black patch of variable size on the throat. The bend of the wing is yellow, and the inner margins of the tail feathers have patches of white.

1. These colors are taken from a book by Smythe (1974), in which he categorized color names. The book is a standard reference on colors in nature.

Females are paler, light spectrum yellow or light drab on the underparts. They have fewer black feathers, if any, and their eye-rings are whitish. The females also have much less yellow on the bend of the wing, and smaller white patches, if any, in the tail feathers. Chapman (1968) and Dingle (*in* Bent 1963) provide excellent descriptions of the plumage.

Foraging Behavior and Diet

Bachman's warblers are primarily insectivorous during the breeding season. Stomach analyses of a small sample of specimens showed remains almost entirely of insects and a few small seeds that may have been taken incidentally (Meanley and Mitchell 1958). Winter diet is probably much the same. Bachman's warbler has also been seen foraging about the flowers of majagua trees (probably *Hibiscus elatus*) (G. Proctor, pers. commun., Gundlach 1876). These observations suggest that the birds' winter diet may include nectar in addition to insects. The related Tennessee warbler (*Vermivora peregrina*) is a fruit and nectar feeder in the winter (Bent 1963).

Foraging behavior has been described in several ways and the accounts leave doubts as to which foraging methods predominate. Brewster and Chapman (1891) wrote that the Bachman's warblers foraged patiently about clumps of dead leaves and wads of drift lodged in cracks in twigs and shrubs. The birds were also observed gleaning from green foliage (Atkins *in* Scott 1890, Dawn 1962). Until birds can be found and observed in some detail, there is no way to identify the relative importance of these or other foraging behaviors to their daily or seasonal diet. Certain North American migrants in the Neotropics are territorial in the winter, such as hooded warblers (*Wilsonia citrina*) and Kentucky warblers (*Oporornis formosus*) (Morton 1980, Powell and Rappole 1986). Some species, such as northern parulas (*Parula americana*) or palm warblers (*Dendroica palmarum*), occur primarily in flocks. Others occur as a single individual/mixed-species flock, for example, golden-winged (*Vermivora chrysoptera*), blue-winged (*V. pinus*), worm-eating (*Helmitheros vermivorus*) (Rappole and Warner 1980), and cerulean warblers (*Dendroica cerulea*) (J. Fitzpatrick and S. Robinson, pers. commun.). Some appear both to flock and to hold territories around defendable food sources, as does the Tennessee (Morton 1980) and, possibly, the Cape May warbler (Hamel, pers. observ.).

Bachman's warblers are apparently related to golden-winged and blue-winged warblers (Hamel 1986); like those species, Bachman's warblers have been observed participating in mixed-species flocks (O. Garrido, pers. commun.). Bachman's warblers are aggressive, at least in migration (Atkins *in* Scott 1890), but no proof exists that they are actually restricted to a single bird per mixed-species flock by intraspecific aggression as are the golden-winged and blue-winged warblers. Nor can any proof be shown that Bachman's warblers are aggressive in defense of nectar resources as are Tennessee warblers. A group of species that occurs about nectar resources in Cuba includes the bee hummingbirds (*Mellisuga helenae*) and the Cuban emerald (*Chlorostilbon ricordii*), the Cape May warbler, and the Caribbean oriole (*Icterus dominicensis*).

The current meager knowledge of foraging behavior can be used to structure hypotheses about the birds, assuming that the competition for food is an important determinant of a species' position in a community. For example, patient probing in clumps of dead leaves is a behavior common to blue-winged and golden-winged warblers. In these species the trait is thought to be associated with a distribution pattern in which one individual defends its mixed-species foraging flock against conspecifics. Were this also true for Bachman's warbler, the number of mixed-species flocks in Cuba would determine the maximum population size of the species. However, if Bachman's warbler also forages on flowers or if it switches to these nectar resources as they become available, the maximum number of birds would be greater.

Breeding Habitat

No biological aspect of the Bachman's warbler has created as much controversy as its breeding habitat. Early observers were not quantitative ecologists, and modern ecologists have not had the opportunity to study populations of the birds. Widmann (1897) provided the clearest description of the breeding grounds of the population in the Mississippi Valley at the turn of the century. Wayne (1910) provided the only descriptions of the birds' breeding grounds on the Atlantic coastal plain (see Figure 1). Elements of the breeding habitat appear to be dense understory of one or more of a variety of shrubs, including *Rubus* sp.

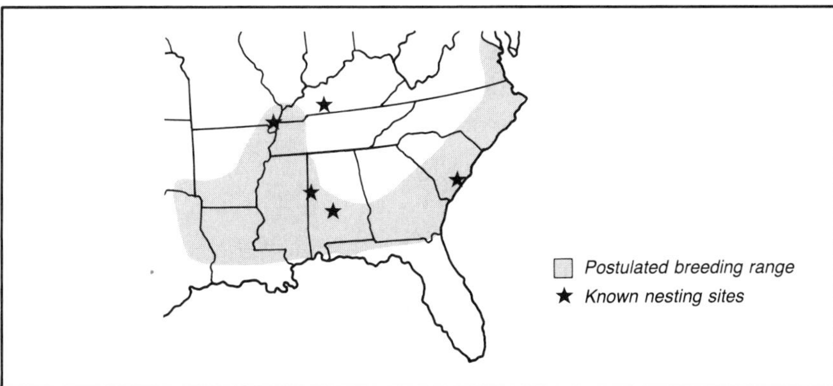

Figure 1. Bachman's warbler breeding range.

cane (*Arundinaria gigantea*) and other species, and the presence of canopy trees. Hooper and Hamel (1977) and Shuler (1977) reached different conclusions from evaluating these same original accounts. Hooper and Hamel identified disturbance to the canopy as the common factor of the observed nesting sites. Shuler believed that the birds were found in old-growth forests. Unfortunately, the nature of the combination of these elements is the important, but undefined, aspect of breeding habi- tat. Hamel (1986) suggested that the habitat might originally have been gap-phase successional openings in forest. Remsen (1986) suggested that the birds were obligate users of canebrakes. Rappole *et al.* (1983) postulated that the birds used secondary successional swamp forest—old-field succession in bottomlands. Individual territorial males have also been studied in dry longleaf-pine stands (Chamberlain 1958).

Range

Bachman's warblers are known to have bred or to have occurred during the breeding season in the Coastal Plain from Virginia to Texas and from Alabama to Oklahoma and Missouri (Dingle *in* Bent 1963). Breeding apparently occurred in forested river bottoms in this region (Widmann 1897, Wayne 1910) and occasionally outside of it (Embody 1907, Stevenson 1938). The birds were not found uniformly throughout that range, but rather only in localized areas of South Carolina, Alabama, Missouri, Arkansas, and Kentucky (Dingle *in* Bent 1963). It is suspected that the warbler occupied many more localities than those, but such sites were not found because of the difficulties of fieldwork encountered by early observers (Widmann 1897, Wayne 1910).

The winter range includes Cuba, the Isle of Pines, and occasionally the Florida mainland (Dingle *in* Bent 1963). One migrant individual was reported in Cay Sal, Bahamas (Riley 1905) (see Figure 2).

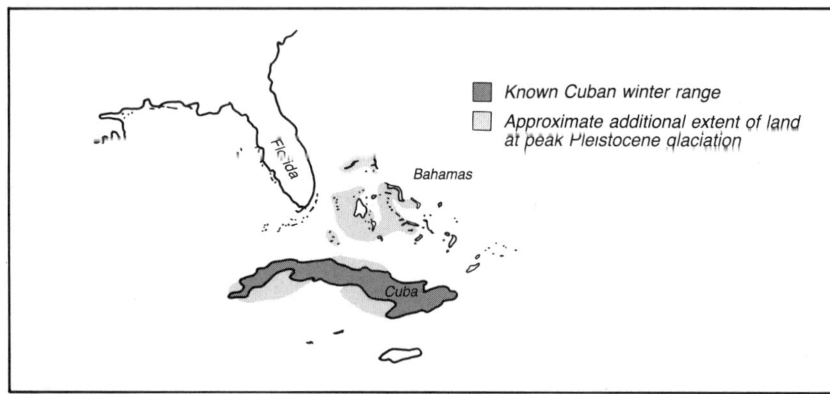

Figure 2. Bachman's warbler winter range.

SIGNIFICANCE OF THE SPECIES AND HISTORICAL PERSPECTIVE

Highly prized by birders, Bachman's warbler is one of the rarest birds in North America and is the least known of all warblers (except for the "lost" species like the carbonated warbler [*Dendroica carbonata*]). The primary value of studying this species lies in understanding the role of history in ecological processes and in conservation. The arguments and propositions raised concerning the history and current status of the species must be speculative, based upon circumstantial evidence, and thus are not scientifically satisfying.

Bachman's warbler has been considered rare since the time of its discovery (Hamel 1986). Because the bird was more numerous at a time when quantitative biological study was uncommon, a historical approach is the primary means of trying to infer its biology. This historical perspective can provide insights into this species and others as well, insights that can be the basis for hypotheses that can be tested later. Unfortunately, historical data cannot be used to refute any particular hypothesis.

The following historical account of the species' decline is speculative. The account begins with past, large-scale factors that Hamel (1986) believes are the cause of the species' rarity and proceeds to more recent and more proximate factors that have further reduced the species' population. The ultimate culprit may be the restriction of the bird's winter range to Cuba by some combination of geologic and ecologic factors. Human-caused changes such as habitat destruction on breeding and wintering grounds, and increased contact with brown-headed cowbirds (*Molothrus ater*), served to accelerate the warbler's decline. At reduced population levels, the bird became more susceptible to a variety of proximate environmental and genetic threats.

The causal factor of the Bachman's rarity is whatever caused the birds to become restricted to Cuba in the winter. This restriction established an upper limit to the birds' winter numbers and hence confined them to a finite population size. Ernst Mayr first raised this point many years ago (Amadon 1953). The cause of the restriction may have been physiological, related to their inability to winter farther north, or the inability to migrate farther (J. Barlow, pers. commun.). It might have been ecological, related to competitors such as orange-crowned warblers (*Vermivora celata*) (Hamel 1981), who were perhaps more efficient at foraging; hence, Bachman's warblers may have been excluded from the mainland parts of its winter range.

One other possibility lies in the recession and progression of sea levels in the Caribbean during the Pleistocene epoch. Presumably the warbler's trait of wintering in Cuba was established during this time. At present, 4 of 332 North American Neotropic migrants (Rappole *et al.* 1983) have winter ranges restricted to the West Indies. All four are wood warblers. The black-throated blue (*Dendroica caerulescens*) and Cape May warblers occur throughout the West Indies and are believed to have some portion of their population wintering on the Central American mainland. The other two species winter in restricted areas in the northeast Caribbean and are both listed as endangered by the U.S. Fish and Wildlife Service.

The current winter ranges of Bachman's and Kirtland's (*Dendroica kirtlandii*) warblers, respectively Cuba and the Bahamas, were both much larger during the Pleistocene than at present. Cuba now makes up almost half the land area of the Caribbean islands, and the Bahamas constitute approximately six percent. At the peak of glaciation, the Bahamas were larger than Cuba is today and constituted about 30 percent of the land area of the West Indies; Cuba more than 35 percent. The relatively great expanse of Cuba and the Bahamas during the glacial maxima in the Pleistocene epoch may be in part responsible for the restriction of winter range of these two species to the islands.

Simultaneous with the maximum enlargement of their island winter ranges, glacial maxima confined the breeding habitats for both species to regions closer to their winter grounds than at present (Webb, in press). Bottomland-hardwood forests probably stretched far down the river basins onto the continental shelf in the Gulf Coast region, making them closer to the winter grounds than is currently true. Under such conditions, a species with a limited physiological ability to migrate over water could have prospered. At the same time, the potentially competing orange-crowned warbler was apparently restricted to western North America (Mengel 1964).

As the glaciers receded, the situation changed in several ways, all of which served to reduce populations. Rising sea levels reduced the area available as winter habitat, slowly at first, but then dramatically. Receding glaciers made breeding habitats available at greater distances, increasing the chances of exposure to mortality on migration. At the same time, orange-crowned warblers presumably moved east with the advancing coniferous forests, and some of them began to winter in the Southeast. This in turn created competition for winter food resources with Bachman's warbler populations that wintered on the mainland.

Shugart (1984) suggests that of all the Caribbean islands, only Cuba may be large enough to support equilibrium vegetation in the dynamic weather system of that area. Hamel proposes that post-glacial Cuba supported smaller populations of Bachman's warblers than previously, that these populations were in dynamic equilibrium with losses to storms in winter and during migration, and that the bird's carrying capacity was shrinking along with the area of Cuba. The winter carrying capacity of the species would be further reduced, perhaps substantially, if a habitat of primary value to the warblers were lost to the island because of natural forces. Breeding populations found adequate habitats in the large swamps and bottomland forests of the major rivers of the south.

After European settlement, conversion of forests to agricultural land, both in Cuba and the United States, was an important factor contributing to the species' decline. Rappole *et al.* (1983) estimates that only 14 percent of native forest land in Cuba remains. It is likely that such forests support far fewer birds than did the island when it was more heavily forested. Hurricanes also may pose a significant threat to current populations.

On the breeding grounds, bottomland-hardwood forests have been reduced to much smaller areas and to much more fragmented conditions than previously. MacDonald *et al.* (1979) estimated that, in Tennessee alone, only 22 percent of the original bottomland forest remained in the late 1970s. The proportion was even less for Missouri and Arkansas.

Storms are a hazard to vegetation and birds in the Caribbean (Huntington and Barbour 1936). A 23-percent decline in Kirtland's warbler numbers from 1973 to 1974 was attributed to Hurricane Gilda (Walkinshaw 1983), which only reached tropical storm intensity when it crossed the Bahamas in October 1973. Ludlow Griscom (1948) was the first to suggest that the decline in Bachman's warbler populations might have been due to hurricanes. Gosselink and Harris (in press) raise the interesting possibility that the warblers were unable to cope with cowbird parasitism. Ample precedent for the effects of this parasitism on other species, such as Kirtland's warbler, exists (Walkinshaw 1983). Cowbirds apparently do not penetrate large tracts of old-growth bottomland hardwoods until after forest clearing has occurred (cf. Hamel in press).

Bachman's populations are presently so low that hurricanes in winter, storms on migration, inability of birds to find mates, genetic problems inherent in small populations (Soule 1986), or other uncontrollable factors may play a significant role in the species' continued decline.

CURRENT TRENDS

Bachman's warbler may be the rarest passerine bird species in North America. No breeding populations are presently known and no winter concentration areas have been identified. The species was listed by the U.S. Fish and Wildlife Service as endangered on March 11, 1967. Hamel (1986) reviewed published reports of the species through 1981. Recently, Dr. Orlando Torres Fundora (pers. commun.) supplied information on four winter sight records he had made as of 1984. Three of the reported sightings were made in the areas of the Zapata Swamp, Matanzas Province, Cuba.

The extensive destruction of forest land that was potential breeding habitat or winter habitat cannot be ignored as a possible cause of the species' low numbers. Harrison (1984) and others have asserted that the destruction of breeding habitat has brought numbers of Bachman's warblers to very low values. Remsen (1986) hypothesizes that the birds require canebrakes (*Arundinaria gigantea*). Holder (1970) notes that such plant communities were among the first to be destroyed as bottomlands were opened to agriculture. Rappole *et al.* (1983) dismisses such breeding habitat hypotheses by saying that the birds used second-growth swamp forests, of which relatively large areas still persist. Hooper and Hamel (1977) and Shuler (1977) use different definitions of breeding habitat to reach different conclusions about breeding habitat.

The inability of individuals to find mates in fragmented landscapes is yet another possible effect of the destruction of breeding habitat. This could cause further population reductions. Any of these breeding-ground-related hypotheses is sufficient to account for a decline in the species. Many of these explanations depend in one way or another on habitat reduction and fragmentation.

Hypotheses concerning destruction of winter habitats are as seductive and conflicting as those concerning breeding habitat. The absence of canebrakes from the Cuban flora suggests that Remsen's (1986) hypothesis may not apply to the birds' winter biology. Rappole *et al.* (1983) points to the drastic reduction of native Cuban forest as the proximate factor responsible for the species' low numbers.

Recent observations suggest that this may not be entirely the case. Bachman's warblers apparently associated with flocks of yellow-headed warblers (*Teretistris fernandinae*) (O. Garrido, pers. commun.). Yellow-headed warblers occur in a wide variety of habitats ranging from mangrove forest to dry scrub forest. The complement of North American migrants associated with the yellow-headed warbler also occur in these habitats (Hamel, pers. observ.). Thus, Bachman's warblers may not be directly habitat-limited in the winter. This is, however, largely speculation.

At the most proximate level, the factors now most likely to affect Bachman's warblers are random natural forces such as disease, predation, and storms.

MANAGEMENT

One habitat manipulation experiment has been conducted on the Francis Marion National Forest in South Carolina involving selective cutting of small groups of trees in the Santee River bottoms. The experiment created habitat that resembled breeding sites described in literature (Hamel 1986, R. Hooper, pers. commun., pers. observ.); hence, it may be possible to manage stands as habitat for Bachman's warblers if sufficient numbers can be found. No Bachman's warblers have begun breeding at the site (J. Cely unpubl. report). Little management can be done until breeding populations or winter concentrations of the birds can be found and studied.

PROGNOSIS

The future of Bachman's warbler appears as bleak today as it did in the 1880s before Charles Galbraith discovered the birds on migration near Mandeville, Louisiana. Stevenson (1972) indicated that the birds may be nearing extinction, but apparently this species has weathered changes in abundance before and may do so again.

RECOMMENDATIONS

It is crucial to attempt to find breeding populations and wintering concentrations. A much larger group of knowledgeable observers now exists than did a century ago to undertake this task. The International Council for Bird Preservation has recently given grants for searches in Tennessee and to support searches in Cuba in the winters of 1986–1987 and 1987–1988.

Further work in several areas is required. First, as Rappole *et al.* (1983) implies, conservation of forest lands in Cuban wintering grounds is important; recent conservation activities of the Cuban government are encouraging (Short and Carbonell 1987). Second, location of breeding populations and conservation of breeding habitats is also important. Substantial tracts of forested wetlands exist in the historic breeding range. Efforts should be undertaken by all groups to search for the birds in large tracts of bottomland forest in the South.[2] Third, systematic searches should be conducted on the Cuban wintering grounds. Fourth, study of other *Vermivora* in winter and of the mixed-species flocks of resident and migrant Cuban birds in winter, will provide important insights into the possibilities for conservation and management of Bachman's warblers when they are found.

2. Any observations should be reported to the appropriate Endangered Species Field Office of FWS, to the nongame wildlife program of the state fish and wildlife agency, and to the state's natural heritage program.

REFERENCES

Amadon, D. 1953. "Migratory birds of relict distribution: some inferences." *Auk* 70:461–469.

Bent, A.C. 1963. *Life Histories of North American Wood Warblers,* part 1. Dover publications. New York, New York.

Brewster, W. and F.M. Chapman. 1891. "Notes on the birds of the lower Suwanee River." *Auk* 8:125–138.

Chamberlain, E.B. 1958. "Bachman's warbler in South Carolina." *Chat* 22:73–74, 77.

Chapman, F.M. 1968. *The Warblers of North America.* Dover reprints. New York, New York.

Dawn, W. 1962. "Rare warbler of southern swamps is more often heard than seen." *Natural History* 71:41–43.

Embody, G.C. 1907. "Bachman's warbler breeding in Logan County, Kentucky." *Auk* 24:41–42.

Gosselink, J.G. and L.D. Harris. "Cumulative impacts of bottomland hardwood forest clearing," *in* R.R. Sharitz and J.W. Gibbons eds., *Freshwater Wetlands and Wildlife.* Savannah River Ecology Laboratory. Aiken, South Carolina. In press.

Griscom, L. 1948. "The changing seasons: a summary of spring migration." *Audubon Field Notes* 2:167–168.

Gundlach, J. 1876. *Contribution a la Ornithologica Cubana.* La Antilla. Habana, Cuba.

Hamel, P.B. 1981. A Hierarchical Approach to Avian Community Structure. Ph.D. dissertation. Department of Zoology. Clemson University. Clemson, South Carolina.

——. 1986. *Bachman's Warbler a Species in Peril.* Smithsonian Institution Press. Washington, D.C.

——. "Breeding bird populations on the Congaree Swamp National Monument, South Carolina," *in* R.R. Sharitz and J.W. Gibbons eds., *Freshwater Wetlands and Wildlife.* Savannah River Ecology Laboratory. Aiken, South Carolina. In press.

——. and S.A. Gauthreaux, Jr. 1982. "The field identification of Bachman's warbler (*Vermivora bachmanii* Audubon)." *American Birds* 36:235–240.

Harrison, H.H. 1984. *Wood Warblers World.* Simon and Schuster. New York, New York.

Holder, T. 1970. *Disappearing Wetlands in Eastern Arkansas.* Arkansas Planning Commission. Little Rock, Arkansas.

Hooper, R.G. and P.B. Hamel. 1977. "Nesting habitat of Bachman's warbler—a review." *Wilson Bulletin* 89:373–379.

Huntington, J.L. and T. Barbour. 1936. "The birds of Soledad, Cuba, after a hurricane." *Auk* 53:436–437.

MacDonald, P.O., W.E. Frayer and J.K. Clauser. 1979. *Documentation, Chronology, and Future Projections of Bottomland Habitat Loss in the Lower Mississippi Alluvial Plain.* U.S. Fish and Wildlife Service. Vicksburg, Mississippi.

Meanley, B. and R.T. Mitchell. 1958. "Food Habits of Bachman's warbler." *Atlantic Naturalist* 13:236–238.

Mengel, R.M. 1964. "The probable history of species formation in some northern wood warblers (Parulidae)." *Living Bird* 3:9–44.

Morton, E.S. 1980. "Adaptations to seasonal changes by migrant land birds in the Panama Canal Zone," pp. 437–453 *in* A. Keast and E.S. Morton eds., *Migrant Birds in the Neotropics: Ecology, Behavior, Distribution, and Conservation.* Smithsonian Institution Press. Washington, D.C.

Powell, G.V.N. and J.H. Rappole. 1986. "The hooded warbler," pp. 827–853 *in* R.L. DiSilvestro ed., *Audubon Wildlife Report 1986.* National Audubon Society. New York, New York. 1,096 pp.

Rappole, J.H. and D.W. Warner. 1980. "Ecological aspects of migrant bird behavior in Veracruz, Mexico," pp. 353–393 *in* A. Keast and E.S Morton eds., *Migrant Birds in the*

Neotropics: Ecology, Behavior, Distribution, and Conservation. Smithsonian Institution Press. Washington, D.C.

——., E.S. Morton, T.E. Lovejoy, III, J.L. Ruos and B. Swift. 1983. *Nearctic Avian Migrants in the Neotropics.* U.S. Department of Interior. Fish and Wildlife Service and World Wildlife Fund. Washington, D.C.

Remsen, J.V., Jr. 1986. "Was Bachman's warbler a bamboo specialist?" *Auk* 103:216–219.

Riley, J.H. 1905. "Birds of the Bahama Islands," pp. 347–368 *in* G.B. Shattuck ed., *The Bahama Islands.* MacMillan company. New York.

Scott, W.E.D. 1890. "A summary of observations on the birds of the Gulf Coast of Florida." *Auk* 7:14–22.

Short, L.L. and M. Carbonell. 1987. "In focus: Cuba." *World Birdwatch* 9:8–9. Autumn.

Shugart, H.H. 1984. *A Theory of Forest Dynamics.* Springer-Verlag. New York, New York.

Shuler, J. 1977. "Bachman's warbler habitat." *Chat* 41:19–23.

Smythe, F.B. 1974, 1981. *Naturalist's Color Guide,* and supplements. American Museum of Natural History. New York, New York.

Soule, M.E. 1986. *Conservation Biology: The Science of Scarcity and Diversity.* Sinauer Associates. Sunderland, Massachusetts.

Stevenson, H.M. 1938. "Bachman's warbler in Alabama." *Wilson Bulletin* 50:36–41.

——. 1972. "The recent history of Bachman's warbler." *Wilson Bulletin* 84:344–347.

Walkinshaw, L.H. 1983. *Kirtland's Warbler: The Natural History of an Endangered Species.* Cranbrook Institute of Science. Bloomfield Hills, Michigan.

Wayne, A.T. 1910. "Birds of South Carolina." *Contributions of the Charleston Museum* 1.

Webb, T. "Vegetational change in eastern North America from 18,000 to 500 yr. B.P." *Proceedings XIX Congressus Internationalis Ornithologicus.* In press.

Widmann, O. 1897. "The summer home of Bachman's warbler no longer unknown." *Auk* 14:305–309.

Paul B. Hamel is a zoologist with the Natural Heritage Program in the Ecological Services Division of the Tennessee Department of Conservation. He has studied Bachman's warbler since 1974.

The author wishes to thank the International Council for Bird Preservation, the Tennessee Department of Conservation, and the Nature Conservancy. Ralph Browning of the Bird Division at the U.S. National Museum kindly made available material for examination, and Larry Harris clarified some ideas in discussion.

Despite loss of habitat, pronghorn antelope numbers have continued an upward trend for 75 years, doubling during the last 10 years. *Marilyn Maring/L.L. Rue Enterprises*

The American Pronghorn

Jim Yoakum
Bureau of Land Management

SPECIES DESCRIPTION AND NATURAL HISTORY

Pronghorn (*Antilocapra americana*) are native only to North America, where they have existed since the middle of the Eocene epoch. This species of antelope is one of the smaller ungulates of North America, ranging in body length from 40 to 60 inches and weighing 90 to 120 pounds. Adult females generally weigh 20 to 30 percent less than males. Both males and females are reddish brown to tan on the upperparts; the underparts, rump, and bands under the neck are white. The top of the neck has a black mane. Males have black cheek patches just below the ears. Both sexes have permanent bone horncores, covered with a sheath of hair tissue that is shed yearly. Adult males' horns average 12 inches and have a branch, or "prong," which protrudes from the upper half of the horn and points forward. Generally, most females have horns, but some may not; horns of does are shorter than the ears.

Pronghorn have exceptionally large eyes, as compared to deer and other antelope, averaging about two inches in diameter. Pronghorn do not have "dew-hoofs"—third and fourth digits on their feet—as is characteristic of deer, and, unlike deer, they have a gall bladder. In contrast to the brownish-tan and white coloring of the adult pronghorn, adult deer are a uniform color. However, the reverse is true with fawns: The deer's coat is spotted while the pronghorn's is not. Both species have a white rump patch. Pronghorn and deer both inhabit many western rangelands concurrently. However, deer are most frequently associated with trees in hilly or mountainous terrain, whereas pronghorn occupy the wide-open, treeless plains and prairies. Although pronghorn may live to be 14 years old (Einarsen 1948), the average life span is from five to seven years.

Taxonomy and Distribution

There are five recognized subspecies of pronghorn. The American pronghorn (*A.a. americana*) are the most abundant and widespread subspecies; more than 90 percent of all antelopes in North America are pronghorn. The pronghorn ranges through the Great Plains of Canada and the United States and inhabits the Great Basin and adjacent mountainous states. Oregon pronghorn (*A.a. oregona*) are located mainly on the sagebrush-grassland steppes of southeast Oregon. This subspecies' peripheral boundaries, however, have not been adequately delineated. Mexican pronghorn (*A.a. mexicana*) are limited to ranges in south Arizona, New Mexico, Texas, and northern Mexico. Peninsular pronghorn (*A.a. peninsularis*) are found in central eastern Lower California. Sonoran pronghorn (*A.a. sonoriensis*) range from the west-central plains of Sonora, Mexico, north to central south Arizona (see Figure 1).

Of these five subspecies, the Peninsular and Sonoran pronghorn are currently classified in the International Union of Conservation and Nature's *Mammal Red Data Book* as endangered (Thornback and Jenkins 1982). Both primarily inhabit Mexico, although Sonoran pronghorn are also found in Arizona. Historical records show that these two subspecies were never as abundant as the other three (Nelson 1925, Yoakum 1978, 1986).

Approximately 54 percent of pronghorn live on private lands. The remaining herds are found on public lands administered by the Bureau of Land Management (13 percent), U.S. Fish and Wildlife Service (8 percent), Army Corps of Engineers (12 percent), military agencies (5 percent), and all other agencies (8 percent) (Colorado State University 1969).

Diet and Habitat

Pronghorn are opportunistic herbivores that select palatable and succulent forage. They graze primarily on grasses and forbs during the spring and summer and browse shrubs heavily during the fall and winter. Grasses consumed are the fine textured species such as

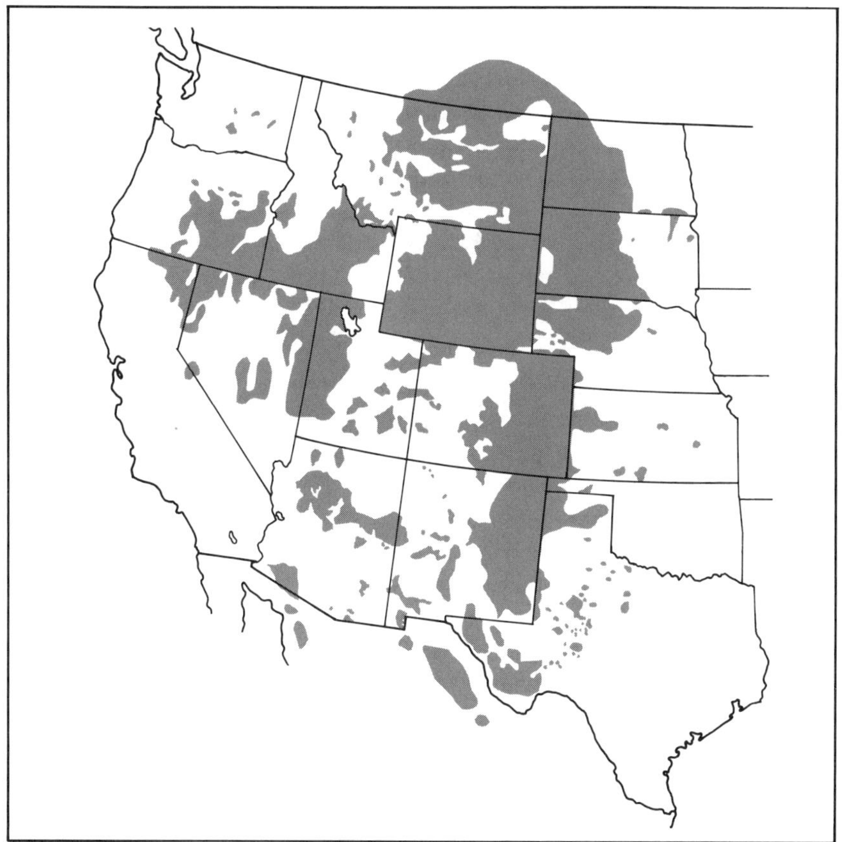

Figure 1. Distribution of the American pronghorn in North America.

Sandberg's bluegrass, not coarse bunch grasses such as bluebunch wheatgrass or ryegrass. Forbs are hightly preferred forage and consumed whenever available. It is postulated that pronghorn population dynamics for many rangelands are related to the availability of forbs. Shrubs, particularly sagebrush, also are highly important to pronghorn survival. This is especially true on rangelands receiving heavy snowfalls up to 24 inches in depth when sagebrush and other shrubs often are the only protruding forage available.

Approximately two-thirds of all pronghorn inhabit grasslands, nearly one-third occupy shrub-grassland, and less than one percent live in the hot deserts (Yoakum 1978).

Their population densities are directly related to the characteristics of the habitat. For example, occupied shrub-grassland steppes are typically large, wide open rangelands with no major physical barriers such as rivers, lakes, and thick forests. The average precipitation in these rangelands is 8 to 15 inches, with a snow level averaging less than

15 inches. It is desirable to have water available within a three- to five-mile radius; pronghorn consume one-quart to one gallon of water daily, especially during the summer.

Vegetation, however, is one of the most important habitat factors. The steppe-dwelling population requires a mixture of grass, forbs, and shrubs that are generally no higher than 24 inches. The preferred height is approximately 15 inches. The area should average about 50 percent nonvegetation and 50 percent vegetation—of which 40 to 60 percent is grass, 10 to 30 percent forbs, and 5 to 10 percent browse. The pronghorn's diet encompasses almost all plant species, with a higher preference toward succulent plants such as clovers, dandelions, evening primrose, some grasses, and preferred browse. Availability of shrubs can be extremely important for winter survival. Pronghorn also use a wide variety of ecosystems, including steppes, grasslands, meadows, forb patches, dry lake beds, and recent wild burns.

Breeding

Generally, an adult female pronghorn, or doe, heavy with young, will leave the herd and seek an isolated area to give birth. This takes place from mid-May to mid-June. Does usually give birth to twin fawns, each weighing about seven pounds. At first, the fawns lie quietly for most of the day, gathering their strength. When they are about one week old, they become more agile and can outrun a human. The fawns will begin to feed on vegetation when they are about three weeks old and feed entirely on plants when they are two months old.

Several weeks after birth, the fawns are taken by the female parent to join other juveniles. In this group, the young pronghorn play and forage under the supervision of two or three does. This period of their lives has a high mortality rate due to inclement weather, predation, disease, and lack of quality forage.

With the approach of fall and the breeding season, the young pronghorn grow rapidly, and it is difficult to distinguish a six-month-old yearling from an adult. At this stage, prime bucks begin to compete for breeding females. Bucks often spar to determine the dominant male, but rarely does this fighting lead to physical injury or death. The dominant buck then breeds with several available females.

Seasonal Activity

Winter is the most difficult time for survival. Preferred forage plants are hard to find, and at times it is difficult for the species to locate enough high-quality nutritious forage to maintain body strength. This is especially true in successive storms, low temperatures, and when deep snows have covered forage plants. When very cold winds and wet snows arrive simultaneously, the devastating chill can stress pronghorn severely. The lack of forage combined with adverse weather often causes high pronghorn losses in many rangelands.

Although some pronghorn, like caribou, migrate yearly, most pronghorn herds do not. However, they frequently make seasonal movements when snows become too deep or when desirable vegetation is more readily available on adjacent areas. For example, a herd in Oregon lives within a 20-square-mile area and spends 90 percent of its time on the higher elevation ranges where preferred forage and water are abundant. Winter snowstorms, however, force it down to the lowest 10 percent of the range, where there is only poor quality forage. But as soon as the snow recedes, the herd moves back to the preferred higher ranges.

Another herd in Oregon moves some 50 to 100 miles, depending on the severity of the winter. Most of the year is spent at the higher elevations because of abundant food and water sources. When the winter has light snows, the herd stays close, within 50 to 75 miles. Harsh winters with repeated heavy snows force the animals to move to lower elevations, but such winters are infrequent.

HISTORICAL PERSPECTIVE

The nineteenth century started with exploration, but ended as a period of heavy exploitation of natural resources. In 1804, when Lewis and Clark crossed the western North American prairies, there were an estimated 30 to 40 million buffalo and possibly the same number, or even more, of pronghorn. During this early period, pronghorn venison was a mainstay of the pioneers' diet and was sold commercially. Pronghorn were killed for sport as well as commercial hunting. The herds decreased drastically because of uncontrolled, yearlong killing regardless of the animal's sex or age. In the latter part of the century, laws were enacted that controlled hunting, but there was little, if any, enforcement.

Consequently, within a 75-year period, the vast herds of buffalo and pronghorn decreased from millions to remnant herds of hundreds. By the turn of the century, the pronghorn's world population had been decimated to a mere 10,000 animals—only a fraction of one percent of their original numbers—and some naturalists predicted that the species would become extinct.

Loss of suitable habitat also contributed to the decline of the pronghorn. As pioneers moved west, millions of acres were plowed for agriculture or grazed intensively by livestock, and water was diverted for irrigation and for use in the burgeoning towns and cities. Thus, the pronghorn could no longer find forage, water, or open space. This loss of habitat caused the herds to become fragmented and restricted to isolated, undeveloped areas.

With the beginning of the twentieth century, however, Americans became increasingly conservation minded. A concerned public demanded, and consequently paid for, implementation of wildlife management. It was around this time that most states implemented laws that forbade the hunting of pronghorn. State and federal wildlife agencies were financed to hire officers to enforce the laws. These agencies were staffed with trained biologists and administrators, resulting in the application of wildlife management principles and practices. Management techniques included a yearly census of herds to document production and the gathering of biological data regarding mortality factors such as disease, predation, and winter kills. From 1923 to 1925, the first extensive inventory of pronghorn was taken, and it was estimated that there were 26,700 in the United States, 1,300 in Canada, and 2,400 in Mexico (Nelson 1925). These numbers reflected a more than 100-percent increase since the early part of the century.

CURRENT TRENDS

Today, every state west of the Mississippi River, as well as the Mexican states of Chihuahua, Lower California, San Luis Potosi, and Sonora, maintain pronghorn (see Table 1). In Canada they are found in Alberta and Saskatchewan. From 1923 to 1983, the total North American pronghorn population increased from a total of 30,400 to 1,051,500 (Yoakum 1986) (see Table 2).

Pronghorn hunting data from 1934 to 1976 shows that regulated harvesting has not interfered with population increases. During this time, herds continued to increase 1,000 percent, although hunters killed more than two million animals. Some states with increasing pronghorn populations permit hunting of all sexes and ages.

SIGNIFICANCE OF THE SPECIES

Pronghorn are classified in a separate family by taxonomists because of two physical characteristics that differentiate this genus from other antelope—the prong and the shedding of the horn sheath every year (Hall and Kelson 1959). The pronghorn maintains a unique distinction

Table 1
Estimated Numbers of Pronghorns in the United States from 1923 to 1983 (Yoakum 1986)

State	1923[a]	1964[b]	1976[c]	1983[d]	Percent Population U.S.	Percent Population North America
Arizona	700	10,000	7,300	9,000	<1	<1
California	1,100	2,700	5,000	6,800	<1	<1
Colorado	1,200	15,200	31,000	57,500	6	5
Idaho	1,500	4,700	13,300	21,500	2	2
Kansas	10	100	1,100	1,200	<1	<1
Montana	3,000	95,000	71,200	161,500	16	15
Nebraska	200	9,000	9,800	9,000	<1	<1
Nevada	4,300	4,500	6,500	9,800	<1	<1
New Mexico	1,700	22,500	26,900	30,000	3	3
North Dakota	200	14,200	8,100	5,700	<1	<1
Oklahoma	20	200	200	400	<1	<1
Oregon	2,000	8,900	11,300	14,00	<1	<1
South Dakota	700	27,400	35,500	67,000	7	6
Texas	2,400	9,400	10,500	12,000	<1	<1
Utah	700	1,000	2,600	6,000	<1	<1
Wyoming	7,000	140,000	168,000	608,000	60	58
TOTAL	26,700	364,800	408,300	1,019,400	96	91

[a] Nelson 1925. All numbers are rounded to nearest 100, except Kansas and Oklahoma.
[b] Yoakum 1978. All numbers rounded to nearest 100.
[c] Yoakum 1978.
[d] Yoakum 1986.
Note: Data for Hawaii and Washington deleted as numbers were less than 100; <1 = less than one percent

Table 2
A Summary of the Estimated Pronghorn Numbers in North America from 1923 to 1983 (Yoakum 1986).

Country	1924[a]	1964[b]	1976[c]	1983[d]	Percent of world population in 1983
Canada	1,300	20,300	22,300	31,500	3
Mexico	2,400	1,200	1,000	600	<1
United States	26,700	364,800	408,300	1,019,400	97
TOTAL	30,400	386,300	431,600	1,051,500	100

[a] Nelson 1925.
[b] Yoakum 1978.
[c] Yoakum 1978.
[d] Yoakum 1986.
Note: All figures rounded to nearest 100; <1 = less than one percent.

among North American big game in that it is the only member of the family and genus. All other antelope in the world are included in the family Bovidae, along with cattle, buffalo, goats, and sheep.

Because of the pronghorn's accelerated population increases during the past decade, it is now second only to deer (all species) as the most abundant big-game animal in the United States. The pronghorn is also second only to deer in the number of animals taken by hunters. The Nevada Department of Wildlife conducted an economic analysis of big-game hunters from 1985 to 1986 and concluded that pronghorn hunters were willing to pay approximately $240 per harvested animal at the current level of population (F. R. Kay, pers. commun.). If this figure was used for pronghorn harvested throughout the United States, the potential economic value of adult males would be approximately $4.5 million.

MANAGEMENT

One of the most important techniques of wildlife management is estimating numbers of wild animals from surveys. Most pronghorn are counted yearly through aerial surveys during the summer and fall to determine production, and are counted again in winter to record mortalities. These counts are often more complete and accurate than those of other big-game species, such as elk and deer, because pronghorn live in open country and are easily seen.

Another wildlife management technique is the translocation of small herds of antelope to unoccupied portions of its historic range. The practice of trapping and translocation started in 1937 in New Mexico. Since then, most states have successfully re-established hundreds of pronghorn on historic rangelands. For example, Colorado transplanted some 1,000 pronghorn in 24 different sites during a 10-year period; Texas captured and released 5,000 pronghorn from 1939 to 1975.

Improved rangeland management practices have also contributed to increasing pronghorn populations. Unproductive farms—thousands of frail prairie lands that were abandoned by homesteaders and unsuitable to intensive agriculture—were returned to native vegetation. The pronghorn has also benefited indirectly from water distribution projects and mixture seedings of grass, forbs, and shrubs. Mixture seedings are more beneficial to the pronghorn than single-grass plantings because they are more nutritious.

Fences designed to be less restrictive to pronghorn movements have also helped the herds. Pronghorn have difficulty jumping over or going through fences constructed to control domestic cattle because, historically, pronghorn habitat contained no similar obstacles. These fences can be a significant factor to pronghorn mortality when they restrict the animal's movements to procure food and water, or to escape from deep snows and enemies. Certain designs, such as three or four strands of barbed wire with the bottom wire at least 15 inches off the ground, enable antelope to move beneath them. Fences constructed of woven-wire to control domestic sheep can be impenetrable barriers that block pronghorn movement from one range to another.

The development and improvement of water availability and distribution is a habitat enhancement technique that has proven successful when applied to pronghorn rangelands. Wildlife agencies have constructed hundreds of water catchments specifically for pronghorn. The most prevalent are "guzzlers," which collect and store precipitation for use during dry seasons. In addition, many water developments built for domestic livestock have provided water for pronghorn and other wildlife. For example, over 1,000 water developments were constructed during a 10-year period for livestock and wildlife, including pronghorn, in Malheur County in southeast Oregon (Heady and Bartolome 1977).

Two organizations meet on a scheduled basis to coordinate and disseminate information on pronghorns. The Interstate Antelope Conference coordinates census methods in California, Idaho, Nevada, and Oregon (Salwasser 1980).[1] Annual meetings have been conducted since 1949, making it one of the earliest and most continuous organizations devoted to management of a single wildlife species in North America. The Pronghorn Antelope Workshop, started in 1965, is dedicated to the biology and management of the species (Autenrieth 1978).[2] Some 50 to 75 wildlife biologists attend, representing provincial, state, and federal wildlife agencies in Canada, Mexico, and the United States. The proceedings of these workshops are an invaluable source of information and include much of the recent field data available on the ecology, biology, and management of the species and its habitat.

Management Guides

There are four sets of management guides for pronghorn and their habitat. Two of these have been developed by the organizations discussed above. A third, Kindschy *et al.* (1982), is keyed to the Great Basin ecosystem but when properly evaluated has application for other pronghorn habitats.[3] The fourth by Yoakum (1980) provides examples

1. Interstate Antelope Conference in care of: Texas Parks and Wildlife Department, 4200 Smith School Road, Austin, Texas 78744.

2. Pronghorn Antelope Workshop in care of: California Department of Fish and Game, P.O. Box 1623, Alturas, California 96101.

3. Wildlife Habitats on Managed Rangelands: U.S. Forest Service, Pacific Northwest Forest and Range Experiment Station, 809 NE Sixth Avenue, Portland, Oregon 97232.

and techniques of maintaining and improving pronghorn habitat management, emphasizing vegetation management, water improvements, fence construction design, and livestock grazing systems.[4]

PROGNOSIS

Pronghorn populations have continued on an upward trend for over 75 years, doubling in numbers during the last 10 years. This increase in numbers has occurred despite loss of habitat to human occupation and development. No wildlife agency at the 1986 Pronghorn Antelope Workshop could definitely explain why this accelerated increase continues. It is apparent that harvest techniques are conservative, and rangelands have sufficient forage and water to support even more animals. It is not known how long this increase in numbers will continue. The normal mortality factors of predation, harsh winters, fences, hunting, and road kills have continued, but not at a pace to check expanding herds. The population peak will be reached eventually, as it is directly related to human population growth and development of western rangelands.

It is apparent that land managers, both private and governmental, understand how to implement range management practices that are compatible with pronghorn habitat needs. Moreover, a current depressed cattle market has decreased livestock use of some western rangelands. This reduced use of forage and waters could be a factor that has favored the pronghorn in recent years.

During the last half of the nineteenth century, uncontrolled hunting and loss of habitat brought about the biocide of the world's population of pronghorn. There is no reason, however, to believe that hunting will be a problem in this century. During the last 50 years, wildlife agencies have proven that conservative hunting programs have been a contributing factor in the increase of pronghorn numbers. However, demands on the western rangelands to meet accelerating human population growth and increased farming and energy development eventually will halt pronghorn increase and even reverse them in some locales. For example, in the Central Valley of California, where pronghorn historically numbered thousands, less than 50 were present as of 1986. Wildlife biologist A. Starker Leopold warned us to "watch out for insidious rates of loss." These slow decreases in numbers are both cumulative and devastating over time. Such decreases already are evident in some valleys of Montana and Wyoming.

4. Habitat Management Guides for the American Pronghorn Antelope: U.S. Bureau of Land Management, Federal Center Building 50, Denver, Colorado 80225.

Wildlife managers need to be aware of the minute changes in habitat condition that also accumulate and cause changes in habitat quality:

> In both the Forest Service and the Bureau of Land Management, fiscal support for wildlife management and research programs has declined in contrast to increased funding for commodity production services. As a result, on-the-ground wildlife managers have difficulty even keeping abreast of developments and have virtually no chance of coping with developmental impacts on important wildlife habitats (*Audubon Wildlife Report 1986*).

With regard to range management practices, it is important to determine whether vegetative stands will be manipulated to the detriment of preferred feeding habitats of the pronghorn and whether fences constructed to contain livestock will limit pronghorn movements and cut them off from critical rangelands. If wildlife agencies do not have the funds or staff to check and control such practices, human development of pronghorn habitat will eventually be harmful to the species' population size.

RECOMMENDATIONS

Present-day management techniques have been good enough to help augment pronghorn populations. The greatest challenge today is to maintain current management strategies which have resulted in quality habitats and increased populations. Some recommendations are:

1. Disseminate and implement the management practices documented in the four management guides discussed. Most of these practices have been used successfully and are readily available. For example, there is a wealth of information showing adverse impacts on antelope of sagebrush conversion, as well as adequate documentation of proper techniques for herd transplants. The challenge will be to keep managers financed adequately to enable them to implement these practices.
2. Studies should be made to determine precisely the reasons for pronghorn population increase. With this information, managers may better understand what to do if population numbers become depressed.
3. The Pronghorn Antelope Workshop and the Interstate Antelope Conference should be encouraged to continue collecting and exchanging vital information on the pronghorn and publishing proceedings of their meetings. In addition, these groups should continue recommending management guidelines for the species and its habitat.

REFERENCES

Audubon Wildlife Report 1986. "Introduction," page XIX, by Roger DiSilvestro, ed., and Amos Eno. National Audubon Society. New York, New York. 1,094 pp.

Autenrieth, R. 1978. "Guidelines for the Management of Pronghorn Antelope," pp. 472–526, *in* M.W. Barrett ed., *Proceedings of the 18th Pronghorn Antelope Workshop.* Jasper, Alberta, Canada.

Colorado State University. 1969. *Fish and Wildlife Resources on the Public Lands.* Public Land Law Review Commission, Chapter V. U.S. Government Printing Office. Washington, D.C.

Einarsen, A.S. 1948. *The Pronghorn and Its Management.* Wildlife Management Institute. Washington, D.C. 235 pp.

Hall, E.R. and K.R. Kelson. 1959. *The Mammals of North America.* Two volumes. Ronald Press Company. New York. 1,083 pp.

Heady, H.F. and J. Bartholome. 1977. *The Vale Rangeland Rehabilitation Program: The Desert Repaired in Southeastern Oregon.* U.S. Department of Agriculture, Forest Service. Pacific Northwest Range and Experiment Station. Resource Bulletin PNW-70. Portland, Oregon. 139 pp.

Kindschy, R.R., C. Sundstrom, and J.D. Yoakum. 1982. Wildlife Habitats in Managed Rangelands—the Great Basin of Southeastern Oregon: Pronghorns. Pacific Northwest Forest and Range Experimental Station. U.S. Department of Agriculture, Forest Service. General Technical Report PNW-145. Portland, Oregon. 18 pp.

Nelson, E.W. 1925. *Status of the Pronghorn Antelope, 1922–24.* U.S. Department of Agriculture Bulletin No. 1346. Washington, D.C. 64 pp.

Salwasser, H. 1980. *Pronghorn Antelope Population and Habitat Management in the Northwestern Great Basin Environments.* Interstate Antelope Conference. Alturas, California. 62 pp.

Thornback, J. and M. Jenkins. 1982. *The International Union of Conservation and Nature (IUCN) Mammal Red Data Book: Part 1.* IUCN. Gresham Press. Surrey, United Kingdom. 516 pp.

Yoakum, J. 1978. "Pronghorn," pp. 103–131, *in* J.L. Schmidt and D.L. Gilbert eds., *Big game of North America, Ecology and Management.* Wildlife Management Institute. Washington, D.C. 494 pp.

——. 1980. *Habitat Management Guides for the American Pronghorn Antelopes.* U.S. Department of Interior, Bureau of Land Management. Technical note 347. Denver, Colorado. 77 pp.

——. 1986. "Trends in Pronghorn Populations: 1800–1983." *Proceedings of the Pronghorn Antelope Workshop.* Reno, Nevada. In press.

Jim Yoakum is a certified wildlife biologist with the Bureau of Land Management and has lived in pronghorn habitat for over 35 years. He is also a wildlife professor at the University of Nevada in Reno.

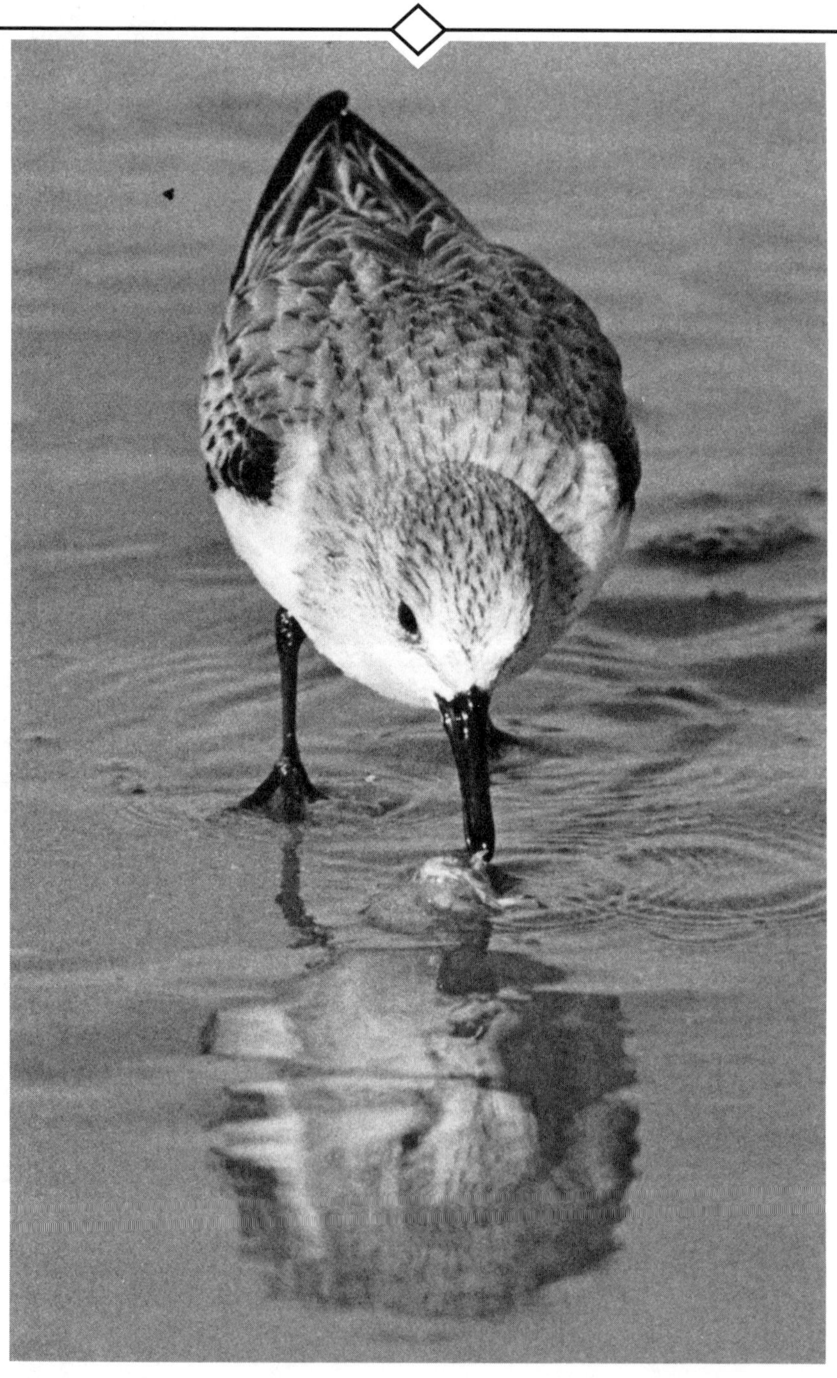

Sanderlings, like many other shorebirds, congregate in migratory staging areas, making them vulnerable to harrassment, development, and pollution. *Kenneth W. Gardiner*

The Sanderling

J.P. Myers
National Audubon Society

SPECIES DESCRIPTION AND NATURAL HISTORY

The sanderling (*Calidris alba*), a member of the sandpiper family (Scolopacidae), is sparrow-like in size, ranging in weight from approximately 40 to 110 grams (1.4 to 3.9 ounces). Most of this variation in weight is seasonal and related to migration. Population average weights in mid-winter typically run between 45 and 60 grams (1.6 and 2 ounces), depending on the latitude (Myers *et al.* 1985). An individual sanderling reaches its peak weight at staging sites during northbound migration. For example, in the Delaware Bay during May, the population average weight rises 55 to 85 grams (1 to 2 ounces) over a three-week period as birds put on weight in preparation for the final leg of migration to arctic nesting grounds.

Sanderlings in basic nonbreeding plumage sport a pale grey, almost white appearance with a contrasting black patch at the bend of the folded wing. In flight, their wings have a conspicuous white wing-bar set off by black leading and trailing wing edges.

Beginning in April, sanderlings start to molt into alternate breeding plumage and by June show a contrasting pattern of rich chestnut on the head, back, and chest, set against pure white on the lower breast and belly. The deepness of the upperparts' coloration varies somewhat, ranging from deep rufous-chestnut to silver gray spotted with black. Even in the lightest breeding-plummaged birds, however, the upper breast and head are clearly and sharply demarcated from the white of the lower breast and belly.

Juvenile sanderlings are readily distinguished from adults after fledging in July through their first month or two on the wintering grounds in September, principally because of the scaled appearance of their back and a pronounced black cap and strong dark eye patch. Gradually through this period, the distinguishing feathers are molted or worn off. The upper breasts of sanderlings early in their first autumn may also be suffused with a grayish wash, but this fades rapidly. Although it is very difficult to distinguish first-winter birds from adults through binoculars past October, in the hand they can be identified reliably until January by the presence of thin terminal bars on their upper rump feathers; these bars wear off by late winter.

The sanderling's bill, legs, and feet are black. Compared with other sandpipers, the sanderling's bill is relatively short and stubby in proportion to body size. The species also differs from all other sandpipers in that it lacks a hind toe. These specializations of bill and foot no doubt represent adaptations to running and feeding on sandy substrates, which are firmer than the muddy surfaces used by most other sandpipers.

Breeding Season

Sanderlings migrate to high arctic tundra for breeding, especially the central Canadian arctic islands in the New World and the Taimyr Peninsula of central Siberia. Along with knots (*Calidris canutus*), sanderlings are one of the most northerly breeding sandpipers (Cramp and Simmons 1983). Sanderlings nest in dry, sparsely vegetated sites that are near ponds or lakes; after hatching, the sanderling young are led to marshy swales associated with these water bodies. Sanderlings eat surface-dwelling insects—craneflies (tipulids) and midges (chironomids)—and spiders. Nesting commences shortly after arrival at the site, when much of the tundra surface is still covered by snow. Sanderlings compress their entire reproductive season, which includes display, nesting, incubation, parental care, and post-fledging preparation for migration, into some 60 days between mid-June and mid-August. Chicks hatched after July 31 have little chance for survival after fledging.

Female sanderlings produce one or two clutches a year; each clutch contains no more than four eggs. Details of the mating system are poorly established and suggest considerable variation among birds and populations (Parmelee 1970, Pienkowski and Green 1976). Monogamy may prevail in some areas. Alternatively, some female sanderlings mate sequentially in a polyandrous fashion: The first clutch is sired by one male, the second by another. Females depart from the breeding site shortly after incubation commences, and the male normally incubates the clutch and cares for the brood. In some cases, the female may lay and then assume care of the second clutch. Around the time when young are capable of flight, the adult caring for that brood departs. As a result, young sanderlings migrate south after all adults have left.

Migration

Southbound migration late in the summer carries sanderlings to temperate and tropical beaches throughout the world (Cramp and Simmons 1983). In the Western Hemisphere from November to February, during the the central core of the nonbreeding season, most sanderlings are in one of three regions (see Figure 1): 1) the Pacific Coast of northwest Chile and southwest Peru; 2) the southeast Atlantic Coast of Brazil; or 3) the U.S. Pacific Coast between central Washington and southern California.

The duration of migration varies considerably among destinations (Myers *et al.* 1985). In general, birds that winter farther south spend less time on the wintering site, arriving and departing earlier. For example, returning birds begin to appear in coastal California in late July, but not until September in Peru or Chile. Among the first arrivals

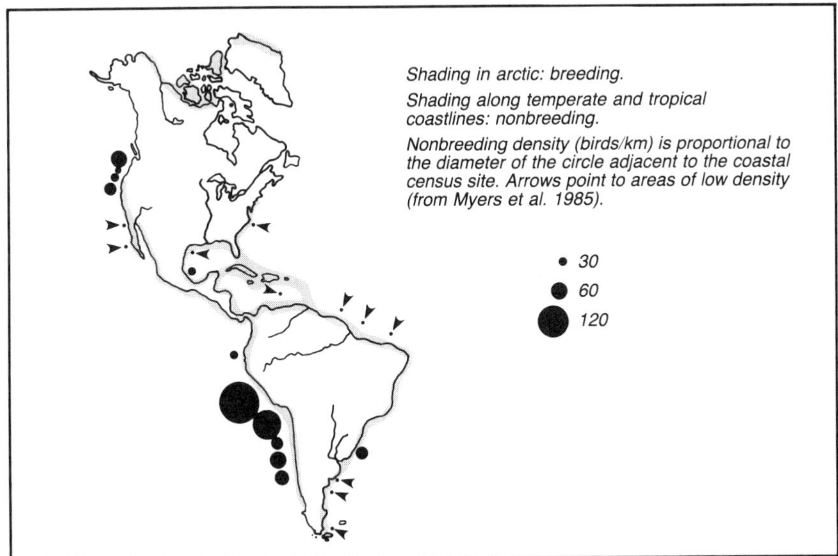

Figure 1. Sanderling distribution in the Western Hemisphere.

in both regions are individuals that will remain at the site until northward migration begins. Yet individual migration schedules differ also, even at a single site. While the first returning birds reach coastal California in July, the bulk do not arrive until August; some do not return until November. Departure schedules on northbound migration are also variable, spread from March through early May.

Almost all sanderlings wintering in North America migrate north in spring. Significant numbers from South American nonbreeding sites, however, do not. These appear to be principally birds hatched in the previous breeding season. None breed while remaining in South America.

Migration routes for sanderlings in the New World are only partially known (Myers *et al.* 1984a). Individuals from wintering populations in Peru and Chile head north along two different routes: 1) via the Pacific Coast, with stopovers in northwest Oregon and southwest Washington; and 2) via the Texas coast and north through the plains. A few sanderlings from Peru and Chile each year also move north along the U.S. Atlantic Coast, pausing in Delaware Bay. Birds from Peru and Chile return south largely along the U.S. East Coast or alternatively back through coastal Texas. A few color-banded individuals migrating north along the Pacific Coast have been observed southbound on the Atlantic. Hence, the sanderlings' route encompasses an immense circumcontinental ellipse.

Color-banded sanderlings from nonbreedings sites in Brazil have been seen on beaches in mid-Atlantic states in spring and in Massachusetts during autumn. Presumably, many of the some 50,000 sanderlings staging in May in Delaware Bay are from Brazil (Dunne *et al.* 1982, Myers 1986); among them are also individuals color-banded on wintering sites in western Florida.

Winter. "Winter" for sanderlings is the period of nonbreeding residency between southbound and northbound migrations. The nonbreeding season is winter only in the Northern Hemisphere.

Whatever the details of climate, ten months of the year find sanderlings away from their breeding grounds, and the majority of this time is spent in residence at a single wintering site. Most of the data on this point come from intensive work with banded sanderlings in California (Myers 1984, Myers *et al.* 1986), Peru (Castro and Myers 1987), and Chile (Tabilo, Sallaberry, and Myers, unpubl. data). Movements within a given winter are quite restricted, with most individual birds spending four to eight months within a single 10-kilometer (six-mile) sector of coast. Individuals in North America also rarely switch their wintering site from one year to the next. Behavioral experiments suggest that birds imprint on a wintering site in the months between October and February following hatching, and normally this site becomes their permanent winter home to which they return throughout their life (Myers *et al.* 1986). Peruvian birds have been observed to be less site-faithful than California birds; they range more broadly within a single season and are more likely to switch sites between years.

Sanderlings' principal prey in migration and during winter are sandy beach invertebrates, especially hippid crabs (*Emerita*), known in the United States as sand crabs or mole crabs and in Peru as *mui-mui*. These crabs live buried in the sand in the wave-washed zone, where they feed on small particles of decomposing plant or animal bodies carried in receding waves. Crabs obtain this food by sticking their frond-like antennae into the waves. Once the wave has washed back, the crabs withdraw its antennae and retreat beneath the surface. This behavior of *Emerita* underlies the sanderling's incessant running up and down in front of waves: the crabs are most accessible to foraging birds at the tail end of the retreating waves, before the crabs retract, but after the water depth diminishes enough to allow the birds access. Sanderlings also take other invertebrates from sandy beaches, including isopods, amphipods, polychaete worms, and small bivalve mollusks, and respond opportunistically to rich food sources. In Delaware Bay each spring, for example, sanderlings join other shorebird species in consuming large quantities of horseshoe crab (*Limulus polyphemus*) eggs. Along beaches in coastal Texas, sanderlings feed on the corn chips and cheese puffs left by people using the beach.

While most sanderlings spend the winter in conspecific flocks, a proportion also defend exclusive feeding territories (Myers *et al.* 1979). The likelihood of defense varies in relation to prey abundance and to the risk of predation by raptors (Myers 1984). Defense is very unlikely when raptors are present. When predators are absent, however, defense is most probable in beach sectors of intermediate prey abundance. The flocks themselves are not coherent social units, but instead aggregations whose composition fluctuates rapidly through time (Myers 1983).

SIGNIFICANCE OF THE SPECIES

Sanderlings share with people a weakness for wave and sand. In August, as people flock toward beaches throughout the Northern Hemisphere, sanderlings also converge upon the wave-washed zone. This means that even if few people can name sanderlings, they recognize the "wind-up toys" that taunt incoming waves on the beach.

To date, no one has measured the direct impact of sanderlings on human economic activity. One might first look to the number of cross-country and cross-hemispheric flights the author has made for ecological studies on the species. A second impact would be the economic sacrifices made by field assistants for the opportunity to participate in field research. Less directly, but perhaps with a broader impact, resorts, motels, and condominiums on each U.S. coastline appeal to potential customers by using the species' name or image. Are such facilities more competitive when named, for example, *The Sanderling Inn* than *The Horseshoe Crab*? Does a beach town attract more visitors because sanderlings cavort in its surf?

Whatever the economic benefit associated with the species, it is not large; hence, the sanderling's significance lies elsewhere. It can be seen first in the bird's contribution to the public's definition of the beach environment and in the educational potential this in turn offers for environmental awareness. This potential is scarcely exploited, save for efforts by the World Wildlife Fund to use the sanderling as a theme species to mobilize contributors to migratory bird conservation. Chilean and Peruvian conservationists have also mounted public awareness campaigns using sanderlings to interest people in coastal zone issues.

Second, sanderlings have proven to be a useful species around which to organize international cooperative efforts in migratory bird conservation research. Over the last seven years, collaborators in six countries have banded together and studied the species, using research as a vehicle for conservation training of resident biologists in each of the countries. This work has catalyzed the genesis of the Western Hemisphere Shorebird Reserve Network (see "Management"). Along the U.S. West Coast, the species has also spawned research that involves volunteers in beach conservation, including many members of National Audubon Society.

Third, sanderlings have become a "white rat" for shorebird research in the New World, Europe, and Africa. Studies have investigated their nesting (Parmelee 1970), migration (Myers *et al.* 1985, Summers and Underhill 1987, Summers *et al.* 1987), population structure (Myers *et al.* 1986), winter spacing behavior (Myers *et al.* 1980, Myers 1984), energetics (Connors *et al.* 1981, Castro 1987), and feeding (Myers *et al.* 1980, Maron and Myers 1985). Collectively, this work makes sanderlings ecologically and behaviorally one of the best known of all shorebirds and hence an important source of guidance in conservation matters.

HISTORICAL PERSPECTIVE

Throughout the early 1900s, market hunters killed shorebirds in large numbers for human consumption. Over the years, this annual take devastated many shorebird populations, pressing several species like the Eskimo curlew[1] (*Numenius borealis*) to the brink of extinction. Sanderlings were among the species hunted. Bent (1927) quotes observers who reported baskets full of sanderlings taken by a single gunner in one tidal cycle in 1872. But few data either document the extent of sanderling kills or describe the populational consequences. U.S. passage of the Migratory Bird Treaty Act of 1918 effectively stopped market hunting (Senner and Howe 1984). Since then, the long-term trend for shorebird numbers has generally been upward.

CURRENT TRENDS

While the long-term trends viewed over a century are positive, recent data spanning the last 15 years suggest that the general upward swing in shorebird numbers has been reversed. Coordinated by Manomet Bird Observatory in collaboration with the U.S. Fish and Wildlife Service, the International Shorebird Survey (ISS) has revealed widespread declines of shorebirds migrating south on the East Coast in autumn (Howe *et al.* 1986). Begun in 1972, the ISS covers 12 species, of which 10 declined duing a decade of monitoring. The average species decreased by 44 percent. Sanderlings showed the most pronounced drop, falling a cumulative 80 percent since 1972; this trend was steady and monotonic.

Along the Atlantic seaboard the survey covers sanderlings that winter in Peru, Chile, and Brazil. Few data from the wintering sites in South America are available to test the downward trend. Preliminary analyses from several sites in Peru and Chile are consistent with the ISS results, except for sites at the southern end of the distribution in Chile, (Castro, Ortiz, Sallaberry, and Myers, unpubl. data) which in fact represent a miniscule portion of birds wintering along that coastline. Complications related to the effects of El Niño current during this period make interpreting these trends problematic without additional study.

Data from the Pacific Coast, the third winter population center of the New World sanderlings, do not suggest a consistent long-term trend. Numbers at one census site in central California held steady through the late 1970s, dropped significantly in the mid-1980s, and then rose again (see Figure 2) (Myers, ms. in prep.).

The ISS results, if true, reflect a decline of alarming proportions, perhaps the largest to be reported of any common, widespread North American species during the middle of this century. Without additional corroboration and further study, the causes of this decline can

1. For a discussion of this species see "The Eskimo Curlew" chapter in this volume.

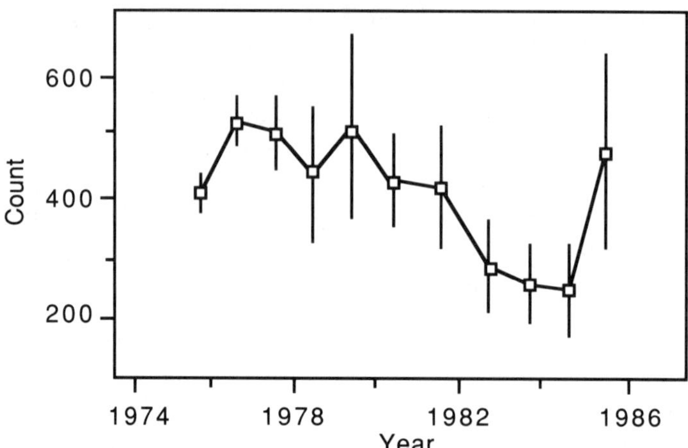

Figure 2. Midwinter average of sanderlings at Bodega Bay, California, 1975 to 1987.

only be speculated. The monotonic nature of the decline would suggest that it is not a result of short-term environmental variations such as El Niño. The fact that California sanderling populations are not declining similarly indicates that the drop does not stem from cumulative environmental change across the arctic; if this were so, Pacific Coast birds would demonstrate the same pattern.

There are, however, two pervasive factors that could account for the decline in sanderling numbers. The first trend involves the widespread application of pesticides in agricultural lands along the Pacific coast of South America, which may interfere with sanderling migratory competency. In the desert coast of Peru, sanderlings congregate around river mouths downstream of agricultural valleys. The river waters are heavily diverted through fields for irrigation and then channeled in ditches and canals to the ocean, where they spill out over the beach where sanderlings often feed, drink, and bathe. These rivulets reek of pesticides. A plausible speculation would be that the birds ingest pesticide-laden foods from these habitats. Were this to occur in April and May, when the birds lay on fat for northward migration, their energy for the journey, stored as lipid reserves, would surely be contaminated. As reserves are used up during migration, the contaminants would be released into the bloodstream and become concentrated in remaining lipid deposits, principally reproductive organs and the brain.

To date, no convincing demonstration has been made of chlorinated hydrocarbon impacts on shorebird populations. Likewise, no studies examine sublethal effects of pesticide contamination on migratory performance of any bird species, such as its competency of orientation. Sublethal effects should be tested for a variety of pesticides using laboratory experiments on orientation, coupled with field observations of pesticide effects during migration.

The second factor that may be affecting sanderling population numbers is the continued degradation and destruction of coastal habitats important to migration. Coastal wetland destruction continues throughout the hemisphere, its pace widely documented in North America (Gosselink and Baumann 1980). The only two known major staging sites in North America for sanderlings, one on beaches near the mouth of the Columbia River in Oregon and Washington and the other on New Jersey beaches in Delaware Bay, have only been discovered in the last 10 years (Dunne *et al.* 1982, Myers *et al.* 1984b). Despite intensive searches, no comparable site has been located on the Gulf Coast of Texas and Louisiana, even though sighting records demonstrate that this pathway is the principal route for sanderlings northbound from Peru and Chile. The Gulf Coast has been the site of widespread construction in coastal beaches and wetlands during the last 30 years.

The second hypothesis of sanderling population decline invokes human disruption of an undocumented staging site along the Texas coast. The fact that Delaware Bay in the heart of megalopolis went so long undiscovered lends credence to a necessary assumption: A Texas site could have been destroyed before it was discovered. Unfortunately, testing this hypothesis may prove impossible.

MANAGEMENT

Sanderlings share with other shorebird species several natural history characteristics that heighten their susceptibility to population loss (Myers *et al.* 1987a). These are: 1) long-distance migration along a chain of critical sites, moving in flights that are demanding in energetic requirements and constrained in time; 2) bottleneck migratory pathways that place large portions of entire sanderling populations at risk at once, violating a fundamental assumption of the "rare = endanered" dogma in conservation biology; 3) low reproductive rates that slow recoveries from population declines; and 4) competition with humans for critical habitats. The combined impact of these four factors places a seemingly numerous species at significant risk to environmental problems. Thus, the recent 80-percent decline in sanderling numbers is not surprising.

Just as these four characteristics compound the environmental risk, they also heighten the challenge for effective management action. This is especially true because of the sanderlings' stepping-stone pattern of migration from one critical staging site to another, and because the migrations are international.

Hence, effective management requires coordinated action at a sequence of sites, each critical to successful migration, yet each lying in nations with different conservation ethics and priorities.

The recognition of these principles of shorebird management has led to the creation of the Western Hemisphere Shorebird Reserve Network, an international program for shorebird conservation. The network's goals are threefold: 1) to create international awareness of the conservation challenges faced by migratory shorebirds and their critical habitats; 2) to link critical sites used by shorebirds during migration in a coordinated management effort; and 3) to provide a network of scientists and conservationists with the technical skills to gather and assess data for guiding shorebird management needs.

The Western Hemisphere Shorebird Reserve Network was formally launched in 1986 when the states of New Jersey and Delaware joined to declare key portions of the Delaware Bay a shorebird conservation area. This ceremonial act brought international recognition to the sites and also spawned local government and private efforts to acquire critical beaches within the bay for protection. The network is now a collaborative venture involving many federal and state wildlife management agencies across the hemisphere (see Figure 3).

The Western Hemisphere Shorebird Reserve Network now operates under the guidance of the International Association of Fish and Wildlife Agencies (which includes Canadian and U.S. representatives) the World Wildlife Fund, Manomet Bird Observatory, and National Audubon Society. In August 1987, representatives from the Surina-

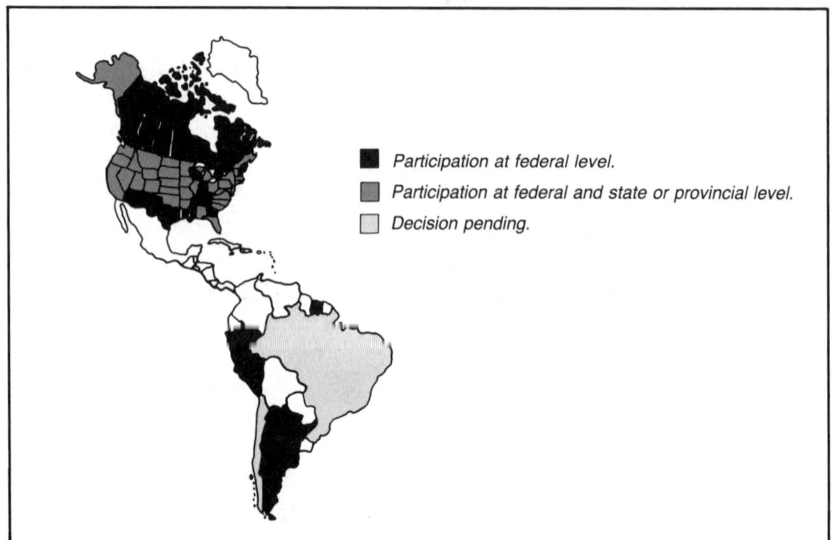

Figure 3. Wildlife agencies currently participating in the Western Hemisphere Shorebird Reserve Network.

mese and Canadian governments met in the Bay of Fundy to nominate critical sites within their countries for membership in the network and to dedicate them to shorebird conservation.

Several sites already in the network are significant to sanderling populations, especially the Delaware Bay and two areas in coastal Peru – the Paracas Peninsula and Mejía Lagoon. Other sites have been identified. The Brazilian government has recently established a national park at Lagoa do Peixe, specifically because of its role as a staging area for shorebird species, including sanderlings, en route to breeding sites in arctic North America. Sanderling staging areas in northwest Oregon and southwest Washington are of special importance to the entire U.S. West Coast sanderling population, but to date these areas lack effective protection.

Because sanderlings are not hunted, management actions for this species fall into two general areas: 1) habitat protection in high-density areas, principally nonbreeding sites used in winter and on migration; and 2) protection of essential resources, especially from chemical contamination. Steps taken to protect habitat should include provisions for minimizing disturbance on beaches used as staging sites by sanderlings. This in now under way in Delaware Bay. New Jersey's Division of Environmental Protection has also established emergency procedures to be used in the event of chemical spills in nearby shipping lanes during critical migratory periods.

Sanderlings may also be amenable to more direct management steps. Experimental fieldwork in California demonstrates that young birds captured shortly after their arrival on wintering grounds (September to December) can be transplanted to other wintering sites (Myers *et al.* 1986). In an initial series of autumn transplants none of the young birds transplanted before January returned to their capture site. Approximately 50 percent of the transplanted birds imprinted on the release site and returned to the release site in subsequent years. While transplanting does not appear to be a necessary management tool at present, its feasibility may prove useful in subsequent years for the sanderling or to employ with other species.

PROGNOSIS

Near-term prospects for sanderlings are uncertain. It would appear that West Coast populations are stable. The weakest link is the Oregon and Washington staging areas where the greatest threat is harrassment and continued recreational development of the coast. Predictions for other New World populations will remain impossible without new information on the reasons for the 80-percent decline.

If near-term prospects are murky, over the long-term they are bleak. Current models of global climate change due to the greenhouse effect predict global average temperature increases of 1.5 to 4°C by 2030 (NRC 1982). This global average will not be distributed evenly, but instead will have less impact in the tropics and more at high latitudes (Hansen *et al.* 1986). High arctic increases are expected to range between 6 to 9°C. Sanderlings breed very far north, in areas where mid-July temperatures do not rise above 5°C (Cramp and Simmons 1983). An increase in temperature of this magnitude may eliminate virtually all sanderling nesting habitat, along with the breeding habitats of a host of other high arctic species.

RECOMMENDATIONS

Recommendations for the management of sanderlings fall into two categories. First, significant questions remain unanswered about the species' biology and population ecology, especially in relation to factors driving population trends. Second, progress in implementing on-the-ground management steps to maintain habitat quality in critical areas is needed.

Recommendations regarding research into sanderling population trends include the following:

1. Further analysis of South American data may enable a test of the International Shorebird Survey results to determine if the 80-percent decline in the sanderling population is real. South American data come only from the Pacific Coast, however, as no systematic censuses are available from southeast Brazil, the other major South American "wintering" region. Except for direct tests using South American data, the only alternative is continued testing and refinement of the statistical procedures used to reveal the current decline. Toward that end, the U.S. Fish and Wildlife Service should expand its support for the International Shorebird Survey and include within that program rigorous field and analytical procedures to test survey methods.
2. The apparent declines of the sanderling and nine other shorebird species make continued population monitoring imperative. North American data from both coasts must be matched with surveys at critical locations in both South American wintering areas.
3. Studies to resolve the speculations regarding the sources of population declines outlined above (see "Current Trends") and

to identify other possible sources should be carried out. Of the two interpretations, the destruction of undiscovered staging sites may reside forever in the netherworld of untestable hypotheses. A decline associated with the impacts of pesticide contamination on migratory competency is readily testable. Moreover, its results would have implications for bird conservation extending far beyond this particular species because it would raise the spectre of pervasive sublethal effects of pesticides on all migratory species.

The specific ecological requirements of sanderlings at winter and migratory stopover sites needs further study.

Of special importance is a family of questions about individual and population traditions versus ecological imperatives. Faced with daunting challenges merely to establish what the biological patterns are, conservation biologists often accept the patterns their research reveals as the only ones possible. In fact, that may often be the case. For example, it would seem unlikely that any other estuary on the East Coast could substitute for Delaware Bay's role in northbound shorebird migration (Myers 1986). But away from the "megacases," arguments that "it must be because it is" become more problematic.

Our abilities as conservation managers will benefit from substantive research that asks how individual and population patterns are established and maintained; to what extent they represent the rut of tradition versus the constraint of ecology; and how accessible to manipulation are the patterns themselves. The need for this information is severe even if all we faced were the "normal" conservation insults like wetland draining for development. The importance of these studies is magnified manyfold by the prospect of climate change and its incumbent habitat displacements. Toward this goal we must identify and exploit the opportunities that "white rat" species like the sanderling offer for basic conservation research.

Specific near-term management objectives for sanderling conservation depend in part on the answers to the research questions discussed above. Even without all the answers, however, several steps are clearly desirable. First, the growth and effectiveness of the Western Hemisphere Shorebird Reserve Network should be promoted. Whatever local challenges the research reveals, it is obvious that international coordination must underpin conservation efforts.

Several sanderling sites that need immediate protective actions include: 1) Delaware Bay, where beach acquisition and protection plans proposed by New Jersey's Division of Environmental Protection must be implemented; 2) the staging sites in northwest Oregon and southwest Washington, from Clatsop Beach, Oregon, to Moclips, Washington, where continued expansion of recreational facilities and activities causes continuous and increasing disturbances of birds refueling for northbound migration; 3) coastal Texas, where condominiums, other developments, and beach vehicular traffic destry more and more of the remaining beach habitats; 4) central Chile, where no conservation management areas yet exist in any coastal habitats; and 5) the barrier island system of the Delmarva Peninsula, a major resting area for migrating sanderlings southbound for Peru and Chile, where human recreational activities in late summer threaten to swamp the natural system.

In Peru, Peruvian environmentalists have just won a major victory in the National Reserve of Paracas by thwarting efforts that would use a major fraction of the reserve for industrial development purposes. Several tens of thousands of sanderlings, along with numbers of other shorebird species, winter in the vicinity of the reserve. Simultaneously, the conservation community in Peru appears to be losing ground over the National Sanctuary of Mejía Lagoon, where agricultural interests increasingly encroach upon that unique patch of coastal wetland. Prospects for conserving both of these sites will improve with international recognition and support.

These management needs are evident now, without any change in climate, yet climate change will affect sanderling populations in at least two very different ways. The first will be through sea level rise and the erosion of beach habitats. Even without human intervention, sea level rise and beach erosion may alter beach topography at such a rate that invertebrate populations—the resources upon which sanderlings depend—will plummet. On the West Coast, many California beaches now backed by cliffs will likely disappear completely. The tension between human developments and sanderling habitat needs are likely to heighten even further as coastal communities respond to beach erosion with sea walls, bulkheads, sand injection, and other intrusive manipulations that degrade the natural environment. "Natural" and human-induced changes in geographic distribution of invertebrates that birds feed on may result in radical alterations in the times and places we find sanderlings. Whether the results will support anything comparable to the current scale of migration remains unknown.

The second impact of the rise in temperature will be through reducing the extent of breeding habitat. The high arctic temperature changes anticipated by the middle of the next century are extreme—6 to 9°C; current projections for future distribution of arctic vegetation (Edlund 1986) do not bode well for sanderling habitat choice. Little suitable habitat is expected to persist if current predictions foretell the future accurately.

Taken together, these two impacts of climate change imply that the most important long-term management steps needed for sanderling conservation involve efforts to slow the pace and moderate the effects of the greenhouse effect. This means that sanderlings, like so many other residents of the Earth, depend upon national and international cooperation in energy conservation and in developing and deploying climate-neutral sources of energy for human use.

REFERENCES

Bent, A.C. 1927. "Life histories of North American shorebirds." Part I. *Smithsonian Institution U.S. National Museum Bulletin* 142.

Castro, G. 1987. "High metabolic rate in Sanderlings (*Calidris alba*)." *Wilson Bulletin* 99:267–268.

——. and J.P. Myers. 1987. "Ecología y conservación del playero blanco." *Boletin de Lima* 52:47–61.

Connors, P.G., J.P. Myers, C.S.W. Connors, and F.A. Pitelka. 1981. "Interhabitat movements by sanderlings in relation to foraging profitability and the tidal cycle." *Auk* 98:49–64.

Cramp, S., and K.E.L. Simmons. 1983. *Handbook of the Birds of Europe, the Middle East, and North Africa.* Vol. III. *Waders to Gulls.* Oxford University Press.

Edlund, S.A. 1986. "Modern arctic vegetation distribution and its congruence with summer climate patterns," pp. 84–99 *in* H.M. French ed., *Impact of Climatic change on the Canadian Arctic.* Environment Canada.

Dunne, P., D. Sibley, C. Sutton, and W. Wander. 1982. "Aerial surveys in Delaware Bay: confirming an enormous spring staging area for shorebirds." *Wader Study Group Bulletin*35:32–33.

Gosselink, J.G. and R.H. Baumann. 1980. "Wetland inventories: wetland loss along the United States coast." *A. Geomorphol. N.F. Supple.* 34:173–187.

Hansen, J., A. Lacis, D. Rind, G. Russell, I. Fung, and S. Lebedeff. 1986. "Evidence for future warming: how large and when," *in* W.E. Shands and J.S. Hoffman eds., *CO2, Climate Change, and Forest Management in the United States.* Conservation Foundation. Washington, D.C. in press.

Harrington, B.A. 1986. "The Red Knot," pp. 870–886 *in* R. DiSilvestro and A. Eno eds, *Audubon Wildlife Report 1986.* National Audubon Society. New York, New York. 1,096 pp.

Howe, M.A., P.H. Geissler, and B.A. Harrington. 1986. "Population trends of North American shorebirds wintering in Central and South America." *Proceedings of the 19th World Conference of the International Council for Bird Preservation.* Kingston, Ontario. June 1986.

Maron, J.L. and J.P. Myers. 1985. "Seasonal changes in feeding success, activity patterns, and weights of nonbreeding Sanderlings *Calidris alba*." *Auk* 102:580–586.

Myers, J.P. 1983. "Space, time, and the pattern of individual associations in a group-living species: sanderlings have no friends." *Behavioral Ecology and Sociobiology* 12:129–134.

——. 1984. "Spacing behavior of nonbreeding shorebirds." *Behavior of Marine Organisms* 6:273–323.

——. 1986. "Sex and gluttony on Delaware Bay." *Natural History* 95:68–77.

——., P.G. Connors, and F.A. Pitelka. 1979. "Territory size in wintering sanderlings: the effects of prey abundance and intruder pressure." *Auk* 96:551–561.

——., S.L. Williams, and F.A. Pitelka. 1980. "An experimental analysis of prey availability for sanderlings *Calidris alba* Pallas feeding on sandy beach crustaceans." *Canadian Journal of Zoology* 58:1564–1574.

——., G. Castro, B. Harrington, M. Howe, J. Maron, E. Ortiz, M. Sallaberry, C.T. Schick, and E. Tabilo. 1984a. "The Panamerican Shorebird Program: a progress report." *Wader Study Group Bulletin* 42:26–31.

——., C.T. Schick, and C.H. Hohenberger. 1984b. "Notes on the 1983 distribution of Sanderling along the United States' Pacific coast." *Wader Study Group Bulletin* 40:22–26.

——., J.L. Maron, and M. Sallaberry. 1985. "Going to extremes: Why do Sanderlings migrate to the Neotropics?" *AOU Monographs* 36:520–535.

——., C.T. Schick, and G. Castro. 1986. "Structure in sanderling populations: The magnitude of intra and inter-year dispersal during the nonbreeding season." *Proceedings of the 19th International Ornithological Congress. In press.*

——., R.I.G. Morrison, P.Z. Antas, B.A. Harrington, T.E. Lovejoy, M. Sallaberry, S.E. Senner, and A. Tarak. 1987a. "Conservation strategy for migratory species." *American Scientist* 75:18–26.

——., P.D. McLain, R.I.G. Morrison, P.Z. Antas, P. Canevari, B.H. Harrington, T.E. Lovejoy, V. Pulido, M. Sallaberry, and S.E. Senner. 1987b. "The Western Hemisphere Shorebird Reserve Network." *Wader Study Group Bulletin* 49, supplement:122–124.

National Research Council. 1982. *Carbon Dioxide and Climate: A Second Assessment.* National Research Council. National Academy Press. Washington, D.C.

Parmelee, D.F. 1970. "Breeding behavior of the sanderling in the Canadian high arctic." *Living Bird* 9:97–146.

——. and R.G. Payne. 1973. "On multiple broods and the breeding strategy of arctic sanderling." *Ibis* 115:218–225.

Pienkowski, M.W. and G.H. Green. 1976. "Breeding biology of sanderlings in north-east Greenland." *British Birds* 69:165–177.

Senner, S.E. and M.A. Howe. 1984. "Conservation of nearctic shorebirds." *Behavior of Marine Organisms* 5:379–421.

Summers, R.W. and L.G. Underhill. 1987. "Factors related to breeding production of Brent Geese *Branta b. bernicula* and waders (charadrii) on the Taimyr Peninsula." *Bird Study* 34:161–171.

——., L.G. Underhill, M. Waltner, and D.A. Whitelaw. 1987. "Population, biometrics, and movement of the Sanderling in southern Africa." *Ostrich* 58:24–39.

J. P. Myers is National Audubon Society's senior vice-president for science and sanctuaries.

In the past, unregulated trapping caused the decline of the otter. Now the major threat to the species is the clearing, draining, and polluting of wetland habitats. *Leonard Lee Rue III.*

The Nearctic River Otter

Paul J. Polechla, Jr.
University of Arkansas

SPECIES DESCRIPTION AND NATURAL HISTORY

The nearctic river otter (*Lutra canadensis*) (hereafter referred to as river otter) can be distinguished from other mammals by a number of characteristics, many of which enhance the river otter's swimming ability (Van Zyll de Jong 1972). River otters have webbed fore and hind feet with well-developed claws. The webbing between the toes enables the otters to paddle through the water. The hind feet have callous outgrowths of skin on the soles, or "plantar pads," which are believed to prevent the otter from slipping when walking on ice. The river otter's legs are short compared to its body length. The tail is long, thick at the base, and tapers toward the tip; it is used for steering and propelling the body through the water. River otters have valvular ears and nostrils that exclude water during a dive. The nose pad, or "rhinarium," is uniquely spade-shaped when viewed anteriorly. Paired projections of the skull located posteriorly to the eye sockets, called the postorbital processes, are poorly developed compared with other otters. The species has a compliment of 36 teeth.

The otter's fur is considered the "diamond" of the fur trade and serves as a standard of comparison for the quality of other furs. Only the sea otter's pelt exceeds the river otter in luster, durability, hair density, and softness. The fur of the river otter consists of long, lustrous guard hairs and short, dense, wool-like hairs which act as insulation by trapping air. As otters swim underwater, a trail of air bubbles escapes from its fur. Upon emerging, water adheres only to the tips of the guard hairs, forming small "spikes."

Reproduction

An analysis of river otter sex ratios indicates that populations contain significantly more males than females (138:100) (Polechla 1987). Male otters are probably capable of breeding year-round, but females have seasonal reproductive activities that vary according to latitude (Audubon and Bachman 1851, Polechla 1987). Breeding occurs from winter to early spring. After fertilization, the zygote divides and forms the blastocyst, a hollow ball of cells. In most mammalian species, the blastocyst implants on the wall of the uterus; however, in the river otter, it floats freely in the uterus for extended periods of time. This delayed implantation lasts for approximately 10 months (Hamilton and Eadie 1964). After implanting, the gestation period begins, lasting about 63 days. The estimated date of implantation in wild river otters varies from November 16 in Florida to March 7 in Alaska. Subsequent estimated parturition dates vary from January 17 in Florida to May 9 in Alaska (Polechla 1987). In most mammals, energy-demanding activities, such as searching for mates and suckling the young, are timed to coincide with peak periods of food availability. The environmental factors that trigger implantation of the river otter blastocyst and the advantages of delayed implantation are still a mystery.

Embryonic litter size ranges from one to six, averaging two to three. Due to attrition, the average number of cubs (or pups) following their parents is fewer than the number of embryos: 2.28 to 2.88 per female (Polechla 1987). Newborn otters are semi-helpless, but soon develop an exploratory behavior, sometimes called play. River otters may first breed at one or two years of age (Hamilton and Eadie 1964, Polechla 1987).

River otters in the wild have lived an estimated 16 years (Matson and Matson 1985); the longevity record in captivity is 23 years (Liers 1966). Mortality rates of otters usually increase substantially at three to five years of age; the reason for this is unknown.

Taxonomy and Distribution

The family of Carnivores known as Mustelidae exemplify a diverse array of adaptations fitting their particular life style. The subfamily Lutrinae is the only subfamily of mustelids that is considered to be semi-aquatic. The nearctic river otter is 1 of 13 species of this subfamily and 1 of 8 members of the genus *Lutra*. Other otters occurring in North America include the sea otter (*Enhydra lutris*), found along the Pacific Coast, and the neotropical river otter (*Lutra longicaudis*), found in South America, Central America, and as far north as Sonora, Mexico. (See the *Audubon Wildlife Report 1987* for a discussion on the southern sea otter.)

In the early settlement days of North America, the river otter had one of the largest distributions of any mammal on the continent (Hall 1981), encompassing 7,720,000 square miles (Anderson 1977) (see Figure 1). Only the distributions of the timber wolf (*Canis lupus*) and the beaver (*Castor canadensis*) approached that of the otter. The otter's range was bounded in the northwest by the Arctic Circle; the northern limits of its range extended across the region of southern Hudson Bay to Quebec. The easternmost boundaries extended along the Atlantic

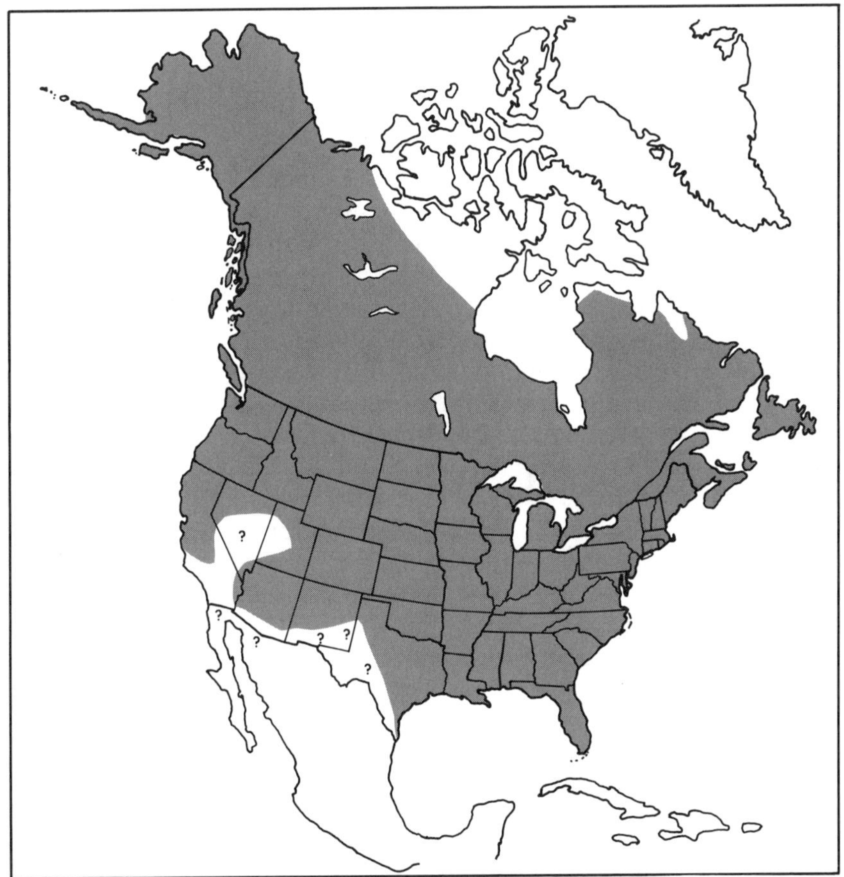

Figure 1. Historic distribution of the nearctic river otter (from Hall 1981).

Coast from the Saint Lawrence River to the tip of the Florida Peninsula. The southern limits ranged along the Gulf Coast from the tip of the Florida Peninsula to the present-day site of Brownsville, Texas, at the mouth of the Rio Grande. The exact distribution of otters in desert regions in North America is not clear. The desert regions are believed to act as barriers to dispersion across drainages (Van Zyll de Jong 1972).

Habitat

Otters occupy many habitat types throughout their range, including swamps, bays, bogs, marshes, pocosins, ponds, lakes, upland streams, lowland rivers, and even coastal regions. Occurrences of river otters in perennial desert rivers of the southwestern United States, for example, the Rio Grande, Gila, Verde, and Colorado rivers, show that although much of the desert is inhospitable to otters, riparian zones along rivers, even those bisecting arid lands, are acceptable semi-aquatic otter habitat.

The size and home range of otters varies according to habitat as well as behavior. In Idaho for example, each otter has a home range of between 1.7 and 3.6 miles of linear riparian habitat along Rocky Mountain streams (Melquist and Hornocker 1983). In coastal marshes of Texas, male otters have an average home range of 1.5 square miles, whereas females average 1.1 square miles (Foy 1984).

Suitable otter habitat seems to be areas with a combination of land and water, with some plant cover bordering the banks or shoreline (Woolington 1984); an abundance of food items, such as fish and crustaceans, must also be available. Poor water quality adversely affects prey densities, which in turn affects otter populations.

Otters are usually abundant in extensive wetland areas and this is especially true in coastal marshes and estuaries. However, in the interior portion of the otter's range, its habitat has been augmented by the activities of the beaver where the two species are sympatric (Tumlison *et al.* 1982, Polechla 1987)—the otter benefits from the beaver's activities but does not require them. Abandoned beaver lodges and natural cavities—brush piles, in between large rocks, and in hollow logs provide temporary resting sites and natal dens for otters. Beaver ponds are noted for their productivity and contain numerous alcoves with fish and crayfish and are retreats often investigated by otters.

Diet

The diet of the river otter is usually restricted to aquatic and semi-aquatic animals (Toweill and Tabor 1982). Fish are the most common food eaten by the otter, occurring in 29 to 100 percent of the studied gastrointestinal tracts and droppings; crustaceans, such as crayfish and crabs, occur anywhere from 0.4 to 98 percent of the time (Pierce 1979). The remainder of the otter's diet consists of insects, mollusks, other invertebrates, amphibians, birds, mammals, reptiles, and some plant materials (Toweill and Tabor 1982).

Few studies have been conducted on the specifics of the otter's feeding behavior. In one Idaho study, otters continually moved to areas of relatively high fish density, consuming fish ranging in size from 0.8 to 19.7 inches or more in length (Melquist and Hornocker 1983). The behavior of species which compose the otter's diet suggests that otters capture slow-moving fish (Ryder 1955).

SIGNIFICANCE OF THE SPECIES

The river otter is considered to be at the top of the food chain because eats fish and crustaceans and has few major predators other than humans. Humans and otters are both dependent upon the aquatic ecosystem. Due to this unique relationship, the otter may serve as an "indicator species," demonstrating the health of the aquatic ecosystem of a particular watershed. If trapping pressure is not substantial, but the otter population is lower than normal, it can be indicative of an unhealthy aquatic environment. In this case, biologists must analyze the components of a debilitated ecosystem to identify the possible causes—for example, siltation, high organic content, heavy metal or PCB pollution, and other problems. Since they inhabit a land-water habitat, otters may also act as important vectors of parasites (Toweill and Tabor 1982).

The river otter is classified as a harvestable furbearer in 27 of 49 of the continental United States and in all 11 Canadian provinces (Deems and Pursley 1978). A total of 52,778 raw pelts worth approximately $3 million were recorded for 1976 (Rue 1981).

The river otter is an appealing species to naturalists, outdoors people, zoo visitors, and laypeople; the aesthetic value of even glimpsing an otter often lasts a lifetime.

HISTORICAL PERSPECTIVE

A number of factors working in concert caused a decline in river otter populations in post-settlement periods in North America. For many generations, Native Americans have snared, trapped, and hunted otters for use as fur, meat, and religious ceremonial items (Swanton 1946,

Jenkins 1983, Polechla 1987). Intense unregulated trapping of otters began when European traders began to hunt commercially. This full-scale harvest was further accelerated by the use of lightweight, compact, leg-hold traps developed in 1848 (Krause n.d.). Thus, trappers were able to carry and set more traps, increasing trapping pressure.

Burgeoning human populations also affected otter populations. After the most suitable land was developed for agriculture and housing, valuable wetlands were drained, channelized, filled, and cleared at a rapid rate. Although the destruction of the otter's wetland habitat affected otters indirectly, it had (and still has) a devastating impact on their populations. Degradation of wetlands reduced both the quality and quantity of available otter habitat. The increasing human presence also brought about pollution of waterways and watersheds with industrial-age waste products such as mine tailings, heavy metals, and organic wastes.

Unregulated trapping, habitat destruction, and pollution took its greatest toll on areas that had the least amount of wetlands. Therefore, otter populations were greatly reduced in interior areas of North America, especially in prairies of the midwestern United States and southern Canada, and arid regions of the southwestern United States. More abundant otter populations occurred on the Atlantic, Gulf, and Pacific coasts, around the Great Lakes, and on the Alaskan Peninsula than in the interior of the continent.

Reintroduction of beavers from the 1920s to the 1960s into the interior of North America had substantially increased the beaver populations. The wetlands created by beavers partially offset the concommitant wetland destruction by humans. Remnant river otter populations responded to this available beaver-augmented habitat. Moreover, the protection of otters from trapping and hunting in some areas may have helped in some cases to increase its population from the low levels of the late 1880s and early 1900s.

CURRENT TRENDS

Biologists feared that populations of the nearctic river otter and of the Central and South American otters, as well as Eurasian, Asian, and African otters, were low (Hill 1978, Jenkins 1983). The Convention on International Trade in Endangered Species of Wild Fauna and Flora (CITES), drafted and signed in the mid-1970s (U.S. Fish and Wildlife Service 1977), has several effects on otter populations of the member nations, which included Canada and the United States (Hill 1978, Jenkins 1983). The river otter was listed in Appendix II of the treaty which required that nations exporting otters tag and record each pelt and cite the state or province of origin. This action temporarily depressed the fur trade market. The treaty also prompted federal, provincial, state, and university organizations to study the status, basic biology, and ecology of the river otter. A large portion of research money was funded under the provisions of the Federal Aid in Wildlife Restoration Act (Pittman-Robertson Act),[1] administered by the U.S. Fish and Wildlife Service. Prior to this, very few basic biological facts about the river otter were known.

In 1976, a total of 17 states gave total protection to the river otter (Deems and Pursley 1978);[2] the otter is considered endangered in 11 states.[3]

MANAGEMENT

The management of otters and other furbearers is in its infancy because biologists are still involved with establishing baseline data on population indices, that is, on whether the population is increasing or decreasing relative to a previous time period. Wildlife agencies in states such as Georgia, Louisiana, Florida, and Texas are determining population trends by conducting scent post surveys (Clark 1982, Humphrey and Zinn 1982). The scent post station is prepared by placing an odiferous lure on an upright dowel rod—a scent post—on a specially prepared tracking surface such as sand or powdered limestone. A number of these scent post stations are prepared for the survey on one day and are examined on the following day to determine the presence or absence of otter tracks and scat. Surveys have been conducted by mailing questionnaires to wildlife biologists, trappers, animal-damage-control personnel ("beaver-control" trappers), commercial fishermen, naturalists, canoe outfitters, back country guides, and other outdoors people (Dubose *et al.* 1980, Polechla and Sealander 1985, Polechla 1987). The distribution of river otters has been plotted from the answers received to questions on these surveys concerning the presence or absence of otters in a particular area.

Another technique used to determine the otter's status in an area where trapping is allowed is to salvage a representative sample of carcasses from trappers, extract a canine tooth from each specimen,

1. Funding for the Pittman-Robertson Act is derived from an excise tax on sporting arms and ammunition.

2. The states are: Arizona, California, Colorado, Idaho, Illinois, Iowa, Missouri, New Jersey, New Mexico, Ohio, Oklahoma, Pennsylvania, South Dakota, Tennessee, Utah, West Virginia, and Wyoming.

3. The states are: Colorado, Illinois, Kentucky, Missouri, Montana, North Dakota, Ohio, Pennsylvania, South Dakota, Tennessee, and Utah.

and then determine the age structure of the entire population (Stephenson 1977). If the sample shows a large population of young individuals approaching sexual maturity, the population is considered to be increasing. If the sample shows a large population of senescent animals, the population is considered to be decreasing. If approximately equal proportions of young and old otters are present in the sample, the population is considered to be stable (Smith 1980). Live trapping and subsequent radio-telemetry of otters has yielded information concerning otter populations (Melquist and Hornocker 1983).

Arizona, Colorado, Iowa, Kansas, Kentucky, Minnesota, Oklahoma, Pennsylvania, Tennessee, and Alberta, Canada, have implemented reintroduction programs. Other states such as Illinois, Indiana, Nebraska, Ohio, and West Virginia are considering reintroducing otters. Management techniques, aside from reintroduction, include giving total protection to the otter, limiting trapping and hunting seasons, limiting export of furs, and regulating the types of traps and the ways in which they can be set. The most important management tool is the purchase and preservation of wetlands. Although most wetlands are conserved explicitly for waterfowl, other wildlife, including furbearing mammals like the river otter, can also benefit.

PROGNOSIS

If reintroduced populations of otters are able to reproduce and recruit new members into the population, then viable or even expanding populations can be re-established in areas where populations are extirpated or extremely low. Another encouraging development is the increase in existing population numbers and the distribution of otters, beginning in the late 1970s and early 1980s, into areas devoid of them. Although there are localities where populations seem to be stable or increasing, there is still cause for concern. Several short-term gains have been made recently, but the promise for viable otter populations in the future is jeopardized by several alarming trends.

The future of the river otter in North America hinges on available wetland habitat. Although beavers can create wetlands with their dams, the positive effect on otter populations can be totally negated by intensive human-caused wetland destruction. Wetland loss continues at a rate of 300,000 to 450,000 acres per year; less than 46 percent of the nation's original wetlands in the lower 48 states remain.[4] The situation

4. See "Federal Wetlands Protection Programs" in the *Audubon Wildlife Report 1986*.

will be critical in the bottomland-hardwood forests of the Mississippi Alluvial Plain, in the riparian corridors along the streams and rivers in the arid lands of the Great Plains and southwestern United States, and in the coastal wetlands of California. However, there has been a glimmer of hope of saving these wetlands with the passage of the 1985 Farm Act, with its "swampbuster" and "sodbuster" provisions, which prohibit payment of farm program benefits to farmers who drain wetlands. This type of temporary incentive is effective only when commodity prices for grains are low. When grain prices increase in the future, there will be a stronger economic incentive to cultivate wetlands.

If pollution abatement programs are weakened, improperly disposed solid and hazardous wastes will leach into surface and ground waters of many drainages. Based on the best available scientific knowledge, the otter is considered to be a top-level carnivore susceptible to bioaccumulation of toxic heavy metals, PCBs, and DDT and its derivatives (O'Connor and Nielson 1981, Clark 1982, Wren 1985). If pollution trends continue, otter populations would probably begin to decline.

If extended periods (three or more years) of high pelt prices for otter and/or beaver occur, the harvest and natural mortality may exceed natality and result in a decline in the otter's population (Dozhier 1987). Precautions must be taken in the future to avoid overhunting and ensure that the river otter continues to be a renewable resource. Although the long-term prognosis is bleak, negative trends can be reversed if we realize that properly managed, unpolluted watersheds are ideal not only for otters, but are also in the best interest of humans.

RECOMMENDATIONS

A synthesis of scientific knowledge from literature (Toweill and Tabor 1982) and the opinions of experts attending national and international symposia indicate a number of research and management needs.

Research Needs

A number of mysteries surrounding river otter biology still remain. In order to be able to accurately determine the status of the species, biologists must know if population indices and estimates are reliable and what factors influence them. Studies using a number of parameters of the population's status are ideal since they offer several kinds of biological evidence to determine if a population is decreasing, increas ing, or remaining stable (Downing 1980, Dixon 1981). These multifaceted approaches also have the advantage of elucidating factors contributing to population status.

The river otter's specific habitat requirements in terms of quantity and quality are not known. Only a few studies document the otter's home range in only a few localities on the entire continent (Melquist and Hornocker 1983, Foy 1984, Woolington 1984). Although the terrestrial vegetation adjacent to the otter's occupied habitat has been described, the otter's preferred aquatic habitat has usually been ignored.Much could be learned about otter ecology by studying both its food habits and the seasonal densities of its prey such as fish and crayfish. This effort would give biologists an opportunity to determine food preferences.

Beaver/otter relations should be investigated more thoroughly by simultaneously radio-tracking a sympatric group of beavers and river otters. More study in this area would shed light on the temporal and spatial interactions between the two species. Since otters are often inadvertently caught in traps set for beavers, controlled experiments should be conducted to determine if the use of aluminum foil strips discourages otters from entering 330 Conibear traps (Polechla and Sealander 1985). Several professional beaver-control trappers claim that the aluminum foil repels otters but has no effect on beavers.

Reproduction is one of the most perplexing aspects of otter biology. The environmental cues responsible for, and the evolutionary advantages of, delayed implantation are poorly understood and require research. The way in which sex, reproductive status, and age influence behavior—scent marking, social interactions, and mate selection—is also largely unknown.

More laboratory-controlled experiments should be conducted (O' Connor and Neilson 1981) to determine the effect of various levels of harmful pollutants, such as PCBs, heavy metals, and DDT and its derivatives. This research is especially needed to ascertain the levels of chemical compounds in otter tissues that have deleterious effects or result in death. In this way, pollutant levels from the tissues of carcasses of wild-trapped otters can be compared with results from lab experiments to determine if the wild otter population, and also the human population, is at risk. By addressing these research questions, biologists can come to a better understanding concerning how otters interact with their environment.

Management Needs

Several management needs must be met regardless of population densities. Remaining wetlands should be identified, classified, and mapped according to quality and quantity of potential and occupied otter habitat. The acquisition and preservation of wetland habitats should be aggressively pursued. When general wetland management plans are drafted and instituted, the river otter should be included with waterfowl, fish, other furbearers, and other wetland wildlife as species to be managed. The drainage and channelization of streams, rivers, and waterways must be curtailed; strips of riparian and shoreline vegetation must be retained and not logged or cleared (Woolington 1984, Polechla and Sealander 1985). Conserving our valuable wetlands for otters and other wildlife will require a concerted effort by private landowners, citizens, biologists, and state and federal government agencies.

Low or decreasing otter populations require a particular type of management plan to increase their densities. In this case, trapping otters should be banned (if not already done). Beaver-control trappers and commercial fishermen should be encouraged to report accidental otter captures. The state conservation agency should then confiscate these carcasses and record the capture data for each specimen. Valuable information concerning reproduction, condition, health, age, and other aspects of otter biology could be learned from necropsies of these salvaged specimens. This would be a way to gather much needed biological data on low populations.

An in-depth survey for these remnant or transient otter populations should be conducted. If some individuals exist in a geographical area, efforts should be made to understand factors limiting their distribution. In the case of a remnant or transient population, it would be better to foster the existing population rather than restock the area with a foreign otter population. If otter populations are extremely low, then beaver-control trapping and commercial fishing with nets should be restricted.

A thorough inventory of habitat should preclude any reintroduction program in order to determine suitability of wetlands for otters. Although some biologists may disagree, some state and provincial agencies use transplanting as a cure-all while ignoring or not identifying the factors limiting populations. Neglecting to assess these factors results in repeated reintroduction failures, unnecessary otter deaths, and unneeded expense. If an area is deemed suitable, groups of 20 otters of approximately equal sex ratios should be released per location (Erickson *et al.* 1984). Releases should be conducted initially on state or federally owned property so that wetlands can be managed appropriately to benefit the otters.

In areas allowing trapping, the tagging of pelts as mandated by CITES must be done to determine the numbers of otters taken. Estimating the number of trappers and trap nights would give an indication of the amount of trapping pressure and therefore trapping success. In addition, the average pelt price of otters should be recorded since it influences otter harvest. In the event otter and/or beaver prices become excessively high, trapping regulations should be altered to prevent overharvest of otters. Reducing bag limits, restricting the number and types of traps and trap sets, shortening the length of the trapping season, and scheduling the season prior to parturition are management strategies that can be used to reduce trapping pressure and numbers taken.

REFERENCES

Anderson, S. 1977. "Geographic ranges of North American terrestrial mammals." *North American Museum Novitates* 2629. 15 pp.

Audubon, J.J. and J. Bachman. 1851. *Quadrupeds of North America.* Vol. 2 V.G. Audubon. New York. Pp. 1–12.

Clark, J.D. 1982. An Evaluation of Censusing Technique and Environmental Pollutant Trends in the River Otter of Georgia. Master's thesis (unpublished). University of Georgia. Athens, Georgia. 96 pp.

Cumbie, P.M. 1975. "Mercury levels in Georgia otter, mink, and freshwater fish." *Bulletin of Environmental Contaminants and Toxicology* 14:193–196.

Deems, E.F., Jr., and D. Pursley. 1978. *North American Furbearers: Their Management, Research, and Harvest Status in 1976.* International Association of Fish and Wildlife Agencies. College Park, Maryland. 171 pp.

Dixon, K.R. 1981. "Data requirements for determining the status of furbearer populations." *Proceedings of the Worldwide Furbearer Conference.* 3:1728–1745.

Downing, R.L. 1980. "Vital statistics of animal populations," pp. 247–267 *in* S.D. Schemnitz ed., *Wildlife Management Techniques Manual.* Wildlife Society. Washington, D.C. 686 pp.

Dozhier, P.L. 1987. "The market: our guess." *The Trapper and Predator Caller* 13(3):78–81.

Dubose, J.S., D.C. Guyunn, Jr., C.E. Mason, and E.J. Hackett. 1980. "Use of trapper harvest survey data to meet ESSA information needs." *Proceedings of the Southeastern Association of Fish and Wildlife Agencies* 34:499–502.

Erickson, D.W., C.R. McCullough and W.R. Poranth. 1984. River Otter Investigations in Missouri: Evaluation of Experimental River Otter Reintroductions. Final Report, Missouri Conservation Department, Federal Aid Project Number W-13-R-38, Study Number 63, Job number 2. 47 pp.

Foy, M.K. 1984. Seasonal Movements, Home Range, and Habitat Utilization by River Otter in Southeastern Texas and Possible Implications for Census. Master's thesis (unpublished) Texas A & M University. College Station, Texas.

Hall, E.R. 1981. *The Mammals of North America.* Second edition. John Wiley and Sons. New York, New York. 601–1181 + 90.

Hamilton, W.J., Jr. and W.R. Eadie. 1964. "Reproduction in the otter, (*Lutra canadensis*)." *Journal of Mammalogy* 45:242–252.

Hill, E.P. 1978. "Current harvest and regulation of trade of river otter in southeastern United States in 1978." pp 164–172. *Proceedings of the Rare and Endangered Wildlife Symposium.*

Humphrey, S.R. and T.L. Zinn. 1982. "Seasonal habitat use by river otters (*Lutra canadensis*) and everglades mink (*Mustela vison evergladensis*) in Florida, USA." *Journal of Wildlife Management* 46:375–381.

Jenkins, J.H. 1983. "The status and management of the river otter (*Lutra canadensis*) in North America." *Acta Zoologica Fennica*. 174:233–235.

Krause, T. n.d. *NTA Trapping Handbook, A Guide for Better Trapping*. Spearman Publishing and Printing. Sutton, Nebraska. 206 pp.

Liers, E.E. 1966. "Notes on breeding the Canadian otter (*Lutra canadensis*) in captivity and longevity records of beavers (*Castor canadensis*)." *International Zoo Yearbook* 6:171–172.

Matson, G.M. and J.K. Matson. 1985. Matson's Tooth Cementum Age Analysis. Progress Report Number 8. Matson's, Milltown, Montana. Unpaginated.

Melquist, W.E. and M.G. Hornocker. 1979. Methods and Techniques for Studying and Censusing River Otter Populations. Forestry, Wildlife, and Range Experimental Station, Technical Report 8. University of Idaho. Moscow, Idaho. 17 pp.

——. and ——. 1983. "Ecology of river otters in west central Idaho." *Wildlife Monographs*. 83:1–60.

Morgan, J. 1980. *Mammalian Status Manual: A State by State Survey of the Endangered and Threatened Mammals of the U.S.* Linton Publishing Company. North Eastham, Massachusetts. 42 pp.

O'Connor, D.J. and S.W. Nielson. 1981. "Environmental survey of methylmercury levels in wild mink (*Mustela vison*) and otter (*Lutra canadensis*) from the northeastern United States and experimental pathology of methlymercurialism in the otter." *Proceedings of the Worldwide Furbearer Conference*. 3:1728–1745.

Pierce, R.M. 1979. Seasonal Feeding Habits of the River Otter (*Lutra canadensis*) in Ditches of the Great Dismal Swamp. Master's thesis (unpublished). Old Dominion University. Norfolk, Virginia. 26 pp.

Polechla, P.J. Jr. 1987. Status of the River Otter (*Lutra canadensis*) Population in Arkansas with Special Reference to Reproductive Biology. Ph.D dissertation (unpublished). University of Arkansas. Fayetteville, Arkansas. 383 pp.

——. and J.A. Sealander. 1985. *An Evaluation of the Status of the River Otter* (Lutra canadensis) *in Arkansas*. Final report, Arkansas Game and Fish Commission, Federal Aid Project Number W-56–23. 157 pp.

Ryder, R.A. 1955. "Fish predation by the otter in Michigan." *Journal of Wildlife Management*. 19:497–498.

Rue, L.L. III, 1981. *Furbearing Animals of North America*. Crown Publishers, Inc. New York, New York. 343 pp.

Smith, R.L. 1980. *Ecology and Field Biology*. Third edition. Harper and Row Publishers. New York, New York. 835 pp.

Stephenson, A.B. 1977. "Age determination and morphological variation of Ontario otters." *Canadian Journal of Zoology*. 55(10):1577–1583.

Swanton, J.R. 1946. *The Indians of the Southeastern United States*. U.S. Government Printing Office. Washington, D.C. 943 pp.

Toweill, D.E. and J.E. Tabor. 1982. "River otter (*Lutra canadensis*)," pp. 688–703 *in* J.A. Chapman and G.A. Feldhamer eds., *Wild Mammals of North America: Biology, Management, and Ecology*. John Hopkins University Press. Baltimore, Maryland. 1,147 pp.

Tumlison, R., M. Karnes and A.W. King. 1982. "The river otter in Arkansas: II. Indications of a beaver-facilitated commensal relationship." *Proceedings of the Arkansas Academy of Science*. 36:73–75.

U.S. Fish and Wildlife Service. 1977. "International trade in endangered species of wild fauna and flora." *Federal Register* 42:10462–10488.

Van Zyll de Jong, C.G. 1972. "A systematic review of the Nearctic and Neotropical river otters (genus *Lutra*, Mustelidae, Carnivora)." *Royal Ontario Museum, Life Science Contributions* 80:1–104.

Woolington, J.D. 1984. Habitat Use and Movements of River Otters at Kelp Bay, Baranof Island, Alaska. Master's thesis (unpublished). University of Alaska. Fairbanks, Alaska. 147 pp.

Wren, C.D. 1985. "Probable case of mercury poisoning in a wild otter, *Lutra canadensis*, in northwestern Ontario." *Canadian Field-Naturalist* 99(1):112–114.

Paul J. Polechla, Jr., studied the Nearctic river otter for five years for his Ph.D dissertation at the University of Arkansas, Fayetteville.

The author would like to thank Michael Pelton for his suggestion to write this account. The author dedicates this species account to John A. Sealander, his major professor, who is retiring in May 1988 after more than 40 years of service in wildlife research and education.

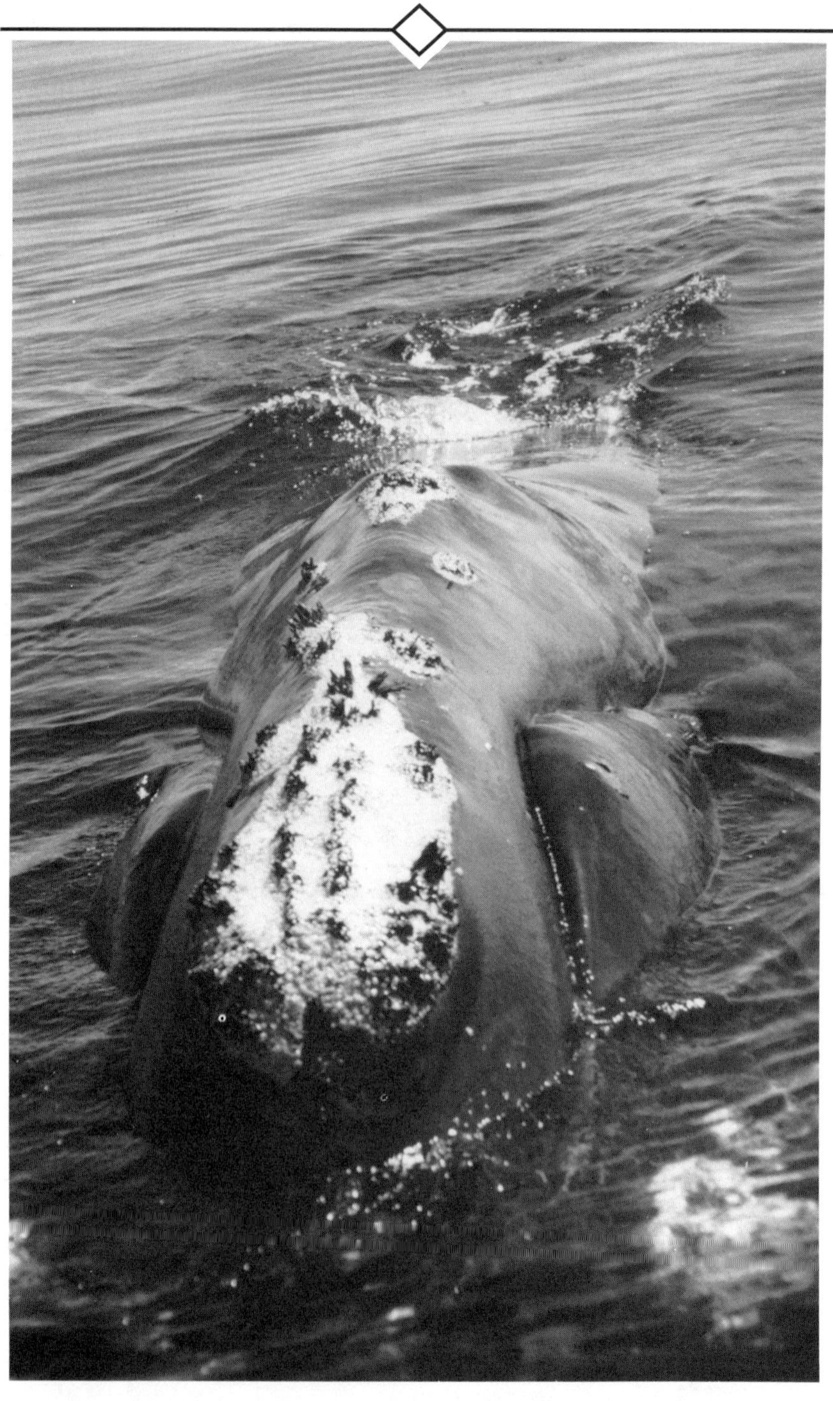

The right whale, intensely pursued by whalers because it was the "right" whale to hunt, may be the only great whale still in danger of extinction. *Amy Knowlton/New England Aquarium*

The North Atlantic Right Whale

Scott D. Kraus, Martie J. Crone, and Amy R. Knowlton
New England Aquarium

SPECIES DESCRIPTION AND NATURAL HISTORY

In the last 50 years, only 15 right whales have been sighted along the west coast of North America, and there is no evidence to indicate that the eastern North Pacific population was ever abundant (Scarff 1986). Therefore, this chapter will focus on the North Atlantic population.

An adult North Atlantic right whale (*Eubalaena glacialis*) ranges between 45 and 55 feet in length and can weigh up to 70 tons. The skin is black, or occasionally mottled gray; many individuals have irregular white patches on the throat and belly. The blubber, which can be eight inches thick, provides insulation and gives the whale buoyancy that causes it to float when dead. Right whales are characterized by the lack of a dorsal fin; short, broad flippers; and wide, deeply notched flukes with a smooth trailing edge. The flukes are often lifted when the whale begins a deep dive. Two widely separated blowholes cause the bushy spout to be V-shaped, allowing the species to be identified from a considerable distance. The massive head, which is one-quarter or more of the body length, has a long, narrow upper jaw and a high-arched lower jaw that covers long (approximately seven feet), dark baleen.

Perhaps the most noticeable feature of the right whale is the growth of tough cornified skin patches on its head called callosities. These patches occur mainly on top of the upper jaw, but also in small areas on the chin, above the eye, immediately behind the blowholes, and, in some individuals, at the upper margin of the lower jaw. Callosities are usually inhabited by small crustaceans called cyamids, or whale lice, which give the patches a creamy or orange coloration. It is suspected that the cyamids are parasitic and feed on the whale's skin (Rowntree 1983). The callosity pattern varies with each whale. In the last decade, scientists have used these patterns, along with scars, pigmentation, and crenulations along the upper margin of the lower jaw, to identify individual right whales (Payne *et al.* 1983, Kraus *et al.* 1986a). Records of over 240 different individuals sighted in the North Atlantic have been compiled into a catalog and resightings of those whales have enabled researchers to learn something of the species' distribution, abundance, biology, and behavior (Kraus *et al.* 1986b).

Taxonomy

The North Atlantic right whale is one of two species in the genus *Eubalaena*. North Pacific and North Atlantic right whales have been combined under the species designation *glacialis*—although some refer to *E. japonica* in the North Pacific as a subspecies. All Southern Hemisphere populations are included under *E. australis*. This chapter will follow Schevill's (1986) recommendation to use *Eubalaena* instead of *Balaena*.

Range and Seasonal Distribution

In the past 20 years, right whales have been sighted in the Gulf of Mexico from the southern tip of Florida to as far north as Newfoundland, and in the Gulf of St. Lawrence. Several areas appear to be especially important habitats for the species (see Figure 1) (Winn *et al.* 1986).

The coastal waters from Savannah, Georgia, to Key Largo, Florida, are a wintering ground for part of the North Atlantic population of right whales. Although a few juveniles, lone adults, and one known adult male have been sighted in the region, most of the sightings consist of mothers with very young calves, indicating that these coastal waters are a major calving ground (Kraus *et al.* 1986b). The annual peak in whale abundance and calving appears to be from January to March. The largest estimate for one season was 34 animals in the waters of coastal Georgia and Florida (out to 40 miles offshore). These whales account for only a small part of the entire population (Kraus 1985). The wintering ground(s) for the majority of the population remains unknown.

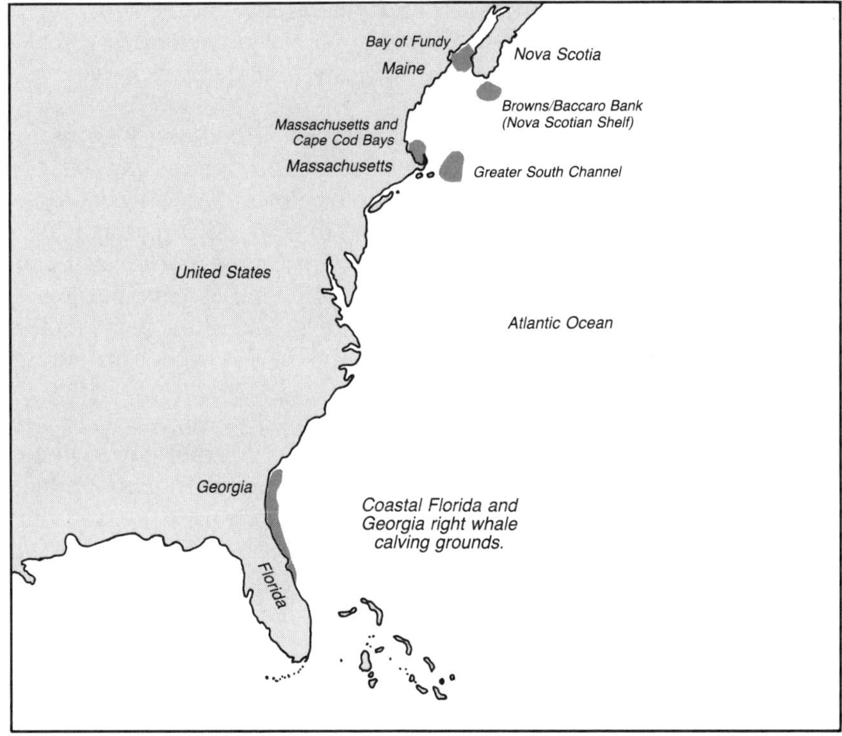

Figure 1. "High-use" habitats of the right whale along the U.S. East Coast.

The Great South Channel, between Cape Cod, Massachusetts, and George's Bank, is an area of right whale concentration each spring (Winn *et al.* 1985). The earliest sightings in the region are in March, the latest in July, and peak numbers occur in May. An estimated 25 to 40 whales, including a few mother/calf pairs and juveniles, use the area each year.

Cape Cod Bay is the location of another spring aggregation of right whales. The peak abundance there occurs late March through April, with occasional sightings in all other months of the year. Recent data show that an average of 35 individuals are seen in the area each year, although seventy or more individuals were seen in one day in 1970 (Watkins and Schevill 1982). Juveniles and mothers with calves are sighted relatively frequently in Cape Cod Bay, and two possible births have been observed in the region (Watkins and Schevill 1982).

In mid- to late-July, right whales begin to congregate in the Bay of Fundy between eastern Maine, New Brunswick, and Nova Scotia (Kraus *et al.* 1982). Abundance peaks there from mid-August to mid-October, with a rapid decrease afterwards. The number of individuals photographically identified each year averages 45; the maximum one-day count for the area was 28. Thirty different mothers with calves have been seen in the Bay of Fundy since 1980. Juveniles are also relatively abundant. This evidence suggests that the area is used as a right whale nursery.

A region on the southern Nova Scotian Shelf, between Browns and Baccaro Banks, 30 miles south of Nova Scotia, is inhabited by relatively large numbers of right whales from June to November (Mitchell *et al.* 1986). Unpublished New England Aquarium data indicate that at least 70 to 100 animals occupy the area yearly. Only three mother/calf pairs have ever been observed in this area. A few juveniles have been seen, but most of the animals observed are adults, including many males. Courtship is commonly seen involving up to 14 whales in surface activity.

Although some of these areas are inhabited by right whales over a period of several months, residence times vary for individual whales within each area. Photographic identification shows that individuals travel between the different regions within a single season, but migration routes remain unknown (Kraus *et al.* 1983, Kraus *et al.* 1986b). Since not all individuals in the right whale catalog are accounted for each year, it is unclear whether the unseen animals are scattered in offshore areas along the Continental Shelf or if there is another undiscovered summering ground. For example, a majority of cows are rarely seen in any area in the years when they are not calving.

Breeding

Surface activities involving several right whales in apparent courtship behavior have been observed in every season throughout most of their range, but precise breeding time and locations are unknown.

A right whale cow gives birth to a single calf that is approximately 14 to 18 feet long. Most calving takes place between December and March after a gestation period estimated to be about 12 months (Klumov 1962). At least 40 percent of the cows that give birth in a year migrate to an area off the coast of Georgia and northeastern Florida where they calve in the winter months. The location of other North Atlantic calving grounds for right whales remains unknown.

Only two females first seen as calves in the western North Atlantic population have been resighted with calves of their own. These two animals gave birth at five and seven years of age. This corresponds well with data from the Argentinian population of South Atlantic right whales, which indicate that *E. australis* reaches sexual maturity at seven years (Payne 1986). A three-year calving interval is predominant in *E. glacialis*, but the range is from two to five years—with only one record of a two-year interval. Known calf production in the western North Atlantic population, obtained from photo identification data, has ranged between 8 and 13 calves per year since 1981.

Diet

Right whales feed on a diet of zooplankton, primarily copepods (calanus) and secondarily on juvenile euphausiids (krill). It is not known how a whale locates a patch of plankton, but when it does, the whale swims through it with its mouth open. There is a gap in the baleen at the front of the mouth that allows the water to flow freely into the mouth. The baleen then strains the plankton from the water, catching the tiny copepods and euphausiids on fine, brushy fringes. The extremely long baleen provides a large surface area for efficient collection of the plankton.

Copepod patches may occur toward the top of the water column in Cape Cod Bay and the Great South Channel, where the whales are often seen skimming as they swim along at the surface.

No surface feeding has been reported south of New York, and it is not known if cows on the Georgia/Florida calving ground feed at all. Most feeding in the northern Gulf of Maine and on the Nova Scotian Shelf apparently occurs at greater depths, where the whales are not visible. Such feeding has been confirmed by the observation and collection of feces that contained copepod mandibles.

Predation

The only suspected natural predator of right whales is the killer whale (*Orcinus orca*). Although six percent of the cataloged right whales have scars from killer whales, no killer whale attacks have ever been observed. It is unknown if any deaths have resulted from such attacks. Small pods of killer whales have been seen near shore in February in Florida, a time when that area is in use by small numbers of right whales (Layne 1965).

SIGNIFICANCE OF THE SPECIES AND HISTORICAL PERSPECTIVE

Scientists have been investigating the basic natural history of this intriguing animal for only 20 years; therefore it is difficult, at this time, to fully understand the importance of right whales to marine ecosystems. However, because the right whale feeds exclusively on zooplankton, it may serve as an indicator of the health of the food chain at lower trophic levels.

Historically, the abundance of the right whale served as the impetus for the development of whaling. The species was considered the "right" whale to kill and derives its common name from this designation. Early whalers found that the species had a number of attractive characteristics that made it highly valuable. The whales inhabited coastal waters, swam slowly, floated when dead (enabling whalers in rowboats to easily catch and tow the animals back to shore stations for flensing), and yielded large quantities of oil and very long baleen. The oil was valuable for its uses in lamps and soaps and the baleen was highly prized by the corset industry. Basque, Dutch, English, and Yankee whalers concentrated their efforts on the right whale so intensely that all stocks in the North Atlantic became severely depleted by the late 1700s. This intense and relentless hunting of the right whale for nearly a thousand years probably brought the species closer to extinction than any other species of large whale that still survives today. Because the right whale has been pushed to this precipice, it has a significant role in raising public awareness and focusing attention on the need to protect marine wildlife and their habitats.

Basque whalers apparently depleted the right whale stock in the northeast Atlantic by 1500 and, by 1530, had established a right whale fishery on the coast of Newfoundland and Labrador (Aquilar 1986). Details concerning the Basque right whale fishery in Labrador are sketchy. However, it has been estimated that between 300 and 500 right whales were taken yearly between 1530 and 1610, totaling 25,000 to 40,000 animals caught over an 80-year period (Aguilar 1986).

In addition to Basque whaling, New England colonists began hunting right whales shortly after they arrived in the New World. Coastal right whale fisheries existed in Massachusetts and Long Island from 1650 to the early 1900s. Data from records of the Long Island fishery account for approximately 550 right whales taken between 1650 and 1924 (Reeves and Mitchell 1986a). The right whale catch in New England waters was not as extensive as that of the Long Island fishery. By 1725, the numbers of right whales in both areas had declined substantially, forcing whalers to sail to other areas and hunt other species for their livelihood. Pelagic right whaling took place on the Cape Farewell Ground approximately 250 miles southeast of Greenland from 1868 to 1897. An estimated 25 animals were taken during this period (Reeves and Mitchell 1986b). Along the southeast United States coast from 1876 to 1882, approximately 25 to 30 right whales were taken (Reeves and Mitchell 1986b). The right whale was considered to be virtually extinct by the early part of the twentieth century.

CURRENT TRENDS

The North Atlantic right whale can be legitimately identified as the only species of large whale still in danger of extinction. Analyses of the current population size range from a minimum count of 240 (New England Aquarium, unpubl. data) to an estimate of 493 (± 1100–95 percent confidence interval) (CeTAP 1982). It is not known how many right whales remained in 1935 when full protection was imposed, but there may have been fewer than 100 animals. If this were the case, then the stock may be displaying a slow rate of growth.

Ongoing research, using primarily photographic "tags," has yielded important information about minimum population counts, habitat use, and migration movements. Since 1980, consistent photo-identification effort in the Bay of Fundy and Browns Bank areas has resulted in a photographic catalog of over 240 different right whales. The number of new animals seen each year, excluding calves, is extremely low, indicating that most of the population that occurs in these areas has been previously identified.

The increase in observer effort in the northeast United States during the last 20 years has resulted in increasing numbers of *E. glacialis* sightings, but may not reflect actual trends in the population. Historical evidence indicates that right whales are no longer abundant in former portions of their range, for example, the Strait of Belle Isle and the coastal waters of Long Island, New York.

All the survey data collected to date are too imprecise to identify any increase or decrease in this population. Better information on calving rates, calving intervals, gestation, longevity, and mortality is needed before assessments about the right whales' status can be considered reliable.

MANAGEMENT

Right whales were protected from commercial whaling by a 1931 League of Nations Resolution that took effect in 1935. This protection has been continued by the International Whaling Commission since 1946. Since then, right whales in U.S. waters have come under the added protection of the Marine Mammal Protection Act of 1972 and the Endangered Species Act of 1973. Right whales are listed as a protected species by the International Whaling Commission, and as endangered (Appendix I) under both the Convention on International Trade in Endangered Species (CITES) and the Committee on the Status of Endangered Wildlife in Canada (Gaskin 1987). They are also protected by the Cetacean Protection Regulations of Canada. With one known exception where a right whale was killed "by mistake" (Sergeant 1966), the international protection laws have been observed in the western North Atlantic.

Within the United States, the Marine Mammal Protection Act of 1972 established a national policy designed to protect marine mammals. The act prohibits the taking of any marine mammal with certain limited exceptions. The Endangered Species Act of 1973 made it a violation to "take, or harass, harm, pursue, hunt, shoot, wound, kill, capture, or collect" endangered species. The act requires that all federal agencies consult with the National Marine Fisheries Service to ensure that any action they take or permit does not jeopardize the continued existence of any species listed as endangered or threatened or adversely affect its critical habitat. (See the "National Marine Fisheries Service" chapter in this volume; for historical background on the service, see the 1985, 1986, and 1987 *Audubon Wildlife Reports*). Almost all activities that may degrade the habitat of the right whale are regulated by some federal agency, hence the act's requirement is an important regulatory tool for protecting the species.

Funding for research to collect essential natural history data on right whales has been sporadic. The federal government, via the National Marine Fisheries Service, has provided limited funding since 1980; private agencies and foundations have helped fill the gaps. State governments of coastal states where right whales are found have recently begun to take an interest in this species. Georgia, Florida, and Massachusetts have each provided financial and/or administrative assistance in the past four years.

In late 1986, five different organizations studying right whales along the East Coast formed the North Atlantic Right Whale Consortium. The consortium includes scientists at the New England Aquarium, University of Rhode Island, The Center for Coastal Studies, Woods Hole Oceanographic Institute, and Marineland of Florida. Congress appropriated funding to the consortium on an annual basis, allowing the organizations to integrate data bases and photo files to create a more complete picture of the species' natural history. With this data, preparation of an effective recovery plan will be more feasible. In 1987, the National Marine Fisheries Service announced the formation of recovery teams for humpback and right whales, with the goal of producing draft recovery plans sometime in 1988.

PROGNOSIS

Assessing the future of the North Atlantic right whale entails balancing incomplete knowledge of its natural history, imprecise population estimates, and apparently significant human effects on this species, against the economic pressures to develop shipping, fisheries, and ocean minerals. Given the low birth rate of the whale, the population's recovery will be a long process even under the best of conditions. However, if natural growth is offset by higher than normal mortality, then the future of this species becomes questionable.

Although 18 dead right whales have been recorded in the western North Atlantic since 1970, the only information available on mortality rates is from animals that wash up on beaches or that are found floating dead. Cataloged animals that have not been resighted for several years may be dead.

Five calves—which constitute 28 percent of the 18 known deaths—including three possible neonates, have stranded on beaches in the southeastern United States. These calves probably represent natural mortality. However, fishing and shipping are two significant human sources of right whale mortality. Six of the 18 (33 percent) documented deaths have been directly attributed to these two factors. (See the chapter on "Plastic Debris and its Effects on Marine Wildlife" in this volume.)

Mortality from Human Activity

Shipping. At least four juveniles and one calf have been killed by ship strikes; five percent of cataloged right whales have scars apparently caused by ships. Right whales engage in several activities that make them susceptible to being struck by vessels, including resting on the surface, surface-swimming while feeding, and courtship. Their susceptibility to collisions with ships is enhanced partly because of the length of time they spend at the surface and partly because they seem to be fairly oblivious to approaching vessels. In addition, because of the tendency of right whales to swim in coastal waters, where vessels are numerous, their chance of being struck is increased.

Fishing. Entanglement of right whales in fishing gear is another cause for concern. Although right whales are not fish eaters, their coastal tendency puts them in areas where fishing activities are common. Ten right whales have been entangled in fishing gear since 1975, primarily gill nets, but also in lines from lobster pots and in fishing weirs. One adult that got caught in a cod trap in Newfoundland swam off with the trap and anchors wrapped around it. It is assumed that the whale died. In addition, 58 percent of the cataloged right whales show scars indicating chafing from previous entanglements.

Other Potential Problems

There are additional potential threats to right whales or their habitat that may adversely affect the species' chance for survival.

Acoustic Disturbance. It is unknown if underwater noise generated by shipping and boat traffic interferes with the communication of right whales. Concern has been expressed about the effects of underwater sounds on the ability of cows and calves to stay together, and on adults to find one another for mating.

Minerals Exploration and Industrial Disturbance. Along the continental shelf of Canada and the United States, seismic exploration and exploratory drilling is under way or planned in several areas within 40 miles of right whale habitat. Gray and bowhead whales change behavior and direction in response to some seismic activity associated with minerals exploration, and bowheads have been shown to alter behavior patterns in response to drill-rig noise and vessel traffic (Malme *et al.* 1983, Richardson *et al.* 1983). The long-term effects of these responses, however, and the applicability of these findings to right whales, are unknown. In addition, major questions still exist regarding the effects of oil spills or the discharge of drilling muds on prey species (copepods), and on the whales themselves (for example, clogging of baleen).

Whale Watching. Right whales are subject to whale watching by people in Cape Cod Bay and to a limited degree in the Bay of Fundy and on the Nova Scotian Shelf. There are no data on the effects of this human activity on any whale species. The National Marine Fisheries Service has issued whale watching guidelines for all species, and the North Atlantic Marine Mammal Association has issued recommendations specifically for right whales. Although it is difficult to monitor private boats—an issue only in Cape Cod Bay—organized whale-watch boat operators are fairly respectful of these guidelines.

Habitat Degradation. Widespread water pollution may prove to be an extremely important factor affecting the recovery of the right whale population. The whale apparently requires extremely dense concentrations of plankton to survive (Kenney *et al.* 1985); a reduction in that food source could have severe effects on the whales' population. Habitat degradation resulting in decreased density of plankton patches may have been a significant cause for right whales' vacating historic habitats such as Delaware Bay, the coastal waters of New York and New Jersey, and Long Island Sound (Reeves *et al.* 1978).

In the final analysis, right whales are extremely vulnerable to the effects of human activities. The low population size and the coastal habits of the species—particularly cows with calves—are significant factors to be considered.

Recommendations

The key to the recovery of the right whale in the western North Atlantic is the establishment of a series of seasonal "sanctuaries" along the east coast of the United States and Canada. During the time of year when these areas are used by the whales, potentially harmful activities to the species should be limited. Recommendations for the areas, seasons, and restrictions are as follows:

1. A January to March sanctuary along the coasts of Georgia and Florida, during which time near shore shipping traffic, dredging, and minerals exploration activities would be restricted.
2. A March to June sanctuary in Cape Cod Bay that will include a ban on fixed fishing gear in the area.
3. A July to November sanctuary in the Bay of Fundy, including a gill net ban.
4. A July to November sanctuary on the Nova Scotian Shelf, during which time shipping lanes would be adjusted to go either north or south of the right whale concentration. Minerals development activities should be banned in the high-use right whale area between Browns and Baccaro banks.

These recommendations follow the spirit of the International Whaling Commission's recommendation that "areas critical to their [right whale] survival and continued recovery should be managed to exclude the effects of [industrial and human-caused] disturbances" (Brownell *et al.* 1986).

However, restricting shipping traffic through Massachusetts Bay in the shipping lanes that lead into Boston is not feasible. Therefore, a program should be implemented to determine the feasibility of using acoustical "scare devices" that would alert whales to the presence of large vessels during the species' time of peak concentration.

A recommendation being considered by the National Marine Fisheries Service is to upgrade whale watching guidelines to regulations. In 1986 in Cape Cod Bay, where whale watching is a multimillion dollar business, the lack of humpback whales led the industry to concentrate on right whales. At one time, as many as seven boats 80 feet or more in length observed a single cow/calf pair. Although there are no data available on the effects of this type of activity on whales, it may be best to give the species all due consideration. Our observations indicate, unfortunately, that "whale to boat distance" or "watching duration" regulations would be nearly unenforceable. An appropriate approach would be to ban all whale watching of mothers and calves, who are the most potentially vulnerable component of the population.

Research

One of the major problems in implementing plans for right whale recovery is that knowledge of the animal's basic biology, as well as its distribution and habitat needs, is incomplete. A high priority, therefore, should be given to continued and additional intensive research as follows:

1. Search for currently unknown habitats and migratory routes, perhaps with the aid of radio and satellite tags.
2. Obtain better population estimates and mortality and reproductive rates in order to detect current trends.
3. Conduct studies on the species' feeding habits, prey requirements, habitat use, and behavioral patterns, and on the effects of human activities upon these factors.
4. Refine knowledge of the right whale's basic biological parameters—gestation, age at sexual maturity, and longevity.
5. Initiate genetic studies to determine the level of inbreeding in this population, provide sex ratio data, and improve information on the effects of inbreeding on the species' ability to recover.
6. Improve understanding of the nature, extent, and effects of right whale encounters with fishing gear.
7. Determine the effects of shipping and other vessel activities, including whale watching, recreational boating, fishing operations, military activities, and minerals exploration and extraction, on right whales.
8. Assess the nature and effects of environmental pollution—lost and discarded fishing gear and other marine debris, chemicals and other pollutants in sewage discharges, runoff, and dredging spoils—on right whale food and habitat.

To ensure survival and recovery of this population, both the United States and Canadian governments must make right whale protection a long-term priority. Because of the complexity of the issues facing right whale managers, effective coordination of activities that affect the species is critical. The active support of states, provinces, conservation groups, marine industries, and concerned individuals will also be essential to the success of any recovery effort.

REFERENCES

Aguilar, A. 1986. "A review of old Basque whaling and its effect on the right whales of the North Atlantic," pp. 191–200 *in* R.L. Brownell, Jr., P.B. Best and J.H. Prescott eds., *Right Whales: Past and Present Status*, special issue no. 10. International Whaling Commission. Cambridge, England.

Brownell, R.L., P.B. Best and J.H. Prescott (eds). 1986. "Report of the Workshop on the Status of right whales," pp. 1–14 in *Right Whales: Past and Present Status*, special issue no. 10. International Whaling Commission. Cambridge, England.

CeTAP. 1982. *A Characterization of Marine Mammals and Turtles in the Mid- and North Atlantic Areas of the U.S. Outer Continental Shelf.* Final report of the Cetacean and Turtle Assessment Program to the U.S. Department of Interior. Contract AA551-CT8–48.

Gaskin, D.E. 1987. "Updated status of the right whale, (*Eubalaena glacialis*), in Canada." *Canadian Field-Naturalist* 101(2):295–309.

Klumov, S.K. 1962. "The right whale in the Pacific ocean," *in* P.I. Usachev ed., *Biological Marine Studies, Trudy Institute Okeanographie* 58: 202–297.

Kraus, S.D. 1985. "A review of the status of right whales (*Eubalaena glacialis*) in the western North Atlantic with a summary of research and management needs." *National Technical Information Services Publication* PB86–154143: 1–61.

——., J.H. Prescott, P.V. Turnbull and R.R. Reeves. 1982. "Preliminary notes on the occurrence of the North Atlantic right whale, (*Eubalaena glacialis*), in the Bay of Fundy." *Report of the International Whaling Commission* 32:407–411.

——., J.H. Prescott and G.S. Stone. 1983. "Right whales in the northern Gulf of Maine." *Whalewatcher* 17(4):18–21.

——., K.E. Moore, C.E. Price, M.J. Crone, W.A. Watkins, H.E. Winn and J.H. Prescott. 1986a. "The use of photographs to identify individual North Atlantic right whales (*Eubalaena glacialis*)," pp. 145–151 *in* R.L. Brownell, Jr., P.B. Best and J.H. Prescott eds., *Right Whales: Past and Present Status*, special issue no. 10. International Whaling Commission. Cambridge, England.

——., J.H. Prescott, A.R. Knowlton and G.S. Stone. 1986b. "Migration and calving of right whales (*Eubalaena glacialis*) in the western North Atlantic," pp. 139–144 *in* R.L. Brownell, Jr., P.B. Best and J.H. Prescott eds., *Right Whales: Past and Present Status*, special issue no. 10. International Whaling Commission. Cambridge, England.

Layne, J.N. 1965. "Observations on marine mammals in Florida waters." *Bulletin of the Florida State Museum* 9:131–181.

Malme, C.I., P.R. Miles, C.W. Clark, P. Tyack and J.E. Bird. 1983. *Investigations of the Potential Effects of Underwater Noise from Petroleum Industry Activities on Migrating Gray Whale Behavior.* Report No. 5366 from BB&N to the U.S. Department of Interior, Minerals Management Service, under contract AA851-CT2–39.

Mitchell, E.D., V.M. Kozicki and R.R. Reeves. 1986. "Sightings of right whales, *Eubalaena glacialis*, on the Scotian Shelf, 1966–1972," *in* R.L. Brownell, Jr., P.B. Best and J.H. Prescott eds., *Right Whales: Past and Present Status*, special issue no. 10. International Whaling Commission. Cambridge, England.

Payne, R., O. Brazier, E.M. Dorsey, J.S. Perkins, V.J. Rowntree and A. Titus. 1983. "External features in southern right whales (*Eubalaena australis*) and their use in identifying individuals," pp. 371–445 *in* R. Payne ed., *Communication and Behavior of Whales*. Westview Press. Boulder, Colorado.

——. 1986. "Long term behavioral studies of the southern right whale (*Eubalaena australis*)," pp. 161–168 *in* R.L. Brownell Jr., P.B. Best, and J.H. Prescott eds., *Right Whales: Past and Present Status*, special issue no. 10. International Whaling Commission. Cambridge, England.

Reeves, R.R., J.G. Mead, and S.K. Katona. 1978. "The right whale, *Eubalaena glacialis*, in the western North Atlantic." *Report of the International Whaling Commission* 28: 303–312.

——. and E. Mitchell. 1986a. "The Long Island (New York) right whale fishery: 1650–1924," pp. 101–220 *in* R.L. Brownell, Jr., P.B. Best and J.H. Prescott eds., *Right Whales: Past and Present Status*, special issue no. 10. International Whaling Commission. Cambridge, England.

——. and ——. 1986b. "American pelagic whaling for right whales in the North Atlantic," pp. 221–254 *in* R.L. Brownell, Jr., P.B. Best and J.H. Prescott eds., *Right Whales: Past and Present Status*, special issue no. 10. International Whaling Commission. Cambridge, England.
Richardson, W.J., R.S. Wells and B. Wuersig. 1983. "Disturbance responses of bowheads, 1982," pp. 117–215 *in* W.J. Richardson ed., *Behavior, Disturbance Responses and Distribution of Bowhead Whales* (Balaena mysticetus) *in the eastern Beaufort Sea, 1982.* Unpublished Report from LGL Ecological Research Association, Inc, Bryan, Texas for U.S. Minerals Management Service, Reston, Virginia.
Rowntree, V. 1983. "Cyamids: The louse that moored." *Whalewatcher* 17(4):14–17.
Scarff, J.E. 1986. "Historic and present distribution of the right whale (*Eubalaena glacialis*) in the eastern North Pacific south of 50′ N and east of 180′ W (SC/35/RW26)" pp. 43–63 *in* R.L. Brownell, Jr., P.B. Best and J.H. Prescott eds., *Right Whales: Past and Present Status*, special issue no. 10. International Whaling Commission. Cambridge, England.
Schevill, W.E. 1986. "Right whale nomenclature," appendix 5: p. 19 *in* R.L. Brownell, Jr., P.B. Best and J.H. Prescott eds., *Right Whales: Past and Present Status*, special issue no. 10. International Whaling Commission. Cambridge, England.
Sergeant, D.E. 1966. Populations of Large Whale Species in the Western North Atlantic with Special Reference to the Fin Whale. Arctic Biological Station Circular no. 9. Fisheries Research Board of Canada. 13 pp.
Watkins, W.A. and W.E. Schevill. 1982. "Observations of right whales, *Eubalaena glacialis*, in Cape Cod waters." *Fisheries Bulletin* 80:875–880.
Winn, H.E. 1984. Development of a Right Whale Sighting Network in the Southeastern U.S. *National Technical Information Services Publication* no. PB84 240548. 12 pp.
——., E.A. Scott and R.D. Kenney. 1985. "Aerial surveys for right whales in the Great South Channel, Spring 1984." *National Technical Information Services Publication* no. PB85–207926.
——., C.A. Price and P.W. Sorensen. 1986. "The distributional biology of the right whale (*Eubalaena glacialis*) in the western North Atlantic," pp. 129–138 *in* R.L. Brownell, Jr., P.B. Best and J.H. Prescott eds., *Right Whales: Past and Present Status*, special issue no. 10. International Whaling Commission. Cambridge, England.

Scott Kraus is director of the New England Aquarium's research program on right whales, now in its ninth year. Martie Crone has worked on the program for five years and is currently responsible for curating the catalog of identified North Atlantic right whales. Amy Knowlton has also been with the program for five years and coordinates all the field research in the calving ground off the southeastern United States.

Populations of the Alaska red king crab (top) and the Dungeness crab, two large and economically important Pacific Coast species, have inexplicably declined in some areas. *Dan Wickham; Oregon Seagrant/Larison*

The Dungeness Crab and the Alaska Red King Crab

Daniel E. Wickham
Bodega Marine Laboratory

SPECIES DESCRIPTION AND NATURAL HISTORY

The Dungeness crab (*Cancer magister*) and Alaska red king crab (*Paralithodes camtschatica*) are two of the largest and most abundant crabs on the Pacific coast of North America. The Dungeness crab is one of seven *Cancer* species on the West Coast (Schmitt 1921). This species can weigh over 4.4 pounds and have a carapace width of 9.6 inches, which is shorter in length than width. The shell is relatively smooth, greenish tan in color, and possesses minute tubercles on top arranged in a distinctive pattern. The underside of the Dungeness crab is creamy white in color. There are nine spines along the antero-lateral border of the shell to the widest part, with no spines behind. The tip of the abdomen is rounded instead of pointed as in the other local *Cancer* species. The digits, or "dactyls," of the claws are white and more delicate than those of the rock crabs of the genus. The underside of the shell's front portion is covered with fine hairs. The abdomen of the male is narrow and approximately the same width over its length. The female has a much wider abdomen, which covers most of the thorax (area between the neck and abdomen) when folded under. Two pairs of abdominal appendages on the male are modified for sperm transfer during mating. The female has four pairs of bristly, or "setaceous," abdominal appendages which are modified for brooding eggs.

The Alaska red king crab is the largest crab in U.S. waters. It is one of four species on the Pacific coast commonly referred to as king crabs (Dawson and Yaldwyn 1985). The red king crab can weigh up to 24 pounds. This crab has a tan-colored, pyramid-shaped carapace which, unlike the carapace of most crabs, is longer than it is wide. The carapace on the adult is knobby while juvenile king crabs are covered by very long, sharp spines. A long rostral spine protrudes in front of the eyes. The legs are very long relative to the length of the carapace; specimens can measure up to six feet in leg span.

Males are distinguished from females by the smaller size of the abdominal fold. Unlike Dungeness crabs, in which the egg clutch is too large to be entirely covered by the fold, king crabs' clutches are completely hidden by the abdomen. The abdomen is made up of many small plates—a leathery matrix arrayed in a twisted asymetric fashion. This characteristic demonstrates their relationship to other anomuran crabs, for example, the hermit crab and the coconut crab.

Distribution

The range of the Dungeness crab extends from Magdalena Bay, Baja California, to the Aleutian Islands, Alaska. To the south, however, it does not occur in any abundance south of Pt. Conception. From Eureka, California, the population extends largely as a single unit along the northern California, Oregon, and Washington coasts. The species extends into Puget Sound, Washington, and continues in abundance along the British Columbia and Alaskan coasts out to the Aleutians (see Figure 1).

The Alaska red king crab ranges from Japan in the western Pacific up through Russian waters into and throughout the Bering Sea, along the Aleutian chain, and into the Gulf of Alaska along the Southwest Peninsula, around Kodiak Island, into Cooks Inlet, and down the eastern shore of the Pacific as far south as British Columbia (see Figure 1).

Life Span

Dungeness crabs molt every one to two months during the first year of life (Butler 1961). In molting, the entire exoskeleton, including the lining of the gills, mouth, and anus, is shed. At this time, crustaceans drink water to expand the new skin so that it enlarges anywhere from 10 to 30 percent in width; calcium carbonate helps to harden it.

The intermolt period lengthens as the crabs mature. As adults they molt once a year. Male Dungeness crabs continue to molt and

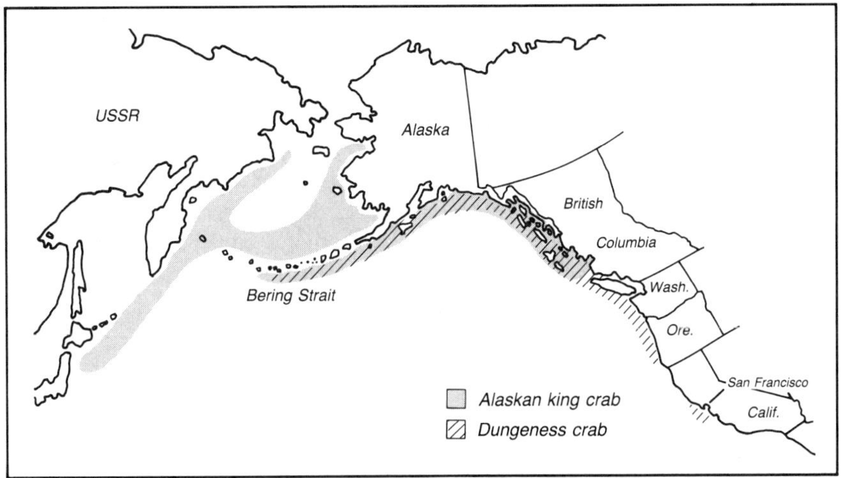

Figure 1. Distribution of Dungeness crab and the Alaska king crab.

grow for approximately eight years. Female growth is not well understood. Recent research suggests that they grow at a similar rate to males during their early lives, but may not live as long (Hankin *et al.* 1985). There are indications that females may become senescent and die at approximately five years of age. Sexual maturity in both males and females occurs when the carapace width is 4 to 4.4 inches and at an age of two- to two-and-a-half years. Red king crabs live up to 15 years, reaching sexual maturity at approximately 5 to 6 years of age and legal harvest size at 8 years.

Breeding

Mating in both Dungeness and king crabs occurs at the time of the female molt, when the male seeks out a female preparing to molt. The female may secrete pheromones at this time to attract the male. The female Dungeness crab normally responds aggressively when approached by another crab. When molt is near, the female becomes aquiescent and allows the male to capture and carry her until she molts. During the molt, the male crab helps her shed the exoskeleton and then copulation ensues. A sperm packet is deposited in the female, and the male carries the female for one or two days while she begins to harden her shell. She escapes from the male when she is able.

The ovarian cycle differs between Dungeness and king crabs, but the eggs of both species hatch into free-swimming larvae called zoea. Dungeness crabs mate in early spring, and females store the sperm while their ovaries develop. In the fall, the females extrude their eggs and use the stored sperm to fertilize them. The eggs flow out of the genital pore under the abdomen as a fluid mass. The female crabs need a sand substrate to successfully deposit their eggs.

The crab burrows in the sand and forms a cup under the abdomen. This depression allows the eggs to stay in place while the female mixes the egg mass with her "pleopods," or abdominal limbs. When the eggs meet with seawater, the membranes become tacky. As the hairs on her limbs pass through the sticky mixture, the eggs adhere to them, forming a cluster which she carries with her. Clutch sizes can range from one to two million eggs. The eggs are brooded from three to four months, depending on temperature.

The eggs hatch in late winter and remain planktonic for three to four months. They pass through five zoeal stages and a final larval stage, or the "megalopa." During the megalopa stage, the larvae are blown inshore by spring winds where they metamorphose into bottomdwelling juveniles. They can be found in bays and estuaries, but also are abundant in shallow coastal waters (Mackay 1942).

Female king crabs extrude their eggs at the same time as mating. The females have no seminal receptacle, hence sperm cannot be stored for later ovulation. Their large abdominal flap covers the entire clutch and therefore the female can cement the eggs to her abdominal limbs without having to burrow in the sediments. The eggs are brooded for approximately 11 months before hatching. Fecundity in this species varies from 150,000 to 400,000 eggs per clutch.

King crab larvae pass through four zoeal stages and one "glaucothoe" stage, which is the functional equivalent of the Dungeness megalopa stage. Larvae are planktonic for one to two months. Juveniles form pods—vast school-like aggregations of spiny young (Powell and Nickerson 1965a). Presumably this behavior provides defense against predation.

Ecological Interactions

Both species of crab, in their respective environments, are among the most abundant and significant predators present. Dungeness crabs prey virtually on any living vertebrate or invertebrate they encounter (Cotshall 1977). Crustaceans, clams, polychaete worms, barnacles, fish, and brittle stars make up a major portion of their diet. Cannibalism by the older crabs on younger crabs, or on soft, recently molted individuals, is also very common. As the young Dungeness crabs mature, they begin to move offshore, but rarely to depths of more than approximately 656 feet. Mayer (1973) demonstrated that this species was significant enough as a benthic predator to play the role of a "keystone species." Their predation on common dominant invertebrates provides room for less competitive invertebrates, thus increasing benthic diversity.

The dramatic effect of this predation was seen in Bodega Bay, California, during the summer of 1985. Unusual spring oceanographic conditions led to a large local settlement of larval crabs. The crabs were so concentrated that they virtually eliminated at least two of the harbor's most abundant invertebrates—the small clam (*Transenella tantilla*) and the tanaid crustacean (*Leptochelia dubia*). Sea gulls rapidly shifted their feeding activity to the heavily concentrated crabs, and, in one or two months, had eaten most of the small crabs. When shorebirds arrived the following winter, their food resources were dramatically reduced. Weights of birds appeared to decline relative to earlier years. Populations of *Leptochelia* and *Transenella* are still dramatically reduced, and is is not clear whether the earlier community will restore itself.

Different sets of predators focus on the Dungeness at different times during its life span. The most dramatic predator is a small ribbon worm (Nemertea). This worm (*Carcinonemertes errans*) lives symbiotically on the exoskeleton of host crabs. On females, the worms prey on the host's eggs. In several populations these worms consume enormous amounts. For example, the crab population on the central California coast can lose from 50 to 90 percent of their eggs to this type of predation (Wickham 1980). Since each of these eggs is a distinct genetic individual, *C. errans* is numerically the single most important predator on this crab population.

Dungeness crab larvae are preyed upon by many fish (for example, coho and chinook salmon) and planktonic predators. Newly settled juveniles are preyed upon extensively by adult Dungeness crabs and other crab species, seagulls and other shorebirds, and several fish species. Rays, small sharks, other large bottom fish (ling cod or halibut) and marine mammals (otters and sea lions) prey on adult crabs. Less is known about the life history of king crabs, but in general it would be similar to that of the Dungeness crab.

HISTORICAL PERSPECTIVE

Information on historical ranges and abundances of both Dungeness and king crabs is largely derived from commercial fishery catch statistics. While these crabs were used by Native Americans prior to European settlement, there is no information on the extensiveness of such use.

A small fishery for the Dungeness crab existed as far south as Morro Bay up to the 1950s. The area from Half Moon Bay (located south of San Francisco Bay) up to the Russian River in the north, makes up the major fishing ground for what is referred to as the central

California fishery. Clark and Bonnot (1940) found that there were two major grounds for this crab in California: the central California grounds and the northern California grounds which commence just north of Ft. Bragg. Very few crabs were found along some 200 miles of coast from the Russian River to Eureka, even prior to the onset of an extensive northern California fishery.

The central California fishery, centered at San Francisco and Bodega bays, was the first large-scale effort mounted for this species. The Dungeness is the well-known edible crab found at fishermen's wharves along the Pacific coast. The early fishery was conducted by small boats in the nearshore waters. Crabs were caught with hoop nets that were dropped and tended by the fishermen and brought back to the surface after a brief soak. A round crab trap introduced in the early 1900s could be left to soak overnight or for longer periods. This allowed larger boats to be used and a greater area to be fished. Clark and Bonnot (1940) showed that a fall off in the "catch per unit effort" occurred as the season progressed in the central California fishery but not in the northern California fishery. This indicated that the harvest rate in central California was high enough to remove most of the legally catchable stock each season.

Management of the fishery began in 1897 when it was made illegal to catch female crabs. In 1903, a season was started and in 1905 a size limit of six inches across the back was established. This was later changed to seven inches (six and a quarter inches if the lateral spines are not included). The biological rationale was primarily to protect the breeding stock. Most of the crabs caught were male crabs which had already had an opportunity to breed. The females were left behind to produce eggs.

The central California fishery proceeded for over half a century with a long-term average catch ranging from four to five million pounds. This poundage fluctuated somewhat cyclically. After a record high catch of over nine million pounds in 1957, the fishery collapsed. Over the past 30 years it has continued at approximately 10 percent of the earlier catches (Dahlstrom and Wild 1983).

The northern California, Oregon, and Washington fisheries did not begin in earnest until 1945. They rapidly built up, and over the past 40 years, fishery effort has increased to very high levels. Often the season lasts for less than a month, ending when there are not enough legal-sized males to harvest economically. Catch size fluctuates over a 9 to 10 year period, consisting of 6 to 7 good years and 2 to 3 bad ones. What drives these cycles is not known and is hotly debated.

Three general explanations have been offered. One theory is that grounds support intense effort for six or seven years and then are depleted; recovery takes three years. This explanation is not likely. Another explanation is large-scale cyclical oceanographic or meteorological phenomena which affect larval distribution, egg survival, or other biological factors. Yet another explanation depends on the species' density. During years of high abundance, new larval or juvenile crabs are crowded out or cannibalized, reducing the next generation. Conversely, when few adults are present, the inherent high fecundity is enough that sufficient eggs will be produced and that resulting juveniles will have no competition from adults, hence will survive well. The cycle is less apparent in British Columbia and Alaska, where the fishery is not operated with the same intensity.

The cause for the collapse of the central California Dungeness crab fishery is a second contentious scientific issue, and several explanations have been advanced. The most prominent concerns pollution coming from San Francisco Bay, but this theory has very little support. The period of highest catches coincided with some of the years of worst water quality. Reduction of fresh water flow from the Sacramento River has coincided with the reduction of crabs, but there is nothing to link the two. Land fill has certainly decreased available juvenile habitat in the Bay, but crab nurseries also exist outside of it. One theory linked an observed increase in ocean temperature in the 1950s to decreased egg survival. However, the ocean temperatures are normal once again and no recovery has occurred.

The only unequivocal data available for an elevated mortality source in natural populations are linked to the symbiotic ribbon worm. These worms are natural predators on crab eggs all over the world but usually cause only incidental mortality. For reasons not yet fully understood, these worms are very abundant in certain populations of both Dungeness and red king crabs. The author feels that apparent epizootics of these worms may relate to changes in the sex ratio brought about by the male only nature of the fisheries for these crabs. Research is currently under way investigating factors contributing to this mortality source.

Like the Dungeness crab, the red king crab occupies a broad geographical range. Information on its abundance is also limited to data available from the commercial fishery. The Alaskan fishery for this crab is relatively recent, with heavy exploitation beginning in the 1950s. By the early 1960s, nearly 180 million pounds of red king crab were being caught each year. Waters around Kodiak Island contributed most of the king crabs. The catches declined in the late 1960s to some 40 million pounds. Catches again increased to a peak of about 180 million pounds during the 1970s, but this time Bristol Bay contributed most of the catch. The Kodiak fishery never recovered to the 1960s level.

Recently there has been a dramatic and alarming decline in abundance of Alaska red king crab in all of the fishery areas. In 1980, the statewide catch was almost 180 million pounds. In 1981, it declined to 65 million pounds, and by 1982 it was only 20 million pounds. Since then, the fishery has been almost completely at a standstill. Many areas have been closed and catches have been less than one million pounds.

As with the collapse of the central California Dungeness crab population, there are more theories to account for the decline of the fishery than data to support them. There is no obvious reason to conclude that the stocks were simply fished out. There have been large increases in the populations of certain predators, such as codfish, in certain Alaskan waters, but it seems unlikely that fish predation could affect king crabs over such a large area. There is little real data to support this.

There are data to suggest that disease could be a factor in the decline. Sparks and Morada (1985) found that a highly pathogenic virus and microsporidian were present in wild stocks of red king crabs. The problem with the study is that it was conducted after the major collapse of the population; hence the authors may have missed the major period of epidemic disease if it occurred.

The ribbon worm is another source of mortality affecting Alaska red king crabs. Several populations of these crabs have been found harboring extremely high densities of several undescribed species of ribbon worms (Wickham *et al.* 1985). Egg losses in populations near Kodiak and Cooks Inlet are total in some cases. As with other disease organisms, epidemic spread could occur during the peak years of abundance.

CURRENT TRENDS

The population of Dungeness crabs along the Pacific coast appear to be continuing in the well-known pattern of cyclic abundance, with the exception of the central California population. The region from Half Moon Bay and extending north to the Russian River continues to have crab populations which are low relative to earlier periods. Research on these declines has not clearly identified the cause.

Populations in northern California, Oregon, and Washington have been low in the early 1980s, after a period of abundance during the 1970s. There was a large settlement of young-of-the-year crabs along the Pacific coast in 1984. If the 1984 settlement leads to an increase in abundance, harvest rates should begin to increase in the 1988 season.

Trends in fishing effort in all fishery regions, excluding central California, are on the increase. Effort is increasing in British Columbia and Alaska as well.

Trends in the king crab fishery suggest that these populations are seriously depleted. Their levels continue to be low and little evidence indicates that an early recovery is in sight. The Bristol Bay population appears to be the only one in which the recruitment of young crabs is sufficient to expect decent catches in the next few years (Blau 1985). A red king crab takes nearly eight years to grow to legal harvest size, so the lack of successful recruitment of small crabs indicates the decline will last for at least that long.

Fishing effort on king crabs is now shifting to two other species, the blue king crab (*Paralithodes platypus*), which occurs in the Bering Sea, and the brown or golden king crab (*Lithodes aequispina*) in the Gulf of Alaska. The limited size of both these populations make it unlikely that either will produce the previously abundant yields of the red king crab.

MANAGEMENT

Dungeness crab management is similar in California, Oregon, and Washington. Females cannot be taken; males must be six and a quarter inches in carapace width to be legally taken. A season is in effect in each region. Economic and biological factors play an important role in regulations. The female ban is partly due to the lower value placed on them. They rarely reach market size and contain much less meat, which is often of lesser quality. The season was instituted in response to the molting seasonality of male crabs. Crabs which have recently molted have thin shells and the meat quantity and quality is reduced. The season is timed to occur when most crabs have hardened and filled out. The size limit is established to ensure that a legal-sized crab will have at least one, and probably two, opportunities to mate. Molting, the process by which crabs grow, results in a stepwise distribution of sizes. The current size limit falls between molt stages 13 and 14 (Butler 1961).

The California Department of Fish and Game collected information on preseason abundance up until the early 1970s. They stopped the assessment due to budget constraints and to pressure caused by conflict between buyers and sellers in reaching a market price at the season opening. There is no attempt to actively manage or to limit fishing effort in this fishery.

Research has addressed the need to ameliorate problems in the central California Dungeness crab fishery. Attempts at developing a hatchery capability for the species have been carried out by the University of California and the California Department of Fish and Game. Neither effort was able to develop an economic method for rearing mass quantites of crab larvae. The only regulatory attempt to protect this species in central California is a ban placed on the sport fishery inside San Francisco Bay.

Experiments to reduce levels of the ribbon worm, by dipping egg-bearing females in fresh water, have shown some success. While fishermen from Bodega Bay occasionally use this technique, no systematic effort to eradicate the worm has been undertaken.

The British Columbia Dungeness crab fishery is managed similarly to the U.S. fisheries, with the exception that females may be caught. Since female crabs rarely attain the minimum legal size, they make up a smaller proportion of the catch than males.

Management of the king crab fisheries in Alaska is more active. As with the Dungeness, management subscribes to the three *s*'s: size, sex, and season. It is a male-only fishery, and males must be greater than six and a half inches in carapace width. Seasons vary from region to region, but quotas are also set on the basis of preseason abundance surveys. The Alaska Department of Fish and Game attempts to restrict catches to no more than 40 percent of the estimated number of legal-sized males. In the last few years they have reduced this to as low as 25 percent. Lately, the fishing effort has been so intense that the individual openings of most crab grounds last for only one or two days. Most of the red king crab populations are now closed to fishing because of insufficient recruitment.

PROGNOSIS

Dungeness crab populations in central California still appear to be relatively low. No current evidence suggests any imminent recovery of the resource, although slight increases in the next year or two may result from increased production of crab larvae farther north. This crab species does not appear to be in danger of extinction. The low level is primarily an economic problem.

Large settlements of juvenile Dungeness crabs were seen in 1984 in northern California, Oregon, and Washington. This should lead to productive fisheries starting in 1988 when these crabs reach market size. If an increase occurs and the crab cycle follows previous ones, five to seven years of high takes can be expected, followed by a decline. It may be that this pattern will continue indefinitely, precluding any change in management policy. The only caution to this prognosis is that the central California population cycled in a similar manner—beginning some 30 years earlier than the northern populations—but collapsed after a record peak of crab abundance in 1957. If this dynamic relates to fishing-induced changes in population (Botsford and Wickham 1978), a similar collapse in northern waters is, at least, possible. If large-scale environmental changes are involved in the central California collapse, no such fear of a broader collapse is warranted.

The prognosis of the red king crab is for continued depression in the fishery in all regions except Bristol Bay. Given the lack of juvenile crabs in most of these regions, the depression could be long term (Blau 1985). Increasing pressure can be expected on the other king crab species. If these alternate crab species are managed similarly to the red king crab, they also may suffer an eventual decline.

RECOMMENDATIONS

Changes in the size limit of Dungeness takes do not appear to be warranted. The only rationale for that would be to increase the males' breeding activity. At this time, however, all data demonstrate that there are sufficient males for breeding and sufficient time for them to breed before they are caught.

The only regulation that may merit change is the ban on females. It is an interesting coincidence that both the Alaska king and Dungeness crab fisheries use this management technique and that they have both experienced wide fluctuations in abundance and collapses in certain populations.

British Columbia has no ban on taking female Dungeness' and experiences much lower levels of population fluctuation. In addition, several other major crustacean fisheries worldwide allow takes of both male and females, with no apparent harm to the resource. McKelvey *et al.* (1980) modeled the crab cycles and believed that female abundance and fecundity was the primary driving force for the fluctuations, but noted that little was known about females in the population.

Researchers have just begun to address the role of the male-only fishery in generating epizootics of *Carcinonemertes*. By reducing the proportion of males in the population it is theoretically possible to increase the number of worms getting to female crabs. Worms need to eat crab eggs to reproduce, so factors that increase the number of worms gaining access to eggs will increase worm reproduction. To the extent that changes in sex-ratio of crabs actually causes increase in worm feeding and reproduction, modifications of crab sex ratios such as opening a female fishery might interrupt worm epizootics.

Disease organisms in the Alaskan red king crab are also probably spread through sexual contact. It is possible that changes in mating systems brought about by sex-specific takes might also facilitate disease spread. To date, however, no serious analyses have addressed disease transmission in commercial crab populations.

One recommendation would be to undertake studies to re-evaluate the efficacy of prohibiting the harvesting of females. Another recommendation could include a more active management of the Dungeness resource. However, an active management strategy has not preserved the red king crab resource. If fishing for female Dungeness crabs is ever allowed, it would be essential to establish some form of quota system to maintain a sufficient level of egg production.

REFERENCES

Blau, S.F. 1985. "Overview and comparison of the major red king crab (*Paralithodes camtschatica*) surveys and fisheries in western Alaska 1969–1984," pp. 23–47 in *Proceedings of the International King Crab Symposium.* Alaska Sea Grant Report No. 85–12. University of Alaska.

Botsford, L.W. and D.E. Wickham. 1978. "Behavior of age-specific density dependent models and the northern California Dungeness crab (*Cancer magister*) fishery." *Journal of the Fisheries Resources Board, Canada* 35:833–843.

——. 1961. "Growth and age determination of the Pacific edible crab *Cancer magister* Dana." *Journal of the Fisheries Resources Board, Canada* 18:873–889.

Clark, G.H. and P. Bonnot. 1940. "The utilization of the California crab resource." *California Fish and Game* 26:374–380

Dahlstrom, W.A. and P.W. Wild. 1983. "A history of Dungeness crab fisheries in California." *California Fish and Game* 172:7–23.

Dawson, W.W. and J.C. Yaldwyn. 1985. "King crabs of the world or the world of the king crabs," pp. 69–106 in *Proceedings of the International King Crab Symposium.* Alaska Sea Grant Report No. 85–12. University of Alaska.

Gotshall, S.W. 1977. "Stomach contents of northern California Dungeness crabs, *Cancer magister.*" *California Fish and Game* 63:43–51.

Hankin, D.G., N. Diamond, M. Mohr and J. Ianelli. 1985. "Molt increments, annual molting probabilities, fecundity and survival rates of adult female Dungeness crabs in northern California," pp. 189–209 in *Proceedings of the Symposium on Dungeness Crab Biology and Management.* Alaska Sea Grant Report No. 85–3. University of Alaska.

MacKay, D.C.G. 1942. "The Pacific edible crab, *Cancer magister.*" *Journal of the Fisheries Resources Board, Canada* 62.

McKelvey, R., D. Hankin, K. Yanosko, and C. Snygg. 1980. "Stable cycles in multistage recruitment models: an application to the northern California Dungeness crab (*Cancer magister*) fishery." *Canadian Journal of Fish. Acquat. Sci.* 37:2323–2344

Powell, G. and R. Nickerson. 1965a. "Aggregation among juvenile king crabs (*Paralithodes camtschatica* Tilesius), Kodiak, Alaska." *Animal Behavior* 13:374–380.

Schmitt, W.L. 1921. "Marine decapod Crustacea of California." *University of California Publication of Zoology* 23:1–470.

Sparks, A.K. and J.F. Morada. 1985. "A preliminary report on the diseases of Alaska king crabs," pp. 333–339 in *Proceedings of the International King Crab Symposium.* Alaska Sea Grant Report No. 85–12. University of Alaska.

Wickham D. 1980. "Aspects of the life history of *Carcinonemertes errans* (Nemertea: Carcinonemertidae), an egg predator of the crab, *Cancer magister.*" *Biological Bulletin* 139:247–257.

——., P. Roe and A.M. Kuris. 1984. "Transfer of nemertean egg predators during host molting and copulation." *Biological Bulletin* 167:331–3387.

——., S.F. Blau and A.M. Kuris. 1985. "Preliminary report on egg mortality in Alaskan king crabs caused by the egg predator Carcinonemertes," pp. 365–370 in *Proceedings of the International King Crab Symposium.* Alaska Sea Grant Report No. 85–12. University of Alaska.

——. 1986. "Epizotic infestations by nemertean brood parasites on commercially important crustaceans." *Canadian Journal Fish. Aquat. Sci.* 43:2295–2302.

Daniel Wickham has been conducting research at the University of California's Bodega Marine Laboratory in Bodega Bay, California, for the past 15 years.

Part Five

Appendices

APPENDIX A

Forest Service Directory

(As of January 1, 1988)

WASHINGTON HEADQUARTERS

Mailing Address:
Forest Service-USDA
P.O. Box 96090
Washington, D.C. 20013-6090

Public Inquiries
202-447-3957

Title	Name	Phone
Chief	F. Dale Robertson	202-447-6661
Associate Chief	George Leonard	202-447-7491
National Forest System		
Deputy Chief	J. Lamar Beasley	202-447-3523
Director, Engineering	Sterling Wilcox	202-235-8035
Director, Lands	Richard Hull	202-235-8212
Director, Land Management Planning	Everett Towle	202-447-6697
Director, Minerals and Geology Management	Buster LaMoure	202-235-8105
Director, Range Management	Robert Williamson	202-235-8139
Director, Recreation Management	John Butruille	202-447-3706
Director, Timber Management	Dave Hessel	202-447-6893
Director, Watershed and Air Management	Gray Reynolds	202-235-8096
Director, Wildlife and Fisheries	Robert Nelson	202-235-8015
State and Private Forestry		
Deputy Chief	Allan West	202-447-6657
Director, Fire and Aviation Management	Lawrence Amicarella	202-235-8039

Title	Name	Phone
Director, Cooperative Forestry	Tony Dorrell	202-235-2212
Director, Forest Pest Management	James Space	202-235-1560
Research		
Deputy Chief	John Ohman	202-447-6665
Director, Forest Environment Research	Richard Smythe	202-235-1071
Director, Forest Fire and Atmospheric Sciences Research	William Sommers	202-235-8195
Director, Forest Insect and Disease Research	James Stewart	202-235-8065
Director, Forest Products and Harvesting Research	Stanley Bean, Jr.	202-235-1203
Director, Forest Inventory and Economics Research	H. Fred Kaiser, Jr.	202-447-2747
Director, International Forestry	David Harcharik	202-235-2743
Director, Timber Management Research	Stanley Krugman	202-235-8200
Programs and Legislation		
Deputy Chief	Jeff Sirmon	202-447-6663
Director, Environmental Coordination	David Ketcham	202-447-4708
Director, Legislative Affairs	Roger Leonard	202-447-7531
Director, Policy Analysis	Vacant	202-447-2775
Director, Program Development and Budget	John Leasure	202-447-6987
Director, Resources Program and Assessment	Thomas Hamilton	202-382-8235
Administration		
Deputy Chief	William Rice	202-447-6707
Office of General Counsel—USDA		
Assistant General Counsel, Natural Resources Division	Clarence Brizee	202-447-7121

REGIONAL HEADQUARTERS AND NATIONAL FORESTS

Region 1—Northern Region (Montana Idaho [northern], North Dakota [northwestern])

Federal Building
P.O. Box 7669
Missoula, MT 59807
406-329-3511

Regional Forester: James Overbay
Director, Wildlife and Fisheries: Kirk Horn

Region 2—Rocky Mountain (Colorado, Kansas, Nebraska, South Dakota [except northwestern], Wyoming [eastern])

11177 West 8th Ave.
P.O. Box 25127
Lakewood, CO 80225
303-236-9427

Regional Forester: Gary Cargill
Director, Range, Wildlife Fisheries and Ecology: Glen Hetzel

Region 3—Southwestern (Arizona, New Mexico)

Federal Building
517 Gold Ave., SW
Albuquerque, NM 87102
505-842-3292

Regional Forester: Sotero Muniz
Director, Wildlife Management: William Zeedyk

Region 4—Intermountain (Idaho [southern], Nevada, Utah, Wyoming [western]).

Federal Building
324 25th Street
Ogden, UT 84401
801-625-5183

Regional Forester: J.S. Tixier
Director, Wildlife and Fisheries Management: William Burbridge

Region 5—Pacific Southwest (California, Guam, Hawaii, Pacific Islands)

630 Sansome Street
San Francisco, CA 94111
415-556-4310

Regional Forester: Paul Barker
Assistant Regional Forester, Fisheries and Wildlife Management: Randall Long

Region 6 —Pacific Northwest (Oregon, Washington)

319 S.W. Pine St.
P.O. Box 3623
Portland, OR 97208
503-221-3625

Regional Forester: James Torrence
Director, Fish and Wildlife: Hugh Black, Jr.

Region 8 —Southern (Alabama, Arkansas, Georgia, Kentucky, Louisiana, Mississippi, North Carolina, Oklahoma, Puerto Rico, South Carolina, Tennessee, Texas)

1720 Peachtree Rd, N.W.
Atlanta, GA 30367
404-347-4177

Regional Forester: John Alcock
Director, Fisheries, Wildlife and Range: Jerry McIlwain

Region 9—Eastern (Connecticut, Delaware, Illinois, Indiana, Iowa, Maine, Maryland, Massachusetts, Michigan, Minnesota, Missouri, New Hampshire, New Jersey, New York, Ohio, Pennsylvania, Rhode Island, Vermont, West Virginia, Wisconsin)

310 West Wisconsin Ave.
Room 500
Milwaukee, WI 53203
414-291-3693

Regional Forester: Floyd Marita
Director, Recreation, Range, Wildlife, and Landscape Management:
Bruce Hronek

Region 10—Alaska

Federal Office Building
P.O. Box 21628
Juneau, AK 99802-1628
907-586-8863

Regional Forester: Michael Barton
Director, Wildlife and Fisheries: Philip Janik

FOREST AND RANGE EXPERIMENT STATIONS

Intermountain Station
Laurence Lassen, Director
324 25th Street
Ogden, UT 84401
801-625-5412

Northeastern Station
Denver Burns, Director
370 Reed Road
Broomall, PA 19008
215-690-3006

Pacific Southwest Station
Roger Bay, Director
1960 Addison Street
P.O. Box 245
Berkeley, CA 94701
415-486-3292

Southeastern Station
Jerry Sesco, Director
200 Weaver Blvd.
P.O. Box 2680
Asheville, NC 28802
704-259-6758

North Central Station
Ronald Lindmark, Director
1992 Folwell Ave.
St. Paul, MN 55108
612-649-5000

Pacific Northwest Station
Robert Ethington, Director
P.O. Box 3890
Portland, OR 97208
503-294-2052

Rocky Mountain Station
Charles Loveless, Director
240 W. Prospect
Fort Collins, CO 80526-2098
303-221-4390

Southern Station
Thomas Ellis, Director
T-10210, U.S. Postal Service Bldg.
701 Loyola Avenue
New Orleans, LA 70113
504-589-6800

Forest Products Labratory
John Erickson, Director
One Gifford Pinchot Drive
Madison, WI 53705-2398
608-264-5600

State and Private Forestry Offices are located in the Regional Headquarters, except for the Eastern Region, where it is at:

Northeastern Area
Thomas Schenarts, Director
370 Reed Road
Broomall, PA 19008
215-461-1660

APPENDIX B

U.S. Fish and Wildlife Service Directory

(As of January 1, 1988)

WASHINGTON HEADQUARTERS

Mailing Address:
Fish and Wildlife Service
Department of the Interior
18th and C Streets, NW
Washington, D.C. 20240

Title	Name	Phone
Director	Frank Dunkle	202-343-4717
Deputy Director	Steven Robinson	202-343-4545
Assistant Director, External Affairs	Sam Marler	202-343-2500
Chief, Legislative Services	Owen Ambor	202-343-5403
Chief, International Affairs	Lawrence Mason	202-343-5188
Chief, Public Affairs	Phil Million	202-343-4131
Assistant Director, Refuges and Wildlife	Marv Plenert (acting)	202-343-5333
Chief, Wildlife Support Staff	Leonard Tinsley	202-343-6351
Chief, Division of Refuges	James Gillet	202-343-4311
Chief, Division of Realty	William Hartwig	202-653-7650
Chief, Office of Migratory Bird Management	Rollin Sparrowe	202-254-3207
Chief, Division of Law Enforcement	Clark Bavin	202-343-9242
Assistant Director, Fish and Wildlife Enhancement	Ronald Lambertson	202-343-4646
Chief, Division of Endangered Species and Habitat Conservation	William Knepp	235-2771
Chief, Division of Federal Aid	Conley Moffett	235-1526
Chief, Office of Management Authority	Marshall Jones	343-4968

Title	Name	Phone
Chief, Division of Environmental Contaminants	John Rogers	235-1904
Assistant Director, Fisheries	Gary Edwards	202-343-6394
Chief, Division of Fish Hatcheries	Vacant	202-653-8746
Chief, Division of Fish and Wildlife Management Assistance	Lynn Starnes	202-632-7463
Assistant Director, Policy, Budgeting, and Administration	Joe Doddridge	202-343-4888
Chief, Division of Budget and Analysis	James Leupold	202-343-2444
Chief, Division of Policy and Directives Management	John Carracciolo	202-343-4633

REGIONAL OFFICES

Region 1 (California, Hawaii, Idaho, Nevada, Oregon, Washington, Pacific Trust Territories)

Fish and Wildlife Service
Lloyd 500 Building, Suite 1692
500 NE Multnomah Street
Portland, OR 97232

Title	Name	Phone
Regional Director	Rolf Wallenstrom	503-231-6118
Assistant Regional Director, Refuges and Wildlife	Lawrence DeBates	503-231-6214
Assistant Regional Director, Fisheries	Vacant	503-231-5967
Assistant Regional Director, Fish and Wildlife Enhancement	David Riley	503-231-6159
Deputy Assistant Regional Director, Fish and Wildlife Enhancement (Federal aid contact)	James Teeter	503-231-6150
Chief, Division of Endangered Species	Wayne White	503-231-6131
Wetlands Coordinator	Dennis Peters	503-231-6154
Assistant Regional Director, Law Enforcement	David McMullen	503-231-6125
Assistant Regional Director, Public Affairs	Diane Hoobler	503-231-6121

Region 2 (Arizona, New Mexico, Oklahoma, Texas)

Fish and Wildlife Service
P.O. Box 1306
Albuquerque, NM 87103

Title	Name	Phone
Regional Director	Michael Spear	505-766-2321
Assistant Regional Director, Refuges and Wildlife	W. Ellis Klett	505-766-1829
Assistant Regional Director, Fisheries and Federal Assistance	Conrad Fjetland	505-766-2323

Title	Name	Phone
Chief, Division of Federal Aid	Donald Kuntzelman	505-766-2095
Assistant Regional Director, Fish and Wildlife Enhancement	James Young	505-766-2324
Chief, Division of Endangered Species	James Johnson	505-766-3972
Wetlands Coordinator	Warren Hagenbuck	505-766-2914
Assistant Regional Director, Law Enforcement	John Cross	505-766-2091
Assistant Regional Director, Public Affairs	Thomas Smylie	505-766-3940

Region 3 (Iowa, Illinois, Indiana, Michigan, Minnesota, Missouri, Ohio, Wisconsin)

Fish and Wildlife Service
Federal Building, Fort Snelling
Twin Cities, MN 55111

Title	Name	Phone
Regional Director	James Gritman	612-725-3563
Assistant Regional Director, Refuges and Wildlife	John Eadie	612-725-3507
Assistant Regional Director, Fisheries and Federal Aid	John Popowski	612-725-3505
Chief, Division of Federal Aid	Joseph Artmann	612-725-3596
Assistant Regional Director, Fish and Wildlife Enhancement	Gerald Lowry	612-725-3510
Chief, Division of Endangered Species	James Engel	612-725-3276
Wetlands Coordinator	Ronald Erickson	612-725-3593
Assistant Regional Director, Law Enforcement	Larry Hood	612-725-3530
Assistant Regional Director, Public Affairs	George Sura	612-725-3520

Region 4 (Alabama, Arkansas, Florida, Georgia, Kentucky, Louisiana, Mississippi, North Carolina, South Carolina, Tennessee, Puerto Rico, and the Virgin Islands)

Fish and Wildlife Service
R.B. Russell Federal Building
75 Spring Street, SW
Atlanta, GA 30303

Title	Name	Phone
Regional Director	James Pulliam, Jr.	404-331-3588
Assistant Regional Director, Refuges and Wildlife	Harold Benson	404-331-0838
Assistant Regional Director, Fisheries and Federal Aid	John Brown	404-331-3576
Assistant Regional Director, Fish and Wildlife Enhancement	Warren Olds, Jr.	404-331-6381
Chief, Division of Federal Aid	Cleophas Cooke, Jr.	404-331-3580
Chief, Division of Endangered Species	Vacant	404-331-3583
Wetlands Coordinator	John Hefner	404-331-6343

Title	Name	Phone
Assistant Regional Director, Law Enforcement	Dan Searcy	404-331-5872
Assistant Regional Director, Public Affairs	Donald Pfitzer	404-331-3594

Region 5 (Connecticut, Delaware, Maine, Maryland, Massachusetts, New Hampshire, New Jersey, New York, Pennsylvania, Rhode Island, Vermont, Virginia, West Virginia)

Fish and Wildlife Service
One Gateway Center, Suite 700
Newton Corner, MA 02158
617-965-5100

Title	Name	Phone
Regional Director	Howard Larsen	x200
Assistant Regional Director, Refuges and Wildlife	Donald Young	x222
Assistant Regional Director, Fisheries and Federal Aid	James Weaver	x208
Chief, Division of Federal Aid	William Hesselton	x212
Assistant Regional Director, Fish and Wildlife Enhancement	Ralph Pisapia	x217
Chief, Division of Endangered Species	Paul Nickerson	x316
Wetlands Coordinator	Ralph Tiner	x379
Assistant Regional Director, Law Enforcement	Eugene Hester	x254
Assistant Regional Director, Public Affairs	Inez Connor	x206

Region 6 (Colorado, Kansas, Montana, Nebraska, North Dakota, South Dakota, Utah, Wyoming)

Fish and Wildlife Service
P.O. Box 25486
Denver Federal Center
Denver, CO 80225

Title	Name	Phone
Regional Director	Galen Buterbaugh	303-236-7920
Assistant Regional Director, Refuges and Wildlife	Nelson Kverno	303-236-8145
Assistant Regional Director, Fisheries and Federal Aid	William Martin	303-236-8154
Chief, Division of Federal Aid	Jerry Blackard	303-236-7392
Assistant Regional Director, Fish and Wildlife Enhancement	Robert Jacobsen	303-236-8189
Chief, Division of Endangered Species and Environmental Contaminants	Larry Shanks	303-236-7398
Wetlands Coordinator	Charles Elliot	303-236-8180
Assistant Regional Director, Law Enforcement	Terry Grosz	303-236-7540
Assistant Regional Director, Public Affairs	Jack Hallowell	303-236-7904

Region 7 (Alaska)

Fish and Wildlife Service
1011 E. Tudor Road
Anchorage, AK 99503

Title	Name	Phone
Regional Director	Walter Stieglitz	907-786-3542
Assistant Regional Director, Refuges and Wildlife	John Rogers	907-786-3545
Assistant Regional Director, Enhancement	Rowan Gould	907-786-3544
Chief, Division of Fisheries	Randy Bailey	907-786-3466
Chief, Division of Federal Aid	William Martin	907-786-3491
Chief, Division of Ecological Services and Endangered Species	Steve Wilson	907-786-3467
Wetlands Coordinator	John Hall	907-786-3403
Assistant Regional Director, Law Enforcement	David Purinton	907-786-3311
Assistant Regional Director, Public Affairs	Bruce Batten	907-786-3486

Region 8 (Research and Development)[1]

Fish and Wildlife Service
U.S. Department of the Interior
Mail Stop: 527 Matomic Bldg.
Washington, D.C. 20240

Title	Name	Phone
Regional Director	Richard Smith	202-653-8791
Office of Scientific Authority	Charles Dane	202-653-5948
Alaska Fish and Wildlife Research Center 1101 East Tudor Road Anchorage, AK 99503	A. William Palmisano	907-786-3448
Cooperative Fish and Wildlife Research Center Fish and Wildlife Service Mail Stop: 527 Matomic Bldg. Washington, D.C. 20240	Edward LaRoe	202-653-8723
National Ecology Research Center Creekside One Bldg. 2627 Redwing Road Fort Collins, CO 80526-2899	Ralph Morgenweck	303-226-9100
National Fisheries Contaminant Research Center Route 1 Columbia, MO 65201	Richard Schoettger	314-875-5399
National Fisheries Research Center 7920 N.W. 71st Street Gainesville, FL 32606	James McCann	904-378-8181

Title	Name	Phone
National Fisheries Research Center—Great Lakes 1451 Green Road Ann Arbor, MI 48105	Jon Stanley	715-682-6163
National Fisheries Research Center—La Crosse P.O. Box 818 La Crosse, WI 54601	Fred Meyer	608-783-6451
National Fisheries Research Center—Leetown Box 700 Kearneysville, WV 25430	Jan Riffe	304-725-8461
National Fisheries Research Center Building 204, Naval Station Seattle, WA 98115	Alfred Fox	206-526-6282
National Wetlands Research Center 1010 Gause Blvd. Slidell, LA 70458	Robert Stewart	504-646-7564
National Wildlife Health Research Center 6006 Schroeder Road Madison, WI 53711	Milton Friend	608-271-4640
Northern Prairie Wildlife Research Center P.O. Box 2096 Jamestown, ND 58401	Rey Stendell	701-252-5363
Patuxent Wildlife Research Center Laurel, MD 20708	Harold O'Connor	301-498-0300
Office of Information Transfer 1025 Pennock Place, Suite 212 Fort Collins, CO 80524[1]	Robert Streeter	303-493-8401

1. Responsible for management of research within the Fish and Wildlife Service.

APPENDIX C

National Park Service Directory

(As of January 1, 1988)

WASHINGTON HEADQUARTERS

Mailing address:
National Park Service
Interior Building
P.O. Box 37127
Washington, D.C. 20013–7127

General Information:
202-343-4747

Title	Name	Phone
Director	Wm. Penn Mott	202-343-4621
Deputy Director	Denis Galvin	202-343-5081
Program Analysis Officer	Carol Aten	202-343-4298
Chief, Public Affairs	George Berklacy	202-343-6843
Assistant Director, Leg. & Congressional Affairs	Rob Wallace	202-343-5[illegible]
Equal Employment Opport. Officer	Marshall Brookes	202-343-6738
Assistant Director, Office of Business and Economic Development	Barbara Gilliard-Payne	202-343-6741
Natural Resources		
Associate Director	Eugene Hester	202-343-3889
Chief, Air Quality Division	John Christiano	202-343-4911
Chief, Water Resources Division	Dan Kimball	303-221-5341
Chief, Wildlife and Vegetation Division[1]	Vacant	
Natural Resources Specialist	Hardy Pearce	

Title	Name	Phone
Ecologist	Craig Shafer	
Science Support Staff	Al Greene	202-343-8114
Senior Scientist	Theodore Sudia	202-343-8121

Park Operations

Associate Director	Robert Stanton	202-343-5651
Chief, Land Resources Division[2]	Willis Kriz	202-523-5252

Cultural Resources

Associate Director	Jerry Rogers	202-343-7625

Planning and Development

Associate Director	Gerald Patten	202-343-1264

Budget and Administration

Associate Director	Edward Davis	202-343-6741

[1] Created in November 1987.
[2] Includes Minerals Resources Section, formerly Energy, Mining and Minerals.

REGIONAL OFFICES

North Atlantic Regional Office (Connecticut, Maine, Massachusetts, New Hampshire, New Jersey, New York, Rhode Island, and Vermont)

Herbert Cables, Jr., Regional Director
National Park Service
15 State Street
Boston, MA 02109
617-565-8800

Chief Scientist: Michael Soukup
Natural Resource Contacts: Nora Mitchel, Len Bobinchock

Mid-Atlantic Regional Office (Delaware, Maryland, Pennsylvania, Virginia, and West Virginia)

James Coleman, Regional Director
National Park Service
143 South Third Street
Philadelphia, PA 19106
215-597-7013

Chief Scientist: John Karish
Natural Resource Contact: William Supernaugh (through Feb. 1988)

National Capital Regional Office (The National Capital Region covers parks in the metropolitan area of Washington, D.C. and certain field areas in Maryland, Virginia, and West Virginia)

Manus Fish, Jr., Regional Director
National Park Service
1100 Ohio Drive, SW
Washington, D.C. 20242
202-426-6612

Chief Scientist: William Anderson
Natural Resource Contact: Stan Lock

Southeast Regional Office (Alabama, Georgia, Kentucky, Mississippi, North Carolina, South Carolina, Tennessee, and Puerto Rico, and the Virgin Islands)

Robert Baker, Regional Director
National Park Service
75 Spring Street, SW
Atlanta, GA 30303
404-331-5185

Chief Scientist: Dominic Dottavio
Natural Resource Contact: Dominic Dottavio

Midwest Regional Office (Illinois, Indiana, Iowa, Kansas, Minnesota, Michigan, Missouri, Nebraska, Ohio, and Wisconsin)

Dan Castleberry, Regional Director
National Park Service
1709 Jackson Street
Omaha, NE 68102
402-221-3431

Chief Scientist: Michael Ruggiero
Natural Resource Contact: Ben Holmes

Rocky Mountain Regional Office (Colorado, Montana, North Dakota, South Dakota, Utah, and Wyoming)

Lorraine Mintzmeyer, Regional Director
National Park Service
12795 West Alameda Parkway
P.O. Box 25287
Denver, CO 80225-0287
303-969-2000

Chief Scientist: Dan Huff
Natural Resource Contact: Cecil Lewis

Southwest Regional Office (Part of Arizona, Arkansas, Louisiana, New Mexico, Oklahoma, and Texas)

John Cook, Regional Director
National Park Service
Old Santa Fe Trail
P.O. Box 728
Santa Fe, NM 87504-0728
505-988-6388

Chief Scientist: Milford Fletcher
Natural Resource Contact: Milford Fletcher

Western Regional Office (Part of Arizona, California, Hawaii, and Nevada)

Stanley Albright, Regional Director
National Park Service
450 Golden Gate Avenue
P.O. Box 36063
San Francisco, CA 94102
415-556-4196

Chief Scientist: Bruce Kilgore
Natural Resource Contact: Bruce Kilgore

Pacific Northwest Regional Office (Idaho, Oregon, and Washington)

Chales Odegaard, Regional Director
National Park Service
83 South King Street
Suite 212
Seattle, WA 98104
206-442-5565

Chief Scientist: James Larson
Natural Resource Contacts: Ed Menning, Janet Edwards

Alaska Regional Office (Alaska)

Boyd Evison, Regional Director
National Park Service
2525 Gambell Street, Room 107
Anchorage, AK 99503-2892
907-271-2690

Chief Scientist: Al Lovaas
Natural Resource Contact: Al Lovaas

APPENDIX D

Bureau of Land Management Directory

(As of January 1, 1988)

WASHINGTON HEADQUARTERS

Mailing Address:
Bureau of Land Management
U.S. Department of the Interior
18th and C Sts., NW
Washington, D.C. 20240

Robert Burford, Director
Bureau of Land Management
202-343-3801

Dean Stepanek, Assistant Director
Land and Renewable Resources
202-343-4896

J. David Almand, Chief
Division of Wildlife and Fisheries, BLM
202-653-9202

STATE OFFICE DIRECTORS AND BIOLOGISTS

Alaska
Michael Penfold, State Director
*Craig Altop, State Office Biologist
Bureau of Land Management
701 C Street, Box 13
Anchorage, AK 99513
907-271-5555

Arizona
D. Dean Bibles, State Director
Carole Hamilton, State Office Biologist
*Gene Dahlem
P.O. Box 16563
Phoenix, AZ 85011
602-241-5504

California
Ed Hastey, State Director
Mike Ferguson, State Office Biologist
*Butch Olendorff
Bureau of Land Management
Federal Bldg.
2800 Cottage Way, E-2841
Sacramento, CA 95825-1889
916-978-4746

Colorado
Neil Morck, State Director
*Lee Upham, State Office Biologist
Bureau of Land Management
2850 Youngfield Street
Lakewood, CO 80215
303-236-1700

Denver Service Center
Bob Moore, Director
*Allen Cooperrider, Service Center Biologist
*Ray Boyd
Bureau of Land Management
Denver Service Center
Denver Federal Center, Bldg. 50
Denver, CO 80225
303-236-0161

Eastern States Office
G. Curtis Jones, Jr., State Director
* Tom Hewitt, State Office Biologist
* Jeff Carroll
Bureau of Land Management
Eastern States Office
350 South Pickett Street
Alexandria, VA 22304
703-274-0190

Idaho
Del Vail, State Director
* Allen Thomas, State Office Biologist
Roger Rosentretter, State Office Botanist
Bureau of Land Management
3380 Americana Terrace
Boise, ID 83706
208-334-1771

Montana (MT, SD, ND)
Marvin LeNoue, State Director (Acting)
Ray Hoem, State Office Biologist
* Dan Hinckley
Bureau of Land Management
222 North 32nd Street
Billings, MT 59107
406-657-6655

Nevada
Ed Spang, State Director
David Goicoechea, State Office Biologist
* Osborne Casey
Bureau of Land Management
P.O. Box 12000
Reno, NV 89520
702-784-5311

New Mexico (KS, NM, OK, TX)
Larry Woodard, State Director
Andy Dimas, State Office Biologist
* Jan Knight
Bureau of Land Management
Montoya Federal Bldg.
South Federal Place
Santa Fe, NM 87504
505-988-6316

Oregon (OR, WA)
Charles Luscher, State Director
Art Oakley, State Office Biologist
* Bill Nietro
Bureau of Land Management
825 NE Multnomah Street
P.O. Box 2965
Portland, OR 97208
503-231-6274

Utah
Kemp Conn, State Director (Acting)
*Jerry Farringer, State Office Biologist
Bureau of Land Management
324 South State Street
Salt Lake City, UT 84111-2303
801-524-5311

Wyoming (WY, NE)
Hillary Oden, State Director
*Dave Roberts, State Office Biologist
Bureau of Land Management
2515 Warren Avenue
Cheyenne, WY 82003
307-772-2111

*Biologist for Endangered Species.

APPENDIX E

Wetlands Management Directory

ENVIRONMENTAL PROTECTION AGENCY

Headquarters
U.S. Environmental Protection Agency
401 M St., SW
Washington, D.C. 20460

Lee Thomas, Administrator
202-382-4700

Larry Jensen
Assistant Administrator for Water
202-382-5700

Rebecca Hanmer, Deputy Assistant
Administrator for Water
202-382-5707

David Davis, Director
Office of Wetlands Protection
202-475-7795

REGIONAL OFFICES

Region 1 (Connecticut, Maine, Massachusetts, New Hampshire, Rhode Island, Vermont)
Michael Deland, Administrator
John F. Kennedy Federal Building
Room 2203
Boston, MA 02203
617-565-3400

Region 2 (New York, New Jersey, Puerto Rico, Virgin Islands)
Christopher Daggett, Administrator
26 Federal Plaza
Room 900
New York, NY 10278
212-264-2525

Region 3 (Delaware, District of Columbia, Maryland, Pennsylvania, West Virginia, Virginia)
James Seif, Administrator
841 Chestnut St.
Philadelphia, PA 19107
215-597-9800

Region 4 (Alabama, Florida, Georgia, Kentucky, Mississippi, North Carolina, South Carolina, Tennessee)
Lee DeHihns, Acting Administrator
345 Courtland St., NE
Atlanta, GA 30365
404-347-4727

Region 5 (Illinois, Indiana, Michigan, Minnesota, Ohio, Wisconsin)
Valdas Adamkus, Administrator
230 S. Dearborn
Chicago, IL 60604
312-353-2000

Region 6 (Arkansas, Louisiana, New Mexico, Oklahoma, Texas)
Robert Layton, Jr., Administrator
Allied Bank Tower at Fountain Place
1445 Ross Avenue
Dallas, TX 75202
214-655-2100

Region 7 (Iowa, Kansas, Missouri, Nebraska)
Morris Kay, Administrator
726 Minnesota Avenue
Kansas City, KS 66101
913-236-2800

Region 8 (Colorado, Montana, North Dakota, South Dakota, Utah, Wyoming)
James Scherer, Administrator
999 18th Street, Suite 500
Denver, CO 80202
303-293-1603

Region 9 (Arizona, California, Hawaii, Nevada, Pacific Trust Territories)
John Wise, Acting Administrator
215 Freemont Street
San Francisco, CA 94105
415-974-8153

Region 10 (Alaska, Idaho, Oregon, Washington)
Robie Russell, Administrator
1200 Sixth Avenue
Seattle, WA 98101
206-442-5810

ARMY CORPS OF ENGINEERS

Headquarters
Army Corps of Engineers
Office of the Chief of Engineers
Casimir Pulaski Building
20 Massachusetts Avenue, NW
Washington, D.C. 20314

Robert Page
Assistant Secretary-Designate, Civil Works
202-697-8986

Lieutenant General Elvin Heiberg III
Chief, Corps of Engineers
202-272-0001

Major General Henry Hatch
Director of Civil Works (DAEN-CWZ)
202-272-0099

Barry Frankel
Director, Real Estate
202-272-0483

John Wallace
Director, Resource Management
202-272-0077

Bernard N. Goode
Chief, Regulatory Branch
202-272-0199

Divisions and Districts

Lower Mississippi Valley Division
Max Reed, Chief, Regulatory Branch
P.O. Box 80
Vicksburg, MS 39180
601-634-5818

Memphis District
David Pitts, Regulatory Chief
Clifford Davis Federal Building
Rm B-202
Memphis, TN 38103-1894
901-521-3471

New Orleans District
Ronald Ventola, Regulatory Chief
P.O. Box 60267
New Orleans, LA 70160-0267
504-838-2255

St. Louis District
Ronald Messerli, Regulatory Chief
210 Tucker Boulevard, N
St. Louis, MO 63101-1986
314-263-5703

Vicksburg District
Edward McGregor, Regulatory Chief
P.O. Box 60
Vicksburg, MS 39180-0060
601-634-5276/89

Missouri River District
Mores Bergman, Chief, Regulatory Branch
P.O. Box 103 Downtown Station
Omaha, NE 68101
402-221-7290

Kansas City District
Mel Jewett, Regulatory Chief
700 Federal Building
601 E. 12th Street
Kansas City, MO 64106-2896
816-374-3645

Omaha District
John Morton, Regulatory Chief
P.O. Box 5
Omaha, NE 68101-0005
402-221-4133

New England Division
William Lawless, Chief,
Regulatory Branch
424 Trapelo Road
Waltham, MA 02254
617-647-8338
(No district offices)

North Atlantic Division
Lenny Kotkiewicz, Chief,
Regulatory Branch
90 Church Street
New York, NY 10077
212-264-7535

Baltimore District
Don Roeske, Regulatory Chief
P.O. Box 1715
Baltimore, MD 21203-1715
301-962-3670

New York District
James Mansky, Regulatory Chief
26 Federal Plaza
New York, NY 10278-0090
212-264-3996

Norfolk District
William Poure, Jr., Regulatory Chief
803 Front Street
Norfolk, VA 23510-1096
804-441-3068

Philadelphia District
Frank Cianfrani, Regulatory Chief
U.S. Customs House
2nd and Chestnut Streets
Philadelphia, PA 19106-2991
215-597-2812

North Central Division
Mitchell Isoe, Chief, Regulatory Branch
536 S. Clark Street
Chicago, IL 60605-1592
312-353-6379

Buffalo District
Paul Leuchner, Regulatory Chief
1776 Niagara Street
Buffalo, NY 14207-3199
716-876-5454

Chicago District
Tom Slowinski, Regulatory Chief
219 S. Dearborn Street
Chicago, IL 60604-1797
312-353-6428

Detroit District
Gary Mannesto, Regulatory Chief
P.O. Box 1027
Detroit, MI 48231-1027
313-226-2218

Rock Island District
Steven Vander Horn, Regulatory Chief
Clock Tower Building
Rock Island, IL 61201-2004
309-788-6361

St. Paul District
Ben Wopat, Regulatory Chief
1135 USPO & Custom House
St. Paul, MN 55101-1479
612-725-5819

North Pacific Division
John Zammit, Chief, Regulatory Branch
P.O. Box 2870
Portland, OR 97208
503-221-3780

Alaska District
Robert Oja, Regulatory Chief
P.O. Box 898
Anchorage, AK 99506-0898
907-753-2712

Portland District
Jerry Newgard, Regulatory Chief
P.O. Box 2946
Portland, OR 97208-2946
503-221-6995

Seattle District
William Baxter, Regulatory Chief
P.O. Box C-3755
Seattle, WA 98124-2255
206-764-3495

Walla Walla District
Dean Hilliard, Regulatory Chief
Building 602
City-County Airport
Walla Walla, WA 93362-9265
509-522-6718

Ohio River Division
Roger Graham, Chief, Regulatory Branch
P.O. Box 1159
Cincinnati, OH 45201-1159
513-684-3972

Huntington District
Gary Watson, Regulatory Chief
508 8th Street
Huntington, WV 25701-2070
304-529-5487

Louisville District
Daniel Evans, Assistant Regulatory Chief
P.O. Box 59
Louisville, KY 40201-0059
502-582-5452

Nashville District
Charles Huddleston, Regulatory Chief
P.O. Box 1070
Nashville, TN 37202-1070
615-251-5487

Pittsburgh District
Eugene Homyak, Regulatory Chief
Federal Building
1000 Liberty Avenue
Pittsburgh, PA 15222-4186
412-644-4204

South Atlantic Division
James Kelly, Jr., Chief, Regulatory Branch
510 Title Building
30 Pryor St., SW
Atlanta, GA 30303
404-331-6744

Charleston District
Clarence Ham, Regulatory Chief
P.O. Box 919
Charleston, SC 29402-0919
803-724-4330

Jacksonville District
John Adams, Regulatory Chief
P.O. Box 4970
Jacksonville, FL 32232-0019
904-791-1659

Mobile District
Ron Krizman, Regulatory Chief
P.O. Box 2288
Mobile, AL 36628-0001
205-690-2658

Savannah District
Steven Osvald, Regulatory Chief
P.O. Box 889
Savannah, GA 31402-0889
912-944-5347

Wilmington District
Charles Hollis, Regulatory Chief
P.O. Box 1890
Wilmington, NC 28402-1890
919-343-4511

South Pacific Division
Theodore Durst, Chief, Regulatory Branch
630 Sansome Street, Room 1216
San Francisco, CA 94111
415-556-2648

Los Angeles District
Charles Holt, Regulatory Chief
P.O. Box 2711
Los Angeles, CA 90053-2325
213-688-5606

Sacramento District
Art Champ, Regulatory Chief
650 Capitol Mall
Sacramento, CA 95814-4794
916-440-2842

San Francisco District
Calvin Fong, Regulatory Chief
211 Main Street
San Francisco, CA 94105-1905
415-974-0416

Southwestern Division
Mark King, Chief, Regulatory Branch
1114 Commerce Street
Dallas, TX 75242
214-767-2432

Albuquerque District
Andrew Rosenau, Regulatory Chief
P.O. Box 1580
Albuquerque, NM 87103-1580
505-766-2776

Fort Worth District
Wayne Lea, Regulatory Chief
P.O. Box 17300
Fort Worth, TX 76102-0300
817-334-2681

Galveston District
Marcos De La Rosa, Regulatory Chief
P.O. Box 1229
Galveston, TX 77553-1229
409-766-5487

Little Rock District
Louie Cockman, Jr., Regulatory Chief
P.O. Box 867
Little Rock, AR 72203-0867
501-378-5295

Tulsa District
Lou Ringeisen, Regulatory Chief
P.O. Box 61
Tulsa, OK 74121-0061
918-581-7261

APPENDIX F

National Marine Fisheries Service (NMFS)

WASHINGTON HEADQUARTERS

Mailing Address:
National Marine Fisheries Service
National Oceanic and Atmospheric Administration (NOAA)
Department of Commerce
1825 Connecticut Avenue, NW
Washington, D.C. 20235

Title	Name	Phone
Assistant Administrator	Dr. William Evans	202-673-5450
Deputy Assistant Administrator	James Douglas, Jr.	202-673-5450
Executive Director	Bill Powell	202-673-5450
Director, Management and Budget Office	Samuel McKeen	202-673-5455
Director, Office of Enforcement	Morris Pallozzi	202-673-5295
Director, Office of Fisheries, Conservation, and Management	Richard Schaefer (acting)	202-673-5263
Director, Office of Research and Environmental Information	Dr. Joseph Angelovic	202-673-5366
Office of Protected Resources	Dr. Nancy Foster	202-673-5348
Office of Trade and Industry Services	Carmen Blondin	202-673-5260
Office of International Affairs	Henry Beasley	202-673-5279
NOAA Constituent Affairs Officer (NMFS)	John Dunnigan	202-673-5429

Regional Offices

Northeast Region (Connecticut, Delaware, Indiana, Illinois, Maine, Massachusetts, Michigan, Minnesota, New Hampshire, New York, New Jersey, New York, Ohio, Pennsylvania, Rhode Island, Vermont, Virginia, West Virginia, Wisconsin)

Richard Roe, Director
National Marine Fisheries Service
14 Elm Street
Federal Building
Gloucester, MA 01930
617-281-3600

Southeast Region (Alabama, Arkansas, Florida, Georgia, Iowa, Kansas, Kentucky, Louisiana, Mississippi, Missouri, Nebraska, New Mexico, North Carolina, Oklahoma, South Carolina, Tennessee, Texas)

Director (Vacant)
National Marine Fisheries Service
9450 Koger Boulevard
St. Petersburg, FL 33702
813-893-3141

Northwest Region (Colorado, Idaho, Montana, North Dakota, South Dakota, Oregon, Utah, Washington, Wyoming)

Rolland Schmitten, Director
National Marine Fisheries Service
7600 Sand Point Way, N.E.
BIN C15700
Seattle, WA 98115-0070
206-526-6150

Southwest Region (Arizona, California, Hawaii, Nevada)

E. Charles Fullerton, Director
National Marine Fisheries Service
300 S. Ferry Street
Terminal Island, CA 90731
213-514-6197

Alaska Region

Robert McVey, Director
National Marine Fisheries Service
P.O. Box 1668
Juneau, AK 99802
907-586-7221

NMFS FISHERIES CENTERS

Northeast Fisheries Center

Allen Peterson, Director
NOAA
Woods Hole, MA 02543
617-548-5123

Northwest and Alaska Fisheries Center

William Aron, Director
7600 Sand Point Way, N.E.
Building 4, BIN NO C15700
Seattle, WA 98115
206-526-4000

Southeast Fisheries Center

Richard Berry, Director
75 Virginia Beach Drive
Miami, FL 33149
305-361-4284

Southwest Fisheries Center

Izadore Barrett, Director
8604 La Jolla Shores Drive
P.O. Box 271
La Jolla, CA 92038
619-546-7000

APPENDIX G

Budget Information Contacts on Federal Fish and Wildlife Programs

(As of January 1, 1988)

Title	Name	Phone
Army Corps of Engineers (Wetlands/404 Program)		
Chief, Programs Division Office of the Corps of Engineers	Don Cluff	202-272-0191
Bureau of Land Management		
Chief, Office of Budget	Roger Hildebeidel	202-343-8571
Budget Analyst, Resource Programs	Phil Moreland	202-343-8571
Environmental Protection Agency (Wetlands/404 Program)		
Director, Budget Office	Alvin Pesachowitz	202-475-8340
Budget Analyst, 404 Program	Edwin Craft	202-382-4170
Fish and Wildlife Service		
Deputy Assistant Director, Policy, Budget, and Administration	Joe Doddridge	202-343-4329
Chief, Budget and Analysis Division	James Leupold	202-343-2444
Forest Service		
Director, Program Development and Budget	John Leasure	202-447-6987
Branch Chief, Program, Planning, and Development	John Skinner	202-447-6987

Title	Name	Phone

Marine Mammal Commission

Title	Name	Phone
Executive Director	John Twiss, Jr.	202-653-6237

National Marine Fisheries Service

Title	Name	Phone
Budget Analyst, Office of Policy and Planning	Donald Wickham	202-673-5430

National Park Service

Title	Name	Phone
Chief, Budget Division	Geary Fisher (acting)	202-343-3313
Supervisory Budget Analyst	Arvid Rumbiatis (acting)	202-343-3084

APPENDIX H

Congressional Contacts and Addresses

Bill Status

To determine the status of legislation in the House or Senate, call the Bill Status Office at 202-225-1772.

Copies of Legislation and Reports

To obtain copies of bills, committee reports, or public laws, write the congressional document office. All requests should list documents in numerical order, lowest to highest, and must include a self-addressed mailing label. You may obtain one free copy each of up to six different documents per request.

Senate Document Room (202-224-7860)
B04, Hart Building
Washington, D.C. 20510

CONGRESSIONAL COMMITTEES

To obtain detailed information about pending wildlife legislation or congressional oversight activity contact the appropriate House or Senate Committee.

HOUSE OF REPRESENTATIVES

COMMITTEE ON AGRICULTURE, 1301 Longworth House Office Bldg., Washington, D.C. 20515 (202-225-2171)

Chairman: E (Kika) de la Garza (TX)
Staff Contact: Jim Lyons
Ranking Minority Member: James Jeffords (VT)
Staff Contact: Charles Hilty

SUBCOMMITTEES

Conservation, Credit and Rural Development
Chairman: Ed Jones (TN)
Staff Contact: Robert Cashdollar (202-225-1867)
Ranking Minority Member: E. Thomas Coleman (MO)
Staff Contact: Susan Adkins (202-225-2342)
Department Operations, Research and Foreign Agriculture
Chairman: George Brown, Jr. (CA)
Staff Contact: William Stiles (202-225-0301)
Ranking Minority Member: Pat Roberts (KS)
Staff Contact: John Aguirre (202-225-0171)
Forests, Family Farms and Energy
Chairman: Harold Volkmer (MO)
Staff Contact: Timothy De Costor (202-225-1867)
Ranking Minority Member: Sid Morrison (WA)
Staff Contact: Carol Dubard (202-225-2342)

COMMITTEE ON APPROPRIATIONS, H-218, Capitol Building Washington, D.C. 20515 (202-225-2771)

Chairman: Jamie Whitten (MS)
Ranking Minority Member: Silvio Conte (MA)

SUBCOMMITTEES

Energy and Water Development, 2362 Rayburn House Office Building, Washington, D.C. 20515 (202-225-3421)
Chairman: Tom Bevill (AL)
Staff Contacts: Hunter Spillan (general); George Urian (Corps of Engineers, Bureau of Reclamation); Aaron Edmondson (Energy); John Mikel (Energy).
Ranking Minority Member: John Meyers (IN)
Staff Contact: Jeff Jacobs (202-225-2471)
Interior and Related Agencies, 2358 Rayburn House Office Building, Washington, D.C. 20515 (202-225-3508)
Chairman: Sidney Yates (IL)
Staff Contacts: Neal Sigmon (general); Bob Kripowicz (Energy).
Ranking Minority Member: Ralph Regula (OH)
Staff Contact: Tim Shea (202-225-6626)

COMMITTEE ON INTERIOR AND INSULAR AFFAIRS, 1324 Longworth House Office Building, Washington, D.C. 20515 (202-225-2761)

Chairman: Morris K. Udall (AZ)
Staff Contacts: Mark Trautwein (Environment, Energy and Public Lands); William Shafer (Mines, Minerals and Public Lands); Michael D. Jackson (Water and Power).
Ranking Minority Member: Don Young (AK)
Staff Contacts: Richard D. Hapke (Energy, 202-226-7397); Manase

Mansur (Insular and International Affairs, 202-226-7397); Stephan Buckner (Mining and Natural Resources, 202-226-2311); Lori Stillman (National Parks, 202-226-2311); William Brooke (Public Lands, 202-226-2311); Delos Cy Jamison (Public Lands, 202-225-6065); Henry Smith (Water and Power Resources, 202-226-2311).

SUBCOMMITTEES

Energy and the Environment, 1327 Longworth House Office Building, Washington, D.C. 20515 (202-225-8331)
Chairman: Morris K. Udall (UT)
Staff Contact: Sam Fowler (Counsel)
Ranking Minority Member: Manuel Lujan, Jr. (NM)
Staff Contact: Richard Hapke (202-226-7397)
Water and Power Resources, 1522 Longworth House Office Building, Washington, D.C. 20515 (202-225-6042)
Chairman: George Miller (CA)
Staff Contact: Daniel Beard
Ranking Minority Member: Charles Pashayan, Jr. (CA)
Staff Contact: Henry Smith (202-226-2311)
Mining and Natural Resources, A819 House Office Building, Annex I, Washington, D.C. 20515 (202-226-7761)
Chairman: Nick Joe Rahall II (WV)
Staff Contact: James H. Zoia
Ranking Minority Member: Larry Craig (ID)
Staff Contact: Stephen Buckner (202-226-2311)
National Parks and Public Lands, A812 House Office Building, Annex I, Washington, D.C. 20515 (202-226-7736)
Chairman: Bruce Vento (MN)
Staff Contact: Dale Crane, James Bradley, Rick Healy, Heather Huyck
Ranking Minority Member: Ron Marlenee (MT)
Staff Contact: Lori Stillman (National Parks); William Brooke (Public Lands); Delos Cy Jamison (Public Lands)
Insular and International Affairs, 1626 Longworth House Office Building, Washington, D.C. 20515 (202-225-9297)
Chairman: Ron de Lugo (VI)
Staff Contact: Jeffrey Farrow
Ranking Minority Member: Robert Lagomarsino (CA)
Staff Contact: Manase Mansur (202-226-7397)

COMMITTEE ON MERCHANT MARINE AND FISHERIES, 1334 Longworth House Office Bldg., Washington, D.C. 20515 (202-225-4047)

Chairman: Walter Jones (NC)
Staff Contacts: Gerald Seifert (General Counsel/Maritime Policy, 202-225-6785); Thomas Kitsos (Oceanography, 202-225-2429); Donald Barry (Counsel/Fisheries and Wildlife, 202-224-3547)
Ranking Minority Member: Robert Davis (MI)
Staff Contacts: George Pence (Staff Director, 202-225-2650); Thomas Melius (Fisheries and Wildlife, 202-226-3520)

SUBCOMMITTEES

Fisheries and Wildlife Conservation and the Environment, H2-543 House Office Building, Annex II, Washington, D.C. 20515 (202-226-3533)
Chairman: Gerry Studds (MA)
Staff Contacts: Will Stelle (Counsel); Jeff Pike
Ranking Minority Member: Don Young (AK)
Staff Contact: Rodney Moore, Jr. (202-226-3520)
Panama Canal/Outer Continental Shelf, H2-579 House Office Buildling, Annex II, Washington, D.C. 20515 (202-226-3514)
Chairman: W.J. (Billy) Tauzin (LA)
Staff Contact: Wallace Henderson
Ranking Minority Member: Jack Fields (TX)
Staff Contact: Harry Burroughs, III (202-226-3540)

SENATE

COMMITTEE ON AGRICULTURE, NUTRITION AND FORESTRY, SR-328A Russell Senate Office Building, Washington, D.C. 20510 (202-224-2035)

Chairman: Patrick Leahy (VT)
Staff Contacts: Charles Riemenschneider (Staff Director, 202-224-2035); John Podesta (Counsel, 202-224-2035); Clarissa Coffin; Mary Dunbar; Michael Dunn; Kathleen Merrigan; Robert Young (Economist)
Ranking Minority Member: Richard Lugar (IN)
Staff Contacts: Charles Conner (Staff Director, 202-224-0005); Thomas Clark (Counsel, 202-224-6923); Charles Oellermann (Economist, 202-224-6901)

SUBCOMMITTEES

Agricultural Research and General Legislation
Chairman: Kent Conrad (ND)
Ranking Minority Member: Pete Wilson (CA)
Conservation and Forestry
Chairman: Wyche Fowler, Jr. (GA)
Ranking Minority Member: Christopher (Kit) Bond (MO)

COMMITTEE ON APPROPRIATIONS, SD-136 Dirksen Senate Office Building, Washington, D.C. 20510 (202-224-3471)

Chairman: John Stennis (MS)
Staff Contacts: Frances Sullivan (Staff Director, 202-224-7254); John Conway (202-224-7222); Robert Jones (202-224-7338); Robert Putnam (202-222-7221);
Ranking Minority Member: Mark Hatfield (OR)

Staff Contacts: Keith Kennedy (Staff Director, 202-224-7335); Gary Barbour (202-224-7241); Juanita Rilling (202-224-7251)

SUBCOMMITTEES

Agriculture, Rural Development and Related Agencies, SD-140 Dirksen Senate Office Building, Washington, D.C. 20510 (202-224-7240)
Chairman: Quentin Burdick (ND)
Staff Contacts: Rocky Kuhn (Staff Director, 202-224-7202); Deborah Dawson (202-224-7252)
Ranking Minority Member: Thad Cochran (MS)
Staff Contact: Irma Hanneman (202-224-7337)
Commerce, Justice, and State, The Judiciary, and Related Agencies, S-146A Capitol Building, Washington, D.C. 20510 (202-224-7277)
Chairman: Ernest Hollings (SC)
Staff Contact: Dorothy Seder (202-224-7244)
Ranking Minority Member: Warren Rudman (NH)
Staff Contact: John Shank (202-224-7244)
Energy and Water Development, SD-131 Dirksen Senate Office Building, Washington, D.C. 20510 (202-224-7260)
Chairman: J. Bennett Johnston (LA)
Staff Contact: David Gwaltney (202-224-7260)
Ranking Minority Member: Mark Hatfield (OR)
Staff Contact: Stephen Crow (202-224-7261)
Interior and Related Agencies, SD-122 Dirksen Senate Office Building, Washington, D.C. 20510 (202-224-7233)
Chairman: Robert Byrd (WV)
Staff Contact: Don Knowles (202-224-7262)
Ranking Minority Member: James McClure (ID)
Staff Contact: Jeff Cilek (202-224-7262)

COMMITTEE ON COMMERCE, SCIENCE AND TRANSPORTATION, SD-508 Dirksen Senate Office Building, Washington, D.C. 20510 (202-224-5115)

Chairman: Ernest Hollings (SC)
Staff Contacts: Ralph Everett (Counsel, 202-224-0427); John Hardy (Merchant Marine, 202-224-4914); Barry Kalinsky (Merchant Marine, 202-224-4919); John Graykowski (Science, Technology and Space, 202-224-9360); Martin Kress (Science, Technology and Space, 202-224-9360); Robert Sneed (Science, Technology and Space, 202-224-9360), Patrick Windham (Science, Technology and Space, 202-224-9360)
Ranking Minority Member: John Danforth (MO)
Staff Contacts: W. Allen Moore (Chief of Staff, 202-224-5183); Mark Farrell (Science, Technology and Space, 202-224-8172); Pete Perkins (Science, Technology and Space, 202-224-8172)

SUBCOMMITTEES

Merchant Marine, SH-245 Hart Senate Office Building, Washington, D.C. 20510 (202-224-4914)

Chairman: John Breau (LA)
Ranking Minority Member: Ted Stevins (AK)
Science, Technology and Space, SH-427 Hart Senate Office Building, Washington, D.C. 20510 (202-224-9360)
Chairman: Donald Riegle, Jr. (MI)
Ranking Minority Member: Larry Pressler (SD)
National Ocean Policy Study, SH-425 Hart Senate Office Building, Washington, D.C. 20510 (202-224-4912)
Chairman: Ernest Hollings (SC)
Ranking Minority Member: John Danforth (MO)

COMMITTEE ON ENERGY AND NATURAL RESOURCES, SD-364 Dirksen Senate Office Building, Washington, D.C. 20510 (202-224-4971)

Chairman: J. Bennett Johnston (LA)
Staff Contacts: Daryl Owen (Staff Director); Mike Harvey (Chief Counsel); Russ Brown; Ben Cooper; Tom Williams
Ranking Minority Member: James McClure (ID)
Staff Contacts: Frank Cushing (Staff Director 202-224-1017); Gary Ellsworth (Counsel 202-224-1017); Richard Grundy (202-224-1017); Howard Useem (Energy Regulation/Conservation 202-224-1017); Marilyn Meigs (Energy Research and Development 202-224-1017); Patty Kennedy (Minerals Resources 202-224-1017); Tony Bevineito (Public Lands 202-224-1017)

SUBCOMMITTEES

Energy Regulation and Conservation, SH-212 Hart Senate Office Building, Washington, D.C. 20510 (202-224-4971)
Chairman: Howard Metzenbaum (OH)
Staff Contacts: Joel Saltzmann (Counsel); Al Stayman
Ranking Minority Member: Don Nickles (OK)
Staff Contacts: Howard Useem
Energy Research and Development, SH-312 Hart Senate Office Building, Washington, D.C. 205100 (202-224-4971)
Chairman: Wendell H. Ford (KY)
Staff Contacts: Cheryl Moss; Mary Louise Wagner
Ranking Minority Member: Pete Domenici (NM)
Staff Contact: Marilyn Meigs
Minerals Resources Development and Production, SD-362 Dirksen Senate Office Building, Washington, D.C. 20510 (202-224-4971)
Chairman: John Melcher (MT)
Staff Contacts: Patricia Beneke (Counsel); Lisa Vehings
Ranking Minority Member: Chic Hecht (NV)
Staff Contact: Patty Kennedy
Public Lands, National Parks and Forests, SD-308 Dirksen Senate Office Building, Washington, D.C. 20510 (202-224-4971)
Chairman: Dale Bumpers (AR)
Staff Contacts: Tom Williams; Beth Norcross
Ranking Minority Member: Malcolm Wallop (WY)
Staff Contacts: Tony Benvinetto (202-224-1017)

Water and Power, SD-306 Dirksen Senate Office Building, Washington, D.C. 20510 (202-224-4971)
Chairman: Bill Bradley (NJ)
Staff Contacts: Bill Conway (Counsel); Russ Brown
Ranking Minority Member: Daniel Evans (WA)
Staff Contacts: Jim Beirne (Counsel)

COMMITTEE ON ENVIRONMENTAL AND PUBLIC WORKS, SD-458 Dirksen Senate Office Building, Washington, D.C. 20510 (202-224-6176)

Chairman: Quentin Burdick (ND)
Staff Contacts: Peter Prowitt (Staff Director, 202-224-7845); Phillip Cummings (Counsel, Environmental, 202-224-7843); Judy Campbell (Special Assistant, 202-224-6176); Stephanie Clough (General Environmental, 202-224-3597); Ron Cooper (Hazardous Wastes and Toxic Substances, 202-224-5031); Robert Davison (Fish and Wildlife, 202-224-7189); Ann Garrabrant (Water Resources, General Public Works, 202-224-6176); Michael Goo (Environmental, 202-224-6691); Nadine Hamilton (Transportation, 202-224-3333); Helen Kalbaugh (General Environmental, 202-224-6176); Jeff Peterson (Environmental, 202-224-7069); Mark Ruter (Environmental, 202-224-6226); Michael Shields (Clean Air, Environmental, 202-224-5031); Thomas Skirbunt (Water Projects, 202-224-3974)
Ranking Minority Member: Robert Stafford (VT)
Staff Contacts: Bailey Guard (Staff Director, 202-224-7854); Katherine Cudlipp (General Counsel, 202-224-5761); Mark Haynes (TVA, Water Projects, 202-224-8218); Jean Lauver (Transportation, 202-224-7863); Jimmie Powell (Budget and Appropriations, Safe Drinking Water, Groundwater, 202-224-8832)

SUBCOMMITTEES

Water Resources, Transportation and Infrastructure
Chairman: Daniel Moynihan (NY)
Staff Contacts: Ann Garrabrant (202-224-6176); Nadine Hamilton (202-224-3333); Thomas Skirbunt (202-224-3597)
Ranking Minority Member: Steven Symms (ID)
Staff Contacts: Mark Haynes (202-224-9218); Jean Lauher (202-224-7863); Steve Swain (202-224-7857); Jimmie Powell (202-224-8832)
Environmental Protection
Chairman: George Mitchell (ME)
Staff Contacts: Bob Davison (202-224-6691); Jeff Peterson (202-224-6691)
Ranking Minority Members: John Chafee (RI)
Staff Contacts: Curtis Moore (202-224-5761); Steven Shimberg (202-224-1063)
Hazardous Wastes and Toxic Substances
Chairman: Max Baucus (MT)
Staff Contacts: Ron Cooper (202-224-5031)
Ranking Minority Member: Dave Durenberger (MN)
Staff Contact: Jimmie Powell (202-224-8832)

Superfund and Environmental Oversight
Chairman: Frank Lautenberg (NJ)
Staff Contacts: Seth Mones (202-224-6691); Mark Reiter (202-224-6226)
Ranking Minority Member: John Warner VA)
Staff Contacts: Katherine Cudlipp (202-224-5761)
Nuclear Regulation
Chairman: John Breaux (LA)
Staff Contacts: Dan Berkovitz (202-224-4039); Tim Smith (202-224-3597)
Ranking Minority Member: Alan Simpson (WY)
Staff Contact: James Curtiss (202-224-2991)

APPENDIX I

Endangered Species List Updates

Proposed Rules: Plants

Species						
Scientific name	Common name	Historic range	Status	When listed	Critical habitat	Special rules
Apocynaceae—Dogbane family: Amosonia Kearneyana	Kearney's blue-star	U.S.A. (AZ)	E	—	NA	NA
Asclepiadaceae—Milkweed family: Asclepias meadii	Mead's milkweed	U.S.A. (IL, IN, IA, KS, MO, WI)	T	—	NA	NA
Asteraceae—Sunflower family: Cirsium pitcheri	Pitcher's thistle	U.S.A.(IL, IN, MI, WI, Canada (Ontario)	T	—	NA	NA
Asteraceae—Aster family: Hymenoxys acaulis var. glabra	Lakeside daisy	U.S.A. (OH, IL), Canada (ONT)	T	—	NA	NA
Asteraceae—Aster family: Marshallia mohrii	Mohr's Barbara's-buttons	U.S.A. (AL, GA)	T	—	NA	NA
Asteraceae—Aster Family: Solidago albopilosa	White-haired goldenrod	U.S.A. (KY)	E	—	NA	NA
Asteraceae—Aster family: Solidago houghtonii	Houghton's goldenrod	U.S.A. (MI), Canada (ONT)	T	—	NA	NA
Bignoniaceae—Bignonia family: Crescentia portoricensis	Higuero de Sierra	U.S.A.(PR)	E	—	NA	NA
Cactaceau—Cactus family: Echinocereus reichenbachii var. chi soensis (=Echinocereus chisoensis)	Chisos Mountain hedgehog cactus	U.S.A. (TX)	T	—	NA	NA
Caryophyllaceae—Pink Family: Arenaria cumberlandensis	Cumberland sandwort	U.S.A. (KY, TN)	E	—	NA	NA

Proposed Rules: Plants

Species						
Scientific name	Common name	Historic range	Status	When listed	Critical habitat	Special rules
Fagaceae—Oak Family: Quercus hinckleyi	Hinckley oak	U.S.A. (TX)	T	—	NA	NA
Isoetaceae—Quillwort family Isoetes melanospora	Black-Spored quillwort	U.S.A. (GA, SC)	E	—	NA	NA
	Mat-forming quill-wort	U.S.A. (GA)	E	—	NA	NA
Isoetes tegetiformans Liliaceae—Lily family Trillium reliquum	Relict trillium	U.S.A. (AL, GA, SC)	E	—	NA	NA
Meliaceae—Mahogany family: Trichilia triacantha	Barisco	U.S.A. (PR)	E	—	NA	NA
Nyctaginaceae—Four-o'clock family: Abronia macrocarpe	Large-fruited sand-verbena	U.S.A. (TX)	E	—	NA	NA
Nyctaginaceae—Four-o'clock family: Boerhavia mathisiana	Mathis spiderling	U.S.A. (TX)	E	—	NA	NA
Papaveraceae—Poppy family: Argemone pleiacantha ssp. pin-natisecta	Sacramento prickly poppy	U.S.A. (NM)	E	—	NA	NA
Polypodiaceae—Fern family						
Polystichum aleuticum	Aleutian Shield-fern	U.S.A. (AK)	E	—	NA	NA
Scrophulariaceae—Snapdragon family: Agalinis acuta	Sandplain gerardia	U.S.A. (CT, MA, MD, NY, RI)	E	—	NA	NA

Proposed Rules: Plants

Species						
Scientific name	Common name	Historic range	Status	When listed	Critical habitat	Special rules
Scrophulariaceae – Snapdragon family: Amphianthus pusillus	Little amphianthus	U.S.A. (AL, GA, SC)	T	–	NA	NA
Solanaceae – Nightshade family: Solanum drymophilum	Erubia	U.S.A. (PR)	E	–	NA	NA
Thymelaeaceae – Mezereum family: Daphnopsis hellerana	none	U.S.A. (PR)	E	–	NA	NA
Verbenaceae – Verbena family: Comutia obovata	Palo de Nigue	U.S.A. (PR)	E	–	NA	NA

Final Rules: Plants

Species						
Scientific name	Common name	Historic range	Status	When listed	Critical habitat	Special rules
Apiaceae – Parsley family: Eryngium cuneifolium	Snakeroot	U.S.A. (FL)	E	256	NA	NA
Aquifoliaceae – Holly family: Ilex cookii	Cook's holly	U.S.A. (PR)	E	277	NA	NA
Asclepiadaceae – Milkweed family: Asclepias welshii	Welsh's milkweed	U.S.A. (UT)	T	295	17.96(a)	NA
Asteraceae – Aster family: Cirsium vinaceum	Sacramento Mountains thistle	U.S.A. (NM)	T	276	NA	NA

Final Rules: Plants

Species						
Scientific name	Common name	Historic range	Status	When listed	Critical habitat	Special rules
Liatris helleri	Heller's blazing star	U.S.A. (NC)	T	300	NA	NA
Brassicaceae—Mustard family: Glaucocarpum suffrutescens	Toad-flax cress	U.S.A. (UT)	E	293	NA	NA
Lesquerella filiformis	Missouri bladder-pod	U.S.A. (MO)	E	252	NA	NA
Lesquerella pallida	White bladderpod	U.S.A. (TX)	E	260	NA	NA
Warea amplexifolia	Wide-leaf warea	U.S.A. (FL)	E	266	NA	NA
Warea carteri	Carter's mustard	U.S.A. (FL)	E	256	NA	NA
Cactaceae—Cactus family: Pediocactus despainii	San Rafael cactus	U.S.A. (UT)	E	286	NA	NA
Caryophyllaceae—Pink family Geocarpon minimum	None	U.S.A. (AR,MO)	T	275	NA	NA
Paronychia chartacea (=Nyachia pulvinata)	Papery whitlow-wort	U.S.A (FL)	T	256	NA	NA
Convolvulaceae—Morning glory family: Bonamia grandiflora	Florida bonamia	U.S.A. (FL)	T	297	NA	NA
Cupressaceae—Cypress family: Cupressus abramsiana	Santa Cruz Cypress	U.S.A. (CA)	E	251	NA	NA
Cyatheaceae—Tree-fern family: Cyathea dryopteroides	Elfin tree fern	U.S.A. (PR)	E	277	NA	NA
Fabaceae—Pea family: Astragalus robbinsii var. jesupi	Jesops milk-vetch	U.S.A. (NH, VT)	E	271	NA	NA
Austragalus montii	Heliotrope milk-vetch	U.S.A. (UT)	T	299	17.96(a)	NA
Lespedeza leptostachya	Prairie bush-clover	U.S.A. (IA, IL, MN, WI)	T	253	NA	NA
Lupinus andorum	Scrub lupine	U.S.A. (FL)	E	264	NA	NA

Final Rules: Plants

Species						
Scientific name	Common name	Historic range	Status	When listed	Critical habitat	Special rules
Serianthes nelsonii	Hayun Lagu (Guam) Tronkon guafi (Rota)	Western Pacific Ocean: U.S.A (Guam, Rota)	257	NA	NA	
Trifolium stoloniferum	Running buffalo clover	U.S.A. (IL, IN, KS, KY, MO, OH, WV)	E	270	NA	NA
Flacourtiaceae – Flacourtia family: Banara vanderbiltii	Palo de Ramon	U.S.A. (PR)	E	254	NA	NA
Hypericaceae – St. John's-Wort family: Hypericum cumulicola	Highlands scrub hypericum	U.S.A. (FL)	E	256	NA	NA
Oleaceae – Olive family: Chionanthus pygmaeus	Pygmy fringe tree	U.S.A. (FL)	E	256	NA	NA
Piperaceae – Pepper family: Peperomia wheeleri	Wheeler's peperomia	U.S.A. (PR)	E	254	NA	NA
Polemoniaceae – Phlox family: Eriastrum densifolium ssp. sanctorum	Santa Ana River Wholly-star	U.S.A. (CA)	E	291	NA	NA
Polygonaceae – Buckwheat family: Centrostegia leptoceras	Slender-horned spine-flower	U.S.A. (CA)	E	291	NA	NA
Polygonella basiramia (= Polygonella ciliata var. basi-ramias)	Wireweed	U.S.A. (FL)	E	256	NA	NA

Final Rules: Plants

Species						
Scientific name	Common name	Historic range	Status	When listed	Critical habitat	Special rules
Primulaceae—Primrose family: Lysimachia asperulaefolia	Rough-leaved loose-strife	U.S.A. (NC, SC)	E	274	NA	NA
Rosaceae—Rose family: Prunus geniculata	Scrub plum	U.S.A. (FL)	E	256	NA	NA
Scrophulariaceae—Snapdragon family: Penstemon haydenii	Blowout penstemon	U.S.A. (NE)	E	—	NA	NA

Proposed Rules: Invertebrates

Species							
Common name	Scientific name	Historic range	Vertebrate Population where endangered or threatened	Status	When listed	Critical habitat	Special rules
CLAMS							
Pearlshell, Louisiana	Margaritifera hembeli	U.S.A. (LA)	NA	E	–	NA	NA
Spinymussel, James (=Virginia spiny mussel)	Pleurobema (=Fusconsia) colina	U.S.A. (VA, WV)	NA	E	–	NA	NA
CRUSTACEANS							
Crayfish, Shasta (=placid crayfish)	Pacifastacus fortis	U.S.A. (CA)	NA	E	–	NA	NA
Shrimp, Alabama cave	Palaemonias alabamae	U.S.A. (AL)	NA		–	NA	NA
Shrimp, California fresh-water	Syncaris pacifica	U.S.A. (CA)	NA	E	–	NA	NA

Final Rules: Invertebrates

Species							
Common name	Scientific name	Historic range	Vertebrate Population where endangered or threatened	Status	When listed	Critical habitat	Special rules
INSECTS							
Butterfly, bay checkerspot	Euphydrayas editha bayensis	U.S.A. (CA)	NA	E	288	NA	NA
Skipper, Pawnee montane	Hesperia leonardus montana	U.S.A. (CO)	NA	T	289	NA	NA
CRUSTACEANS Crayfish (no common name)	Cambarus zophonastes	U.S.A. (AR)	NA	E	263	NA	NA
CLAMS Mussel, Curtis'	Pleurobema curtum	U.S.A. (AL, MS)	NA	E	262	NA	NA
Mussel, Judge Tait's	Pleurobema taitianum	U.S.A. (AL, MS)	NA	E	262	NA	NA
Mussel, Marshall's	Pleurobema marshalli	U.S.A. (AL, MS)	NA	E	262	NA	NA
Mussel, penitent	Epioblasma (=Dysomia) penita	U.S.A. (AL, MS)	E	262	NA	NA	
Stirrup shell	Quadrula stapes	U.S.A. (AL, MS)	NA	E	262	NA	NA

Proposed Rules: Birds/Mammals

Species							
Common name	Scientific name	Historic range	Vertebrate Population where endangered or threatened	Status	When listed	Critical habitat	Special rules
MAMMALS							
Bat, Mexican long-nosed	Leptonychteris nivalis	U.S.A. (NM, TX); Mexico; Central America	Entire	E	–	NA	NA
Bat, Sanborn's long-nosed	Leptonycteris sanborni (=L. yerbabuenae)	U.S.A. (AZ, NM); Mexico; Central America	Entire	E	–	NA	NA
Deer, Visayan	Cervus alfredi	Philippines	Entire	E	–	NA	NA
Rat, Stephens' kangaroo	Dipodomys stephensi	U.S.A. (CA)	Entire	E	–	NA	NA
Rat, Tipton kangaroo	Dipodomys nitratoides nitratoides	U.S.A. (CA)	Entire	–	NA	NA	

Final Rules: Birds and Mammals

Species							
Common name	Scientific name	Historic range	Vertebrate Population where endangered or threatened	Status	When listed	Critical habitat	Special rules
REPTILES							
Alligator, American	Alligator missis-sippiensis	Southeastern U.S.A.	Entire	T(S/A)	1, 11, 20, 47, 51, 60, 113, 134, 186, 269, 3, 279	NA	17.42(a)
Crocodile, Nile	Crocodylus nilo-ticus	Africa; Middle East	Entire (Except ranched populations in Zimbabwe)	E		NA	NA
Crocodile, Nile	Crocodylus nilo-ticus	Africa; Middle East	Zimbabwe (ranched populations only)	279	NA	17.42(c)	
Tortoise, gopher	Gopherus poly-phemus	U.S.A. (AL, FL, GA, LA, MS, SC)	Wherever found west of Mobile and Tombigbee Rivers in AL, MS, LA).	T	261	NA	NA
Turtle, Alabama red-bellied	Pseudemys alaba-mensis	U.S.A. (AL)	Entire	E	278	NA	NA

Final Rules: Birds and Mammals

Species							
Common name	Scientific name	Historic range	Vertebrate Population where endangered or threatened	Status	When listed	Critical habitat	Special rules
Turtle, flattened musk	Stemotherus depressus	U.S.A. (AL)	Black Warrior River System upstream from Bankhead Dam	T	272	NA	NA
Skink, blue-tailed mole	Eumeces egregius lividus	U.S.A. (FL)	Entire	T	298	NA	17.42(d)
Skink, Sand	Neoseps reynoldsi	U.S.A. (FL)	Entire	T	298	NA	17.42(d)
BIRDS							
Caracara, Audubon's crested	Polyborus plancus audubonii	U.S.A. (AZ, FL, LA, TX, NM); south to Panama; Cuba	U.S.A. (FL)	T	280	NA	NA
Tern, roseate	Sterna dougallii dougallii	Tropical and temperate coasts of Atlantic Basin and East Africa	U.S.A. (Atlantic Coast south to NC); Canada (NF, NS, QU); Bermuda	E	296	NA	NA

Final Rules: Birds and Mammals

Species			Vertebrate Population where endangered or threatened				
Common name	Scientific name	Historic range		Status	When listed	Critical habitat	Special rules
Do	do	do	Western Hemisphere and adjacent oceans, incl. U.S.A. (FL, PR, VI), where not listed as endangered.	T	296	NA	NA
Towhee, Inyo brown	Pipilo fuscus eremophilus	U.S.A. (CA)	Entire	T	262	17.95(b)	NA
Vireo, black-capped	Vireo atricapillus	U.S.A. (KS, LA, NE, OK, TX); Mexico	Entire	E	294	NA	NA
MAMMALS							
Rat, giant kangaroo	Dipodomys ingens	U.S.A. (CA)	Entire	E	250	NA	NA
Squirrel, Mount Graham red	Tamiasciurus hudsonicus grahamensis	U.S.A. (AZ)	Entire	E	268	NA	NA
Vole, Hualapai	Microtus mexicanus hualpaiensis	U.S.A. (AZ)	Entire	E	292	NA	NA

Final Rules: Birds and Mammals

Species							
Common name	Scientific name	Historic range	Vertebrate Population where endangered or threatened	Status	When listed	Critical habitat	Special rules
AMPHIBIANS							
Toad, Puerto Rican crested	Peltophryne lemus	U.S.A. (PR); British Virgin Islands	Entire	T	283	NA	NA

Proposed Rules: Fishes

Common name	Scientific name	Historic range	Vertebrate Population where endangered or threatened	Status	When listed	Critical habitat	Special rules
FISHES							
Dace, Clover Valley speckled	Rhinichthys osculus oligoporus	U.S.A. (NV)	Entire	E	–	NA	NA
Dace, Independence Valley speckled	Rhinichthys oculus lethroporus	U.S.A. (NV)	Entire	E	–	NA	NA
Darter, boulder	Etheostoma (Nothonotus) sp.	U.S.A. (TN, AL)	Entire	E	–	NA	NA
Sucker, Lost River	Deltistes luxatus	U.S.A. (OR, CA)	Entire	E	–	NA	NA
Sucker, Shortnose	Chasmistes brevirostris	U.S.A. (OR, CA)	Entire	E	–	NA	NA

Final Rules: Fishes

Species		Historic range	Vertebrate Population where endangered or threatened	Status	When listed	Critical habitat	Special rules
Common name	Scientific name						
FISHES							
Dace, Blackside	Phoxinus cumberlandensis	U.S.A. (TN, KY)	NA	T	273	NA	NA
Shiner, Cape Fear	Notropis mekistochelas	U.S.A. (NC)	Entire	T	290	17.95(e)	NA
Shiner, Pecos bluntnose	Notropis simus pecosensis	U.S.A. (NM)	Entire	T	258	17.95(a)	17.44(r)
Silverside, Waccamaw	Menidia extensa	U.S.A. (NC)	Entire	T	265	17.95(E) ERR81	17.44(s)
Spinedace, Little Colorado	Lepidomeda vittata	U.S.A. (AZ)	Entire	T	287	17.95(e)	17.44(t)

APPENDIX J

Federal Fish and Wildlife Program Budgets

Cynthia Lenhart

INTRODUCTION

Five federal agencies are primarily responsible for the management of the nation's fish and wildlife resources: the Fish and Wildlife Service (FWS), Forest Service, Bureau of Land Management (BLM), National Park Service (NPS), and National Marine Fisheries Service (NMFS). In 1988, the budgets for these agencies range from about $160 million to $2.5 billion.[1] However, except for FWS, these budgets include funding for activities other than those related to fish and wildlife conservation.

All of the agencies received modest increases in 1988 total appropriations over 1987 levels, ranging from nine percent for FWS to one percent for NMFS. In the past six or seven years the budgets of the Forest Service, BLM, and NPS have declined in spending power;[2] NMFS' budget has kept steady; the FWS budget has increased. Since 1981, the FWS budget has increased by 34 percent in constant dollars; the NMFS budget has remained fairly even since 1982.[3]

1. All budget years cited are federal fiscal years.

2. Throughout this chapter, comparisons in funding levels between different years are made in constant dollars to account for inflation and allow more accurate comparisons of purchasing power. Constant dollar conversions were made using the Gross National Product implicit price deflators reported by the Bureau of Economic Analysis for the years 1981 through 1986 and an estimated Gross National Product price deflator of 4.2 for the fourth quarter of 1987. Percentage changes are calculated by converting fiscal year appropriations into dollar values of the fiscal year with which they are being compared. For example, in comparisons with 1982 appropriations, 1988 appropriations are converted into 1982 dollars.

3. Budget trends are based on 1981 figures, except for NMFS and NPS, which had structural budget changes that make comparisons difficult for years prior to 1982.

While the total budget of some agencies has declined, funding for the wildlife programs has generally increased in constant dollars. The most significant increase has occurred in the NPS natural resources management account, which is up 65 percent in constant dollars since 1982. Fish and wildlife habitat management on the National Forest System has increased 18 percent in constant dollars since 1981. BLM wildlife habitat management, on the other hand, has registered more than a nine percent decline in spending power since 1981, the year of President Carter's last budget.

Thus, with the exception of BLM, wildlife-related federal spending has basically survived the Reagan Administration. In 1988, most federal wildlife programs are funded at levels comparable to or somewhat above those of 1981 or 1982. Congress has steadfastly refused to accept annual administration budget proposals to slash funding for natural resource management. Nevertheless, many federal fish and wildlife programs, with an ever-increasing list of responsibilities, continue to be hampered by limitations on personnel imposed by the Reagan Administration.

FISH AND WILDLIFE SERVICE

The U.S. Fish and Wildlife Service is the leading federal agency responsible for the conservation and management of fish and wildlife resources. It has principal responsibility and authority for migratory birds, threatened and endangered species, and certain marine mammals. FWS manages 440 national wildlife refuges—more than 90 million acres—as well as 71 national fish hatcheries. With a personnel roster of just over 6,300, the Service's 1988 total budget is about $743 million, of which some 43 percent is in permanent and trust funds; the remainder of the budget is discretionary in nature and must receive congressional approval each year.

The spending levels of permanent and trust funds generally are not subject to annual congressional direction, but for 1988 the appropriations committees decisively rejected an administration proposal to transfer $25 million from the Dingell-Johnson account to FWS' primary operating account, resource management. The transfer would have been used to offset decreases slated in the administration's 1988 FWS budget request. Congress opposed this budgetary sleight of hand, citing the need to maintain the financial support of fishermen who voluntarily pay the excise tax on fishing equipment to fund sport fish programs.

Congress also rejected typical administration proposals to halt land acquisition and significantly reduce refuge maintenance. Altogether Congress appropriated some $426 million for discretionary programs—34 percent more than the president's request—an amount just about equal to what was spent in 1987.

The FWS 1988 budget shows a 34-percent increase above the 1981 level in constant dollars. Much of this increase, however, reflects the 1984 legislative expansion of the Dingell-Johnson account, which led to a significant increase in spending for state grants for fish restoration. Not including federal grants-in-aid and other permanent and trust funds, the FWS budget has increased 16 percent in constant dollars over the past seven years.

FWS underwent a major reorganization in 1986, and the budget structure was changed as well. Resource management, which has been divided into five new subcategories, is the largest account in the total budget, receiving 46 percent of the total. Federal grants-in-aid, funded primarily by excise taxes on certain kinds of sporting equipment and on motorboat fuel, constitute 37 percent of the total budget; land acquisition, supported by monies from the Land and Water Conservation Fund and the Migratory Bird Conservation Account, constitutes 11 percent; the "construction and anadromous fish" account forms three percent; and other miscellaneous permanent funds make up the remaining two percent of the FWS 1988 budget (see Figure 1).

Fish and Wildlife Enhancement

This new budget subcategory of resource management includes certain aspects of the endangered species management program (listing, consultation, permit review, recovery actions on off-refuge lands, and grants to states), ecological services, environmental contaminants, and the national wetlands inventory. Congress appropriated nearly $50 million for this program in 1988, a 20-percent increase from the president's budget, and about $3 million more than in 1987 (see Figure 2). Specific congressional add-ons to the president's budget request included $250,000 for endangered species listing, and $150,000 for Section 7 consultation activities to accomodate an expected jump in the number of project reviews. Congress rejected the administration's oft-repeated proposal to zero-fund federal grants to states for endangered species recovery, and appropriated $4.3 million to maintain that program at the 1987 spending level.

Endangered species recovery received a lump-sum $1.5 million increase in 1988. Concerned that a large percentage of recovery monies are allocated to a relatively few, high-visibility species, Congress refused to make species-specific allocations, and basically left it to the discretion of FWS. Several high-priority projects may be funded with the $1.5 million add-on. For example, the president's budget provided less than $525,000 for both domestic and international sea turtle

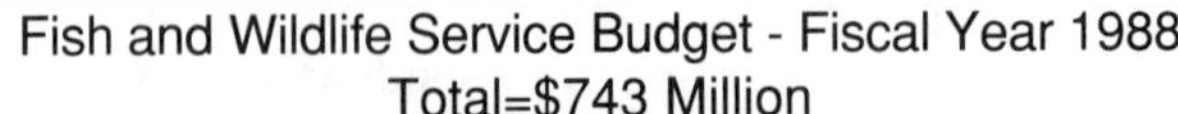

Fish and Wildlife Service Budget - Fiscal Year 1988
Total=$743 Million

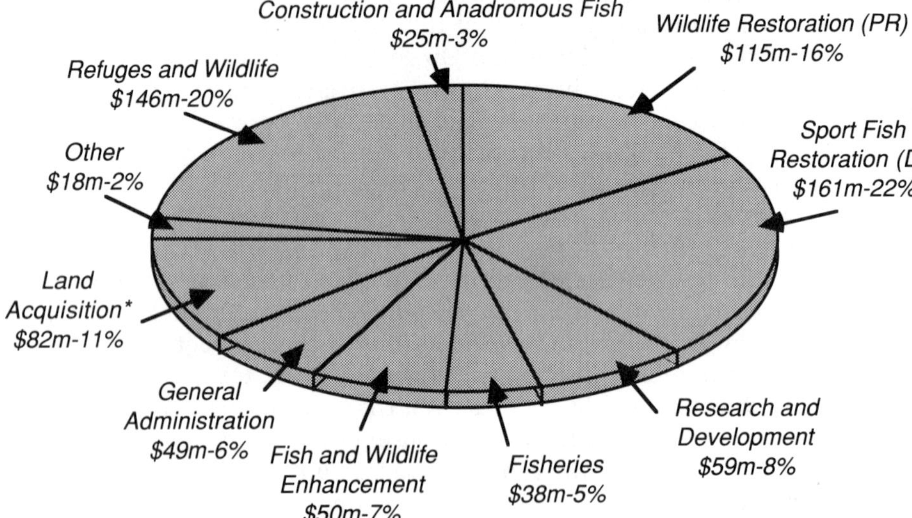

*Land acquisition includes $51.8 million appropriated from the Land and Water Conservation Fund, $1 million appropriated under the Wetlands Loan Act, and $28.9 million from the Migratory Bird Conservation Account.

Figure 1.

recovery work. FWS has responsibility for promoting the recovery of seven species of sea turtles that feed and nest on U.S. territory. As nesting beaches are destroyed and foreign exploitation continues, population declines are outstripping existing service resources. FWS estimates that it could use at least $700,000 in additional funds in 1988 to carry out telemetry studies to determine habitat preferences of hawksbill and loggerhead turtles, to survey populations, and to protect nesting beaches in the southeastern United States.

In response to requests from some conservation groups that Congress appropriate money to buy water rights in the Colorado River for endangered fish, the appropriations committees directed FWS to prepare a report regarding instream flow requirements and water acquisition needs in that drainage.

Another significant increase of $1.2 million was provided for FWS to assist in implementing the Food Security Act of 1985, generally referred to as the Farm Bill. Several conservation provisions of that law are critically important to the preservation of wildlife habitat. FWS

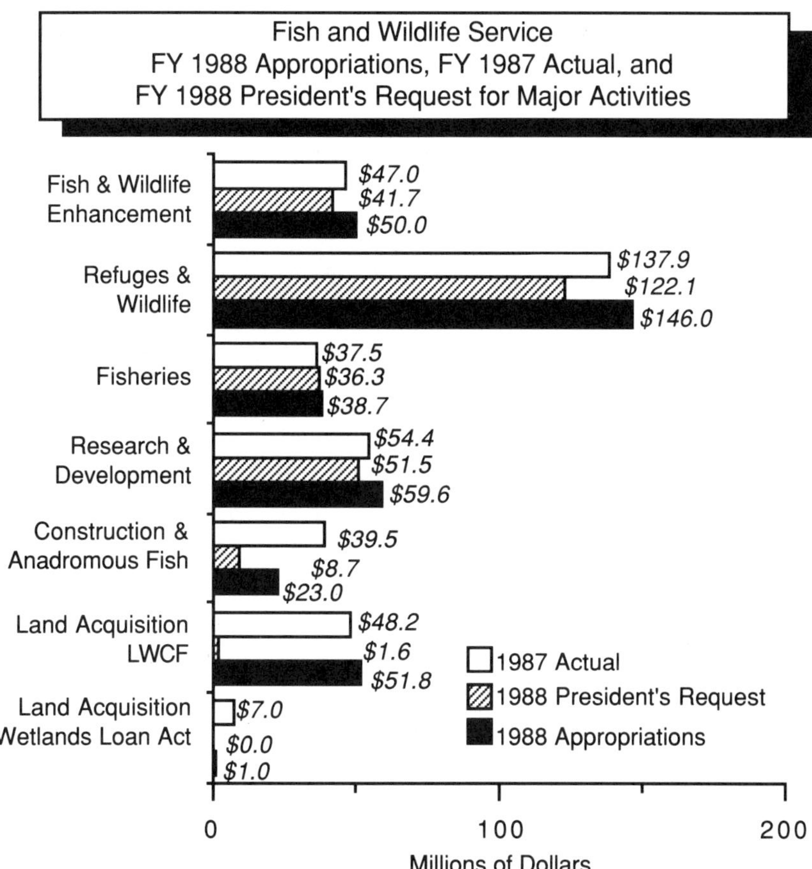

Figure 2.

will use the money to ensure that the provisions are implemented to benefit wildlife and preserve wetlands.

Concerned with a 1986 FWS report detailing widespread refuge contamination problems, Congress in 1987 added $4.5 million for the agency to deal with contaminant issues; $2 million was expressly allocated for refuges. In 1988, Congress added another $1 million to FWS' budget to improve the agency's ability to analyze the large volume of samples now being generated through this aggressive monitoring program.

Refuges and Wildlife

This new budget subcategory of resources management covers expenses related to the administration of the refuge system, migratory bird and marine mammal management, and law enforcement. Congress appropriated $146.7 million for this program in 1988, a 20-percent increase from the president's budget, and almost $9 million more than in 1987.

Much of this increase went to support the Accelerated Refuge Maintenance and Management (ARMM) program, as Congress again rejected an administration proposal to slash ARMM funding by 42 percent. FWS estimates that some $60 million per year is needed to protect its $2 billion investment in refuge facilities, but the administration's ARMM program has fallen far short of this goal. Congress also added increases to the president's budget for defense of refuge water rights, start-up costs for new refuges, implementation of refuge fishery management plans, and a challenge grant program for projects on refuges.

Law enforcement increases included more than $2 million to raise the number of agents from about 188 to 202; $300,000 for personnel and operational start-up costs associated with FWS' new forensics laboratory; $50,000 for law enforcement in the Caribbean; and $200,000 for law enforcement in the Southwest.

Under migratory bird management, Congress added $500,000 for nongame birds. Conservationists viewed this as a small but significant step in broadening the conservation horizon of the Fish and Wildlife Service. While charged with the conservation of some 832 species of migratory birds, FWS tends to concentrate its management efforts on those species that are either hunted or endangered. This focus can be partly explained by funding realities. Research and management of species of economic or sport value is supported by hunters through excise taxes on firearms, ammunition, and archery equipment (which go to the Pittman-Robertson Fund) and duck stamps for waterfowl hunting. Threatened and endangered species recovery funds are made available under the Endangered Species Act. Nongame species funding is supposed to be provided by the Fish and Wildlife Conservation Act of 1980, which authorizes the appropriation of up to $5 million per year for state nongame grants. The act has yet to be implemented, however; no money has ever been appropriated and no politically viable funding mechanism has been created.

The nongame funds provided by Congress in 1988 will go for implementation of a nongame plan developed by FWS in 1983. Conservationists believe that implementation of the nongame bird plan may help to arrest the decline of some 28 species before they reach endangered status. While some states have shown initiative in launching nongame conservation programs, critical information gaps on declining species persist due to lack of federal guidance. Noting this, Congress directed FWS to use $100,000 for regional and national coordination of state nongame activities. Congress designated the remaining $400,000 for population monitoring activities, to be conducted in cooperation with state and private agencies and volunteer networks, many of which already carry out nationwide population surveys. Also under migratory bird management, Congress provided $200,000 for implementation of the North American Waterfowl Management Plan; to cooperate with states and interested organizations in habitat protection efforts; and to work with Canadian officials in building up declining waterfowl populations.

Fisheries

The fisheries account, a subcategory of resources management, supports operation and maintenance of federal fish hatcheries, management of refuge fish populations, technical assistance to Indian tribes and others, and implementation of the Lower Snake River Compensation Plan. Congress provided $38.7 million for fishery resources in 1988, a three percent increase over the president's request and about $2.4 million more than in 1987. Excluding funds for the Lower Snake River Compensation Plan, initiated in 1984, fishery resources funding has declined about 30 percent in constant dollars since 1981.

In response to proposals for funding major rehabilitation programs at a number of hatcheries, Congress directed the service to conduct a review of all fish hatchery operational plans and to request funds for essential maintenance needs in a more orderly fashion commencing with the 1989 budget. Congress cut the administration's proposed budget for the Lower Snake River Compensation Fund—a program to mitigate damage to fishery resources caused by four federal dams in Washington—more than $1 million, noting that the Clearwater fish hatchery would not come on line in 1988 as originally expected. Two national fish hatcheries and three fishery assistance offices were transferred from the Bureau of Indian Affairs to FWS, with related funding adjustments. Congress restored hatchery maintenance to the base funding level, and provided minor increases for operations and improvements at a fishery research lab and an endangered fish handling facility.

Research and Development

All of FWS' research activities were consolidated into research and development, a new budget subcategory of resources management. Congress appropriated $59.6 million to the research account, a 16-percent increase from the president's request, and just over $5 million more than in 1987. This increase included $2 million for studies on the Arctic National Wildlife Refuge relating to impacts of proposed oil and gas development; $500,000 for waterfowl research relating to implementation of the North American Waterfowl Management Plan; and $100,000 to address the brown tree snake problem in Guam and to prevent its spread to Hawaii.[4]

Congress also provided $650,000 for Alaska mammal research, which will aid in determining the impact of subsistence hunting on polar bear and walrus populations.

General Administration

The fifth subcategory of the resources management account, general administration, covers the costs of running the central office in Washington D.C., seven regional offices, and research facilities. In one action with direct bearing on wildlife conservation, Congress provided $500,000 for matching grants to the National Fish and Wildlife Foundation. The foundation was established by Congress in 1984 as an independent, nonprofit organization devoted to the development of innovative conservation projects. The foundation creates partnerships with private organizations and public agencies, and encourages and administers donations in support of priority projects. In 1987, the foundation raised more than $1.5 million in private funds and administered 30 projects.

Construction and Anadromous Fish

Congress appropriated $25.1 million for this account, a 189-percent increase from the president's budget. The administration had proposed no new construction projects on refuges and hatcheries, but Congress provided a little over $5 million for this purpose. Funding for research facilitities and dam rehabilitation was increased, and monies were included for construction of a wildlife forensics laboratory in Oregon. Congress rejected the administration's proposal to halt anadromous fish grants to the states, providing $1.5 million for the program, and continued support for an ongoing striped bass study.

Land Acquisition

FWS has two main sources of fiscal support for land acquisition: the Land and Water Conservation Fund and Migratory Bird Conservation Account. In 1988, the president's budget proposed no funding for new land acquisition except for lands acquired with duck-stamp receipts, projected to yield about $17 million in 1988. (Other revenue sources—recreation fee receipts and import duties on firearms—are expected to

4. Predation by the introduced brown tree snake has caused a serious decline in numbers of seven endemic bird species in Guam.

yield another $12 million in 1988.) Congress rejected this proposal and appropriated an additional $1 million under the Wetlands Loan Act (leaving a balance of $2.6 million of the authorized $200 million loan advance), and $51.8 million from the Land and Water Conservation Fund. The 1988 Land and Water Conservation Fund appropriation is about 7.5 percent above the 1987 level. while significantly more than the annual average over the past decade of $32.8 million, it is still approximately equal in purchasing power to appropriations provided in the late 1970s (see Figure 3).

FOREST SERVICE

The U.S. Forest Service is the largest federal agency responsible for natural resources, with an operating budget in 1988 of $2.5 billion. In 1987 the Forest Service employed the equivalent of 37,735 full-time workers; 889 of these—two percent of the total staff—were wildlife and fish management personnel, including 564 biologists.

The Forest Service manages 191 million acres of land constituting the National Forest System. The forest, range land, and aquatic habitats within the system support more than 3,000 wildlife species,

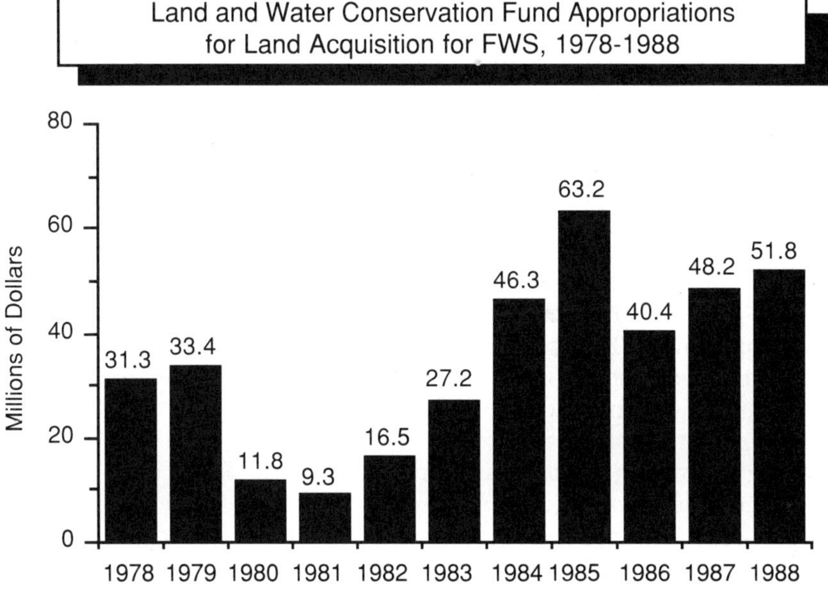

Figure 3.

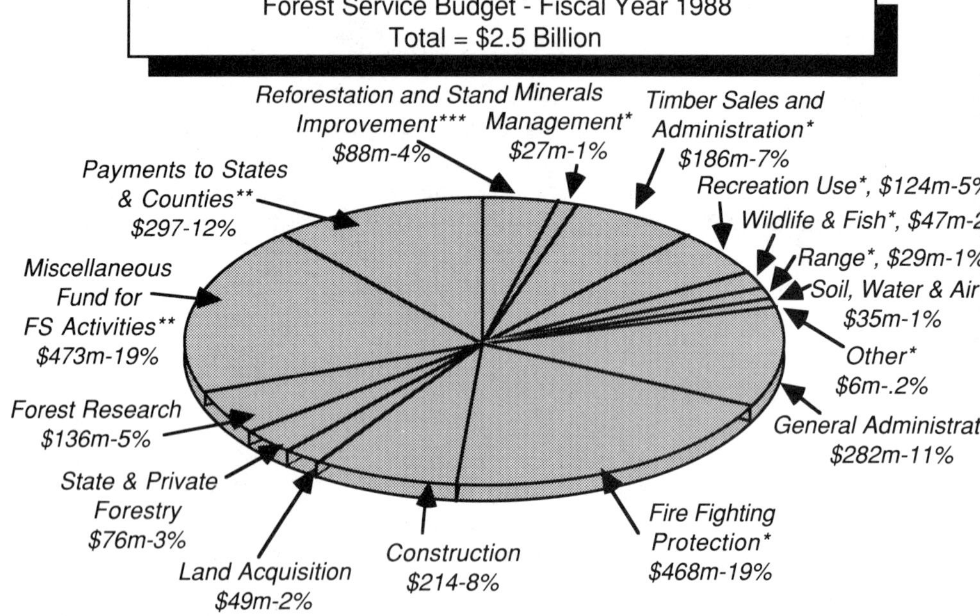

Figure 4.

and are critical to the maintenance and recovery of many threatened and endangered species, such as the grizzly bear, gray wolf, and California condor. The system contains more than half of the big-game habitat in the United States, and more than a quarter of the spawning and rearing habitat for salmon and steelhead in the Pacific Northwest and Alaska. National Forest lands include or affect most of the nation's premier trout streams.

The total 1988 Forest Service budget is about eight percent higher than in 1987. This total includes $799 million in permanent and trust funds, representing 31 percent of the total budget. More than half of the permanent and trust funds is used to support the National Forest System, and the remainder is used to pay states and counties their share of receipts from commercial activities on forest system lands. Excluding permanent and trust funds, the Forest Service has $1.7 billion to divide among five major accounts in 1988: National Forest System, Construction, Forest Research, State and Private Forestry, and Land Acquisition (see Figure 4).

In 1988, about 50 percent of the total Forest Service budget will be used to fund activities on the National Forest System. A minimum of

$456.8 million, or 18 percent of the total budget, will be used to support the timber program. (This amount includes road construction, but not mitigation activities, which are supported by several accounts.) In comparison, $47.4 million will be used in 1988 for the wildlife and fish habitat management program, representing a mere two percent of the total budget.

The 1980 Resources Planning Act (RPA) directed the Forest Service to establish its own funding and program goals. The 1985 RPA update, which set such guidelines through 1990, projected a need for substantial increases in appropriations for most programs. The only exceptions were timber sales and administration, which were slated for a steady level of funding in constant dollars. Appropriations trends since 1980 have failed, however, to meet the somewhat lofty goals of the Forest Service's planning process. While timber spending has remained relatively steady, as prescribed, wildlife and fish budgets in the last three years have averaged just over half of the 1985 RPA updated goal.

Wildlife and Fish Habitat Management

The wildlife and fish habitat management program receives funds from more than one account. Most of its funding comes from the National Forest System account, which includes funds for timber support activities, for fish and wildlife biologists' participation in forest planning and coordination with other commodity development activities, and for direct habitat improvement. Additional wildlife and fish funds come from Knutson-Vandenberg deposits made by timber purchasers for reforestation and resource improvements. Knutson-Vandenberg monies are used to mitigate habitat loss and for habitat enhancement on specific timber-sale areas. In 1988 the administration proposed to offset its proposed decrease in appropriations for wildlife and fish management by using $6.2 million from the Knutson-Vandenberg fund; Congress rejected this proposal.

The Multiple-Use Sustained-Yield Act of 1960 requires the Forest Service to give wildlife and fish due consideration in National Forest System management, and Forest Service policy requires that wildlife and fish receive "co-equal" consideration with other resources. In reality, wildlife and fish play minor roles in the system's management compared to commodity uses. Wildlife and fish habitat management on the National Forest System has become increasingly more difficult as development pressures, public use, and legal requirements have grown while funding and staff have shrunk. As more money is needed to mitigate the effects of resource development activities such as timber harvest and grazing, less money has been allocated to direct habitat improvement; in the past six years, the number of acres directly improved for wildlife has declined by more than 60 percent.

The president's 1988 budget proposed a nine percent reduction from the 1987 funding level for the wildlife and fish habitat management program. "Coordination" (a euphemism for mitigation activities) would have received a modest increase of $1.6 million, but habitat improvement would have suffered a particularly severe cut. If the president's budget had been accepted by Congress, anadromous fish habitat improvement allocations would have been reduced by over 50 percent; endangered species by 37 percent. Congress,however, rejected the president's proposal and appropriated $47.4 million for wildlife and fish habitat management in 1988, a 25 percent increase over the president's request of $37.9 million and a 14 percent increase over the 1987 level of $41.5 million (see Figure 5).

Specific increases for 1988 included $2 million for inventory and monitoring of the northern spotted owl. The owl is considered an indicator species for the old-growth forests of the Pacific Northwest, and has become the symbol of the raging controversy over timber management in those forests. Given the level of development activity in its preferred habitat, the owl must be monitored closely to assure that forest management plans do not threaten it—or other old growth/

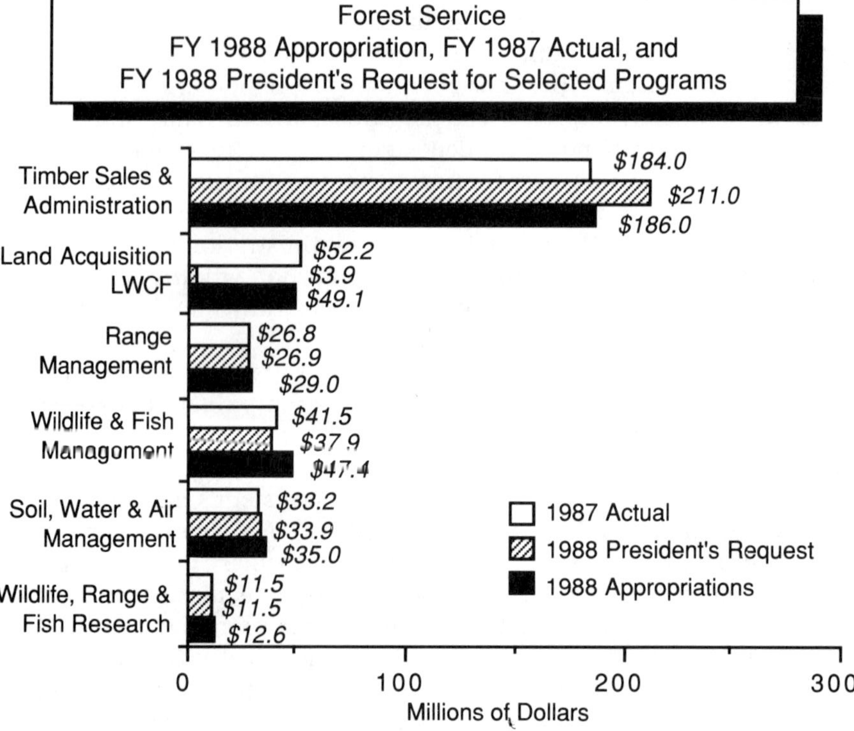

Figure 5.

mature forest species—to the point where listing under the Endangered Species Act would be warranted. A petition to list the owl was submitted to the Fish and Wildlife Service in January of 1987; in December FWS decided that listing was not warranted at that time, but that additional research was needed.

In 1987, Congress recognized the critical need for more information on the spotted owl, and appropriated $1 million to the Forest Service to increase its effort to inventory and monitor the status of the species, and to help resolve management controversies. The agency appointed a spotted owl activities coordinator, and initiated a program that standardized field survey techniques. Inventories have just begun on many of the forests involved. Covering all of the owl-network sites on any given forest may take several years; owls do not always respond to calls, so determining their presence often requires several visits to each site. Inventory of wilderness and roadless area sites is especially time-consuming due to access problems. So far, monitoring has been limited to designated spotted owl habitat areas in those forests that have completed the inventory process. The $2 million add-on in 1988 will allow the Forest Service to continue to implement this ambitious program.

Congress also provided an additional $2.5 million above the president's request to bring the anadromous fish habitat improvement program up to the 1987 spending level in constant dollars. These monies will be used to restore in-stream habitats in the Northwest. Salmon stocks there are at an all-time low, primarily due to dam construction, but more recently to habitat degradation caused by timber cutting. The productivity of resident fish habitat has also declined dramatically in the last decade, particularly in the West, because of timber harvesting and livestock grazing. The president's budget had proposed a $300,000 cut in the resident fish habitat improvement program, which Congress restored.

There are 162 animal and plant species in National Forest System that are federally listed as threatened or endangered, or proposed for listing. Congress provided an increase of $2.5 million for endangered species habitat management, bringing the total budget for this aspect of the wildlife program to $4.5 million, 28 percent more than in 1987.

Congress also added $2 million to the president's budget to continue the Forest Service's Cost-Share Program, which serves to promote partnerships with the public in improving wildlife and fisheries habitat in the National Forest System. Federally appropriated dollars are matched by state, private or other federal funds, to carry out projects that otherwise would not get done. In 1987, some 200 entities entered into partnerships with the Forest Service to improve wildlife and fish habitat on over 40,000 acres. These cooperators financed over $2.6 million worth of projects, far surpassing the $1.5 million available in federal matching funds. The following examples of organizations cooperating with the Forest Service in 1987 typify the activity generated by this program:

- In cooperation with Ducks Unlimited, 200 artificial nesting islands were installed for the dusky Canada goose on the Copper River Delta in Alaska's Chugach National Forest. Populations of this subspecies have declined sharply in the last few years due to predation by mammals. The Delta is the dusky's only nesting place.
- The Rocky Mountain Elk Foundation helped revitalize elk habitat on the Coconino National Forest in Arizona by improving water sources and revegetating old road corridors.
- The Florida Game and Fresh Water Fish Commission cooperated in a prescribed burn project involving 2,000 acres of longleaf pine stands in Ocala National Forest to maintain the open, park-like setting required by the endangered red-cockaded woodpecker.
- Trout Unlimited, the Colorado Division of Wildlife, and the Forest Service placed logs and management structures in the Delores River of the San Juan National Forest to improve rainbow and cutthroat trout habitat.

Wildlife and Fish Habitat Research

Research for wildlife, range, and fish habitat was funded at $12.6 million in 1988, compared to the president's request of $11.4 million, and up nine percent from the 1987 level. Congress allocated increases for research on the threatened grizzly bear and the endangered Puerto Rican parrot. It also provided funds for several old-growth related research projects, on spotted owl habitat requirements in the western United States, Sitka black-tailed deer in the forests of southeastern Alaska, and Douglas-fir habitat in the Pacific Northwest and Alaska. The $1.2 million congressional increase also permits acceleration into research on the effects of timber management on deer and elk in Oregon and on various wildlife species in eastern and southern hardwood forests; the effects of grazing on anadromous fish habitat in Idaho; and the effects of timber management on cold water fish habitat in Minnesota.

Land Acquisition

Congress once again rejected the administration's proposal to halt new land acquisition, and appropriated $49 million from the Land and

Water Conservation Fund for land additions to the National Forest System. This amount is a six percent decrease from the 1987 level of $52.2 million. Over the past decade, Forest Service land acquisition annual funding has averaged $46.3 million (see Figure 6).

BUREAU OF LAND MANAGEMENT

The Bureau of Land Management manages 272 million acres of public land and administers mineral-leasing and development laws on an additional 300 million acres managed by other agencies and on lands where the subsurface mineral rights are federally owned. Although BLM ostensibly manages its lands for multiple uses, during the Reagan Administration the agency has been under intense pressure to favor commodity resources at the expense of other resources such as fish and wildlife.

While BLM is responsible for managing more land than any other federal agency, it is supported by relatively few employees and far fewer dollars per acre managed. In 1988, Congress appropriated a total of $499 million for BLM, and the agency was staffed with about 9,600 full-time personnel. About half of the BLM budget is spent on general

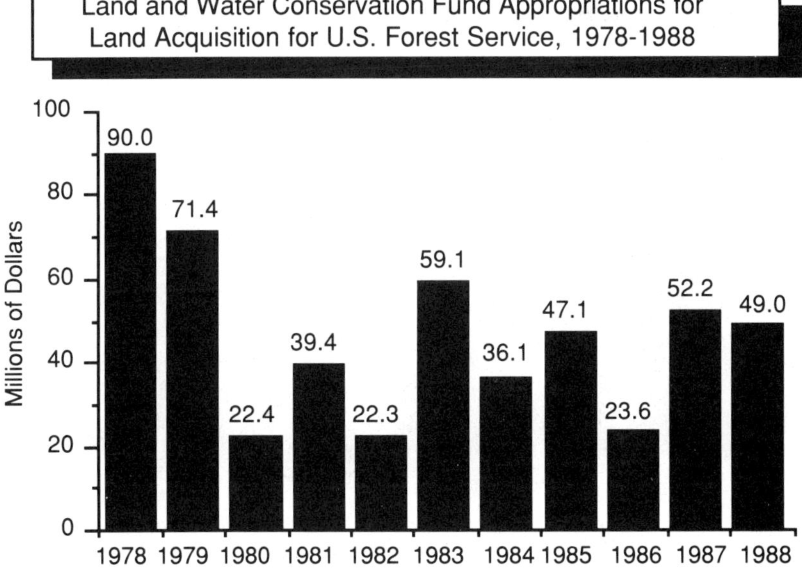

Figure 6.

administration, firefighting, and payments in lieu of taxes to states and counties; the other half is allocated to land management activities. Of the total 1988 BLM budget, renewable resources management (which includes management of range, recreation, forest, fish and wildlife habitat, fire, soil, water, and air), accounts for 19 percent; energy and minerals management, 12 percent; and management of timber harvesting on BLM lands in western Oregon, 8 percent (see Figure 7). The Reagan budget years have wreaked particular havoc on BLM's renewable resource programs, which have suffered greater budget reductions than those of any other federal agency with wildlife management responsibilities.

Wildlife Habitat Management

With over 270 million acres of habitat to manage, the Bureau's wildlife program must conduct resource inventories; prepare, implement, and monitor plans to improve habitat; make recommendations on all BLM activities to help mitigate adverse impacts of land development; and provide for the recovery of threatened and endangered species on its land. To carry out these responsibilities, BLM staffs a total of 220 offices nationwide. In 1980, there were 363 biologists employed by the wildlife habitat management program; the Reagan Administration has

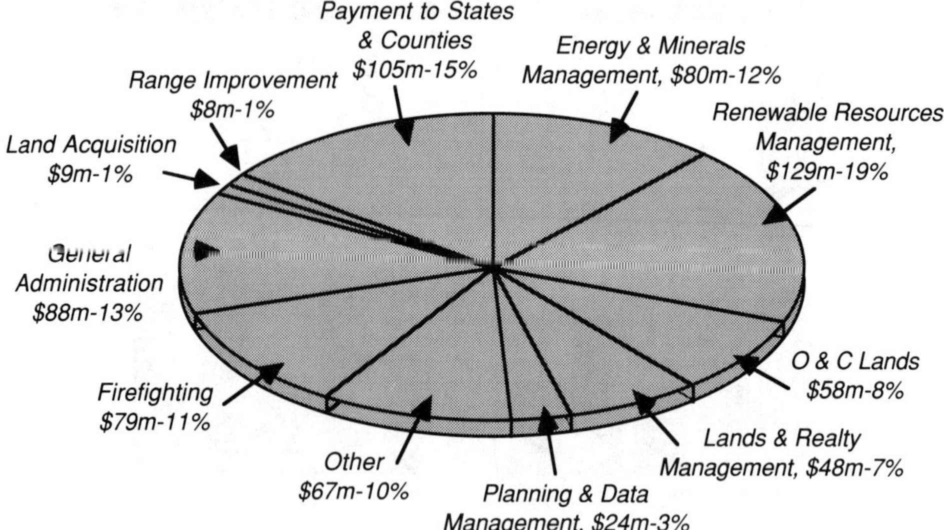

Figure 7.

reduced this number by over 30 percent, to just 244 in 1988. This dramatic reduction in biologists has been felt most acutely in metropolitan BLM districts and districts with high energy development activity. For example, each year the one biologist in Wyoming's Casper District must process an average of 900 applications for oil and gas drilling—in addition to basic program responsibilities of monitoring grazing, developing and implementing habitat improvement plans, and screening projects for impacts on threatened and endangered species.

The loss of 119 biologists has caused many district and area offices to assign fish and wildlife program responsibilities to other resource professionals, most of whom lack sufficient wildlife and fish expertise to identify the impacts of, and alternatives to, various land-use actions. As a result, BLM offices often find it difficult to provide basic National Environmental Policy Act compliance on land-use decisions because of inadequate analysis of fish and wildlife impacts.

The president's 1988 budget proposed a decrease of over $2.3 million from the wildlife program's 1987 base level and a reduction in 20 full-time equivalents. Congress rejected this proposal, and provided a total of $18.4 million for fish and wildlife habitat management in 1988, a 20-percent increase above the president's request and $2.3 million more than the 1987 appropriation (see Figure 8). An all-time high for the program, this funding level is still more than nine percent below the 1981 level in constant dollars.

Roughly 60 percent of the Congressional add-on simply represented a restoration of funds to the 1987 level. Specific increases for 1988 included $250,000 to accelerate habitat management activities in riparian zones. Many riparian areas managed by BLM are seriously degraded because of excessive livestock grazing, mining activities, and road construction. With so few fisheries biologists (25 in 1988), the bureau is seriously constrained in its implementation of habitat improvement projects prescribed in existing riparian and fisheries habitat management plans. In February 1987 BLM released its new "Riparian Policy," which was designed to publicly demonstrate its commitment to long-term management of riparian areas on public lands. With additional funding in 1988, the bureau's wildlife program will intensify efforts to inventory, monitor, and complete management plans for various riparian areas in the arid West. In Arizona, for example, BLM's Phoenix and Yuma districts plan to conduct a multidisciplinary survey of 21 miles of the Bill Williams River. The state will acquire about 2,000 acres of riparian habitat on the San Pedro River adjacent to Mexico, and BLM's Safford district will prepare a management plan for the area. Several districts plan to construct more fences for livestock control and are reviewing 13 riparian areas for designation as areas of critical environmental concern.

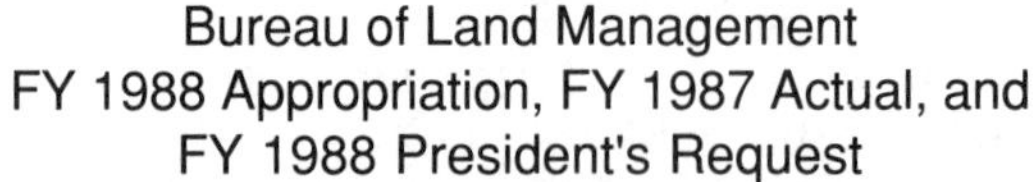

Bureau of Land Management
FY 1988 Appropriation, FY 1987 Actual, and
FY 1988 President's Request

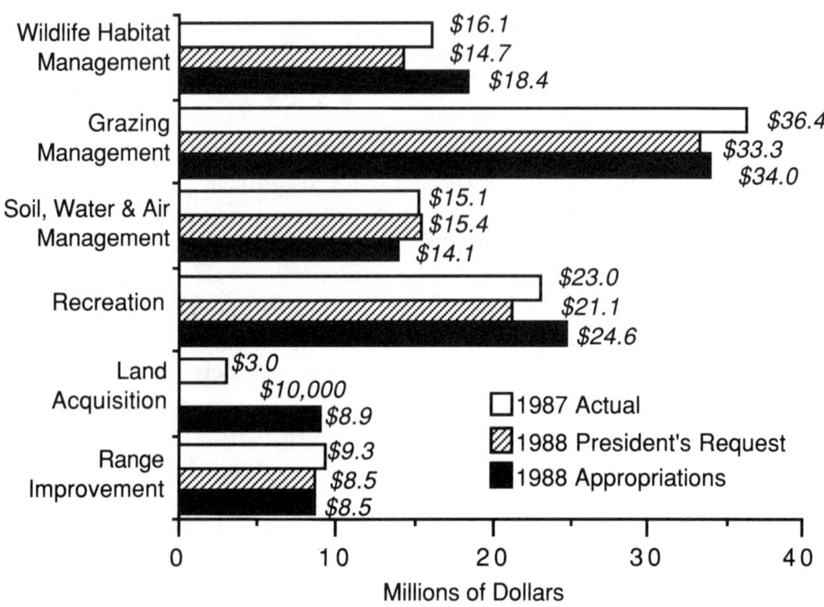

Figure 8.

BLM's endangered species program also received a minor boost in funding, with a $300,000 increase over the 1987 level, bringing the total program budget to $4.3 million. BLM lands provide habitat for 127 species that are federally listed as threatened or endangered. Recovery plans have been developed for just 73 of these species, and only 56 plans are actually being implemented in the field. BLM is far behind schedule in carrying out the habitat improvement projects for which it is responsible.

With the increase in endangered species funding, BLM plans, among other things, to focus more attention on the desert tortoise, which is a candidate for listing. California and Utah will both receive additional funds to implement management designed to prevent further deterioration of tortoise habitat, with the hope that this action will preclude the need to list the species. Arizona will use $60,000 in "new" funds for desert tortoise surveys. Endangered plant species will also benefit from the 1988 increase. Oregon and Utah will fund a total of three new botanist positions, in response to congressional concern about staffing levels as expressed in the Senate appropriations committee report.

A final major initiative that will be supported by the 1988 wildlife budget increase is the challenge grant program. Since 1985, Congress has provided BLM with a modest amount of money to use as matching funds to encourage private and state government cooperators to help with habitat improvement projects. In 1988, Congress appropriated $900,000 for such grants. In Oregon, for instance, potential challenge grant work includes a spotted owl study that would be partially supported by the National Council and Paper Industry for Air and Stream Improvement. In Wyoming, the North American Wild Sheep Foundation and the state game and fish department may cooperate to manipulate vegetation to improve bighorn sheep winter range. Several bighorn projects are proposed in Utah and Nevada as well. Also in Wyoming, BLM will use challenge grant money to work with various organizations, including the National Audubon Society, to study the impact of human disturbance on nesting white pelicans at Pathfinder Reservoir. In New Mexico, volunteers will work with the bureau to complete a major raptor nest inventory, encompassing 10,000 acres. In Montana, Ducks Unlimited may offer a substantial amount of matching funds to help support major wetland development projects.

Land Acquisition

Over the past decade, annual appropriations from the Land and Water Conservation Fund for BLM land acquisition have averaged a modest $2.4 million (see Figure 9). The president's budget proposed a $10,000 funding level for BLM land acquisition in 1988. Congress appropriated a total of $8.9 million, which included $600,000 to acquire desert tortoise habitat in California and $4 million to begin federal acquisition in the Carrizo Plain of California. The Carrizo Plain, which provides habitat for eight listed species, including the San Joaquin kit fox and the California condor, has long been the site of conflict over oil and gas development. Representatives of federal and state agencies, The Nature Conservancy, and several energy companies have agreed on a proposal to establish an 180,000-acre reserve in the area, to be acquired over the next decade through a combination of federal, state, and private funding. The plan for the area would allow multiple-use activities, including mineral development, that are designed in a manner compatible with the conservation of the area's endangered species. In its 1988 appropriations report, Congress directed the Fish and Wildlife Service to enter into a memorandum of understanding with the California Department of Fish and Game and others to coordinate endangered species recovery actions in the San Joaquin Valley. Congress stated that it expected that this appropriation and related actions would resolve endangered species issues in the area. An additional $250,000 was appropriated to BLM for acquisition management expenses related to the project.

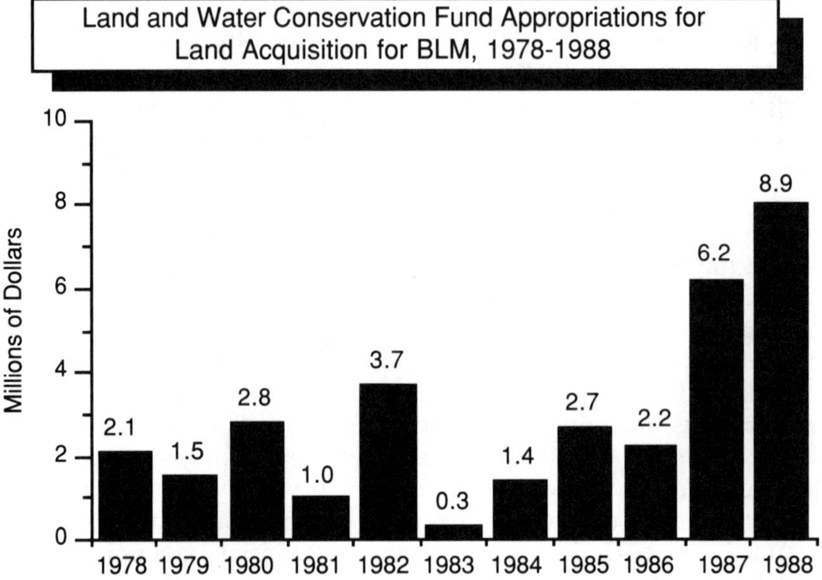

Figure 9.

NATIONAL PARK SERVICE

The National Park Service is responsible for some 79.6 million acres of land distributed among 338 units in 49 states and representing most of the significant ecosystems in the nation. The 1916 National Park System Organic Act mandated the protection of all park resources, including wildlife. NPS emphasizes an "ecosystem approach" to land management that rarely focuses exclusively on wildlife.

Congress appropriated a total of $931 million for NPS in 1988, 17 percent above the president's request of $774 million, and somewhat higher than the 1987 appropriation of $909 million. As it has in the past, Congress rejected administration proposals to halt new land acquisition, terminate state-assistance grants under the Land and Water Conservation Fund, eliminate funding for the Historic Preservation Fund, and defer most construction. In the 1988 budget, park management received 79 percent of the funds; construction, 10 percent; land acquisition, 7 percent; and the Historic Preservation Fund, 3 percent (see Figure 10). The 1988 level is substantially below the agency's budgets from 1983 to 1985, when land acquisition, construction, and maintenance were all funded at much higher levels. Since that time, these accounts have decreased, while funding for park management has increased. Congress appropriated $731 million for park management in 1988, a 17-percent increase over actual 1987

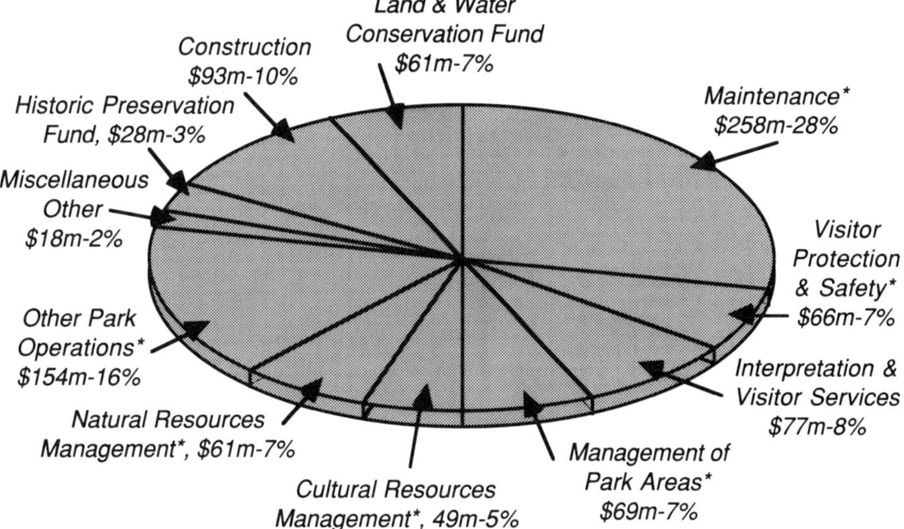

Figure 10.

expenditures of $605 million. In constant dollars, the 1988 park management budget is 31 percent above the 1982 level of $470 million.

Natural Resources Management

The National Park Service's ecosystem approach to management theoretically integrates wildlife concerns into all management activities, which makes it extremely difficult to track specific wildlife-related expenditures in NPS' budget. Most funding for direct wildlife-related activities, however, is appropriated under natural resources management, a subcategory of the park management account. Natural resources management was funded at a level of $60.5 million in 1988, a slight increase over the president's request and $3.3 million more than in 1987. This activity constitutes just seven percent of the total NPS budget in 1988. Although the funding level for natural resources management has increased over the years relative to the rest of the budget (for example, it was just 4.8 percent of the 1982 budget), it is still a remarkably small portion of the budget for an agency whose mission is to preserve some of the most spectacular and unique natural resources in the nation. Of about 16,000 full-time personnel, only 71 professional scientists are currently employed by NPS to monitor and manage the natural resources of the park system. Congress, concerned that the agency's research program is "being developed in a haphazard fashion in response to specific problems and absent any general framework" (House committee report), provided $100,000 in 1988 for an analysis of the current research program and for recommendations regarding its future direction.

The natural resources management program is subdivided into several accounts; Natural Resources Preservation Program funds the most discernible wildlife-related activities. Funds from this subaccount are used for research, monitoring, and mitigation projects—many focusing on important wildlife issues in the parks.

NPS will spend about $7.6 million on the Natural Resources Preservation Program in 1988. Some of this money will be used to conclude a three-year study of the Florida panther—a survey of the population dynamics, habitat preferences, and prey base for this critically endangered resident of Everglades National Park and Big Cypress National Preserve. Another research project that will be completed in 1988 concerns the effects of hunters on brown bear populations in the Katmai National Park and Preserve in Alaska.

NPS also plans, beginning in 1988, to allocate a permanent budget increase for grizzly bear management in Glacier and Yellowstone national parks. For the past three years, the Natural Resources Preservation Program has provided funding to develop and field test various ways to improve waste handling and storage, visitor management, interpretation, and backcountry patrol needs in Glacier and Yellowstone. Based on the results of this experiment, the agency proposes to use an additional $82,000 per year at Glacier and $268,000 at Yellowstone to intensify efforts to educate visitors about grizzly bears, enforce bear-related regulations, and monitor bear activity.

Land Acquisition

Land and Water Conservation Fund appropriations are used to acquire additional acreage for the National Park System and for matching grants to states for outdoor recreation programs. Congress ignored the administration's proposal to zero-fund both accounts, and appropriated $40.7 million for federal land acquisition and $20 million for matching grants to states in 1988, a 30 percent decrease from the 1987 level of $87.2 million. The 1988 appropriation is substantially below historic levels for Park Service land acquisition, which was funded at $129 million in 1982 and at an average of $290 million in the late 1970s (see Figure 11).

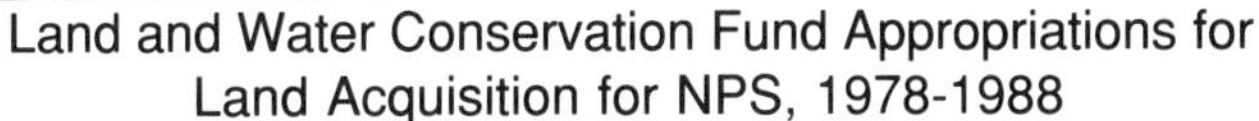

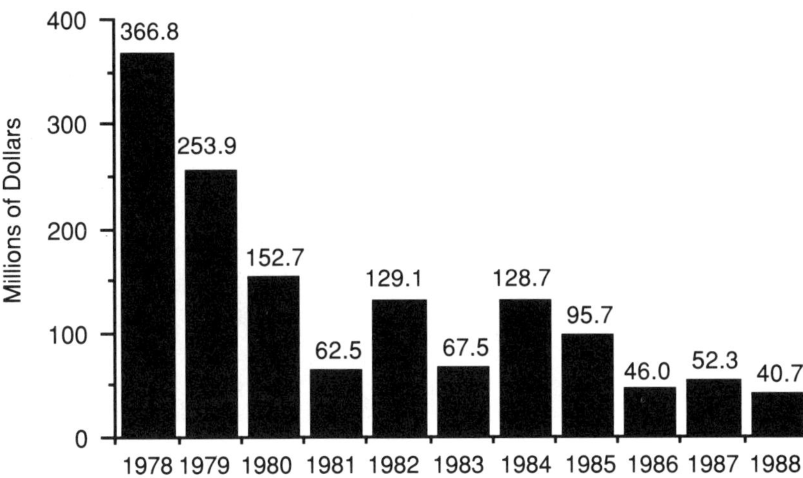

Figure 11.

NATIONAL MARINE FISHERIES SERVICE

The National Marine Fisheries Service manages marine fisheries within the U.S. exclusive economic zone, which extends from the seaward boundary of state territorial waters to 200 miles off the U.S. coast. NMFS is also responsible for managing and protecting marine mammals (under the Marine Mammal Protection Act), and marine endangered and threatened species. NMFS shares with FWS the responsibility for conserving marine mammals. NMFS is responsible for whales, dolphins, seals, and sea lions, while the Fish and Wildlife Service manages polar bears, walruses, sea otters, and manatees.

NMFS is funded as part of the the National Oceanic and Atmospheric Administration. The NMFS budget is divided into three major categories: information collection and analysis; conservation and management operations; and state and industry programs. Research activities account for 61 percent of the 1988 NMFS budget, reflecting the agency's traditional focus on fisheries research. Conservation and management operations form just over a quarter of the 1988 budget, and state and industry programs constitute 13 percent (see Figure 12).

Congress appropriated a total of $163 million for NMFS in 1988, a 21-percent increase from the president's request, and about the same as the $163 million level appropriated in 1987. Of all the federal agencies with fish and wildlife management responsibilities, NMFS has been

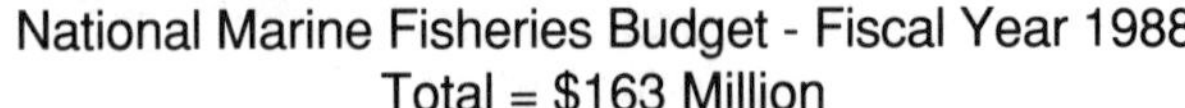

National Marine Fisheries Budget - Fiscal Year 1988
Total = $163 Million

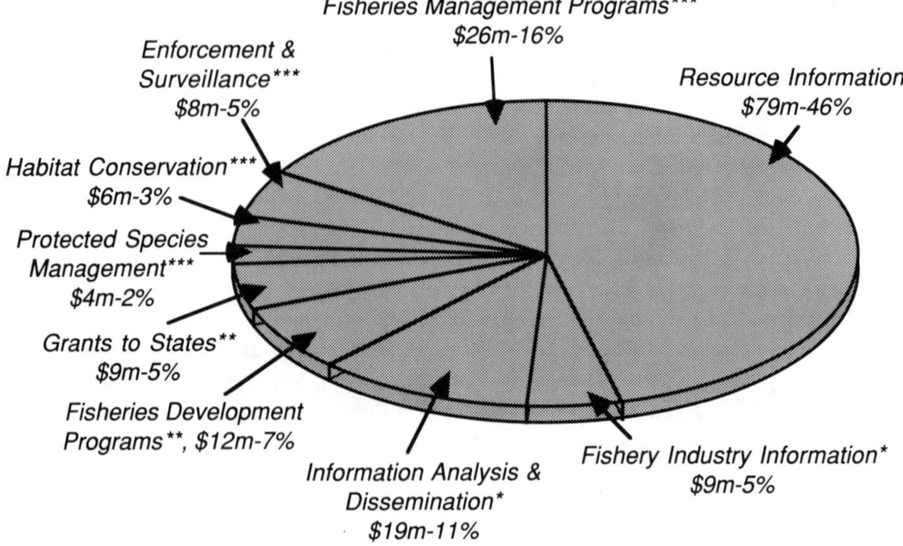

Figure 12.

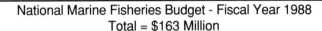

the target of the sharpest budget reduction proposals by the Reagan Administration. Congress has rejected these proposals year after year, and has provided NMFS with modest annual increases to keep pace with inflation. The 1988 NMFS budget is about even with the 1981 level in constant dollars.

Information Collection and Analysis

In 1988 Congress appropriated $106 million for information collection and analysis, which includes research on the marine environment and its biological resources, as well as on the fishing industry. In contrast, the president's budget had proposed a funding level of $65 million, with a reduction of about 160 full-time personnel (see Figure 13). Congressional research add-ons to the president's request included $1.3 million for protected species, $1.6 million for marine mammals, $1.7 million for Chesapeake Bay, and $5.1 million for fisheries habitat studies. Congress allocated $10,000 of the total amount provided for

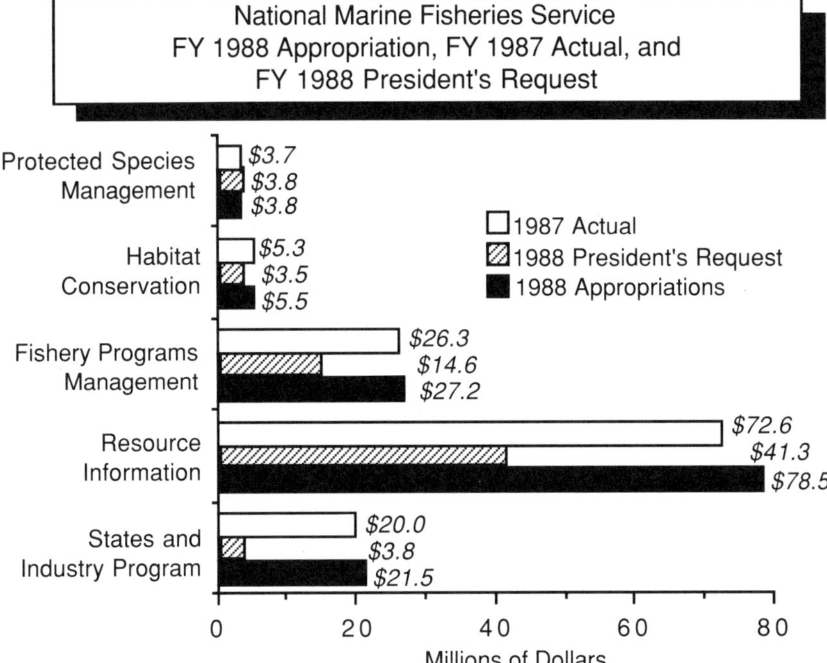

Figure 13.

protected species to continue research on the Kemp's Ridley sea turtle, citing the need to determine the role of Long Island Sound in the turtle's development.

Conservation and Management Operations

Congress provided $45 million for conservation and management operations in 1988; the president's budget had proposed a level of $30.5 million. This program funds species management, habitat conservation, and law enforcement. Among other add-ons, Congress allocated $250,000 for development and implementation of recovery plans for endangered species of porpoise, whale, and fish, and $38,000 in matching funds for the state of Oregon to develop a management plan for harbor seals and California sea lions.

State and Industry Assistance Programs

Congress appropriated a total of $21.5 million for this budget category in 1988. State programs received $9 million, which included $4 million in grants to support research and development efforts on commercial fisheries, $2 million in disaster aid, $2.5 million for anadromous fish conservation projects, and $500,000 for striped bass research. Industry programs, which support various activities to promote the development of U.S. fisheries and to ensure the quality of U.S. fish products, were allocated $12.5 million. The president's budget had proposed no funding for state programs, and just $3.8 million for fisheries product quality and safety research. The Reagan Administration has repeatedly tried to terminate funding for these activities, maintaining that states, industry, and the private sector could implement them more efficiently. This attempt has failed, however, to have much impact on these programs, which have received a fairly even level of funding in constant dollars since 1982.

Turtle Excluder Device Controversy

The controversy over NMFS regulations requiring the use of turtle excluder devices (TEDs) on shrimp trawls rose to a higher level of acrimony between environmentalists and the shrimp industry in 1987. While thousands of shrimpers gathered at rallies throughout the Gulf Coast protesting that TEDs would put them out of business, environmentalists worked hard to inform the public and Congress of the dire situation facing endangered sea turtles such as the Kemp's ridley.

Representative Bob Livingston (R-LA) sought relief for the shrimpers by offering an amendment to the 1987 supplemental appropriations bill that would have exempted shrimpers in the Western Gulf from the requirment to use TEDs. When this measure was rejected, opponents of TEDs attempted to amend the Endangered Species Act reauthorization bill to delay for two years the mandatory use of TEDs in offshore waters in the Gulf. This amendment also failed. The Senate will consider the Endangered Species Act reauthorization in 1988 and may come under similar pressure to waive the TED requirements.

In its 1988 appropriations report, Congress directed NMFS to continue its present studies of TEDs and to include new data and analyses of the full economic impact of TEDs on the amount of shrimpers' catch that is lost through TED use; the impact of TEDs when used in near shore and inshore waters; and the turtle mortality rate in these waters. Congress ordered NMFS to give a progress report on this research to the appropriations committee every 60 days.

Cynthia Lenhart is a wildlife specialist with National Audubon Society's Washington, D.C., office.

Index

World Wildlife Fund, CITES ivory trade control system and, 348
Wyoming Resource Area, Pinedale, 161